Handbook of Gifted Education

THIRD EDITION

EDITORS

Nicholas Colangelo

The University of Iowa

Gary A. Davis

University of Wisconsin—Madison

Boston • New York • San Francisco
Mexico City • Montreal • Toronto • London • Madrid • Munich • Paris
Hong Kong • Singapore • Tokyo • Cape Town • Sydney

We dedicate this book to
Kay and Joe

and

Tony, Alyssa, Nick,
Marie, Jeanie, and Lina.

and

on the Davis side to
Cathy, Kirsten, Sonja, Richard, Ingrid,
Bonnie, and the memory of Michael Frost,
Dan Davis, Terry Davis, and Allen Nielsen.

and

In Memoriam
to Jacqueline N. Blank,
a founder of the Belin-Blank Center
and tremendous friend of gifted education,
who died April 26, 2002.

Executive Editor: *Virginia Lanigan*
Series Editorial Assistant: *Robert Champagne*
Marketing Manager: *Taryn Wahlquist*
Production Editor: *Michael Granger*
Editorial Production Service: *Modern Graphics*
Composition Buyer: *Linda Cox*
Manufacturing Buyer: *JoAnne Sweeney*
Cover Administrator: *Kristina Mose-Libon*
Electronic Composition: *Modern Graphics*

For related titles and support materials, visit our online catalog at www.ablongman.com.

Library of Congress Cataloging-in-Publication Data

Handbook of gifted education / edited by Nicholas Colangelo and Gary A. Davis.—3rd ed.
    p. cm.
  Includes bibliographical references and index.
  ISBN 0-205-34063-6
   1. Gifted children—Education—United States—Handbooks, manuals, etc. 2. Talented students—Education—United States—Handbooks, manuals, etc. I. Colangelo, Nicholas. II. Davis, Gary A.

LC3993.9 .H35 2003
371.95—dc21

2002071097

Printed in the United States of America

10 9 8 7 6 5 4 3 2   07 06 05 04 03

Contents

*O*ur vision for this third edition of *Handbook of Gifted Education* was twofold. First, we wanted new insights and updates to the dynamic thinking of most of our eminent authors from the previous edition. All have thoughtfully built upon and extended their work further into forefronts of gifted education.

Second, we wanted the book to extend its coverage to include further exciting and central topics. This third edition includes nineteen new authors and nine new topics. For example, new in this edition are chapters looking at social policy, teaching thinking skills, artistic giftedness, the gifted delinquent, giftedness in spatial abilities, and two long-overdue topics—educating gifted students in rural areas and the use of computer technology in gifted education.

These new topics nicely complement the stimulating and insightful topics—too many to list here—from our previous edition. With 47 chapters, each of which condenses at least a book-length topic, the chapters necessarily are concise—a distinct benefit to the reader.

More thorough than before, the book remains a scholarly handbook. It provides authoritative knowledge, insights, and recommendations that make the book suitable, at once, for college senior and graduate courses and as a sound resource for university educators and scholar-practitioners in the field.

The history of gifted education has shown an ebb-and-flow pattern with both educators and the general public. The educational pendulum swings between excellence and equity; between cultivating talents of the brightest and most talented—while aiding all children—versus helping below-average children to become more proficient.

The current "flow" was born in the 1970s. The 1980s saw a rapid expansion of interest in meeting the academic needs of gifted youngsters. The interest has been worldwide, with legislation and programs sprouting not only in the United States and Canada, but in Mexico, England, Scotland, Ireland, Italy, Australia, Indonesia, Micronesia, the Dominican Republic, Costa Rica, Brazil, Colombia, Israel, Egypt, Saudi Arabia, India, China, Taiwan, Japan, Hong Kong, the Philippines, Guam, South Africa, and (at least before the dissolution of Communist bloc countries), Russia, Poland, Bulgaria, and elsewhere.

At the beginning of the twenty-first century, the gifted movement remains strong. However, "ebbing" still happens in some school districts because of budget difficulties, the de-tracking movement, and indecisive state and district mandates. The 1994 publication of *The Bell Curve* by Herrnstein and Murray, which argued for a genetic basis of social class differences in intelligence, helped reduce interest in promoting intellectual giftedness.

On the upside, the 1980s, 1990s, and current twenty-first-century years have brought a finer focus on social and psychological issues pertaining to the gifted. Such issues concern, for example, minority, female, handicapped, very young, and rural gifted children; extraordinarily precocious children and youth; families of the gifted; the use of technology; the role of counseling; strong gifts in specific intellectual areas; and subtle dynamics such as extreme sensitivity, excitability, empathy, and near-neurotic levels of perfectionism.

Also on the upside, in the midst of ebbing, the 1993 publication of the national report *National Excellence: A Case for Developing America's Talent* helped raise awareness that, yes, America *is* facing a "quiet crisis." We face a quiet crisis when we ignore our top students, when we ignore their educational needs and preparation, when we ignore their futures and ours.

At present, support for programs and services for the gifted and talented remain enthusiastic and progressive—with exceptions. Some critics continue to see gifted education as an undemocratic and elitist effort to "give to the rich." Some teachers and principals install programs only in begrudging response to state mandates or the demands of parents. Some politicians demand competency testing in the basics—leading to narrow and sometimes fearful efforts to raise classroom competency scores, at the cost of richer depth and breadth. Most colleges and universities are too

slow in providing coursework and professional training.

Most of the strong interest in—indeed, demand
for—college work in gifted education comes from
teachers, counselors, and administrators. After experiencing the realities of schools and classrooms, they
realize that gifted children present a unique and unmet
challenge to the entire educational system. It is these
enthusiastic educators who want a better understanding of gifted students and a better repertoire of strategies for teaching them.

We developed this text and resource book to assist
teachers, counselors, and administrators in their day-
to-day work with gifted youngsters in schools. We
hope this third edition will enrich their professional
development.

With a group of unusually authoritative authors,
this book also provides form and substance, in depth,
for scholars who need an up-to-date resource. Those
who study these chapters will become familiar with
today's issues in the field and with the seasoned ideas
and unique insights expected of a resource volume.

This book is divided into seven main sections: (1)
an overview and presentation of issues; (2) conceptions and identification; (3) instructional models and
practices; (4) creativity, thinking skills, and genius
and eminence; (5) psychological and counseling issues; (6) populations of giftedness; and (7) special
topics, a potpourri that includes teacher training, technology, legal issues, international perspectives, and
government policy. We believe this book is a comprehensive and readable text, covering issues, problems,
and practical strategies in all central components of
gifted education.

We wish to especially recognize Rachelle Hansen,
secretary at The Connie Belin & Jacqueline N. Blank
International Center for Gifted Education and Talent
Development, for her extensive and valuable assis-
tance. We also recognize the staff at the Belin-Blank
Center for their proofreading and editorial assistance,
particularly the work of Jerilyn Fisher. We thank
Allyn & Bacon editor Virginia Lanigan for her sup-
port as well as the reviewers of this edition: M. Gail
Hickey, Indiana University, Fort Wayne; James E.
Green, University of Tulsa; Nancy S. Breard,
Converse College; and Judith Slater, Florida
International University. Finally, we are grateful and
indebted to our contributing authors who generously
collaborated with us in realizing our vision for this
third and expanded edition.

N.C.
G.A.D.

Susan G. Assouline is the Belin-Blank Center's Associate Director and Clinical Supervisor. She received her B.S. in general science with a teaching endorsement, her Ed.S. in School Psychology, and her Ph.D. in Psychological and Quantitative Foundations, all from The University of Iowa. Upon completion of her doctorate, she was awarded a two-year post-doctoral fellowship at the Study of Mathematically Precocious Youth (SMPY) at Johns Hopkins University, and upon completion joined the Belin-Blank Center in 1990. She is especially interested in identification of aca-demic talent in elementary students and is co-author of the books *Jane and Johnny Love Math: Recognizing and Encouraging Mathematical Talent in Elementary Students (A Guidebook for Educators and Parents);* and *Extraordinary Math: An Exceptional Approach to Educating Mathematically Excellent Stu-dents,* which is in press. As well, she is co-editor with Nicholas Colangelo of the series *Talent Development: Proceedings from the WallaceResearch Symposia on Giftedness and Talent Development,* and co-developer of *The Iowa Acceleration Scale.*

Clar M. Baldus is the Administrator for Rural Schools Programs and Inventiveness Programs at the Belin-Blank Center and the State Coordinator for Invent Iowa, an invention program that serves K–12. She also administers the Iowa Online Advanced Placement Academy. Clar received her B.A. in Art Education from Mount Mercy College, Cedar Rapids, IA, and her M.A. as a Master of Education: Applied Research from Marycrest College, Davenport, IA. She completed a Ph.D. in Educational Psychology (with emphasis in visual/spatial abilities) at The University of Iowa. Her research has been guided by her passion for art, interest in creative processes, and commitment to talent development. Before joining the Belin-Blank Center, Clar was a resource specialist and assessment facilitator for elementary gifted and talented students in Cedar Rapids Community Schools.

Camilla Persson Benbow from 1981–1986 was an associate research scientist at Johns Hopkins University. In 1986, she moved to Iowa State University, where she became Department Chair in 1992 and Distinguished Professor in 1995. In 1996, she became Interim Dean of Education and remained in that position until she was named Dean of Peabody College, Nashville. While Dean Benbow's scholarship has concentrated predominantly on academically talented children, her efforts in the arena of educational policy

are broader. She works on such issues as equity and ensuring the optimal development of all children through individualized educational services that capitalize on strengths, build on high expectations, promote competence, and focus on outcomes. She has published over 100 articles in journals and magazines, edited two books, and received both the Early Scholar Award and the Distinguished Scholar Award from the National Association for Gifted Children.

James H. Borland is Professor of Education and Chair of the Department of Curriculum and Teaching at Teachers College, Columbia University, where he also directs the graduate programs in the education of gifted students. He is author of the book *Planning and Implementing Programs for the Gifted* and numerous journal articles and book chapters. Professor Borland also is editor the forthcoming book *Rethinking Gifted Education,* editor of the *Education and Psychology of the Gifted* series of books from Teachers College Press, and is past co-editor of the Section on Teaching, Learning, and Human Development of the *American Educational Research Journal.* He has lectured on the education of gifted students across the United States and abroad.

Linda E. Brody is Director of the Study of Exceptional Talent and Co-Director of the Diagnostic and Counseling Center at the Johns Hopkins University Center for Talented Youth (CTY). Her research interests focus on highly gifted students, gifted girls, and gifted students with learning disabilities. She has published numerous articles on these and other topics and is co-editor of two books: *Women and the Mathematical Mystique* and *Learning Disabled Gifted Students: Identification and Programming.* She also teaches graduate courses in gifted education at Johns Hopkins.

Donna Rae Clasen is Professor Emeritus at the University of Wisconsin, Whitewater, Department of Educational Foundations, where she developed and taught a series of undergraduate and graduate courses in the education of the gifted, including two telecourses, *Creativity in the Class0room* and *Teaching for Thinking.* With a three-year Jacob Javits grant, she developed Project STREAM, which she directed for thirteen years, that identifies high-ability minority students and gives them valuable school and university experiences. Professor Clasen has published numerous articles in *Gifted Child Quarterly, Roeper Review, Middle School Journal, Journal of Youth and Adolescence,* and *Develop-*

mental Psychology. She is a former President of the Wisconsin Association of Educators of Gifted and Talented. In 1987, she was named Wisconsin Teacher Educator of the Year by the Wisconsin Department of Public Instruction.

Robert E. Clasen is Professor Emeritus at the University of Wisconsin, Madison, Depart-ment of Educational Psychology. He was Director of Education Outreach for UW-Madison and Director of Outreach to the Talented and Gifted (UTAG). He produced, wrote, and hosted three tele-courses for the gifted, including *Simple Gifts: Programming for the Gifted* and *Educating Able Learners.* In addition to compiling a number of books of readings to accompany the telecourses, he wrote and revised several telecourse study guides and published articles in the *Journal of Educational Research, Gifted Child Quarterly,* and *Roeper Review.*

Nicholas Colangelo is the Myron and Jacqueline Blank Professor of Gifted Education at The University of Iowa. He is also Director of The Connie Belin & Jacqueline N. Blank International Center for Gifted Education and Talent Development. He is author of numerous articles on counseling gifted students and the affective development of gifted. He has edited two texts: *New Voices in Counseling the Gifted* (with Ronald Zaffrann) and *Handbook of Gifted Education, Editions I, II, and III* (with Gary A. Davis). He has served on the editorial boards of major journals including *Counseling and Development, Gifted Child Quarterly, Journal of Creative Behavior, Journal for the Education of the Gifted,* and *Roeper Review.* In 1991, he was presented with the Distinguished Scholar Award by the National Association for Gifted Children; in 1993, he received the Distinguished Service Award from the Iowa Talented and Gifted Association; and in 1995, he received the Alumni Achievement Award presented by the School of Education, University of Wisconsin—Madison. In 1996–1997, he served as Executive Administrator for the World Council for Gifted and Talented Children. In 2000, he received the State of Iowa Regents Award for Faculty Excellence.

Arthur L. Costa is Emeritus Professor of Education at California State University, Sacramento, and Co-Director of the Institute for Intelligent Behavior in Berkeley. He has served as a classroom teacher, curriculum consultant, assistant superintendent for instruction, and Director of Educational Programs for the National Aeronautics and Space Administration. Author of numerous journal articles, he edited the book *Developing Minds: A Resource Book for Teaching Thinking* and is author of *The Enabling Behaviors, Teaching for Intelligent Behaviors,* and *The School as a Home for the Mind.* He is co-author of *Cognitive Coaching: A Foundation for Renaissance Schools,* and co-editor of *The Role of Assessment in the Learning Organization: Shifting the Paradigm* and *If Minds Matter.* Active in many profes-

sional organizations, Professor Costa served as President of the California Association for Supervision and Curriculum Development and (national) President of the Association for Supervision and Curriculum Development.

Laurie J. Croft taught at the University of Tulsa School for Gifted Children. At The Connie Belin & Jacqueline N. Blank International Center for Gifted Education and Talent Development, Dr. Croft coordinates summer workshops in gifted education for educators, supervises practicum experiences for teachers of the gifted, and develops professional educational opportunities for teachers. Representing the Belin-Blank Center, she serves on the Iowa Advanced Placement Advisory Committee, the University's Honors Opportunity Program Advisory Committee, and the College of Education Diversity Committee. Dr. Croft has presented at the Iowa Talented and Gifted Association; Oklahoma Association for the Gifted, Creative, and Talented; Wallace National Research Symposium on Talent Development; College of William and Mary National Curriculum Network Conference; and to parent groups and educators in Iowa and other Midwestern states. In Chile, Santiago, she gave keynote presentations at the Seminario Internacional: Niños y Jóvenes con Talentos Académicos.

Gary A. Davis is Professor Emeritus of Educational Psychology at the University of Wisconsin, Madison He is author of many articles in the areas of creativity, problem solving, character education, and effective schooling, and of several books, including *Education of the Gifted and Talented* (with Sylvia Rimm, in 5th edition), *Creativity Is Forever* (in 4th edition), *Psychology of Problem Solving, Effective Schools and Effective Teachers, Educational Psychology, Teaching Values,* and *Values Are Forever.* He is co-editor of *Training Creative Thinking, Psychology of Education: New Looks,* and *Handbook of Gifted Education* (with Nicholas Colangelo, in 3rd edition). In 1999, he received the E. Paul Torrance Creativity Award from the Creativity Division of the National Association for Gifted Children. He served on the Wisconsin State Superintendent's Advisory Committee on the Gifted and Talented and as Director of the College for Kids summer program (1985). He is a current or former reviewer for *Journal of Creative Behavior, Creativity Research Journal, Roeper Review,* and *Gifted Child Quarterly.*

James R. Delisle is Professor of Education at Kent State University, where he directs the undergraduate and graduate programs in gifted child education. He is the author of nine books, including the best-selling *Gifted Kids Survival Guide: A Teen Handbook* (with Judy Galbraith) and *Once Upon a Mind: The Stories and Scholars of Gifted Child Education.* Professor Delisle also directs a program for gifted students in grades 7–8 in the Twinsburg, Ohio, Public Schools.

John F. Feldhusen is Robert B. Kane Distinguished Professor of Education Emeritus at Purdue University and Director Emeritus of the Purdue Gifted Education Resource Institute. He is the former editor of *Gifted Child Quarterly* and *Gifted and Talented International*. He received a Distinguished Scholar award from the National Association for Gifted Children and was awarded an honorary doctorate by Purdue University in 1998.

David H. Feldman is Professor in the Eliot-Pearson Department of Child Development and Director of the Developmental Science Group at Tufts University. His research focuses on extreme forms of giftedness and creativity, cognitive developmental transitions of large-scale, and nonuniversal theory, a broad framework that integrates giftedness and creativity into developmental theory. Among his books are *Beyond Universals in Cognitive Development* (2nd edition), *Changing the World: A Framework for the Study of Creativity* (with Mihalyi Csikszentmihalyi and Howard Gardner), and *Nature's Gambit: Child Prodigies and the Development of Human Potential*. With Howard Gardner, he also edits a series of books from Project Zero at Harvard University on early childhood education. Professor Feldman was a Fulbright Fellow in 1981 and a Distinguished Scholar of the National Association for Gifted Children in 1988.

Donna Y. Ford is Professor of Special Education at The Ohio State University, where she teaches courses in gifted education. She conducts research on recruiting and retaining culturally diverse students in gifted education, minority student achievement and underachievement, and other topics in multicultural and urban education. Professor Ford received a Research Award from the Shannon Center for Advanced Studies, an Early Career Achievement Award from the American Educational Research Association, an Early Scholar Award from the National Association for Gifted Children (NAGC), and the Esteemed Scholarship Award from the National Association of Black Psychologists. She has published over 80 articles and is the author of *Reversing Underachievement Among Gifted Black Students* and *Multicultural Gifted Education*. Professor Ford is a former Board Member of NAGC and has served on the editorial boards of *Gifted Child Quarterly, Journal of Negro Education,* and *Roeper Review.*

Françoys Gagné is Professor of Psychology (Educational Psychology) at the Université du Quebéc à Montréal. He authored a book (in French) reviewing the literature on acceleration and has published numerous articles in both French and English. He is best known in the United States and abroad for his Differentiated Model of Giftedness and Talent, as well as his psychometric studies of peer nominations. Professor Gagné was the founding president of Giftedness Quebec, a bilingual advocacy group, and is an active consultant in public schools. Among other awards, in 1993 and 1998 he received awards from the American Mensa Association for his research in gifted education, in 1994 he received an award from the *Gifted Child Quarterly* for "Best Article of the Year"; and in 1996 he received the Distinguished Scholar Award from the National Association for Gifted Children.

James J. Gallagher is William Rand Kenan, Jr., Professor of Education at the University of North Carolina at Chapel Hill and a senior investigator in the Frank Porter Graham Child Development Center at that University. He has held numerous leadership positions, including the presidencies of the Association for the Gifted, the World Council for the Gifted and Talented, and the National Association for Gifted Children. In addition to numerous articles and monographs, he recently co-authored, with his daughter, Shelagh, the fourth edition of *Teaching the Gifted Child.*

Howard Gardner is John H. and Elisabeth A. Hobbs Professor in Cognition and Education at the Harvard Graduate School of Education. He also holds positions as Adjunct Professor of Psychology at Harvard University, Adjunct Professor of eurology at the Boston University School of Medicine, and Co-Director of Harvard Project Zero. Among numerous honors, Professor Gardner received a MacArthur Prize Fellowship in 1981. In 1990, he was the first American to receive the University of Louisville's Grawemeyer Award in education. He has received sixteen honorary degrees. The John S. Guggenheim Memorial Foundation awarded him a Fellowship for 2000. He is best known in educational circles for his theory of multiple intelligences, a critique of the notion that there exists but a single human intelligence that can be assessed by standard tests. During the past fifteen years, he and colleagues at Project Zero have been working on the design of performance-based assessments, education for understanding, and the use of multiple intelligences to achieve more personalized curriculum, instruction, and assessment. Most recently, Professor Gardner has carried out intensive case studies of exemplary creators and leaders. He is the author of eighteen books, which have been translated into twenty languages, and several hundred articles. His two most recent books are *The Disciplined Mind: What All Students Should Understand* and *Intelligence Reframed: Multiple Intelligences for the 21st Century.*

Linda S. Gottfredson is Professor of Education and Affiliate Faculty of the Honors Program at the University of Delaware. She also co-directs the Delaware–Johns Hopkins Project for the Study of Intelligence and Society. Professor Gottfredson has published extensively in the fields of intelligence, employment testing, and vocational psychology. She is also frequently called on to summarize the research on general intelligence in lectures (e.g., in Israel, Russia) and publications for non-experts (e.g., *Scientific American, Cerebrum, The American Scholar,* and Borgatta's *Encyclopedia of Sociology*). Her focus on the social dilemmas and controversies created by individual and group differences in intelligence is illustrated in three special journal issues she edited: "The *g* Factor in Employment" (*Journal of Vocational Behavior,* 1986), "Fairness in Employment Testing" (*Journal of Vocational Behavior,* 1988), and "Intelligence and Social Policy" (*Intelligence,* 1997).

Miraca U. M. Gross is Professor of Gifted Education and Director of the Gifted Education Research, Resource and Information Centre at the University of New South Wales in Sydney, Australia. Her research, which focuses on the socio-affective development of intellectually gifted children, the highly gifted, and the academic and affective outcomes of programs of ability grouping and acceleration, won her the Hollingworth Award for Research in the Education and Psychology of the Gifted in 1987, and a Mensa Education and Research Foundation Award for Excellence in 1988 and 1990. The (American) National Association for Gifted Children honored her with their Early Scholar Award in 1995. In 1997, the Australian Federal Government conferred on her the inaugural Australian Award for University Teaching in Education. She has authored three books, *Exceptionally Gifted Children, Gifted Students in Primary Schools: Differentiating the Curriculum* (with Bronwyn MacLeod, Diana Drummond, and Caroline Merrick), and *Gifted Students in Secondary Schools: Differentiating the Curriculum* (with Bronwyn MacLeod and Marilyn Pretorius).

Nancy Ewald Jackson is Professor of Educational Psychology in the Division of Psychological and Quantitative Foundations, College of Education, The University of Iowa. Recent publications include the book *Routes to Reading Success and Failure: Toward an Integrated Cognitive Psychology of Reading* (with Max Coltheart) and the chapter "Strategies for modeling the development of giftedness in children" in the 2000 American Psychological Association book, *Talents Unfold-ing: Cognition and Development.* Her empirical work includes several longitudinal studies of the development of precocious readers and young children with other intellectual gifts. Professor Jackson has been especially concerned with integrating the study of giftedness with broader theoretical accounts of cognition and development. She is a charter member of the Iowa Academy of Education.

Frances A. Karnes is Professor of Special Education at the University of Southern Mississippi, Director of the Frances A. Karnes Center for Gifted Studies, and Co-Director of the Institute for Law and Gifted Education. She is author or co-author of over 200 articles and co-author of 15 books on gifted education and related areas, including *Gifted Children and the Law, Gifted Children and Legal Issues in Education,*

and, in 2000, *Gifted Children and Legal Issues: An Update* (all three with Ronald G. Marquardt). She currently serves on the board of the National Association for Gifted Children. Honors include a Faculty Research Award, granted by the University of Southern Mississippi Alumni Association; an Honorary Doctor of Education degree from Quincy University, her alma mater; an award presented by the Mississippi Legislature for outstanding contributions to academic excellence in higher education; and, recently, the Power of One Award from the Governor of Mississippi.

Barbara A. Kerr is Professor of Counseling Psychology at Arizona State University, adjunct faculty at Frank Lloyd Wright School of Architecture-Taliesin West and a Fellow of the American Psychological Association. Her research concerns the extraordinary talent in all of its forms. She is the author of *Smart Girls, The Handbook for Counseling Gifted and Talented, Smart Boys,* and *Letters to the Medicine Man,* as well as over 100 articles and papers in the area of talent development. At ASU, she teaches courses in counseling, gender issues, alternative therapies, and gifted education. At the Cascabel Retreat Center, she founded in Scottsdale, Arizona, she provides a place for educators, scholars, and practitioners to explore issues in giftedness, creativity, and spirituality.

Penny Britton Kolloff is Associate Professor at Illinois State University. She served two terms on the Board of Directors of the National Association for Gifted Children and currently serves on the Board of Directors of the Illinois Association for Gifted Children. She also is a member of the advisory boards for the Center for Talent Development, Northwestern University, and the Indiana Academy for Science, Mathematics, and Humanities. She received the Early Leader award (1987) and the Outstanding Research Paper award (1985) from the National Association for Gifted Children.

James A. Kulik is Research Scientist and Director of the University of Michigan's Office of Evaluations and Examinations. His research specialty is use of quantitative methods to review and analyze collections of research findings on educational issues. Since 1976, he has applied quantitative methods to the research literature on instructional technology, on classroom organization, and in other areas. He is the author of more than 150 journal articles, book chapters, and conference reports describing the results of his research efforts. Kulik's applied interests include the design of evaluation and examination instruments and analysis, and interpretation of data collected with such instruments.

David Lubinski is Professor and Director of Graduate Studies in the Department of Psychology and Human Development, Vanderbilt University, and Associate Editor, *Journal of Personality and Social Psychology: Personality Processes and Individual Differences.* With Camilla

Benbow, he co-directs Study of Mathematically Precocious Youth (SMPY), a planned fifty-year longitudinal study of over 5,000 intellectually talented SMPY participants, begun in 1971. His work, published in two books and nine APA journals, has earned him the American Psychological Association's (APA) 1996 Distinguished Scientific Award for Early Career Contribution to Psychology (Applied Research/Psychometrics), APA's 1996 George A. Miller Award (Outstanding Article in General Psychology), the 1995 American Educational Research Association's Research Excellence Award (Counseling/Human Development), and, most recently, APA's Templeton Award (2000) for Positive Psychology. He was elected to the Society for Multivariate Experimental Psychology in 1998.

Ann Lupkowski-Shoplik is Director of the Carnegie Mellon Institute for Talented Elementary Students at Carnegie Mellon University. She conducts the annual Elementary Student Talent Search and oversees the C-MITES summer program and Weekend Workshops for academically talented kindergarten-through-seventh-grade children. She co-authored *Jane and Johnny Love Math: Recognizing and Encouraging Mathematical Talent in Elementary Students* (with Susan G. Assouline) and *Extraordinary Math: An Exceptional Approach to Educating Mathematically Excellent Students* (also with Susan G. Assouline).

C. June Maker is Professor of Special Education at the University of Arizona, Tucson, and Director of the government-funded DISCOVER Projects. She served on the Board of Directors of NAGC for nineteen years, and as officer and chair of various committees in organizations such as TAG and WCGT. Professor Maker's recent research, conducted in the United States, Mexico, and abroad, has produced a unique performance-based assessment of problem solving in multiple domains, plus curricula designed to enhance the strengths and talents of all students. She serves on editorial boards for journals in gifted education and special education, and is editor of the book series *Critical Issues in Gifted Education.* She has served as a school teacher, regional supervisor for a state department of education, and as an administrative intern in the federal office for the gifted.

Ronald G. Marquardt is Professor of Political Science at the University of Southern Mississippi. A specialist in constitutional and administrative law, he has published in such diverse journals as the *Law and Policy Quarterly, Midwest Quarterly, Mississippi Folklore Register, Law Library Journal, Administrative Law Review, Roeper Review,* and the *Peabody Journal of Education.* He is co-author of *Gifted Children and the Law: Mediation, Due Process, and Court Cases; Gifted Children and Legal Issues in Education;* and *Gifted Children and Legal Issues: An Update* (all with Frances A. Karnes). He has presented at national and international gifted association meetings and has published numerous articles related to the law and gifted students.

Gail Martino is Senior Research Scientist at the Gillette Advanced Technology Center, Boston. Prior to joining Gillette, she was Assistant Professor at Colgate University. Dr. Martino was educated at Syracuse University and Boston College and earned an NIH postdoctoral fellowship to study sensory science at the John B. Pierce Laboratory of Yale University School of Medicine. She has published articles on the nature of giftedness, neuropsychology, and sensory science.

Terry McNabb is Associate Professor of Teacher Education at Coe College in Cedar Rapids, Iowa, where she teaches classes in Child and Adolescent Development. She worked previously at the Connie Belin & Jacqueline N. Blank International Center for Gifted Education and Talent Development, The University of Iowa, and the American College Testing Program. Her research interests are in academic motivation, gender differences, and academic self-concept.

Sidney M. Moon is Professor of Educational Studies and Director of the Gifted Education Resource Institute at Purdue University. She also is a licensed family therapist and a National Certified Counselor. She has been active in gifted education as a parent, counselor, teacher, administrator, and researcher for twenty-five years. Professor Moon's research focuses on personal and environmental influences on academic talent development. She is a past President of the Research and Evaluation Division of the National Association for Gifted Children.

Martha J. Morelock is Assistant Professor of Psychology at Elmira College, Elmira, New York. She received a Hollingworth Award for her Ph.D. thesis on children above 200 IQ. With David Henry Feldman, she has co-authored several articles, including chapters in both editions of the *International Handbook of Giftedness and Talent.* Professor Morelock's article "On the Nature of Giftedness and Talent: Imposing Order on Chaos" (*Roeper Review*) and her chapter "A Sociohistorical Perspective on Exceptionally High-IQ Children," published by the American Psychological Association, received international recognition. The latter influenced the Columbus Group definition of giftedness. Her Australian book *Gifted Children Have Talents Too!* (with Karin Morrison) received wide media attention and is used as a text for teacher education in Australia.

Jennifer K. New is a freelance writer and business owner living in Iowa City. She has an M.A. in English from the University of Washington, Seattle, and a teaching certificate from Antioch University, Yellow Springs, Ohio. She is a co-founder and partner of Synapse Learning Design, a curriculum design and educational consulting firm. Her writing has appeared in national publications, including *salon.com* and *Teacher Magazine.* Her first book, a biography of the artist/journalist Dan Eldon, was published by Chronicle Books, in autumn 2001.

Megan Foley Nicpon is a doctoral student in the Counseling Psychology program at Arizona State University and a graduate assistant for the National Science Foundation Gender Equity Options in Science (GEOS) Project. She has taught freshman seminar courses and assisted in teaching the Helping Relationships course at ASU. Her research interests center on issues of talent development, academic persistence, and health psychology. She has experience in the counseling and assessment of gifted and chronically ill children.

Patricia O'Connell is director of the Javits Gifted and Talented Education Program in the U.S. Department of Education. She served for three years as Director of Academic Programs at the Center for Talented Youth at Johns Hopkins University and for ten years as the State Director for Gifted Programs in Maine. She was president of the Council of state Directors of Programs for the Gifted and secretary of the Association for the Gifted. She holds undergraduate and advanced degrees in anthropology and museum studies, as well as a master's degree in Education Policy Studies from Harvard University.

Paula Olszewski-Kubilius is Associate Professor in the School of Education and Social Policy at Northwestern University and Direc-tor of the Center for Talent Development. She serves on the editorial boards of *Roeper Review, Gifted International,* and the *Journal for the Education of the Gifted.* She is co-editor of the *Journal of Secondary Gifted Education.* She has headed several grant-supported intervention programs for developing the abilities of academically talented low-income minority children. Professor Olszewski-Kubilius is co-editor of several books, including *Current Research Methods for Studying Creativity in Youth* and *Patterns of Influence on Gifted Learners: The Home, the Self and the School,* and co-authored the handbook *Helping Gifted Children and Their Families Prepare for College: A Handbook Designed to Assist Economically Disadvantaged and First Generation College Attendees.* In 1987, she received an Early Scholar Award from the National Association for Gifted Children.

Michael M. Piechowski is a Senior Fellow of the Institute for Educational Advancement and Professor Emeritus of Education and Psychology, Northland College, Ashland, Wisconsin, where he introduced a course in transpersonal psychology. He is co-author of *Theory of Levels of Emotional Development* (2 volumes) with Kazimierz Dabrowski. His article "Overexcitabilities" appears in the *Encyclopedia of Creativity.* He has made studies of self-actualizing people and moral exemplars: A. de Saint-Exupéry, Eleanor Roosevelt, Leta Hollingworth, Etty Hillesum, and Peace Pilgrim, as well as contemporary individuals. His most recent pieces are "From William James to Maslow and Dabrowski: Excitability of Character and Self-Actualization," published in *Creative Intelligence: Toward a Theoretic Integration,* edited by Ambrose, Cohen, and Tannenbaum, and "Childhood Experiences and Spiritual Giftedness," published in *Advanced Develop-ment.* He lives in Madison, Wisconsin, where he laments the separation from his trees in the north.

Robert Plomin is MRC Research Professor of Behavioural Genetics and Deputy Director of the Research Centre for Social, Genetic and Developmental Psychiatry at the Institute of Psychiatry in London. The Research Centre aims to bring together research strategies on nature and nurture in the investigation of behavioral dimensions and disorders, a theme that has been the focus of his research. He is first author of the textbook, *Behavioral Genetics* (in 4th edition, 2001). He has written eight other books, including *Genetics and Experience: The Developmental Interplay Between Nature and Nurture,* and edited several others.

Thomas S. Price is a doctoral student working with Robert Plomin at the Research Centre for Social, Genetic and Developmental Psychiatry at the Institute of Psychiatry in London. His interests include the application of behavior genetic methodologies to the study of cognitive development, including the relationships among causal factors in normal and extreme ability.

Michael C. Pyryt is Associate Professor of Applied Psychology and Director of the Centre for Gifted Education at the University of Calgary. Professor Pyryt has presented numerous papers at national and international conferences in North America, Europe, and Australia, and has published articles on a variety of topics related to gifted individuals and gifted education. He is currently an Associate Editor of the *Journal for the Education of the Gifted* and a member of the Editorial Advisory Board of the *Gifted Child Quarterly* and the *Journal for Secondary Gifted Education.*

Valerie Ramos-Ford is an independent educational consultant and an Assistant Professor of Early Elementary Education at The College of New Jersey. Her expertise is in the areas of Multiple Intelligences, at-risk populations, curriculum development, facility and program design, teacher training, and administrative development and support. Professor Ramos-Ford is a former research project manager and researcher for Howard Gardner's Project Zero/Project Spectrum at Harvard University.

Sally M. Reis is Professor of Educational Psychology at the University of Connecticut, where she also serves as Principal Investigator for the National Research Center on the Gifted and Talented. Her research interests relate to special populations of gifted and talented students, including students with learning disabilities, gifted females, and diverse groups of talented students. Professor Reis is also interested in extensions of the Schoolwide Enrichment Model to expand offerings and provide enrichment to talented students not previously identified as gifted. She is co-author of *The Schoolwide Enrichment Model, The Secondary Triad Model, Dilemmas in Talent Development in the Middle Years,* and *Work Left Undone: Choices and Compromises of Talented Females,* a book about women's talent development. She serves on several editorial boards, including the *Gifted Child Quarterly,* and at this writing is President of the National Association for Gifted Children.

Joseph S. Renzulli is Neag Professor of Gifted Education and Talent Development and Director of the National Research Center on the Gifted and Talented at the University of Connecticut. He recently was named Distinguished Professor by the Board of Trustees at the University of Connecticut, and earlier received a Distinguished Scholar Award from the National Association for Gifted Children. He has served as Senior Research Associate for the White House Task Force on Education for the Gifted and Talented, and on editorial boards in gifted education, educational psychology, and law and education. His Enrichment Triad Model is the most widely used guide for developing gifted programs, and his well-known Three Ring conception helps identify and develop high potential with young people. Author of numerous books and articles, and a series author with the Houghton Mifflin Reading Series, his three most recent books are *Schools for Talent Development, The Schoolwide Enrichment Model* (with Sally M. Reis), and *The Total Talent Portfolio* (with Jeanne H. Purcell). His proudest accomplishments are the annual Confratute Program, which since 1978 has served over 18,000 persons from around the world, and the UConn Mentor Connection, a summer program that pairs high school students with leading scientists, historians, artists, and other faculty at the University of Connecticut.

E. Susanne Richert is President of the Global Institute for Maximizing Potential, whose mission is to support international advancement of student and teacher intellectual, emotional, social, and ethical development. Her ©Maximizing Student Potential Model has produced significant gains in critical thinking, self-esteem, school achievement, and improvements on state performance assessments, and an over 50% reduction in discipline problems. Elements of her model are in use in over sixty districts, from Pre-K to high school, nationally impacting over 83,000 students of diverse demographics. Dr. Richert has served as consultant to the U.S. Supreme Court and the U.S. Information Agency. She has trained hundreds of teachers around the globe in urban, rural, and suburban schools. She has presented at gifted education conferences throughout North American and in Asia, Europe, and the Middle East. Among more than sixty publications is the widely used *National Report on Identification,* written for the U.S. Department of Education, and her forthcoming

book *Maximizing Student Potential,* based on fifteen years of research on staff development.

Sylvia B. Rimm is Clinical Professor at Case Western Reserve University, School of Medicine, and Director of the Family Achievement Clinic in Cleveland. She is co-author of *Education of the Gifted and Talented* (with Gary A. Davis) and has authored twelve other books, creativity tests, and many articles. Her interests include parenting, gifted children, underachievement, and girls and women's issues. She appears regularly on NBC's Today Show and Weekend Today, and her column *Sylvia Rimm on Raising Kids* is syndicated by Creators Syndicate. Her book *Why Bright Kids Get Poor Grades* focuses on how to reverse underachievement in gifted children, and her book *See Jane Win* was a *New York Times* best seller. She is a member of the Board of Directors of the National Association for Gifted Children.

Ann Robinson is Professor in the Department of Educational Leadership and Director of Gifted Programs at the University of Arkansas at Little Rock. She has served on the Board of Directors of the National Association for Gifted Children, was the first Editor of the NAGC Service Publications, and from 1992 to 1997 was Editor of the *Gifted Child Quarterly.* Among her publications is *Recommended Practices in Gifted Education* (with Bruce Shore, Dewey Cornell, and Virgil Ward), a standard research reference in the field. In 1996, Professor Robinson founded the Advanced Placement Teacher Institutes at the University of Arkansas at Little Rock. She has received both the Early Scholar Award and the Early Leaders Award from NAGC. In 1999, she received the Distinguished Alumni Award of Distinction from the School of Education at Purdue University.

Shirley W. Schiever is the Curriculum Specialist at Madge Utterback Middle School, the fine arts magnet middle school in the Tucson Unified School District. She is author of *A Comprehensive Approach to Teaching Thinking* and co-editor of *Critical Issues in Gifted Education: Volume II. Defensible Programs for Cultural Ethnic Minorities.* Her interests focus on problem solving within an integrated curriculum designed to develop higher-level thinking in students, and on recognizing and capitalizing on strengths within the multiple intelligences, especially in ethnic and cultural minority populations.

Robert A. Schultz is Assistant Professor of Gifted Education and Curriculum Studies at the University of Toledo. His work addresses the social and emotional needs of gifted individuals at the secondary school level, including teacher education, individualization, and program design, delivery, and evaluation. He is Chair of the Conceptual Foundations Divisions of the National Association of Gifted Children and serves as a Contributing Editor to *Roeper Review.* In 1998 he received the Doctoral Student Award from NAGC for current impact and potential to enhance the field of gifted education.

Ken Seeley is President of the Colorado Foundation for Families and Children. He served as Principal of the Laboratory School at the University of Northern Colorado and was Professor of Education at the University of Denver. While at the University of Denver, Dr. Seeley initiated the first teacher education program in gifted education in the Rocky Mountain region. He served as Editor of the *Journal for the Education of the Gifted* and has extensive experience in the evaluation of gifted programs. He was Director of Programs at the Clayton Foundation, which provides direct services to high-risk families and children.

Linda Kreger Silverman, a licensed psychologist, is Director of the Institute for the Study of Advanced Development and its subsidiary, the Gifted Development Center, both in Denver. She served for nine years on the faculty of the University of Denver in Counseling Psychology and Gifted Education. Her textbook *Counseling the Gifted and Talented* has been adopted by over fifty colleges and universities. She recently authored *Upside-down Brilliance: The Visual-Spatial Learner.* Professor Silverman is founder and Editor of *Advanced Development,* the only journal on adult giftedness. She conducts research on profoundly gifted children, visual-spatial learners, introversion, and the comparative assessment of the gifted on various instruments. She serves on the American Psychological Association Task Force on Giftedness, the National Associa-tion for Gifted Children Task Force on Social and Emotional Needs of the Gifted, and the panel guiding the next revision of the Stanford-Binet Intelligence Scale.

Dean Keith Simonton is Professor of Psychol-ogy at the University of California, Davis. He has authored more than 200 articles and chapters plus eight books, including *Genius, Creativity, and Leadership; Scientific Genius; Greatness; Genius and Creativity; Great Psychologists;* and *Origins of Genius,* which received the William James Book Award from the American Psychological Association. Other honors include the Sir Francis Galton Award for Outstanding Contributions to the Study of Creativity, the Rudolf Arnheim Award for Outstanding Contributions to Psychology and the Arts, and the George A. Miller Outstanding Article Award. He serves on several editorial boards, such as *Creativity Research Journal, Empirical Studies of the Arts, Leadership Quarterly,* and *Journal of Creative Behavior,* which he edited from 1993 to 1999. Professor Simonton's research focuses on the cognitive, personality, developmental, and sociocultural factors behind exceptional creativity, leadership, genius, and talent.

Lauren A. Sosniak is Professor of Education in the Division of Teacher Education at San José State University. Her work has appeared in *Teachers College Record, Journal of Curriculum Studies, Theory Into Practice, Educational Evaluation and Policy Analy-sis, Elementary School Journal,* and the *Interna-tional Encyclopedia of Education.* Professor Sosniak has served as book review editor for *Educational Researcher* and as a member of the editorial boards for the *Journal of Curriculum Studies, Teachers College Record,* and the *American Journal of Education.*

Julian C. Stanley is Professor Emeritus of Psychology and Director of the Study of Mathematically Precocious Youth, founded by him in 1971, in the Center for Talented Youth (CTY) at Johns Hopkins University. His research, development, and service have involved chiefly finding boys and girls who reason exceptionally well mathematically and helping them get the special, supplemental, accelerative educational opportunities they need and deserve. SMPY has sparked the creation of large annual regional talent search-es and residential summer academic programs across the nation, especially at Johns Hopkins University, Duke University, Northwestern University, Iowa State University, and the University of Denver. He edited, co-edited, or sponsored *Mathematical Talent, Intellectual Talent, The Gifted and the Creative, Educating the Gifted, Women and the Mathematical Mystique,* and *Academic Precocity.* He is a former president of the American Educational Research Association, the National Council on Measurement in Education, and the Divisions of Educational Psychology and Evaluation and Measurement of the American Psychological Association.

Robert J. Sternberg is IBM Professor of Psychology and Education in the Department of Psychology at Yale University. He is author of *Beyond IQ, Metaphors of Mind,* and *Successful Intelligence* and co-edited *Conceptions of Giftedness* (with Janet Davidson). He is Associate Director of the National Center for Research on the Gifted and Talented, funded by the U.S. Office of Educational Research and Improvement, and is currently involved in a number of research projects on gifted education. His particular interests are in abilities, creativity, and learning styles. Professor Sternberg has received numerous awards, including the Distinguished Scholar Award of the National Association for Gifted Children. He has also served as President of the American Psychological Association.

Abraham J. Tannenbaum is Professor Emeritus of Education and Psychology at Teachers College, Columbia University, Department of Special Education. As a Fulbright Professor, he spent one year at Hebrew University in Jerusalem teaching and conducting research on his school-readiness program for disadvantaged children. Among many publications, two books are *Adolescent Attitudes Toward Academic Brilliance* (1962) and *Gifted Children: Psychological and Educational Per-spectives* (1983). He served as President of the Metropolitan Association for the Gifted and President of the National Council for Children with Behavioral

Disorders. Among many plaques he received are Intertel's Award for Research on the Gifted and the Distinguished Scholar Award from the National Association for Gifted Children.

Joyce VanTassel-Baska is Jody and Layton Smith Professor of Education at the College of William and Mary, where she has developed a graduate program and a research and development center in gifted education. Formerly, she founded and directed the Center for Talent Development at Northwestern University. She has served as State Director of Gifted Programs in Illinois, as Regional Director of a gifted service center in the Chicago area, as Coordinator of Gifted Programs for the Toledo, Ohio, Public School system, and as a teacher of gifted high school students in English and Latin. She has been a consultant on gifted education in over forty states and for the U.S. Department of Education, National Association of Secondary School Principals, and American Association of School Administrators. She is a past President of the Association for the Gifted of the Council for Exceptional Children, and a past member of the Board of Directors of the National Association for Gifted children. Professor VanTassel-Baska has published over 150 monographs, book chapters, and articles, plus the four recent books *Excellence in Educating the Gifted, Developing Verbal Talent* (with Dana Johnson and Linda Boyce), *Comprehensive Curriculum for Gifted Learners,* and *Planning Effective Curriculum for the Gifted.* She is Editor of *Gifted and Talented International.* Numerous awards include an Outstanding Faculty Award from the State Council for Higher Education in Virginia, a Faculty Award from Phi Beta Kappa, and a Distinguished Scholar Award from the National Association for Gifted Children.

Catya von Károlyi is a doctoral candidate in psychology at Boston College, where she works with Ellen Winner. She investigates atypical development, including cognitive and socio-emotional correlates of extreme intellectual giftedness, visual-spatial processing in dyslexia, and children's awareness of issues. She is a past President, Vice President, and Member of the Board of Directors of the Hollingworth Center for Highly Gifted Children and has served on advisory committees on gifted education.

Herbert J. Walberg is Research Professor of Education at the University of Illinois at Chicago. He has written or edited more than fifty books and contributed more than 380 articles to educational and psychological research journals on such topics as educational effectiveness and exceptional human accomplishments. Professor Walberg currently is studying winners of the International Olympiad of Mathematics from Japan, the People's Republic of China, and the United States. He has testified before U.S. congressional committees and state and federal courts. A Fellow of four academic organizations, Professor Walberg has won a number of awards for his scholarship and is one of a dozen U.S. Fellows of the International Academy of Education.

Deborah B. Williams currently is Research Evaluator for the Gifted, Talented and Enriched Academic Programs for the Chicago Public Schools. She previously was Associate Professor of Education at North Park University, Chicago. Dr. Williams has presented papers in South Africa, Italy, Venezuela, Canada, and the United States. She received her Ph.D. in Public Policy Analysis from the University of Illinois at Chicago.

Ellen Winner is Professor of Psychology at Boston College and Senior Research Associate at Project Zero, Harvard Graduate School of Education. She is the author of *Invented Worlds: The Psychology of the Arts, The Point of Words: Children's Understanding of Metaphor and Irony,* and *Gifted Children: Myths and Realities,* for which she received the Alpha Sigma Nu National Jesuit Book Award in Science. She was the co-editor of a double issue of the *Journal of Aesthetic Education* entitled "The Arts and Academic Achievement: What the Evidence Shows." Professor Winner is a past President of Division 10 (Psychology and the Arts) of the American Psychological Association, which in 2000 awarded her the Rudolf Arnheim Award for Outstanding Research by a Senior Scholar. Her research focuses on the psychology of the arts, creativity, and giftedness.

Susie Zeiser is a doctoral student in Educational Psychology at the University of Illinois at Chicago. Formerly a teacher of gifted children, she is engaged in the study of eminent girls and women. She participates with a group of a dozen scholars who study the early childhood traits and conditions of notable American women, and is concentrating on those renowned for their anthropological and feminist contributions.

Guest Foreword: The Third Edition Is Longer and Better Than its Two Predecessors

JULIAN C. STANLEY, *Director of the Study of Mathematically Precocious Youth (SMPY), Johns Hopkins University*

*T*his distinguished standard of the gifted-child field is enlarged a bit (31 chapters in the first edition, 44 chapters in the second edition, and 47 now), pruned a little, and supplemented appropriately. The ten new chapters are "The Science and Politics of Intelligence in Gifted Education," by Linda S. Gottfredson of the University of Delaware; "Transforming Gifts into Talents: The DMGT as a Developmental Theory," by Françoys Gagné of the Université du Quebéc à Montréal, Canada; "A Conception of Giftedness and Its Relationship to the Development of Social Capital," by Joseph S. Renzulli of the University of Connecticut; "In the Habit of Skillful Thinking," by Arthur Costa of the California State University—Sacramento; "Artistic Giftedness," by Ellen Winner of the Harvard Graduate School and Boston College, and Gail Martino of the Gillette Advanced Technology Center; "High Risk Gifted Learners," by Ken Seeley of the Colorado Foundation for Families and Children in Denver; "Gifted Education in Rural Schools," by Nicholas Colangelo, Susan G. Assouline, Clar M. Baldus, and Jennifer K. New of The University of Iowa; "Teachers of the Gifted: Gifted Teachers," by Laurie J. Croft of The University of Iowa; "Exceptional Spatial Abilities," by David Lubinski of Vanderbilt University; and "Technology and the Gifted," by Michael C. Pyryt of the University of Calgary in Canada.

Six chapters from the second edition have been eliminated or incorporated into new chapters. Miraca U. M. Gross from Australia has taken over the late A. Harry Passow's excellent "International Perspective on Gifted Education," renamed simply "International Perspectives." All of the chapters retained from the second edition have been edited, revised, and updated by their authors.

Because of its extensive coverage and high standards, this unique handbook can be used well, albeit selectively, as the most comprehensive textbook for courses in the education of gifted, talented, and creative youth. It is also invaluable for gifted-child specialists, graduate students, teachers at all levels, school administrators, educational-policy makers (oh, how I wish the U.S. Department of Education would absorb its contents!), school-board members, parents of the gifted, Mensa members, program officers of philanthropic foundations, journalists, TV anchors, and even intellectually curious kids themselves. I can think of no one even remotely concerned with talent and creativity who would not benefit from at least some of its contents.

Well done, editors of this revision! It should stand as the jewel in the crown of the field for a number of years, until you foresighted, energetic specialists produce the fourth edition.

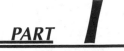

Introduction

We begin this volume with three chapters that survey themes, problems, and significant events and contributions in gifted education, with a close look at that most central concept in giftedness, intelligence.

Chapter 1 by Nicholas Colangelo and Gary A. Davis highlights the need for special services and programs for gifted students—"our most precious natural resource"—and some traditional and contemporary issues and topics; for example, the equity–excellence dilemma, elitism, anti-intellectualism, the National Excellence report, and the detracking and cooperative learning movements. Brief historical overviews of gifted education worldwide and in America, along with momentous developments in intelligence testing, put today's investment in gifted education into its larger context. The chapter ends with a summary description of the seven sections of this book.

In Chapter 2, James J. Gallagher reiterates that America's students are less well educated than foreign students. He notes that gifted students have richer knowledge structures and superior metathinking skills, and acknowledges the impact of Gardner's and Sternberg's multiple types of intelligence. Some, not all, gifted students are creative, notes Gallagher, which requires favorable personality traits. While gifted students are above average on social and emotional adjustment, some face depression, anxiety, and even suicide. Gallagher mentions the increasing concern for identifying and teaching ethnically diverse and economically disadvantaged gifted students. He notes also the challenges of working with gifted un-derachievers, gifted females, and "twice exceptional" (gifted/disabled) students; the benefits of acceleration; other strategies for differentiating the curriculum (enrichment, deeper sophistication, problem-based learning); grouping gifted students for improved achievement and self-concepts; homeschooling the gifted; and the potential of technology.

In Chapter 3, Linda S. Gottfredson reviews research and conclusions on general intelligence (g). Such research is unpopular, she notes, because it confirms that only some people can achieve at high levels. An underlying g is common to all broad and specific mental abilities. Looking at the normal, bell-shaped distribution of intelligence, Gottfredson reminds us that IQ 160 is double the distance between IQ 100 and 130, and that such a child should not be educated with age mates. IQs are stable through childhood and adolescence, but decline with age. Racial-ethnic differences also are stable. One's processing power versus accumulated knowledge are reflected in *fluid* versus *crystallized* intelligence. Despite logic and popular belief, heritability increases with age; that is, the influence of environment on IQ decreases over the years. The niche-seeking theory states that our environments are partly selected by our g. Also, our family's collective genes influence our sensitivity (e.g., to drugs) and exposure to other aspects of our environments (gene–environment interactions). Intelligence predicts important life outcomes, for example, education, occupational level, and, as children, assignment to special education or gifted programs.

Introduction and Overview

NICHOLAS COLANGELO, *University of Iowa*
GARY A. DAVIS, *University of Wisconsin, Madison*

Nurturing the talents of our most gifted and talented children is one of the most exciting yet controversial issues in education today. The base of the controversy is society's "love–hate" relationship with giftedness and talent (e.g., Benbow & Stanley, 1996; Gallagher & Weiss, 1979). On one hand, we admire the talent and drive of individuals who rise from humble backgrounds. On the other, our nation has a long-standing commitment to egalitarianism, reflected in that mighty phrase "All men are created equal." Both educators and people on the street are caught in the confusing tension between encouraging yet restraining individual accomplishment (Gardner, 1982).

Society swings back and forth between the goals of equity versus excellence. When excellence is of concern—as in 1957 when the Russians' Sputnik beat America into space and 1983 when the *A Nation at Risk* report jolted American educators—programs for the brightest quickly receive priority. When equity is the primary concern, as in the 1960s, early 1970s, and resurfacing in the 1990s, planning suitable educational programs for gifted students is put on a back burner or in the closet. *Equity* typically is translated as helping slow-learning, disadvantaged, and other at-risk students become more equal. Unfortunately, treating issues of equity and excellence as antagonistic and mutually exclusive is destructive to the development of sound educational practices that meet the educational needs of every individual student.

It seems that educators, politicians, and others either defend or attack gifted education with enthusiasm, yet typically with little or no factual information. The following are some themes that help account for the ambivalent, even hostile reactions to gifted education, or otherwise lead educators and others to ignore the needs of the gifted.

Giving to the "Haves"

Some resent giving special educational privileges to those already basking in talent and who appear to succeed with little or no effort. In fact, it is damaging to talented children and youth to require them to cope with a system that ignores their capabilities, ignores their true educational needs, and requires them to proceed at the pace of below-average students. It also is an unfortunate misperception to equate giftedness with effortlessness. Regardless of native ability, achieving excellence in school or any career field takes hard work—gifted students in G/T programs are not "getting something for nothing." The excellent research by Bloom and Sosniak (1981) and studies of eminent individuals emphasize the effort and commitment required to develop high talent.[1]

The Detracking Movement

Jeannie Oakes (1985), Samuel Roundfield Lucas (1999), and others have argued that tracking plans are racist and discriminatory, deprive slow-track students of educational opportunities, and damage their self-concepts. Such arguments certainly touch the heartstrings of democratic-minded persons. Unfortunately, this "national hysteria" (Reis et al., 1992) has led some districts not only to abolish their accelerated classes, but special classes for the gifted and gifted programs themselves. Said Renzulli (1991a), with heterogeneous grouping "bright kids learn nothing new until January."[2]

---

1. See Chapter 19 by Sosniak, Chapter 27 by Walberg, Williams, and Zeiser, and Chapter 28 by Simonton.

2. See Chapter 21 by Kulik for a discussion of tracking, ability grouping and the gifted.

Cooperative Learning

Detracking is one recent damaging reform movement, cooperative learning is the other. A prototype cooperative learning group consists of four students—two average students, a slower learner, and a fast learner—who work together to complete a worksheet, solve a problem, or otherwise master material. Proponents, who believe cooperative learning should be the primary teaching strategy, cite gains in achievement, motivation, cognitive growth, social skills, and self-confidence, as well as reduced classroom management problems (e.g., Slavin, Madden, & Stevens, 1990). The teaching strategy probably is highly effective—except for gifted students, who (1) prefer not to work in groups because they can learn faster alone; (2) typically get stuck doing most of the work; (3) mainly teach the others, and, most importantly; (4) miss opportunities for accelerated or enriched work that matches their abilities, particularly with other gifted students. In short, cooperative learning diverts attention from more valid educational needs of gifted students.[3]

Perhaps, surprisingly, a benefit of the detracking and cooperative learning movements is the growing attention to building the skills and talents of *all* students, including gifted ones. Dubbed *talent development,* the best-known strategy is to bring creativity, thinking skills, and other enrichment into the regular classroom for everyone—while still selecting the top 15 or 20 percent for more specialized work (Renzulli, 1994; Renzulli & Reis, 1985).[4] Using the phrase *talent development* also circumvents the awkward social problem of labeling some students "gifted" and, by exclusion, the others "not gifted" (Treffinger & Feldhusen, 1996).

Elitism and Anti-Intellectualism

Elitism includes the fear that one person or group may be perceived as inherently superior or of more value than others. Fear of elitism, however, sometimes leads to a false equation of recognizing differences with holding an elitist point of view. For example, recognizing the skill of a piano virtuoso does not indicate a belief that this skill makes the person "better" than others as a human being. Youngsters sometimes are perceived as "elite" for a variety of reasons, such as outstanding athletic abilities, good looks, or family wealth. The children themselves may act elitist—egotistical and self-important. However, elitism in these areas somehow is considered more acceptable than in children who are intellectually gifted. As a group, gifted youngsters tend to be more understanding and modest than others (e.g., Goldberg, 1965), although snobbishness of gifted students has been reported (Starko, 1990).

Anti-intellectualism is expressed by some who are hostile to the intellectually gifted and to intellectual pursuits generally. Note that if a youngster excels in sports, dance, art, music, or school politics, anti-intellectualism does not arise. However, if a student is labeled *intellectually gifted* and achieves at high levels, that is another matter. While society allows and applauds certain areas of talent, high intellectual ability spurs ambivalence. Intellectual giftedness appears to threaten the self-esteem of others, both youngsters and adults, in a way that other talents do not.

Pretending We Don't Know

In the field of gifted education we focus on issues of individual differences in intelligence. The popular media and commentators in the field have led the public to believe that there is little definite knowledge about intelligence. Often, when there is controversy regarding intelligence, the public is presented with information that proclaims "there is much we don't know about intelligence" and that studies that make definitive statements about intelligence and individual and group differences in intelligence are either flawed or inconsistent with other research that provides opposite results. Since our second edition of the *Handbook,* an excellent special issue of the journal *Intelligence* has appeared, guest edited by Linda Gottfredson,[5] titled Special Issue: Intelligence and Social Policy (*Intelligence, 24*(1), 1997). The lead article includes a statement signed by fifty-two experts regarding what is mainstream science regarding intelligence. These experts agree that intelligence has a genetic component, that real differences in intelligence exist, that these can be measured fairly by intelligence tests, that differences are found between races, and that intelligence influences life outcomes (Gottfredson, 1997).

It is important to maintain the distinction between science and politics. It can be the case that science

---

3. See Chapter 22 by Robinson.

4. See Chapter 14 by Renzulli and Reis for an overview of the talent development approach.

5. See Chapter 3 by Gottfredson.

provides us with evidence counter to our values or politics. Gifted education is a field with politically charged issues, and it must strive to recognize these issues while at the same time providing the most accurate information as we know it.

"They Will Make It on Their Own"

One common argument against special educational programs for the gifted is the belief that these students "will make it on their own." A corollary is "Give the help to students who really need it." However, many students labeled *gifted* do *not* make it on their own. Inadequate curriculum, unsupportive educators, social and emotional difficulties, peer pressures, and inadequate parenting all can extinguish the potentially high accomplishment of gifted children and adolescents.

The Excitement of Educating Gifted Students

The above are some problems confronting gifted education and gifted students. More difficulties will be noted in later chapters. Nonetheless, there exists tremendous excitement about giftedness. As Sternberg and Davidson (1986) stated, "Giftedness is arguably the most precious natural resource a civilization can have" (p. ix). Children who produce and create well beyond our expectations invigorate us and show us the possibilities of human potential. Adults of eminence have left their mark in helping societies develop technologically, aesthetically, and morally. Your authors have never met teachers more excited about teaching than those who work with groups of gifted children.

Historical Overview of Giftedness and Gifted Education

Giftedness Around the World

Identifying and educating gifted youth has intrigued virtually all societies in recorded history. In ancient Sparta, military skills were valued so exclusively that "giftedness" was defined by outstanding skills in combat, warfare, and leadership. In Athens, upper-class young boys went to private schools for academics and physical fitness training. Older boys were taught mathematics, logic, rhetoric, politics, culture, and "disputation" by sophists. Plato's Academy selected both young men and women based on intelligence and physical stamina, rather than social position. In Rome, although higher education was reserved for males, some gifted women emerged who greatly affected Roman society—for example, the Roman matron Cornelia, mother of statesmen Gaius and Tiberius Gracchus (Good, 1960).

Renaissance Europe sought out and rewarded its gifted artists, architects, and writers with wealth and honor, for example, Michelangelo, Leonardo da Vinci, Boccacio, Bernini, and Dante.

Beginning with the Tang Dynasty (A.D. 618), early China brought its child prodigies to the imperial court, where their gifts were nurtured. China at this time anticipated four principles of contemporary gifted education (Tsuin-Chen, 1961). First, the Chinese accepted a multiple-talent conception of giftedness, valuing literary ability, leadership, imagination, reading speed, reasoning, and other talents. Second, they recognized that some precocious youth would grow up to be average; some average youth would later show gifts; and true child prodigies would show gifts and talents throughout their lives. Third, they realized that abilities of even the most gifted would not develop fully without special training. Fourth, they believed that education should be available to children of all social classes, but that they should be educated according to their abilities.

During the Tokugawa period in Japan (1604–1868), Samurai children received training in history, the Confucian classics, composition, calligraphy, moral values, etiquette, and martial arts, whereas poor children learned loyalty, obedience, and diligence.

Gifted Education in America

In early America, some gifted youth were accommodated only in the sense that attending secondary school and college was based on both academic achievement and the ability to pay the fees (Newland, 1976). With compulsory attendance laws, schooling became available to all children, but few special services were available for the gifted. Some noteworthy exceptions are these:

- In 1870 St. Louis initiated tracking, allowing some students to complete the first eight grades in less than eight years.
- In 1884 Woburn, Massachusetts, created the "Doubled Tillage Plan": After the first semester of

first grade, bright children were accelerated directly into the second semester of second grade.

- In 1886 Elizabeth, New Jersey, began a tracking system that permitted bright students to progress more rapidly than others.
- In 1891 schools in Cambridge, Massachusetts, developed a similar double-track plan. Students capable of even more accelerated work were taught by special tutors.
- About 1900 some "rapid progress" classes telescoped three years of school work into two.
- In 1902 Worcester, Massachusetts, opened the first special school for gifted children.
- In 1916 special classes for gifted children were created in Los Angeles and Cincinnati; Urbana, Illinois, followed in 1919, and Manhattan and Cleveland in 1922.

By about 1920 approximately two-thirds of all large cities had created some type of program for gifted students. In the 1920s and 1930s, however, interest in gifted education took a nose dive for two reasons. First, equity and democracy took center stage. Dean Worcester referred to the 1920s as "the age of the common man" and "the age of mediocrity, when the idea was to have everybody just as near alike as they could be . . . administrators had as their ideal to bring everyone to the standard, but they had no interest in carrying anybody beyond the standard" (Getzels, 1977, p. 264). Second, the Great Depression reduced most people's concern to survival. Providing special opportunities for gifted youngsters was not a priority.

Significant Events Preceding Gifted Education Today

Historical events underlying today's strong interest in gifted education centers on a half-dozen people, an intelligence test, one Russian satellite, and three national reports.

Sir Francis Galton (1822–1911), younger cousin to Charles Darwin, is credited with the earliest significant research and writing on intelligence and intelligence testing. Impressed by cousin Charles's *Origin of the Species,* Galton reasoned that intelligence was related to the keenness of one's senses, which would have survival value. His efforts to measure intelligence therefore involved tests of visual and auditory acuity, tactile sensitivity, and reaction time. A hereditary basis of intelligence appeared to be confirmed by

his observation that distinguished persons seemed to come from distinguished families, a conclusion reported in his most famous book *Hereditary Genius* (Galton, 1869).

At the turn of the century, Alfred Binet, with his colleague T. Simon, was hired by government officials in Paris to devise a test to identify dull children who would not benefit from regular classes and therefore required special training. At the time, some children were placed in schools for the retarded because they were too quiet, too aggressive, or had problems with speech, hearing, or vision. A direct test of intelligence was needed.

A number of Binet's tests failed—hand-squeezing strength, hand speed in moving 50 cm, the amount of forehead pressure that causes pain, detecting differences in hand-held weights, and reaction time to sounds or in naming colors. However, scores on tests of memory, judgment, reasoning, comprehension, and the ability to pay attention tended to agree with the criterion, teachers' judgments of intelligence.

Binet gave us the concept of *mental age,* the notion that children grow in intelligence and that any given child may be measurably ahead or behind the typical intellectual level for his or her actual age. A related notion is that at any given chronological age, children who learn the most do so partly because of greater intelligence.

In 1910, Henry Goddard successfully identified the intelligence of 400 "feebleminded" children with the Binet-Simon tests, and in 1911 he summarized his evaluation of 2,000 normal children (Stanley, 1976). The tests successfully measured intelligence not only at below-average levels, but at average and above-average levels as well.

Stanford psychologist Lewis Terman made two historically significant contributions to gifted education, which earned him the title of father of the gifted education movement. First, he supervised the modification of the Binet-Simon tests, producing in 1916 the grandfather of all American intelligence tests, the Stanford-Binet Intelligence Scale. The test was revised in 1937, 1960, and 1986.

Terman's second contribution was his identification and longitudinal study of 1,528 gifted children, 856 boys and 672 girls, published in four volumes of *Genetic Studies of Genius* (Terman, 1925; Terman Burks, & Jensen, 1930; Terman & Oden, 1947, 1959). They have been the most studied group of gifted individuals in the world. In 1921, Terman and his colleagues began administering the Stanford-

Binet test to students initially identified by teachers as highly intelligent. The final sample consisted of students from Los Angeles, San Francisco, Oakland, Berkeley, and Alameda, with an average age of 12, who scored above IQ 135, although most were above 140. Jewish children tended to be overrepresented; minority children were underrepresented (e.g., there were two Armenians and one Native American). Chinese children were excluded because they attended special Asian schools at the time. Nearly one-third were from professional families. Thus far, nine major contacts—field studies or mailings—across more than a half century have traced their educational, professional, psychological, social, and even physical development. As a group, they were above average in all of these areas, although no geniuses of the stature of Einstein or Picasso emerged (see, e.g., Goleman, 1980; Sears, 1979; Sears & Barbee, 1977).

According to Stanley (1976), Galton was the grandfather of the gifted-child movement, Binet the midwife, Terman the father, and Columbia University's Leta Hollingworth the nurturant mother. Her pioneering contributions consisted of personal efforts supporting gifted education and gifted students in the New York City area, from about 1916 until her death in 1939, and the publication of two major books, *Gifted Children: Their Nature and Nurture* (Hollingworth, 1926) and *Children above 180 IQ Stanford-Binet: Origin and Development* (Hollingworth, 1942). In contrast with Terman's accurate conclusion that gifted children, as a group, are more emotionally stable, Hollingworth drew attention to the strong emotional problems and counseling needs of many gifted students, arguing that the greater the gift, the greater the need for "emotional education."

The last significant historical event to predate the mid-1970s resurgence of interest in gifted education was the launching in 1957 of the Soviet satellite Sputnik. To many, this represented a clear technological defeat—Soviet scientific minds had beaten ours hands down. Popular reports criticized American education, compared it with Russian education, or emphasized that America ignored gifted children. For example, a 1959 report entitled *Soviet Commitment to Education* (First Official U.S. Education Mission to the USSR, 1959) claimed that the typical Russian high school graduate had completed ten years of math, five years of physics, five years of biology, five years of a foreign language, four years of chemistry, and one year of astronomy. Tannenbaum (1979) described the aftermath of Sputnik as a "total talent mo-bilization." Academic coursework was telescoped (condensed) for bright students; college courses were offered in high school; and foreign languages were taught in elementary classes. Acceleration and ability grouping were used, efforts were made to identify gifted and talented minority children, and new math and science curricula were developed. High schools glowed with new concern for high scholastic standards and career-mindedness. Bright students were expected to take tough courses—to fulfill their potential and submit their developed abilities for service to the nation (Tannenbaum, 1979). The scare of Sputnik and the interest in educating gifted and talented students wore off in about five years.

Today's interest in giftedness began in the early 1970s and has been heavily influenced by the publication of three national reports. The first report in 1972 was to the Congress of the United States, titled *Education of the Gifted and Talented*. This report is commonly known as the "Marland Report" in recognition of the U.S. Commissioner of Education S. P. Marland, who spearheaded the report. The Marland Report brought gifted education to the national forefront. Among other things, it indicated that 3 to 5 percent of the nation's students could be considered gifted, that most gifted students were not having their educational needs met, that differential education for the gifted was a low national priority, and that gifted children without a suitable education could suffer psychological damage and permanent impairment of their abilities. One outcome was an aggressive role by the federal government in promoting and financially supporting programs for gifted and talented students. Probably the most lasting influence of the report was the federal definition of gifted and talented, which delineated six areas of giftedness based on achievement or potential: general intellectual ability, specific academic aptitude, creative or productive thinking, leadership ability, ability in the visual and performing arts, and psychomotor ability. This definition in its various modifications and adaptations still provides the bases for many of today's school programs.

In 1983 the *A Nation at Risk* report by the National Commission on Excellence in Education held up an unforgiving mirror to the nation. A brief but critical report, the Commission took the nation's education to task for low standards, loss of academic focus, and losing ground to other nations in educating its youth. While the report was not about gifted education per se, many of its comments spoke to neglect of high academic standards and abandonment of top academic students. The result of the *A Nation at Risk* report was a positive attention to gifted education, at least briefly.

The third of the reports was in 1993 (the United States apparently works in decade cycles when it comes to reports affecting gifted education), titled *National Excellence: A Case for Developing America's Talent,* by the U.S. Department of Education (1993) with Patricia O'Connell Ross as Project Director (see O'Connell Ross, Chapter 47). This latest report indicated that America had a "quiet crisis" in educating its talented students. A number of issues were highlighted, including America's ambivalence toward intellect, the importance of social/emotional issues, issues of rural schools and urban schools, the challenges of identifying culturally diverse students, and again the warning of international competition especially in science and mathematics. The 1993 report recognized the very limited role of the federal government since the years immediately following the Marland report. In 1988, the Jacob K. Javits Gifted and Talented Education Act reestablished a federal presence, albeit a limited one. *The National Excellence* report supported the Javits Act and promoted as the new federal definition the definition in the Javits Gifted and Talented Education Act:

> Children and youth with outstanding talent perform or show the potential for performing at remarkably high levels of accomplishment when compared with others of their, age, experience, or environment.
>
> These children and youth exhibit high performance capability in intellectual, creative, and/or artistic areas, possess an unusual leadership capacity, or excel in specific academic fields. They require services or activities not ordinarily provided by the schools.
>
> Outstanding talents are present in children and youth from all cultural groups, across the economic strata, and in all areas of human endeavor. (U.S. Department of Education, 1993, p. 3)

The current federal definition emphasizes different areas of giftedness, similar to the Marland definition, determining giftedness in comparison to peers in their environment, and acknowledges giftedness across cultures and economic strata. The *National Excellence* report has not had the dramatic effects of its two predecessors in part because its tone and message are "quiet," much like its assessment of the national crisis.

Handbook of Gifted Education

The book is divided into seven main sections. We believe they cover the major topic areas and issues in gifted education.

1. An "Introduction" focuses on the need for gifted education, a brief history, issues and trends, needs of special groups, and current social policies relating to gifted students and gifted education.

2. "Conceptions and Identification" presents definitions of talents, gifts, and giftedness; intellectual and affective components of giftedness; explanations and interpretations of intelligence and their implications for the gifted; and fairness issues and methods in identifying gifted and talented students.

3. "Instructional Models and Practices" is an extensive section that covers acceleration and enrichment programs, procedures, philosophies, and activities that foster academic and creative growth. More specifically, this section includes curriculum models that structure and guide acceleration and enrichment practices; mentorships; secondary school programs; parent influence; examinations of ability grouping and cooperative learning as they relate to gifted students; and an often neglected but vital component, evaluating gifted programs.

4. "Creativity and Thinking Skills," as the name suggests, includes discussions of interpretations of creativity, the challenge of identifying and teaching the creatively gifted, a taxonomy of thinking skills that guides teaching, creativity in the arts, and components and precursors of eminence and genius.

5. "Psychological and Counseling Services" focuses on the personal, educational, and career counseling needs of the gifted and how to plan suitable counseling for gifted students and their families. The section includes a close look at the interrelated topics of motivation, underachievement, the delinquent gifted, perfectionism, and emotional giftedness—an intriguing phenomena of high excitability, sensitivity, emotional understanding, and moral and ethical concern by some highly gifted students.

6. While many sections address differences among gifted groups, "Populations of Giftedness" looks specifically at young children, adolescents, girls and women, minority students, and students in rural areas. One chapter addresses extreme precocity and IQ and the illogical savant syndrome.

7. Finally, "Special Topics" presents a potpourri of pertinent subjects: for example, an international focus in teaching gifted students, teacher training, students with extraordinary spatial capabilities, the uses and benefits of computers with gifted students, legal and ethical issues, and the U.S. government's view of giftedness and its implications for the future.

SUMMARY AND CONCLUSIONS

Gifted education has had an uneven history in American education. The "love–hate" relationship society has had with gifted education has led to both an energetic focus on gifted students and a near total ignoring of their needs. Important events such as Sputnik and reports such as the *Marland Report, A Nation at Risk,* and the *National Excellence* report have been markers in the history of gifted education. It is important to stabilize the educational focus on gifted and talented students so that their needs are met on a continuing basis rather than for political expediency. The *Handbook of Gifted Education* since 1991 has been a statement for the importance of continued educational attention to gifted and talented students.

QUESTIONS FOR THOUGHT AND DISCUSSION

1. Explain the equity–excellence issue in education. What do you see as the trend today?

2. On one hand, gifted education faces criticisms of "giving to the haves," "elitism," and "They will make it on their own"—which suggest eliminating gifted programs. On the other hand is the core issue: Should we ignore the educational needs of bright and talented students—and let them be bored, frustrated, and educated below their capabilities? What is your resolution? What should be the future trend?

3. Briefly summarize the historic Galton, Binet/Simon, and Terman contributions to the concepts of intelligence and giftedness.

4. Do you agree with the briefly summarized central conclusions of the *National Excellence* report—especially the often-cited "quiet crisis" phrase? Explain.

REFERENCES

Benbow, C. P., & Stanley, J. C. (1996). Inequality in equity: How "equity" can lead to inequity for high potential students. *Psychology, Public Policy, and Law, 2,* 249–292.

Bloom, B. S., & Sosniak, L. A. (1981). Talent development vs. schooling. *Educational Leadership, 39,* 86–94.

First Official U.S. Education Mission to the USSR. (1959). *Soviet commitment to education.* Bulletin 1959, No. 16. Washington, DC: Office of Education, U.S. Department of Health, Education and Welfare.

Gallagher, J. J., & Weiss, P. (1979). *The education of gifted and talented children and youth.* Washington, DC: Council for Basic Education.

Gardner, J. W. (1982). *Excellence: Can we be equal and excellent too?* (2nd ed.). New York: Norton.

Getzels, J. W. (1977). General discussion immediately after the Terman Memorial Symposium. In J. C. Stanley, W. C. George, & C. H. Solano (Eds.), *The gifted and the creative: A fifty-year perspective* (pp. 225–269). Baltimore: Johns Hopkins University Press.

Gottfredson, L. S. (1997). Mainstream silence on intelligence: An editorial with 52 signatures, history, and bibliography. *Intelligence, 24*(1), 13–22.

Goldberg, M. L. (1956). *Research on the talented.* New York: Bureau of Publications, Columbia University.

Goleman, D. (1980). 1,528 little geniuses and how they grew. *Psychology Today, 13*(9), 28–43.

Good, H. G. (1960). *A history of western education* (2nd ed.). New York: Macmillan.

Hollingworth, L. S. (1926). *Gifted children: Their nature and nurture.* New York: Macmillan.

Hollingworth, L. S. (1942). *Children above 180 IQ Stanford-Binet: Origin and development.* New York: World Book.

Lucas, S. R. (1999). *Tracking inequality: Stratification and mobility in American high schools.* New York: Teachers College Press.

Newland, T. E. (1976). *The gifted in historical perspective.* Englewood Cliffs, NJ: Prentice-Hall.

Oakes, J. (1985). *Keeping track.* New Haven, CT: Yale University Press.

Reis, S. M., Westberg, K., Kulikowich, J., Caillard, F., Herbert, T., Purcell, J., Rogers, J., & Smist, J. (1992, April). Modifying regular classroom instruction with curriculum compacting. In J. S. Renzulli (Chair), *Regular classroom practices with gifted students: Findings from the National Research Center on the Gifted and Talented.* Symposium conducted at the annual meeting of the American Educational Research Association, San Francisco.

Renzulli, J. S. (1991). The National Research Center on the Gifted and Talented: The dream, the design, and the destination. *Gifted Children Quarterly, 35,* 73–80.

Renzulli, J. S. (1994). *Schools for talent development: A practical plan for total school improvement.* Mansfield Center, CT: Creative Learning Press.

Renzulli, J. S., & Reis, S. M. (1985). *The schoolwide enrichment model: A comprehensive plan for educational excellence.* Mansfield Center, CT: Creative Learning Press.

Sears, P. S. (1979). The Terman genetic studies of genius, 1922–1972. In A. H. Passow (Ed.), *The gifted and the talented* (pp. 75–96). Chicago: National Society for the Study of Education.

Sears P. S., & Barbee, A. H. (1977). Career and life satisfactions among Terman's gifted women. In J. C. Stanley, W. C. George, & C. H. Solano (Eds.), *The gifted and the creative: A fifty-year perspective* (pp. 28–65). Baltimore: Johns Hopkins University Press.

Slavin, R. E., Madden, N. A., & Stevens, R. J. (1990). Cooperative learning models for the 3 R's. *Educational Leadership, 47*(4), 22–29.

Stanley, J. C. (1976). Concern for intellectually talented youths: How it originated. and fluctuated. *Journal of Clinical Child Psychology, 5,* 38–42.

Starko, A. J. (1990). Life and death of a gifted program: Lessons not yet learned. *Roeper Review, 13,* 33–38.

Sternberg, R. J., & Davidson, J. E. (Eds.). (1986). *Conceptions of giftedness.* New York: Cambridge University Press.

Tannenbaum, A. J. (1979). Pre-Sputnik to post-Watergate concern about the gifted. In A. H. Passow (Ed.), *The gifted and the talented* (pp. 5–27). Chicago: National Society for the Study of Education.

Terman, L. M. (1925). *Genetic studies of genius: Vol. 1. Mental and physical traits of a thousand gifted children.* Stanford: Stanford University Press.

Terman, L. M., Burks, B. S., & Jensen, D. W. (1930). *Genetic studies of genius: Vol. 3. The promise of youth: Follow-up studies of a thousand gifted children.* Stanford, CA: Stanford University Press.

Terman, L. M., & Oden, M. H. (1947). *Genetic studies of genius: Vol. 4. The gifted child grows up.* Stanford: Stanford University Press.

Terman, L. M., & Oden, M. H. (1959). *Genetic studies of genius: Vol. 5. The gifted group at midlife: Thirty-five years' follow-up of a superior group.* Stanford: Stanford University Press.

Treffinger, D. J., & Feldhusen, J. F. (1996). Talent recognition and development: Successor to gifted education. *Journal for the Education of the Gifted, 19,* 181–193.

Tsuin-Chen, O. (1961). Some facts and ideas about talent and genius in Chinese history. In G. Z. F. Bereday & J. A. Lauwerys (Eds.), *Concepts of excellence in education: The yearbook of education.* New York: Harcourt, Brace and World.

U.S. Department of Health, Education, and Welfare. (1972). *Education of the gifted and talented.* Washington, DC: Author.

U.S. Department of Education, National Commission on Excellence in Education. (1983). *A Nation at Risk: The imperative for educational reform.* Washington, DC: Author.

U.S. Department of Education, Office of Educational Research and Improvement. *National Excellence: A case for developing America's talent.* Washington, DC: Author.

2

Issues and Challenges in the Education of Gifted Students

JAMES J. GALLAGHER, *University of North Carolina—Chapel Hill*

The education of gifted children in the twenty-first century surely will be shaped by many forces at large in society and in the broader field of education. In the past, this field has prospered from rivalry with the Soviet Union and suffered from issues of cultural diversity. Perhaps the growing realization of the importance of the information society will trigger new initiatives.

In public policy parlance, education of gifted students is a "cool" problem, one that has long-term consequences for society but does not demand the sort of short-term action and allocation of resources required by "hot" problems such as school violence or segregation (Gallagher, 2000).

One of the nagging problems that do bother thoughtful people is the consistent finding that American students, even the best American students, are not competitive with students from other countries in areas such as mathematics and science. The *National Excellence* report (Ross, 1993) summarized this finding as follows:

- Only a small percentage of students are prepared for challenging college-level work, as measured by tests that are not very exacting or difficult.
- The highest achieving U.S. students fare poorly when compared with similar students in other nations.
- Students going on to a university education in other countries are expected to know more than U.S. students and to be able to think and write analytically about that knowledge on challenging exams.

A similar story was told by the Third International Mathematics and Science Study (TIMSS, 1997), which stressed the low performance of American students compared with students in other countries. Even twelfth-grade students enrolled in advanced calculus and physics classes could perform only at the level of average students from other countries in mathematics and science.

Major Issues

The following are my candidates for significant issues, and there are many subissues within these broad areas of concern.

- How do we now understand intelligence, and how does that view affect educational programs for gifted students?
- How do cultural differences affect our identification processes and special programs for gifted students?
- How do we plan for special subgroups of gifted students?
- How do we adapt educational programs and goals for gifted students?

The Nature of Intelligence

As our knowledge of intelligence increases and expands, a portrait of intelligence as a huge storehouse of information has been replaced by a construct of intelligence as a series of interconnected knowledge structures, a network of interrelationships. The gifted student is one who has richer and more complex knowledge structures and, more important, the meta-thinking skills necessary to continue building those knowledge structures. The more complex the knowledge structure, the more likely it is that new information can be usefully inserted into that structure or across structures.

A new challenge appears to be how to measure knowledge structures in these various domains. How does one determine the relationships among concepts? A number of methods being tried include word association, ordered recall, and sorting and ratings of degrees of relatedness. Such devices can produce a matrix of proximity values (Goldsmith, Johnson, & Acton, 1991).

Another way of judging contrasting knowledge structures is the series of comparisons of the behaviors of "experts" versus "novices" in areas from physics to medical diagnosis to chess. Chi, Glaser, and Farr (1988) summarize that literature as follows:

1. Experts excel mainly in their own domains.
2. Experts perceive large meaningful patterns in their domains.
3. Experts are faster than novices at performing the skills of their domains, and they quickly solve problems with little error.
4. Experts have superior short-term and long-term memory.
5. Experts see and represent problems in their domains at a deeper level than do novices; novices tend to represent problems at a superficial level.
6. Experts spend a great deal of time analyzing problems qualitatively.
7. Experts have strong self-monitoring skills.

In other words, experts have knowledge structures that allow them to respond to new experiences in a more thoughtful and analytic fashion, freed from the immediacy of the particular experience.

Several different models of intelligence have burst upon the scene, each changing our view of giftedness. Gardner's multiple intelligences in linguistic, logical-mathematical, spatial, bodily kinesthetic, musical, interpersonal, and intrapersonal areas have broadened the concept of intelligence and diversified the differentiated lessons being provided for gifted students (Ramos-Ford & Gardner, 1997).[1]

Sternberg (2000) presented his triarchic theory of intelligence, which features the executive and control functions of intelligence—the decision-making functions of intelligence that have not been well addressed by past intelligence tests of Terman and Wechsler.

Perkins (1995) presented three intelligence models of the past: *neural intelligence, experiential intelligence,* and *reflective intelligence,* all of which he believes need to be combined into a single new model. The last two of these suggest that experience and education can play a role in the development of intelligence.

We have moved some distance from the notion that intelligence was purely hereditary (Plomin, 1997), while still finding a substantial influence from heredity.[2] Even the shape of the "normal curve of intelligence" has been challenged (Robinson, Zigler, & Gallagher, 2000). It turns out that the distribution of intelligence scores ends at the bottom of the "normal curve" at IQ 70, except for those with serious pathologies, while the distribution at the high end of the scale can go well over 200 when the scale permits it. The number of students at the upper end is several times what would be predicted on the basis of the "normal curve." In addition, Flynn (1999) reported consistent improvements in IQ scores across generations; measured intelligence appears to be growing over time in Western societies.

All of this suggests that intelligence is malleable and capable of improvement if we pay appropriate attention to it. We are not limited to 2 percent or 5 percent of the population being gifted—a message that should be exciting to educators and parents alike (Gallagher, 2000).

It has become increasingly accepted that there are personality patterns that link to creative performance. Sternberg and Lubart (1993) reviewed the literature on this topic and found that tolerance of ambiguity, moderate risk taking, the willingness to surmount obstacles and persevere, the willingness to grow (to admit that old ideas were incomplete or even wrong), and a substantial amount of self-esteem all seem to predispose a person of high mental ability to be creative. It concerns many educators that these characteristics are not often stimulated or supported in the typical public school program, whether for gifted students or for others.

Creativity and Giftedness

What is the link between high intelligence and creativity? These terms have become separated in the past because of the accident of measurement. The intelligence test measures past knowledge and reasoning ability, whereas creativity represents the process by which students and adults produce unique

---

1. See Chapter 8 by von Károlyi, Ramos-Ford, and Gardner.

2. See Chapter 9 by Plomin and Price.

products of value to themselves and society (Csikszentmihalyi, 1996). Not everyone who scores high on intelligence tests will be creative, though many will. So what are the characteristics that tend to make some students manifestly creative? What can we as educators do to enhance it?

Simonton (1999) has contributed some thoughts on the process of creativity, identifying it as Darwinian in nature. His definition of creativity is that the product (1) must be original and (2) must prove adaptive in some sense. An original idea or product is judged adaptive not by the originator but by the recipients. There is another reason for maintaining that creativity entails an interpersonal or sociocultural evaluation. "Not only must others decide whether something seems original, but they are also the ultimate judges of whether something appears workable" (p. 6).

Darwin, Mozart, and Shakespeare are judged creative geniuses because their ideas have had such widespread application. Darwin studied variation in life forms, found some life forms better adapted to the environment than others, and concluded that those life forms will succeed in the struggle for existence and reproduce their kind. In each successive generation, the more adaptive variants will gradually replace the less-fit variants and will be better adapted to a particular environment.

The analogy to the creative person is that creativity begins with the production of many ideational variants; there is a selection from among the variants, and this results in the creative idea. Also required is a memory system and the ability to communicate the stored ideas to others. The investigation of creativity, then, involves how the variants are produced and the manner in which they are selected to obtain the final product.

Simonton (1999) generated a list of creativity facilitators that gives clues as to how creativity comes about:

a. A wide range of interests providing a base for unique associations
b. Open to novel experiences that can stimulate creativity
c. Allow unrelated ideas to be thought of at the same time
d. Flexible both cognitively and behaviorally to go in unconventional paths
e. Introverted, allowing for solitary contemplation
f. Independent, autonomous, and nonconventional

Social and Emotional Adjustment

There have been two conflicting views expressed over the years regarding the social and emotional adjustment of gifted students. One of these suggests that gifted students are more at risk for adjustment problems and more vulnerable for adjustment difficulties. Their giftedness gives rise to a greater risk for emotional and social problems.

A second view suggests that gifted children are better adjusted than their nongifted peers because their giftedness protects the child from maladjustment (Neihart, 1999). Several reviews of the literature in recent years have tried to determine the relative merit of these two opposing views (Gust-Brey & Cross, 1999; Neihart, 1999).

All of these reviews essentially agree that there is little difference in emotional adjustment when comparing groups of gifted students to students of average ability. If there is an advantage, it tilts in the direction of the gifted students. On the other hand, it is clear that giftedness does not immunize a student from social or emotional problems. They are as susceptible to depression, anxiety, and suicide as are their nongifted colleagues. These findings are clouded, to some extent, by the fact that the gifted students in the studies from Terman were selected in a way that was favorable to the students. That is, if we select students from summer programs such as the Talent Search Program, we will not randomly pick from the gifted population; rather, we will pick the very best and most effective of those students. This would tend to make these particular gifted populations look slightly better adjusted than any unselected gifted population.

Gust-Brey and Cross (1999) pointed out that the incidence of suicide is going up among adolescents in general, and that would seem to mean that the incidence is increasing in the gifted populations as well. There is some indication that youngsters who are extremely creative artistically have more vulnerability to mental illness than their academically gifted classmates. It goes without saying that teachers and counselors should be alert to the signs of depression or anxiety on the part of these students, and to see that they receive appropriate attention whether gifted or nongifted.

For years, there has been a continuing dialogue between psychologists and educators as to whether a positive self-image builds a more effective learner, or whether effective learning builds a more positive self-image. Research evidence suggests that these two constructs are highly interactive. Schunk (1991) pointed out that feelings of self-efficacy is a predictor of such diverse outcomes as academic achievement, social skills, smoking cessation, pain tolerance, athletic performance, career choices, assertiveness, coping with feared events, recovery from heart attack, and sales performance. Even more important, it is evident that self-image can be modified by success or failure, by attributions, and by the timing of rewards and feedback from others, particularly teachers.

Cultural Differences and Giftedness

Cultural and Ethnic Minorities

One increasing concern is the particular needs of racial, ethnic, and cultural subgroups of gifted children. Black, Hispanic, and Native American children appear in gifted programs at only about one-half or less their prevalence in the larger society, whereas Asian Americans appear at twice their percentage in the U.S. population.

Identification

Considerable attention is being paid to possible bias of measuring instruments, which are often held responsible for these differential prevalence rates. Various tests, such as the Raven Progressive Matrices, have been suggested as freer from cultural bias than the usual Binet and Wechsler measures. However, an alternative explanation is available. Instead of clinging to the discredited idea that intelligence is totally genetically based and impervious to environmental effects, which would be the only reason we might expect equal prevalence of giftedness across ethnic and racial groups, we should consider whether such differential prevalence rates might be explainable through the differential environmental advantages or disadvantages that such subpopulations have had in our society (see Gallagher & Gallagher, 1994; Perkins & Simmons, 1988).

Of course, it is easier to change the identifying tests than to change the uneven societal playing field on which these children must compete. The development of the federal Javits Program, designed to aid culturally different gifted students, has substantially expanded the search for alternative identification protocols and instructional strategies. A number of alternative methods and procedures have been suggested by which students from minority populations could be more accurately assessed for their learning potential than by traditional IQ or achievement tests.

Characteristics

Another way of studying talented economically disadvantaged children is to identify the top performers in a particular group and then compare them with the remainder of the group. One hundred and fifty-four graduates from Head Start programs (the top 3 percent in achievement of the entire sample of 5,142 children) were examined at the end of first grade and comparisons made between this top echelon and the larger groups (Robinson, Weinberg, Redden, Ramey, & Ramey, 1998). This elite group of Head Start graduates were judged by their teachers to be superior to the rest of the group in cooperation, assertiveness, self-control, and academic competence.

Similarly, the parents described these top 3 percent Head Start children as being higher in assertiveness, responsibility, and self-control than did the parents of children in the larger group. The parents of the top group also reported parenting practices that were more responsible, flexible, and less restrictive than those of the other parents, and they communicated to their children how important it was to do well in school!

Of course, children with these favorable personal characteristics received more favorable interactions with their teachers and their parents. Just as unfavorable perceptions tend to lead to negative consequences, so favorable perceptions lead to positive consequences. In this way, *how* the child begins in school has a great deal to do with how they will progress in future educational settings. There is no doubt that this top group of Head Start students is clearly different in personality and school behavior from their same age group with similar Head Start experience.

Special Programming. A further question now being explored is what kind of special program would be desired for minority gifted students, once identified. A number of observers have pointed out that the special needs of these subgroups call for differential educational approaches.

Maker and Schiever (1989, p. 301) summarized program suggestions from a wide variety of specialists concerned with Hispanic, Black, Native American, and Asian American gifted children as follows:

1. Identify students' strengths and plan a curriculum to develop these abilities.
2. Provide for the development of basic skills and other abilities students may lack.
3. Regard differences as positive rather than negative attributes.
4. Provide for involvement of parents, the community, and mentors or role models.
5. Create and maintain classrooms with a multicultural emphasis.

Although these precepts would seem to be good advice for all students and teachers, increased attention and emphasis should be considered for these factors when planning for multicultural gifted students. We are sure to see an increase in such differential planning in the future as our sensitivity to the special needs of these subgroups intensifies.

What are the differentiated programs or experiences that such minority gifted students should have? One suggestion has been to introduce them to multicultural literature as a way of promoting self-understanding, awareness, and pride. Ford, Tyson, Howard, and Harris (2000) provide an annotated bibliography of ten books with gifted Black students as the main character. They note that such books also can provide White students with an increased understanding of the dilemmas facing able Black students.

Cross-Cultural Studies. Considerable attention has been given to cross-cultural comparisons of academic performance because of concern that U.S. students are not competing successfully with students in other countries. Stevenson, Lee, and Chen (1994) report on the treatment of gifted students in Japan, China, and Taiwan. While China and Taiwan have developed special programs for gifted students with the specific purpose of fulfilling the need for well-educated citizens for economic growth, Japan, aware of its past elitist military background, has been careful to maintain equity as an educational philosophy. Although Japan has special high schools for high-achieving students, such schools are justified on the grounds that some students have earned this treatment through their hard work, not their native abilities.

Japanese parents, well aware of the importance of attending the right school, have invested heavily in *jukus,* supplementary schools to improve students' mastery and prepare them for higher education entrance examinations. The *jukus* are a $6 billion industry in Japan. The emphasis in all of these cultures has been on *student effort* as a key element of performance, although innate differences in intelligence are accepted as fact.

These cultures believe an emphasis on hard work and attainment helps all students, both average and gifted, and hence they downplay the importance of innate ability.

Special Subgroups of Gifted Students

Gifted Underachievers

One subgroup that has received little attention over the past decade is that of *gifted underachievers,* students who possess considerable intellectual potential, but who perform in a mediocre fashion, or worse, in the educational setting (Rimm, 1997).[3] In part, this lack of attention would seem to be due to the tendency of many communities and states to accept the definition of a *gifted* student as one who is productive and effective. Such a definition removes the underachiever from the gifted category since they are neither productive nor effective. Still, many educators wish to find ways to stimulate and encourage such youngsters so as to release the vast potential that they seem to have.

We are still searching for characteristics that separate underachievers from achievers. In a study using a database of over 30,000 high school juniors and seniors, giftedness was measured as a composite score over the 95th percentile on the American College Testing program. Underachievement was defined as a high school grade-point average of less than 2.25 on a 4-point scale. Gifted underachievers defined in this fashion had significantly fewer out-of-class accomplishments in areas of leadership, music, writing, and athletics, and had a significantly lower opinion of their high school education than the high achievers. Colangelo, Kerr, Christensen, and Maxey (1993) describe the sample as follows: "They are, for the most part, white, male, middle-class young people with some dissatisfactions about their school and some concerns about their own behavior" (p. 160). For these students, the lack of fulfillment of academic promise continues to be a frustrating situation that resists easy solution.

It is a difficult matter to change the maladapted patterns of students who have had eight or ten years of developing precisely the wrong approach to aca-

3. See Chapter 33 by Rimm.

emic stress or challenge. When one takes on this task, it is certain to require prolonged and great intensity of effort on the part of both the student and those trying to help that student change. The most well known educational intervention strategies have established either part-time or full-time special classrooms for gifted underachievers (Butler-Por, 1987; Whitmore, 1980). In these classrooms, as reported by Reis and McCoach (2000):

> educators strive to create a favorable environment for student achievement by altering the traditional classroom organization. A smaller student-teacher ratio exists, teachers create less conventional types of teaching and learning activities, teachers give students some choice and freedom in exercising control over their atmosphere, and students are encouraged to utilize different learning strategies. (p. 164)

Gifted Girls

One subgroup of gifted students that is attracting more and more attention is that of gifted girls and women. The first major indicator of differences between gifted girls and women, compared with gifted males, was found in the longitudinal study of Lewis Terman and his colleagues (Terman & Oden, 1947). From a career perspective, the women in the sample were much less productive than the men.

Although there clearly are complicating factors that explain such differences, particularly the multiple responsibilities of homemaking and child rearing, there are a number of other factors inhibiting the full intellectual development of gifted girls and women in our society as well (Jacklin, 1989). Reis and Callahan (1989) asked whether women have really come such a long way, given their poor representation in legislative halls, the courts, and major corporations.

While some believe there may be a constitutional difference between males and females in such specific aptitudes as mathematics (Stanley & Benbow, 1986), the mainstream of thought today focuses on the social environment and how it can be modified to encourage gifted female students. Adolescence seems to be a particularly difficult period for gifted girls. It is the time when their self-esteem seems to be weakest and their concerns about social acceptance at their peak (Kerr, 1997).[4] One suggestion is that gifted girls

be encouraged to take risks: engage in physical activities that are challenging, take the most challenging courses available, and speak out and defend their points of view.

Many teachers have not often encouraged these as feminine traits. Kerr recommends that specific comments be made on girls' performance rather than a general "very good." For example, a statement such as, "Your writing lately seems to me to be showing that you are finding your voice as a writer. I can always identify your work by its vivid descriptions and sharp humor" (Kerr, 1997, p. 494), can be highly self-enhancing for the student, girl or boy.

In recognition of the potential intimidation by males in the classroom at the adolescent age level, some attempts have been made to develop single-sex classes or schools, and these seem to have real advantages in freeing up girls' self-expression and confidence (Hollinger, 1993).

Twice Exceptional Children

The emergence of gifted students with individual disabilities, such as Helen Keller, Franklin Roosevelt, and Woodrow Wilson, reminds us that there also may be substantial hidden talent in individuals whose disabilities have cloaked their giftedness from their teachers, parents, and friends.

Baum and Owen (1988) compared high ability students with learning disabilities (LD) with a group of average-ability students with learning disabilities and found major differences between the two groups. The gifted LD students were seen as disruptive in class but showing more creativity than the average LD students. The gifted LD students attributed their poor school performance to shyness.

Coleman (1992) carried out a similar study comparing elementary-aged gifted LD and average LD students on coping skills. The gifted LD students revealed significantly more planful problem solving when responding to problem scenarios presented to them. Coleman proposed that coping strategies be directly taught to all LD students, in addition to having a general counseling program.

Groups Versus Individuals. Whenever people wish to know about the characteristics of gifted students, or to compare subgroups of gifted students to other samples, they ask questions such as "Are they loners?" or "Do they have emotional difficulties?" or "Are they snobbish?" The answers to these ques-

---

4. See Chapter 38 by Kerr and Nicpon.

tions can come either through *group statistics,* the average, or *individual cases,* the variance. The answer can vary depending on which choice is made. Group statistics will reveal that gifted students are generally quite socially adept, popular with their peers, and emotionally stable. However, if you focus on one particular child, you may discover that, for example, Burton is emotionally disturbed to the point of suicide and desperately needs help. There are no contradictions between these two statements. We merely need to recognize and take into account the wide variance in this population around any personal characteristic, from height and weight to social skills.

Educational Adaptations for Gifted Students

One of the most common suggestions made for gifted students in the schools is that they should receive a differentiated program, something different from that presented to typical students. There are three ways to modify the educational program. We can change the learning environment, change the curriculum content, stress the development of cognitive or learning strategies and approaches, or use any combination of these three modifications.

Learning Environments

Acceleration. One way to change the environment is to move the student more rapidly through the standard sequence. One of the motivations to accelerate a gifted student involves the length of time required to finish a professional or technical program. It is not unreasonable to conceive of students beginning kindergarten at age five and not completing their graduate or professional program until age 30 or beyond—spending a quarter of a century in school! Anything that will shorten that period without affecting the program or student should receive consideration. But can acceleration create harmful conditions that outweigh the savings?

One concern about students who have been accelerated is that such an academic move could result in socioemotional problems. The educational practitioners surveyed by Southern and Jones (1991) *believed* that there were a wide range of potential problems for students who were accelerated. However, Sayler and Brookshire (1993), drawing from a base of almost

25,000 eighth-grade students from the National Education Longitudinal Study, identified those students within this larger sample who were accelerated or gifted. Comparisons of accelerated students, gifted students, and a randomly selected group of regular students revealed that the accelerated students appeared, on average, to be popular, to have a positive self-concept and internal locus of control, and to be seen as troublemakers significantly less often than the regular group. The authors concluded that the fear that acceleration usually or inevitably leads to academic, social, or emotional maladjustment was not supported. The accelerated students displayed levels of emotional adjustment and feelings of acceptance by others that were higher than those of regular students and about the same as those of older students identified as gifted.

What actually happens to students who have been accelerated? One answer to this question came from a study of sixty-five students who entered college two years younger than the norm. These early entrants graduated earlier, and a greater percentage graduated Phi Beta Kappa than was true of the general college population. All but four of the sixty-five accelerated students completed their programs (Brody, Assouline, & Stanley, 1990). There was little evidence of any academic malfunctioning in this special group because of their accelerated status. The authors cautioned, however, that such acceleration seems successful when the students have aptitude scores at least equal to the average for college students.

One of the major contributions to this field has been made by Julian Stanley and his Study of Mathematically Precocious Youth (SMPY). Its original purpose was to identify youth with extraordinary talent in mathematics through tests given in the early teens. SMPY has become a base for student acceleration, and through special summer programs talented students can earn credit for advanced mathematics courses.

Benbow and Lubinski (1996) have begun a long-term evaluation of SMPY students, and preliminary findings indicate substantial later academic success and student satisfaction. SMPY also was one of the first to document gender differences in advanced mathematics and to build special programs for gifted girls (Lubinski & Benbow, 1994).

One special condition of acceleration can involve children with very high IQ scores. They may be accelerated more than the one or two grades that is the usual practice. What happens then? Gross (1992) described several students who were radically accelerated and reported that they were more stimulated intellectually, enjoyed closer and more productive social relationships, and displayed healthier levels of social self-esteem than did gifted students who remained with their own age group.

Gallagher (1993) pointed out that a regular classroom teacher has a primary responsibility to average students and then to students who have fallen behind. Time often runs out before a well-meaning teacher can organize special experiences for gifted students. Teachers also often lack special training in teaching advanced thinking skills.

Growing evidence supports the value of peer stimulation of gifted students. In a review of mathematically gifted students, Sowell (1993) found that "Precocious students enjoy working alongside others who are precocious; the fast pace appears to be invigorating. . . . Situations in which students spend greater amounts of time together appear to be conducive to greater achievement and more positive attitudes than situations in which time with peers is limited" (p. 128). The problem that faces educational leaders and administrators is how to put these pieces of information together in view of the strong current trend toward inclusion and heterogeneous grouping.

The educational reform movement that stresses *equity* has appeared to result in a reduction in the number of special classes for young gifted students and the number of pull-out or resource room settings. This, in turn, increases the need to study gifted students' performance in regular classrooms. Westberg, Archambault, Dobyns, and Salvin (1993) performed an observational study of forty-six third- and fourth-grade classrooms across the country. They looked at the teacher-student interactions with one gifted and one average-ability student for a two-day period in each of the classrooms. They found no instructional or curricular differentiation in 84 percent of the instructional activities. The greatest amount of differentiation appeared in mathematics, in which gifted students were given advanced content materials. The majority of gifted students who were observed were not provided with instructional or curricular experiences commensurate with their abilities.

On the other hand, there is evidence that attending and participating in special programs does change the perceptions, attitudes, and motivation of many gifted students. Barnett and Durden (1993) studied students who had taken special academic advanced courses from the Center for Talented Youth (CTY) at Johns Hopkins University. They found that the CTY students took more advanced college courses at an earlier age and enrolled in more college courses than a comparable group of students who did not attend such courses. On a sadder note, Purcell (1993) reported a sharp decline in energy, curiosity, and intrinsic motivation to achieve among students who had been in a gifted program that was eliminated by their school system.

Homeschooling. One phenomenon of late twentieth century has been a movement towards homeschooling, with over one million children receiving their education at home (Ray, 1997). Although homeschooling originated with parents anxious to maintain a religious element in their child's education, it now has become a vehicle for many parents of gifted and talented students. Many of these parents have despaired of the public schools' failure to meet the needs of their exceptional children.

Such an education has now become feasible through the use of the Internet. No longer is the school the gatekeeper or exclusive dispenser of knowledge. Access to the Internet opens wide the door to knowledge of all sorts. Students can focus on a particular project without having to stop at fifty-minute intervals to change classes, nor do they have to limit themselves to grade-level books or texts or curricula.

The concern that such homeschooled children would be deprived of social opportunities has largely been proven untrue as parents make plans to involve their children in clubs, recreational sports, and other activities (Kearney, 1998).

There have been few serious efforts to evaluate the overall impact of homeschooling on students, but there have been enough favorable reports from parents to get the attention of other parents seeking an educational alternative for their gifted child. It has also caught the attention of educational administrators who are aware that they are losing some of their better students to this alternative and seek ways to entice these children back into public school programs.

Curriculum Differentiation

More concrete examples are now available of just what "differentiated curriculum for gifted students" means (see VanTassel-Baska, 1997).[5] Gallagher and Gallagher (1994) presented four major ways to adapt current curriculum to the special needs of gifted students:

Acceleration: Speeding up curriculum so that, for example, eighth-grade algebra might be presented in sixth grade.

Enrichment: Extending normal curriculum with differing examples and associations that build complex ideas on the regular curriculum.

Sophistication: Direct instruction in complex networks of ideas, such as theories in the sciences or larger generalizations in the humanities.

Novelty: Introducing into the curriculum unique ideas not normally found in standard programs, such as the interdisciplinary impact of technology on the society.

The choice of which approach or which combination of approaches would be desirable is based on the particular group of students and the preferences of the teacher.

VanTassel-Baska (1997) produced her Integrated Curriculum Model that stresses three dimensions: (1) emphasizing advanced content knowledge central to disciplines of study, (2) providing higher-order thinking and processing, and (3) focusing learning experiences around major issues, themes, and ideas that define both real world applications and theoretical modeling within and across areas of study.

Differentiated curriculum seems to be pursued less often in the humanities than in the sciences. Brandwein (1987) proposed a curriculum in the humanities for gifted students in elementary schools that focuses on exploration of such concepts as *truth, beauty, justice, love,* and *faith.* This is similar to some of the curricular suggestions of Adler (1984), focusing on important concepts and values as the organizing rubric for the gifted curriculum.

There are beginning to appear some systematic efforts to evaluate the impact of various curricula changes. A secondary program of mathematics and science, which incorporated higher-level thinking skills and real-life laboratory experiences into mutu-

ally reinforcing mathematics and science content, was used with a group of students with high potential for math and science (Tyler-Wood, Mortenson, Putney, & Cass, 2000). After two years, the American College Test (ACT) was administered to the special class of 32 students and a matched control group of 32 students from nearby communities. The special group was superior on all subtests of the ACT in math and science.

Instructional Strategies

One of the growing instructional strategies used in American education is Problem Based Learning (PBL). There are three critical features to the PBL approach (Stepien, Gallagher, & Workman, 1993):

- *Learning is initiated with an ill-structured problem.* The solution is not embedded in the statement of the problem itself, as would be true in an arithmetic reasoning problem.
- *The student is made a stakeholder in the situation.* He or she may be asked to play the role of a legislator or scientist who must make a decision about the situation.
- *The instructor plays the role of metacognitive coach.* "Helps" guide students in their search for important knowledge by helping with the organization of information.

The PBL approach appears to heighten student interest and motivation without losing content mastery for the subject matter. It can be used to instruct a wide ability range of students simultaneously.

One consistent strategy has been to provide opportunities for students to problem-solve, problem-find, and create unique and original products. Such thinking skills can lead students to a more independent approach to problems. There probably has never been a more intensive effort in gifted education than the focus on stimulating creative thinking. Despite the continuing interest, there has grown a new realization that such strategies cannot and should not be considered apart from the knowledge base of the student. There is an increasing realization that you cannot be creative in the abstract. You must be creative in something, in mathematics or art or historical research, and to do that you must have some organization of knowledge in that content field (Gallagher & Gallagher, 1994).

---

5. See Chapter 13 by VanTassel-Baska.

One other mental operation that has received attention recently is that by which controlled mental processes are made automatic. Whether in athletics or in intellectual striving, the ability to make complex processes automatic allows easier access to relevant knowledge and frees up attentional resources that can be directed toward other aspects of the task. A strong knowledge base allows more effective *automaticity.* In short, cognitive skills or strategies are most useful when they are combined with an effective associative network of concepts and systems of ideas. Such a network increases the effectiveness of memory, allows a better organization of a hierarchy of ideas, and makes it easier to access the information on demand. Obviously, the educational question of moment is how to develop most effectively such an associative network.

Only in quite recent times has attention been paid to the development of a problem-finding curriculum with students. Even the education of gifted students has been largely confined to a series of problem-solving exercises, with the teacher carefully constructing the problem in such a way as to ensure the students' mastery.

Problem-based learning was included in an introductory course on Science, Society and the Future for high-aptitude secondary students (Gallagher, Stepien, & Rosenthal, 1992). The students showed significant gains in fact finding and problem finding over students of comparable ability lacking the special training. There seems little doubt that it is possible to train students in metacognitive processes to the point that such skills can become functional in the classroom.

Technology. The potential for the uses of technology is far greater than is realized in classrooms or schools. Barr (1990) pointed out that "intuitive learning" (learning through nonrational or nonlogical means) can be enhanced through the use of high-resolution graphics programs that allow students to explore the structure of complex molecules in three dimensions, or through programs that translate complex calculus equations into visual representations that allow for intuitive understandings not possible in two-dimensional print pages.

The most significant addition to technology for gifted students has been their recent access to the Internet. These students are no longer tied to their teachers or their school in the search for knowledge. They can and do "surf" the net for all manner of in-formation. Each new innovation brings its own problems, and one problem with the Internet is the suspect validity of the information that the student gains access to. How to separate the valid from the invalid is, as yet, an unsolved problem and one that is worrisome to many persons.

Equity–Excellence Influences on Programming

Two contradictory values have been competing for predominance in American education: *equity versus excellence.* Those who stress *equity* focus on the vastly different opportunities that exist from one subculture to another in the United States. They focus on bringing the economically disadvantaged students up to a higher performance level. Those who stress *equity* as a premium value see evil designs in the attempt to provide special help for gifted students (*excellence*). Margolin (1996) suggested that we are providing aid and comfort to the "oppressors" of our society by establishing special programs for gifted students.

Those supporting *equity* (see Margolin, 1996; Oakes, 1985; Sapon-Shevin, 1996) are particularly concerned that many minority students have not had the chance to show what they can do, and may be kept out of special services for gifted students because of their limited scores on aptitude tests. In this way, they observe, the majority of high-income parents will continue to see to it that their children dominate the special programs for gifted students.

One of the most influential of trends over the past decade has been the move toward *inclusion.* This is a term from special education, describing the proposed integration of children with disabilities with other students in the same classroom. This inclusion philosophy has been replacing the resource room as the primary model for educating children with disabilities (Kirk, Gallagher, & Anastasiow, 2000).

Part of the reason for this inclusion movement has stemmed from the overrepresentation of minority children in pull-out programs for children with disabilities, leading to suggestions that minority children were being discriminated against and given an inferior education. Inclusion would at least put such children in the same environment as the mainstream children (Stainback & Stainback, 1996).

There is a similar push for inclusion of gifted students because of under-representation of minorities in separate educational settings for gifted children, again leading to the suspicion that minority students were being kept out of desirable educational experiences (Sapon-Shevin, 1996). Regardless, there seems to be a trend toward educating gifted students in the regular classroom, with help from a consultant teacher or by organizing *cluster groups* (6 to 10 gifted students forming a subgroup in the regular classroom).

SUMMARY AND CONCLUSIONS

Any attempt to predict the future about education of gifted students must, of necessity, predict the future of American education, since gifted education is a small boat on a huge educational ocean and will be moved around depending on the other societal or professional forces at work. We have already seen in this review how programs for gifted students have been influenced by societal issues of equity and by national politics.

The presence and full implications of the Internet for the future of education have not been grasped yet. We, in the educational enterprise, are no longer the exclusive gatekeepers to knowledge, and our control over available knowledge will probably decrease gradually over the next few decades. At the same time, increased access to all sorts of information can have a wonderful liberating effect on gifted students who can use their own search skills to seek out information at their own pace.

One other current conflict that we should be able to leave behind us is the issue of cultural differences in ability, aptitude, and membership in programs for gifted students. We have been going through some intellectual gymnastics regarding "equity" to try and equalize our various ethnic and cultural groups on knowledge and skills, if not in reality, by some type of artificial rules.

Imagine the same procedures and rules being applied to basketball teams that we now use in gifted education. The membership on the team would be decided by proportions of membership in the larger student body. If there are 70 percent White males, then 70 percent of the basketball team will be reserved for White males, regardless of skill or ability.

The various running and shooting tests that the coach uses to select students for the team will be identified as culturally biased, since White males did comparatively poorly on them. There will be stories of inferior basketball genes possessed by the White males to account for their poor performance—instead of identifying *motivation, willingness to practice long and hard,* and *desire* as the possible cause of these cultural differences. It doesn't take much imagination to see our successful basketball coach going out the door along with our hopes of a winning season if we choose our basketball team, our school orchestra, or our school play participants in this fashion.

Since we now know that intelligence can be developed as well as discovered, we have a special responsibility to see to it that everyone gets a fair chance at such development. This responsibility includes parents as well as teachers, to see that all our youths are the best that they can be.

One of the determining factors about the future of gifted education lies in personnel preparation (Gallagher, 2000). There are few higher education centers currently preparing educational specialists in this field. Universities have found that it is not financially feasible to support an area that has only a few students. The many programs for specialists in teaching students with disabilities was made possible through large federal subsidies, and there are currently no such subsidies for teachers of gifted students. Either some way of supporting such training programs must be found, or alternative methods such as distance learning, short-term modules, summer programs, etc., need to be employed. If there are no systematic approaches to special personnel preparation, then there will be no profession of gifted education.

We certainly now realize that the information age carries its own special responsibilities, and that we will need the full complement of high ability students from all cultures and ethnic backgrounds to be able to reach higher plateaus of understanding and creativity in the future.

QUESTIONS FOR THOUGHT AND DISCUSSION

1. Gallagher reviews a wide range of issues, challenges, problems, and teaching recommendations. List five that he mentions. Prioritize them according to which seem most pressing or important.

2. Compared with students in other countries, does the apparently lower educational level of Americans concern you? Why or why not?

3. Gallagher mentions that some schools define a gifted student as "one who is productive and effective." Should gifted underachievers therefore be excluded from gifted programs and services? Why or why not?

4. In discussing the acceleration and grouping of gifted students, Gallagher briefly mentions a central issue today: "How to put these pieces of information together in view of the strong current trend toward inclusions and heterogeneous grouping" [i.e., detracking]. Explain how "equity versus excellence" relates to this issue.

REFERENCES

Adler, M. (1984). *The Paidaia program: An educational syllabus.* New York: Macmillan.

Barnett, L., & Durden, W. (1993). Education patterns of academically talented youth. *Gifted Child Quarterly, 37,* 161–168.

Barr, D. (1990). A solution in search of a problem: The role of technology in educational reform. *Journal for the Education of the Gifted, 14,* 79–95.

Baum, S., & Owen, S. (1988). High ability/learning disabled students: How are they different? *Gifted Child Quarterly, 32, 321–326.*

Benbow, C. P., & Lubinski, D. (1996). *Intellectual talent: Psychometric and social issues.* Baltimore: Johns Hopkins University Press.

Brandwein, P. (1987). *The permanent agenda of man: The humanities.* New York: Harcourt Brace Jovanovich.

Brody, L., Assouline, S., & Stanley, J. (1990). Five years of early entrants: Predicting successful achievement in college. *Gifted Child Quarterly, 34,* 138–142.

Butler-Por, N. (1987). *Underachievers in school: Issues and intervention.* New York: Wiley.

Chi, M., Glaser, R., & Farr, M. (Eds.) (1988). *The nature of expertise.* Hillsdale, NJ: Erlbaum.

Colangelo, N., Kerr, B., Christensen, P., & Maxey, J. (1993). A comparison of gifted underachievers and gifted high achievers. *Gifted Child Quarterly, 37,* 155–160.

Coleman, M. (1992). A comparison of how gifted/LD and average-LD boys cope with school frustration. *Journal for the Education of the Gifted, 15,* 239–265.

Csikszentmihalyi, M. (1996). *Creativity.* New York: Harper Collins.

Flynn, J. (1999). Searching for justice: The discovery of IQ gains over time. *American Psychologist, 54,* 5–20.

Ford, D., Tyson, C., Howard, T., Harris, J. (2000). Multicultural literature and gifted Black students: Promoting self-understanding, awareness, and pride. *Roeper Review, 22,* 235–240.

Gallagher, J. (1993). An intersection of public policy and social science: Gifted students and education in mathematics and science. In L. Penner, G. Batsche, H. Knoff, & D. Nelson (Eds.), *The challenge in mathematics and science education* (pp. 15–47). Washington, DC: American Psychological Association.

Gallagher, J. (2000). Unthinkable thoughts: Education of gifted students. *Gifted Child Quarterly, 44,* 5–12.

Gallagher, J., & Gallagher, S. (1994). *Teaching the gifted child* (4th ed.). Boston: Allyn & Bacon.

Gallagher, S., Stepien, W. & Rosenthal, H. (1992). The effects of problem-based learning on problem solving. *Gifted Child Quarterly, 35,* 12–19.

Goldsmith, T., Johnson, P., & Acton, W. (1991). Assessing structural knowledge. *Journal of Educational Psychology, 83,* 88–96.

Gross, M. (1992). The use of radical acceleration in cases of extreme intellectual precocity. *Gifted Child Quarterly, 36,* 91–99.

Gust-Brey, K., & Cross, T. (1999). An examination of the literature base on the suicidal behaviors of gifted students. *Roeper Review, 22,* 28–35.

Hollinger, D. (Ed.). (1993). *Single-sex schooling: Perspectives from practice and research.* Washington, DC: U.S. Department of Education.

Jacklin, C. (1989). Female and male: Issues of gender. *American Psychologist, 44,* 127–133.

Kearney, K. (1998). Gifted children and homeschooling: Historical and contemporary perspectives. In S. Cline & K. Hegeman (Eds.), *Gifted Education in the Twenty-First Century* (pp. 175–194). Delray Beach, FL: Winslow Press.

Kerr, B. (1997). Developing talents in girls and young women. In N. Colangelo & G. Davis (Eds.), *Handbook of Gifted Education* (2nd ed., pp. 483–497). Boston: Allyn & Bacon.

Kirk, S., Gallagher, J., & Anastasiow, N. (2000). *Educating Exceptional Children (9th ed.).* Boston: Houghton Mifflin.

Lubinski, D., & Benbow, C. (1994). The study of mathematically precocious youth (SMPY): The first three decades of a planned fifty-year longitudinal study of intellectual talent. In R. Subotnik & K. Arnold (Eds.), *Beyond Terman: Longitudinal studies in contemporary gifted education* (pp. 255–281). Norwood, NJ: Ablex.

Maker C. J., & Schiever S. W. (Eds.). (1989) *Critical issues in gifted education: Defensible programs for cultural and ethnic minorities.* Austin, TX: Pro-Ed.

Margolin, L. (1996). A pedagogy of privilege. *Journal for the Education of the Gifted, 19*(2), 164–180.

Neihart, M. (1999). The impact of giftedness on psychological well-being: What does the empirical literature say? *Roeper Review, 22,* 10–17.

Oakes, J. (1985). *Keeping track.* New Haven, CT: Yale University Press.

Perkins, D. (1995). *Outsmarting IQ: The emerging science of learnable intelligence.* New York: The Free Press.

Perkins, D., & Simmons, R. (1988). *The cognitive roots of scientific and mathematical ability.* Washington, DC: U.S. Department of Education.

Plomin, R. (1997). Genetics and intelligence. In N. Colangelo & G. Davis (Eds.), *Handbook of gifted education* (2nd ed., pp. 67–74). Boston: Allyn & Bacon.

Purcell, J. (1993). The effects of the elimination of gifted and talented programs on participating students and their parents. *Gifted Child Quarterly, 37,* 177–187.

Ramos-Ford, V., & Gardner, H. (1997). Giftedness from a multiple intelligences perspective. In N. Colangelo & G. Davis (Eds.), *Handbook of gifted education* (2nd ed., pp. 54–74). Boston: Allyn & Bacon.

Ray, B. (1997). *Home education across the United States: Family characteristics, student achievement, longitudinal traits.* Purcellville, VA: Home School Legal Defense Association.

Reis, S. M., & Callahan, C. (1989). Gifted females: They've come a long way—or have they? *Journal for the Education of the Gifted, 12,* 99–117.

Reis, S., & McCoach, B. (2000). The underachievement of gifted students: What do we know and where do we go? *Gifted Child Quarterly, 44,* 152–170.

Rimm, S. (1997). Underachievement syndrome: A national epidemic. In N. Colangelo & G. Davis (Eds.), *Handbook of gifted education* (2nd ed., pp. 416–434). Boston: Allyn & Bacon.

Robinson, N. M., Weinberg, R. A., Redden, D., Ramey, S. L., & Ramey, C. T. (1998). Factors associated with high academic competence among former Head Start children. *Gifted Child Quarterly, 42,* 148–156.

Robinson, N., Zigler, E., & Gallagher, J. (2000). Two tails of the normal curve: Similarities and differences in the study of mental retardation and giftedness. *American Psychologist, 55,* 1413–1424.

Ross, P. (1993). *National excellence: The case for developing America's talent.* Washington, DC: U.S. Department of Education.

Sapon-Shevin, M. (1996). Beyond gifted education: Building a shared agenda for school reform. *Journal for the Education of the Gifted, 19,* 194–214.

Sayler, M., & Brookshire, W. (1993). Social, emotional, and behavioral adjustment of accelerated students, students in gifted classes, and regular students in eighth grade. *Gifted Child Quarterly, 37,* 150–154.

Schunk, D. (1991). Self-efficacy and academic motivation. *Journal of Educational Psychology, 26,* 337–345.

Simonton, D. K. (1999). *Origins of genius: Darwinian perspectives on creativity.* New York: Oxford University Press.

Southern, W., & Jones, E. (1991). *The academic acceleration of gifted children.* New York: Teachers College Press.

Sowell, E. (1993). Programs for mathematically gifted students: A review of empirical research. *Gifted Child Quarterly, 37,* 124–132.

Stainback, S., & Stainback, W. (1996). *Inclusion: A guide for educators.* Baltimore, MD: Paul H. Brookes.

Stanley, J. C., & Benbow, C. P. (1986). Youths who reason exceptionally well mathematically. In R. J. Sternberg & J. E. Davidson (Eds.), *Conceptions of giftedness* (pp. 361–387). New York: Cambridge University Press.

Stepien, W., Gallagher, S. A., & Workman, D. (1993). Problem-based learning for traditional and interdisciplinary classrooms. *Journal for the Education of the Gifted, 16*(4), 5–17.

Sternberg, R. (2000). Patterns of giftedness: A triarchic analysis. *Roeper Review, 22,* 231–240.

Sternberg, R., & Lubart, T. (1993). Creative giftedness: A multivariate investment approach. *Gifted Child Quarterly, 37,* 7–15.

Stevenson, H., Lee, S., & Chen, C. (1994). Education of gifted and talented students in mainland China, Taiwan, and Japan. *Journal for the Education of the Gifted, 17,* 104–130.

Terman, L., & Oden, M. H. (1947). *The gifted child grows up: Twenty-five years follow-up of a superior group* (Vol. 4). Stanford, CA: Stanford University Press.

The Third International Mathematics and Science Study (TIMSS). (1997). Washington, DC: U.S. Department of Education.

Tyler-Wood, T., Mortenson, M., Putney, D., & Cass, M. (2000). An effective mathematics and sciences curriculum option for secondary gifted education. *Roeper Review, 22*(4), 266–269.

VanTassel-Baska, J. (1997). What matters in curriculum for gifted learners: Reflections on theory, research and practice. In N. Colangelo & G. Davis (Eds.), *Handbook of gifted education* (2nd ed., pp. 126–135). Boston: Allyn & Bacon.

Westberg, K., Archambault, F., Dobyns, S., & Salvin, T. (1993). The classroom practices observation study. *Journal for the Education of the Gifted, 16,* 120–146.

Whitmore, J. (1980). The etiology of underachievement in highly gifted young children. *Journal for the Education of the Gifted, 3,* 38–51.

3

The Science and Politics of Intelligence in Gifted Education

LINDA S. GOTTFREDSON, *University of Delaware*

g is probably the most controversial single result in psychology, as well as being one of the most important.
—Deary, 2000, p. 8

Why is it so hard to persuade schools that gifted children have special needs? Why are people who advocate their needs tagged as elitists—even *antidemocratic*—for doing so ("To group or not to group: Is that really the question?" was the title of a 1995 debate between William Durden and Robert Slavin)? And why do public schools often treat exceptionally gifted students as, literally, an embarrassment of riches? The full list of laments is long and all too familiar to educators of gifted children.

Nor are the critics persuaded when gifted educators cite the research evidence—for example, that ability grouping and accelerated instruction enhance the performance of intellectually gifted students without harming the less able (Kulik & Kulik, 1997; Page & Keith, 1994). Or that gifted children thrive on the challenge of more demanding work and, on the other hand, resent being exploited in mixed-ability classrooms as either as tutors or workhorses in cooperative-learning groups (Colangelo & Davis, 1997; Robinson, 1997).

As in other arenas of political life, the scientific facts often carry little weight. Indeed the facts are often shaped to fit the political claims being argued. Hence, textbooks regularly report, falsely, that ability grouping harms less able students (e.g., Mulkey, 1993, p. 132) and that more "democratic" instructional strategies (e.g., cooperative learning in mixed ability groups) are more effective for student learning (Glazer, 1990). To argue the facts that cooperative learning does not help everyone is

itself sometimes greeted as a cover for elitism, or worse.[1]

The Political Reality

These political realities are not unique to gifted education, for they reflect an ambivalence about talent that pervades employee selection, admissions to college, and many other aspects of American life where talent matters (Colangelo & Davis, 1997; Gottfredson, 2000a; Tannenbaum, 1996). Since this nation's early days (deTocqueville, 1990/1835; Gardner, 1984), Americans at once celebrate the self-made man who rises through sheer talent and grit, and deplore the inequalities that the freedom to advance (or fall behind) on one's own merits allows. Wanting to believe that "all men are created equal" in talent as well as basic rights, Americans are made uneasy by the consequences of people having the liberty to capitalize on their unequal strengths. They nourish the myth that with hard work *anyone* can rise to great heights if given the opportunity. Of special relevance to gifted education, Americans look to the schools to be the Great Equalizer; hence the sensitivities over gifted education—it seems to help the rich get richer.

Because educational policy makers tend to equate democracy more with equality than with freedom, they generally give priority to equal *results* in academic achievement over equal *opportunity* to reach one's potential. They relax this priority when there is external political pressure to use the "best and brightest" for some collective national purpose, such as competing with the Soviet Union in space or with

---

1. See Chapter 22 by Robinson.

24

Japan in the marketplace. Their usual preferences thus create special challenges for those advocating programs for gifted children.

How is one to respond? Clearly, not by thoughtlessly accepting *or* dismissing the politics or science of gifted education's critics—say, the political preference that equal results be our first principle, or the (false) claim that equality of endowment is a fact. There is no scientific fact that can tell us how much we should value equality of results over equality of opportunity, or vice versa, when the two conflict. Rather, this is an important social debate that gifted educators should enter with political awareness but a confident voice.

Equality of endowment is, however, a scientific issue, and there is much evidence on the matter. Unfortunately, the scientific facts are often either unknown by or misrepresented to the public. Nowhere is this truer than on the topic of intelligence. Differences in general intelligence are the core fact relating to giftedness, but are also its biggest political millstone. Sometimes, it seems as if the more researchers learn about intelligence and ways of measuring it, the louder skeptics complain.

Accordingly, it may help to lay out the basics of what is known about intelligence as it relates to key questions in gifted education. For instance, are there multiple, independent kinds of giftedness, or of intelligence itself? Does intellectual giftedness result mostly from nature or nurture? If giftedness is to some extent innate, doesn't nurture supersede nature anyway as children advance through school? Can IQ tests predict great cultural achievement? Is a high IQ even necessary for it? And what abilities does an IQ score even represent, in the first place? Can all students develop high abilities if given proper instruction and sufficient opportunity to practice? Could we all be Mozarts?

Journalists opined on these questions at length after publication in 1994 of *The Bell Curve: Intelligence and Class Structure in American Life* (Herrnstein & Murray, 1994). Most of them asserted the answers to be, respectively, "yes" (intelligence is multidimensional), nurture dominates, any impact of the genes recedes with age, great cultural achievement is unrelated to and does not require high intelligence, IQ tests measure only narrow academic skills, and all students could develop such skills if given the opportunity and encouragement. Moreover, they often described claims to the contrary as already discredited views of ideologically driven pseudo-scientists.

What does the scientific research actually show? Just the opposite. Alarmed at the crescendo of disinformation, fifty-two leading intelligence researchers issued a statement in 1994 ("Mainstream Science on Intelligence"), first published in the *Wall Street Journal* (December 13, 1994), and later republished as an editorial in the journal *Intelligence* (Gottfredson, 1997a). Its twenty-five ABCs of confirmed knowledge on intelligence can be found in the major textbooks and scientific treatises on the topic (e.g., Brody, 1992; Carroll, 1993; Deary, 2000; Jensen, 1980, 1998; Plomin, DeFries, McClearn, & McGuffin, 2001), as well as in an American Psychological Association (APA) task force report published soon after (Neisser et al., 1996). I echo their main points below and elaborate on their relevance to the debate over gifted education. The truth, as we shall see, is more complex and far more interesting than most people might suspect.

The Scientific ABCs of Intelligence: Its Generality, Demographics, Genetics, and Pragmatics

Generality

Perhaps the single most important fact about general intelligence is its great generality. People who are high in one mental aptitude tend to be high in all. The positive correlations among all mental tests, despite their vast differences in format (e.g., written versus oral; group-administered versus individually administered) and manifest content (e.g., words, figures, numbers, drawings), indicate that all mental tests tend to measure something in common. That common factor can be extracted from the scores on any large, diverse battery of mental tests by applying the statistical technique of factor analysis. The resulting common factor, which can be separated from other components of the tests, is called *g* (short for the general mental ability factor). Most mental tests measure *g* more than anything else, and researchers have been unable to develop meaningful mental tests that do not measure mostly *g*. Moreover, virtually identical *g* factors emerge from different test batteries (as long as they are large and diverse) and from different age, racial-ethnic, sex, and national groups (Bouchard, 1998; Jensen, 1998, chap. 4), which suggests that there exists a single, humanity-wide ladder of general mental competence.

Because the *g* continuum is common to all tests and human groups, despite their superficial dissimilarities, the variations in mental competence that the *g* factor represents must be fairly independent of the vagaries of culture and context. Indeed, intelligence has often been verbally defined in precisely such terms—as the ability to learn, think abstractly, reason, and solve problems. In more colloquial terms, it is the ability to catch on, make sense of things, and figure out what to do. Most globally, *g* is the ability to process information of any sort.

g as the Common Core of All Mental Abilities.
The existence of a strong *general* factor does not mean that intelligence is the only mental ability or a unitary mental process. People rightly have a broader conception of human talent, and the argument for a *g* factor—a general intelligence factor—should not be misconstrued as an argument that intellectual ability or achievement itself is unidimensional. Different mental abilities are only moderately to moderately highly correlated, and factor analyses show that the *g* factor accounts for only about half the variance in scores in any broad battery of mental tests. In addition, although more specific mental abilities such as verbal and spatial aptitude share mostly the same genetic roots as does *g,* they still tend to be somewhat genetically distinct from *g* (Bouchard, 1998; Plomin et al., 2001, Chap. 10).[2]

The point is that a highly general intelligence factor forms the common core for all mental abilities yet studied. It is therefore likely that a favorable *g* level forms an essential foundation for most, if not all, highly valued forms of cultural achievement, such as in music, the arts, science, and politics. High intelligence obviously is not sufficient for high levels of achievement, but it may be necessary. Howard Gardner (1983), the proponent of multiple intelligence theory, has himself said that all the exemplars of his seven or more "intelligences" probably exceeded IQ 120 (Jensen, 1998, p. 128), which is the 90th percentile in intelligence.[3] On the other hand, as I discuss later, high intelligence is not a *sufficient* condition for greatness. But, to repeat, although intellectual potential is not unidimensional and potential must be accompanied by other personal traits and opportunities to result in actual achievement, higher than average *g* may be *necessary* for high levels of either potential or actual achievement.

---

2. See Chapter 9 by Plomin and Price.

3. See Chapter 8 by von Károlyi, Ramos-Ford, and Gardner.

Hierarchical Model of Mental Abilities.
Intelligence researchers now favor what they call the *hierarchical* model of cognitive abilities (Deary, 2000). It is a major advance in the field of intelligence because it unifies major theories that had once been thought irreconcilable. It does so, first, by distinguishing abilities according to how broad versus narrow they are and, second, by showing how the more general abilities actually form the foundation of the more specific ones. This unified model helps to clarify (even settle) the debate over whether there exists one intelligence or many. It also helps clarify the derivative debate over giftedness—is there one form or many?

As shown in Figure 3.1, the hierarchical model consists of three strata or layers of abilities, where the higher strata represent the more general abilities (Carroll, 1993, Chap. 16). The crowded bottom layer includes many specific abilities, the middle layer about ten broad abilities, and the top stratum only highly general capabilities. If *giftedness* represents fairly broad abilities and *talent* more specific ones, then talents appear lower in the hierarchy than do different forms of giftedness. The many highly specific Stratum I abilities are measured by tests with names such as lexical knowledge, reading comprehension, associative memory, free recall memory, spatial relations, spatial scanning, and musical discrimination. All the tests correlate among themselves, but some more strongly than others based on like content (verbal, spatial, numerical, etc.). This indicates that the individual tests within a cluster are all tapping some common ability—some *broad ability factor*—in addition to whatever they each may measure uniquely, but that different clusters reflect different broad ability factors.

It is this set of broad ability factors, statistically derived from the Stratum I tests, that constitute the middle layer of the hierarchy. Examples of these Stratum II factors include "general memory and learning," "broad spatial perception," and "broad auditory perception." Factors at this level of generality tap the broad sorts of distinctions in talent that we commonly observe among students: for instance, a quantitative versus a verbal bent.

Stratum II factors are themselves moderately to highly correlated among themselves, indicating that they, in turn, measure something even more general. Stratum III, the apex of the hierarchy, includes these most general capabilities that, because they are so general, fit the description of intelligences. The big question has been: How many are there? Independent analyses have determined there to be just *one*. It is,

Level of generality

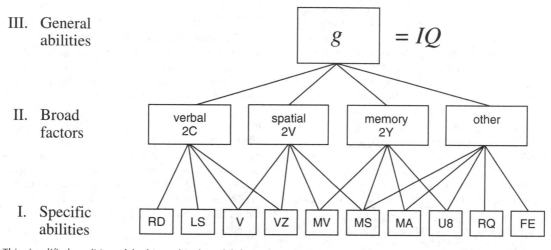

This simplified rendition of the hierarchical model draws from Carroll's (1993, Chap. 15) three-stratum summary of the evidence. Verbal, spatial, and memory represent three of his eight Stratum II factors, respectively, crystallized intelligence (2C), broad visual perception (2V), and general memory and learning (2Y). The Stratum I abilities sampled here are reading decoding (RD), listening ability (LS), verbal (printed) language comprehension (V), visualization (VZ), visual memory (MV), memory span (MS), associative memory (MA), maintaining and judging rhythm (U8), quantitative reasoning (RQ), and expressional fluency (FE). See Carroll (1993, p. 626) for the five other Stratum II factors in his summary model, as well as for the other Stratum III factors that are correlated with the Stratum II factors shown here.

Figure 3.1   Hierarchical Model of Mental Abilities.

moreover, the same general mental ability factor, *g,* that was discovered in the first years of intelligence research a century ago. As well as researchers can tell, it is a general capacity—perhaps even a property of the brain—that reflects the speed and efficiency with which we process information of any sort. Stratum II abilities are composed mostly of this single Stratum III factor, *g,* and relatively little remains when *g* is statistically partialled out of them.

Multiple Intelligences: Where Do They Fit In?
But how can there be only one highly general ability? Hasn't Howard Gardner (1983) shown that there are at least seven (linguistic, logical-mathematical, spatial, bodily-kinesthetic, musical, interpersonal, and intrapersonal)? And doesn't Robert Sternberg argue that intelligence researchers have found just one general intelligence only because they have not looked for any others (Sternberg et al., 2000, p. xii)?[4] He proposes a triarchic theory in which there are three types

of intelligence, academic, practical, and creative, which he sometimes combines under the umbrella concept "successful intelligence" (Sternberg, 1997). Both Gardner and Sternberg argue that g may infuse one or so of their "intelligences" (e.g., Gardner's logical-analytical and Sternberg's academic), but that the others reflect independent kinds of intellectual prowess.

Both of their theories are popular among educators for reasons explained earlier—they are widely interpreted as promises that everyone can be smart in some way, that Mother Nature is an egalitarian after all. However, intelligence researchers have explored many kinds of abilities over the years, intellectual and not, also in a quest for major mental abilities that are independent of *g*. Their searches have yielded none. Many hundreds of studies have analyzed the structure of mental abilities, that is, the relations among them. John B. Carroll (1993) painstakingly gathered and reanalyzed 450 such studies, the best of nearly a century's worldwide research on the topic. His reanalysis yields only one highly general ability, *g*. Carroll (1993) concluded, moreover, that four of Gardner's

4. See Chapter 7 by Sternberg.

"intelligences" (linguistic, logical-mathematical, spatial, and perhaps musical) probably represent broad abilities at the Stratum II level, all of which, it should be recalled, consist primarily of *g*. Gardner's other three intelligences do not seem to be as clearly cognitive in nature, and may mostly reflect traits that have already been studied under other rubrics, such as personality and emotions. Gardner's claims about his intelligences could be easily tested were Gardner or others actually to measure the proposed intelligences and to correlate them with one another as well as with other oft-measured psychological traits such as *g*. This has never been done (Hunt, 2001). In contrast to Gardner, Sternberg and his colleagues claim to have performed such research and successfully demonstrated that there exist separate academic and practical intelligences. However, their evidence turns out to be scanty and to crumble altogether when it is independently examined (Gottfredson, in press a). In short, there is much evidence supporting the claim for only one highly general mental ability, *g*, but none for claims for several co-equal general intelligences.

Research has, however, discovered a kernel of truth to multiple intelligence theory that is relevant to gifted education. Although different abilities tend to come bundled together (if you are high in one you tend to be high in all others), this linkage seems to get looser at higher IQ levels (Detterman & Daniel, 1989; see literature review by Jensen, 1998). That is, whereas low-IQ people tend to be low in all mental abilities, high-IQ people are not as likely to be high in all abilities. The latter's ability profiles are more uneven. To paraphrase past summaries of the finding, "dullness is general but giftedness is not." This conclusion is consistent with descriptions of gifted children. Ellen Winner (1996), for instance, describes amazingly gifted children whose unusual gifts seem confined to one realm of endeavor—art, or mathematics, or reading.[5] Nonetheless, with few exceptions (idiot savants), highly gifted children are above average in IQ. If multiple intelligences exist in this limited sense, they are the playground of the cognitively rich.

In sum, there are different forms of giftedness, but these different gifts do not represent independent intelligences. Rather, they are more like differently flavored ice creams—wonderfully different but all depending on the same basic ingredient. Each form may require a different means of identification and

different environmental supports (Stanley, 1997), but none will be found or flourish independent of *g*.

Demographics

Differences Along the IQ Continuum. The most important fact about the distribution of general intelligence is this: Most people cluster around the average IQ and are therefore much alike, but there is a significant minority of individuals at the extremes of high and low intelligence and who are thus quite unlike the average person. As with height and many other human traits, IQ is distributed according to the bell-shaped curve. The range of normal IQ is shown in Figure 3.2. It is referred to as the "normal" range because IQ 70 is often considered the threshold for borderline mental retardation and IQ 130 the threshold for intellectual giftedness. This 60-point IQ range includes about 95% of the general American population.

Fully half of the population is found within just 10 IQ points of the average, IQ 100. People in this large middle cluster (IQ 90–110) probably do not appear terribly different from one another in intellectual competence in most day-to-day encounters. The same cannot be said, however, of individuals even halfway toward the boundaries of "normal" intelligence, that is, at IQ 85 versus IQ 115 (about the sixteenth and eighty-fourth percentiles). As shown in the figure, individuals of IQ 115 are usually capable of learning abstract information in a college (semi-independent) format, whereas individuals of IQ 85 generally require hands-on instruction for even concrete tasks. At the ends of the normal range (IQs 70 and 130), learning ability differs markedly—and so too, therefore, must education if it is to meet the distinctive needs of the individuals involved.

Note that we have just compared people of only *mild* retardation or giftedness. Imagine now the extremely gifted. Consider children of IQ 160, for instance, who are hardly the most extremely gifted. Were they to be represented in Figure 3.2, they would be placed as far to the right of the threshold for giftedness (IQ 130) as the latter is from the average IQ (IQ 100)—that is, off the book's page altogether. It is no wonder that children of extraordinarily high IQ are sometimes viewed as alien or freaky. They *are* outside our normal range of experience. They can do things—read, draw, master algebra—that we had thought impossible for anyone their age, even for persons years older! Children of IQ 160 differ as much

---

5. See Chapter 26 by Winner and Martino.

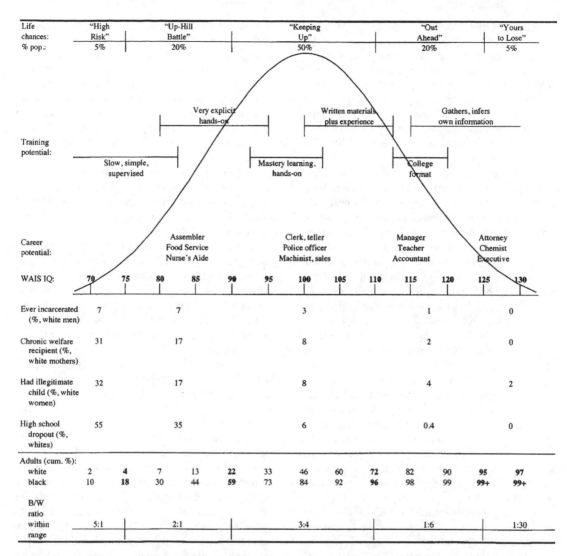

Cumulative percentages for adults were based on mean Wechsler Adult Intelligence Scale (WAIS) IQs of 101.4 for whites and 86.9 for blacks and SDs of 14.7 for whites and 13.0 for blacks (Reynolds, Chastain, Kaufman, & McLean, 1987, p. 330). Percentiles for IQ scores were estimated by use of cumulative normal probability tables. Copyright 1997 by Elsevier Science. Reprinted with permission.

Figure 3.2 The Distribution of People and Life Chances Along the IQ Continuum.

from the average child intellectually as the average child does from one of IQ 40, which is near the border between "moderate" (Wechsler IQ 40–54) and "severe" mental retardation (Wechsler IQ 25–39). With moderate retardation, a child usually "can learn functional academic skills to approximately fourth grade level by late teens if given special education"

(Matarazzo, 1972). Below that IQ level, children usually "cannot learn functional academic skills."

No one would ever claim that a moderately retarded child will thrive in a regular classroom without special attention, but schools regularly presume as much for the moderately gifted child. This (mis)treatment is akin to placing a child of average intelligence in a class for the moderately retarded, or putting a child of IQ 130 in a special education class for the mildly retarded, and then dismissing complaints of inappropriate placement by asserting that the "gifted" child will "succeed in any case." Educating a profoundly gifted child (of, say, IQ 180–200) in a regular classroom may be as intellectually stultifying as the unthinkable proposition of educating a normal child among the "profoundly" retarded (below IQ 20).

Age Differences. Age, gender, and ethnic differences raise other concerns in gifted education. With regard to age, there are two key issues. Obviously, *absolute* mental capability increases with age, quickly in early childhood and more slowly in adolescence, at which point it begins to level off. Eighteen-year-olds are much more facile at processing information than are eight-year-olds. The IQ score does not capture this growth in mental age, however, because it measures mental competence only *relative* to one's agemates. Thus, an IQ of 100 represents considerably greater mental horsepower at age eighteen than at age eight.

The first issue involving age is whether IQ (i.e., rank in IQ) is stable during development. Do smart children become smart adolescents? For the most part, yes. In one of the best studies to date, Moffitt, Caspi, Harkness, and Silva (1993) followed 800 children every two years from ages seven to thirteen and found "negligible" IQ change for most. Even in the minority of cases where changes were "marked and real," they were "variable in timing, idiosyncratic in source, and transient in course" (p. 455)—that is, unpredictable.

A recent study (Deary, 2000) of IQ stability across the longest age span yet, ages eleven to seventy-seven, reported a correlation of 0.73 (0.63 when not corrected for statistical artifacts). This is among the lower correlations reported for key studies, which often range into the 0.80s and 0.90s. The overall picture, then, is one in which large shifts in IQ rank are the exception and stability the rule. In fact, behavioral geneticists have devoted considerable attention to explaining this stability: Is it owing mostly to genetics or environment? The estimates they derive from large, longitudinal studies indicate that genes account for most of the stability but also some of the change (Plomin et al., 2001). Therefore, although high intellectual ability may not always be noticed or nourished, it is probably fairly continuous from early childhood and seldom, if ever, springs forth entirely anew at some later age.

The second age-related issue concerns later-life declines in mental power. Sadly, what goes up during youth also tends to come down in adulthood. It is well known that the facility to learn and reason declines with age, beginning in the twenties to thirties. According to Salthouse (2000), the decline from age eighteen to eighty in such abilities is comparable to their increase from age eight to eighteen. Moreover, he and others describe how specific information-processing abilities all tend to decline together, suggesting either that all specific abilities depend on a single general mental ability that is vulnerable to aging, or else that there is a general aging process that affects distinct abilities in the same way (see Deary, 2000, Chap. 8; Schaie, 1996).

The relevance of this fact to giftedness concerns its expression in adulthood. Extraordinary achievement in some fields (physics, mathematics) may depend more on raw reasoning ability than it does in others, where notable advances require the accumulation and synthesis of vast amounts of information and personal experience (e.g., literature, history, philosophy). Whereas so-called processing power declines, stores of knowledge continue to grow until very old age, when they may begin to decay. This may partly account for why "best contributions" tend to be made at earlier ages in the former than the latter fields (Simonton, 1994).

This distinction between the vulnerable raw processing power and the sustainable mental skills that have distilled from the many years of exercising that power is the distinction between *fluid* and *crystallized* intelligence. Fluid intelligence (Gf) represents the ability to learn new things, while crystallized intelligence (Gc) is the *general* knowledge (e.g., vocabulary) that has crystallized from past learning. The two are highly correlated Stratum II abilities (although fluid *g* turns out to be identical to *g* itself), but with advancing age crystallized intelligence becomes a better indicator of past than current fluid intelligence. That is why crystallized intelligence is sometimes referred to as "hollow" in old age. Others (Baltes, 1993) draw essentially the same distinction when they refer to the *mechanics* versus the *pragmatics* of intelligence: The latter is maintained even as its original basis—the mechanics—wanes.

Racial-Ethnic Differences. Perhaps the most contentious question in the field of intelligence is whether genders or racial-ethnic groups differ in mental ability. If there truly are average group differences in general ability (*g*) or group factors (e.g., quantitative or spatial abilities), then we can expect any gifted program that targets those abilities to result in differential selection by gender or ethnicity. Racial-ethnic differences in selection are rife in employment, college admissions, and assignment to special education, and these differentials have provoked much litigation. The question is whether the test score differences reflect *real* differences in developed competence or the result of test bias and, even if tests are *not* biased, whether intelligence and its surrogates (SAT scores, grades, and so on) are *legitimate* bases for selection. I deal here with the "Are they real?" question, and leave the "Are they a valid basis for selection?" question until later.

Looking first at the racial-ethnic disparities, the answer to the first question is that the major mental tests are *not* biased against native-born, English-speaking Americans, including Black Americans. This question was scientifically settled in 1980 (Jensen, 1980). The same mental test score *does* mean the same thing, on the average, for all individuals meeting the foregoing description, regardless of group membership. The average IQ differences represent real differences in the higher-order thinking skills that people have developed.

Individuals in all racial-ethnic groups span the full range of intelligence, of course. The average group differences result from their members tending to cluster along different stretches of the IQ continuum: Among Americans, Blacks tend to cluster around IQ 85, gentile Whites around IQ 100, and Ashkenazi Jews around IQ 115. The averages for Hispanics and Native Americans tend to fall between those for Blacks and gentile Whites; those for Asian-Americans between gentile Whites and Jews. Each racial-ethnic group can itself be further divided into subgroups, whose IQ averages also reliably differ. For instance, Blacks from the Caribbean tend to have higher IQs than do other subgroups of American Blacks; Cuban Americans tend to score higher than other Hispanic groups; and gentile Whites differ somewhat among themselves depending on country of family origin. Regardless of what causes these average group differences (they remain unexplained), group differences are the rule and not the exception within the United States as well as around the world.

This partial separation of IQ bell curves might not matter much except for two reasons. First, some of the average differences are quite large. I focus here on the average Black-White difference because it has

been of most concern. For instance, the average for American Blacks is located near the White 15th percentile. If we take IQ 130 as the threshold for intellectual giftedness, this corresponds to about the 97th–98th percentile among Whites, as shown in the lower rows of Figure 3.2. The 98th percentile among Blacks, in contrast, is around IQ 115 (which is about the 82nd percentile for Whites and 50th for Jews). In terms of learning ability, Figure 3.2 shows that this is the difference between gathering and inferring information on one's own (being self-instructing, so to speak) and relying on a college format. If we were to select the top two percent (or five percent or ten percent) of the two populations, the two selected groups would therefore differ noticeably in their ability to handle challenging instruction (cf. Gottfredson, 2000b).

Second, giftedness concerns not averages, but one extreme of the IQ distribution. Because of the shape of the bell curve, with its tapering tails, any average group difference is magnified at the tails of the respective distributions. The further out the tails we look, the more magnified becomes the group difference. This is illustrated in the last line of Figure 3.2. Take, for instance, the per capita ratio of Blacks to Whites in different segments of the IQ distribution. For IQs 91–110, the Black:White ratio is 3:4, or close to even. For IQs 111–125, the ratio falls to 1:6, and for IQs above 125, it is 1:30.

Clearly, if IQ level plays even a major role in selection for gifted instruction, Blacks will be greatly underrepresented when the same criteria are used to select Blacks and Whites from representative samples of their respective populations. Nationwide, it would result in only a tiny proportion of Blacks in gifted education programs. Asian-American and Jewish-American children, however, would be overrepresented, owing to their greater representation at the higher reaches of IQ. Such racially-disparate results also occur in selection for elite occupations and graduate education; they have created considerable legal and political turmoil there, too.

Many school systems have broadened their definitions of giftedness by not restricting their programs to academic talents, and thereby obtaining a more representative demographic mix of students. Others have opened the selection process, for example, by admitting students based on nominations from parents and teachers, regardless of test scores (Stanley, 1997). Neither change can accommodate the accelerated instruction that is beneficial for highly able students, because many students in the broadened pools cannot cope with such acceleration. This democratization of gifted education, therefore, has the frequent result of transforming gifted education into generic pull-out enrichment programs that only supplement, not accelerate, regular instruction. Although enrichment can enhance performance as well as relieve the boredom of regular instruction, it falls far short of the results of acceleration.

Gender Differences. The story on gender differences is not as clear, partly because any average sex difference is small (at most several IQ points). The most direct test of the sex-difference-in-*g* hypothesis failed to support it (Jensen, 1998). There are other gender differences, however, that are relevant to gifted education. One is that the variance in many abilities, including IQ, is greater for males than females, which means that we might expect more males at the retarded and gifted extremes of the ability distribution. Selection ratios for both types of program are consistent with this expectation (Gallagher, 1995).

Of equal or greater importance are the well-documented sex differences in *profiles* of mental ability, even when controlling for interest and instruction in the relevant areas. Males tend to score better in spatial and mathematical reasoning and females in certain verbal proficiencies. In terms of the hierarchical model of human mental ability, these are differences in Stratum II abilities. Males average about one-third to one-half standard deviation higher than females in spatial ability (which is analogous to 5–8 IQ points). The *average* sex difference in mathematical reasoning is small, but the disproportion becomes dramatic among the most talented. To illustrate, male:female ratios among gifted seventh and eighth graders are 2:1 above SAT-M 500, 4:1 above SAT-M 600, and 13:1 above SAT-M 700 (Lubinski & Benbow, 1992). Thus, although such sex differences may not be very noticeable for the bulk of the population, they can become stark at the level from which workers are recruited to high-level math and science occupations requiring these aptitudes (e.g., physics).

In short, average group disparities in mental abilities are common, and they can reflect differences in either profile or magnitude. Each group disparity poses a political challenge to school systems. Because average differences have bigger effects at the "tails" of any ability distribution, they become glar-ing and pose especially prickly political challenges for gifted and special education.

Genetics

Most people view the unusually high abilities of some children as "gifts"—as windfalls that owe little or nothing to the efforts of the children themselves. The disagreement has been over whether such gifts come from nature or nurture. While the origins of extremely high intelligence are far less understood than the origins of retardation and dementia, research on the genetics of normal intelligence (IQ differences in general) provides a useful guide to the debate. The following discussion deals only with *individual* differences in intelligence, because the causes of average *group* differences remain unknown. It also focuses on general intelligence, *g,* rather than special aptitudes, because the genetic sources of the latter turn out to be mostly shared with *g,* as noted earlier.

Heritability of *g*. When behavioral geneticists speak of the *heritability* of a trait, they are actually using a short-hand phrase that can be easily misunderstood. Degree of heritability—say, 40 percent or 80 percent—is not a physical constant, free of time and place, like absolute zero in temperature. Heritability is simply the proportion of (a) phenotypic (observed) variation in an attribute that can be attributed to (b) genotypic variation in the group studied. Heritability estimates therefore apply only to environments and populations *like the ones studied,* not to all possible ones. Eliminating all environmental differences among us, for example, would reduce our differences in intelligence, with the result (perhaps counterintuitive) that all remaining differences in IQ would be genetic—that is, 100% heritable. Our genes will not have changed, but heritabilities will have. Conversely, greater differences among environments are likely to *reduce* heritability by simply adding more environmentally induced variation to a trait's phenotypic pot (the denominator of the heritability ratio). Current estimates of heritability have been derived from populations in rich and poor, Western and non-Western populations, but not often from the extremes of environmental privilege or deprivation. The emerging pattern of estimates, therefore, may not apply to all human groups.

With that caveat in mind, the estimates have brought startling news. They tell us that all sides of the nature-nurture debate had badly misunderstood how genes and environments affect our behavior. Because Robert Plomin discusses the topic in Chapter 9, I shall highlight only a few of the more pertinent surprises from the large corpus of behavioral genetic studies of intelligence.

Heritability of *g Rises* with Age. Even among geneticists, the common expectation had been that any genetic effects would fade with age owing to greater exposure to the vicissitudes of life, good and bad. In actuality, the heritability of intelligence rises with age, from about 20 percent in infancy, to 40 percent in the preschool years, to 60 percent by adolescence, to 80 percent in adulthood. With age, phenotypic differences therefore come to correlate about 0.9 (the square root of 0.80) with genotypic differences in IQ. This is a truly astonishing finding. Recent evidence shows that the heritabilities of school achievement and the narrower Stratum II abilities likewise increase with age (Plomin et al., 2001). This may follow from the fact that, although they have lower heritabilities than does *g,* their heritable components mostly overlap those for *g* (Bouchard, 1998; Plomin et al., 2001).

Shared Family Effects *Disappear* with Age. A second big surprise concerns *environmental* influences on IQ. It had long been assumed, by behavioral geneticists too, that they consist largely of the family influences that siblings share but which differ between families (parents' child-rearing style, income, education, and the like). Such shared family influences do, in fact, rival genetic influences in early childhood, but they virtually disappear by adolescence. Only *non-shared* environments—aspects of environments that affect one individual at a time (e.g., illness, injury)—continue to influence IQ. Their effect is to make siblings in the same home *less* alike over time.

Siblings by adoption illustrate the two surprising findings simultaneously. With age, they become less like their environmental siblings and parents but *more* like the biological ones they have never met. By adolescence, adoptive siblings are no more alike than strangers. In contrast, identical twins reared apart correlate almost as highly in adult IQ (0.72–0.78) as do identical twins who were reared together (.86; Plomin et al., 2001, p. 168). What is true for *g* is also true of personality and virtually all other traits and behaviors

yet studied, including height and weight (but excluding juvenile delinquency).

How could it be that intelligence becomes more genetic with age while the influences of family advantage and disadvantage vanish? Currently, the major theory is that people to some extent seek out and create their own environments based on their genetic proclivities. Scarr's "niche-seeking" theory (Scarr & McCartney, 1983), which is similar to Bouchard and colleagues' "genes-drive-experience" theory (Bouchard, Lykken, Tellegen, & McGue, 1994), is that children increasingly choose and change their own environments as they become more independent of their families. They bring their environments more in line with their latent tastes and abilities, which further enhances the development of those tastes and abilities. Early *shared* family influences cease to operate about the age when children leave home.

The genes-drive-experience-and-niche-seeking theory supports the notion that individuals have a hand in creating themselves and their own destiny. It tells us that we are not the hapless putty of *either* nature or nurture. It also seems consistent with observations of gifted children. Many of them are relentless in reshaping their environments. Winner (1996), for example, describes how "David" enlisted his mother's help to learn to read at age three. "By the time he was three and a half, the library waived the limit on how many books David could take out so that his mother would not have to bring him in every day" (p. 18). Nor would he "rest until he had an answer that satisfied him," such as "where wind came from" (p. 20). Or consider three-year-old "Michael," who "exhausted his parents" with his rage for mastering mathematics, greeting his father every day after work with an insistent request that they "go do work" with his math books (p. 21).

The Nature of Nurture. In fact, behavioral genetic research has shown that many of the environments (e.g., rearing conditions) and events (marital history, job loss, and so on) that we experience are to some extent genetic in origin, that is, the product of our own genotypes (Plomin et al., 2001). Environments are thus not entirely external or "out there." Rather, to some degree they represent our *extended phenotypes*—the expression of our own genes. Accordingly, many of life's environments and events also turn out to be somewhat heritable (Plomin, 1994;

Plomin & Bergeman, 1991). Although environments can shape us, they themselves are partly shaped by our family's collective genes. As behavioral geneticists say, this is the operation of nature *via* nurture.

The real question, then, is not whether nature or nurture dominates, but how the two work together. The two forces are not independent and parallel, but the venue for each other's operation. Two phenomena that illustrate this are highly relevant to understanding giftedness: First, our genotypes influence our *sensitivity* to environments and, second, they influence our *exposure* to them. With regard to sensitivity, genetic differences often make people differentially susceptible or responsive to identical drugs, life stresses, instruction in reading, and the like. As physicians and educators know first-hand, treatments that help some individuals do not help others, and may even hurt them. In the parlance of behavioral genetics, these are gene-environment *interactions*. Their practical implication for gifted education is that the optimal school environment is one that provides a *menu of opportunity* for a wide range of genotypes. This is hardly news, of course, to parents and educators. They know that children don't all react in the same way to the same treatment, educational or otherwise. And it is a consistent theme in gifted education, in particular. What behavioral genetics research adds is evidence that our individuality stems in part from the unique genotypes with which we all are born (except identical twins) and that, like plants, some of us wither in environments where others may thrive. Thus, although schools may not be able to create giftedness, they can provide the conditions essential for it to flower into high accomplishment.

The second phenomenon, which is genetically driven exposure to environments, refers to gene-environment *correlation*. This is simply the fact that genetically distinct individuals (different genotypes) are not randomly distributed across environments. Rather, they tend to be clustered in different environments. This happens partly because the same parental genes that produce the child's genotype also influence the environment the parents create for the child. This is called *passive* gene-environment correlation. But the most interesting reasons for gene-environment correlations are that people with different genotypes (shyness, aggressiveness, high intelligence, and so on) *evoke* different responses from their environments, and they also actively *create* different environments for themselves. These are labeled, respectively, "evocative" (or reactive) and "active"

gene-environment correlations. Winner's (1996) David and Michael exhibited both of these processes, as do we all.

The active-organism portrait painted by behavioral genetic research has important practical implications. The phenomenon of gene-environment interaction makes it unwise to try imposing identical environments. Such effort is unwise because instruction that is helpful for low-*g* students can stall the progress of high-*g* students, and vice versa. It suggests that, ideally, genetically appropriate environments may be key in capitalizing on children's different potentials.

The phenomenon of gene–environment correlation actually makes the effort to equalize environments futile. Genetically different individuals will use, misuse, modify, and interpret the same environments in different ways. It is literally impossible to provide identical environments to genetically different people.

But futile or not, much educational policy seems directed at just that—leveling all distinctions in the services that schools provide to all but the learning disabled, where the ultimate criterion of success is that all students succeed in mastering the same material. This is the strong educational tide against which advocates for the gifted must perennially row. Worse yet, in stressing the distinctive educational needs of gifted students, advocates must necessarily stress what makes them distinctive, which is their superior intellectual potential. It is exactly the "innate superiority" of some individuals over others, however, that schools seem loathe to recognize, let alone nourish. Genetic reality runs headlong into today's political reality. The political challenge, then, is to create the educational conditions for individuality to express itself and for gifted potential to be realized *despite* the fact that such conditions will produce greater inequality of result.

Pragmatics

Researchers will continue to puzzle for decades over what *g* "really" is, biologically and psychologically, but there is no doubt that having more of it rather than less provides an individual enormous advantages in life. As reported elsewhere, "IQ is strongly related, probably more so than any other single measurable human trait, to many important educational, occupational, economic, and social outcomes" (Gottfredson, 1997a, p. 14).

The most important fact about *g*—its generality—accounts for its pervasive and lifelong practical utility. Recall that the general intelligence factor, *g,* reflects a highly content- and context-independent capacity for apprehending, comprehending, integrating, and drawing inferences from information of any type. This includes all learning beyond rote memorization, as well as applying old learning to new situations. Life is a long train of activities that constantly requires just this—learning, thinking, problem solving, and decision making of some sort—in short, the exercise of *g*. General intelligence is not just a narrow "academic" ability, but one of global, life-long value. People may not use it fully or to good purpose, but *g* is perhaps the most versatile tool in the toolkit of human abilities.

g Has Pervasive Practical Consequences. The *g* factor is the best single predictor—and a better one than social class background—of standardized school achievement, years of education obtained, occupational level achieved, performance in job training, performance once on the job, delinquency, and more (Brody, 1992; Gottfredson, 1997b). This is why mental tests have been so useful in educational and occupational settings. They help predict who will perform best and therefore can raise the average performance in a student body or workforce when they are used to select among applicants. Many decades of research (e.g., Schmidt & Hunter, 1998) confirm that they are valid—legitimate—for this purpose, and that average performance falls when selection procedures disregard *g*.

g's ability to predict important life outcomes ranges from strong (standardized school achievement), to moderate (job performance), to weak (law-abidingness), but it seems to predict to some degree just about everything people value. From reading restaurant menus to using medicines correctly, higher *g* helps in the daily activities of life. It is thus a constant headwind making it difficult for people of below average IQ to prosper and get ahead in life—or even keep up. As functional literacy and health literacy researchers have documented, poor comprehension of life's daily tasks and opportunities—managing everything from money, an educational career, a family, and a chronic illness such as diabetes or hypertension—can accumulate to produce poverty, poor health, and other bad outcomes. A large longitudinal study of Australian servicemen showed, for instance, that the risk of death from auto accidents doubled for

men of IQ 85–100 compared to men of IQ 100–115, and it tripled for men of IQ 80–85 (O'Toole, 1990). To take another example, a large study of Medicaid patients found that annual health costs were four times higher for those with inadequate literacy than for the average Medicaid patient (Weiss et al., 1994), suggesting they had worse health as well.

Just as low *g* is at the center of a nexus of bad life outcomes (poverty, illegitimacy, school dropout, and crime), so too high *g* is at the center of a nexus of good outcomes (high education, occupation, and income) (Gottfredson, in press b; Herrnstein & Murray, 1994). This can be seen in Figure 3.2. Whereas adults who are somewhat above average in IQ (IQ 111–125) are "out ahead" in terms of competing for college admission and high-level jobs and having low rates of poverty, illegitimacy, school dropout, and incarceration, people of somewhat below average IQ (IQ 76–90) struggle in an up-hill battle. They are competitive only for low-level jobs, and they experience various social pathologies at many times the rate of their brethren of merely somewhat above average IQ: from four times the rate for bearing illegitimate children to about 80 times the rate for dropping out of school. The different risk rates stem from differences in intelligence rather than social class, because essentially the same inequalities are found among siblings of different IQ growing up in the very same home (Murray, 1997).

This is not to say, of course, that *g* is the only risk factor in life outcomes, nor even that it is the major one in many cases. Other advantages, such as favorable family circumstances, lengthy practice or experience, persistence, or a winning personality can compensate for below-average *g* in some realms of life. None, however, can substitute for missing information-processing skills when people confront life's relentless flow of demands and opportunities for learning and decision making. For instance, army research has shown that experienced soldiers in the 10th–30th percentiles of general mental ability can outperform brighter soldiers with little or no experience, but that their superiority disappears once the brighter men get a few months of experience (Wigdor & Green, 1991). In other words, no matter what else might increase a person's odds for success, lower *g* always lowers them. The reverse is also true, of course. High *g* always raises one's odds of success, but other traits or conditions (fecklessness, illness, lack of opportunity) can harm them. High *g* is no guarantee of success, but, like money, it certainly helps to have more rather than less. Simonton (1994, p. 226) has shown this to be true for the very highest levels of cultural achievement, too.

Narrower Abilities Have Narrower Effects. One might reasonably suppose that tests of math ability would predict achievement in math better than in reading, and that tests of verbal ability would do the opposite. Much research has disconfirmed this hypothesis. Specialized abilities seldom add much, if anything, to the prediction of performance beyond that afforded by g, regardless of academic subject or occupation. Generally, tests of narrower abilities (such as verbal or quantitative aptitudes) tend to predict performance in all academic subjects about equally well, or poorly, in broad samples of students (Jencks et al., 1979; Thorndike, 1986). Job performance researchers find the same thing. It seldom matters much which aptitude test you use as long as it is a good measure of g (Schmidt & Hunter, 1998, 2000; Thorndike, 1986). It is always the g component of a test or test battery that carries the freight of prediction, and tests that measure g less well tend to predict performance less well. Where special abilities do add noticeably to prediction, their value seems limited to a narrow domain of tasks (clerical speed in clerical jobs).

As with the genetic research, then, research in education and personnel selection psychology finds that the special aptitudes have some independent influence, but that it is small relative to g. They are bit players in the drama of social inequality. Because they are largely coincident with g itself in composition as well as consequence, domain-specific talents are not likely ever to provide a multiple-intelligences route to greater social equality. This does not mean that we should expect gifted individuals to be uniformly gifted, but—once again—only that we should not expect there to be routes to giftedness and high achievement that are independent of g. Specific talents can add to, but not substitute for, g.

Where and Why g Matters Most. Just as the question of whether differences in g "result from nature *or* nurture" is passé, so too is the question of whether they "matter in real life." The interesting question, instead, is where g matters most and least, and why. The clearest evidence on g's gradients of effect comes from the century of research in personnel selection psychology. The research documents four important factors that increase the correlations we observe between g and performance: (1) the task is more complex, (2) the task is instrumental rather than socioemotional in character, (3) the group has not already been winnowed on the basis of g (say, owing to selection on test scores or educational level), and (4) the people involved have similar levels of *relative* experience at the task. The first two get at the heart of why higher levels of g are more useful in some activities than others, whereas the latter two concern artifacts that can camouflage the impact of g by artificially lowering its correlation with other variables.

The importance of task complexity is well established. Complexity is the key distinction between high and low-level jobs, difficult and easy functional literacy tasks, and difficult and easy IQ test items—*regardless* of their manifest content (Gottfredson, 1997b). The more complex a job is, the better g tends to predict differences in worker performance (with validities rising from about 0.2 to about 0.8 for individual jobs).

Predictive validities are uniformly lower, however, for activities with a high socioemotional content, for instance, the citizenship (reliability, teamwork) rather than core-technical aspects of jobs (engine repair, architectural design). It appears then, that g probably predicts best when activities are instrumental ones that people perform as individuals, but that other personal traits (e.g., extraversion) become increasingly important when tasks depend more on emotional or interpersonal behaviors.

The greater utility of g in complex or instrumental tasks emerges clearly when individuals are drawn from a wide range of intelligence but similar task-relevant experience, as would generally be the case among applicants for entry-level jobs or college admissions. g's utility can be totally disguised, however, by the other two factors that affect IQ correlations by artificially depressing them, namely, when individuals represent only a truncated segment of the ability distribution or differ widely in relevant experience. The latter was illustrated by the situation, discussed earlier, where dull but experienced soldiers were found to (temporarily) outperform bright but inexperienced soldiers. The impact of restriction in range can be seen in the correlations of IQ with standardized academic achievement. The observed correlations fall from 0.6–0.7 in elementary school to 0.3–0.4 in graduate school, not because higher education is less intellectually demanding (it certainly is not!), but because more people of below-average (and then average) IQ fall by the wayside at each successive step up the educational ladder (Jensen, 1980, p. 319).

A practical implication of the "complexity effect" is that more intellectually demanding programs will produce bigger differences in student performance and leave more students behind than will less demanding ones, especially when selection into the program deemphasizes *g*. However, the "instrumental versus socioemotional task effect" predicts that *g* level will have relatively less effect when the programs involve task domains that are less strictly intellectual because they call for emotional maturity or life experience, as is the case in writing rather than mathematics. A practical implication of the third, "restriction in range effect" is that it is easy to debunk the importance of IQ for gifted levels of achievement by correlating IQ with performance in a group of gifted students, National Merit Finalists, or the like. Other traits are guaranteed to loom large compared to *g* in accounting for differences in performance in such groups, but it hardly means that less able students would succeed in the program were they to be admitted. Another false but effective debunking strategy is to capitalize on the fourth, "differential experience effect" by correlating IQ with performance when some students in the sample have already had instruction or experience (say, with a musical instrument) but others not. This is sure to obscure the value of higher *g* in mastering the task.

Relation Between *g* and Great Achievement. The foregoing evidence dealt with what might be called garden-variety success—a graduate or professional degree, a high-level job, and a good income. Such were the outcomes of Terman's highly able sample of men and women, for instance (Oden, 1968). But what about the ability of *g* to predict remarkably high levels of achievement—of culturally recognized greatness? Dean Keith Simonton's chapter deals with this question, so I will comment only briefly.[6]

In some sense, the story of greatness is the same as for garden-variety success in a culture. Above-average intelligence is probably essential; additional increments are helpful; but even the highest levels of intelligence are not by themselves sufficient. Simonton's (1994) discussion of famous Western artists, intellectuals, and political leaders illustrates

how higher increments of intelligence have some value, albeit limited, in predicting different degrees of greatness.

Genius or greatness depends on a confluence of several favorable traits, high intelligence being only one among them. Discussions of extraordinarily gifted children refer, for instance, to their precocity, insistence on marching to their own drummer, and a rage to master (Winner, 1996); to adult genius as the product of high ability, high productivity, and high creativity (Eysenck, 1995; Jensen, 1996); and to greatness as involving high intelligence, determination, and energy (Simonton, 1994). Simonton captures the crucial role of non-intellectual traits:

> [M]aking it big ["becoming a star"] is a career. People who wish to do so must organize their whole lives around a single enterprise. They must be monomaniacs, even megalomaniacs, about their pursuits. They must start early, labor continuously, and never give up the cause. Success is not for the lazy, procrastinating, or mercurial (p. 181).

As Simonton (2001) points out, greatness may be a genetically emergenic phenomenon. *Emergenesis* is a lucky combination in the genetic lottery that does not run in families precisely because it is the *rare conjunction* of traits inherited separately (Lykken, 1982). If greatness is thus *multiplicative* in nature, the lack of any single component—including high intelligence—dooms one to nongreatness.

Greatness also tends to be domain-specific rather than general. Mozart was not a Gauss or Shakespeare too. Whatever role environmental influences and opportunities play in tilting individuals toward one form of greatness or another, the direction that greatness takes is probably also influenced by the person's particular confluence of abilities, general and specific. But like *g* itself, specific talents would not be sufficient for greatness. No ability, no matter how strong or versatile, is more than a tool. It must be honed and wielded with enormous dedication and long practice to produce anything extraordinary.

SUMMARY AND CONCLUSIONS

The general mental ability factor, *g,* is a general capacity for processing information of any type. It is manifested in daily life as the ability to learn, reason, and solve problems, and it therefore corresponds to

---

6. See Chapter 28 by Simonton.

what many people think of as intelligence. This general ability is measured well by IQ tests; it is highly practical in daily affairs; and it helps predict many valued life outcomes. Higher levels of g provide bigger advantages when the task is more complex. The g factor is the major component of all broad mental abilities and is therefore probably a crucial component of all forms of intellectual giftedness. The genetic heritability of IQ increases from 40 percent in the early elementary school years to 80 percent in adulthood, but appropriate environments are necessary for high levels of g to blossom into actual achievement. Moderately high levels of g are generally necessary but not sufficient for high levels of educational and occupational achievement. The same seems to be true for cultural greatness or genius. Moderately high intelligence is necessary, but must be accompanied by other highly favorable attributes, such as great zeal, tenacity, and perhaps a special verbal, quantitative, spatial, musical, or other talent in order for extraordinary achievement to result.

The fact that differences in intelligence are real, stable, and important creates a political dilemma for Americans. Although providing everyone equal opportunity to achieve on the basis of their talents and efforts will not produce equal results, Americans tend to want both forms of equality. The belief of many educational policy makers that schools should be used to decrease social inequality makes it difficult to advocate special programs for the gifted. While regular academic programs may harm the development of the gifted, programs that meet their needs are often criticized as only helping the "rich to get richer." Behavioral genetic research on the genetic and environmental sources of individuality are consistent with a call for schools to provide a large menu of opportunities that corresponds to the full diversity of their students.

QUESTIONS FOR THOUGHT AND DISCUSSION

1. Examine some major published debate or disagreement over gifted education. To what extent were the arguments over goals and values (politics), and to what extent were they over empirical facts (scientific evidence)? For the politics, what were the key points of implicit or explicit contention? For the science, how much and what kind of evidence was actually provided?

2. Explain the three-tiered hierarchical (pyramid) model of intelligence that Gottfredson says is widely accepted.

How can the model (or Gottfredson) account for extraordinary musical, mathematical, or other highly specific capability?

3. Explain Gottfredson's criticism of multiple types of intelligence (i.e., those of Gardner and Sternberg).

4. In fact, many schools and districts continue to use IQ tests (g) for G/T program selection. Consider political realities, political correctness, and your conscience. What do you think about other selection criteria, such as self-nominations, parent nominations, teacher nominations, grades (achievement), observed art or science talent, or even a high interest in program participation? Also, would different students be selected? Explain.

5. Explain "gene-environment interaction" and implications for teaching gifted students.

REFERENCES

Baltes, P. B. (1993). The aging mind: Potential and limits. *The Gerontologist, 33*(5), 580–594.

Bouchard, T. J., Jr. (1998). Genetic and environmental influences on adult intelligence and special mental abilities. *Human Biology, 70*(2), 257–279.

Bouchard, T. J., Jr., Lykken, D. T., Tellegen, A., & McGue, M. (1994). Genes, drives, environment, and experience: EPD theory revised. In C. P. Benbow & D. Lubinski (Eds.), *Intellectual talent: Psychometric and social issues* (pp. 5–43). Baltimore: Johns Hopkins University Press.

Brody, N. (1992). *Intelligence* (2nd ed.). San Diego: Academic Press.

Carroll, J. B. (1993). *Human cognitive abilities: A survey of factor-analytic studies.* Cambridge: Cambridge University Press.

Colangelo, N., & Davis, G. A. (1997). Introduction and overview. In N. Colangelo & G. A. Davis (Eds.), *Handbook of gifted education* (2nd ed., pp. 3–9). Boston: Allyn & Bacon.

Deary, I. J. (2000). *Looking down on intelligence: From psychometrics to the brain.* Oxford: Oxford University Press.

de Tocqueville, A. (1990/1835). *Democracy in America.* New York: Vintage.

Detterman, D. K., & Daniel, M. H. (1989). Correlations of mental tests with each other and with cognitive variables are highest for low IQ groups. *Intelligence, 13,* 349–359.

Eysenck, H. J. (1995). *Genius: The natural history of creativity.* Cambridge: Cambridge University Press.

Gallagher, J. J. (1995, January). Education of gifted students: A civil rights issue? *Phi Delta Kappan,* 408–410.

Gardner, H. (1983). *Frames of mind: The theory of multiple intelligences.* New York: Basic Books.

Gardner, J. W. (1984). *Excellence: Can we be equal and excellent too?* (2nd ed.). New York: Norton.

Glazer, S. (1990). Why schools still have tracking. *Congressional Quarterly's Editorial Research Reports,* 1(48), 746–759.

Gottfredson, L. S. (1997a). Editorial: Mainstream science on intelligence: An editorial with 52 signatories, history, and bibliography. *Intelligence, 24*(1), 25–52.

Gottfredson, L. S. (1997b). Why g matters: The complexity of everyday life. *Intelligence, 24*(1), 79–132.

Gottfredson, L. S. (2000a). Pretending that intelligence doesn't matter. *Cerebrum, 2*(3), 75–96.

Gottfredson, L. S. (2000b). Skills gaps, not tests, make racial proportionality impossible. *Psychology, Public Policy, and Law, 6*(1), 129–143.

Gottfredson, L. S. (in press a). Dissecting practical intelligence: Its claims and evidence. *Intelligence.*

Gottfredson, L. S. (in press b). g, jobs, and life. In H. Nyborg (Ed.), *The scientific study of mental ability: Tribute to Arthur R. Jensen.* New York: Pergamon.

Herrnstein, R. J., & Murray, C. (1994). *The bell curve: Intelligence and class structure in American life.* New York: Free Press.

Hunt, E. B. (2001). Multiple views of multiple intelligence [Review of *Intelligence reframed: Multiple intelligence in the 21st century*]. *Contemporary Psychology, 46*(1), 5–7.

Jencks, C., Bartlett, S., Corcoran, M., Crouse, J., Eaglesfield, D., Jackson, G., McClelland, K., Mueser, P., Olneck, M., Schwartz, J., Ward, S., & Williams, J. (1979). *Who gets ahead? The determinants of economic success in America.* New York: Basic Books.

Jensen, A. R. (1980). *Bias in mental testing.* New York: Free Press.

Jensen, A. R. (1996). Giftedness and genius: Crucial differences. In C. P. Benbow & D. Lubinski (Eds.), *Intellectual talent: Psychometric and social issues* (pp. 393–411). Baltimore: Johns Hopkins University Press.

Jensen, A. R. (1998). *The g factor: The science of mental ability.* Westport, CT: Praeger.

Kulik, J. A., & Kulik, C.-L. C. (1997). Ability grouping. In N. Colangelo & G. A. Davis (Eds.), *Handbook of gifted education* (2nd ed., pp. 230–242). Boston: Allyn & Bacon.

Lubinski, D., & Benbow, C. P. (1992). Gender differences in abilities and preferences among the gifted: Implications for the math-science pipeline. *Current Directions in Psychological Science, 1*(2), 61–66.

Lykken, D. T. (1982). Research with twins: The concept of emergenesis. *Psychophysiology, 19,* 361–373.

Matarazzo, J. D. (1972). *Wechsler's measurement and appraisal of adult intelligence.* Baltimore: Williams & Wilkins.

Moffitt, T. E., Caspi, A., Harkness, A. R., & Silva, P. A. (1993). The natural history of change in intellectual performance: Who changes? How much? Is it meaningful? *Journal of Child Psychology and Psychiatry, 34*(4), 455–506.

Mulkey, L. M. (1993). *Sociology of education: Theoretical and empirical investigations.* New York: Harcourt Brace Jovanovich.

Murray, C. (1997). IQ will put you in your place. *Sunday London Times,* May 25.

Neisser, U., Boodoo, G., Bouchard, T. J., Jr., Boykin, A. W., Brody, N., Ceci, S. J., Halpern, D. F., Loehlin, J. C., Perloff, R., Sternberg, R. J., & Urbina, S. (1996). Intelligence: Knowns and unknowns: *American Psychologist, 51,* 77–101.

Oden, M. H. (1968). The fulfillment of promise: Forty-year follow-up of the Terman gifted group. *Genetic Psychology Monographs, 77,* 3–93.

O'Toole, B. J. (1990). Intelligence and behavior and motor vehicle accident mortality. *Accident Analysis and Prevention, 22,* 211–221.

Page, E. B., & Keith, T. Z. (1994). The elephant in the classroom: Ability grouping and the gifted. In C. P. Benbow & D. Lubinski (Eds.), *Intellectual talent: Psychometric and social issues* (pp. 192–210). Baltimore: Johns Hopkins University Press.

Plomin, R. (1994). *Genetics and experience: The interplay between nature and nurture.* Thousand Oaks, CA: Sage.

Plomin, R., & Bergeman, C. S. (1991). The nature of nurture: Genetic influence on "environmental" measures. *Behavioral and Brain Sciences, 14,* 373–427.

Plomin, R., DeFries, J. C., McClearn, G. E., & McGuffin, P. (2001). *Behavioral genetics* (4th ed.). New York: Worth.

Reynolds, C. R., Chastain, R. L., Kaufman, A. S., & McLean, J. E. (1987). Demographic characteristics and IQ among adults: Analysis of the WAIS-R standardization sample as a function of the stratification variables. *Journal of School Psychology, 25,* 323–342.

Robinson, A. (1997). Cooperative learning for talented students: Emergent issues and implications. In N. Colangelo & G. A. Davis (Eds.), *Handbook of gifted education* (2nd ed., pp. 243–252). Boston: Allyn & Bacon.

Salthouse, T. (2000, December). Analytic models of intellectual aging. Invited address to the annual meeting of the International Society for Intelligence Research, Cleveland, OH.

Scarr, S., & McCartney, K. (1983). How people make their own environments: A theory of genotype → environmental effects. *Child Development, 54,* 424–435.

Schaie, K. W. (1996). Intellectual development in adulthood. In J. E. Birren & K. W. Schaie (Eds.), *Handbook of the psychology of aging* (4th ed.). San Diego: Academic Press.

Schmidt, F. L., & Hunter, J. E. (1998). The validity and utility of selection methods in personnel psychology: Practical and theoretical implications of 85 years of research findings. *Psychological Bulletin, 124*(2), 262–274.

Schmidt, F. L., & Hunter, J. E. (2000). Select on intelligence. In E. A. Locke (Ed.), *The Blackwell handbook of principles of organizational behavior* (pp. 3–14). Malden, MA: Blackwell.

Simonton, D. K. (1994). *Greatness: Who makes history and why.* New York: Guilford.

Simonton, D. K. (2001). Talent development as a multidimensional, multiplicative, and dynamic process. *Current Directions in Psychological Science, 10*(2), 39–43.

Stanley, J. C. (1997). Varieties of intellectual talent. *The Journal of Creative Behavior, 31*(2), 93–119.

Sternberg, R. J. (1997). *Successful intelligence.* New York: Plume.

Sternberg, R. J., Forsythe, G. B., Horvath, J. A., Wagner, R. K., Williams, W. M., Snook, S. A., & Grigorenko, E. L. (2000). *Practical intelligence in everyday life.* New York: Cambridge University Press.

Tannenbaum, A. J. (1996). The IQ controversy and the gifted. In C. P. Benbow & D. Lubinski (Eds.), *Intellectual talent: Psychometric and social issues* (pp. 44–77). Baltimore: Johns Hopkins University Press.

Thorndike, R. (1986). The role of general ability in prediction. *Journal of Vocational Behavior, 29,* 332–339.

"To group or not to group: Is that really the question?" (1995, September). *Johns Hopkins Magazine,* pp. 46, 48–52.

Weiss, B. D., Blanchard, J. S., McGee, D. L., Hart, G., Warren, B., Burgoon, M., & Smith, K. (1994). Illiteracy among Medicaid recipients and its relationship to health care costs. *Journal of Health Care for the Poor and Underserved, 5,* 99–111.

Wigdor, A. K., & Green, B. F., Jr. (Eds.) (1991). *Performance for the workplace. Volume 1.* Washington, DC: National Academy Press.

Winner, E. (1996). *Gifted children: Myths and realities.* New York: Basic Books.

Conceptions and Identification

Part II focuses on how *giftedness* is defined and conceptualized, and ways gifted students are—or should be—identified. Several themes emerge. One is that diverse conceptualizations of "giftedness" exist, emphasizing, for example, different combinations of traits that create different varieties of giftedness; differentiating gifts versus talents; and proposing multiple types of intelligence. A second theme describes a growing trend toward using one's talents to help others, and teaching gifted students to do so. A third theme explores the genetic substrate of intelligence and giftedness. A fourth examines a key step in every G/T program—the identification of gifted students, including issues, methods, problems, principles, and common mistakes.

In Chapter 4 Abraham J. Tannenbaum first presents a taxonomic definition of giftedness comprised of eight combinations that essentially reflect *who, what,* and *how:* Producers of thoughts or tangibles may work creatively or proficiently; performers of staged artistry or human services also may work creatively or proficiently. Tannenbaum's *sea star* model emphasizes five cognitive and noncognitive factors that link high promise with productive adult giftedness. Each of the five factors—general ability, special aptitudes, nonintellectual (especially personality) factors, environmental supports, and chance—have both static (status criteria at a given time) and dynamic (changing processes) subfactors. Then Tannenbaum elaborates on the nature of and issues related to these five factors: recent conclusions relating to IQ, including arguments against the use of IQ scores in education and the nature-nurture problem; the nature and importance of special aptitudes, with special attention to mathematical abilities and the nature and role of multipotentiality.

Françoys Gagné in Chapter 5 outlines his Differentiated Model of Giftedness and Talent, a theory that defines *gifts* as untrained natural abilities that become developed into measurable *talents* via learning and practice. Gifts break down into intellectual, creative, socioaffective, and sensorimotor domains; talents into academics, arts, business, leisure, social action, sports, and technology. The transformation from gifts to talents involves three types of catalysts, which positively or negatively impact learning: intrapersonal (e.g., physical, motivational, and personality factors), environmental (e.g., persons, events, and one's social milieu), and chance, whose two "rolls of the dice" determine one's genetic and family circumstances. From most to least impact on talent development, Gagné lists chance, the innate gifts themselves, intrapersonal catalysts, learning/practice, and lastly environmental catalysts. His metric model of levels of giftedness includes *mildly* (1 in 10), *moderately* (1 in 100), *highly* (1 in 1,000), *exceptionally* (1 in 10,000), and *extremely gifted* (1 in 100,000).

Joseph S. Renzulli's best-known theoretical and practical contributions to gifted education include his Enrichment Triad Model, Revolving Door Identification Model (with Sally Reis and Linda Smith), and Schoolwide Enrichment Model (with Sally Reis)—profound contributions indeed! In Chapter 6, under the umbrella phrase *social capital,* Renzulli explains that gifted education should not simply help students become educated and successful for their own personal benefit. Rather, gifted education should help raise bright students' awareness of how they can—and should—focus their intellectual, motivational, and creative talents on improving the lives of others. He cites Nelson Mandela, Rachel Carson, Martin Luther King, Jr., and Mother Teresa as examples. Renzulli explains his Operation Houndstooth at the University of Connecticut, which aims at educational interventions for developing social capital. Operation Houndstooth components include, for example, optimism, courage, sensitivity to human concerns, and feelings of vision and destiny.

The project shares much with positive psychology and, while not specifically named, character education.

One revolution in education in the past two decades is the broadening of our definition of intelligence. Whenever this topic is discussed, Robert J. Sternberg and Howard Gardner are the first (often the only) names mentioned. In Chapter 7 Sternberg reviews his Triarchic Theory of successful intelligence: *Analytic* giftedness is exhibited by persons who do well on intelligence and achievement tests; *synthetic* giftedness is displayed by unconventional, creative, and intuitive thinkers; and *practical* giftedness is shown by persons superior in adapting to and coping with everyday problems and job challenges. *Giftedness* is a well-managed balance of these three types of intelligence. Sternberg notes that children with high synthetic and practical intelligence are rarely taught, or evaluated, in ways that match their strength. Also, success is most likely when one capitalizes on strengths and corrects or compensates for one's weaknesses. Giftedness is not fixed, but capable of improvement—by capitalizing on strengths and improving weaknesses.

Like Sternberg, Catya von Károlyi, Valerie Ramos-Ford, and Howard Gardner in Chapter 8 review another alternative to traditional IQ conceptions of intelligence and giftedness. Gardner's theory of Multiple Intelligences (MI) currently includes eight intelligences: linguistic, logical-mathematical, spatial, musical, bodily-kinesthetic, interpersonal, intrapersonal, and naturalist. An individual may be gifted in any combination of the intelligences, which work in concert with one another in virtually any domain. Gardner's MI perspective influences how we conceive of and identify giftedness, and how we educate "traditionally" gifted students as well as students gifted in other types of his intelligences. Project Spectrum provides an example of MI assessment and instruction in action. Another example illustrates how an MI perspective can enhance students' learning and understanding of core ideas in various domains of knowledge through multiple entry (starting) points. MI theory has opened the eyes of many educators regarding conceptions of intelligence and giftedness and the teaching of all students.

In Chapter 9, which revolves around the nature-nurture problem, Robert Plomin and Thomas S. Price review developments in genetics research related to general cognitive ability and giftedness; that is, to intelligence. While genetics plays a "significant and substantial" role in one's intelligence, Plomin agrees that environmental factors—such as educational interventions—also contribute to intellectual development and behavior. Further, knowledge of genetic influence does not dictate specific gifted programming directions, say the authors, but "better decisions ought to be made with knowledge than without it." Adoption studies and twin research indicate heritability estimates—the proportion of differences in IQ due to genetics, not environment—of about 50 percent. As Gottfredson noted, heritability estimates are higher for adults than for children; environmental influence actually decreases with age. According to Plomin and Price, any difference between intelligence test and achievement test scores—as with underachievement—is due to environmental factors.

Susan G. Assouline in Chapter 10 elaborates on assessment, which includes testing, interviews, and observation to identify gifted students and to plan programs and curriculum for them. She explains differences between and uses of authentic, criterion-referenced, and standardized (norm-referenced) tests. Assouline notes that critics pan intelligence testing, for example, for presenting one number that provides no guidance for improvement. A brief history of intelligence testing in gifted education includes mainly Galton, Binet and Simon, and Terman, who represent the psychometric tradition, and more recently the cognitive modifiability and information-processing uses of testing. Assouline explains some limitations of group IQ tests, and recommends the individually administered Stanford-Binet and WISC tests, plus the relatively new Differential Aptitude Scales. In one case study, a Psychological Interpretive Report describes how an assessment of "Fred" led to accelerating him several grades. A second case study used the Iowa Acceleration Scale to evaluate "Jenny," also for acceleration. Assouline's Consumer Guidelines describe the sensible selection and use of tests, including attention to who administers the test and the specific form of recommendations.

E. Susanne Richert in Chapter 11 reviews several related educational trends and political problems. Especially, charges of elitism and discrimination have led to heterogeneous classes and the elimination of gifted programs—which have been overloaded with White middle-class students. Much of her chapter describes her equitable and remarkably successful solution. Working mainly in New Jersey and Connecticut schools with large proportions of minority and poor students, Richert's Project APOGEE, which includes her Maximizing Potential Strategies, used self, parent, and teacher nominations and renorming to select the top 20–25% in each ethnic group for special programs. Instead of using multiple (combined) criteria or cutoff scores, both of which are discriminatory, Richert's identification procedure requires just one high rating, resulting in up to an 800 percent increase in minority/poor student participation in special programs. Her strategy includes strong teacher training and many other options, including homogeneous grouping for required subjects (e.g., reading) and, in secondary school, advanced and honors classes. Richert reviews remarkable results, including strong increases in thinking skills, reading ability, reduced behavior problems—and performance on state achievement tests.

4

Nature and Nurture of Giftedness

ABRAHAM J. TANNENBAUM, *Columbia University*

Behavioral scientists never tire of searching for *the* childhood abilities that guarantee superior accomplishment later in life. The fact is, besides intellect and artistry, *many* attributes of the human psyche interweave with its surroundings to shape a child's future. Except for rare cases of young prodigies, children generally never attain the status of being gifted by adult standards. At best, they are more advanced in learning and in creativity than their age peers and thereby show promise of excelling in later life. But "promise" implies risks in prediction, not assurances.

A Definition of Giftedness

Keeping in mind that developed talent exists primarily in adults, I propose a definition of giftedness in children to denote their potential for becoming critically acclaimed performers or exemplary producers of ideas in spheres of activity that enhance the moral, physical, emotional, social, intellectual, or aesthetic life of humanity.

In detailing this proposed definition as it pertains to childhood *promise,* it is useful to answer three basic questions about giftedness in its *maturity,* most often in adulthood:

1. *Who* qualifies to join the pool of *possibly* gifted individuals?
2. *What* broad realms of achievement among pool members are judged for signs of excellence?
3. *How* do pool members demonstrate their giftedness in these domains of human accomplishment?

As illustrated in Figure 4.1, the answer to the *who* question is that there are two types of gifted people: *producers* and *performers.* What do *producers* pro-

duce? *Thoughts* and *tangibles.* What do *performers* perform? *Staged artistry* and *human services. How* do *producers* of *thoughts, producers* of *tangibles, performers* of *staged artistry* and *performers* of *human services* go about proving their excellence? By working *creatively* or *proficiently.*

Accordingly, there are eight groups of individuals who are recognized by Western societies for the quality of their work, as follows:

1. The producer of thoughts, creatively. This is the philosopher, not the professor of other people's philosophies; the brilliant poet, novelist, essayist, or dramatist, not the voracious reader of literature; the acclaimed painter, composer, or choreographer, not just the lover of the arts; the theoretical or experimental scientist, not the science enthusiast; the historian, not the history buff.

2. The producer of thoughts, proficiently. This is the expert who can solve complex problems, as in math or science, with the deep insight (rather than innovation) needed to work out a solution. Included are the masters of computer programs who use the technology for retrieval and analysis of complex data. Also included are the talented editors who can turn chaotic manuscripts into fine literature. Among the most prominent in this category are the efficiency experts, the great troubleshooters with superior critical skills, which they use to correct existing schemes.

3. The producer of tangibles, creatively. This is the inventor with enough imagination in science and technology to develop such patentable products as the light bulb, the refrigerator, computer hardware, medical equipment, sophisticated communication devices, and the proverbial better mousetrap. In the arts, they are the sculptors, architects, and design engi-

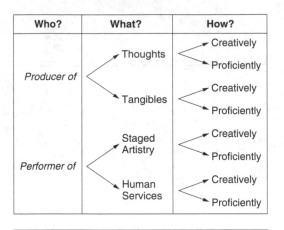

Who?	What?	How?
Producer of	Thoughts	Creatively / Proficiently
	Tangibles	Creatively / Proficiently
Performer of	Staged Artistry	Creatively / Proficiently
	Human Services	Creatively / Proficiently

Figure 4.1 Defining *who* may show signs of giftedness, through *what* media it reveals itself, and *how* it can be expressed.

neers whose main talents lie in developing new products that are either aesthetically or functionally appreciated.

4. The producer of tangibles, proficiently. This is the precision worker whose strength lies in meticulousness rather than originality. Included are diamond polishers whose perfect facets reflect light brilliantly; stonecutters who chisel intricate figures and ornaments for a cathedral's exterior; wood craftspersons who reproduce traditional furniture faithfully in all its complicated design; toolmakers who work by hand to reproduce precision instruments; and machinists capable of constructing sophisticated, problem-free machines and equipment. Master forgers of great art might be included in this category.

5. The performer of staged artistry, creatively. This is the interpreter or recreator. Included are the musical recitalists presenting their own understanding of composers' works; dramatic actors breathing life into a character in a play; dancers communicating their idiosyncratic rendition of a choreographed piece; poetry readers; and orchestral conductors whose brilliance lies in their unique renditions of others' works. Oratory and debate can also be fitted into this category, although some may count them among the lost arts.

6. The performer of staged artistry, proficiently. Included are dancers who translate the choreographer's art into motion faithfully, not inter-

pretively; orchestral musicians whose technique and self-discipline enable the conductor to recreate the wishes of the composer; movie actors who carry out the will of the director and thus turn movie drama into a "director's art"; and chorus members whose precise musical or dance performances blend easily with that of other members.

7. The performer of human services, creatively. Included are innovative teachers, political leaders, social workers, clinical psychologists, and other members of the helping professions. Also deserving mention are action researchers in medicine, the behavioral and social sciences, education, and any other fields that can help the human-to-human condition.

8. The performer of human services, proficiently. These are the classroom teachers who follow guidelines faithfully and successfully; physicians with a keen mind for diagnosis and treatment; psychiatrists who are sensitive to the needs of patients; and administrators of large corporations and service institutions who demonstrate superior managerial skills that require following a predesigned administrative plan competently, rather than designing and executing an original plan.

The Linkages Between Promise and Fulfillment

Having defined giftedness in its maturity as comprising eight broad categories, let us now take up the question of what intrapsychic attributes and external circumstances enable a child *over time* to qualify as gifted. As emphasized in the beginning of this chapter, ability alone at an early age is a fair but far from perfect forerunner of eventual success. Much happens in children's life experiences throughout the school years and beyond that helps to account for what these growing individuals may or may not become.

Mental power by itself is not only a limited predictor of *eventual* adult achievement; it is a far from perfect correlate *during* adulthood, for even then there are traces of mediocrity in high places. Some people get ahead on little more than captivating charm or good looks; on aggressive ambition; on nepotism or "nephewism"; or on affiliation with the "right" race, color, or creed. These booster variables propel them through open doors of opportunity, which close immediately behind them. Others enter through merit at a time when career openings happen to be available. These life circumstances can prevent or delay a person's opportunity to enter an advanced-level career, despite outstanding qualifications through ability and training.

Antecedents and Concomitants of Demonstrated Giftedness: The Star Model

There are no simple, foolproof causes of *demonstrated* giftedness. The antecedents and concomitants are complex, elusive, and not entirely known. However, they lie within the filigree of interweaving, interacting factors—five in all—which may be depicted in the form of a sea star (see Figure 4.2).

The five elements that contribute to the critical center mesh that accounts for gifted behavior are (1) superior general intellect, (2) distinctive special aptitudes, (3) a supportive array of nonintellective traits, (4) a challenging and facilitative environment, and (5) chance—the smile of good fortune at critical periods of life. Each factor consists of *static* and *dynamic* subfactors.

Static subfactors denote individual status, usually relating to group norms, group identity, or other external criteria. They tend to portray humans in snap-

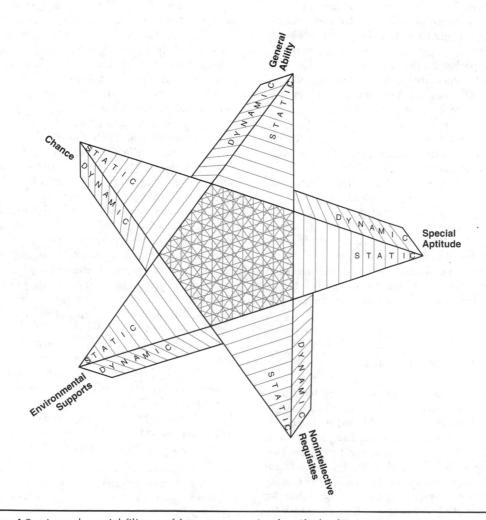

Figure 4.2   A psychosocial filigree of factors accounting for gifted achievements.

shot-like assessments, single impressions frozen in time and place. What these reveal corresponds to what is seen in an aerial photo of forest land, which is descriptive rather than analytic; it records a panorama of color, density, and variety of trees, without exploring what makes them appear the way they do. Similarly, a static view of children and their life circumstances provides a useful impression of where they stand in comparison to others at a particular moment in time. Such assessment relating to giftedness often comprises survey methods and standardized measures.

Dynamic subfactors, on the other hand, refer to processes of human functioning and of the situational contexts in which individual behavior is shaped. Unlike static impressions, which are basically molar, dynamic processes are of a molecular nature and can be discerned only through diagnosis at levels below the surface. The objective is to elucidate the individuality of people and the uniqueness of the surroundings with which they interact. Most theories of dynamic processes in gifted children have been validated only through clinical insights and wise armchair speculation.

No combination of any four factors can compensate for a serious deficiency in the fifth. Also, the minimal essentials, or threshold levels, for all five vary with every talent domain. For example, giftedness in theoretical physics requires higher general ability but fewer interpersonal skills than does giftedness in the social services professions. Therefore, no single set of criteria can be equally effective and efficient for identifying, for example, both "hard" scientists and politicians. The five factors interact in different ways for separate talent domains, but *all* are represented in some way in every form of giftedness.

Superior General Ability

General intellectual ability, or *g,* may be defined roughly as some kind of mysterious mental strength denoting abstract thinking ability and is shared by a variety of specific competencies. The *g* factor, as revealed in tested general intelligence, figures on a sliding scale in all high-level areas. That is, different threshold IQs are required for various kinds of accomplishment, higher in academic subjects than, for example, in the performing arts. There is no basis for

making extreme assertions about the IQ, whether to discount its relevance to giftedness entirely or to accept it without reservation. Instead, positions along this continuum should be adjusted according to the talent area, which means taking a stance closer to one extreme for some kinds of giftedness and nearer the opposite extreme for others.

Interpretations and Criticisms of IQ Differences

Some heated disputes on what to make of IQ assessments never cool down, for example, the long-standing debate on whether IQ tests are culturally biased, per se, or reflect society's bias against some minority cultures (Tannenbaum, 1996). Equally persistent is the conflict on how broadly to interpret an IQ score. Winner (1996) declares that "global giftedness" is a myth, especially if it derives from tests of general intelligence. First, she cites anecdotal encounters with children whose abilities in a single discipline are extraordinary, but who function at an ordinary level in other school subjects. Second, she regards IQ tests as measuring a narrow range of skills that are relevant only to mastering school curricula.

As for the need to regard intelligence more broadly, Sternberg (1999) has proposed a theory of what he calls "successful intelligence."[1] The concept distinguishes between being smart at school as against dealing competently with the wider world of real life. According to Sternberg, IQ scores reveal abilities that are "general only with respect to the academic or analytical aspect of intelligence. Once one includes creative and practical abilities in an assessment, the general factor is greatly diminished or disappears" (p. 16). In other words, conventional measures of intelligence tell part of the story quite well, but only part of the story.

In his widely popular theory of multiple intelligences (MI), Gardner (1983, 1997, 1999) has drawn attention away from the general ability *g* factor to promote the existence of fairly discreet mental strengths, or "intelligences," which he posits through logical impression rather than on the basis of formal data collection and analysis.[2] Despite criticism from psychologists who fault Gardner for failing to rein-

---

1. See Chapter 7 by Sternberg.
2. See Chapter 8 by von Károlyi, Ramos-Ford, and Gardner.

force MI's heuristic reasonableness with objective empiricism (Stanley, 1997; Traub, 1998), the model has gained wide acceptance among educators who plan curricula for the gifted and among publishers who distribute vast amounts of MI-inspired instructional material.

MI theory also leads to radical departures from convention in its way of testing for high potential in children. Existing measures of aptitudes, especially in non-academic domains, are notoriously weak in internal consistency and predictive validity. Gardner (1997) therefore expresses his preference for another approach, as follows: "I favor mechanisms that allow individuals to show what it is that they can already accomplish in a domain" (p. 123). This is done by closely observing children and their productivity in natural learning environments, such as classrooms, rather than at formal testing sessions in an examiner's office (Ramos-Ford & Gardner, 1997). Gardner's rejection of *g*-centrism and IQ testing in favor of a more inclusive, "real-life" orientation has a welcome democratic live-and-let-live ring to it, which helps account for its immense popularity, although he distances himself from those who use MI theory to justify their belief that "everyone is gifted" (Gardner, 1997, p. 123).

For those who would like to abandon any kind of mental testing altogether, Howe (1999) offers encouragement by declaring that innate abilities don't figure at all in talent development. What really counts instead is hard, persistent work at self-advancement over a long period of time (i.e., at least ten distraction-free years).[3] Is this theory a case of pie-in-the-sky idealism or head-in-the-sand escapism? Probably either or both.

IQ Does Tell Us What We Want To Know

Advocates of IQ measures and measurement are as uncompromising in their defense as critics are in their attacks. Gottfredson (1997) quotes a statement on defining intelligence and how to assess it, signed by no fewer than 52 "experts in the study of intelligence" (p. 1).[4] The document makes the following assertions, among others:

---

3. See a related view by Sosniak in Chapter 19.
4. See Chapter 3 by Gottfredson.

(a) Intelligence denotes the ability to reason, think abstractly, learn quickly, learn from experience, and comprehend and solve complex problems. Contrary to the belief that it refers merely to school smarts, book learning, test-taking cleverness, or even acquiring academic skills in their narrow, superficial versions, it relates, instead, to broad and deep insights into the world of ideas.

(b) Intelligence is measurable by IQ tests, which are extremely reliable and valid. However, these instruments have not been designed to assess creativity, personality, character, or other kinds of human differences.

(c) Different types of intelligence tests all measure the same general intelligence. Some emphasize verbal skills; others concentrate on nonverbal shapes and designs; others evaluate knowledge of such basics as many/few, open/closed, and up/down.

(d) The range of IQ in a population can be represented in a bell (normal) curve, with most people clustering around IQ 100, which is therefore considered average. Only about 3 percent earn IQs above 130, the threshold for "giftedness" in many cases.

(e) Intelligence tests are not biased against Blacks or other minority, English-speaking, native-born people in the United States. IQ scores predict equally well for all of these American subpopulations.

(f) IQ is probably the single most valid indicator of potential in educational, occupational, economic, and social endeavors. Its predictive power varies from very strong (in education and military training) to robust (in social competence) to modest but consistent (in law-abiding behavior).

(g) A high IQ is advantageous in virtually all activities in everyday life because nearly all of them require the kinds of reasoning and decision-making strength that IQ tests measure.

(h) While differences in intelligence are not the exclusive influences on capability in education, training, or complex work, they are often the most important. Since individuals are selected on the basis of high intelligence for advanced academic or preprofessional study, differences in their IQ scores are necessarily narrow. Other influences therefore loom larger on the range of achievement in these disciplines.

(i) Personality traits, special talents, physical capabilities, experience, and similar factors affect success in many tasks. However, they are not as transferable or applicable from one kind of task to another as is general intelligence (*g*).

There are also some beginning steps taken to determine more precisely the predictive validity of *g*, in comparison and in conjunction with specific abilities, as they relate to particular scholastic skills. For example, the results of the McGrew, Keith, Flanagan, and Vanderwood (1997) study of children in five grade-level categories (i.e., grades 1–2, 3–4, 5–6, 7–9, 10–12) showed that the *combined* outcomes on tests of *g* and of special aptitudes are powerful forecasters of children's mastery of several basic school-related skills. The researchers therefore endorse the use of reliable and valid measures of specific abilities to reinforce the predictive power of *g*.

Far more evidence is needed to confirm and expand on the little that is known about the relative predictive strengths of general and special abilities as they affect at least some kinds of success in, as well as out of, classrooms. With the full picture still fairly clouded, critics of IQ remain stubborn in their cynicism, while defenders of IQ remain hardened in their orthodoxies.

Rapprochement? Or a Pox on Extremism of Either Kind?

It is hard to imagine any hope for conciliation in this IQ debate since the combatants are entrenched in seemingly snug and smug positions. As in so many instances where beliefs are polarized, the truth probably lies somewhere between the extremes. Many critics denounce IQ testing as morally wrong on grounds that a single metric labels and pigeonholes young children for life as *retarded, average,* or *gifted* in violation of democratic beliefs in the rights of individuals to be captains of their own destinies. As if to reinforce their view of the illegitimacy of IQ testing, these commentators often consider the measurement instruments to lack validity. In other words, it is not only *wrong* to predict the future from one test score, it is *impossible* to do so as well. One is reminded of the disgruntled restaurant guest's concerns that the food tastes like poison and the portions are too small.

Legitimacy and validity don't go together; in fact, they move in opposite directions, which means that we cannot have it both ways. The more progress made in doctoring IQ tests or in devising substitute measures to improve predictability (validity) in academics or other criteria (e.g., street smarts and the like), the more difficult it will be to defend their legitimacy.

Regarding IQ, Meyer et al. (2001) found these correlations: between SAT and subsequent college GPA, 0.20 ($n = 3,816$); GRE Quantitative and subsequent graduate GPA, 0.22 ($n = 5,186$); GRE Verbal and subsequent graduate GPA, 0.28 ($n = 5,816$); general intelligence and success in pilot training, 0.13 ($n = 15,403$); and general intelligence and functional effectiveness across jobs, 0.25 ($n = 40,230$).

In another large-scale meta-analysis dealing exclusively with the predictive validity of the GRE, Kuncel, Hezlett, & Ones (2001) found similar correlations with grades in graduate school and recommended that GRE be combined with other measures to improve prediction. Their advice would also be appropriate for studies of children, if reliable and valid supplementary measures were available.

Nature Versus Nurture

More than a half century ago, Pastore (1949) found that the nature/nurture controversy concerning IQ related closely to differences in political orientation. Liberals in general favored the influence of nurture, which they saw as basically malleable; conservatives tended to vote on the side of nature, which they viewed as basically durable. Today's conflicting opinions on the relative influence of heredity and environment on IQ may not be as closely tied to political ideologies as they once were; there is now more empirical evidence than ever on the amount of variance explained by each variable.

In their statement on IQ and its measurement, the 52 behavioral scientists mentioned earlier were clearly persuaded by research indicating that heredity exerts a stronger influence than environment on IQ differences (Gottfredson, 1997). The evidence favoring nature over nurture is extensive, persuasive, even decisive, or so it seems. It focuses on various dyads, including biologically related and unrelated siblings, monozygotic (MZ) and dizygotic (DZ) twins, each pair reared together or apart from infancy or later in life, in any of several kinds of home settings.

A leading exponent of the powerful influence of nature, compared to nurture, has been Thomas J. Bouchard (1995, 1997; Bouchard, Lykken, Tellegen, & McGue, 1996), whose research on the issue began in 1979 with a study of 100 sets of twins and triplets reared apart. He examined the nature/nurture relationships in several key aspects of human psychology and physiology, cognition being but one of them. However, he is most widely respected—and debated—in regard to his finding that heredity accounts for as much as 70 percent of the variance in IQ. Much less discussed is his equally startling discovery that heredity also figures prominently in many aspects of human behavior and systems of belief that IQ does not influence.

Another prolific contributor to the substantial research literature on the relative impact of genes and environment on IQ has been Robert Plomin, who initiated the well-known Colorado Adoption Project in 1975.[5] Plomin and DeFries's (1983) "longitudinal, prospective, multivariate adoption study of behavioral development" (p. 276) involved 152 one- and two-year olds adopted in the first month of life and designated as experimentals, along with 120 non-adopted age-mates who served as controls. Plomin and colleagues (e.g., Thompson & Plomin, 2000) concluded that heredity accounts for 50 percent of the variance, 20 percent less than the variance reported by Bouchard.

The idea that environment is not necessarily an additive to heritability, but often derives from it, is argued forcefully by researchers. With a population of 707 10–18-year-old dyads (twins, related and unrelated siblings), Plomin, Reiss, Hetherington, and Howe (1994) found that more than a quarter of the differences in nearly all 18 measures of social surroundings could be explained by genetic differences in the sample population.

Also, Scarr (1996) pointed to children's tendencies to choose as friends those who are like-minded, like-spirited, and like them in abilities, interests, and general lifestyles. Thus, hereditary factors affecting the nature of young people also shape the nature of their peer associations. Rowe (1994, 2001) and Harris (1998) argue that parents influence their offspring's socialization not just through genes, but also by electing to live in neighborhoods where other families with similar genetic endowments choose to re-

side. In sum, heredity determines children's individualities and, by extension, their choices of socio-geographic and school settings that are most likely to reinforce these individualities.

An unfortunate consequence of nature versus nurture research is the danger of using it for racial profiling and stereotyping. One of the most prolific writers on such matters is J. Philippe Rushton, whose book *Race, Evolution and Behavior* (1995) is a major treatise on the subject. It is not, as some would suspect from the title, a racist diatribe to be discounted as a rallying call to the bigoted. But unfortunately, it can be used for such purposes. Racists can quickly extrapolate from his comments on racial variation in intelligence that high IQ is a "condition of worth," to borrow Carl Rogers's term. For after all, Rushton quotes *The Bell Curve* (Herrnstein & Murray, 1994) to show that IQ predicts school achievement, job and training success, and as well as low frequencies of child abuse, crime and delinquency, health problems, accident proneness, having a child out of wedlock, getting a divorce before five years of marriage, and smoking during pregnancy.

One cannot help but suspect that the degrees of self-destructive and antisocial tendencies are not exclusive consequences of IQ scores, but also are mediated by differential social climates. Furthermore, Rushton's thesis should be balanced by some sobering weak associations. For example, high IQ is hardly related to effective political leadership, social skills, moral behavior, emotional intelligence (Goleman, 1995), successful intelligence (Sternberg, 1996), or talent in art, music, dance, and theater, among other forms of creativity.

As for discerning intimations of immortality, neither the Stanford-Binet in Terman's longitudinal study (Feldman, 1984; Holahan & Sears, 1985; Oden, 1968) nor the Scholastic Aptitude Test, administered to pre-adolescents in Stanley's Study of Mathematically Precocious Youth (Lubinski, Webb, Morelock, & Benbow, 2001) have determined who, if anyone, would deserve to qualify for that level of renown.

Conventional wisdom avers that, in the best of all worlds, where teaching and environments for learning are perfected, heredity will account for 100 percent of the variance in human performance or production. The rationale for this assertion would appear self-evident and ironclad, except that it fails to recognize the existence of the accidental and inscrutable. Biographies and autobiographies of high

---

5. See Chapter 9 by Plomin and Price.

achievers often report unexpected, life-changing experiences that have galvanized their career commitments and their pursuit of excellence. By definition, these critical events—which include, for example, chance encounters with inspiring individuals or peer groups, with print or audio material, or with performances on stage or in lecture halls—have no rational antecedents and therefore cannot be explained by nature, nurture, or even error variance through known testing procedures. Instead, they amount to the "special chemistry" between an able and impressionable learner and a mind-stirring teacher, counselor, coach, essay, poem, novel, musical composition, or experience with nature.

Which is more influential, heredity versus environment? It is not a sign of fence sitting to conclude that nature and nurture are complementary forces in determining IQ scores and lifetime achievement. Not only is the complementarity necessary, but in a practical sense it doesn't matter which of the two is stronger. Neither can function without the other. The strength of both have to be maximized to realize maximal effect.

Special Abilities

A general factor may predominate, but children also possess special aptitudes, some of which are much more fully developed than others, especially in gifted individuals. Furthermore, there are signs of extraordinary aptitudes even among children who are too young to undergo formal, standardized testing in *any* domain of specialization. Consider, for example, the case of child prodigies, some of them not yet of school age.[6]

As for those who are of school age, formal testing for precocity in special abilities has proven consistently successful only in mathematics, as demonstrated mainly in the SMPY project.[7] For example, in a study of 1,996 SMPY seventh and eighth graders, Benbow (1992) found that the SAT-Mathematics test predicted mathematics-achievement differences ten years later, even with students in an extremely restricted range of scores at and beyond the 99th percentile of the normative distribution.

No screening measure of special talent in other disciplines has yet proven as sage as the SMPY instrument in forecasting fulfillment of early promise. The best that can be done in art and music, for instance, is to theorize about the distinctive characteristics of young, promising talent, based on retrospective accounts of developmental indicators among adult artists and musicians (Winner and Martino, 2000).[8]

A lingering question is whether high-functioning children in one domain tend to possess multiple talents as well. Achter, Lubinski, and Benbow (1995) studied more than 1,000 academically gifted adolescents and found that elevated levels of performance on the SMPY battery did not generalize to other measures. Their conclusion seems reasonable in light of the facts that John Milton's theology, Louis Pasteur's art, and Albert Einstein's performances on the violin, while superior, never measured up to their contributions to poetry, biology, and physics, respectively. William Blake was a rarity among geniuses because he achieved immortality as both an artist and a poet.

Far more important regarding multipotentiality is the question of whether *moderately* high aptitude in one domain is required to reinforce *extremely* high aptitude in another in order to fulfill creative potential. As Root-Bernstein (1989) concluded from biographical evidence, the lesser advanced of two impressive aptitudes informs the other in ingenious ways to enhance the latter's promise and fulfillment. If so, then the leavening effects of secondary talent is what separates the truly innovative philosopher, scientist, mathematician, or research psychologist from professors of other people's philosophy, science, mathematics, or psychological research.

What Achter, Lubinski, and Benbow (1995) might address through mass data analysis are the Root-Bernstein hypotheses concerning the consequences of possessing fairly uneven multitalents, as against narrowly focused high aptitudes. Such a study would yield vital and obvious implications for nurturing special abilities at school.

Special aptitudes can help a child excel in a specific discipline, *if* she or he also shows evidence of

---

6. See Chapter 35 by Morelock and Feldman.

7. See Chapter 15 by Lupkowski-Shoplik, Benbow, Assouline, and Brody.

8. See Chapter 26 by Winner and Martino.

superior general ability. But to bring giftedness fully to life, these cognitive faculties have to be energized by an encouraging disposition, an enriching environment, and timely elements of chance.

Nonintellective Factors

Relating personality traits to giftedness is a chicken-and-egg problem. Nobody knows whether, and to what extent, these attributes are *causes, concomitants,* or *consequences* of successful achievement. There may be links involving creativity (C), psychopathology (P), or such third factors (T) as perfectionism, reluctance to take intellectual risks, proneness to distraction, or others that do not fall into the category of creativity or psychopathology but can affect either or both.

Richards (1981) found a fairly consistent C-P link and posited five major (and several minor) possible relationships among C, P, and T as follows: P→C, for example, pathological deviance drives a person to cultivate offbeat, creative behavior; P←C, for example, creative impulses that are difficult to harness lead to emotional distress or a non-adaptive life style; P→T→C, for example, abnormal obsessive compulsion, combined with easy distraction by generally ignored stimuli, facilitate innovative accomplishment; P←T←C, for example, creative productivity that becomes stereotyped, for fear of taking risks results in ever-growing frustration and ego threat; and P←T→C, that is, psychopathology and creativity have no direct impact on each other, but respond instead to a third cluster of traits that affect, and also mediate, the association.

Does recent research support Richards's (1981) findings? Holden (1987) cited several scholars who "used modern psychiatric diagnostic criteria to explore the relationship between mental illness and creativity" (p. 9), mainly with artists and writers. The results showed clear signs of mental disorder in a disproportionate number of the adult subjects. Ludwig's (1995) investigation of eminent people in a wide variety of professions also concluded that greatness is far more often accompanied by emotional handicap than is averageness.

However, research by Vaillant (2000) included a Terman (1925) group of 90 women born about 1910 and distinguished by their high IQ in childhood (mean in 150 range), rather than by their eminence

later in life (Terman & Oden, 1959). Vaillant concluded that their superior tested intelligence "was a social asset. Their mental health was demonstrably better than that of their [randomly selected] California classmates" (p. 92). High achievement would seem to be bolstered by mental health via such attributes as emotional intelligence (Goleman, 1995), emotion regulation (Salovey & Sluyter, 1997), and constructive thinking (Epstein, 1998). Such attributes promote positive attitudes towards life's challenges and a "can do" self-confidence in advanced learning and creative activities.

Is it possible to reconcile the association between creativity and psychopathology, on one hand, with creativity's link to mental health, on the other? Perhaps the solution is to distinguish "big C" from "little c" brands of creativity. "Big C," by definition, shakes up a discipline in a revolutionary way, thus attracting renown to those who demonstrate such excellence. This requires extreme iconoclastic emotions that may be aberrant but necessary to trigger the dramatic "Big C" talent. "Little c" reflects good, but not great, ideas that show enough originality to impress neighbors and friends who feel mildly edified by them. For this level and kind of activity, a healthy, happy outlook may be an advantage to the creative process.

Regarding "little c" creatives of all ages, Amabile (1996, 2001) considered the question of whether internal, self-starting inclinations or external rewards are better motivators. Her evidence favors internal motivation clearly and consistently. Lens and Rand (2000) confirmed its importance and listed several types, including curiosity, need for competency and efficiency, and achievement motivation.

Whether extrinsic motivation enhances intrinsic motivation remains a subject of intensive debate. Cameron & Pierce (1994) concluded from their meta-analysis of 96 relevant studies that it definitely does. Yet the following remain intriguing mysteries to be answered by research on internal and external modes of motivation: Whatever happened to John Milton's dictum, "Fame is the spur"? Has not the patronage of great artists and composers inspired treasurable creative efforts? Did this external blandishment merely facilitate the release of internally motivated energies? Do external stimulants work their magic only on "big C" immortals? Or is motivation a matter of individuality, which prompts most people, young and old, to respond best to urges from within, while the rest are galvanized into action primarily by external pressure from admired or feared others? If so, then studying internal and external motivation by calculating central tendencies produces only a partial picture that must be completed by clinical research that teases out the contrasting typologies.

Motivation can help the gifted reach high production and performance goals, provided their self-concepts are clear and strong. Colangelo and Assouline (2000) quoted several studies that confirm a positive relationship between strong self-concept and giftedness. However, there is a persistent chicken-and-egg question: Does a healthy image of oneself stimulate gifted behavior? Or does gifted behavior elevate the self image? Probably both are mutually reinforcing.

Research shows that self-concept connects best with achievement when its focus is domain-specific. Marsh (1992) reported a relationship between subject-related, academic self-concept ratings and performances in eight academic school subjects. Some of the correlations are impressively high. Further evidence of the effectiveness of domain-specific self-concept, even in non-academic disciplines, was demonstrated by Vispoel's (1995) study of over 800 college students in the areas of dance, dramatic art, visual art, and music. In a survey of sixth and eighth grade Norwegian students, Skaalvik and Rankin (1995) found that math- and verbal-related self-concepts correlated significantly with both intrinsic motivation and achievement in these subject areas.

In still another contribution to knowledge of how self-concept works, Marsh, Chessor, Craven, and Roche (1995) found that children in special elementary school programs for the gifted experienced a lowering of self-concept in reading, math, and general school success, as compared to equally able students in regular programs. Is the high self-concept of those who excel in heterogeneous classes a natural and realistic assessment of personal ability? Or is self-concept unduly inflated because of the relatively weak competition from fellow students?

Of the non-intellective factors that enable individual excellence to flourish, the ones that are explicated here are only a small sample of what actually exist. The intention is to be illustrative, not exhaustive, in the discussion of traits that help shape and direct gifted behavior. Still, even the present small sample should be enough to show that a rude awakening awaits those who ignore the map of personal idiosyncrasy and rely only on cognitive perspectives and their measures to forecast later success.

The Environment

Giftedness requires social context that enables it to mature. These contexts are as broad as society itself and as restricted as the sociology of the classroom. Human potential needs nurturance, urgings, encouragement, and even pressures from a world that cares. The most serious societal threat to the cultivation of giftedness occurs when excellence of performance or productivity is no longer deemed a standard.

Environment plays such an important role in shaping creative activity that Csikszentmihalyi (1988) gives it prominent attention among three forces that initiate creative behavior: (1) the *domain* in which productivity or performance is acceptable and which undergoes substantive and stylistic change from one period in history to another; (2) the *field* of teachers, critics, patrons, and creative peers who judge individual contributions to each domain; and (3) the *person* who creates within the limits of a domain and sometimes revolutionizes it to the satisfaction of the field. Thus, giftedness does not develop in an environmental vacuum but, rather, interacts with a particular domain and field in a sensitive, meaningful partnership.

School and community definitely stimulate gifted development, although it is not known how much of the variance they explain nor to what extent they are free of genetic antecedents. For example, Winner (1997) reviewed studies of differentiated instruction and found the results generally favorable—but only a limited number of gifted school-age children were offered such opportunities. The educational modifications that seem to work include acceleration, lateral enrichment, and special grouping (provided there is something special in the curricula of special groups). Even with our present incomplete knowledge, evidence shows that special education for the gifted is measurably effective, be it in the form of fast-paced instruction, in-depth studies of conventional subjects, or add-on course work to broaden the curriculum. The reason is simple, as my mentor once remarked: Teach Sanskrit to students capable of learning it, and they will learn more Sanskrit than will comparably capable students who are not taught Sanskrit.

Outside the walls of home and school there are other vital environmental forces, especially the neighborhood where the child lives and the child's peer group, each with its own structures and dynamics (Leventhal & Brooks-Gunn, 2000). Of course, factors that complicate research on the influence of neighborhoods and peers are the residents' genetic inheritance of intellective powers and their non-intellective identity in choosing to live where they do.

Pressures on children to conform to peer leadership and majority consensus are powerful and often decisive. It is therefore necessary for a teacher to take into account the feelings of schoolmates and neighborhood friends about the desirability of being gifted before attempting to encourage the ablest to "reach for the stars." In a study by Schroeder-Davis (1996), 3,514 junior and senior high school students responded to the question of whether they would rather be the best-looking, smartest, or most athletic students in class. Fifty-three percent chose to be the smartest, although only 0.3 percent stated that the reason for desiring to be most intelligent was to gain popularity.

In a replication of Tannenbaum's (1962) study of students' attitudes towards academic brilliance, studiousness, and interest in athletics, Udvari & Rubin (1996) found academic brilliance more acceptable than average achievement at school. Compared with the Tannenbaum data, and similar to the Schroeder-Davis (1996) report, this study showed a marked improvement in the brightest children's status among cohorts.

If there is a technical reason for the discrepancy in results, it may be because the Udvari and Rubin population was of elementary school age while the Tannenbaum survey was confined to high school juniors. Adolescence could signal changes in attitudes that existed earlier in life. Otherwise, it is legitimate to exult in the inter-generational elevation of children's feelings about those described as the best and the brightest at school.

However, if attitudes toward the gifted have improved in some ways over time, there are other forces in society that continue to discourage interest in this minority. Some negativism comes from educators who worry about elitism in school and society, or believe that the gifted can fend for themselves without special help. Perhaps more inhibiting is the influence of cultural values that place a premium on equality, even at the expense of excellence. As a result, the social and educational environments send mixed messages to the gifted, some inspiriting and some dispiriting, but all of them significant enough to make their mark on the lives of these exceptional children.

Chance Factors

The influence of the unexpected and unpredictable on the course of human development is a largely neglected subject in studies of giftedness. This aversion is understandable, because what is there to say about luck—except that it exists and that it can make a difference between success and failure? Nobody knows what forms it will take, or when or how often it will strike. It is treated almost as if it were a supernatural force, and therefore outside the pale of science. Nonetheless, no one can deny its power to facilitate or inhibit, and to direct or redirect, a creative act.

It is hard for educators, parents, and members of the helping professions to realize that their best efforts on behalf of potentially gifted children can be enhanced or nullified by circumstances over which they have no control. Even when a person seems a sure bet for success, bad fortune can turn matters around completely.

According to Atkinson's (1978) view, all human behavior and accomplishment can be ascribed to "two crucial rolls of the dice over which no individual exerts any personal control: the accidents of birth and background. One roll of the dice determines an individual's heredity; the other his formative environment" (p. 221).

Chance factors should never be trivialized or neglected in the study of giftedness, especially given that so many eminent people emphasize unpredictable events that helped them reach the top.

Is chance simply a stroke of luck, a random event in the life of an individual, totally unrelated to the lawful functioning of the psyche or the environment? Is it a static condition, improbable and fateful? Or can a person reach out and develop a dynamic relationship with it?

According to Austin (1978), there are four levels of chance factors. The first is simply luck, good or bad, that befalls a passive person who is in the right (or wrong) place at the right (or wrong) time. At the second level, a person increases the likelihood of being struck with good fortune by setting the mind and body into constant motion, although the activity is ill defined, restless, and aimlessly driven. Though mostly wasteful, such behavior "stirs the pot of random ideas" constantly so that a few will connect in unanticipated combinations. The third level of chance connects an unforeseen experience with a person who is uniquely equipped to grasp its significance. Social and psychological factors interact to illustrate Louis Pasteur's dictum that "chance favors the prepared mind." Luck strikes rarely, and it is a rare person who can make the most of it. Finally, there is a fourth level of chance, which Austin calls *altamirage,* a facility for becoming lucky because of the highly individualized action taken by a person. It is the kind of good fortune "experienced by only *one* quixotic rider cantering in on his own homemade hobby-horse to intercept the problem at an odd angle" (p. 77). Such rare and often eccentric individuals patiently and persistently tinker with ideas and materials until a rare combination clicks brilliantly into place, sometimes without warning.

Of the four levels suggested by Austin, the second and fourth suggest interactions between the individual and "luck." "Stirring the pot" helps persons somehow to place themselves in the right positions when fortune strikes. Altamirage also runs counter to passivity and gives the edge to people who tickle fate with particular off-beat mannerisms that somehow invite the smile of good fortune.

No matter how chance factors are defined, one truism seems irrefutable: Luck interacts with inspiration and perspiration in a mutually dependent way. Without high potential, no amount of good fortune can help the mediocre person achieve greatness; conversely, without some good fortune, no amount of potential can be truly realized.

SUMMARY AND CONCLUSIONS

This chapter defines giftedness operationally and elaborates on the factors that combine to account for gifted behavior. The portrait is of eight types of developed talent, only a few of which are ever demonstrated in childhood. But children can grow up to be gifted in the way adults are if they are made of the right stuff in general ability, special aptitudes, and personality and can make the most of a supportive environment punctuated by timely strokes of luck as

they grow older. Until maturation and nurturance are allowed to run their courses, all that can be said for bright and talented children, even the prodigies among them, is that they are *potentially* gifted. Whether, and in what ways, early promise will be fulfilled, only time can tell.

QUESTIONS FOR THOUGHT AND DISCUSSION

1. Look at Tannenbaum's Figure 4.1, which summarizes his eight varieties of giftedness. Where do you fit?
2. Briefly explain each of the five "points" on Tannenbaum's sea star model of "factors accounting for gifted achievement." Did he leave anything out? Explain.
3. Explain Tannenbaum's interpretation of multipotentiality that assumes unequal levels of talent in different areas.
4. Explain Tannenbaum's reconciliation of (a) the link between psychoses and creativity and (b) Terman's finding of high mental health in high-IQ young people. Do you agree?
5. What chance factors have helped you achieve in your life?

REFERENCES

Achter, J. A., Lubinski, D., & Benbow, C. P. (1996). Multipotentiality among the intellectually gifted: It was never there and already it's vanishing. *Journal of Counseling Psychology, 43,* 65–76.

Amabile, T. M. (1996). *Creativity in context: Update to "The Social Psychology of Creativity."* Boulder, CO: Westview Press.

Amabile, T. M. (2001). Beyond talent: John Irving and the passionate craft of creativity. *American Psychologist, 56,* 333–336.

Atkinson, J. W. (1978). Motivational determinants of intellective performance and cumulative achievement. In J. W. Atkinson & J. O. Raynor (Eds.), *Personality, motivation, and achievement* (pp. 221–242). New York: Wiley.

Austin, J. H. (1978). *Chase, chance, and creativity.* New York: Columbia University Press.

Benbow, C. P. (1992). Academic achievement in mathematics and science of students between ages 13 and 23: Are there differences among students in the top one percent of mathematical ability? *Journal of Educational Psychology, 84,* 51–61.

Bouchard, T. J., Jr. (1995). Longitudinal studies of personality and intelligence: A behavior genetic and evolutionary psychology perspective. In D. H. Saklofske

& M. Zeidner (Eds.), *International handbook of personality and intelligence* (pp. 81–106). New York: Plenum.

Bouchard, T. J., Jr. (1997). IQ similarity in twins reared apart: Findings and responses to critics. In R. J. Sternberg & E. L. Grigorenko (Eds.), *Intelligence, heredity, and environment* (pp. 126–160). New York: Cambridge University Press.

Bouchard, T. J., Jr., Lykken, D. T., Tellegen, R., McGue, M. (1996). Genes, drives, environment, and experience: EPD theory revised. In C. P. Benbow & D. Lubinski (Eds.), *Intellectual talent* (pp. 5–43). Baltimore: Johns Hopkins University Press.

Cameron, J., & Pierce, W. D. (1994). Reinforcement, reward, and intrinsic motivation: A meta-analysis. *Review of Educational Research, 64,* 363–423.

Colangelo, N., & Assouline, S. G. (2000). Counseling gifted students. In K. A. Heller, F. J. Mönks, R. J. Sternberg, & R. F. Subotnik (Eds.), *International handbook of giftedness and talent* (2nd ed., pp. 595–607). Oxford: Elsevier.

Csikszentmihalyi, M. (1988). Society, culture, and person: A systems view of creativity. In R. J. Sternberg (Ed.), *The nature of creativity* (pp. 325–339). New York: Cambridge University Press.

Epstein, S. (1998). *Constructive thinking: The key to emotional intelligence.* Westport, CT: Praeger.

Feldman, D. H. (1984). A follow-up of subjects scoring above 180 IQ in Terman's genetic studies of genius. *Exceptional Children, 50,* 518–523.

Gardner, H. (1983). *Frames of mind.* New York: Basic Books.

Gardner, H. (1997). Six afterthoughts: Comments on "Varieties of intellectual talents." *Journal of Creative Behavior, 31,* 120–124.

Gardner, H. (1999). *Intelligence reframed: Multiple intelligences in the 21st century.* New York: Basic Books.

Goleman, D. (1995). *Emotional Intelligence: Why it can matter more than IQ.* New York: Bantam Books.

Gottfredson, L. S. (1997). Mainstream science on intelligence: An editorial with 52 signatories, history, and bibliography. *Intelligence, 24,* 13–23.

Harris, J. R. (1998). *The nurture assumption: Why children turn out the way they do.* New York: Free Press.

Herrnstein, R. J., & Murray, C. (1994). *The bell curve: Intelligence and class structure in American life.* New York: Free Press.

Holahan, C. K., & Sears, R. S. (1995). *The gifted group in later maturity.* Stanford: Stanford University Press.

Holden, C. (1987, April). Creativity and the troubled mind. *Psychology Today, 21,* 9–10.

Howe, M. J. A. (1999). *Psychology of high abilities.* New York: New York University Press.

Kuncel, N. R., Hezlett, S. A., & Ones, D. S. (2001). A comprehensive meta-analysis of the predictive validity of the graduate record examinations: Implications for graduate student selection and performance. *Psychological bulletin, 127,* 162–181.

Lens, W., & Rand, P. (2000). Motivation and cognition: Their role in the development of giftedness. In K. A. Heller, F. J. Mönks, R. J. Sternberg, & R. F. Subotnik (Eds.), *International handbook of giftedness and talent* (2nd ed., pp. 193–202). Oxford: Elsevier.

Leventhal, T., & Brooks-Gunn, J. (2000). The neighborhoods they live in: The effects of neighborhood residence on child and adolescent outcomes. *Psychological Bulletin, 126,* 309–337.

Lubinski, D., Webb, R. M., Morelock, M. J., & Benbow, C. P. (2001). Top 1 in 10,000: A 10-year follow-up of the profoundly gifted. *Journal of Applied Psychology, 86,* 718–729.

Ludwig, A. M. (1995). *The price of greatness: Resolving the creativity and madness controversy.* New York: Guilford Press.

Marsh, H. W. (1992). Content specificity of relations between academic achievement and academic self-concept. *Journal of Educational Psychology, 84,* 35–42.

Marsh, H. W., Chessor, D., Craven, R., & Roche, L. (1995). The effects of gifted and talented programs on academic self-concept: The big fish strikes again. *American Educational Research Journal, 32,* 285–319.

McGrew, K. S., Keith, T. Z., Flanagan, D. P., & Vanderwood, M. (1997). Beyond g: The impact of gf-gc specific cognitive abilities research on the future use and interpretation of intelligence tests in schools. *School Psychology Review, 26,* 189–210.

Meyer, G. J., Finn, S. E., Eyde, L. D., Kay, G. G., Moreand, K. L., Dies, R. R., Eisman, E. J., Kubiszin, T. W., & Reed, G. M. (2001). Psychological testing and psychological assessment: A review of evidence and issues. *American Psychologist, 56,* 128–165.

Oden, M. H. (1968). The fulfillment of promise: Forty-year follow up of the Terman group. *Genetic Psychology Monographs, 77,* 3–93.

Pastore, N. (1949). *The nature-nurture controversy.* New York: Kings Crown Press.

Plomin, R., & DeFries, J. C. (1983). The Colorado adoption project. *Child Development, 54,* 276–289.

Plomin, R., Reiss, D., Hetherington, E. M., & Howe, G. W. (1994). Nature and nurture: Genetic contributions to measures of the family environment. *Developmental Psychology, 3,* 32–43.

Ramos-Ford, V., & Gardner, H. (1997). Giftedness from a multiple intelligences perspective. In N. Colangelo & G. A. Davis (Eds.), *Handbook of gifted education* (2nd ed., pp. 54–66). Boston: Allyn & Bacon.

Richards, R. L. (1981). Relationships between creativity and psychopathology: An evaluation and interpretation of the evidence. *Genetic Psychology Monographs, 103,* 261–324.

Root-Bernstein, R. S. (1989). *Discovering.* Cambridge: Harvard University Press.

Rowe, D. C. (1994). *The limits of family influence.* New York: Guilford.

Rowe, D. C. (2001). The nurture assumption persists. *American Psychologist, 56,* 168–169.

Rushton, J. P. (1995). *Race, evolution, and behavior.* New Brunswick, NJ: Transaction Publishers.

Salovey, P., & Sluyter, D. J. (Eds). (1997). *Emotional development and emotional intelligence: Educational implications.* New York: Basic Books.

Scarr, S. (1996). How people make their own environments: Implications for parents and policy makers. *Psychology, Public Policy, and Law, 2*(2), 204–228.

Schroeder-Davis, S. (1996). Anti-intellectualism in secondary schools: The problem continues. *Gifted Education Press Quarterly, 10*(2), 2–8.

Skaalvik, E. M., & Rankin, R. J. (1995). A test of the internal/external frame of reference model at different levels of math and verbal self-perception. *American Educational Research Journal, 32,* 161–184.

Stanley, J. C. (1997). Varieties of intellectual talent. *Journal of Creative Behavior, 31,* 93–119.

Sternberg, R. J. (1996). *Successful intelligence.* New York: Simon and Schuster.

Sternberg, R. J. (1999). The theory of successful intelligence. *Review of General Psychology, 3,* 1–25.

Tannenbaum, A. J. (1962). *Adolescent attitudes toward academic brilliance.* New York: Bureau of Publications, Teachers College, Columbia University.

Tannenbaum, A. J. (1996). The IQ controversy and the gifted. In C. P. Benbow & D. Lubinski (Eds.), *Intellectual talent* (pp. 44–77). Baltimore: Johns Hopkins University Press.

Terman, L. M. (1925). *Genetic studies of genius: Vol. 1. Mental and physical traits of a thousand gifted children.* Stanford: Stanford University Press.

Terman, L. M., & Oden, M. H. (1959). *Genetic studies of genius: Vol. 5. Thirty-five years follow-up of the superior child.* Stanford: Stanford University Press.

Thompson, L. A., & Plomin, R. (2000). Genetic tools for exploring individual differences in intelligence. In K. A. Heller, F. J. Mönks, R. J. Sternberg, and R. F. Subotnik (Eds.), *International handbook of giftedness and talent* (2nd ed., pp. 157–164). Oxford: Elsevier.

Traub, J. (1998, October 26). Multiple intelligence disorder. *The New Republic* (pp. 20–23).

Udvari, S. J., & Rubin, K. H. (1996). Gifted and non-selected children's perceptions of academic achievement, academic effort, and athleticism. *Gifted Child Quarterly, 40,* 211–219.

Vaillant, G. E. (2000). Adaptive mental mechanisms: Their role in a positive psychology. *American Psychologist, 55,* 89–98.

Vispoel, W. P. (1995). Self-concept in artistic domains: An extension of the Shavelson, Hubner, and Stanton (1976) model. *Journal of Educational Psychology, 87,* 134–153.

Winner, E. (1996). *Gifted children: Myths and realities.* New York: Basic Books.

Winner, E. (1997). Exceptionally high intelligence and schooling. *American Psychologist, 52,* 1070–1081.

Winner, E., & Martino, G. (2000). Giftedness in non-academic domains: The case of the visual arts and music. In K. A. Heller, F. J. Mönks, R. J. Sternberg, & R. F. Subotnik (Eds.), *International handbook of giftedness and talent* (2nd ed., pp. 95–110). Oxford: Elsevier.

BIBLIOGRAPHY

Carroll, J. B. (1993). *Human cognitive abilities.* New York: Cambridge University Press.

Carroll, J. B. (1997). Psychometrics, intelligence, and public perception. *Intelligence, 24*(1), 25–52.

Collins, W. A., Maccoby, E. E., Steinberg, L., Hetherington, E. M., & Bornstein, M. H. (2000). Contemporary research on parenting: The case for nature and nurture. *American Psychologist, 55,* 218–232.

Flynn, J. R. (1999). The discovery of IQ gains over time. *American Psychologist, 54,* 5–20.

Gardner, H. (1993). *Multiple Intelligences: The theory in practice.* New York: Basic Books.

Jensen, A. R. (1998). *The g factor.* Westport CT: Praeger.

Okagaki, L., & Frensch, P. A. (1998). Parenting and children's achievement: A multiethnic perspective. *American Educational Research Journal, 35,* 123–144.

Rolfhus, E. L., & Ackerman, P. L. (1999). Assessing individual differences in knowledge: Knowledge, intelligence, and related traits. *Journal of Educational Psychology, 91,* 511–526.

Saudino, K. J., Plomin, R., Pedersen, N. L., & McClearn, G. E. (1994). The etiology of low and high cognitive ability during the second half of the life span. *Intelligence, 19,* 359–371.

Simonton, D. K. (1988). Creativity, leadership, and chance. In R. J. Sternberg (Ed.), *The nature of creativity* (pp. 386–426). New York: Cambridge University Press.

Spearman, C. E. (1927). *Human cognitive abilities: A survey of factor-analytic studies.* New York: Cambridge University Press.

Terman, L. M., & Merrill, M. A. (1937). *Measuring intelligence.* Cambridge, MA: The Riverside Press.

Thompson, L. A., Tiu, R., Spinks, R., & Detterman, D. K. (1999). Unpublished manuscript cited by L. A. Thompson & R. Plomin (2000) on p. 159 in K. A. Heller, F. J. Mönks, R. J. Sternberg, & R. F. Subotnik

(Eds.), *International handbook of giftedness and talent* (2nd ed.). Oxford: Elsevier.

Thorndike, R. L. (1985). The critical role of general ability in prediction. *Multivariate Behavioral Research, 20,* 241–254.

Trost, G. (2000). Prediction of excellence in school, higher education, and work. In K. A. Heller, F. J. Mönks, R. J.

Sternberg, & R. F. Subotnik (Eds.), *International handbook of giftedness and talent* (2nd ed., pp. 317–327). Oxford: Elsevier.

Wechsler, D. (1944). *Measurement of adult intelligence.* Baltimore: Williams & Wilkins.

5

Transforming Gifts into Talents:
The DMGT as a Developmental Theory

FRANÇOYS GAGNÉ, *Université du Québec à Montréal*

Most professionals in gifted education do not distinguish between *giftedness* and *talent,* the two central constructs that define this special population. Almost everyone uses these two words as synonyms in sentences such as "the gifted and talented are . . . ." Over the last four decades, only a few scholars have proposed distinctions (e.g., Feldhusen, 1986, 1992; Gagné, 1985; Morelock, 1996; U.S. Department of Education, 1993). In most cases, these concepts suffered from major flaws (see Gagné, 1985, 1997, 1999a). Yet, as I recently argued (Gagné, 1999a), these two different concepts can be usefully discriminated in the field's literature, justifying the need for two distinct labels. They roughly correspond to the ideas of potential/aptitude and achievement or, in other words, to the distinction between natural abilities and systematically developed skills. The *Differentiated Model of Giftedness and Talent* (DMGT) uses that distinction to anchor its definitions of the two concepts.

Giftedness designates the possession and use of untrained and spontaneously expressed natural abilities (called aptitudes or gifts), in at least one ability domain, to a degree that places an individual at least among the top 10 percent of age peers.

Talent designates the superior mastery of systematically developed abilities (or skills) and knowledge in at least one field of human activity to a degree that places an individual at least among the top 10 percent of age peers who are or have been active in that field or fields.

These definitions reveal that the two concepts share three characteristics: (a) both refer to human abilities; (b) both are normative, in the sense that they target individuals who differ from the norm or average; (c) both refer to individuals who are "nonnormal" because of their outstanding behaviors. These commonalities help understand why they are confounded by most professionals in the field, as well as in common language.

In order to represent more accurately the complexity of the talent development process, the DMGT introduces four other components (see Figure 5.1): intrapersonal catalysts (IC), environmental catalysts (EC), learning/practice (LP), and chance (C). As seen in the formal definitions above, precise thresholds specify what is meant by "outstanding" behaviors. These thresholds are part of a five-unit metric-based system of levels within the population of gifted or talented individuals (Gagné, 1998c). Finally, the DMGT proposes a theory of talent development in the form of a set of dynamic interactions among the six components; some interactions have strong empirical bases, others remain assumptions or hypothetical statements. The present overview is structured around the three themes identified above: (a) the six components, (b) the prevalence question, and (c) the dynamics of talent development in DMGT.

A Componential Survey

The six components of the DMGT can be subdivided into two trios. The first describes the core of the talent development process, that is, the transformation of outstanding natural abilities (or gifts) into the high-level skills (or talents) of a particular occupational field through a long process of learning and practice (LP). The members of the second trio have in common the concept of *catalyst,* since they act as facilitators or

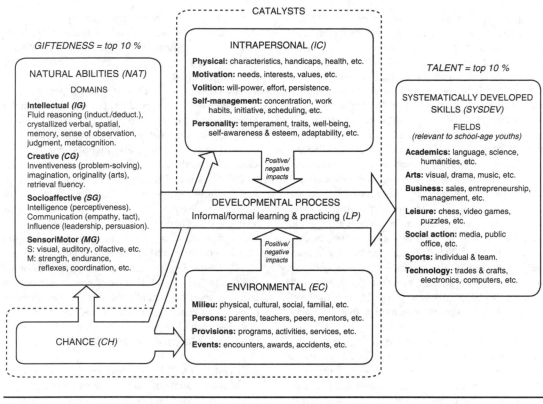

Figure 5.1 Gagné's Differentiated Model of Giftedness and Talent.

inhibitors of the talent development process. Because it is considered an essential part of a complete definition of giftedness and talent, the 10 percent prevalence estimate will be discussed at the end of this survey.

The Talent Development Trio

The DMGT's delineation between gifts and talents is a particular case of the general distinction between aptitude (or potential) and achievement. The relevance and validity of the concept of aptitude has been questioned by some prominent scholars (e.g., Anastasi, 1980). In counterpoint, Angoff (1988) built a strong defense for such a distinction, using the following differentiating characteristics: (a) slow growth for aptitudes versus rapid growth for achievement; (b) informal versus formal learning; (c) resistance to stimulation versus susceptibility to it; (d) major genetic substratum versus a major practice component; (e) more general content versus more circumscribed

content; (f) "old formal" learning versus recent acquisitions; (g) more generalizable versus narrower transfer; (h) prospective use (predicting future learning) versus retrospective use (assessing amount learned); and (i) usable for general population evaluation versus limited to systematically exposed individuals. All of these characteristics apply perfectly to the DMGT's differentiation between gifts and talents.

Gifts (G). The DMGT proposes four aptitude *domains* (see Figure 5.1): intellectual, creative, socioaffective, and sensorimotor. Each can be divided into any number of categories. Figure 5.1 shows exemplars borrowed from various sources. These subdivisions should not be considered essential subcomponents of the model since, within each of the four domains, many competing classification systems exist. Just with regard to cognitive abilities, some of the better known taxonomies include Carroll's (1993) three-level hierarchy of abilities, Gardner's (1983) multiple intelligences, and Sternberg's (1985) tri-archic theory.[1] As knowledge progresses within each ability domain, no doubt new taxonomies will be proposed. For instance, recent work related to the concept of emotional intelligence (e.g., Mayer, Caruso, & Salovey, 2000) could give birth to a new category system within the socioaffective domain.

Natural (NAT) abilities can be observed through the various tasks that confront children in the course of their development. These include the intellectual abilities needed when learning to read, speak a foreign language, or understand new mathematical concepts, and the creative abilities applied to solving various technical problems or producing original work in science, literature, and art. There are also the physical abilities involved in sports, music, or carpentry, or the social abilities that children use in their daily interactions with classmates, teachers, and parents. These natural abilities manifest themselves in all children to a variable degree. It is only when the level of expression becomes outstanding that the label *gifted* may be used. High aptitudes or gifts can be observed more easily and directly in young children because environmental influences and systematic learning have exerted their moderating influence in a limited way. However, gifts still manifest themselves in older children, even in adults, through the facility and speed with which some individuals acquire new skills in any given field of human activity; the easier or faster the learning process, the greater the natural abilities. The *gifted* label appears specific to the field of education; rarely does one see the term employed by educators in arts or by professionals in sports; there, the common expressions for giftedness are "talent" or "natural talent."

Two domains, the intellectual and the psychomotor, have developed psychometrically valid measures of natural abilities. IQ tests, group or individually administered, are generally recognized as the most reliable and valid assessments of general cognitive functioning, often referred to as the "*g*" factor (Jensen, 1998). In the psychomotor domain, one finds complex batteries of tests to assess the physical fitness of children in elementary or junior high schools (President's Council on Physical Fitness and Sports, 2001; Australian Sports Commission, 1994). The creative domain also has tests, but their psychometric qualities remain far below those of IQ tests, espe-

cially in terms of convergent validity. The socioaffective domain lags behind in terms of psychometrically sound measures; available instruments predominantly revolve around self-assessments or peer judgments.

Is there still any need to defend the genetic basis of natural abilities? Nowadays, few researchers in the social sciences deny the significant contribution of hereditary factors to human characteristics, including physical and mental abilities, interests, and temperament. The two domains with the best measures of natural abilities are also those with the most extensive analysis of the nature-nurture question. Especially in the last two decades, hundreds of studies have examined the contribution of genes to individual differences in general cognitive functioning, comparing identical twins reared together or apart (Bouchard, 1997), identical twins with fraternal ones, or adopted siblings (Rowe, 1994). If any degree of contention is left, it concerns essentially the relative contributions of nature and nurture. Similar proofs have been accumulating with regard to psychomotor abilities (Bouchard, Malina, & Pérusse, 1997).

Talents (T). Talents progressively emerge from the transformation of high aptitudes into the well-trained (or systematically developed—SYSDEV) skills characteristic of a particular field of human activity. These fields can be extremely diverse (see Figure 5.1); indeed, *any* occupational field in which a series of skills needs to be mastered generates large individual differences in performance, ranging from minimum competence to high-level expertise. Any individuals whose outstanding skill mastery places them among the top 10 percent within their occupational field should be recognized as talented. In many of these fields, individuals pursue the development of their skills as a leisure activity (e.g., cooking, gardening, handyman); in some others, leisurely pursuits may even characterize a majority of the participants (e.g., chess, bridge, music, and most sports).

Measuring talent is a straightforward enterprise: It simply corresponds to outstanding performance in the specific skills of any occupational field. During the developmental phase of any talent, whether academic, artistic, technological, or athletic, many occasions for normative assessments present themselves: teacher exams, achievement tests, competitions, scholarships, and so forth. But after individuals have completed their training, performance rankings usu-

---

1. See Chapter 3 by Gottfredson.

ally disappear. How will you know if the plumber you have called is below or above average compared to peers? How about the mechanic working on your car, the dentist repairing a filling, the accountant preparing your income tax return, the coach managing your child's hockey team? Most of the time, the only guideline will be word of mouth. Even when assessments are available, their validity is often questionable because they rely mostly on peer or superiors' ratings (Anastasi & Urbina, 1997). Only professional athletes have to deal with constant normative comparisons of their performances!

There is no direct bilateral relationship between gift domains and talent fields. A given natural ability can express itself in many different ways, depending on the field of activity. Manual dexterity can be modeled into the particular skills of a pianist, a painter, or a video-game player; similarly, intelligence can be modeled into the scientific reasoning of a chemist, the game analysis of a chess player, or the strategic planning of an athlete. Yet some occupational fields are associated more directly with specific ability domains. For instance, sports skills are built on the foundations of motor abilities; wine tasting develops from sensory acuity; knowledge-dependent fields (e.g., traditional professions, technical occupations, mental sports, like chess or bridge) build their expertise from natural cognitive abilities; and talent in social-interaction occupations (e.g., sales, teaching, health services) is closely associated with high socioaffective abilities.

Talent is a developmental construct. That statement means that soon after youngsters have begun learning a new set of skills, it becomes possible to assess their performances normatively, comparing them with others who have been learning for an approximately equal amount of time. In schools, such assessments can begin as early as kindergarten. Assessments also exist for beginners in music, dance, visual arts, or sports. Note that the level of achievement can change as learning progresses. During the first years in school, a student can obtain grades within the top 10 percent of his or her class and, consequently, be labeled *academically talented*. Then, for whatever reason, the student's progress may slow, justifying a decision to remove the person from the talented group. The reverse is equally possible. However, because of high correlations between yearly achievements, most talented students correctly maintain their label for the whole of their formal schooling.

Learning and Practicing (LP). The talent development process consists in transforming specific natural abilities into the skills that define competence or expertise in a given occupational field. Competence corresponds to levels of mastery ranging from minimally acceptable to well above average, yet below the defined threshold for talented or expert behavior. Thus, talent is to gifted education what competence is to general education. As usually defined (see Ericsson, 1996), the concept of *expertise* largely overlaps the DMGT's concept of *talent*.

Developmental processes can take four different forms: (a) maturation; (b) informal learning; (c) formal non-institutional learning; (d) formal institutional learning. *Maturation* is a process totally controlled by the genome. It ensures the growth and transformation of all biological structures: bones, internal organs, brain, etc. That developmental process in turn impacts other functions at the phenotypic level. For instance, research has shown that major changes in brain physiology directly coincide with parallel changes in cognitive achievements (Gazzaniga, Ivry, & Mangun, 1998).

Informal learning corresponds essentially to knowledge and skills acquired during daily activities. Much of what is called *practical intelligence* (see Sternberg & Wagner, 1986) is the result of such informal or unstructured learning activities. The general knowledge, language skills, social skills, and manual skills mastered by young children before they enter the school system result almost totally from such unstructured activities.

The last two developmental or learning processes are formal in the sense that (a) there is a conscious intention to attain specific learning goals, and (b) there is a systematically planned sequence of learning steps to achieve these goals. The first case, that of *formal noninstitutional learning,* corresponds to autodidactic or self-taught learning. Many individuals, young and old, decide to develop competencies in a particular occupational field, most of the time as a leisure activity. Few will achieve performances that would compare with the best in these fields. But it may sometimes happen, for example, that a self-taught pianist will outperform music students who have trained for five or six years. In the DMGT framework, these outstanding autodidacts would be labeled as *talented* (Gagné, 1993). Still, the most common learning process remains institutionally based and leads to some form of official recognition of competency: going to school, joining a sports team, or enrolling in a music school, a cooking academy, or a public-speaking program, that is, by *formal institutional learning*.

Theoretically, both gifts and talents can use all four types of the developmental processes described above. In practice, some types appear much more appropriate to gifts than talents, or vice-versa. For instance, maturation affects the growth of talents only indirectly, that is, through its action on natural abilities, the real building blocks of talents. On the other hand, early stimulation programs like Head Start (Haskins, 1989) can be catalogued as formal institutional attempts to develop general cognitive abilities (intellectual giftedness). However, such systematic interventions are uncommon. Consequently, only a small percentage of at-risk children will have their natural abilities influenced by these programs.

As a general rule, these four processes contribute to the development of gifts in inverse proportion to their degree of formality. In other words, the major developmental agent for gifts is maturation, closely followed by informal learning. In the case of talents, it is the opposite, with formal institutional learning accounting for most of the developmental impact.

The Trio of Catalysts

A term from chemistry, *catalyst* designates chemical substances introduced into a chemical reaction usually to accelerate it. At the end, these contributors regain their initial state. In other words, catalysts contribute to a reaction without being constituents of the final product. In the case of talent development, the constituent elements are the natural abilities, which are slowly transformed into specific skills. Talent is strictly measured through the level of skill mastery; neither the type of the contributing catalysts nor the strength of their contribution has relevance for that assessment. The DMGT recognizes three types of catalysts: intrapersonal, environmental, and chance factors. Each of them may be examined with regard to two dimensions: *direction*—positive/facilitating versus negative/hindering—and *strength* of causal impact on the developmental process.

Intrapersonal Catalysts. The intrapersonal catalysts are subdivided into physical and psychological factors, all of them under the partial influence of genetic endowment. *Physical* characteristics may take many forms. For instance, when elite dance schools select young candidates for training, they often use physical parameters (e.g., height, slenderness, leg length) to determine the chances that a young student may attain high performance levels. In music, hand span directly affects the repertoire of a young musician. The same applies to sports, where physical templates have been defined for many sports (e.g., jockey versus basketball player).

The psychological constructs associated with talent development are so numerous that the list of intrapersonal catalysts could cover many pages; Figure 5.1 shows only a carefully chosen few. To date, four categories have been created: *motivation, volition, self-management,* and *personality*. Concerning the first two categories, most of the scientific literature in psychology confounds goal-defining and goal implementing behaviors. Borrowing from Kuhl's work (e.g., Kuhl & Beckmann, 1985), Corno (1993; see also Corno & Kanfer, 1993) proposed a clear distinction between these two constructs, naming them *motivation* (e.g., interests, needs, intrinsic/extrinsic motivation) and *volition* (e.g., effort, perseverance, self-control, regular monitoring), respectively. Both constructs appear to play a significant role in initiating the process of talent development, guiding it, and sustaining it through obstacles, boredom, and occasional failure.

The introduction of *self-management* as a distinct category results from my recent research on multitalented individuals (Gagné, 1999b; Gagné, Neveu, Simard, & St Père, 1996), in which high-level self-management was perceived by virtually all parent interviewees to be one of the most typical characteristics of their multitalented adolescent. Its definition encompasses a large group of constructs commonly found in the scientific literature; the most popular within the last decade is the concept of self-regulation (Zimmerman, 1998). A closely related concept, labeled "personal talent," was recently proposed by Moon (in press). The four descriptors (see Figure 5.1) attempt to convey the breadth of self-management. *Concentration* refers to the ability to shut out extraneous stimuli and to keep working on the same task for hours—or days—on end. The concept of *work habits* refers to process activities—and their monitoring—during learning. *Initiative* is understood here as the ability to "boot" oneself to work; it overlaps to some extent the concept of autonomy. It also overlaps some aspects of volition, namely, finding in oneself the energy to begin and maintain an activity, especially when motivation is low. Finally, *scheduling* corresponds to the efficient planning of one's daily or weekly activities. It is a very useful ability when one's personal program includes a large number of such activities, and when frequent juggling is required.

Personality is also a widely encompassing construct. There is some agreement for a need to separate innate and acquired characteristics. These could be labeled *temperament* and *personality traits,* respectively, or basic tendencies and characteristic adaptations (McCrae et al., 2000). Recent research has led to the proposal of five basic bipolar personality dimensions called "The Big Five" (Digman, 1990) or the Five-Factor Model (FFM). They are commonly labeled as follows: Neuroticism (N), Extraversion (E), Openness (O), Agreeableness (A), and Conscientiousness (C). McCrae and Costa (1999) affirm: "Much of what psychologists mean by the term *personality* is summarized by the FFM, and the model has been of great utility to the field by integrating and systematizing diverse conceptions and measures" (p. 139). There is growing evidence for a close relationship between temperament dimensions and adult personality traits (Rothbart, Ahadi, & Evans, 2000), two terms of frequent use as variables in research on characteristics of gifted and talented individuals.

Environmental Catalysts. The environment exerts its positive or negative impact in many different ways. In the DMGT, four distinct environmental inputs are distinguished (see Figure 5.1). The *milieu* or surroundings can be examined both at a macroscopic level (e.g., geographic, demographic, sociological) and a microscopic level (e.g., size of family, socioeconomic status, neighborhood services). For example, young gifted persons who live far from large urban centers do not have easy access to appropriate learning resources (e.g., sports training centers, music conservatories, magnet schools). Within the child's home environment, the parents' financial comfort, the absence of one of the caregivers, the number and age distribution of siblings within the family, as well as many other elements of the immediate environment can have some degree of impact on the child's talent development. Psychological factors, for instance the parents' value of educational pursuits or their personal psychological health, are included in the "persons" category below.

The concept of environmental input brings to mind spontaneously significant *persons,* be they parents, siblings, the extended family, friends, educators, mentors, idols, etc. The significant impact of persons on other persons is probably easier to imagine than that of any other source of influence within the environment. Moreover, the traditional environmentalist beliefs of most professionals in the social sciences,

for whom nurture is a more powerful agent than nature (see Cohen's, 1999, critique), emphasizes the importance of humans as significant agents in the lives of their fellow humans. Thus, it is not surprising that a good percentage of the professional literature on talent development, not only in academics, but also in arts, business, or sports, examines the potential influence of significant individuals in the immediate environment of gifted or talented youngsters. This statement applies equally well to the larger literature on human development. Similarly, retrospective interviews of eminent individuals frequently leave the impression that they attribute to significant persons, especially their parents, the lion's share of environmental influences (Bloom, 1985; Cox, Daniel, & Boston, 1985; Hemery, 1986). In brief, according to a recently proposed label, the explanation of human behavior through environmental causes is the *Standard Social Science Model* or SSSM (Tooby & Cosmides, 1992).

The *provisions* category includes a wide diversity of individual or group interventions specifically targeted at talent development. In the field of gifted education, provisions have been traditionally subdivided into three groups: enrichment, grouping, and acceleration. This triarchic distinction suffers from two major logical flaws. First, it unduly opposes enrichment and acceleration, encouraging the stereotypic image that acceleration practices are not enriching. Second, the categories are not mutually exclusive, since many accelerative practices require ability grouping, for instance, in Advanced Placement courses (College Board, 2001). Massé and Gagné (1983) proposed instead that enrichment be considered the general goal of *all* provisions offered to gifted or talented youngsters, whatever the talent field. Common administrative formats would then be categorized according to two criteria: (a) the presence or absence of ability grouping; (b) the presence or absence of acceleration. In this way, four major types of formats are distinguished, all of them potentially enriching, on condition of course that their content be of good quality!

Finally, significant *events* (e.g., the death of a parent, winning a prize or award, suffering a major accident or illness) can markedly influence the course of talent development.

Chance. Tannenbaum (1983) can be credited with the first extensive examination of the role of chance as a contributing factor to talent development. Borrowed from that model, chance was originally introduced in the DMGT as a fifth element among the environmental catalysts. It soon became clear, however, that chance influences all the environmental catalysts. For example, children have no control over the socio-economic status of the family in which they are raised, the quality of the parenting they receive, nor over the existence of talent development programs in the neighborhood school. Moreover, chance manifests itself in one other major event, namely the transmission of hereditary characteristics. Few human phenomena are more dependent on chance than the specific mix of genes resulting from the random meeting of a particular ovum and one among millions of spermatozoids. Atkinson (1978) claimed that all human accomplishments can be ascribed to "two crucial rolls of the dice over which no individual exerts any personal control. These are the accidents of birth and background" (p. 221). Atkinson's "accidents of birth" stress the role of chance outside the EC zone, especially through the action of genetic endowment in the G and IC components. In brief, as shown in Figure 5.1, there is some degree of chance in all the causal components of the model, except the LP process.

The Prevalence Estimate

This section explains why a prevalence estimate should be included in a complete definition of the giftedness and talent concepts, and why the 10 percent threshold was chosen for the DMGT.

Background and Proposal. The term *prevalence* refers to the percentage of a subgroup within a larger population. Concepts like talent and giftedness require a prevalence estimate for their definitions to be complete because they target atypical subgroups within a general population. Similar concepts, like poverty, obesity, mental deficiency, genius, deafness, and countless others also base their definition on normative judgments. By introducing either a percentage estimate (e.g., 5 percent of the population) or a threshold (e.g., IQ ≥ 130), the scholar specifies the boundaries separating those who belong to that category from those who don't. In turn, the size of the population further clarifies the meaning of the concept. For instance, if we defined the gifted as the top 1 percent of the population it would convey a totally different message about their exceptionality than if they were defined as the top 20 percent of the general

population. Note that there are twenty times more individuals in the more generous estimate.

Identifying appropriate thresholds is not an easy task because there are no clear and objective markers on a measurement scale to indicate the passage from one category (e.g., average ability, normal weight) to the next (e.g., gifted, overweight). Any proposed threshold is localized somewhere within a grey zone, with some experts showing more openness—proposing larger percentages—and others maintaining stricter positions. Scholars' proposals range from the 1 percent adopted by Terman (1925) with his threshold of a 135 IQ, or the 3 percent to 5 percent in the U.S. Office of Education Marland definition, to the 20 percent advanced by Renzulli (1986) to create the talent pools in his Revolving Door model. What about the ratios used in school districts? In a survey of state policies, Mitchell (1988) pointed out that "states using intelligence and achievement test scores for identification generally use cutoff points which range between the 95th and 98th percentile levels" (p. 240).

I use a five-level system of cutoffs—based on the metric system—with its lowest level fixed at 10 percent (Gagné, 1998c). Although that minimum leans toward the generous pole of the continuum, it is counterbalanced by the introduction of five degrees of giftedness or talent, labeled *mildly, moderately, highly, exceptionally,* and *extremely,* respectively. Following metric system rules, each group represents the top 10 percent of the previous group. Table 5.1 shows these five groups with their corresponding ratio in the general population, standard deviation scores, as well as approximate IQ equivalents. Note that the 10 percent estimate applies to each natural ability domain and each talent field. Since there is only partial overlap between ability domains and talent fields, it follows that the *total* percentage of gifted and talented individuals far exceeds 10 percent. Indeed, using a peer nomination form to identify multiple abilities, a recent study produced an estimate of almost 50 percent within a large ($n = 2500$) sample of elementary school children (Gagné, 1998b).

Comments. A first comment concerns the reference group to be considered when deciding who will be labeled *gifted* or *talented.* In other words, giftedness and talent represent the top 10 percent of what population? As argued elsewhere (Gagné, 1993), different reference groups should be adopted for gifts versus talents. In a nutshell, since everyone possesses some degree of every natural ability, it follows that

Table 5.1 Gagné's Metric-Based (MB) System of Levels within the Gifted/Talented Population

Level	Label	Ratio in General Population	IQ Equivalents	Standard Deviation
5	Extremely	1:100,000	165	+4.3
4	Exceptionally	1:10,000	155	+3.7
3	Highly	1:1,000	145	+3.0
2	Moderately	1:100	135	+2.3
1	Mildly	1:10	120	+1.3

the whole population should serve as the reference base to select the top 10 percent for any form of giftedness. The only caveat is age. Because natural abilities have strong developmental curves, at least until early adulthood, the comparison must be made with individuals of the same age. In the case of talents, the reference group should be composed of all those who (a) have attempted to master the specific skills of a talent field, and (b) have learned and practiced for approximately the same amount of time. The second criterion intends to control for individual differences in amount of learning time, independent of achieved competence.

Let us apply the system to a concrete situation. An unfortunate habit of many keynote speakers is to illustrate their presentations with examples of gifted or talented behaviors of children who show exceptional precocity in verbal, mathematical, scientific, moral, or social development. As attractive as such examples may be, they illustrate behaviors that the vast majority of gifted students identified in school districts— the *mildly* gifted or talented between the 90th and 99th percentiles—will rarely show. Think about it. The prevalence of *exceptionally* gifted individuals (intellectually), those with IQs of 155 or more, is approximately 1:10,100 within the general population. Since the DMGT defines the total gifted population as the top 10 percent (IQs ≥ 120) of the same-age general population, the prevalence of exceptionally gifted individuals *within the gifted population* does not exceed 1:10,000. It corresponds to one such student in thirty to forty homogeneous groups of gifted students. Even full-time teachers of the gifted would, in the course of their whole career, encounter at best just a few of them. In short, *exceptional* giftedness is a rare phenomenon indeed. Consequently, when we present extreme examples of behavior to groups of parents or teachers, we risk conveying a distorted image of who the "garden variety" of gifted and tal-

ented individuals really are. Further, if we present giftedness and talent as very exceptional phenomena, we might tempt school administrators to judge that such a rare population does not require large investments of time and money to cater to their special needs.

Toward a Talent Development Theory

The third part of this chapter addresses two major questions. First, using existing literature, what types of relationships can be observed among the six components of the DMGT? Second, is it possible to create a hierarchy of the five factors in terms of their relative influence on talent development? In other words, where lies the difference between those who become talented and those who don't? Answers to both questions will include empirical evidence and hypotheses, as well as educated guesses.

A Complex Pattern of Interactions

Five major groups of causal factors have been described: gifts (G), intrapersonal (IC) and environmental (EC) catalysts, the learning and practicing process (LP), as well as chance (C). Although a detailed examination of the complex relationships among them is not possible here, I will give at least a glimpse of their dynamic interactions.

The Basic Connection. The most fundamental relationship involves the concepts of *gifts* and *talents*. As described earlier, talent development corresponds to the transformation of outstanding natural abilities—or aptitudes—into the skills characteristic of a particular occupational field. In the DMGT, natural abilities are treated as the "raw materials" or the constituent elements of talents. For instance, the research skills of a chemist are assumed to derive directly from general cognitive abilities related to memorizing information, analyzing data, creating relationships—causal or otherwise—among concepts, extrapolating judgments from observed facts, and so forth. Similarly, the skills of a young pianist derive from general sensorimotor abilities, among them two-hand coordination, finger dexterity, motor reaction time, rhythm, and auditory discrimination. Because of that basic relationship, the presence of talent necessarily implies the possession of well above average natural abilities; one cannot become talented without first being gifted, or almost so.

The reverse is not true, however. It is possible for outstanding gifts to remain potentialities, as witnessed by the well-known phenomenon of academic underachievement. In other fields, like arts or sports, those who possess outstanding natural abilities but find little interest in the pursuit of excellence can drop out at any time, unless forced by outside agents (e.g., parents) to maintain their involvement. Because school is compulsory, dropping out can be done only metaphorically!

How strong is the relationship between gifts and talents, especially with respect to the causal influence of the four other components? That crucial question will be examined later.

Learning/Practice (LP) as a Go Between. The arrows in Figure 5.1 indicate that ICs and ECs typically act through the LP process. For instance, bright and highly motivated students will study more to get better grades. Parents will offer help that will improve the study habits of their children, or will pay for a summer camp in sports that, by offering advanced learning/training opportunities, will help improve their child's performance. The moderator role of the LP process is quite normal; it confirms that talent does not manifest itself overnight. The skills have to be built, even when, thanks to very high natural abilities, the first achievements seem almost instantaneous and effortless. Sometimes, environmental influences do not act directly on the learning process, but through an intrapersonal catalyst. For instance, when parents or teachers attempt to increase the motivation of children so that they will study more—and, hopefully, improve their academic performance—their intervention will impact the LP component through the modification of an IC component. Similarly, when coaches help their athletes develop visualization abilities (Orlick, 1986), they are trying to improve a specific IC component that will in turn improve the effectiveness of the training process. A more effective LP process usually means better performances leading to an increased talent level. As we will see later, the usual role of the learning process as a go between does not automatically mean more causal importance.

Bi-Directional Interactions. Interactions can be very complex. Indeed, empirical evidence exists to support causal interactions between *any* pairing of the five components, and in both directions in each case. We have already mentioned examples of EC → IC influences; the reverse is also common. For example, if some parents observe that their child is expressing a strong interest in astronomy, they might invest in a high-quality telescope. Similarly, the strong anxiety reactions of a young musician before a performance might encourage his music teacher to introduce special pre-performance relaxation exercises. The impact—positive or negative—on one's self-concept of being labeled *gifted* or *talented* is a typical case of G → IC interaction. Conversely, ICs may exert an impact on the development of natural abilities. Persons with little motivation to take care of their health will avoid physical activities. Compared to individuals who do regular workouts, their physical fitness will no doubt decrease as the years go by. As a last example, the EC → LP causal relationship is easy to visualize: It can be the impact of a new coach's training plan on daily practice activities, of parents moving closer to a music conservatory to allow more regular contact with a master teacher, or the impact of a school's policy changes on the students' amount of homework. Conversely, a poor LP process that manifests itself through a child's unsatisfactory homework may lead the parents and the teacher (EC) to offer closer supervision.

Talent as a Retroactive Cause. Usually, talent is a dependent variable in most empirical studies devoted to the prediction of outstanding performance. But it can become an independent variable, for instance, when talent enters into a feedback loop and influences the performers and/or influential persons in their environment. No doubt, the early successes of young students, young artists, or young athletes serve to heighten their motivation to pursue their training, even increase its intensity. Similarly, parents will become more motivated to maintain or increase their support, coaches will feel more eager to supervise young athletes whose early outstanding performances reveal high talent promise, and even sponsors will open their purse wider! As the saying goes: "Success breeds success."

In summary, no causal component stands alone. They all interact with each other and with the learning process in complex ways; and these interactions will differ significantly from one person to the next. Individual talent emerges from complex and unique choreographies between the five groups of causal influences.

What Makes a Difference?

Even though all five causal components are active, this does not mean that they are equally powerful as agents of talent emergence. Each talented person follows a unique path toward excellence. But what about averages? Are some factors generally recognized as more powerful influences on outstanding performance? For those involved in the search for and development of gifted individuals, this is a critical question.

Literature Review. In spite of its theoretical and practical importance, the "causal hierarchy" question has yet to receive a clear answer. In the field of education alone, thousands of empirical studies have compared achieving students with less performing ones, hoping to unravel the network of causal factors leading to academic success. Dozens of variables, covering every category and subcategory of the DMGT, have been measured. Unfortunately, individual studies include too few independent variables to bring even a semblance of answer to this question.

Perhaps a meta-analytic look at a large sample of empirical studies would point in the right direction. Walberg and his colleagues did just that, synthesizing almost 3,000 published studies on the causes of academic achievement (Walberg, 1984).[2] They identified nine groups of significant factors, which they organized under three major headings: (a) *Aptitude* (1. ability; 2. development; 3. motivation); (b) *Instruction* (4. amount; 5. quality); and (c) *Environment* (6. home; 7. classroom; 8. peers; 9. television). In terms of effect sizes, ability (IQ) came well in front of all other factors with an average correlation of .70 with academic achievement. By contrast, the best predictors within the Instruction category had average effect sizes around 1.0 *SD,* equivalent to a correlation of about .45 (Cohen, 1969); and the best predictors

in the Environment category had average effect sizes around .70 *SD,* equivalent to a correlation of .33. Walberg did not mention that obvious explanatory hierarchy among factors. He stated instead: "The first five essential factors appear to substitute, compensate, or trade-off for one another at diminishing rates of return. . . . Thus, no single essential factor overwhelms the others; all appear important" (p. 22).

Simonton (1994) also adopted a macroscopic perspective when he examined the lives of great historical figures and tried to tease out the characteristics that might explain why and how they attained the pinnacles in their respective fields, including science, arts, and politics. He surveyed a large variety of psychological constructs "that participate in the making of geniuses of all species. Genetic endowment, reinforcement schedules, motivation, birth order, childhood trauma, marginality, age, intelligence, risk taking, self-actualization, depression, social learning, authoritarianism, and emulation—I could cite many more instances" (p. 412). Unfortunately, nowhere does one find an attempt to rank them according to their relative causal power. When presenting the various factors, Simonton gives each some degree of prominence, leaving the clear impression that most have equal importance in the emergence of greatness (Gagné, 1999c).[3]

What is my personal answer to the question "what makes a difference"? Again, because of space limitations, the following paragraphs will barely scratch the surface of my arguments in defense of the proposed hierarchy.

C.GIPE and the Primacy of Chance. My present view could be summarized with the acronym *C.GIPE* (pronounced "seagype"). Using one letter per component picked clockwise from the bottom left of Figure 5.1, it shows the decreasing order of causal impact: from chance at the top of the hierarchy to environmental catalysts at the bottom. Why is chance given such a predominant role? The answer lies in Atkinson's two rolls of the dice: the genetic roll and the parental roll. Note that the genetic endowment affects not only the G component, but also the IC component, as shown by the arrows in Figure 5.1. Two additional facts, both related to the genetic endowment, increase the significance of the chance factor. First, the importance of the genotype as a determinant

---

2. See Chapter 27 by Walberg, Williams, and Zeiser.

3. See Chapter 28 by Simonton.

of human individual differences has grown over the last two decades; second, chance directly impacts the next two factors in my proposed hierarchy, G and IC.

The Major Role of Gifts. My arguments for giving *gifts* a second rank rest essentially on data from two giftedness domains: cognitive and physical abilities. In the first case, research has shown that IQ measures are, by far, the best predictor of academic achievement (Jensen, 1980, 1998). In grade school, most correlations between IQ scores and standardized achievement tests range between .60 and .70. Even in high school settings, the correlations usually remain around .50, while they decrease to the .30s and .40s when college achievement is assessed. Moreover, there is ample evidence for a primary role of IQ measures as predictors of work performance (Gottfredson, 1997; Schmidt & Hunter, 1998). In the case of physical abilities, there is also growing evidence that "natural talent" (giftedness) is a major differentiator between those who can attain excellence in sports and those who cannot. For instance, the Australian Institute of Sport (AIS) supervises the administration of tests of physical fitness to middle school students in most Australian states. They use a two-step system. First, a general fitness test with eight components is offered to a number of students in eighth and ninth grades. Only those who outperform 97 percent of their peers on any one of these eight components are invited to take a second battery. Again, only those in the top 10 percent on subgroups of these tests—depending on the competitive sport chosen—will be invited to an advanced training program. Such a selection procedure leaves aside over 99.5 percent of all adolescents, an eloquent testimony of the AIS belief that very high natural abilities are required for athletes to develop their talent to national standards.

The Importance of Intrapersonal Catalysts. The placement of intrapersonal catalysts in third rank brings up two questions: (a) Why do they follow gifts and (b) why do they precede learning and practice? With regard to cognitive gifts, the research literature suggests that the best "contenders" to prominence among IC factors would be motivation-related constructs. As Hemery (1986) said in the last sentence of his book: "They [sports' highest achievers] tell us all something about ourselves and what we may be capable of achieving, if we dream and make the commitment to work hard towards that vision" (p. 204).

But what does research say about these contenders? Virtually every comparative study of the relative explanatory power of motivational constructs versus IQ measures has shown a clear superiority of the latter. After reviewing the literature, Gagné and St Père (2002) concluded as follows:

> Motivation's independent contribution to the prediction of scholastic or occupational achievement appears limited. It is frequently non-existent . . . or much less powerful than the independent contribution of cognitive abilities. . . . The 4:1 and 6:1 ratios, respectively, extracted from Walberg's (1984) and Schmidt and Hunter's (1998) syntheses, probably upper-limit estimates, are more or less equidistant from the two extremes. (p. 74)

In other words, when compared directly to *any* measure of motivation or volition, IQ scores "explain" on average *five times* more achievement variance. As for other constructs included in the IC component, there is little literature on their unique contribution to talent development. The term *unique* means the percentage of variance they account for after the impact of natural abilities has been controlled. My guess is that we would find an even higher ratio in favor of IQ measures than the ones reported by Gagné and St Père.

A Modest Practice Component. The next question concerns the priority of intrapersonal catalysts over the LP component. A group of scholars, led by K. A. Ericsson (e.g., 1996), would strongly oppose such a low ranking. Over the last decade, they have been arguing for a strong causal relationship between level of talent and amount—and quality—of practice, almost to the exclusion of other causal sources, especially natural abilities (Ericsson & Charness, 1994; Howe, Davidson, & Sloboda, 1998). Their extreme position has triggered numerous objections in the scholarly world. What they repeatedly overlook in their studies is the large individual differences *within* the groups they compare (e.g., amateurs versus professionals; or music soloists versus music teachers). Let's look at one example related to academic achievement. Time spent in school is a relevant measure of the learning and practice component. Standardized achievement test scores show that the range of performances among large cohorts of same-grade students actually covers many grade levels. For instance, data from the norm manuals of the Iowa Tests of Basic Skills (Hoover, Hieronymus, Frisbie, & Dunbar, 1993) reveal that the range of achievement scores of grade 5 students extends from a first grade average to beyond a ninth grade average (Gagné, 1998a). In other words, Ericsson's "road to excellence" requires much more than just "practice makes perfect."

Two additional arguments support the placement of the LP component below that of IC factors. First, the IC group comprises a large number of variables that have been linked to achievement, whereas the LP process offers just a few measures, both quantitative and qualitative. I have yet to find a single study that assesses the predictive validity of a large group of variables belonging to the IC versus LP components. But I strongly believe that the combined contribution of almost any group of IC factors will outpredict any combination of LP measures. Second, to use a common metaphor, the LP "motor" needs fuel to run, and that fuel comes directly from the intrapersonal and environmental catalysts. It is either passion, competitiveness, parental support, coach admonitions, or any other IC or EC element that helps maintain a steady regimen of learning and practice, especially when the learner encounters obstacles.

Scaled-Down Environmental Influences. Relegating the environmental catalysts to the bottom of the causal hierarchy contradicts common sense, as well as much of the social sciences literature. As stated earlier, environmentalism is the leading ideology in the behavioral sciences (Cohen, 1999; Harris, 1998; Pinker, 1997; Tooby & Cosmides, 1992). Yet over the last two decades, researchers in behavioral genetics have strongly questioned the causal importance of environmental inputs, thus triggering a heated debate (see Collins, Maccoby, Steinberg, Hetherington, & Bornstein, 2000).

Four major arguments are advanced. The first one, commonly labeled "the nature of nurture," states that most environmental measures are partly influenced by the genotype, which artificially inflates their contribution. For example, Scarr and Carter-Saltzman (1982) demonstrated that the teaching abilities of mothers were strongly associated with their intelligence level. The second argument is based on the recurrent observation in twin and adoption studies that *shared* family influences—the family environment that affects all siblings similarly—account for a very small percentage of individual differences in cognitive abilities and personality. In other words, the parents' rearing behaviors have little to do with what makes their children similar and, at the same time,

different from those of other families. In line with other specialists in behavioral genetics (e.g., Scarr, 1992), Rowe (1994) gave the following interpretation:

> Some three-quarters of American families fall into this range of social class categories, where rearing effects have been proven weak, despite massive differences in levels of funding for their public schools and massive differences in home intellectual environments. Of course, I do not intend to imply that intelligence develops without exposure to schools, books, television shows, magazines, and good conversations. I mean simply that these exposures can be found in three-quarters of American society in significant abundance to support full intellectual growth. (pp. 124–125).

A third argument invokes the phenomenological perspective, according to which EC influences are continuously filtered through the eyes of the persons who are targeted by them. That perceptual filtering gives more importance to ICs, strengthening the argument in favor of their placement immediately after the G component. Perceptual differences might explain why environmental inputs contribute much more to *differences* between siblings—called *nonshared* environmental influences—than to similarities between them (Plomin & McClearn, 1993).

Fourth, the growing interest in the study of resilience (O'Connell Higgins, 1994), the ability of some individuals to achieve high personal maturity in spite of having suffered exceptionally negative environmental influences, suggests that detrimental environmental obstacles can be surmounted (see Bartholomew, 1997; Gagné, 2000).

In summary, the EC component has been placed in last position not because such influences are not important, but mostly because EC differences found in "normal" environments (at least 75 percent of North American families, as argued by Rowe) do not make the difference between outstanding achievements and more average ones.

SUMMARY AND CONCLUSIONS

So much more would need to be said to faithfully convey the complexity of the DMGT as it now exists in the thoughts and (unpublished!) notes of its author. And those ideas constantly evolve, as would clearly appear by comparing this chapter with the original one (Gagné, 1991). Now that the contents and internal structure of the components are well stabilized, future efforts will focus on the developmental theory itself. Two major directions will be pursued. The first will consist in searching the scientific literature for additional empirical evidence in support of the present developmental hypotheses, and for additional hypotheses and corollaries. The second research path will consist in examining possible modifications to the C.GIPE causal hierarchy with regard to (a) stages of talent development, (b) fields of talent, (c) levels of excellence, (d) gender differences, (e) cultural differences, and so forth. The past decades of slow progress to clearly identify "what makes a difference" should be a humbling reminder that there is still a long distance to cover to get close to that lofty goal. Still, what an exciting challenge it offers to all scholars who dream of unearthing the roots of excellence!

The *Differentiated Model of Giftedness and Talent* (DMGT) is a developmental theory of talent emergence, in which outstanding natural abilities (gifts) are transformed into the specific expert skills (talents) of a particular occupational field through a slow process of learning and training. The learning can be informal (daily use) or formal (self-managed or institution-based). This development is either facilitated or hindered by three types of catalysts: chance (genotype, accidents), intrapersonal (motiviation, willpower, self-management, personality) and environmental (milieu, significant others, provisions, special events). The labels *gifted* or *talented* are reserved for those who perform among at least the top 10 percent on relevant measures. Five levels are proposed within a metric-type system: mild (1:10), moderate (1:100), high (1:1,000), exceptional (1:10,000), extreme (1:100,000).

The relationships among the six components (G, CH, IC, EC, LP, and T) are expressed through a complex pattern of interactions. The most fundamental interaction is the causal impact of gifts on talents, gifts being the constituent elements (or raw materials) of talents, the presence of talent(s) implies underlying gift(s). But the reverse is not true: Gifts can remain undeveloped (e.g., academic underachievement). The causal components usually act through the LP process, facilitating or hindering the learning activities, and thus the performance. But any pair of components can interact, in both directions (e.g., gifts influencing IC, and vice-versa); talents can even have a feedback effect on the other components. The DMGT's answer to the crucial question "What makes the difference between becoming or not becoming talented?" places the five components in the following decreasing order of causal impact on talent emergence: chance, gifts, intrapersonal, learning/practice, and environmental (C.GIPE). Each component's position in this hierarchy is buttressed by empirical data.

QUESTIONS FOR THOUGHT AND DISCUSSION

1. Think of any field of expertise. What might be the requisite natural abilities (gifts)? What are the observable skills (talents)? How are they related?

2. Compare Gagné's four domains of giftedness and six fields of talent with Sternberg's Triarchic Theory (Chapter 7) and Gardner's Theory of Multiple Intelligences theory (Chapter 8). What are the similarities and differences?

3. Choose any occupational (perhaps artistic) field. What are examples of "performances" that would correspond to each of Gagné's five metrically defined levels of giftedness/talent?

4. Look again at Gagné's hierarchy of influence on talent development—his C.GIPE model (e.g., chance is the most important determiner of great achievement, environmental conditions the least important.) What counter-arguments might you propose to defend changes to that hierarchy?

REFERENCES

Anastasi, A. (1980). Abilities and the measurement of achievement. In W. B. Schrader (Ed.), *Measuring achievement: Progress over a decade* (pp. 1–10). San Francisco: Jossey-Bass.

Anastasi, A., & Urbina, S. (1997). *Psychological testing* (7th ed.). Upper Saddle River, NJ: Prentice-Hall.

Angoff, W. H. (1988). The nature-nurture debate, aptitudes, and group differences. *American Psychologist, 41,* 713–720.

Atkinson, J. W. (1978). Motivational determinants of intellective performance and cumulative achievement. In J. W. Atkinson & J. O. Raynor (Eds.), *Personality, motivation, and achievement* (pp. 221–242). New York: Wiley.

Australian Sports Commission. (1994). *The search is over: Norms for sport related fitness tests in Australian students aged 12–17 years.* Canberra, Australia: Author.

Bartholomew, A. (1997, March). The gift of music was his passport. *Readers' Digest,* 149–154.

Bloom, B. S. (1985). *Developing talent in young people.* New York: Ballantine Books.

Bouchard, C., Malina, R. M., & Pérusse, L. (1997). *Genetics of fitness and physical performance.* Champaign, IL: Human Kinetics.

Bouchard, T. J. (1997). IQ similarity in twins reared apart: Findings and responses to critics. In R. J. Sternberg & E. Grigorenko (Eds.), *Intelligence, heredity, and environment*, pp. 126–160. New York: Cambridge University Press.

Carroll, J. B. (1993). *Human cognitive abilities: A survey of factor-analytic studies.* New York: Cambridge University Press.

Cohen, D. B. (1999). *Stranger in the nest.* New York: Wiley.

Cohen, J. (1969). *Statistical power analysis for the behavioral sciences.* New York: Academic Press.

College Board. (2001). *Advanced placement program.* [Available at: www.collegeboard.org/ap/].

Collins, W. A., Maccoby, E. E., Steinberg, L., Hetherington, E. M., & Bornstein, M. H. (2000). Contemporary research on parenting: The case for Nature and Nurture. *American Psychologist, 55,* 218–232.

Corno, L. (1993). The best-laid plans: Modern conceptions of volition and educational research. *Educational Researcher, 22,* 14–22.

Corno, L., & Kanfer, R. (1993). The role of volition in learning and performance. *Review of Research in Education, 19,* 301–341.

Cox, J., Daniel, N., & Boston, B. O. (1985). *Educating able learners: Programs and promising practices.* Austin: University of Texas Press.

Digman, J. M. (1990). Personality structure: Emergence of the five-factor model. In M. R. Rosenzweig & L. W. Porter (Eds.), *Annual Review of Psychology* (Vol. 41, pp. 417–440). Palo Alto, CA: Annual Reviews.

Ericsson, K. A. (Ed.) (1996). *The road to excellence: The acquisition of expert performance in the arts and sciences, sports, and games.* Mahwah, NJ: Erlbaum.

Ericsson, K. A., & Charness, N. (1994). Expert performance: Its structure and acquisition. *American Psychologist, 49,* 725–747.

Feldhusen, J. F. (1986). A conception of giftedness. In R. J. Sternberg & J. E. Davidson (Eds.), *Conceptions of giftedness* (pp. 112–127). New York: Cambridge University Press.

Feldhusen, J. F. (1992). *Talent identification and development in education (TIDE).* Sarasota, FL: Center for Creative Learning.

Gagné, F. (1985). Giftedness and talent: Reexamining a reexamination of the definitions. *Gifted Child Quarterly, 29,* 103–112.

Gagné, F. (1991). Toward a differentiated model of giftedness and talent. In N. Colangelo & G. A. Davis (Eds.), *Handbook of gifted education* (pp. 65–80). Boston: Allyn and Bacon.

Gagné, F. (1993). Constructs and models pertaining to exceptional human abilities. In K. A. Heller, F. J. Mönks, & A. H. Passow (Eds.), *International handbook of research and development of giftedness and talent* (pp. 63–85). Oxford: Pergamon Press.

Gagné, F. (1997). Critique of Morelock's (1996) definitions of giftedness and talent. *Roeper Review, 20,* 76–85.

Gagné, F. (1998a, November). *Individual differences are MUCH larger than you think!* Paper presented at the meeting of the National Association for Gifted Children, Louisville, KY.

Gagné, F. (1998b). The prevalence of gifted, talented, and multitalented individuals: Estimates from peer and teacher nominations. In R. C. Friedman & K. B. Rogers (Eds.), *Talent in context: Historical and social perspectives on giftedness* (pp. 101–126). Washington, DC: American Psychological Association.

Gagné, F. (1998c). A proposal for subcategories within the gifted or talented populations. *Gifted Child Quarterly, 42,* 87–95.

Gagné, F. (1999a). Is there any light at the end of the tunnel? *Journal for the Education of the Gifted, 22,* 191–234.

Gagné, F. (1999b). The multigifts of multitalented individuals. In S. Cline & K. T. Hegeman (Eds.), *Gifted education in the twenty-first century: Issues and concerns* (pp. 17–45). Delray Beach, FL: Winslow Press.

Gagné, F. (1999c). Review of D. K. Simonton's (1994) "Greatness: Who makes history and why." *High Ability Studies, 10,* 113–115.

Gagné, F. (2000). Understanding the complex choreography of talent development through DMGT-based analysis. In K. A. Heller, F. J. Mönks, R. J. Sternberg, & R. Subotnik (Eds.), *International handbook for research on giftedness and talent* (2nd ed., pp. 67–79). Oxford: Pergamon Press.

Gagné, F., Neveu, F., Simard, L., & St Père, F. (1996). How a search for multitalented individuals challenged the concept itself. *Gifted and Talented International, 11,* 4–10.

Gagné, F., & St Père, F. (2002). When IQ is controlled, does motivation still predict achievement? *Intelligence, 30,* 71–100.

Gardner, H. (1983). *Frames of mind: The theory of multiple intelligences.* New York: Basic Books.

Gazzaniga, M. S., Ivry, R. B., & Mangun, G. R. (1998). *Cognitive neuroscience: The biology of mind.* New York: Norton.

Gottfredson, L. S. (1997). Why g matters: The complexity of everyday life. *Intelligence, 24,* 79–132.

Harris, J. R. (1998). *The nurture assumption.* New York: Free Press.

Haskins, R. (1989). Beyond metaphor: The efficacy of early childhood education. *American Psychologist, 44,* 274–282.

Hemery, D. (1986). *The pursuit of sporting excellence: A study of sport's highest achievers.* London: Willow Books.

Hoover, H. D., Hieronymus, A. N., Frisbie, D. A., & Dunbar, S. B. (1993). *Norms and score conversions: Form K, levels 7–14 of the ITBS Survey Battery.* Chicago: Riverside.

Howe, M. J. A., Davidson, J. W., & Sloboda, J. A. (1998). Innate talents: Reality or myth? *Behavioral and Brain Sciences, 21,* 399–442.

Jensen, A. R. (1980). *Bias in mental testing.* New York: Free Press.

Jensen, A. R. (1998). *The "g" factor: The science of mental ability.* Westport, CT: Praeger.

Kuhl, J., & Beckmann, J. (Eds.). (1985). *Action control: From cognition to behavior.* New York: Springer-Verlag.

Marland, S. P. (1972). *Education of the gifted and talented: Report to the Congress of the United States by the U.S. Commissioner of Education.* Washington, DC: U.S. Government Printing Office.

Massé, P., & Gagné, F. (1983). Observations on enrichment and acceleration. In B. M. Shore, F. Gagné, S. Larivée, R. H. Tali, & R. E. Tremblay (Eds.), *Face to face with giftedness* (pp. 395–413). Monroe, NY: Trillium Press.

Mayer, J. D., Caruso, D. R., & Salovey, P. (2000). Emotional intelligence meets traditional standards for an intelligence. *Intelligence, 27,* 267–298.

McCrae, R. R., & Costa, P. T. Jr. (1999). A five-factor theory of personality. In L. A. Pervin & O. P. John (Eds.), *Handbook of personality: Theory and research* (2nd ed., pp. 139–153). New York: Guilford Press.

McCrae, R. R., Costa, P. T. Jr., Ostendorf, F., Angleitner, A., Hrebickova, M., Avia, M. D., Sanz, J., Sanchez-Bernardos, M. L., Kusdil, M. E., Woodfield, R., Saunders, P. R., & Smith, P. B. (2000). Nature over nurture: Temperament, personality, and life span development. *Journal of Personality and Social Psychology, 78,* 173–186.

Mitchell, B. M. (1988). The latest National Assessment of Gifted Education. *Roeper Review, 10,* 239–240.

Moon, S. (in press). Personal talent: What is it and how can we study it? In N. Colangelo & S. Assouline (Eds.), *Talent Development VI: Proceedings from the 2000 Henry B. and Jocelyn Wallace National Research Symposium on Talent Development.* Scottsdale, AZ: Gifted Psychology Press.

Morelock, M. (1996). On the nature of giftedness and talent: Imposing order on chaos. *Roeper Review, 19,* 4–12.

O'Connell Higgins, G. (1994). *Resilient adults: Overcoming a cruel past.* San Francisco: Jossey-Bass.

Orlick, T. (1986). *Psyching for sport: Mental training for athletes.* Champaign, IL: Human Kinetics.

Pinker, S. (1997). *How the mind works.* New York: Norton.

Plomin, R., & McClearn, G. E. (Eds.) (1993). *Nature, nurture, and psychology.* Washington, DC: American Psychological Association.

President's Council on Physical Fitness and Sports (2001). *President's challenge: Physical fitness program packet.* Retrieved from http://www.fitness.gov/challenge/challenge.html.

Renzulli, J. S. (1986). The three-ring conception of gifted-ness: A developmental model for creative productivity. In R. J. Sternberg and J. E. Davidson (Eds.), *Conceptions of giftedness* (pp. 53–92). New York: Cambridge University Press.

Rothbart, M. K., Ahadi, S. A., & Evans, D. E. (2000). Temperament and personality: Origins and outcomes. *Journal of Personality and Social Psychology, 78,* 122–135.

Rowe, D. C. (1994). *The limits of family influence: genes, experience, and behavior.* New York: Guilford Press.

Scarr, S. (1992). Developmental theories for the 1990s: Development and individual differences. *Developmental Psychology, 63,* 1–19.

Scarr, S., & Carter-Saltzman, L. (1982). Genetics and intelligence. In R. J. Sternberg (Ed.), *Handbook of human intelligence* (p. 792–896). New York: Cambridge University Press.

Schmidt, F. L., & Hunter, J. E. (1998). The validity and utility of selection methods in personnel psychology: Practical and theoretical implications of 85 years of research findings. *Psychological Bulletin, 124,* 262–274.

Simonton, D. K. (1994). *Who makes history and why.* New York: Guilford Press.

Sternberg, R. J. (1985). *Beyond IQ: A triarchic theory of human intelligence.* New York: Cambridge University Press.

Sternberg, R. J., & Wagner, R. K. (Eds.) (1986). *Practical intelligence: Nature and origins of competence in the everyday world.* New York: Cambridge University Press.

Tannenbaum, A. J. (1983). *Gifted children: Psychological and educational perspectives.* New York: Macmillan.

Terman, L. M. (1925). *Genetic studies of genius: Vol. 1. Mental and physical traits of a thousand gifted children.* Stanford: Stanford University Press.

Tooby, J., & Cosmides, L. (1992). The psychological foundations of culture. In J. M. Barkow, L. Cosmides, & J. Tooby (Eds.), *The adapted mind: Evolutionary psychology and the generation of culture* (pp. 19–136). New York: Oxford University Press.

U.S. Department of Education. (1993). *National Excellence: A case for developing America's talent.* Washington, DC: U.S. Government Printing Office.

Walberg, H. J. (1984). Improving the productivity of America's schools. *Educational Leadership, 41*(8), 19–27.

Zimmerman, B. J. (1998). Academic studying and the development of personal skill: A self-regulatory perspective. *Educational Psychologist, 33,* 73–86.

6

Conception of Giftedness and Its Relationship to the Development of Social Capital[1]

JOSEPH S. RENZULLI, *University of Connecticut*

The good we secure for ourselves is precarious and uncertain until it is secured for all of us and incorporated into our common life.

—Jane Addams

Changing the World . . . One Life at a Time

After repeatedly observing the little boy crying on the school bus, Melanie, a fifth-grade student, took a seat next to him and struck up a conversation. "You don't understand," said Tony, a first grader whose face was practically hidden behind the thickest eyeglasses Melanie had ever seen. "You see these glasses? I'm partially sighted. The kids trip me and make fun of me; I have special books for my subjects, but there are no books in the library that I can read."

Later that day Melanie approached her enrichment teacher and asked if she could make Tony her "Type III" Project for the year.[2] Over the next several days, Melanie and the enrichment teacher drew up a plan that began with some "friendly persuasion" for the boys that were harassing Tony. A few of the school's bigger, well-respected boys and girls escorted him from the school bus and sat with him in the lunch room.

Melanie then asked Tony a series of questions from an instrument called the Interest-A-Lyzer to determine what some of his reading interests might be. She reecruited a number of the school's best writers to work on large print "big books" books that dealt with Tony's interests in sports and adventure stories. She also recruited the school's best artists to illustrate the books, and served as the editor and production manager for the series.

As the project progressed over the next several months, a remarkable change took place in Tony's attitude toward school. He became a local celebrity, and other students even signed out books from Tony's special section of the library. Melanie's creative idea and her task commitment resulted in the development of profound empathy and sensitivity to human concerns and the application of her talents to an unselfish cause. When questioned about her work, Melanie explained simply, "It didn't change the world, but it changed the world of one little boy."

Background

In the early 1970s I began work on a conception of giftedness that challenged the traditional view of this concept as mainly a function of high scores on intelligence tests. This work met a less-than-enthusiastic reception from the gifted establishment of the time, including rejections of my writing by all the main journals in the field of gifted education. My convictions about a broadened view of human potential caused me to seek an audience elsewhere, and in 1978 the *Kappan* published my article entitled, "What Makes Giftedness: Reexamining a Definition" (Renzulli, 1978). In the ensuing years scholars, practitioners, and policy makers began to gain a more flexible attitude toward the meaning of this complex phenomenon called *giftedness,* and the 1978 *Kappan* article is now the most widely cited publication in the field. I mention this fortunate turn of events mainly to

1. The work reported in this chapter was supported under the Javits Act Program as administrered by the Office of Educational Research and Improvement, U.S. Department of Education (grant No. R-206R-00001), but the opinions expressed are those of the author. The author gratefully acknowledges contributions to this work by Rachel E. Sytsma and Kristin B. Berman.

2. Type III Enrichment is a self-selected individual or small group investigation of a real problem.

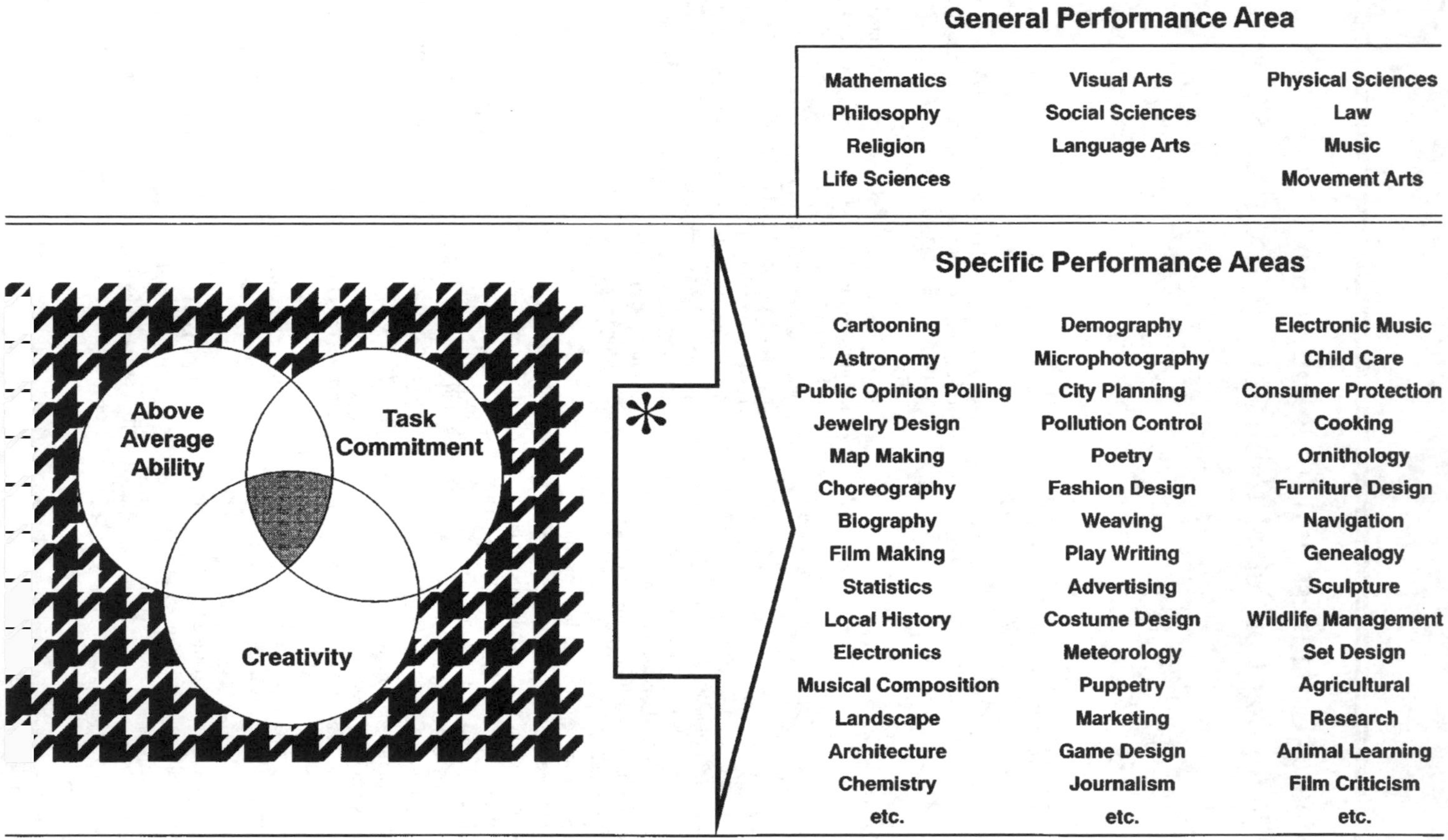

General Performance Area

Mathematics	Visual Arts	Physical Sciences
Philosophy	Social Sciences	Law
Religion	Language Arts	Music
Life Sciences		Movement Arts

Specific Performance Areas

Cartooning	Demography	Electronic Music
Astronomy	Microphotography	Child Care
Public Opinion Polling	City Planning	Consumer Protection
Jewelry Design	Pollution Control	Cooking
Map Making	Poetry	Ornithology
Choreography	Fashion Design	Furniture Design
Biography	Weaving	Navigation
Film Making	Play Writing	Genealogy
Statistics	Advertising	Sculpture
Local History	Costume Design	Wildlife Management
Electronics	Meteorology	Set Design
Musical Composition	Puppetry	Agricultural
Landscape	Marketing	Research
Architecture	Game Design	Animal Learning
Chemistry	Journalism	Film Criticism
etc.	etc.	etc.

*

Task Commitment

Above Average Ability

Creativity

* This arrow should read as " ... brought to bear upon ... "

Figure 6.1 Graphic Representation of the Three-Ring Definition of Giftedness.

call attention to the always expectant hope that people can change their minds about a long cherished belief and that leaders and practitioners in the field will once again be willing to examine an extension to today's more flexible conceptions of giftedness.

In what is now popularly known as the three-ring conception of giftedness (above average but not necessarily superior ability, creativity, and task commitment), I embedded the three rings in a houndstooth background that represents the interactions between personality and environment (see Figure 6.1). These factors aid in the development of three clusters of traits that represent gifted behaviors. What I recognized but did not emphasize at the time was that a scientific examination of a more focused set of background components is necessary in order for us to understand the sources of gifted behaviors and, more importantly, the ways in which people transform their gifted assets into constructive action.[3] Why did Melanie devote her time and energy to a socially responsible project that would improve the life of one little boy? And can a better understanding of people who use their gifts in socially constructive ways help us create conditions that expand the number of people who contribute to the growth of social as well as economic capital? Can our education system produce future corporate leaders who are as sensitive to aesthetic and environmental concerns as they are to the corporate bottom line? Can we influence the ethics and morality of future industrial and political leaders so that they place gross national happiness on an equal or higher scale of values than gross national product? These are some of the questions we are attempting to address in an ongoing series of research studies that examine the relationship between noncognitive personal characteristics and the role that these characteristics play in the development of social capital.

What Is Social Capital and Why Is It Important?

Financial and intellectual capital are the well-known forces that drive the economy and generate highly valued material assets, wealth production, and professional advancement—all important goals in a capitalist economic system. *Social capital,* on the other hand, is a set of intangible assets that address the collective needs and problems of other individuals and our communities at large. Although social capital cannot be defined as precisely as corporate earnings or gross domestic product, LaBonte (1999) eloquently defines it as: "something going on 'out there' in peoples day-to-day relationships that is an important determinant to the quality of their lives, if not society's healthy functioning. It is the 'gluey stuff' that binds individuals to groups, groups to organizations, citizens to societies" (p. 431). This kind of capital generally enhances community life and the network of obligations we have to one another. Investments in social capital benefit society as a whole because they help to create the values, norms, networks, and social trust that facilitate coordination and cooperation geared toward the greater public good.

Striking evidence indicates a marked decline in American social capital over the latter half of the twentieth century. National surveys show declines over the last few decades in voter turnout and political participation, membership in service clubs, church-related groups, parent-teacher associations, unions, and fraternal groups.

What is perhaps most striking when examining the commentary of leading scholars about the differences between economic and social capital is that investments in *both* types of national assets can result in greater prosperity and improved physical and mental health, as well as a society that honors freedom, happiness, justice, civic participation, and the dignity of a diverse population. Putnam (1993, 1995) pointed out that the aggregation of social capital has contributed to economic development. He found that widespread participation in group activities, social trust, and cooperation created conditions for both good government and prosperity. Putnam traced the roots of investments in social capital to medieval times and concluded that communities did not become civil because they were rich, but rather they became rich because they were civil.

Researchers who have studied social capital point out that it is created largely by the actions of individuals. They also have reported that *leadership* is a necessary condition for the creation of social capital. Although numerous studies and a great deal of commentary about leadership have been discussed in the gifted education literature, no one has yet examined the relationship between the characteristics of gifted leaders and their motivation to use their gifts for the production of social capital.

3. I prefer to use the word "gifted" as an adjective rather than a noun.

Operation Houndstooth

One of the more fortunate new directions in the social sciences in recent years has been the development of the *positive psychology* movement. Championed by Martin E. P. Seligman, this movement focuses on enhancing what is good in life rather than fixing what is maladaptive behavior. The goal of positive psychology is to create a science of human strengths that will help us to understand and learn how to foster socially constructive virtues in young people. Although all of society's institutions need to be involved in helping to shape positive values and virtues, schools play an especially important part today because of changes in family structures and because people of all ages now spend more than a fifth of their lives in some kind of schooling. In a study dealing with developing excellence in young people, Larson (2000) found that average students report being bored about one-third of the time. He speculated that participation in civic and socially engaging activities might hold the key to overcoming some of the disengagement and disaffection that is rampant among American youth. Larson argued that components of positive development such as initiative, creativity, leadership, altruism, and civic engagement can result from early and continuous opportunities to participate in experiences that promote characteristics associated with the production of social capital.

This chapter examines the scientific research that defines several categories of personal characteristics found in the houndstooth background underlying the three-ring conception of giftedness. Collectively referred to as Operation Houndstooth, these categories include, but may not be limited to, Optimism, Courage, Romance with a Topic or Discipline, Sensitivity to Human Concerns, Physical/Mental Energy, and Vision/Sense of Destiny (Figure 6.2). Empirical research and anecdotal exemplars of adults and young people who have displayed these concerns will be described, current research studies and instrument development initiatives will be reported, and an agenda for programmatic research that, hopefully, will lead to a better understanding of positive human concerns will be discussed. Finally, suggestions will be made regarding how parents, schools, and society at large might take a more active part in providing opportunities, resources, and encouragement for participation in experiences that promote the kinds of positive human concerns that are the raw material of increased social capital.

Before discussing the Houndstooth components, it is important to point out that we are in the early stages of trying to understand a very complex concept. Quick and easy answers about promoting larger amounts of social capital as a national goal may be years away, but it is my hope that this chapter will motivate other investigators to sense the importance of this challenge and pursue studies that will contribute to our understanding of this complex concept. I also hope that school personnel will begin to think about steps that they can take now to make changes in the ways we promote in young people some of the virtues discussed below. And earlier is better! Howard Gardner has commented on the importance of early experiences in acquiring enduring habits of mind: "Research shows that when children are young they develop what you call intuitive theories. It's like powerful engravings on your brain. Teachers don't realize how powerful they are, but early theories don't disappear, they stay on the ground" (Gardner, quoted in Kogan, 2000, p. 66). Wouldn't it be nice if we began engravings that might lead to societal improvements rather than the status and materialism markers so prevalent in the life styles of many of our young people?

The goals of Operation Houndstooth are twofold. First, we examine the scientific research that has been conducted on the components in Figure 6.2. The second phase consists of a series of experimental studies to determine how various school-related interventions can promote the types of behavior defined within the respective components.

Optimism

The most widely investigated Houndstooth component is *optimism*. The advent of positive psychology and multidimensional research approaches to health and wellness have created an environment ripe for the resurgence of research on optimism. Although difficult to define with absolute parameters, Peterson (2000) described it as an amoeba-like "velcro" concept to which everything seems to stick. The reason for optimism's amoebic and adhesive nature is its complexity. Peterson encourages a shift from a purely cognitive approach toward conceptualizing optimism as a cognitive characteristic with strong emotional and motivational overtones. Culture appears pivotal, in that social values influence individuals, and individual differences in the measurement of optimism are prominent within positive psychology research. As we move forward with experiments to promote

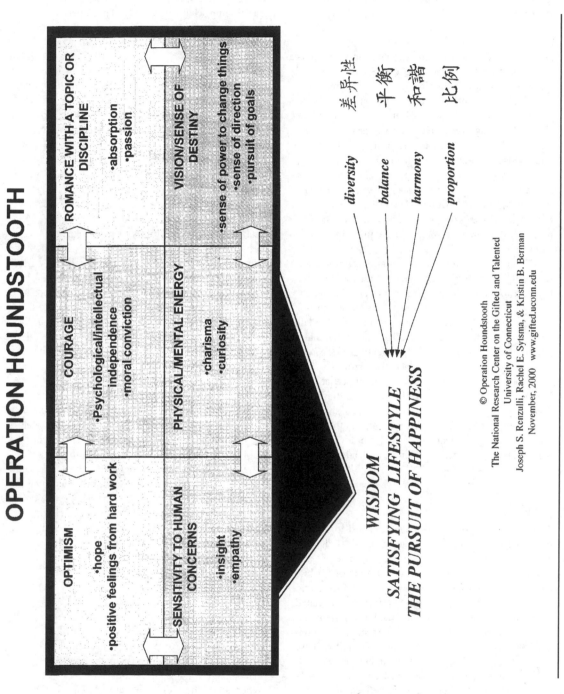

Figure 6.2 Operation Houndstooth.

optimism, this observation reminds us that opportunities should be sought to capitalize on the cultural strengths of diverse groups.

Optimism is something we all have to a certain degree; it is a personal, dispositional trait that appears to mediate between external events and individual interpretation of those events (Seligman & Csikszentmihalyi, 2000). Yet work by Seligman and his colleagues (1991, 1995) has illustrated that those optimistic behaviors or mindsets can be modified (learned) through reflective self-awareness and intervention strategies. While optimism may be based on one's sense of competence or learned ways of coping, it also may be rooted in a variety of beliefs in powers that transcend the individual, such as spiritual or religious beliefs. In fact, Lionel Tiger (1979), in his book *Optimism: The Biology of Hope,* argued that religions may have arisen in response to people's biological need to be optimistic.

Given the present state of affairs, in combination with ample literature explaining optimism's positive benefits to well-being, coping, perseverance, health, and happiness, it is essential that we expand our understanding of the power of optimism to develop talent. It is difficult to maximize an individual's potential when hampered by physical disorders, depleted energy levels, and negative attitudes and expectations, let alone if one is ill equipped at coping and has difficulty persevering. Perhaps those students with high measures of optimism in combination with other co-cognitive factors presented in this chapter are the very students most likely to develop into the creative producers and eminent leaders of tomorrow.

Courage

The factor of *courage* has been described in various contexts: physical courage, facing physical danger; psychological courage, facing one's own fears; and moral courage, maintaining moral integrity while overcoming the fear of being rejected by the group (Putman, 1997). Moral courage is strongly correlated with other Houndstooth factors such as empathy, altruism, and sensitivity to human concerns. The concept of *sensitivity to human concerns* combines these concepts into action, in that through heartfelt feeling for another's plight, one will act courageously for the benefit of others, even in the face of societal disapproval.

Courage also has been discussed in connection with the emergence of creativity, so much so that MacKinnon (1978) recognized it as the most significant characteristic of a creative person. This includes questioning what's accepted, being open to new experiences, listening to one's own intuition, imagining the impossible, and standing aside, or against, the group if necessary. Berman (1997) agreed with MacKinnon, pointing out that the job of teachers is not so much to teach traits such as courage, but rather to model them. Berman's work deals with the development of prosocial behaviors inherent in growth of moral courage. His work reflects a body of literature that documents the early natural ability of children to feel empathetic toward others, and at very early ages (Gove & Keating, 1979; Zahn-Waxler & Radke-Yarrow, 1982).[4]

Often the creative person must grapple with internal blocks or fears that must be overcome in order to seek and express the truths of new ideas, popular or not. Copernicus drew on great psychological courage to resist the overwhelming sense of perception and tradition that told men of his time how the sun rises and sets. As the individual power of his mind began to discover the illusion of the popular thinking, he struggled with the conflict between his pious religious faith and the truth of his profound discovery. He found solace for his seemingly heretical thinking in the very faith that posed his conflict: "All I can do is to adore when I behold this unfailing regularity, this miraculous balance and perfect adaptation. The majesty of it all humbles me to the dust" (Barnes, 1979, p. 112). This man, along with those who followed his lead—Kepler, Bruno, and Galileo—exemplified great psychological courage in pursuit of the truth.

Many people are blocked when they find themselves in psychological servitude, or under the emotional manipulation of another being. Psychological courage must be developed to live a normal life of individuating from parents and developing healthy relationships that do not interfere with independent functioning.

Romance with a Topic or Discipline

The concept of *romance with a topic* can be explored through the notions of passion, peak experience, or flow. This relates to physical and mental energy, in that intrinsic motivation exists in the context of topics that are appealing or interesting (Ryan & Deci, 2000). When all of these elements are present, the original

---

4. See Chapter 31 by Piechowski.

meaning of the word *passion* becomes relevant. The Latin root of the word is *pati,* meaning *to suffer.* One is willing to suffer for that which one loves. The concept of suffering also implies the connection with effort, exertion, and intense action (Kaufmann, 2000).

Passion has stimulated interest among philosophers and poets for millennia. The connection to the creative spirit has always been a target of inquiry in Socrates' writings:

> There is a . . . form of madness or possession of which the Muses are the source. This seizes a tender, virgin soul and stimulates it to rapt, passionate expression . . . glorifying the countless glorious deeds of ancient times for the instruction of posterity (Eliot, 1909, Vol. 7, p. 422).

And Burke wrote in the 1700s:

> The passion . . . is that state of the soul, in which all its motions are suspended . . . in this case the mind is so entirely filled with its object that it cannot contain any other (Eliot, 1909, Vol. 24, p. 47).

This description precedes the theory of flow as described by Csikszentmihalyi (1990, 1996). When one becomes thoroughly engaged in an activity in which the balance of ability and challenge meshes, the resulting experience is one of total absorption and self-actualization.

In the study of creative and eminent adults, the love of a topic usually began at an early age and blossomed under nurturing circumstances. Talent, personality, and ability are often not enough to succeed without the ingredient of the "labor of love" (Amabile, 1983). Popular wisdom encourages counselors of young people to advise them to do what they love, yet we may need to go beyond this traditional advice. Without emphasis also on the difficulty and sometimes pain of achievement—and an acknowledgment of the darker emotions of fear, anxiety, disillusionment, and rage that are part of real passions, along with strategies to cope with this part of the passionate experience—the concept of romance with a topic becomes only a romantic fantasy (Kaufmann, 2000).

Sensitivity to Human Concerns

Sensitivity to human concerns deals with the concept of moral courage and its correlates of empathy and altruism. The roots of these words give a universal basis for their definition: empathy (Greek, *pathos*—feeling), altruism (Latin, *alter*—other). The concept of sensitivity to human concerns combines these concepts into action in that through heartfelt feeling for another's plight, one will act, even in the face of societal disapproval, for the benefit of others.

Danish and Kagan (1971) found significant changes on the Scale of Affective Sensitivity in a control group after an intensive counseling intervention. Other researchers have found a relationship between empathic or altruistic tendencies and helping behaviors (Eisenberg-Berg, 1979; Eisenberg & Miller, 1987; Mehrabian & Epstein, 1972; Reis, 1995). These connections suggest the importance of developing ways to increase empathic tendencies if sensitivity to human concerns is a trait of value. This appears particularly important in our current climate; a number of studies have pointed to a decrease in knowledge and caring about social concerns among young people (Fowler, 1990; Hart Research Associates, 1989; Times Mirror Center for the People and the Press, 1990). The need for developing these traits is best summarized by the social psychologist Uri Bronfenbrenner (1979):

> No society can sustain itself unless its members have learned the sensitivities, motivations, and skills involved in assisting and caring for other human beings. Yet the school, which is carrying the primary responsibility for preparing young people for effective participation in adult life, does not, at least in American society, give high priority to providing opportunities in which such learning could take place (p. 8).

Research suggests that the environment can influence the nurturing of these traits (Battistich, Watson, Solomon, Schaps, & Solomon, 1991; Berman, 1997; Danish & Kagan, 1971; Zahn-Waxler & Radke-Yarrow, 1982), and the indications are that as a society, this must become an imperative.

Physical/Mental Energy

Physical and mental energy are more difficult to define, and are best understood in the context of several related factors that have been discussed in research literature. The nature of *charisma,* defined often as nonverbal emotional expressiveness and the ability to inspire followers with admiration (Lindholm, 1990), implies a high level of physical and mental energy. Curiosity, or inquisitiveness, also manifests in high levels of energy or intensity. In her study of eminent older women, Reis (1995) found a sense of vitality and energy to be an essential personal characteristic.

The importance of this energy level to creative production has been identified and described by several different theorists. John-Steiner (1997) stated: "Creativity requires a continuity of concern, an intense awareness of one's active inner life combined with sensitivity to the external world . . . intensity is then the one universal given in this account of creative thinking" (p. 219). Dabrowski (1977) identified five specific areas of sensitivity that are described as *overexcitabilities.* Some children exhibit intense energy levels in one or more of these five areas: psychomotor, intellectual, emotional, imaginational, and sensual. Many of the great leaders and producers of history (e.g., Leonardo da Vinci, Albert Einstein, Margaret Sanger, Booker T. Washington) displayed such intensities.

Charismatic figures such as Nietzche and Weber are represented to be more vivid than ordinary mortals; they appear to exist in an altered and intensified state of consciousness that is outside of ordinary emotional life (Lindholm, 1990). The power of a charismatic leader can be used for positive or negative ends. Examples are seen in Martin Luther King, Jr., and John F. Kennedy on one end of the spectrum, and Adolf Hitler, Charles Manson, and David Koresh on the other. Much work needs to be done in developing moral courage and sensitivity to human concerns so that these abilities can be used for societal good and advancement, rather than for personal power or even crimes against humanity.

Curiosity or inquisitiveness, another component of physical and mental energy, can fuel one's desire for learning even when the application of the knowledge is not readily apparent. Extensive curiosity can lead to dangerous behaviors, yet studies also show a positive relationship between curiosity and creativity (Padhee & Das, 1987). Identification of social or environmental factors that nurture these traits concerns many researchers. Nonpunitive environments open to exploration—rather than those which exert excessive control, provide low levels of challenge, or lack connectedness—allow for optimizing potential in the expression of physical and mental energy (Berman, 1997; Ryan & Deci, 2000). Finally, the first of the seven da Vincian principles representative of that energetic icon is *curiosita*—an insatiably curious approach to life and an unrelenting quest for continuous learning (Gelb, 1998).

Vision/Sense of Destiny

Vision/sense of destiny is the least researched component of Operation Houndstooth, and yet we know

from the history of civilization that persons with vision and a sense of destiny have truly made the modern world. Although there is a paucity of literature directly associated with destiny, the life histories of individuals eminent in their respective fields strongly suggest that vision and destiny are integral to the development of extraordinarily high levels of performance and success. Individuals possessing a sense of vision or destiny are apparent not only in retrospect but during early development. Consider the boy who is currently youth spokesperson for the World Centers of Compassion for Children, an organization to which he is devoted and for which he has traveled, encouraging education and policy for global nonviolence (Silverman, Roeper, & Smith, 2000). While identification and description of the characteristics setting these individuals apart from simple performance or success is difficult, the manifestation of those characteristics is quite obvious.

Despite the dearth of research literature in these areas, possible components of vision and destiny seem to be emerging from a few well-researched areas of psychology and education. These include achievement motivation, competence motivation, locus of control, intrinsic motivation, self-determination theory, and self-regulation theory (Ambrose, 2000; Rea, 2000; Rotter, 1966; Ryan & Deci, 2000; Schwartz, 2000; Wicker, Lambert, Richardson, & Kahler, 1984; Williams, 1998; Wong & Csikszentmihalyi, 1991). Erikson (1964) spoke of the *will* as the unbroken determination to exercise free choice as well as self-restraint. He also spoke of *purpose* as the courage to envision and pursue valued goals, and of *competence* as that which eventually becomes "workmanship." Almost all research on gifted contributors to all walks of life points out that eminent individuals possess an urge not to settle, conform, or become complacent. This research consistently recognizes the task commitment of these individuals for continuing their efforts, sometimes under the most adverse circumstances.

A *sense of direction* falls under the vision and sense of destiny component in Operation Houndstooth, as does a *sense of power to change things* (Figure 6.2). In research about gifted women, Reis (1995, 1998) found that a sense of destiny characterized virtually all those who achieved eminence.

If we assume that those individuals with high measures of internal locus of control are also likely to have high measures of some combination of curiosity, personal interest, and achievement motivation, then we can infer that having a highly internal locus of control may lead to a "sense of purpose." With a sense of purpose, self-determination would seem reinforced, perhaps magnified, leading to a sense of direction. As individuals begin to possess that sense of direction, they will be more apt to develop a vision for the future. With a sense of vision comes the feeling that one has the power to make a difference (a sense of power to change things), and once that is in place, it seems a natural conclusion that a sense of destiny arises.

Writing on optimal motivation, Rea (2000) offered a formula-like definition for *achievement motivation.* Achievement motivation, as he presents it, is comprised of expectancy, value, and affect, which, when optimized, produce optimal achievement evidenced as Csikszentmihalyi's concept of *flow.* Rea relates "serious fun" to flow, and says that students are optimally motivated to develop their talents when in flow because their physical and mental well-being and their performance levels are high. If Rea is correct that flow (seen as optimal achievement motivation) is the ideal situation for talent development, and if achievement motivation (along with intrinsic motivation, self-determination, and internal locus of control) is a foundational precursor to vision and destiny, then one can begin to illustrate how talent development relates to the co-cognitive factors and their subcomponents described herein.

The Role of Gifted and General Education

The history and culture of mankind can be charted to a large extent by the creative contributions of the world's most gifted and talented men and women. Advocates for special services for the gifted regularly invoke the names of persons such as Thomas Edison, Marie Curie, Jonas Salk, Isadora Duncan, and Albert Einstein as a rationale for providing supplementary resources to improve the educational experience of potentially gifted young people. If we assume that it has, indeed, been people like these who have created the science, culture, and wisdom of centuries past, then it is also safe to assume that persons who are the stewards and nurturers of today's potentially able young people can have a profound affect on shaping the values and directions toward which future contributors of remarkable accomplishments devote their energies.

Such stewardship is an awesome responsibility, and yet it has some intriguing overtones, because the persons who will be added to the lists of Edisons and Einsteins are in our homes and classrooms today. Note that this stewardship does not rest solely with teachers who are responsible for gifted programs. Melanie did, in fact, do her work as part of a special program for the gifted, but many other instances of creative productivity and problem solving by young people are guided by teachers in general education programs. In spite of our best efforts to identify students for special programs, predicting who will be our most gifted contributors is still an inexact science. What is even more significant, so far as our work on Operation Houndstooth is concerned, is that by expanding the conception of giftedness beyond the traditional high-scoring test-takers and good lesson-learners paradigm, we will find as rich a source of potentially gifted contributors in a broad and diverse population of nonselected students as we find in students traditionally selected for gifted programs.

Said another way, does anybody really care about the test scores or grade point average of people like Melanie or Martin Luther King, Jr.?

Are the Goals of Operation Houndstooth Realistic?

There have been times in the history of civilization when the *zeitgeist* has resulted in elevating a society's values toward social capital. The focus on democracy in ancient Greece, the ascendancy of the arts during the Renaissance, and the elevation of man as a logical and rational thinker during the Reformation are examples of times when entire cultures and societies brought new ways of thinking to bear on issues that enriched people's lives. Even in our own country, there have been times when our culture placed a high value on a sense of community and the dedication of individual and group efforts toward improvement of the greater good.

In 1830, Alexis de Tocqueville, the French philosopher and celebrated commentator on our emerging democracy, wrote about the need and desire for civil associations of all kinds on the part of Americans who, he observed, worked together with their fellow citizens toward common goals. "Americans of all ages, all conditions, and all dispositions constantly form associations. . . . Nothing in my opinion is more deserving of our attention than the intellectual and moral associations of America" (de Tocqueville, 1945, p. 109). de Tocqueville went so far as to say that the key to making democracy work in America was the propensity of our ancestors to form all kinds of civic associations—to view the building of community as important as personal success and prosperity.

If, as studies have shown, self-interest has replaced some of the values that created a more socially conscious early America, and if the negative trends of young people's overindulgences and disassociations are growing, then we must ask: Is there a role that schools can play in gently influencing future citizens and, especially, future leaders toward a value system that assumes greater responsibility for the production of social capital? Modern society is barraging our young people with messages that emphasize fast-paced life, material gain, selfishness, and rampant consumerism.

Can we create the future CEOs of automobile and energy companies who are as committed to safety and emission control as they are to shareholder's profits, sexier cars, and the corporate bottom line? Could some of the endless pitches for commercial products at least be interspersed with advocacy for more time with our children, a greater tolerance for diversity, and more concern for the rapid depletion of the earth's resources? Can the strips that flow across the bottom of our television screens carry messages that relate to gross national happiness as well as gross national product?

It is intriguing to consider that the men and women who will decide the content of these messages are the boys and girls who are in our classrooms today.

The general goal of our work is to infuse into the process of schooling experiences related to the Houndstooth components that will contribute to the development of wisdom and a satisfying lifestyle. It would be naïve to think that a redirection of educational goals can take place without a commitment at all levels to examine the purposes of education in a democracy. It is also naïve to think that experiences directed toward the production of social capital can, or are even intended to, replace our present day focus on material productivity and intellectual capital. Rather, this work seeks to enhance the development of wisdom and a satisfying lifestyle that are paralleled by concerns for diversity, balance, harmony, and proportion in all of the choices and in the decisions that young people make in the process of growing up. What people think and decide to do drives society's best ideas and achievements. If we want leaders who will promote ideas and achievements that take into consideration the components we have identified in Operation Houndstooth, then giftedness in the new century will have to be redefined in ways that take these co-cognitive components into account. And the strategies that are used to develop giftedness in young people will need to give as much attention to the co-cognitive conditions of development as we presently give to cognitive development.

Although there is no silver bullet or quick institutional fix for infusing these components into the curriculum or creating a greater awareness of the need to produce more social capital, there is support for this endeavor. First, the entire positive psychology movement is growing in popularity and promises to enhance research of the type we are pursuing. Second, already completed research in psychology, sociology, and anthropology clearly indicates that the environment in general, and schooling in particular, can nurture and influence the co-cognitive traits we have identified in Operation Houndstooth. Third, economists have pointed out the benefits of a reciprocal relationship between material and social capital, and many social, political, spiritual, and educational commentators have indicated that nurturing these traits must become an imperative.

My colleagues and I are only in the early stages on this path toward once again attempting to expand the definition of giftedness. We believe that an expanded definition will not only help us understand the unique contributions of persons who have used their talents to make the world a better place, it will also help us to extend supplementary opportunities and services to potentially able young people who have been overlooked because of the overemphasis on cognitive traits in the identification of giftedness. Each area of inquiry brings us closer to understanding the complexity of the concepts, identifying promising practices and assessment techniques, and bringing this message forward to interested educators. While the whole notion of changing the big picture seems awesome and overwhelming, the words of Margaret Mead remind us that it can be done: "*Never doubt that a small group of thoughtful, committed citizens can change the world . . . indeed, it is the only thing that ever does.*"

SUMMARY AND CONCLUSIONS

Material about Operation Houndstooth is being shared through presentations and postings on our website and we are developing an ongoing database that will make methods and materials for co-cognitive development available to educators and parents. There are many ways in which interested persons can become involved in our research, and I invite these readers to visit the Operation Houndstooth section of our website (www.gifted.uconn.edu), where they can share their experiences and communicate their interest in possible research and field test opportunities.

QUESTIONS FOR THOUGHT AND DISCUSSION

1. How might schools identify students—for example, for G/T programs—who will contribute to growth in "social capital"? That is, how can we select students with strong feelings of fairness, kindness, justice, and a strong willingness to help others?

2. In gifted programs, do you see a conflict between fostering educational excellence versus helping students become concerned for the welfare of others? Explain.

3. How would you rate yourself in ethics, sensitivity to the welfare of others, and in actively making changes to help others? Explain. How might you improve?

4. Explain "positive psychology."

5. What do you think of Renzulli's Operation Houndstooth? What concepts might be added? Explain.

REFERENCES

Amabile, T. (1983). *The social psychology of creativity.* New York: Springer Verlag.

Ambrose, D. (2000). World-view entrapment: Moral-ethical implications for gifted education. *Journal for the Education of the Gifted, 23*(2), 159–186.

Barnes, H. (1979). History teaching—dramatic art. In E. Piening & N. Lyons (Eds.), *Education as an art.* New York: Rudolf Steiner School Press.

Battistich, B., Watson, M., Solomon, D., Schaps, E., & Solomon, J. (1991). The child development project: Program for the development of prosocial character. In W. Kurtines and J. Gewirtz (Eds.), *Handbook of moral behavior and development, Volume 3: Application* (pp. 1–34). Hillsdale, NJ: Erlbaum.

Berman, S. (1997). *Children's social consciousness and the development of social responsibility.* Albany: State University of New York Press.

Bronfenbrenner, U. (1979). *The ecology of human development.* Cambridge: Harvard University Press.

Csikszentmilhalyi, M. (1990). *Flow: The psychology of optimal experience.* New York: HarperCollins.

Csikszentmialyi, M. (1996). *Creativity: Flow and the psychology of discovery and invention.* New York: HarperCollins.

Dabrowski, K., & Piechowski, M. M. (1977). *Theory of levels of emotional development,* Vols. 1 & 2. Oceanside, NY: Dabor Science.

Danish, S. J., & Kagan, N. (1971). Measurement of affective sensitivity: Toward a valid measure of interpersonal perception. *Journal of Counseling Psychology 18,* 51–54.

de Tocqueville, A. (1945). *Democracy in America,* Vol. 2. New York: Knopf.

Eisenberg-Berg, N. (1979). Development of children's prosocial moral judgment. *Developmental Psychology, 15,* 128–137.

Eisenberg, N., Miller, P. A. (1987). The relation of empathy to prosocial and related behaviors. *Psychological Bulletin, 101,* 91–119.

Eliot, C. W. (Ed.). (1909). *The Harvard Classics.* New York: Collier.

Erikson, E. H. (1964). *Insight and responsibility: Lectures on the ethical implications of psychoanalytic insight.* New York: Norton.

Fowler, D. (1990). Democracy's next generation. *Educational Leadership 48*(3), 10–15.

Gove, F. L., & Keating, D. P. (1979). Empathic role-taking precursors. *Developmental Psychology 15,* 594–600.

Hart Research Associates. (1989). *Democracy's next generation: A study of youth and teachers.* Washington, DC: People for the American Way.

John-Steiner, V. (1997). *Notebooks of the mind: Explorations of thinking.* New York: Oxford University Press.

Kauffmann, F. (2000). Gifted Education and romance of passion. *Communicator 31*(3), 1.

Kogan, M. (2000). Teaching truth, beauty, and goodness. (An interview with Howard Gardner). *Monitor on Psychology, 31*(12), 66–67.

LaBonte, R. (1999). Social capital and community development: Practitioner emptor. *Australian and New Zealand Journal of Public Health, 23*(4), 430–433.

Larson, R. W. (2000). Toward a psychology of positive youth development. *American Psychologist, 15,* 170–183.

Lindholm, C. (1990). *Charisma.* Cambridge, MA: Basil Blackwell.

MacKinnon, D. W. (1978). *In search of human effectiveness.* Buffalo, NY: Creative Education Foundation.

Mehrabian, A., & Epstein, N. (1972). A measure of emotional empathy. *Journal of Personality 40,* 525–543.

Padhee, B., & Das, S. (1987). Reliability of an adapted curiosity scale. *Social Science International 3,* 27–30.

Peterson, C. (2000). The future of optimism. *American Psychologist, 55,* 44–55.

Putman, D. (1997). Psychological Courage. *Philosophy, Psychiatry, & Psychology 4*(1) 1–11.

Putnam, R. (1993). *Making democracy work: Civic traditions in modern Italy.* Princeton: Princeton University Press.

Putnam, R. (1995). Bowling alone: America's declining social capital. *Journal of Democracy, 6*(1) 65–78.

Rea, D. W. (2000). Optimal motivation for talent development. *Journal for the Education of the Gifted, 23*(2),

187–216.

Reis, S. M. (1995). Older women's reflections on eminence: Obstacles and opportunities. *Roeper Review, 18,* 66–72.

Reis, S. M. (1998). *Work left undone: Choices and compromises of talented females.* Mansfield Center, CT: Creative Learning Press.

Renzulli, J. S. (1978). What makes giftedness? Re-examining a definition. *Phi Delta Kappan, 60,* 180–184.

Rotter, J. B. (1966). Generalized expectancies for internal versus external control of reinforcement. *Psychological Monographs, 81*(1, Whole No. 609).

Ryan, R. M., & Deci, E. L. (2000). Self-determination theory and the facilitation of intrinsic motivation, social development, and well-being. *American Psychologist, 55,* 68–78.

Schwartz, B. (2000). Self-determination: The tyranny of freedom. *American Psychologist, 55,* 79–88.

Seligman, M. E. P. (1991). *Learned optimism.* New York: Knopf.

Seligman, M. E. P., & Csikszentmihalyi, M. (2000). Positive psychology. *American Psychologist, 55,* 5–14.

Seligman, M. E. P., Reivich, K., Jaycox, L., & Gillham, J. (1995). *The optimistic child.* New York: Houghton Mifflin.

Silverman, L., Roeper, A., & Smith, G. (2000, November). *A child shall lead them: Children for nonviolence.* Paper presented at the meeting of the National Association of Gifted Children, Atlanta, GA.

Tiger, L. (1979). *Optimism: The biology of hope.* New York: Simon & Schuster.

Times Mirror Center for the People and the Press (1990). *The age of indifference: A study of young Americans and how they view the news.* Washington, DC: Author.

Wicker, F. W., Lambert, F. B., Richardson, F. C., & Kahler, J. (1984). Categorical goal hierarchies and classification of the human motives. *Journal of Personality, 52*(3), 285–305.

Williams, J. (1998). Self-concept–performance congruence: An exploration of patterns among high-achieving adolescents. *Journal for the Education of the Gifted, 21*(4), 415–422.

Wong, M. M., & Csikszentmihalyi, M. (1991). Motivation and academic achievement: The effects of personality traits and the quality of experience. *Journal of Personality, 59,* 539–574.

Zahn-Waxler, C., & Radke-Yarrow, M. (1982). The development of altruism: Alternative research strategies. In N. Eisenberg-Berg (Ed.), *The development of pro-social behavior* (pp. 109–137). New York: Academic Press.

BIBLIOGRAPHY

Aspinwall, L. G., & Richter, L. (1999). Optimism and self-mastery predict more rapid disengagement from unsolvable tasks in the presence of alternatives. *Motivation and Emotion, 23*(3), 221–245.

Baum, S. M., Olenchak, F. R., & Owen, S. V. (1998). Gifted students with attention deficits: Fact and/or fiction? Or, can we see the forest for the trees? *Gifted Child Quarterly, 42*(2), 96–104.

Chang, E. C. (Ed.). (2001). *Optimism and pessimism: Implications for theory, research, and practice.* Washington, DC: American Psychological Association.

Cholpan, B. E., McCain, M. L., Caronell, J. L., & Hagen, R. L. (1985). Empathy: Review of available measures. *Journal of Personality and Social Psychology 48,* 635–653.

Feshback, N. D., & Hoffman, M. L. (1978, April). Sex differences in children's reports of emotion-arousing situations. In D. McGuiness (chair), Symposium conducted at the meeting of the Western Psychological Association, San Francisco.

Fredrickson, B. (2000, March 7). Cultivating positive emotions to optimize health and well-being. *Prevention and Treatment* [On-line], 1–26. Available on the Internet at: *http://journals.apa.org/prevention/volume3/pre0030001a.html*

Friedman, H. S. (1980). Understanding and assessing nonverbal expressiveness: The affective communication test. *Journal of Personality and Social Psychology, 39,* 333–351.

Gagné, F. (1985). Giftedness and talent: Reexamining a re-examination of the definitions. *Gifted Child Quarterly, 29,* 103–112.

Gardner, H. (1983). *Frames of mind: The theory of multiple intelligences.* New York: Basic Books.

Gelb, M. J. (1998). *How to think like Leonardo da Vinci.* New York: Delacorte Press.

George, P. G., & Scheft, T. (1998). Children's thoughts about the future: Comparing gifted and nongifted students after 20 years. *Journal for the Education of the Gifted, 21*(2), 224–239.

Gottfried, A. E. (1982). *Children's academic intrinsic motivation inventory.* Princeton, NJ: Educational Testing Service.

Kreitler, S., Kreitler, H., & Zigler, E. (1974). Cognitive orientation and curiosity. *British Journal of Psychology 65,* 43–52.

Maslow, A. (1954). *Motivation and personality.* New York: Harper.

Mönks, F. J. (1991). Kann wissenschäftliche argumentation auf aktulität verzichten? (Are scientific arguments dispensable in the discussion on identification of the gifted?) *Zeitschrift für Entwicklungspsychologie und Pädagogische Psychologie, 23,* 232–240.

Moon, S. M. (2000, May). *Personal talent: What is it and how can we study it?* Paper presented at the Fifth Biennial Henry B. and Joycelyn Wallace National Research Symposium on Talent Development, Iowa City.

Naylor, F. D. (1981). Melbourne curiosity inventory. *Australian Psychologist, 16,* 172–183.

Portes, A. (1998). Social capital: Its origins and applications in modern sociology. *Annual Review of Sociology, 24,* 1–24.

Scheier, M. F., & Carver, C. S. (1985). Optimism, coping, and health: Assessment and implications of generalized outcome expectancies. *Health Psychology, 4,* 219–247.

Sternberg, R. J., & Davidson, J. E. (1986). *Conceptions of giftedness.* New York: Cambridge University Press.

Stipek, D. J., Lamb, M. E., & Zigler, E. F. (1981). OPTI: A measure of children's optimism. *Educational and Psychological Measurement, 41,* 131–143.

Tannenbaum, A. J. (1986). Giftedness: A psychosocial approach. In R. J. Sternberg & J. E. Davidson (Eds.), *Conceptions of giftedness.* New York: Cambridge University Press.

Underwood, B., & Moore, B. (1982). Perspective-taking and altruism. *Psychological Bulletin, 91,* 143–173.

7

Giftedness According to the Theory of Successful Intelligence[1]

ROBERT J. STERNBERG, *Yale University*

Throughout most of the 20th century, intellectual giftedness has been defined as a unidimensional construct. The most frequently used measure of that dimension has been the IQ. Underlying the use of this measure is the belief that intelligence is a single thing and that IQ provides a reasonably good, although not perfect, measure of it. Sometimes, achievement test scores as well as IQ test scores are used in the identification of children as gifted. However, achievement test scores tend to be highly correlated with IQ test scores and measure almost the same thing. The basic thesis of this chapter is that we ought to define intellectual giftedness in a broader way that goes beyond what is measured by either IQ or achievement tests.

Kinds of Intellectual Giftedness

In my *Theory of Successful Intelligence* (Sternberg, 1985, 1988b, 1997, 1999), there are multiple loci of intellectual giftedness. Giftedness cannot possibly be captured by a single number. Unless we examine the multiple sources of giftedness, we risk missing identification of large numbers of gifted individuals.

  1. *Intelligence is defined in terms of the ability to achieve success in life in terms of one's personal standards, within one's sociocultural context.* The field of intelligence has at times tended to put "the cart before the horse," defining the construct conceptually on the basis of how it is operationalized, rather than vice versa. This practice has resulted in tests that stress the academic aspect of intelligence, as one might expect, given the origins of modern intelligence testing in the work of Binet and Simon (1916) in designing an instrument that would distinguish children who would succeed from those who would fail in school. But the construct of intelligence needs to serve a broader purpose, accounting for the bases of success in all of one's life.

  The use of societal criteria of success (e.g., school grades, personal income) can obscure the fact that these operationalizations often do not capture people's personal notions of success. Some people choose to concentrate on extracurricular activities such as athletics or music and pay less attention to grades in school; others may choose occupations that are personally meaningful to them but that never will yield the income they could gain doing work that is less personally meaningful. Although scientific analysis of some kinds requires nomothetic (common) operationalizations, the definition of success for an individual is idiographic (individual).

  In the theory of successful intelligence, however, the conceptualization of intelligence is always within a sociocultural context. Although the processes of intelligence may be common across such contexts, what constitutes success is not. Being a successful member of the clergy of a particular religion may be highly rewarded in one society and viewed as a worthless pursuit in another culture.

  1. Preparation of this chapter was supported by grant REC-9979843 from the U.S. National Science Foundation and the Javits Act Program (Grant No. R206R950001) as administered by the Office of Educational Research and Improvement, U.S. Department of Education. Grantees undertaking such projects are encouraged to express freely their professional judgment. This article, therefore, does not necessarily represent the position or policies of the Office of Educational Research and Improvement or the U.S. Department of Education, and no official endorsement should be inferred.

2. *One's ability to achieve success depends on capitalizing on one's strengths and correcting or compensating for one's weaknesses.* Theories of intelligence typically specify some relatively fixed set of abilities, whether one general factor and a number of specific factors (Spearman, 1904), seven multiple factors (Thurstone, 1938), or eight multiple intelligences (Gardner, 1999). Such a nomothetic specification is useful in establishing a common set of skills to be tested. But people achieve success, even within a given occupation, in many different ways. For example, successful teachers and researchers achieve success through many different blendings of skills rather than through any single formula that works for all of them.

3. *One is successfully intelligent by virtue of how one adapts to, shapes, and selects environments.* Definitions of intelligence traditionally have emphasized the role of adaptation to the environment (Intelligence and its measurement, 1921; Sternberg & Detterman, 1986). But intelligence involves not only modifying oneself to suit the environment (adaptation), but also modifying the environment to suit oneself (shaping), and sometimes, finding a new environment that is a better match to one's skills, values, or desires (selection).

Not all people have equal opportunities to adapt to, shape, and select environments. In general, people of higher socioeconomic standing tend to have more opportunities, while people of lower socioeconomic standing have fewer. The economy or political situation of the society also can be factors. Other variables that may affect such opportunities are education and especially literacy, political party, race, religion, and so forth. For example, someone with a college education typically has many more possible career options than does someone who has dropped out of high school in order to support a family. Thus, how and how well an individual adapts to, shapes, and selects environments must always be viewed in terms of the opportunities the individual has.

4. *Success is attained through a balance of analytical, creative, and practical abilities.* Analytical abilities are the abilities primarily measured by traditional tests of abilities. But success in life requires one not only to analyze one's own ideas as well as the ideas of others, but also to generate ideas and to persuade other people of their value. This necessity occurs in the world of work, as when a subordinate tries to convince a superior of the value of his or her plan; in the world of personal relationships, as when a child attempts to convince a parent to do what he or she

wants or when a spouse tries to convince the other spouse to do things his or her preferred way; and in the world of the school, as when a student writes an essay arguing for a point of view. The three main kinds of giftedness are in terms of *analytic, synthetic,* and *practical* abilities, and the ways in which they are balanced.

Analytic Giftedness

Giftedness in analytic skills involves being able to dissect a problem and understand its parts. People who are strong in this area of intellectual functioning tend to do well on conventional tests of intelligence because these tests place a premium on analytic reasoning. For example, analogy items require analysis of relations between pairs of terms and pairs of relations; synonym items require analysis of which of several answer options most closely corresponds to a given target word; reading comprehension involves analysis of reading passages; matrix problems involve analysis of interrelations among rows and columns of figures, numbers, or whatever. In other words, analytic giftedness is the kind best measured by existing tests.

I frequently give the example of one of my past students, "Alice," who was a prime example of analytic giftedness. Her test scores were excellent, her undergraduate grades were excellent, her teachers thought that she was extremely smart, and she did well in almost all the things that are traditionally viewed as part of intellectual giftedness. However, Alice proved to have difficulty in her later years of graduate school. Although she was excellent at analyzing ideas, she was not nearly so good at coming up with clever ideas of her own.

Synthetic Giftedness

Synthetic giftedness is seen in people who are insightful, intuitive, creative, or simply adept at coping with novel situations. People who are synthetically gifted do not necessarily do well on conventional measures of intelligence. Indeed, if they see more in a problem than did the test constructor or read different things into the problem, they may get answers wrong because they don't see things the way many others do. Thus, people with synthetic giftedness may not be the ones with the highest IQs, but they may be the ones who ultimately make the greatest contributions to various pursuits, such as science, literature, art, and drama. Synthetic giftedness is important not only in science and the arts. People who make money in the stock market tend to be contrarians: They can see market phenomena in ways different from those of others analyzing the market. Similarly, people who succeed in business tend to be those who see a need for a new product or service or see a new way of delivering it. Synthetic giftedness is important for success in the world but is hardly measured at all by existing tests.

I sometimes give as an example of synthetic giftedness my graduate student "Barbara," who did not do well at all on tests but who was recommended to us at Yale as having unusual creative and insight skills. Despite her low test scores, Barbara proved herself to be enormously creative in producing ideas for new research. Thus, although she may not have been as strong as Alice in analyzing problems, she was much better at coming up with new problems of her own.

Practical Giftedness

A third kind of intellectual giftedness is practical giftedness, which involves applying whatever analytic or synthetic ability one may have to everyday, pragmatic situations. The practically gifted person can go into a setting, figure out what needs to be done to succeed in that setting, and then do it. Many people have strong analytic or synthetic abilities but are unable to apply these abilities to negotiating successful relations with other people, or to getting ahead in their careers. The practically gifted person specializes in these uses of abilities.

I sometimes give as an example of a practically gifted individual my graduate student "Celia," who had neither Alice's analytic ability nor Barbara's synthetic ability, but who was highly successful in figuring out what she needed to do in order to succeed in an academic environment. She knew what kind of research was valued, how to get articles into journals, how to impress people at job interviews, and the like. Although she did not have the skills of an Alice or a Barbara, she could turn the skills she had to her advantage in practical settings.

Combining Analytic, Synthetic, and Practical Giftedness

Of course, people do not possess just one of these different kinds of skills; rather they have some blend of the three. Moreover, this blend can change over time because intelligence can be developed in various directions. People who are extreme in just one of these kinds of giftedness without having at least some skill in the others tend to be less successful in ultimately convincing people of their worth. For example, someone who is highly creative but cannot demonstrate it in practical settings and cannot convince people of the worth of his or her ideas may encounter frustration at every turn. Thus, an important part of giftedness is being able to coordinate these three aspects of abilities, and knowing when to use which. Giftedness is as much a well-managed balance of these three abilities as it is a high score on any one or more of them. I therefore sometimes refer to a gifted person as a good "mental self-manager."

Loci of Intellectual Giftedness

The three kinds of intellectual giftedness described above are general categories of superiority. In order to understand giftedness more fully, one would wish to understand the loci of information processing that contribute to these kinds of giftedness.

Components of Intelligence

Metacomponents. In the preceding triarchic theory of intelligence, executive processes used to plan, monitor, and evaluate problem solving and decision making are referred to as *metacomponents*. Metacomponents are essential to successful problem solving and decision making. I usually refer to eight of them, although the list may not be exhaustive.

1. *Problem recognition.* One cannot solve a problem of which one is unaware. Some people excel in problem solving because they are quick to recognize when they have problems or else are good at generating important problems to study. Problem recognition therefore precedes the normal problem-solving cycle, in that it is prerequisite for it.

2. *Problem definition.* It is not enough to recognize a problem: One also has to figure out the nature of the problem being confronted. Problem definition involves figuring out just what a given problem is. Some people may be good problem solvers but frequently are solving the wrong problem. People who excel in problem definition are those who, when confronted with a set of environmental contingencies, can figure out exactly what the problem is that needs to be solved.

I believe it somewhat ironic that schools tend to present children, even gifted children, with the problems that they are supposed to solve. In everyday life and in the contributions of great discoverers and inventors, problem recognition and problem definition are key. Therefore, I believe we should give more emphasis to having students figure out problems rather than having us define the problems for them.

3. *Selection of lower-order components for problem solving.* This metacomponent involves the choosing of a set of processes to solve a problem. We have a large array of mental processes at our disposal. No matter how well we may execute any one or more of these processes, the processes may not be effective for us if we don't know when to use them. Good problem solvers tend to be people who know which processes to use and when.

4. *Ordering of lower-order processes into a strategy.* Having chosen a set of processes, it is necessary to sequence them in a way that will lead from the formulation of the problem to its solution. One may choose the correct processes but misorder their execution, with the result that a problem proves to be insoluble. Individuals who excel in this metacomponent are able to sequence steps correctly.

5. *Mental representation of problems.* In order to solve a problem, one needs somehow to represent it mentally. Alternative forms of mental representation are available. For example, linear syllogisms such as "John is taller than Mary. Mary is taller than Susan. Who is tallest?" are soluble through either a linguistic representation of information, a spatial representation of information, or a combination of the two (Sternberg, 1985). Thus, in this and other problems, options are available for the representation of information. However, not all representations of a given problem are equally useful, and how useful a given representation is depends not only on the problem but on the strengths and weaknesses of the individual in exploiting different representations. Hence, someone who excels in mental representation is not someone who is necessarily the best utilizer of every representation, but rather someone who knows what representations to use when, given the constraints of the problem, the time to solve the problem, and that person's abilities.

6. *Allocation of processing resources.* In life, we often have too many things to do in the amount of time we have to do them. Thus, it is necessary to allocate our time and mental processing resources to make as effective use as possible of the time and resources we have at our command. People who excel in this meta-component are able to set aside the amounts of time and processing resources that best suit a particular problem. Other people may be good problem solvers but spend too long on problems that do not deserve a lot of time and not enough time on problems that deserve more. Effective resource allocation is extremely important for successful performance in the complex stream of everyday life.

7. *Solution monitoring.* Solution monitoring refers to keeping track of how problem solving is going as one is solving a particular problem. It often happens that we start going down a garden path in our problem solving, or else start on a path that may ultimately lead to solution but only after a long uphill battle. Good solution monitors keep track of where their problem solving is leading them, and as they see that the path they are on is not taking them where they want to go, they consider using an alternative strategy.

8. *Solution evaluation.* After one has solved a problem and found a solution, the problem-solving cycle is not complete. One still needs to evaluate the quality and appropriateness of the solution. Students in various levels of schooling often make errors in their work because their solutions are unacceptable. Students may never bother to check whether their work even makes sense, much less whether it is exact. We need to evaluate our solution against the original constraints of the problem. People who excel in this metacomponent are not necessarily the best in the other metacomponents. However, they recognize when a solution isn't what it should be and therefore can persevere until they come up with a solution that fits the constraints of the problem.

The metacomponents are interactive with each other. In my experience, it is almost impossible to measure them singly, as almost any task that requires one of them also requires at least several others. We have had some success in measuring metacomponents (Sternberg, 1985), but I doubt that any of our measures or anyone else's are pure. An important locus of giftedness is not only in how adept a person is at executing each of the metacomponents but in how adept the person is at combining them and utilizing them in a well-integrated way.

Performance Components. Performance components are the processes used to solve a problem. Thus, the metacomponents decide what to do, whereas the performance components actually do it. The number of performance components is quite large, since somewhat different performance components are used in the solution of different problems. Nevertheless, there is overlap within classes of tasks. Here, I will discuss some of the performance components involved in inductive reasoning. It is important to note, however, that they represent only a small subset of the total number of performance components in human information processing.

1. *Encoding.* In order to solve a problem, one first has to perceive the terms of the problem and retrieve information in long-term memory relevant to those perceptions. The process involved is encoding. My own work, as well as that of others (e.g., Siegler, 1978), suggests that encoding is a particularly important process in the solution of problems. If one mis-encodes the terms of a problem, it doesn't matter how well one operates on the encodings: The answer will be wrong, because the problem was incorrectly perceived. Excellent encoders tend to be people with large knowledge bases, who see more in the terms of a problem than a novice might. Expert encoders do not always encode more quickly than novices. Indeed, some of our research suggests that expert encoders may encode the terms more slowly, in part because they have more knowledge to call on, and in part because strong encoding can facilitate later operations on those encodings (see Sternberg & Rifkin, 1979; S. Sternberg, 1969).

2. *Inference.* Inference is involved in seeing the relation between two terms or objects. It is used in a large variety of tasks. Excellent inferers are good at comparing and contrasting, in that they easily see relations between different things. The inferences that are made depend in part on how well the relevant objects are encoded. One may not be able to infer a relation between two objects if one doesn't know the relevant attributes about which the inference needs to be made.

3. *Mapping.* This process is used to determine relations among relations. For example, it forms the basis for analogical reasoning. We have found that mapping appears somewhat later than other components of performance, perhaps because it involves second-order relations (Sternberg & Rifkin, 1979). It

is possible to map relations of successively higher orders. Work with adolescents shows that the acquisition of mapping of successively higher-order relations continues throughout adolescence (Case, 1978; Sternberg & Downing, 1982).

4. *Application.* Application is the carrying over of a relation from one set of terms to another. For example, in analogies, it is used to apply a relation previously inferred (Sternberg, 1977). Good appliers are able to carry over relations they have inferred in one setting to another setting.

Knowledge Acquisition Components. Knowledge acquisition components are used to learn new information. Gifted individuals are often particularly effective in the use of these components because they are so often adept at learning new information. We have proposed three knowledge-acquisition components that are particularly important in learning (Sternberg & Davidson, 1983).

1. *Selective encoding.* Selective encoding is used to separate information that is relevant to one's purposes from information that is not relevant. For example, when a scientist receives a computer output of data from an experiment, a seemingly bewildering array of numbers may appear. The good selective encoder knows which of these numbers are important to the particular scientific purposes. Indeed, selective encoding is important in all walks of life. For example, a business executive needs to know which factors are relevant in making a management decision and which factors are of less consequence. A writer needs to know which details to include in an article or a book and which details are of little or no interest. An artist must decide how detailed to make a particular painting or sculpture. Selective encoding, therefore, is important to giftedness in many different walks of life.

2. *Selective combination.* Often, it is not enough just to decide what details are relevant for a particular purpose. One needs to know how to put those relevant pieces of information together. For example, in doing a mathematical proof, the greatest difficulty often is not in figuring out which postulates or theorems are relevant, but in figuring out how to sequence them together to reach the desired conclusion. In any aspect of science, one frequently needs to put together the pieces of a difficult puzzle, much as a detective would when trying to analyze clues at the scene of a crime.

Similarly, a doctor needs to figure out how a set of symptoms can be used in combination to help understand the particular presenting syndrome.

3. *Selective comparison.* Selective comparison is the use of old information for new purposes; for example, recognizing how information one has used in one experiment could be carried over to another. Kekule's dream about a snake dancing around and biting its tail was a selective comparison in that it provided the basis for his figuring out the structure of the benzene molecule. Good selective comparers not only see analogies between present problems and past ones, they also see sources of disanalogy between sets of problems. In other words, they see the dissimilarities as well as the similarities between the old situation and the new one.

The Role of Experience

The components of intelligence described above are always applied in a task that is either relatively *novel* or relatively *familiar.* In some cases, the components of problem solving change as the problem solver becomes more familiar with the task and sees better ways of doing it. However, my research has shown that more often the components are executed more rapidly or efficiently, but these components do not change as one becomes more familiar with the problem-solving tasks. Two regions of experience for the application of components to tasks are particularly relevant for understanding intelligence (Sternberg, 1985; Sternberg & Lubart, 1995, 1996).

Relative Novelty. Insightful people are often particularly adept at applying components of information processing to problems that are relatively novel. They can take a problem that is quite different from ones they have solved before and see a new way of solving it that most other people would not see. The student Barbara, described above, would be a case in point. Coping with relative novelty is an important part of synthetic intelligence. I emphasize the word *relatively* because problems that are extremely novel do not measure intelligence well at all. For example, it would be pointless to give calculus problems to second graders. The region of interest for measuring synthetic ability is the region in which a problem is new, but not completely so. In assessing these skills, we use insight problems (Davidson & Sternberg, 1984), analogies that require novel reasoning (e.g., MAN : (SKIN, PETS) :: (DOG, TREE) : BARK; Sternberg, 1982; Tetewsky & Sternberg, 1986), and counterfactual analogies (involving, e.g., dancers who eat their shoes; Sternberg & Gastel, 1989a, 1989b). People who are gifted in coping with relative novelty tend to be our most creative contributors to society.

Relative Familiarity. The region of relative familiarity is the area in which task performance starts to be automatized. Automatization is a critical part of intelligence, in that many of the problem-solving behaviors we need to perform are executed again and again. They can be executed efficiently because they do not consume many resources and can even be executed in parallel. For example, reading is initially a difficult and halting process but becomes smooth and rapid once the bottom-up processing of words and sentences becomes automatized. Driving, speaking, and writing are all processes that become increasingly automatized with practice. People who are good automatizers have an edge in problem solving over people who are not, in that their automatization frees processing resources that can be used to cope with novelty. People who do not automatize need to devote processing resources to the basics of a problem, with the result that these resources are not free for dealing with the more novel aspects.

There is no guarantee that people who are good at coping with relative novelty will be good automatizers. That is, giftedness does not necessarily apply at all levels of the experiential continuum. A person might be gifted at one level of this continuum or at several levels. I suggested earlier that superior automatization frees resources for coping with novelty. However, there can also be costs associated with automatization. Sometimes, as experts become more and more routinized in their solution of a problem or a class of problems, they lose flexibility. They begin to have difficulty seeing things in new ways. Our research has even found that this loss of flexibility can impede experts more than novices when a task that is familiar to the experts is changed in its essential aspects (Frensch & Sternberg, 1989).

Contextual Functions

The components of intelligence are applied to various levels of experience in order to serve three different functions in everyday contexts. Understanding practical giftedness of the kind demonstrated by Celia requires understanding the three functions that intelligent thinking and behavior can serve.

1. *Adaptation.* *Adaptation* refers to the adjustment of one's self and one's behavior to make a good fit with the environment. When one takes on a new job, a new school, a new relationship, or any kind of new environment, it is usually necessary to adapt in some degree. Our research suggests that practically intelligent people are often good adapters (Sternberg et al., 2000; Sternberg, Wagner, Williams, & Horvath, 1995; Wagner & Sternberg, 1985). People who are practically gifted are not necessarily those who are the most superior in executing the components of intelligence. Rather, their superiority is in exploiting these components in practical settings. Others may be better at executing the components in the abstract but do not know how to apply them in everyday life.

Our research suggests that a critical aspect of environmental adaptation is the acquisition and utilization of tacit knowledge (Sternberg et al., 2000; Wagner & Sternberg, 1985). Tacit knowledge is what one needs to know in order to adapt to an environment when that knowledge is not explicitly taught and often not even verbalized. Tacit knowledge comprises the "tricks of the trade" or "rules of thumb" that lead to successful performance in a given domain. It is possible to identify the tacit knowledge within a given domain (see, e.g., Sternberg, 1988b, for identification of tacit knowledge relevant to business management). Practically intelligent people are adept at picking up this knowledge. The ability to pick up and also to exploit tacit knowledge does not appear to be much related to conventional IQ.

2. *Selection.* It is not always practically intelligent to adapt to an environment. Sometimes, the smart thing is to get out. If you can see that a job, problem, relationship, or whatever is not one that is suitable for you, it may be best to put it behind you. Practically intelligent people know when to get out. The practically intelligent person is someone who achieves a balance between adaptation and selection. He or she knows when to try to conform to an environment but also when to leave it.

3. *Shaping.* One does not always leave an environment when it is not just so. For example, one may be in a job that is nonideal but see ways to make the job better. I believe that if there is a pinnacle of practical intelligence, it is in the ability of an individual to shape an environment. Practically intelligent people

have a knack for turning environments into what they want them to be. Great scientists, artists, writers, politicians, and others are people who succeed in shaping their environments. They set the paradigms that others follow, rather than merely following those paradigms. Hence, a practically gifted person is able to set standards, not just conform to them.

Capitalization on Strengths and Compensation for and Remediation of Weaknesses

There is one thing that people who are intellectually gifted throughout their lives have in common: They know what they are good at, know what they are not good at, and are able to capitalize on their strengths and compensate for their weaknesses. They also may remediate their weaknesses to the point where these weaknesses no longer get in their way.

This view of giftedness is quite different from the standard one. This view suggests that people who are intellectually gifted are not necessarily good at lots of things. One cannot add up the scores on a bunch of subtests or items and measure giftedness simply in terms of the number of items correctly answered. A person may show up as far more gifted by being good in one thing than by being good in a large number of things. The big question is not how many things a person is good at, but how well a person can exploit whatever he or she is good at and find ways around the things that he or she is not good at.

Measurement of Intellectual Giftedness

The kinds of skills described here are not measured well by conventional tests of intelligence or other cognitive abilities. At best, such tests measure analytic skills, but they do not measure synthetic and practical skills. Conventional tests of creativity attempt to measure divergent thinking abilities, but they do not measure synthetic intelligence in a way that I consider adequate.

We use the Sternberg Triarchic Abilities Test (Sternberg, 1993) to measure analytical, creative, and practical abilities. It provides seven separate scores: analytic, synthetic, automatization, and practical abilities, as well as verbal, quantitative, and figural processing. One special use of the test is for identifying gifted individuals. The idea is that someone may be gifted with respect to some aspects of the theory but not others. Indeed, few people will be gifted with respect to all aspects of the triarchic theory.

How does the newly developed test differ from a conventional intelligence test? It differs in several respects.

First, it is broader, providing measurement of synthetic and practical skills as well as analytic skills. Moreover, separate scores are provided for verbal, quantitative, and figural processing. Thus, it can potentially identify as gifted some children not now being so identified.

Second, even for measuring conventional analytic abilities, I believe the test is more progressive than most existing ones. For example, many existing tests measure vocabulary. However, vocabulary is highly dependent on background. It is a measure of the products rather than the processes of learning. Students from diverse backgrounds may not do equally well, not because of differences in abilities, but because of differences in opportunities provided by diverse environments. In the triarchic test, verbal analytic abilities are measured by learning words from context. Students receive unknown words (neologisms) embedded in context and need to use the context to figure out the meanings of the words. In this way, we measure the precursor to vocabulary—learning from context—and hence zero in on the processes rather than the products of learning.

Third, only the automatization subtest is severely timed. Current tests confound speed with quality of information processing. I believe it is more effective to separate the measurement of mental speed from the measurement of power. Hence, the measurement of speed is through automatization, while other subtests are liberally timed so that children will have enough time to finish the items.

Fourth, the test is based on a theory of intelligence, rather than being wholly empirically derived. Most existing intelligence tests are atheoretical, or only weakly based on a theory of intelligence. The triarchic test is an attempt to undergird the measurement of intelligence with a theory, rather than to proceed entirely on an empirical and atheoretical basis.

How does one actually measure some of the new kinds of abilities not covered on previous tests? Consider, for example, coping with novelty—synthetic ability. In the verbal subtest, subjects are given reasoning problems preceded by either factual or counterfactual statements. For example, a verbal analogy might be preceded by a statement such as "Balloons are filled with air" or, by contrast,

"Balloons are evil." Subjects have to solve the reasoning problems by assuming that the preceding premise is true. Half the premises are true and half are not. We have found that while analytic "Alice types" are better at solving standard, verbal analogies, synthetic thinking "Barbara types" are better at solving these novel analogies; they can more freely assume something that is counterfactual to be true. Alice types have trouble escaping their everyday presuppositions. The quantitative test consists of number matrices in which some of the entries are conventional numerals and some are numbers represented by new numeration systems. Examinees are given the equivalencies between the old and new number systems and have to convert back and forth between them in order to solve the matrix problems.

Practical abilities are measured by a variety of item types as well. For example, the verbal subtest consists of informal reasoning items in which examinees must recognize inferential fallacies in advertisements, political slogans, everyday statements, and the like. The idea is for students to show their skill in reasoning with everyday formal reasoning material rather than with academic formal reasoning material. The figural test consists of maps and diagrams, for example, a subway map or a map of the city, and subjects must use the information in the maps to plan efficient routes. Again, the idea is to assess the application of the components of intelligence to practical settings.

Thus, the idea of testing is to expand our notion of giftedness and then be able to identify as gifted those individuals who may be adept in skills that are not measured by conventional tests. These individuals may actually be the ones who later in life make the more important contributions. Analytic abilities alone are generally not enough to enable one to make important contributions. There is a need for synthetic and practical thinking as well.

Developing Intellectual Giftedness

I do not believe that intellectual giftedness is necessarily something with which one is born. It is generally accepted by psychologists that there is some hereditary component to intelligence; at the same time, it also is accepted that there is more to intelligence than just the effects of heredity. Although one probably cannot take a mentally retarded individual and turn him or her into a budding genius, I believe that it is possible to increase our intellectual skills, and we have collected evidence that suggests as much (Davidson & Sternberg, 1984; Sternberg, 1987, 1997; Sternberg & Grigorenko, 2000). We have developed a program for teaching intellectual skills at the high school and college levels (Sternberg, 1984, 1986; Sternberg & Grigorenko, in press) and have worked as well with younger children. The idea of development ought to be combined with the idea of testing: One gives a first form of an intelligence test, then training, then a second form of the intelligence test in order to assess improvement.

What abilities, exactly, should be tapped? Practical intelligence involves capitalization on strengths and compensation for (or remediation of) weaknesses. We need to teach students to make the most of their strengths and to find ways around or ways to improve their weaknesses. We cannot render enormous changes for everyone. What we can do is help students more effectively exploit their intellectual abilities at the same time that they increase those abilities in need of enhancement.

Our experience is that the teaching of intellectual skills does not eliminate individual differences. We will not end up with everyone performing at the same level. To the contrary, when we have trained both children identified as gifted and children not so identified, almost all the children will have improved, but the difference at the end of training is about the same as the difference at the beginning. In other words, the learning curves for gifted and nongifted children are roughly parallel.

Intelligence is not the whole story to giftedness. Creativity is important (see Sternberg, 1988a; Sternberg & Lubart, 1995), as are personality dispositions and motivational states. Hence, we have focused mainly on its intellectual side, not on all sides. We should not believe that the only possible kind of giftedness is with respect to intelligence.

Using the Theory of Successful Intelligence to Improve School Performance

We have done a number of research studies to show that the theory of successful intelligence can make a difference to school performance. In the first set of studies, we explored the question of whether conventional education in school systematically discriminates against children with creative and practical gifts (Sternberg & Clinkenbeard, 1995; Sternberg, Ferrari, Clinkenbeard, & Grigorenko, 1996; Sternberg, Grigorenko, Ferrari, & Clinkenbeard, 1999). Motivating this work was the belief that the systems in schools strongly tend to favor children with strengths in memory and analytical abilities.

We used the Sternberg Triarchic Abilities Test, as described above. The test was administered to 326 children around the United States and in some other countries who were identified by their schools as gifted according to local criteria. Children were selected for a summer program in (college-level) psychology if they fell into one of five ability groupings: high analytical, high creative, high practical, high balanced (high in all three abilities), or low balanced (low in all three abilities). Students who came to Yale were then divided into four instructional groups. Students in all four instructional groups used the same introductory psychology textbook (a preliminary version of Sternberg [1995]) and listened to the same psychology lectures. What differed among them was the type of afternoon discussion section to which they were assigned. They were assigned to an instructional condition that emphasized either memory, analytical, creative, or practical instruction. For example, in the memory condition, they might be asked to describe the main tenets of a major theory of depression. In the analytical condition, they might be asked to compare and contrast two theories of depression. In the creative condition, they might be asked to formulate their own theory of depression. In the practical condition, they might be asked how they could use what they had learned about depression to help a friend who was depressed.

Students in all four instructional conditions were evaluated in terms of their performance on homework, a midterm exam, a final exam, and an independent project. Each type of work was evaluated for memory, analytical, creative, and practical quality. Thus, all students were evaluated in exactly the same way.

Our results suggested the utility of the theory of successful intelligence. When the students first arrived at Yale, we observed that the students in the high creative and high practical groups were much more diverse in terms of racial, ethnic, socioeconomic, and educational backgrounds than were students in the high-analytical group, suggesting that correlations of measured intelligence with status variables such as these may be reduced by using a broader conception of intelligence. Thus, the kinds of students identified as strong differed in terms of populations from which they were drawn in comparison with students identified as strong solely by analytical measures. More important, just by expanding the range of abilities we measured, we discovered intellectual strengths that might not have been apparent through a conventional test.

We found that all three ability tests—analytical, creative, and practical—significantly predicted course performance. When multiple-regression analysis was used, at least two of these ability measures contributed significantly to the prediction of each of the measures of achievement. Perhaps as a reflection of the difficulty of deemphasizing the analytical way of teaching, one of the significant predictors was always the analytical score.[2] Most important, there was an aptitude-treatment interaction whereby students who were placed in instructional conditions that better matched their pattern of abilities outperformed students who were mismatched. That is, when students are taught in a way that fits how they think, they do better in school. Children with creative and practical abilities—who are almost never taught or assessed in a way that matches their pattern of abilities—may be at a disadvantage in course after course, year after year.

In a follow-up study (Sternberg, Torff, & Grigorenko, 1998a, 1998b), we looked at learning of social studies and science by third-grade and eighth-grade students. The 225 third-graders were students in a very low-income neighborhood in Raleigh, North Carolina. The 142 eighth-graders were students who were largely middle to upper-middle class studying in Baltimore, Maryland, and Fresno, California. In this study, students were assigned to one of three instructional conditions. In the first condition, they were taught the course that basically they would have learned had we not intervened. The emphasis in the course was on memory. In a second condition, they were taught in a way that emphasized critical (analytical) thinking. In the third condition, they were taught in a way that emphasized analytical, creative, and practical thinking. All students' performance was assessed for memory learning (through multiple-choice assessments) as well as for analytical, creative, and practical learning (through performance assessments).

As expected, we found that students in the successful-intelligence (analytical, creative, practical) condition outperformed the other students in terms of the performance assessments. One could argue that this result merely reflected the way they were taught. Nevertheless, the result suggested that teaching for these kinds of thinking succeeded. More important, however, was the finding that children in the successful-intelligence condition outperformed the other children even on the multiple-choice memory tests. In other words, to the extent that one's goal is just to maximize children's memory for information, teaching for successful intelligence is still superior. It enables children to capitalize on their strengths and to correct or to compensate for their weaknesses, and it allows children to encode material in a variety of interesting ways.

We have now extended these results to reading curricula at the middle-school and high-school levels. In a study of 871 middle-school students and 432 high school students, we taught reading either triarchically or through the regular curriculum. At the middle-school level, reading was taught explicitly. At the high-school level, reading was infused into instruction in mathematics, physical sciences, social sciences, English, history, foreign languages, and the arts. In all settings, students who were taught triarchically substantially outperformed students who were taught in standard ways (Grigorenko, Jarvin, & Sternberg, 2000).

SUMMARY AND CONCLUSIONS

It is possible to understand intellectual giftedness in a way that transcends the bounds of our usual conceptions of intelligence. I propose in this chapter one model of extending these bounds, the triarchic theory of human intelligence. I believe this theory provides us with a firmer and broader base for understanding intellectual giftedness than we have through existing

---

2. However, in a replication of our study with low-income African-American students in New York, Deborah Coates of the City University of New York found a different pattern of results. Her data indicated that the tests of practical abilities were better predictors of course performance than were the analytical measures, suggesting that which ability test predicts which criterion depends on population as well as mode of teaching.

theories and tests designed to measure intellectual excellence.

QUESTIONS FOR THOUGHT AND DISCUSSION

1. In what ways is the theory of successful intelligence consistent with conventional theories of intelligence with respect to its characterization of giftedness? In what ways is it different?

2. Howard Gardner has proposed a theory of multiple intelligences, according to which there are multiple intelligences including linguistic, logical-mathematical, spatial, musical, bodily-kinesthetic, interpersonal, intrapersonal, and naturalistic intelligences. The theory of successful intelligence might be viewed as, in some ways, compatible with Gardner's theory rather than competitive to it. How might the theory of successful intelligence be integrated with Gardner's theory?

3. In what ways might one implement the theory of successful intelligence in programming for gifted students?

4. Sometimes students are identified as gifted by one model (e.g., the model of successful intelligence) and then instructed and assessed for their achievement by another model (e.g., a simple acceleration model that presents the usual material, but more rapidly). What are some potential problems that arise when the model of identification of the gifted does not match the model for their instruction and assessment of achievement?

5. If you were to construct your own model of giftedness, perhaps building on existing models such as that of successful intelligence, but going beyond them, what would you put into your model?

REFERENCES

Binet, A., & Simon, T. (1916). *The development of intelligence in children.* Baltimore: Williams & Wilkins. (Originally published in 1905).

Case, R. (1978). Intellectual development from birth to adulthood: A neo-Piagetian interpretation. In R. Siegler (Ed.), *Children's thinking: What develops?* (pp. 37–71). Hillsdale, NJ: Erlbaum.

Davidson, J. E., & Sternberg, R. J. (1984). The role of insight in intellectual giftedness. *Gifted Child Quarterly, 28,* 58–64.

Frensch, P. A., & Sternberg, R. J. (1989). Expertise and intelligent thinking: When is it worse to know better? In R. J. Sternberg (Ed.), *Advances in the psychology of human intelligence* (Vol. 5, pp. 157–188). Hillsdale, NJ: Erlbaum.

Gardner, H. (1999). *Intelligence reframed: Multiple intelligences for the 21st century.* New York: Basic Books.

Grigorenko, E. L., Jarvin, L., & Sternberg, R. J. (2000). *School-based tests of the triarchic theory of human intelligence: Three settings, three samples, three syllabi.* Manuscript submitted for publication.

"Intelligence and its measurement": A symposium (1921). *Journal of Educational Psychology, 12,* 123–147, 195–216, 271–275.

Siegler, R. S. (1978). The origins of scientific reasoning. In R. S. Siegler (Ed.), *Children's thinking: What develops?* (pp. 109–149). Hillsdale, NJ: Erlbaum.

Spearman, C. (1904). "General intelligence," objectively determined and measured. *American Journal of Psychology, 15*(2), 201–293.

Sternberg, R. J. (1977). *Intelligence, information processing, and analogical reasoning: The componential analysis of human abilities.* Hillsdale, NJ: Erlbaum.

Sternberg, R. J. (1982). Nonentrenchment in the assessment of intellectual giftedness. *Gifted Child Quarterly, 26,* 63–67.

Sternberg, R. J. (1984). What should intelligence tests test? Implications of a triarchic theory of intelligence for intelligence testing. *Educational Researcher, 13,* 5–15.

Sternberg, R. J. (1985). *Beyond IQ: A triarchic theory of human intelligence.* New York: Cambridge University Press.

Sternberg, R. J. (1986). *Intelligence applied: Understanding and increasing your intellectual skills.* San Diego: Harcourt Brace Jovanovich.

Sternberg, R. J. (1987). Most vocabulary is learned from context. In M. G. McKeown & M. E. Curtis (Eds.), *The nature of vocabulary acquisition* (pp. 89–105). Hillsdale, NJ: Erlbaum.

Sternberg, R. J. (Ed.). (1988a). *The nature of creativity.* New York: Cambridge University Press.

Sternberg, R. J. (1988b). *The triarchic mind.* New York: Viking.

Sternberg, R. J. (1993). *Sternberg Triarchic Abilities Test.* Unpublished test.

Sternberg, R. J. (1995). *In search of the human mind.* Orlando, FL: Harcourt Brace College Publishers.

Sternberg, R. J. (1997). *Successful intelligence.* New York: Plume.

Sternberg, R. J. (1999). The theory of successful intelligence. *Review of General Psychology, 3,* 292–316.

Sternberg, R. J., & Clinkenbeard, P. R. (1995). A triarchic model applied to identifying, teaching, and assessing gifted children. *Roeper Review, 17,* 255–260.

Sternberg, R. J., & Davidson, J. E. (1983). Insight in the gifted. *Educational Psychologist, 18,* 51–57.

Sternberg, R. J., & Detterman, D. K. (Eds.). (1986). *What is intelligence?* Norwood, NJ: Ablex.

Sternberg, R. J., & Downing, C. J. (1982). The development of higher-order reasoning in adolescence. *Child Development, 53,* 209–221.

Sternberg, R. J., Ferrari, M., Clinkenbeard, P. R., & Grigorenko, E. L. (1996). Identification, instruction, and assessment of gifted children: A construct validation of a triarchic model. *Gifted Child Quarterly, 40,* 129–137.

Sternberg, R. J., & Gastel, J. (1989a). If dancers ate their shoes: Inductive reasoning with factual and counterfactual premises. *Memory and Cognition, 17,* 1–10.

Sternberg, R. J., & Gastel, J. (1989b). Coping with novelty in human intelligence: An empirical investigation. *Intelligence, 13,* 187–197.

Sternberg, R. J., & Grigorenko, E. L. (in press). *Intelligence applied* (2nd ed.) New York: Oxford University Press.

Sternberg, R. J., & Grigorenko, E. L. (2000). *Teaching for successful intelligence.* Arlington Heights, IL: Skylight Training and Publishing Inc.

Sternberg, R. J., Grigorenko, E. L., Ferrari, M., & Clinkenbeard, P. (1999). A triarchic analysis of an aptitude-treatment interaction. *European Journal of Psychological Assessment, 15*(1), 1–11.

Sternberg, R. J., & Lubart, T. I. (1995). *Defying the crowd: Cultivating creativity in a culture of conformity.* New York: Free Press.

Sternberg, R. J., & Lubart, T. I. (1996). Investing in creativity. *American Psychologist, 51*(7), 677–688.

Sternberg, R. J., & Rifkin, B. (1979). The development of analogical reasoning processes. *Journal of Experimental Child Psychology, 27,* 195–232.

Sternberg, R. J., Torff, B., & Grigorenko, E. L. (1998a). Teaching for successful intelligence raises school achievement. *Phi Delta Kappan, 79,* 667–669.

Sternberg, R. J., Torff, B., & Grigorenko, E. L. (1998b). Teaching triarchically improves school achievement. *Journal of Educational Psychology, 90,* 374–384.

Sternberg, R. J., Wagner, R. K., Williams, W. M., & Horvath, J. A. (1995). Testing common sense. *American Psychologist, 50*(11), 912–927.

Sternberg, S. (1969). Memory-scanning: Mental processes revealed by reaction-time experiments. *American Scientist, 4,* 421–457.

Tetewsky, S. J., & Sternberg, R. J. (1986). Conceptual and lexical determinants of nonentrenched thinking. *Journal of Memory and Language, 25,* 202–225.

Thurstone, L. L. (1938). *Primary mental abilities.* Chicago: University of Chicago Press.

Wagner, R. K., & Sternberg, R. J. (1985). Practical intelligence in real-world pursuits: The role of tacit knowledge. *Journal of Personality and Social Psychology, 49,* 436–458.

8

Multiple Intelligences: A Perspective on Giftedness

CATYA VON KÁROLYI, *Boston College*
VALERIE RAMOS-FORD, *College of New Jersey*
HOWARD GARDNER, *Harvard University*

Giftedness: A Multiple Intelligences Perspective

There exists an extensive history of approaches to the identification of gifted and talented individuals. One of the most widely implemented methods has been the administration of a standardized test of intelligence, a practice that can be traced principally to the work of Alfred Binet. In light of the expansion of public education in Paris in the early twentieth century, this pioneering psychologist and his colleagues were asked to devise measurements that could assist in identifying students who were likely to fail in elementary school (Binet & Simon, 1905). In response, they created the first successful measure of scholastic intelligence. Binet's concept of *mental age* soon led to its influential by-product, the *intelligence quotient* (IQ).

Binet's ideas made their way swiftly across the Atlantic and were embraced particularly by Lewis Terman and his colleagues at Stanford University, who in 1916 created the Stanford-Binet Intelligence Scale. Although IQ measures were indisputably of value, they led to a narrow view of intelligence—one inextricably tied to those skills that were most valued in the schools of the time, linguistic and logical-mathematical skill.

Nearly a century later, many educators, scientists, and lay persons still subscribe to this limited view of intelligence. Although many tests in this tradition are useful as a means to specific ends, their proponents often describe the instruments as revealing far more about an individual's capabilities and characteristics than they actually do. Most of these tests rely heavily on a series of short-answer or multiple-choice questions that call on linguistic and logical-mathematical abilities. What results is a snapshot of the individual's capabilities at a precise point in time, in a limited range of intellectual spheres, as discerned in the often stressful test-taking situation (see Steele, 1997, for more about the influence of testing situations; also Spencer, Steele, & Quinn, 1999; Steele & Aronson, 1995).

The use of IQ tests has had particularly strong impact on the identification and education of the gifted and talented in our society. Taking a lead from Terman's (1925) widely known longitudinal study of California children with high IQs, the terms *giftedness* and *high IQ* had become virtually synonymous by the 1930s. Despite efforts over the last several decades to broaden how intelligence is defined and appraised (Ceci, 1990; Feldman, 1980; Gardner, 1983/1994; Getzels & Jackson, 1961, 1962; Guilford, 1967; Sternberg 1986; Thurstone, 1938; Torrance, 1981), a high IQ score remains the most common standard for admission to specialized programs for the gifted and talented.

Gardner's (1983/1994) theory of Multiple Intelligences (MI) added momentum to the movement to broaden how we define intelligence and, in turn, how we educate children. MI theory calls for a conception of human abilities that includes multiple areas of intelligence and, by extension, for a broadened conception of the role of schools in service to the development of students' interests and competencies. MI theory presents a challenge to traditional education's overwhelming emphases on *scholastic intelligence* and on assessing giftedness through the use of IQ tests.

An MI perspective influences how we conceive and measure giftedness and how we educate all kinds of gifted students—students who are gifted in the traditional sense of the word as well as students who are gifted in one or more of the intelligences framed in

Gardner's theory. It calls on society to value a greater variety of patterns of ability and to educate children using approaches that are sensitive to each *individual's* profile of abilities. This chapter, however, is not a "How-To" manual for educating gifted students.[1] Instead, we provide starting points for using a Multiple Intelligences (MI) perspective to educating students with unusually high levels of promise or performance in one or more culturally valued areas.

Changes in instruction and curricula, purported to be motivated by MI theory, vary widely in their fidelity to it. Many teachers have applied MI theory with successful and productive results, but others have misconstrued and misapplied MI theory (Kornhaber, Fierros, & Veenemam, in press). For example, some teachers have labeled children as possessing one type of intelligence (i.e., "Suzy's a Spatial and Timmy's an Interpersonal"; see Gardner, 1999, for more myths and realities); and some teachers have misused Multiple Intelligences theory to deny services to traditionally gifted students or as ill-conceived support for the notion that "all of our students are gifted."

There is no endorsed MI school or MI test (Gardner, 1993, 1999). MI theory is not intended to categorize or label people. Individualizing children's education strikes us as the best solution to meeting the needs of both typical and atypical learners. Be they gifted, disabled, or typical, children deserve personalized educational experiences that provide a wide range of new learning opportunities and that take into account each child's needs, interests, strengths, and weaknesses. Project Spectrum, described below, provides some examples of how this might be accomplished within an MI perspective. We also discuss some ways in which an MI perspective can be employed to enhance understanding of core ideas in domains of knowledge. Throughout, we will explore ways that MI theory can influence both how we educate gifted students and how we conceive of giftedness. We begin with a brief description of the theory as it now stands.

Theory of Multiple Intelligences—Reframed

From its outset, the theory of multiple intelligences, first presented in *Frames of Mind* (Gardner,

1983/1994), threw into question the idea that an individual's intellectual capacities can be captured in a single measure of intelligence. Although the theory does not directly dispute the notion of "*g,*" it does challenge the scope and dominion of its explanatory power (Gardner, 1999). MI theory moves beyond this narrow approach to one that actively seeks to identify what may be unique about an individual's proclivities and capabilities in a number of spheres.

Gardner (1983/1994, 1999) defines *intelligence* as a biopsychological potential to process information in certain ways: Each intelligence can be activated in an appropriate cultural setting. An intelligence permits an individual to solve problems and fashion products that are of value within a cultural context. To be included in MI theory, a candidate intelligence must meet a set of criteria. These criteria were deliberately drawn from several disparate sources: the developmental trajectories of typical and gifted individuals; exceptional populations including prodigies and savants; the breakdown of skills under conditions of brain damage; psychometric studies and psychological experiments; and studies of the training and generalization of particular skills. Consideration was also given to whether an intelligence had a plausible evolutionary history and an identifiable *core operation,* or set of operations, with potential for definable expert *end-state performance.* The phrase *core operations* refers to capacities and processes that seem central to an intelligence (see Table 8.1) and *end-state performance* refers to accomplishments that rely on highly developed and efficiently harnessed core operations of a given intelligence.

Initially, Gardner (1983, 1999) delineated seven relatively autonomous intelligences—a count that was recently updated to eight or possibly nine intelligences (Gardner, 1999; see Table 8.1). The seven intelligences that originally met the criteria were *linguistic, logical-mathematical, spatial, musical, bodily-kinesthetic,* and two areas of person-related understanding, *interpersonal* and *intrapersonal.* Later, Gardner (1999) added *naturalist* intelligence and proposed that *existentialist* intelligence be considered for future inclusion. At present, existentialist intelligence—the intelligence that poses big questions—has not been sufficiently studied to determine whether it meets the criteria for inclusion in MI theory. We include it here because of its potential usefulness in the identification and education of gifted students (von Károlyi, 2001). These eight or

---

1. For a list of resources, see the appendices in Gardner (1999).

Table 8.1 Multiple Intelligences

Category	Core Operations	Example
Linguistic		
Mastery, sensitivity, desire to explore, and love of words, spoken, and written language(s).	Comprehension and expression of written and oral language, syntax, semantics, pragmatics.	William Shakespeare, Toni Morrison.
Logical-Mathematical		
Confront, logically analyze, assess and empirically investigate objects, abstractions, and problems, discern relations and underlying principles, carry out mathematical operations, handle long chains of reasoning.	Computation, deductive reasoning, inductive reasoning.	Paul Erdos, Isaac Newton.
Musical		
Skill in producing, composing, performing, listening, discerning, and sensitivity to the components of music and sound.	Pitch, melody, rhythm, texture, timbre, musical, themes, harmony.	Charlie Parker, Wolfgang Amadeus Mozart.
Spatial		
Accurately perceive, recognize, manipulate, modify and transform shape, form, and pattern.	Design, color, form, perspective, balance, contrast, match.	Leonardo da Vinci, Frank Lloyd Wright.
Bodily-Kinesthetic		
Orchestrate and control body motions and handle objects, skillfully, to perform tasks or fashion products.	Control & coordination, stamina, balance, locating self or objects in space.	Martha Graham, Tiger Woods.
Interpersonal		
Be sensitive to, accurately assess, and understand other's actions, motivations, moods, feelings, and other mental states and act productively on the basis of that knowledge.	Ability to inspire, instruct, or lead others and respond to their actions, emotions, motivations, opinions, and situations.	Virginia Woolf, Dalai Lama.
Intrapersonal		
Be sensitive to, accurately assess, understand and regulate oneself and act productively on the basis of one's actions, motivations, moods, feelings, and other mental states.	Knowledge and understanding of one's strengths and weaknesses, styles, emotions, motivations, self-orientation.	Mahatma Gandhi, Oprah Winfrey.
Naturalist		
Expertise in recognition and classification of natural objects, i.e., flora & fauna, or artifacts, i.e., cars, coins, or stamps.	Noting the differences that are key to discriminating among several categories or species of objects in the natural world.	Charles Darwin, Jane Goodall.
Existential*		
Capturing and pondering the fundamental questions of existence; an interest and concern with "ultimate" issues.	Capacity to raise big questions about one's place in the cosmos.	Soren Kierkegaard, Martin Luther King, Jr.

Adapted from Gardner, 1985, 1998, 1999.
*Note: *Unconfirmed ninth intelligence.*

nine intelligences are not the only possible ones—others may emerge. The intelligences proposed so far are intended to support the notion of a pluralistic view of intelligence, not to restrict its scope or define it in its entirety.

The Distinction Between Domains and Intelligences

Whereas an intelligence is defined as biopsychological potential or capacity within the context of a species, a domain exists within the context of a culture (Csikszentmihalyi, 1988; Feldman, 1980; Gardner, 1999). It is a social construct. A domain is a discipline or set of activities and operations within which practitioners can be arrayed in terms of expertise. It is usually associated with a (more or less) dedicated symbol system (Gardner, 1999). Generally, more than one intelligence will be implemented in work within any given domain. Activities in the domain of mathematics, for example, tend to harness logical-mathematical and often spatial intelligence. However, there is more than one way to become skillful in a domain: With little reliance on spatial intelligence, some individuals might perform at high levels on spatial tasks by employing semantic strategies—relying primarily on verbal and logical-mathematical intelligences. A student can be considered gifted in any domain that draws on one or more of the intelligences (Gardner, 1993). Educators of gifted students will likely run into idiosyncratic application of intelligences to domains. For example, some children who become competent in billiards may rely on logical-mathematical rather than bodily kinesthetic intelligence. It is, therefore, particularly important for educators of gifted students to keep the distinction between domains and intelligences in mind.

The Autonomy of the Intelligences

According to MI theory, each intelligence is a relatively autonomous intellectual potential capable of functioning independently of the others. Particularly convincing support for this claim has been found in the neuropsychological literature. For example, research with brain-damaged adults has repeatedly demonstrated that particular faculties can be lost while others remain relatively or even wholly unaffected (Gardner, 1975). To be sure, we are not suggesting that normally functioning individuals will demonstrate intelligences that work completely independently of one another. In fact, it can be assumed that in most cases the intelligences work in concert with one another. What differs among individuals is their profile of intelligences at a given moment. Theoretically, there could be individuals who perform at the same level or even excel in all of the intelligences. In most cases, however, individuals exhibit a more jagged profile of abilities, exhibiting various strengths and weaknesses. Being gifted in

one intelligence does not, and should not, foretell (or preclude) a similarly high level of ability in another.

The notion of autonomy of intelligences has important implications for the field of gifted education. It cannot be assumed that an individual who demonstrates exceptional linguistic and logical-mathematical skills—abilities tapped by IQ tests—will also display exceptional ability (or even interest) in activities relying on interpersonal or kinesthetic intelligence, for example. Neither can it be assumed that a child who performs poorly on an IQ test or a standardized achievement test will fail to excel in activities relying on one or more of the other intelligences. There are many examples that support the proceeding claims: the child with an overall IQ of 130 who has difficulty understanding spatial problems; the ten-year-old violin prodigy who performs poorly in academic subjects; or the poet who has little skill or understanding in the logical-mathematical domain. Given the precious and limited resources for gifted programs and the autonomy of the intelligences, it makes sense to target the *specific* areas in which individual students are gifted for special educational programming and enrichment.

Each intelligence proceeds along its own developmental trajectory. Individuals will differ with regard to the areas in which they are considered to be "at promise" or "at risk" and the extent to which they are considered to be so in each area. The field of gifted education is beginning to focus on the impact that developmental asynchrony (uneven maturity in different areas of development) has on the gifted child (Morelock, 1992). Although most of the emphasis has been placed on the impact of asynchronous cognitive, social-emotional, and physical development, the concept of asynchrony can also be applied to uneven development across intelligences. From an MI perspective, intellectual asynchrony is an expected characteristic of the gifted child. In other words, although most children will have an uneven profile of abilities, and thus some level of intellectual asynchrony, children who are deemed gifted according to one or another criteria are likely to have greater than average levels of intellectual asynchrony. From an MI perspective, however, such children and typical children can be educated using the same basic approach: Educators should first seek to identify children's profiles of ability and then seek the best means by which they can be supported and developed.

Assessing Intelligences: Considerations

We hold that each child deserves a personalized educational experience that provides a wide range of new learning opportunities and that fully takes into account each child's individual needs, interests, strengths, and weaknesses. Although the same basic approach may be taken in educating a variety of children, because no two children are likely to have the same profile of abilities, an individual-centered approach to education should take these differences into account. Such an approach can benefit both typical and atypical learners.

In all too many school settings, however, one can only remotely approach the goal of individualizing children's education. In such situations, gifted programs can diminish the gap between the child's educational needs and the available educational opportunities. If one is to provide differentiated services to gifted students, whether their gift is in music or science, languages or sports, some criteria for identifying giftedness are needed. Given this less than ideal situation, we offer some thoughts for those who would assess children's intelligences and suitability for participation in gifted programs.

There are clearly many areas of human capabilities that contemporary constructs of intelligence simply fail to explain: for example, the piano virtuoso, the world-class athlete, or the skilled architect. The intelligences most involved in each of these individuals' areas of expertise are unlikely to be measured by an intelligence test limited to logical-mathematical and linguistic capabilities. We do not dispute the value of considering IQ as one factor in the identification in placement of the gifted individual; however, other factors deserve to be taken into account as well. We are not alone in suggesting that giftedness need not be limited to high IQ. Sternberg (1986) suggests we include practical intelligence and consider information processing components, such as automaticity and response to novelty, in our constructs of intelligence and giftedness. In addition to higher than average ability and creativity, Renzulli and Smith (1980) and his colleagues suggest we consider the role that task commitment plays in producing gifted behaviors. Here, we focus on giftedness from a Multiple Intelligences perspective. Whichever perspective or combination of perspectives one employs, those who are involved in identifying participants for gifted programming may wish to contemplate the following matters.

In selecting students, consider the match of the program to the child's profile of abilities and areas of interest, desire and reasons for wishing to participate in the program, the quality of products that the child has already fashioned, as well as the student's performance during the trial week or two with other comparable children. In addition to employing multiple approaches, include multiple opportunities to be identified as gifted in one's assessment strategy. Different abilities will be evident in different situations and at different points of development. When, for example, a school limits its identification process to a group IQ test in the fourth grade—i.e., relying on a single measure at a single point in time—we do a disservice to untold numbers of children with all sorts of gifts. In contrast, employing a combination of approaches at multiple observation points will uncover more gifted individuals with more diverse capabilities than can be found using a single test, a single observation, or a single selection criterion.

Short answer standardized testing has become increasingly prominent in society. Tests determine who will be admitted into academic settings from preschool to law school and into professions ranging from police work to teaching, and they often dictate who will be promoted and who held back. Most standardized tests used in educational placement decisions primarily tap linguistic and logical-mathematical abilities. And even if they are explicitly targeted to non-standard intelligences, the format is biased toward logical analyses (e.g., "On what basis can I eliminate two possibilities?"). As we stated earlier, what results is a snapshot of a narrow slice of the individual's capabilities. Although properly constructed tests can be useful for certain applications with certain populations, tests are all too often misapplied, misinterpreted, and overemphasized.

Among others, Steele (Steele, 1997; Steele & Aronson, 1995) has studied the effect of what he calls stereotype threat on test performance. Test performance is affected by stereotyped threat when a member of a racial or ethnic group that has been stereotyped as having lower than average abilities in a given area knows that those abilities are being tested. When the same test is characterized as one that assesses an ability that is not included in this negative stereotype, the student's performance will, generally, be much higher.

Another example of the effect of stereotyping on test performance comes from studies of Asian women's math performance (Shih, Pittinsky, &

Ambady, 1999). When these students' gender was emphasized, their math test performance was lower than a control group's performance; but when their identity as Asian was emphasized, they performed at a higher level than the control group. The students' math abilities were equal, but the testing situations were not. Explicit and implicit labeling and stereotyping can have either a beneficial or a stigmatizing effect on performance in a testing situation. If various groups perform differently in various testing situations, can we say that any given testing situation is equitable in its assessment across groups? This question is particularly relevant to traditional gifted education, which, to a large extent and for various reasons, has failed to provide gifted programming equitably across diverse racial and socio-economic groups. Those who develop or employ tests of MI must also be mindful of the effects of observation on the observed.

In addition, when observing children's interactions with materials and ideas in a domain, one should keep in mind that enthusiasm does not necessarily reflect skill in that domain. When assessing children for participation in a gifted program, one must keep in mind the distinction between preferences and capacities. For example, a child who is gifted in logical-mathematical intelligence and not particularly gifted in bodily-kinesthetic intelligence may, nevertheless, enthusiastically engage in sports activities and avoid mathematics. Such a situation could easily occur in a school setting where athletic prowess is valued by other students and the community, but mathematical prowess is not. Such a situation could also occur in cases where instruction in athletics is well matched to the student's ability level, but the instruction in mathematics is inadequate. Yet another opportunity could be lost when a child is highly gifted in linguistic intelligence, for example, but only moderately gifted in spatial intelligence. Because of the relative weakness of spatial intelligence in the child's profile of abilities, such a child might avoid activities biased towards spatial intelligence in spite of her spatial giftedness.

Some consideration should be given to the problems inherent in assessing special populations of gifted students, such as those who are traditionally gifted but also have learning disorders. Learning disorders and traditional giftedness can mask each other in such a manner that typical assessment approaches fail to identify either the giftedness or the learning disorder. In a similar manner, learning disorders and

giftedness in nontraditional areas may also mask each other. Here, again, is reason to employ multiple approaches to assessing gifted children.

Intelligence Fair Assessment

From an MI perspective, assessment approaches must be "intelligence fair." To the greatest extent possible, assessment instruments should attempt to access the intelligence-in-operation[2] and should not confound intelligences. For example, a measure of spatial abilities should primarily engage spatial abilities in both comprehending the task and producing the response. If it is to be *intelligence fair,* a measure of spatial abilities should not presuppose linguistic and logical-mathematical ones. Although it may not be possible to develop completely *intelligence-fair* methods, any progress in this direction increases the validity of the assessment. For example, rather than trying to access a child's understanding of numbers by assessing a verbal response to a word problem, such as, "If Nick has two apples and Emma has three, how many apples do they have altogether?", provide a board game designed to demonstrate skill and understanding of numbers and number concepts and watch the child play. Assessing a child's social understanding by observing classroom interactions is not only more *intelligence fair,* it also has much more ecological validity.

Evaluations will be most informed and useful when they occur in situations closely resembling actual working conditions. Classrooms rich with engaging and enjoyable materials and activities that are designed to activate each intelligence will maximize opportunities to observe and evaluate students' capacities in contexts that are more ecologically valid than those found in traditional classrooms. Evaluation can become an ongoing, unobtrusive part of the child's natural learning environment. Gifted education should strive towards making assessment as engaging, enjoyable, and meaningful for the child as it is informative.

Both educators and students should engage in regular and appropriate reflection on their goals and the means to achieving these goals; they should assess and use such assessments for revising or rethinking goals and procedures (Gardner, 1991b). One way to assess one's success or progress towards a goal is

---

2. Here, again, it is important to keep in mind the distinctions between intelligences and domains.

through the use of portfolios or, more accurately, "process folios": meaningful collections of student work that illustrate both exploration of and progress in a particular domain of inquiry and also include examples of a student's best work (see, e.g., Wolf, Bixby, Glenn, & Gardner, 1991).

We find it useful to distinguish between tests and assessment. Whereas tests generally gather bits of information in a decontextualized setting on some sort of predetermined schedule, assessment is a broader, more flexible approach. Assessment is an ongoing process of reflection and observation that should work hand in hand with a well designed curriculum—one that exposes the child to a wide variety of materials and takes place in a meaningful context. Assessment includes methods and measures that elicit information during the ordinary course of performances in their usual contexts and can occur any time an individual is involved in a domain.

A rough profile of the student's intelligences can be gleaned from assessments. It should be noted that this profile can be expected to change with experiences and over time. A profile of intelligences serves as a guide to formal educational opportunities as well as to less formal activities that can nurture and support the particular array of capabilities that a student exhibits. In addition, attention to a student's profile may suggest ways in which instruction in a particular topic can be adapted to maximize the student's access to important points. Project Spectrum's more structured approach to developing a student profile is discussed below.

MI Theory in Action

MI theory is not a prescription for assessment approaches or educational programs, but a provocation to think differently about assessment and education. In this capacity, it has inspired numerous educational programs, among them Project Spectrum (Chen, Isberg, & Krechevsky, 1998; Chen, Krechevsky, Viens, & Isberg, 1998; Krechevsky, 1998). We will briefly describe some ways in which Project Spectrum demonstrates MI theory in action; we hope that the description can catalyze the design of gifted programs that take an MI Perspective. Parenthetical comments will note applications and adaptations for gifted children.

Project Spectrum

At Project Spectrum, Mara Krechevsky, David Feldman, Howard Gardner, and colleagues developed methods of assessment and an approach to instruction based on MI theory's pluralistic view of human cognition. Project Spectrum provides a rich child-friendly environment in which a wide range of abilities in young children can be comfortably and unobtrusively observed and assessed in a meaningful context. Activities and materials are linked to adult roles or *endpoints,* and children's strengths are cultivated in ecologically valid ways. Through the Spectrum approach, teachers gather a wealth of information about the intellectual strengths and working styles of each child. This information becomes the basis of Spectrum Profiles, which in turn become the basis for decisions shaping each student's classroom experience.

The Spectrum-Inspired Classroom. The Spectrum classroom features a wide variety of materials, games, puzzles, and learning areas that were designed to engage and interest young children. In addition, there are regularly scheduled activities such as creative movement sessions and a class newspaper in which children can demonstrate their language skills by reporting on events of interest. Of course, social interactions take place throughout the classroom. In many ways, Spectrum is reminiscent of what can be found in many well-implemented preschool classrooms—a rich and diverse environment in which to explore and learn.

Spectrum Materials. Rather than label materials *spatial* or *logical-mathematical,* Project Spectrum provides centers stocked with materials aligned with particular adult roles or *endpoints.* For example, there is a space for music, creative movement, and story telling; an area for building; a naturalists' corner; etc. Each center induces the application of a number of intelligences in the context of a culturally valued domain.

Theme-based materials can also tap a range of intelligences and provide both learning and opportunities to assess understanding. Project Spectrum employs theme-based kits furnished with materials intended to evoke and exercise multiple intelligences. A kit might accompany children to a museum and be used to help emphasize and draw children's attention to particular aspects of the museum experience. (When working with gifted children in an area of strength it is important to provide materials with a sufficient range of sophistication and complexity.)

Spectrum Assessment. Spectrum's assessment measures employ a variety of methods for recording and scoring a child's performance in various activities. These methods range from the use of fully quantified score sheets to more holistic, observational checklists. A strength of the Spectrum approach is that it provides several means of organizing and recording observations. (This approach provides many opportunities to locate and monitor the progress of young gifted children.)

The Spectrum Profile. Relatively brief individualized written reports generated from the child's formal and informal engagement with Spectrum materials over the course of the school year make up the Spectrum Profile. The profile describes the particular pattern of intellectual capabilities and working styles exhibited by each child. Consistent with the idea that assessment should be in service of individuals and not simply a means of ranking them, the profile provides concrete yet informal suggestions for follow-up activities for each child. The Spectrum Profile is intended as a guide to the child's profile of cognitive capabilities and working styles and the specific needs and opportunities that accompany such a profile. It addresses *relative* strengths and weaknesses within a child's own range of capabilities; and when the child's performance stands out in relation to the larger profile of preschoolers, it records *absolute* strengths. (It is easy to see how this approach might be employed to help teachers identify and serve young gifted children.)

A Multiple Intelligences Approach to Teacher Training

MI theory can serve as a powerful framework for teacher training and development. First, it can help a teacher look at his own profile of strengths and weaknesses. This self-examination enables a teacher to see where to improve his level of understanding in order to teach more effectively and where his or her strengths and weaknesses might interact with those of students. Second, the theory has spawned a number

of methods that a teacher can employ to observe individual children closely and to put those observations to educational use. Finally, MI theory offers a starting point from which teachers can think more concretely about curriculum development and how to employ the children's profiles of intelligences to maximize understanding. MI theory does not presume to offer one way in which children of any age or level of cognitive capability should be taught. Rather, it serves as a catalyst, and perhaps a challenge, to teachers to find what is best *in* each child and *for* each child (Gardner, 1993, 1998, 2000b).

In relation to the identification and education of gifted children, MI theory broadens our notion of intelligence and giftedness and expands our means of assessing and nurturing promise and achievement in many different cognitive domains. MI theory has encouraged educators, parents, and others to abandon the notion that "the cream always rises to the top." There are cases of youth who reveal their extraordinary talent to the world with little or no provocation, but these are rare (Feldman, 1992; Winner, 1996). MI theory suggests that children should be given many opportunities to experience, explore, and develop interests and proficiencies. Thus, it reduces the chance that a potential musical prodigy will never have access to a musical instrument or a potentially gifted dancer will never try moving creatively.

With its emphasis on a child-centered education designed to develop an array of abilities, Project Spectrum offers a flexible framework within which educators can develop customized programs that more effectively serve all children in their care—be they gifted or more typical. The assumption of an MI perspective might improve gifted education's success with underachieving or disadvantaged gifted students. Such students need to experience successes and build upon those experiences, and an MI-influenced classroom can provide a much wider range of areas for success than is found in a traditional classroom.

Project Spectrum's major focus is early childhood education. Traditional schools frequently neglect very young traditionally gifted students' educational needs. It is our hope that providing examples of MI theory in action from early childhood onward will stimulate an increase of individual-centered instruction for children of all ages and all ability levels—gifted as well as typical children.

Educating for Understanding: A Few Key Points

The goal of education, according to Gardner (1991a, 2000a), is enhanced understanding—understanding of the physical and biological worlds and understanding of the worlds of self and others. Across time and across civilizations, these various "worlds"—or culturally meaningful domains—pose important questions that an educated person should understand. It is important to distinguish, here, between real and surface understanding. Genuine understanding consists in mastery of core concepts that lie at the heart of disciplines as well as mastery of the procedures by which disciplinary experts proceed with their work. Real understanding—"big-U" Understanding—transfers across situations. It carries from the school setting to new real world and theoretical venues.

While each intelligence has core operations,[3] each *world* has core ideas. For example, a core idea in biology is the theory of evolution; a core idea in American history is the effect on the nation of successive waves of immigrants; a core idea in music is the development of themes and variations. Familiarity and facility with these core ideas is at the root of (big-U) Understanding. Educators and communities must come together to develop a dynamic agreement of what constitutes suitable core ideas for Understanding our various *worlds* through an ongoing process of successive approximations. The pedagogy for facilitating Understanding follows this same dynamic and uncertain path.

MI theory provides some possible entry points to help teachers draw students closer to Understanding. Entry points benefit children by employing their preferred ways of knowing. Although suitable for all students, the entry point approach provides an especially powerful means of engaging gifted students by presenting multiple opportunities and multiple means of access to understanding. This ensemble of entries benefits the child who grasps a core idea quickly by providing rich opportunity for integrating, synthesizing, and assessing the fidelity of these various windows to understanding. In addition, through multiple entry points, a core idea can be presented in many different ways without undue redundancy—the mind-numbing bane of the traditionally gifted child's school experience.

An Application of Multiple Entry Points

Entry points are biased towards harnessing and engaging particular intelligences. Roughly, Gardner's intelligences map onto these entry points: Narrational, Quantitative/Numerical, Logical, Foundational/Existential, Aesthetic, Hands-On, and Social/Personal (for more about entry points, see Gardner, 1991a, 1999, 2000a). It is important to keep in mind that not every topic can be accessed through each entry point. With a little creativity, however, the entry point approach can be used to enhance understanding of core ideas in most domains. The following example illustrates how multiple entry points might be applied to the study of evolution.

Narrational

Tell a "Just-So" story about one of the following topics: (1) Why the walking catfish walks; (2) An example of convergent evolution; (3) Successive generations of bats and moths adapting to environmental demands of their roles as predator and prey. Be creative with your character development, but be certain that the role of evolutionary adaptation is central to your plot and that your fable is true to the major scientific points.

Logical/Quantitative/Numerical

Pick one of the following: (1) Breed multiple generations of two strains of fruit fly. Count, record, graph, and compare rates of mutation. (2) Select two points of time—one just prior to and the other during the Cambrian Explosion. For each time, consider what we know about the numbers of species versus the numbers of individuals in a species and graph this relationship. What adaptive purposes might these two types of variety (within species versus across species) serve?

Foundational/Existential

Pick one topic for exploration: (1) From an evolutionary perspective what are the implications of mass cloning on the adaptability of a species? (2) What is

---

3. In practice, these operations are seldom called on solely by a single intelligence, but rather work conjointly and variously with other intelligences.

the relation between survival of the individual, survival of the group or species, and prosocial behavior?

Aesthetic

(1) Consider the adaptive purposes of plumage on different sexes and species of birds and represent (draw, sculpt, film, etc.) a real or imagined male-female pair of birds. Be prepared to explain, or find some other way to represent, how your plumage choices are adaptive to the birds' environment. (2) Create and represent a new type of migrating bird (north to south and back again) that has adapted to an environment in which the wind blows hard and constantly from the east. (3) Imagine that each musical instrument is an environment and that a melody is a species. Develop a four-note theme and specific variations that, by analogy, represent evolutionary adaptation from one instrument to another. For example, if you composed the theme on a piano, one variation might be an adaptation for flute, another for drum, etc.

Hands-On/Experiential

(1) Breed multiple generations of fruit flies and watch for and record mutations. What adaptive purpose does mutation serve, and how might this apply to the specific mutations you observed? (2) At a natural history museum, map the evolution of the modern-day horse from its predecessors. How has the horse changed over time, and what environmental changes might have influenced the horse's evolution?

Social/Personal

Imagine you are part of a team that has been called upon to explain the potential long-term effect of global warming on one habitat to the Global Warming Council (made up of your classmates). Each of you will be the "spokesperson" for one species. As a group, the team selects which habitat, and then the students pair up. Each pair selects two species that share some component or niche in that habitat. One student of each pair should concentrate on a species for which it is likely that global warming increases adaptive advantage, and one should concentrate on a species for which it likely decreases their adaptive advantage. Although the focus of each student thus differs, student pairs should work together to (a) research the two species, (b) write an executive summary of their findings, adding each student's specula-

tions on their species' possible future adaptations that might result from global warming, and (c) prepare a presentation to the Global Warming Council about the effects of global warming on the habitat you selected using your two species as examples.

To prepare for this presentation, take turns role playing "spokesperson" and council member. Pretend the council member is a cartoon or stereotypical of one of the following roles: (a) journalist, (b) scientist, (c) musician, (d) computer programmer, (e) fireperson, (f) conservative politician, (g) liberal politician, (h) corporate executive, (i) veterinarian, or (j) poet. How do you adapt your presentation to the role of the council member? What changes and what stays constant? For the *actual* presentation, each member of the council is secretly assigned one of these roles. During your presentation, watch the members of the Global Warming Council's reactions. Try to figure out which role each member is playing and how to slant your presentation to influence the most council members. The Global Warming Council rates each presentation.

And so on . . .

Here, clearly, the overriding theme, the core idea, is evolutionary adaptation. For a given core idea, the complexity of entry points should be matched to students' readiness. Thus, the tried and true strategy of individualizing traditionally gifted student's education is built into the entry point adaptation of MI theory. Other strategies particularly suitable for educating traditionally gifted students, such as tapping higher reasoning skills, creative problem finding and solving, and employing theme-based approaches, are implicit in the construct of using multiple entry points to understand core ideas.

Single entry points can be used to entice students into a domain. Multiple entry points can be employed to promote transfer of understanding. In addition, the use of multiple entry points can help to bridge between students' areas of strength and weakness: For example, by first engaging the students' proclivities, one then may be able to harness their attention toward avoided areas. At the same time, such bridging entails the kind of cognitive stretch that is necessary for enhanced understanding.

Performances of Understanding

The original purpose of measuring intelligence via the IQ test was to find suitable educational placements for atypical students by *predicting* their performance. Instead of predicting performance, why not assess performance directly and adapt curricula and placement accordingly? Gardner's (1991a) *performances of understanding* provides not only a means of appraising students' current level of understanding, regular use of such performances also increases the likelihood that students will be able to transfer their understanding to novel situations, while also developing skills in transmitting their understanding to others.

Performances of understanding provide a means to observe students' progress towards mastery of an area. Student performances of understanding can take a variety of forms. They might be portfolios or *process folios,* records of accomplishments relating to the execution and completion of large-scale projects, productions and exhibitions, debates or arguments from *both* sides of a controversial issue, models, journals, inventions, etc. Students should be encouraged to avoid performances of a rote, ritualized, or conventional nature, which often provide the illusion of understanding without any evidence that this knowledge can be used appropriately in new contexts (Gardner, 1991a, 1999).

There are a number of points to consider as one assesses performances for understanding, though not all will apply to all performances or all domains of learning. One might appraise a student's level of understanding in terms of its depth, its breadth, number of dimensions considered, identification of trends or tendencies and exceptions to these, ability to override naïve theories and responses, and the all-important ability to transfer understanding from a familiar situation to a novel one. In appraising a student's performance of understanding, one might also consider originality, sense of genre or aesthetic form, capacity to connect a concept to others that are related, synthesizing capacity, and expressiveness. Often, when we communicate something to others, gaps in our understanding come to light: Thus performance *of* understanding also serves as performance *for* understanding.

Ideally, assessments should be as engaging and valuable to the student as they are informative to the teacher. Assessment of understanding should be an ongoing dynamic process of sampling a student's level of understanding from both the teacher's and the student's perspectives. In addition, where appropriate and available, perspectives on students' progress towards mastery of an area can be sought from the community or from experts in the field. The former might be best called upon to respond to such things as performances (i.e., music, theatre, dance), demonstrations, debates, and exhibitions; the latter might be necessary to assess highly gifted (or highly creative) students' performances—particularly in cases where the gifted students' level of understanding in a domain approaches or exceeds that of the classroom teacher.

Struggle for Understanding

Just as the good teacher takes into account her understanding in an area of student inquiry, he or she also takes into account the relation between the classroom activities and materials and the students' readiness to encounter them. What gifted students of all sorts deeply need, and what often is missing for them, are opportunities to work with like-minded peers and opportunities to engage in new learning—to experience the struggles involved in reaching new Understanding in their areas of strength.

Gifted students should not be denied their right to struggle for understanding (Moreale, 1995) in their areas of giftedness. Students who go through school without struggle fail to develop attitudes and skills needed to tackle difficult tasks and may acquire mental laziness. Course work is as ill suited to students who only revisit existing knowledge and never stretch to understand new ideas, as it is ill suited to students who spend the majority of their time in a conceptual swamp sinking from the weight of ideas or tasks presented in a manner too advanced for their level of readiness. It is critical to find a suitable match between the student's readiness for new understanding and the tasks at hand. Here, again, MI theory and the profile of intelligences can provide a framework for developing appropriate education for *all* students *including* gifted students of all descriptions.

One impact of MI theory on the field of giftedness has been to broaden the construct from traditional giftedness to one that is more *intelligence fair*—one that values a wider range of culturally meaningful human potentials. Although some have misinterpreted MI theory and misused it to deny suitable educational efforts to traditionally gifted students, such an approach misses the point of MI theory. Taking an MI perspective should enhance educational opportunities for all students—including gifted students of all descriptions. For students gifted in intelligences not typically recognized in the traditional classroom, as well as for traditionally gifted students, applying an MI perspective should give them suitable challenges in their area(s) of strength, a wider range of educational experiences and areas for exploration (and thus added opportunities for success in school), and potentially, the discovery that they have other areas of giftedness. Educators, in turn, may improve their own effectiveness to the extent that they can draw on several of their own intelligences and stimulate a wider spectrum of intelligences in their students.

SUMMARY AND CONCLUSIONS

Gardner's theory of Multiple Intelligence (MI) calls for a conception of human abilities that includes multiple areas of intelligence. An MI perspective influences how we conceive and measure giftedness, and how we educate all kinds of gifted students—students who are gifted in the traditional sense of the word as well as students who are gifted in one or more culturally valued areas. At Project Spectrum, an example of MI theory in action, learning centers based on adult roles or *endpoints* provide a range of learning opportunities designed to exercise each intelligence. Observing students engaging in a wide range of activities and interacting with a variety of materials allows teachers at Project Spectrum to develop students' profiles of abilities. These provide bases for individualizing each student's educational experience.

While each intelligence has core operations, each domain has core ideas. For true Understanding of a core idea to occur, students must be able to transfer understanding from a familiar situation to a novel one. An MI perspective can enhance understanding through application of multiple *entry points*. Performances of understanding provide a means of appraising students' current levels of understanding and increase the likelihood that they will transfer their understanding to novel situations.

It is critical to find a suitable match between the students' readiness for new understanding and the tasks at hand. MI theory and the profile of intelligences can provide a framework for developing appropriate education for *all* students, *including* gifted students of all descriptions. Entry points or endpoints

can serve as starting points for applying an MI perspective on giftedness to your classroom.

QUESTIONS FOR THOUGHT AND DISCUSSION

1. Explain how the MI view of giftedness differs from a traditional IQ view. To what extent can a traditional view of giftedness account for (explain) students who are gifted from an MI perspective? To what extent can MI Theory account for traditionally gifted students?

2. How might you develop and use a profile of MI abilities for all students in a classroom?

3. What is an *endpoint*? How might you incorporate endpoints in classroom teaching? What benefit would gifted and typical students derive from employing this approach?

4. After reading about Gardner's eight intelligences, what do you think of traditional IQ scores—which many schools, districts, and states require and use?

5. Evaluate yourself on the eight intelligences. What do you conclude?

REFERENCES

Binet, A., & Simon, T. (1905). Méthodes nouvelles pour le diagnostique du niveau intellectuel des anormaux. *L'année Psychologique, 11,* 245–336.

Ceci, S. J. (1990). *On intelligence—more or less: A bio-ecological treatise on intellectual development.* Englewood Cliffs, NJ: Prentice Hall.

Chen, J.-Q., Krechevsky, M., Viens, J., & Isberg, E. (1998). *Building on children's strengths: The experience of Project Spectrum. Project Zero frameworks for early childhood education.* (Vol. 1). Williston, VT: Teachers College Press.

Chen, J.-Q., Isberg, E., & Krechevsky, M. (Eds.). (1998). *Project Spectrum: Early learning activities. Project Zero frameworks for early childhood education.* (Vol. 2). Williston, VT: Teachers College Press.

Csikszentmihalyi, M. (1988). Society, culture, and person: A systems view of creativity. In R. J. Sternberg (Ed.), *The nature of creativity: Contemporary psychological perspectives* (pp. 325–339). New York: Cambridge University Press.

Feldman, D. H. (1980). *Beyond universals in cognitive development.* New York: Ablex.

Feldman, D. H. (1992). The theory of co-incidence: How giftedness develops in extreme and less extreme cases. In F. J. Mönks & W. A. M. Peters (Eds.), *Talent for the future* (pp. 10–22). Maastricht, The Netherlands: Van Gorcum, Assen.

Gardner, H. (1975). *The shattered mind: The person after brain damage.* New York: Basic Books.

Gardner, H. (1983/1994). *Frames of mind: The theory of multiple intelligences.* New York: Basic Books.

Gardner, H. (1991a). *The unschooled mind: How children think and how schools should teach.* New York: Basic Books.

Gardner, H. (1991b). Assessment in context: The alternative to standardized testing. In B. Gifford & M. C. O'Connor (Eds.), *Future assessments: Changing views of aptitude, achievement, and instruction* (pp. 77–119). Boston: Kluwer.

Gardner, H. (1993). *Multiple intelligences: The theory in practice.* New York: Basic Books.

Gardner, H. (1998). A multiplicity of intelligences. *Scientific American, 9*(4), 19–23.

Gardner, H. (1999). *Intelligence reframed: Multiple intelligences for the 21st century.* New York: Basic Books.

Gardner, H. (2000a). *The disciplined mind: Beyond facts and standardized tests, the K-12 education that every child deserves.* New York: Penguin USA.

Gardner, H. (2000b). The giftedness matrix: A developmental perspective. In R. C. Friedman, B. M. Shore, et al. (Eds.), *Talents unfolding: Cognition and development* (pp. 77–88). Washington, DC: American Psychological Association.

Getzels, J. W., & Jackson, P. W. (1961). Family environment and cognitive style: A study of the sources of highly intelligent and of highly creative adolescents. *American Sociological Review, 26*(3), 351–359.

Getzels, J. W., & Jackson, P. W. (1962). *Creativity and intelligence: Explorations with gifted students.* New York: Wiley.

Guilford, J. P. (1967). *The nature of human intelligence.* New York: McGraw-Hill.

Kornhaber, M., Fierros, E., & Veenemam, S. (in press). Multiple intelligences: Best ideas from practice and Project Zero. Boston: Allyn & Bacon.

Krechevsky, M. (1998). *Project Spectrum: Preschool assessment handbook. Project Zero frameworks for early childhood education.* (Vol. 3). Williston, VT: Teachers College Press.

Moreale, C. (1995). An equal opportunity to struggle. *Highly Gifted Children, 10*(4), 4.

Morelock, M. J. (1992). Giftedness: The view from within.

Understanding Our Gifted, 4(3), 11–15.

Renzulli, J. S., & Smith, L. H. (1980, Nov.–Dec.). An alternative approach to identifying and programming for gifted and talented students. *Gifted Child Today, 15,* 4–11.

Shih, M., Pittinsky, T. L., & Ambady, N. (1999). Stereotype susceptibility: Identity salience and shifts in quantitative performance. *Psychological Science, 10*(1), 80–83.

Spencer, S. J., Steele, C. M., & Quinn, D. M. (1999). Stereotype threat and women's math performance. *Journal of Experimental Social Psychology, 35*(1), 4–28.

Steele, C. M. (1997). A threat in the air: How stereotypes shape intellectual identity and performance. *American Psychologist, 52,* 613–629.

Steele, C. M., & Aronson, J. (1995). Stereotype threat and the intellectual test performance of African Americans. *Journal of Personality & Social Psychology, 69,* 797–811.

Sternberg, R. J. (1986). A triarchic theory of intellectual giftedness. In R. J. Sternberg & J. E. Davidson (Eds.), *Conceptions of giftedness* (pp. 223–243). New York: Cambridge University Press.

Terman, L. M. (1925). *Genetic studies of genius.* (Vol. 1). Stanford: Stanford University Press.

Thurstone, L. (1938). *Primary mental abilities.* Chicago: University of Chicago Press.

Torrance, E. P. (1981). Emerging conceptions of giftedness. In W. B. Barbe & J. S. Renzulli (Eds.), *Psychology and the education of the gifted* (3rd ed., pp. 47–54). New York: Irvington.

von Károlyi, C. (2001). Early issue awareness in young highly gifted children: Do the claims hold up? In C. von Károlyi (Chair), *Issue awareness and the highly gifted: Following up on Leta Hollingworth's work.* Symposium for the Biennial meeting of the Society for Research in Child Development (SRCD). Minneapolis, Minnesota.

Winner, E. (1996). *Gifted children: Myths and realities.* New York: Basic Books.

Wolf, D. P., Bixby, J., Glenn, J., & Gardner, H. (1991). To use their minds well: Investigating new forms of student assessment. In G. Grant (Ed.), *Review of research in education* (Vol. 17, pp. 31–74). Washington, DC: American Educational Research Association.

9

The Relationship Between Genetics and Intelligence

ROBERT PLOMIN, *King's College, London*
THOMAS S. PRICE, *King's College, London*

In the field of gifted education, the contribution of genetics has long been neglected. The purpose of this chapter is to suggest that the field has much to gain by taking a more balanced view that recognizes nature (genetics) as well as nurture (environment) on the origins of giftedness. The chapter focuses on the domain about which most is known, intelligence, and emphasizes the important contributions that genetic research can make toward understanding nurture as well as nature. Properly understood, genetic research on intelligence does not threaten gifted education but, rather, provides fundamental facts on which the field can grow in exciting new directions.

At the outset, it should be emphasized that we focus on intelligence in part because it is central to many theories of giftedness, but primarily because more genetic research has been conducted on intelligence than on any other human characteristic—much more than all of the other areas of giftedness put together. Genetic research on other aspects of giftedness as well as their relationship to intelligence is needed (Simonton, 2001). For example, as explained later, we are especially interested in motivational issues and have come to view genetic propensities more in terms of *appetites* than *aptitudes*. We predict that most of the genetic findings that we discuss in relation to intelligence—beginning with the finding of significant and substantial genetic influence—will be relevant as well to other aspects of giftedness.

Nature and Nurture

The neglect of genetics in contemporary discussions of giftedness is striking. Part of the reason for this neglect is the legacy of behaviorism in the behavioral sciences, which led to environmentalism (you are what you learn) and which conditioned behavioral scientists to be uncomfortable with biology. The major reason, however, is that many fear that finding genetic influence will mean that nothing can be done environmentally.

This notion is wrong for three reasons. First, to recognize genetic influence does not imply that a trait is due entirely to genetics. Rarely do genetic factors account for more than half of the variance of behavioral traits. Second, the phrase *genetic influence* in relation to complex traits like intelligence denotes probabilistic propensities, not predetermined programming. Disorders caused by a single gene, such as Huntington's disease or thousands of other rare single-gene disorders, may run their course regardless of other genes or the environment. Complex traits, however, involve many genes and many environmental influences. For this reason, genetic influences on complex traits are not hard-wired, mechanistic determinants. Rather, genes merely contribute to the odds that development will proceed in a certain direction. In summary, *genetic* does not mean innate. *Innate* implies hard-wired, fixed action patterns of a species that are impervious to experience. Third, genetic research only describes genetic and environmental influences as they exist on average in a particular population at a particular time. Even if a trait were highly heritable, an intervention could have a dramatic effect. For example, a type of mental retardation called phenylketonuria (PKU) is caused by inheriting a single gene, but its damaging consequences can be avoided by dietary restriction (Plomin, DeFries, McClearn, & McGuffin, 2001). PKU and its dietary treatment is an example of the general principle that a new intervention, which did not previously contribute to environmental influences in the population, could have a major effect in the population.

Heritability does not imply immutability. In other words, genetic research describes "what is," but it does not predict "what could be." This is where interpretations of expert training go wrong (Bussell et al., 1999; Howe, Davidson, & Sloboda, 1998). Giftedness is not just a gift—much practice is required. Moreover, most individuals profit enormously from intensive training. However, these facts should not be taken to imply that environmental factors are responsible for the origins of individual differences or that genetic factors are not important. The extent to which genetic factors contribute to individual differences early in the development of talents or after much practice is an empirical issue. An apt demonstration of this point shows that the heritability of performance on a motor task is substantial before, during, and after training (Fox, Hershberger, & Bouchard, Jr., 1996).

In relation to unease in thinking about genetic influences, it should also be noted that genetic research does not prescribe or proscribe "what should be." Concerns about political implications lie at the core of uneasiness about finding genetic influence. The most general fear is that finding genes associated with intellectual performance will undermine support for social programs because it will legitimate social inequality as "natural." The unwelcome truth is that equal opportunity will not produce equality of outcome because people differ in ability in part for genetic reasons. However, when the U.S. founding fathers said that all men are created equal they did not mean that all people are identical, but, rather, that they should be equal before the law. Democracy is needed to ensure that all people are treated equally *despite* their differences. However, finding genetic influence is compatible with a wide range of actions, including no action at all. Values come into play when decisions are made concerning what is to be done with such knowledge.

If genetic research describes "what is" rather than predicting "what could be" or prescribing "what should be," what does it matter whether genetic factors are important? Many educational programs for the gifted would proceed largely unchanged whether or not heredity is important. Moreover, knowledge of genetic influences is unlikely to be of much specific help to the educator confronted with a particular gifted child. Genetic research is, however, likely to contribute to the field in more general ways. Although finding genetic influences bears no necessary implications for social action, better decisions ought to be made with knowledge than without it.

That is, knowing "what is" should help guide the search for "what could be."

Nonetheless, the major reason for wanting to understand the genetic and environmental origins of individual differences in intelligence is the basic science goal of explanation. Although basic science carries no promise of practical application, it often leads to novel and important applications. The driving force behind science is simply curiosity, a curiosity that is shared by educators and parents who wonder why children develop the way they do.

Intelligence (General Cognitive Ability, *g*)

Another preliminary issue concerns *intelligence,* a word that is almost as contentious as the word *genetics* in the world of gifted education. The word *intelligence* has so many different meanings that it is preferable to use a more specific label in order to avoid confusion. What is meant by *intelligence* in this chapter is general cognitive ability, which represents the well-established fact that nearly all reliable measures of cognitive abilities (such as tests of verbal, spatial, and memory abilities) intercorrelate at least moderately. General cognitive ability is what such tests have in common. In a meta-analysis of 322 studies that included hundreds of different kinds of cognitive tests, the average correlation among the tests was about 0.30 (Carroll, 1993). A technique called factor analysis, in which a composite score is created that represents what is shared in common among the measures, indicates that a general factor (first principal component) accounts for about 40 percent of the total variance of cognitive tests (Jensen, 1998b). However, this commonality is not just a statistical abstraction—one can simply look at a matrix of correlations among such measures and see that there is a positive relationship among all tests and that some measures (such as spatial and verbal ability) intercorrelate more highly on average than do other measures (such as nonverbal memory tests). Because all of these measures intercorrelate to some extent, the general factor is also indexed reasonably well by a simple total score on a diverse set of cognitive measures, as in IQ tests. This overlap emerges not only for traditional measures of reasoning, spatial, verbal, and memory abilities, but also for information-processing tasks that rely on reaction time and other cognitive tasks used to assess, for example, working memory (Anderson, 1992).

General cognitive ability was recognised in 1904 by Charles Spearman who used *g* as a neutral signifier that avoided the many connotations of the word *intelligence*. As such, *g* is one of the most reliable and valid traits in the behavioral domain (Jensen, 1998a); its long-term stability after childhood is greater than for any other behavioural trait (Deary, Whalley, Lemmon, Crawford, & Starr, 2000); it predicts important social outcomes such as educational and occupational levels far better than any other trait (Gottfredson, 1997); and it is a key factor in cognitive aging (Salthouse & Czaja, 2000). There are, of course, many other important noncognitive abilities, such as athletic ability, but there seems to be little to be gained but confusion by lumping all such abilities together as is done with the popular notion of "multiple intelligences" (Gardner, 1983; see Chapter 8 by von Károlyi, Ramos-Ford, and Gardner). Also, *g* by no means guarantees success either in school or in the workplace—achievement also requires personality, motivation, and social skills, currently referred to as "emotional intelligence" (Goleman, 1995). (See Chapter 31 by Piechowski.)

Although the concept of *g* is widely accepted (Carroll, 1997; Neisser et al., 1996; Snyderman & Rothman, 1987), acceptance is not universal. The arguments against *g* have been reviewed (Jensen, 1998a). They include ideological issues such as political concerns and the notion that *g* merely reflects knowledge and skills that happen to be valued by the dominant culture (Gould, 1996). Objections of a more scientific nature include theories that focus on specific abilities (Gardner, 1983; Sternberg, 1985; see Chapter 7 by Sternberg). However, when these theories are examined empirically, *g* shines through. For example, one of the major advocates of a "componential" view of cognitive processing conceded: "We interpret the preponderance of evidence as overwhelmingly supporting the existence of some kind of general factor in human intelligence. Indeed, we are unable to find any convincing evidence at all that militates against this view" (Sternberg & M. K. Gardner, 1983). But *g* is not the whole story—group factors representing specific abilities are also important levels of analysis—but trying to tell the story of cognitive abilities without *g* loses the plot entirely.

Although *g* is important, there is much more to cognitive functioning. Cognitive abilities are usually considered in a hierarchical model (Carroll, 1993).

General cognitive ability is at the top of the hierarchy, representing what all tests of cognitive ability have in common. Below general cognitive ability in the hierarchy are broad factors of more specific cognitive abilities, such as verbal ability, spatial ability, memory, and speed of processing. These broad factors are indexed by several tests. In addition, the lower part of the hierarchy can also be considered in terms of elementary processes that are thought to be involved in information processing.

The Genetic and Environmental Origins of *g*

Family studies show that *g* runs in families. The average correlation of *g* scores for parents and offspring and for siblings is about 0.45. The question is whether *g* runs in families for reasons of nature or nurture. Adoption and twin studies provide a kind of natural experiment to disentangle genetic and environmental influences. (For details about genetic methods, see Plomin et al., 2001). If family resemblance is due to heredity, then genetically related individuals adopted apart should be similar, even though they do not share the same family environment. If family resemblance is due to shared family environment, then genetically unrelated individuals adopted together should be similar even though they do not share heredity.

The results of dozens of studies indicate that both nature and nurture are important. First-degree relatives include parents and their offspring and siblings, who are related 50 percent genetically. For 1,017 pairs of first-degree relatives who were adopted apart, the average *g* correlation is 0.22, suggesting that genetic factors account for about half of the *g* correlation of 0.45 for first-degree relatives who lived together (Bouchard, Jr., & McGue, 1981). For 2,101 pairs of genetically unrelated adoptive parents and their adopted children and pairs of unrelated children adopted together, the average *g* correlation is about 0.23, suggesting that shared family environment also makes a contribution.

Thus, in rough summary, "genetic" relatives adopted apart correlate about 0.22, "environmental" relatives correlate about 0.23, and "genetic-plus-environmental" relatives correlate about 0.45. Of the *g* resemblance between first-degree relatives, about half appears to be due to nature and the other half to nurture. *Heritability* is a statistic that describes the proportion of variance in the population that can be attributed to genetic differences among individuals. The heritability estimate from these adoption data is 44 percent, which means that of the differences among individuals in g scores, genetic differences can account for approximately 44 percent of this variance. (The correlation of 0.22 is doubled to estimate heritability because first-degree relatives are only 50 percent similar genetically, as explained elsewhere [Plomin et al., 2001].) This means that about half of the g differences among individuals in the population can be accounted for by genetic differences among them. Nurture, shared family environment, accounts for an additional 23 percent of the variance. The rest of the variance of g scores can be attributed to error of measurement (about 10 percent) and to environmental influences that are not shared by individuals in the same family (about 23 percent).

Twin studies provide another kind of natural experiment in which the resemblance of identical twins, who are identical genetically, is compared to the resemblance of fraternal twins, first-degree relatives whose genetic relatedness is 0.50. If heredity affects a trait, identical twins should be more similar for the trait than fraternal twins. For g, the average twin correlations are 0.86 for identical twins (4,672 pairs) and 0.60 for fraternal twins (5,546 pairs; Bouchard, Jr., & McGue, 1981). Because identical twins are twice as similar genetically as fraternal twins, a rough estimate of heritability doubles the difference between the identical and fraternal twin correlations. This estimate of heritability is 52 percent $((0.86 - 0.60) \times 2)$, similar to the estimate of 44 percent from adoption studies. It should be noted that the correlation of 0.60 for fraternal twins exceeds the correlation of 0.45 for non-twin siblings, which suggests that shared environmental factors contribute more to the resemblance of twins than to non-twin siblings, an issue to which we shall return.

One of the most dramatic adoption designs involves reared-apart identical twins, although the number of such twin pairs is small for obvious reasons. For several small studies involving a total of 65 pairs of identical twins reared apart, the average g correlation was 0.72 (Bouchard, Jr., & McGue, 1981). Because they are genetically identical but are not reared in the same family, the correlation for identical twins reared apart provides a direct estimate of heritability. This heritability estimate of 72 percent is higher than the estimate of 44 percent from adoption studies and 52 percent from twin studies, and it has

been replicated in two modern studies totalling 95 pairs of identical twins reared apart (Bouchard, Jr., Lykken, McGue, Segal, & Tellegen, 1990; Pedersen, Plomin, Nesselroade, & McClearn, 1992). A possible explanation for this higher heritability estimate is that, unlike most adoption and twin studies, studies of twins reared apart focused on adults rather than children and adolescents. As explained later, heritability appears to be greater later in life.

Model-fitting meta-analyses that simultaneously analyze all of the family, adoption, and twin data yield heritability estimates of about 0.50 (Chipuer, Rovine, & Plomin, 1990; Loehlin, 1989). Few scientists any longer dispute the conclusion that g shows significant genetic influence (Snyderman & Rothman, 1987). It should be noted that the total variance of g scores includes error of measurement. Corrected for unreliability of measurement, heritability estimates would be higher. Also, as will be discussed, adults show even greater heritability than children. Regardless of the precise estimate of heritability, genetic influence on g scores is not only statistically significant, it is also very substantial.

What About High g? It cannot be assumed that the etiology of high g is the same as the etiology of the normal range of individual differences (Plomin, 1991). It is surprising that so little is known about the genetic and environmental origins of high g. The issue is whether genetic factors affect high ability, which is different from the usual focus on genetic contributions to intelligence differences among individuals in the population. That is, the reasons that one child has an IQ of 150 and another an IQ of 145 are less important than understanding why both children have such high IQ scores, compared with the rest of the population.

The first family study of gifted individuals was published by Francis Galton, the father of behavioral genetics, in *Hereditary Genius: An Inquiry into Its Laws and Consequences* (Galton, 1869/1992). Since there was no satisfactory way at the time to measure mental ability, Galton had to rely on reputation as an index. Galton identified approximately 1000 "eminent" men and found that they belonged to only 300 families, suggesting that the tendency toward eminence is familial. Galton was aware of the possible objection that relatives of eminent men share social, educational, and financial advantages. Nonetheless, Galton concluded that genius is solely a matter of nature (heredity) rather than nurture (environment).

Family studies by themselves cannot disentangle genetic and environmental factors. Galton (1883) set up a needless battle by pitting nature against nurture, arguing that "there is no escape from the conclusion that nature prevails enormously over nurture" (p. 241). Nonetheless, his work was pivotal in documenting the range of variation in human behavior and in suggesting that heredity underlies behavioral variation.

A more modern family study of high *g* involved a follow-up study of Terman's gifted individuals. The average IQ of their offspring was 133, a score in the top few percentile of the distribution of IQ scores (Oden, 1968). This result suggests that familial factors contribute importantly to high *g*, but, again, a family study cannot disentangle the effects of nature and nurture.

A new genetic approach to this issue has been developed to analyze twin data for the extremes of the distribution; it is essentially an analysis of means. The method, called *DF analysis* after its developers (DeFries & Fulker, 1985), compares the mean scores of the partners (co-twins) of high scoring twin individuals for identical and fraternal twin pairs. If familial (genetic and environmental) factors are not important, co-twins of high-scoring twins should have an average IQ near the population mean of 100. If familial factors are important, co-twins will have an average score that lies between the high-scoring twins and the population average. If genetic factors are important, co-twins of identical twins will have an average score closer to the high-scoring twins than will the co-twins of fraternal twins. The first attempts to apply this approach to high *g* suggest that genetic factors are as important at the high end of the distribution of IQ scores as they are for the rest of the distribution (Plomin & Thompson, 1993).

Although more work needs to be done to feel confident about this conclusion, these results suggest an important hypothesis: In terms of genetic influence, high intelligence might merely be the high extreme of the continuous dimension of intelligence. That is, the same genetic deck of cards might be dealt to everyone, but individuals at the high end of the distribution have been dealt a better hand. It should be noted that these results refer only to the top few percentiles of *g* scores, not to the rare one-in-a-million genius. Lykken and colleagues (Lykken, McGue, Tellegen, & Bouchard, Jr., 1992) have speculated that genetic influences on genius are different from those that affect the normal range in intelligence in that particular rare combinations of many genes may be necessary for genius.

The issue of nature and nurture for high *g* was taken up for this chapter in an analysis of data from a longitudinal cohort of young twins, the Twins Early Development Study (TEDS), whose large sample size provides greatly increased power as compared to previous studies. The measure of *g* employed was the first principal component of verbal and nonverbal cognitive tests assessed at two, three, and four years of age using parent-report instruments. Genetic analyses on this sample consisting of 2,339 MZ pairs and 2,303 same-sex DZ pairs at age four indicate moderate heritability of a general factor abstracted from these measures (Price, Eley, Petrill, & Plomin, 2001). Employing only the same-sex pairs in this sample, the heritability of this cognitive composite is 0.24 (0.20, 0.29) at age two, 0.25 (0.20, 0.30) at age three, and 0.21 (0.16, 0.27) at age four (95 percent confidence intervals in parentheses). DF analyses on the 15 percent highest scorers at each age indicate group heritability of 0.25 (0.12, 0.38) at age two, 0.16 (0.03, 0.29) at age three, and 0.06 (−0.08, 0.19) at age four. As can be seen from the confidence intervals, these heritabilities of high *g* are not significantly different at two, three, and four years, nor are they significantly different at any age from the heritabilities of individual differences throughout the distribution. Thus, the most parsimonious interpretation of these results is that high *g* merely represents the high extreme of the same genetic factors that operate throughout the distribution of *g*. However, the downward trend of heritability of high *g* from two to three to four years warrants further exploration.

Specific Cognitive Abilities. Genetic research suggests that broad factors of verbal abilities and spatial abilities are more heritable than other broad factors such as memory and processing speed, but not enough research has been done even to be certain about this simple conclusion. More research is needed that focuses on each specific cognitive ability (Plomin & DeFries, 1998). For example, the broad factor of spatial ability shows moderate heritability, but it seems that this factor includes tests of some of the most highly heritable cognitive abilities and some tests of the least heritable abilities. In contrast, for the broad factor of verbal ability, which also shows moderate heritability, most tests—including tests as diverse as vocabulary and word fluency—show moderate heritability. For memory, tests that involve words seem to be more heritable than other types of memory tests. In addition to questions about the heritability of such traditional specific cognitive abilities, genetic research has just begun to investigate information-processing measures, as well as newer measures of neuroscience such as electroencephalographic evoked potentials, positron emission tomography scans, and functional magnetic resonance imaging (Kosslyn & Plomin, 2001; Vernon, 1993).

Beyond Heritability

The conclusion that genetic contributions to individual differences in IQ test scores are significant and substantial is one of the most important facts that has been uncovered in research on intelligence. Even when this conclusion is fully accepted, however, we are much closer to the beginning than to the end of the story of heredity and intelligence (Plomin, 1999). The rest of the story requires going beyond anonymous genetic and environmental components of variance. Three other genetic discoveries deserve mention.

The first discovery is that the heritability of *g* increases with age (McCartney, Harris, & Bernieri, 1990; McGue, Bouchard, Jr., Iacono, & Lykken, 1993; Plomin, 1986). Sorting the results by age indicates that heritability increases from about 0.20 in infancy to about 0.40 in childhood to 0.60 or higher later in life (McGue et al., 1993), even for individuals over 80 years old (McClearn et al., 1997). This increase in heritability throughout the life span is interesting because it is counterintuitive in relation to the widely held assumption that the effects of experiences—Shakespeare's "slings and arrows of outrageous fortune"—accumulate over time. This finding suggests that people actively select, modify, and even create environments conducive to the development of their genetic proclivities. For this reason, it may be more appropriate to think about *g* as an *appetite* rather than an *aptitude*.

The second developmental discovery comes from genetic analyses of age-to-age change and continuity. These analyses show that genetic factors contribute to change as well as continuity, especially during the transition from early to middle childhood (Fulker, Cherny, & Cardon, 1993). What this means

is that genetic factors that contribute to individual differences in *g* in early childhood differ to some extent from genetic factors that affect intelligence in middle childhood. Although this could mean that new genes are turned on in middle childhood, it is more likely that the same genes have different effects in the brains of eight-year-olds as compared to four-year-olds (Plomin, 1986). Genetic influence on age-to-age change could be part of the reason for "nipped buds" and "late bloomers." (See Chapter 28 by Simonton.)

The third discovery involves multivariate genetic analysis, which makes it possible to estimate the extent to which genetic effects on one trait overlap with genetic effects on another trait. Multivariate genetic analysis yields a statistic called the *genetic correlation,* which is an estimate of the extent to which genetic effects on one trait correlate with genetic effects on another trait independent of the heritability of the two traits. That is, although all cognitive abilities are moderately heritable, the genetic correlations between them could be anywhere from 0.0, indicating complete independence, to 1.0, indicating that the same genes influence different cognitive abilities. In the case of cognitive abilities, multivariate genetic analyses have consistently found that genetic correlations among cognitive abilities are very high—close to 1.0 (Petrill, 1997). In other words, if a gene were found that is associated with a particular cognitive ability, the same gene would be expected to be associated with all other cognitive abilities as well. As noted earlier, *g* accounts for about 40 percent of the total phenotypic variance of cognitive tests. In contrast, multivariate genetic research indicates that *g* accounts for nearly *all* of the genetic variance of cognitive tests. This finding has the interesting converse implication that what is specific to each cognitive test is largely environmental (Petrill, 1997)—that is, what makes us good at all tests is largely genetic but what makes us better at some tests than others is largely environmental.

Another example of multivariate genetic analysis involves tests of school achievement, which also show substantial genetic influence. Multivariate genetic analyses have consistently shown that genetic effects on intelligence tests account completely for genetic effects on tests of school achievement (Thompson, Detterman, & Plomin, 1991; Wadsworth, 1994). Conversely, differences between scores on intelligence tests and tests of school achievement are exclusively environmental in origin. This finding illustrates the possibility of unanticipated applications of basic research. First, the finding suggests that school achievement scores independent of intelligence test scores are largely devoid of genetic influence, and would thus provide a better measure of the effectiveness of the child's environment in fostering achievement. Second, the finding suggests that underachievement, defined as a discrepancy between ability and achievement, is largely due to environmental factors. These environmental factors may reflect motivational processes, since the discrepancy between ability and achievement is most prominent in poorly motivated individuals. Research to identify specific environmental factors that lead to underachievement deserves a high priority in order to foster the development of gifted underachievers. (See Chapter 41 by Silverman and Chapter 33 by Rimm.)

Identifying Genes

The twentieth century began with the rediscovery of Mendel's laws of heredity. The word *genetics* was only invented in 1903. Fifty years later it was understood that DNA was the mechanism of heredity. The genetic code was cracked in 1966—the four-letter alphabet (G, A, T, C) of DNA is read as three-letter words that code for the 20 amino acids that are the building blocks of proteins. The crowning glory of the century and a tremendous start to the new century is the Human Genome Project, which has provided a working draft of the sequence of the 3 billion letters of DNA in the human genome.

The most exciting development for behavioral genetics is the identification of the DNA sequences that make us different from each other. There is no human genome sequence—we each have a unique genome. Indeed, about one in every thousand DNA letters differs, about 3 million variations in total. Many of these DNA differences have already been identified. The Human Genome Project has spawned new technologies that will make it possible to investigate simultaneously thousands of DNA variants as they relate to behavioral traits. These DNA differences are responsible for the widespread heritability of psychological disorders and dimensions. That is, when we say that a trait is heritable, we mean that variations in DNA exist that cause differences in behaviour. The challenge is to use the thousands of new DNA markers to find genes in complex systems that involve multiple genes as well as multiple nongenetic factors (Plomin, Owen, & McGuffin, 1994). However, no genes have as yet been found that contribute to *g,* although research on this topic is in progress that focuses on high *g* (Plomin et al., 1994). Despite the allure of molecular genetic strategies, this chapter forgoes further discussion of this topic because of its promissory nature (Plomin, 1986).

Identifying Environments

It is not sufficiently appreciated that genetically sensitive designs that recognize the importance of both nature and nurture are uniquely well suited to investigate environmental influences. Two of the most important discoveries from behavioral genetic research involve nurture rather than nature. The first is the topic of shared and nonshared environments mentioned earlier. The obvious fact that intelligence runs in families has reasonably but wrongly been attributed to shared family environment. The "nurture assumption" (Harris, 1998)—that the home is the most important part of the child's environment—implies that children growing up in the same home should be similar to one another because they share these environmental influences. To some extent, this is the case prior to adolescence; but in the long run, growing up in the same family does not make children similar in IQ scores. Genetically related children in the same family are indeed similar, but heredity accounts for this familial resemblance. Environmental influences relevant to cognitive development make children in the same family *different,* not similar. This type of environmental influence has been called *non-shared environment,* because environmental influences of this type are not shared by children growing up in the same family (Plomin & Daniels, 1987).

As mentioned earlier, heritability of intelligence appears to increase during the life span. As heritability increases, the effect of shared environment appears to decrease. Also discussed earlier, genetic research involving young children and twins suggests substantial influence of shared environment. However, research during the past two decades indicates that shared environmental influence is much less after adolescence. Further, as also mentioned earlier, twin studies yield inflated estimates of shared environmental influence (Plomin, 1988).

The strongest evidence for the importance of shared environment comes from the correlation for adoptive siblings—that is, pairs of genetically unrelated children adopted into the same families. Their average *g* correlation is about 0.30 across studies. However, these studies happen to assess adoptive siblings as children. In 1978, the first study of older adoptive siblings yielded a strikingly different result: The *g* correlation was –0.03 for 84 pairs of adoptive siblings from sixteen to twenty-two years of age (Scarr & Weinberg, 1978). Other studies of older adoptive siblings have also found similarly low *g* correlations. The most impressive evidence comes from a ten-year longitudinal follow-up study of over two hundred pairs of adoptive siblings. At the average age of eight years, the *g* correlation was 0.26. Ten years later, their *g* correlation was near zero (Loehlin, Horn, & Willerman, 1989). These results suggest that shared environment is important for *g* scores during childhood when children are living at home, then fades in importance after adolescence.

These results suggest that a priority for research should be the identification of nonshared experiences that account for long-term environmental influences on *g*. The nonshared environmental factors that make children in the same family different (such as differences in parental treatment, differences in school experiences, and different experiences with peers) indicate the long-term consequences of environmental influence for *g*. The key is to study more than one child per family in order to ask what environmental experiences make children growing up in the same family so different. Some steps have been taken toward distinguishing *g*-relevant environmental measures that assess nonshared environment (Chipuer & Plomin, 1992). Measures of shared environment can be expected to correlate with *g* scores in childhood but not later, at least not for environmental reasons (see below). Measures of nonshared environment, on the other hand, are not expected to correlate with *g* scores during childhood but are the best hope for predicting later *g* scores from earlier experiences.

The second important discovery from genetic research concerning the environment has been called the *nature of nurture* (Plomin & Bergeman, 1991). The phenomenon is this: Measures widely used to assess the environment in fact show genetic influence in twin and adoption studies conducted in recent years (Plomin, 1994). Although this seems paradoxical, what it means at its simplest level is that ostensible measures of the environment inadvertently assess genetically influenced characteristics of individuals. For example, one of the most widely used observation/interview measures of the home environment

(parental behavior) as it is related to cognitive development is a measure called the Home Observation for Measurement of the Environment (HOME; Caldwell & Bradley, 1978).

In an adoption study, mothers' behavior toward each child was assessed using the HOME for nonadoptive and adoptive siblings. Separate HOME scores were obtained for mothers' behavior toward each child when the child was twelve months old and again when each child was twenty-four months (Plomin, DeFries, & Fulker, 1988). The question was whether mothers were more similar in their behavior toward genetically related nonadoptive siblings as compared to genetically unrelated adoptive siblings. If so, this pattern of results would suggest genetic influence. Sibling correlations for HOME total scores were 0.50 and 0.36, respectively, for nonadoptive and adoptive siblings at twelve months. At twenty-four months, the pattern of sibling correlations was similar: 0.50 for nonadoptive siblings and 0.32 for adoptive siblings. Thus, these data suggest that parental behavior assessed by the HOME substantially reflects genetic differences among children.

If genetic factors contribute to environmental measures such as the HOME, genetic factors might also be involved in the correlation between the HOME and children's cognitive development. This appears to be the case—about half of the HOME's prediction of children's cognitive development can be accounted for by genetic factors (Braungart, Plomin, DeFries, & Fulker, 1992).

These findings on the nature of nurture suggest that research on family environment needs to be embedded in genetic designs that can disentangle nurture from nature (Rowe, 1994). More generally, research on the developmental interface between nature and nurture needs to consider a more active role of children in selecting, modifying, and creating their own environments (Scarr, 1992). Bright children select and are selected by peers and educational programs that foster their abilities. They read and think more. This is the profound meaning of finding genetic influence on measures of the environment. Genes contribute to experience itself (Plomin, 1994).

SUMMARY AND CONCLUSIONS

The convergence of evidence from numerous family, twin, and adoption studies makes it clear that genetics plays a major role in the origins of individual differences in the normal range of intelligence and probably in high intelligence as well. There is still much to be learned about this rudimentary nature-nurture question, especially in relation to specific cognitive abilities.

Although more research of this sort is needed, the theme of this chapter is that genetic research can go far beyond estimating heritability. The emerging ability to identify specific genes involved in intelligence is a particularly exciting possibility that will revolutionize genetic research, for example, by making it possible to identify relevant genotypes directly from a few drops of blood or a few cells scraped from the lining of the cheek. However, most of what is currently known about the genetics of intelligence comes from twin and adoption studies, and such studies will continue to provide valuable information even when molecular genetic research comes on line.

More research is needed that takes advantage of new developmental, multivariate, and environmental approaches to genetic analysis. Although such research has just begun, it already has yielded findings of great importance. For example, developmental genetic research indicates that the heritability of intelligence increases with age, and that genetic factors also contribute to age-to-age change, especially during the transition to middle childhood. Multivariate genetic research has indicated that genetic effects on cognitive abilities are general to *g* rather than specific to more modular processes. It has also suggested that the overlap between intelligence and scholastic achievement is due entirely to genetic factors, whereas the differences between them are environmental in origin. Perhaps most important of all are the environmental findings concerning the importance of nonshared environment and genetic influences on experience. Another important direction for research is to investigate environmental factors, including instructional practices, as they interact with genetic propensities.

Incorporating genetic strategies in research on gifted education promises to be stimulating for both fields and synergistic in its contributions towards understanding the development of giftedness.

QUESTIONS FOR THOUGHT AND DISCUSSION

1. Consider Plomin and Price's strong emphasis on general cognitive ability, or *g,* and Gardner's theory of multiple intelligences. Is there a conflict? Explain.

2. *g* runs in families. Use twin research to explain the nature and the nurture sides of this generalization.

3. In Plomin and Price's section entitled Beyond Heritability, what do they mean when they say "it may be more appropriate to think about *g* as an *appetite* rather than an *aptitude*."?

4. What is meant by "nonshared environment"?

REFERENCES

Anderson, M. (1992). *The development of intelligence: Studies in developmental psychology.* Hove, UK: Psychology Press.

Bouchard, T. J., Jr., Lykken, D. T., McGue, M., Segal, N. L., & Tellegen, A. (1990). Sources of human psychological differences: The Minnesota Study of Twins Reared Apart. *Science, 250,* 223–228.

Bouchard, T. J., Jr., & McGue, M. (1981). Familial studies of intelligence: A review. *Science, 212,* 1055–1059.

Braungart, J. M., Plomin, R., DeFries, J. C., & Fulker, D. W. (1992). Genetic influence on tester-rated infant temperament as assessed by Bayley's Infant Behavior Record: Nonadoptive and adoptive siblings and twins. *Developmental Psychology, 28,* 40–47.

Bussell, D. A., Neiderhiser, J. M., Pike, A., Plomin, R., Simmens, S. J., Howe, G. W., Hetherington, E. M., Carroll, E., & Reiss, D. (1999). Adolescents' relationships to siblings and mothers: A multivariate genetic analysis. *Developmental Psychology, 35,* 1248–1259.

Caldwell, B. M., & Bradley, R. H. (1978). *Home observation for measurement of the environment.* Little Rock: University of Arkansas.

Carroll, J. B. (1993). *Human cognitive abilities.* New York: Cambridge University Press.

Carroll, J. B. (1997). Psychometrics, intelligence, and public policy. *Intelligence, 24,* 25–52.

Chipuer, H. M., & Plomin, R. (1992). Using siblings to identify shared and non-shared HOME items. *British Journal of Developmental Psychology, 10,* 165–178.

Chipuer, H. M., Rovine, M. J., & Plomin, R. (1990). LISREL modeling: Genetic and environmental influences on IQ revisited. *Intelligence, 14,* 11–29.

Deary, I. J., Whalley, L. J., Lemmon, H., Crawford, J. R., & Starr, J. M. (2000). The stability of individual differences in mental ability from childhood to old age: Follow-up of the 1932 Scottish Mental Survey. *Intelligence, 28,* 49–55.

DeFries, J. C., & Fulker, D. W. (1985). Multiple regression analysis of twin data. *Behavior Genetics, 15,* 467–473.

Fox, P. W., Hershberger, S. L., & Bouchard, T. J., Jr. (1996). Genetic and environmental contributions to the acquisition of a motor skill. *Nature, 384,* 356–357.

Fulker, D. W., Cherny, S. S., & Cardon, L. R. (1993). Continuity and change in cognitive development. In R. Plomin & G. E. McClearn (Eds.), *Nature, nurture, and psychology* (pp. 77–97). Washington, DC: American Psychological Association.

Galton, F. (1869/1992). *Heredity genius: An enquiry into its laws and consequences.* Cleveland: World.

Galton, F. (1883). *Inquiries into human faculty and its development.* London: Macmillan.

Gardner, H. (1983). *Frames of mind: The theory of multiple intelligences.* New York: Basic Books.

Goleman, D. (1995). *Emotional intelligence.* New York: Bantam Books.

Gottfredson, L. S. (1997). Why *g* matters: The complexity of everyday life. *Intelligence, 24,* 79–132.

Gould, S. J. (1996). *The mismeasure of man* (2nd ed.). New York: Norton.

Harris, J. R. (1998). *The nurture assumption: Why children turn out the way they do.* New York: The Free Press.

Howe, M. J. A., Davidson, J. W., & Sloboda, J. A. (1998). Innate talents: Reality or myth? *Behavioral and Brain Sciences, 21,* 399–442.

Jensen, A. R. (1998a). *The g factor: The science of mental ability.* Westport, CT: Praeger.

Jensen, A. R. (1998b). The puzzle of nongenetic variance. In R. J. Sternberg & E. L. Grigorenko (Eds.), *Intelligence, heredity and environment* (pp. 42–88).

Kosslyn, S., & Plomin, R. (2001). Towards a neurocognitive genetics: Goals and issues. In D. Dougherty, S. L. Rauch, & J. F. Rosenbaum (Eds.), *Psychiatric neuroimaging research: Contemporary strategies* (pp. 491–515). Washington, DC: American Psychiatric Press.

Loehlin, J. C. (1989). Partitioning environmental and genetic contributions to behavioral development. *American Psychologist, 44,* 1285–1292.

Loehlin, J. C., Horn, J. M., & Willerman, L. (1989). Modeling IQ change: Evidence from the Texas Adoption Project. *Child Development, 60,* 993–1004.

Lykken, D. T., McGue, M., Tellegen, A., & Bouchard, T. J., Jr. (1992). Emergenesis: Genetic traits that may not run in families. *American Psychologist, 47,* 1565–1577.

McCartney, K., Harris, M. J., & Bernieri, F. (1990). Growing up and growing apart: A developmental meta-analysis of twin studies. *Psychological Bulletin, 107,* 226–237.

McClearn, G. E., Johansson, B., Berg, S., Pedersen, N. L., Ahern, F., Petrill, S. A., & Plomin, R. (1997). Substantial genetic influence on cognitive abilities in twins 80+ years old. *Science, 276,* 1560–1563.

McGue, M., Bouchard, T. J., Jr., Iacono, W. G., & Lykken, D. T. (1993). Behavioral genetics of cognitive ability: A life-span perspective. In R. Plomin & G. E. McClearn (Eds.), *Nature, nurture, and psychology* (pp. 59–76). Washington, DC: American Psychological Association.

Neisser, U., Boodoo, G., Bouchard, T. J., Jr., Boykin, A. W., Brody, N., Ceci, S. J., Halpern, D. F., Loehlin, J. C., Perloff, R., Sternberg, R. J., & Urbina, S. (1996). Intelligence: Knowns and unknowns. *American Psychologist, 51,* 77–101.

Oden, M. H. (1968). The fullfillment of promise: 40 year follow-up of the Terman gifted group. *Genetic Psychology Monographs, 77,* 3–93.

Pedersen, N. L., Plomin, R., Nesselroade, J. R., & McClearn, G. E. (1992). A quantitative genetic analysis of cognitive abilities during the second half of the life span. *Psychological Science, 3,* 346–353.

Petrill, S. A. (1997). Molarity versus modularity of cognitive functioning? A behavioral genetic perspective. *Current Directions in Psychological Science, 6,* 96–99.

Plomin, R. (1986). *Development, genetics, and psychology.* Hillsdale, NJ: Erlbaum.

Plomin, R. (1988). The nature and nurture of cognitive abilities. In R. J. Sternberg (Ed.), *Advances in the psychology of human intelligence. Vol. 4* (pp. 1–33). Hillsdale, NJ: Erlbaum.

Plomin, R. (1991). Genetic risk and psychosocial disorders: Links between the normal and abnormal. In M. Rutter & P. Casaer (Eds.), *Biological risk factors for psychosocial disorders* (pp. 101–138). Cambridge: Cambridge University Press.

Plomin, R. (1994). *Genetics and experience: The interplay between nature and nurture.* Thousand Oaks, CA: Sage Publications.

Plomin, R. (1999). Genetics and general cognitive ability. *Nature, 402,* C25–C29.

Plomin, R., & Bergeman, C. S. (1991). The nature of nurture: Genetic influences on "environmental" measures. *Behavioral and Brain Sciences, 14,* 373–427.

Plomin, R., & Daniels, D. (1987). Why are children in the same family so different from each other? *Behavioral and Brain Sciences, 10,* 1–16.

Plomin, R., & DeFries, J. C. (1998, May). Genetics of cognitive abilities and disabilities. *Scientific American,* 62–69.

Plomin, R., DeFries, J. C., & Fulker, D. W. (1988). *Nature and nurture during infancy and early childhood.* Cambridge: Cambridge University Press.

Plomin, R., DeFries, J. C., McClearn, G. E., & McGuffin, P. (2001). *Behavioral genetics* (4th ed.). New York: Worth.

Plomin, R., Owen, M. J., & McGuffin, P. (1994). The genetic basis of complex human behaviors. *Science, 264,* 1733–1739.

Plomin, R., & Thompson, L. A. (1993). Genetics and high cognitive ability. In G. R. Bock & K. Ackrill (Eds.), *The origins and development of high ability* (pp. 62–84). Chichester, UK: Wiley (CIBA Foundation Symposium 178).

Price, T. S., Eley, T. C., Petrill, S. A., & Plomin, R. (2001). Longitudinal genetic analysis of specific cognitive abilities in pre-school children. *Submitted.*

Rowe, D. C. (1994). *The limits of family influence: Genes, experience, and behaviour.* New York: Guilford.

Salthouse, T. A., & Czaja, S. J. (2000). Structural constraints on process explanations in cognitive aging. *Psychology and Aging, 15,* 44–55.

Scarr, S. (1992). Developmental theories for the 1990s: Development and individual differences. *Child Development, 63,* 1–19.

Scarr, S., & Weinberg, R. A. (1978). The influence of "family background" on intellectual attainment. *American Sociological Review, 43,* 674–692.

Simonton, D. K. (2001). Talent development as a multidimensional, multiplicative, and dynamic process. *Current Directions in Psychological Science, 10,* 39–43.

Snyderman, M., & Rothman, S. (1987). Survey of expert opinion on intelligence and aptitude testing. *American Psychologist, 42,* 137–144.

Sternberg, R. J. (1985). *Beyond IQ: A triarchic theory of human intelligence.* Cambridge: Cambridge University Press.

Sternberg, R. J., & Gardner, M. K. (1983). A componential interpretation of the general factor in human intelligence. In H. J. Eysenck (Ed.), *A model for intelligence.* Berlin: Springer Verlag.

Thompson, L. A., Detterman, D. K., & Plomin, R. (1991). Associations between cognitive abilities and scholastic achievement: Genetic overlap but environmental differences. *Psychological Science, 2,* 158–165.

Vernon, P. A. (1993). *Biological approaches to the study of human intelligence.* Norwood, NJ: Ablex.

Wadsworth, S. J. (1994). School achievement. In R. Plomin & D. W. Fulker (Eds.), *Nature and nurture during middle childhood* (pp. 86–101). Oxford: Blackwell.

10

Psychological and Educational Assessment of Gifted Children

SUSAN G, ASSOULINE, *The University of Iowa*

An *assessment* is a data-gathering process designed to help answer questions and make decisions. Many assume that assessment and testing are synonymous; however, testing is but one of four components of an educational and/or psychological assessment. The four components are (a) standardized tests, (b) interviews, (c) structured or unstructured observations, and (d) informal procedures (Sattler, 2001). As components of a comprehensive assessment, interviews, observations, and informal procedures will be briefly addressed, but the emphasis and purpose of this chapter is to highlight and confirm testing, and standardized testing in particular, as the primary component of an assessment of a gifted student.

It is important for the reader to know what I mean by "test." The simple response is that a test is a *sample* of behavior. However, a more complex answer lies in the pages that follow.

Anastasi (1988) defined *psychological tests* as, "like other tests in science, insofar as observations are made on a small but carefully chosen *sample* of an individual's behavior" (p. 24). She described the function of psychological tests as the "measure [of] differences between individuals or between the reactions of the same individual on different occasions" (p. 3). In other words, psychological tests measure individual differences in samples of behavior. The behaviors being measured may be sampled from broad domains, such as intelligence or personality.

Educational tests are also measures of samples of behavior, but, as defined by Anastasi, "have been specifically developed for use in educational contexts" (1988, p. 411). Because the distinction between psychological and educational tests is not always clear, the term *psychoeducational* has come to mean

that the information used will include results from psychological as well as educational tests.

Many adjectives have been placed in front of the word *test,* for example, authentic, criterion-referenced, standardized, or norm-referenced. *Criterion-referenced tests* differ in significant ways from norm-referenced or standardized tests. Criterion-referenced tests (e.g., spelling tests) are designed to yield information that suggests an individual's degree of competency or mastery of a pre-established level of performance or criterion. Criterion-referenced tests are an example of the informal component of an assessment. The information from a criterion-referenced test can be helpful in determining curriculum.

An *authentic assessment* analyzes a student's work. Authentic assessments are especially subjective in nature. Often, the student's work, as well as the analysis of the work, is kept in a portfolio or folder, and sometimes an authentic assessment is called a *portfolio assessment.* Although the adjective *authentic* implies that this form of assessment is more valid than a standardized or norm-referenced test, that is not the case. Authentic assessments also represent the informal component of an assessment and can be rich with information about a learner.

Norm-referenced tests are developed so that a score can be compared to a representative group of individuals referred to as a *normative sample.* In order for the comparison to be valid, a norm-referenced test must be administered under the same (i.e., standardized) conditions for everybody. In this chapter, the terms *norm-referenced* and *standardized* are used interchangeably. Both large-group administered tests of achievement, such as the Iowa Tests of Basic Skills (ITBS), and individually administered intelligence tests are examples of norm-referenced or standardized tests.

Norm-referenced or standardized tests are perennially criticized. Wiggins (1993), for example, criticizes testing with the assertion that:

> Students are tested not on the way they use, extend, or criticize "knowledge" but on their ability to generate a superficially correct response on cue. They are allowed one attempt at a test they know nothing about until they begin taking it. For their efforts, they receive—and are judged by—a single numerical score that tells them little about their current level of progress and gives them no help in improving (p. 2).

Similar attacks are found in a variety of publications, including professional educational publications such as *Phi Delta Kappan*. For example, in the September 2001 issue, Wassermann laments that both the practice of standardized testing as well as criticisms of standardized testing have remained consistent throughout the latter half of the twentieth century, and argues that we should be suspicious of the motives of those advocating standardized testing. Wassermann asserts that educators should omit testing from the assessment process and revert to, "the use of informed, evaluative observations by teachers," even though these observations may be "flawed . . . subjective . . . [and] it's true that teachers' judgments about students' performance could be wrong, misguided, or biased" (p. 36).

In this chapter, I propose that the responsible educator should ignore Wiggins' and Wasserman's advice and (a) recognize that standardized tests can be extremely useful in understanding the learning needs of a gifted student, and (b) advocate for the synthesis of information from standardized tests as well as from informal assessment procedures to develop programs for gifted students.

The first part of this chapter provides the reader with an appreciation of standardized testing through the presentation of a brief history of norm-referenced testing, theories of intelligence, and giftedness. The second part presents two case studies and discusses testing issues as they relate to the field of gifted education. The case studies demonstrate clearly the value of information from standardized testing for making programming and placement decisions about gifted students. The chapter concludes with a list of "consumer guidelines" that summarize important issues when assessing gifted children.

How Has the History of Testing Influenced Today's Practices in Gifted Education?

In 1869 Sir Francis Galton published *Hereditary Genius,* which established the link between the terms *intelligence* and *genius.* Lewis Terman published in 1916 the U.S. version of Binet and Simon's individual intelligence test. Terman called his version of Binet and Simon's test the Stanford-Binet Intelligence Scale and, in 1922, used this scale to launch a study of 1,528 gifted children. The results of Terman's study were published in a series entitled *The Genetic Studies of Genius,* the first volume of which was published in 1925 (Terman, 1925). In Terman's work, we see the shift in terminology from *genius* to *gifted* (Feldhusen & Jarwan, 1993). Also, through Terman's work we see the forging of the strong link between intelligence testing and gifted.

Terman's extensive longitudinal studies established the foundation for identifying gifted students on the basis of intellectual potential as measured by individualized intelligence tests. However, Terman was sensitive to the limitations of measuring "intelligence," and early in the days of developing the Stanford-Binet Terman cautioned test users:

> We must guard against defining intelligence solely in terms of ability to pass the tests of a given intelligence scale. It should go without saying that no existing scale is capable of adequately measuring the ability to deal with all possible kinds of material on all intelligence levels. (Terman, 1921, p. 131)

Terman's precautionary statements were prescient to the theoretical work dominating the last quarter of the 20th century. During the twentieth century, the conceptualization of intelligence evolved from a single point of view (i.e., Terman's Stanford-Binet) into a complex perspective with several different orientations, three of which are described below: psychometric, cognitive modifiability, and information processing. Each orientation has influenced educational practice; at the same time, educational practice has influenced our views about the usefulness of intelligence tests.

The oldest and most research-based tradition of measuring intelligence is the psychometric approach (McGrew & Flanagan, 1998). *Psychometrics* is defined as the quantitative measure of psychological traits or attributes (Sattler, 2001). The psychometric approach has resulted in thousands of tests; according to the 1999 edition of *Tests in Print,* there were 2,939 commercially available tests. Each test is concerned with measurement issues of reliability and validity. *Reliability* refers to the consistency and stability (accuracy) of scores earned by test-takers. *Validity* is a more esoteric concept, but a brief definition of validity refers to its "appropriateness" to the domain being measured. (See Anastasi, 1988, or Hammill, Brown, & Bryant, 1992, for more detailed explanations of reliability and validity.)

The psychometric approach to testing dominates the present-day educational system, and with good reason, as the information from norm-referenced testing can be tremendously useful in both placement and programming decisions. The psychometric approach continues to evolve. Some types of psychometric testing, for example, Galton's measurement of sensory discrimination abilities as a way of measuring intelligence, are now extinct. Other types of psychometric tests have evolved, for example, individualized intelligence tests; and their evolution is complemented (not replaced) by the cognitive modifiability and information-processing approaches.

Assessing how an individual functions within an environment represents an interactive or dynamic approach to assessment (as opposed to the more "static" nature of the psychometric approach) and characterizes *cognitive modifiability* theories of intelligence. McGrew and Flanagan (1998) associate cognitive modifiability theories with Vygotsky's *zone of proximal development* (ZPD). ZPD is defined as, "the difference between a person's . . . performance in isolation and one's performance when mediated by hints, guided instruction, and suggestions by another individual" (p. 30). Dynamic assessments evolved from cognitive modifiability theory, and, by their nature, dynamic assessments correspond to the gifted educator's vision of diagnostically assessing a student's learning needs and matching those needs with an appropriate prescription for instruction.

The *information processing* approach to intelligence is characterized by analyses of how information is received and mentally operated upon during problem solving and everyday tasks. Information processing is still relatively new; it only entered the psychological scene in the 1960s. Naglieri and Kaufman (2001) refer to tests that have been developed from the information processing tradition as a new breed of instruments that provide, "cognitively-based alternatives to traditional IQ test technology that has dominated the field during most of the 20th century" (p. 152). Measurement of processing components by this new breed of instruments still relies on psychometric procedures and principles.

Sattler (2001) provides a fascinating timeline that reviews the historical markers in cognitive and educational assessment. The timeline presented in Table 10.1 includes important dates and notes about the evolution of theories of intelligence testing as they relate to gifted education. Much of the information in Table 10.1 draws heavily from Sattler and McGrew and Flanagan (1998).

What Types of Educational Decisions Are Conducive to Assessment?

The purpose of an assessment is to gather information relevant to making a decision. In gifted education, decisions about students usually involve (a) placement into a program and/or level and (b) type of curriculum to use within the program. Until recently, the primary reason for assessing an academically talented child was to make a decision regarding placement. For gifted children, this traditionally has been to obtain a measure of general intellectual ability (IQ).

Group intelligence tests are often used as a way of initially screening for students of high academic ability, but beyond that their uses with individual students are limited. Two tests widely used are the Otis-Lennon School Ability Test (OLSAT)—7th Edition, published in 1995, and the newly revised Cognitive Abilities Test (CogAT) Form 6 (Lohman & Hagen, 2001). Both tests were concurrently normed with a group-administered achievement battery. The OLSAT, which yields a verbal score, a nonverbal score, and a total score, was normed at the same time as the Stanford Achievement Tests and the Metropolitan Achievement Tests. The CogAT, which yields a score measuring reasoning in three domains—verbal, quantitative, and nonverbal—was normed along with the Iowa Tests of Basic Skills. Combining the information, for example, from the CogAT and the ITBS, can help educators in their decision making.

Despite improvements in the group-administered tests of general ability, an individually administered intelligence test remains the best instrument for identifying gifted children on the criterion of *general ability* (see Table 10.2, Part A). Sattler (2001) tecom-

Table 10.1   Twentieth Century Timeline of Cognitive and Educational Assessment

1904	Spearman introduced the concept of a two-factor theory of intelligence—a general factor (g) of intelligence and one or more specific factors (s). Spearman's g emphasized intelligence—mental ability—as a unitary trait.
1905	Alfred Binet and Theodore Simon developed a 30-item test intended to measure judgment, comprehension, and reasoning of school-aged children (based upon testing that began in the early 1890s). This effort resulted in the Binet-Simon Scale.
1916	Stanford University Professor Lewis Terman published an extended standardized form of the Binet-Simon Scale under the name of the Stanford Revision and Extension of the Binet-Simon Scale. Terman's scale served as the foundation for future applications of the psychometric theory of intelligence testing to measurement. This scale and its subsequent revisions represent the classic application of Spearman's theory of intelligence to measurement. The concept of IQ (intelligence quotient), as a ratio of mental age to chronological age, was introduced with Terman's scale. IQ was essentially an operational definition of general mental ability, i.e., Spearman's g.
1936	The Iowa Every-Pupil Tests of Basic Skills (later renamed the Iowa Tests of Basic Skills) were developed by E. F. Lindquist and his colleagues at the University of Iowa. The ITBS represents a large-scale achievement-testing program. Many gifted programs use scores from tests like the ITBS to identify students for programs.
1937	The 1916 version of the Binet-Simon Scales was revised by Lewis Terman and his colleague Maude Merrill and renamed the Stanford-Binet Intelligence Scale.
1938	Louis Thurstone introduced a "multiple" intelligences theory. In direct contrast to Spearman's g, Thurstone's theory, and the resultant test, the Primary Mental Abilities Tests, portrayed intelligence as equally weighted multiple abilities, including, verbal, number, and space ability.
1939	David Wechsler published the Wechsler-Bellevue Intelligence Scale. Revisions of this scale, as the Wechsler Adult Intelligence Scale (WAIS) were published in 1955, 1981, and 1997. (Note: in 1914 David Wechsler was introduced to the measurement of intelligence through his experience as a U.S. Army private in the Army's large-scale testing program.)
1949	The Wechsler Intelligence Scale for Children (WISC), designed for children ages 6 to 16, was published. The Wechsler tests use a point-scale format. The underlying assumption of a point-scale format is that items are designed to measure specific functions or aspects of behavior at every age. In 1967 the Wechsler Preschool and Primary Scale of Intelligence (WPPSI), designed for children ages 3 to 7, was published; a revision (WPPSI-R) was published in 1991. In 1974 the WISC was revised and renamed the WISC-R; and in 1991 the WISC-R was revised and renamed the WISC-III.
	Wechsler considered IQ, defined as the ratio of mental age to chronological age, as unsuitable, especially for adults. He developed the notion of a *deviation IQ* in which the examinee's score is compared with scores earned by other individuals of the examinee's age.
1960	The best items from the two 1937 forms of the Stanford Binet Intelligence Scale were selected and combined into one form, the Stanford-Binet Form L-M (*L* is for Lewis Terman and *M* is for Maude Merrill, Terman's colleague and co-developer of the Stanford Binet). New norms for the 1960 form were published in 1972. For the next 25 years, the Stanford-Binet (Form L-M) was regarded as an extremely reliable and valid instrument for use in predicting academic success. It was designed to be used with individuals as young as two years of age through adult.
1970	Congress mandated Secretary of Education Sidney Marland to generate a report on the *Education of Gifted and Talented* (published in 1972 and commonly called the *Marland Report*). From this report, a national definition of gifted and talented students was generated (see Table 10.2). This definition is still used in many states, and given its nature seems to ensure that standardized tests—especially tests of intelligence—will continue to play a role in the identification of gifted students.
1972	Professor Julian C. Stanley initiated the Talent Search Model. Although the Talent Search only tested a few hundred students in the early 1970s, by the beginning of the twenty-first century, hundreds of thousands of students are participating annually in the Talent Search.
1975	U.S. PL 94-142, protecting the right to equal education for all handicapped children, was passed. In 1990 this law was updated and renamed the Individuals with Disabilities Education Act—IDEA. There was a reauthorization in 1997, and amendments in 1999. PL 94-142 was a watershed in education; educators and parents are now more aware of assessment and special needs, as well as the requirement to accommodate students with special needs.
1983	Howard Gardner proposed a Theory of Multiple Intelligences. Gardner's theory resulted in a variety of instructional and assessment strategies; however, no standardized test exists to measure the multiple intelligences.
1985	Robert Sternberg introduced a Triarchic Theory of Intelligence. Sternberg's theory, like Gardner's, is also in contrast to a single, unitary view of intelligence. McGrew and Flanagan (1998) stated that Sternberg's theory has not held up well when judged against established standards of validity.

(continued)

Table 10.1 Continued

1986	The Stanford-Binet Intelligence Scale: Fourth Edition (SB: IV) was developed by R. L. Thorndike, E. Hagen, and J. Sattler. The SB: IV introduced users to a factor structure, which includes a general intelligence factor, several general memory factors, and several specific factors such as verbal, quantitative, and abstract visual reasoning factors.
	Note: Silverman and Kearney (1992) made a strong case for continuing to use the Stanford-Binet (L-M) with extraordinarily able students because it is more effective at differentiating exceptionally gifted from moderately gifted children. However, Robinson (1992) countered Silverman and Kearney with two important points. First, the norms of the SB: IV are superior when compared to the 1972 norms of the Stanford-Binet (L-M). In fact, with the publication of this chapter we are now over fifteen years beyond the 1986 norms of the SB: IV. When the Stanford Binet 5 is published (scheduled for release after 2003), the availability of more recent norms will make a compelling argument for its use. Robinson's (1992) second point concerned the usefulness of the factoral structure (e.g., memory, verbal, quantitative, and abstract visual reasoning) of the SB: IV, and the "power" of that structure for understanding a child's pattern of abilities.
1988	The Jacob K. Javits Gifted and Talented Students Act reestablished modest (not exceeding 10 million dollars on an annual basis) federal funding for gifted programs.
1990	The Differential Abilities Scale, a revision and extension of the 1980 British Ability Scales (Elliott, 1990) was published. This is a relatively new instrument and reflects information-processing theories and approaches to understanding human abilities.
1993	*The National Excellence Report: A Case for Developing America's Talent* (Ross, 1993) was published by the U.S. Department of Education's Office of Educational Research and Improvement. The report offers a new federal definition which has been adopted by several states (see Table 10.2, Part B).

Table 10.2 1972 and 1993 Federal Definitions of Gifted and Talented

Part A: 1972 Marland Definition (Public Law 91-230, section 806)

Gifted and talented children are those identified by professionally qualified persons, who by virtue of outstanding abilities are capable of high performance. These are children who require differentiated educational programs and/or services beyond those normally provided by the regular school program in order to realize their contribution to self and society.

Children capable of high performance include those with demonstrated achievement and/or potential ability in any of the following areas, singly or in combination:

1. general intellectual ability
2. specific academic aptitude
3. creative or productive thinking
4. leadership ability
5. visual and performing arts
6. psychomotor ability*

It can be assumed that utilization of these criteria for identification of the gifted and talented will encompass a minimum of 3 to 5% of the school population.

Part B: 1993 National Excellence Report Definition (Based upon the Federal Javits Gifted and Talented Education Act)

Children and youth with outstanding talent perform or [who] show the potential for performing at remarkably high levels of accomplishment when compared with others of their age, experience, or environment.

These children and youth exhibit high performance capability in intellectual, creative, and/or artistic areas, possess an unusual leadership capacity, or excel in specific academic fields. They require services or activities not ordinarily provided by the schools.

Outstanding talents are present in children and youth from all cultural groups, across all economic strata, and in all areas of human endeavor.

This was later removed.

mends that placement decisions be based only on the Wechsler Scales (Wechsler, 1991), the Stanford-Binet Intelligence Scale: IV (Thorndike, Hagen, & Sattler, 1986), or the Differential Ability Scales (Elliott, 1990).

Placement is important, but it should not eclipse the equally important goal of programming. An assessment of a gifted child must go well beyond the administration of an intelligence test (a measure of general school ability), and should include measures of achievement, as well as the other components of an assessment: interviews, structured or unstructured observations, and informal procedures. In sum: the assessment should go beyond placement and should provide information that can assist in educational programming decisions. The application of assessment information for both placement and programming is demonstrated in two case studies (see Figures 10.1 and 10.2).

Two Case Studies

The two separate cases in Figures 10.1 and 10.2 demonstrate the usefulness of tests as part of the assessment process for gifted placement and programming. Figure 10.1 is a report of an assessment of Fred, an extremely able student. At the time of the report, Fred was placed in first grade in accordance with his age. However, as noted throughout the report, the first grade curriculum was so underchallenging that Fred was very frustrated, and his parents requested a grade-skip from first to seventh grade! Parents and school officials were each intractable in their positions and were ready to go to court for a placement ruling.

Throughout the report, there is a *School Psychologist's Perspective of the Assessment (SPPA),* which details the motivation for which tests were selected as well as the interpretation of the results. The purpose of reproducing the assessment report and the *SPPA* is not to recommend specific tests, but demonstrate how the tests "saved the school day" for this very gifted student.

For Fred, both the immediate as well as the long-term indicators of success were extremely positive. Six months after the results from the psychoeducational assessment were used to accelerate Fred from first grade to a third/fourth grade class, the unanimous conclusion was that the placement and the program were tremendously successful. The school personnel gained a new appreciation of Fred's ability and achievement, and the discussions about Fred opened up new opportunities for other gifted students.

Fred entered Purdue University at the age of eleven. He graduated from Purdue with a Doctor of Pharmacy degree at the age of 17, and enrolled in a Ph.D. program at Rockefeller University in New York.

Fred's case was litigious for two reasons: (a) he was extremely capable, and (b) there was a great deal of defensive reluctance by the educators because the results from the screening were incongruent with their informal observations. Cases like Fred's do not have to be controversial if educators and psychologists use the information from tests of ability, aptitude, and achievement to make decisions about placement and programming. Fred's assessment occurred prior to the development of the *Iowa Acceleration Scale* (IAS), which is discussed below and sections of which are presented in Figure 10.2. However, a discussion similar to that promoted by the process of using the IAS occurred with Fred, and it was that group discussion, based upon assessment data, that fostered an appropriate placement and program for this extremely gifted student.

An essential component to Fred's assessment was the professional administration and interpretation of the tests within the context of the information that had been gathered informally. An appreciation for the special programming needs of academically able students also is crucial. Additionally, it was important to convey this information to parents and educators in a way that would serve the child.

What Is the Role of Assessment in Whole-Grade Acceleration Decisions?

Despite the unequivocal evidence (DeHaan & Havighurst, 1961; Gallagher, 1996; Kulik & Kulik, 1984) supporting whole-grade acceleration as a programming option for gifted students, acceleration—or grade-skipping—remains a contentious issue.[1] Prior to the publication of guidelines for grade advancement (Feldhusen, Proctor, & Black, 1986), most decisions concerning grade acceleration were based upon the selective biases of a school administrator. In some instances, discussion about acceleration is precluded by a district's extant policy *against* acceleration. The Feldhusen et al. article was helpful to many gifted educators and parents of gifted students who found themselves in the role of advocate for acceleration without the tools to advocate effectively.

---

1. See Chapter 21 by Kulik.

The Connie Belin & Jacqueline N. Blank International Center
for Gifted Education and Talent Development

STUDENT: Fred D.
BIRTHDATE: April, 11
AGE: 6 years, 7 months
REPORT DATE: December 1
EVALUATION DATE: November 12–14
SCHOOL PSYCHOLOGIST: Susan G. Assouline, Ed.S., Ph.D.

Reason for Referral:

The superintendent of schools recommended that Dr. D. refer his son, Fred, to the Belin-Blank Center for an evaluation of Fred's academic achievement and for recommendations based upon that evaluation. At the time of the referral, Fred had been withdrawn from first grade in the local public school and was home-schooled.

School Psychologist's Perspective of the Assessment (SPPA): A good assessment begins with a question to be answered. There are two questions concerning this student: (1) What is the appropriate grade placement? (2) What is the appropriate academic program?

Background Information and Observations:
Fred had been evaluated previously at the age of 5 years, 2 months, and 6 years, 5 months. Each of these evaluations included the administration of an individual intelligence test (Stanford-Binet: Fourth Edition and the Wechsler Intelligence Scale for Children—Revised), and each evaluation resulted in confirmation of Fred's superior intellectual ability. The academic achievement tests administered during the previous evaluations were designed to provide a general indication of Fred's achievement in reading, mathematics, and spelling. The tests administered at the age of 6 years, 1 month were the Wide Range Achievement Test—Revised (WRAT-R) and the Basic Achievement Skills Individual Screener. *On these screening instruments, Fred performed at the seventh-grade level for reading, math, and spelling.* The two prior assessments resulted in two reports, and the primary recommendation from each of those reports was that consideration be given to Fred's program of study to determine the best way in which to meet his needs for academic stimulation and appropriate socialization with his schoolmates.

(SPPA): Two individual administrations of an intelligence test had been administered within a sixteen-month period, and each had yielded similar results. (At the time of this assessment, these were the most current results available.) There was no need for a third administration of an intelligence test.

However, the information from the previous administrations of measures of achievement was insufficient. The measures used were designed for screening; the information from them was inappropriate for a placement or a program decision. This is obvious in the vague recommendations that were presented with the results of these previous assessments.

Reports from the previous evaluations indicated that Fred had excellent concentration and attention, and my observations of Fred's ability to concentrate and attend to tasks verified the previously reported observations.

The statement concerning Fred's ability to concentrate is an example of nontest data that was part of the assessment. This observation is used in the recommendations.

Fred is right-handed and has worn corrective lenses for four months.

Interpretation of Results:
Tests Used

> Raven's Progressive Matrices (RPM)
> Stanford Diagnostic Reading Test (Green Level, Form A)
> Standard Reading Inventory (SRI)
> Stanford Diagnostic Mathematics Test (Green Level, Form A)
> Sequential Tests of Educational Progress (STEP): Basic Concepts and Computation

One of the goals of the present evaluation was to determine Fred's academic progress relative to his ability. Fred was asked to complete the Raven's Progressive Matrices (RPM), an untimed nonverbal test of figural reasoning. For this test, the individual is presented with 60 meaningless figures and is asked to discern the nature of the pattern for each figure and complete the relations. Fred correctly completed 41 out of 60 figures in 35 minutes and earned a score surpassing 98% of the *8-year-olds* in the normative sample (the highest raw score earned by the 6 ½-year-olds in the normative sample was 34). Thus, compared to the highest score earned by his *age-mates* in the normative sample, he was able to answer correctly 7 more items than the top-scoring individual(s). This is a significant discrepancy from the highest score earned by his age-mates and confirms that Fred's ability to form comparisons, reason by analogy, and organize spatial perceptions into systematically related wholes, as measured by this well-standardized instrument, is superior—even when compared to children two years older than he.

During an interview with Fred's father, Dr. D, he described Fred's routine at home. The family chose not to have a television in their home, and evenings were devoted to study and exploration of world events. It was obvious that Fred had been presented with considerable factual knowledge; however, all evidence indicated that he was ready not only for the exposure to this knowledge, but to process the information with reasoning skills that surpass those of bright students in higher grades. The results of the RPM support this observation.

Superior ability to process information and to attend to learning tasks is rare and requires careful tailor-

SSPA:
It was extremely important to determine how Fred's abstract reasoning skills compared to his age-mates as well as to older children. The comparison to age-mates responded to educators' concerns that there are "lots of bright children" in Fred's class, and Fred's academic needs are no different from theirs. The comparison to older children was equally important because abstract reasoning skills are part of an advanced curriculum that was under consideration.

In the parent interview, Dr. D. mentioned to the school psychologist that some educators believed that Fred was being pushed at home and that Fred was not ready for advanced material. During the presentation of the results to Fred's educators, the school psychologist corrected this misconception. On the contrary, Fred was doing what he was able to do. His parents were responding to his academic needs and were requesting that the school find an optimal match between the curriculum and Fred's ability and achievement.

Finding the optimal match between Fred's ability and achievement was the reason for completing the

ing of an individualized educational plan that will provide an optimal match between Fred's ability and achievement. The two previous psychoeducational reports included a screening of spelling, reading, and mathematics. The present assessment of reading and mathematics was more diagnostic in nature.

Reading: The Green Level (Form A) of the Stanford Diagnostic Reading Test was administered. The Green Level is designed for students in grades 3, 4, and 5 and provides comparative scores for a sample of students in those grades. Fred worked quickly through the sub-tests. The final passages were to be read silently, but Fred subvocalized each of those passages. Even though he worked quickly, he was not impulsive in his responses and he rechecked his answers to the questions.

When compared to fourth graders, Fred earned the percentile rankings reported below. Grade equivalent scores represent the typical performance of students in a specified grade. Because Fred is not a typical student, grade equivalents are not generally good comparative indicators; however, for our purpose of determining where to begin instruction, it was appropriate.

Stanford Diagnostic Reading	*Per-centile*	*Grade Equivalent*
(Green Level—Form A)	(Compared to fourth graders)	
Auditory discrimination	92	7.3
Phonetic analysis	95	>12
Structural analysis	83	6.8
Auditory analysis	51	3.9
Literal comprehension	74	4.7
Inferential comprehension	43	3.7

The "lowest" grade equivalent score (earned for inferential comprehension) was two grade levels above his present placement. The highest (earned for phonetic analysis) was beyond grade 12. Relatively speaking, Fred's auditory vocabulary, literal comprehension, and inferential comprehension, as measured by these subtests of the Stanford Diagnostic Reading Test, are not as well developed as his ability to discriminate auditorily, analyze the relationships between sounds and letters (phonetic

assessment. The screening instruments from the previous assessments were inadequate for this task. The tests that were chosen were diagnostic in nature and were administered so that specific suggestions regarding programming could be made.

analysis), and decode words through the analysis of word parts (structural analysis). In other words, the skills measured by the cognitively less demanding tasks of recognizing words and decoding them are more advanced than his *understanding* of common words and his general reading comprehension, especially his inferential comprehension.

The Standard Reading Inventory (SRI) was also administered, and the hypothesis that Fred's decoding skills were more developed than his comprehension skills was confirmed by the results of the SRI. He orally read the fourth- and fifth-grade passages with only a few minor pronunciation errors. It was noted that he read in a monotone. We did not go beyond the fourth- and fifth-grade passages, but he could probably read passages at a much higher grade level. However, it is unlikely that he could comprehend passages at the junior high grade levels. His silent reading speed was at the instructional level for grade 4, but not for grade 5.

Instructionally, Fred reached frustration (correctly answered four out of ten comprehension questions for both silent and oral reading) at the fourth grade level. He correctly answered four of the ten comprehension questions for the fifth-grade oral reading passage, but he answered only two of the ten comprehension questions correctly for the fifth-grade silent reading passage. He subvocalized while he was reading this passage.

Coupled with the information from the Stanford Diagnostic Reading Test, it appears that providing material at an advanced third- or fourth-grade level would be instructionally appropriate. Fred's ability to decode written words will continue to be far superior to his ability to comprehend for several more years. Fred could probably read a sixth- or seventh-grade social studies text, but his thinking is not yet sophisticated enough to comprehend the material fully and draw inferences. He needs time to allow underlying cognitive functions necessary for comprehending to develop and mature.

Reading: Fred needs only limited instruction in decoding or phonics. It is recommended that an instructional program emphasize the development of his comprehension skills. His overall comprehension is at an advanced third-grade or beginning fourth-grade level, and instruction with materials at

SSPA:
Since reading is one of the most important elementary school activities, a careful assessment of Fred's reading skills was critical. Additionally, this case almost went to court because the initial screening information suggested a "reading level of seventh grade," and the parents used that information to advocate that Fred be placed in grade 7. School personnel reacted strongly against this and wanted to keep Fred in grade 1.

The distinction between Fred's decoding skills and his comprehension skills was important because it begins to explain why parents and educators had seemingly incompatible programming goals. The parents were focusing on the highly developed decoding skills (especially as reported in a previous screening assessment), but the educators were convinced that Fred would not survive in seventh-grade classes—even though he could "read" the material.

All of the above information, which was based upon data from the assessment, leads to the recommendation below.

these levels would probably provide sufficient challenge. To continue developing his comprehension skills, Fred needs: (1) time for the underlying cognitive processes to mature, and (2) the opportunity to interact with students who are at a similar level of comprehension. These students will likely be found in higher grades. If Fred is accelerated into third or fourth grade, it would be appropriate to place him with the most advanced reading group.

Although his reading comprehension skills are (relatively) not as superior as his skills at decoding words, they are still superior when compared to those of his age- or grade-mates. The fact that his ability to comprehend ranges from two to four grade levels above his age-mates means he will need special arrangements for reading instruction. A whole-language approach to reading and writing instruction might foster Fred's progress in each of these areas. However, it would be important *not* to use a grade-level basal for whole-language instruction. Rather, Fred will need exposure to literature such as that provided by the Great Books Series.

Mathematics: Mathematics was the other curriculum area for which programming recommendations were needed. Three mathematics tests were administered before finding one that was appropriately difficult. The Green Level (Form A) of the Stanford Diagnostic Mathematics Test was the first test administered. The green level was developed for students in grades 4, 5, or 6. Fred finished the whole test in less than an hour (95 minutes is allowed). When compared to fifth graders, he earned the following percentiles for the three sub-tests:

Stanford Diagnostic Mathematics Test

Subtest	Percentile Rank Compared to Fifth Grader
Number system and numeration	86
Computation	85
Applications	94

The Stanford Diagnostic Mathematics Test did not appear to be sensitive enough to prescribe specific instruction. Therefore, the Basic Concepts and Computation tests of the Sequential Tests of Educational Progress (STEP) were administered.

The Basic Concepts test designed for grades 6–9 was too difficult, as evidenced by his performance: Fred required all 40 minutes to answer 24 of the 50 questions; and he correctly answered only 14 questions, which placed him at the 8th percentile when compared to ninth graders. It was decided not to give him the middle school/junior high level of the Computation test. There was concern that he would be unnecessarily frustrated.

Therefore, the lower level of the STEP Basic Concepts and Computation tests, which were designed for grades 3–5, was administered. On this level of the Basic Concepts test, Fred correctly answered 38 out of 50 items in 35 minutes. When compared to second-semester fifth graders, this score is at the 83rd percentile. Eight of the 12 missed items required manipulation of number concepts. On the Computation subtest, Fred correctly answered 53 out of 60 items in 28 minutes. This score is at the 90th percentile when compared to second-semester fifth graders.

Recommendation for Mathematics: The fact that Fred did so well on both of the tests designed for third through fifth graders indicates that he has relatively few, if any, gaps in his mathematics knowledge base. The biggest concern is that he not rush too quickly into pre-algebra and algebra because he needs time to allow for the development of the necessary cognitive structures that will foster success in more abstract mathematics such as algebra and geometry. Unlike many extremely precocious students, Fred has not developed sloppy habits. He did not do all of his work in his head; rather, he was careful to work out the problems on scratch paper. However, if he remains unchallenged, he will most likely develop poor work habits because performing computations mentally will be one of the only ways that he can mentally challenge himself.

Summary and General Recommendations:
Given Fred's superior performance on the two previously administered individual intelligence tests, as well as his superior performance on the RPM, one would predict that his academic achievement would be at least two grade levels above that of his age- or grade-mates. Indeed, Fred has fully utilized his superior academic ability and has achieved at a level commensurate with that ability. Fred has excellent concentration and attending skills and could easily

SSPA:
For a more complete discussion of elementary students who are mathematically talented, see *Jane and Johnny Love Math: Recognizing and Encouraging Mathematical Talent in Elementary Students* (Lupkowski & Assouline, 1992) and *Developing Mathematical Talent: A Guide for Teachers and Parents of Gifted Students* (Assouline & Lupkowski-Shoplik, in press).

succeed in third- or fourth-grade material. For some tasks, such as decoding and basic computation, even fourth-grade material will be too easy for him.

The more routine school tasks (i.e., decoding of words and basic mathematics computation) are about as fully developed as can be expected for a 6 ½-year-old child, and his ability to concentrate and attend has been well honed. *Fred is at a critical point in his academic development. He will not lose his ability to learn, but if he is not sufficiently challenged he may lose his love for learning and will likely develop poor study habits.*

- With regard to his general reading comprehension, placing him in an advanced third-, fourth-, or fifth-grade class seems most appropriate.
- Because his reading and math comprehension skills seem to be equally developed, it would make sense to consider whole-grade rather than subject-matter acceleration. For subjects such as science and social studies, Fred is probably ready to begin receiving instruction at a third-, fourth-, or even fifth-grade level. Pre-testing in these subject areas would be appropriate.

The school system is fortunate that Fred's parents are able and willing to fill in any gaps in Fred's instruction that might occur as a result of accelerating Fred by two or more grades. When students who have superb ability to learn are tutored at home, it is sometimes believed that the parents' opinion is suspect because parents have invested so much in their child's education. My sense of the situation is that Dr. D has tapped into his son's strengths and has helped his son realize those strengths. Fred took the tests at the Belin-Blank Center by himself and demonstrated extremely mature behavior. His behavior was more similar to that of a mature, extremely intelligent eight- or nine-year-old. His demeanor is like that of a well-behaved upper elementary student.

Fred has achieved through home schooling provided by his parents, but he needs the opportunity to interact with peers. He also needs exposure to extracurricular activities and contests, such as spelling bees, the Mathematical Olympiad for Elementary Students, and science projects that are typically assigned in the upper elementary grades. In determining an appropriate placement for Fred, attention should be paid to the most academically comfortable setting, that is, third, fourth, or fifth grade, as well as the most emotionally comfortably setting. The receiving teacher(s), parents, and administrator(s) should discuss the most appropriate setting.

An understanding teacher who can adequately prepare his or her class to welcome a new student (who is younger, yet equally or more able), and who can communicate effectively with the parents is most important.

- I have recommended that Dr. and Mrs. D continue to provide enriching educational experiences for their son. However, it was suggested that these experiences might focus on opportunities that are not traditionally offered in the public school. For example, Fred would probably do well if exposed to one or two foreign languages, as well as a musical instrument. Activities in sports and social groups such as Cub Scouts are also to be encouraged. When he is old enough (probably around age 11 or 12), Fred would probably benefit from summer academic programs offered by universities such as the University of Iowa.
- Follow-up every three or four months with the Belin-Blank Center Staff, to be initiated by Dr. and Mrs. D, is strongly recommended.

SSPA:
Follow-up is a critical component of a successful assessment and intervention.

Figure 10.1   Psychological Interpretive Report.

Southern and Jones (1991) and Passow (1993) moved the debate about the advantages of acceleration forward. In 1993 Assouline, Colangelo, and Lupkowski published the *Iowa Acceleration Scale (IAS),* a guidance tool designed to facilitate discussions and decisions about acceleration. In 1999 the manual for the *Iowa Acceleration Scale* (IAS) (Assouline, Colangelo, Lupkowski-Shoplik, & Lipscomb, 1999) was published. The *Iowa Acceleration Scale (IAS)* and the accompanying manual were developed to guide educators in making recommendations about accelerating a student. Because no single definition exists as to what qualifies a student for whole-grade acceleration, one goal of the IAS is to provide exclusionary indicators of the appropriateness of acceleration as an educational option for students in kindergarten through eighth grade.

The indicators of the IAS include school-related issues, such as class attendance and the student's attitude toward learning; developmental factors, such as body size and fine and gross motor coordination; interpersonal skills, which assess how effectively a student interacts with others; and attitude and support of the principal individuals involved in the student's academic life. These issues represent the informal components of the IAS.

The IAS also requires information from tests of academic achievement and ability. With respect to academic ability, a formal measure of intelligence is one of the critical aspects underlying acceleration decisions using the IAS. Both group-administered and individually administered test scores can be used. A score representing superior intelligence is required before other indicators on the IAS can even be

Figure 10.2 The Iowa Acceleration Scale.

IAS Example: Jenny
The Iowa Acceleration Scale Form*

Section I: General Information

Part A: Student Information

Student Name _Jenny_

Student Address __1234 Small Road_

_____ _Mid-Sized Town, Midwestern State 12345_

Student Phone Number _123-4567_ Gender _Female_

Present School _Presidential Elementary_ Present Grade _3rd_ Proposed Grade _5th_

School Address _5678 Main Street_

_____ _Mid-Sized Town, Midwestern State 12345_

	Year	Month	Day
Date of IAS Completion (Today's Date)	__	_12_	_3_
Student's Date of Birth	__	_3_	_14_
Student's Chronological Age	_8_	_8_	_19_

Part B: Family Information

Father: _Steve_ Occupation: _Banker_

Does parent live with child? Yes _X_ No ___ Sometimes ___

Mother: _Cindi_ Occupation: _Teacher_

Does parent live with child? Yes _X_ No ___ Sometimes ___

Names of Siblings	Gender	Age	School Grade Name of School
Ken	_Male_	_8_	_Junior High_

Part C: Child Study Team Information

Names/Position of Individuals Participating in Acceleration/Decision/Planning:

Principal _Mrs. S._ Parent (Guardian) _Steve & Cindi_

Present Teacher _Mrs. P_ Receiving Teacher _Mrs. R._

Other (e.g., Gifted Ed. Coordinator, School Counselor, School Psychologist) _Mrs. E. (G/T Coordinator)_

---

*Sections of the Iowa Acceleration Scale (IAS) have been reprinted with permission of Great Potential Press (formerly Gifted Psychology Press). This publication, or parts thereof, may not be reproduced in any form without written permission of Great Potential Press.

Name of Person Completing this Form: ___*Mrs. E.*___

        Position: ___*G/T Coordinator*___

Who initiated the consideration of acceleration?   Student _X_ (see attached letter) Parents ____

        Educator _____ (Please indicate name: _____ and position: _____)

(Sections II through V have been omitted from this figure. See the IAS manual for a detailed description of these Sections.)

Section VI: Academic Ability and Achievement

Part A: Ability Test Results

NOTE: although an IQ score is not a perfect measure of ability, research has shown that individualized intelligence test scores are excellent predictors of academic success.

For each item below, *circle the number* to the right of the response that best describes the results of tests which the student has completed.

On an individualized intelligence test (name of test:___*WISC-III*___) administered within the last three years, the student's overall IQ score was:

                                                               Please circle one

Between one and two standard deviations above the mean (115–129)   1

Between two and three standard deviations above the mean (130–144)   ②

Three or more standard deviations above the mean (145–above)   4

If a score is unavailable, an individualized IQ test, such as the WISC-III, Binet IV, or W-J Cognitive Ability Scale, should be administered and the results incorporated into this decision-making process about acceleration. (If the score is below 115, see Section II, Critical Items.)

Comments or concerns: *Verbal Score in Superior Range, Performance Score in High Average to Above Average Range. This is NOT a concern.*

Part B: Achievement Test Results

Grade level achievement test administered within the last year:

    Name of test: ___*ITBS*___

    Please indicate the type of test used: Individual ____ Group _X_

Above-grade level achievement test administered within the last year (if available):

    Name of test: _____

    Please indicate the type of test used: Individual ____ Group _X_

Please *circle one number* in each category for #1 (i.e., grade level test results). Then *circle one number* in each category for #2 (i.e., above-grade level test results), *or circle the option given for #3* if above-grade level test results are not available.

	Vocab-ulary	Total Reading	Total Math	Total Language	Social Studies	Science	Other (Math Concepts)
1. On a grade level test, the student:							
Performed at < 90th Percentile:	0	0	0	0	⓪	⓪	0
Performed at > 90th Percentile	②	②	②	②	2	2	②
2. On an above-grade level test, the student:							
Performed at < 90th Percentile:	0	0	0	0	0	0	0
Performed at ≥ 90th Percentile:	2	2	2	2	2	2	2
3. Above-grade level test results not available	-	-	-	-	-	-	-

Comments or concerns: *Language Total from Grade 1 not available for Grade 2*

Add all of the numbers circled from Part A and Part B to calculate the Academic Ability and Achievement (AAA) Subtotal: *12*
If this (AAA) subtotal score is < 10, whole-grade acceleration is *not recommended.*
If the score is ≥ 10, continue on to the next section of this form.

Section VII: School and Academic Factors

Please *circle the number* to the right of the statement that best describes the student.
1. Grade Placement Under Consideration

Please circle one

Acceleration would result in a change in building at the beginning of the first semester of the academic year (e.g., elementary to junior high). In this case, a plan for transition is needed. — ⓪

Acceleration would require the student to attend some classes in another building. — 1

Early entrance would be to kindergarten. — 3

Early entrance would be to first grade. — 4

Comments or concerns: *Acceleration would mean a change in building.*

(The following items have been omitted from Figure 10.2: items 2–7 from Sections VII: School and Academic Factors; Section VIII: Developmental Factors; Section IX: Interpersonal Skills; and items 16–18 of Section X: Attitude and Support.)

Section X: Attitude and Support

19. Planning for Acceleration Prior to Completing the IAS Form

Please circle one

No prior planning or gathering of information has taken place or been shared
regarding this student's acceleration   0

Limited staffing, information sharing, and planning have occurred regarding
this student's acceleration   ①

Extensive staffing, planning, and discussion have occurred regarding this
student's acceleration   2

Comments or concerns: _____

Section XI: Scale Subtotals, IAS Grand Total, and Guidelines

Is the Academic Ability and Achievement (AAA) Subtotal Score ≥10? Yes __X__ No ____
    If AAA Subtotal is <10, *do not* consider whole-grade acceleration.

Academic Ability and Achievement Subtotal   *12* of a possible 32 points

School and Academic Factors Subtotal   *15* of a possible 22 points

Developmental Factors Subtotal   *6* of a possible 9 points

Interpersonal Skills Subtotal   *14* of a possible 16 points

Attitude and Support Subtotal   *8* of a possible 11 points

Add the above five scale subtotals together to equal the IAS Grand Total:

Iowa Acceleration Scale Grand Total __55__ of a possible 90 points

Guideline for Interpreting the Iowa Acceleration Scale Grand Total:

70 to 90 total points	Student is an excellent candidate for whole-grade acceleration. Acceleration is recommended.
54 to 69 total points	Student is a good candidate for whole-grade acceleration. Acceleration is recommended.
43 to 53 total points	Student is a marginal candidate for whole-grade acceleration. There is no clear recommendation. Review materials closely and carefully consider alternatives.
42 or fewer total points	Whole-grade acceleration is *not recommended.* Consider single-subject acceleration, mentoring, enrichment, or other alternatives.

Analysis of Team Decision and Outcome

Jenny:
Current Grade: 3rd Grade, with acceleration in Reading and Language Arts
Proposed Grade for Acceleration: 5th Grade
IAS Score: 55 (Good Candidate for Whole-Grade Acceleration)

Overall, Jenny is a good candidate for acceleration into the fifth grade. One concern did suppress her score, and this was indicated in Section VII, Item 1, Grade Placement Under Consideration. Jenny earned a zero on this item, because acceleration at this point in time would result in a mid-year change in buildings—she would be moved from the elementary school to the junior high school. Because the acceleration is still recommended, however, a plan needs to be in place so that Jenny can make the necessary adjustments in the new environment. This plan includes specifically implementing some of the typical transition activities experienced by fourth graders.

Note: In reality, Jenny's acceleration took place several years ago. Because of this, we have been able to track her progress. At the beginning of the trial period, Jenny was treated much like a transfer student and was given special consideration regarding the change in her routine. In no time, though, her mother reported that Jenny had adapted to the new setting like "a fish to water." A critical factor to the success of this intervention was the receiving teacher's willingness and openness to having Jenny in her class. This set the tone for the rest of the class. Additionally, the receiving teacher was involved in the planning phase of the acceleration process, which eased some of Jenny's anxieties. It was clear from the beginning of the process that Jenny knew what she wanted and was willing to work with the teachers to assure that she was in a challenging setting.

Jenny was very satisfied with her school experience as a result of the acceleration. She was appropriately challenged, and her enthusiasm for school remained undiminished throughout high school and into college. All indicators continue to confirm that the acceleration was a successful educational intervention.

Jenny's Letter to the Principal

Dear Mrs. S

I find that the work I'm being given Is very discouraging because its much to easy.
Most of it I know so I do the work catch on and I have to wait for the others to catch on.
The grade I'd like to go to best would be college but since I can't could I have something
more challenging. Say for Instence I could go to any Grade I want as long as Long as
its in Presidential Elementary Or Presidential Middle School. I like to trie 5th Grade
I dout it but it would be nice to go ther and see what its like. I don't care if I leave
Presidential Elementary cause I really don't have any thing really Inporntant or true
friends that I'd miss

Sincerely, Jenny

considered. As demonstrated in the sample case (see Figure 10.2), and in addition to the required information from an IQ test, the IAS asks for achievement results from both grade-level and above-grade-level testing. A student *must* have grade-level test results; and although above-grade-level testing is not required, it is strongly recommended. (With the increase in participation in talent searches of both elementary and middle school students, above-level test results are more readily available.)

Figure 10.2 includes an example of items from an actual case in which the IAS was used to make a whole-grade acceleration decision. "Jenny" is a real student who is currently in her first year of college. Included in Figure 10.2 is a letter that is reproduced exactly as Jenny wrote it. In this letter,

Jenny expressed her desire to be skipped into a higher grade. Her motivation and advanced language skills are apparent in this poignant letter. The absence of above-level testing information should be noted. When Jenny's case was presented, the availability of above-level testing through elementary talent searches was relatively limited, and Jenny's school district was not participating at that time. Nonetheless, the team's ultimate decision was that she be accelerated.[2]

When Is an Assessment Important for a Gifted Student?

Identification and Programming

The National Association for Gifted Children (1998) *Pre-K—Grade 12 Gifted Program Standards* includes five guiding principles, two of which are relevant to a discussion about assessment. Principle 3 states that, "A student assessment profile of individual strengths and needs must be developed to plan appropriate intervention." Exemplary standards for this principle state that "Individual assessment plans should be developed for all gifted learners who need gifted education. An assessment profile should reflect the gifted learner's interests, learning style, and educational needs." Principle 4 states that, "All student identification procedures and instruments must be based on current theory and research." The exemplary standards for this principle include: "Student assessment data should come from multiple sources and include multiple assessment methods. . . . Student assessment data should represent an appropriate balance of reliable and valid quantitative and qualitative measures."

Although these standards are well intentioned, they do not provide the typical educator of the gifted with a great deal of guidance about specific steps to take. Educators need to be thoroughly informed before embarking on an assessment. However, only through an assessment will educators be able to provide students with a curriculum that is based upon the learner's needs.

The Twice-Exceptional Student

The twice-exceptional student is exceptional in at least two ways: (a) Giftedness is one of the exceptionalities, and (b) one or more disabilities, for example, a physical, learning, and/or emotional disability, represents the second exceptionality. Combining the terms *gifted* and *learning disabled* may seem to pose a conflict to some, especially to those who may still adhere to Terman's (1925) conclusions. Although Terman's work was important because it dispelled the myth of the sickly, socially awkward child and introduced us to the gifted child as an individual with superior intelligence, in good health, and socially well adjusted, these same conclusions masked our awareness that some gifted children also had physical, learning, or social-emotional exceptionalities that needed to be addressed.

Since the 1975 passage of PL 94-142, there is increased public awareness regarding the characteristics of all students with disabilities. Public awareness has grown to recognize that many students with disabilities are also gifted, and vice versa. For comprehensive discussions on students who are gifted and learning disabled, see Brody and Mills (1997) and Coben and Vaughn (1994). Kaufmann and Castellanos (2001) provide an excellent review of the gifted student with ADHD, and Neihart (2000) posits that gifted children with Asperger's Syndrome are under-identified because some of their behaviors are incorrectly attributed to learning disabilities.

For most students who are twice-exceptional, an IQ test is a critical first step to discovering their giftedness, but the analysis of the IQ test profile must go beyond the score to look at patterns of strengths and weaknesses, especially within the context of the newer theories of intelligences.[3]

Which Tests Are Recommended for the Assessment of Gifted Students?

Assouline and Lupkowski-Shoplik (in press) have developed for educators and parents "Consumer Guidelines for Educational Assessments," which includes:

1. The assessment question guides the selection of tests and drives the recommendations. Parents should be

---

2. In the IAS manual, Jenny's case is reproduced in its entirety. Sections of Jenny's case have been reprinted in Figure 10.2 with permission of the publisher, Great Potential Press, formerly Gifted Psychology Press.

---

3. See Chapter 7 by Sternberg and Chapter 8 by von Károlyi, Ramos-Ford, and Gardner.

involved in formulating the assessment question.

2. Know what types of tests are appropriate and useful for obtaining the needed information. A general ability test can be helpful in predicting success in school, but won't give enough specific information about a child's specific aptitude, for example, mathematics, to determine placement in a mathematics class or programming within that class.

3. Confirm that the person conducting the assessment has appropriate training. A teacher who is familiar with the directions can administer some tests. Other tests require extensive training, and the person administering them usually has an advanced degree.

4. Test results should be reported in written form. This report should include the actual test scores, which should be presented within an educational context. A test score, by itself, is of little value.

5. Verify that the report will include several specific recommendations individualized to the child who was tested. A photocopied list of pre-published educational practices is not acceptable.

6. Reports should be completed and sent in a timely fashion, that is, within one month after the assessment has been completed. Parents should be notified of any delays.

7. Parents should know whether a test will be administered as a group or individually. If the test is individually administered, parents should know in advance whether the test is designed for electronic response, paper and pencil response, or whether the student will respond orally.

8. Cost may be an issue for some parents. At one end of the cost-continuum, testing might be done through the school district at no cost to parents. At the other end of the cost-continuum, parents might pay several hundred dollars, especially for a thorough assessment that includes an individualized intelligence test.

SUMMARY AND CONCLUSIONS

This chapter highlighted the brief history of testing and its role in the educational lives of gifted children. Much of the chapter was a defense of testing as the primary way in which psychologists and educators obtain the information necessary for placement and programming. Although the general public, as well as some educators, sometimes criticize testing as an unnecessary educational practice, there is strong evidence that testing should continue to be an integral part of the education of all students, and gifted students in particular. The two case studies demonstrated the importance of a professional interpretation of the results from testing to the educational decision-making process.

QUESTIONS FOR THOUGHT AND DISCUSSION

1. What can an individualized intelligence test tell you about a student? How important is the score from an IQ test to the understanding of a student's learning needs?

2. According to Assouline, testing is one of four components of an assessment. Why was testing described as the most important component? How do the other three components fit into an assessment?

3. Imagine that a school board member wants to eliminate testing from the gifted education program to save money. The person believes that testing should be replaced with "portfolio assessment." List five to seven points from this chapter that would be your response to this board member's recommendation.

4. Think of an elementary student in your school district who needs accelerated experiences. How would testing fit into curricular planning for that student?

5. Some gifted students also have a learning and/or social emotional disability. How can an assessment help educators and parents achieve a better understanding of such a student?

REFERENCES

American Heritage College Dictionary (3rd ed.). (1993). Boston: Houghton Mifflin Co.

Anastasi, A. (1988). *Psychological testing* (6th ed.). New York: Macmillan.

Assouline, S. G., Colangelo, N., & Lupkowski, L. (1993). *The Iowa acceleration scale.* Belin-Blank Center, The University of Iowa, Iowa City.

Assouline, S. G., Colangelo, N., Lupkowski-Shoplik, A. E., & Lipscomb, J. (1999). *The Iowa Acceleration Scale manual.* Scottsdale, AZ: Gifted Psychology Press.

Assouline, S. G., & Lupkowski-Shoplik, A. E. (In press). *Developing mathematical talent: A guide for teachers and parents of gifted students.* Waco, TX: Prufrock Press.

Brody, L. E., & Mills, C. J. (1997). Gifted children with learning disabilities. *Journal of Learning Disabilities, 30,* 282–296.

Coben, S. S., & Vaughn, S. (1994). Gifted students with learning disabilities: What does the research say? *Learning Disabilities: A Multidisciplinary Journal, 5*(2), 87–94.

DeHaan, R. F., & Havighurst, R. (1961). Educating gifted children (rev. ed.). Chicago: University of Chicago Press.

Elliott, C. D. (1990). *Differential ability scales.* San Antonio, TX: Psychological Corporation.

Feldhusen, J. F., & Jarwan, F. A. (1993). Identification of gifted and talented youth for educational programs. In K. A. Heller, F. J. Mönks, & A. H. Passow

(Eds.), *International handbook of research and development of giftedness and talent* (pp. 233–252). Oxford: Pergamon.

Feldhusen, J. F., Proctor, T. B., & Black, K. N. (1986). Guidelines for grade advancement of precocious children. *Roeper Review, 9,* 25–27.

Gallagher, J. J. (1996). Educational research and education policy: The strange case of acceleration. In C. P. Benbow & D. Lubinski (Eds.), *Intellectual talent: Psychometric and social issues* (pp. 83–92). Baltimore: Johns Hopkins University Press.

Galton, F. (1869). *Hereditary genius.* New York: Macmillan.

Hammill, D. D., Brown, L., & Bryant, B. R. (1992). A consumer's guide to tests in print (2nd ed.). Austin, TX: Pro-Ed.

Kaufmann, F. A., & Castellanos, F. X. (2001). Attention-Deficit/Hyperactivity disorder in gifted students. In K. A. Heller, F. J. Mönks, R. J. Sternberg, & R. Subotnik (Eds.), *International handbook for research on giftedness* (2nd ed., pp. 621–632). New York: Elsevier.

Kulik, J. A., & Kulik, C. C. (1984). The effects of accelerated instruction on students. *Review of Educational Research, 54,* 409–425.

Lohman, D. F., & Hagen, E. P. (2001). The Cognitive Abilities Test (Form 6). Chicago: Riverside Publishing.

Lupkowski, A. E., & Assouline, S. G. (1992). *Jane and Johnny love math: Recognizing and encouraging mathematical talent in elementary students.* Unionville, NY: Trillium Press.

McGrew, K. S., & Flanagan, D. P. (1998). *The intelligence test desk reference.* Boston: Allyn and Bacon.

Murphy, L. L., Impara, J. C., & Plake, B. S. (Eds.). (1999). *Tests in print V.* Lincoln, NE: Buros Institute of Mental Measurements.

Naglieri, J. A., & Kaufman, J. C. (2001). Understanding intelligence, giftedness and creativity using the PASS Theory. *Roeper Review, 23,* 151–156.

National Association for Gifted Children. (1998). *Pre-K—grade 12 gifted program standards* [Electronic version]. Retrieved from http://www.nagc.org/webprek12.htm.

Neihart, M. (2000). Gifted children with Asperger's Syndrome. *Gifted Child Quarterly, 44,* 222–230.

Otis, A. S., & Lennon, R. T. (1995). *The Otis-Lennon school ability test* (7th ed.). San Antonio: Hartcourt Brace Educational Measurement.

Passow, H. (1993). Nation/state policies regarding education of the gifted. In K. A. Heller, F. J. Mönks, & A. H. Passow (Eds.), *International handbook of research and development of giftedness and talent* (pp. 29–46). Oxford: Pergamon.

Robinson, N. M. (1992). Stanford-Binet IV, of course! Time marches on! *Roeper Review, 15,* 32–34.

Ross, P. O. (1993). *National excellence: A case for developing America's talent.* Washington, DC: U.S. Department of Education.

Sattler, J. M. (2001). *Assessment of children* (4th ed.). San Diego: Sattler.

Silverman, L. K., & Kearney, K. (1992). The case for the Stanford-Binet L-M as a supplemental test. *Roeper Review, 15,* 34–37.

Southern, W. T., & Jones, E. D. (1991). *The academic acceleration of gifted children.* New York: Teachers College Press.

Terman, L. M. (1921). A symposium: Intelligence and its measurement. *Journal of Educational Psychology, 12,* 127–133.

Terman, L. M. (1925). *Genetic studies of genius* (vol. 1). Stanford: Stanford University Press.

Thorndike, R. L., Hagen, E. P., & Sattler, J. M. (1986). *Stanford-Binet intelligence scale* (4th ed.). Chicago: Riverside.

U.S. Commissioner of Education. (1972). *Education of the gifted and talented* (Report to the Congress). Washington, DC: U.S. Government Printing Office.

Wassermann, S. (2001). Quantum theory, the uncertainty principle, and the alchemy of standardized testing. *Phi Delta Kappan, 83*(1), 28–40.

Wechsler, D. (1991). *Manual for the Wechsler Intelligence Scale for Children—third edition.* San Antonio: The Psychological Corporation.

Wiggins, G. P. (1993). *Assessing student performance.* San Francisco: Jossey-Bass.

11

Excellence with Justice in Identification and Programming

E. SUSANNE RICHERT, *Global Institute for Maximizing Potential, Ocean Grove, New Jersey[1]*

At the beginning of this millennium, economically disadvantaged and socially or linguistically diverse gifted students in the United States are less and less likely to have their needs met in public schools because of the confluence of several national trends. First, the heterogeneous grouping movement, a misguided democratic effort, has had a devastating effect especially on elementary and middle school programs for the gifted, and especially in states without rigorous mandates or generous funding for programs for the gifted. Second, the political movement for "excellence" in education based on increasingly demanding "standards" which some leaders in our field initially lauded as expanding opportunities for advanced learners, has had a negative impact on gifted education. Under the guise of "excellence for all," excellence for the minority of students with gifted potential, regardless of social background, has too often been sacrificed, especially in elementary and middle schools (Ortiz, 2000). Furthermore, increased reliance on culturally biased norm-referenced or performance tests at all grade levels, but particularly at the secondary level, has reduced the proportion of culturally diverse students in "honors" or advanced placement classes. Third, the national impetus for school reform has led many schools to adopt reform models that eliminate programs for the gifted, especially in economically disadvantaged districts, which further exacerbates inequity (Office of Educational Research and Improvement, 1998; Northwest Regional Education Laboratory, 1998). This misguided reform effort deprives students with the most urgent need for programs of opportunities to achieve their highest potential.

Unless we can offer models for the education of the gifted that do not violate equity, gifted programs will continue to be eliminated in public schools. This chapter offers three pragmatic approaches, on which I have been conducting research over the last decade in order to counteract the devastating trends:

1. Identification procedures that equitably find giftedness in all populations;
2. Cost-effective program designs that guarantee equity in who is served;
3. Curriculum for all students that can both foster equity in identification and guarantee effective strategies in heterogeneous grouping.

These approaches guarantee equity, since they result in demographic heterogeneity in who is served. They satisfy the quest for excellence as well as cost-effectiveness in program design, since they have been demonstrated to result in statistically significant cognitive, affective, and social benefits to the students served, regardless of culture, economic class, or gender.

Problems in Programs for the Gifted

Elitism in Programs

Beginning with the National Report on Identification (Richert, 1985, 1987; Richert, Alvino, & McDonnel, 1982), I have been criticizing the following elitist practices that continue to jeopardize support for gifted programs: (1) elitist and distorted definitions of giftedness, (2) confusion about the purpose of identification, (3) violation of educational equity, (4) misuse and abuse of tests and test results, (5) cosmetic

---

1. www.globalinst.com.

and improper use of multiple criteria, and (6) elitist program design.

Also, these three problems have made gifted education vulnerable to attack from many sources, and are not easy to refute:

1. Elitist identification practices and definitions of giftedness create school segregation by economic class and cultural groups;
2. The most motivating and challenging curriculum is found in programs for the gifted, while curriculum for other programs is often monotonous and devoid of interest;
3. The best trained and most effective teachers work with the gifted, denying the benefits of these teachers to students of other abilities.

These serious problems have been raised by many educators and parents. Many national education associations have taken formal positions against tracking and various forms of ability grouping. The problems are polarizing champions of heterogeneous grouping versus advocates of differentiated educational provisions for the gifted. The result has been drastically reduced programs for the gifted in many districts, especially those with large culturally diverse populations.

The responses of most educators of the gifted to this relentless trend toward heterogeneous grouping have fallen into two extremes, neither of which is satisfactory. One position makes uncompromising elitist arguments for serving at least the "most gifted" students, who tend to be defined as exceptionally high IQ students and who most often are White with "disposable incomes," to use Sapon-Shevin's term (1994). This elitist stance has unfortunately generated fodder for the "egalitarian" positions of Oakes (1985), Goodlad and Oakes (1988), and Sapon-Shevin (1994), among others, as well as, ironically, the irresponsible policy recommendations against efforts at equity in education for the poor or culturally diverse made by Herrnstein and Murray (1994) in their controversial book *The Bell Curve.*

The other strategy is to yield to school reform efforts in a misguided attempt to serve the gifted in full-time heterogeneous classes, or to offer the panacea of "enrichment for all." This approach ignores the research-based needs of the gifted for various kinds of homogeneous grouping so effectively analyzed by

Kulik and Kulik (Kulik, 1992: Kulik & Kulik, 1987; see Chapter 21).

Elitist Definitions of Giftedness

Many districts and states continue to use elitist definitions of giftedness that result in the inclusion of only certain kinds of gifted students, most often those who are White, middle class, and academically achieving. A major purpose of the 1972 federal definition of giftedness (Marland, 1972), as well as the more recent *National Excellence: The Case for Developing America's Talent* (U.S. Department of Education, 1993), was to expand the concept of giftedness beyond IQ. Yet in practice, limited definitions are still applied, especially in states where *gifted* is a special education category and relies on special education funding.

Some state and local definitions distort the intention of these federal definitions by inappropriately distinguishing between *gifted* and *talented* students. This creates an elitist hierarchy. It uses the former term for general intellectual ability, as measured primarily by intelligence tests, and the latter for other gifted abilities referred to in the federal definition— that is, specific academic aptitude, creativity, leadership, and ability in the visual and performing arts. Some state departments of education, for example, that of New York, distort Renzulli's (1978) concept of giftedness (the interaction of above-average ability, creativity, and motivation) by designating as *gifted,* and thereby eligible for programs, those students who demonstrate all three abilities, and as *talented* those students who exhibit only two abilities (New York State Department of Education, n.d., p. 2).

Such distinctions ignore the differences between the manifestations of giftedness studied in adults and the potential for giftedness in children that gifted programs are designed to develop. False distinctions between *talented* and *gifted* among children or designating degrees of giftedness ("highly," "severely," "profoundly," or "exotically" gifted) create implicit hierarchies, engender elitism within programs, and exclude many students with gifted potential. Such hierarchies also ignore the fact that giftedness emerges through the interaction of innate abilities and learning or experience.

The major bias that impels these practices is the prevalent myth that academic achievement is directly related to adult eminence. Various studies (e.g., Baird, 1982; Munday & Davis, 1974; Taylor, Albo,

Holland, & Brandt, 1985) have found no correlation, or even a small negative correlation, between academic achievement and adult giftedness in a broad range of fields. This should not be surprising, because many of the evaluation criteria for determining grades, such as propensity for convergent thinking, conformity to expectations of teachers or test makers, and meeting externally determined deadlines, are inversely correlated with adult eminence or original contributions to most fields. These studies demonstrate that test scores predict test scores; grades predict grades. As Nairn (Nairn & Associates, 1980) and others have argued, socioeconomic status predicts both. Giftedness, or original contribution to a field, requires nonacademic abilities unrelated or inversely related to school achievement, such as creativity, passion, and intrinsic motivation.

Confusion about the Purposes of Identification

Confusion about the purposes of identification is often related to the needs and values of those involved in the process. The interest of some researchers has been in designating traits that will predict giftedness in adults, rather than in specifying necessary educational provisions. There also are educators who want the identification criteria (such as high grades and teacher recommendations) to reaffirm the values of conformity inherent in their school system. Some parents want to have a label for their children to affirm their own self-esteem (Miller, 1981).

But these are distortions of the purpose of programs for the gifted, which should be the development of latent and manifest potential in all areas. The identification process should be a *needs assessment* whose primary purpose is the placement of students into educational programs designed to develop their intellectual, emotional, and social potential.

Violation of Educational Equity

Typical identification procedures violate educational equity by consistently excluding large proportions of poor and culturally diverse gifted students. The conclusion of the *National Report on Identification* (Richert, Alvino, & McDonnel, 1982) is still accurate: measures of academic achievement most frequently used by schools are teacher recommendations, grades, and standardized tests (Ford, 1998). Demanding state performance assessments are also

still being used. These identification data, especially the latter, often screen out sub-populations that especially need programs, such as underachieving, learning-disabled, handicapped, and culturally diverse students with gifted potential. A significant finding of the *National Report* is unfortunately still true: Poor students are most consistently screened out of gifted programs, and their disadvantage cuts across every other sub-population. In addition, as Torrance (1979) argued, the majority of creative and divergent thinkers are excluded by using IQ as a criterion.

The U.S. Department of Education (1979), Richert et al. (1982), and Zappia (1989) reported a 30 to 70 percent underrepresentation of culturally different students in programs for the gifted in the United States, which has not improved in the last decade (Ford, 1998; see Chapter 39). Typical of the national pattern, the eight demographically diverse New Jersey districts that participated in Project APOGEE (Academic Programs for the Gifted with Excellence and Equity) originally had 10 to 75 percent underrepresentation of culturally diverse students (Richert & Wilson, 1995). Even more dramatic were the data on economic bias. The APOGEE districts started with 75 to 600 percent underrepresentation of economically disadvantaged students (defined as receiving free or reduced-priced lunch) in their programs for the gifted. The underrepresentation of poor African-American males, the group most at risk in U.S. schools, was over 800 percent in some districts. The shocking inequity is a problem not only for those excluded from gifted programs, it also has made programs vulnerable to charges of elitism.

Inappropriate, Cosmetic, and Distorting Use of Multiple Identification Criteria

The trend to use data from a variety of sources can actually be counterproductive. Many practitioners use combinations of test scores (IQ, achievement, or both), teacher observations, and sometimes parent observations in the identification process (Richert et al., 1982). The data, however, are often misused in several ways: The data may be unreliable, used at an inappropriate stage or sequence in the identification process, weighted in indefensible ways, or placed without validity in a matrix with other data.

Adding the results of various procedures, measures, and test scores and using the sum as the criterion for selection is the statistical equivalent of adding apples and oranges. The ranges, standard deviations, reliability, and construct and content validity of different measures, whether formal or informal, are not necessarily equivalent.

The statistically unsound, but widely used practice of giving equal weighting to data from multiple sources, or even using weighted-scoring procedures, was strongly criticized by a national panel of experts (Richert et al., 1982). Such combinations of data tend to screen out poor and culturally diverse students who might show giftedness in a single area. Combining data inappropriately tends to identify Jacks-of-all-trades. It may eliminate the "masters of some" and the current "masters of none"—those underachieving students who particularly need a gifted program to develop their unmanifested potential.

Even when multiple measures are used, standardized test scores tend to be given disproportionate weight. Also, the more measures that are used and combined inappropriately, the more likely it becomes that disadvantaged students (poor, minority, creative, and others who tend to be underachievers in schools) will be excluded. The recent move toward procedures that include "authentic" or "alternative" assessment is not necessarily helpful to the poor or culturally different, because, as Asa Hilliard (1993) forcefully argued, such procedures rely primarily on subjective, White, middle-class expectations.

In sum, the use of multiple measures, which may create the appearance of inclusiveness, may reinforce a narrow concept of giftedness and exacerbate the problem of elitism in identification. Another problem is the sequence in which multiple sources of data are used. If parents or teachers assess the creativity or motivation of students only *after* they have qualified for a talent pool with a high standardized achievement test score, then disadvantaged students already would have been screened out. If individualized IQ tests are given to students only *after* they qualify through a group IQ or achievement test, then underachieving students already will have been excluded. Such procedures are merely cosmetic efforts at equity, which actually may reinforce the exclusion of disadvantaged groups.

Those without training in characteristics of the gifted are often unreliable sources of identification data. Other sources of information that lead to bias and exclusion include locally designed check-lists and observation forms that are not research based (Richert, 1987; Richert et al., 1982).

Elitist Program Models

Limited school resources may set up counterproductive competition among groups vying for funds and services. Administrators often argue that limited funds allow only small numbers of gifted students to be served. As a result, parents whose children are being served tend to defend the status quo; they fear that their children will be excluded if culturally different and disadvantaged children are included. Similarly, parents of children who are not served in such programs are against allocating funds for programs that exclude their children. This kind of polarization, dramatized by Sapon-Shevin (1994), is used to argue that programs for the gifted cause a "disruption of community" and therefore should be eliminated.

One unfortunate outcome of educational reforms attempting to foster "excellence" has been the creation of elitist programs that serve as few as 1 to 3 percent of students. These programs look for and establish services for the "highly gifted." Program models that delineate a hierarchical pattern (pyramids or ladders; e.g., Cox, Daniel, & Boston, 1985) of degrees of giftedness, rather than an egalitarian and pluralistic model that simply acknowledges various kinds of gifted potential, polarize support for gifted programs.

Project APOGEE

In Project APOGEE, ethical principles and equitable identification procedures that I have been recommending since 1982 (Richert, 1987, 1990, 1994, 1995; Richert et al., 1982) were used in over 30 schools in 8 New Jersey school districts of various sizes and demographics. These rural, urban, and suburban districts included student populations that ranged from 185 to 28,461. The proportions of poor and culturally diverse students ranged from 2 to 87 percent. The more than 3,000 students identified for services included over 60 percent poor or culturally diverse students with gifted potential.

Principles of Identification

APOGEE applied these six identification principles that emerged through the deliberations of the national panel of experts as part of the *National Report on Identification* (Richert et al., 1982):

1. *Defensibility:* Procedures should be based on the best available research and recommendations.

2. *Advocacy:* Identification should be designed in the best interests of all students. Students should not be harmed by the procedures.

3. *Equity*

- Procedures should guarantee that no one is overlooked. Students from all groups should be considered for representation according to their demographic representation in the district.
- The civil rights of students to equal access to programs should be protected.
- Strategies should be specified for identifying the disadvantaged gifted.
- Cutoff scores should be avoided because they are the most common way that disadvantaged students are discriminated against. (High scores should be used to include students, but if students meet other criteria—through self or parent nominations, for example—then a lower test score should not be used to exclude them.)

4. *Pluralism:* The broadest defensible definition of giftedness should be used.

5. *Comprehensiveness:* As many learners with gifted potential as possible should be identified and served.

6. *Pragmatism:* Procedures should allow for cost-effective modification of available instruments and personnel.

Defensible Definitions

The *National Report on Identification* (Richert et al., 1982) analyzed a strong trend in the United States over the last half of this century toward broadening definitions to include multiple abilities and factors of giftedness. A few of the contributions to that direction include Guilford's (1967) multifactored structure-of-intellect model; Torrance's (1964) research in creativity; Renzulli's (1978) explanation of motivational factors in giftedness; Tannenbaum's (1983; see Chapter 4) emphasis on nonintellectual and social variables of giftedness; and my own insistence on the ethical component of giftedness (Richert, 1986, 1994).

In the area of cognitive science, Gardner (1983; see Chapter 8), Sternberg (1985; see Chapter 7), and Gagné (1985; see Chapter 5), as well as a special issue of the *Roeper Review* (Silverman, 1986), emphasize the recognition of diverse, discrete cognitive abilities in the identification of giftedness. In addition, I have argued for a comprehensive and pluralistic definition, one that not only acknowledges the

existence of various exceptional abilities, but also is ethical and will neither harm nor limit the potential of exceptional students from diverse backgrounds (Richert, 1986, 1987, 1994, 2000). It is more defensible in terms of the research, and more acceptable in terms of students' self-concepts, to view the identification process as a needs assessment that targets untapped gifted potential.

The pragmatic definition that was applied in APOGEE from 1990 to 1993 was to identify up to 25 percent of students within each demographic group. The 1993 federal definition supports this approach by arguing that "Children and youth of outstanding talent perform or show the potential for performing at remarkably high levels of accomplishment when *compared with others of their age, experience or environment* (U.S. Department of Education, 1993 italics added).

Selection of Tests and Instruments

In APOGEE, these precautions and recommendations of the panel of experts for the *National Report* about the appropriateness of tests for different abilities, populations, and stages of identification were followed:

1. Selection of different measures and procedures to identify each gifted ability;

2. Addressing the following issues before using any test:

- Is the test appropriate for the ability being sought?
- Is the test being used at the appropriate stage of identification (i.e., nomination into a broad talent pool; assessment for a specific program option; evaluation within a program)?
- Is the test appropriate for any disadvantaged groups in the district that are typically discriminated against in measures of academic achievement (e.g., poor, minority, creative, underachieving)?

Three Approaches to Equitable Identification of Disadvantaged Groups

While most states formally subscribe to the comprehensive federal definition of giftedness, in practice many local districts tend to seek—and to find—White, middle-class academic achievers. Measures of academic achievement that are most often used by schools, including teacher recommendations, grades, and especially standardized tests, have been amply demonstrated to have cultural biases (e.g., Black, 1963; Hoffman, 1962; Miller, 1974; Samuda, 1975). The *National Report on Identification* specified the following groups as being severely underrepresented in programs for the gifted:

• Poor students (e.g., students qualifying for free or reduced-price lunch)
• Culturally diverse students
• Students with minimal proficiency in English
• Males (when identifying verbal ability below the fifth grade)
• Females (when identifying mathematical ability)
• Intellectually creative, academically under-achieving, physically handicapped, and learning-disabled students

The approach used in the APOGEE Project acknowledges both the bias in typical standardized tests and the differences among the various cultural groups (Richert & Wilson, 1995). The goal is to compare students only to their demographic peers or within their social environment. The effect is to create local norms for each sub-population by disaggregating all data, including tests and various forms of nominations. This method is relatively simple and cost-effective in that it relies primarily on existing data and uses the same instruments for all students.

VanTassel-Baska and Willis (1982) found that test scores of economically disadvantaged students tended to underestimate their potential for success in an academically advanced program. This means that admitting poor students with gifted potential who have lower scores is both justifiable and defensible. The improved performance of the identified students from all demographic groups in APOGEE classes (to be discussed) provides ample support for the effectiveness of this strategy.

Identification Strategies Used in APOGEE

Project APOGEE used a procedure approved by the U.S. Office of Civil Rights (U.S. Department of Education, 1979). The available test scores, teacher nominations (grades K–11), parent nominations (grades K–3), and self-nominations (grades 6–11) were separated according to their various demographic groups, including categories for economic class, cultural group, and gender. Economic groupings were based on whether students were "disadvan-

taged," using the federal standard of qualifying for free or reduced-price lunch, or "advantaged," that is, not qualifying for free or reduced-price lunch.

Cultural groups varied by district, but included African American, Hispanic, Indian (from Asia), Asian, Native American, White, Limited English Proficient, and several others. If there was a greater than 15 percent gender inequity, which often occurred among African American and Hispanic groups, data were renormed for gender. Students were then selected on the basis of their highest score on any one of the rank-ordered lists of various instruments used by the school, which included at least two of the following: standardized achievement tests, teacher recommendations, parent recommendations, and self-nominations.

Such renorming guarantees the selection of the same percentage of students from *within* each sub-population present in the school. Selecting up to 25 percent of students from each group allowed expanded opportunities for students from all demographic groups, including the White middle class. This strategy therefore avoids polarizing demographic groups and generates advocacy among parents of students with diverse backgrounds.

Multiple Sources of Data Should Complement, Not Confirm Each Other

Data from different sources should be used independently, and a high score on any one source should be sufficient to include a student in a program. Cutoff scores should not be used because they tend to exclude creative, underachieving, and disadvantaged students. Creative or disadvantaged students should not be excluded from a program solely on the basis of a test score if there are other indicators of exceptional potential (such as teacher, parent, or self-nominations). Students should be able to qualify for a program by scoring high on any of several measures, rather than on most or all. In the APOGEE project, all formal and informal data were renormed, and students qualified by scoring among the top 25 percent of their demographic group on any test score or by teacher, parent, or self-nomination.

Appropriate Use of Data from Students, Parents, Teachers, and Peers

Checklists and other informal data from parents, teachers, and peers are especially important to ensure identification of students from disadvantaged populations. At the primary (K–3) level, parents are good sources of information about a child's strengths and intrinsic motivations, sometimes demonstrated by extracurricular activities. At all grade levels, teachers trained in identifying characteristics, positive and negative, of the gifted are particularly good sources of observations about creative behaviors. Without such training, data from teachers may offer information that is even less useful than a standardized test (Gear, 1976, 1978).

Peer nominations are also useful, especially in finding students with leadership potential. It is from peers that leaders emerge and by peers that leaders must first be recognized. Peer nominations also are useful in the area of creativity, because peers have a good basis for judging the imaginativeness and uniqueness of a fellow student's ideas.

Nomination forms should produce different scores for diverse abilities. For example, a minimum requirement would be for teacher observation check-lists to evaluate both specific academic abilities that the program addresses and intellectual creativity.

Achievement and IQ tests tend to screen out the most creative students, and teachers often have biases against nonconforming students. For this reason, nominations for creativity are especially crucial.[2]

The APOGEE Project used easily implemented, research-based, self, teacher, and parent nomination forms, which then were renormed for the various demographic groups in each district (Richert, 1993).

Self-Nominations

Starting at about grade 4, self-nominations can be very successful identification instruments. Their disadvantage is that students who have high potential but poor self-esteem, or who are underachieving, may not nominate themselves if they have traditional views of giftedness. Therefore, instead of identifying themselves as "gifted," students are asked to express their level of interest in various program options that allow for intrinsic motivation, creativity, and risk taking. Students first are informed about the curriculum and objectives, and then are invited to visit various program options. They apply for those that they want to pursue. This method taps into the intrinsic motivation and intense interests of the gifted and was, after renorming, a highly successful indicator of gifted potential in the APOGEE Project.

Use of Data on Student Progress for Evaluation

The identification process is not concluded upon determination of a list of students to receive services. The last stage of identification is ongoing evaluation and assessment of students' performance and interests. Students should be assessed annually, not to determine whether they are "still gifted," but to determine whether they should remain in a particular program option or would be better served in another option or in the regular classroom. The focus is on the best interests of the student, not those of the teacher, parent, or school. The same data gathered to evaluate individual students may be used in aggregate for program evaluation and improvement.

Data on student progress in a program option (related to the program's curriculum objectives to develop higher level cognitive abilities, creative and critical thinking, or higher-level emotional and ethical potentials), rather than changes in standardized test scores, should determine whether a student continues in the program each year.[3]

The few standardized tests appropriate at this stage are specified in the *National Report on Identification* (Richert et al., 1982). These tests may provide some assessment of progress. However, teacher, self, and peer evaluations of product and process are better indicators of progress. Product evaluations should include assessments of critical thinking and other higher-level cognitive skills such as creativity, complexity, and pragmatism (does it work?). Process evaluations by self and teacher should address higher-level affective and social skills, such as independence, intrinsic motivation, risk taking, persistence, decision making, and cooperation. Product and process evaluations may be carried out during the year with various criterion-referenced scales and check-lists that address the goals of the

---

2. Several instruments are included in Chapter 6 of the *National Report* and are available from the Global Institute.

3. See Richert (1986, 1990, 1994, 1995) for sources and analyses of the higher levels of cognitive, affective, and ethical taxonomies appropriate for curriculum objectives.

program. Many have been collected in a training handbook (Richert, 2001).

Using Strategies to Develop Potential in the Regular Classroom

The long-range educational goal of schools should be to train all teachers in methods that develop the highest-level cognitive, affective, and ethical potential of all students (Richert, 1995, 1996). Then, whatever their background, characteristics, or diverse potentials, students could be identified for various program options because their abilities would become manifest in the classroom. The APOGEE Project was designed to train teachers to upgrade instruction not only in classes where identified students were homogeneously grouped, but also in regular heterogeneous classes.

Equitable Result of APOGEE's Identification Procedures

The result of renorming the data in the APOGEE Project was an overall increased representation of culturally diverse students by 500 percent, an increase of economically disadvantaged students by 600 percent, and an increase of up to 800 percent of poor, culturally diverse males in program options designed to evoke gifted potential (Richert, 1995). Proportionate representation was achieved for all demographic groups in each district.

Low-Cost Program Demonstrates Excellence with Equity

Because of inevitable competition for resources, an inexpensive program design that uses primarily existing resources, rather than hiring many new staff, is necessary to serve the 20 to 25 percent of students with gifted potential. Without a practical and comprehensive program design, broad-based and equitable identification cannot be supported. A crucial advocacy issue is that identifying fewer than about 20 percent of students tends to polarize parents of high-achieving students versus parents of disadvantaged or culturally different students in the competition for places in a program.

In order to develop a high-quality program that can serve the diverse needs of up to 20 or 25 percent of a student population, I have recommended a five-step plan for modifying the diversity of existing district resources. It includes homogeneous grouping in required subject areas, the regular classroom, cocurricular activities, and electives, among many others (Richert et al., 1982).

The APOGEE Program design modified existing resources to serve the top 25 percent within each demographic group. Depending on the number of classes per grade level in each building, the top 20 to 25 percent of students in grades K–11 (for placement in grades 1–12) from *within* each sub-population was selected for a class that would meet daily for at least one required subject area. Instruction for teachers in differentiating subject areas for individual interests, learning styles, and achievement levels was provided by offering training in my Maximizing Potential Model (Richert, 1994, 1995; Richert & Wilson, 1995).

In the elementary grades, which had self-contained classes, identified students were regrouped across classes at each grade level, a minimum of 45 minutes a day, for at least their reading class. Some districts chose to have one to three-hour reading/language arts blocks. Other districts added math or a math-science block. At the middle or secondary levels, additional advanced or honors sections were taught by trained teachers. The net effect is that at least *twice* the original number of students take advanced courses, and those courses now include representative numbers of students from all demographic groups. Equity is not violated; economic or cultural groups are not "segregated."

As a major caution, equitable identification and placement by themselves are not sufficient to meet the needs of nontraditional students. Fragmented pull-out programs cannot meet the needs of under-achieving students who need modification of required subject areas where they are not excelling. Without intensive staff development for teachers who will be serving students with gifted potential who are not usually identified (such as highly creative, culturally diverse, and poor students), these students will be set up for failure.

Intensive training to meet the needs of the gifted in required subject areas was offered through the APOGEE Project to over 150 regular classroom teachers, grades 1 to 12. The process included three kinds of instruction over a two-year period: (1) 45 hours of direct training, (2) from 10 to 30 hours of follow-up Sessions, and (3) on-site, in-class coaching sessions for each teacher. Trained teachers then used 36 Strategies for Maximizing Cognitive, Affective and Ethical Potential (Richert, 1995) not only with classes of identified students, but also with their heterogeneously grouped classes. The training included many strategies for individualizing instruction for students' interests, learning styles, abilities, and emotional and academic needs over a wide range of achievement levels. The staff development ensured that excellence was not sacrificed for equity. This approach is cost-effective and overcomes the objection that only the highest achieving students get the most effective instruction or the best trained teachers (Oakes, 1985; Sapon-Shevin, 1994).

Administrative support for the program model and staff development was most often based on its benefits for all students, not just those with gifted potential. For example, in one New Jersey district, in which over 20 percent of the students are economically disadvantaged, now has almost 40 percent of its students in advanced or honors classes. Parents of students with gifted potential become strong program advocates because students are being served consistently in academic subject areas where they get credit for their work, rather than in fragmented enrichment or pull-out programs that do not improve their academic performance. This approach also avoids the politically correct, but cosmetic and ineffective, approach of "enrichment for all," which sacrifices excellence for equity.

Programming for Excellence and Justice

Counteracting Negative Trends in Programs for Disadvantaged Populations

At the conclusion of the APOGEE Project, the Global Institute for Maximizing Potential determined to expand equity and justice in public schools by developing services and research to counteract the increasingly negative impact of some national trends. These trends include elitist identification, which excludes the disadvantaged; the egalitarian heterogeneous grouping movement, which has eliminated many effective programs for the gifted; and increasingly demanding and biased standards based assessment, which underestimate the abilities of many students in poor schools.

We have been taking advantage of the regular classroom, where most disadvantaged students with exceptional potential have been relegated, for several purposes. First, it can be used as a vehicle to demonstrate untapped abilities among all students, but especially the disadvantaged, so more will be included in programs. Second, where political agendas have eliminated programs for the gifted, it is necessary to modify instruction to overcome the underachievement of talented students in heterogeneous contexts.

Impact on High Stakes State Performance Assessments

My Maximizing Cognitive, Affective and Ethical Potential Professional Development and Instructional Model™ is being used to improve scores on demanding high-stakes performance assessments in more than thirty schools in several states.

In Connecticut, this model has been successful with 35 K–6 teachers, instructing more than 560 students. Over the last six years, students in urban Hartford's mostly bilingual Sanchez Elementary School have made steady gains in the number of students who achieve proficiency on the Connecticut Mastery Tests (CMTs). Analysis of data since 1993 shows that Sanchez Elementary School's rate of gain for students achieving mastery on CMTs has been 16 percent greater than the districts' overall improvement over the same period.

In Evangeline Parish, Louisiana, one school with trained teachers using our instructional strategies reported an increase from 25 to 75 percent (a 300 percent gain) in students achieving mastery in math in a difficult state math assessment.

Most recent impact data, however, are from New Jersey (NJ), which is in the vanguard of the school reform movement and is aggressively responding to the political demand for higher standards (Walker & Gutmore, 2000). The New Jersey Department of Education (NJDE) mandated school reform in thirty underfunded, traditionally low performing urban districts. In these thirty districts, the NJDE "approved" reform models have eliminated the majority of K–8 programs for the gifted, including five that were successfully initiated through APOGEE. Gifted students of all demographics have therefore been denied academic programs.

The impact of my Maximizing Potential Strategies™ in urban schools had been demonstrated on New Jersey's extremely demanding state performance assessments. Based on national norms, only the top 15 percent of fourth and eighth grade American students would achieve the proficiency levels required on NJDE tests. This percentage is important, since it is from within this group that gifted students of all demographics may be identified.

From 1997 to 1998, in one of the thirty urban multicultural New Jersey districts, we conducted thirty hours of intensive training in my Maximizing Potential™ instructional model, followed by on-site coaching for about two hundred teachers. Students in these fifteen schools, in comparison to nine control schools, made dramatic gains in the major subjects tested on New Jersey's eighth grade performance assessment, the Early Warning Test (EWT). Two of the fifteen schools received awards from NJDE for achieving the greatest gains statewide on the EWT.

- *Mathematics:* Schools using our model averaged 20 percent rates of gain compared to –2 percent for schools we were not working with. Two schools that most effectively used Maximizing Potential strategies made dramatic gains of 29 percent and 38 percent.
- *Reading:* Schools we worked with averaged 10 percent rates of gain compared to –2 percent for schools we were not working with. Three schools using Maximizing Potential strategies made gains of 20–27 percent.
- *Writing:* There was little time to address writing, but four schools effectively using our strategies made gains of 8 to 17 percent in writing scores. Scores stayed about the same for other schools in the district.

In 1997–1998, a predominantly African American middle school in an urban New Jersey district increased the percentage of students passing EWT writing from 44 to 77 percent, which is a phenomenal 75 percent rate of gain. High school students in the same urban district made a comparative gain of 9 percent in New Jersey's High School Proficiency Test in reading and writing.

In 1999 the NJDE instituted new and even more demanding state performance assessments with devastating impact on scores statewide, particularly in economically disadvantaged schools. After revising our strategies to accommodate the new standards, we worked intensively in 1999–2000 with three schools in one urban district with a high proportion of bilingual students.

The results in 2000 demonstrated a dramatic impact in these three schools, as compared to three control schools with similar demographics.

- *Mathematics:* Schools we were working with averaged 45 percent rates of gain compared to –20% for schools not receiving services, a net difference of 64 percent. Our three schools had dramatic rates of gain of 19–81 percent.
- *Literacy* (includes reading and writing): Schools we were working with averaged 13 percent rates of gain compared to 2.5 percent for schools we were not working with. One school gained 27 percent.

The district's middle school was one of the very few New Jersey urban schools with 75 percent of students achieving proficiency in both subjects, which is the NJDE standard. In math, they achieved one of the best urban results in the state: 84 percent of students passing.

NJDE data released for the same district in June and August of 2001 continues to demonstrate the high effectiveness of our Maximizing Potential Strategies. Overall, these results demonstrate that with intensive staff development and on site follow-up in Strategies that Maximize students' cognitive, affective and ethical potential:

- Regular classroom instruction can be made much more effective in evoking and demonstrating the abilities of disadvantaged and culturally diverse students;
- Economically disadvantaged students can achieve demanding standards; and
- The limitations of some comprehensive school reform models in serving students with high potential can be overcome.

Finally, it must be emphasized that these regular classroom approaches are still not a substitute for programs that provide some homogeneous grouping in required subjects for students with gifted potential.

SUMMARY AND CONCLUSIONS

The tragic events of September 11, 2001, demonstrated again our planet's great need for developing the highest intellectual, emotional, and ethical potential of everyone, especially those with gifted potential who will be leaders and opinion-makers in every field and nation—and who will determine whether our future will be filled with justice or devastation. The field of the education of the gifted has a significant responsibility to ensure that those with exceptional potential from every nation and demographic group have the support they need to become productive citizens of our world, rather than efficient destroyers of life and hope for our planet. Our field's contribution can and should be to ensure, first, that equity is assured in who is served by programs for the gifted and, second, that programs promote the development among practitioners and students of the the universal ethical principles that transcend cultural differences: compassion, justice, service, and taking responsibility for the consequences of our actions—on ourselves and others.

Elitism in identification, programming, and curriculum for the gifted has long excluded economically disadvantaged and culturally diverse students from programs. Over the last decade, inequitable practices have made our field especially vulnerable to attack from diverse angles: the antielitist detracking groups, "proexcellence" standards-based political agendas, and publicly funded comprehensive reform for schools in poor districts. The most pernicious effect, which is certainly ironic for the "antielitists," has been in the elimination of most programs at the elementary and middle school levels in poor, rather than affluent, schools.

My twenty years of research on the demonstrated impact of equitable identification, comprehensive and low-cost program design, and intensive staff development using my Maximizing Potential Strategies has taught me a great deal. First, there is enormous underachievement among students of all cultures and economic circumstances—but it can be overcome! Second, if programs for the gifted are to survive, it is essential that we offer equitable, practical models for both identification and programming, along with intensive staff development for all teachers. Third, we will never know how many students are capable of high-level work unless we first meet their needs in the regular classroom. Therefore, at this critical juncture when disadvantaged students in ailing public schools are likely not to have any differentiated programs available to them, training of all teachers in methods to maximize students' cognitive, affective, and ethical potential is essential.

Programs for students with gifted potential can be equitable, defensible, pragmatic, and serve the needs of both students and our planet if we follow these practices:

1. Adopt a comprehensive and pluralistic definition that includes diverse potential among all demographic and ethnic groups;
2. Develop cost-effective, multiple program options that integrate emotional and ethical, as well as intellectual potential, in required subject areas, rather that just nonessential enrichment;
3. Recognize that the purpose of identification and programmatic provisions for the gifted is not to label or to reward achievement or conformity to local school expectations, but to find and develop exceptional potential to serve humanity;
4. Use appropriate data from multiple sources about cognitive, creative, and other abilities from sources beyond academic achievement to identify gifted abilities;
5. Renorm academic achievement and other instruments to overcome bias against various disadvantaged groups, particularly the poor and the culturally diverse;
6. Identify up to 25 percent of a school's student population so that if errors are made, they are errors of inclusion rather than exclusion;
7. Fund intensive staff development to improve the effectiveness of all teachers in evoking maximum cognitive, emotional, and ethical potential.

QUESTIONS FOR THOUGHT AND DISCUSSION

1. How will an examination of student population demographics reveal if a gifted program seems elitist?

2. You may be planning to enter the field of gifted education. How will you defend yourself against charges of elitism?

3. Should programs for the gifted include proportional representation of all demographic groups? What are the various ways this can be achieved?

4. Against—and for—which populations are standardized tests, teacher recommendations, and grades biased? Which students (including students from the majority culture) are most underserved in programs for the gifted? Explain.

5. Gottfredson in Chapter 3 emphasizes genetic differences in IQ (and giftedness), which is accurately measured

by IQ tests. Can you summarize and reconcile the differences between her perceptions and conclusions and those of Richert in Chapter 11?

REFERENCES

Baird, L. L. (1982). *The role of academic ability in high level accomplishment and general success.* College Board Report No. 82. New York: College Board Publications.

Black, H. (1963). *They shall not pass.* New York: Morrow.

Coopersmith, S. (1967). *The antecedents of self-esteem.* San Francisco: Freeman.

Cox, J., Daniel, N., & Boston, B. O. (1985). *Educating able learners.* Austin: University of Texas Press.

Ford, D. Y. (1998, Spring). The underrepresentation of minority students in gifted education: Problems and promises in recruitment and retention. *The Journal of Special Education, 32,* 4–14.

Gagne, F. (1985). Giftedness and talent: Reexamining a reexamination of the definitions. *Gifted Child Quarterly, 29,* 103–112.

Gardner, H. (1983). *Frames of mind.* New York: Basic Books.

Gear, G. H. (1976). Teacher judgment in identification of gifted children. *Gifted Child Quarterly, 10,* 478–489.

Gear, G. H. (1978). Effects of training on teachers' accuracy in identifying gifted children. *Gifted Child Quarterly, 12,* 90–97.

Goodlad, J. I., & Oakes, J. (1988, February). We must offer equal access to knowledge. *Educational Leadership,* 16–22.

Guilford, J. P. (1967). *The nature of human intelligence.* New York: McGraw-Hill.

Herrnstein, R. J., & Murray, C. (1994). *The bell curve.* New York: Simon & Schuster.

Hilliard, A. (1993). Presentation at the National Association for Black School Educators. Houston, Texas.

Kulik, J. A. (1992). *An analysis of the research on ability grouping: Historical and contemporary perspectives.* Storrs: National Research Center on the Gifted and Talented, University of Connecticut.

Kulik, J. A., & Kulik, C. (1987). Effects of ability grouping on student achievement. *Equity and Excellence, 23,* 22–30.

Marland, S. P., Jr. (1972). *Education of the gifted and talented.* Report to the Congress of the United States by the U.S. Commissioner of Education. Washington, DC: U.S. Department of Health, Education, and Welfare.

Miller, A. (1981). *Prisoners of childhood: How narcissistic parents form and deform the emotional lives of their gifted children.* New York: Basic Books.

Miller, L. P. (Ed.). (1974). *The testing of black students. A symposium.* Englewood Cliffs, NJ: Prentice-Hall.

Munday, L. S., & Davis, J. C. (1974). *Varieties of accomplishment after college: Perspective of the meaning of academic talent* (ACT Research Report No. 7). Iowa City: American College Testing Program.

Nairn, A., & Associates. (1980). *The reign of ETS: The corporation that makes up minds* (the Ralph Nader report on the Educational Testing Service). Washington, DC: Ralph Nader.

Northwest Regional Educational Laboratory. (1998). *A catalog of school reform models.* Portland, Oregon: Author.

Oakes, J. (1985). *Keeping track: How schools structure inequality.* New Haven: Yale University Press.

Office of Educational Research and Improvement, U.S. Department of Education (1998). Tools for schools: School reform model supported by the National Institute on the Education for At-Risk students. Washington, DC: Author.

Ortiz, A. (2000). *Including students with special needs in standards based reform: Issues associated with the alignment of standards, curriculum and instruction.* Aurora, CO: Mid-Continent Research Lab.

Renzulli, J. S. (1978). What makes giftedness?: Reexamining a definition. *Phi Delta Kappan, 60,* 108–184.

Richert, E. S. (1985). The state of the art of identification of gifted students in the United States. *Gifted Education International, 3,* 47–51.

Richert, E. S. (1986). Toward the Tao of giftedness. *Roeper Review, 8,* 197–204.

Richert, E. S. (1987). Rampant problems and promising practices in the identification of disadvantaged gifted students. *Gifted Child Quarterly, 31,* 149–154.

Richert, E. S. (1990). Patterns of underachievement among gifted adolescents. In J. Genshaft & M. Bireley (Eds.), *The gifted adolescent: Personal and educational issues.* New York: Teachers College Press.

Richert, E. S. (1993). *Richert teacher, parent and self nomination forms.* Ocean Grove, NJ: Global Institute for Maximizing Potential.

Richert, E. S. (1994). *Training handbook for maximizing student potential.* Ocean Grove, NJ: Global Institute for Maximizing Potential.

Richert, E. S. (1995). *Maximizing student potential.* Ocean Grove, NJ: Global Institute for Maximizing Potential.

Richert, E. S. (1996). Maximizing student and teacher potentials: Preliminary research results. In J. Chan, R. Li, & J. Spinks (Eds.), *Maximizing student potential: Lengthening our stride.* Hong Kong: University of Hong Kong, Social Science Research Center.

Richert, E. S. (2000). *Maximizing gifted potential for the 21st century.* Paper presented at the Arab Council for the Gifted & Talented Conference, Amman, Jordan.

Richert, E. S. (2001). *Maximizing student potential.* Ocean Grove NJ: Global Institute for Maximizing Potential.

Richert, E. S., Alvino, J., & McDonnel, R. (1982). *National report on identification: Assessment and recommendations for comprehensive identification of gifted and talented youth* (for the U.S. Department of Education). Sewell, NJ: Educational Information and Resource Center.

Richert, E. S., & Wilson, R. B. (1995). Maximizing urban student and teacher potentials: Preliminary research results. In G. Ohwheri (Ed.), *Developing strategies for excellence in urban education.* New York: Nova.

Samuda, R. J. (1975). Alternatives to traditional standardized tests, introduction. In R. J. Samuda (Ed.), *Psychological testing of American minorities* (pp. 13–157). New York: Dodd, Mead.

Sapon-Shevin, M. (1994). *Playing favorites: Gifted education and the disruption of community.* Ithaca: State University of New York Press.

Silverman, L. K. (Ed.). (1986). The IQ controversy (Special Issue). *Roeper Review, 8.*

Sternberg, R. (1985). *Beyond IQ.* Cambridge: Cambridge University Press.

Tannenbaum, A. J. (1983). *Gifted children: Psychological and educational perspectives.* New York: Macmillan.

Taylor, C. W., Albo, D., Holland, J., & Brandt, C. (1985). Attributes of excellence in various professions: Their relevance to the selection of gifted/talented persons. *Gifted Child Quarterly, 29,* 29–34.

Torrance, E. P. (1979). *The search for Satori and creativity.* Buffalo, NY: Creative Education Foundation.

Torrance, E. P., & Ball, O. E. (1984). *Torrance tests of creative thinking: Streamlined* (Revised manual, Figural A and B). Bensenville, IL: Scholastic Testing Service.

U.S. Department of Education. (1979). *Office of Civil Rights report.* Washington, DC: Author.

U.S. Department of Education. (1993). *National excellence: A case for developing American Talent.* Washington, DC: Author.

VanTassel-Baska, J., & Willis, G. (1982). A three year study of the effects of low income on SAT scores among the academically able. *Gifted Child Quarterly, 31,* 4.

Walker, M., & Gutmore, D. (2000). The quest for equity and excellence in education: A study on whole school reform in New Jersey special needs districts. South Orange, NJ: Seton Hall, Center for Urban Leadership.

Zappia, I. (1989). Identification of gifted Hispanic students. In C. J. Maker & S. Scheiver (Eds.), *Critical issues in gifted education: Defensible programs for cultural and ethnic minorities* (Vol. 2, pp. 19–261). Austin, TX: Pro-Ed.

BIBLIOGRAPHY

Davidson, K. L. (1992). A comparison of Native American and White students as measured by the Kaufman Assessment Battery for children. *Roeper Review, 14,* 111–115.

Ennis, R. H., Millman, J., & Tomro, T. N. (1990). *Cornell critical thinking tests.* Costa Mesa, CA: Critical Thinking Press.

Hoffman, B. (1962). *The tyranny of testing.* New York: Crowell-Collier.

Kauffman, A., & Kauffman, N. (1983). *Kauffman assessment battery for children.* Circle Pines, MN: American Guidance Service.

Maker, J. (1992). Intelligence and creativity in multiple intelligences: Identification and development. *Educating Able Learners, 17*(4) 12–19.

Meeker, M. N., Meeker, R., & Roid, G. (1985). *Structure of the intellect learning abilities test* (SOI-LA). Los Angeles: Western Psychological Services.

New York State Department of Education. (n.d.). *Guidelines for the identification of the gifted and talented.* Albany: New York State Department of Education.

Passow, A. H. (1988). Educating gifted persons who are caring and concerned. *Roeper Review, 11,* 13–15.

Piechowski, M. M., & Colangelo, N. (1984). Developmental potential of the gifted. *Gifted Child Quarterly, 8,* 80–88.

Raven, J. C. (1958). *Standard progressive matrices.* London: H. K. Lewis.

Roeper, A. (1982). How the gifted cope with their emotions. *Roeper Review, 5,* 21–24.

Toffler, A. (1984) *Future Shock.* New York: Bantam Doubleday Dell Publishing Group.

Torrance, E. P. (1964). *Education amid the creative potential.* Minneapolis: University of Minnesota Press.

U.S. Department of Education. (1994). *Identifying outstanding talent in American Indian and Alaska Native students.* Washington, DC: Author.

Weiner, L. (1995). *Diminished discourse and impoverished schools: Urban legacies of the "excellence" reforms.* New York: Nova.

Instructional Models and Practices

Part III presents strategies for meeting the educational needs of gifted youngsters. There is indeed a wide array of enrichment and acceleration programs and practices. We will examine curriculum considerations, a program model that helps all students, the talent search strategy, Saturday and summer programs, recommendations for gifted high school students, residential high schools, conditions that create intense involvement, mentoring, ability grouping, and the pluses and minuses of cooperative learning. Finally, we take a broad look at a critical but often ignored step: evaluating your gifted program.

All G/T planners emphasize thinking skills and problem solving. In Chapter 12 Shirley W. Schiever and C. June Maker define a gifted person as one who can solve complex problems in "efficient, effective, ethical, elegant, or economical ways." They note that *enrichment* can refer either to the curriculum or to such program delivery services as Saturday classes or resource room programs. *Acceleration* also can refer to either (advanced) curriculum or to delivery services such as grade skipping or early admission. A sensible program will include both acceleration and enrichment, according to student characteristics and needs. Using the analogy of catastrophe theory, the authors describe how content, process, and product—if accelerated and enriched—can combine to produce a qualitatively different curriculum. The authors especially emphasize how their five Problem Types can stimulate progressively higher levels of thinking skills and hence the desired qualitative change.

In Chapter 13 Joyce VanTassel-Baska describes her Integrated Curriculum Model (ICM), which draws from leading gifted curriculum approaches such as developing thinking skills in the production of a product (process-product approach) and the acceleration of existing curriculum. She notes that some shortcomings of these models include a lack of comprehensiveness and cohesiveness, an absence of rich content knowledge, and inadequate differentiation for the gifted. Three key curricular dimensions of her ICM thus include advanced content; higher-order thinking; and a focus on major issues, concepts, themes, and ideas. Such features cater to gifted students' traits of precocity, intensity, and capacity for higher-level thinking (complexity). VanTassel-Baska describes the translation of ICM into her successful National Language Arts Curriculum Project, National Science Curriculum Project for High Ability Learners, and a social studies curriculum, all of which employ interdisciplinary, concept-based curriculum and higher-order thinking.

With a focus on creative productivity, Joseph S. Renzulli and Sally M. Reis in Chapter 14 summarize Renzulli's 1977 Enrichment Triad Model, including the Three Ring conception of giftedness; their 1981 Revolving Door Identification Model; and based on both of these, their thoughtful and high-impact Schoolwide Enrichment Model. A three-dimensional summary of the SEM, with 63 cells, encompasses *School Structures,* including the regular curriculum (modified with compacting and textbook modification), enrichment clusters (nongraded investigative activities for small groups of students with a common interest), and a continuum of special services (e.g., counseling, acceleration, mentorships); *School Delivery Components,* which include total talent portfolios (abilities, interests, learning styles), curriculum modification techniques (e.g., challenging, in-depth enrichment experiences and curriculum compacting) and the Triad Model itself; and seven topics under the heading *Organizational Components*. Despite site-specific variations, the SEM is well received.

In Chapter 15 Ann Lupkowski-Shoplik, Camilla Persson Benbow, Susan G. Assouline, and Linda E. Brody give well-deserved credit to Julian Stanley for creating the Talent Search concept. Originating as the Study of Mathematically Precocious Youth, SMPY used the high-school-level SAT-M to identify mathematically talented seventh graders in the Baltimore area for special summer courses and, perhaps years later, a "smorgasbord" of other educational options, for example, grade skipping, independent study, Advanced Placement courses, dual enrollment in high school and college, early college entrance, and educational and career counseling. The successful strategy now includes verbally and mathematically precocious seventh graders in university-based Talent Search programs across the United States and in other countries. Further, the concept has stimulated Elementary Talent Searches, in which bright elementary students are identified with middle-school aptitude tests. The authors review uniformly supportive research, including Benbow's fifty-year longitudinal study of SMPY participants.

Paula Olszewski-Kubilius in Chapter 16 explains how summer, Saturday, and other special outside-of-school programs and competitions supply vital learning experiences for gifted students. Such programs offer high-level accelerated courses, enrichment opportunities, career exploration, and/or introductions to various subject areas. Other benefits are social support from gifted peers, positive feelings from a suitable academic challenge, improved study and academic skills, high achievement, sometimes high school or college course credit, and helpful educational and career information. At first, however, self-concepts may be slightly depressed due to social comparison. Research by Olszewski-Kubilius and others found that accelerated summer math classes helped gifted girls compete well with mathematically motivated boys. Continuing problems, notes Olszewski-Kubilius are the overlap with regular school curriculum and awarding course credit to students who succeed in the special programs.

In Chapter 17 John F. Feldhusen raises our eyebrows by recommending that for middle and high school students, we discard the concepts of *gifted* and *gifted program*. Rather, we should focus on identifying talented students and developing their capabilities. Identification might include SAT scores, achievement tests, and rating scales such as Renzulli's Scales for Rating the Behavior Characteristics of Superior Students and Feldhusen's own Purdue Academic Rating Scales and Purdue Vocational Talent Scales. Instead of "a program," Feldhusen recommends that talent development include a diversity of well-selected courses, extra-school opportunities, and other services, for example, academic and career counseling; honors, AP, accelerated, enriched, and college classes; Saturday and summer programs; concurrent enrollment in college; mentorships; independent study; and working with talented peers. Feldhusen's Growth Plan includes statements of one's experiences, strengths, interests, goals, and educational plans. His *Purdue Pyramid* illustrates educational experiences that lead to an understanding of one's talents and a commitment to their development.

Penny Britton Kolloff in Chapter 18 describes a growing strategy for meeting the educational needs of high school students with exceptional math and science abilities. Usually located on college campuses, residential high schools foster excellence, especially in math and science, but also in the arts, literature, English, foreign languages, and other humanities areas. Beginning with the North Carolina School of Science and Mathematics, Kolloff describes several specific schools, objective and subjective admission criteria, student diversity, faculty (which includes teachers, professors, and other professionals), curriculum (including AP courses, college courses, and research opportunities), and extracurricular activities. Especially, Kolloff explains why the schools have been superbly successful and why all states should examine this growing concept.

In Chapter 19 Lauren A. Sosniak outlines some thought-provoking findings from Benjamin Bloom's Development of Talent Research Project, in which she played a key role. She especially stresses the issues of *time, task,* and *context* for high-level development of artistic/musical, athletic, or scientific talent. Under *time,* Sosniak describes the long-term and intense involvement with a field, which produces transformations in the individuals, the perceived domain content, and the young persons' interaction with teachers and content. *Task* refers primarily to the authentic nature of the artistic, athletic, or scientific tasks, compared with typical schoolwork. Finally, she discusses the all-important social *context* that supports long-term engagement. Called *communities of practice,* the social context supplies the models, resources, and encouragement that reinforce the development of one's talent. Finally, Sosniak emphasizes the challenge of making talent development a deliberate choice, rather than a fortuitous combination of opportunities and communities of practice.

We typically imagine mentorships as a high school plan—placing interested students on the job with local engineers, doctors, or executives for a few hours per week to learn about the profession, preparation, and the mentors' skills, training, and lifestyle. In Chapter 20 Donna Rae and Robert E. Clasen describe how teachers of the gifted can—and definitely should—organize mentoring programs for both secondary and elementary students. They review such features as the age of protégé; duration of mentorships; characteristics and roles of the mentor and protégé (and critical matching considerations); special benefits for gifted minority, disadvantaged, and female students, and students with disabilities; features of successful programs; telementoring; planning, organizing, and evaluating mentorships; and thoughtful cautions and caveats, including what to do if the mentorship falls apart.

The past two decades have seen a trend toward eliminating high school tracking, ability grouping at all levels, and even gifted programs. Such plans, say critics, give lower-ability students an inferior education and low self-esteem. In Chapter 21 James A. Kulik explains why the movement appears to be failing. Almost all schools in the United States, both elementary and secondary, successfully use grouping or tracking to adjust teaching pace and content to student needs. Further, based on meta-analysis of "mountains of studies," only the XYZ plan—grouping by ability without differentiating the curriculum—gives little benefit. Cross-grade and within-class grouping in reading and arithmetic produce substantial benefits, as do enriched, accelerated, and advanced classes. The few schools that have totally eliminated tracking usually suffer educationally. Kulik noted that in 250 schools nominated as our "most restructured," over half of the students spend "substantial" amounts of time in ability groups or tracks. Nearly all high schools still track students in math. Elementary schools still use separate (lower or higher ability) classes or within-class grouping. Even "highly reformed" elementary schools, with hetero-geneous classes, continue to use within-class groups and pullout programs. Some pressures for grouping—parents demand differentiation, and colleges prefer students with strong preparation.

In Chapter 22, Ann Robinson reviews developments in cooperative learning research. The continuing dilemma is that cooperative learning does indeed benefit most students—but gifted students may wind up as tutors, and they miss more suitable opportunities. Research with high ability learners in cooperative groups has mushroomed; there also is an increase in higher-level learning outcomes. With the "free rider" and "sucker" effects, higher ability kids do most of the work—until they feel like suckers and disengage, sometimes preferring to fail. Generally, people in groups work less hard. Recent research, as in the past, still compares homogeneous versus heterogeneous (in ability) grouping, also various group sizes. A new trend is dyads, which produce greater participation, helpfulness, and achievement. Robinson explains the difference between task structure (working conditions—individual, cooperative, or competitive) and goal/incentive structure. With bright learners, competition may simply be a challenge to improve oneself. One problem is that satisfactory group performance does not guarantee individual learning.

James H. Borland in Chapter 23 addresses the evaluation of gifted programs. In contrast with most such evaluations, he recommends that we take a wider view—one that considers social, political, and moral and ethical implications for all persons in the school and community. He explains that evaluation may be conceived as judgmental, descriptive (goal-oriented or goal-free), or improvement-oriented. Postpositivist evaluation stresses qualitative and naturalistic studies, and recognizes different perceptions, values, and realities. Functions of evaluation are summative, formative, and sometimes psychological or sociopolitical. Some problems include ambiguous goals (e.g., "to create leaders"), a lack of suitable tests, ceiling effects, and inappropriate norms. Although outside evaluators bring objectivity, they have limited inside knowledge. Evaluation issues include authentic assessment and serving minority students. Borland's five-step evaluation procedure requires no psychometric training.

12

New Directions in Enrichment and Acceleration

SHIRLEY W. SCHIEVER, *Tucson United School District*
C. JUNE MAKER, *University of Arizona—Tucson*

The question "Is this an enrichment or an acceleration program?" is indicative of two of the problems associated with these terms. First is the implication that no program could be both enriched and accelerated, that one mode must be chosen and adhered to, and that never the twain shall meet. Second, referring to "enrichment" or "acceleration" programs creates confusion. Does enrichment refer to the curriculum or the service delivery of the program? Does an acceleration program deliver an accelerated curriculum, or does it provide for the (grade) acceleration of students?

The purpose of this chapter is to clarify the confusion that exists and to make a case for the complementary nature of enrichment and acceleration, and the necessity for inclusion of both in curriculum for gifted students. To this end, a brief overview of enrichment and acceleration practices will be provided, an application of catastrophe theory to curriculum for the gifted offered, and a structure for developing and examining curricula presented.

Definition of Giftedness

We define giftedness in a different way from traditional definitions, particularly the view of a gifted person as one who scores high on an IQ test. To us, that is a limited viewpoint and does not capture the richness nor complexity of giftedness. In keeping with our many experiences and our educational philosophy, we believe that the key concept in giftedness is the ability (as well as interest and willingness) to solve complex problems. Gifted people are those who can solve the most complex problems in the most efficient, effective, ethical, elegant, or economical ways. These individuals may solve simple problems;

they may find complexity within a seemingly simple problem; or they may find a complex problem to be simple. The key element is enjoyment of challenges and complexity.

This propensity for solving complex problems can be manifested in several domains of ability, and both Howard Gardner's and Robert Sternberg's theories of intelligence give us insights into different areas in which people can be gifted.[1] Gardner (1983) defined seven different intelligences in his first book: linguistic, logical-mathematical, spatial, interpersonal, intrapersonal, musical, and bodily-kinesthetic. Later, he added a naturalist intelligence, a spiritual intelligence, and an existential intelligence (Gardner, 1999). Further, he suggested that others exist and that we should be open to discovering and defining them. Sternberg (1985) defined three basic types of intelligence: analytic, synthetic, and practical. The three types can be seen across each of Gardner's intelligences, resulting in many different ways in which giftedness can be expressed.

We are not suggesting that all children are gifted in ways that demand a special program, but we do believe that complex problem-solving abilities can be seen in many and varied ways. For example, a person who is gifted in spatial ability will demonstrate characteristics of giftedness such as communication/expressiveness through visual products rather than verbal ones (unless, of course, she is gifted in linguistic ability as well). If this person tends to have high abilities in synthetic intelligence, she may create beautiful paintings, while someone gifted in practical intelligence may tend to express her spatial abilities

---

1. See Chapter 7 by Sternberg and Chapter 8 by von Károlyi, Ramos-Ford, and Gardner.

through interior decorating. The characteristics of giftedness and the way they are defined in Maker and Nielson's (1996) book fit well within our definition of giftedness as the ability and willingness to solve complex problems in a variety of domains and in a variety of ways: humor, motivation, interests, communication/expressiveness, inquiry, problem solving, sensitivity, intuition, reasoning, imagination/creativity, learning ability, or memory/knowledge/understanding.

Enrichment

The term *enrichment* is used to refer to curriculum as well as program delivery services. *Enriched curriculum* refers to richer, more varied educational experiences, a curriculum that has been modified or added to in some way (Davis & Rimm, 1989; Howley, Howley, & Pendarvis, 1986). These modifications or additions may be in content or teaching strategies, and ideally they are based on the characteristics of the learners for whom they are designed.

The goal of an enrichment program is to offer students curriculum that is greater in depth or breadth than that generally provided; that is, to challenge and offer growth in the area of the student's giftedness. After-school or Saturday classes, resource rooms, additions to regular classroom curriculum, or special interest clubs may be used as ways to implement an enrichment program. The key element for an enrichment program should be a *systematic* plan for extended student learning. Such programs as Future Problem Solving, Odyssey of the Mind, and Science Olympics provide a systematic plan for extended learning through problem solving, but they cannot be considered sufficient within themselves as a program for gifted students.

Howley, Howley, and Pendarvis (1986) describe three approaches to enrichment: process-oriented, content-oriented, and product-oriented. Each of these approaches will be considered briefly as it applies to curriculum.

The process-oriented approach to enrichment is designed to develop students' higher mental processes and, in some cases, their creative production as well. Students usually are taught the steps or components of one or more models, such as Bloom's Taxonomy of Cognitive Objectives (Bloom, Englehart, Furst, Hill, & Krathwohl, 1956); Creative Problem Solving (Parnes, 1981); or the Structure of Intellect

(Guilford, 1967), and are required or encouraged to apply the focus skills through using learning centers, engaging in discussions, and/or conducting independent studies on topics of interest to them.

One concern regarding this approach is that the thinking processes frequently are taught and/or practiced in isolation from content, or subject matter. The resulting fragmentation is not likely to promote the transfer of the higher thinking skills to other content areas or to daily problems or situations. For example, games that require strategic planning or problem solving are often used to "teach" thinking. Thinking processes are best taught and practiced using substantive content. If students are expected to think, they need something to think *about*.

Content-oriented approaches to enrichment stress the presentation of a particular content area. Generally, the curriculum for mathematics, science, language arts, or the social sciences is treated with a greater breadth and depth than is possible in the regular curriculum. Offerings may be in the form of mini-courses, museum and science center programs, college options for pre-college students, and mentorships (Howley et al., 1986). For example, at the elementary level, students might be offered a mini-course in pre-algebra; at the middle school level students could be offered a mentorship with an astronomer; or at the high school level students might enroll in Advanced Placement (AP) biology, calculus, chemistry, English, or American history or in classes held on a college campus. AP classes and college classes also are considered to be content acceleration methods.

The disadvantage of mini-courses and special programs is that usually the enrichment is separated from the curriculum students are exposed to on a consistent basis in the regular classroom. This violates developmental and curricular principles. From a developmental standpoint, learning experiences should be sequential if skills and the information base are to develop in a logical progression and rest on a solid foundation. Such detached offerings also violate the curriculum principle of *organization for learning value* (Maker, 1982a, 1982b; Maker & Nielson, 1996); that is, all or major portions of instruction and learning experiences should be organized around basic concepts or abstract generalizations that enable students to learn efficiently and to see the interconnectedness among concepts and disciplines.

Product-oriented enrichment programs emphasize primarily the *result* or *product* of instruction rather than the content or processes involved. Products may be tangible, such as a report, painting, novel, or presentation, or intangible, such as improved mental health (Howley et al., 1986) or coping skills. Commonly, enrichment programs purportedly emphasize processes (i.e., higher levels of thinking), but in reality, process instruction is directed toward demonstrating the processes learned by developing products. This situation may result from the pressure exerted on teacher and student alike to "show" what happens in the program for the gifted, that is, to produce evidence that learning is occurring and that it *is* different from regular class activities.

The criticism of product-oriented enrichment is that frequently it results in a "make it and take it" expectation; students churn out products without establishing a knowledge base or striving for accuracy and excellence in the product; quantity becomes the yardstick rather than quality. Such situations represent a lack of understanding of the necessity for, and role of, process, content, *and* product in curriculum enrichment for gifted students.

Certain models or approaches to enrichment are comprehensive in integrating content, process, and product. These include the Parallel Curriculum Model, Schoolwide Enrichment Model (Renzulli & Reis, 1985, 1997) and the Autonomous Learner Model (Betts, 1985).[2] Other models include Group Investigations (Sharan & Sharan, 1992) and Problem-Based Learning (Stepien, Gallagher, & Workman, 1993).

Problem-Based Learning may at first seem to be a content model, but much more is involved. Students are presented with complex, real-life problems and are expected to solve them, using the methods and thinking processes of the professionals who grapple with these types of "ill-structured" problems on a daily basis. Processes and products different from the regular curriculum are natural outcomes of the focus on realistic interdisciplinary situations.

Adopting approaches in which the three dimensions of content, process, and product are integrated, or making a conscious effort to combine methods from the three orientations, will better address the needs of gifted students through comprehensive enrichment.

Research on Enrichment

Because so many varied approaches are labeled "enrichment," research on this general practice is difficult to summarize. However, one body of research is available and provides strong support for the practice. Since the debate on ability grouping has continued for many years and has become somewhat heated, several meta-analyses of research and best-evidence syntheses have been conducted in an attempt to bring a scientific perspective to these arguments. The research indicates clearly that programs in which all ability groups follow the same curriculum have little or no effect on student achievement, while grouping programs that involve a more substantial adjustment of curriculum to ability have clear positive effects on children (Kulik, 1992).[3] Rogers (1991) concluded that ability grouping for curriculum extension in a pullout program produces an academic effect size of .65 (.30 is considered substantial), which is reflected in general achievement, critical thinking, and creativity; and Kulik (1992) reported that talented students from enriched classes "outperform initially equivalent students from conventional classes by 4 to 5 months on grade equivalent scales" (p. v).

Evidence for the success of enrichment practices also can be found in research on individual models and approaches advocated for use with gifted students. Reviews of several of these models can be found in Maker and Nielson (1995).

Acceleration

The term *acceleration* commonly is used both to denote models of service delivery and curriculum delivery. Acceleration as a *service delivery* model includes early entrance to kindergarten or to college; grade-skipping; or part-time grade acceleration, in which a student enters a higher grade level for part of the school day to receive advanced instruction in one or more content areas. Service delivery acceleration offers standard curricular experiences to students at a younger-than-usual age or lower-than-usual grade level.

Acceleration as a curriculum model involves speeding up the pace at which material is presented and/or expected to be mastered. Such acceleration

---

2. See Chapter 14 by Renzulli and Reis.

3. See Chapter 21 by Kulik.

may occur in a regular classroom, a resource room, or in special classes. It may take the form of telescoping, so that students complete two or more years' work in one year, or self-paced studies. While each type of acceleration has advantages, certain disadvantages also exist; both will be discussed briefly.

Early entrance to kindergarten or first grade allows children who are ready for the academic rigors and structure of school to encounter learning that may be challenging. Early entrance also allows students to complete schooling at a relatively young age, leaving more time for career and professional development. However, early entrance may tax the physical maturity of some children. They may tire before older students, or experience frustration due to the level of their psychomotor development. That is, their fine motor coordination may be underdeveloped by kindergarten standards, and they may have difficulty manipulating crayons or pencils. Additionally, this placement does not provide intellectual peers for the gifted child; average five-year-old children do not think in the same ways or about the same topics as gifted four-year-old children. Early entrance to college usually holds fewer perils than early entrance to kindergarten, unless the gifted students hope to socialize with college students of normal college age. However, the intellectual stimulation and challenges of good college courses may override this disappointment.

Full-time grade acceleration (grade-skipping) is an economical way to provide for gifted students. For some students, usually those in the primary grades, parents and students may find grade-skipping to offer sufficient challenges, and therefore to be a viable placement. However, grade-skipping may put older gifted students at a maturational disadvantage similar to that of the young kindergartner. This disadvantage becomes more pronounced during the middle and high school years, when physical maturation determines athletic prowess and influences heavily an individual's self-confidence.

As a general problem, acceleration as a service delivery model fails to provide a differentiated curriculum for gifted learners. Students receive instruction and have learning experiences that are designed for average students who are *older* than the gifted students, but the curriculum is not changed to match the needs of the gifted. The pace and content remain unchanged, the learner merely experiences them at an earlier age than usual. In addition, no provision is made for the different ways in which a student may be gifted. Acceleration as a service delivery model is based on the assumption that a student needs instruction at the same pace in all content areas and all activities. This assumption does not include understanding and recognition of the fact that many gifted children's development is "asynchronous" (Silverman, 1997).

Telescoping curriculum content so that gifted students may cover more material in less time and self-paced learning are types of curriculum acceleration. Bright students may master material rapidly and feel good about their accomplishments in this type of acceleration, and it is an economical plan. Telescoping and content acceleration generally present more problems to teachers and administrators than to students. Teachers need the requisite skills and time to telescope curriculum; and self-paced content acceleration for individual students requires planning time and special management techniques.

As with acceleration as a service delivery model, acceleration as a curriculum model offers "the same but sooner and/or faster" to gifted students. The content, learning processes, and expected products remain the same for students, whether they are gifted or not; only the onset and pace change.

Research on Acceleration

Researchers have studied acceleration of the various types and at different grade levels, and generally have reported academic achievement and social adjustment equal to or better than nonaccelerated, similar-ability peers, with no discernible negative effects from the acceleration. Kulik (1992), for instance, concluded from his meta-analyses of research that "talented students from accelerated classes outperform non-accelerates of the same age and IQ by almost one full year on achievement tests" (p. v). Other reported advantages of acceleration include (1) improved motivation, confidence, and scholarship; (2) prevention of lazy mental habits; (3) early completion of professional training, and (4) reduction of the cost of education (VanTassel-Baska, 1986).

In spite of evidence supporting the efficacy of acceleration for gifted students, widespread resistance to the concept and practice exists. The current organizational structure of most schools is geared to average students, with few provisions for the gifted; many teachers and administrators are reluctant to allow or create variances for individual students. Service delivery acceleration and individually paced learning also challenge the purpose of school, in terms of the democratic ideal and the concept of socialization with age peers. Additionally, acceleration as it has been practiced frequently has meant only covering more material faster. Also, the beliefs exist that acceleration is responsible for social maladjustment or that it creates skill gaps in core areas (VanTassel-Baska, 1986).

Enrichment and Acceleration as Complementary Program Components

Combining or integrating enrichment and acceleration for gifted students is not a radical nor revolutionary idea. In practice, meeting the needs of gifted students as determined by their learning characteristics and areas of giftedness requires that abstract and complex concepts be taught (enrichment) and that students proceed at a pace that is more rapid than that of the average learner (acceleration) in their area(s) of giftedness. Additionally, support for such integration may be found in the literature. Fox (1979) believes that acceleration means the adjustment of learning time to meet student capabilities and this adjustment will lead to higher levels of abstraction, more creative thinking, and mastery of more difficult content. VanTassel-Baska (1981) has stated that the term *enrichment* has no meaning for the gifted unless it is inextricably bound to good acceleration practices. Davis and Rimm (1989), in asking whether a special math, computer, or foreign language class in the elementary school is considered enrichment or acceleration, implied that in many cases the dichotomy is a false one.

As evidenced by practice and the literature, enrichment and acceleration are complementary components of a comprehensive curriculum for gifted learners. In the remainder of this chapter, using the concept of catastrophe theory as rationale and organizer, we will make a case for the necessity of including both enrichment and acceleration components in curriculum for gifted students.

Catastrophe Theory and Curriculum for Gifted Students

As explained by Berliner (1986), catastrophe theory is a mathematical system to account for abrupt changes in the nature of objects. It was developed by René Thom, a topological mathematician, and first published in 1968 in France. The theory may be applied to phenomena that are discontinuous, sudden,

and unpredictable, wherein change occurs imperceptibly or gradually to a point, and then suddenly a new state occurs. The simplest example from the physical world is the change of water into steam. As water heats, at some point (depending on the interaction of temperature, volume, pressure, and chemical particles), the water changes from liquid to gas. More heat has become the agent of a qualitative change; an interaction among factors has occurred. In Berliner's (1986) words, "more leads to different" (p. 34).

When applying catastrophe theory to curriculum, the critical factors are curriculum content, process, and product and acceleration and enrichment. Curriculum content, processes, and products must be accelerated and enriched to that point at which *more* becomes *different*. This is the point when an interaction occurs; the curriculum becomes *qualitatively differentiated*. Further discussion and examples of this concept follow.

One recommended modification to the content of curriculum for gifted students is an increase in the level of abstractness (Maker, 1982a; Maker & Nielson, 1996). The concepts selected to be taught should be abstract rather than concrete; thus they should be concepts such as culture, values, and mathematical patterns. Choosing abstract concepts *enriches* the curriculum, but the presentation and exploration of the concepts also must be *accelerated* if the dynamic of catastrophe theory is to be activated, that is, if the curriculum is to become qualitatively different.

For example, a regular sixth grade curriculum might include a study of the eastern hemisphere. Gifted students need to establish a factual information base, just as others do. However, gifted students should spend the majority of their time dealing with abstract concepts such as *culture, cause-effect relationships, political systems,* and *economic systems.* Concrete manifestations of abstract ideas always must be connected with and used to understand the overarching "big ideas." The abstractness of the content provides a type of enrichment, as this is beyond the regular curriculum, but the pace of presentation also must be accelerated.

The processes of instruction and learning included in curriculum for gifted students should be modified in a variety of ways, including an emphasis on higher levels of thinking (Maker, 1982a; Maker & Nielson, 1996). For example, gifted students should spend the majority of their time critically examining, synthesizing, and evaluating ideas, rather than memorizing and applying information and procedures. Focusing on the higher thought processes enriches the curriculum; these skills should be taught and practiced at an accelerated rate as well. Acceleration involves teaching the skills to students at younger than usual ages as well as pacing the instruction more rapidly than normal.

Student products reflect content learned and processes engaged in before and during the creation of the product. Products of gifted students should demonstrate the results of enrichment and acceleration of content, and process instruction by the sophistication of the concepts included and the presentation, form, or format of the finished product. For example, average fourth grade students, on completion of a unit of study on their state of residence, might submit reports of factual information about the state, and include a map and drawings of the state flag, flower, and bird. A more abstract approach suitable for gifted fourth grade students might focus on the effects of political forces on their state's government and economic climate. After examining and evaluating these forces, these students might even develop and give presentations to state legislators regarding the effect of, for example, underfunding educational programs or the attraction of new industry to the state. If their areas of giftedness were spatial, they might choose to present a photographic essay or a highly visual PowerPoint presentation, while linguistically gifted students might give an impassioned speech. Several students working together might combine their talents and interests into a multimedia presentation.

Applying catastrophe theory to the acceleration and enrichment of the content, processes, and products of the curriculum for gifted students provides a conceptual framework for differentiating such curriculum. The critical point is that all three factors—content, process, and product—must be both enriched *and* accelerated. Without both enrichment and acceleration, more is simply more; the point of the interaction that produces a qualitative difference is not reached. Acceleration and enrichment are necessary but not sufficient factors in developing and presenting curriculum to gifted learners. The catastrophic change that produces qualitatively different curriculum occurs only when all factors are present to a sufficient degree.

Curriculum for the Gifted

Experts in the field (e.g., Clark, 1988; Kaplan, 1979) agree that curriculum for gifted students should be differentiated from that offered to other students, according to the characteristics and needs of the individual. A number of models and checklists have been developed as ways to approach developing such differentiated curricula (Feldhusen & Wyman, 1980; Kaplan, 1974; Maker & Nielson, 1995, 1996; Sato & Johnson, 1978). Based on current research, preferred practices, and catastrophe theory, we offer a new approach. This approach illustrates the interdependent and interactive nature and roles of enrichment and acceleration in developing curricula for gifted students.

Problem Solving and the Curriculum

As educators focus more intensely on thinking skills and the thinking process, problem solving is mentioned frequently. Anderson's (1980) definition of problem solving as any goal-directed sequence of cognitive operations is very broad, but he is not alone in believing that thinking is problem solving. This belief leads to a natural progression of examining and/or planning curriculum for gifted students from a problem-solving perspective.

Types of Problems

Getzels (1964) makes a distinction between a *presented problem* and a *discovered problem situation*. A presented problem has a known formulation, method of solution, and solution. A discovered problem situation does not yet have a known formulation, and therefore no known method of solution and no known solution. Based on this concept, Getzels and Csikszentmihalyi (1967) developed a conceptual distinction between types of problems. According to these researchers, one can distinguish problem situations on the basis of (1) how clearly and completely the problem is stated at the beginning, (2) how much of the method for reaching the solution is available to the solver, and (3) how general is the agreement about an acceptable solution. Two ends of a continuum can be identified. At one end is a situation in which the problem, method, and the solution are known to the presenter. The problem solver needs only to employ the appropriate steps to arrive at the correct solution. At the other end of the continuum is a situation in which the problem is not formulated, and no solution or known method of solution exists. Most problems, or tasks and projects in people's personal and professional lives, are of the latter type. Maker (1986) expanded a model produced by Getzels and

Csikszentmihalyi (1967, p. 81), producing four problem types, and Schiever (1990) identified a fifth type. These problem types differ in what is known both to the problem presenter and the problem solver:

1. The problem and the method of solution are known to the problem presenter and the problem solver, but the solution is known only to the problem presenter.
2. The problem is known by the presenter and the solver, but the method of solution and solution are known only to the presenter.
3. The problem is known to the presenter and the solver, more than one method may be used to solve the problem, and the solution or range of solutions is known to the presenter.
4. The problem is known to the presenter and the solver, but the method and the solution are unknown to both the presenter and the solver.
5. The problem is undefined or unknown, and the method and the solution are unknown to both the presenter and the solver (see Table 12.1). In the classroom setting, situations that include this type of problem may be presented so that students use the skills necessary to solve real-life problems.

If thinking is considered to be problem solving, the utility of this conceptualization for curriculum development is readily apparent. School learning experiences typically consist of primarily Type I problems, wherein students are presented a clearly defined problem (such as in math) and taught the steps necessary to reach a solution. However, if one believes that the goal of curricula is to prepare students to be adults who cope successfully with and solve both personal and career problems, curricula also must include solving problems of types II, III, IV, and V if the necessary skills are to be taught and practiced. If gifted students are to become leaders and professionals with the capabilities society wants and needs and/or self-fulfilled adults, their school experiences must prepare them to be effective solvers of undefined, real-life problems.

Problem Solving as a Structure for Curriculum

Schiever (1990) suggested that thinking is developmental and that developmental processes include classification, concept development, derivation of principles, drawing conclusions, and making generalizations. These developmental processes each can be considered in light of problem types; that is, in what ways can, for example, classification be taught within the structure of a Type I, II, III, IV, or V problem? Curriculum content provides the context for teaching the developmental processes within the problem-solving perspective. Examples of such an approach to curriculum development follow. These examples are based on the belief that requiring students to memorize the results of other people's thinking is not a preferred teaching practice. Rather, students should be allowed and enabled to develop their own classification categories, concept delineations, principles, conclusions, and generalizations.

The National Standards for Civics and Government (1994) includes both content and performance

Table 12.1   Types of Problem Situations

Type	Problem Presenter	Problem Solver	Method Presenter	Method Solver	Solution Presenter	Solution Solver
I	K	K	K	K	K	U
II	K	K	K	U	K	U
III	K	K	R	U	R	U
IV	K	K	U	U	U	U
V	U	U	U	U	U	U

Source: Adapted with permission from The Creative Vision *by J. W. Getzels and M. Csikszentmihalyi, 1976, page 80, Table 6.1. Copyright © 1976 by John Wiley & Sons, New York. Note: K = Known, U = Unknown, R = Range.*

standards for students, as well as standards for teachers, schools, and state and local education agencies. The content standards specify not only the content to be mastered, but the intellectual and participatory skills students should acquire as well. For our purposes, we will use the Content Standard V, for grades 5–8, the responsibilities of citizens. Within this set of standards, Content Standard 1, personal responsibilities, is as follows: "Students should be able to evaluate, take, and defend positions on the importance of personal responsibilities to the individual and to society" (p. 78).

A Type I activity might require that students list five ways in which a person their age should be expected to take care of themselves. Following this, a comprehensive list could be put on the chalk board based on the students' personal lists. Students could then group the actions as "pleasant," "annoying," "difficult," or "easy." This activity primarily requires recall, which is low-level thinking, and the classification also is at a low level because the categories were provided.

A Type II activity might require students to extend the idea of self-care to the family. In what ways should persons their age be responsible for "taking care" of their families? In teams of two or three, students could develop lists of "within the family" and "outside world" actions appropriate for their ages. The list could be posted, and students asked to note which actions they perform daily, weekly, monthly, or not at all. The teacher, while drawing on students' experiences and beliefs, has defined the problem and provided the categories. While asking students to rank order the actions from most important to least and to support the ranking requires evaluation, the structure of the preceding tasks limits the thinking, and the curriculum is not enriched.

A Type III problem could center on accepting responsibility for the consequences of one's actions. A scenario of an adolescent who makes an unwise choice, steals something of moderate value, or violates a significant family rule could be presented to the class. Students could be instructed to develop two subsequent scenarios, one in which the young person assumes responsibility for the action and takes steps to rectify the situation and the other in which he or she tries to cover up, deny, or blame another for the problem. Following each scenario to its logical conclusion would provide ample material for discussions requiring analysis and evaluation, but the parameters set by the teacher at each step limit the level and complexity of thinking required of the students.

A Type IV problem might be presented through a question such as, "How might we determine the necessary components of a functional society?" The problem is known to the teacher and the students, but the method(s) and solution(s) are unknown and probably will evolve as the process unfolds. Students must generalize about the essence of functional groups, analyze components, and evaluate the importance of each. Information will be processed prior to naming components as necessary, and therefore the thinking will be at a higher level of abstraction than for problem Types I and II. In this example, content and processes are enriched. If accelerated pacing is included, as well as enriched and advanced student products, the interaction necessary for a differentiated curriculum will occur.

The key question for a Type V activity could be, "What current issues are related to personal responsibility?" Students need to define the problem in a way that gives them a direction in which to move toward solution. Conceivably, students could engage in most or all of the developmental processes and complex thinking strategies as they solve the problem. For example, students would have to (1) make conclusions and arrive at decisions before they gather data, (2) examine critically and evaluate the data, (3) derive principles of personal responsibility, and (4) generalize to determine the nature and parameters of personal responsibility within the global community. Drawing on their individual concepts, students might attempt to derive principles that would enable them to select (draw conclusions, make decisions) and convey the essence of what they had generalized about personal responsibility. The developmental processes would be applied as needed to fit the content and the task to be performed. As in the Type IV task, the levels of thinking will reflect the prior processing of information. The structure of this Type V problem assuredly would allow students to meet the content standard previously stated: "Students should be able to evaluate, take, and defend positions on the importance of personal responsibilities to the individual and to society." Additionally, as with the Type IV problem, curriculum content and processes have been enriched. Accelerated pacing and enriched and advanced products should result in qualitatively different learning experiences.

Curriculum Development

Developmental thinking processes may be examined and taught through superimposing the concept of problem type on the skill in the context of content to be learned, and structuring learning experiences accordingly. We are not suggesting that each skill should be taught as each of the four problem types; our purpose is to suggest a way to approach curriculum design or to evaluate existing curriculum. The reader should note that Type V problems necessarily move the thinker to high levels of thought processes, where undefined and real-life problems are found. Type V problems, by definition, entail developmental thinking processes and require complex thinking strategies. Classification or any other developmental process may be used or taught in a Type V format, but the skill will not be used in isolation. The interrelatedness of complex cognitive operations is apparent in the above analysis of Type V situations; teaching a developmental process within a Type V format necessarily requires complex thinking strategies.

Enrichment. Using the problem types as a structure for planning curriculum enables teachers to examine the thinking processes being taught, practiced, and learned, and facilitates the enrichment of curriculum content. As increasing numbers of Types III, IV, and V problems are used, thematic organization and more abstract and complex content may be included. By moving away from the clearly defined, rote-memory and comprehension-based activities and concept attainment, the progression naturally is toward bigger ideas that are more inclusive and more abstract. For example, to develop *chronological thinking,* (National Standards for Civics, 1994), students might examine patterns of historical succession and duration through a variety of independent methods (Type IV). A natural progression would occur toward being able to explain historical continuity and change. This progression toward the abstract and complex occurs when the structure for curriculum design incorporates higher levels of thinking and problem solving within the context of the content to be taught and learned.

Acceleration. Acceleration of learning experiences for gifted students must occur in two ways. First, gifted students are developmentally advanced, and the intellectually gifted can process more abstract ideas at an earlier age than other students. This means

that the concept of the constitutional balance of power, designed to be taught in grades 5–8 (National Standards for Civics, 1994), probably is appropriate for third or fourth grade gifted students.

Secondly, gifted students can move through, or process, information and ideas more quickly in their areas of giftedness than can other students. For example, students gifted in interpersonal or linguistic intelligence may not only begin processing abstract concepts such as *conflict* at an earlier age than their peers, but they also may move more quickly through developmental process activities and be able to apply the concept to undefined or real-life problems far sooner than their age-mates (Gallagher & Gallagher, 1994). An instructional unit that might require six weeks for most students to complete not only should be taught earlier and at a higher or more abstract level, but also may be completed by gifted students within three or four weeks.

Level of material and pace of instruction are dimensions of acceleration that mesh with the inclusion of enriched learning within a problem-solving approach to curriculum development. The problem types may be used as an infrastructure for acceleration and enrichment of content, process, and product. When these factors are in place, the stage is set for the catastrophic event, the desired change, and the emergence of a qualitatively different curriculum.

SUMMARY AND CONCLUSIONS

Acceleration and enrichment are terms used to describe both curriculum and service-delivery models. The primary focus of this chapter is on the curricular aspects of both, and their necessarily complementary nature. Components of curriculum, the content, instructional and learning processes, and expected student products—all must be enriched *and* accelerated. Catastrophe Theory provides a framework for understanding how enrichment and acceleration must come together to create appropriately differentiated curriculum for the gifted learner. Problem solving as a structure for curriculum is presented within a framework of problem types ranging from simple to complex. Examples drawn from the National Standards for History and for Civics and Government illustrate the use of problem types as a means of differentiating curriculum. The resulting curriculum is not just enriched, nor is it just accelerated. Through a dynamic interaction of factors, it has become differentiated for gifted learners.

QUESTIONS FOR THOUGHT AND DISCUSSION

1. In what ways is Schiever and Maker's definition of *giftedness* different from that commonly held by most educators?

2. How might you explain or demonstrate to a group of parents how catastrophe theory is applied to curriculum for the gifted?

3. How well do Schiever and Maker's Problem Types fit (or not fit) with other models or structures used to develop curriculum for the gifted (e.g., Bloom's Taxonomy; Renzulli and Reis's enrichment Types I, II, and III described in Chapter 14)? What combinations of the Problem Types with other models might you develop that are comfortable for your teaching style? For your students' learning styles?

4. What from this chapter was most useful or interesting to you? Why? What was least useful or interesting to you? Why?

REFERENCES

Anderson, J. R. (1980). *Cognitive psychology and its implications.* San Francisco: Freeman.

Berliner, D. C. (1986). Catastrophes and interactions: Comments on "the mistaken metaphor." In C. J. Maker (Ed.), *Critical issues in gifted education: Defensible programs for the gifted* (pp. 31–38). Rockville, MD: Aspen.

Betts, G. (1985). *Autonomous learner model for the gifted and talented.* Greeley, CO: Autonomous Learning Publications and Specialists.

Bloom, B. S., Englehart, M. D., Furst, E., Hill, W. H., & Krathwohl, D. R. (1956). *Taxonomy of educational objectives, handbook J: Cognitive domain.* New York: McKay.

Clark, B. (1988). *Growing up gifted* (3rd ed.). Columbus, OH: Merrill.

Davis, G. A., & Rimm, S. B. (1989). *Education of the gifted and talented* (2nd ed.). Englewood Cliffs, NJ: Prentice-Hall.

Feldhusen, J. F., & Wyman, A. R. (1980). Super Saturday: Design and implementation of Purdue's special program for gifted children. *Gifted Child Quarterly, 24,* 15–21.

Fox, L. H. (1979). Programs for the gifted and talented: An overview. In A. H. Passow (Ed.), *The gifted and the talented* (pp. 104–126). Chicago: National Society for the Study of Education.

Gallagher, J. J., & Gallagher, S. A. (1994). *Teaching the gifted child* (4th ed.) Boston: Allyn & Bacon.

Gardner, H. (1983). *Frames of mind.* New York: Basic Books.

Gardner, H. (1999). *Intelligence reframed.* New York: Basic Books.

Getzels, J. W. (1964). Creative thinking, problem solving, and instruction. In E. R. Hilgard (Ed.), *Theories of learning and instruction* (pp. 240–267). NSSE 66th Yearbook. Chicago: University of Chicago Press.

Getzels, J. W., & Csikszentmihalyi, M. (1967). Scientific creativity. *Science Journal, 3,*(9), 80–84.

Guilford, J. P. (1967). *The nature of human intelligence.* New York: McGraw-Hill.

Howley, A., Howley, C. B., & Pendarvis, E. D. (1986). *Teaching gifted children.* Boston: Little, Brown.

Kaplan, S. N. (1974). *Providing programs for the gifted and talented.* Ventura, CA: Office of the Ventura County Superintendent of Schools.

Kaplan, S. N. (1979). *Inservice training manual: Activities for developing curriculum for the gifted and talented.* Ventura, CA: Office of the Ventura County Superintendent of Schools.

Kulik, J. A. (1992). *An analysis of the research on ability grouping: Historical and contemporary perspectives.* Storrs, CT: National Research Center on the Gifted and Talented, University of Connecticut.

Maker, C. J. (1982a). *Curriculum development for the gifted.* Austin: PRO-ED.

Maker, C. J. (1982b). *Teaching models in education of the gifted.* Austin: PRO-ED.

Maker, C. J. (1986). *Frames of discovery: A process approach to identifying talent in special populations.* Unpublished paper available from author, Department of Special Education and Rehabilitation, University of Arizona.

Maker, C. J., & Nielson, A. B. (1995). Teaching models in education of the gifted (2nd ed.). Austin: Pro-Ed.

Maker, C. J., & Nielson, A. B. (1996). *Curriculum development and teaching strategies for gifted learners* (2nd ed.). Austin, TX: Pro-Ed.

National Standards for Civics and Government. (1994). Calabasas, CA: Center for Civic Education.

Parnes, S. J. (1981). CPSI: The general system. In W. B. Barbe and J. S. Renzulli (Eds.), *Psychology and education of the gifted.* New York: Irvington.

Renzulli, J. S., & Reis, S. A. (1985). *The school-wide enrichment model: A comprehensive plan for educational excellence.* Mansfield Center, CT: Creative Learning Press.

Renzulli, J. S., & Reis, S. M. (1997). *The schoolwide enrichment model: A how-to guide for educational excellence.* Mansfield Center, CT: Creative Learning Press.

Rogers, K. B. (1991). *The relationship of grouping practices to the education of the gifted and talented learner.* Storrs, CT: The National Research Center on the Gifted and Talented, University of Connecticut.

Sato, I. S., & Johnson, B. (1978). Multifaceted training meets multidimensionally gifted. *Journal of Creative Behavior, 12,* 63–71.

Schiever, S. W. (1990). *A comprehensive approach to teaching thinking.* Boston: Allyn and Bacon.

Sharan, Y., & Sharan, S. (1992). *Expanding cooperative learning through group investigations.* New York: Teachers College Press.

Silverman, L. S. (1997). The construct of asynchrony. *Peabody Journal of Education 72*(3 & 4), 36–58.

Stepien, W. J., Gallagher, S. A., & Workman, D. (1993). Problem-based learning for traditional and interdisciplinary classrooms. *Journal for the Education of the Gifted, 16*(4), 338–357.

Sternberg, R. J. (1985). *Beyond IQ: A triarchic theory of human intelligence.* New York: Cambridge University Press.

Taba, H., Durkin, M. C., Fraenkel, J. R., & McNaughton, A. H. (1971). *A teacher's handbook for elementary social studies: An inductive approach.* Reading, MA: Addison-Wesley.

VanTassel-Baska, J. (1981, December). *The great debates: For acceleration.* Speech presented at the CEC/TAG National Topical Conference on the Gifted and Talented Child, Orlando, FL.

VanTassel-Baska, J. (1986). Acceleration. In C. J. Maker (Ed.), *Critical issues in gifted education. Defensible programs for the gifted* (pp. 179–196). Austin: PRO-ED.

13

What Matters in Curriculum for Gifted Learners: Reflections on Theory, Research, and Practice

JOYCE VANTASSEL-BASKA, *College of William and Mary*

How can educators help a gifted student to excel? The answer to this question is complicated; much of our research on what has an impact on the lives of gifted individuals relates, for example, to the role of parents (Bloom, 1985; Feldman, 1985), the role of internal factors and significant others (VanTassel-Baska & Olszewski-Kubilius, 1989), the role of crystallizing experiences (Gardner, 1985), and even the role of chance (Tannenbaum, 1983). Yet the quality and character of a school's curriculum are vital ingredients to the eventual realization of a child's capacity. Gifted and talented students, like all students, have the right to a continuity of educational experience that meets their present and future academic needs. When an organized, thoughtful curriculum plan is in place and when that curriculum is supported by articulate, informed educational leadership, the probability of capturing the interest and energy of our ablest young thinkers is markedly enhanced. Certainly an organized curriculum is a key ingredient in the complex blending of circumstances so central to the transformation of a gifted learner's initial capacity for intellectual activity into a mature competence for academic and professional accomplishment.

Several key beliefs and assumptions have guided the thinking of most recent curriculum theory in gifted education (Gallagher & Gallagher, 1994; Maker & Nielson, 1996; Passow, 1982; VanTassel-Baska, 2000). These beliefs may be stated succinctly as follows:

1. All learners should be provided curriculum opportunities that allow them to attain optimum levels of learning.
2. Gifted learners have different learning needs compared with typical learners. Therefore, curriculum must be adapted or designed to accommodate these needs.
3. The needs of gifted learners cut across cognitive, affective, social, and aesthetic areas of curriculum experiences.
4. Gifted learners are best served by a confluent approach that allows for both accelerated and enriched learning.
5. Curriculum experiences for gifted learners need to be carefully planned, written down, implemented, and evaluated in order to maximize potential effect.

The purpose of this chapter is to present a view of curriculum for the gifted that is consonant with these assumptions and also recognizes key characteristics of the learner, the research and development evidence for curricular approaches, and the application of coherent curriculum theory to practice. The Integrated Curriculum Model (ICM) described in this chapter represents a synthesis of several approaches, forged to create greater complementarity in translating appropriate curriculum for the gifted learner into meaningful practice.

Historical Development of Curriculum in Gifted Education

For twenty-five years, the field of gifted education has favored a process-product orientation to curriculum. Fueled by the practical application of the Enrichment Triad Model (Renzulli, 1977) in pullout resource classrooms primarily at the elementary level, this approach gained further support as the cognitive science movement developed, calling for higher-order thinking skills, relevant real-world products, and emphasis on different modes of thinking (Gardner, 1983; Sternberg, 1985). The Autonomous Learner Model (Betts, 1991), the Purdue Three-Stage Model (Feldhusen & Kolloff, 1978), and the IPPM (Individualized Programming Planning Model; Treffinger, 1986) all made the underlying assumption that good curriculum for gifted learners was developed on the basis of individual learner interest, and all models emphasized higher-order skills used in the service of creating meaningful products.

This dominance in thinking about curriculum for the gifted has limited the development and use of models of curriculum derived from the disciplines of knowledge themselves. Thus, many gifted programs have lacked the rich substance that only the world of content knowledge might bring when linked to important ideas and issues.

Another approach to curriculum began to find favor in the late 1970s as a reaction against the trivialization of curriculum spawned by the misapplication of process-product models. Stanley's diagnostic-prescriptive content-based approach to curriculum (Stanley, Keating, & Fox, 1974; see also Keating, 1976) was concerned about students' learning important subject matter, but did not advocate radical reorganization of existing school curriculum, merely its speeding up or acceleration for gifted learners. Based on Scholastic Aptitude Test scores derived from national talent searches that identify over 120,000 talented middle-school-age students each year, this curriculum approach has been widely implemented in university-based summer and academic year offerings. Begun initially as a fast-paced, credit-producing series of course options primarily in mathematics, this model has now spread to all content areas. It offered nothing new in curriculum substance, only a prescription for flexible pacing of what already existed.

Rationale for an Integrated Curriculum Model

What the field has lacked is a comprehensive and cohesive curriculum framework that is sensitive to what good curriculum design contains, that honors the disciplines under study, and that sufficiently differentiates for gifted students. Thus it is time to support an integrated model of curriculum for gifted learners, one that draws the best from each curriculum approach already advocated.

There are other important reasons for advocating an integrated model for curriculum for the gifted. One stems from the need to address all salient characteristics of the gifted learner simultaneously, attending to precocity, intensity, and complexity as integrated characteristics that represent cognitive and affective dimensions of the learner. Integrating curriculum approaches allows for this broad-based response to student needs. A second reason relates to current delivery models for curriculum. As pullout programs have decreased in number, more gifted students are served in heterogeneous or self-contained (special class) settings, contexts in which integrated curriculum approaches can work well if applied diligently and systematically. An integrated curriculum may be thought of as a total curriculum package in an area of learning rather than an "add-on" curriculum.

A third reason for an integrated approach rests with the current research on learning. Studies have documented that better transfer of learning occurs when higher-order thinking skills are embedded in subject matter (Perkins & Saloman, 1989), and that teaching concepts of a discipline is a better way to produce long-term learning than teaching facts and rules (Marzano, 1992).

A fourth reason for using an integrated model for curriculum is related to a clear shift of emphasis from the focus on the individual gifted learner to the process of collective talent development for all learners. As this shift has occurred, the wedding of curriculum principles important for the gifted has been seen as the province of all learners as they develop talents in both traditional and nontraditional domains. This is accomplished through interdisciplinary, concept-based curriculum and higher-order thinking. For all of these reasons, the integrated curriculum model offers a cogent guide for curriculum design and development for gifted learners.

The Integrated Curriculum Model

The Integrated Curriculum Model (ICM) includes three interrelated curriculum dimensions, each responsive to a very different aspect of the gifted learner. These curriculum dimensions may be thought of as (1) emphasizing advanced content that frames disciplines of study, (2) providing higher order thinking and processing, and (3) focusing learning experiences around major issues, themes, and ideas that define both real-world applications and theoretical modeling within and across areas of study (see Figure 13.1).

The ICM synthesizes the three best approaches to curriculum development and implementation documented in the literature (i.e., Benbow & Stanley, 1983; Maker & Nielson, 1996; Ward, 1981). The fusion of these approaches is central to the development of coherent curriculum that is responsive to the diverse needs of gifted students, yet provides rich challenges for optimal learning.

The Talent Development Approach in Action

One approach to the talent development of all learners has been explored through national curriculum projects in science, social studies, and language arts, developed to respond to the needs of gifted learners for a challenging curriculum and to demonstrate alignment with the new curriculum reform paradigm (VanTassel-Baska, in press). Funded through the U.S. Department of Education Javits Act, these curriculum development projects at the College of William and Mary provide field-validated units for direct use in classrooms or as models for further development. Each set of units was developed by a team of curriculum specialists that included a classroom teacher, a content expert, and others with both curriculum and gifted and talented expertise.

The translation of the ICM to the National Language Arts Curriculum Project was accomplished by developing a curriculum framework addressing each of the dimensions. To satisfy the need for *advanced content,* the language arts curriculum used advanced literature selections, works that were at a reading level two years beyond grade level and so-phisticated in meaning. The writing emphasis was on persuasive essays—developing argument in written form—a more advanced form of writing than is typically taught at elementary levels. Advanced vocabulary and mastery of English syntax at the elementary level were also stressed. The *process-product* dimension of the curriculum was addressed by the embedded model of reasoning developed by Paul (1992) and the use of a research model developed to aid students in generating original work. Products were encouraged through both written and oral work. The *issue/theme* dimension of the curriculum included focusing on the theme of *change* as it applied to works of literature selected for the units, the writing process, language study, and learners' reflections on their own learning throughout the unit. Additionally, selecting an issue of significance to study was emphasized as a part of the research project for each unit. To date, six units have been developed, validated, piloted, and revised using this framework.

The translation of the ICM to the National Science Curriculum Project for High Ability Learners was driven by the overarching theme of *systems,* which became the conceptual organizing influence in each of seven units of study. Students learned the elements, boundaries, inputs, and outputs as well as interactions of selected systems. Through a problem-based learning approach, they also learned how science systems interact with real-world social, political, and economic systems. The *process-product* dimension of the curriculum model was addressed by engaging students in a scientific research process that led them to create their own experiments and to design their own solutions to the unit's central problem. The *content* dimension was addressed by selecting advanced science content for each unit and encouraging in-depth study of selected content relevant to understanding the central problem of the unit. These units are currently used in classrooms across the country to incor-

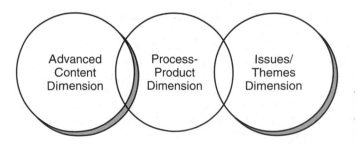

Figure 13.1 The Integrated Curriculum Model for Gifted Learners.

porate the new science emphasis and have been found successful in heterogeneous as well as more restricted settings.

The translation of the ICM to social studies was also driven by the theme or concept of *systems,* with additional emphasis on *change* and *cause and effect* for six units of study. Several units asked students to apply an understanding of systems to structures of society such as economic, political, and cultural systems. Other units focused on change and cause and effect, emphasizing connected chains of causes and effects to help students to understand multiple causation in history and to recognize that historical events are not inevitable. The *process-product* dimension of the model, as in the language arts, was addressed primarily through embedding the Paul (1992) model of reasoning and through questioning and writing projects that encourage analysis of issues. This dimension was also addressed through a heavy emphasis on historical analysis, using a specific model to help students understand the importance of context as well as content in analyzing primary sources. Products included written and oral presentations of research efforts and other activities. The *advanced content* dimension was addressed through the selection of advanced reading materials, in terms of specific documents and historical fiction extensions, and through early introduction of skills and ideas in social studies, such as primary source analysis and a heavy focus on issues and unpredictability in history.

Curriculum Reform Design Elements

These national curriculum projects for high-ability learners were developed with an understanding of appropriate curriculum dimensions for gifted students. They also include key design features of curriculum reform strongly advocated by the national standards projects (O'Day & Smith, 1993) and the middle school movement (Erb, 1994). Thus the projects employ the following emphases:

- The curriculum is *meaning-based* in that it emphasizes depth over breadth and concepts over facts. It also is grounded in real-world issues and problems that students care about or need to know. For example, in science, students study the implications of daily occurrences like acid spills on interstate highway systems. In language arts, they relate to the impact of the treatment of minorities in this country as it has changed over a sixty-year period.

- The curriculum incorporates *higher-order thinking* as integral to all content areas. The units provide students opportunities to demonstrate their understanding of advanced content and interdisciplinary ideas through strategies such as concept mapping, persuasive writing, and designing experiments.

- The curriculum emphasizes *intra-* and *interdisciplinary connections* through overarching concepts, issues, and themes as major organizers. Thus, students study systems of cities, of government, of economies, and of language as well as chemistry and biology.

- The curriculum provides opportunities for *metacognition,* student reflection on learning processes. Students are involved in consciously planning, monitoring, and assessing their own learning for efficient and effective use of time and resources.

- The curriculum develops *habits of mind* through cultivating modes of thinking that resemble those of professionals in various fields with respect to skills, predispositions, and attitudes. For example, in science, curiosity, objectivity, and skepticism are openly nurtured.

- The curriculum promotes *active learning* and *problem solving* by putting students in charge of their own learning. In the problem-based science units, students find out what they know, what they need to know, and how to pursue important knowledge in working on a real-world problem in small investigatory teams. In social studies, students work together to explore different aspects of a culture and then to share findings.

- The curriculum is *technology-relevant* in that it uses various new technologies as tools for the learning process, from doing research via the Internet, to composing at the word processor, to communicating with students across the world by e-mail.

- The curriculum sets *learner outcomes of significance.* Expectations for learning reflect the priorities of the new curriculum for being broad-based, conceptual, and relevant to real-world application. In each set of units, learner outcomes reflect content, process, and concept emphases.

- The curriculum employs *authentic assessment* by tapping into what students know as a result of meaningful instruction. Using approaches like portfolios and performance-based activities, the units engage learners in assessment as an active part of the learning process.

All of these reform elements formed the basis for the initial curriculum development work. Tailoring the curriculum for gifted learners occurred through ensuring the following kinds of emphasis: provisions for acceleration and compression of content; use of higher-order thinking skills (e.g., analysis, synthesis, evaluation); integration of content by key ideas, issues, and themes; advanced reading level; opportunities for students to develop advanced products; opportunities for independent learning based on student capacity and interest; and use of inquiry-based instructional techniques.

Implementation Considerations

Implementation of the Integrated Curriculum Model (ICM) is based on several considerations. Most important among them is the nature of the gifted learner.

The Learner: Characteristics, Aptitudes, and Predispositions

There are many characteristics of gifted learners on which one might focus to create an optimal match between learner and curriculum. In our studies it has become apparent that three characteristics remain pivotal for curriculum planning and development.

The *precocity* of the learner is a key characteristic. Most students identified for gifted programs are at least two years advanced in mathematical, verbal, or both areas. For very gifted learners, there is a powerful motivation to "learn fast and move ahead."

In addition to precocity, another key characteristic is the *intensity* of gifted learners. This intensity may be manifested affectively in emotional responsiveness, as when students react strongly to the death of a pet or a classroom injustice committed by a teacher. But this characteristic also has saliency in the cognitive realm. Students exhibit intensity through the capacity to focus and concentrate for long periods of time on a subject or an idea that fascinates them. Such a characteristic can just as quickly become dissipated in uninteresting busywork or lack of depth in the exploration even of a subject of interest. Intensity, like precocity, needs curricular attention.

The third learner characteristic of curricular interest is *complexity*, the capacity of gifted learners to engage in higher-level and abstract thinking even at young ages. It also refers to their preference for hard

and challenging work, often at levels beyond their current functioning. They also enjoy working on multiple levels simultaneously, as when solving complex real-world problems that have many parts and perspectives to study. Just as with precocity and intensity, the characteristic of complexity in the gifted demands curriculum responsiveness. It is openly desired by the learner as well as indicated by student behavior.

Curriculum models for the gifted have responded variously to these characteristics. The Integrated Curriculum Model represents a fusion of these approaches, such that the most powerful characteristics of the gifted are directly reflected in the curriculum intervention.

Context Variables

While the need for a match between the learner and the intervention has already been described, it is also important to highlight contextual considerations that could have an impact on the successful use of this curriculum model. At least four variables must be considered.

Flexibility in Student Placement and Progress

Even an enriched and accelerated curriculum developed for high-ability learners cannot be used without careful consideration of entry skills, rate of learning, and special interests and needs. Thus, ungraded multi-age contexts in which high-ability learners may access appropriate work groups and curriculum stations are crucial components of implementation. Pretesting students on relevant skills is a central part of many new curriculum projects, and diagnosing unusual readiness or developmental spurts that may occur in a curriculum sequence is also important. Schools may notice and use such data as a basis for more in-depth work in an area of a particular teaching unit.

Grouping

Attention must be paid to the beneficial impact of grouping for instruction. Forming instructional groups of gifted students is clearly the most effective and efficient way to deliver differentiated curriculum. Whether such grouping occurs in separately designated classes or in regular classrooms is a local consideration.

Trained Teachers

There is little reason not to place gifted students with teachers who have received at least 12 hours of professional training. The benefits to gifted learners become greater when differentiated curriculum is handled by those sensitive to the nature and needs of such students.

A Climate of Excellence

For gifted learners to perform at optimal levels, the educational context must offer challenging opportunities that provide generative situations (VanTassel-Baska, 1998), yet also demand high standards of excellence. More than ever, a climate of excellence matters if curriculum standards are to be raised successfully for any student. For gifted students in particular, such a climate must be in place to ensure optimal development, positive attitudes toward learning, and high engagement. Such a climate is also essential for disadvantaged gifted youth, who are put more at risk by lowered expectations for performance (House & Lapan, 1994).

Research Results and Implications

Studies continue to assess the cognitive and affective impacts of the Integrated Curriculum Model in the three content domains. Results from six years of data in language arts and five years in science are summarized in the following sections; social studies data collection remains in early stages.

Science Curriculum Effectiveness Data

The problem-based science curriculum units for high ability learners in grades 2–8 have been rigorously evaluated to ensure both effectiveness in promoting student learning gains and acceptance by teachers.

Although the units are designed to have assessments address all three of the major science learning goals—content, process, and concept—the research design focused explicitly on student application of the scientific method. Findings related to two of the units, *Acid, Acid Everywhere* and *What a Find,* are presented here for illustrative purposes.

Design

The sample was composed of volunteer teachers and their classrooms from our national network of schools, including districts from Illinois, Florida, Connecticut, South Carolina, Ohio, Indiana, and Virginia. All seventy-five teachers who participated in the field-testing of units received implementation training lasting two to five days.

Students included in the sample were all average, above average, or high ability learners and were drawn from urban, suburban, and rural districts. All pullout and self-contained classrooms contained only high ability learners, but other organizational models were also represented in the sample.

Experimental and comparison classrooms were assessed on a pre- and post-test basis. Post-tests were administered at the conclusion of the implementation process, after approximately twenty to thirty-six hours of instruction.

Instruments and Procedures

The claims made regarding the evidence of effectiveness of this project in promoting student learning are based on the use of the Cain (1990) Diet Cola Test. The Diet Cola Test measures a student's ability to apply the scientific method and to demonstrate scientific reasoning skills.

The instrument has alternate forms, which made it very useful for the pre/post-test design. It is an open-ended, performance-based assessment using a rubric that has a ceiling of twenty-one points for rating student responses. Administration takes only thirty–forty minutes.

Data Analysis and Results

Using the classroom as the unit of analysis, an analysis of covariance yielded statistically significant differences between treatment and comparison groups on both units ($p < .05$). For Acid, Acid Everywhere, the test yielded a significant F value of 32.86 ($p < .001$); experimental classrooms had an adjusted mean post-test score of 6.81, while the adjusted mean score for the comparison group was 5.41. For What a Find, the adjusted mean on the Diet Cola Test for the experimental group was 5.95, and for the comparison group, 4.07 ($F = 4.72$; $p < .05$). The effect sizes also demonstrated that the differences were educationally important.

Teacher Questionnaire Results

In addition to student test data, the effectiveness of the science units was assessed by asking teachers to respond to a *Curriculum Unit Evaluation Questionnaire.* Forty-two teachers from fifteen school districts completed the questionnaire for *Acid, Acid Everywhere.* Demographic data from this form indicated that the range of classes included various grouping patterns, from self-contained gifted classes to heterogeneous classrooms, and that the teachers were generally experienced, with several years of working with gifted and talented students and in teaching science.

The questionnaire asked teachers to indicate their perceptions about a number of items concerning the unit, based on their experience teaching it. Most teachers reported positive perceptions. Teachers found the unit to be highly appropriate for high ability students in terms of goals and outcomes as well as exercises and activities; felt that it promoted active student involvement; and felt that it was motivating for students.

The overall judgment of the units by pilot teachers seemed to center on four main points:

- The units had applicability across a broad range of learners.
- The units were well designed and documented important curriculum elements for teachers.
- The units were enjoyable and motivating for both students and teachers.
- Teachers would use the units again.

Language Arts Curriculum Effectiveness Data

The study focused on the effectiveness of the William and Mary language arts curriculum for teaching literary analysis and interpretation and persuasive writing as language arts manifestations of higher-level thinking. Thus, it contributes to our understanding of the importance of embedding higher-order skills into content.

Design and Sample

In all, forty-six schools in ten states participated in the study. Students (N = 2,189) were all pre-identified gifted learners in grades 2–8 in their local school district.

Instrumentation

The two assessments measured literary analysis and persuasive writing skills. At the beginning and at the end of each unit, students were asked to read a selection and to complete the two assessments based on that selection. The first assessment was a performance-based test of literary analysis and interpretation. This test included four questions addressing the following topics: (1) main idea, (2) analysis of a quote, (3) relationship of the concept of change to the selection, and (4) creating a title with a rationale to support it. The second assessment was a performance-based persuasive writing assessment that asked students to develop an argument to support whether or not they would require all the students in their grade to read the given selection. In each unit, students read and responded to a different selection in the pre-test than in the post-test, although the two selections in each unit represented the same genre.

The rubric for the literature test gave a range of zero to three points for each of the four questions, for a total score range of zero to twelve. The rubric for the writing test gave a range of zero to twenty total points, with a zero to six range for each of the elements of claim, data, and warrant, and a zero to two range for conclusion.

Data Analysis and Results

The results of analyses of covariance indicated statistically significant differences favoring the treatment group on the post-tests for literary analysis and interpretation ($F = 17.75$; $p < 0.001$) and for persuasive writing ($F = 70$; $p < 0.001$). For the literary analysis test, the adjusted mean score on the post-test for the treatment group was 6.86, while the comparison group had an adjusted mean score of 5.88. On the persuasive writing test, differences were even more dramatic, with the treatment group achieving an adjusted mean post-test score of 11.34, while the comparison group had an adjusted mean score of 7.59, The effect sizes were also medium to large, again indicating educational importance of the results as well as statistical significance.

These analyses were conducted across four units; the results of separate analyses, conducted at the unit level, are consistent with the results combined across units. In other words, virtually any language arts unit within the William and Mary curriculum can be implemented and produce a significant treatment effect.

Additional tests were run to compare performance by gender and by socio-economic status (SES) within the treatment group. The results showed no differences by gender for literature, but found a statistically significant difference for persuasive writing favoring girls ($p < 0.01$). However, that difference was found to be of little practical importance when effect size was computed. This suggests that boys and girls benefited relatively equally from their exposure to the curriculum. The SES comparison used school-wide data on students on free or reduced lunch to categorize schools as high SES or lower SES. This comparison yielded no statistically significant differences between groups and demonstrated clearly, especially in writing, that students from high and low SES groups can benefit from the curriculum.

Discussion of Results

The data suggest that the William and Mary language arts units produces significant and important gains for gifted learners in key aspects of the language arts as assessed by demonstration of high level thinking on performance-based measures. The treatment was effective with both economically disadvantaged as well as more advantaged students. It was also effective with males and females. The grouping model used showed minimal evidence of impact on student performance, with all group-ing models showing strong evidence of learning gains.

Clearly, students benefited from their exposure to the William and Mary curriculum in language arts. Furthermore, this study showed how curriculum derived from standards-based reform can be assessed using instruments that require demonstration of higher-order reasoning in the language arts domain.

SUMMARY AND CONCLUSIONS

The Integrated Curriculum Model offers the best combinational approach to date for restructuring curriculum for gifted learners at the same time that it responds to the curriculum reform agenda. It offers practitioners concrete units of study to implement in classrooms nationally. By meeting the criteria for exemplary curriculum design, exemplary content considerations, and differentiation for gifted learners, the units developed at the College of William and Mary provide the translation from theoretical principles to practice.

QUESTIONS FOR THOUGHT AND DISCUSSION

1. Explain why VanTassel-Baska believes her Integrated Curriculum Model (ICM) is superior to past curriculum models for the gifted.

2. VanTassel-Baska criticizes process-product orientations to gifted curriculum (e.g., Renzulli's Enrichment Triad Model, Chapter 14) for not providing rich content knowledge. Is this criticism is justified? Explain.

3. Itemize and explain what VanTassel-Baska believes are necessary "Curriculum Reform Design Elements."

4. Which do you believe are the most important elements? Explain.

REFERENCES

Benbow, C. P., & Stanley, J. C. (Eds.). (1983). *Academic precocity: Aspects of its development.* Baltimore: Johns Hopkins University Press.

Betts, G. (1991). The autonomous learner model for the gifted and talented. In N. Colangelo & G. A. Davis (Eds.), *Handbook of gifted education* (pp. 142–153). Boston: Allyn & Bacon.

Bloom, B. (1985). *Developing talent in young people.* New York: Ballantine.

Cain, M. F. (1990). The Diet Cola Test. *Science Scope, 13* (4), 32–34.

Erb, T. (1994). The middle school: Mimicking the success routes of the information age. *Journal for the Education of the Gifted, 17,* 385–408.

Feldhusen, J., & Kolloff, P. (1978, January–February). A three stage model for gifted education. *G/C/T,* 3–5, 53–57.

Feldman, D. (1985). *Nature's gambit.* New York: Basic Books.

Gallagher, J. J., & Gallagher, S. A. (1994). *Teaching the gifted child* (4th ed.). Boston: Allyn & Bacon.

Gardner, H. (1983). *Frames of mind.* New York: Basic Books.

Gardner, H. (1985). The role of crystallizing experience. In F. Horowitz & M. O'Brien (Eds.), *Developmental perspectives on the education of the gifted.* Washington, DC: American Psychological Association.

Hillocks, G., Jr. (1986). *Research on written composition: New directions for teaching.* Urbana, IL: ERIC Clearinghouse on Reading and Communication Skills and National Conference on Research in English.

House, E., & Lapan, S. (1994). Evaluation of programs for disadvantaged gifted students. *Journal for the Education of the Gifted, 17,* 441–466.

Keating, D. (1976). *Intellectual talent.* Baltimore: Johns Hopkins University Press.

Maker, C. J., & Nielson, A. B. (1996). *Curriculum development and teaching strategies for gifted learners.* Austin: Pro-Ed.

Marzano, R. (1992). *Cultivating thinking in English.* Urbana, IL: National Council of Teachers of English.

O'Day, J. A., & Smith, M. S. (1993). Systemic reform and educational opportunity. In S. H. Fuhrman (Ed.), *Designing coherent education policy* (pp. 250–311). San Francisco: Jossey-Bass.

Passow, A. H. (1982). *Differentiated curriculum for the gifted/talented.* Ventura County, CA: Office of the Superintendent of Schools.

Paul, R. (1992). *Critical thinking: What every person needs to survive in a rapidly changing world.* Rohnert Park, CA: Critical Thinking Foundation.

Perkins, D., & Saloman, G. (1989). Are cognitive skills context bound? *Educational Research, 18*(1), 16–25.

Renzulli, J. (1977). *The enrichment triad.* Mansfield Center, CT: Creative Learning Press.

Stanley, J., Keating, D., & Fox, L. (1974). *Mathematical talent.* Baltimore: Johns Hopkins University Press.

Sternbaum, R. J. (1985). *Beyond IQ.* New York: Basic Books.

Tannenbaum, A. (1983). *Gifted children.* New York: Macmillan.

Toulmin, S. E. (1958). *The uses of argument.* Cambridge: Cambridge University Press.

Treffinger, D. (1986). Fostering effective, independent learning through individualized programming. In J. S. Renzulli (Ed.), *Systems and models for developing programs for the gifted and talented* (pp. 429–468). Mansfield Center, CT: Creative Learning Press.

VanTassel-Baska, J. (Ed.). (1998). *Excellence in educating gifted and talented learners* (3rd ed.). Denver, CO: Love.

VanTassel-Baska, J. (2000). Theory and research on curriculum development for the gifted. In K. A. Heller, F. Mönks, R. J. Sternberg, & R. F. Subotnik (Eds.), *International handbook on giftedness and talent* (2nd ed., pp. 345–365). London: Pergamon Press.

VanTassel-Baska, J. (in press). *Curriculum planning and instructional design for gifted learners* (2nd ed.). Denver, CO: Love.

VanTassel-Baska, J., & Olszewski-Kubilius, P. (1989). *Patterns of influence: The home, the self, and the school.* New York: Teachers College Press.

Ward, V. (1981). *Differential education for the gifted.* Ventura County, CA: Office of the Superintendent of Schools.

BIBLIOGRAPHY

Adams, C. M., & Callahan, C. M. (1995). The reliability and validity of a performance task for evaluating science process skills. *Gifted Child Quarterly, 39,* 14–20.

Amabile, T. (1996). *Creativity in context.* Boulder, CO: Westview Press.

Archambault, F. X., Westberg, K. L., Brown, S., Hallmark, B. W., Zhang, W., & Emmons, C. (1993). Regular classroom practices with gifted students: Findings from the classroom practices survey. *Journal for the Education of the Gifted, 16,* 103–119.

Bolanos, P. (1991). *Curriculum for the key school.* Presentation at a meeting of the National Javits Project Directors, Washington, DC.

Burkhalter, N. (1995). A Vygotsky-based curriculum for teaching persuasive writing in the elementary grades. *Language Arts, 72,* 192–196.

Gardner, H. (1993). *Multiple intelligences: The theory in practice.* New York: Basic Books.

Hansen, J., & Feldhusen, J. (1994). Comparison of trained and untrained teachers of gifted students. *Gifted Child Quarterly, 38,* 115–123.

Karnes, F. A., & Stephens, K. R. (2000). State definitions for the gifted and talented revisited. *Exceptional Children, 66,* 219–238.

Kulik, J. (1993). *An analysis of the research on ability grouping: Historical and contemporary perspectives.* Storrs, CT: National Research Center on the Gifted and Talented, University of Connecticut.

Maker, C. J. (1982). *Curriculum development for the gifted.* Rockville, MD: Aspen.

National Assessment Governing Board. (1992). *Reading framework for the 1992 national assessment of education progress.* Washington, DC: U.S. Department of Education.

Parker, J., & Karnes, F. (1991). Graduate degree programs and resource centers in gifted education: An update and analysis. *Gifted Child Quarterly, 35,* 43–48.

Reis, S. M., & Purcell, J. H. (1993). An analysis of content elimination and strategies used by elementary classroom teachers and the curriculum compacting process. *Journal for the Education the Gifted, 16,* 147–170.

Schlichter, C. (1986). Talents Unlimited: An inservice education model for teaching thinking skills. *Gifted Child Quarterly, 30,* 119–123.

Schlichter, C. (1997). Talents Unlimited Model in programs for gifted students. In N. Colangelo & G. A. Davis (Eds.), *Handbook of gifted education* (2nd ed., pp. 318–327). Boston: Allyn & Bacon.

VanTassel-Baska, J. (1986). Effective curriculum and instructional models for the gifted. *Gifted Child Quarterly, 30,* 164–169.

VanTassel-Baska, J. (1992). *Effective curriculum planning for gifted learners.* Denver, CO: Love.

VanTassel-Baska, J. (1994a). *Comprehensive curriculum for gifted learners* (2nd ed.). Boston: Allyn & Bacon.

VanTassel-Baska, J. (1994b). Development and assessment of integrated curriculum: A worthy challenge. *Quest, 5*(2), 1–5.

VanTassel-Baska, J. (1995). The development of talent through curriculum. *Roeper Review, 18,* 98–102.

VanTassel-Baska, J., Bass, G., Ries, R., Poland, D., & Avery, L. D. (1998). A national study of science curriculum effectiveness with high ability students. *Gifted Child Quarterly, 42,* 200–211.

VanTassel-Baska, J., & Feldhusen, J. (Eds.). (1981). *Concept curriculum for the gifted K-8.* Matteson, IL: Matteson School District #162.

VanTassel-Baska, J., Johnson, D. T., Hughes, C. E., & Boyce, L. N. (1996). A study of language arts curriculum effectiveness with high ability learners. *Journal for the Education of the Gifted, 19,* 461–480.

VanTassel-Baska, J., & Little, C. A. (in press). *Reform-based content curriculum for high-ability learners.* Waco, TX: Prufrock.

VanTassel-Baska, J., Zuo, L., Avery, L. D., & Little, C. A. (in press). A curriculum study of gifted student learning in the language arts. *Gifted Child Quarterly.*

Westberg, K. L., Archambault, F. X., Dobyns, S. M., & Salvin, T. J. (1993). An observational study of classroom practices used with third- and fourth-grade students. *Journal for the Education of the Gifted, 16,* 120–146.

14

The Schoolwide Enrichment Model: Developing Creative and Productive Giftedness

JOSEPH S. RENZULLI AND SALLY M. REIS, *University of Connecticut*

How can we develop the creative potential of young people and inspire creative productivity in a time period in which fast is considered good and faster is considered even better? How can we help children to learn to think creatively, and to value opportunities for quiet reflection and creative work of their choice? The Schoolwide Enrichment Model (SEM) gives each school the flexibility to develop unique programs for talent development and creative productivity based on local resources, student demographics, and school dynamics as well as faculty strengths and creativity. The major goal of SEM is to promote both challenging and enjoyable high-end learning across a wide range of school types, levels, and demographic differences. The idea is to create a repertoire of services that can be integrated to create "a rising tide lifts all ships" approach.

The SEM suggests that educators examine ways to make schools more inviting, friendly, and enjoyable places that encourage talent development—instead of regarding students as repositories for information that will be assessed with the next round of standardized tests. Not only has this model been successful in addressing the problem of high potential students who have been under-challenged, it also provides additional important learning paths for gifted and talented students who find success in more traditional learning environments.

At the heart of the SEM is the Enrichment Triad Model (Renzulli, 1976) developed in the mid-1970s and initially implemented by school districts primarily in Connecticut. The model proved to be quite popular. A book about the Enrichment Triad Model (Renzulli, 1977) was published, and even more districts began asking for help in implementing this approach. At this point, a clear need was established for research about the effectiveness of the model and for practical procedures that could provide technical assistance to help interested educators develop programs in their schools. We became fascinated by the wide range of Triad programs developed by different teachers in different school districts, some urban, rural, and suburban. In some programs, for example, teachers consistently elicited high levels of creative productivity in students, while others had few students who engaged in this type of work. In some districts, many enrichment opportunities were regularly offered to students not formally identified for the program, while in other districts only identified gifted students had access to enrichment experiences.

In the more than two decades since the Enrichment Triad Model was first used, an unusually large number of examples of creative productivity have been produced by young people whose educational experiences were guided by this programming approach. Perhaps we did not fully understand at the onset of our work the full implications of the model for encouraging and developing creative productivity in young people. These implications relate most directly to teacher training, resource procurement and management, product evaluation, and other theoretical concerns (such as motivation, task commitment, self-efficacy) that probably would have gone unexamined, undeveloped, and unrefined without the favorable results that were reported to us by early implementers of the model. We became increasingly interested in how and why the model was working, and how we could further expand the theoretical rationale underlying our work and enlarge the population to which services could be provided. Thus, several years of conceptual analysis, practical experience, and an examination of the work of other theorists brought us to the point of tying together the material in this chapter, which represents approximately twenty-three years of field-testing, research, evolution, and dissemination.

This chapter provides an overview of the conception of giftedness upon which this model is based. It also provides a description of the original Enrichment Triad Model along with a chronology of how the model has expanded and changed. Selected research about the SEM is discussed and a brief summary of the research dealing with the SEM is provided.

A Broadened Conception of Giftedness

Restrictiveness in determining who is eligible for special programs and services can be expressed in two ways. First, a definition can limit the number of specific performance areas that are considered in determining eligibility for special services. A conservative definition, for example, might limit eligibility to academic performance only and exclude other areas such as music, art, drama, leadership, public speaking, social service, creative writing, or skills in interpersonal relations. Second, a definition can limit the degree or level of excellence that one must attain by establishing extremely high cutoff points.

In recent years, very few educators cling tenaciously to a "straight IQ" or purely academic definition of giftedness. "Multiple talent" and "multiple criteria" are almost the bywords of the present-day gifted education movement, and most people have little difficulty in accepting a definition that includes most areas of human activity that are manifested in socially useful forms of expression.

Two Kinds of Giftedness

Schoolhouse Giftedness

Schoolhouse giftedness might also be called *test-taking* or *lesson-learning* giftedness. It is the kind most easily measured by IQ or other cognitive ability tests, and for this reason it is also the type most often used for selecting students for entrance into special programs. The abilities people display on IQ and aptitude tests are exactly the kinds of abilities most valued in traditional school learning situations.

A large body of research tells us that students who score high on IQ tests are also likely to get high grades in school, and that these test-taking and lesson-learning abilities generally remain stable over time. The results of this research should lead to some very obvious conclusions about schoolhouse giftedness: It exists in varying degrees, it can be identified through standardized assessment techniques, and we should therefore do everything in our power to make appropriate modifications for students who have the ability to cover regular curricular material at advanced rates and levels of understanding.

Curriculum compacting (Renzulli, Smith, & Reis, 1982; Reis, Burns, & Renzulli, 1992) is a procedure used for modifying standard curricular content to accommodate advanced learners. Other acceleration techniques should represent essential parts of every school program that strives to respect the individual differences that are clearly evident from classroom performance and/or scores yielded by cognitive ability tests.

Creative-Productive Giftedness

Scores on IQ tests and other measures of cognitive ability do not tell the whole story when it comes to making predictions about creative-productive giftedness. Creative-productive giftedness describes human activity and involvement in which a premium is placed on the development of original material and products that are purposefully designed to have an impact on one or more target audiences. Learning situations that are designed to promote creative-productive giftedness emphasize the application of information (content) and thinking skills (process) in an integrated, inductive, and real-problem oriented manner. The role of the student is transformed from that of a learner of prescribed lessons to one in which she or he uses the *modus operandi* of a firsthand inquirer. This approach is quite different from the development of lesson-learning giftedness, which tends to emphasize deductive learning, structured training in the development of thinking processes, and the acquisition, storage, and retrieval of information. In other words, creative-productive giftedness is simply putting one's abilities to work on problems and areas of study that have personal relevance to the student and that can be escalated to appropriately challenging levels of investigative activity.

Why is creative-productive giftedness important enough for us to question the "tidy" and relatively easy approach that has traditionally been used to select students on the basis of test scores? Why do some people want to rock the boat by challenging a conception of giftedness that can be numerically defined by simply giving a test? The answers to these questions are simple yet compelling.

There is much more to identifying human potential than the abilities revealed on traditional tests of intelligence, aptitude, and achievement. Furthermore, history tells us it has been the creative and productive people of the world—the producers rather than consumers of knowledge, the reconstructionists of thought in all areas of human endeavor—who have become recognized as "truly gifted" individuals. History does not remember persons who merely scored well on IQ tests or those who learned their lessons well.

The definition of giftedness (see Figure 14.1) that characterizes creative productive giftedness and serves as part of the rationale for the Enrichment Triad Model is the three-ring conception of giftedness (Renzulli, 1978, 1986), in which giftedness consists of an interaction among three basic clusters, above average general ability, high levels of creativity, and high task commitment. Gifted and talented students capable of developing this composite set of potentially valuable areas of human performance require a variety of educational opportunities and services not normally provided through regular instructional programming.

An Overview of the Enrichment Triad Model

The Enrichment Triad Model was designed to encourage creative productivity on the part of young

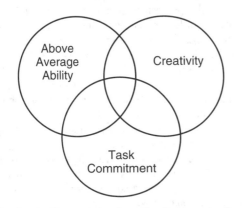

Reprinted with permission from Creative Learning Press.

Figure 14.1 The Three-Ring Conception of Giftedness.

people by exposing them to various topics, areas of interest, and fields of study, and to further train them to *apply* advanced content, process-training skills, and methodology training to self-selected areas of interest. Accordingly, three types of enrichment are included in the Triad Model (see Figure 14.2).

Type I enrichment is designed to expose students to a wide variety of disciplines, topics, occupations, hobbies, persons, places, and events that would not ordinarily be covered in the regular curriculum. In schools that use this model, an enrichment team consisting of parents, teachers, and students often organizes and plans Type I experiences by contacting speakers, arranging minicourses, demonstrations, or performances, or by ordering and distributing films, slides, videotapes, or other print or non-print media.

Type II enrichment consists of materials and methods designed to promote the development of thinking and feeling processes. Some Type II training is general and is usually carried out both in classrooms and in enrichment programs. Training activities include the development of (1) creative thinking and problem solving, critical thinking, and affective processes; (2) a wide variety of specific learning-how-to-learn skills; (3) skills in the appropriate use of advanced-level reference materials; and (4) written, oral, and visual communication skills. Other Type II enrichment is specific; it cannot be planned in advance, and it usually involves advanced methodological instruction in an area of interest selected by the student. For example, students who become interested in botany after a Type I experience might pursue additional training in this area by doing advanced reading in botany; compiling, planning, and carrying out plant experiments; and seeking more advanced methods training if they wish to go further.

Type III enrichment involves students who become interested in pursuing a self-selected area and are willing to commit the time necessary for advanced content acquisition and process training in which they assume the role of a first-hand inquirer. The goals of Type III enrichment include:

• Providing opportunities for applying interests, knowledge, creative ideas and task commitment to a self-selected problem or area of study;
• Acquiring advanced level understanding of the knowledge (content) and methodology (process) that are used within particular disciplines, artistic areas of expression, and interdisciplinary studies;

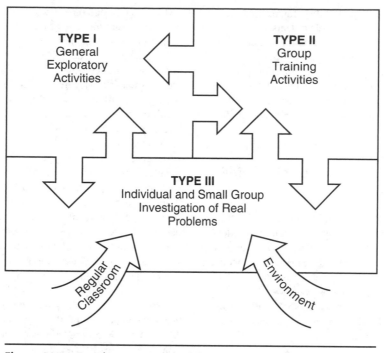

Figure 14.2   Enrichment Triad Model.

- Developing authentic products that are primarily directed to bring about a desired impact upon a specified audience;
- Developing self-directed learning skills in the areas of planning, organization, resource utilization, time management, decision making, and self-evaluation; and
- Developing task commitment, self-confidence, and feelings of creative accomplishment.

Schoolwide Enrichment Model (SEM)

In the SEM, a *talent pool* of 10–15 percent of above average ability/high potential students is identified through a variety of measures, including achievement tests, teacher nominations, assessment of potential for creativity and task commitment, as well as alternative pathways of entrance (self-nomination, parent nomination, etc.). High achievement test and IQ test scores automatically include a student in the talent pool, enabling those students who are underachieving in their academic schoolwork to be included.

Once students are identified for the talent pool, they are eligible for several kinds of services. First,

interest and learning styles assessments are used. Informal and formal methods identify or create students' interests and encourage them to further develop and pursue these interests in various ways. Learning style preferences that are assessed include projects, independent study, teaching games, simulations, peer teaching, programmed instruction, lecture, drill and recitation, and discussion.

Second, curriculum compacting is provided to all eligible students for whom the regular curriculum is modified by eliminating portions of previously mastered content. This elimination or streamlining of curriculum enables above average students to avoid repetition of previously mastered work while simultaneously finding time for more appropriately challenging activities (Reis, Burns, & Renzulli, 1992; Renzulli, Smith, & Reis, 1982). A form entitled The Compactor (Renzulli & Smith, 1978) is used to document which content areas have been compacted and what alternative work has been substituted.

Third, the Enrichment Triad Model offers three types of enrichment experiences. Type I, II, and III Enrichment are offered to all students; however, Type III enrichment is usually more appropriate for students with higher levels of ability, interest, and task commitment, that is, talent pool students.

Separate studies on the SEM demonstrated its effectiveness in schools with widely differing socioeconomic levels and program organization patterns (Olenchak, 1988; Olenchak & Renzulli, 1989). The SEM has been implemented in thousands of school districts across the country (Burns, 1998) and interest continues to grow.

Newest Directions for the Schoolwide Enrichment Model

The present reform initiatives in general education have created a more receptive atmosphere for flexible approaches that challenge *all* students. Accordingly, the Schoolwide Enrichment Model (SEM; see Figure 14.3) has been expanded to address three major goals that we believe will accommodate the needs of gifted students, and at the same time provide challenging learning experiences for all students. These goals are:

- To maintain and expand a continuum of special services that will challenge students with demonstrated superior performance or the potential for superior performance in any and all aspects of the school and extracurricular program.
- To infuse into the general education program a broad range of activities for high-end learning that will (a) challenge all students to perform at advanced levels and (b) allow teachers to determine which students should be given extended opportunities, resources, and encouragement in particular areas where superior interest and performance are demonstrated.
- To preserve and protect the positions of gifted education specialists and any other specialized personnel necessary for carrying out the first two goals.

School Structures

Regular Curriculum. The regular curriculum consists of everything that is a part of the predetermined goals, schedules, learning outcomes, and delivery systems of the school. The regular curriculum might be traditional, innovative, or in the process of transition, but its predominant feature is that authoritative forces (i.e., policy makers, school councils,

textbook adoption committees, state regulators) have determined that the regular curriculum should be the "centerpiece" of student learning.

Application of the SEM influences the regular curriculum in three ways. First, the challenge level of required material is differentiated through processes such as curriculum compacting and textbook content modification procedures. Second, systematic content intensification procedures should be used to replace eliminated content with selected, in-depth learning experiences. Third, the types of enrichment recommended in the Enrichment Triad Model are integrated selectively into regular curriculum activities. Although our goal in the SEM is to influence rather than replace the regular curriculum, application of certain SEM components and related staff development activities has resulted in substantial changes in both the content and instructional processes of the entire regular curriculum.

Enrichment Clusters. The enrichment clusters, a second component of the Schoolwide Enrichment Model, are non-graded groups of students who share common interests. They come together during specially designated time blocks during school to work with an adult who shares their interests and who has some degree of advanced knowledge and expertise in the area. The enrichment clusters usually meet for a block of time weekly during a semester. All students complete an interest inventory developed to assess their interests, and an enrichment team of parents and teachers tally all of the major families of interests. Adults from the faculty, staff, parents, and community are recruited to facilitate enrichment clusters based on these interests, for example, creative writing, drawing, sculpting, or archeology. Training is provided to the facilitators who agree to offer the clusters. A brochure is developed and sent to all parents and students that discusses student interests and asks parents and students to select choices of enrichment clusters. The following is a title and description that appeared in one brochure:

Invention Convention

Are you an inventive thinker? Would you like to be? Brainstorm a problem, try to identify many solutions, and design an invention to solve the problem, as an inventor might give birth to a real invention. Create your invention individually or with a partner under the guidance of Bob Erikson and his students, who work at the Connecticut Science Fair. You may decide to share your

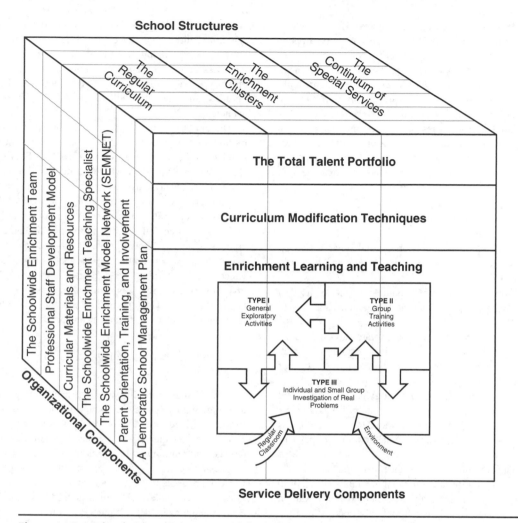

Figure 14.3 Schoolwide Enrichment Model.

final product at the Young Inventors' Fair on March 25th, a statewide daylong celebration of creativity.

Students select their top three choices for the clusters, and scheduling attempts to place all children into their first or, in some cases, second choice. Like extracurricular activities and programs such as 4-H and Junior Achievement, the main rationale for participation in one or more clusters is that *students and teachers want to be there.* All teachers (including music, art, physical education, etc.) are involved in teaching the clusters; and their involvement in any particular cluster is based on the same type of interest assess-

ment that is used for students in selecting clusters of choice.

The model for learning used with enrichment clusters is based on an inductive approach to solving real-world problems through the development of authentic products and services. Unlike traditional, didactic modes of teaching, this approach, known as *enrichment learning and teaching* (described more fully in a later section), uses the Enrichment Triad Model to create a learning situation that uses suitable methodology, develops higher-order thinking skills, and authentically applies these skills in creative and productive situations. Enrichment clusters promote cooperativeness within the context of real-world problem solving, and they provide superlative opportunities for promoting students' self-concepts. "A major assumption underlying the use of enrichment clusters is that *every child is special if we create conditions in which that child can be a specialist within a specialty group*" (Renzulli, 1994, p. 70).

A detailed set of lesson plans or unit plans are not prepared in advance by the cluster facilitator; rather, direction is provided by three key questions addressed in the cluster by the facilitator and the students:

1. What do people with an interest in this area (such as film making) do?
2. What knowledge, materials, and other resources do they need to do it in an excellent and authentic way?
3. In what ways can the product or service be used to have an impact on an intended audience?

Enrichment clusters incorporate advanced content, providing students with information about particular fields of knowledge—such as the structure of a field as well as its basic principles and the functional concepts. The methodology used within a field is also considered advanced content, and involves knowledge of the structures and tools of fields, as well as knowledge about the methodology of particular fields.

The enrichment clusters are not intended to be the total program for talent development in a school, or to replace existing programs for talented youth. Rather, they are one vehicle for stimulating interests and developing talent potentials across the entire school population. They are also vehicles for staff development, in that they provide teachers an opportunity to participate in enrichment teaching, and subsequently to analyze and compare this type of teaching with traditional methods of instruction.

Continuum of Special Services. A broad range of special services is the third school structure targeted by the SEM model; a diagram representing these services is presented in Figure 14.4. Although the enrichment clusters and the SEM-based modifications of the regular curriculum provide a broad range of services to meet individual needs, a program for total talent development still requires supplementary services that challenge our most academically talented young people. These services typically include individual or small-group counseling, various types of acceleration, direct assistance in facilitating advanced level work, arranging for mentorships with faculty members or people in the community, and making other types of connections between students, their families, and out-of-school persons, resources, and agencies.

Direct assistance also involves setting up and promoting student, faculty, and parental involvement in special programs such as Future Problem Solving, Odyssey of the Mind, the Model United Nations program, state and national essay competitions, and mathematics, art, and history contests. Another type of direct assistance arranges out-of-school involvement for individual students in summer programs, on-campus courses, special schools, theatrical groups, scientific expeditions, and apprenticeships at places where advanced level learning opportunities are available. Provision of these services is one of the responsibilities of the schoolwide enrichment teaching specialist or an enrichment team of teachers and parents.

Service Delivery Components

Total Talent Portfolio. Our approach to targeting learning characteristics uses both traditional and performance-based assessment to compile information about three dimensions of the learner—abilities, interests, and learning styles. This information, which focuses on strengths rather than deficits, is compiled in a management form called the *Total Talent Portfolio* (see Table 14.1) which is used to make decisions about talent development opportunities in regular classes, enrichment clusters, and in the continuum of special services.

This expanded approach to identifying talent potentials is essential if we are to make genuine efforts to include more under-represented students in a plan for *total* talent development. This approach is also consistent with the more flexible conception of *developing* gifts and talents that has been a cornerstone of our work and our concerns for promoting equity in special programs.

Curriculum Modification (and Differentiation) Techniques. The second service delivery component of the SEM is a series of curriculum modification techniques designed to (1) adjust levels of required learning so that all students are challenged, (2) increase the number of in-depth learning experiences,

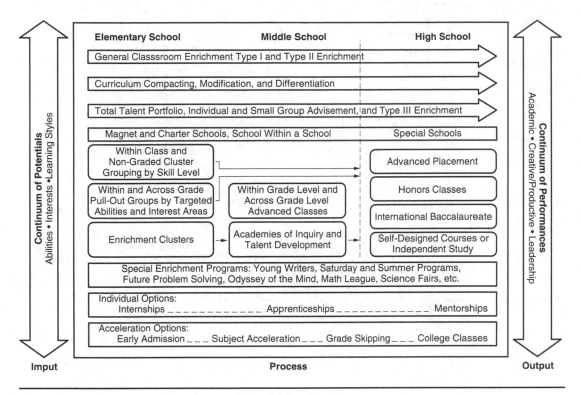

Figure 14.4 The Integrated Continuum of Special Services.

and (3) introduce various types of enrichment into regular curricular experiences. The procedures used to carry out curriculum modification are curriculum compacting, textbook analysis and removal of repetitious material, and a planned approach for introducing greater depth into regular curricular material. Due to space restrictions, curriculum compacting is described in depth here, and other modification techniques are described in detail in other publications (see, for example, Renzulli, 1994; Reis et al., 1993).

How to Use the Compacting Process. The first of three phases of the compacting process consists of *defining the goals and outcomes* of a given unit or segment of instruction. This information is readily available in most subjects because specific goals and outcomes can usually be found in teachers' manuals, curriculum guides, scope-and-sequence charts, and some of the new curricular frameworks that are

emerging in connection with outcome-based education models. The scope and sequence charts prepared by publishers—or a simple comparison of the table of contents of a basal series—will provide a quick overview of new versus repeated material.

The second phase of curriculum compacting is *identifying students* who have already mastered the objectives or outcomes of a unit or segment of instruction that is about to be taught. This first step of this phase consists of estimating which students have the potential to master new material at a faster than normal pace. Scores on previous tests, completed assignments, and classroom participation are the best ways of identifying highly likely candidates for compacting. Standardized achievement tests can serve as a good general screen for this step because they make it possible to list the names of all students who are scoring one or more years above grade level in particular subject areas.

Table 14.1   The Total Talent Portfolio.

Abilities	Interests	Style Preferences			
Maximum Performance Indicators[1]	Interest Areas[2]	Instructional Styles Preferences[3]	Learning Environment Preferences[4]	Thinking Styles Preferences[5]	Expression Style Preferences[6]
Tests	Fine Arts	Recitation & drill	*Inter/Intra*	Analytic	Written
• Standardized	Crafts	Peer tutoring	*Personal*	(School smart)	
• Teacher-made	Literary	Lecture	• Self-Oriented		Oral
Course grades	Historical	Lecture/discussion	• Peer-Oriented	Synthetic/	
Teacher ratings	Mathematical/	Discussion	• Adult-Oriented	Creative	Manipulative
Product evalua-	Logical	Guided indepen-	• Combined	(Creative,	
tion	Physical Sciences	dent study*	*Physical*	inventive)	Discussion
• Written	Life Sciences	Learning/interest	• Sound		
• Oral	Political/Judicial	center	• Heat	Practical/	Display
• Visual	Athletic/	Simulation, role	• Light	Contextual	
• Musical	Recreation	playing, drama-	• Design	(Street smart)	Dramatization
• Constructed	Marketing/	tization, guided	• Mobility		
(Note differences	Business	fantasy	• Time of day	Legislative	Artistic
between assigned	Drama/Dance	Learning games	• Food intake		
and self-selected	Musical	Replicative re-	• Seating	Executive	Graphic
products)	Performance	ports or proj-			
Level of participa-	Musical	ects*		Judicial	Commercial
tion in learning	Composition	Investigative re-			
activities	Managerial/	ports or proj-			Service
Degree of interac-	Business	ects*			
tion with others	Photography	Unguided inde-			
	Film/Video	pendent study*			
	Computers	Internship*			
	Other (Specify)	Apprenticeship*			
		*With or without a mentor			

1. Source: General Tests and Measurements Literature
2. Source: Renzulli & Reis, 1997
3. Source: Renzulli & Smith, 1978
4. Source: Amabile, 1983; Dunn, Dunn, & Price, 1977; Gardner, 1983
5. Source: Sternberg, 1984, 1988, 1990
6. Source: Kettle, Renzulli, & Rizza, 1998; Renzulli & Reis, 1985

Being a candidate for compacting does not necessarily mean that a student knows the material under consideration. Therefore, the second step of identifying candidates consists of finding or developing appropriate tests or other assessment techniques that can be used to evaluate specific learning outcomes. Unit pre-tests or end-of-unit tests that can be administered as pre-tests are appropriate for this task, especially when it comes to the assessment of basic skills. An analysis of pre-test results enables the teacher to document performance in specific skills, and to select instructional activities or practice material necessary to bring the student up to a higher level of proficiency.

The process is slightly modified for compacting content areas that are not as easily assessed as basic skills, and for students who have not mastered the material, but are judged to be candidates for more rapid coverage. First, students should have a thorough understanding of the goals and procedures of compacting, including the nature of the replacement process. A given segment of material should be discussed with the student (e.g., a unit that includes a series of chapters in a social studies text), and the procedures for verifying mastery at a high level should be specified. These procedures might consist of answering questions based on the chapters, writing an essay, or taking a standard end-of-unit test. Of course, an examination of potential acceleration and/or enrichment replacement activities should be a part of this discussion.

Another alternative is to assess or pre-test *all* students in a class when a new unit or topic is introduced. Although this may seem like more work for the teacher, it provides the opportunity for all students to demonstrate their strengths or previous mastery in a given area. Using a matrix of learning objectives, teachers can fill in test results and establish small, flexible, and temporary groups for skill instruction and replacement activities.

The final phase of the compacting process, providing acceleration and enrichment options, can be one of the most exciting aspects of teaching because it is based on cooperative decision making and creativity on the parts of both teachers and students. They can gather enrichment materials from classroom teachers, librarians, media specialists, and content area or gifted education specialists. These materials may include self-directed learning activities, instructional materials that focus on particular thinking skills, and a variety of individual and group project-oriented activities that are designed to promote hands-on research and investigative skills.

The time made available through compacting provides opportunities for exciting learning experiences, such as small group, special topic seminars that might be directed by students or community resource persons; community-based apprenticeships or opportunities to work with a mentor; peer tutoring situations; involvement in community service activities; or opportunities to rotate through a series of self-selected mini-courses.

Enrichment strategies might include a variety of Type I, II, or III activities or a number of the options included on the continuum of special services (Figure 14.4). Acceleration might include the use of material from the next unit or chapter, the use of the next chronological grade level textbook, or the completion of even more advanced work. Alternative activities should reflect an appropriate level of challenge and rigor that is commensurate with the student's abilities and interests.

We have observed another interesting occurrence that results from curriculum compacting. When some bright but underachieving students realized that they could both economize on regularly assigned material

and "earn time" to pursue self-selected interests, their motivation to complete regular assignments increased. As one student put it, "Everyone understands a good deal!"

The best way to get an overview of the curriculum compacting process is to examine an actual example of how the management form that guides this process is used. This form, The Compactor, presented in Figure 14.5, serves as both an organizational and record keeping tool. Teachers should fill out one form per student, or one form for a small group of students who are working at approximately the same level (e.g., a reading or math group). The Compactor is divided into three sections:

- The first column should include information on learning objectives and student strengths in those areas. Teachers should list the objectives for a particular unit of study, followed by data on students' proficiency in those objectives, including test scores, behavioral profiles, and past academic records.
- In the second column, teachers should detail the pre-test vehicles they select, along with test results. The pretest instruments can be formal measures, such as pencil-and-paper tests, or informal measures, such as performance assessments based on observations of class participation and written assignments. Specificity is extremely important; recording an overall score of 85 percent on ten objectives, for example, sheds little light on what portion of the material can be compacted, since students might show limited mastery of some objectives and high levels of mastery on others.
- Column three is used to record information about acceleration or enrichment options. In determining these options, teachers must be fully aware of students' individual interests and learning styles. We should never replace compacted regular curriculum work with harder, more advanced material that is solely determined by the teacher; instead, students' interests should be taken into account. If, for example, a student loves working on science fair projects, that option may be used to replace material that has been compacted from the regular curriculum. We should also be careful to help monitor the challenge level of the material that is being substituted. We want students to understand the nature of effort and challenge, and we should ensure that students are not simply replacing the compacted material with basic reading or other work that is not advanced.

INDIVIDUAL EDUCATIONAL PROGRAMMING GUIDE
The Compactor

Prepared by Joseph S. Renzulli
Linda M. Smith

NAME_____ AGE _____ TEACHER(S)_____

SCHOOL _____ GRADE_____ PARENT(S) _____

Individual Conference Dates And Persons
Participating in Planning Of IEP

_____ _____ _____ _____

CURRICULUM AREAS TO BE CONSIDERED FOR COMPACTING Provide a brief description of basic material to be covered during this marking period and the assessment information or evidence that suggests the need for compacting.	PROCEDURES FOR COMPACTING BASIC MATERIAL Describe activities that will be used to guarantee proficiency in basic curricular areas.	ACCELERATION AND/OR ENRICHMENT ACTIVITIES Describe activities that will be used to provide advanced level learning experiences in each area of the regular curriculum.

☐ Check here if additional information is recorded on the reverse side.

Copyright © 1978 by Creative Learning Press, Inc. P.O. Box 320 Mansfield Center, CT 06250. All rights reserved.

Figure 14.5 The Compactor.

As a case study in curriculum compacting, Rosa is a fifth grader in a self-contained heterogeneous classroom; her school is located in a lower socio-economic urban school district. While Rosa's reading and language scores range between four and five years above grade level, most of her 29 classmates are reading one to two years below grade level. This presented Rosa's teacher with a common problem: What was the best way to instruct Rosa? He agreed to compact her curriculum. Taking the easiest approach possible, he administered all of the appropriate unit tests for the grade level in the Basal Language Arts program and excused Rosa from completing the activities and worksheets in the units where she showed proficiency (80 percent and above). When Rosa missed one or two questions, the teacher checked for trends in those items and provided instruction and practice materials to ensure concept mastery.

Compacting spared Rosa up to six or eight hours a week with language arts skills that were simply beneath her level. She joined the class instruction only when her pre-tests indicated she had not fully acquired the skills or to take part in a discussion that her teacher thought she would enjoy. In the time saved through compacting, Rosa spent as many as five hours a week in a resource room for high ability students. This time was usually scheduled during her language arts class, benefiting both Rosa and her teacher, since he didn't have to search for all of the enrichment options himself. The best part of the process for Rosa was that she didn't have to make up regular classroom assignments because she was not missing essential work.

Rosa also visited a regional science center with other students who had expressed a high interest and aptitude for science. Science was a second area of strength for Rosa, and based on the results of her *Interest-A-Lyzer,* a decision was made for Rosa to proceed with a science fair project on growing plants under various conditions. Rosa's Compactor, which covered an entire semester, was updated in January. Her teacher remarked that compacting her curriculum had actually saved him time—time he would have spent correcting papers needlessly assigned! The value of compacting for Rosa convinced him that he should continue the process. The Compactor was also used as a vehicle for explaining to Rosa's parents how specific modifications were being made to accommodate her advanced language arts achievement level and her interest in science. A copy of the Compactor was also passed on to Rosa's sixth grade teacher, and a conference between the fifth and sixth grade teachers and the resource teacher helped to ensure continuity in dealing with Rosa's special needs.

The many changes that are taking place in our schools require all educators to examine a broad range of techniques for providing equitably for *all* students. Curriculum compacting is one such process. It is adaptable to any school configuration or curricular framework, and it is flexible enough to be used within the context of rapidly changing approaches to general education. The case study described above, and practical experience gained through several years of field testing and refining the compacting process, have demonstrated many positive benefits for both students and teachers.

Enrichment Learning and Teaching. The third service delivery component of the SEM, which is based on the Enrichment Triad Model, is enrichment learning and teaching. The best way to define this concept is with the following four principles:

1. Each learner is unique, and therefore all learning experiences must be examined in ways that take into account the abilities, interests, and learning styles of the individual.
2. Learning is more effective when students enjoy what they are doing, and therefore learning experiences should be constructed and assessed with as much concern for enjoyment as for other goals.
3. Learning is more meaningful and enjoyable when content (i.e., knowledge) and process (i.e., thinking skills, methods of inquiry) are learned within the context of a real and present problem. Therefore, attention should be given to opportuni-

ties to personalize (1) student choice in problem selection, (2) the relevance of the problem for individual students at the time the problem is being addressed, and (3) authentic strategies for addressing the problem.
4. Some formal instruction may be used in enrichment learning and teaching, but a major goal is to enhance knowledge and thinking skill acquisition (gained through formal instruction) with applications that result in students' own construction of meaning (Renzulli, 1994, p. 204).

The ultimate goal of learning that is guided by these principles is to replace dependent and passive learning with independence and engaged learning. Over the years, however, we have achieved success by gaining faculty, administrative, and parental consensus on a small number of easy-to-understand concepts and related services, and by providing resources and training related to each concept and service delivery procedure.

Numerous research studies and field tests in schools with widely varying demographics have been carried out and are summarized in Table 14.2 (Renzulli & Reis, 1994). These studies and field tests provided opportunities for the development of large amounts of practical know-how that are available to schools that would like to implement the SEM. They also have shown that the SEM can be implemented in a wide variety of settings and used with various populations of students, including high ability students with learning disabilities or who underachieve in school.

Concluding Thoughts

We are pleased to conclude this chapter with some non-negotiables about the SEM. First, we have advocated a larger talent pool than traditionally has been the practice in gifted education, a talent pool that includes students who gain entrance on *both* test and non-test criteria (Renzulli, 1988a, b). Still, we firmly maintain that the concentration of services necessary for the development of high level potentials cannot take place without targeting and documenting individual student abilities. Targeting and documenting are part of an ongoing process that produces a comprehensive and always evolving Total Talent Portfolio about student abilities, interests, and learning styles. The most important thing to keep in mind about this

Table 14.2 Research Related to Schoolwide Enrichment Model

Author, Date	Title of Study	Samples*	Major Finding
Cooper, 1983	Administrator's attitudes toward gifted programs based on the Enrichment Triad/Revolving Door Identification Model: Case studies in decision-making.	8 districts $n = 32$	Administrator perceptions regarding the model included greater staff participation in education of high ability students, more positive staff attitudes toward the program, fewer concerns about identification, positive changes in how the guidance department worked with students, more incentives for students to work toward higher goals. Administrators found SEM to have significant impact on all students.
Baum, 1985	Learning-disabled students with superior cognitive abilities: A validation study of descriptive behaviors.	E $n = 112$	SEM recommended as one vehicle to meet the unique needs of gifted students with learning disabilities because of the emphasis on strengths, interests, and learning styles.
Karafelis, 1986	The effects of the tri-art drama curriculum on the reading comprehension of students with varying levels of cognitive ability.	E, M $n = 80$	Students receiving experimental treatment did equally well on achievement tests as the control group.
Schack, 1986	Creative productivity and self-efficacy in children.	E, M $n = 294$	Self-efficacy was a significant predictor of initiation of an independent investigation, and self-efficacy at the end of treatment was higher in students who participated in Type III projects.
Starko, 1986	The effects of the Revolving Door Identification Model on creative productivity and self-efficacy.	E $n = 103$	Students who became involved with self-selected independent studies in SEM programs initiated their own creative products both inside and outside school more often than students who qualified for the program but did not receive services. Students in the enrichment group reported over twice as many creative projects per student (3.37) as the comparison group (.50) and showed greater diversity and sophistication in projects.

			The number of creative products completed in school (Type IIIs) was a highly significant predictor of self-efficacy.
Burns, 1987	The effects of group training activities on students' creative productivity.	E *n* = 515	Students receiving process skill training were 64% more likely to initiate self-selected projects (Type IIIs) than the students who did not receive the training.
Skaught, 1987	The social acceptability of talent pool students in an elementary school using the Schoolwide Enrichment Model.	E *n* =	Students identified as above average for an SEM program were positively accepted by their peers.
			In schools where SEM had been implemented, a "condition of separateness" did not exist for students in the program.
Baum, 1988	An enrichment program for gifted learning disabled students.	E *n* = 7	The Type III independent study, when used as an intervention with high ability, learning disabled students, was associated with improvement in the students' behavior, specifically the ability to self-regulate time on task; improvement in self-esteem; and the development of specific instructional strategies to enhance the potential of high potential, learning disabled students.
Delcourt, 1988	Characteristics related to high levels of creative/productive behavior in secondary school students: A multi-case study.	S *n* = 18	Students completing self-selected investigations (Type IIIs) displayed positive changes in the following: personal skills required for project completion (e.g., writing), personal characteristics (e.g., increased patience), and decisions related to career choices.
Emerick, 1988	Academic underachievement among the gifted: Students' perceptions of factors relating to the reversal of academic underachievement patterns.	H+ *n* = 10	Reversal of academic underachievement through use of various components of SEM including curriculum compacting, exposure to Type I experiences, opportunities to be involved in Type III studies, and an appropriate assessment of learning styles to provide a match between students and teachers.

(continued)

Table 14.2 continued

Author, Date	Title of Study	Samples*	Major Finding
Olenchak, 1988	The Schoolwide Enrichment Model in elementary schools: A study of implementation stages and effects on educational excellence.	P, E $n = 236$ teacher $n = 1,698$ student	SEM contributed to improved teachers', parents', and administrators' attitudes toward education for high ability students.
Heal, 1989	Student perceptions of labeling the gifted: A comparative case study analysis.	E $n = 149$	SEM was associated with a reduction in the negative effects of labeling.
Olenchak, 1990	School change through gifted education: Effects on elementary students' attitudes toward learning.	P, E $n = 1,935$	Positive changes in student attitudes toward learning as well as toward gifted education and school in general.
Imbeau, 1991	Teachers' attitudes toward curriculum compacting with regard to the implementation of the procedure.	P, E, M, S $n = 166$	Group membership (peer coaching) was a significant predictor of post-test teachers' attitudes.
Newman, 1991	The effects of the Talents Unlimited Model on students' creative productivity.	E $n = 147$	Students with training in the Talents Unlimited Model were more likely to complete independent investigations (Type IIIs) than the students who did not receive the training.
Olenchak, 1991	Assessing program effects for gifted/learning disabled students.	P, E $n = 108$	Supported use of SEM as a means of meeting educational needs of a wide variety of high ability students. SEM, when used as an intervention, was associated with improved attitudes toward learning among elementary, high ability students with learning disabilities. Furthermore, the same students, who completed a high percentage of Type III projects, made positive gains with respect to self-concept.
Taylor, 1992	The effects of the Secondary Enrichment Triad Model on the career development of vocational-technical school students.	S $n = 60$	Involvement in Type III studies substantially increased post-secondary education plans of students (from attending 2.6 years to attending 4.0 years).
Delcourt, 1993	Creative productivity among secondary school students: Combining energy, interest, and imagination.	S $n = 18$ (longitudinal)	Students who participated in Type III projects, both in and out of school, maintained interests in

college and career aspirations that were similar to those manifested during their public school years as opposed to previous reports of little or no relation between personally initiated and assigned school projects.

Supports the concept that adolescents and young adults can be producers of information, as well as consumers.

Hébert, 1993	Reflections at graduation: The long-term impact of elementary school experiences in creative productivity.	S $n = 9$ (longitudinal)	Five major findings: Type III interests of students affect postsecondary plans; creative outlets are needed in high school; a decrease in creative Type III productivity occurs during the junior high experience; the Type III process serves as important training for later productivity; nonintellectual characteristics with students remain consistent.
Kettle, Renzulli, & Rizza, 1998	Products of mind: exploring student preferences for product development using My Way . . . an expression style instrument.	E, M $n = 3,532$	Students' preferences for creating potential products were explored through the use of an expression style inventory. Factor analytic procedures yielded the following 11 factors: computer, service, dramatization, artistic, audio/visual, written, commercial, oral, manipulative, musical, and vocal.
Reis, Westberg, Kulikowich, & Purcell, 1998	Curriculum compacting and achievement test scores: What does the research say?	K, E, M $n = 336$	Using curriculum compacting to eliminate between 40–50% of curricula for students with demonstrated advanced content knowledge and superior ability resulted in no decline in achievement test scores.

P = primary grades, K–2; E = elementary grades, 3–5; M = middle grades, 6–8; S = secondary grades, 9–12.

approach is that *all information should be used to make individual programming decisions about present and future activities, and about ways in which we can enhance and build upon documented strengths.* Documented information will enable us (1) to recommend enrollment in advanced courses or special programs (such as summer programs and college courses), and (2) it will provide direction in taking extraordinary steps to develop specific interests and projects within advanced topics or subject matter areas.

Enrichment specialists must devote a *majority* of their time to working directly with talent pool students, and this time should mainly be devoted to facilitating individual and small group investigations (i.e., Type IIIs). Some of their time with talent pool students can be devoted to stimulating interest in potential Type IIIs through *advanced* Type I experiences and *advanced* Type II training that focuses on learning research skills necessary to carry out investigations in various disciplines.

A second non-negotiable is that SEM programs must have specialized personnel to work directly with talent pool students, to teach advanced courses, and to coordinate enrichment services in cooperation with a schoolwide enrichment team. The old cliché, "Something that is the responsibility of everyone ends up being the responsibility of no one," has never been more applicable than when it comes to enrichment specialists. The demands made upon regular classroom teachers, especially during these times of mainstreaming and heterogeneous grouping, leave precious little time to challenge our most able learners and to accommodate interests that are above and beyond the regular curriculum. In a study recently completed by the National Research Center on the Gifted and Talented (Westberg, 1995), it was found that in 84 percent of regular classroom activities, *no differentiation was provided for identified high ability students.*

Related to this non-negotiable are the issues of teacher selection and training, and the scheduling of special program teachers. Providing unusually high levels of challenge requires advanced training in the discipline(s) that one is teaching, in the application of process skills, and in the management and facilitation of individual and small group investigations. It is these characteristics of enrichment specialists, rather than the mere grouping of students, that have resulted in achievement gains and high levels of creative productivity by program students.

Every profession is defined in part by its identifiable specializations, according to the task(s) to be accomplished. But specialization means more than the acquisition of particular skills. It also means affiliation with others who share common goals; the promotion of one's field; participation in professional activities, organizations, and research; and contributions to the advancement of the field. It also means the kinds of continued study and growth that make a difference between a job and a career. Now, more

than ever, it is essential to fight for the special program positions that are falling prey to budget cuts and the "heterogenization" of education. All professionals in the field should work to establish standards and specialized certification for enrichment specialists. They should also help parents organize a task force that will be ready at a moment's notice to call in the support of every parent (past as well as present) whose child has been served in a special program.

SUMMARY AND CONCLUSIONS

The Schoolwide Enrichment Model (SEM) provides a detailed plan to develop talents and gifts and encourage creative productivity in students. A talent pool of 10–15 percent of the general population is established using a flexible identification system that enables students to receive a continuum of services including acceleration, enrichment, counseling, and opportunities for individual talent development based on their interests, learning styles, and academic strengths. Each school that has an SEM program has the flexibility to develop its own unique programs, based on local resources, student demographics, and school dynamics as well as faculty strengths and creativity. The idea is to create a repertoire of services that can be integrated to create "a rising tide lifts all ships" approach. The model includes a continuum of services, enrichment opportunities, and three distinct services: curriculum modification and differentiation, enrichment opportunities of various types, and opportunities for the development of individual portfolios that include interests, learning styles, product styles, and other information about student strengths. Not only has this model been successful in addressing the problem of high potential students who have been under-challenged, it also provides additional important learning paths for gifted and talented students who find success in more traditional learning environments.

There may never have been a time when so much debate about what should be taught has existed in American schools. The current emphasis on testing, the standardization of curriculum, and the drive to increase achievement scores has produced major changes in education during the last two decades. Yet at the same time, our society continues to need to develop creativity in our students. As overpopulation, disease, pollution, and starvation increase both here and throughout the rest of the world, the need for creative solutions to these and other problems seems clear. The absence of opportunities to develop creativity in all young people, and especially in talented students, is troubling. In the SEM, students are encouraged to become responsible partners in their own education and to develop a passion and joy for learning. As students pursue creative enrichment opportunities, they learn communication skills and to enjoy creative challenges. The SEM provides the opportunity for students to develop their gifts and talents and to begin the process of life-long learning, culminating, we hope, in creative productive work of their own selection as adults.

QUESTIONS FOR THOUGHT AND DISCUSSION

1. How can enrichment clusters and compacting in the SEM help develop both academic giftedness and creative/productive giftedness?

2. How does the "Rising Tide" philosophy underlying the SEM fit with current educational reform efforts—especially heterogeneous grouping?

3. Look at the summary three-dimensional model of the SEM in Figure 14.3. Which are probably the most challenging components to implement?

4. Do conflicts exist related to teaching creative productivity and teaching advanced content? Is the (often political) competency testing movement relevant? Explain.

REFERENCES

Amabile, T. (1983). *The social psychology of creativity.* New York. Springer-Verlag.

Baum, S. (1985). *Learning disabled students with superior cognitive abilities: A validation study of descriptive behaviors.* Unpublished doctoral dissertation, University of Connecticut, Storrs.

Baum, S. (1988). An enrichment program for the gifted learning disabled students. *Gifted Child Quarterly, 32,* 226–230.

Burns, D. E. (1998). *SEM network directory.* Storrs, CT: University of Connecticut, Neag Center for Gifted Education and Talent Development.

Burns, D. E. (1987). *The effects of group training activities on students' creative productivity.* Unpublished doctoral dissertation, The University of Connecticut, Storrs.

Cooper, C. (1983). *Administrators' attitudes toward gifted programs based on the enrichment triad/revolving door identification model: Case studies in decision making.* Unpublished doctoral dissertation, University of Connecticut, Storrs.

Delcourt, M. A. B. (1988). *Characteristics related to high levels of creative/productive behavior in secondary school students: A multicase study.* Unpublished doctoral dissertation, University of Connecticut, Storrs.

Delcourt, M. A. B. (1993). Creative productivity among secondary school students: Combining energy, interest, and imagination. *Gifted Child Quarterly, 37,* 23–31.

Dunn, R., Dunn, K., & Price, G. E. (1977). Diagnosing learning styles: Avoiding malpractice suits against school systems. *Phi Delta Kappan, 58*(5), 418–420.

Emerick, L. (1988). *Academic underachievement among the gifted: Students' perceptions of factors relating to the reversal of the academic underachievement pattern.* Unpublished doctoral dissertation, University of Connecticut, Storrs.

Gardner, H. (1983). *Frames of mind.* New York: Basic Books.

Heal, M. M. (1989). *Student perceptions of labeling the gifted: A comparative case study analysis.* Unpublished doctoral dissertation, University of Connecticut, Storrs.

Hébert, T. P. (1993). Reflections at graduation: The long-term impact of elementary school experiences in creative productivity. *Roeper Review, 16,* 22–28.

Imbeau, M. B. (1991). *Teachers' attitudes toward curriculum compacting: A comparison of different inservice strategies.* Unpublished doctoral dissertation, University of Connecticut, Storrs.

Karafelis, P. (1986). *The effects of the tri-art drama curriculum on the reading comprehension of students with varying levels of cognitive ability.* Unpublished doctoral dissertation, University of Connecticut, Storrs.

Kettle, K., Renzulli, J. S., & Rizza, M. G. (1998). Products of mind: Exploring student preferences for product development using My Way . . . An Expression Style Instrument. *Gifted Child Quarterly, 42,* 49–60.

Newman, J. L. (1991). *The effects of the talents unlimited model on students' creative productivity.* Unpublished doctoral dissertation, University of Alabama, Tuscaloosa.

Olenchak, F. R. (1988). The schoolwide enrichment model in the elementary schools: A study of implementation stages and effects on educational excellence. In J. S. Renzulli (Ed.), *Technical report on research studies relating to the revolving door identification model* (2nd ed., pp. 201–247). Storrs, CT: The University of Connecticut, Bureau of Educational Research.

Olenchak, F. R. (1990). School change through gifted education: Effects on elementary students' attitudes toward learning. *Journal for the Education of the Gifted, 14*(1), 66–78.

Olenchak, F. R. (1991). Assessing program effects for gifted/learning disabled students. In R. Swassing & A. Robinson (Eds.), *NAGC 1991 Research Briefs*. Washington, DC: National Association for Gifted Children.

Olenchak, F. R., & Renzulli, J. S. (1989). The effectiveness of the schoolwide enrichment model on selected aspects of elementary school change. *Gifted Child Quarterly, 32*, 44–57.

Reis, S. M., Burns, D. E., & Renzulli, J. S. (1992). *Curriculum compacting: The complete guide to modifying the regular curriculum for high ability students*. Mansfield Center, CT: Creative Learning Press.

Reis, S. M., Westberg, K. L., Kulikowich, J., Caillard, F., Hébert, T. P., Plucker, J. A., Purcell, J. H., Rogers, J., & Smist, J. (1993). *Why not let high ability students start school in January? The curriculum compacting study* (Research Monograph 93106). Storrs, CT: University of Connecticut, National Research Center on the Gifted and Talented.

Renzulli, J. S. (1976). The enrichment triad model: A guide for developing defensible programs for the gifted and talented. *Gifted Child Quarterly, 20*, 303–326.

Renzulli, J. S. (1977). *The enrichment triad model: A guide for developing defensible programs for the gifted and talented*. Mansfield Center, CT: Creative Learning Press.

Renzulli, J. S. (1978). What makes giftedness? Re-examining a definition. *Phi Delta Kappan, 60*, 180–184, 261.

Renzulli, J. S. (1982). What makes a problem real: Stalking the elusive meaning of qualitative differences in gifted education. *Gifted Child Quarterly, 26*, 147–156.

Renzulli, J. S. (1986). The three ring conception of giftedness: A developmental model for creative productivity. In R. J. Sternberg & J. E. Davidson (Eds.), *Conceptions of giftedness* (pp. 53–92). New York: Cambridge University Press.

Renzulli, J. S. (1988a). The multiple menu model for developing differentiated curriculum for the gifted and talented. *Gifted Child Quarterly, 32*, 298–309.

Renzulli, J. S. (Ed.). (1988b). *Technical report of research studies related to the enrichment triad/revolving door model* (3rd ed.). Storrs, CT: University of Connecticut, Teaching the Talented Program.

Renzulli, J. S. (1994). *Schools for talent development: A practical plan for total school improvement*. Mansfield Center, CT: Creative Learning Press.

Renzulli, J. S., & Reis, S. M. (1985). *The schoolwide enrichment model: A comprehensive plan for educational excellence*. Mansfield Center, CT: Creative Learning Press.

Renzulli, J. S., & Reis, S. M. (1994). Research related to the schoolwide enrichment model. *Gifted Child Quarterly, 38*, 2–14.

Renzulli, J. S., & Reis, S. M. (1997). *The schoolwide enrichment model: A how-to guide for educational excellence*. Mansfield Center, CT: Creative Learning Press.

Renzulli, J. S., & Smith, L. H. (1978). *The compactor*. Mansfield Center, CT: Creative Learning Press.

Renzulli, J. S., Smith, L. H., & Reis, S. M. (1982). Curriculum compacting: An essential strategy for working with gifted students. *The Elementary School Journal, 82*, 185–194.

Schack, G. D. (1986). *Creative productivity and self-efficacy in children*. Unpublished doctoral dissertation, University of Connecticut, Storrs.

Skaught, B. J. (1987). *The social acceptability of talent pool students in an elementary school using the schoolwide enrichment model*. Unpublished doctoral dissertation, University of Connecticut, Storrs.

Starko, A. J. (1986). *The effects of the revolving door identification model on creative productivity and self-efficacy*. Unpublished doctoral dissertation, University of Connecticut, Storrs.

Sternberg, R. J. (1984). Toward a triarchic theory of human intelligence. *Behavioral and Brain Sciences, 7*, 269–287.

Sternberg, R. J. (1988). Three facet model of creativity. In R. J. Sternberg (Ed.), *The Nature of Creativity* (pp. 125–147). Boston: Cambridge University Press.

Sternberg, R. J. (1990). Thinking styles: Keys to understanding student performance. *Phi Delta Kappan, 71*(5), 366–371.

Taylor, L. A. (1992). *The effects of the secondary enrichment triad model and a career counseling component on the career development of vocational-technical school students*. Unpublished doctoral dissertation, University of Connecticut, Storrs.

Westberg, K. L. (1995). Meeting the needs of the gifted in the regular classroom: The practices of exemplary teachers and schools. *Gifted Child Today, 18*, 27–29.

BIBLIOGRAPHY

Bruner, J. S. (1960). *The process of education*. Cambridge: Harvard University Press.

Bruner, J. S. (1966). *Toward a theory of instruction*. Cambridge: Harvard University Press.

Dewey, J. (1913). *Interest and effort in education*. New York: Houghton Mifflin.

Dewey, J. (1916). *Democracy and education*. New York: Macmillan.

James, W. (1885). On the functions of cognition. *Mind, 10*, 27–44.

Kirschenbaum, R. J., & Siegle, D. (1993, April). *Predicting creative performance in an enrichment program*. Paper presented at the Association for the Education of Gifted Underachieving Students 6th Annual Conference, Portland, OR.

Neisser, U. (1979). The concept of intelligence. In R. J. Sternberg & D. K. Detterman (Eds.), *Human Intelligence* (pp. 179–189). Norwood, NJ: Ablex.

Piaget, J. (1975). *The development of thought: Equilibration of cognitive structures.* New York: Viking.

Reis, S. M., & Renzulli, J. S. (1982, May). *A case for the broadened conception of giftedness. Phi Delta Kappan,* 619–620.

Renzulli, J. S., Reis, S. M., & Smith, L. H. (1981). *The revolving door identification model.* Mansfield Center, CT: Creative Learning Press.

Thorndike, E. L. (1921). Intelligence and its measurement. *Journal of Educational Psychology, 12,* 124–127.

Torrance, E. P. (1962). *Guiding creative talent.* Englewood Cliffs, NJ: Prentice-Hall.

Torrance, E. P. (1974). *Norms-technical manual: Torrance tests of creative thinking.* Bensenville, IL: Scholastic Testing Service.

Ward, V. S. (1960). Systematic intensification and extensification of the school curriculum. *Exceptional Children, 28,* 67–71, 77.

15

Talent Searches: Meeting the Needs of Academically Talented Youth

ANN LUPKOWSKI-SHOPLIK, *Carnegie Mellon University*
CAMILLA P. BENBOW, *Vanderbilt University*
SUSAN G. ASSOULINE, *The University of Iowa*
LINDA E. BRODY, *Johns Hopkins University*

This chapter is dedicated to Dr. Julian C. Stanley, founder of the Talent Search Model.

The Talent Search concept, pioneered by Julian C. Stanley in the 1970s, is elegant and bold in its simplicity: Offer a challenging test designed for older students to bright, motivated younger students as a means of identifying exceptional talent in a specific domain. Inspired by Leta Hollingworth's use of above-level tests and his own experimental work with young math prodigies, Stanley held the first large-scale testing of seventh and eighth graders under the auspices of the Study of Mathematically Precocious Youth (SMPY) at the Johns Hopkins University in January, 1972. He used the Scholastic Aptitude Test (now SAT-I), a test designed for college-bound twelfth graders, to identify advanced mathematical reasoning abilities in middle school students (Stanley, 1996).

Today, over 300,000 students from every state and many countries around the world participate in annual university-based Talent Searches. These Talent Search programs offer several testing options, serve a broad age group, and identify talent in the areas of mathematical, verbal, and scientific reasoning abilities. They also offer a variety of programmatic opportunities to serve the students they identify. In spite of this incredible growth, the model remains true to the principles and practices established by Stanley over three decades ago. This chapter presents an overview of the Talent Search model: its philosophy, its approach to helping talented students achieve their full potential, and evidence for its effectiveness.[1]

How Does the Talent Search Work?

Talent Searches offer a systematic assessment program using aptitude tests rather than achievement tests or IQ tests to identify talent. The tests used by Talent Searches were selected to allow talented students to use their reasoning abilitites to solve a problem, even if the content is unfamiliar.

The Talent Search begins with a two-step process. The initial screening is designed to identify students who will benefit from the information they will gain from an above-level assessment. It is based on an in-grade standardized test such as the Iowa Tests of Basic Skills. Students who score at a designated level or higher (usually 95th or 97th percentile, depending on the program) on a grade-level standardized achievement test are invited to take an above-level test as a measure of their aptitude.[2]

1. See Benbow (1991), Cohn (1991), Keating (1976), Keating and Stanley (1972), Lubinski and Benbow (1994), Stanley (1977), Stanley (1996), Stanley and Benbow (1986), Stanley, George, and Solano (1977), and Stanley, Keating, and Fox (1974) for a more detailed presentation of the history of the Talent Searches.

2. See Stanley and Brody (1989) for a discussion of the merits of the history and rationale of cut-off scores for middle school students participating in the Talent Search, and Lupkowski-Shoplik and Swiatek (1999) for a study concerning cut-off scores for elementary students taking the EXPLORE assessment.

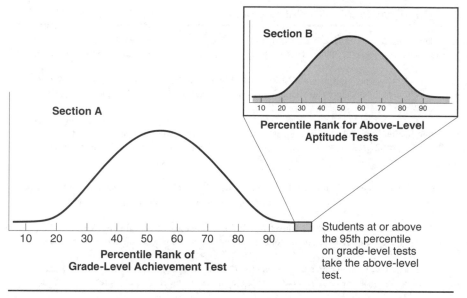

Figure 15.1   Normal curves illustrating how an above-level test "spreads out" the scores of academically talented students.

The second step in this process is to administer the above-level test to the eligible students. The assessments used by the Talent Searches were developed for students two to four years older than the students' present grade placement, thus allowing those who have hit the ceiling on an in-grade achievement test to demonstrate their advanced abilities. The bell curve shown in Figure 15.1, Section A, is the distribution that is typically found when a general group of students takes an in-grade test. Figure 15.1, Section B, shows that when the students in the upper tail of the typical normal curve take a test designed for older students, a new bell curve results. Some students do very well on the new test, some earn low scores, and most earn scores in the middle range. Administering an above-level test to students at the upper end of the bell curve helps discriminate able students from exceptionally able students, and it provides a more precise assessment of aptitude and readiness for additional academic challenges.

The discriminatory power of this identification model has been demonstrated by Benbow (1992). In a follow-up study of Talent Search participants after ten years, all of whom were in the top 1 percent in mathematical reasoning ability and generally high achievers, the academic achievements of those individuals in the top quarter of this group were still more impressive than the achievements of those in the bottom quarter of this group. The same has been found for verbal ability (Lubinski, Webb, Morelock, & Benbow, 2001).[3]

Students who participate in Talent Searches receive information about how to interpret their scores and, depending on their performance, are eligible for a range of opportunities and services offered by the Talent Searches. These include recognition in award ceremonies, invitations to take classes and participate in programs, and information about other programmatic opportunities that might be appropriate to meet their educational needs. See Table 15.1 for a list of university-based Talent Search programs.

Which Above-Level Tests Are Used by Talent Searches?

Several tests are now used by the Talent Searches for above-level testing. The SAT was the original Talent Search instrument used for seventh and eighth grade students, and the SAT-I is still the most widely

---

3. Interested readers may consult Achter, Lubinski, Benbow, and Eftekhari-Sanjani (1999) for further discussions of validity.

Table 15.1   University-Based Talent Search Programs

Academic Talent Search, California State University, 6000 J St., Sacramento, CA 95819, (916) 278-7032, *http://edweb.csus.edu/projects/ATS/;* Talent Searches for elementary and middle school students in northern California.

The Belin-Blank Center, The University of Iowa, 210 Lindquist Center, Iowa City, IA 52242, (319) 335-6196, *www.uiowa.edu/~belinctr/;* elementary and middle-school Talent Searches for third through ninth graders offered in many states.

Carnegie Mellon Institute for Talented Elementary Students, Carnegie Mellon University, 4902 Forbes Ave., #6261, Pittsburgh, PA 15213, (412) 268-1629, *www.cmu.edu/cmites;* elementary Talent Search for third through sixth graders in Pennsylvania.

Center for Talent Development, Northwestern University, 617 Dartmouth Pl., Evanston, IL 60208, (847) 491-3782, *http://ctdnet.acns.nwu.edu/;* Talent Searches for third through eighth graders offered in many states.

Center for Talented Youth, Johns Hopkins University, 3400 N. Charles St., Baltimore, MD 21218, (410) 516-0337, *www.jhu.edu/~gifted/index.html;* Talent Searches for second through eighth graders offered in many states.

Centre for Gifted Education, 170 Education Block, University of Calgary, 2500 University Dr. NW, Calgary, Alberta, Canada T2N 1N4, (403) 220-7799, *www.acs.ucalgary.ca/~gifteduc;* elementary student Talent Search.

Gifted Education Research, Resource and Information Centre, 14th Floor, Mathews Building, University of New South Wales, Kensington Campus, Sydney 2052, Australia 612-9385-1972, *www.arts.unsw.edu.au/gerric;* elementary student Talent Search.

Iowa Talent Search, Office of Precollegiate Programs for Talented & Gifted, 310 Pearson Hall, Iowa State University, Ames, IA 50011, (515) 294-1772, *http://www.public.iastate.edu/~opptag_info/mainpage.htm;* second through ninth grade Talent Searches.

Irish Centre for Talented Youth, Dublin City University, Dublin 9, Ireland, 353-1-7005634, *http://www.dcu.ie/ctyi/;* Talent Searches for twelve- through sixteen-year-olds.

Halbert and Nancy Robinson Center for Young Scholars, University of Washington, Box 351630, Seattle, WA 98195, (206) 543-4160, *http://depts.washington.edu/cscy/;* Talent Searches for fifth through ninth graders offered in Washington State.

Rocky Mountain Talent Search, University of Denver, Denver, CO 80208, (303) 871-2983, *www.du.edu/education/ces/rmts.html;* Talent Searches for fifth through ninth graders offered in many states.

Talent Identification Program, Duke University, Box 90747, Durham, NC 27708, (919) 684-3847, *www.tip.duke.edu/;* Talent Searches for upper elementary and middle school students offered in many states.

---

used above-level test for middle school students. However, several of the Talent Searches also offer the ACT Assessment or the Spatial Test Battery. The School and College Abilities Test (SCAT) has forms that make it an option as an above-level test for elementary or middle school students. The PLUS was specifically developed for use with fifth and sixth grade Talent Search students. Another widely used test for Talent Search students in elementary school is EXPLORE.

Scholastic Assessment Test (SAT-I)

When Stanley started the Talent Search in the early 1970s, he was initially interested in finding students who were exceptionally talented in mathematics. He looked for a test that would measure high-level mathematical reasoning abilities and that was professionally prepared, standardized, secure, reliable, and had several forms. He also needed a test that would be so challenging for his young students that virtually none of them would earn perfect scores, and the average Talent Search examinee would score halfway between a perfect score and a chance score. He also needed a test with well-known, meaningful, normative interpretations of scores available. Stanley selected the mathematics section of the Scholastic Aptitude Test (SAT-M), a test designed to assess the reasoning abilities of college-bound eleventh and twelfth graders. After pilot-testing the SAT-M with several large groups of talented seventh graders, Stanley and his colleagues hypothesized that, "the SAT-M must function far more at an analytic reasoning level for Talent Search participants than it does for high-school juniors and seniors" (Stanley & Benbow, 1986, p. 362).

In 1994, the SAT was revised and renamed the Scholastic Assessment Test (SAT I). Scores on the mathematical and verbal sections are reported on a scale of 200 to 800, and Talent Search participants typically score across the full range from 200 to 800. The SAT is used by the majority of the seventh and eighth grade Talent Searches listed in Table 15.1.

It is amazing how well many students perform on this difficult above-level assessment. For example, in 2000 the average male college-bound high school senior (representing the 50th percentile) earned a score of 507 on the verbal section. In the 2001 Talent Search sponsored by the Center for Talented Youth (CTY) at Johns Hopkins University, approximately 22 percent of seventh grade males and 45 percent of eighth grade males did as well or better than this. For females, the average college-bound high school student scored 504 on the verbal section, and 24% of female 7th grade Talent Search participants and 47% of the eighth grade cohort did this well or better. Similarly, in mathematics, the mean score in 2000 for college-bound students was 533 for males, and 27 percent of seventh grade and 50 percent of eighth grade males in CTY's 2001 Talent Search did this well or better. Among females, the college-bound students averaged 498, and 32 percent of seventh grade and 59 percent of eighth grade Talent Search females scored at least this high (Center for Talented Youth, 2001).

ACT Assessment

The ACT Assessment, a college entrance exam developed by ACT (formerly the American College Testing Program), was pilot-tested as a potential Talent Search instrument in 1987 (Sawyer & Brounstein, 1988) and was found to be a valid above-level instrument for identifying academically talented seventh and eighth graders (Dreyden & Stanley, 1988; Maxey & Dreyden, 1988; Stanley & York, 1988). It is currently administered by most of the seventh and eighth grade Talent Searches listed in Table 15.1. The ACT Assessment includes four tests: mathematics, English, reading, and science reasoning. Scores from these four tests are averaged to produce a composite score. Scores on each of the ACT tests, as well as the composite score, are reported on a scale of 1 to 36. During the 2000–2001 academic year, the average college-bound high school senior earned a composite score of 21. Approximately 11 percent (n = 29,409) of the 2000–2001 Talent Search seventh graders earned a composite score of 21 or higher, and 40 percent (n = 6,178) of 2000–2001 Talent Search eighth graders performed that well (personal communication, Richard Sawyer, ACT, August 13, 2001).

School and College Abilities Test (SCAT)

Although the earliest Talent Searches focused on middle school students, it seemed that the same concept that worked so well for seventh graders could be adapted for younger students. In 1981 Sanford J. Cohn, at Arizona State University, adapted the Talent Search process to academically talented students as young as age 7 (Cohn, 1991). He then brought this concept to the CTY at Johns Hopkins University. CTY now uses the SCAT as the vehicle of discovery for its elementary Talent Search for second to fourth graders.

The SCAT includes two subtests that measure quantitative and verbal reasoning ability. There are three levels available: elementary, intermediate, and advanced, with the advanced form providing norms through high school level. Iowa State University's Talent Search also uses the SCAT for second to fourth graders. The Academic Talent Search at California State University Sacramento uses the SCAT to identify fifth to ninth graders for its programs.

PLUS Academic Abilities Assessment

The PLUS, developed by Educational Testing Service, reports verbal and quantitative scores. Fifth graders who take this test in a Talent Search are compared to the national sample of eighth graders, while sixth graders are compared to a national sample of ninth graders. The Center for Talented Youth at Johns Hopkins University originally developed this test and was the first to use the PLUS Academic Abilities Assessment in its search for exceptionally talented fifth and sixth graders. The PLUS is currently offered by a number of other Talent Searches.

EXPLORE

The EXPLORE, developed by American College Testing for eighth graders, consists of four multiple-choice tests: English, mathematics, reading, and science reasoning. It also reports a composite score, which is the average of the four scores. ACT developed EXPLORE to measure students' curriculum-related knowledge as well as complex cognitive skills. It was first used in The University of Iowa and Carnegie Mellon University Elementary Student Talent Searches in 1993 (Colangelo, Assouline, & Lu, 1994), and has been adopted by other university based Talent Searches at Northwestern University and Duke University (see Lupkowski-Shoplik & Swiatek, 1999). Elementary students have done extremely well on EXPLORE. For example, sixth graders have consistently exceeded the average eighth graders' performance on EXPLORE and, with the exception of mathematics, the fifth graders also exceeded the average eighth graders' performance.

Spatial Test Battery

Since 1996 a computerized Spatial Test Battery (STB) has been offered as an optional part of CTY's Talent Search for seventh and eighth graders (Stumpf & Mills, 1999a). A version for younger students is being piloted. This test was developed by CTY after seven years of research on the critical components of scientific innovation and increasing recognition of the important role spatial abilities play in many career fields today.[4] The STB includes four subtests: visual memory, surface development, block rotation, and perspectives. When taken in conjunction with the SAT-I, it has been shown to provide an enhanced prediction of success in CTY's mathematics and science courses (Stumpf & Mills, 1999b). Therefore, CTY expanded its eligibility criteria for math and scienc courses to includea combination of STB and SAT-I

scores for students who miss eligibility on SAT-I alone.

The Smorgasbord of Educational Options

In its commitment to furthering students' educational development, SMPY experimented with developing educational options to challenge the students with whom they worked. Initially, accelerative options such as fast-paced mathematics classes and early entrance to college were consistent with the existing research (Stanley, Keating, & Fox, 1974). Over time, SMPY and the Talent Searches identified a wide variety of ways to accelerate and/or supplement a gifted student's educational program so that challenge and rigor are provided. Researchers have referred to the list of options as a *smorgasbord* from which students should choose the options appropriate for their unique educational needs (Benbow, 1979, 1986; Stanley, 1991).

The goal is to create an optimal match between a gifted student's demonstrated abilities, achievements, and interests and his or her educational program (Benbow & Stanley, 1996; Robinson & Robinson, 1982; Durden & Tangherlini, 1993).

Among the accelerative options to be considered are:

- Early entrance to kindergarten
- Grade skipping
- Taking selected classes with an older age group
- Independent study/tutoring in advanced subject matter
- Testing out of courses
- Distance learning courses
- Fast-paced classes or compressed curricula
- The International Baccalaureate Program
- Advanced Placement courses
- Summer courses
- Dual enrollment in high school and college
- Early entrance to college
- Concurrent undergraduate and graduate programs.

Most of these options utilize resources, curricula, or programs for older students, which are already available and thus are highly cost-effective. Research supports the efficacy of these programs to promote learning among gifted students (e.g., Benbow & Lubinski, 1996; Benbow & Stanley, 1996; Brody &

---

4. See Chapter 40 by Lubinski.

Blackburn, 1996; Brody & Stanley, 1991; Kolitch & Brody, 1992; Olszewski-Kubilius, 1998a; Reis et al., 1993; Swiatek & Benbow, 1991a, 1991b).

The smorgasbord also includes enrichment options, that is, coursework and experiences that broaden a student's experiences. Individual projects, courses in areas outside of the typical school curriculum, and extracurricular activities are appropriate ways to provide additional challenges to a gifted child. Research and internship opportunities seem especially promising as these students become older (Lubinski, Webb, Morelock, & Benbow, 2001).

The Pyramid of Educational Options

Individual Talent Searches provide guidelines to assist students with interpreting their scores and identifying educational strategies and opportunities that might be appropriate for their needs. Figure 15.2 presents the Pyramid of Educational Options (Assouline & Lupkowski-Shoplik, 1997), the goal of which is to provide guidance for educators and families in selecting appropriate options for their talented students.

The options listed, which were compiled from Boatman, Davis, and Benbow (1995), Cohn (1991), and VanTassel-Baska (1996), are in ascending order, with enrichment-based options at the bottom and accelerative options at the top. All Talent Search students would benefit from the options listed at the bottom of the Pyramid, while the more accelerative options would be recommended for those students earning higher scores on the above-level tests. Of course, motivation, past achievement, maturity, interest, and availability of resources also play an important role in making programming decisions.

The DT-PI Model

One of Julian Stanley's most significant contributions, in addition to the Talent Search concept itself, was the development of the Diagnostic Testing-Prescriptive Instruction (DT-PI) model (Benbow, 1986; Lupkowski & Assouline, 1992; Lupkowski, Assouline, & Vestal, 1992; Stanley, 1978, 1979, 2000). Used by SMPY and the Talent Searches primarily in mathematics classes, the DT-PI model includes pre-testing students to determine what they already know and what they don't know. Class time is spent on the concepts they have not yet mastered, rather than on concepts they already understand well. After studying a topic, students take a post-test to demonstrate mastery. In this way, bright students are encouraged to move ahead at an individualized pace. They are guided by able mentors, whose classrooms are composed of students studying several different levels of mathematics. For example, Algebra I, Algebra II, and Geometry courses might be taught in the same room at the same time.

This model has demonstrated great success in mathematics (Lupkowski & Assouline, 1992; Stanley, 2001) and other subjects (Stanley & Stanley, 1985). The DT-PI classes have demonstrated that not only could talented youth learn mathematics extremely rapidly, but that many of the students had already learned mathematical concepts that had not been formally taught to them (Bartkovich & George, 1980; Bartkovich & Mezynski, 1981; Stanley, 2000; Stanley et al., 1974). The beauty of this model is that it offers a way to differentiate curriculum for bright students, since the educators working with these exceptional youngsters have found a wide range of ability in their classrooms, even though all students demonstrated exceptional abilities.

Thousands of students each year participate in fast-paced classes using the DT-PI model. Students as young as age 6 have used the DT-PI model successfully (Benbow & Lubinski, 1997).

Using the Information from Above-Level Tests: The Cases of Lisa and Fran

As we have seen grade-level test results have limited use for exceptionally talented students, because these students reach the ceiling of a too-easy test, and they cannot show the extent of their abilities. The results from above-level testing offer much more information. The following example of two students, Lisa and Fran, illustrates this.

As third graders, both students took the Iowa Tests of Basic Skills (ITBS), and they both performed exceptionally well on the mathematics sections of this test (see Table 15.2). Their grade-level ITBS scores were nearly identical, which might lead educators to believe that they would need similar curricular adjustments in mathematics. When those two students took the above-level EXPLORE test in fourth grade, however, they presented very different profiles. Lisa's EXPLORE-Math scale score placed her at the 96th percentile when compared to the eighth grade norm group, while Fran's scale score placed her at the

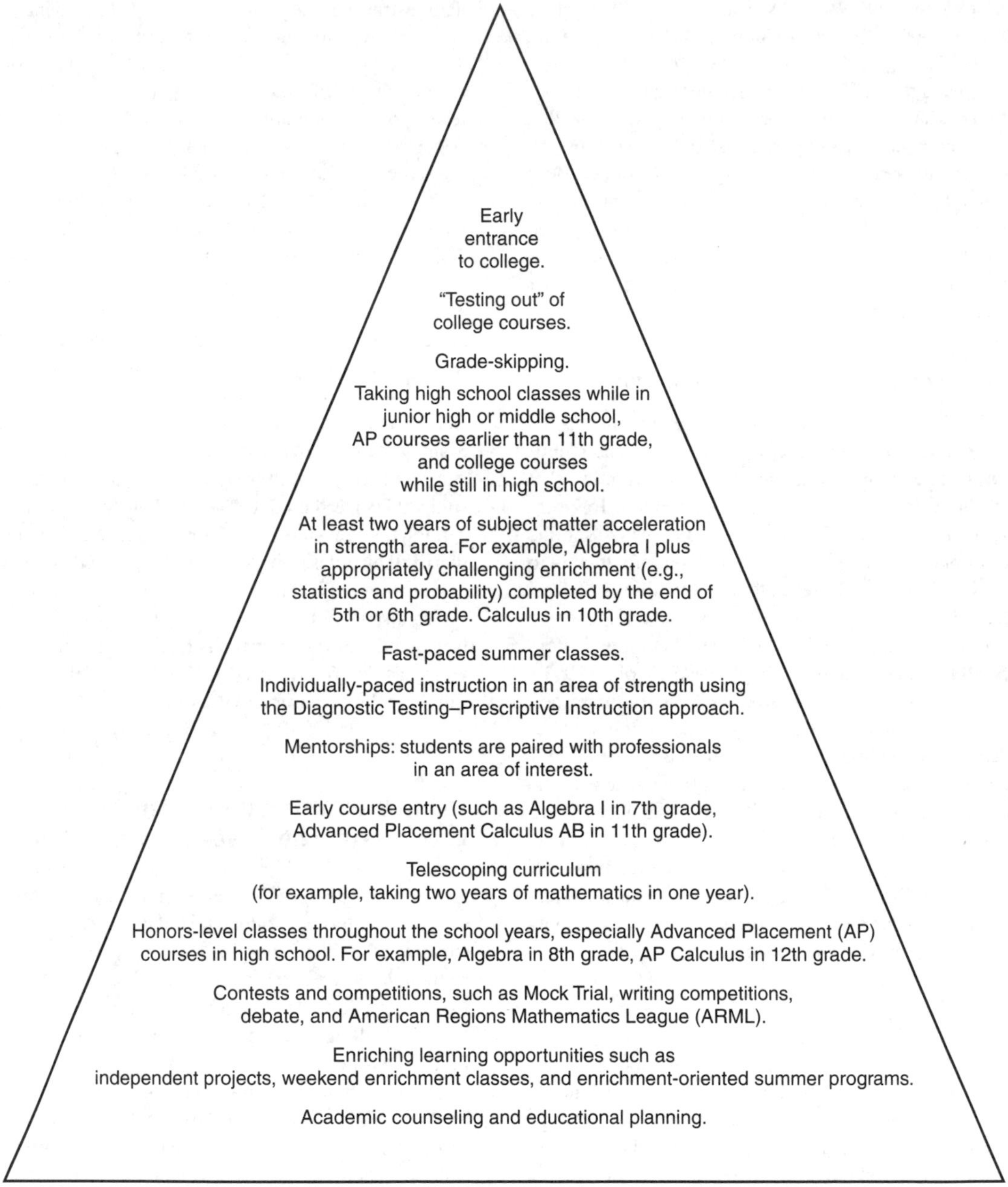

Early
entrance
to college.

"Testing out" of
college courses.

Grade-skipping.

Taking high school classes while in
junior high or middle school,
AP courses earlier than 11th grade,
and college courses
while still in high school.

At least two years of subject matter acceleration
in strength area. For example, Algebra I plus
appropriately challenging enrichment (e.g.,
statistics and probability) completed by the end of
5th or 6th grade. Calculus in 10th grade.

Fast-paced summer classes.

Individually-paced instruction in an area of strength using
the Diagnostic Testing–Prescriptive Instruction approach.

Mentorships: students are paired with professionals
in an area of interest.

Early course entry (such as Algebra I in 7th grade,
Advanced Placement Calculus AB in 11th grade).

Telescoping curriculum
(for example, taking two years of mathematics in one year).

Honors-level classes throughout the school years, especially Advanced Placement (AP)
courses in high school. For example, Algebra in 8th grade, AP Calculus in 12th grade.

Contests and competitions, such as Mock Trial, writing competitions,
debate, and American Regions Mathematics League (ARML).

Enriching learning opportunities such as
independent projects, weekend enrichment classes, and enrichment-oriented summer programs.

Academic counseling and educational planning.

Figure 15.2 Pyramid of Educational Options.

26th percentile when compared to the eighth grade norm group.

Although the two students demonstrated very similar profiles on the grade-level test (Iowa Tests of Basic Skills), their abilities and needs in mathematics are clearly very different, as shown by their dramatically different performances on the above-level mathematics test of EXPLORE. Both students would certainly benefit from additional challenges in mathematics, including participating in contests and com-

Table 15.2 Grade-Level Test Percentiles and Above-Level Test Scores and Percentiles for Two Students

Test	Lisa	Fran
Grade-Level Test, 3rd grade		
Iowa Tests of Basic Skills, Math Concepts	99th percentile	99th percentile
Iowa Tests of Basic Skills, Math Problems	96th percentile	99th percentile
Iowa Tests of Basic Skills Test, Math Total	99th percentile	99th percentile
Above-Level Test, 4th grade, EXPLORE-Mathematics (percentile compared to 8th graders)	Scale score = 21 of 25 (96th percentile)	Scale score = 11 of 25 (26th percentile)

petitions, being grouped with other talented students for mathematics instruction, and perhaps compacting a course sequence by taking two years of mathematics in one year. But, as demonstrated by her performance on EXPLORE-Mathematics, Lisa has more pronounced needs in mathematics than Fran. Not only would Lisa benefit from all of the options previously suggested, she might also consider participation in an individually paced instructional program for mathematics during the school year or summer, accelerating in mathematics, or even skipping a grade if all academic areas are advanced.

What Are the Benefits of Participating in Talent Searches?

Talent Search programs offer many benefits. As described by Rotigel and Lupkowski-Shoplik (1999), these benefits include:

1. *Educational diagnosis.* Above-level tests measure talented students' abilities more accurately than do grade-level achievement tests. They spread out the scores of academically talented students, resulting in a bell-shaped distribution such as the one shown in Figure 15.1. Having an accurate measure of students' abilities enables educators to offer specific recommendations for students' educational programs.

2. *Educational recommendations tailored to the abilities of the student.* Researchers who have used the SAT, EXPLORE, and other tests with thousands of youngsters have developed guidelines for educational recommendations for students scoring at par-

ticular levels (Assouline & Lupkowski-Shoplik, in press; Cohn, 1991; Olszewski-Kubilius, 1998a, 1998b). These recommendations range from enrichment options to accelerative options, and they represent a continuum of modifications, which best match a child's demonstrated ability and achievement. A consistent goal of Talent Search programs is to match the level and pace of the curriculum to the child's needs by finding the "optimal match."

3. *Educational opportunities provided by university-based talent searches.* University-based Talent Searches offer enriching and accelerative classes during the summer, on weekends, and through correspondence courses and on-line courses (Olszewski-Kubilius, 1998b). These special programs offer students the opportunity to study topics that might not be offered at their local schools. Residential programs offer opportunities for emotional and social growth, in addition to the obvious academic benefits (VanTassel-Baska, 1996). Through these special programs, students are given the opportunity to meet and study with other talented youngsters.

4. *Appropriate educational information.* Through participation in a Talent Search, students obtain a more accurate measure of their academic abilities and learn more about their own capabilities. Participation in specially designed programs helps students to be better informed about their own achievements and abilities when it is time to select a college or a career.

5. *Honors, awards, and scholarships.* Talent Searches often give students a variety of awards based on their excellent performance on a Talent Search measure (Cohn, 1991). Additionally, students who perform well on the above-level test may have special opportunities at some of the university-based programs, such as a merit scholarship, to attend university courses.

Research Findings on the Talent Searches

In the early 1980s, the Talent Search model was adopted by several other universities in addition to Johns Hopkins, and the Study of Mathematically Precocious Youth (SMPY) refocused and extended its efforts on research and nurturing the exceptionally talented student. In particular, SMPY, through its planned fifty-year longitudinal study, began to examine the impact of the Talent Search identification process and educational options upon student development (Lubinski & Benbow, 1994, 2000).

SMPY's longitudinal study is now located at Vanderbilt's Peabody College of Education and Human Development, where, coincidentally, Julian Stanley began his career. This project involves studying, throughout their lives, over 5,000 mathematically and/or verbally precocious students. SMPY is now in its fourth decade; it continues to provide data for the evaluation and refinement of Talent Search programs. The data provide information about the development, needs, and characteristics of intellectually precocious youth. The primary long-term goal of the longitudinal study is to characterize the key factors that lead to creative work, adult productivity, and high academic achievement, primarily in mathematics and the sciences.

The data collected during SMPY's first three decades have shown that most Talent Search students do achieve their potential for high academic success in high school, college, and even graduate school. They are off to a great start as productive adults. Yet it is also clear that intellectually talented students will not necessarily achieve their full potential unless provided with appropriate educational opportunities.

Because the SMPY longitudinal study and the research studies completed by other university-sponsored Talent Searches have generated such a wealth of data and information, we limit our discussion here to only four questions.

What Evidence Supports the Validity of the Talent Search Tests? Benbow and Wolins (1996),

Brody and Benbow (1990), Minor and Benbow (1996), and Stanley (1977–1978) all support the notion that the SAT-M is indeed an aptitude test that measures mathematical reasoning ability especially well among gifted seventh graders. The SAT measures a specific aptitude that develops over time. Educational experiences in math and science, over a protracted period, are correlated with higher SAT-M performance. Similarly, experiences in the humanities are correlated with enhanced verbal scores (Brody & Benbow, 1990).

The SAT was the first Talent Search instrument used, and consequently there is considerably more research reported on student performance on that test than on other tests currently in use. Research with the SAT has shown that talented students can be identified before age 13, and that the SAT has predictive validity for achievements in college, graduate school, and careers. Also important is the finding that those individuals with exceptional mathematical abilities relative to verbal abilities tend to gravitate toward mathematics, engineering, and the physical sciences, while those with the inverse pattern are more attracted to the humanities, law, and social sciences. Studies of other tests used in Talent Searches have demonstrated that talented students can be identified as early as third grade, and these Talent Search instruments (e.g., EXPLORE) also help to differentiate talented from exceptionally talented students (Colangelo, Assouline, & Lu, 1994; Lupkowski-Shoplik & Swiatek, 1999; Mills & Barnett, 1992).

What Have We Learned about Talented Individuals from Studies of Talent Search Participants? Studies in both the psychometric and cognitive traditions indicate that extraordinary intellectual talent is best conceptualized in terms of precocity (Dark & Benbow, 1994; Jackson & Butterfield, 1986). The problem-solving strategies used by intellectually precocious students seem to be reflections of what emerges developmentally several years later for most individuals. Mathematically talented individuals seem especially adept at manipulating information in working memory, especially numeric/spatial stimuli, while verbally talented students excel in retrieving information from long-term memory and in representing word stimuli in working memory (Dark & Benbow, 1994).

Intellectually talented students tend to be socially well adjusted and have positive self-concepts, self-esteem, and attitudes toward school (Swiatek, 1993).

They possess an internal locus of control, and on average their psychological health does not differ much from that of normative or socio-economically privileged samples (Jensen, 1994). There are indications, however, that modestly gifted students appear to be somewhat better adjusted than the highly gifted, and that verbally gifted females are at a somewhat greater risk for emotional distress than verbally gifted males (Brody & Benbow, 1986). Highly talented individuals' vocational preferences are dominated by theoretical and investigative interests, and they tend to come from advantaged and stimulating homes (Benbow, 1992).

The Talent Searches have given us evidence that gifted students are underchallenged, beginning as early as elementary school. In one study (Assouline & Doellinger, 2001), academically able students in sixth grade and younger performed as well as or better than average eighth graders on the EXPLORE. Further analysis of the data revealed that talented elementary students performed well in the content areas of Statistics and Probability, Geometry, and Pre-algebra.

A huge amount of research has been conducted on gender differences using the Talent Search data, and some of these findings have been striking. More males than females score extremely high on the mathematics sections of the SAT, EXPLORE, and SCAT (Benbow, 1988; Benbow & Stanley, 1980, 1982, 1983; Mills, Ablard, & Stumpf, 1993; Swiatek, Lupkowski-Shoplik, & O'Donoghue, 2000). Highly able males and females have different ability and preference profiles (Lubinski & Benbow, 1992, 1994; Lubinski, Benbow, & Ryan, 1995; Lubinski, Schmidt, & Benbow, 1996). The psychological profiles of mathematically talented males are more likely to be congruent with studying in the physical sciences than are the profiles of similarly talented females, and these predictions have been supported by SMPY's longitudinal study (Lubinski & Benbow, 1992; Lubinski, Benbow, & Sanders, 1993). As adults, mathematically talented males are more heavily represented in the physical sciences and at the highest educational levels than their female counterparts. However, males and females who select math/science have similar psychological profiles (Benbow, Lubinski, Shea, & Eftekhari-Sanjani, 2000; Lubinski & Benbow, 1992; Lubinski, Benbow, & Sanders, 1993; Lubinski et al., 2001).

While it has long been thought that intellectually talented youth struggle with multi-potentiality issues—swimming in a sea of possibilities—further

analysis has revealed that not to be the case (Achter, Lubinski, & Benbow, 1996). Vocational preferences assessed at age 13, which clearly are differentiated, are stable over 20 years and add incremental validity beyond ability measures in predicting educational outcomes (Achter, Lubinski, Benbow, & Eftekhari-Sanjani, 1999).

What Do Longitudinal Studies Tell Us about Talent Search Participants Over Time? One study involved two cohorts of intellectually talented individuals who were identified by SMPY in the early and late 1970s and then tracked. After 20 years, at age 33, they demonstrated exceptional academic achievements—90 percent earned a bachelor's degree and over 25 percent earned a doctorate (Benbow, Lubinski, Shea, & Eftekhari-Sanjani, 2000). (In the general population, about 1 percent earn doctorates.) The men and women in the study demonstrated equivalent educational achievement, earning the same percentages of both bachelor's and doctoral degrees. On the whole, males were heavily invested in the inorganic sciences and engineering, whereas greater female participation was in the medical and biological sciences, as well as in the social sciences, arts, and humanities. On all indicators examined, these males and females reported feeling equally good about themselves and their success, even though the males, on average, reported higher incomes (but they also reported working longer hours). Perhaps this income finding emerged because the males and females differed somewhat in how they preferred to allocate their time. Males seemed to place greater emphasis on securing career success, while their female counterparts were more balanced in their priorities involving career, family, and friends. Overall, the men and women appear to have constructed equally satisfying and meaningful lives that took somewhat different forms.

In a second study we learned clearly that identifying profound precocity during adolescence isolates a group at promise for truly exceptional adult achievement and creative production. Lubinski, Webb, Morelock, and Benbow (2001) surveyed Talent Search participants who had been identified in the early 1980s as scoring in the top .01 percent in ability. Over half of these individuals were pursuing doctorates and, almost without exception, were attending some of the most elite universities in the world—twice the rate of the top 1% sample (described above). By their mid-twenties, many of these exceptionally talented individuals had published scientific articles, written for literary publications, created video games, or secured patents for their inventions. A sizable number had won prestigious awards or secured fellowships. One of these individuals had become a full professor before age 25 at a major research university.

This group of profoundly gifted individuals had, as students, strongly preferred educational opportunities tailored to their precocious rate of learning (i.e., appropriate developmental placement) and they were able to experience this optimal match.

What Evidence Supports the Programmatic Options Advocated by Talent Searches? The results of studies evaluating the Talent Searches' programmatic innovations have been uniformly positive (e.g., Benbow & Lubinski, 1996; Benbow & Stanley, 1983; Brody & Benbow, 1987; Kolitch & Brody, 1992; Olszewski-Kubilius, 1998a; Richardson & Benbow, 1990; Stanley & Benbow, 1983; Swiatek & Benbow, 1991a, 1991b, 1992). Even though intellectually gifted students as a group achieve academically at a high level, it does appear they do *not* achieve as highly if deprived of a developmentally appropriate education. Moreover, Talent Search students evaluate these programs positively, seeing them as satisfying and beneficial even several years later. Especially valuable, beyond the sheer intellectual stimulation, was the acknowledgment of their abilities and the contact with intellectual peers. This seems to be particularly true for the young women.

Although the sheer number of studies on the short-term and long-term effects of the variety of accelerative experiences that are promoted by the various Talent Search programs is voluminous (Benbow & Stanley, 1996), the results can be summarized rather succinctly. When differences are found, they favor the accelerates over nonaccelerates irrespective of the mode of acceleration. And, Terman's data indicate that this is true even 50 years after the acceleration occurred (Cronbach, 1996).

SUMMARY AND CONCLUSIONS

Both elementary and secondary students may participate in a Talent Search at one of many universities. Academically talented students take an above-level test. Talented youngsters who perform well on the above-level test may participate in many academically challenging opportunities the Talent Searches offer, including fast-paced academic summer programs, distance learning classes, and enrichment programs.

Talent Searches have conducted extensive research studies on the characteristics and needs of academically talented youth. These studies have indicated that the Talent Search model effectively identifies profoundly talented youth, who later demonstrate truly exceptional adult achievements. These studies also highlight the fact that talented youth benefit from academic experiences that are tailored to their needs and that the impact of Talent Search programs on students extends well beyond high school.

Since the first Talent Search in 1972, millions of students have been identified through the Talent Searches and have benefited from the early identification and special programming options that they offer. There also has been an exponential increase in the opportunities available to gifted students.

. . . [T]he accomplishments of thousands of these academically able young people are dramatically large. They are accomplishments unheard of prior to the start of the Talent Searches. In research studies documenting the value of the SAT as a predictor of academic success, the findings are not merely statistically significant. The programs are *profound* in their capacity to enable highly able and eager students to proceed educationally as fast and in as great a depth and breadth as they wish (Cohn, 1993, p. 170).

Since 1972, the impact of Julian Stanley's ideas has been tremendous. Literally millions of students' lives have been touched by his work. We can only imagine how the Talent Search model and the programs the Talent Searches offer will influence the lives of future students. We owe this to the vision of Julian Stanley.

QUESTIONS FOR THOUGHT AND DISCUSSION

1. What is meant by "above-level testing"? How and why is it useful for identifying students with exceptional abilities?

2. How might a local school district use the concept of above-level testing to help identify students for its gifted programs? (Do you see problems?)

3. Beyond identifying G/T students for a program, how might a school system use the information about their students provided by the Talent Searches?

4. Consider two bright eighth graders. One performed extremely well on the SAT in a Talent Search (e.g., top 1 percent). The other student also qualified to participate in

the Talent Search but did poorly on the SAT. How might educational recommendations differ for these two students?

5. Why has longitudinal research been an important component of the Talent Searches? What have we learned from research on former Talent Search participants?

The authors want to thank Mary Ann Swiatek for helpful comments on an earlier version of this chapter.

REFERENCES

Achter, J. A., Lubinski, D., & Benbow, C. P. (1996). Multipotentiality among intellectually gifted: "It was never there and already it's vanishing." *Journal of Counseling Psychology, 43,* 65–76.

Achter, J. A., Lubinski, D., Benbow, C. P., & Eftekhari-Sanjani, H. (1999). Assessing vocational preferences among intellectually gifted adolescents adds incremental validity to abilities: A discriminant analysis of educational outcomes over a 10-year interval. *Journal of Educational Psychology, 91,* 777–786.

Assouline, S. G., & Doellinger, H. L. (2001). Elementary students who can do junior high mathematics: Policy or pedagogy. In N. Colangelo & S. G. Assouline (Eds.), *Talent development IV: Proceedings from the 1998 Henry B. and Jocelyn Wallace National Research Symposium on Talent Development* (pp. 123–134). Scottsdale, AZ: Great Potential Press, Inc.

Assouline, S. G., & Lupkowski-Shoplik, A. (1997). Talent searches: A model for the discovery and development of academic talent. In N. Colangelo & G. A. Davis (Eds.), *Handbook of gifted education* (2nd ed., pp. 170–179). Boston: Allyn & Bacon.

Assouline, S. G., & Lupkowski-Shoplik, A. (In press). *Developing mathematical talent: A guide for teachers and parents of gifted students.* Waco, TX: Prufrock Press.

Bartkovich, K. G., & George, W. C. (1980). *Teaching the gifted and talented in the mathematics classroom.* Washington, DC: National Education Association.

Bartkovich, K. G., & Mezynski, K. (1981). Fast-paced precalculus mathematics for talented junior-high students: Two recent SMPY programs. *Gifted Child Quarterly, 25,* 73–80.

Benbow, C. P. (1979). The components of SMPY's smorgasbord of accelerative options. *Intellectually Talented Youth Bulletin, 5*(10), 21–23.

Benbow, C. P. (1986). SMPY's model for teaching mathematically precocious students. In J. S. Renzulli (Ed.), *Systems and models for developing programs for the gifted and talented* (pp. 2–26). Mansfield Center, CT: Creative Learning Press.

Benbow, C. P. (1988). Sex differences in mathematical reasoning ability in intellectually talented preadolescents: Their nature, effects, and possible causes. *Behavioral and Brain Sciences, 11,* 169–232.

Benbow, C. P. (1991). Meeting the needs of gifted students through the use of acceleration: A neglected resource. In M. C. Wang, M. C. Reynolds, & H. J. Walberg (Eds.), *Handbook of special education, Vol. 4* (pp. 23–36). Elmsford, NY: Pergamon Press.

Benbow, C. P. (1992). Academic achievement in math and science between ages 13 and 23: Are there differences in the top one percent of ability? *Journal of Educational Psychology, 84,* 51–61.

Benbow, C. P., & Lubinski, D. (1996). *Intellectual talent: Psychometric and social issues.* Baltimore: Johns Hopkins University Press.

Benbow, C. P., & Lubinski, D. (1997). Intellectually talented children: How can we best meet their needs? In N. Colangelo & G. A. Davis (Eds.), *Handbook of gifted education* (2nd ed., pp. 155–169). Boston: Allyn & Bacon.

Benbow, C. P., Lubinski, D., Shea, D. L., & Eftekhari-Sanjani, H. (2000). Sex differences in mathematical reasoning: Their status 20 years later. *Psychological Science, 11,* 474–480.

Benbow, C. P., & Stanley, J. C. (1980). Sex differences in mathematical ability: Fact or artifact? *Science, 210,* 1262–1264.

Benbow, C. P., & Stanley, J. C. (1982). Consequences in high school and college of sex differences in mathematical reasoning ability: A longitudinal perspective. *American Educational Research Journal, 19,* 598–622.

Benbow, C. P., & Stanley, J. C. (1983). *Academic precocity: Aspects of its development.* Baltimore: Johns Hopkins University Press.

Benbow, C. P., & Stanley, J. C. (1996). Inequity in equity: How "equity" can lead to inequity for high-potential students. *Psychology, Public Policy, and Law, 2,* 249–292.

Benbow, C. P., & Wolins, L. (1996). Utility of out-of-level testing for gifted 7th and 8th graders using SAT-M: An examination of item bias. In C. P. Benbow & D. Lubinski (Eds.), *Intellectual talent: Psychometric and social issues* (pp. 333–346). Baltimore: Johns Hopkins University Press.

Boatman, T. A., Davis, K. G., & Benbow, C. P. (1995). Best practices in gifted education. In A. Thomas & J. Grimes (Eds.), *Best practices in school psychology* (Vol 3, pp. 1083–1096). Washington, DC: National Association of School Psychologists.

Brody, L. E., & Benbow, C. P. (1986). Social and emotional adjustment of adolescents extremely talented in verbal or mathematical reasoning. *Journal of Youth and Adolescence, 15*(1), 1–18.

Brody, L. E., & Benbow, C. P. (1987). Accelerative strategies: How effective are they for the gifted? *Gifted Child Quarterly, 31,* 105–110.

Brody, L. E., & Benbow, C. P. (1990). Effects of high school course-work and time on SAT scores. *Journal of Educational Psychology, 82,* 866–875.

Brody, L. E., & Blackburn, C. (1996). Nurturing exceptional talent: SET as a legacy of SMPY. In C. P. Benbow & D.

Lubinski (Eds.), *Intellectual Talent: Psychometric and Social Issues* (pp. 246–265). Baltimore: Johns Hopkins University Press.

Brody, L. E., & Stanley, J. C. (1991). Young college students: Assessing factors that contribute to success. In W. T. Southern & E. D. Jones (Eds.), *The academic acceleration of gifted children* (pp. 103–131). New York: Teachers College Press.

Center for Talented Youth. (2001). *CTY Talent Search 2001: Seventh and eighth grades Talent Search report.* Baltimore: Center for Talented Youth, Johns Hopkins University.

Cohn, S. J. (1991). Talent searches. In N. Colangelo & G. A. Davis (Eds.), *Handbook of gifted education* (pp. 166–177). Boston: Allyn and Bacon.

Colangelo, N., Assouline, S. G., & Lu, W.-H. (1994). Using EXPLORE as an above-level instrument in the search for elementary student talent. In N. Colangelo, S. G. Assouline, & D. L. Ambroson (Eds.), *Talent development: Proceedings from the 1993 Henry B. and Jocelyn Wallace National Research Symposium on Talent Development* (pp. 281–297). Dayton, OH: Ohio Psychology Press.

Cronbach, L. (1996). Acceleration among the Terman males: Correlates in midlife and after. In C. P. Benbow & D. Lubinski (Eds.), *Intellectual talent: Psychometric and social issues* (pp. 179–191). Baltimore: Johns Hopkins University Press.

Dark, V. J., & Benbow, C. P. (1994). Type of stimulus mediates the relationship between performance and type of precocity. *Intelligence, 19,* 337–357.

Dreyden, J. I., & Stanley, G. E. (1988, April). *College entrance test scores and demographic profile information for talented seventh grade youth.* Paper presented at the annual meeting of the National Council on Measurement in Education, New Orleans.

Durden, W. G., & Tangherlini, A. E. (1993). *Smart kids.* Seattle: Hogrefe & Huber.

Jackson, N. E., & Butterfield, E. C. (1986). A conception of giftedness designed to promote research. In R. J. Sternberg & J. E. Davidson (Eds.), *Conceptions of giftedness* (pp. 151–181). New York: Cambridge University Press.

Jensen, M. B. (1994). *Psychological well-being of intellectually precocious youth and peers at commensurate levels of socio-economic status.* Unpublished master's thesis, Iowa State University.

Keating, D. P. (1976). *Intellectual talent: Research and development.* Baltimore: Johns Hopkins University Press.

Keating, D. P., & Stanley, J. C. (1972). Extreme measures for the exceptionally gifted in mathematics and science. *Educational Researcher, 1*(9), 3–7.

Kolitch, E. R., & Brody, L. E. (1992). Mathematics acceleration of highly talented students: An evaluation. *Gifted Child Quarterly, 36,* 78–86.

Lubinski, D., & Benbow, C. P. (1992). Gender differences in abilities and preferences among the gifted: Implications for the math/science pipeline. *Current Directions in Psychological Science, 1,* 61–66.

Lubinski, D., & Benbow, C. P. (1994). The study of mathematically precocious youth: The first three decades of a planned 50-year study of intellectual talent. In R. F. Subotnik & K. D. Arnold (Eds.), *Beyond Terman: Contemporary longitudinal studies of giftedness and talent* (pp. 255–281). Norwood, NJ: Ablex.

Lubinski, D., & Benbow, C. P. (2000). States of excellence. *American Psychologist, 55,* 137–150.

Lubinski, D., Benbow, C. P., & Ryan, J. (1995). Stability of vocational interest among the intellectually gifted from adolescence to adulthood: A 15-year longitudinal study. *Journal of Applied Psychology, 80,* 90–94.

Lubinski, D., Benbow, C. P., & Sanders, C. E. (1993). Reconceptualizing gender differences in achievement among the gifted: An outcome of contrasting attributes for personal fulfillment in the world of work. In K. A. Heller, F. J. Monks, & A. H. Passow (Eds.), *International handbook for research on giftedness and talent* (pp. 575–602). Oxford: Pergamon Press.

Lubinski, D., Benbow, C. P., Shea, D. L., Eftekhari-Sanjani, H., & Halvorson, M. B. J. (2001). Men and woman at promise for scientific excellence: Similarity not dissimilarity. *Psychological Science, 12,* 309–317.

Lubinski, D., Schmidt, D. B., & Benbow, C. P. (1996). A 20-year stability analysis of the Study of Values for intellectually gifted individuals from adolescence to adulthood. *Journal of Applied Psychology, 81,* 443–451.

Lubinski, D., Webb, R. M., Morelock, M. J., & Benbow, C. P. (2001). Top 1 in 10,000: A 10-year follow up of the profoundly gifted. *Journal of Applied Psychology, 86,* 718–729.

Lupkowski, A. E., & Assouline, S. G. (1992). *Jane and Johnny love math: Recognizing and encouraging mathematical talent in elementary students.* Unionville, NY: Trillium.

Lupkowski, A. E., Assouline, S. G., & Vestal, J. (1992). Mentors in math. *Gifted Child Today, 15*(3), 26–31.

Lupkowski-Shoplik, A., & Swiatek, M. A. (1999). Elementary Student Talent Searches: Establishing appropriate guidelines for qualifying test scores. *Gifted Child Quarterly, 43,* 265–272.

Maxey, E. J., & Dreyden, J. I. (1988, April). *Measures of validity between the ACT Assessment and other achievement variables for talented seventh grade youth.* Paper presented at the annual meeting of the National Council on Measurement in Education, New Orleans.

Mills, C. J., Ablard, K. E., & Stumpf, H. (1993). Gender differences in academically talented young students' mathematical reasoning: Patterns across age and subskills. *Journal of Educational Psychology, 85,* 340–346.

Mills, C. J., & Barnett, L. B. (1992). The use of the Secondary School Admission Test (SSAT) to identify academically talented elementary school students. *Gifted Child Quarterly, 36*, 155–159.

Minor, L. L., & Benbow, C. P. (1996). Construct validity of the SAT-M: A comparative study of high school students and gifted seventh graders. In C. P. Benbow & D. Lubinski (Eds.), *Intellectual talent: Psychometric and social issues* (pp. 347–361). Baltimore: Johns Hopkins University Press.

Olszewski-Kubilius, P. (1998a). Research evidence regarding the validity and effects of talent search educational programs. *Journal of Secondary Education, 9*(3), 134–138.

Olszewski-Kubilius, P. (1998b). Talent Search: Purposes, rationale, and role in gifted education. *Journal of Secondary Gifted Education, 9*(3), 106–113.

Reis, S. M., Westburg, K. L., Kulikowich, J., Caillard, F., Hebert, T., Plucker, J., Purcell, J. H., Rogers, J. B., & Smits, J. M. (1993, July). Why not let high ability students start school in January? The curriculum compacting study (Research Monograph No. 93105). Storrs, CT: University of Connecticut, National Research Center on the Gifted and Talented.

Richardson, T. M., & Benbow, C. P. (1990). Long-term effects of acceleration on social and emotional adjustment of mathematically precocious youth. *Journal of Educational Psychology, 82*, 464–470.

Robinson, N. S., & Robinson, H. B. (1982). The optimal match: Devising the best compromise for the highly gifted student. In D. Feldman (Ed.), *New directions for child development: Developmental approaches to giftedness and creativity* (pp. 79–94). San Francisco: Jossey-Bass.

Rotigel, J. V., & Lupkowski-Shoplik, A. (1999). Using talent searches to identify and meet the educational needs of mathematically talented youngsters. *School Science and Mathematics, 99*(6), 330–337.

Sawyer, R., & Brounstein, P. (1988, April). *The relationship between ACT and SAT scores among academically talented seventh grade students.* Paper presented at the annual meeting of the National Council on Measurement in Education, New Orleans.

Stanley, G. E., & York, A. V. (1988, April). The ACT Assessment as a measure for identifying talented seventh grade youth. Paper presented at the annual meeting of the National Council on Measurement in Education, New Orleans.

Stanley, J. C. (1977). Rationale of the Study of Mathematically Precocious Youth (SMPY) during its first five years of promoting educational acceleration. In J. C. Stanley, W. C. George, & C. H. Solano (Eds.), *The gifted and the creative: A fifty-year perspective* (pp. 75–112). Baltimore: Johns Hopkins University Press.

Stanley, J. C. (1977–1978). The predictive value of the SAT for brilliant seventh and eighth graders. *College Board Review*, No. 106.

Stanley, J. C. (1978). SMPY's DT-PI mentor model: Diagnostic testing followed by prescriptive instruction. *Intellectually Talented Youth Bulletin, 4*(10), 7–8.

Stanley, J. C. (1979a). How to use a fast-pacing math mentor. *Intellectually Talented Youth Bulletin, 5*(6), 1–2.

Stanley, J. C. (1991). A better model for residential high schools for talented youths. *Phi Delta Kappan, 72*, 471–473.

Stanley, J. C. (1996). In the beginning: The study of mathematically precocious youth. In C. P. Benbow and D. Lubinski (Eds.), *Intellectual talent: Psychometric and social issues* (pp. 225–235). Baltimore: Johns Hopkins University Press.

Stanley, J. C. (2000). Helping students learn only what they don't already know. *Psychology, Public Policy and Law, 6*(1), 216–222.

Stanley, J. C. (2001). Helping students learn only what they don't already know. In N. Colangelo and S. G. Assouline (Eds.), *Proceedings from the 1998 Henry B. and Jocelyn Wallace National Research Symposium on Talent Development* (pp. 293–301). Scottsdale, AZ: Great Potential Press.

Stanley, J. C., & Benbow, C. P. (1983). Intellectually talented students: The key is curricular flexibility. In S. Paris, G. Olson, & H. Stevenson (Eds.), *Learning and motivation in the classroom* (pp. 259–281). Hillsdale, NJ: Erlbaum.

Stanley, J. C., & Benbow, C. P. (1986). Youths who reason exceptionally well mathematically. In R. J. Sternberg & J. E. Davidson (Eds.), *Conceptions of giftedness,* (pp. 361–387). New York: Cambridge University Press.

Stanley, J. C., & Brody, L. E. (1989). Comment about Ebmeier and Schmulbach's "An examination of the selection practices used in the talent search program." *Gifted Child Quarterly. 33*, 142–143.

Stanley, J. C., George, W. C., & Solano, C. H. (Eds.). (1977). *The gifted and the creative: A fifty-year perspective.* Baltimore: Johns Hopkins University Press.

Stanley, J. C., Keating, D. P., & Fox, L. H. (1974). *Mathematical talent: Discovery, description, and development.* Baltimore: Johns Hopkins University Press.

Stanley, J. C., & Stanley, B. S. K. (1985). High-school biology, chemistry, or physics learned well in three weeks. *Journal of Research in Science Teaching, 23*, 237–250.

Stumpf, H., & Mills, C. (1999a). *Psychometric properties of the 1997/1998 version of the computerized IAAY Spatial Test Battery (STB) and its impact on the CTY and CAA Talent Searches.* Technical Report No. 22. Baltimore: Johns Hopkins University, Center for Talented Youth.

Stumpf, H., & Mills, C. J. (1999b). *Predictive validity of the Scholastic Assessment Test I and the Spatial Test Battery with respect to study success in CTY and CAA mathematics and science courses.* Technical Report No. 23. Baltimore: Johns Hopkins University, Center for Talented Youth.

Swiatek, M. A. (1993). A decade of longitudinal research on academic acceleration through the study of mathematically precocious youth. *Roeper Review, 15,* 120–123.

Swiatek, M. A., & Benbow, C. P. (1991a). A ten-year longitudinal follow-up of ability-matched accelerated and unaccelerated gifted students. *Journal of Educational Psychology, 83,* 528–538.

Swiatek, M. A., & Benbow, C. P. (1991b). A ten-year longitudinal follow-up of participants in a fast-paced mathematics course. *Journal for Research in Mathematics Education, 22,* 138–150.

Swiatek, M. A., & Benbow, C. P. (1992). Nonacademic correlates of satisfaction with accelerative programs. *Journal of Youth and Adolescence, 21,* 699–723.

Swiatek, M. A., Lupkowski-Shoplik, A., & O'Donoghue, C. C. (2000). Gender differences in above-level EXPLORE scores of gifted third- through sixth-graders. *Journal of Educational Psychology, 92,* 718–723.

VanTassel-Baska, J. L. (1996). Contributions to gifted education of the talent search concept. In C. P. Benbow & D. Lubinski (Eds.), *Psychometric and social issues concerning intellect and talent* (pp. 236–245). Baltimore: Johns Hopkins University Press.

BIBLIOGRAPHY

Benbow, C. P., & Arjmand, O. (1990). Predictors of high academic achievement in mathematics and science by mathematically talented students. *Journal of Educational Psychology, 82,* 430–441.

Benbow, C. P., Perkins, S., & Stanley, J. C. (1983). Mathematics taught at a fast pace: A longitudinal evaluation of SMPY's first class. In C. P. Benbow & J. C. Stanley (Eds.), *Academic precocity: Aspects of its development* (pp. 51–78). Baltimore: Johns Hopkins University Press.

Colangelo, N., & Assouline, S. G. (2000). Counseling gifted students. In K. A. Heller, F. J. Monks, R. J. Sternberg, & R. F. Subotnik (Eds.), *International handbook of giftedness and talent* (2nd ed., pp. 595–607). New York: Elsevier.

Feldhusen, J. F., Winkel, L. V., & Ehle, D. A. (1996, Spring). Is it acceleration or simply appropriate instruction for precocious youth? *Teaching Exceptional Children,* 48–51.

Fox, L. H. (1974). A mathematics program for fostering precocious achievement In J. C. Stanley, D. P. Keating, & L. H. Fox (Eds.), Mathematical talent: Discovery, description, and development (pp. 101–125). Baltimore: Johns Hopkins University Press.

Fox, L. H., & Cohn, S. J. (1980). Sex differences in the development of precocious mathematical talent. In L. H. Fox, L. Brody, & D. Tobin (Eds.), *Women and the mathematical mystique.* Baltimore: Johns Hopkins University Press.

George, W. C., Cohn, S. J., & Stanley, J. C. (1979). *Educating the gifted: Acceleration and enrichment.* Baltimore: Johns Hopkins University Press.

Lubinski, D., & Humphreys, L. G. (1990a). A broadly based analysis of mathematical giftedness. *Intelligence, 14,* 327–355.

Lubinski, D., & Humphreys, L. G. (1990b). Assessing spurious "moderator effects": Illustrated substantively with the hypothesized ("synergistic") relation between spatial visualization and mathematical ability. *Psychological Bulletin, 107,* 385–393.

Robinson, N. M. (1996). Acceleration as an option for the highly gifted adolescent. In C. P. Benbow & D. Lubinski (Eds.), *Intellectual talent* (pp. 169–178). Baltimore: Johns Hopkins University Press.

Shore, B. M., Cornell, D. G., Robinson, A., & Ward, V. S. (1991). *Recommended practices in gifted education: A critical analysis.* New York: Teachers College Press.

Stanley, J. C. (1979b). The study and facilitation of talent in mathematics. In A. H. Passow (Ed.), *The gifted and the talented. 78th yearbook of the National Society for the Study of Education* (pp. 169–185). Chicago: University of Chicago Press.

Stanley, J. C. (1989). Guiding gifted students in their academic planning. In J. L. VanTassel-Baska & P. Olszewski-Kubilius (Eds.), *Patterns of influence on gifted learners: The home, the self, and the school* (pp. 192–200). New York: Teachers College Press.

Stanley, J. C., & George, W. C. (1980). SMPY's ever-increasing D4. *Gifted Child Quarterly, 24,* 41–48.

VanTassel-Baska, J. L., & Olszewski-Kubilius, P. (Eds.). (1989). *Patterns of influence on gifted learners.* New York: Teachers College Press.

16

Special Summer and Saturday Programs for Gifted Students

PAULA OLSZEWSKI-KUBILIUS, *Northwestern University*

There is a history of cultural institutions offering academic programs for children who live in their communities. These include museums and arts organizations, among others. Generally, these programs are geared for children of all ability areas. Increasingly, however, special programs that occur outside typical school hours are being developed for academically gifted students, especially by universities and colleges. This chapter will explore some of the issues involved with programming outside of school and the role such programs play in talent development. Research results about the long- and short-term effects of such programs will also be presented briefly.

Why Special Programs?

One important question is why special programs should exist for gifted learners. Are they needed? If so, why? Many individuals believe that educational programs outside of school are absolutely necessary for gifted children because of their special learning needs (Olszewski-Kubilius, 1989). Typically, these programs provide a level of challenge and a pace of learning that is more suitable to the intellectual capabilities of gifted students and very different from what they encounter in school. There are more opportunities for independent inquiry, in-depth study, and accelerated learning. For many gifted children, this is the first time they are placed in a learning situation that requires concentrated study and work.

Further, the talent-development process may require additional intensive instruction beyond what schools can or are willing to provide (Bloom, 1985). It is widely accepted that developing musical or athletic talent to a high level requires lessons, special teachers, and long hours of devoted study and practice over a period of years. Research has indicated that gifted scientists, writers, and others spent considerable time learning in their talent area from parents and mentors or tinkering and studying on their own (Bloom, 1985).[1] As with musical and athletic talent, however, parents may not be knowledgeable enough to instruct their child in other talent areas beyond a certain point. Even in the best schools, the amount of instruction in an area for a gifted child may not be sufficient to develop his or her talent or to satisfy the child's hunger for learning (Thompson, 2001).

Even if a parent or mentor is capable of providing additional instruction, academically gifted children need to have friends and interact with intellectual peers. Most academically gifted children spend little of their time in school in homogeneous classes with other gifted children (Archambault, Westberg, Brown, Hallmark, Emmons, & Zhang, 1993; Cox, Daniel, & Boston, 1985). However, classes with other gifted children are more likely to foster friendships based on common interests and priorities and general social support for educational pursuits and talent development (Olszewski-Kubilius, Grant, & Seibert, 1993). In addition, these settings provide a greater degree of intellectual stimulation and challenge.

Finally, special programs for some academically gifted children may be necessary to save them from a pattern of underachievement or poor study habits that can result from "easy" or "boring" classes (Rimm, 1991) and lack of peer support for academic achievement. Thus, special programs outside of school are becoming vital to the education of gifted youth.

---

1. See Chapter 19 by Sosniak.

Special summer programs for gifted students have proliferated with the advent and growth of regional talent search programs in the United States. Programs such as Northwestern University's Center for Talent Development, Duke University's Talent Identification Program, Johns Hopkins University's Center for Talented Youth, Denver University's Rocky Mountain Talent Search, and others conduct regionally based academic talent searches using above-level testing for elementary and middle school students. These programs have contributed to the growth of other summer programs for gifted students by providing an efficient and economical identification system involving over 150,000 students annually. The talent search programs produce compendiums of other summer programs and make them available to talent search participants, thereby increasing knowledge about and access to such outside-of-school opportunities.

General Issues with Special Programs

Regardless of who sponsors special programs or their content, some general issues result from their existence.

Relationship to In-School Programs. A frequent concern of educators is the articulation between in-school programs and outside-of-school programs. While many extra-school educational programs offer enrichment-type courses only, some summer and Saturday programs enable gifted students to take courses they would normally take in school (e.g., algebra). When students accelerate themselves in a content area at the seventh or eighth grade through a special program, there can be both immediate and long-term consequences. Immediate consequences include how to respond to the course just completed and what kind of course the student should now be placed in. Long-term consequences include how to accommodate a high school junior who has completed all of the mathematics courses that the high school has to offer.

Schools may actively discourage students from participating in special programs because of these articulation issues, or they may indirectly discourage them by not responding appropriately after the experience. Research has shown that students who complete high school coursework in summer programs often do not receive credit for such work, and many are not subsequently placed appropriately in the content area (Olszewski-Kubilius, Laubscher, Wohl, &

Grant, 1996), despite the fact that such students are well prepared for subsequent courses and typically succeed in them (Kolitch & Brody, 1992; Mills, Ablard, & Lynch, 1992). Some students even repeat their courses in their home schools (Olszewski-Kubilius, 1989). Nothing is more demoralizing to a good student, especially one who seeks challenging courses in special programs, than being required to retake a course or not allowed to go on to the next course in the sequence.

Access to Special Programs. Special summer and Saturday programs are most often sponsored by institutions of higher education. Most charge tuition. As a result, many are simply out of reach for academically gifted children who are economically disadvantaged. Minority children are less likely to be identified as gifted and less likely to be placed in special programs within their schools (Alamprese, Erlanger, & Brigham, 1988; VanTassel-Baska, Patton, & Prillamon, 1990). They are also underrepresented in talent search and other outside-of-school educational programs. But gifted minority students, especially those who are economically disadvantaged, are in dire need of the services provided by special programs. The costs of residential summer programs are often too high for even moderate-income families. And commuter programs may be too distant, especially in more rural areas. Thus, though special summer and Saturday programs are increasingly seen as vital to talent development, access to them is too often limited to the more economically advantaged gifted students and those in resource-rich geographic locations.

Distance-learning programs, particularly web-based courses, are becoming increasingly available in our technologically oriented society, but these also typically involve tuition, making them inaccessible to many of the same students (Adams & Cross, 1999/2000).

Instructional Models and Program Types. Summer and Saturday programs vary on many dimensions, such as content, duration, intensity, sponsorship, and overall purpose. There are many different program and instructional models. Program attributes are important because they determine the type of student for whom the experience is most appropriate. Summer programs that offer intensive accelerated courses are a good match for very able students with good study skills and an ability to learn independently (Bartkovich & Mezynski, 1981; Benbow & Stanley, 1983; Lynch, 1992; Olszewski-Kubilius, Kulieke,

Willis, & Krasney, 1989). These programs typically use techniques such as telescoping or curriculum compacting to reduce the amount of time students spend on a course by as much as 50%.

Programs that offer students an opportunity to study a single subject in great depth are more suited to students with intense, focused interests (VanTassel-Baska, 1988) and specific talent areas. Some programs give students the chance to sample several different courses (e.g., students take one class in the morning and one in the afternoon). Some Saturday programs are single-shot events that focus on career awareness or introduce students to a field of study; some summer programs include this as a small component of their academic classes. Some programs offer typical elementary, high school, or college classes with the goal of accelerating students in the content area, while others offer enrichment types of classes that pose fewer articulation problems for local schools (Feldhusen & Sokol, 1982). Some programs consist of mentorships, internships, or shadowing an adult professional on the job. Some summer programs even offer study abroad opportunities (Limburg-Weber, 1999/2000).

Summer and Saturday programs meet both the intellectual needs of children and their social-emotional needs. For some children, the desire for an intellectual peer group may be the most important reason for pursuing summer or Saturday programs. Summer programs that are residential and at least two weeks in duration, and Saturday programs that offer eight to ten weeks of contact, will best provide a social context for the development of sustained peer relationships and friendships.

Study abroad during the summer or the academic year is an option for high school students. School-year programs are organized as a "homestay" with attendance at a local school and special foreign language classes (Olszewski-Kubilius & Limburg-Weber, 1999; Limburg-Weber, 1999/2000). Summer programs typically consist of travel combined with study of the host country's culture and language. The benefits of study abroad include increased facility with another language and broadened cultural perspectives (Olszewski-Kubilius & Limburg-Weber, 1999).

Other types of pre-college programs include dual enrollment, in which high school students take high school and college classes simultaneously (McCarthy, 1999); by-mail correspondence programs and various other distance-learning options (e.g., web-based courses, CD-ROM-based courses, one- or two-way audio and video transmission teaching) for both high school (Sawyer, DeLong, & von Brock, 1987; Olszewki-Kubilius & Limburg-Weber, 1999; Adams & Cross, 1999/2000) and college-level courses; early-entrance programs to college; and memberships in organizations or clubs that offer informational newsletters and other opportunities (e.g., Study of Exceptional Talent at Johns Hopkins University).

Some programs attempt to serve gifted students with a wide range of above-average abilities; others focus on a more homogeneous group, for example, highly gifted students. These latter types of programs typically use off-level testing as a way of discerning high levels of talent within an area. Some programs target students typically underrepresented in gifted programs, such as minority or economically disadvantaged students or females (Brody & Fox, 1980; Fox, Brody, & Tobin, 1985; Haensly & Lehmann, 1998). Characteristics of special programs are important to educators who often must respond to students' experiences at the local school level, to parents who are seeking programs that will further their child's talent development, and to gifted students who desire suitable, supportive, and enjoyable learning environments.

Benefits of Special Programs

Organizers of special programs believe that gifted students benefit greatly from them. Research evidence actually exists on very few of these proposed benefits, and this body of research will be reviewed in the next section. However, the purported benefits of special programs include the following (Olszewski-Kubilius, 1989):

- Perceptions of increased social support for learning and achievement due to homogeneous grouping with other gifted students and support from teachers and counselors;
- Positive feelings resulting from a learning situation that presents a more appropriate match between the students' intellectual abilities and the challenge or rigor of a course;
- Development of study skills as a result of immersion in an intellectually challenging course;
- Development of independence and enhancement of general living skills because of living away from home on one's own;
- Increased knowledge about university programs and college life;

- Raising expectations and aspirations for educational achievement due to success in a challenging learning environment;
- Reinforcement for risk taking as a result of extending oneself both intellectually and socially;
- Growth in acceptance of others, knowledge of different cultures, and an enhanced world view as a result of living and socializing with a more diverse group of students; and
- Self-testing of abilities due to placement in an intellectually challenging situation, and subsequent re-evaluations and new goal setting that can further a student's progress in attaining excellence.

Research on the Effects of Special Programs

Self-Esteem, Self-Concept, and Self-Perceptions

Parents, educators, and researchers are interested in the effects of special programs on gifted students' self-concepts, self-esteem, and self-perceptions. Students and parents seek out these programs because they believe the programs will provide a better and more appropriate environment—socially, emotionally, and academically. In general, the research suggests that special programs are positive experiences for most students.

Previous research had shown that gifted children tend to have higher scores on global self-concept measures compared with non-gifted children (see Olszewski, Kulieke, & Willis, 1987, and Hoge & Renzulli, 1993, for reviews of this literature). Thus, while giftedness per se is not associated with reduced levels of self-esteem, the question is whether placement in a special program for gifted students results in changes in self-esteem or self-perceptions. As Olszewski et al. (1987) noted, a change in environment, which involves a change in friends, social climate, or academic rigor or challenge, can impact on self-perceptions. Such changes result from a re-evaluation of one's competence in a particular area based on a new reference group. The gifted student is no longer "a big fish in a little pond."

Previous research on in-school programs has shown varied results. Maddux, Scheiber, and Bass (1982) found no statistically significant differences on a self-concept measure for children enrolled in a totally segregated or partially segregated gifted program versus those not enrolled in any special program, although segregated children did have higher scores. These authors also found that segregated children in the first year of the program were rated less positively by peers, but this finding was transitory and disappeared by year two.

In contrast, research by Coleman and Fults (1982, 1985) showed that gifted fourth, fifth, and sixth grade children who were enrolled in a segregated, one-day-a-week pullout program had lower self-concept scores than gifted children in the regular classroom. Scores fluctuated over time and were more positive upon return to the regular classroom for sixth graders and prior to placement in the segregated program for fourth graders. These results substantiate the social comparison basis for changes in self-concept for in-school programs.

Delcourt, Lloyd, Cornell, and Goldberg (1994) compared the self-esteem of students in four different program arrangements, separate classes, special schools, pullout programs, and within-class groupings. The students in the separate classes had the highest levels of achievement across the comparison groups and other program types, but the lowest perceptions of their academic competence and sense of acceptance by peers. Students in the special schools also had lower perceptions of their academic competence than the other groups of children. Delcourt et al. also concluded that lowered self-esteem or perceptions of academic competence, which appear after initial placement and last for about two years, is a result of social comparison. Students in all the groups studied reported that they felt comfortable with the number of friends they had in their own school and their popularity. "The type of grouping arrangement did not influence student perceptions of their social relations for gifted or nongifted students" (Delcourt et al., 1994, p. xix).

Studies specifically conducted on children enrolled in special summer or Saturday programs also show varied results. Kolloff and Moore (1989) measured the self-concepts of fifth through tenth graders attending three different two-week summer residential programs. Their results indicated that students' self-concepts were more positive at the end of the program than at the beginning, as measured by two separate instruments. Changes, however, were small to moderate on the average. The authors speculate that an enhanced self-concept is the result of a more appropriate academic setting and greater peer acceptance.

Olszewski-Kubilius et al. (1987) used an instrument that assessed various domains of self-concept with seventh through ninth-grade students participating in two summer residential programs. Students were measured before the programs and on the first and last days of the programs. Results showed declines in academic self-concept over time, an initial decline then increase in social acceptance, and positive changes for physical and athletic self-concepts over the course of the three-week programs.

Cooley, Cornell, and Lee (1991) report that African American students who attended a predominantly White university summer enrichment program were accepted by other students and were comparable in self-concept and academic self-esteem as assessed by teachers. These authors concluded that summer programs for gifted students that are White-dominated can provide a supportive environment for gifted Black students.

In summary, although the research results are mixed, it appears that negative effects of placement in special programs on self-esteem, self-concept, and self-perceptions, due to a higher-level comparison group, are slight to moderate and probably transitory.

Effects of Fast-Paced Summer Programs

One instructional model, which is used extensively in summer programs across the United States, involves fast-paced courses. These programs emerged subsequent to the creation of the regional talent searches for seventh and eighth graders, which began over twenty years ago. Fast-paced summer courses are typically open to students scoring at the mean for high school seniors who plan to attend college (roughly, 500 SAT-Mathematics [SAT-M] and 500 SAT-Verbal [SAT-V]). They include an array of honors-level high school courses that students seek to complete in a reduced time frame—150 hours of in-school instruction is reduced to 75 hours of instruction during the summer—and they encourage excellence, hard work, and a positive attitude towards academic accomplishment.

Research has shown that the SAT scores used as cutoffs for entrance into these types of programs are valid and select students who will succeed academically (Olszewski-Kubilius, 1998; Olszewski-Kubilius, Kulieke, Willis, & Krasney, 1989). Research has also shown that student achievement is high. On average, students complete two courses in precalculus mathematics within 50 hours of instruction (Bartkovich & Mezynski, 1981) and perform

higher on standardized tests than students who spend an entire year in similar mathematics classes (Stanley, 1976). Similar achievement levels have been found for fast-paced science classes (Lynch, 1992). Better performance, especially in mathematics, is associated with well-developed, independent study skills (Olszewski-Kubilius et al., 1989).

Students who take fast-paced courses differ in their motivations for participating in them (Brounstein, Holahan, & Sawyer, 1988). Some students are primarily motivated by academic interests and concerns, while others have modest academic expectations and are interested in the social value of the experience (i.e., relationships with other students and staff). A relatively small group of students are motivated equally by academic and social outcomes (Brounstein et al., 1988).

The evidence regarding how schools respond to fast-paced classes is equivocal. Lynch (1990) reported that 80% of students who asked for credit for high school courses completed in a summer program received it, although many schools required the students to take a school exam. Appropriate placement in the content area subsequent to a summer course was a more frequent response by schools (Lynch, 1990).

However, Olszewski-Kubilius (1989) found that only 50% of students who achieved proficiency (i.e., scored at or above the mean for high school seniors on a standardized test) in summer fast-paced classes received credit or appropriate placement in their home schools. Additionally, these rates varied by subject area. They were higher for cumulatively organized subjects such as algebra or Latin, and lower for verbal classes such as writing or literature.

The awarding of credit by schools for summer courses is facilitated by accreditation of the program by an outside educational agency. Olszewski-Kubilius, Laubscher, Wohl, and Grant (1996) reported that after a summer program at a major midwestern university had been accredited by the North Central Association of Colleges and Schools, and thus was able to award credit to middle and high school students who successfully completed high school courses, the numbers of students whose schools honored the credit increased significantly. This study also found that most schools do not have policies against awarding credit for outside coursework, and that factors that facilitate credit include notice of the child's intent to take a summer course and petitions by parents for credit.

Research indicates that fast-paced, accelerative summer programs can significantly influence many aspects of students' academic careers, occupational choices, and aspirations. A five-year study by the Center for Talented Youth of Johns Hopkins University compared talent search participants who took an accelerated summer class to a similar group, matched on gender and SAT scores, who participated in the talent search selection process but did not take courses (Barnett & Durden, 1993). The summer program participants took Advanced Placement (AP) calculus and the calculus AB and BC exams earlier than talent search-only participants, were more likely to take college courses while still in high school, and entered more academically competitive colleges.

Olszewski-Kubilius and Grant (1996) found that students who had participated in an accelerated summer program continued a pattern of high academic achievement throughout high school and college. Students, especially females, who took a mathematics class benefited more than students who took other subjects in the summer. Specifically, math females had accelerated themselves more in mathematics, earned more honors in math, took more AP classes of any type in high school and more math classes in college, participated more in math clubs, more often majored in math or science in college, and had higher educational aspirations. Females who took non-math courses consistently reported the least acceleration and relatively lower levels of achievement and lower aspirations than other students (Olszewski-Kubilius & Grant, 1994).[2]

Because of the underrepresentation of females in advanced math courses and math and science careers, several studies have specifically examined gender differences in the effects of summer programs on academically talented students' educational and vocational decisions and achievements. Fox, Brody, and Tobin (1985) and Brody and Fox (1980) reported on the effects of a fast-paced, noncompetitive summer algebra class designed for seventh-grade females talented in mathematics. The experimental girls were compared to control groups of males and females who had participated in a talent search, females who had participated in a career awareness program, and students who had participated in school-based math programs. Two to three years after the intervention,

the experimental girls were more accelerated in mathematics than the control boys or girls. But by grade 11, the number of accelerated experimental girls remained stable, the number of accelerated control girls declined, and the number of accelerated control boys increased dramatically. The authors suggested that the intervention helped mathematically talented girls to keep even with boys. Additional effects of the summer program for girls included a greater commitment to consistent full-time work in the future and higher educational aspirations (Fox, Brody, & Tobin, 1985).

Several studies have shown that intensive outside-of-school academic programs other than summer programs can have powerful, positive effects. As described in Benbow, Perkins, and Stanley (1983) and Swiatek and Benbow (1991), students in an accelerative math program that compressed four-and-a-half years of high school mathematics into two years were compared to three other groups of students: those who qualified for the program but did not participate, those who entered the program but dropped out, and those who were initially in the program but later were placed in a slower-paced mathematics class. Students who completed the program had higher SAT-M scores at the end of high school and were more likely to have completed calculus and taken AP Calculus AB and the Calculus BC exam. They took high school math classes earlier; took more college-level classes in high school; scored higher on the College Board Achievement tests; were more likely to earn at least a National Merit Letter of Commendation and to participate in math competitions; attended more prestigious colleges; were more likely to enter college early; and were more likely to study applied math in graduate school.

In summary, special intensive programs in mathematics, particularly summer programs, can positively affect students' educational and career progress or decisions.

Effects of Other Programs

Research on the effects of other kinds of special programs for gifted children is generally sparse. Sawyer, DeLong, and von Brock (1987) reported that 98% of students who studied Advanced Placement (AP) courses by correspondence scored a 3 or above on the AP exam (a score of 3 generally earns college credit). This is especially impressive, given that these students were younger than typical high school students who take AP exams. Distance-education

---

2. See Olszewski-Kubilius (1998) for a summary of research on fast-paced summer programs.

courses are a good alternative for gifted students whose schools do not offer AP classes or only a limited number of them.

Colson (1980) investigated the effects of a community-based career guidance program on gifted high school students. The program included educational awareness, career awareness, self-awareness, planning and decision making, shadowing a university professor, and an active, hands-on internship. Participants queried one year later felt that the career education program was the single most significant event of their senior year, and that it was the best preparation for later decision making.

Several outside-of-school programs focus on groups of gifted students underrepresented in gifted programs. For example, Lynch and Mills (1990) provided Saturday and summer classes to sixth-grade low-income, minority students. The classes provided instruction in mathematics and language arts. The results showed that students made greater gains on standardized tests in mathematics, although not in reading, compared to a group of similar students who did not receive special instruction. The authors reported that as a result of the gains, some students qualified for their in-school gifted program.

Confessore (1991) reported on adolescent students who participated in a university-based summer arts program ten years earlier. The students took college-level classes in art, music, dance, theater, or creative writing. The surveys showed that, in general, students remained active in the arts, and 83% stated that the program helped them confirm their identity as artists. Participants also reported that contact with other artistically talented adolescents was a major benefit of the program. Special outside-of-school programs in the arts also can have positive long-term effects for gifted students.

Contests and Competitions

Other programs in which gifted students can participate are contests, competitions, and olympiads. Many such programs exist in the United States and across Europe (see Goldstein & Wagner, 1993; Tallent-Runnel, & Candler-Lotven, 1996; Karnes & Riley, 1996). These programs give students advanced training and skills, opportunities to meet with other students with similar interests and abilities, and opportunities to receive feedback from and interact with adult professionals (Olszewski-Kubilius & Limburg-Weber, 1999; Subotnik, Miserandino, &

Olszewski-Kubilius, 1996). Some programs, like the Westinghouse Science Talent Search, involve years of preparation, significant cash prizes, and several levels of competitions (i.e., state, regional, and national).

Little research exists on the effects of contests and competitions. Longitudinal follow-ups on participants in the Westinghouse Science Talent Search found that most had continued to pursue mathematics- and science-related fields (Subotnik & Steiner, 1994). However, more females left these fields than males, although their reasons for doing so did not differ. It appears that some students who received a great deal of support from mentors in preparation for the Westinghouse competition did not receive the same level of support when in college (Subotnik & Steiner, 1994).

The Future of Special Programs

The demand for outside-of-school programs for gifted students likely will increase. The form these programs take may change, however. Computer technology offers exciting possibilities for delivery of special courses and programs using several distance education formats, including telementoring (Lewis, 1989; McBride & Lewis, 1993; Adams & Cross, 1999/2000). These technologies can increase access for gifted students, especially those who are geographically isolated or in schools with limited instructional resources.

Research must continue to assess the long-term effects and benefits of special programs for students and the validity of entrance and selection criteria against student performance. These are needed to convince educators and policy makers that gifted children can learn at faster rates than other children, and they need and profit from special educational services.

Finally, as the number of summer and extra-school programs for gifted students rises, the articulation between these programs and in-school programs and curricula will likely become a greater issue. The increase in the variety of different types of supplemental programs, the number of institutions that offer them, and the number of students that participate in them has had some negative consequences for students. Rather than deal with the myriad of programs, schools sometimes opt for general blanket policies that do not allow credit for any "outside" courses or programs. However, with a growing number of states instituting legislation to support dual enrollment, the precedent is set to accept credits from outside institutions, particularly institutions of higher education.

Summer and Saturday programs have become vital to the talent development of academically gifted students. The educational models they embody, for example, fast-paced instruction or problem-based learning, need to become an essential part of the local school curriculum. These programs have the potential to link schools, universities, and other institutions in significant and highly beneficial ways.

SUMMARY AND CONCLUSIONS

Special summer and Saturday programs for gifted students have proliferated over the last decade. Outside of school programs play a unique role in the talent development process providing students challenging coursework, unique kinds of educational experiences, and access to intellectual peers.

Summer and Saturday programs raise issues such as the relationship between outside of school programs and in-school curricula and programs. Such programs typically operate quite independently of school programs with little articulation regarding issues such as credit and placement. Summer programs, while beneficial to students, are not accessible to all students since many involve tuition and other costs. Outside of school programs vary greatly in type and include fast-paced, accelerated courses, dual enrollment in college and high school courses, competitions and contests, study abroad, mentorships or internships, and distance-learning courses.

Research on summer programs indicates that gifted students achieve at appropriate levels in fast-paced classes and subsequently tend to take more advanced high school and college courses and generally pursue a more rigorous course of study. These effects are particularly potent for gifted girls. Homogeneous grouping with other gifted students in summer or Saturday programs has no long-term negative effects on students' self-esteem or self-concept.

Summer programs are likely to continue to grow as an important component of talent development. More research is needed to document the proposed benefits of programs as well as increased efforts to insure access for all students and articulation between outside-of-school and in-school programs.

QUESTIONS FOR THOUGHT AND DISCUSSION

1. Imagine you are a middle- or high-school teacher interested in special, out-of-school opportunities for gifted students. How would you learn what is available for your students?

2. On average, working with other gifted students in special programs seems to depress self-concepts and self-esteem, at least temporarily. Is this a problem? How might students' loss of self-esteem be lessened or removed?

3. Imagine that a summer math course truly duplicates a regular high school math course. How could you convince school administrators to award high school credit for successfully completing the challenging summer course? Are positive and negative effects on students relevant here? Are AP tests relevant? Is a policy change in order? Explain.

REFERENCES

Adams, C. M., & Cross, T. L. (1999/2000). Distance learning opportunities for academically gifted students. *Journal of Secondary Gifted Education, 11*(2), 88–96.

Alamprese, J. A., Erlanger, W. J., & Brigham, N. (1988). *No gift wasted: Effective strategies for educating highly able disadvantaged students in math and science.* (Vols. 1–2). USOE contract #300-87-0152.

Archambault Jr., F. X., Westberg, K. L., Brown, S. W., Hallmark, B. W., Emmons, C. L., & Zhang, W. (1993). *Regular classroom practices with gifted students: Results of a national survey of classroom teachers.* Storrs, CT: National Research Center on the Gifted and Talented.

Barnett, L. B., & Durden, W. G. (1993). Education patterns of academically talented youth. *Gifted Child Quarterly, 37,* 161–168.

Bartkovich, K. G., & Mezynski, K. (1981). Fast-paced precalculus mathematics for talented junior-high students: Two recent SMPY programs. *Gifted Child Quarterly, 25,* 73–80.

Benbow, C. P., Perkins, S., & Stanley, J. C. (1983). Mathematics taught at a fast pace: A longitudinal evaluation of SMPY's first class. In C. P. Benbow & J. C. Stanley (Eds.), *Academic Precocity: Aspects of Its Development* (pp. 51–78). Baltimore: Johns Hopkins University Press.

Benbow, C. P., & Stanley, J. C. (Eds.). (1983). *Academic precocity: Aspects of its development.* Baltimore: Johns Hopkins University Press.

Bloom, B. S. (Ed.). (1985). *Developing talent in young people.* New York: Ballantine.

Brody, L., & Fox, L. H. (1980). An accelerative intervention program for mathematically gifted girls. In L. H. Fox, L.

Brody, & D. Tobin (Eds.), *Women and the mathematical mystique* (pp. 164–178). Hillsdale, NJ: Erlbaum.

Brounstein, P. J., Holahan, W., & Sawyer, R. (1988). The expectations and motivations of gifted students in a residential academic program: A study of individual differences. *Journal for the Education of the Gifted, 11,* 36–52.

Coleman, J., & Fults, B. (1982). Self-concept and the gifted classroom: The role of social comparisons. *Gifted Child Quarterly, 26,* 116–120.

Coleman, J., & Fults, B. (1985). Special-class placement, level of intelligence, and the self-concepts of gifted children: A social comparison perspective. *Remedial and Special Education, 6*(1), 7–12.

Colson, S. (1980). The evaluation of a community-based career education program for gifted and talented students as an administrative model for an alternative program. *Gifted Child Quarterly, 24,* 101–106.

Confessore, G. J. (1991). What became of the kids who participated in the 1981 Johnson Early College Summer Arts Program? *Journal for the Education of the Gifted, 15,* 64–82.

Cooley, M. R., Cornell, D. G., & Lee, C. C. (1991). Peer acceptance and self-concept of Black students in a summer gifted program. *Journal for the Education of the Gifted, 14,* 166–170.

Cox, J., Daniel, N., & Boston, B. O. (1985). *Educating able learners: Programs and promising practices.* Austin: University of Texas Press.

Delcourt, M. A. B., Lloyd, B. H., Cornell, D. G., & Goldberg, M. D. (1994). *Evaluation of the effects of programming arrangements on student learning outcomes.* Storrs, CT: National Research Center on the Gifted and Talented.

Feldhusen, J., & Sokol, L. (1982). Extra-school programming to meet the needs of gifted youth: Super Saturday. *Gifted Child Quarterly, 26,* 51–56.

Ford, D. Y. (1996). *Reversing underachievement among gifted Black students.* New York: Teachers College Press.

Fox, L. H., Brody, L., & Tobin, D. (1985). The impact of early intervention programs upon course-taking and attitudes in high school. In S. F. Chipman, L. R. Brush, & D. M. Wilson (Eds.), *Women and mathematics: Balancing the equation* (pp. 249–274). Hillsdale, NJ: Erlbaum.

Goldstein, D., & Wagner, H. (1993). After school programs, competitions, school olympics, and summer programs. In K. A. Heller, F. J. Monks, & A. H. Passow (Eds.), *International handbook of research and development of giftedness and talent* (pp. 593–604). New York: Pergamon Press.

Haensly, P. A., & Lehmann, P. (1998). Nurturing giftedness while minority adolescents juggle change spheres. *Journal of Secondary Gifted Education, 9,* 163–178.

Hoge, R. D., & Renzulli, J. S. (1993). Exploring the link between giftedness and self-concept. *Review of Educational Research, 63,* 449–465.

Karnes, F. A., & Riley, T. L. (1996). *Competitions: Maximizing your abilities.* Waco, TX: Prufrock.

Kolitch, E. R., & Brody, L. (1992). Mathematics acceleration of highly talented students: An evaluation. *Gifted Child Quarterly, 39,* 78–96.

Kolloff, P. B., & Moore, A. D. (1989). Effects of summer programs on the self-concepts of gifted children. *Journal for the Education of the Gifted, 12,* 268–276.

Lewis, G. (1989). Serving the gifted in rural areas. Telelearning: Making maximum use of the medium. *Roeper Review, 11,* 195–202.

Limburg-Weber, L. (1999/2000). Send them packing: Study abroad as an option for gifted students. *Journal of Secondary Gifted Education, 11*(2), 43–51.

Lynch, S. J. (1992). Fast-paced high school science for the academically talented: A six-year perspective. *Gifted Child Quarterly, 36,* 147–154.

Lynch, S. J. (1990). Credit and placement issues for the academically talented following summer studies in science and mathematics. *Gifted Child Quarterly, 34,* 27–30.

Lynch, S. J., & Mills, C. J. (1990). The Skills Reinforcement Project (SRP): An academic program for high potential minority youth. *Journal for the Education of the Gifted, 13,* 364–379.

Maddux, C. D., Scheiber, L. M., & Bass, J. E. (1982). Self-concept and social distance in gifted children. *Gifted Child Quarterly, 26,* 77–81.

McBride, R. O., & Lewis, G. (1993). Sharing the resources: Electronic outreach programs. *Journal for the Education of the Gifted, 16,* 372–386.

McCarthy, C. R. (1999). Dual enrollment programs: Legislation helps high school students enroll in college courses. *Journal of Secondary Gifted Education, 11,* 24–32.

Mills, C. J. Ablard, K. E., & Lynch, S. J. (1992). Academically talented students' preparation for advanced-level courses after an individually-paced precalculus class. *Journal for the Education of the Gifted, 16,* 3–17.

Olszewski-Kubilius, P. (1998). Research evidence regarding the validity and effects of talent search educational programs. *Journal of Secondary Gifted Education, 7,* 134–138.

Olszewski-Kubilius, P. (1989). Development of academic talent: The role of summer programs. In J. VanTassel-Baska & P. Olszewski-Kubilius (Eds.), *Patterns of influence on gifted learners: The home, the self and the school* (pp. 214–230). New York: Teachers College Press.

Olszewski-Kubilius P., & Grant, B. (1996). Academically talented females in mathematics: The role of special programs and support from others in acceleration, achievement and aspiration. In K. D. Noble & R. F. Subotnik (Eds.), *Remarkable women: Perspectives on female talent development* (pp. 281–291). Cresskill, NJ: Hampton Press.

Olszewski-Kubilius P., Grant, B., & Seibert, C. (1993). Social support systems and the disadvantaged gifted: A framework for developing programs and services. *Roeper Review, 17,* 20–25.

Olszewski, P., Kulieke, M., & Willis, G. B. (1987, Summer). Changes in the self-perceptions of gifted students who participate in rigorous academic programs. *Journal for the Education of the Gifted, 10,* 287–303.

Olszewski-Kubilius, P., Kulieke, M. J., Willis, G. B., & Krasney, N. (1989). An analysis of the validity of SAT entrance scores for accelerated classes. *Journal for the Education of the Gifted, 13,* 37–54.

Olszewski-Kubilius, P., Laubscher, L., Wohl, V., & Grant, B. (1996). Issues and factors involved in credit and placement for accelerated summer coursework. *Journal of Secondary Gifted Education, 8*(1), 5–15.

Olszewski-Kubilius, P., & Limburg-Weber, L. (1999). *Designs for excellence: A guide to educational program options for academically talented middle and secondary students.* Evanston, IL: Center for Talent Development, Northwestern University.

Rimm, S. (1991). Underachievement and superachievement: Flip sides of the same psychological coin. In N. Colangelo & G. A. Davis (Eds.), *Handbook of gifted education* (2nd Ed.) (pp. 416–434). Boston: Allyn & Bacon.

Sawyer, R. N., DeLong, M. R., & von Brock, A. B. (1987). By-mail learning options for academically talented middle-school youth. *Gifted Child Quarterly, 3,* 118–120.

Stanley, J. C. (1976). Special fast-mathematics classes taught by college professors to fourth through twelfth graders. In D. P. Keating (Ed.), *Intellectual talent: research and development.* Baltimore: Johns Hopkins University Press.

Subotnik, R. F., Miserandino, A. D., & Olszewski-Kubilius, P. (1996). Implications of the olympiad studies for the development of mathematics talent in schools. *International Journal of Educational Research, 25,* 563–573.

Subotnik, R. F., & Steiner, C. L. (1994). Adult manifestations of adolescent talent in science: A longitudinal study of 1983 Westinghouse Science Talent Search winners. In R. F. Subotnik and K. D. Arnold (Eds.), *Beyond Terman: Contemporary longitudinal studies of giftedness and talent.* (pp. 52–76). Norwood, NJ: Ablex.

Swiatek, M. A., & Benbow, C. P. (1991). Ten-year longitudinal follow-up of ability matched accelerated and unaccelerated gifted students. *Journal of Educational Psychology, 3,* 528–538.

Tallent-Runnels, M. K., & Candler-Lotven, A. C. (1996). *Academic competitions for gifted students: A resource book for teachers and parents.* Thousand Oaks, CA: Corwin Press.

Thompson, M. (2001). Developing verbal talent. Evanston, IL: Center for Talent Development, Northwestern University.

VanTassel-Baska, J. (1988). Curriculum esign issues in developing a curriculum for the gifted. In J. VanTassel-Baska (Ed.), *Comprehensive currciulum for gifted learners.* Boston: Allyn & Bacon.

VanTassel-Baska, J., Patton, J., & Prillaman, D. (1990). The nature and extent of programs for the disadvantaged gifted in the United States and territories. *Gifted Child Quarterly, 34,* 94–96.

17

Talented Youth at the Secondary Level

JOHN F. FELDHUSEN, *Purdue University*

Academically talented youth need curriculum and instruction, at a level and pace commensurate with their precocity; freedom from social pressure to be normal and average in personality and adjustment, like everybody else; clarification of their emerging talent strengths; and motivation to strive for high-level creative achievements. School, family, and the whole community can provide support in achieving these needs. However, there is often very little such support, and even opposition or resistance, for fulfilling these needs.

Two major shifts in orientation are needed if we hope to enhance or facilitate the development of talent among adolescents during the middle school and high school years. One is to abandon the *program* concept and the other is to abandon the *gifted* concept. *Program* often connotes a specific and restricted set of activities exclusively for an explicitly identified group of students labeled *gifted*. The extent of activities is often limited to an hour or two of pullout time from a math, English, or science class for some bland and often worthless enrichment activities (Cox, Daniel, & Boston, 1985). Little good is accomplished with such "programs."

The full development of youth talents calls for a wide diversity of experiences in accelerated courses of instruction, extracurricular activities, and extra-school experiences in the wider community. The latter, extra-school activities, might include participation in special Saturday or summer programs (Feldhusen, 1991), concurrent enrollment in college or university courses, or work with a local drama or historical society. Talent development calls for a rich variety of experiences through which highly able youth carry out a self-identification process to under-

stand better their special aptitudes and talents, grow in knowledge in the fields related to their talents, and increasingly commit themselves to the full development of their talents.

The second shift is away from the concept and label *gifted* to a *talent* orientation. A report from the U.S. Department of Education (1993) concluded that "The term 'gifted' connotes a mature power rather than a developing ability and, therefore, is antithetic to recent research findings about children" (p. 26). The report used the term *talent* or *talented* rather than *gift* or *gifted* and offered the following definition: "Children and youth with outstanding talent perform or show the potential for performing at remarkably high levels" (p. 26).

It is clear, then, that our task is to find youth who are precocious in their talent development and to identify their specific talent strength or strengths. Some will possess multiple talents, calling for several accelerated learning experiences; others will have only one or two talent strengths and a more limited need for special educational opportunities. In any event, these are youth who *need* accelerated, enriched, fast-paced, challenging instruction to sustain their talent development (Feldhusen, 2000).

Efforts to search for and identify talented youth have become excessively formal, statistical, and dependent on tests. The process of identification also has resulted in excessive labeling behavior on the part of school personnel, especially in so-called gifted programs. A process of searching for and selecting youth for special educational opportunities to meet their particular needs surely can be carried out without the intermediate step of labeling them as gifted. Rather than labeling and categorizing them, it is preferable to use the language of special education and denote them as children with special talents, aptitudes, abilities, or needs (Feldhusen, 2000).

Search and Selection

A variety of methods can be used to search for talented youth. Regional talent searches using the SAT and ACT (Assouline & Lupkowski-Shoplik, 1997) serve well to identify youth with high-level aptitude.[1] An elementary version of the ACT, EXPLORE, is also now available (Assouline & Lupkowski-Shoplik, 1997). A variety of other competitions also serve to identify talented, precocious youth. Standardized achievement test results also can be used to identify special talents, but we recognize that low ceilings on such tests often impose severe restrictions on the highest score levels attainable by talented youth.

Teachers can be trained to structure educational activities and opportunities in their classrooms to allow youth to reveal their talents. Teachers typically need training to enable them to recognize the behavioral signs that reveal special talent strengths (Feldhusen & Jin, 2000).

Preliminary screening in the talent search can be facilitated with rating scales such as the Scales for Rating the Behavioral Characteristics of Superior Students (SRBCSS; Renzulli, Smith, White, Callahan, Hartman, & Westberg, 2002) and the Purdue Academic Rating Scales (Feldhusen, Hoover, & Sayler, 1990). Interest inventories such as the Interest-A-Lyzer (Renzulli, Hébert, & Sorenson, 1994) also can be useful in the search for talent strengths.

The ten scales of the SRBCSS include several of particular interest for talent assessment, namely Leadership, Art, Music, Creativity, Expressiveness, Drama, and Planning. The Purdue Academic Rating Scales focus on five talent domains: science, mathematics, English, social studies, and foreign languages. The Purdue Vocational Talent Scales assess special aptitude in home economics, trade and industrial areas, vocational agriculture, and business. All of these instruments are useful as preliminary indicators of talent.

---

1. See Chapter 15 by Lupkowski-Shoplik, Benbow, Assouline, and Brody.

Ultimately, youth talents are best revealed in challenging, rich learning situations and best assessed by teachers who create learning experiences in which talent can be shown and who recognize the superior talents manifested by their students. The process is then cyclical, in that preliminary identification by a teacher leads to increasingly well tailored instruction to sustain the challenge and to keep the talent growing and developing (Feldhusen, 2000).

Secondary Services, Opportunities, and Activities

The locus of educational provision for talented adolescents is in classes, extracurricular activities, counseling, and extra-school opportunities (Feldhusen, 1999). A wide variety of services should be available to meet the special needs of talented youth for enriched, advanced, and challenging learning experiences. Table 17.1 presents a smorgasbord of educational services that are appropriate at the middle and high school levels for talented youth. The lists are suggestive and not limiting. Talented students should have many opportunities to study and learn with other talented, precocious youth, and to accelerate their learning program to fit their own precocity (Feldhusen, Van Winkle, & Ehle, 1996).

Although there has been much debate in recent years about special high-track classes, as well as some shifting to heterogeneous grouping, we agree wholeheartedly with Kulik and Kulik (1997), who concluded: "Benefits for higher aptitude students are usually largest in special accelerated and enriched classes" (p. 240).

Talented youth *need* the stimulation and challenge that can only come with advanced and enriched instruction, highly knowledgeable teachers, and equally talented/precocious peers. It is of no academic value to bide one's time in low-level, slow-paced instruction or cooperative-learning activities. Grouping for special classes should be on a subject-by-subject basis and based on youth talents and precocity, not on a general tracking plan. However, it is clear that some youth are talented in so many areas—multitalented—that their entire program should be advanced in all subjects and in the company of other talented students (Feldhusen & Bogess, 2000).

Talented youth should be allowed, encouraged, and counseled to take Advanced Placement (AP) courses whenever and wherever they are available

Table 17.1 Talent Development Services

Junior High or Middle School Services	*High School Services*

1. Counseling
  a. Group
  b. Individual
2. Honors Classes
3. Future Problem Solving
4. Junior Great Books
5. Odyssey of the Mind
6. Career Education
7. Seminars
8. Mentors
9. AP or College Classes
10. Acceleration
  a. Math
  b. Science
  c. English
11. Special Opportunities
  a. Art
  b. Music
  c. Drama
  d. Dance
12. Special Projects
13. Foreign Language
14. Correspondence Study
15. Independent Study
	1. Counseling
	  a. Group
	  b. Individual
	2. Honors Classes
	3. Advanced Placement Classes
	4. Foreign Languages
	5. Seminars
	6. Mentorships
	7. Internships
	8. Concurrent College Enrollment
	9. College Classes in High School
	10. Special Opportunities
	  a. Art
	  b. Music
	  c. Drama
	  d. Dance
	11. Special Projects for Vocationally Talented
	12. Debate
	13. Correspondence Study
	14. Independent Study
	15. Math Olympiad
	16. U.S. Academic Triathlon
	17. Academy for Creative Exploration

(Curry, MacDonald, & Morgan, 1999; Pyryt, 2000). The AP exams also offer excellent tests of talent strengths as well as college credit for those students who score well.

Concurrent college or university enrollment affords another way for talented youth to experience higher level academic challenges. The student also earns college credit for courses completed successfully. Several state education departments now require high schools to award academic credit toward high school graduation for college courses that parallel high school courses.

Extracurricular activities afford many opportunities for talent development. For verbally talented youth, debate and other forensic activities afford excellent opportunities to develop talents in public speaking, group leadership, library research, writing, planning, and organizing. Language clubs make it possible to learn a foreign language. Youth organizations in vocational subjects provide many opportunities for talent development in project work, leadership, and artistic design. Most high schools offer an abundance of extracurricular opportunities.

Counselors should be able to identify youth with special talents and provide educational and career guidance for their optimum development (see, e.g., Colangelo & Assouline, 2000). Academic records in junior and senior high schools should serve to identify the specific talent strengths of students and should be used in writing short- and long-range talent development plans for individual students. The Growth Plan concept (Feldhusen & Wood, 1997) will be presented in the next section.

Talented youth need to select courses wisely in junior and senior high school to ready themselves for college programs. Some should plan to attend one of the residential high schools of mathematics and science now operating in 12 states (Feldhusen & Bogess, 2000).[2] Early admission to college,

2. See Chapter 18 by Kolloff.

preferably a major university, affords many talented youth the *only* route to challenging learning experiences that sustain talent development. Counselors can and should provide guidance to the right courses in middle school and the freshman and sophomore years of high school to ensure readiness of talented youth for concurrent college enrollment, early admission to college, or admission to one of the residential high schools.

Extra-school opportunities also can contribute significantly to the process of talent development. These are the educational opportunities, resources, and activities in the community, state, and region that are accessible after school, evenings, weekends, and summers (Feldhusen, 1991) or by distance learning (Adams & Cross, 2000).[3] Some schools and chambers of commerce have published catalogs of such opportunities for their areas. The offerings also are reported in newspapers or brochures distributed in the community. The activities often center at colleges, universities, museums, libraries, historical sites, or institutes and may consist of public lectures, classes, courses, exhibits, and the like (Campbell, Wagner, & Walberg, 2000).

Mentorships with college professors, special classes on Saturdays and in summers, research internships, use of library and computer facilities, and association with the college theater are some of the resources that are often open to talented youth who live near colleges and universities.

Mentorships afford excellent opportunities for students to learn about careers that match their own talent profiles, to begin to emulate the professional behaviors that characterize the occupations to which they aspire, to develop the motivation for appropriate educational services for targeted professional fields, and to set goals for high-level achievement in those fields.[4] Pleiss and Feldhusen (1995) reported that without mentors who model high-level achievement in fields related to youth's specific talents, many youth simply take on popular athletic or entertainment figures as their vicarious mentors. Mentors must be carefully selected and trained to model appropriate high-level achievements in youth academic talent domains.

We conclude that effective talent development depends on a wide variety of resources in both school and community and on the motivation of talented youth and their parents (Olszewski-Kubilius & Limburg-Weber, 1999), with guidance from school teachers and counselors, to make optimum use of the available resources. Too often, programs for the gifted have conveyed the message that only the special services offered in the program qualify as educational provision for the gifted. In contrast, our view is an eclectic one: use *all* available resources, even though they are not officially designated "gifted programs," and add services as needed, such as Advanced Placement classes, seminars, honors classes, and special clubs. Absence of a formal gifted program often leads to hand wringing and desperation on the part of parents of talented youth. Ideally, their responses should be (1) to seek out the best current options for their talented child and (2) to press the school to offer more advanced, challenging learning opportunities.

Growth Plans

Talents grow into full-blown, mature expertise or competence when there is explicit planning during childhood and adolescence for their development. The process begins when parents, teachers, counselors, or others recognize the young person's special talents, aptitudes, and abilities as well as the intense interest that often accompanies special talent. Ultimately, it is the children and then the adolescents who must come to see and understand their own talent strengths and commit to the development of their talents (Feldhusen, Wood, & Dai, 1997). Parents and school personnel can help a great deal, but they cannot force children to become motivated to develop their own talents. Challenging and exciting teachers in the early years and increasingly competent, expert teachers in the middle years (Bloom, 1985), along with supportive and knowledgeable parents, can provide the initial impetus for the eventual takeover of the task by talented youth themselves.

The concept of a Growth Plan (Feldhusen & Wood, 1997) is a formal mechanism or procedure for inducing more specific thought about talent development. A Growth Plan for an eighth-grade adolescent is presented in Figure 17.1. The planning process is best carried out in school, led by a counselor or talent development coordinator, in a series of four to eight meetings of 40 to 60 minutes each with students in small groups of 12 to 20. The students develop the Growth Plan with assistance from the counselor or coordinator.

---

3. See Chapter 45 by Pyryt.

4. See Chapter 20 by Clasen and Clasen.

Name: K. M.

Grade level: Entering 8th grade.

Current courses: STAR 1: A Voyage Through the Digestive System of Mammals and The Chemistry of Aquatics Environments. At home school: Most Abled Math and Most Abled Language Arts.

Clubs, organizations: Science Olympiad and Sports Teams.

Awards, Honors: Science Olympiad State Finalist; Highest Math Student in the Seventh Grade; Scholastic Awards in Math, Science, Social Studies, and Language.

Test scores: SAT V = 540, Q = 490; Ach: Science: 97%; Math: 92%; IQ: 147.

Prior experience in gifted program: Has been enrolled in Most Abled (accelerated) classes at his home school.

Interest analysis: K. M. has a wide variety of interests, including writing, sciences, and reading. He enjoys going to movies and investigating science topics.

Learning styles: K. M. likes to learn in a hands-on, highly active environment. He prefers tasks and projects that are highly structured and that allow him to examine the components carefully. He likes to work in groups and by himself.

Student's Own Goals	Recommended Classes for Next Year
Short-term:	Continue in Most Abled (accelerated) classes.
Raise SAT scores.	
Progress faster in science studies	
Become more responsible (i.e., getting homework completed).	
Long-term:	
Pursue career interests in radiology, ecology, or chemistry.	

Recommended Activity in School	Recommended Extra-School Activities
Continue participation in Science Olympiad.	Visit more aquariums to continue studies in ecology.
Pursue athletic activities as determined by K. M. and his parents.	Contact and/or secure mentor to assist with further ecological studies.
Pursue interests in mathematics, science, and ecology through school clubs.	

Final plan_____

Figure 17.1 Growth Plan.

The first section of the Growth Plan is an inventory or review of self, abilities, interests, and accomplishments to date. The planning process often is carried out in the late spring as a preparation for the next school year and beyond. Test scores are made available to students as much as possible for their age, and are interpreted with the assistance of the counselor or coordinator to help students achieve as much self-understanding as possible.

A critical aspect of the review of self and accomplishments is to help the student become aware of major achievements as definers of superior talent. Kay (1999) developed a system to help students define the categories and levels of their accomplishments from year to year as they move through school. Hopefully, such inventorying will help students not only become increasingly aware of the importance of such achievements, but also more and more able to see the link between those achievements and their emerging talents.

The next phase of Growth Plan activity is goal setting. Students are led in the process of developing and/or clarifying their short- and long-term personal, social, academic, and career goals. This may require class and out-of-class time for students to reflect on the directions of their lives and their aspirations for the future. The goals are recorded on the Growth Plan.

The next phase is selecting classes, courses, and academic experiences for the year ahead and possibly several years ahead if they contemplate early college admission. Counselors should be ready to guide students in linking their goals to the necessary academic steps. Extracurricular activities are also planned and incorporated into the Growth Plan. Finally, educational opportunities outside of school, especially in colleges or universities in the area, are reviewed as possible resources in the Growth Plan. Throughout this planning process, the counselor's role includes making students aware of appropriate resources and activities.

After a tentative draft of the Growth Plan has been written, it should be taken home for discussion with parents and revised according to the realities that flow from students' perceptions of parent feedback and suggestions. In most cases, talented students will be dependent on parent support, especially for extra-school activities, such as Saturday and summer programs or concurrent college enrollment that involve additional costs.

The Growth Plan process should increasingly be guided by students themselves. Hopefully, they will come to see themselves as capable of planning for and guiding their own talent development.

Purdue Pyramid Model of Talent Development

Figure 17.2 presents a summary pyramid model of the talent development process. The base suggests that talented youth, like all youth, need acceptance as legitimate, valid human beings. Peer pressure to be normal or average is a major problem for talented teenagers. Typically, they can best achieve peer acceptance in the company of other talented youth. The model then suggests, in the vertical segments, a variety of educational experiences that facilitate talent development. The suggestions represent a sampling, a definitive list.

Out of the educational opportunities, as a result of challenging educational experiences, talented youth come to better understand their talents, aptitudes, abilities, interests, motivation, potentials, and limitations. Self-understanding is a necessary prelude to the final pyramid stage, commitment to the full development of one's talents and abilities. Such a commitment is linked to an awareness of career goals as well as knowledge of the educational routes to those goals.

Personality, adjustment, and motivation of talented youth are also special problems facing teachers and parents. While the Terman (1925) research seemed to suggest that gifted youth are normally adjusted and possessed of healthy personalities, Hollingworth (1929) found that highly gifted youth were often at odds with other youth, sometimes had trouble "bearing fools gladly," and had unique motivational patterns. Simonton (1999), in an analysis of creative geniuses, found that many were severely maladjusted and even suffering from severe mental disorders.[5] Feldhusen and Nimlos-Hippen (1992), Delisle (1990), Silverman (1993), Hayes and Sloat (1990), and Harkavy and Asnis (1985) report that suicidal tendencies and depression may characterize many gifted youth. Thus, school pressures to be well adjusted and normal like everybody else may be contradictory to emerging patterns in some gifted youth and may be closely linked to their emerging talents and achievement goals. Surely, we cannot accept nor encourage maladjustment or psychological problems among talented youth, but we can recognize that adjustment patterns among talented youth may be quite different from those that characterize youth of average ability and call for unique modes of counseling. Silverman (1993) presented a number of special techniques that seem to work well with talented youth and that meet their special needs.

Throughout the teenage years, parent support is a vital ingredient of talent development. Parents provide the financial resources for the extra-school opportunities; they are the sounding board for discussion of opportunities; they provide guidance and motivation; and they afford emotional support throughout the process.

SUMMARY AND CONCLUSIONS

Three major research projects have yielded insights about the talent development process. The first was conducted by Benjamin Bloom and reported in 1985 in *Developing Talent in Young People.*[6] Studying

---

5. See Chapter 28 by Simonton.
6. See Chapter 19 by Sosniak.

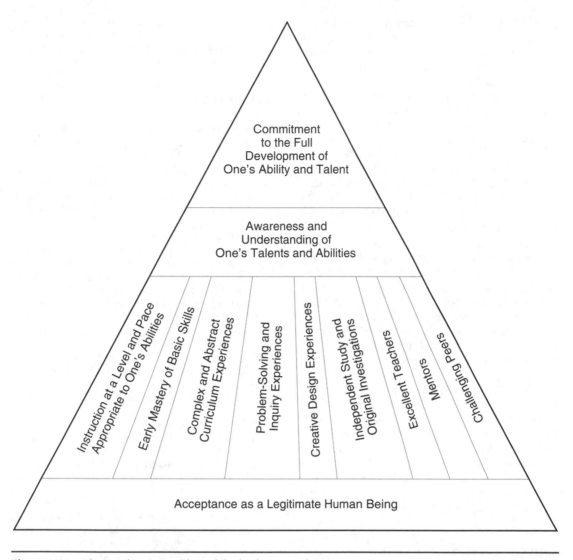

Figure 17.2 The Purdue Pyramid Model of Talent Development.

athletes, artists, and scientists who had achieved world-class recognition, Bloom tried to find the conditions in youth that facilitated their talent development. He found that early identification of talent strengths, highly supportive and encouraging parents, and stimulating and knowledgeable teachers were key elements in their early development. The youth themselves showed early capacity to learn rapidly and well. Long-term commitment of the youth themselves to the development of their talent emerged in later adolescence and characterized those who went on to high-level achievement.

In *Multiple Intelligences: The Theory in Practice*, Gardner (1993) reminds us of the emerging role of the multiple talents conception, first presented by him in 1983 and now having a powerful impact on school reform in the United States.[7] As opposed to the old conception of a single general intelligence, or *g*, Gardner's theory proposes seven basic talents or intelligences: logical-mathematical, linguistic, musical,

---

7. See Chapter 8 by von Károlyi, Ramos-Ford, and Gardner.

spatial, bodily-kinesthetic, interpersonal, and intrapersonal. Implementation of the theory in schools is being carried out and evaluated. Gardner, Walters, and Hatch (1992) concluded: "Within the area of education, the applications of the theory are . . . tentative and speculative" (p. 35). Nevertheless, observers are almost uniformly optimistic that the multiple intelligences approach in education bodes well for talent development in schools.

Csikszentmihalyi, Rathunde, and Whalen (1993), described research that followed 208 youth through their high school years. The students showed talent precocity in mathematics, science, music, art, and athletics. The researchers concluded that talents continue to grow in youth through the adolescent years if students develop productive work and study habits, have positive personality traits, enjoy strong family support, have teachers who model professional identity and love of their field, and have a conservative sexual orientation. They also concluded that talent development is a complex process involving differentiation of one's talents, aptitudes, and abilities, and integration of one's capacities into a unified persona that experiences "flow" or total absorption in the talent field activities.

The junior and senior high school years are critical times for talent recognition and development. A report from the U.S. Department of Education, (1993) *National Excellence: A Case for Developing America's Talent* stresses the need for a new view and conception of youth talents and urges abandonment of the term and conception *gifted*. It seems likely that this transition will lead to more effective ways of discovering and nurturing youth talents.

QUESTIONS FOR THOUGHT AND DISCUSSION

1. Feldhusen describes methods for *identifying* talented secondary students. Others (e.g., Schultz & Delisle, Chapter 38) strictly recommend self-selection. What do you think?

2. Feldhusen argues that pullout types of programs include "bland and often worthless enrichment activities" and "little good is accomplished with such programs." Does his focus on secondary students have anything to do with this opinion? Think about Renzulli's Enrichment Triad Model (Chapter 14). Is Feldhusen correct? What do you think?

3. Consider the talent development services listed in Figure 17.1 and the various activities and teaching principle listed in the second-to-bottom level of the Purdue Pyramid Model of Talent Development (Figure 17.2). On a scale of 1 to 10, rate the likely value of each activity or teaching principle for talent development with (a) elementary students, (b) middle school students, and (c) high school students. Can you think of additional valuable activities or considerations?

REFERENCES

Adams, C. M., & Cross, T. L. (2000). Distance learning opportunities for academically gifted students. *Journal of Secondary Gifted Education, 11*(1), 88–96.

Assouline, S. G., & Lupkowski-Shoplik, A. (1997). Talent searches: A model for the discovery and development of academic talent. In N. Colangelo & G. A. Davis (Eds.), *Handbook of gifted education,* (pp. 170–179). Boston: Allyn & Bacon.

Bloom, B. S. (1985). Generalizations about talent development. In B. S. Bloom (Ed.), *Developing talent in young people* (pp. 507–549). New York: Ballantine Books.

Campbell, J. R., Wagner, H., & Walberg, H. J. (2000). Academic competitions and programs designed to challenge the exceptionally talented. In K. Heller, F. J. Mönks, R. J. Sternberg, & R. F. Subotnik (Eds.), *International handbook of giftedness and talent* (pp. 523–535). New York: Pergamon Press.

Colangelo, N., & Assouline, S. G. (2000). Counseling gifted students. In K. Heller, F. J. Mönks, R. J. Sternberg, & R. F. Subotnik (Eds.), *International handbook of giftedness and talent* (pp. 595–607). New York: Pergamon Press.

Cox, J., Daniel, N., & Boston, B. O. (1985). *Educating able learners: Programs and promising practices.* Austin: University of Texas Press.

Csikszentmihalyi, M., Rathunde, K., & Whalen, S. (1993). *Talented teenagers.* New York: Cambridge University Press.

Curry, W., MacDonald, W., & Morgan, R. (1999). The Advanced Placement Program: Access to excellence. *Journal of Secondary Gifted Education, 11*(1), 17–23.

Delisle, J. R. (1990). The gifted adolescent at risk: Strategies and resources for suicide prevention among gifted youth. *Journal for the Education of the Gifted, 13,* 212–228.

Feldhusen, J. F. (1991). Saturday and summer programs. In N. Colangelo & G. A. Davis (Eds.), *Handbook of gifted education* (pp. 197–208). Boston: Allyn & Bacon.

Feldhusen, J. F. (1999). Talent identification and development in education: The basic tenets. In S. Kline & K. T. Hegeman (Eds.), *Gifted education in the twenty-first century* (pp. 89–100). New York: Winslow Press.

Feldhusen, J. F. (2000, winter). From talent recognition and development to creative achievement and expertise. *Mensa Research Journal, 43,* 8–11.

Feldhusen, J. F., & Bogess, J. (2000). Secondary schools for academically talented youth. *Gifted Education International, 14*(2), 170–176.

Feldhusen, J. F., & Cobb, S. J. (1989). College courses for high school credit. *G/T Indiana, 1*(6), 2.

Feldhusen, J. F., Hoover, S. M., & Sayler, M. F. (1990). *Identification and education of the gifted and talented at the secondary level.* Monroe, NY: Trillium Press.

Feldhusen, J. F., & Jin, S. U. (2000). Assessing the knowledge base of educators who work with gifted students. *Understanding Our Gifted, 12*(2), 23–24.

Feldhusen, J. F., & Nimlos-Hippen, A. L. (1992). An exploratory study of self concepts and depression among the gifted. *Gifted Education International, 8,* 136–138.

Feldhusen, J. F., Van Winkle, L., & Ehle, D. (1996). Is it acceleration or simply appropriate instruction for precocious youth? *Teaching Exceptional Children, 28*(3), 48–51.

Feldhusen, J. F., Wood, B. K., & Dai, D. Y. (1997). Gifted students' perceptions of their talents. *Gifted and Talented International, 12*(1), 42–45.

Feldhusen, J. F., & Wood, B. K. (1997). Developing growth plans for gifted students. *Gifted Child Today, 20*(6), 24–26, 48–49.

Gardner, H. (1983). *Frames of mind: The theory of multiple intelligences.* New York: Basic Books.

Gardner, H. (1993). *Multiple intelligences: The theory in practice.* New York: Basic Books.

Gardner, H., Walters, J., & Hatch, T. (1992). If teaching had looked beyond the classroom: The development and education of intelligences. *Innotech Journal, 16*(1), 18–36.

Goldstein, D., & Wagner, H. (1993). After school programs, competitions, school olympics, and summer programs. In K. Heller, F. J. Mönks, & A. H. Passow (Eds.), *International handbook of giftedness and talent* (pp. 593–604). New York: Pergamon Press.

Harkavy, J., & Asnis, G. (1985). Suicide attempts in adolescence: Prevalence and implications. *New England Journal of Medicine, 313,* 1290–1291.

Hayes, M. L., & Sloat, R. S. (1990). Suicide and the gifted adolescent. *Journal for the Education of the Gifted, 13,* 229–244.

Hollingworth, L. S. (1929). *Gifted children: Their nature and nurture.* New York: Macmillan.

Kay, S. I. (1999). The talent profile as a curricular tool for academics, the arts, and athletics. In S. Kline & K. T. Hegeman (Eds.), *Gifted education in the twenty-first century* (pp. 47–59). New York: Winslow Press.

Kulik, J. A., & Kulik, C. C. (1997). Ability grouping. In N. Colangelo & G. A. Davis (Eds.), *Handbook of gifted education* (2nd ed.) (pp. 230–242). Boston: Allyn & Bacon.

Olszewski-Kubilius, P., & Limburg-Weber, L. L. (1999). Options for middle school and secondary level gifted students. *Journal of Secondary Gifted Education, 11*(1), 4–10.

Pleiss, M. K., & Feldhusen, J. F. (1995). Mentors, role models, and heroes in the lives of gifted children. *Educational Psychologist, 30*(3), 159–169.

Pyryt, M. C. (2000). Talent development in science and technology. In K. Heller, F. J. Mönks, R. J. Sternberg, & R. F. Subotnik (Eds.), *International handbook of giftedness and talent* (pp. 427–437). New York: Pergamon Press.

Renzulli, J. S., Hébert, T. P., & Sorenson, M. F. (1994). *Secondary interest-a-lyzer.* Mansfield Center, CT: Creative Learning Press.

Renzulli, J. S., Smith, L. H., White, A. J., Callahan, C. M., Hartman, R. K. & Westberg, K. L. (2002). *Scales for rating the behavioral characteristics of superior students.* (rev. ed.). Mansfield Center, CT: Creative Learning Press.

Silverman, L. K. (1993). *Counseling the gifted and talented.* Denver: Love.

Simonton, D. K. (1999). *Origins of genius.* New York: Oxford University Press.

Terman, L. M. (1925). *Genetic studies of genius: Vol. 1. Mental and physical traits of a thousand gifted children.* Stanford: Stanford University Press.

U.S. Department of Education. (1993). *National excellence: A case for developing America's talent.* Washington, DC: U.S. Government Printing Office.

18

State-Supported Residential High Schools

PENNY BRITTON KOLLOFF, *Illinois State University—Normal*

This chapter describes a national trend in the education of gifted students, the development of state-supported special residential high schools for young people of exceptional intellectual and academic ability. The first of these high schools appeared in 1980 in North Carolina. Between 1980 and 1990, nine more states created these schools. In the years since, these original ten schools have flourished, and three more states have established schools with the mission of providing an appropriate education to their most academically talented high school students. Although there currently are more than 13 residential schools and programs throughout the country, this chapter focuses on those chartered by the legislatures of the states in which they exist. Stanley (1987) recommended that any state that has at least 300 National Merit semifinalists each year should explore the possibility of a residential high school.

Rationale

Since the early 1970s, programs for gifted students have proliferated across the United States as local schools have created various accommodations for their high-ability learners. Approaches for high school students have usually taken the form of advanced or honors courses, opportunities for acceleration to higher level classes, or in some cases enrollment in college classes while still in high school (Cox, Daniel, & Boston, 1985; Robinson, 1999). Depending on the local or state definition of *gifted,* programs of these types usually strive to meet the needs of 10–15 percent of the students in a school. However, if these students are considered a homogeneous group, then the most academically and intellectually advanced among them will still have unmet needs.

The typical high school is unable to offer the number of advanced courses or a sufficiently diverse curriculum to provide for the gifted learner who, for example, is capable of mastering all the mathematics courses the school has to offer within a year or two of entrance. VanTassel-Baska (1998) noted additional obstacles to providing appropriate educational programs for gifted learners at the secondary level, including inflexible schedules, curricula that fail to allow for the depth required by gifted learners, and the inability to provide an articulated, differentiated set of experiences. Robinson (1999) observed that typical high school curricula are so packed with subjects beyond traditional disciplines (e.g., driver education, ESL) that the schools are unable to offer special courses for gifted students. At a time when many of the nation's secondary schools do not offer a physics course, some do not include a course in chemistry, and many students do not have an opportunity to go beyond the second year of a foreign language, concern must focus on making advanced courses accessible to the most intellectually capable students. When schools, often small or rural, do not have sufficient enrollments to offer the most advanced classes or cannot provide teachers for such courses, then educators, parents, and students must seek alternatives for students who need such experiences. It is this most advanced group of students for whom special schools are developed.

Certain characteristics define students for whom a special residential school may be appropriate. They are individuals capable of mastering content in much less time than is required by other students, and who are able to engage in complex processes at high levels of abstraction. Because of these capabilities, gifted students often exhaust the curricular offerings of their local high school well before they graduate.

238

In short, these students need an educational experience different from that offered by most schools.

In addition to advanced course offerings, these students require faculty who are specialists in areas of advanced content and who can deliver appropriately fast-paced, high-level instruction. Again, most schools—necessarily addressing the needs of the majority of their students—do not have such faculty available.

There is another recognized need of gifted students, that of interacting with others of similar ability in a supportive climate. At best, typical high schools provide these opportunities on a limited basis, perhaps just several hours a week, perhaps just in one or two classes in which students are grouped by ability. Fears of elitism, strong feelings against tracking or ability grouping, and parent or teacher resistance prevent schools from going farther to group students for large portions of their time. Backlash against grouping students by ability has led some school districts to eliminate special programs and classes for gifted students (Purcell, 1993; Renzulli & Reis, 1991).

These conditions—combined with the goals of (1) achieving academic excellence in our country's educational systems, (2) developing the talented as a source of future economic and social leadership, and (3) establishing highly visible partnerships linking political, economic, and educational institutions— have led to the realization that special residential schools are indeed an appropriate way to meet the needs of many of the nation's most talented young people. Recognizing the importance of meeting these needs, and acknowledging that long-term benefits may accrue from an investment in the education of the exceptionally gifted, have resulted in proposals to state legislatures to create and sustain residential high schools for highly gifted students within their states.

Almost a decade ago, the U.S. Department of Education released *National Excellence: A Case for Developing America's Talent* (Ross, 1993). The report cited six broad recommendations for ensuring that education in this country will meet the needs of our students as they fulfill their potential and as they compare to students in other countries. Five of these recommendations relate directly to the goals and activities of state residential high schools for gifted students. The recommendations call for an appropriately challenging curriculum, high-level learning opportunities, opportunities for disadvantaged and minority students, appropriate teacher training and technical assistance, and the attainment of world class performance (pp. 28–29).

States with residential high schools for high-ability students have positioned themselves well to respond to the above recommendations. Each state with a school for gifted students has the opportunity to create a program that both benefits its own students and provides leadership in the state educational community. This leadership emerges as curricula are developed and tested with the residential students, as programs bring teachers from local schools to the campus to work with the students and faculty, and through activities that spread the resources of the residential school to other schools and students in the state. A sense of commitment to the larger community—stemming from the need to return some of the investment by the state—keeps the residential school from becoming insular. In many cases, initiatives for educational reform and innovation begin in such a school and spread throughout the state.

An Early Example

In 1978 then Governor James B. Hunt, Jr., and the General Assembly of North Carolina proposed the first residential high school for gifted students of that state. In the fall of 1980, the North Carolina School of Science and Mathematics, in Durham, accepted its first class of junior-year students and began a program designed to meet the academic, social, and emotional needs of a cross-section of the brightest students in the state. In addition to the direct benefits to the students who have attended and graduated from the school, the North Carolina school has pioneered ways for developing and disseminating new curricula and teaching methods to other schools throughout the state.

The North Carolina school has served as a model for similar schools throughout the country, drawing a racially and economically diverse student body of juniors and seniors from all geographic areas of the state. Faculty members have a high degree of academic expertise; many hold doctoral degrees. The curriculum offers opportunities for students to accelerate and enrich their academic programs. The overall program incorporates independent study, community service, and other extracurricular elements, and seeks to provide a balanced experience for students.

This successful school also can point to benefits to the state that invested in the plan. A large number of graduates elect to attend colleges and universities in North Carolina, and many of them choose to remain in the state to enter professional careers and raise their families. Businesses and industries have chosen to locate in North Carolina in part because of the state's demonstrated commitment to excellence in education. These are persuasive arguments that have influenced other state legislatures considering similar plans.

Characteristics of Special Residential Schools

The Students

Most residential high schools admit students at grade 11 for the beginning of a two-year experience. Illinois and Alabama admit students who are beginning grade 10, and North Carolina is considering tenth grade admission. Because they are established through legislative action supported by state funds, the schools are committed to enrolling a student body that represents the population of the state. Consideration is given to mirroring the demographic profile of the state. School size ranges from under 100 to over 600.

Identification and selection of students for participation in a special residential school is a complex process that starts well before the beginning of the academic year in which a student enters. Applicants take standardized tests such as the SAT-I: Reasoning Tests (formerly the Scholastic Aptitude Test or SAT), the PSAT, the ACT, or similar above-level tests. Most schools use a combination of test scores, high school grades, recommendations, writing samples, portfolios of art work or auditions in other talent areas, and interviews to assemble a profile of each applicant. Subjective and objective assessments are combined to arrive at admissions decisions.

In addition to evidence of academic achievement and ability, residential schools look for students who show potential to succeed in a program that requires independent work and who demonstrate the maturity to live away from home while attending a rigorous academic school.

Research by Jarwan and Feldhusen (1993) affirms the importance of linking the identification and selection process to the particular curriculum and program of the school. A good match between student and program will help ensure that both the students and the school will be successful. Systematic training for those involved in the identification and selection process also is critical, so that later subjective assessments of prospective students by a group of professionals will achieve maximum reliability.

The Faculty

Instructors for these exceptionally talented students come from high schools, colleges and universities, and the private sector. Most residential schools report that their faculties hold advanced degrees, with a substantial number having earned doctorates. In cases where the residential school is affiliated with a college or university, faculty may teach both college and high school students. There is considerable flexibility concerning the requirements for "certification" of teachers in these schools. Efforts are made to recruit teachers with outstanding academic credentials *and* the ability to work well with gifted students. Schools want individuals who can inspire gifted students, both inside and outside of the classroom, create and deliver high level instruction, offer support for creative ideas, and become role models as productive adults.

Residential schools often have special visiting teacher/scholar programs that bring teachers from around the state to the residential site to work with the students. These individuals teach, develop curricula, observe and implement teaching methods, and return home to adapt the techniques and materials for their high-ability students and to share them with other teachers.

Facilities

Special residential schools require special facilities. Because of the nature of the schools, there must be a complex of buildings that accommodates both the instructional and living components of the programs. Existing residential schools have addressed this need in several ways. The first of these special schools for gifted students, the North Carolina School of Science and Mathematics, is located in a former hospital complex that was converted into dormitories, classrooms, laboratories, a library, and recreational areas. The Arkansas residential high school also is housed in a former hospital in Hot Springs. The Illinois Math and Science Academy moved into a high school building that had been vacated. Initially, some classrooms were turned into dormitory rooms while others remained classrooms or became laboratories or other needed spaces. Dormitories have since been constructed on the academy campus.

Several residential high schools are located on college or university campuses where the needed facilities already exist with little need for modification. The

Louisiana School for Math, Science, and the Arts is located on the campus of Northwestern State University in Nachitoches. The Texas Academy of Mathematics and Science is part of the University of North Texas, located in Denton. The Indiana Academy for Science, Mathematics and Humanities is on the campus of Ball State University in Muncie. The Mississippi School for Math and Science is on the campus of the Mississippi University for Women in Columbus. The South Carolina Governors' School for Science and Mathematics is located at Coker College in Hartsville. The Missouri Academy of Science, Mathematics and Computing recently opened at Northwest Missouri State University. Worcester Polytechnic Institute is the site for the Massachusetts Academy of Mathematics and Science.

In most of these situations, while the residential high school and the college or university exist on the same campus, there are separate facilities for the two student bodies. Dormitories house only high school students, and restrictions are placed on the interaction of high school and older students. A unique situation exists at the Indiana Academy where the residential high school, Ball State University, and the Burris Laboratory School (a K–12 public school affiliated with the university) share some facilities and provide students with flexibility in course taking and extracurricular choices while still preserving certain limitations.

The Curriculum

At the heart of residential schools for gifted students are the curricula especially designed to meet their needs. With an emphasis on mathematics and science in virtually all programs, students usually advance rapidly through high-level course work in these and other areas. Curricular offerings in these schools may fit one of several different models. For some, the College Board Advanced Placement (AP) program is the foundation of the curriculum. Students who spend two years in a residential high school may take many AP classes and/or exams, thus enabling them to begin college or university with a year or more of credit in several areas. Stanley (1987), in fact, urged that the curriculum for a school of this kind include courses that prepare students to take AP exams in calculus, physics, chemistry, computer science, and biology. At the Illinois Mathematics and Science Academy, the completion of the three-year program takes students through a

beginning university curriculum and prepares them to take a variety of AP exams in mathematics, sciences, English, and foreign languages.

Residential schools located on college or university campuses also incorporate university courses into the curriculum of the high school. Students may take courses (e.g., languages, arts) not offered in the residential school curriculum or other specialized college courses that balance and supplement the curriculum of the high school. The curriculum of the Texas Academy of Mathematics and Science consists of university honors courses, for which the students earn college credit in addition to completing the requirements for high school graduation. In their two years at Texas Academy, students simultaneously complete the last two years of high school and the first two years of college. Students at the Indiana Academy for Science, Mathematics and Humanities may take, for example, Greek or fine arts courses at Ball State University or music at Burris Laboratory School (Dixon, 1993).

Although the typical emphasis of special residential high schools is science and mathematics, these schools also incorporate strong communications and arts programs into the curriculum. The Louisiana School for Math, Science, and the Arts goes a step further in offering students the opportunity to focus on math/science, humanities, or the creative and performing arts. A student may select one or more of these areas in which to concentrate. The Indiana Academy incorporated *humanities* into the name of the school, and the curriculum reflects this emphasis.

Most special high schools also develop unique curricular offerings beyond the AP and college courses. Humanities, English, and social studies courses may be organized in ways different from the traditional secondary curriculum. The nature of the learners and faculty lend themselves to the development of courses that explore broad, interdisciplinary themes, epistemology, and the historical and philosophical foundations of disciplines.

The Illinois Mathematics and Science Academy developed an approach known as Problem-Based Learning in which students are given realistic problems to investigate. The "fuzzy situations" require students to exercise their question-asking, information-gathering, and hypothesis-formulating and testing skills while their teachers play the roles of facilitators and coaches. These experiences engage students in studying the content of various disciplines in nontraditional, but real-world ways (Stepien &

Gallagher, 1993; Stepien, Gallagher & Workman, 1993).

The curriculum at the Indiana Academy for Science, Mathematics and Humanities includes a number of thematic interdisciplinary courses that focus on history and English. Examples include Civitas/Human Struggles (a three-semester interdisciplinary English and Social Studies course), Russian Literature (a history, literature, and culture course), and Lost Generation Literature (a study of the culture and literature of the American expatriates in Paris in the 1920s). In addition to these courses, all students enroll in a course called Colloquium, which meets once a week to discuss selected great issues (Indiana Academy for Science, Mathematics and Humanities (n.d.)).

Course offerings are not the only area in which the curriculum of these schools may differ from traditional programs. Approaches to assessment may also be innovative, using such techniques as test analysis, where students analyze, correct, and critique their tests, which the instructor has returned to them ungraded but with errors marked (Carter, 1997/1998), or discussion examinations, which allow students to prepare for group interactions that are assessed by the instructor (Dixon, 2000).

Overall, the curriculum of special residential high schools is characterized by its appropriateness to the education of gifted students. These schools offer a program of advanced courses in a curriculum with considerable breadth and depth. Students can pursue a sequence of courses in mathematics and sciences that includes advanced courses rarely available in high schools. Both advanced and nontraditional offerings in other areas may be available, for example, in languages, thematic humanities courses, and independent studies.

In addition, mentorships, internships, and research opportunities are incorporated into the program to allow various degrees of individualization for students. In many of the schools, students are encouraged to pursue original research projects. Residential schools located on university campuses may arrange for students to work on projects with faculty mentors. Schools located near research and medical facilities, high-tech centers, or other industries in the scientific field are able to place students in mentorships and internships where they experience involvement in the actual workings of these organizations. For example, the Oklahoma School of Science and Mathematics offers a wide range of mentorships, with research and

project opportunities in science and technology that usually take one or more semesters and result in a written and oral report (Oklahoma School of Science and Mathematics, 2001).

Extracurricular Program

Beyond the academic day, residential students may be involved in community service activities, recreational programs, faculty-student projects, clubs, and competitions and contests. Residential schools offer many of the same activities students would find in their local schools, including musical and theatrical performance groups; individual and team sports; foreign language, science, and math organizations; and service clubs. The campuses develop diverse extracurricular programs based on the students' interests and talents. Students often have opportunities to attend seminars, lectures, symposia, and other events that take place at the schools themselves and on nearby college campuses.

Following the example set by the North Carolina school, most other institutions have established a requirement that students become involved in campus and community service. Projects include activities such as tutoring, volunteering in hospitals or similar institutions, or assisting local agencies and organizations.

Benefits of Special Residential Schools

A number of groups benefit from special residential schools for gifted students. Most important, of course, are the students themselves who are challenged at their levels by an appropriately rigorous curriculum. These students experience an education designed for them. They are taught by faculty who are experts in their fields and who are committed to providing appropriate education for the gifted. The students are in an environment where they are energized and sparked by other students with similar abilities and interests. They often earn college credit through Advanced Placement or college courses completed while still in high school. Thus they are able to save both time and money as they enter a university ready to begin upper-level courses.

Because there is potential for wider benefits to education in the state, the majority of residential schools have extensive outreach programs. Many schools bring teachers from schools around the state to the residential site as visiting scholars and instructors for a semester or a full academic year. These teachers then return to their home schools with teaching methods and curriculum that may be adopted or adapted for local students.

A growing trend finds residential schools using distance learning to transmit courses to schools throughout the state, where other students may take advantage of the curriculum. The Indiana Academy provides courses such as High School Physics, Russian, Japanese, AP Physics B, AP Chemistry, AP Biology, AP Calculus AB, and Human/Molecular Genetics to schools where there is student interest but no teacher is available or enrollment is too low to offer the class. The Indiana Academy offers French, German, Japanese, and Spanish, by distance learning to elementary schools.

Technology supports another innovative outreach effort by the Indiana Academy for Science, Mathematics and Humanities. Each year the Academy develops a series of "electronic field trips," which are broadcast live from various on-site locations to millions of school children throughout the country and rebroadcast to even wider audiences. These field trips include such diverse topics as the migration of sea turtles, the Dead Sea Scrolls, presidential elections, African voices, and the history of controlled flight (Adams & Cross, 2000).

Still other outreach efforts include workshops and institutes at the residential schools or other sites that bring teachers together to learn about techniques and materials for educating the gifted. The Illinois Mathematics and Science Academy hosts conferences on special topics, for example, a Great Minds series that reached students, teachers, and community members throughout the state. They engaged in dialogues with visiting scholars who are leaders in the sciences, media, technology, and ethics. Other IMSA initiatives include conducting summer and academic year programs for students from underrepresented groups to develop and nurture the talents of potential candidates for admission (Illinois Mathematics and Science Academy, 2001a, 2001b).

Special Issues

The establishment of special residential high schools raises a number of issues that must be resolved before such a school can open. One of the first is a concern of communities that the residential schools will take their top students away from the local high schools in a kind of "brain drain." This fear is unfounded, generally, because residential schools enroll students from throughout the state, and no one community or local area sends a disproportionate number of students.

A second issue, raised by legislators, parents, and local schools, is that of young people leaving home two or three years before they ordinarily would leave to attend college. For residential high schools located at colleges and universities, there are additional concerns related to placing high school-age students on campuses with older students. Existing residential high schools have limited the interactions between high school and college students by housing them separately and segregating the two groups for social and, in most cases, academic activities.

Another often repeated concern is that placing the most talented students together in a school of this type will lead to feelings of superiority among the selected students and a perception that they are entitled to receive special opportunities and benefits with nothing expected in return. Schools address this concern by structuring involvement in outside community and volunteer activities, and by requiring that students share responsibility for maintaining their school. Most schools communicate to the students the expectation that the students will repay in these ways the state's investment in their education.

When considering state-supported residential high schools, questions always are raised about the composition of the student body. Legislators and funding groups ask schools to ensure that the classes will be balanced in terms of geographic, racial, ethnic, gender, and socioeconomic representation. This brings up the question—often unspoken—of quotas. How does a school balance the student body while homogeneously grouping the students in terms of academic and intellectual ability? Most of the schools specify in their written materials that they are committed to achieving a diversified student body and that geographic and other variables are considered by the admissions committee.

Stanley (1987), however, in discussing residential high schools for mathematically talented youth, urged that minimum ability levels be established for selection and that these levels not be modified to accommodate outside pressures. According to Stanley, these minimum levels should be developed by each state and should use as a reference point the average SAT scores achieved by male college-bound seniors in that state. In accord with Stanley's view, the Texas

Academy of Mathematics and Science set a minimum acceptable score of 600 on the mathematics portion of the SAT-I with an overall minimum of 1100 on the combined verbal and mathematics parts of the test (Boothe et al., 1999). The North Carolina School of Science and Mathematics, in contrast, publishes no minimum scores, believing that admissions criteria must be flexible to allow for special situations—for example, a student who has recently immigrated to this country and is not yet fluent enough in English to achieve the minimum scores on the SAT (Eilber, 1987). Efforts to ensure diversity among the classes at the Illinois Mathematics and Science Academy resulted in slightly more than half of the student body in 1999–2000 reporting ethnicity other than Caucasian (Illinois Mathematics and Science Academy, 2001a).

Despite the intention of state residential high schools for gifted students to reflect the demographics of the population, Jarwan and Feldhusen (1993) found that representation of ethnic groups in the composition of these schools does not mirror the representation of these groups in the general population: African American, Hispanic, and Native American groups are underrepresented in these schools and Asian students are overrepresented.

Another consideration affecting the establishment of special residential schools is the provision of a total, rounded experience for the students. This involves support services, such as academic and personal counseling, and a program of extracurricular opportunities including athletics, recreation, arts clubs and performing groups, and social activities. Because students are on campus twenty-four hours a day, seven days a week for most weeks of the year, planning must be comprehensive and must address the needs of the total student. Residential staff must be prepared to assist students as they adjust to living away from home for the first time, encountering an extremely demanding curriculum, and balancing their academic and social interests and commitments in a new community.

Existing residential high schools for the gifted carefully plan their calendars to include long weekends at home, as well as opportunities for students to become involved in outside interests at the school. Staff members are alert to signs of stress, depression, and homesickness, and they are attuned to student behaviors that reveal problems in adjusting to the new environment, such as missing classes, failing to complete assignments, excessive socializing, or withdrawing from interactions with others. Although there may be relatively few instances of these types of difficulties, they are the kinds of issues that set residential schools apart from other high schools and must be addressed in planning for and staffing such a school.

Judging Success of Residential Schools

The impact of special residential schools is assessed in several ways. A number of the residential high schools evaluate aspects of the program that originally were stated as potential benefits. One of these is the percentage of graduates remaining in the state to attend colleges and universities. For example, surveys taken ten years after the establishment of the North Carolina School of Science and Mathematics revealed that 67% of the graduates had enrolled at in-state colleges and universities for their freshman year; by their junior year 73% were registered at in-state colleges and universities (Johnston, 1988); and 82% were studying science or mathematics. The Indiana Academy for Science, Mathematics and Humanities reports that 64% of the year 2000 graduating class chose to remain in Indiana to attend a college or university, thus fulfilling one of the proposed benefits to the state—that of retaining a group of its most talented young people (T. Cross, personal communication, May 15, 2001).

Additional benefits to the state's educational system were evidenced in the number and scope of the outreach programs. Academically talented students from throughout the state attend the North Carolina school in the summer for advanced instruction in math and science. Teachers from the state spend summer months on campus working with the school's faculty to learn techniques that can be used in their home schools.

Graduating classes of residential schools typically have produced large numbers of National Merit Scholar semifinalists and finalists. For example, in the 2000 Illinois Mathematics and Science Academy graduating class, 23% of the students were National Merit semifinalists (Illinois Mathematics and Science Academy, 2001b).

A final indicator of success is that students graduating from residential high schools have attracted millions of dollars in scholarship offers as well as recognition for their outstanding performance in academic competitions. Individual awards and recognition have included student-designed experiments for the NASA space shuttle program and membership on the International Physics Olympiad. Illinois Mathematics and Science Academy students have placed first in the 1993 Westinghouse Science Talent Search, first in the American High School Math Exam, and as individuals and teams have placed in numerous national and international mathematics, computer science, and science competitions. Three North Carolina School of Science and Mathematics students won the top Siemens Westinghouse Science and Technology award in 2000. The Texas Academy for Math and Science (TAMS) reports that between 1993 and 2001, 20 TAMS students were named as finalists in the prestigious Westinghouse/Intel talent searches.

SUMMARY AND CONCLUSIONS

The establishment of state-supported residential high schools for gifted students is a movement whose time has come. The schools offer high-level, intellectually rigorous experiences to students whose educational needs usually cannot be met in their home schools. Most residential high schools emphasize mathematics and science. Most are located on college campuses. Students typically spend their last two years of high school in these schools, and they often earn AP and/or college credit.

Beginning with the North Carolina School of Science and Mathematics and the Louisiana School for Math, Science and the Arts, the movement has gained momentum. At present, 13 states have established academic-year residential high schools for gifted students. The issue is under study by other states.

As perceptions of the success and the return on investment increase, more states are likely to follow the example of those that already have created residential high schools. Particularly meaningful and convincing will be evidence that these schools benefit not only the gifted students who attend, but also other schools within their state. For example, residential high schools develop curriculum and instructional methods that are exported to other state schools, provide courses using distance education, and bring in visiting teachers who learn skills that benefit students in their local schools. Further support will come from evidence that such schools contribute to the long-term economic growth of the states in which they exist. In fact, most students attend college and remain in their home states.

As a final comment, different kinds of services and programs correspond to different types and levels of giftedness. Many schools will continue to address these needs through cluster groups, pullout programs, self-contained classrooms, honors courses, and other options. At the same time, state leaders hopefully will heed the recommendations of experts and the examples of states already with residential high schools, and establish such schools for their most talented and perhaps most underserved population of gifted students.

QUESTIONS FOR THOUGHT AND DISCUSSION

1. What factors might influence students to apply to the residential high school program in their state?

2. In what ways are the needs of students who attend residential schools for gifted different from the needs of their age-peers who attend traditional high schools?

3. What kinds of resistance would likely be raised by state legislators who are considering establishing a school of this type? What responses might prove to be effective in overcoming this resistance?

4. Why do most of these schools focus so completely on mathematics and science? What other areas might need special residential schools?

5. What concerns would parents of students seeking admission to residential high schools be likely to have? If you were their child, how would you answer their concerns?

REFERENCES

Adams, C. M., & Cross, T. L. (2000). Distance learning opportunities for academically gifted students. *Journal of Secondary Gifted Education, 11,* 88–96.

Boothe, D., Sethna, B. N., Stanley, J. C., & Colgate, S. D. (1999). Special opportunities for exceptionally able high school students. *Journal of Secondary Gifted Education, 10,* 195–202.

Carter, C. R. (1997/1998). Assessment: Shifting the responsibility. *Journal of Secondary Gifted Education, 9,* 68–75.

Cox, J., Daniel, N., & Boston, B. (1985). *Educating able learners.* Austin: University of Texas Press.

Dixon, F. A. (1993). *History of the Indiana Academy for Science, Mathematics and the Humanities.* Unpublished manuscript.

Dixon, F. A. (2000). The discussion examination: Making assessment match instructional strategy. *Roeper Review, 23,* 104–108.

Eilber, C. R. (1987). The North Carolina School of Science and Mathematics. *Phi Delta Kappan, 68,* 773–777.

Illinois Mathematics and Science Academy (2001a). 1999–2000 IMSA annual report. Aurora, IL: Illinois Mathematics and Science Academy.

Illinois Mathematics and Science Academy. (2001b). Internal report.

Indiana Academy for Science, Mathematics and Humanities. (n.d.). *2000–2001 Course Catalogue.* (Available from the Indiana Academy for Science, Mathematics and Humanities, Ball State University, Muncie, IN 47306.)

Jarwan, F. A., & Feldhusen, J. F. (1993). *Residential schools of mathematics and science for academically talented youth: An analysis of admission programs.* Storrs, CT: National Research Center for Gifted and Talented.

Johnston, F. (1988, March 14). School of science and math—10 years old and growing. *The Durham Morning Herald.*

Oklahoma School of Science and Mathematics. (2001). Retrieved May 14, 2001, from: *http://www.ossm.edu/ mentor/mentor.htm.*

Purcell, J. H. (1993). The effects of elimination of gifted and talented programs on participating students and their parents. *Gifted Child Quarterly, 37,* 177–187.

Renzulli, J. S., & Reis, S. M. (1991). The reform movement and the quiet crisis in gifted education. *Gifted Child Quarterly, 35,* 26–35.

Robinson, N. M. (1999). Necessity is the mother of invention: The roots of our "system" of providing educational alternatives for gifted students. *Journal of Secondary Gifted Education, 10,* 120–128.

Ross, P. O. (1993). *National excellence: A case for developing America's talent.* Washington, DC: U.S. Department of Education.

Stanley, J. C. (1987). State residential high schools for mathematically talented youth. *Phi Delta Kappan, 68,* 770–772.

Stepien, W. J., & Gallagher, S. A. (1993). Problem-based learning: As authentic as it gets. *Educational Leadership, 50,* 25–28.

Stepien, W. J., Gallagher, S. A., & Workman, D. (1993). Problem-based learning for traditional and interdisciplinary classrooms. *Journal for the Education of the Gifted, 16,* 338–357.

VanTassel-Baska, J. (1998). Key issues and problems in secondary programming. In J. VanTassel-Baska (Ed.), *Excellence in educating gifted and talented learners* (3rd ed.) (pp. 241–259). Denver: Love Publishing.

19

Developing Talent: Time, Task, and Context

LAUREN A. SOSNIAK, *San José State University*

There was a time not too long ago when many people—professional educators and laymen alike—believed that the development of talent was principally a matter of identifying talent as early as possible and then providing support for its development and removing distractions. A person either was born with certain talents or gifts, which with the right support could blossom, or else was not likely ever to realize great accomplishments (Howe, 1990).

Many of us think differently now. Whatever the innate characteristics of an individual that might support exceptional accomplishment, we realize that we are far from being able to identify them. Even if we could identify innate characteristics helpful for exceptional development of one sort or another, they are likely to account for only a very small amount of a person's ultimate accomplishments. Further, we believe that current efforts at early identification are likely to be futile; we appear to be looking for the wrong things, in the wrong ways. Most importantly, we are quite confident that extraordinary levels of accomplishment are possible for individuals who do not necessarily show early promise.

I realized the import of this change of perspective when it became clear to me that Benjamin Bloom, Director of the Development of Talent Research Project (Bloom, 1985), faced findings from his study that he did not expect, findings that were counter to what he would have predicted earlier, and he was able to change his mind about what he believed he knew. At the start of the Development of Talent Research Project, Bloom (1982) expected that the individuals we studied "would be initially identified as possessing special gifts or qualities and then provided with special instruction and encouragement" (p. 520) as a result of these gifts or qualities. But the data from the study made it clear that his initial assumption of early discovery followed by instruction and support was wrong (Bloom, 1982, 1985).

The individuals in the sample for the Development of Talent Research Project typically did *not* show unusual promise at the start. And, typically, there was no early intention of working toward a standard of excellence in a particular field. Instead of early discovery followed by development, we found that the individuals were encouraged and supported in considerable learning—often informal but also formal—before they were identified as special and accorded even more encouragement and support. More time and interest invested in the talent field resulted in further identification of special qualities that, in turn, were again rewarded with more encouragement and support. Aptitudes, attitudes, and expectations grew in concert with one another and were mutually confirming (Sosniak, 1985a). As Bloom once told a reporter, "We were looking for exceptional kids and what we found were exceptional conditions" (Carlson, 1985, p. 49).

This chapter tells the story of findings from the Development of Talent Research Project. The project was a study of groups of individuals who, though relatively young (under the age of 35), had realized exceptional levels of accomplishment in one of six fields: concert piano, sculpture, swimming, tennis, mathematics, and research neurology (two artistic disciplines, two psychomotor activities, and two academic/intellectual fields). The project explored the lives of 120 talented individuals in all, approximately 20 in each field. We conducted face-to-face interviews with the individuals and interviewed parents of almost all. The plan was to search for regularities and recurrent patterns in the educational histories of groups of clearly accomplished individuals, hoping that such consistencies might shed light on how the development of high levels of talent is achieved.

I had the good fortune to serve as the research coordinator for a team of graduate students working under Ben Bloom's direction on the Development of Talent Research Project. I interviewed many of the talented individuals myself. In this chapter I outline the exceptional conditions Bloom referred to, as I understand them now after some years of reflection and further study. The central issues can be summarized under the headings of *time, task,* and *context*. Of course, each is intimately connected with the others, and I speak of them separately only for analytic purposes; I often will refer to one in relation to another.

Time (and Opportunity to Learn)

The Development of Talent Research Project confirmed what many scholars had suspected and some researchers already had demonstrated in smaller contexts like playing chess: developing exceptional abilities takes a lot of time. We found, for example, that internationally recognized concert pianists worked for an average of 17 years from their first formal lessons to their first international recognition; the "quickest" in the group went from novice to virtuoso in a dozen years. For Olympic swimmers, 15 years elapsed, on average, between the time they began swimming just for fun and the time they earned a place on an Olympic team.

The consequences of a long-term perspective for teaching and learning—a truly long-term perspective—are huge. There are implications for educators, parents, and society, and especially for the children and youth with whom we work. The long-term perspective that the Development of Talent Research Project offers is quite different from thinking about teaching and learning for a semester-long or year-long course, or even for, say, high school success. A dozen years or more of involvement and investment in learning something raises important questions about teaching, learning, and nurturing talent, some of which I will turn to later in this chapter.

In the Development of Talent Research Project, we learned a fair amount about the nature of the very long time individuals spent working toward what would eventually be a demonstration of exceptional accomplishment. And we frequently were jolted by

the multiple and overlapping arenas for time spent learning: children and youth not only received instruction in a talent area, they also "played at" the talent area quite informally, they read about and watched or listened to others working at the talent area, and they demonstrated their involvement with the talent area to others. For the individuals who formed the sample for the Development of Talent Research Project, the development of talent was a process of learning that grew from and threaded around their everyday lives. It was both formal and informal, structured and casual, self-conscious and matter-of-fact, special and ordinary, and all at the same time. Time spent learning had a vertical dimension as well as a horizontal one, and an affective dimension as well as a cognitive one.

We came to understand that the long-term process of developing talent was not simply a matter of becoming quantitatively more knowledgeable and skilled over time, or of working more intensely for longer hours. It was predominantly a matter of qualitative and evolutionary transformations. The individuals were transformed; the substance of what was being learned was transformed; and the manner in which individuals engaged with teachers and field-specific content was transformed. Students progressively adopted different views of who they were, of what their fields of expertise were about, and of how the field fitted into their lives (Sosniak, 1987). These transformations followed a pattern reminiscent of Whitehead's (1929) "rhythms of learning"—phases of romance, precision, and generalization—over the course of their long years of work in their respective fields.

Task

Following from this, we came to realize that time spent learning needs to be understood in the context of the tasks individuals engage in. Perhaps most obviously, the tasks for the development of talent do need to be *subject specific*. Considerable exposure to domain-specific content is an essential early component of the development of human competence. Rich exposure to domain-specific knowledge is said to have important consequences for the development of automaticity, which in turn is believed to help explain the impressive coding and chunking abilities of experts (Glaser & Chi, 1988).

Perhaps less obviously, it appears that tasks for the development of talent need to be appropriate to the amount of *experience* a student has had with a field of study. In other words, tasks need to take into account the long-term nature of the experience of developing talent. They may need to be particularly engaging at the start, encouraging and supporting any and all involvement with a field. They may need to emphasize precision only after an individual has been hooked on the idea of study and has come to realize the value of precision. They may need to allow for individual expression and style only in relation to a strong knowledge base for making decisions about appropriate deviations from standard practices. We know that the individuals we studied moved through a sequence of decidedly different central tasks at different points in the long process of developing expertise (Sosniak, 1985b).

Another core idea about tasks is the importance of the link between the tasks youth are encouraged to engage in and the tasks that represent the field itself in its contemporary social construction. The word *authentic* is used too often these days, but it does seem to capture the nature of the tasks that were revealed in the Development of Talent Research Project study. The tasks were genuine; they were real in an everyday, common sense way. Children and youth did things they knew other people of various ages from various settings also were doing.

Children and youth used materials that are part of our social technologies—they played pianos that adults used also, swam in Olympic-sized pools, and read field-specific books and magazines that were created for the consuming public. Both the tasks the youth engaged in and the materials they used to pursue their tasks were connected to tasks valued by significant portions of society. And youth knew these tasks and materials were valued because they saw them being displayed—by others in their family, in their community, and in ever larger arenas.

In other words, less flattering words, the work that children and youth did in the pursuit of the development of talent was not merely "schoolwork." Schoolwork too often involves tasks that hold little value for the public at large, and does not support conversation outside of school classrooms. School tasks too often are tasks that people outside of school would not, themselves, engage in voluntarily and would not willingly observe as spectators. In the process of the development of talent, in contrast with much of schoolwork, the tasks that children and

youth engaged in linked their lives and conversations with the lives and conversations of many other people of varied age groups, from many communities, and even across historical time.

One of the most important challenges we face in the years to come is to identify tasks that support and sustain a learner through the many years of learning necessary to realize exceptional accomplishment. These tasks need to be appropriate both to a learner's experience and to the social construction of the talent fields. These tasks need to be responsive to a full range of curriculum considerations—including attention to the development of knowledge, skills, and dispositions. And these tasks need to balance challenge with reward, encouraging students to care about what they "don't know" and "can't do" yet, but that will hold them in good stead over the long-term process of developing talent.

Social Context

Just as talent fields are themselves social constructions, the development of talent appears to require enormously supportive social contexts. One of the lessons from the Development of Talent Research Project is that no one develops talent on his or her own—without the support, encouragement, advice, insight, guidance, and good will of many others. The development of talent is a tribute of many people working for the accomplishments of one.

For the individuals in the sample of the Development of Talent Research Project, their many years of work on the way to international recognition involved increasing exposure to and participation in *communities of practice* for their respective talent fields. Communities of practice are, at their root, groups of people who share a substantive focus that is important to their lives, and who share a willingness to invest time and effort around work in that substantive area. Communities of practice may be formal or informal, vocational or avocational (or some of each, for different participants). Communities of practice may inhabit a physical place, or they may be "virtual," connecting people through writing, radio, television, or the Internet for example.

Perhaps the best way to communicate my understanding of communities of practice is to provide some examples. For the individuals in the sample of the Development of Talent Research Project, in most instances families were the first communities of practice that the youth encountered. Individuals who would, many years later, demonstrate exceptional accomplishment as concert pianists typically grew up in homes where music was valued, and this value was expressed on a daily basis. Individuals who would, many years later, demonstrate exceptional accomplishment as Olympic athletes typically grew up in homes where sports were valued, and this value was expressed on a daily basis. The more we knew about the everyday life of the children who would grow up to be concert pianists, Olympic swimmers, or research mathematicians, the more obvious it became that pianists were not likely to come from swimmers' homes, swimmers were not likely to come from the pianists' homes, and so on.

For the most part, the parents of the individuals in the study were not professionally involved in the areas in which their children would later excel; however, they did, typically, hold an avocational interest in that field or in a closely related activity. Parents may have worked as accountants, or salesmen, or lawyers, or fruit vendors, but they loved music, or sports, or the world of science. As a consequence, young children were exposed regularly to activities connected with their subsequent talent fields; they were supported and rewarded for behaviors related to the fields; and they learned in informal ways about knowledge and skills of the activity in which they would eventually excel. The talent area provided activities and amusement for children and their parents—and an interest for them to share.

In other words, the communities of practice in these homes had a substantive focus and offered support, encouragement, and reward for work with that substantive area. Children could choose to join in with these adult interests, or not join in, or join in at different levels of involvement. But if a child's interest was significantly different from that of the adults in the home, he or she was not likely to find all of the formal and informal avenues for learning about an alternative substantive area. Further, if a child's interest was significantly different from that of the adults in the home, he or she was not likely to secure as many and as varied rewards for work with the alternative substantive focus.

Many more communities of practice exist outside the home. In the Development of Talent Research Project, we found, for example, that pianists who began lessons with a local music teacher typically became members of a group of students involved in small recitals once or twice a year. Swimmers who

took lessons at the local "Y" or the community pool join that group of swimmers in local swim clubs. Young scientists had backyard or basement pals with whom they studied the ecology of their area or conducted experiments with chemicals found in youth science sets.

The talent areas themselves create communities of practice. The individuals interviewed in our study reported that as youth they had the opportunity to move from formal and informal lessons into music adjudications and other age-group competitions. They took part in music groups, art shows, math or science clubs, and so forth. They were introduced to collections of books, magazines, and recordings related to their talent area. They took part in after school programs and summer programs and camps associated with their talent field. There were public events for youth learning the field to demonstrate their growing expertise. (For example, they played piano at school performances or exhibited their work at community art shows and school science fairs.) There also were public events that youth attended as observers—watching more advanced students or even the most advanced practitioners of the field.

The communities of practice create their own activities, their own ways of reporting on their work, and their own events to identify and honor the best among themselves. The multiple, overlapping communities of practice that the individuals were introduced to seem to have exerted a pull on the youth, shaping interests and educational needs, and initiating the youth into the existing social groups that each of the talent fields represents.

The picture I have been describing has, I hope, communicated visions of groups of people with a shared substantive focus that was important to their lives, and a shared willingness to invest time and effort around work in that substantive area. These communities of practice offered *models* for development, and they offered *resources* for support, inspiration, and sustenance. Communities of practice created *standards* for work—for work by the novice, the knowledgeable layman, and for the expert. At their best, communities of practice modelled and inspired excellence; they defined and gave meaning to significant educative tasks; and they supported and sustained work over the long periods necessary for the development of talent. The youth and young adults in the Development of Talent Research Project were fortunate to be welcomed into, or to find their way into, communities that shaped and inspired their work.

They had many varied opportunities to see themselves as members of field-specific communities, to come to know the commitments, and to watch and live out for themselves the process of a community renewing itself.

Unanswered Questions

As much as the data from the Development of Talent Research Project have to offer us as educators, they also leave unanswered questions. In this section I will raise briefly two issues around which I find myself troubled or perplexed.

One of the questions that has become especially important to me in recent years has to do with why the individuals in the sample for the Development of Talent Research project typically did *not* show unusual promise at the start. Why did we hear so frequently from our interviewees and their parents about other children and youth in their communities who, early on, were so much better than the individuals who eventually demonstrated the exceptional adult achievement that included them in our study? What happened to those sprinters in the course of the marathon that the development of talent turned out to be? I have no firm answers for these questions, but I think they are important for our community of educators to pursue.

My own inclinations, of course, are that answers to these questions will hinge around the issues of *time, task,* and *context.* I suspect that some students who are identified early as having unusual potential find themselves valuing the peculiarities of being first, fastest, and smartest, at the cost of being able to stay with tasks that are difficult, that take a long time to master, or that do not offer significant immediate rewards. For example, we learned from the tennis players in our study that young male tennis players can excel in age-group competition by playing the strongest baseline game. But unless these young boys are willing to lose many matches in order to learn to play a serve-and-volley game, even when they do not yet have the height and arm-span to support such a strategy, they are unlikely to realize exceptional adult accomplishment.

I suspect also that social support for being early or advanced at something is quite different from social support for long-term involvement and for making multiple connections. In other words, being

applauded and rewarded for being first may be very different from being applauded and rewarded for involvement with a field of study and for involvement with other people who share the same field-specific interests.

These are, of course, only my hypotheses. I am prepared, as Benjamin Bloom was, to be convinced by research in the years to come that my inclinations are wrong. I am prepared to accept compelling alternative explanations for how best to understand and support the development of exceptional accomplishment in a wide variety of fields over the long-term. Importantly, though, the question still remains: Why did we hear so frequently from our interviewees and their parents about other children and youth in their communities who, early on, were so much better than the individuals who eventually demonstrated the exceptional adult achievement that included them in our study?

The final issue I would like to raise, which troubles me most, is the matter of chance and choice. The picture I have tried to convey about time, task, and context for the development of talent is, in many ways, a hopeful one. It suggests that with persistence at substantively meaningful and experientially appropriate tasks, significant accomplishment is possible. It suggests that individuals and communities can provide support to encourage persistence, even (or especially) in the face of difficult tasks that are not easily learned and demonstrated. It suggests that increasing levels of accomplishment are possible for ever larger numbers of youth, if we work to rethink teaching and learning over long periods of time and across multiple contexts.

Still, the picture from the Development of Talent Research Project has its discouraging aspects also. For the youth in the Development of Talent Research Project, the opportunities to get involved with a talent area, and to find meaningful communities of practice for development over time, were largely a matter of *chance.* These opportunities had to do with fortunate circumstances of birth and fortunate matches between a child and his or her proximal communities. While all of us certainly are grateful for such fortunate outcomes of chance, I doubt any of us rests comfortably with the idea that the development of talent is *inevitably* a result only of such fortuitous circumstances.

What would we have to do as educators, and as members of our own substantive communities of practice, to create conditions that allow ever larger portions of our youth to work toward the development of talent, irrespective of where and to whom they are born? How can we help children and youth find the fit between their own interests and inclinations and the possibilities that are available to them in our broader society? In other words, how can we work to ensure that the development of talent is more a matter of choice than chance?

My own hypotheses are that we need to think about curriculum possibilities for both school and out-of-school settings. We need to think about how to take better advantage of the many years children and youth are required to attend school, to examine how we might make field-specific possibilities and communities of practice embedded in school work. Importantly, we need to recognize that school is just a small part of the lives of children and youth and that talent development apparently grows from and around everyday life. The access we offer to multiple field-specific communities of practice outside of school is as critical as anything we might do in school. The questions, however, about how to provide access and long-term support and encouragement are numerous.

The fact that we know the development of talent is possible for larger numbers of youth than we had imagined in the past opens educational possibilities previously unexplored. Our challenge in the future years is to learn to nurture talent over the long term. We need to learn more about the tasks and the social contexts that support the development of talent. And in the process I hope we learn to make the development of talent much more a matter of choice rather than chance.

SUMMARY AND CONCLUSIONS

This chapter outlines findings from the Development of Talent Research Project (Bloom, 1985), especially the issues of time, task, and context.

It addresses issues of both long-term involvement with a field of study and comprehensive involvement across multiple dimensions of everyday life. I speak about the process of developing talent as not simply a matter of becoming quantitatively more knowledgeable and skilled over time, or of working more intensely for longer hours, but especially as a matter of qualitative and evolutionary transformations of indi-

viduals, the substance of what is being learned, and the manner in which individuals engage with teachers and field-specific content. I address the substantive and "authentic" aspects of tasks for the development of talent, as well as the issue of shaping tasks with regard for the learner's experience with the subject matter. And I discuss social contexts supporting long-term engagement and offering models, resources, and standards that reveal to youth the nature and desirability of the development of talent.

In the end I raise questions about the youth we know already that we are losing in our efforts to develop talent. In particular, I note the challenge of making the development of talent a matter of choice rather than one of chance.

QUESTIONS FOR THOUGHT AND DISCUSSION

1. Is the development of talent more like a marathon than a sprint? Explain.

2. Based on Sosniak's chapter, what changes might we suggest in gifted education that would better support the long-term process of talent development?

3. Regarding academic talent:
  a. Are there some academic areas where an early start is important—perhaps essential—for the development of exceptional accomplishment? Explain.
  b. Do some academic areas have multiple entry points that allow for later starts without sacrificing access to the top levels of accomplishment? Explain.

4. Consider the "choice versus chance" issue. How might we help the development of talent move beyond fortunate circumstances of birth or the fortunate chance fit between a child and his or her proximal community?

5. Current trends in gifted education focus on acceleration and enrichment, including compacting. Given this chapter's argument for authentic tasks with supportive communities of practice, how might a gifted and talented program respond to these challenges?

REFERENCES

Bloom, B. S. (1982). The role of gifts and markers in the development of talent. *Exceptional Children, 48,* 510–521.

Bloom, B. S. (Ed.). (1985). *Developing talent in young people.* New York: Ballantine.

Carlson, B. (1985, Fall). Exceptional conditions, not exceptional talent, produce high achievers. *University of Chicago Magazine, 78*(1), 18–19, 49.

Glaser, R., & Chi, M. T. H. (1988). Overview. In M. T. H. Chi, R. Glaser, & M. J. Farr (Eds.), *The nature of expertise.* Hillsdale, NJ: Erlbaum.

Howe, M. J. A. (Ed.). (1990). *Encouraging the development of exceptional skills and talents.* Leicester, UK: British Psychological Society.

Sosniak, L. A. (1985a). A long-term commitment to learning. In B. S. Bloom (Ed.), *Developing talent in young people* (pp. 477–506). New York: Ballantine.

Sosniak, L. A. (1985b). Phases of learning. In B. S. Bloom (Ed.), *Developing talent in young people* (pp. 409–438). New York: Ballantine.

Sosniak, L. A. (1987). The nature of change in successful learning. *Teachers College Record, 88,* 519–535.

Whitehead, A. N. (1929). *The aims of education.* New York: Macmillan.

20

Mentoring the Gifted and Talented

DONNA RAE CLASEN, *University of Wisconsin—Whitewater*
ROBERT E. CLASEN, *University of Wisconsin—Madison*

The mentor has another function, and this is developmentally the most crucial one: To support and facilitate the realization of the Dream.

—Levinson et al. (1978)

Mentoring is a timeless and universal means of nurturing potential and advancing the Dream. It comes to us across centuries and from almost all cultures in which examples exist of a master taking on the role of mentor to a promising novice. Since ancient times, great leaders have counseled and instructed young protégés who show promise of maintaining the leader's legacy; master artisans have worked with talented novices to develop their skills; philosophers and spiritual leaders have attended to like-minded young intellectuals. In all these mentoring relationships, the master transfers the knowledge, expertise, and experiences of a science, art, skill, or philosophy to a protégé who may eventually establish new frontiers in the field, break existing records, and create new traditions.

While mentoring increasingly is recognized as a valuable process for guiding youth with varied academic, behavioral, and social needs (see, e.g., Sipe & Roder, 1999), it is also a time-honored means of educating and encouraging the gifted and talented. For extremely high-ability young people whose recognized skills and ability levels extend far beyond the scope of usual school resources, a mentorship can be the most successful means of meeting their specific needs (Reilly, 1992). The matching of a promising novice with an established expert provides the novice with challenge and continued encouragement in the development of his or her talent. Mentorships can

also be effective in developing talent where the gift may be less readily recognized, for example, with economically disadvantaged youth (Torrance, Goff, & Satterfield, 1998), underachieving gifted (Hébert & Olenchak, 2000), and students with learning disabilities (Yoshimoto, 2000).

A mentorship can be a productive and meaningful experience for both mentor and mentee, offering the potential of a successful, long-term relationship. Mentorships, however, have their pitfalls and particular challenges. Without a strong infrastructure, allowances for systematic feedback, and a good match between mentor and mentee, the mentorship may flounder, disappointing all concerned. While mentorships vary greatly in description and implementation, the probability of their success is likely to be increased when several aspects of mentoring are taken into consideration.

What Is Mentoring?

Tradition holds that the term *mentor* comes from Classical Greek, where Homer tells us that Mentor (believed to be Athena in disguise) became teacher and counselor to Odysseus' son Telemachus during the father's Odyssey and long absence from his family. Mentor guided the boy Telemachus in becoming a man.

While definitions and practices of mentorships vary substantially in the current gifted and talented field, characteristics of the classical mentoring model are informative. The classical mentorship was a one-on-one relationship; a wise, experienced person guided a neophyte; a long-term commitment was made by both individuals; and both found satisfaction in the mentorship. However, Powell (1999) noted one flaw in the original Greek model. The goddess-endowed power of Athena gave her the ability to control and shape her protégé's expectations, placing in jeopardy one of the most desirable features of a good mentorship, the opportunity for the mentee to have full participation in determining the development of his or her unique talents and in controlling the personal dream.

In current gifted and talented mentorships, vestiges of the traditional mentorship remain, with varying degrees of differences. Most mentorships involving the gifted and talented are one-on-one, the relationship most supportive for providing specialized, individual attention to a protégé's development. However, more than one mentor can enhance a mentorship if mentor roles are noncompetitive. Arnold and Subotnik (1995) suggested that high-ability youth might profit from multiple mentors, including peer mentors who can offer "emotional support, competition, and comparison" (p. 120) at all stages of an individual's development. Clasen and Hanson (1987) proposed double mentoring as a means of assuring that both talent development and psychosocial needs are addressed in a mentorship. One mentor is a specialist who focuses on talent development while the second mentor attends to affective and social developmental needs of the mentee, particularly as they are impacted by the first mentorship.

Duration of the relationship also varies. Although a minimum of a year is expected for a traditional mentorship (Guetzloe, 1997; Zorman, 1993), the time span depends upon the purpose of the mentorship and the age and maturity of the mentee. Mentorships for elementary students frequently range in time from several weeks to a semester (Reisner, Petry, & Armitage, 1990). High school students are often engaged for at least a year, particularly in mentorships with a strong academic focus (Lupkowski, Assouline, & Stanley, 1990). However, mentorships for secondary school students that range from 10 to 20 weeks are also reported (Beck, 1989; Marlow & Marlow, 1996). Regardless of the time involvement, commitment to the undertaking by both mentor and mentee is required for a successful experience.

The classical expectation was that the mentor would help a neophyte grow and develop affectively and psychosocially as well as in intellectual and talent areas. While this expectation may be less realistic in some current, short-term mentorships, the concept is still embraced. Casey and Shore (2000) reported that "the mentoring literature highlights the importance in educational success of a link between the basically academic process of imparting knowledge and skills, and the need to provide guidance toward the life to follow" (p. 229). Cox and Daniel (1983) regarded the goal of mentoring as the shaping of the mentee's life outlook. Freedman's (1993) view was similar; he noted that many mentors delve "deeply into the requirements of growing up" (p. 71). The value of a mentor's attention to affective and social development also is recognized by mentees. For example, Presidential Scholars reported that they found role modeling, support, and encouragement the most valuable contributions of their mentors (Kaufmann, Harrel, Milam, Woolverton, & Miller, 1986).

While modeling and emotional support are often regarded as essential in initial stages of the mentorship, career socialization is crucial for older students as the mentorship evolves. As the mentee becomes more skilled and self-determining, the mentor helps the mentee become increasingly more professional. In this case, the mentor introduces the mentee to the professional "playbook" or tacit understandings regarding career and professional management in a specific domain (Arnold & Subotnik, 1995).

Need for Mentorships

Unless a young person has access to a well-ordered domain and to a responsive and accessible field, potentials will probably never reach full flower.
    Csikszentmihalyi, Rathunde, & Whalen (1993)

Giftedness alone does not assure realization of the gift nor the Dream. At some time, intervention by an adult or a series of adults is essential to the development of the gift. Mentorships are especially recommended for extremely precocious students (Lupkowski et al., 1990; Stanley, 1979), for gifted students who have exhausted the resources of the school (Reilly, 1992), and for children of disadvantaged circumstances whose potential may never be realized without special opportunities (Arnold & Subotnik, 1995; Goff & Torrance, 1999).

One recommendation from the report *National Excellence: A Case for Developing America's Talent*

(O'Connell Ross, 1993), clearly called for mentoring or mentoring-like activities to open doors of opportunities for high-ability youth: Recommendations are for the establishment of high-level learning opportunities that are as "diverse as the talents of the children" and that permit more in-depth work, appropriate pacing, and work in community settings. The report urged strong school-community links and the use of the valuable resources within the community. Mentorships respond to these recommendations.

Characteristics and Roles of a Mentor

Much of the success of a mentorship will be determined by the mentor. Not everyone who is an expert can be a mentor; expertise and skill in a field are necessary but not sufficient. The mentor must be willing—even eager—to share expertise with a novice whose energy and questions may be taxing and with whom patience and understanding will likely be required. Sensitivity to the mentee's developmental needs in areas such as socialization and peer affiliations is essential. Strong personal integrity is crucial. Other desirable qualities include good communication and problem-solving skills, creativity, flexibility—and a sense of humor.

Good mentors are akin to the "flow" teachers described by Csikszentmihalyi, Rathunde, and Whalen (1993) in their study of talented teenagers. Flow teachers are those who provide students with optimal learning experiences in which the student becomes entirely engrossed in something that is enjoyable, challenging, and intrinsically rewarding. Flow teachers had three dimensions that especially encouraged the development of talent: (1) They systematically nurtured their own interests and skills professionally, that is, performers performed, artists created. (2) They focused on intrinsic rewards, seeking a balance between critique and encouragement and providing feedback most likely to increase the joy of developing the talent. (3) They read the shifting needs of students and sought a harmony between their expectations and other competing demands on students (pp. 190–195).

During a mentorship, the mentor will assume several interlocking roles:

1. Teacher: As teacher, the mentor helps the mentee push the boundaries of knowledge and skills. The mentor provides systematic feedback on work and helps the novice analyze and evaluate progress and products.

2. Expert: The mentor has the ability and experience to create unique learning opportunities, to share traditional accumulated wisdom, and to introduce the novice to an expert's view of a domain.

3. Guide: The mentor knows the path to success and the obstacles to reaching goals and shows the way, while allowing for individual exploration.

4. Advisor: The mentor advises the mentee regarding expectations and possibilities, introduces the mores and standards of the field, and helps in problem solving and decision making. As advisor, the mentor confronts the novice if behavior is inappropriate.

5. Friend: The mentor is a source of emotional support, someone the mentee can trust and with whom feelings can be shared.

6. Role model: As a role model, the mentor becomes an exemplar of certain values, attitudes, and behavioral patterns that the mentee will often strive to emulate.

The mentor has the opportunity to promote a young person's vision and to encourage the confronting of the unknown. Some argue that the mentor's most important role is to support the young person's dream and to facilitate its realization (Levinson, Darrow, Klein, Levinson, & McKee, 1978). While many short-term mentorships in gifted education may not be expected to have such impact on an individual's life, the influence of a mentor should never be underestimated. Even a short-term partnership can impact upon self-esteem, feelings of competence, and sense of worth (Reisner et al., 1990).

Characteristics and Roles of the Mentee

While mentor characteristics must be given careful consideration in establishing a mentorship, it is equally important to attend to characteristics of the mentee. All gifted and talented students are not ready or able to enter into a mentorship. Readiness should be carefully assessed before the mentorship begins. Readiness involves possessing exceptional ability and potential to excel in a domain, abiding interest and enthusiasm for an area of study, perseverance, and willingness to commit time and energy to study and exploration. Commitment, in particular, is a prominent factor in evaluating readiness (Atkinson, Hansen, & Passman, 1992; Clasen & Hanson, 1987).

Age is also an issue. Boston (1979) maintained that most elementary students lack the developmental maturity for a one-to-one relationship with an adult and for the required autonomous study. However, Lengel (1989) argued that early attention is essential for underachieving high-ability students and described a successful mentorship program involving underachieving students in grades 3 through 6 who worked with teacher mentors throughout the school year. Other successful programs involving students as early as fourth and fifth grade have been reported by Ellingson, Haeger, and Feldhusen (1986), Hébert and Speirs Neumeister (2000/2001), and Reisner et al. (1990). Stanley (1979) and Lupkowski et al. (1990) found that successful mentorships could be developed for precocious math students as young as six and ten years old.

Reilly (1992) asserted that a protégé is not ready for a mentorship until all available school opportunities have been exhausted. While admitting that determining readiness for a mentor "is a judgment call at best," Reilly outlined an 11-step process for reaching the decision to arrange for a professional mentor. Several of these steps focus on accessing school resources. Reilly cautioned that a student's desire to study "on my own" may be interpreted incorrectly as indicating a need for a mentor when in fact, there may be another valid interpretation, such as a desire to explore a subject in more depth and breadth. Another translation not mentioned by Reilly is that the student is saying, "I'm bored." In this case as well, it would be appropriate to try other approaches before suggesting a mentorship.

In all cases, the mentee must be mature enough to fulfill age-appropriate responsibilities. Commitment to appointments, schedules, and timelines is essential. A strong drive to explore the chosen domain will help the mentee sustain the mentorship despite likely conflicts of interests. The mentee should be able to keep the lines of communication open with mentor, teachers, and parents or guardians, and inform them if demands of the mentorship become overwhelming or if unexpected obstacles to success emerge.

Profiles of Mentorships

There is great diversity in mentorship profiles. What is considered a mentorship in one school district might not be identified as such in another. Broadened definitions of mentoring have resulted in tutoring, after-school projects, community service activities, and "shadowing." In fact, Healy and Welchert (1990) argued that "short-term, cost-effective arrangements of limited significance . . . have, in the minds of some, sullied and usurped the title *mentoring*" (p. 18). Struchen and Porta (1997) added that short-term, "drive-by mentoring" also might pose risks for students. In partnerships where a "mentor" appears for a short time and then disappears, a student may feel rejected or confused by the experience, especially if the mentorship term had created unrealistic student expectations, such as a new friendship or in-depth attention to the student's interests and abilities. An additional effect might be the young person's unwillingness to later enter into a more traditional mentorship.

Short-term partnerships might have the potential of becoming a true mentorship but do not qualify as such without certain critical components, basic among them being a one-on-one relationship with an expert in the field serving as guide, advisor, and teacher along with sufficient time for a productive mentor-mentee relationship to develop. Following a review of the mentoring literature, Zorman (1993) concluded that five characteristics distinguish mentoring from other relationships: (1) mutual passion for a specific area of interest; (2) a match of teaching and learning styles; (3) lifelong trust; (4) mutual perceptions of symmetry, that is, a movement toward equality in the relationship as the protégé advances in knowledge and skill; and (5) a sharing of lifestyle as the novice gradually adopts patterns of the engineer, teacher, artist, or other professional.

One characteristic, lifelong trust, may be problematic. While trust is necessary for building a mentorship, lifelong trust cannot be assured. Levinson et al. (1978), for example, reported that a rupture in the relationship was not unusual later in life when the mentee's need for complete autonomy reaches its zenith. Also, many mentors will be surpassed in fame and fortune by the protégé and must be comfortable with this possibility if trust is to be maintained.

Although mentorships are frequently recommended as a component of gifted programming, mentorships involving gifted students are not that common. Of the 913 articles on mentoring annotated by Noller and Frey (1994), only 68 were categorized for gifted students and these included descriptions of mentorships for gifted students in other countries. Other reviews of the literature on mentoring the gifted and talented indicate that most mentorships involve junior and senior high school students (Christie, 1995; Davalos & Haensly, 1997; Goh & Goh, 1996; Lupkowski et al., 1990). The foci of most mentorships for older students was on career exploration or development of talent in a specific discipline but also included leadership, critical thinking, underachievement, research, and creative writing.

Mentoring programs for elementary students appear to be increasing (Hébert & Speirs Neumeister, 2000/2001; Lupkowski, Assouline, & Vestal, 1992). Mentorships for younger children center on talent development, academic achievement, exploration of interests, self-perception, and interpersonal relations. Tan-Willman's (1992) Canadian program for elementary students focused on highly creative students. The Gifted Handicapped Mentor Program in New York was built around specific abilities of gifted students who had special learning or physical challenges (Levey & Dolan, 1988).

Across programs, mentors come from a variety of fields. They include teachers, university faculty and students, professionals, business people, and retirees—individuals desirous of sharing skill or knowledge with a young novice. Many mentorships rely on community volunteers (Atkinson et al., 1992; Davalos & Haensly, 1997; Milam & Schwartz, 1992). Mentorships also recruit mentors from within the school district to work with a student outside their usual grade-level (Lengel, 1989) or draw upon both school and community volunteers (White-Hood, 1993). University students have served as mentors to younger students in a number of successful programs (Duln, Lammers, Mason, & Graves, 1994; Hébert & Speirs Neumeister, 2000/2001; Prillaman & Richardson, 1989), with university students usually receiving college credit for their involvement.

In several instances, cross-age peer mentorships prove successful. Wright and Borland (1992) reported positive results when gifted urban middle school students served as mentors for young, disadvantaged kindergarten children. In another instance, a brilliant ten-year-old math student served as a mentor for a precocious six-year-old math prodigy (Stanley, 1979). High school seniors served as mentors in a unique program pairing physics seniors and second graders in an engineering project to produce aerodynamic rocket models (Roper-Davis, 1999). In addition to providing students with hands-on experiences, the seniors developed storybooks explaining Newton's laws at a second-grade level. The mentorship accommodated the needs of gifted learners while introducing the second graders to physics.

Wright and Borland (1992) noted that adolescent mentors could make valuable contributions, but emphasized that "clearly structured and explicit expectations for their behavior must be established early on" (p. 129) and that their developmental needs for socialization and recreational activities should be taken into account.

The majority of mentorships are collaborations between school and university or school and community. Many university faculty become mentors to precocious young people, nurturing their "rage to know" and their ability to excel. University-school partnerships also link university students as mentors with gifted students in a school or school district (Duln et al., 1994; Hébert & Speirs Neumeister, 2000/2001). University mentors received training, often as part of a class, and the partnership extended at least one semester. In one collaboration the university played a unique role. In Project Synergy, the partnership between Teachers College, Columbia University, and Public School 149/207 in Harlem, New York City, university staff trained gifted middle school students to be mentors to potentially gifted kindergarten students who were economically disadvantaged (Wright & Borland, 1992).

Mentorships developed from community-school collaborations are often innovative and broad-based, providing a wide range of experiences (Christie, 1995; Duff, 2000). One example is a year-long, high school Independent Study Mentorship (ISM) class in a large southwestern school district (Davalos & Haensly, 1997). As part of the district's gifted program, juniors and seniors in the two-hour ISM block class were linked with community mentors in sites such as medical centers, architectural firms, or art studios. Students and mentors sometimes met during the class period as well as after school and on weekends. Student work centered on research following the professional guidelines of their domain and included a final product and oral and written reports. Student surveys indicated that mentees perceived benefits from the mentorship in academic, personal, and career areas.

In some instances volunteers stepped forward to create mentorships in response to community needs. One such example was the Mentors in the 'Hood program in New Orleans where musical artists created mentorships for talented young musicians, training them musically and modeling appropriate behavior and attitudes (Berry, 1996). In Pittsburgh in 1986, Bill Strickland founded the Manchester Craftsmen's Guild in his inner-city neighborhood (Guetzloe, 1997). His goal was to provide mentoring and to offer art and photography opportunities as means of developing a college-orientation in participants. The program's success resulted in funding from the corporate sector and a "genius award" for Strickland from the MacArthur Foundation. Participants, numbering 300 each week, attend free of charge and work with acclaimed artists who are trained as mentors.

Community-based organizations can also step forward. The Wisconsin Center for Academically Talented Youth (WCATY) in Madison supports summer mentorships for selected middle school students who have participated in the Midwest Talent Search or Midwest Talent Search for Young Students. Applicants are chosen on the basis of a project proposal, which must include a mentor statement of intent and a reference from a school staff member. Projects or final reports are required at the end of the summer. Mentorships have ranged from Norwegian wood carving to genetics to chamber music (Schatz, 1999/2000).

Descriptions of mentoring collaborations suggest several advantages. Organization and implementation of the program usually were shared; limited resources were used effectively; and the likelihood of more mentors and mentees being involved increased. One serious limitation was the lack of consistent funding from school districts for mentorship support.

Mentorships for Disadvantaged Students and Students with Disabilities

Increasingly, mentorships have been recommended as a means of helping students who may face extraordinary obstacles in realizing their potential (Goff & Torrance, 1999; Hamilton & Hamilton, 1992; Olszewski-Kubilius & Scott, 1992; Struchen & Porta, 1997). For many students the support, encouragement, and opportunity necessary for talent development are missing or minimal in their lives.

Mentorships can help provide these critical elements. They also can impact upon negative attitudes that can limit a student's orientation toward education, achievement, and success. More importantly, the mentorship may enhance the young person's sense of self-worth and an appreciation of the potential to be tapped.

Reisner et al. (1990) described several programs for disadvantaged youth in which college students served as mentors. The City University of New York (CUNY) Student Mentor Program was one of the more extensive, and serves as a good example. CUNY'S program involved 226 college mentors matched with an equal number of high school students from disadvantaged backgrounds. Partners met once a week for two hours over a semester's time. The curriculum base was career-oriented, but also stressed personal goal development and decision-making skills. Program evaluations indicated the mentorships were especially helpful in empowering students to establish educational and career goals.

Mentoring also has been recommended for gifted students with a learning or behavioral disability. Yoshimoto (2000) reviewed a mentorship for dyslexic students, which involved community and school mentors for high school students and selected intermediate students with dyslexia. Coordinated with a program based on Renzulli's (1977) Enrichment Triad Model, the mentorship was designed to help students identify their talents and interests and to apply academic skills in developing projects in real world settings. In another program, gifted adolescents who had achieved in school while coping with the challenge of Emotional Behavior Disorders (EBD) were matched with elementary students with EBD (Burrell, Wood, Pikes, & Holliday, 2001). The mentorships proved successful in helping the younger students adjust in school and in improving their self-perception.

While research on the effectiveness of mentoring disadvantaged youth is limited, findings from several studies support their value. A 22-year longitudinal study of creative achievement in adults indicated that a mentor was a critical component for facilitating achievement in the economically disadvantaged (Torrance, Goff, & Satterfield, 1998). Reisner et al. (1990) reported that their survey of evaluations of mentorships presented evidence of improvement in three areas: (1) academic performance, (2) motivation and attitude toward school, and (3) self-esteem and confidence. In their review of research on mentoring, Flaxman, Ascher, and Harrington (1988) concluded that carefully planned, intensive mentoring could "solve some of the contradictions" disadvantaged youth experience in realizing their potential.

Mentorships for Females

Several reviews of mentorships stress the importance of mentors for girls and women (Collins, 1983; Grau, 1985; Kaufmann et al., 1986). Women who are leaders in their field provide much needed role modeling for young women as well as insight and advice regarding career experiences and expectations. Despite the obvious benefits of same-sex mentoring, many gifted and talented girls are paired with male mentors, due in part to the lack of available female mentors (Beck, 1989).

While research is needed to explore possible differences between the effectiveness of gifted students in same-gender and cross-gender mentorships, several studies confirm the general importance of mentors for girls and women. Kaufmann et al. (1986) found that having a mentor resulted in equality of earning power between career men and women. Beck (1989) reported that young women in high school paired with female college mentors concluded that the mentorship promoted their risk-taking and their ability to work independently. It also helped them to consider ways to integrate career and family. Beck pointed out that female mentors can be particularly helpful in aiding young women to overcome psychological barriers to achievement since they had confronted those barriers successfully themselves. Duff (2000) described the mentoring program at Ursuline Academy, a Texas preparatory high school for girls. Student interactions with knowledgeable and successful professional women so impacted their career and academic interests that after two years the program was substantially extended.

Mentorships for Males

Given increasing evidence that gifted young men, especially Black and Hispanic, may be especially at risk for realizing their potential (Ford, 1996; Torrance, Goff, & Satterfield, 1998, p. 7), mentorships seem an attractive option for enhancing their possibilities for success. Hébert and Olenchak (2000) reviewed three case studies in which mentoring relationships were established with the intent of reversing underachievement. Each mentorship was a year or more in duration and included gifted underachieving students

from elementary school to college. The authors concluded that mentor relationships could be effective in reversing the pattern of underachievement in gifted young men, as well as positively impacting both attitude toward school and peer relationships. A school-based mentorship pairing secondary male students with elementary males identified with Emotional Behavior Disorders (EBD) found the mentorship to be effective in mitigating problematic behaviors, while increasing positive social interaction skills and self-perceptions (Burrell et al., 2001).

Telementoring

Although mentorships are being extended to serve a broader base of gifted and talented students, it seems apparent that most mentorships retain essential aspects of the traditional model. One major innovation, however, is changing the traditional concept substantially: telementoring. Telementoring establishes the mentorship over the Internet. In this arrangement, it is possible, even likely, that mentor and mentee will never actually meet. This mentoring arrangement carries obvious advantages and disadvantages. Since face-to-face interaction between mentor and mentee is unlikely, the close personal contact is absent. The most serious concerns center on the potential absence of an infrastructure that screens mentors, matches mentor and mentee, and provides for systematic and appropriate feedback.

There are advantages to telementoring. Both mentors and gifted and talented may find the flexibility attractive; communication can take place as one's schedule permits. The time flexibility may encourage more mentors and mentees to get involved. There is also the potential for mentorships with national and international experts and professionals who would otherwise be unavailable.

A fairly extensive review of mentorships offered online indicated that detailed study of a site and its offerings should be undertaken before getting students involved. Some sites, however, offer credible mentorship opportunities as well as sound information on designing and implementing a mentorship program. For example, The National Mentoring Partnership site, funded in part by the U.S. Department of Education, offers online mentorship opportunities, program resources, information from state partnership affiliates, and up-to-date news on mentoring. Online mentorships available for students are developed with well-defined mission statements and well-established operating principles. Comprehensive reports, such as a review of national mentorships (Sipe & Roder, 1999), are available online from the website at *http://www.mentoring.org*. Sites such as The National Mentoring Center at the Northwest Regional Educational Laboratory at *http://www.nwrel.org* also provide publications and a wide range of resources. One caution is in order: Websites disappear, often with no farewell and usually with no forwarding address.

A variety of companies and agencies also sponsor telementoring opportunities. Hewlett Packard's program is an example of a well-designed, company-school mentoring partnership. The Hewlett Packard Email Mentor Program provides one-on-one mentorships between Hewlett Packard employees and students from fifth to twelfth grade. The company provides mentor training. The program requires commitment and participation from a classroom teacher before a mentorship will be established, thus ensuring the presence of an intermediary to monitor the process and to provide feedback and support. Information on Hewlett Packard mentorship programs as well as their materials on training mentors and developing programs can be found at the International Telementor Program site: *http://www.telementor.org*. The site also provides access to other companies and organizations that offer program-based mentorships with national and international experts in areas such as meteorology, physics, and engineering.

Telementoring for gifted and talented students has also been established at universities. The SET (Study of Exceptional Talent) Mentor Program Center for Talented Youth at the Johns Hopkins University provides a model for developing mentorships between graduates or older members of the program and new, younger members. Older SET members provide mentoring that may center on school concerns, career choices, or academic issues. Information on the SET Mentoring Program is available at *http://www.jhu.edu/~gifted/set*. University-school partnerships have also gone online. One mentorship at the University of Minnesota involved university students and ninth-graders in a mentorship using telecommunications (Duln et al., 1994). Mentors responded to student writing, offering suggestions and raising questions intended to advance the mentee's writing capability.

Ursuline Academy, a private school for girls in Dallas, Texas, offers online mentoring for high school students in a wide variety of career fields (Duff, 2000). Starting with a small group of upper-level students and mentors at Texas Instruments, the telementoring program later expanded to include students from all grade levels and mentors drawn from a pool of professionals developed by the school, including many alumnae.

Structuring a Mentorship

Matching Mentor and Mentee

The success of a mentorship often will depend upon the match between mentor and mentee, and the time spent in finding a compatible partnership will be rewarded. Frequently, a gifted and talented coordinator, teacher, or counselor will make the match in consultation with mentor and mentee. Background information, interest surveys, and interviews often are used in determining the match. In some instances, however, students and mentors have an opportunity to select each other. The CUNY Student Mentor program is a good example. In this program, before mentoring began, high school students and university mentors met after school for several weeks where they engaged in informal conversation, games, and interviews. By the fifth week, when mentoring started, a mutual selection usually had occurred (Reisner et al., 1990). Because matching in such a case is more spontaneous and natural, the partnership is likely to be strong and enduring (Flaxman et al., 1988).

Depending upon the purpose of the mentorship, pairing according to gender and cultural and ethnic backgrounds may also be important. For example, social distance between mentor and mentee may be an obstacle to a successful relationship; the mentor may initially establish unrealistic goals for the young person and the mentee may regard the mentor's world as remote and unaccessible (Struchen & Porta, 1997). When role models are a priority, it is desirable to match mentees with successful mentors with whom they can relate and who can help them see themselves in comparable successful positions in the future, for example, pairing girls with successful women and young minority students with minority leaders (Beck, 1989; Guetzloe, 1997; Reisner et al., 1990). However, the number of available mentors will not always allow this choice. Furthermore, many successful mentorships have been cross-gender and cross-cultural.

Preparation and Implementation

Mentorships, like all partner relationships, are more likely to succeed when they are entered into purposefully, with commitment on both sides, and with a reasonably clear understanding of the roles and responsibilities of each partner. To increase the likelihood of success, several mentor programs have established well-defined guidelines for structuring a partnership. A ten-step process involving three phases incorporates the most frequently suggested components.

Phase 1: The Preparation

1. *Establish need and student readiness.* The first step is to determine whether or not a mentorship is the best educational option for a student or group of students at the present time. The answer must consider a student's age, maturity, and work habits as well as alternative educational possibilities. Student desire and ability to commit to a mentorship are considered in the initial assessment.

2. *Recruit potential mentors.* Mentors are recruited from universities, businesses, community groups and organizations, and by individual recommendation. Often, mentors who have been involved in a successful mentorship will recommend other potential mentors. Recruitment is usually by personal contact by someone familiar with mentorship principles and the potential benefits of a mentorship to both mentee and mentor. Once a program becomes established, it is likely that a pool of potential mentors will always be available. Creation of a Mentorship Directory, updated regularly, is extremely helpful.

3. *Select mentors.* Screening of mentors varies in intensity, but often includes an interview, recommendations by peers, and reviews of their previous experiences working with young people. (See the Caveats section.)

4. *Match mentee and mentor.* The compatibility of the mentor and mentee will be a major factor in the success of the mentorship. Whenever possible, mentor and mentee should meet and chat informally before the final decision is made. A visit to the mentor's place of work is also helpful.

5. *Provide training and orientation.* Training of mentors is almost universally recommended. Mentor training should include information on effective mentoring practices and activities that produce a productive mentoring relationship. For mentors working with young people, training frequently will review developmental issues, raising awareness of stresses and other demands on the mentee and their potential impact on the mentorship.

For university students or adolescents mentoring younger students, classes or workshops should be part of the process. Reisner et al. (1990) noted that orientation may be especially important "when there are racial, cultural and socioeconomic differences between . . . mentors and the students they serve" (p. 39). Equally important are orientation sessions for mentees (Atkinson et al., 1992; Milam & Schwartz, 1992) and for their parents (Prillaman & Richardson, 1989).

Phase Two: The Mentorship

6. *Determine the conceptual contract and work plan.* Together, the mentor and mentee identify their roles and responsibilities, often with a facilitating third party, such as a teacher or program director. The purpose of the mentorship is reviewed. In an early meeting a work plan or schedule is agreed upon by the mentor and mentee, and, when appropriate, a specific area of study is outlined. Academic needs of the student are considered as well as other demands on the mentee's time. Asking the mentee to keep a journal of activities, thoughts, and learning experiences is common in many mentorships.

7. *Arrange for systematic feedback.* Systematic feedback allows for mentor and mentee to regulate the mentorship, maintain an open relationship, and make changes as needed. A line of communication should also be established for feedback between mentor and program coordinator as well as between mentee and coordinator. As the mentorship progresses, some arrangement should allow for input from the mentee's teachers and parents.

8. *Allow the mentorship to take its course.* The mentorship usually will include some planned activities; but often it is shaped by emerging needs, interests, and special opportunities as mentor and mentee explore a domain. Ideally, it will allow for time to go forward, to back up, to retrench, to reflect—and especially to dream.

Phase Three: The Culmination

9. *Realize a final product.* Whether it is a written report, a science project, an art show or an exhibition, a final product brings closure to a mentorship and creates a sense of satisfaction for all involved. A culminating activity also offers the mentee an opportunity to share his or her work and the mentoring experience with an audience.

10. *Evaluate the mentorship.* The question of program quality always should be addressed. Evaluations should reflect the goals of the program. Thus, designers of mentoring programs must determine how well outcomes and expectations match. Teasing out the factors leading to success (or failure) is also necessary for defensible mentorships.

Formative evaluation of the mentorship is provided by systematic feedback during the partnership, but a summative or final assessment should be done by all interested parties: mentor and mentee, school personnel, parents, and other involved individuals. Evaluations might include case studies, questionnaires, surveys, and self-reports from mentor and mentee regarding the process and effectiveness of the mentorship. Mentorships for underachievers or disadvantaged students might assess changes in attitude, achievement, or self-concept (Reisner et al., 1990). Academic mentorships might assess skill development, academic acceleration, or the quality of a final product (Atkinson et al., 1992; Lupkowski et al., 1990).

Wright and Borland (1992) noted that in many mentorships the impact of a mentorship upon the future success of the mentee will not be known for some time, especially in mentorships with young children. As a result, more informal evaluations relying on participants' perceptions of the immediate experience constitute a reasonable approach to assessment.

Caveats: Fundamentals to Keep in Mind when Setting up Mentorships

With the proliferation of mentorships to meet the needs of a wide variety of students comes increased potential for collateral damage. Sometime, somewhere, there may be an individual volunteering for a mentoring position who has a powerful personal agenda far from that expected by the instrumentalist who is arranging the mentorship. Therefore, the school district must have a written policy regarding mentorships, including selection and screening of mentors; and the district's legal consultants should approve any contracts or documents related to mentoring, including telementoring. It is also necessary that parents or guardians be fully informed of the mentorship and give written permission for mentoring arrangements.

While our review of mentorships encountered no reported aberrations, the potential for such occurrences is recognized, especially in the screening of potential mentors. The National Mentoring Partnership at *http://www.mentoringworks.org* recommends some sort of background check, the most preferred being a state and federal check. Although background screening may inhibit some potential mentors from volunteering, Struchen and Porta (1997) advised that the "welfare of the children outweighs the increased difficulty of recruitment and the potential loss of mentors." The Mentoring Partnership of Minnesota specifically addressed the issue of background checks as well as concerns related to risk management. Five basic steps were suggested for designing a liability and risk management system: (1) identification of potential risk, for example, in transportation of students; (2) measurement of risk, that is, how big is the risk?; (3) control of risk, for example, by training volunteers and carrying insurance; (4) management of claims through systematic supervision; and (5) improvement of policy, that is, changing liability as programs change. Information on background checks, insurance, and liability is available from most state departments of education.

These cautions are not intended to dissuade the development of mentorships. It is the authors' intent to insure continuation of the exceptional opportunities for students provided by mentorships by noting those safeguards which increase the likelihood of a successful mentorship experience for all involved.

Attention to several additional critical factors also can mitigate or eliminate later program difficulties, whether setting up a mentoring program or a single mentorship.

1. Setting the Numbers. Individuals responsible for establishing mentorships must determine how many relationships can effectively be managed over a given period of time. Additional resources should be required before expanding beyond the magic number.

2. The Tender Years. The developmental level of the student is a major consideration. Some elementary students are ready for a mentorship; some high school students are not. Instrumental mentorships arranged for younger students must stand the test of reasonableness and prudence. Obviously, parental or guardian permission is required for any deviation from the normal school routine; and this permission should be gathered in face-to-face contact, not the return of a signed form.

3. Developmental Needs. Some mentors, while skilled experts in their fields, may be unable or unwilling to handle some of the critical developmental needs of the mentee. This is as important for adolescents as for elementary-age children. Clasen and Hanson (1987) argued that success of a mentorship often depended upon attention to developmental needs. They recommended double mentoring where a second mentor, often a teacher, helped the student in areas important to both the student's personal growth and to the success of the mentorship. They identified several areas in which the second mentor could be particularly effective, including the development of skills for communicating with adults, especially those in power positions; time management; personal reflection on the mentorship; and providing opportunities for mentees to interact with peers engaged in mentorships.

4. Support Systems. In addition to support for the mentee, four additional kinds of continuing support must be considered.

- *Support for the mentor.* Mentors must be valued and supported, and their contribution should receive formal recognition from the school. Further, the mentor may need help in learning how to cope with the mentee in terms of age difference, cultural background, or attitude and value differences (Freedman, 1993). Communication links among mentor, mentee, someone from the school, and parents by phone, email, or personal visits should be established. As the relationship advances, changes in equity within the relationship will affect the mentor, who may need support in effectively empowering the mentee, rather than realizing the mentor's own dream.
- *Support for the coordinator.* Beyond being matchmaker in instrumental mentorships, the coordinator often becomes a communicator, a negotiator, a second mentor, and a counselor. Much of the scaffolding of the mentorship is done by the coordinator, and as a result she or he may be held accountable by the school for the success or failure of the mentorship. This is an awesome responsibility, and the individual assigned the task should be supplied with the necessary time, space and resources to take on the job.

- *Support for the family.* Parents or significant family members may feel threatened by the role of the mentor in the life of their child. As much as possible, they should share in the process by being kept informed, attending occasional meetings, and visiting the mentor and student during a mutually agreed upon time.
- *Support for the mentorship.* Most mentorships are not part of the school budget. Mentors usually contribute their services, and their institutions or agencies provide access to resources such as libraries or laboratories. Money should be budgeted, however, for possible transportation costs, incidental expenses, and fees for special events or special resources. School districts can give additional support by providing school credit to students involved in long-term, productive mentorships.

5. What if the mentorship falls apart? Sometimes the mentorship will not work. It could be that one or both of the partners finds the relationship incompatible. Mentor and mentee need to know that they are expected to work at the relationship and do all they can to make it succeed, but they also need the reassurance that they are free to dissolve the mentorship if absolutely necessary. In such a case, both should be able to leave the mentorship without assigning blame, but they should also be helped to evaluate what happened.

Labors Rewarded: Benefits of Mentorships

Much of the staying power of mentorships is due to a broad range of mentoring benefits. Among them, seven are especially compelling.

1. Meeting superior ability needs. Mentorships provide high-level learning experiences for students with the need and the readiness to move beyond the regular school provisions and into a relationship that will motivate, stimulate, and challenge the ability and interest levels of the student. For students with a passion for an area of development, it is an opportunity to meet others who share the passion and who can nurture the interest in a broader context.

2. Career exploration and development. The proliferation of mentorships with a career emphasis indicates the value placed on mentoring for career development across disciplines. Merriam's (1983) review indicated that the mentor is often the principal force in a successful person's career. The mentorship is especially valuable when young people are still questioning their abilities and interests, for the mentorship can "affirm their specialness without limiting it too early" (Albert, 1981, p. 4).

3. Development of potential. The abilities of many talented young people will be realized only through special opportunities such as a mentorship. In many cases talent development will depend entirely upon opportunity; capabilities and interests alone do not suffice. A mentoring relationship may provide the necessary environment for a change in attitude and in achievement for students screened out of gifted and talented programs or accelerated classes. These include underachieving, learning-disabled, handicapped, economically disadvantaged, and minority students (Richert, 1991).

4. Psychosocial advancement. During the mentorship, self-reliance, personal responsibility, and self-directed learning are encouraged and enhanced. From the mentor, the mentee can learn interpersonal skills, self-monitoring of feelings, and ways of interacting with others (Moore, 1992). The total experience can increase self-esteem, feelings of competence, and a sense of identity.

5. Connections with the larger world. Mentorships can help students see that they and their interests are part of a larger world and that their work contributes to a number of domains that interlock with their particular field of study.

6. Shared rewards. While mentees garner emotional support, advanced knowledge and skills, and insights into careers, the mentor has the satisfaction of passing on tradition to a new generation. And through the views of the novice, the mentor may find renewed energy and enthusiasm for the field.

7. Community and school collaborations. Collaborations involving the schools and the public and private sectors provide access to many untapped resources that can supplement the needs of gifted and talented students (Atkinson et al., 1992; Davalos & Haensly, 1997). The partnerships can develop positive public relations; and as school personnel, community leaders, university faculty, and area experts work together on behalf of students, a bond is forged between school and community.

SUMMARY AND CONCLUSIONS

A mentorship involves a young novice learning from an experienced and successful master in a relationship in which both are committed to exploring a mutual interest in depth. The mentor serves as teacher, advisor, and role model, guiding the youth toward excellence and helping validate both the individual and the talent. The young student gains knowledge and skills, explores career choices, confronts new challenges, develops a keener understanding of life's possibilities, and enjoys enhanced self-understanding, self-confidence, and self-esteem.

Mentorships have pitfalls but many of these can be avoided by thoughtful planning, including a careful matching of mentor and mentee. A mentorship is not for all gifted and talented students, but for those of demonstrated capacity in a domain who are ready to push the frontiers of their knowledge and skills. Mentorships are an option that should be available to gifted and talented students who have demonstrated the creativity and task commitment required of a mentoring relationship, particularly if they have exhausted programs available in their schools. Whether the mentorship focuses on advancing a super talent or nurturing promising potential, a mentorship may mean the difference between a dream withered and a dream realized.

QUESTIONS FOR THOUGHT AND DISCUSSION

1. Reflect on your own educational experiences. (a) When would it have been beneficial to have had a mentor? (b) If you had had a mentor at a critical time, how might the mentor have impacted your life?

2. Imagine a varied group for four or five gifted students (including minority, disabled, and female students) at the age level you expect to teach. How would mentoring benefit each student?

3. The chapter mentioned several caveats, including a background check for mentors. Are the cautions justified? Why or why not?

4. What would you predict for the future of telementoring?

REFERENCES

Albert, R. (1981). Special programs require special people. *Roeper Review, 4*(2), 2–4.

Arnold, K. D., & Subotnik, R. F. (1995). Mentoring the gifted: A differentiated model. *Educational Horizons, 73*(3), 118–123.

Atkinson, C., Hansen, D., & Passman, B. (1992). The Mentorship Academy Program: A school-community partnership for developing talent. *Gifted Child Today, 15*(3), 18–22.

Beck, L. (1989). Mentorships: Benefits and effects on career development. *Gifted Child Quarterly, 33,* 22–28.

Berry, J. (1996). New Orleans' brass bands: Mentors in the 'hood. *Youth Today, 1,* 11–15.

Boston, B. O. (1979). Developing a community based mentorship program for the gifted and talented. (Contract No. 300-78-0530). Washington, DC: U.S. Office of Education.

Burrell, B., Wood, S., Pikes, T. & Holliday, C. (2001). Student mentors and proteges learning together. *Teaching Exceptional Children, 33,*(3), 24–29.

Casey, K. M., & Shore, B. M. (2000). Mentors' contributions to gifted adolescents' affective, social, and vocational development. *Roeper Review, 22,* 227–230.

Christie, W. (1995). Mentoring at Meriden: The Parnassus Program. *The Educational Forum, 59,* 393–398.

Clasen, D. R., & Hanson, M. (1987). Double mentoring: A process for facilitating mentorships for gifted students. *Roeper Review, 10,* 107–110.

Collins, N. (1983). *Professional women and their mentors.* Englewood Cliffs, NJ: Prentice Hall.

Cox, J., & Daniel, N. (1983, September/October). The role of the mentor. *G/C/T,* 54–61.

Csikszentmihalyi, M., Rathunde, K., & Whalen, S. (1993). *Talented teenagers: The roots of success and failure.* New York: Cambridge Press.

Davalos, R. A., & Haensly, P. A. (1997). After the dust has settled: Youth reflect on their high school mentored research experience. *Roeper Review, 19,* 204–207.

Duff, C. (2000). Online mentoring. *Educational Leadership, 58*(2), 49–52.

Duln, A., Lammers, E., Mason, L., & Graves, M. (1994). Responding to ninth-grade students via telecommunications: College mentor strategies and development over time. *Research in the Teaching of English, 28,* 117–153.

Ellingson, M. K., Haeger, W. W., Feldhusen, J. F. (1986). The Purdue mentor program: A university-based mentorship program for G/C/T children. *G/C/T, 9*(2), 2–5.

Flaxman, E., Ascher, C., & Harrington, C. (1988, September). *Mentoring programs and practices: An analysis of the literature.* New York: Institute for Urban and Minority Education, Columbia University.

Ford, D. Y. (1996). *Reversing underachievement among gifted Black students.* New York: Teachers College Press.

Freedman, M. (1993). *The kindness of strangers: Adult mentors, urban youth, and the new volunteerism.* San Francisco: Jossey-Bass.

Goff, K., & Torrance, E. P. (1999). Discovering and developing giftedness through mentoring. *Gifted Child Today, 22*(3), 14–15, 52–53.

Goh, B. E., & Goh, D. (1996). Developing creative writing talent through a mentorship program. *Gifted Education International, 11,* 156–159.

Grau, P. (1985). Counseling the gifted girl. *Gifted Child Today, 24*(3), 8–12.

Guetzloe, E. (1997). The power of positive relationships: Mentoring programs in the school and community. *Preventing School Failure, 41*(3), 100–104.

Hamilton, S. F., & Hamilton, M. A. (1992). Mentoring programs: Promise and paradox. *Phi Delta Kappan, 73,* 546–550.

Healy, C. C., & Welchert, A. J. (1990). Mentoring relations: A definition to advance research and practice. *Educational Researcher, 19*(9), 17–21.

Hébert, T. P., & Olenchak, F. R. (2000). Mentors for gifted underachieving males: Developing potential and realizing promise. *Gifted Child Quarterly, 44,* 196–207.

Hébert, T. P., & Speirs Neumeister, K. L. (Winter 2000/2001). University mentors in the elementary classroom: Supporting the intellectual, motivational, and emotional needs of high-ability students. *Journal for the Education of the Gifted, 24*(2), 122–148.

Kaufmann, F. A., Harrel, G., Milam, C. P., Woolverton, N., & Miller, J. (1986). The nature, role, and influence of mentors in the lives of gifted adults. *Journal of Counseling and Development, 64,* 576–578.

Lengel, A. (1989). Mentee/mentor: Someone in my corner. *Gifted Child Today, 12*(1), 27–29.

Levey, S., & Dolan, J. (1988). Addressing specific learning abilities in gifted students. *Gifted Child Today, 11*(3), 10–11.

Levinson, D., Darrow, C., Klein, E., Levinson, M., & McKee, B. (1978). *The seasons of a man's life.* New York: Ballantine Books.

Lupkowski, A. E., Assouline, S. G., & Stanley, J. C. (1990). Applying a mentor model for young mathematically talented students. *Gifted Child Today, 13*(2), 15–19.

Lupkowski, A. E., Assouline, S. G., & Vestal, J. (1992). Mentors in math. *Gifted Child Today, 15*(3), 26–31.

Marlow, S. E., & Marlow, M. P. (1996). Sharing voices of experience in mathematics and science: Beginning a mentorship program for middle school girls. *Focus on Learning Problems in Mathematics, 18,* 146–154.

Milam, C. P., & Schwartz, B. (1992). Mentorship connection. *Gifted Child Today, 15*(3), 9–13.

Moore, K. M. (1992). The role of mentors in developing leaders in academe. *Educational Record, 63*(1), 23–28.

Noller, R. B., & Frey, R. (1994). *Mentoring: Annotated bibliography (1982–1992).* Sarasota, FL: Center for Creative Learning.

Olszewski-Kubilius, P. M., & Scott, J. M. (1992). An investigation of the college and career counseling needs of economically disadvantaged, minority gifted students. *Roeper Review, 14,* 141–148.

Powell, B. J. (1999). Mentoring: One of the master's tools. *Initiatives, 59,* 19–31.

Prillaman, D., & Richardson, R. (1989). The William and Mary Mentorship Model: College students as a resource for the gifted. *Roeper Review, 12,* 114–118.

Reilly, J. (1992). When does a student really need a professional mentor? *Gifted Child Today, 15*(3), 2–8.

Reisner, E., Petry, C., & Armitage, M. (1990, April). *A review of programs involving college students as tutors or mentors in grades K-12.* (Vol. 1) (Contract No. LC 89089001). Washington, DC: Policy Studies Associates.

Renzulli, J. S. (1977). *The enrichment triad model.* Mansfield Center, CT: Creative Learning Press.

Richert, E. S. (1991). Rampant problems and promising practices in identification. In N. Colangelo & G. Davis (Eds.), *Handbook of gifted education* (pp. 81–96). Boston: Allyn & Bacon.

Roper-Davis, S. (1999). Reaching for the Stars. *Gifted Child Today, 22*(1), 22–24.

Ross, P. O. (Ed.). (1993). *National excellence: A case for developing America's talent.* Washington, DC: U.S. Department of Education.

Schatz, E. (Winter 1999/2000). Mentors: Matchmaking for young people. *Journal of Secondary Gifted Education, 11*(2), 67–87.

Sipe, C. L., & Roder, A. E. (1999). *Mentoring school-age children: A classification of programs.* Prepared for the Public Policy Council of the National Mentoring Partnership. Philadelphia, PA: Public/Private Ventures. (Available from Public/Private Ventures, 399 Market Street, Philadelphia, PA 19106.)

Stanley, J. C. (1979). How to use a fast-pacing math mentor. *Intellectually Talented Youth Bulletin, 5*(6), 1–2.

Struchen, W., & Porta, M. (1997). From role-modeling to mentoring for African American youth: Ingredients for successful relationships. *Preventing School Failure, 41*(3), 119–123.

Tan-Willman, C. (1992). The prime mentors of Canada: A junior-senior partnership for the development of creative potential. In W. Wu, C. Kuo, J. Steeves (Eds.), *The Second Asian Conference on Giftedness Proceedings* (pp. 351–357). Taipei, Taiwan: National Taiwan Normal University.

Torrance, E. P., Goff, K., & Satterfield, N. (1998). *Multicultural mentoring of the gifted and talented.* Waco, TX: Prufrock Press.

White-Hood, M. (1993). Taking up the mentoring challenge. *Educational Leadership, 5*(3), 76–78.

Wright, L., & Borland, J. H. (1992). A special friend: Adolescent mentors for young, economically disadvantaged, potentially gifted students. *Roeper Review, 14,* 124–129.

Yoshimoto, R. (2000). Celebrating strengths and talents of dyslexic children: An educational model. *Perspectives, 26*(2), 34–36.

Zorman, R. (1993). The life-stage mentoring model for the gifted. *Gifted International, 8*(1), 4–8.

BIBLIOGRAPHY

Callahan, C. M. (1993). The performance of high ability students in the United States on national and international tests. *Monograph of the National Association for Gifted Children.* Washington, DC: National Association for Gifted Children.

Clasen, D. R. (1993). Resolving Inequities: Discovery and development of talents in student populations traditionally underrepresented in gifted and talented programming. *Journal of the California Association for the Gifted, 23*(4), 25–29.

Clasen, D. R. (2001, March). Twice-exceptional children: Gifted children with learning differences. *Unique Gifts/Hidden Talents.* (Available from the International Dyslexia Association, Wisconsin Branch, 1614, Laurel Crest, Madison, WI 53705.)

Comer, R. (1989). A mentorship program for gifted students. *The School Counselor, 36,* 224–228.

Edlind, E. P., & Haensly, P. A. (1985). Gifts of mentorships. *Gifted Child Quarterly, 29,* 55–60.

Emerson-Stonnell, S., & Carter, C. (1994). Math mentor programs. *Gifted Child Today, 17*(1), 34–36, 41.

Erikson, E. (1968). *Identity: Youth and crisis.* New York: Norton.

Evertson, C. M., & Smithey, M. W. (2000). Mentoring effects on proteges' classroom practice: An experimental field study. *Journal of Educational Research, 93,* 294–304.

Feldman, D. H. (1991). (With Goldsmith, L. T.). *Nature's Gambit: Child prodigies and the development of human potential.* New York: Teachers College Press.

Merriam, S. (1983). Mentors and proteges: A critical review of the literature. *Adult Education Quarterly, 33,* 161–173.

Runions, T., & Smyth, E. (1985). Gifted adolescents as co-learners in mentorships. *Journal for the Education of the Gifted, 8*(2), 127–132.

Torrance, E. P. (1984). *Mentor relationships: How they aid creative achievement, endure, change and die.* New York: Bearly Limited.

West, T. G. (1997). *In the mind's eye: Visual thinkers, gifted people with dyslexia and other learning difficulties, computer images and the ironies of creativity.* Amherst, NY: Prometheus Books.

West, T. G. (2001). On ground that they understand—Awakening strengths that non-dyslexics don't know exist. *Unique Gifts/Hidden Talents.* (Available from the International Dyslexia Association, Wisconsin Branch, 1614, Laurel Crest, Madison, WI 53705.)

21

Grouping and Tracking

JAMES A. KULIK, *University of Michigan*

Ability grouping and tracking were controversial practices when they were first used in American schools a century ago, and they remain contentious issues today. Parents, teachers, and school administrators argue about these topics in school meetings. Experts write about them in professional journals. Professional associations take stands on these practices. And newspaper reporters write articles about the tracking wars in American education.

Grouping and tracking are not only controversial topics, but they are also confusing. People disagree about what the terms mean, and they also argue about such basic facts as *why* and *how often* schools group and track students. Most important, people disagree about how grouping and tracking affect children. Some say that grouping and tracking can be beneficial, since they help schools achieve excellence in education. Others say that grouping and tracking are harmful, since they keep schools from achieving educational equality.

Loveless (1998, 1999) has written a good description of these tracking wars. On one side of the battle line are the *detrackers,* who are committed to ridding American schools of all grouping and tracking. Detrackers view tracking and grouping as forms of segregation, and they view elimination of these practices as a necessary step in the nation's march toward educational equality. On the other side are those who oppose the idea of one-track schools and defend school programs that sometimes group children for instruction by skills and interests. Opponents of detracking think that single-track schools will never accommodate a diverse student body or provide an excellent education for all.

Like it or not, teachers of the gifted and talented have become embroiled in the tracking wars.

Although gifted education is not synonymous with grouping and tracking, most programs for the gifted attract a select group of high-aptitude students, and these students usually receive some of their instruction separately from other students. Grouping is thus a part of many programs for the gifted, and the idea of gifted education thus offends detrackers. Some would like to eliminate from the schools all special programs for gifted and talented students so that all students could follow a common curriculum.

Fortunately, research results on grouping and tracking have been accumulating for three-quarters of a century, and they can clear up some of the confusion about grouping. But research studies do not automatically lead to understanding. When research findings are selectively quoted and inaccurately summarized, they only add complications to the puzzle. For research findings to be enlightening, they must be carefully organized, summarized, and analyzed.

My purpose in this chapter is to provide a clear summary and analysis of research findings on grouping and tracking. My main focus is on experimental, ethnographic, and correlational evidence on grouping and tracking effects. But before summarizing and analyzing this evidence, I consider basic questions about terminology, extent of grouping and tracking in American schools, and historical perspectives.

Definition of Terms

The term *ability grouping* means different things to different people. In a broad sense, *ability grouping* is a characteristic of any program in which school personnel use test scores or school performance to assign same-grade children to groups or classes with markedly different levels of academic preparation. Ability grouping is thus a characteristic of a number of different school programs. It occurs when schools assign children to high, middle, and low classes in the elementary grades; when they assign children to reading groups according to reading level rather than school grade or age; when they form teachable groups within arithmetic or reading classes on the basis of arithmetic skills; when they assign middle and high school students to different classes in core subjects such as English and mathematics; and when they provide special classes for the gifted and talented.

It is worth noting that not every writer on the topic uses the term *ability grouping* in this way. In the older literature on ability grouping, the term refers to programs in which children of a given grade level are assigned to separate classes based on their test scores (e.g., Keliher, 1931). The term thus referred to what is today called *ability-based class assignments.* The term *ability grouping* was gradually broadened to cover the within-class and cross-grade grouping programs that were introduced into American education during the 1940s and 1950s. In the recent literature, however, some writers are again using the term in a narrow way. Loveless (1998), for example, restricts the term to within-class programs that separate elementary school students by reading or arithmetic levels into separate instructional groups (e.g., "redbirds" and "bluebirds").

In this chapter, I use the term *ability grouping* in the broad rather than the narrow sense. I have at least two reasons for not restricting the term to within-class programs. First, within-class grouping programs were introduced into American education about fifty years ago, whereas the term *ability grouping* has been used in American education for nearly 100 years. Restricting the term *ability grouping* to within-class programs restricts discussions to the recent literature and deprives us of important lessons learned during the first fifty years of ability grouping. Second, within-class programs are almost exclusively a feature of elementary schools. Equating ability grouping with programs of within-class grouping deprives us of lessons about grouping from middle and high schools.

Tracking is not the same thing as grouping, and it is important to know where the two practices differ. Most researchers use the term *tracking* to refer to high school programs in which students choose among college-preparatory, general, or vocational classes on the basis of their preparation and goals.

Some current writers use the term *tracking* in a broader sense. Oakes (1985), for example, uses the term to describe all instructional programs that provide differentiated instruction for students. Other writers use the term to refer to the most rigid and onerous forms of ability grouping. For example, Singal (1991) restricts the term *tracking* to programs in which students are sorted at an early age by intelligence test scores into separate inflexible tracks for fast, medium, and slow learners, where they remain through high school. In this report, I use the term *tracking* in the widely accepted narrower sense of the term. I use it to refer to high school programs that provide students with college preparatory, vocational, and general tracks.

It is especially important to note that ability grouping and tracking are also different from curricular differentiation. A differentiated curriculum provides different courses of study for same-age children with different learning needs and preferences. Programs of bilingual education and special education, for example, involve curricular differentiation. It is important to note that a school may have curricular differentiation without ability grouping. For example, the general and vocational programs in a high school are different curricular programs, but the students who follow them usually score at about the same level on tests of school aptitude. It is also important to note that ability grouping can occur without curricular differentiation. That is, schools sometimes prescribe the same course of study for high, middle, and low groups.

Extent of Grouping in American Schools

The most widely cited statistics on grouping in high schools are those from the Office of Educational Research and Improvement's National Educational Longitudinal Survey (NELS) of 1988 (Ingels et al., 1998). The most widely cited statistics on extent of grouping in elementary and middle schools are those from the Johns Hopkins Center for Research on Elementary and Middle Schools (Braddock, 1990; McPartland, Coldiron, & Braddock, 1987).

High Schools

The NELS of 1988 is a national survey of 25,000 students in nearly 1,000 schools (Ingels et al., 1998).

NELS researchers asked the students' teachers if the achievement level of a student's class was above average, average, below average, or heterogeneous when compared to the achievement level of the whole school.

Teachers in both eighth and tenth grade reported that most students were being taught in homogeneous classes (Rees, Argys, & Brewer, 1996). In the tenth grade, for example, teachers characterized as homogeneous 85% of English classes, 89% of mathematics classes, 88% of science classes, and 82% of social studies classes. Heterogeneous classes were therefore a clear minority at the high school level. Of the homogeneous classes, roughly 30% were considered above average in aptitude; 50% were middle-level aptitude; and 20% were below average in aptitude. Clearly, most high school students were in homogeneous classes most of the time, and heterogeneous classes were the exception rather than the rule.

Middle Schools

The Center for Research on Elementary and Middle Schools at Johns Hopkins University in 1988 asked principals in nearly 1,800 middle schools about grouping practices (Braddock, 1990; Loveless, 1998). One of the survey questions was: "For which academic subjects are students assigned to homogeneous classes on the basis of similar abilities or achievement levels?" Results showed that middle schools typically group pupils in some subjects, but not all. In the seventh grade, for example, 22% of all students were in homogeneous classes for all subjects; 47% were in homogeneous classes for some subjects; and 31% were in no homogeneous classes. Distinct levels of curriculum were typical in English and mathematics, but were less common in science and social studies. Overall, grouping was less common in middle schools than in high schools, but grouping was still a very common practice in middle schools.

Elementary Schools

McPartland, Coldiron, and Braddock (1987) described grouping patterns based on a comprehensive survey of elementary schools in the state of Pennsylvania. McPartland and his colleagues found that within-class grouping by ability was used in well over 90% of the schools at the primary level and in 85% to 90% of the schools at the upper elementary level. In addition, McPartland and his colleagues

found that the majority of schools in their sample (almost 70%) also grouped children by skill into separate classes (between-class grouping) in at least one subject.

Overall Patterns

The best available evidence suggests that almost all schools in this country use some form of homogeneity grouping for at least some classes, and most children are grouped homogeneously for some or all of their work, either within classes or in separate classrooms. Separate classes for faster and slower students are most common at the high school level and least common at the elementary school level. Within-class grouping appears to be very widely used in elementary schools. The evidence on these points is not definitive, however. Survey data at all educational levels need to be updated, and only regional survey data—not national data—are available from elementary schools.

Early Research Reviews

During the four decades from the 1930s through the 1960s, reviewers painted at least four pictures of research results on grouping. The pictures differed as much as the decades that produced them.

The first picture of the research comes from the late 1920s when the mental testing movement was at its height in American education. Reviewers of the time felt optimistic about the testing movement, and they had positive things to say about ability grouping. Their most important conclusion, repeated in review after review in the early 1930s, was that grouping led to better school outcomes when ability groups worked with methods and materials that suited their aptitude levels (e.g., Miller & Otto, 1930; Turney, 1931).

In the 1930s, the second picture, John Dewey's philosophy of progressive education became an important influence on American schools, and with its rise, enthusiasm about grouping began to fade. Progressive educators held that the social spirit of the classroom did as much for children as formal instruction did, and they criticized grouping programs both for fostering undemocratic feelings in children and for promoting traditional content teaching. Their reviews (e.g., Keliher, 1931) focused on negative effects of grouping. They reported that students learned less and also declined in self-concept and leadership skills in grouped classes.

In the third picture, during the 1950s, the United States and Russia were fighting a cold war for scientific and technological supremacy, and American schools were expected to contribute to the struggle by emphasizing academic and scientific excellence. The new reviews (e.g., Ekstrom, 1961; Goldberg, 1958; Passow, 1958) reported that higher aptitude youngsters made notable gains when taught in special enriched and accelerated classes. The reviewers reported that accelerated and enriched classes helped talented children academically and also seemed to have no detrimental effects on their social and emotional adjustment.

Finally, the civil rights movement of the 1960s led to still another re-evaluation of grouping research. After the 1960s a number of reviewers (e.g., Eash, 1961, Findley & Bryan, 1971; Heathers, 1969) reported that no one benefits from ability grouping and that children who are in the middle and lower groups clearly suffer a loss in achievement, academic motivation, and self-esteem.

Four educational eras thus produced four pictures of grouping effects. Reviewers saw one thing in one era and something entirely different in the next era. Reviewers are notorious for finding fault with and dismissing study results that do not support their viewpoints. But other factors were also obstacles to consensus. It is clear, for example, that reviewers in different eras were looking at different types of grouping programs and different types of evaluation studies. To make sense of findings, one has to distinguish carefully among types of evaluation studies and types of programs.

In this review, I examine results from three different types of evaluation studies. *Experimental* studies examine educational outcomes for equivalent students assigned to grouped and non-grouped classes. *Ethnographic* studies provide narrative descriptions of classroom processes in upper and lower tracks. *Correlational* analyses examine performance differences in upper and lower tracks when characteristics of students selecting the tracks are statistically controlled.

Experimental Studies of Grouping

The most comprehensive reviews of experimental evidence on grouping are reports by Robert Slavin at Johns Hopkins University (e.g., Slavin, 1987, 1990b) and by my research group at the University of Michigan (e.g., C.-L. Kulik & J. Kulik, 1982, 1984; J. Kulik, 1992; J. Kulik & C.-L. Kulik, 1984, 1987, 1992). Both the Johns Hopkins and Michigan researchers used versions of Glass's (1976) meta-analytic methodology in their reviews. Reviewers using meta-analytic methods usually carry out computer searches of library databases to locate as many credible studies of an issue as they can; they describe features and outcomes of studies using quantitative or quasi-quantitative methods; and they use statistical methods to summarize study results and to relate study features to outcomes. Working independently, the Johns Hopkins and Michigan researchers used these meta-analytic methods to examine five major types of grouping: (a) XYZ programs; (b) cross-grade programs; (c) within-class programs; (d) advanced and accelerated classes; and (e) enriched classes.

XYZ Grouping

In 1919 Detroit became the first large city in America to introduce into its schools a formal plan of ability grouping (Courtis, 1925). The Detroit plan called for intelligence testing of all school children at the start of grade 1 and then placement of children into X, Y, and Z groups on the basis of test results. The top 20 per cent went to the X classes, the middle 60 per cent to Y classes, and the bottom 20 per cent to Z classes. Standard materials and methods were used in all classes, and all classes covered material at the same grade level.

Many school systems followed the Detroit model in subsequent years and instituted their own plans of multilevel grouping. Some developed comprehensive XYZ plans, in which the groups remained separate for the whole day. Other schools used single-subject grouping. Few of the plans relied as much as the Detroit plan on intelligence tests for initial placements, and few separated students at such an early age. Most plans, however, were like the Detroit plan in their basic goal. They were designed to make the teacher's job easier by reducing pupil variation in their classes, and they were not used as a way of providing highly differentiated curricula to ability groups.

The Michigan meta-analyses covered 22 studies of comprehensive XYZ programs and 29 studies of single-subject XYZ grouping (J. Kulik, 1992). The Johns Hopkins analyses covered 30 studies of comprehensive XYZ grouping and 19 studies of single-subject XYZ grouping (Slavin, 1987, 1990b).

Like other meta-analysts, the Hopkins and Michigan reviewers expressed treatment effects as effect sizes, or in standard deviation units. In principle, the computation of effect sizes is simple. A reviewer usually finds the difference between an experimental group's gain on an outcome measure and a control group's gain. The reviewer then divides this difference by an estimate of the population standard deviation on the measure. The effect size is thus simply a standardized measure of the treatment effect. An effect size is positive when the treatment makes a contribution, negative when the treatment has a harmful effect. An effect size is large when its absolute value is around 0.8, medium when around 0.5, and small when around 0.2 (Cohen, 1977). Glass (1976) noted that an effect size of one standard deviation is equivalent to an effect of one grade-equivalent unit.

The Michigan meta-analyses found that lower and middle aptitude students learn about the same amount in grouped and mixed classes. Middle and lower aptitude students who gain about one year on a grade-equivalent scale after a year in a mixed class would also gain about one year on the scale when taught in a homogeneous class. The Michigan meta-analysis also showed that XYZ grouping has a slight positive effect on the achievement of higher aptitude students. The average effect of XYZ grouping on high-aptitude students was an increase in test scores of 0.13 standard deviations. A higher aptitude student who gained 1.0 year on a grade-equivalent scale in a mixed class thus would have gained about 1.1 years in a homogeneous class.

The Johns Hopkins results were similar. Slavin found near-zero effects of grouping on lower, middle, and higher aptitude students. He found that a student who gains one year on a grade-equivalent scale after a year in a mixed-ability class would also gain one year if taught in a homogeneous class. Slavin's analysis suggested that this result is equally true for higher, middle, and lower aptitude students.

Why were contributions of XYZ grouping to student achievement so small? It may be because the XYZ programs did not provide a differentiated curriculum for the stratified classes. While school personnel were careful to place children into XYZ classes by aptitude, they did not adjust the curriculum to the aptitude levels of the classes. All groups worked with the same materials and followed the same course of study. The programs were therefore programs of differential placement without differentiated curricula.

Some studies of comprehensive XYZ classes also looked at grouping effects on student self-esteem. The Michigan meta-analyses covered results from 13 such studies (J. Kulik, 1992). On average, self-esteem scores went up slightly for low-aptitude learners in XYZ programs, and they went down slightly for high-aptitude learners. Thus, brighter children appeared to lose a little of their self-assurance when they were put into classes with equally talented children, whereas slower children gained a little in self-confidence when they were taught in classes with other slower learners.

How can we explain these self-esteem effects? Social factors probably have a direct influence on a child's self-image. Children appear to judge their abilities by comparing themselves to the children they see around them. Social comparison theory thus predicts a drop in self-esteem for a high-achieving student placed in a homogeneous group of high-achievers, since the student will stand out less in such company. Social comparison theory also predicts a rise in self-esteem for low achievers placed in a group of slow learners, since low-aptitude students will less often be overshadowed in a homogeneous group. Labeling theory, on the other hand, says that self-esteem will rise for children who are put into a group labeled as high-ability and self-esteem will fall for children in a group labeled as low-ability. The evidence does not support the predictions of labeling theory. Labels are apparently a less powerful influence on self-conceptions than are the conclusions that people draw by themselves from their own comparisons with those around them.

Loveless (1999) criticized the evidence on XYZ grouping on the basis of its age. XYZ studies included in the Michigan meta-analyses date from 1928 to 1986, and XYZ studies included in the Johns Hopkins meta-analyses are no more current. Some experts believe that schools have largely abandoned XYZ grouping in recent decades because XYZ programs do not adjust curricula to fit student needs. According to Loveless, studies of XYZ grouping are yesterday's studies, and no one should draw conclusions about today's programs on the basis of yesterday's results.

Nonetheless, I believe that findings on XYZ programs are still relevant for us today. Over the course of six decades, XYZ programs have made only small and largely insignificant contributions to improving schools. Administrators of schools that are still using XYZ grouping should be aware of its weak evaluation record, and administrators of schools that are considering reorganization should keep in mind that little will be gained by instituting XYZ grouping without curricular differentiation.

Cross-Grade Grouping

Unlike XYZ plans, programs of cross-grade grouping provide different curricula for children at different ability levels. The best-known approach to cross-grade grouping is the Joplin plan, which was first used during the 1950s for reading instruction in the Joplin, Missouri, elementary schools. During the hour reserved for reading in the Joplin schools, children in grades 4, 5, and 6 broke into nine different groups that were reading at anything from the Grade 2 to Grade 9 level. The children went to their reading classes without regard to their regular grade placement but returned to their age-graded classrooms at the end of the reading period. Almost all formal evaluations of cross-grade grouping involve the Joplin plan for reading instruction in elementary schools.

Both the Michigan and Johns Hopkins meta-analyses found that cross-grade programs in elementary and middle schools usually produce positive results (J. Kulik, 1992; Slavin, 1987). The Michigan analysis, for example, covered 14 studies of cross-grade grouping. More than 80 percent of these studies found positive effects from grouping. The average effect size was 0.33 standard deviations. While the typical pupil in a mixed-ability class would gain one year on a grade-equivalent scale in a school year, the typical pupil in a cross-grade program would gain 1.3 years. Effects were positive for high, middle, and low groups in cross-grade programs.

Such findings inspired Slavin to make cross-grade grouping a basic feature in a reading program that he introduced into the Baltimore schools in 1987 (Slavin & Madden, 2000). The reading program now appears to be one of the most successful of all recent innovations in elementary schools. Called Success for All (SFA), Slavin's program is now used in reading classes by about one million students in 1,800 schools. Program participants are grouped for reading instruction across age lines by reading skill so that each reading class contains students at different grade levels but at the same reading level. Reading skills are assessed regularly for all students, and these assessments are used for regrouping

students and for assigning students for special tutoring when needed.

Slavin and Madden reported results from nearly 200 comparisons of SFA and control groups in grades 1 through 5. For SFA students in general, effect sizes averaged around one-half standard deviation at all grade levels. Program benefits were especially strong for students in the lowest 25% of their grades. They ranged from an improvement in reading test scores of 1.03 standard deviations for first graders to 1.68 standard deviations for fourth graders. A follow-up study of Baltimore schools found that positive program effects continued into grades 6 and 7, when students were in middle schools.

These strong SFA results help bring the cross-grade grouping story into the present. Evaluations of SFA show that cross-grade grouping programs are contributing importantly to school reform efforts today. The SFA evaluations are especially important because they suggest that cross-grade grouping can be very helpful for slower students. Eliminating cross-grade programs from schools could hurt the students about whom detrackers are most concerned.

Within-Class Grouping

Within-class grouping programs also provide different curricula for children at different ability levels. The most popular model for within-class grouping was developed in the 1950s for teaching arithmetic in elementary schools. A teacher following the model would use test scores and school records to divide her class into three groups for their arithmetic lessons, and she would use textbook material from several grade levels to instruct the groups. The high group in grade 6, for example, might use materials from grades 6, 7, and 8; the middle group might use materials from grades 5, 6, and 7; and the low group might use materials from grades 4, 5, and 6. The teacher would present material to one group for approximately 15 minutes before moving on to another group. Other approaches to within-class grouping are possible, but almost all controlled evaluations examine within-class programs that follow this model.

Both the Michigan and Johns Hopkins meta-analyses found that within-class programs in elementary and middle schools usually produce positive results (J. Kulik, 1992; Slavin, 1987). The Michigan analysis, for example, covered 11 studies of within-class grouping. Most of these studies reported clear positive results. Average effect size was 0.25; the average gain attributable to within-class grouping was thus between 2 and 3 months on a grade equivalent scale. Effects were similar for high, middle, and low groups.

An important recent report by Linchevski and Kutscher (1998) suggests that within-class grouping can produce dramatic improvements in school performance. Linchevski and Kutscher investigated the effects of a teaching program that included both homogeneous and heterogeneous grouping. Each junior high school student in this program learned math in both homogeneous and heterogeneous groups. The study compared achievement scores of students in this program, called the TAP program, to achievement of students in traditional homogeneous classes. At the end of two years of instruction, all students took tests of mathematics achievement. Lower and middle aptitude students in TAP classes outscored equivalent control students by at least 20 percentage points, and high-aptitude students performed at about the same level as equivalent controls. Note that gains from the TAP program were especially high for students in the lower and middle tracks. Far from being a drag on achievement of low- and middle-aptitude students, this program used within-class homogeneous and heterogeneous grouping to narrow the gap between high- and lower-aptitude learners.

For the full story of effectiveness of within-class programs, we must put together the older meta-analytic evidence and the newer evidence from studies such as the one by Linchevski and Kutscher. The results show that within-class grouping can raise class achievement in arithmetic and that it may also have especially dramatic effects on the performance of slower students. Findings on within-class programs thus seem to parallel findings on cross-grade grouping. Carefully designed programs that use within-class or cross-grade grouping appear to benefit all students, and they can be especially helpful for slower students.

Advanced and Accelerated Classes for the Gifted and Talented

American education has a long tradition of providing special classes for children whose educational needs differ from those of the majority. Special classes have been formed of children who are physically handicapped, emotionally or socially maladjusted, lacking in proficiency in English, and so on. One of the longest traditions is providing special classes for gifted and talented children.

The first classes devised especially for gifted and talented children were accelerated ones (Tannenbaum, 1958). The Cambridge Double Track Plan of 1891 put bright children into special classes that covered the work of six years in four, and the special-progress classes of New York City, established in 1900, allowed pupils to complete the work of three years in two. The basic idea of educational acceleration is to modify a school program so that students complete standard courses at an earlier age or in less time than is usual.

The Michigan meta-analyses covered 23 studies in which achievement of students in accelerated classes was compared to achievement of equivalent students in non-accelerated (control) classes (J. Kulik, 1992). All of the studies examined moderate acceleration of a whole class of students rather than acceleration of individual children. In each of the comparisons, involving students who were initially equivalent in age and intelligence, the students in accelerated classes outperformed the students in non-accelerated classes. In the typical study, the test scores of accelerated students were about one standard deviation higher than the scores of equivalent non-accelerates. On a grade-equivalent scale, the accelerates thus outperformed the non-accelerates by about one year.

The strong effects of accelerated and advanced classes are probably due to curricular differentiation. If curricular adjustment is at a minimum in XYZ classes, it is probably at a maximum in accelerated classes. High-aptitude students benefit from taking these advanced classes, and they suffer when they are held back in classes that work on material suited to average learners.

Enriched Classes for the Gifted and Talented

Accelerated programs were the first accommodation made for gifted and talented students in age-graded schools. But by the 1920s educators were becoming concerned that accelerated programs did not meet the emotional and social needs of gifted youngsters. To some, enriched classes of the sort that Leta Hollingworth had set up in the New York City schools in 1916 seemed an attractive alternative to acceleration. In these classes, children spent about half of their school hours working on the prescribed curriculum, and about half pursuing enriching activities. In classes that Hollingworth created for seven- to nine-year-olds, for example, enrichment activities included conversational French; the study of biography; study of the history of civilization; and a good deal of extra work in science, mathematics, English composition, and music (Gray & Hollingworth, 1931).

The Michigan meta-analyses covered 25 studies of enriched classes for talented students. Twenty-two of the 25 studies found that talented students achieved more when they were taught in enriched rather than regular mixed-ability classes. In the average study, students in the enriched classes outperformed equivalent students in mixed classes by 0.41 standard deviations, equivalent to about 4 months on a grade-equivalent scale.

The effects of enriched classes seem remarkable to me, given the goals of most enrichment programs and the criterion tests used to measure their effects. Most enrichment programs are meant to give students varied experiences that would not be available in regular classrooms; they do not ordinarily try to provide more work on the basic skills. However, the standardized achievement tests used to evaluate the effects of most enrichment programs stress basic skills. When children from enriched and regular classes are compared on standardized tests, the two groups may seem to be competing on an uneven field, with the test bias favoring the children from the regular classrooms. It seems likely, however, that enriched curricula almost invariably involve above-grade-level materials.

Conclusions from Experimental Studies

Different grouping and tracking programs have different effects on student achievement. Decades of experimental studies show, for example, that school achievement hardly changes with the introduction of XYZ grouping. Test scores of high groups may go up a small amount, but test scores of low and middle groups go neither up nor down with a switch from mixed-ability to XYZ classes. XYZ grouping also has only small effects on student self-esteem. Slower students may show a slight rise in self-esteem, but quicker students often show a slight decline in self-esteem when assigned to homogeneous classes.

Evaluation results are very different for programs in which groups follow curricula adjusted to their skill levels. Evaluation studies show, for example, that elementary school students benefit academically from cross-grade and within-class grouping in reading and arithmetic. According to recent studies, these cross-grade and within-class programs may be especially helpful for slower students. Studies also show that enriched, accelerated, and advanced classes are very beneficial for high-aptitude learners.

Overall, therefore, experimental studies provide strong evidence that grouping programs are often very effective when they are used to provide appropriate curricular materials for students with different educational needs. Studies also provide strong evidence that grouping contributes little to educational improvement efforts when it is used as an end in itself.

Correlational Analyses of Tracking

A study by Jencks and his colleagues illustrates the correlational approach (Jencks, 1972). To investigate the effects of high school tracking, Jencks and his colleagues looked at 91 predominantly White high schools throughout the United States that had tested their students for Project Talent in both the ninth grade and the twelfth grade. With statistical techniques, the researchers showed that students who reported that they were in the college preparatory curriculum averaged slightly higher on grade 12 tests than did students of comparable aptitude in other tracks.

Correlational studies of survey data on tracking address two main questions. First, what factors influence students to enroll in different curricular tracks? Researchers have been especially interested in determining whether academic ability or socioeconomic status plays a more important role in track placement. Second, how much do curricular tracks influence students? Researchers have explored the influence of tracks on such educational outcomes as high school achievement, postsecondary attainment, and self-esteem.

Jencks (1972) has written one of the best summaries of results on the first question. He drew four main conclusions about determinants of track placement:

- Personal preference is the most important determinant. The Equality of Educational Opportunity Survey, for example, found that 85% of all high school seniors were in the curriculum they want to be in (Coleman et al., 1966).
- After personal preference, the next most important determinant of curriculum placement seems to be academic ability. Jencks reported that the

correlation between test scores and curriculum assignment is around 0.50.
- Social class does not seem to play an important role in high school curriculum placement, except insofar as it influences test scores.
- Race plays an even smaller role in track placement. Blacks have a higher probability of ending up in the college preparatory track than do whites of equivalent aptitude and socioeconomic status.

The effects of track placement on student achievement are less clear. Gamoran and Berends (1987) reviewed 16 national or statewide studies with relevant data. Some studies found that track membership accounted for a significant amount of variation in test scores; others found that it accounted for a nonsignificant amount. The effects of tracking on educational attainment were more clear. Gamoran and Berends reported that all studies found that track membership influences educational attainment after high school. That is, students who are in college preparatory programs are more likely to enroll in college than are equally able students from the general and nonacademic tracks.

It is possible to be more precise about the size of these tracking effects (J. Kulik, 1998). It should be noted, first of all, that test scores of high school students completing academic and nonacademic programs are clearly different. Academic students on the average score at the 71st percentile on standardized achievement tests given at the end of high school (or 0.56 standard deviations above the mean); nonacademic students score on the average at the 33rd percentile (or 0.44 standard deviations below the mean). The achievement gap at high school graduation is therefore equivalent to about one standard deviation.

Only part of this gap is an effect of curricular track. Correlational analyses show that the most important cause of the achievement gap is self-selection (J. Kulik, 1998). The results suggest that if similar students selected academic and nonacademic programs, the gap would be only about 0.2 standard deviations. Thus, 80% of the difference in test scores of academic and nonacademic students at the end of high school is due to the difference in aptitude of the students who entered the programs.

Slavin (1990a) discussed problems with drawing conclusions from correlational analyses like these, and he concluded that the problems are severe. He believes, first of all, that the statistical controls in the correlational analyses are inadequate:

One problem is statistical; when groups are very different on a covariate, the covariate does not adequately "control" for group differences. . . . When comparing high- to low-ability groups, pretest or covariate differences of one to two standard deviations are typical. No statistician on earth would expect that analysis of covariance or regression could adequately control for such large differences. (p. 506)

Another problem in correlational analyses is failure to measure all differences between high tracks and low tracks. Many factors determine track placement, including a student's achievement level, behavior, attitudes, motivation, and prior course selection. These factors also affect student achievement in both tracked and untracked classes. Researchers cannot adequately measure and control all such factors, however, and unmeasured and uncontrolled input factors may produce the outcome differences that are assumed to be tracking effects.

If Slavin's criticisms are correct, conclusions from correlational analyses are undependable because the analyses are methodologically inadequate. But even if the study methodology is flawed, the study results are hardly damning to curricular tracking. The studies simply show that most of the variability in achievement observed at the time of high school graduation is the result of differences among students that were apparent at the start of high school. Some variation in achievement, however, is associated with the differentiated curricula that high schools offer. This conclusion is consistent with the experimental evidence on the effects of advanced, accelerated, and enriched classes.

Ethnographic Studies of Tracking

A first generation of ethnographic studies focused on teacher and student behaviors in upper and lower tracks. The earliest studies of this type examined British streamed schools (Ball, 1981; Hargreaves, 1967; Lacey, 1970), but later influential studies focused on American schools and classes (Oakes, 1985; Page, 1991; Rosenbaum, 1976). A newer generation of studies has examined the success of recent efforts to untrack American schools (Gamoran & Weinstein, 1998; Wells & Oakes, 1996).

The study described by Jeannie Oakes (1985) in her book *Keeping Track* is the best known of all ethnographic studies of tracking. Oakes and her coworkers made their observations in 299 English and math classes (75 high track, 85 average track, 64 low track, and 75 heterogeneous classes) in a national sample of 25 junior and senior high schools. The observations covered course content, quality of instruction, classroom climate, and student attitudes in each of the classes.

To Oakes, instruction seemed to be better in the higher tracks. In English classes, for example, the percentage of time spent on instruction was 81 for the high track and 75 for the low track; in math classes, percentage of time spent on instruction was 81 for the high track and 78 for the low track. In English classes, percentage of time off-task was 2 for the high track and 4 for the low; in math classes, it was 1 for the high track and 4 for the low. In all, more time was spent on instruction and less time was spent off-task in the high tracks.

Oakes also reported that there were curricular differences in high- and low-track classes. For example, low-track classes seemed to cover less-demanding topics, whereas high-track classes covered more complex material. High-track teachers also seemed to encourage competent and autonomous thinking, whereas low-track teachers stressed low-level skills and conformity to rules and expectations.

Gamoran and Berends (1987) summarized the main results from ethnographic studies of track differences. They reported that ethnographers have reached four main conclusions: (a) instruction is conceptually simplified and proceeds more slowly in lower tracks; (b) teachers with more experience and those regarded as more successful seem to be disproportionately assigned to the higher tracks; (c) teachers view high-track students positively and low-track students negatively; and (d) most of a student's friends are found in the same track.

Gamoran and Berends noted, however, that most of the track differences found by ethnographers, when quantified, appear to be tiny. The difference of 2 or 3 percent in time on instruction or time off-task, for example, is not large. It amounts to a difference of less than ten minutes per day in time on-instruction or off-task for low- versus high-track classes.

Critics have also noted that ethnographic analyses do not disentangle the effects due to grouping and those due to student characteristics. Slavin (1990a) suggests that high- and low-aptitude students might differ as much or more in ungrouped situations as they do in grouped ones. Noting that time on task is reportedly lower in low-track classes, he asks, "Might it be that low-achieving students are more likely to be off-task no matter where they are?" (p. 505).

Finally, critics have suggested that ethnographers may be misinterpreting some of their observations. Slavin (1990a) makes the following point:

> On the quality of instruction issue, the variables typically found to differentiate high- and low-track classes are ones that cannot be separated from the nature of the students themselves. For example, many studies find that there is less content covered in low-track classes. But is this by its nature an indication of low quality? Might it be that low-track classes need a slower pace of instruction? The whole idea of ability grouping is to provide students with a level and pace of instruction appropriate to their different needs. (p. 505)

That is, the teacher and curricular differences described by Oakes may represent appropriate responses to the different educational and emotional needs of different school children.

A new generation of ethnographic studies is focusing on progress that school reformers have made in untracking American schools. Notable reports on untracking have been written by Gamoran and Weinstein (1998) and by Wells and Oakes (1996). Both reports suggest that school reformers are *not* achieving their goal of improving American schools by eliminating tracking. Few schools have been able to eliminate tracking completely, and those that have sometimes suffered a loss in instructional quality as a result.

Gamoran and Weinstein's (1998) report provides concrete information on these points. These researchers conducted phone interviews with more than 250 schools nominated as being among the most restructured in the country. Although administrators at these schools reported that students spent most of their time in heterogeneous groups, the researchers determined that in more than half the schools students spent substantial amounts of time in ability groups or tracks. At the high school and middle school levels, for example, almost all schools assigned students to math classes based on test and school performance. Elementary schools varied in their grouping patterns. Some grouped children by ability into separate classes, and some grouped children by ability within classes.

Gamoran and his colleagues also made site visits to a sample of 24 of the nominated schools: eight high schools, eight middle schools, and eight elementary schools. Their observations in these 24 schools confirmed findings from the larger study. Only three of the eight high schools had eliminated tracking, for example. One of the three untracked schools seemed to offer rigorous, academically challenging work in mixed-ability classes, but in the other two schools mixed-ability grouping appeared to lead to a loss of academic rigor. Among the eight middle schools, only one used mixed-ability grouping exclusively in all subjects. The site visitors reported that work in this school seldom called for higher-order thinking or deep analysis. Thus, of the 16 middle and high schools visited by Gamoran and Weinstein's team, only one provided evidence of consistently high-quality instruction in untracked classes. Gamoran and Weinstein drew few conclusions about elementary school untracking because the grouping situation in these schools seemed complex to them. They found that most children in the highly reformed elementary schools were in mixed-ability classes for most of the day, but pullout programs and within-class groups introduced some degree of differentiation in students' work in these schools.

Oakes and her colleagues visited ten geographically diverse schools three times over a two-year period to determine what happens to schools that decide to reduce ability grouping and tracking (Wells and Oakes, 1996). According to these observers, two obstacles are especially clear. One is the demand for differentiation from parents. The parents argued that same-age children differ too much in their preparation, skills, and interests to fit into a single mold, and they demanded differentiated curricula in the schools. According to Wells and Oakes, the other major obstacle to detracking is the pressure for differentiation from higher education. Colleges and universities give preference to students whose course choices reflect strong academic motivation and good academic preparation. Overall, Wells and Oakes's detracking vignettes are stories of difficulty and failure.

Although the first generation of ethnographic studies raised provocative questions about ability grouping, they did not provide scientific answers. The studies were simply too casual. Ethnographers documented some surface differences between tracks, but their conclusions about tracking differences were sometimes overstated, and their conclusions about causes of low achievement in vocational and general tracks were speculative at best. Ethnographers designed a second generation of studies to chart progress of untracking efforts, but their reports are largely a story of unfulfilled expectations. The studies suggest that untracking is a complicated and difficult business. On the basis of their recent ethnographic observations, for example, Gamoran and Weinstein (1998) concluded that untracking is a goal that is often desired but rarely achieved. According to Gamoran and Weinstein, when untracking is achieved, it brings no guarantee of high-quality instruction for everyone but instead may bring a low-level equality to all.

SUMMARY AND CONCLUSIONS

Grouping and tracking a studies come in all shapes and sizes. They vary in methodology, quality, and interpretation. Reviewers therefore must search a cluttered landscape to find out what the research says about grouping and tracking. When study results have been carefully summarized and organized, however, conclusions start to become clear.

The ethnographic studies of grouping appear to be higher in rhetorical than scientific value. Ethnographers have reported, for example, that in low-track classes the pace of instruction is slow, the curriculum is debased, and teachers are inexperienced. But careful scrutiny shows that the evidence for such charges is weak. Differences in instructional pace in tracked and untracked classes, for example, may be an appropriate teacher response to the preparation of students in these classes.

Findings from correlational analyses are also uncertain. Correlational analyses show that the achievement gap between students in upper and lower tracks is due mostly to student self-selection. A second, less important factor that may contribute to track differences in achievement is the different number of advanced courses in core subjects taken by students in collegiate versus noncollegiate tracks. A third factor may be the difference in the way that the same courses are taught for collegiate and noncollegiate students. Correlational analyses do not provide conclusive evidence on the second and third factors, however.

Experimental studies still seem to be the best guide to understanding the effects of grouping on children. Most of the older narrative reviews are nonquantitative and imprecise, and review conclusions seem to reflect the educational philosophies of their times. Careful meta-analytic reviews of the experimental evidence on grouping provide a sounder basis for conclusions.

These meta-analyses show that effects of grouping and tracking vary by program and by student. XYZ grouping effects are clearly different from effects of other grouping programs. XYZ programs usually have negligible effects on the achievement of students in middle and low groups and small effects on the achievement of students in high groups. In addition, slower students may show a slight rise in self-esteem when placed in homogeneous classes while faster students may suffer a slight drop in self-esteem when placed with other high achievers. The lack of differentiated curricula in high, middle, and low groups likely accounts for the limited effects of XYZ programs on student achievement.

Evaluation results are very different for programs in which groups follow curricula adjusted to their skill levels. Cross-grade and within-class grouping programs in reading and arithmetic, for example, adjust curricula to group skills, and these programs make important contributions to student achievement. Gains of one standard deviation in test scores of slower students are common.

The gains associated with advanced and accelerated classes are especially large. Classes in which talented children cover four grades in three years, for example, boost achievement levels a good deal. Enriched classes boost student achievement by more moderate amounts. The average boost from these classes is four months on a grade-equivalent scale.

These conclusions are obviously quite different from the well-known conclusions about grouping reached by Oakes (1985). Oakes concluded that students in the top tracks gain nothing from grouping and that other students suffer clear and consistent disadvantages, including loss of academic ground, self-esteem, and ambition. Oakes also concluded that tracking is unfair to students because it denies them their right to a common curriculum. She therefore called for the detracking of American schools.

Tracking and grouping effects are far more variable than Oakes suggests. Sweeping statements about *the* effect of grouping and tracking may make good rhetoric but poor science. Recent ethnographic studies show that school administrators who embrace detracking as a goal have seldom been able to implement it in their schools. Opposition from stakeholders and requirements of American colleges and universities have proved to be major obstacles to detracking. On the basis of site visits, experts have concluded that untracking brings no guarantee of high-quality instruction for everyone but may instead lead all to a common level of educational mediocrity.

QUESTIONS FOR THOUGHT AND DISCUSSION

1. Summarize the four twentieth-century "pictures" of educational trends/fads that affected tracking and grouping.

2. What are the differences between ethnographic, correlational, and experimental studies?

3. What's the difference between XYZ grouping, within-class grouping, between-class grouping, and tracking?

4. Comment on the evidence used by Jeannie Oakes (and others) to argue for the detracking movement. Do you feel it is sound? Do you agree with her arguments (or part of her arguments)?

5. Based on Kulik's article and your own feelings, what do you conclude about the virtues of tracking and ability grouping—especially in regard to gifted students?

REFERENCES

Ball, S. J. (1981). *Beachside Comprehensive: A case-study of a secondary school.* Cambridge: Cambridge University Press.

Braddock II, J. H. (1990). Tracking the middle grades: National patterns of grouping for instruction. *Phi Delta Kappan, 71,* 445–449.

Cohen, J. (1977). *Statistical power analysis for the behavioral sciences* (rev. ed.). New York: Academic Press.

Coleman, J., Campbell, E., Hobson, C., McPartland, J., Mood, A., Wienfield, F., & York, R. (1966). *Equality of educational opportunity.* Washington, DC: U.S. Government Printing Office.

Courtis, S. A. (1925). Ability-grouping in Detroit schools. In G. M. Whipple (Ed.), *The ability grouping of pupils.* 35th Yearbook of the National Society for the Study of Education (Part I, pp. 44–47). Bloomington, IL: Public School Publishing.

Eash, M. J. (1961). Grouping: What have we learned. *Educational Leadership, 18,* 429–434.

Ekstrom, R. B. (1961). Experimental studies of homogeneous grouping: A critical review. *School Review, 69,* 216–226.

Findley, W. G., & Bryan, M. (1971). *Ability grouping: 1970 Status, impact, and alternatives.* Athens: Center for Educational Improvement, University of Georgia. (ERIC Document Reproduction Service No. Ed 060–595).

Gamoran, A., & Berends, M. (1987). The effects of stratification in secondary schools: Synthesis of survey and ethnographic research. *Review of Educational Research, 57,* 415–435.

Gamoran, A., & Weinstein, M. (1998). Differentiation and opportunity in restructured schools. *American Journal of Education, 106,* 385–415.

Glass, G. V. (1976). Primary, secondary, and meta-analysis of research. *Educational Researcher, 5,* 3–8.

Goldberg, M. L. (1958). Recent research on the talented. *Teachers College Record, 60,* 150–163.

Gray, H. A., & Hollingworth, L. S. (1931). The achievement of gifted children enrolled and not enrolled in special opportunity classes. *Journal of Educational Research, 24,* 255–261.

Hargreaves, D. H. (1967). *Social relations in a secondary school.* London: Tinling.

Heathers, G. (1969). Grouping. In R. Ebel (Ed.), *Encyclopedia of educational research* (4th ed., pp. 559–570). New York: Macmillan.

Ingels, S. J., Scott, L. A., Taylor, J. R., Owings, J., & Quinn, P. (1998). *National Education Longitudinal Study of 1988 (NELS: 88), base year through second follow-up: Final methodology report.* Working paper series. Washington, DC: U.S. Department of Education, Office of Educational Research and Improvement, National Center for Education Statistics (ERIC Document Reproduction Service No. ED 434 129).

Jencks, C. (1972). *Inequality.* New York: Basic Books.

Keliher, A. C. (1931). *A critical study of homogeneous grouping.* New York: Bureau of Publications, Teachers College, Columbia University.

Kulik, C.-L. C., & Kulik, J. A. (1982). Effects of ability grouping on secondary school students: A meta-analysis of evaluation findings. *American Educational Research Journal, 19,* 415–428.

Kulik, C.-L. C., & Kulik, J. A. (1984, August). *Effects of ability grouping on elementary school pupils: A meta-analysis.* Paper presented at the annual meeting of the American Psychological Association, Toronto (ERIC Document Reproduction Service No. ED 255 329).

Kulik, J. A. (1992). *An analysis of the research on ability grouping: Historical and contemporary perspectives.* Research-based decision making series. Storrs, CT: National Research Center on the Gifted and Talented, University of Connecticut (ERIC Document Reproduction Service No. ED 350777).

Kulik, J. A., & Kulik, C.-L. C. (1984). Effects of accelerated instruction on students. *Review of Educational Research, 54,* 409–426.

Kulik, J. A., & Kulik, C.-L. C. (1987). Effects of ability grouping on student achievement. *Equity and Excellence, 23,* 22–30.

Kulik, J. A., & Kulik, C.-L. C. (1992). Meta-analytic findings on grouping programs. *Gifted Child Quarterly, 36,* 73–77.

Lacey, C. (1970). *Hightown Grammar.* Manchester, England: Manchester University Press.

Linchevski, L., & Kutscher, B. (1998). Tell me with whom you're learning, and I'll tell you how much you've learned: Mixed-ability versus same-ability grouping in mathematics. *Journal for Research in Mathematics Education, 29,* 533–554.

Loveless, T. (1998). *The tracking and ability grouping debate.* Washington, DC: Thomas B. Fordham Foundation (ERIC Document Reproduction Service No. ED 422 445).

Loveless, T. (1999). *The tracking wars: State reform meets school policy.* Washington, DC: Brookings Institution.

McPartland, J. M., Coldiron, J. R., & Braddock, J. H. (1987). *School structures and classroom practices in elementary, middle, and secondary schools.* Baltimore: Center for Research on Elementary and Middle Schools, Johns Hopkins University (ERIC Document Reproduction Service No. ED 291 703).

Miller, W. S., & Otto, H. J. (1930). Analysis of experimental studies in homogeneous grouping. *Journal of Educational Research, 21,* 95–102.

Oakes, J. (1985). *Keeping track: How schools structure inequality.* New Haven: Yale University.

Page, R. N. (1991). *Lower-track classrooms: A curricular and cultural perspective.* New York: Teachers College Press.

Passow, A. H. (1958). Enrichment of education for the gifted. In N. Henry (Ed.), *Education for the gifted.* 57th Yearbook of the National Society for the Study of Education (part II, pp. 193–221). Chicago: University of Chicago Press.

Rees, D., Argys, L. M., & Brewer, D. J. (1996). Tracking in the United States: Descriptive statistics from NELS. *Economics of Education Review, 15*(1), 83–89.

Rosenbaum, J. E. (1976). *Making inequality.* New York: Wiley.

Singal, D. J. (1991, November). The other crisis in American education. *The Atlantic Monthly, 268,* 59–74.

Slavin, R. E. (1987). Ability grouping and student achievement in elementary schools: A best evidence synthesis. *Review of Educational Research, 57,* 293–336.

Slavin, R. E. (1990a). Ability grouping in secondary schools: A response to Hallinan. *Review of Educational Research, 60,* 505–507.

Slavin, R. E. (1990b). Achievement effects of ability grouping in secondary schools: A best evidence synthesis. *Review of Educational Research, 60,* 471–499.

Slavin, R. E., & Madden, N. A. (2000). Research on achievement outcomes of Success For All: A summary and response to critics. *Phi Delta Kappan, 82,* 38–40, 59–66.

Tannenbaum, A. J. (1958). History of interest in the gifted. In N. Henry (Ed.), *Education for the gifted.* 57th Yearbook of the National Society for the Study of Education (part II, pp. 21–38). Chicago: University of Chicago Press.

Turney, A. H. (1931). The status of ability grouping. *Educational Administration and Supervision, 17,* 110–127.

Wells, A. S., & Oakes, J. (1996). Potential pitfalls of systemic reform: Early lessons from research on detracking. *Sociology of Education, Special Issue,* 135–143.

BIBLIOGRAPHY

Alexander, K. L., Cook, M. A., & McDill, E. L. (1978). Curriculum tracking and educational stratification. *American Sociological Review, 43,* 47–66.

Gamoran, A., & Mare, R. D. (1989). Secondary school tracking and educational inequality: Compensation, reinforcement, or neutrality. *American Journal of Sociology, 94,* 146–183.

Garet, M. S., & DeLany, B. (1988). Students courses, and stratification. *Sociology of Education, 61,* 61–77.

Goodlad, J. I. (1984). *A place called school.* New York: McGraw-Hill.

Hauser, R. M., Sewell, w. H., & Alwin, D. F. (1976). High school effect on achievement. In W. H. Sewell, R. M. Hauser & D. Featherman (Eds.), *Schooling and achievement in American society.* New York: Academic Press.

Heyns, B. (1974). Social selection and stratification within schools. *American Journal of Sociology, 79,* 1434–1451.

Kulik, J. A. (1998). Curricular tracks and high school vocational education. In A. Gamoran (Ed.), *The quality of vocational education. Background papers from the 1994 National Assessment of Vocational Education* (pp. 65–132). Washington, DC: U.S. Department of Education, Office of Educational Research and Improvement, National Institute on Postsecondary Education, Libraries, and Lifelong Learning.

Mosteller, F., Light, R. J., & Sachs, J. A. (1996). Sustained inquiry in education: Lessons from skill grouping and class size. *Harvard Educational Review, 66,* 797–842.

Rosenbaum, J. E. (1980). Track misperceptions and frustrated college plans: An analysis of the effects of tracks and track perceptions in the National Longitudinal Survey. *Sociology of Education, 53,* 74–88.

Worlton, J. T. (1928). The effect of homogeneous classification on the scholastic achievement of bright pupils. *Elementary School Journal, 28,* 336–345.

22

Cooperative Learning and High Ability Students

ANN ROBINSON,   *University of Arkansas-Little Rock*

It has been slightly over a decade since Robinson (1990b) and Slavin (1990) debated the issue of cooperative learning and talented students. At that time, little attention was given to the effects of this grouping strategy on high ability learners by the general research community or by advocates of cooperative learning. In the interval, what new research, observations, or insights have emerged to inform our thinking and our practices in the future?

This chapter will trace developments in the research focus on cooperative learning and talented learners from 1990 to the present, review some recent studies that inform previously examined issues, and pose new questions for gifted educators and for cooperative learning advocates.

Changes in Focus and Frequency of Research on Cooperative Learning and High Ability Learners

In 1990, the research on the effects of cooperative learning on talented students, or the more generally defined high ability learners, was virtually nonexistent (Robinson, 1990a, 1991). In a search of the PSYCHINFO and ERIC databases prior to 1990, only one empirical study was located (Smith, Johnson, & Johnson, 1982). It did not focus on the needs, effects, or issues of talented learners and contained only a subsample of fourteen talented students. In an update, these two databases were searched again from the years 1989 through July 1994 (Robinson, 1997). The combined PSYCHINFO and ERIC searches located six published articles with qualitative or quantitative data. A third search from 1994 to 2001, conducted for this chapter, resulted in

twenty-two data-based journal articles. The three searches chart an increase in the number of empirical studies that address the effects of cooperative learning on talented students. On closer inspection, the development of the research base across time also reveals shifts in the focus of the research as well as some constants. These trends are summarized in Table 22.1.

When examined across time, some issues have diminished in importance; some have held steady. Other issues have moved to center stage within the last five years. First, high ability learners and identified gifted students have received increased attention from researchers and cooperative learning advocates. Second, the general research literature on cooperative learning has begun to include higher, level achievement outcomes. While early research was overwhelmingly dependent on basic skill definitions of achievement, some recent studies (e.g., Barron, 2000; Fuchs et al., 2000) used a "complex task." Thus, these two early concerns have diminished in importance because they are beginning to be addressed.

One area of concern that has been steady since the early 1990s is the motivation loss in groups and the concomitant problem of debilitating experiences for high ability learners. These motivational concerns are best captured by the "free rider" and "sucker" effects. Also, classic social psychology studies have led to newer research on student interactions and behavior (Fuchs et al., 1996; Webb, Nemer, Chizhik, & Sugrue, 1998), cooperative and competitive goal structures (Feldhusen, Dai, & Clinkenbeard, 2000), and student preferences (Li & Adamson, 1992; Ramsay & Richards, 1997; Rizza, 1998).

Table 22.1   Trends in the Research on Cooperative Learning and Talented Students.

	Prior to 1990	*1989 to 1994*	*1994 to 2001*
Data bases searched	PSYCHINFO and ERIC	PSYCHINFO and ERIC	PSYCHINFO and ERIC
No. of entries	6	41	58
No. of published entries with data	1	6	10
Representative published studies	Smith, Johnson, & Johnson, 1982	Clinkenbeard, 1991 Elmore & Zenus, 1994 Li & Adamson, 1992 Matthews, 1992	Feldhusen, Dai, & Clinkenbeard, 2000 Kenny et al., 1994 Fuchs et al., 1998 Melser, 1999
Issues and concerns related to talented learners	Lack of attention to high ability learners in the research Poorly defined samples of high achievers Weak comparisons Emphasis on low level outcomes Contradictory results for higher level outcomes (summarized in Robinson, 1990a) Time is a fixed resource; other opportunities are lost (summarized in Robinson, 1990b)	Curriculum access; time in cooperative learning groups may restrict accelerated pace (Robinson, 1991 & 1994) Student interactions reveal negative responses to group learning from some learners Motivation losses from free rider and sucker effects Use of cooperative assessments may mask individual student learning (summarized in Robinson, 1997)	Increased use of cooperative learning dyads with high achiever tutoring low achiever Focus on ability composition of dyads and groups Prevalence in classrooms Implementation fidelity No studies of sucker effects or other sources of motivation loss for high ability learners

Finally, one issue is neither new nor unexpected: Grouping again takes center stage in discussions of cooperative learning and high ability students. Studies of group composition (Fuchs et al., 2000; Melser, 1999; Webb et al., 1998; Webb, Welner, & Zuniga, 2001) take at least three directions: homogeneous versus heterogeneous groups, dyads versus triads and other size conformations, and structured (assigning roles to children) versus unstructured groups.

Differences in Motivation and Behavior in Groups

Motivation of students in groups has been a steady concern of both cooperative learning advocates and critics. Not all students respond the same to cooperative learning groups. Some students are active; others are passive. Because engagement can affect achievement and because engagement is an overt marker of student motivation, the conditions that underlie student disengagement and passivity in groups are important considerations. A related concern is what leads some students to dominate groups. Because dominance, control, and "advantaging themselves" are frequent criticisms leveled at talented learners (Johnson & Johnson, 1992, 1993; King, 1993), interactions and behaviors of high ability students in cooperative learning groups are also of interest.

Lessons from Social Psychology

In terms of disengagement and passivity, the body of literature that examines motivation losses in groups has relevance for the ways in which cooperative learning operates in classroom practice. Early researchers in group process noted that under certain conditions, persons working in groups tended to exert less effort. Reduced effort or motivation in turn resulted in lowered productivity.

Social Loafing. One branch of the research on group behavior and motivation losses in groups was based on the concept of *social loafing* (Karau & Williams, 1993). In a series of experiments involving persons pulling on ropes in a tug-of-war task, a German psychologist, Ringelmann (after whom the Ringelmann Effect was named) noted that as the size of the group increased, individual members of the team reduced their efforts (Latane, Williams, & Harkins, 1979). Other researchers noted that in matters of altruism, bystanders in large groups were less likely to assist someone in distress if the bystanding group was large rather than small. It was assumed that the diffusion of individual responsibility encouraged people to let others step forward, or at least inhibited them from doing so themselves.

Ringelmann's work was further developed by social psychologists who proposed two related phenomena to explain the loss of motivation in groups. These are the *free-rider effect* and the less frequently cited *sucker effect*. Both are relevant to the experiences of talented learners in cooperative learning groups.

Free-rider effect. The free-rider effect occurs when the possibility arises that some other member of the group can and will provide what is needed, thus making one's own contribution to the group unnecessary. In other words, an individual group member

may not contribute because he or she does not perceive a need to do so. Both Johnson and Johnson (1992) and Slavin (1992) noted the possibility of free-rider effects, particularly in cooperative learning models in which there is little individual accountability. Slavin (1992) commented that filling out one copy of a worksheet or turning in one group product are examples of cooperative learning practices that invite free riding.

While the free rider is usually assumed to be the lowest performing or least motivated member of the group, a series of experiments by Kerr and Bruun (1983) demonstrated that different group members exerted effort or free rode under different task conditions. When the group's evaluation depended on the highest score, high ability members worked harder; when the worst score defined the group's evaluation, the low ability members worked harder. Thus, both high and low ability members would free ride under certain conditions, even when their contributions were identifiable.

Sucker Effect. The sucker effect was suggested by Orbell and Dawes (1981) to explain a second source of motivation loss in groups. If there is a possibility that a member can free ride, there is also a danger that other group members will feel forced to carry the free rider. Orbell and Dawes hypothesized that people find it so aversive to be played for a sucker that they will reduce their own contributions to the group in order to avoid exploitation.

Kerr (1983) designed a series of experiments to determine the existence of such an effect. Although he studied college students working with a motor task rather than an academic one, the sucker effect clearly operated. In fact, it was so potent that capable partners "sometimes preferred to fail at the task rather than to be a sucker and carry a free rider" (p. 823). Further, while the free-rider effect was most likely to operate at the beginning of a set of learning tasks, *the sucker effect was more powerful at the end of them.*

It should be noted that most group members were tolerant of low-performing individuals when they perceived the low performance to be due to low ability rather than low effort. In short-term tasks, they willingly carried a low-performing, low-ability member. However, *high performing* members did not carry low performing, low-effort members and would fail themselves rather than exert effort.

Robinson and Clinkenbeard (1993) suggested that the sucker effect has implications for the motivation of high-attaining students in several cooperative learning models. A plausible, though untested, hypothesis is that the cumulative effects over time of a free-riding member in a cooperative learning group might depress the performance or encourage the disengagement of previously high achieving, highly motivated members. The effect might be especially potent if a high achieving member felt powerless to affect unmotivated members of the group or to change group affiliation.

What is the state of the evidence concerning the operation of free-rider and sucker effects in cooperative learning groups? Studies that specifically examine these effects in a tightly controlled setting or in a naturalistic classroom environment are yet to emerge. However, the evidence continues to mount in some field studies of cooperative learning that student passivity does occur in groups (King, 1993; Mandel, 1991), and that it occurs for a variety of reasons. For example, Mulryan (1992) reported that fifth- and sixth-grade students responded differentially to cooperative learning. The major finding of her study was that "some students, mainly low achievers, manifested a high level of passive behavior in cooperative small groups" (p. 261). However, she identified some high achieving students who also were passive. According to Mulryan, these students could be characterized as despondent, bored, or "intellectual snobs." Interview transcripts indicate that one despondent student was passive because another group member "says mean things." A bored student indicated that the task was too easy. A student that Mulryan characterized as an intellectual snob expressed frustration because the task was easy for him but difficult for others in the group, thus slowing him down.

In a participant observation study, Mandel (1991) noted that students in the Group Investigation model of cooperative learning presented both high and low interaction in both cooperative learning individual work and in more traditional kinds of individual work. Those who emerged as leaders in the group discussion portion of the Group Investigation model tended to be highly interactive in both cooperative and noncooperative, traditional individual work periods. Students who were nonparticipants in the group discussion portion of the model tended to exhibit low interaction with other students in both cooperative and individual work. Mandel (1991) concluded that students' cooperative behaviors in the group were influenced by their personality rather than by their participation in cooperative learning.

Task Structures and Goal Structures

The way a teacher organizes a cooperative learning group can affect the disengagement or participation of members in the group. In terms of organizing students for learning in the classroom, teachers can vary the structure of the task and the kind of goal or incentive they wish to use. These differences have implications for all learners, and high ability learners are no exception.

Specifically, one aspect of cooperative learning is often confused; task structure and goal structure are frequently confounded. It is important to disentangle these two aspects of learning organization because some combinations of task and goal structures may better address the needs of talented learners than others. Good and Brophy (2000) provide a useful framework for understanding the differences between cooperative tasks and cooperative goals. By constructing a three by three matrix, they clarify that individual, cooperative, and competitive tasks can have a variety of goal structures—also individual, cooperative, and competitive (Good & Brophy, 2000).

According to Good and Brophy (2000), task structures are defined as the nature of the task and its accompanying working conditions. For example, an individual task structure requires students to work alone. In the early work of Johnson and Johnson (1992), a student was given a packet of materials, instructed not to talk with anyone, and asked to complete the work on his or her own. A cooperative task structure requires students to work together, to assist one another, and on many occasions to complete a group product. The third type of task structure is competitive. These types of tasks are usually contests, and they can be completed individually (e.g., a spelling bee) or as a group (e.g., debate teams).

Task structures differ from goal structures. These differences are important and are a source of disagreement among cooperative learning advocates. For example, the Johnsons are opposed to competitive goal structures; Slavin incorporates competitive goal structures into some of his models, in particular Teams-Games-Tournaments.

Goal structures are less obvious in the classroom than task structures, but they are crucial to understanding the effects of cooperative learning on the motivation of learners. Like tasks, goal structures can be individual, cooperative, or competitive. If a goal structure is competitive, the reward that a student receives (a grade, a certificate, praise from the teacher) *depends upon the outcome of the competition.* Winners receive rewards; losers do not. If a goal structure is cooperative, the reward that a student receives *depends on group performance.* For example, if a student's grade depends upon her own individual quiz score *and* the added quiz scores of everyone else in the team, the goal structure is cooperative.

If the goal structure is individual, the reward that a student receives *depends upon her own performance.* For example, if a student completes an assignment and does well, she will receive a high grade based on that performance irrespective of the performances of other students on that task. The reward for this student is completely independent of others. If all students in this classroom complete an assignment and if all students do well, all students will receive a high grade. In the individual goal structure, students are not competing for scarce resources, as is the case in being graded "on the curve." The task structure–goal structure matrix in Table 22.2 demonstrates how an individual goal structure can be accomplished through all three types of tasks—individual, cooperative, and competitive. Table 22.2 illustrates the relationship between task structure and goal structure, and gives an example classroom activity for each possible combination.

In regard to the task structures and the goal structures, the key issue for educators concerned about high ability learners is to identify which combinations of structures are least likely to invite free-rider and sucker effects, and which are most likely to preserve some elements of choice in topic, materials, and interaction. It is clear from examining Table 22.2 that individual goal structures do not have to be operationalized in a lonely and punishing way, as is generally the case in the research carried out by the Johnsons and their associates. Many students enjoy reading a self-selected book quietly and completing a related art project for display; both task and goal are individually structured. Students retain choice over subject matter and pacing in the reading activity.

In terms of a cooperative task with an individual goal structure, many students enjoy group brainstorming and discussions, but prefer to work on an independent investigation related to the group's overall presentation. They have the opportunity to offer and receive explanations concerning the material, to pro-

vide feedback, and to get assistance. However, their grade depends upon their own presentation and therefore upon their own effort. It is likely that high ability learners will worry less about shouldering the workload in a group task structure that permits an individual goal structure. Again, students retain some choice over subject matter and pacing in the combination group and independent investigation activity. They are more likely to feel they have control over the quality of their final product and do not have to compensate for a low effort member.

Competitive tasks and goal structures are the least favored options of cooperative learning advocates, but even competitive structures have some interesting implications for high ability learners. There is evidence that high ability learners hold a differentiated view of competition. In a factor analysis study of preferences for cooperation and competition, high ability learners attending a university summer program responded to a goal orientation questionnaire (Feldhusen, Dai, & Clinkenbeard, 2000). Two factors emerged: Competition-Outcome and Competition-Process. Competition-Outcome is the more standard interpretation of competition by cooperative learning advocates; it is the positive feeling associated with outperforming others. However, the second factor, Competition-Process, emphasized feelings of being challenged to improve oneself or of enjoying the excitement of competition rather than the ultimate outcome. Given the more elaborate structure of competition for high ability learners, Feldhusen, Dai, and Clinkenbeard suggested that further research should investigate student interpretations of individualistic learning as well.

Rather than viewing individual learning as lonely, high ability learners may have a richer interpretation of individual tasks and individual goal structures. Given the stated preferences and positive effects of individual learning for high ability students (Clinkenbeard, 1989; Csikszentmihalyi, Rathunde, & Whalen, 1993; Li & Adamson, 1992), this would be an important area for investigation.

Differences in the Composition of Groups

As research on cooperative learning progresses, more studies are available on the effects of group composition and related behaviors of the members to outcomes such as individual achievement, group

Table 22.2   Example Activities by Task Structure and Goal Structure

Task Structures	Goal Structures		
	Individual Goal	Cooperative Goal	Competitive Goal
Individual (Student works alone)	Student selects a book to read and completes a diorama based on the book. Dioramas, which have been assessed with a rubric, are displayed to encourage classmates to read other students' book selections.	Students in a cooperative base group individually investigate mapmaking at a computer terminal. Then each student in the support groups designs and completes a map on her own for an individual grade. Individual grades are summed for a team score. All teams who have all members completing the map receive a certificate.	Each student in class completes her mathematics seatwork. The student who finishes first and has all answers correct receives praise and a small prize from the teacher.
Cooperative (Students work in groups)	A group of five students brainstorms subtopics for a unit on the Harlem Renaissance. Each student in the group selects a subtopic (artists, jazz musicians, a specific author, race relations, New York neighborhoods) for investigation and reports the findings back to the group. The teacher assesses each student's oral report individually with a rubric.	Groups of students read a common set of materials on the Harlem Renaissance and are directed by the teacher to become an expert on an assigned subtopic. Students meet as experts to discuss their topic and return to their group to teach their topic to their group mates. Each student in the group completes a quiz and all scores are summed for a team grade which each student receives.	After the teacher presents material on the Harlem Renaissance, heterogeneous groups of students study the material together, tutor, and quiz one another for the week. On Friday, students are assigned to tables and compete against one another on written questions. Students earn points by answering correctly or challenging others at their table. Points won by each student in the study group are summed to determine the team score.
Competitive (Students compete with one another)	Students participate in an old-fashioned spelling bee. The winner of the bee gets to select the kind of treat provided to the class.	Groups of students select a subtopic on the Harlem Renaissance and complete a group product. Student judges organize a "product fair" and recognize the highest rated team with applause and a blue ribbon.	After studying the Harlem Renaissance, teams of students compete in a Quiz Bowl competition on the topic. The winning team selects the kind of treat provided to the class.

productivity, and student cognitive and social interactions. Two areas of research on group composition have particular implications for talented students: the ability differences in the group and the size of the group.

Cooperative Learning Group Membership

Research on group membership has mixed effects depending on the student population of interest. Most standard cooperative learning models expect that students will be grouped heterogeneously; in fact, such grouping is a stated goal of many advocates. However, grouping arrangements do not have uniform effects on all students. In a review, Webb and Palincsar (1996) concluded that when a high ability, low ability, and medium ability student were grouped together, the high ability student tutored the low ability student, and the medium ability student was left out of the group interaction. They concluded that medium ability students learn most in homogeneous groups.

Some studies that analyzed for ability differences reported that high ability students performed better in homogeneous than in heterogeneous groups (Fuchs et al., 1998; Hooper & Hannafin, 1988; Webb et al., 1998). Another study reported that high ability students perform equally well in both kinds of grouping arrangements (Kenny, Archambault, & Hallmark, 1995), although talented students completed more work; that is, the group was more productive in the homogeneous condition.

It is important to note that the studies comparing the effects of group composition on achievement in cooperative learning groups employ the same tasks, curriculum, or assessments for all students. Thus, the effects of accelerative opportunities on the achievement of homogeneously composed groups or dyads are not known. Given that acceleration without cooperative learning produces large effects for talented learners (Kulik & Kulik, 1984; Swiatek & Benbow, 1991), it might be hypothesized that homogeneously composed high ability cooperative learning groups engaged in an accelerated curriculum would produce even greater achievement gains than those groups working on common grade level tasks.

Group Size, Cooperative Learning, and Talented Learners

In contrast to the earlier reviews of cooperative learning, which focused on models that used groups of three or more (Robinson, 1990b, 1991), recent research has included dyads. Fuchs et al. (2000) noted that the research on group size is small; however, the researchers noted that dyads tended to score higher on measures of participation, helpfulness, cooperation, quality of talk, and quality of task performance. Dyads in which a high achieving student was paired with a low achieving student produced more gains than when a medium achieving student supplied the explanations to the low attaining student. In contrast, cognitive conflict and resolution were more likely for non-high ability students in larger groups where there were opportunities for high attaining students to interact with those who challenged their thinking. Fuchs et al. concluded that "high achievers, when working on complex material, should have ample opportunity to work in small groups with fellow high achievers so that cognitive conflict and resolution can occur" (p. 206).

In the move from groups to dyads, particularly dyads that include a high attaining and a low attaining student, the assurances by cooperative learning advocates that all students contribute equally to the achievement of the group is contradicted by some of their own studies. A comparative review of literature on peer tutoring and cooperative learning studies employing dyads would serve to identify the similarities and the differences between these two lines of investigation.

Group Productivity and Cooperative Learning Groups

Increasingly, group productivity is suggested as a reason for cooperative learning in the school setting (Webb et al., 1998). However, not all cooperative learning researchers view group productivity as the outcome of interest. In a review, Slavin (1992) commented that some cooperative learning studies confuse group productivity with individual learning. His example has much resonance for educators concerned with high ability learners. He explained,

> Leonard Bernstein and I could write a brilliant concerto together, about twice as good as the average of the concerto he could write and the one I could write working separately (I can barely read music). But how much would we *learn* from working cooperatively? I doubt that Leonard Bernstein would learn much about writing concertos from me, and I might do better to take a course on music than to start by watching a composer write a concerto. The point of this example is to illustrative that *learning is completely different from "group" productivity.* It may well be that working in a

group under certain circumstances does increase the learning of the individuals in that group more than would working under other arrangements, but a measure of group productivity provides no evidence one way or the other on this; only an individual learning measure that cannot be influenced by group help can indicate which incentive or task structure is best. Learning takes place only between the ears of the learner. If a group produces a beautiful lab report, but only a few students really contributed to it, it is unlikely that the group as a whole learned more than they might have learned had they each had to write their own (perhaps less beautiful) lab reports under an individualistic or competitive incentive structure. In fact, what often happens in cooperative groups that produce a single report, worksheet, or other group product is that the most able group members simply do the work or give the answers to their teammates, which may be the most efficient strategy for group productivity but is a poor strategy for individual learning (pp. 150–151).

In other words, if a teacher wants to know what a student knows and is able to do, a measure of individual learning is necessary. Hiding the low achievement of individual students by placing them in cooperative learning groups with a high ability member who can and will do the work for a group grade or a group product will make the class averages look better. However, it won't help the low attaining student (who still doesn't know the material) or the high attaining student (who might develop resentment for carrying the instructional load).

Group productivity is useful in adult work groups in corporate America, where the goal is to maximize productivity and company profits. However, classrooms are not board rooms. Educators are able to assist students only when they know what *each* student is able to do, so they can plan instruction to take every student, including the talented learner, further along an educational trajectory. In a learning setting with children and adolescents, group productivity measures can mask a multitude of mistakes and passive responses from students.

Prevalence and Teacher Fidelity

Given that both cooperative learning advocates and critics voice concerns about motivation losses and other problems, if models are not implemented properly, how extensive might the problem be for high ability youth? Is cooperative learning being used in a balanced way? How often are teachers implementing cooperative learning in the classroom? How are they

doing it? Prevalence studies are not numerous, but two recent surveys are suggestive.

McManus and Gettinger (1996) surveyed a small sample of third grade teachers and found widespread and daily use of cooperative learning. In terms of content areas, reading was most frequently mentioned with 24 out of 26 teachers (92 percent) reporting its use. In addition, 88 percent of the teachers reported they received formal training. However, when teachers were surveyed about their use of two features considered important, their responses diverged. The two features were heterogeneous grouping and an interdependent reward structure (group rewards depend on individual achievement), a feature considered crucial by Slavin. The teachers reported using homogeneous grouping "very often." In contrast, they reported using group rewards for individual contributions infrequently. They were more likely to implement group rewards for a group product.

Similar findings were reported in a study of 85 elementary teachers by Antil, Jenkins, Wayne, and Vadasy (1998). Again, teachers reported using cooperative learning widely, but without the forms of individual accountability designed to document individual learning and minimize free-rider effects. One intriguing survey result is that in an observational study, Meloth and Deering (1994) concluded that children were likely to share their learning strategies with one another if simply asked to do so. The complex interdependent reward structure limited student communication in the groups.

Given that teachers do not often implement the complexities of cooperative learning, and that some of the procedures for invoking goal structures reduce choices for students, further thought is necessary to uncover which aspects of cooperative learning are truly necessary.

SUMMARY AND CONCLUSIONS

Research on cooperative learning continues to be important to our understanding of the effects of this grouping strategy on talented learners. While high ability students are not the population of interest to cooperative learning advocates, there has been an increase in the numbers of studies that investigate the effects on students identified as "gifted" or described as "high ability."

First, some areas originally identified as weaknesses in the research literature on cooperative learning have begun to be addressed. Although the majority of the studies continue to use basic skill achievement outcomes, a few of the newer studies have included complex learning tasks.

Second, some concerns suggested in an earlier review (see Robinson, 1997) continue to emerge as problems for high ability learners. Studies that document student passivity in groups lend research support to the concern that free-rider effects operate in cooperative learning groups. Unfortunately, a second type of motivation loss, disengagement due to the sucker effect, has not been systematically investigated. Whether the sucker effect manifests itself in the strict sense of failure to participate and complete assignments or whether it takes the form of resentment, avoidance of interaction, or cheating is not known.

Third, some pesky issues appear without fail. The studies of group composition indicate that on common tasks, homogeneous high ability dyads and groups outperform other small-group arrangements. In addition, high ability learners in homogeneous groups generally, but not always, outperform high ability learners in heterogeneous groups. Given the concerns by cooperative learning advocates that high ability learners "advantage" themselves by taking over the explainer function in heterogeneous groups, perhaps the balance of power in terms of intellectual leadership on a task might be more easily obtained in homogeneously grouped, high ability dyads.

Finally, new questions about cooperative learning and high ability learners have emerged. For example, surveys and interviews documenting the use of cooperative learning in classrooms, along with the confusion of task structures and goal structures, support concern for the neglect of individual task structures with talented learners. Specifically, can some of the benefits touted for cooperative learning be achieved for talented students without the cooperative goal structure? For example, could a cooperative task foster social construction of knowledge even if the cooperative task is paired with an individual rather than a cooperative goal structure? Could a cooperative task with an individual goal structure ameliorate some of the burdensome aspects of group work for high ability learners? Could individual accountability be achieved for all students through a cooperative task with an individual goal structure?

There is much to understand about the complex dynamics of cooperative learning. Children may appear to be busily engaged, but on closer inspection their interactions may or may not be productive. Also, if asked about their preferences for cooperative learning, few socially aware children will give answers that make them look unfriendly to others or that might encourage the teacher to restrict their access to chatting with their mates. Future research should include observational studies in the classroom. Additional focus is needed on the ways and the reasons that free-rider and sucker effects develop and manifest themselves. Features of cooperative learning like heterogeneous grouping and interdependent rewards, which have been deemed crucial by cooperative learning advocates, need to be examined more critically, particularly in light of emerging evidence that teachers do not implement the models strictly. To date, it may be that we have treated cooperative learning as if it were a sausage. It is cheap and can be tasty if the diner does not think too much about what's in it. On closer inspection, however, not all of its questionable ingredients should be ingested.

QUESTIONS FOR THOUGHT AND DISCUSSION

1. Summarize the key features of cooperative learning and contrast them with another type of small-group learning activity, such as creative problem solving.

2. Explain the 3×3 matrix summarizing task structure and goal structure (Table 22.1). Which two or three combinations would suit your teaching style and personality the best? Explain.

3. Imagine you are a teacher who loves to use cooperative learning groups. How might you try to accommodate the needs and abilities of gifted students in using cooperative groups?

4. Itemize every advantage and disadvantage of cooperative groups for high ability students that you can find in Robinson's chapter. Explain each briefly. Feel free to add some of your own.

5. Explain the advantages of dyads.

REFERENCES

Antil, L. R., Jenkins, J. R., Wayne, S. K., & Vadasy, P. F. (1998). Cooperative learning: Prevalence, conceptualizations, and the relation between research and practice. *American Educational Research Journal, 35,* 419–454.

Barron, B. (2000). Problem solving in video-based microworld: Collaborative and individual outcomes of high-achieving sixth-grade students. *Journal of Educational Psychology, 92,* 391–398.

Clinkenbeard, P. R. (1989). Motivation to win: Negative aspects of success at competition. *Journal for the Education of the Gifted, 12,* 293–305.

Csikszentmihalyi, M., Rathunde, K., & Whalen, S. (1993). *Talented teenagers: The roots of success and failure.* Cambridge: Cambridge University Press.

Feldhusen, J. F., Dai, D. Y., & Clinkenbeard, P. R. (2000). Dimensions of competitive and cooperative learning among gifted learners. *Journal for the Education of the Gifted, 23,* 328–342.

Fuchs, L. S., Fuchs, D., Hamlett, C. L., & Karns, K. (1998). High-achieving students' interactions and performance on complex mathematical tasks as a function of homogeneous and heterogeneous pairings. *American Educational Research Journal, 35,* 227–268.

Fuchs, L. S., Fuchs, D., Karns, K., Hamlett, C. L., Dutka, S., & Katzaroff, M. (1996). The relation between student ability and the quality and effectiveness of explanations. *American Educational Research Journal, 33,* 631–664.

Fuchs, L. S., Fuchs, D., Kazdan, S., Karns, K., Calhoon, M. B., Hamlett, C. L., & Hewlett, S. (2000). Effects of workgroup structure and size on student productivity during collaborative work on complex tasks. *Elementary School Journal, 100*(3), 183–212.

Good, T. L., & Brophy, J. L. (2000). *Looking in classrooms.* (8th ed.). New York: Longman.

Hooper, S., & Hannafin, M. J. (1988). Cooperative CBI: The effects of heterogeneous versus homogeneous grouping on the learning of progressively complex concepts. *Journal of Educational Computing Research, 4,* 413–424.

Johnson, D. W., & Johnson, R. T. (1992). Positive interdependence: Key to effective cooperation. In R. Hertz-Lazarowitz & N. Miller (Eds.), *Interaction in cooperative groups: The theoretical anatomy of group learning* (pp. 174–199). New York: Cambridge University Press.

Johnson, D. W., & Johnson, R. T. (1993). Gifted students illustrate what isn't cooperative learning. *Educational Leadership, 50,* 60–61.

Karau, S. J., & Williams, K. D. (1993). Social loafing: A meta-analytic review and theoretical integration. *Journal of Personality and Social Psychology, 65,* 681–706.

Kenny, D. A., Archambault, F. X., & Hallmark, B. W. (1995). The effects of group composition on gifted and non-gifted elementary students in cooperative learning groups. Storrs, CT: National Research Center on the Gifted and Talented, University of Connecticut.

Kerr, N. L. (1983). Motivation losses in small groups: A social dilemma analysis. *Journal of Personality and Social Psychology, 45,* 819–828.

Kerr, N. L., & Bruun, S. E. (1983). The dispensability of member effort and group motivation losses: Free-rider effects. *Journal of Personality and Social Psychology, 44,* 78–94.

King, L. H. (1993). High and low achievers' perceptions and cooperative learning in two small groups. *Elementary School Journal, 93,* 399–416.

Kulik, J. A., & Kulik, C.-L. C. (1984). Effects of accelerated instruction on students. *Review of Educational Research, 54,* 409–426.

Latane, B., Williams, K., & Harkins, S. (1979). Many hands make light the work: The causes and consequences of social loafing. *Journal of Personality and Social Psychology, 37,* 822–832.

Li, A. K. F., & Adamson, G. (1992). Gifted secondary students preferred learning style: Cooperative, competitive, or individualistic? *Journal for the Education of the Gifted, 16,* 46–54.

Mandel, S. (1991). *Responses to cooperative learning processes among elementary-age students.* Paper presented at the meeting of the American Educational Research Association.

McManus, S. M., & Gettinger, M. (1996). Teacher and students' evaluations of cooperative learning and observed interactive behaviors. *Journal of Educational Research, 90*(1), 13–31.

Meloth, M. S., & Deering, P. D. (1994). Task talk and task awareness under different cooperative learning conditions. *American Educational Research Journal, 31,* 138–165.

Melser, N. A. (1999). Gifted students and cooperative learning: A study of grouping strategies. *Roeper Review, 21,* 315.

Mulryan, C. M. (1992). Student passivity during cooperative small groups in mathematics. *Journal of Educational Research, 85,* 261–273.

Orbell, J., & Dawes, R. (1981). Social dilemmas. In G. Stephenson & J. H. Davis (Eds.), *Progress in applied social psychology, vol. 1,* (pp. 37–65). Chichester, UK: Wiley.

Ramsay, S. G., & Richards, H. C. (1997). Cooperative learning environments: Effects on academic attitudes of gifted students. *Gifted Child Quarterly, 41,* 160–168.

Rizza, M. G. (1998). Exploring successful learning with talented female adolescents. *Dissertation Absracts International, Section A., 58*(8-A): 3003.

Robinson, A. (1990a). Cooperation or exploitation? The argument against cooperative learning for talented students. *Journal for the Education of the Gifted, 14,* 9–27.

Robinson, A. (1990b). Response to Slavin: Cooperation, consistency, and challenge for academically talented youth. *Journal for the Education of the Gifted, 14,* 31–36.

Robinson, A. (1991). *Cooperative learning and the academically talented student.* Storrs, CT: National Research Center on the Gifted and Talented.

Robinson, A. (1997). Cooperative learning for talented students: Emergent issues and implications. In N. Colangelo & G. A. Davis (Eds.), *Handbook of gifted education* (2nd ed., pp. 243–252). Boston: Allyn & Bacon.

Robinson, A., & Clinkenbeard, P. R. (1993). *Cooperative learning and theories of motivation.* Paper presented at the Henry B. and Jocelyn Wallace National Research Symposium on Talent Development, Iowa City.

Slavin, R. E. (1990). Ability grouping, cooperative learning and the gifted. *Journal for the Education of the Gifted, 14,* 3–8.

Slavin, R. E. (1992). When and why does cooperative learning increase achievement? Theoretical and empirical perspectives. In R. Hertz-Lazarowitz & N. Miller (Eds.), *Interaction in cooperative groups: The theoretical anatomy of group learning* (pp. 145–173). New York: Cambridge University Press.

Smith, K., Johnson, D. W., & Johnson, R. (1982). The effects of cooperative and individualistic instruction on the achievement of handicapped, regular, and gifted students. *Journal of Social Psychology, 116,* 277–283.

Swiatek, M. A., & Benbow, C. P. (1991). A ten-year longitudinal follow-up of ability-matched accelerated and unaccelerated gifted students. *Journal of Educational Psychology, 83,* 528–538.

Webb, N. M., Nemer, K. M., Chizhik, A. W., & Sugrue, B. (1998). Equity issues in collaborative group assessment: Group composition and performance. *American Educational Research Journal, 35,* 607–651.

Webb, N. M., & Palincscar, A. S. (1996). Group processes in the classroom. In D. Berliner & R. Calfee (Eds.), *Handbook of Educational Psychology* (3rd ed., pp. 841–873). New York: Macmilan.

Webb, N., Welner, K. M., & Zuniga, S. (2001). *Short circuits or superconductors? Examining factors that encourage or undermine group learning and collaboration among high-ability students.* Paper presented at the meeting of the American Educational Research Association, Seattle, WA.

23

Evaluating Gifted Programs: A Broader Perspective

JAMES H. BORLAND, *Columbia University*

In preparing to write a chapter on evaluating gifted programs for this third edition of the *Handbook of Gifted Education*, I read the chapter on the same topic I wrote for the second edition. By and large, I liked what I had written, as far as it went. However, that was the problem; it did not go far enough. By "it" I mean my conception of what program evaluation was and what it properly encompassed. At the time I wrote the earlier chapter, I subscribed to a traditional and still prevalent view of evaluation as an activity whose focus and proper sphere of concern is bounded by the dimensions of the program targeted for evaluation.

According to this traditional view, if one were evaluating a gifted program in a certain school district, one's task would consist of learning what the goals of the program are (unless one were to undertake a goal-free evaluation, described later) and determining the extent to which the program meets those goals. Human and other factors external to the program itself (e.g., regular classroom teachers, administrators, the regular curriculum) would be considered only to the extent that they supply data that bear on the focal issue of program effectiveness, materially contribute to the program, or in some other way affect its ability to reach its goals. Summative conclusions, whether their intent be judgmental, informational, or facilitative of program improvement, are always in relation to the program itself: whether it is meeting *its* goals, what it is doing in relation to *its* mission, how it or the surrounding culture can be modified to help it come closer being what is described in *its* program plan.

Implicit in this was the notion that the proper focus was on how the program affected the students it served, and, to some extent, the program staff and parents of identified students. If the program met its goals, then, to quote Robert Browning, "God's in His heaven / All's right with the world!"

So what is wrong with this picture? What is wrong is the idea that a gifted program, or any other program for that matter, is a universe unto itself and that if a particular program is doing what it was created to do, that is all we ought to be concerned with. I have come to what should have been an obvious realization all along: Like any human enterprise, gifted programs exist in contexts, and these contexts matter. As Migotsky et al. (1997) argue, in discussing program evaluation,

> Evaluands should not be viewed as amoral objects that we prod and probe to squeeze out indicators of merit or worth. We concur with Schwandt (1997) that "evaluation practice now acknowledges the fact that programs are social, political, and moral constructions that embody the different (and often conflicting) interests and values of stakeholders." (p. 466)

What this suggests to me is that, in evaluating gifted programs, we need to broaden our focus beyond the program itself and to examine the larger effects the program is having on the system within which it operates (the school, the school district, the community) and on individuals not usually thought of as stakeholders (e.g., students not in the program but whose share of district resources is affected by allocation of resources to the gifted program). Let me give you an example of an experience, one of many, that has brought me to this view.

A few years ago, along with my Teachers College colleague Lisa Wright, I was asked to evaluate a gifted program in a school district in New York State. One unusual component of the program was a series of four Friday-through-Sunday field trips to such places as Boston and Washington, DC, during which the students stayed in hotels, took tours of historical sites, and wrote of their experiences. In the context established by the goals of this program, the field trips made sense.

However, these trips were also expensive. Since this was not an unusually wealthy school district, the allocation of resources was significant in the district-wide scheme of things. I believe that the educational benefits of these trips were such that they would not be limited only to students identified as gifted and that, given the opportunity, most, if not all, of the district's students would have enjoyed and learned from these trips. Thus, in the larger context of the school district as a whole, where resource allocation is essentially a zero-sum game, different questions arise that go beyond whether these trips are an effective means to the end of meeting the goals of the gifted program. These questions bear on how the trips affect others in the district and whether it is morally justifiable to limit participation in activities underwritten by public moneys to a small segment of all the students who would enjoy and benefit from those activities.

What I am suggesting is that the evaluation of gifted programs should be an expanded activity that looks not only at how well the program is functioning on its own terms, but what collateral effects the program is having in the larger contexts within which it operates and that, directly or indirectly, it affects. The danger of focusing only on the program itself and not the larger context is summed up in the title of an article on program evaluation by McCorkle (1986), "The Operation Was a Success but the Patient Died."

My conception of program evaluation requires, among other things, a reconceptualization of the term "stakeholder" as it is usually used in discussions of program evaluation. For example, students not in the gifted program described above might not have thought of themselves as stakeholders in the program, but since the lavish field-trip expenditures reduced the resources available to students not in the program, they clearly had an "interest" in the program.

Moreover, I want to suggest that we should expand the context of evaluation in another manner. Rather than limiting our focus to the merely instrumental—to such things as program effectiveness—we should take seriously the assertion of Migotsky et al. (1997) that programs are not "amoral objects" and Schwandt's (1997) statement that "evaluation prac-

tice now acknowledges the fact that programs are social, political, and moral constructions" (p. 10). In other words, I am arguing that, in gifted program evaluation, in addition to asking whether a program is meeting its goals and what effect it is having on the larger context, we should also assess the ethical and moral consequences of the program. It is not enough to ask whether the program is doing what it set out to do. It is also necessary to ask, I now believe, whether the program *ought to* do what it set out to do and whether the cost is worth the outcome in moral, as well as material, terms.

Thus, instead of advocating strictly program-focused, amoral, value-free evaluation, which I think is what I was doing in the last edition of this *Handbook,* I am now arguing that (a) program evaluation should be contextual (it should assess program outcomes as they relate to the program's goals and traditional stakeholders *and* as they relate to the system or systems within which the program is embedded and to any individuals who are nontraditional but effective stakeholders) and (b) it should be concerned with values and moral questions. This is similar to Vedung's (1997) conception of evaluation as a comprehensive assessment of programs in light of their historical, political, economic, and social contexts with the goal of ascertaining the "whole pattern of causal interdependencies" (p. 210).

For lack of a better term, what I am advocating could be called "contextually focused, value-sensitive program evaluation" (I will not attempt an acronym). I will return to this concept at the end of this chapter and briefly address how it affects the process of evaluating gifted programs. Before doing that, let me discuss some of the problems, issues, and methods relevant to evaluating programs for gifted students.

Why Evaluate Gifted Programs?

The evaluation of programs for gifted students poses some unique and daunting problems for both practitioners and scholars, problems that are conceptual (what exactly *is* program evaluation?), psychological (who really *wants* to be evaluated?), and practical (for example, how do you measure growth in students who start out at the ceiling level of a test?). Too often, confronted by this welter of difficulties, educators throw in the towel and decide that a systematic evaluation is unnecessary, unfeasible, or unaffordable, or that distributing questionnaires to students and parents to gauge how happy they are with the program will suffice.

This is unfortunate for several reasons, three of which are particularly salient. First, the infrequency with which programs for gifted students are subjected to careful, systematic evaluations impoverishes us as a field. If program evaluation were to be done on a routine and widespread basis, we would have a broader database on which to draw in order to answer some important questions concerning our practice. Most basic among these is the simple question, "Do gifted programs work?" I find this question to be very embarrassing because, although I think the answer is a qualified *yes,* I cannot adduce much in the way of good empirical evidence to substantiate my belief. The absence of data on outcomes leaves programs for gifted students open to serious questions regarding their efficacy. This, in turn, can make such programs vulnerable, especially when school authorities must contend with the pressures of economic exigency and questions about the fairness of special programs for gifted students (see, e.g., Margolin, 1994, 1996; Sapon-Shevin, 1994, 1996).

The second problem is perhaps even more critical. It is difficult to maintain and increase the quality of a program that does not undergo frequent systematic assessment. As Fetterman (1993) writes, "gifted and talented education programs, perhaps more acutely than most educational programs, require a clear-sighted and self-critical awareness of program strengths and goals" (p. 1). Improving the programs we offer our students is a professional and moral obligation, one we cannot discharge effectively unless we assess the programs in the first place. Thus, on both the national and the local level, we suffer when we neglect the important task of evaluating programs for gifted students.

The third reason is related to the discussion with which I began this chapter. Gifted programs can have wide-ranging effects beyond the bounds of the programs themselves, and an effective evaluation of a program must, I believe, attempt to discover and assess the sum total of its effects. If a gifted program is providing demonstrable benefits to its target population but is having negative collateral consequences, an effective evaluation ought to reveal that. If evaluations are to be utilization-focused (Patton, 1986), if they are going to serve the stakeholders who commission them, stakeholders whose responsibilities almost always extend beyond the gifted program itself,

they cannot look at the program as a isolated, decontextualized entity.

This may seem to be counter to the interests of the gifted program, its students, and its staff if, successful as a program might be in isolation, an evaluation calls attention to negative impacts within the larger context. However, such a state of affairs cannot contribute to the stability or security of the program. And we surely can do much better than thinking of education in such zero-sum terms, in which benefits to some must result in corresponding liabilities for others.

Similarly, the need to consider the moral and ethical outcomes of gifted programs is unattended to when we neglect to engage in program evaluation. Education is, among other things, a moral enterprise, and to the extent that we fail to keep an eye on the moral consequences of educational programs we and the students in our charge are the worse for our failure. A good part of the controversy surrounding gifted education relates to moral and ethical issues, issues that are not as clear-cut as some critics or defenders of the field insist and whose ambiguity argues for disciplined inquiry. Ignoring issues that are very prominent in the discourse surrounding gifted education when we evaluate gifted programs makes very little sense, and it raises moral and ethical questions in itself.

The foregoing assumes some consensus on the issue of what program evaluation is, what its functions are, and other concerns—a consensus that does not, in fact, exist. Let us now turn to some of those issues, starting with the most basic, what program evaluation is.

What Is Program Evaluation?

There are numerous conceptions of program evaluation, many of which are valid, each of which has its own implications with respect to purposes and practices.

Evaluation as Judgment

People typically think of program evaluation as a judgmental process, and there are, indeed, definitions of evaluation that stress this dimension. For example, the definition put forth by the Joint Committee on Standards for Educational Evaluation (1981) defines evaluation simply as, "the systematic investigation of the merit or worth of some object" (p. 12). The Joint

Committee's definition implies a distinction between a program's *merit* (its intrinsic quality or degree of excellence) and its *worth* (its value or importance to somebody or some group), qualities that can be independent of each other.

For example, I have seen programs for gifted students that, although high in merit, have been regarded by school authorities as having little worth. Such programs, when budgets become tight or educational trends unfavorable, face elimination if they are not mandated, marginalization if they are. It must also be admitted that programs of questionable merit can have undeniable worth to school districts for their public relations value or their ability to mollify assertive parents. Whether the emphasis is on merit, worth, or both, evaluation can be conceived of as largely judgmental, especially in its summative function (see below). There are, however, other ways of conceiving of the process.

Evaluation as Description

Evaluation can be descriptive instead of, or as well as, being judgmental, as Stake (1967) acknowledges when he writes that evaluation is "an activity comprised of both description and evaluation" (p. 525). Guba and Lincoln (1989), recounting the history of educational evaluation, describe the "second generation of evaluation" as "an approach characterized by *description* of patterns of strengths and weaknesses with respect to certain stated objectives" (p. 28). The central figure of this generation was Ralph Tyler, the so-called "Father of Evaluation."

Objective, or Goal-Oriented Evaluation. Tyler (1950) defined evaluation as "the process of determining to what extent . . . educational objectives are actually being realized" (p. 69). This is a classic conception of the evaluation process, one with considerable utility since it is straightforward both in conception (a program is successful to the extent that it satisfies its objectives) and execution (one focuses one's efforts on gathering information on whether or not established objectives have been met).

Goal-Free Evaluation. In contrast, Michael Scriven has proposed a form of evaluation in which the evaluator ignores program goals and objectives altogether, one that involves "gathering data directly on program effects and effectiveness without risking contamination by goals" (Patton, 1986, p. 111).

According to Scriven (1972), knowledge of program goals is not only "an unnecessary but also a possibly contaminating step" (p. 2) in the evaluation process. Knowledge of goals and objectives can introduce "perceptual biases" that may make the evaluator oblivious to important unanticipated program outcomes, whereas being unaware of the goals and objectives can "maintain evaluator objectivity and independence through goal-free conditions" (Patton, 1986, p. 112).

Whether one focuses on program goals and objectives or chooses to remain completely ignorant of them, the broader conception of evaluation implied here is descriptive. The evaluator either describes what was intended, what was accomplished, and the gap between the two or, ignoring program goals, describes what happened as a result of program implementation.

Evaluation as Program Improvement

The Stanford Evaluation Consortium (Cronbach et al., 1980) defines evaluation as a "systematic examination of events occurring in and consequent of a contemporary program . . . conducted to assist in improving this program and other programs having the same general purpose" (p. 14). No mention is made of judging or describing, although these activities are not necessarily antithetical to program improvement.

Program improvement is one of the most important outcomes of program evaluation and may be the most compelling reason to undertake the process. As I suggest above, improving programs for gifted students is one of our imperatives, and this goal ought to be part of our general conception of the purposes of program evaluation.

Utilization-Focused Evaluation

Patton (1986) argues that "much of what passes for program evaluation is not very useful" and, sensibly, that "evaluation ought to be useful" (p. 7). What he calls the "utilization crisis" in program evaluation was caused by the practice of commissioning evaluations and then ignoring their findings in future decision making. This experience led him to the concept of *utilization-focused evaluation.*

Patton stresses the importance of identifying the stakeholders, those who have an interest in the outcome of the evaluation, determining what they want or need to know, and providing information that they are likely to use in making decisions about the program under review. In Patton's approach, the overriding concern is whether "there is an immediate, concrete, and observable effect on specific decisions and program activities resulting directly from evaluation findings" (p. 30); in other words, whether evaluation data are used.

Postpositivist Evaluation

Postpositivist evaluation refers to the increased application of qualitative, naturalistic, constructivist, critical, or hermeneutic inquiry to the problems of educational evaluation (see, for example, Denzin & Lincoln, 1998; Guba & Lincoln, 1989; Patton, 1986). The axioms and methods of postpositivism are quite compatible with inquiry into and assessment of giftedness, which is, in many ways, a socially constructed concept.

It is not possible to describe postpositivism in a few sentences (see Borland, 1990; Guba, 1991; Lincoln & Guba, 1985), but at its core is a rejection of the positivist notion that the methods that characterize inquiry in the physical sciences are applicable to the study of human beings, their behavior, and their institutions. Among its axioms are the belief that realities are multiple and constructed; that the act of observation affects that which is being observed; that generalization is undesirable and perhaps impossible; and that inquiry cannot be, and should not pretend to be, objective and value free. Methodologically, postpositivists stress qualitative methods; purposive instead of random sampling; human beings as data-gathering instruments; letting one's research or evaluation design emerge as one progresses instead of following a prespecified design; allowing theory to emerge from one's engagement with one's respondents instead of starting with or testing a theory; close description of specific settings (ideographic interpretation) instead of generalizable findings (nomothetic laws); negotiating outcomes with respondents; and case-study reporting.

In the realm of evaluation, this means that the relevant data, what are usually taken as the results of the evaluation, are not, in Guba and Lincoln's (1989) words, " 'discovered' as if they had always been 'out there.' . . . [Instead,] the results are *literally*—we stress *literally*—*created* . . . as a product of an interaction between humans" (p. 67). As a result, "different stakeholders will have different constructions" (p. 67). Therefore, evaluation should in part involve forc-

ing various stakeholders in a program to confront their own and others' constructed knowledge about the program, resulting in "more informed and sophisticated personal constructions" (p. 67).

As should be clear, there are many ways to conceive of program evaluation, each of which has important considerations for practice. This may seem to be more confusing than helpful, but it reflects the true state of the art. Some clarification may come from considering the various functions that program evaluation can serve.

What Are the Functions of Evaluation?

Scriven (1967) drew a well-known and useful distinction between two major functions of program evaluation—the summative and the formative—which is useful in understanding how evaluation can be used. I will discuss this distinction, as well as two other functions of evaluation.

The Summative Function

Summative evaluation is what comes to mind when most people think of program evaluation. The focus in summative evaluation is on program outcomes at or near the end of a program's lifespan or after some significant period of time (such as an academic year). The major concern is with issues of program efficacy and accountability. Summative evaluation has both a retrospective and a prospective aspect. It is retrospective in attempting to determine whether a program has been effective. It is prospective in that it is frequently used to make major decisions about a program's future, such as whether to continue or terminate a program, increase or decrease its funding, and so forth. Because summative evaluations are often the basis for administrative decisions, the audience for these data is usually higher-level administrators who have the responsibility for such decisions.

The Formative Function

Formative evaluation differs from summative evaluation chiefly in that it serves a diagnostic function. This form of evaluation involves the collection of data at various points during the life of a program—during an academic year, for example—so that problems can be detected and responded to while the program is still operating, not after the fact, as is usually the case with summative evaluation. The goal is to improve the program now, not to answer questions of accountability or the program's long-term fate. For this reason, formative data are probably of more interest to those in the program's day-to-day management and decision making than they are to higher-level administrators. This distinction is, however, not absolute. For one thing, formative data can be incorporated into a summative evaluation. Moreover, a formative evaluation, by helping educators identify and alleviate problems, can affect overall program effectiveness and, thus, the results of summative evaluation. In this sense, provisions for formative evaluation are a program component that, like other program components, should be a focus of a summative evaluation.

Other Functions of Evaluation

Nevo (1983) mentions two other functions that deserve brief attention. The *psychological,* or *sociopolitical,* function is just that: evaluation whose intended ends are either psychological or sociopolitical. The goal is either to affect the thinking or behavior of one or more people or to achieve some objective with respect to the status of an individual, group, or program within a particular social structure, such as a school, school district, academic department, or state bureaucracy. I have, on occasion, been hired as an evaluator for a program for gifted students only to learn that the intent of the evaluation was psychological (for example, to remind program staff that they are accountable to administrators or the school board) or sociopolitical (for example, to enhance the program's stature within a school district).

There is also an *administrative* evaluation function, whereby X evaluates Y for no reason other than as a statement or reminder that X *can* evaluate Y by virtue of a higher position in the administrative hierarchy. It is difficult to regard this as a legitimate function of evaluation, but it does occur and should be noted.

Not only can program evaluation be defined in different ways, it can serve a variety of functions. These are obviously related; evaluation as judgment is more likely to be summative, whereas evaluation as program improvement is more likely to be formative. All this is important, I believe, because a clear conception of the forms and functions of program evaluation helps one to plan and carry out an effective evaluation.

Problems in Evaluating Programs for Gifted Students

Problems with Goals and Objectives

Clear, unambiguous program goals and objectives are useful, although, as we have seen, not indispensable, in evaluation. This is especially true if the evaluation effort focuses on whether the program has met, or is meeting, its stated goals. Even when conducting a goal-free evaluation, knowledge of program goals is useful when stakeholders try to interpret the evaluation results.

Problems with goals and objectives come in a variety of forms. One of these is the goal-free program. It has, unfortunately, not been uncommon in my experience with public school programs for gifted students to receive nothing but blank stares in response to the question, "What are the goals of your program?" In a surprising number of cases, the implicit but overriding goal seems to be, "To have a gifted program." That goal has the undeniable virtue of being easily met. The problem here is obvious. If nobody knows why the program exists, not only can evaluation be problematic, so can nearly every aspect of the program.

Even when there are program goals, there can be problems. For example, some goals are so grand and lofty as to make it extremely unlikely that a mere educational program could reach them. Wanting to have a positive effect on "the future of our country" or aspiring to "create a cadre of leaders for the world of tomorrow" certainly do not bode well for a positive summative evaluation.

Other goals are just the opposite; they are so trivial as to prompt a response of "So what?". Establishing as a program goal the identification of a certain percentage of the student body as gifted or the delivery of in-service education to a certain number of teachers is to substitute administrative responsibilities for program objectives. These goals are easily met, a fact that has little, if any, bearing on the merit, worth, or effectiveness of the program. Goals are of little use in program evaluation if they do not specify what benefits will accrue to students and what the program will do for students that would not be done were the program not to exist.

Problems with Measurement

Evaluation nearly always involves some form of measurement or assessment, although not necessarily through tests. This presents a host of problems.

Lack of Adequate Tests. One problem, or apparent problem, is the paucity of valid tests for measuring a number of the things we would like to assess in programs for gifted students. One example of this is creativity, valid measures of which have been the Holy Grail for some test constructors for a number of years. This is understandable, for creativity looms large in the goals and activities of a number of programs. However, attempts to capture this elusive construct with standardized paper-and-pencil measures have been largely unsuccessful (see, for example, Crockenberg, 1972; Perkins, 1981; Wallach, 1985; see Torrance, 1975, 1988, for a different view).

Now, for a number of people, often including stakeholders in program evaluations, the only valid way to measure something is through the use of an objective test. As House (1993) wrote, although "standardized test scores are not entirely suitable for this purpose [program evaluation]" (p. 2), "there is a demand for test results from policy makers and legislatures that cannot be denied" (p. 11). This is because, for many people, the terms *objective* and *valid* have become conflated, which is unfortunate, for whether a test is objective or not has nothing to do with its validity. Furthermore, frankly subjective methods can outperform objective ones, as is shown by the success Amabile (e.g., 1983) has had with consensual assessment relative to the poor record achieved by objective tests of creativity.

The absence of valid tests does not imply the absence of tests altogether, as the existence of a number of measures with the words *Creativity Test* on their covers demonstrates. Moreover, many of us are so awed by tests that, however skeptical we may be as consumers of other products, we become very credulous test consumers, ignoring or not reading what is written in the research journals or the *Mental Measurements Yearbooks*. Thus, legitimate program goals that refer to psychometrically elusive constructs can have two unhappy outcomes. One, resulting from the belief that valid assessment requires a test, and reinforced by a tendency to believe that if a test is published it must be valid, is to use objective but invalid measures. The second is to conclude that no assessment is possible. There is an alternative, as I implied above by referring to Amabile's work, and I will return to this later when I discuss authentic assessment.

Lack of Sufficient Ceiling on Tests. Another measurement problem is caused by ceiling effects on tests. On some tests, especially, but not only, achievement measures, the test ceiling may be too low for advanced students. All this means is that the test is not difficult enough for the ablest students or that there is not enough range at the top end of the score distribution to reveal true differences among the highest scorers.

This problem can affect evaluations in which there is an attempt to assess growth due to program intervention by computing gain scores, that is, differences between pretest scores and post-test scores (not a good idea because it can compound measurement error, but it is often done). If a test with a low ceiling is used as a pretest to assess students' status prior to exposure to the program, many students may start out with the highest score possible, making it impossible for them to show gains, should there be any. As a group, they may even show small decreases in their mean score, purely as a result of regression toward the mean, a measurement artifact (explained in the next section).

Because of ceiling effects, some educators have recommended out-of-level testing for gifted students. This simply means switching to a test designed for chronologically older students. If too many gifted third graders are scoring at the ceiling level on a given test, one could administer, say, the fifth-grade test instead. Probably the best example of this approach is found in the work of the Johns Hopkins Study of Mathematically Precocious Youth (e.g., Benbow, 1986; Stanley, 1981), in which the mathematics section of the Scholastic Aptitude Test, as it was called then, was used to assess mathematical precocity among middle school students.[1] One thing to keep in mind, as the SMPY researchers themselves point out, is that a test may be qualitatively different when used

---

1. See Chapter 15 by Lupkowski-Shoplik, Benbow, Assouline, and Brody.

with an age group other than the one for which it was designed or on which it was normed. The SAT-M, for example, may be an achievement test for high school seniors who have been exposed to the mathematics curriculum it covers, but for younger students who have had no such exposure, it may function as a test of problem solving, creativity, persistence, or risk-taking.

Regression Effects. Regression toward the mean is a phenomenon whereby groups of individuals selected because of very high or very low scores on a test, such as students selected for gifted programs or remedial programs, when tested again, achieve, as a group, mean scores that are closer to the population mean. This is a by-product of the fact that tests are not completely reliable, that chance plays a part in the score one earns even on the most precise psychometric instrument, and that, when there is some random fluctuation of scores, those at the top can only go down and those at the bottom can only go up a bit.

Meaningless as this error variance is, it can pose problems for those interested in the assessment of gifted learners. For students in highly selective programs, regression effects can work against the measurement of real gains, attenuating them if not canceling them out. For this reason, it is important not to use the same instrument for identifying gifted students and later for assessing their progress. By the same token, if a test used as a post-test measure of student growth or status correlates strongly with the test (or battery of indicators) used for identifying students, regression effects can also occur.

Inappropriate Norms. In this field, more often than not, we are concerned with test scores at the upper extreme of the score distribution. Since this is where we often want to make distinctions between students, we need to be confident that when test raw scores are translated into percentiles, normal curve equivalents, or some other normative score, these latter scores are reliable. Unfortunately, this is not always the case.

To distinguish accurately between the percentile rankings of high scorers at the upper extremes of the score distribution, one needs quite a few subjects in the norming sample who score at the upper extremes, and since these subjects represent a small percentage of the total, the total norming sample must be large indeed. If the test in question needs to be in different forms so that it can be used with various ages and

levels of achievement, aptitude, or ability, the size requirements for the sample increase markedly.

Because of these demands, it is frequently the case that norms at the upper end of the score distribution are derived from a subsample of the norming sample that is too small for the task. Put simply, many tests used to assess gifted students have had too few gifted students in their norming samples. Scores in the upper range may, therefore, be less reliable. Or a range of raw scores may be pegged to a single ceiling percentile, so that true differences between students are obscured. This phenomenon, which is related to ceiling effects, is such that the reliability of high scores on a test should be treated with skepticism until one consults the test manual to learn about the norming sample and the standard error of scores over the range of the score distribution.

Problems with Evaluation Designs

It is difficult to design program evaluations in the way one would like to design a good experiment. To build in appropriate controls, it is useful to have, in addition to a treatment group (in this case a group of students who experience the gifted program), a control group (one that does not). Moreover, these groups should be randomly constituted from a pool of students, all of whom qualify for the program in question. One can quickly see why there might be objections from parents and others were there to be a control group consisting of students who qualified for the program in question but who, for evaluation purposes, were excluded from it. Thus, when evaluators attempt to employ or approximate experimental designs, they typically resort to one-group designs, with no control or comparison group, which are problematic.

There are some ways around this without the ethical and political problems of asking some parents to place their gifted students in the "no-program" control group. One is to use some variation of a counterbalanced design (Campbell & Stanley, 1963) in which parts of the program, such as exposure to different curricular components, are presented to different groups of students at different times. For example, students in a program might be divided into two groups, ideally through a random process, with one group receiving exposure to one curricular component, with distinct objectives and methods, while the other group receives exposure to another component altogether. When this phase of the program concludes, the two groups can be assessed, with each group serving as the control for the other in a quasi-experimental two-group design. Then each group can be exposed to the curriculum component it missed the first time, and additional comparisons can be made.

Design problems can be daunting, but they can be overcome. Nonetheless, evaluating programs for gifted students is, I believe, more difficult than evaluating most other programs

Using an Outside Evaluator

One approach to program evaluation is to bring in an outsider, or a group of outsiders, to conduct an evaluation. This could be someone from academia, perhaps with a specialization in evaluation or the education of gifted students; a professional evaluator; an educational consultant; or, if one is near a college with a graduate program in education, students conducting a supervised practicum. Whoever is engaged to conduct an outside evaluation, the approach has some things to recommend it.

One advantage an outsider brings is a greater degree of objectivity than is possible for someone inside the system. One can, at times, be too close to a program to see what someone with a fresher perspective can see. Of course, complete objectivity is impossible, but at least someone from outside brings a different subjectivity to the task. In addition, an outsider is, or should be, able to carry out an evaluation without concern for the future consequences of certain findings. Since outsiders do not owe their livelihood to the powers that be, an outside evaluator possesses a degree of independence of thought and expression not enjoyed by those on the inside. Finally, an experienced evaluator brings a breadth of experience derived from work with many types of programs. Knowing what has and has not worked in other settings can be of great value, especially when significant changes are being considered. In short, an outside evaluator can provide a valuable service.

However, total reliance on outsiders is a mistake. For one thing, some of the very virtues of an outside evaluator—an outside perspective, freedom from negative repercussions from evaluation findings—have their negative sides. An outside perspective, although affording greater breadth, affords limited depth and precludes the sort of local knowledge that accrues to someone with long experience in a given setting. In addition, freedom from the consequences of evaluation findings is counterbalanced by lower

commitment, less of a stake in how the evaluation improves the program.

Another problem is that outside evaluations tend to be summative only, neglecting the formative function that is so important for program improvement. This does not have to be the case, but it is not unusual for an evaluator to be approached in the spring of the school year when all that can be done is some form of summative evaluation. The best time to begin discussing an evaluation with a consultant is well before the school year begins, so that a careful evaluation plan, with provisions for formative evaluation, can be developed.

Finally, few schools and school districts have the resources to commission evaluations by outsiders on an annual basis. Frequent evaluation is important for improvement, and this requires that evaluation, *conducted internally,* be built into the program as an essential component. As I argue in my book on program planning (Borland, 1989), evaluation ought to be an integral component of every program for gifted students, one that is no less necessary than, say, identification.

Other Issues Related to the Evaluation of Gifted Programs

Authentic Assessment and Program Evaluation

Much has been written on the topic of *authentic assessment,* assessment that more closely resembles the actual curriculum and instruction whose effects are being measured (see, for example, Darling-Hammond, Ancess, & Falk, 1995; *Using Performance Assessment,* 1992; Wiggins, 1989). An obvious example is the use of essays instead of multiple-choice examinations to assess writing ability.

This is a promising area that has borne fruit in the field of gifted education in the form of Amabile's (1983) work on *consensual assessment.* According to Ebersole (1994), consensual assessment is the judgment, by consensus, of creative products within a specific domain, such as the essays mentioned above, by individuals who have expertise in that domain. There is an obvious advantage to this method. It mirrors the way we do things in the real world, in which the work of individuals working in, say, various artistic domains is assessed by individuals and groups within those domains—critics, gallery owners, curators, editors, conductors, directors, and so forth. It is, in that respect, truly authentic assessment.

These ideas can be brought into the realm of program evaluation quite readily. To the extent that programs exist to assist students in acquiring certain skills, assessing those skills as part of program evaluation can, and arguably should, be done in as authentic a manner as possible. For example, if enhancing students' creativity is a major goal of the program, rather than basing evaluation on gains on paper-and-pencil tests of creativity, one could place students in situations that require them to respond creatively to problems in relevant domains.

Evaluation of Programs Designed to Serve Traditionally Underrepresented Gifted Students

Unfortunately, there is ample evidence (e.g., Borland, Schnur, & Wright, 2000; Borland & Wright, 1994; Ford & Harris, 1999; Richert, 1987; VanTassel-Baska, Patton, & Prillaman, 1989) that, despite good intentions, we have failed to do enough to identify and serve gifted students who are outside society's mainstream, including students who are economically disadvantaged, especially students of color. There has been progress, however, as evidenced by the programs for underrepresented students funded though the provisions of the Jacob Javits Gifted and Talented Students Program. But with progress comes new concerns related to program evaluation.

Some problems are obvious, such as the need to accommodate the needs of students with limited English proficiency. Others, however, are less so. One problem is *cultural inversion,* in which mainstream values, such as striving for academic success, are seen as emblematic of an oppressive majority. Fordham (1991) discusses "the burden of acting White," with which academically successful minority students frequently must contend, and how this can create considerable distress since, although it facilitates academic success and upward mobility, it can alienate minority students from their peers and family members.[2]

Successful evaluation of programs specifically for underrepresented gifted students or of mainstream programs that are more inclusive will require an understanding that giftedness manifests itself in different ways in different cultures and settings and that,

in order to understand these manifestations, one must understand the culture and the setting. As Armour-Thomas (1992) argues, cognitive potential and cultural experience cannot be understood apart from each other.

A Framework for Program Evaluation

How, then, can one carry out the evaluation of a gifted program? The following is a straightforward, practicable approach that requires no statistical or psychometric expertise and is designed for teachers, program coordinators, and other practitioners. It revolves around program goals.

Step One: Defining or Clarifying Program Goals

Clear, sensible goals greatly facilitate evaluation. The first step, therefore, is to review and to *clarify the goals* of the program, making certain they refer to benefits that will accrue to students as a result of program intervention.

Step Two: Selecting Goals for the Current Evaluation

Typically, programs come with quite a few goals, and to try to make them all the focus of any single evaluation effort could make the process too unwieldy. Therefore, it makes sense to *focus on a few goals,* perhaps three or four—maybe fewer, maybe more—in any annual evaluation. Which goals are chosen depends on various factors, perhaps special emphases for the upcoming year or perceived program deficiencies that need work. There is no need, nor is it advisable, to try to cover every goal every year. At this point, forms can be made, perhaps something like the one shown in Figure 23.1, on which the goals can be written and additional information noted. This should be done before the beginning of the academic year so that formative as well as summative data can be planned.

Step Three: Identifying Program Activities, Outcomes, and Criteria Related to the Selected Goals

Throughout the coming year, various program activities will take place that are designed to achieve

---

2. See Chapter 39 by Ford.

Program Goal:

Activity	Behavior or Outcome	Observation Points	Criterion	Performance	Analysis

Synthesis:

Figure 23.1   Form for planning goal-based program evaluation.

goals or that involve students in behaviors that reflect on goal attainment. The next step, therefore, is to list on each form those *activities* in which student behavior can be observed that will shed light on progress toward the goal. For example, if a targeted goal is for students to develop research skills, student work on independent projects is one obvious activity in which to observe students for behavior that indicates how they are progressing. For each goal, then, one should list as many activities as can be anticipated, and one can add activities as they are planned during the year.

Each of these activities will have a *behavior or outcome* that is to some extent observable, and these should also be listed, as should the *observation points,* when the behaviors or outcomes will be observed. Finally, the *criteria,* or desired level of performance, should be specified. Using the above example, depending on past experience, one might stipulate a certain percentage of students completing projects as one criterion for the goal.

Step Four: Recording and Analyzing Student Performance

As each activity related to the program goal takes place, one can record the students' actual level of *performance.* Then, comparing this with the previously established criterion, one can record a few *analytical comments* relating to the degree to which the criterion was met and what this implies. Once this is done for all activities listed in the first column, one or two synthesizing paragraphs can be written commenting on the degree to which the goal was met and what should be done in the future. Once these have been done for all targeted goals, they can be integrated into an evaluation report.

The purpose of this stage of the process is to gather as much evidence as possible from direct observation of student work and behavior to shed light on the degree of progress toward selected program goals. It is likely that most of the information collected will not be test data, and many of the data will be subjective. This should not be a concern. The important thing is to gather as many data as possible and to make the evaluation practicable within the constraints posed by available resources. It should be clear that no particular expertise in program evaluation is required to carry out an evaluation of this sort, and that is by design.

Step Five: Writing the Report

The preceding four steps of this evaluation process are very positivistic in nature, relying on a traditional Tylerian conception of evaluation as an assessment of inputs and outputs relative to clear, unambiguous program goals. I am offering this more for the sake of simplicity and as an aid to those intimidated by program evaluation than as a reflection of my beliefs about teaching and learning, the nature of reality, and how inquiry should be conducted.

I believe that the evaluation report should not be merely a summary of the progress made toward the goals targeted for assessment in the year in question. Rather, the information gathered from the process described above can, and should, be incorporated into an evaluation report that takes into account (a) the multiple constructed realities of the various program stakeholders, (b) the effects of the program on the larger context in which it is embedded, and (c) the moral and ethical consequences of the program's activities.

Acknowledging Multiple Constructed Realities. Diffrent stakeholders not only hold different opinions and views concerning the program and its various components, but they construct different realities and, to the extent that they are informants in the evaluation process, co-construct evaluation findings with the evaluator(s). These findings have no fixed immutable meanings that can be generalized across all people and all settings, and a useful evaluation report that is not grounded completely in the positivist paradigm ought to reflect these ontological and epistemological positions.

Analyzing Effects on the Larger Context. The report should also apply the findings about program goals to the broader setting in which the program operates. In the case of a gifted program in a school district, this involves such things as looking for consistency or conflict between program goals and district philosophy and policies; reciprocal impacts of program activities and other district educational activities on each other; effects on the totality of the gifted students' school lives, not just that part played out in the gifted program; effects on district-wide resource allocation; and relationships between the gifted program and other programs, gifted program faculty and other faculty; gifted students and other students, school, and parents.

Addressing Moral and Ethical Consequences.
The moral and ethical consequences of the program
should be part of a comprehensive utilization-focused
evaluation. Among the ethical questions that commonly arise in the context of gifted programs are the
following: Does the program provide students in the
gifted program with experiences that are appropriate
for them only, or are students in the program given
opportunities that other students would enjoy and
from which they would derive benefits? Are the program's identification procedures equitable? Is the
program serving a reasonably representative cross-
section of the district's population, or are there pronounced racial and socioeconomic differences
between students in the gifted program and those in
the general school population? Are there unfair benefits or social liabilities to the label, however implicit,
"gifted student"? Do some parents wield disproportionate power over program decisions by virtue of
their social or economic standing in the community?
And, to adopt a utilitarian perspective, does the program do more good than harm?

SUMMARY AND CONCLUSIONS

I hope I have not emphasized the difficulties of program evaluation too much, for, as I hope the framework I present above indicates, evaluation is a
practicable and necessary part of operating a program for gifted students. If planning and conducting
a program evaluation appears to be daunting keep in
mind that maintaining and improving a program that
is not evaluated is even more daunting. Evaluation
is a form of inquiry, which is a search after knowledge. If we do not even attempt to evaluate our programs, we are stating implicitly that we are content
to remain ignorant. How could we justify this to our
students and to ourselves?

QUESTIONS FOR THOUGHT
AND DISCUSSION

1. According to Borland, program evaluations are
(a) judgmental, (b) descriptive, (c) improvement-oriented,
(d) utilization (usefulness) oriented, and/or (e) postpositivist. On a scale of 1 to 10, how would you rate Borland's
own five-step model on each of these five overlapping conceptions of evaluation?

2. What are the differences between summative, formative, psychological/sociopolitical, and administrative functions of evaluation? As a teacher of the gifted, which are you
likely to be concerned with?

3. Imagine you are evaluating a gifted program. Look at
Figure 23.1. List just one important goal, then practice filling out the rest of the form.

4. Discuss the advantages and disadvantages of a postpositivist evaluation.

5. Following Borland's concern for the wider context,
how might you evaluate the program's impact on other
students? Other teachers? Administrators? Parents? The
wider community?

REFERENCES

Amabile, T. M. (1983). *The social psychology of creativity.*
New York: Springer-Verlag.

Armour-Thomas, E. (1992). Intellectual assessment of children from culturally diverse backgrounds. *School
Psychology Review, 21,* 552–565.

Benbow, C. P. (1986). SMPY's model for teaching mathematically precocious students. In J. S. Renzulli (Ed.),
*Systems and models for developing programs for the
gifted and talented* (pp. 1–26). Mansfield Center, CT:
Creative Learning Press.

Borland, J. H. (1989). *Planning and implementing programs
for the gifted.* New York: Teachers College Press.

Borland, J. H. (1990). Postpositivist inquiry: Implications
of the "new philosophy of science" for the field of the education of the gifted. *Gifted Child Quarterly, 34,*
161–167.

Borland, J. H., Schnur, R., & Wright, L. (2000).
Economically disadvantaged students in a school for the
academically gifted: A postpositivist inquiry into individual and family adjustment. *Gifted Child Quarterly,
44,* 13–32.

Borland, J. H., & Wright, L. (1994). Identifying young, potentially gifted, economically disadvantaged students.
Gifted Child Quarterly, 38, 164–171.

Campbell, D. T., & Stanley, J. C. (1963). *Experimental and
quasi-experimental designs for research.* Chicago: Rand
McNally.

Crockenberg, S. (1972). Creativity tests: Boon or boon-
doggle for education? *Review of Educational Research,
42,* 27–45.

Cronbach, L. J., Ambron, S. R., Dornbusch, S. M., Hess,
R. D., Hornik, R. C., Phillips, D. C., Walker, D. E., &
Weiner, S. S. (1980). *Toward reform of program evalua-
tion.* San Francisco: Jossey-Bass.

Darling-Hammond, L., Ancess, J., & Falk, B. (1995).
Authentic assessment in action. New York: Teachers
College Press.

Denzin, N. K., & Lincoln, Y. S. (Eds.). (1998). *The landscape of qualitative research: Theories and issues.* Thousand Oaks, CA: Sage.

Ebersole, D. G. (1994). Connoisseurship, critical community, and consensual assessment: The role of subjective judgment in the identification of young, disadvantaged gifted students. Unpublished doctoral dissertation, Teachers College, Columbia University.

Fetterman, D. M. (1993). *Evaluate yourself.* Storrs, CT: National Research Center on the Gifted and Talented.

Ford, D. Y., & Harris J. J. III. (1999). *Multicultural gifted education.* New York: Teachers College Press.

Fordham, S. (1991). Peer proofing academic competition among Black adolescents: "Acting White" Black American style. In C. E. Sleeter (Ed.), *Empowerment through multicultural education* (pp. 69–93). Albany: State University of New York Press.

Guba, E. G. (1991). *The paradigm dialog.* Beverly Hills, CA: Sage.

Guba, E. G., & Lincoln, Y. S. (1989). *Fourth generation evaluation.* Beverly Hills, CA: Sage.

House, E. R. (1993). *Evaluation of programs for disadvantaged gifted students.* Unpublished manuscript, University of Colorado, Boulder.

Joint Committee on Standards for Educational Evaluation. (1981). *Standards for evaluations of educational programs, projects, and materials.* New York: McGraw-Hill.

Lincoln, Y. S., & Guba, E. G. (1985). *Naturalistic inquiry.* Beverly Hills, CA: Sage.

Margolin, L. (1996). A pedagogy of privilege. *Journal for the Education of the Gifted, 19,* 164–180.

Margolin, L. (1994). *Goodness personified: The emergence of gifted children.* New York: Aldine de Gruyter.

Migotsky, C., Stake, R., Davis, R., Williams, B., DePaul, G., Cisneros, E. J., Johnson, E., & Feltovich, J. (1997). Probative, dialectic, and moral reasoning in program evaluation. *Qualitative Inquiry, 3,* 453–467.

McCorkle, M. D. (1986). The operation was a success but the patient died: A critique of "The implementation and evaluation of a problem-solving training program for adolescents." *Evaluation and Program Planning, 7,* 193–198.

Nevo, D. (1983). The conceptualization of educational evaluation: An analytical review of the literature. *Review of Educational Research, 53,* 117–128.

Patton, M. Q. (1986). *Utilization-focused evaluation* (2nd ed.). Beverly Hills, CA: Sage.

Perkins, D. N. (1981). *The mind's best work.* Cambridge: Harvard University Press.

Richert, E. S. (1987). Rampant problems and promising practices in the identification of disadvantaged gifted students. *Gifted Child Quarterly, 31,* 149–154.

Sapon-Shevin, M. (1994). *Playing favorites: Gifted education and the disruption of community.* Ithaca: State University of New York Press.

Sapon-Shevin, M. (1996). Beyond gifted education: Building a shared agenda for school reform. *Journal for the Education of the Gifted, 19,* 194–214.

Schwandt, T. A. (1997). Reading the "problem of evaluation" in social inquiry. *Qualitative Inquiry, 3,* 4–25.

Scriven, M. (1967). The methodology of evaluation. In R. E. Stake (Ed.), *AERA monograph series on curriculum evaluation,* No. 1. Chicago: Rand McNally.

Scriven, M. (1972). Pros and cons about goal-free evaluation. *Evaluation Comment: The Journal of Educational Evaluation, 3*(4), 1–7.

Stake, R. E. (1967). The countenance of educational evaluation. *Teachers College Record, 68,* 523–540.

Stanley, J. C. (1981). Rationale of the study of mathematically precocious youth (SMPY) during its first five years of promoting educational acceleration. In W. B. Barbe & J. S. Renzulli (Eds.), *Psychology and education of the gifted* (pp. 248–283). New York: Irvington.

Torrance, E. P. (1975). Creativity research in education: Still alive. In I. A. Taylor and J. W. Getzels (Eds.), *Perspectives in creativity* (pp. 278–296). Chicago: Aldine.

Torrance, E. P. (1988). The nature of creativity as manifested in testing. In R. J. Sternberg (Ed.), *The nature of creativity* (pp. 43–75). New York: Cambridge University Press.

Tyler, R. W. (1950). *Basic principles of curriculum and instruction.* Chicago: University of Chicago Press.

Using Performance Assessment [Special issue]. (1992). *Educational Leadership, 49*(8).

VanTassel-Baska, J., Patton, J., & Prillaman, D. (1989). Disadvantaged gifted learners: At risk for educational attention. *Focus on Exceptional Children, 22*(3), 1–15.

Vedung, E. (1997). Public policy and program evaluation. New Brunswick, NJ: Transaction.

Wallach, M. A. (1985). Creativity testing and giftedness. In F. D. Horowitz & M. O'Brien (Eds.), *The gifted and talented: Developmental perspectives* (pp. 99–123). Washington, DC: American Psychological Association.

Wiggins, G. (1989). A true test: Toward more authentic and equitable assessment. *Phi Delta Kappan, 70*(9), 703–713.

BIBLIOGRAPHY

Bennett, C. F. (1979). *Analyzing impacts of extension programs.* Washington, DC: U.S. Department of Agriculture.

Bennett, C. F. (1982). *Reflective appraisal of programs.* Ithaca: Cornell University.

Cross, T. (1994). A commentary: Alternative inquiry and its potential contribution to gifted education. *Roeper Review, 16,* 284–285.

Eisner, E. W. (1979). *The educational imagination.* New York: Macmillan.

Ford, D. Y. (1992). Determinants of underachievement as perceived by gifted, above-average and average black students. *Roeper Review, 14,* 130–136.

Ford, D. Y. (1993). An investigation of the paradox of underachievement among gifted black students. *Roeper Review, 16,* 78–84.

Ford, D. Y. (1996). *Reversing underachievement among gifted Black students.* New York: Teachers College Press.

Fordham, S. (1988). Racelessness as a strategy in Black students' school success: Pragmatic strategy or pyrrhic victory? *Harvard Educational Review, 58*(1), 54–84.

Fordham, S., & Ogbu, J. U. (1986). Black students' school success: Coping with the burden of "acting White." *The Urban Review, 18,* 176–206.

Gage, N. L. (1989). The paradigm wars and their aftermath: A "historical" sketch of research on teaching since 1989. *Educational Researcher, 18,* 4–10.

Glass, G. V. (1969). *The growth of evaluation methodology* (Research Paper No. 27). Boulder: Laboratory of Educational Research, University of Colorado.

Goldenberg, C., & Gallimore, R. (1991). Local knowledge, research knowledge, and educational change: A case study of early Spanish reading improvement. *Educational Researcher, 20*(8), 2–14.

House, E. R. (1980). *Evaluating with validity.* Beverly Hills, CA: Sage.

Ogbu, J. U. (1978). *Minority education and caste: The American system in cross-cultural perspective.* New York: Academic Press.

Ogbu, J. U. (1985). Minority education and caste. In N. Yetman (Eds.), *Majority and minority: The dynamic of race and ethnicity in American life.* (4th ed., pp. 370–383). Boston: Allyn and Bacon.

Ogbu, J. U. (1992). Understanding cultural diversity and learning. *Educational Researcher, 21*(8), 5–14.

Passow, A. H. (1989). Needed research and development in educating high ability children. *Roeper Review, 11,* 223–229.

Scriven, M. (1991). *Evaluation thesaurus* (4th ed.). Newbury Park, CA: Sage.

Shaklee, B. D. (1992). Identification of young gifted students. *Journal for the Education of the Gifted, 15,* 134–144.

Stufflebeam, D. L. (1974). *Meta-evaluation* (Occasional Paper No. 3). Kalamazoo: Western Michigan University.

Wright, L. & Borland, J. H. (1993). Using early childhood developmental portfolios in the identification and education of young, economically disadvantaged, potentially gifted students. *Roeper Review, 15,* 205–210.

Creativity, Thinking Skills, and Eminence

Every statement of goals for gifted programs names growth in creative thinking and other thinking skills as prime objectives. Part IV helps clarify these complex topics by looking at theories of creativity, how to identify creative students and inspire creative thinking, the nature of artistic giftedness, and factors that contribute to high achievement, productivity, and adult eminence.

In Chapter 24 Gary A. Davis itemizes complexities of creativity, stressing that current creativity tests therefore cannot be highly valid. Some creative students will be easily recognized by their high energy, lively imaginations, curiosity, humor, and creative involvement. Creative personality/motivation inventories, divergent thinking tests, creativity ratings/nominations, and, especially, evaluations of past creative activities will help identify creative students. At least two of these criteria of creativeness should be used. Davis's suggestions for promoting creativity include developing creativity consciousness and creative attitudes, improving students' understanding of creativity, exercising creative abilities, teaching creative thinking techniques, and above all involving students in activities that require creative thinking.

Arthur L. Costa in Chapter 25 describes the impact of today's broadened definitions of intelligence, which emphasize trainable skills and habits. He describes four components of a thoughtful thinking-skills program: selecting suitable content; instructing students in the thinking skills; practicing with complex tasks, such as problem solving, creativity, and decision making, that require skillful thinking; and developing *habits of mind,* conceived as inclinations, dispositions, and capabilities to use a variety of thinking skills. The thrust of Costa's chapter elaborates on his 16 habits of mind, for example, persisting,

managing impulsiveness, listening with empathy, flexible thinking, metacognition, striving for accuracy, questioning and finding problems, applying past learning to new problems, imagining and creating, taking risks, using humor, and remaining open to new learning.

In Chapter 26 Ellen Winner and Gail Martino point out commonalities of artistic and scholastic giftedness-precocity, intense motivation, and high creativity. Then they review unique characteristics of artistically gifted children. The authors emphasize that drawing skills not only emerge early, but are qualitatively different from the art skills of typical children. Most notably, the artistically gifted see things differently, have superior visual memories, and attend carefully to the act of drawing. They draw quickly, with details and asymmetry. The result can be remarkable realism—a Western indicator of artistic giftedness. Turning to origins, Winner and Martino concede that intense motivation and training combine with giftedness to produce high achievement, but these cannot explain innate artistic giftedness and "big-C" creativity. Finally, artistic inventiveness in adulthood enables a few precocious artists to "change their domain" and achieve high recognition.

Herbert J. Walberg, Deborah B. Williams, and Susie Zeiser in Chapter 27 itemize nine educational productivity factors that increase efficiency in academic learning and contribute to developing exceptional talent. The interacting productivity factors, identified partly from two decades of studying talented adolescents and eminent adults, include, for example, ability, time engaged in learning, quality of instruction, a home life that supports intellectual development, peers outside of school, and the negatively related factor of exposure to mass media and popular culture—particularly TV. They stress the key role of motivation, which leads to sustained effort, feelings of satisfaction, and motivation for further learning. Walberg's studies of traits of talented adolescents and eminent women essentially duplicated factors leading to eminence in men—for example, intelligence, perseverance, inquisitiveness, creativity, and stimulating social environments.

In Chapter 28 Dean Keith Simonton elaborates on the complicated relationship of giftedness and genius. The core dilemma is that many of Terman's high IQ children did not achieve at high levels; and many of the eminent adults in Cox's biographical study would not have met Terman's IQ criterion. Simonton proposes a multiplicative relationship—among, for example, intellect, motivation, personality, childhood experience, and education—which predicts the disproportionate number of lifetime achievements by just a handful of persons. High drive and dedication are essential, notes Simonton, but mental disturbance and childhood emotional trauma also are common among eminent persons. Further, first borns are more likely to be successful in traditional areas, later borns in artistic and nontraditional areas. In many fields, extensive education apparently provides no great advantage.

24

Identifying Creative Students, Teaching for Creative Growth

GARY A. DAVIS, *University of Wisconsin—Madison*

Before looking at strategies for identifying and developing creativity, let's consider some complexities.

- We can be creative in any single part, several parts, or virtually all parts of our personal, educational, leisure, and professional lives.
- Creative capability may or may not be content-specific. Ability in one area, such as music, may be independent of creative talent in another, for example, science.
- The size of creative accomplishment lies on a continuum. We have almost incidental insights, as when a child invents a play activity, and large-scale creative achievements with endless subproblems, as with the creative landmarks by Frank Lloyd Wright.
- Three prerequisites for creativity are suitable (1) intellectual and information-processing abilities; (2) personality and motivational traits; and (3) family, educational, and cultural experiences. An incomplete list of important abilities appears in Table 24.1. Table 24.2 itemizes some favorable personality and motivational characteristics. The recurrent negative traits in Table 24.3—although helpful identifiers—are not often appreciated.
- Maslow (1954) distinguished between *self-actualized* creative people, who are mentally healthy and habitually creative in all aspects of their lives, and *special talent* creative people, who achieve eminence in an area but may be neurotic or psychotic. Richards (1990) also described *everyday creativity* and *eminent creativity.* While the former are mentally healthy, the majority of eminent artists and riters suffer most commonly from manic-depressive disorders. Richards once noted that if Vincent van Gogh had been given antidepressants, he might have painted happy clowns on black velvet.

- Creative innovation arises from *lengthy* training, experience, planning, and lots of heady problem solving. It also happens *suddenly,* as when Cartoonist Gary Larson substitutes house flies for adoring mothers to produce, "Oh my, what a cute little maggot!"
- Moderately high motivation (arousal seeking, adventurousness) is essential for creative productivity (Farley, 1986). Said Richards (1990), "There is enough disruption to stir the waters without sinking the boat" (p. 312).
- Creative endeavor often first requires irrational and unrestrained fantasy, followed in a second stage by cold logic, analysis, and evaluation.
- Creative thinking can be "forced," as when we set a time and place for brainstorming. Creative inspiration also happens unpredictably—problem solutions, poetry, and even symphonies pop into consciousness. Hemingway once said, "The stuff comes alive and turns crazy on ya' " (Bass, 1968).
- Problem *finding* can be as important as later problem *solving.* Torrance called it sensing gaps in information. Others call it problem sensitivity, problem discovery, or problem defining. If one defines a problem well, the rest may be easy, said Einstein.
- We can study creativity at the level of the individual (e.g., ability, motivation), family (e.g., genetics, child rearing, instruction, birth order, disruption), professional group (e.g., existing knowledge), or society (e.g., supportive or repressive; Richards, 1990).[1]

---

1. See Chapter 35 by Morelock and Feldman and Chapter 28 by Simonton.

Table 24.1 Some Helpful Creative Abilities

Idea fluency	Synthesize
Flexibility	Evaluate
Originality	Think critically
Elaboration	Think logically
Sensitivity to problems and missing information	Think analogically
Define and redefine problems	Think aesthetically
Identify the "real" problem	Reason
Identify subproblems	See relationships
Intuition, Perceptiveness	Make Inferences
Concentrate	Transform
Visualize	Plan
See structure in chaos	Predict outcomes
Detect gaps in information	Anticipate consequences
Resist premature closure	Extend boundaries, go beyond the usual
Regress—think with an uncluttered, perhaps childlike mind	Ask good questions
Avoid habits, mental sets, perceptual sets	Make good decisions
Separate relevant from irrelevant	Understand complex issues
Analyze	Use present knowledge to solve problems

Such complexities remind us of the depth and mystery of creativity. A bad news implication is that current creativity tests cannot achieve high validity (accuracy) in predicting student creativeness. Further, creativity tests may never predict outstanding adult creative achievement.[2]

The good news is that there are many promising ways to identify students with creative personality dispositions, creative abilities, and visible creative talent. There also are lots of ways to raise creativity consciousness, encourage young people to use their creative abilities, and strengthen pivotal abilities and personality traits.

Measuring Creativity and Identifying Creative Students

Using tests, inventories, or rating scales to measure creativeness is just one way to identify students with above-average to high creative potential. Sometimes the identification problem is much simpler.

Many children and adolescents are obviously creative. They are visibly intelligent, energetic, inquisitive, imaginative, and humorous. They relish their creative involvement in art, science, writing, computers, or other academic areas or hobbies. In secondary school we might find strong interests in theater, music composition, creative writing, political or committee leadership, social action, entrepreneurship, as well as in more academic areas.

Two disarmingly simple questions are solid indicators of creative talent in secondary students or adults: (1) Did you have an imaginary playmate as a child? (2) Have you been involved in theater? Some adults will laughingly concede, "I still have an imaginary playmate!" The young child would play with and blame things on the imaginary playmate, and insist that Mom (or the restaurant server) set an extra place at the table. The imaginary friend usually disappears after children enter kindergarten.

Adults who had an imaginary playmate or have a background in theater—they often admit to *both*—will always show creative personality traits, creative abilities (Tables 24.1 and 24.2), and a history of creative involvement. Could a theater teacher help you identify creative high school students?

Informal and Formal Identification of Creativity

As with identifying gifted students generally, recognizing creative talent can be based on *informal,*

---

2. Our best intelligence tests cannot predict outstanding professional achievement either.

Table 24.2 Personality Characteristics Related to Creativity

Positive Traits	*Approximate Synonyms*
Original	Imaginative, resourceful, unconventional, challenges assumptions, asks "what if?", irritated and bored by the obvious
Aware of creativeness	Creativity conscious, values originality, values own creativity
Independent	Self-confident, individualistic, sets own rules, unconcerned with impressing others, resists societal demands
Risk-taking	Not afraid to be different or try something new, willing to cope with hostility, willing to cope with failure
Motivated	Adventurous, sensation seeking, enthusiastic, excitable, spontaneous, impulsive, goes beyond assigned tasks
Curious	Questioning, experimenting, inquisitive, wide interests
Sense of humor	Playful, plays with ideas, childlike freshness in thinking
Attracted to complexity	Attracted to novelty, asymmetry, the mysterious; is a complex person; tolerant of ambiguity, disorder, incongruity
Artistic	Artistic and aesthetic interests
Open-minded	Receptive to new ideas, other viewpoints, new experiences, and growth; liberal, altruistic
Needs time alone	Reflective, introspective, internally preoccupied, sensitive, may be withdrawn, likes to work alone
Intuitive	Perceptive, sees relationships, uses all senses in observing

subjective evaluations by teachers, parents, peers, or the students themselves, or on *formal* creativity test or inventory scores. Sometimes, formal-looking assessments (e.g., rating scales) are used to record informal impressions of students' creative abilities, personality traits, or creative achievements.

Table 24.3 Negative Traits of Some Creative Persons

Overactive physically and mentally
Temperamental, emotional
Indifferent to conventions and courtesies
Questions rules, laws, and authority
Resists domination
Egocentric, intolerant, tactless
Rebellious, uncooperative, stubborn, demanding
Capricious, careless, disorderly
Cynical, sarcastic
Absentminded, forgetful, mind wanders
Argumentative, argues that everyone else is wrong
Sloppy and disorganized with details and unimportant
    matters

Source: Primarily from Smith (1966) and Torrance (1962).

Biographical Information

A *certain*—but little used—way to locate creative students at any grade level is to examine students' past and present creative activities (e.g., Bull & Davis, 1980; Holland, 1961; Lees-Haley, 1978; Plucker, 1999b; Okuda, Runco, & Berger, 1991). Face validity is high. For example, Holland identified high school students who were creatively talented in art or science by soliciting their history of creative activities. *He concluded that past creative achievement is the single best predictor of future creative achievement.*

Creativity tests are incomplete. As we will see, creative personality inventories measure personality and motivational dispositions. Divergent thinking tests measure some divergent thinking abilities. But information about students' real creative involvement covers both—and more.

Does the elementary child have unusually wide interests, unique hobbies, strange collections? Perhaps dinosaurs, magic, Egyptology, Charlie Chaplin impressions, or a collection of animal bones? Does the child have unusual experience or talent in art, poetry, creative writing, handicrafts, building things, music, dance, computers, or a science area? Perhaps you know a "dinosaur kid," a "photography kid," or a child who knows more about Picasso, Wynton Marsalis, Russian cosmonauts, DNA, hostas, or the insides of computers than do most teachers. Maybe the child or adolescent is a theater kid or had an imaginary playmate.

Torrance's "Things Done on Your Own." Torrance's (1962) "Things Done on Your Own" is a checklist of 100 creative activities in language arts, science, social studies, art, "and other fields." Students are asked to "Indicate . . . only the things you have done on your own, not the things you have been assigned or made to do" (p. 251; see Table 24.4).

Renzulli's Action Information. Renzulli's Action Information (Renzulli & Reis, 1997) helps se-

lect motivated, creative students to work on independent projects.[3] Action Information is either (1) student ideas for an independent research project or (2) teacher observations of students' strong interests and high motivation. A few of examples of Action Information appear in Table 24.5.

Consensual Assessment Technique, Detroit Public Schools Creativity Scales. With Amabile's consensual assessment strategy, teachers elicit samples of students' creative work and then rate its creativeness. For example, in one study five- to ten-year-old children made up a ten-minute story to fit a

Table 24.4   Sample Items from Torrance's (1962) Things Done On Your Own Inventory

Wrote a poem, story, or play
Produced a puppet show
Acted in, directed, organized, or designed stage settings for a play or skit
Made up a song, dance, musical composition, or new game
Explored a cave
Read a science magazine
Printed photographs
Made an electric motor, musical instrument, ink, or leaf prints
Planned an experiment, dissected an animal
Grafted a plant or rooted one from a cutting
Collected insects, rocks, stamps, postmarks, or wild flowers
Kept a daily record of weather
Organized or helped to organize a club
Figured out a way of improving the way we do something at home or in school
Found out how some government agency (post office, court, etc.) operates
Made a poster for a club, school, or other event
Organized or helped organize paper drive, rummage sale, etc.
Sketched a landscape, designed jewelry
Illustrated a story, drew cartoons
Made linoleum cuts, watercolor, oil painting
Made a toy for a child (or a wood or soap carving, ornamental basket)
Drew up plans for (or constructed) an invention or apparatus
Made up recipe

Table 24.5   Examples of Renzulli's Action Information

Goes "above and beyond the call of duty" in completing, for example, an art, writing, or science project that shows superlative quality.
Is obsessed with a particular topic or area of study.
Is sought out by others because he or she is an expert in a particular area.
Is labeled by others (not always in complimentary ways) as the "math marvel," "computer whiz kid," "poet in residence," or "mad scientist."
Wants to "get something going," for example, a class newspaper, money-raising project, field trip, or action on a social problem.
Has extracurricular activities that are more important than regular school work.
May start a club, interest group, or project (e.g., film making) on his or her own.
Typically is the class clown or lackadaisical, but becomes very serious and immersed in a particular topic area.
Voluntarily visits museums, laboratories, power plants, etc., on his or her own.
Forgets to come back to class or is always late when returning from a particular course or special interest area, for example, the computer, art, or industrial arts room.
Is a clever humorist—sees whimsical implications of otherwise serious situations.
Has set up a laboratory, photography darkroom, or other special interest area at home on his or her own.
Feels compulsion to begin work on a topic ("I have to write it down before I go nuts").

Source: From Renzulli and Reis (1997). Reprinted by permission of Creative Learning Press.

---

3. See Chapter 14 by Renzulli and Reis.

wordless picture book adventure of a boy and his dog at a pond (Amabile & Hennessey, 1988). With high interrater reliability, three teachers rated the stories on *creativity, how well they liked the story, novelty, imagination, logic, emotion, grammar, detail, vocabulary,* and *"straightforwardness."*

With the similar Detroit Public Schools Creativity Scales (Parke & Byrnes, 1984), community experts in a subject area evaluated the creativeness of music compositions, music performances, dance, art, short story and novel writing, drama, poetry, or speeches.

Using or Building a Creative Activities Inventory. One could adapt Torrance's 100-item checklist, Renzulli's Action Information strategy; Amabile's consensual assessment technique; the Detroit Public Schools strategy; Holland's creative activity checklist; the Okuda, Runco, and Berger Creative Activities Check List; the Lees-Haley Creative Behavior Inventory, or the Bull and Davis Statement of Past Creative Activities to help identify creatively gifted students.

One also could create a brief and original inventory, to be completed by students or parents, that simply asks about a student's past or present strong interests and hobbies. For example:

> Describe any hobbies, collections, or strong interests that you [your child may] have had. For example, have you [has your child] been really interested in writing poetry or stories, magic, theater, computers, Ancient Athens, reptiles or dinosaurs, collections, science, space travel, art, handicrafts, or music? Other hobbies or collections? If so, list them.

A few statements reflecting outstanding past or present creative involvement likely will emerge. A good relationship exists between past, present, and future creativity.

Personality and Motivation Inventories

Creative people are unique individuals, but they have a lot in common. They necessarily have personality and motivational dispositions that help them think in unconventional ways, become absorbed in their projects, and risk failure and making fools of themselves. Inventories that assess creative traits can be administered and scored relatively easily.

As a shining example of on-target efficiency, teachers can use Renzulli's thoughtfully constructed ten-item creativity rating scale, part of his Scales for Rating the Behavioral Characteristics of Superior Students (Renzulli & Reis, 1997; Table 24.6).

My How Do You Think (HDYT) test (Davis, 1975; Davis & Bull, 1978) evaluates most of the traits in Table 24.2, along with belief in ESP and flying saucers.[4] HDYT was validated against actual creative products (art, writing, invention) required for a college creativity class and consistently shows high internal reliability (about 0.93). It works well with high school students and even middle school students (who occasionally need a word defined; Lees-Haley & Swords, 1981). With gifted nine- to twelve-year-old children, Lees-Haley and Sutton (1982) found correlations of 0.42 and 0.59 between HDYT scores and scores on their Creative Behavior Inventory, a checklist of creative activities. The children found HDYT quite interesting.

Published spin-offs from HDYT include the high school Group Inventory for Finding Interests II (GIFFI II; Davis & Rimm, 1982), a shortened version of HDYT. The Group Inventory for Finding Interests I (GIFFI I), for middle school students, takes items from HDYT and Rimm's elementary school Group Inventory for Finding (Creative) Talent (GIFT; Rimm & Davis, 1976). Rimm (1983) also developed the Preschool and Kindergarten Interest Descriptor (PRIDE), which parents fill out to describe their four- or five-year-old child.

Given the complexities of creativity, HDYT, GIFFI I and II, and Rimm's GIFT and PRIDE show reasonable validity and high internal reliability.

As with the Davis and Rimm tests, Schaefer's (1971) Creativity Attitude Survey, with 32 yes-no items normed on fourth- and fifth-grade children, measures humor, confidence in one's ideas, appreciation for novelty and fantasy, interest in art and writing, and attraction to the abstract and magical.

Feldhusen, Denny, and Condon (1965) created their unpublished Creativity Self-Report Scale for use with middle and high school students. It includes 67 phrases considered by Torrance (1962) "to be descriptive of the behaviors and attributes of creative persons." A sample of the items/characteristics appears in Table 24.7.

Gough (1979) validated an easily used creativity scale for his 300-item Adjective Check List (ACL;

---

4. HDYT is available from the author.

Table 24.6   Creativity Characteristics

	1	2	3	4
1. Displays a great deal of curiosity about many things; is constantly asking questions about anything and everything.	___	___	___	___
2. Generates a large number of ideas or solutions to problems and questions; often offers unusual ("way out"), unique, clever responses.	___	___	___	___
3. Is uninhibited in expressing opinion; is sometimes radical and spirited in disagreement; is tenacious.	___	___	___	___
4. Is a high risk taker; is adventurous and speculative.	___	___	___	___
5. Displays a good deal of intellectual playfulness; fantasizes; imagines ("I wonder what would happen if . . ."); manipulates ideas (i.e., changes, elaborates upon them); is often concerned with adapting, improving, and modifying institutions, objects, and systems.	___	___	___	___
6. Displays a keen sense of humor and sees humor in situations that may not appear to be humorous to others.	___	___	___	___
7. Is unusually aware of his or her impulses and more open to the irrational in himself or herself (freer expression of feminine interest for boys, greater than usual amount of independence for girls); shows emotional sensitivity.	___	___	___	___
8. Is sensitive to beauty; attends to aesthetic characteristics of things.	___	___	___	___
9. Is nonconforming; accepts disorder; is not interested in details; is individualistic; does not mind being different.	___	___	___	___
10. Criticizes constructively; is unwilling to accept authoritarian pronouncements without critical examination.	___	___	___	___

Total Score _____

Scoring Weights: 1 = Seldom or never; 2 = Occasionally; 3 = Considerably; 4 = Almost always.

Source: From Scales for Rating Behavioral Characteristics of Superior Students (Renzulli et al, 2001). Reprinted by permission of Creative Learning Press.

Gough & Heilbrun, 1965). The creativity score is simply the number of positive items checked minus the number of negative items checked. The 18 positive items are *capable, clever, confident, egotistical, humorous, individualistic, informal, insightful, intelligent, interests wide, inventive, original, reflective, resourceful, self-confident, sexy, snobbish,* and *unconventional.* The 12 negative items are *affected, cautious, commonplace, conservative, conventional, dissatisfied, honest, interests narrow, mannerly, sincere, submissive,* and *suspicious.*

Divergent Thinking Tests

The Torrance Tests of Creative Thinking (TTCT; Torrance, 1966a) remain the most popular creativity tests of any kind. Torrance may have inadvertently led others to believe that his tests measure creativity, all creativity, and nothing but creativity, but he never deluded himself. From his original technical manual (Torrance, 1966b, p. 23):

Since a person can behave creatively in an almost infinite number of ways, in the opinion of the author it

Table 24.7   Sample of Items from the Creativity Self-Report Scale

Instructions: Indicate which phrases are descriptive of you:

Not bothered by mess or disorder	Like adventure
Like things that are mysterious	Full of energy
Like working with ideas	Full of curiosity
Like to be independent	Have some odd habits
Get lost in a problem	Like complicated ideas
Ask many questions	Like to hear other people's ideas
Act childish or silly sometimes	A self-starter
Self-confident	Good sense of humor
See beauty in some things	Sometimes stubborn
Persistent	Willing to take risks
Sometimes sloppy	Sometimes act without planning
Question authority and rules	Open-minded
Enjoy taking things apart	Cannot write fast enough to keep up with thoughts
Stick with a project to completion	Seen by some students as being different
Look for new ways of doing things	Not afraid of being thought to be "different"
Sometimes question or disagree with statements made by the teacher	

Source: From Feldhusen, Denny, & Condon, 1965.

would be ridiculous even to try to develop a comprehensive battery of tests of creative thinking that would sample any kind of universe of creative thinking abilities. . . . He does believe that the sets of test tasks assembled in the [TTCT] sample a rather wide range of the abilities in such a universe.

The TTCT were ten years in development and have the most complete administration and (updated) scoring guides and norms (Torrance 1990a, 1990b). Multitudes of validation studies exist, including a twenty-two-year longitudinal validation by Torrance (1981a). Plucker's (1999a) reanalysis of Torrance's longitudinal data indicated that the TTCT predicted adult creativeness three times better than IQ scores.

The TTCT verbal battery includes seven subtests in each of two forms. For example, students ask questions about an odd picture, list unusual uses for a cardboard box or tin can, list improvements for a stuffed elephant or monkey, or list consequences of an unlikely event (e.g., clouds are so low you can only see people's feet). The nonverbal/figural battery includes three subtests, also in two forms. These require the test taker to create a meaningful drawing from an incomplete or abstract form.

Verbal tests may be group administered from fourth grade through graduate school, but administered individually from kindergarten through third grade. Figural tests may be group administered at any age level. Figural tests are more culture-fair.

Originally, the TTCT produced four scores: for idea *fluency, flexibility, originality,* and *elaboration.* In 1984 Torrance and Ball produced a "streamlined" scoring system for the figural tests, intended to both expedite scoring and evaluate a total of eighteen creative abilities (Torrance, 1990b). In addition to *fluency, originality,* and *elaboration,* the streamlined scoring evaluates *abstractness of title, resistance to premature closure, emotional expressiveness, story telling articulateness, movement or action, synthesis of incomplete figures, unusual visualization, extending or breaking boundaries, internal visualization, humor, richness of imagery, colorfulness of imagery,* and *fantasy.*

The Getzels and Jackson (1962) five tests include Word Association, Uses for Things, Hidden Shapes, Fables, and Make-up Problems. These are scored for number of ideas, number of categories of ideas, originality, correctness (in finding hidden geometric shapes), appropriateness (of fable endings and made-up problems), and complexity (of made-up problems). Some consider the Make-up Problems test, in which subjects create mathematical problems based on numerical statements, to be a test of mathematical creativity.

The five Wallach and Kogan (1965) tests, Instances (e.g., "Name all the round things that you can think of"), Alternate Uses, Similarities (e.g., between a cat and a mouse), Pattern Meanings, and Line Meanings, are scored for originality and fluency. Both the Getzels and Jackson and the Wallach and Kogan batteries are published only in their respective books and apparently may be used without charge.

Torrance's (1981b) Thinking Creatively in Action and Movement is unique in that it was designed for children ages three to eight. For example, subtests ask children to show as many ways as they can to walk or run from one spot to another or put a paper cup in a waste basket.

Thinking Creatively with Sounds and Words (Torrance, Khatena, & Cunnington, 1973) includes two different tests (sets of audio recordings). With Onomatopoeia and Images, the test taker writes one idea stimulated by each of the ten word stimuli (e.g., *zoom, moan, fizzy, jingle*). The words are repeated. With Sounds and Images, the person describes one idea stimulated by each of four abstract sounds, which also are repeated. Responses to both tests are scored only for *originality*, according to norms.

One unique newcomer is Urban and Jellen's (1993) Test for Creative Thinking–Drawing Production (TCT-DP). The TCT-DP most resembles Torrance's figural tests, and is said to evaluate both creative abilities and personality traits. A favorable 1990 evaluation led Polish researchers to recommend that the TCT-DP test be used as an official screening instrument in Poland for identifying gifted and creative students.

Forms A and B both include a single six-inch square frame with six "figural fragments": a 90-degree angle, a half-circle, a squiggly line, a dot, a short dotted line, and outside the frame a small square with one open side. The test can be used with subjects "between 5 and 95 years of age." Administration is untimed, but usually requires fifteen minutes or less. Scoring is claimed to require one to two minutes.

Eleven scores are based on extensions of the figural fragments; additions to the used or extended figural fragments; new figures, symbols, or elements; connections made between one figural fragment and another; connections made to produce a theme; extensions of the small open square; other drawing extensions that break the boundary or lie outside the large square frame; breaking away from two-dimensionality; drawings that show humor or emotion; surrealistic, fictional, abstract, or unconventional elements or figures; and speed.

The authors claim that the TDT-CP is different from and superior to other divergent thinking tests. However, both the TDT-CP and the streamlined scoring of the Torrance figural tests award points for unconventionality and fantasy (originality), humor, affectivity (emotional expressiveness), producing a theme (story telling articulateness), and extending or breaking boundaries.

Two other published divergent thinking tests are the original Guilford (1970) tests and the Monitor Test of Creative Potential, for age seven and older (Hoepfner & Hemenway, 1973).

Other Creativity Tests

The unique Percept Generic Test (Smith & Carlsson, 1987) repeatedly presents a picture at ever-shorter exposure times until the original is quite unrecognizable. Creative people more quickly break away from the dominant ("correct") perception and construct an imaginative, subjective interpretation. The Creative Processes Rating Scales evaluates elementary school children's creative processes in the visual arts (Kulp & Tarter, 1986). A Test of Musical Divergent Production evaluates *fluency, flexibility, originality, elaboration,* and *quality* with instrumental music students (Gorder, 1980). The Judging Criteria Instrument (Eichenberger, 1978) evaluates creativity in a physics class, with rating scales that evaluate fluency, flexibility, originality, elaboration, usefulness, social acceptance, and worth to science.[5]

Recommendations

In this section I mentioned informal ways to recognize creativeness, along with inventories of past creative activities, personality/motivation inventories, and divergent thinking tests. To these I might add simple "creativeness" ratings or nominations by teachers, parents, peers, or the students themselves.

---

5. Lists of mostly obscure tests for particular subject areas or purposes may be found in Dacey (1989), Davis (1971, 1973, 1989), Kaltsoonis (1971, 1972), Kaltsoonis and Honeywell (1980), and especially Runco (1999).

Generally, to have confidence in identifying creative talent, one should use *at least* two criteria. If a student scores high on both, a teacher can be reasonably certain of valid identification. Tests, inventories, or ratings—especially divergent thinking tests—can be misleading; a student might easily be creative in areas not evaluated by the instrument or the rater.

Personality/biographical inventories and divergent thinking tests both work reasonably well—given such limitations as the complexity of creativity and evaluating just part of human creativeness (i.e., a sample of personality traits or divergent thinking abilities). Renzulli's creativity rating scale, How Do You Think, GIFFI I and II, GIFT, PRIDE, and Schaefer's Creativity Attitude Survey show good track records for predicting student creativeness.

Regarding divergent thinking tests, the Torrance Tests must remain at the top of the list, although Urban and Jellen's TCT-DP seems promising. If cost is an issue, the Getzels and Jackson and Wallach and Kogan tests have careful development histories and may be used apparently without charge.

As a final reminder, tests and inventories that try to *measure* personality dispositions and creative abilities are just one way to *identify* creative children and youth. An awareness of creative characteristics, creative abilities, and especially students' backgrounds of creative activities can help teachers and others recognize creative students with accuracy and validity—without using tests or inventories.

Teaching for Creative Growth

An elementary issue is: Can creativity be taught? Or are you born with it? The answer is *yes* and *yes.* Some people are born with a combination of creative genius, intelligence, extraordinary motivation, and a sense of destiny that leads them to eminent creative achievement. Mozart, Picasso, Marie Curie, George Washington Carver, and Thomas Edison come to mind.

At the same time, it is absolutely true that everyone's creative ability, creative productivity, and creative living can be elevated. At the very least, we all can make better use of the creative abilities with which we were born. Sternberg (2000) argued that high creativity stems from conscious decisions, for example, to redefine problems, overcome obstacles, do what you love to do—and believe in yourself.

Goals of Creativity Training

We will organize creativity training concepts under five headings:

- Fostering creativity consciousness and creative attitudes
- Improving students' understanding of creativity and creative people
- Exercising creative abilities
- Teaching creative thinking techniques
- Involving students in creative activities

Fostering Creativity Consciousness and Creative Attitudes

Carl Rogers (1962) gave us the popular phrase *psychologically safe environment.* Others have called it a *creative environment* or *creative atmosphere.* By any name, it's basic to promoting creativity consciousness and creative attitudes.

Creativity consciousness is crucial to becoming a more creative person, yet it's the easiest to teach. Creativity consciousness will be aided by virtually any classroom creativity activity—especially if the activity begins with an unambiguous and reinforcing, "Now let's be creative!"

With *creative attitudes,* students will value creative ideas and innovation; they will be receptive to the unusual, perhaps far-fetched ideas of others; and they will be consciously disposed to think creatively, play with ideas, and become involved in creative activities. An awareness of blocks to their creative thinking—mental sets, perceptual sets, rules, traditions, and especially conformity pressures—will help students dare to be different.

Every creativity course and professional workshop emphasizes creativity consciousness, appropriate creative attitudes, and everyday blocks to creativity and imagination. So do creativity-conscious teachers.

Creativity consciousness and creative attitudes may be helped if learners understand that the history of civilization is a chain of creative innovations in every area. Innovation never stops.

Hopefully, students can grasp the importance of creativity for their own personal growth and development—their *self-actualization.* Self-actualization means developing your potential and becoming what you are capable of becoming. This includes being an independent, forward-growing, fully functioning, democratic-minded, and mentally healthy individual. After many thoughtful years, both Rogers (1962) and Maslow (1954) concluded that self-actualization and creative development were essentially identical. Most creativity scholars agree.

Fleith (2000) and Rejskind (2000) suggested how teachers can raise creativity consciousness and creative attitudes. For example:

- Maintain a psychologically safe classroom environment;
- Help students become aware of their creativity;
- Recognize and reward each child's creativity;
- Encourage fantasy and imagination;
- Accept students as they are;
- Give positive, constructive evaluation;
- Help students resist peer pressure to conform;
- Recognize students' strengths, abilities, and interests;
- Encourage questions, different responses, humor, and risk-taking;
- Be aware that a child's "difficult" behavior could be a manifestation of creativity.

Fleith described an atmosphere that inhibits creativity: Students cannot share ideas, ideas are ignored, mistakes are not allowed, one right answer is required, competition is extreme, fear may exist, and the class has a "controlling teacher."

Importantly, creativity consciousness and creative attitudes also can be raised by a teacher who models creative attitudes and creative behavior. Look in the mirror. How should you think and act to model creativity? To stimulate creativity in students? What type of questions can you ask so that students must think creatively?

Improving Students' Understanding of Creativity and Creative People

If students better understand the topic of creativity, it will help raise creativity consciousness, demystify creativity, and convince students that they are perfectly capable—with interest and effort—of hatching creative ideas and doing creative things. Although discussions must be tailored to students' ages and abilities, students can be helped to understand:

- The nature of creative ideas as *modifications* of existing ideas (e.g., ever-evolving computers, automobiles, and athletic shoes), *new combinations* of

ideas (e.g., Reese's Peanut Butter Cups, TV and VCR combinations), and products of *analogical thinking* (e.g., Andrew Lloyd Weber's Broadway shows, inspired by Jesus, Evita Peron, and T. S. Eliot's poetry about cats).
- Attitudes and personality traits that contribute to creative imagination and creative productivity–creativity consciousness and the traits in Table 24.2, 24.6, and 24.7.
- Deliberate creativity techniques that extend intuition and spontaneous imagination (described later in this chapter).
- Divergent thinking tests, personality/motivation inventories, and assessments of past creative activities.
- Speculations on the creative process, for example, the Wallas (1926) stages of *preparation, incubation, illumination,* and *verification,* and the Creative Problem Solving steps of *fact finding, problem finding, idea finding, solution finding* (idea evaluation), and *acceptance finding* (idea implementation). The creative process also may be seen as a mental transformation or change in perception, which can be illustrated with optical illusions and *Far Side* cartoons.

Depending on ages and abilities, students also can learn about definitions and theories of creativity, abilities that underlie creative expression, habits and traditions that block creativity, and the importance of creativity to themselves and to the evolution of society.[6]

Exercising Creative Abilities

As with any other mental or physical ability, we can strengthen creative abilities with practice. For example, classroom brainstorming sessions can focus on local school problems—traffic safety, hall and grounds cleanliness, overcrowding, under funding, smoking, drugs, guns, bullying, raising money, or increasing attendance at parents' night—as well as on subject-related topics. "How can we improve this?" "What would happen if . . . ?"

Independent and small-group projects in academic or high interest areas nurture such complex abilities as independent thinking, clarifying and defining

---

6. See Davis (1998) for more details.

problems, generating ideas, analyzing, organizing, thinking critically, evaluating, making decisions, and communicating results. Such projects also improve technical skills, library and information retrieval skills, and social skills.

If one wished to focus on specific creative abilities (e.g., those in Table 25.2), *fluency* would be exercised by encouraging students to, for example, "Think of all the ideas you can"; *flexibility* by "How else could we do this?" or "How else could we solve this problem?"; *originality* by "Can you think of a new approach?", "New ideas?", "Combine some ideas?", "Where could we borrow ideas?", "What else is like this?"; and *elaboration* by encouraging students to add, embellish, and extend initial ideas and solutions.

Problem sensitivity can be exercised with open-ended questions that ask, "What *don't* I know about (the Civil War, clouds, history of women's rights, mixing paints, dinosaurs, global warming)?"; *predicting outcomes* by asking, "What will happen if we do it this way?"; *visualization* ability with guided visualization activities (see Bagley & Hess, 1984; Eberle, 1995; Leff, 1984). Some creativity workbooks present exercises for strengthening *analogical thinking* (e.g., Gordon, 1968; Stanish, 1977, 1988). For example: How are you like a rubber band? A candle? A doorknob? What does this poetry or music suggest?

Idea evaluation can made objective with an evaluation matrix. Problem solutions are listed vertically on the left axis of a matrix, evaluation criteria are listed along the top axis. Each idea is rated on each criteria; rating totals appear at the right side. Or a teacher can simply ask: "Is this a good idea?", "Which idea will work best?", or "What would our president (or your mother) say about this?"

An imaginative teacher can create exercises for strengthening *analysis* ("What's wrong here?"); *synthesis* ("Can we combine some of these ideas?"); *logical reasoning* ("If all ants are insects, are all insects ants?"); *planning* ("What do we need to do in order to put on a class play?"); *prioritizing* ("In what order should we do these things?"); *recognizing relevancy* ("What doesn't matter?" "What's most important?"); *making inferences* ("What can we learn from this?"); *critical thinking* ("What's wrong with doing it this way?"); *futuristic thinking* ("How might this be done in another 100 years?"); *raising awareness of blocks and barriers* ("How did laws and habits affect this innovation?"). The three dozen creative abilities in

Table 24.2 will suggest further open-ended creativity-stimulating questions. Be imaginative.

Teaching Creative Thinking Techniques

It is not easy for adults or children to adopt an unfamiliar thinking technique. Nonetheless, creative people do use creativity techniques, consciously or unconsciously. Personally, I have found ideas for comical (more-or-less) dialogues by creating checklists of well-known children's stories (e.g., Alice in Wonderland, Cinderella), famous people and comedians (e.g., Sigmund Freud, Woody Allen), and myths (e.g., Frankenstein), and analogically drawing ideas from these sources (see Davis, 1998). I also used the morphological synthesis technique, a matrix method, to create hundreds of character education exercises that use brainstorming, analogical thinking, "What would happen if . . .?", and visualization (Davis, 1996a, 1996b).

Perhaps the most common idea-finding technique is deliberate analogical thinking. As a few examples, every issue of every newspaper includes political cartoons and/or cartoon strips analogically inspired by popular movies, TV commercials, historical or biblical events, or current news incidents. From today's newspaper, comical-looking Frank stands between two shoulder-high shrubs exclaiming, "Call me Bill Clinton!" Ernest happily asks, "Why's that?" "I'm between two bushes!" Liszt's Hungarian Rhapsodies stem from Gypsy folk tunes, and the *Star Spangled Banner* melody came from an English drinking song. Shakespeare's plays are rooted in historical events or other plays or literature. Darwin's natural selection idea came from English cattle breeding. Velcro was inspired by cockleburs. Examples are endless (see Davis, 1998, Gordon, 1974).

Brainstorming—with its deferred judgment and deliberately looking for wild ideas—is a household word. Its creator, Alex Osborn (1963), observed that one cannot be critical and creative at the same time. Brainstorming produces a creative atmosphere, encourages imagination, teaches creativity consciousness and creative attitudes (e.g., receptiveness to wild ideas), and teaches students to consider many ideas before settling on a solution. A fun spin-off is reverse brainstorming—thinking of ways to make the situation *worse* ("How can we increase vandalism?"). With brainwriting, a sheet of paper is circulated around a small group, each person adding an idea to the growing list.

Attribute listing is taught in design engineering classes as a simple way to change or improve anything. One lists important attributes of a product (e.g., size, shape, material, color, name, function, intended market, etc.) and then itemizes ways to modify each attribute. Fran Stryker, creator of the mid-century Lone Ranger series, modified characteristics of *characters, goals, obstacles,* and *outcomes.*

Morphological synthesis is a simple extension of attribute listing. Ideas for one attribute of a problem (e.g., "How can we stimulate creativity?") appear on one axis of a matrix, and ideas for another attribute (e.g., "Who should do it?") appear on the other. Matrix cells represent idea combinations—some preposterous and some creatively suitable.

Osborn's idea checklist lies at the core of his classic brainstorming book *Applied Imagination.* His "73 idea-spurring questions" include, for example, *adapt, modify, magnify, split up, substitute, reverse, new twist, new form, other process, other ingredient, turn it upside down,* and *combine ideas.* The checklist stimulates ideas for many kinds of problems.[7]

Finally, three imagination-prodding techniques based in analogical thinking—broadly defined—are found in Gordon's (1961, 1968, 1974; see also Stanish, 1988) synectics methods. Direct Analogy is looking for analogically related problems (and solutions) in nature. Personal Analogy is imagining oneself to be a problem object. Fantasy Analogy is thinking of how, in one's wildest imagination, one would like the problem to be solved. Your refrigerator's ice maker was born in a synectics session.

Involving Students in Creative Activities

The most logically sound way to "teach creativity" is to involve students in creative activities and projects, including individual and small group projects.[8] Two national creativity-stimulating programs are *Future Problem Solving* and *Odyssey of the Mind.* Both were designed to teach creativity by involving students in challenging problems and projects.

In the report by Fleith (2000), classroom strategies and activities that elementary teachers believed would increase creative growth included

- Cooperative groups, which expose students to differing points of view;
- Cluster groups, based on student interests and strengths;
- Allowing students to select what they want to do;
- Arts centers;
- Drawing;
- Giving options;
- Brainstorming;
- Open-ended activities;
- Hands-on activities;
- Creative writing.

Also, currently available creativity-stimulating opportunities should be examined and perhaps expanded. Are music, science, and art programs adequate? Are students encouraged to become involved in scientific, aesthetic, and independent research activities? Are community resources and mentors used to good advantage?

SUMMARY AND CONCLUSIONS

Identifying creative students might be simple. They will show enthusiasm, curiosity, humor, and lots of creative interests and activities. Surveys of students' past creative behavior, creative personality/motivation inventories, divergent thinking tests, and teacher-, parent-, or self-ratings of creativeness can help identification. To offset reliability and validity problems, at least two criteria of creativeness should be used.

Fostering creative development is a core goal of most G/T programs. A teacher can strengthen creativity consciousness and favorable creative attitudes, help students understand creativity and creative people, exercise simple and complex creative abilities, teach creative thinking techniques and their related principles, and most importantly engage students in activities that stimulate the development of creative thinking abilities and proclivities.

QUESTIONS FOR THOUGHT AND DISCUSSION

1. Consider the grade level of students you expect to teach. Based on your own conception of creativity and Davis's chapter, how would you identify students with high creative potential?

---

7. This and other idea checklists appear in Davis (1998).
8. See Chapter 14 by Renzulli and Reis.

2. With these same students in mind, how might you:
   a. Create a "psychologically safe" creative atmosphere?
   b. Exercise simple and complex creative abilities?
   c. Promote creative involvement?

3. Will the complexities of creativity outlined at the beginning of Davis's chapter complicate or interfere with your efforts to identify or strengthen creativity? Explain.

4. Rate yourself on Renzulli's Creativity Characteristics (Table 24.6). What do you learn about yourself?

REFERENCES

Amabile, T. M., & Hennessey, B. A. (1988). Story-telling: A method for assessing children's creativity. *Journal of Creative Behavior, 22,* 235–246.

Bagley, M. T., & Hess, K. K. (1984). *200 ways of using imagery in the classroom.* New York: Trillium.

Bass, S. (1968). *Why man creates* (film). Oakland, CA: Kaiser Aluminum.

Bull, K. S., & Davis, G. A. (1980). Evaluating creative potential using the statement of past creative activities. *Journal of Creative Behavior, 14,* 249–257.

Davis, G. A. (1975). In frumious pursuit of the creative person. *Journal of Creative Behavior, 9,* 75–87.

Davis, G. A. (1996a). *Teaching values.* Cross Plains, WI: Westwood.

Davis, G. A. (1996b). *Values are forever.* Cross Plains, WI: Westwood.

Davis, G. A. (1998). *Creativity is forever* (4th ed.). Dubuque, IA: Kendall/Hunt.

Davis, G. A., & Bull, K. S. (1978). Strengthening affective components of creativity in a college course. *Journal of Educational Psychology, 70,* 833–836.

Davis, G. A., & Rimm, S. (1982). Group inventory for finding interests (GIFFI) I and II: Instruments for identifying creative potential in the junior and senior high school. *Journal of Creative Behavior, 16,* 50–57.

Eberle, B. (1995). *Scamper.* Waco, TX: Prufrock.

Eichenberger, R. J. (1978). Creativity measurement through use of judgment criteria in physics. *Educational and Psychological Measurement, 38,* 221–227.

Farley, F. H. (1986, May). The big T in personality. *Psychology Today,* 47–52.

Feldhusen, J. F., Denny, T., & Condon, C. F. (1965). *Manual for the creativity self-report scale.* Unpublished manuscript, Purdue University, West Lafayette, IN.

Fleith, D. (2000). Teacher and students perceptions of creativity in the classroom environment. *Roeper Review, 22,* 148–157.

Getzels, J. W., & Jackson, P. W. (1962). *Creativity and intelligence.* New York: Wiley.

Gorder, W. D. (1980). Divergent production abilities as constructs of musical creativity. *Journal of Research in Music Education, 28*(1), 38–42.

Gordon, W. J. J. (1961). *Synectics.* New York: Harper & Row.

Gordon, W. J. J. (1968). *Making it strange* (books 1–4). New York: Harper & Row.

Gordon, W. J. J. (1974). Some source material in discovery by analogy. *Journal of Creative Behavior, 8,* 239–257.

Gough, H. G. (1979). A creative personality scale for the Adjective Check List. *Journal of Personality and Social Psychology, 37,* 1398–1405.

Gough, H. G., & Heilbrun, A. B., Jr. (1965). *The Adjective Check List manual.* Palo Alto, CA: Consulting Psychologists Press.

Guilford, J. P. (1970). *Creativity tests for children: A manual of interpretation.* Orange, CA: Sheridan Psychological Services.

Hoepfner, R., & Hemenway, J. (1973). *Test of creative potential.* Hollywood, CA: Monitor.

Holland, J. L. (1961). Creative and academic performance among talented adolescents. *Journal of Educational Psychology, 52,* 136–147.

Kulp, M., & Tarter, B. J. (1986). The creative processes rating scale. *Creative Child and Adult Quarterly, 11,* 166–173.

Lees-Haley, P. R. (1978). *Creative behavior inventory.* Huntsville, AL: Basic Research, Inc.

Lees-Haley, P. R., & Sutton, J. (1982). An extension of Davis' *How Do You Think* test to elementary school students. *Roeper Review, 4*(3), 43.

Lees-Haley, P. R., & Swords, M. (1981). A validation study of Davis' *How Do You Think* (HDYT) test with middle school students. *Journal for the Education of the Gifted, 4*(2), 144–146.

Leff, H. L. (1984). *Playful perception.* Burlington, VT: Waterfront Books.

Maslow, A. H. (1954). *Motivation and personality.* New York: Harper & Row.

Okuda, S. M., Runco, M. A., & Berger, D. E. (1991). Creativity and the finding and solving of real-world problems. *Journal of Psychoeducational Assessment, 9,* 45–53.

Osborn, A. F. (1963). *Applied imagination* (3rd ed.). New York: Scribners.

Parke, B. N., & Byrnes, P. (1984). Toward objectifying the measurement of creativity. *Roeper Review, 6,* 216–218.

Plucker, J. A. (1999a). Is the proof in the pudding? Reanalyses of Torrance's (1958 to present) longitudinal data. *Creativity Research Journal, 12,* 103–114.

Plucker, J. A. (1999b). Reanalysis of student responses to creativity checklists: Evidence of content generality. *Journal of Creative Behavior, 33,* 126–137.

Renzulli, J. S., & Reis, S. M. (1997). *Schoolwide enrichment model: A how-to guide for educational excellence.* Mansfield Center, CT: Creative Learning Press.

Renzulli, J. S., Smith, L., White, A., Callahan, C., Hartman, R., & Westberg, K. (2001). *Scales for rating the behavioral characteristics of superior students* [manual and 10 rating scales]. Mansfield Center, CT: Creative Learning Press.

Rejskind, G. (2000). TAG teachers: Only the creative need apply. *Roeper Review, 22,* 153–157.

Richards, R. (1990). Everyday creativity, eminent creativity, and health. *Creativity Research Journal, 3,* 300–326.

Rimm, S. B. (1983). *Preschool and kindergarten interest descriptor.* Watertown, WI: Educational Assessment Service.

Rimm, S. B., & Davis, G. A. (1976). GIFT: An instrument for the identification of creativity. *Journal of Creative Behavior, 10,* 178–182.

Rogers, C. R. (1962). Toward a theory of creativity. In S. J. Parnes & H. F. Harding (Eds.), *A source book for creative thinking* (pp. 63–72). New York: Scribners.

Schaefer, C. E. (1971). *Creativity attitude survey.* Jacksonville, IL: Psychologists and Educators, Inc.

Smith, G. J. W., & Carlsson, I. (1987). A new creativity test. *Journal of Creative Behavior, 21,* 7–14.

Stanish, B. (1977). *Sunflowering.* Carthage, IL: Good Apple.

Stanish, B. (1988). *Lessons from the hearthstone traveler.* Carthage, IL: Good Apple.

Sternberg, R. S. (2000). Identifying and developing creative giftedness. *Roeper Review, 23,* 60–64.

Torrance, E. P. (1962). *Guiding creative talent.* Englewood Cliffs, NJ: Prentice-Hall.

Torrance, E. P. (1966a). *Torrance tests of creative thinking.* Bensenville, IL: Scholastic Testing Service.

Torrance, E. P. (1966b). *Torrance tests of creative thinking: Norms-technical manual.* Princeton, NJ: Personnel Press.

Torrance, E. P. (1981a). Empirical validation of criterion-referenced indicators of creative ability through a longitudinal study. *Creative Child and Adult Quarterly, 6,* 146–150.

Torrance, E. P. (1981b). *Thinking creatively in action and movement.* Bensenville, IL: Scholastic Testing Service.

Torrance, E. P. (1990a). *Torrance tests of creative thinking: Manual for scoring and interpreting results. Verbal, forms A and B.* Bensenville, IL: Scholastic Testing Service.

Torrance, E. P. (1990b). *Torrance tests of creative thinking: Norms-technical manual. Figural (streamlined) forms A and B.* Bensenville, IL: Scholastic Testing Service.

Torrance, E. P., & Ball, O. E. (1984). *Torrance tests of creative thinking: Streamlined (revised) manual, figural A and B.* Bensenville, IL: Scholastic Testing Service.

Torrance, E. P., Khatena, J., & Cunnington, B. F. (1973). *Thinking creatively with sounds and words.* Bensenville, IL: Scholastic Testing Service.

Urban, K. K., & Jellen, H. G. (1993). *Manual for the Test for Creative Thinking: Drawing production.* Hannover, Germany: University of Hannover.

Wallach, M. A., & Kogan, N. (1965). *Modes of thinking in young children.* New York: Holt.

Wallas, G. (1926). *The art of thought.* New York: Harcourt.

BIBLIOGRAPHY

Dacey, J. S. (1989). *Fundamentals of creative thinking.* Lexington, MA: Lexington Books.

Davis, G. A. (1971). Instruments useful in studying creative behavior and creative talents: Part II. *Journal of Creative Behavior, 5,* 162–165.

Davis, G. A. (1973). *Psychology of problem solving.* New York: Basic Books.

Davis, G. A. (1989). Testing for creative potential. *Contemporary Educational Psychology, 14,* 257–274.

Kaltsoonis, B. (1971). Instruments useful in studying creative behavior and creative talents: Part I. Commercially available instruments. *Journal of Creative Behavior, 5,* 117–126.

Kaltsoonis, B. (1972). Additional instruments useful in studying creative behavior and creative talents: Part III. Noncommercially available instruments. *Journal of Creative Behavior, 6,* 268–274.

Kaltsoonis, B., & Honeywell, L. (1980). Additional instruments useful in studying creative behavior and creative talent: Part IV. Noncommercially available instruments. *Journal of Creative Behavior, 14,* 56–67.

Runco, M. A. (1999). Appendix II: Tests of creativity. In M. A. Runco & S. R. Pritzker (Eds.), *Encyclopedia of creativity* (pp. 755–760). San Diego, CA: Academic Press.

Smith, J. M. (1966). *Setting conditions for creative teaching in the elementary school.* Needham Heights, MA: Allyn & Bacon.

25

In the Habit of Skillful Thinking

ARTHUR L. COSTA, *California State University, Sacramento, and Institute for Intelligent Behavior, El Dorado Hills, California*

Education today is trapped in the belief that high test scores have something to do with becoming a wise, intelligent, and well-educated person. It assumes that if teachers teach academic subjects and if students learn and are evaluated on how well they learn the minute sub-skills in each content area, they will somehow become the kind of people we want them to become.

Lord Kelvin, a nineteenth-century physicist/astronomer, once said, "If you cannot measure it, if you cannot express it in numbers, your knowledge is of a very meager and unsatisfactory kind." This mechanistic mentality still serves educators as a rationale for justifying such standard operating procedures as tracking students according to high and low aptitude, the bell curve, drill and practice, competition, frequent testing, using IQ scores as a basis for ability grouping, task-analyzing learning into discrete skills, and reinforcing learning with rewards and external motivations (Resnick & Hall, 1998).

Being Intelligent and Becoming Intelligent

Operating under this obsolescent paradigm, many still believe that "native" intelligence and other forms of talent are fixed, quantifiable, and unchangeable; that intelligence is an entity displayed in one's measurable performance. Doing well means that one has ability; doing poorly means that one doesn't have ability. This negative view of the intelligent self influences effort. When people view their intelligence as fixed, they strive to obtain positive evaluations of their ability and to avoid displaying evidence of inadequacies in comparison to others.

More recently, a transformation of our conception of intelligence has provided one of the most refreshing, liberating, and powerful forces in the restructuring of our schools, of education, and of society (Costa & Kallick, 2001; Fogarty, 1998; Gardner, 1983; Perkins, 1995; Sternberg, 1986). We have come to believe that intelligence can be learned, nurtured, and grown. Ability is a repertoire of skills and habits that continuously and incrementally expands through one's efforts. When students and teachers adopt this belief, they tend to invest energy to learn something new and to increase their understanding and mastery.

As American schools break out of this aptitude-centered traditional mentality, they make it possible for learners to acquire the kinds of mental habits needed for productive and fulfilling lives. This new definition of intelligence is as attentive to robust habits of mind as it is to the specifics of knowledge structures, thinking skills, and solving challenging problems. Standards of learning are beginning to reflect the belief that ability is a continuously expandable repertoire of mental habits and that, through one's efforts, intelligence grows incrementally (Marzano & Pollock, 2001). When confronted with difficult, challenging tasks, efficacious thinkers apply self-regulatory, metacognitive skills, focus on analyzing the task, and try to generate and execute alternative strategies.

One's intelligence is the sum of one's habits of mind.
—Lauren B. Resnick (2001)

Components of a Well-Developed Thinking Skills Program

Over the past fifteen years, there has been a strong emphasis on infusing thinking skills into curriculum and instruction (Costa, 1985). The results have generally proven positive (Beyer, 2001). A well balanced thinking skills curriculum includes at least four components: (1) judiciously selected content, (2) instruction in thinking skills, (3) providing challenging tasks that require the application of and reflection on skillful thinking, all of which lead to (4) habituating certain dispositions toward thinking or habits of mind. The relationship of these four components might be illustrated as in Figure 25.1.

1. *Judiciously selected content.* The center circle represents the content or subject within which the problem is being solved. The selection of relevant content is important; first, because skillful thinking cannot be performed in a vacuum—there must be something to think about; and second, the nature of the discipline imposes constraints on the procedures of problem solving. Scientific problems, in which the control of experimental variables is paramount, differ from social and aesthetic problems in which ethics and artistic judgment play a significant role. Also, student motivation to learn a new or complex cognitive skill is sharply enhanced when instruction in how to do it is provided at a point where students perceive a need to use the skill to understand the content.

Content, therefore, should be selected judiciously for its generative contribution to employing and practicing the thinking skills and strategies. Content is not an end but rather a vehicle that activates and engages the inquiring mind.

2. *Thinking skills.* The next larger circle represents such skills of thinking as comparing, inferring,

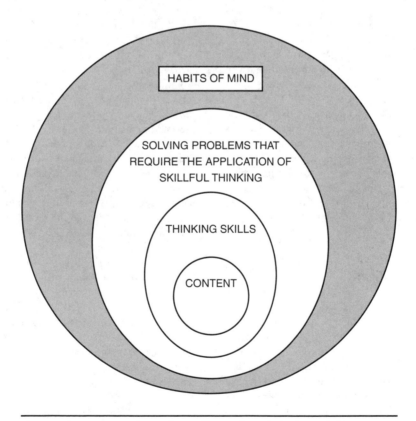

Figure 25.1 Components of a Well-Developed Thinking Skills Program.

analyzing, sequencing, synthesizing, and predicting. Researchers and specialists agree that such skills are the basic tools of effective thinking. Success in school, at work and in life depends upon acquiring and performing certain basic, discrete cognitive functions such as recalling, comparing, classifying, inferring, generalizing, evaluating, experimenting, and analyzing. While these capacities are innate, their refinement, procedures, and applications may need to be brought to the conscious level through direct instruction.

3. *Performance on tasks requiring skillful thinking.* Such cognitive skills are seldom performed in isolation. Few people simply go out and observe, compare, or synthesize. Thinking skills are employed within a larger context in response to some challenging condition: dichotomies, anomalies, dilemmas, ambiguities, paradoxes, conflicts, enigmas, or obstacles for which resolutions are not immediately apparent. To resolve such tasks, larger mental operations comprising clusters of numerous cognitive subskills are employed over time. The skills are combined and organized into strategies and sequences that we refer to as problem solving, decision making, creativity, or knowledge generation. For example, decision making may require observing accurately, generating data, inferring causality, comparing and contrasting alternative choices, and predicting consequences (Ennis, 1985; Swartz & Parks, 1994; Treffinger & Isaksen, 2001).

4. *Habits of mind (dispositions).* Even though persons may possess these skills and operational capacities, they must also be alert to opportunities to apply them. Performing *habits of mind,* therefore, requires not only possessing these basic skills and capacities to carry out the strategy, but also the inclinations, proclivities and dispositions to do so in situations that demand their application (Perkins, Jay, & Tishman, 1993; Tishman, 2000). A habit of mind includes:

- Valuing: Choosing to employ a pattern of intellectual behaviors rather than other, less productive patterns.
- Having the inclination: Feeling the tendency toward employing a pattern of intellectual behaviors.
- Being alert: Perceiving opportunities for, and appropriateness of employing the pattern of behavior.
- Being capable: Possessing the basic thinking skills and capacities to carry through with the behaviors.

- Making a commitment: Reflecting on and constantly striving to improve performance of the pattern of intellectual behavior.

Getting into the Habit of Behaving Intelligently

Habit is a cable. We weave a thread of it each day, and at last we cannot break it.
 —Horace Mann

While intelligent human beings are capable of thinking skillfully, it is their habits of mind that provide the fuel to activate strategic thinking. In order to engage skillfully in problem solving, decision making, or knowledge generation, they must possess the inclination to decrease impulsivity, display empathy, and be inquisitive and persistent. Habits of mind provide the dispositions necessary to do the skillful thinking required within and beyond the classroom walls.[1]

Research in effective thinking and intelligent behavior by such authors as Feuerstein et al. (1980), Glatthorn and Baron (1985), Sternberg (1984), Ennis (2001), Goleman (1995), Perkins (1995), and Coles (1997) indicates that there are identifiable characteristics of effective thinkers. It is not necessarily scientists, artists, mathematicians, or the wealthy that demonstrate these behaviors. These characteristics have been identified in successful mechanics, teachers, entrepreneurs, salespeople, and parents—people in all walks of life.

While there is not a finite number of habits of mind, a list of 16 has been synthesized. Habits of mind transcend all subject matters commonly taught in school. Furthermore, these habits of mind are not just "kid stuff" applied to adults. They are ageless developmental qualities. Along with some of the capabilities they encompass, the 16 habits of mind are as follows (Costa, 2000):

---

1. After years of implementing both the Habits of Mind and the Swartz and Parks (1994) Thinking Model, Mary Anne Kiser, Principal of Meadowglens Elementary School in Naperville, Illinois, described this relationship.

1. Persisting When the Solution to a Problem Is Not Readily Apparent

Effective people stick to a task until it is completed. They don't give up easily. They are able to analyze a problem and to develop a system, structure, or strategy to attack it. They employ a range and have a repertoire of alternative strategies for problem solving. If one strategy doesn't work, they know how to back up and try another. They have systematic methods of analyzing a problem: knowing how to begin, knowing what steps must be performed, and knowing what data need to be generated or collected. They are comfortable with ambiguous situations.

Some students give up in despair when the answer to a problem is not immediately known. Some have difficulty staying focused for any length of time, are easily distracted, and may give up because they have a limited repertoire of problem solving strategies.

2. Managing Impulsivity

Effective problem solvers have a sense of deliberativeness. They think before they act. They intentionally form a vision of a product, plan of action, goal, or destination before they begin. They strive to clarify and understand directions, develop a strategy for approaching a problem, and withhold immediate value judgments about an idea before fully understanding it. Reflective individuals consider alternatives and consequences of several possible directions before taking action. They decrease their need for trial and error by gathering information, taking time to reflect on an answer before giving it, making sure they understand directions, and listening to alternative points of view (Goleman, 1995).

Often students blurt the first answer that comes to mind, start to work without fully understanding the directions, lack an organized plan or strategy for approaching a problem, or make immediate value judgments about an idea—criticizing or praising it—before fully understanding it. They are gullible and may take the first suggestion given or operate on the first idea that comes to mind rather than consider alternatives and consequences of several possible directions.

3. Listening to Others with Understanding and Empathy

Highly effective people spend an inordinate amount of time and energy listening (Covey, 1989).

Paraphrasing another person's ideas, detecting indicators (cues) of their feelings or emotional states in their oral and body language, accurately expressing another person's concepts, emotions, and problems—all are indications of listening behavior. Skillful listeners gently attend to another person, demonstrating their understanding of and empathy for an idea or feeling by paraphrasing it accurately, building upon it, clarifying it, or giving an example of it.

We spend 55 percent of our lives listening, yet it is one of the least taught skills in school. We often say we are listening, but in actuality we are rehearsing in our head what we are going to say next when our partner is finished. Some students ridicule, laugh at, or put down others' ideas. They interrupt and are unable to build upon, consider the merits of, or operate on another person's ideas. Good listeners try to understand what the other person is saying. In the end they may disagree sharply, but because they disagree, they want to know exactly what it is they are disagreeing with.

4. Thinking Flexibly

Flexible people have the capacity to change their mind as they receive additional data. They engage in multiple and simultaneous outcomes and activities, draw upon a repertoire of problem-solving strategies, and practice "style flexibility," knowing when it is appropriate to be broad in their thinking and when a situation requires detailed precision. They envision a range of consequences, create and seek novel approaches, and have a well-developed sense of humor.

Flexible people can approach a problem from a new angle using a novel approach (de Bono, 1991, refers to this as *lateral thinking*). They consider alternative points of view or deal with several sources of information simultaneously. Their minds are open to change based on additional information, opinions, data, or reasoning, which may contradict their beliefs. They have and can develop options and alternatives to consider.

Flexible thinkers are able to shift, at will, perceiving from our own point of view or, by contrast, perceiving through another person's orientation. We operate from this second position when we empathize with others' feelings, predict how others are thinking, and anticipate potential misunderstandings.

Flexible thinkers display confidence in their intuition. They tolerate confusion and ambiguity, up to a point. Flexibility is the cradle of humor, creativity, and repertoire.

Some students have difficulty in considering alternative points of view or dealing with more than one classification system simultaneously. *Their* way to solve a problem seems to be the *only* way. Their mind is made up: "Don't confuse me with facts; that's it."

5. Thinking about Our Own Thinking: Metacognition

Metacognition is our ability to know what we know and what we don't know. It is our ability to develop a plan of action, maintain that plan in mind over a period of time, then reflect back and evaluate the plan upon its completion. Planning a strategy before embarking on a course of action assists us in keeping track of the steps in the sequence of planned behaviors. It facilitates making temporal and comparative judgments, assessing readiness for more or different activities, and monitoring our interpretations, perceptions, decisions, and behaviors.

Metacognition means becoming increasingly aware of our actions and the effect of those actions on others and on the environment; forming internal questions; developing mental maps or plans of action; mentally rehearsing prior to performance; monitoring those plans as they are employed—being conscious of the need for midcourse corrections if the plan does not meet expectations; evaluating the plan upon completion and editing mental pictures for improved performance.

Many students do not take the time to wonder why we are doing what we are doing. They seldom question themselves about their own learning strategies or evaluate the efficiency of their own performance. Some students have virtually no idea of what they should do when they confront a problem and are often unable to explain their strategies of decision making (Sternberg & Wagner, n.d.).

6. Striving for Accuracy and Precision

Embodied in the stamina, grace, and elegance of an accomplished ballerina, surgeon, or shoemaker is the desire for craftsmanship, mastery, flawlessness, and the economy of energy to produce exceptional results. People who value accuracy, precision, and craftsmanship take time to check over their products. They review their criteria of excellence and confirm that their finished product matches the criteria exactly. To be craftsmanlike means knowing that one can continually perfect one's craft by working to attain the highest possible standards. They take pride in their work and have a desire for accuracy, fidelity, and elegance as they invest time to refine their products.

Some students turn in sloppy, incomplete, or uncorrected work. They are more anxious to get rid of the assignment than to check it over for accuracy and precision. They are more interested in expedience rather than excellence.

7. Asking Questions and Posing Problems

One of the characteristics distinguishing humans from other forms of life is our inclination and ability to *find* problems to solve. Effective problem solvers know how to ask questions to fill in the gaps between what they know and what they don't know. Effective questioners are inclined to ask a range of questions, for example, for data to support others' conclusions and assumptions:

"What evidence do you have . . . ?"
"How do you know that's true?"

They pose questions about alternative points of view:

"From whose viewpoint are we seeing, reading, or hearing?"
"From what angle, what perspective are we viewing this situation?"

Students pose questions about causal connections and relationships:

"How are these people (events, situations) related to each other?"
"What produced this connection?"

They pose hypothetical problems:

"What do you think would happen if . . . ?"
"If that is true, then what might happen if . . . ?"

Inquirers recognize discrepancies and unusual phenomena in their environment and probe into their causes: "Why do cats purr?" "What are some alternative solutions to international conflicts other than wars?"

Some students may be unaware of the functions, in productive questions. When confronted with a discrepancy, they may lack an overall questioning strategy.

8. Applying Past Knowledge to New Situations

Human beings learn from experience. When confronted with a new and perplexing problem they will often draw experiences from their past. They ask themselves, "What does this remind me of?" or "When have I been in a situation like this before? What worked for me then?"

Too often, students begin a new task as if it were being approached for the very first time. It is as if each experience is encapsulated and has no relationship to what has come before or what comes afterward.

9. Thinking and Communicating with Clarity and Precision

Fuzzy language is a reflection of fuzzy thinking. Intelligent people strive to communicate accurately in both written and oral form, taking care to use precise language, define terms, use correct names and universal labels, and make correct analogies. They strive to avoid overgeneralizations, deletions, and distortions. Instead, they support their statements with explanations, comparisons, quantification, and evidence.

We sometimes hear students and other adults using vague and imprecise language. They call specific objects such non-descriptive names as "*stuff*," "*junk*," and "*things*." They punctuate sentences with meaningless interjections, such as "*ya know*," "*er*," and "*uh*." They use vague or general nouns and pronouns: "*They* told me to do it." "*Everybody* has one."

10. Gathering Data through All Senses

We know that information gets into the brain through the sensory pathways: gustatory, olfactory, tactile, kinesthetic, auditory, and visual. Most linguistic, cultural, and physical learning is derived from the environment by observing or taking in through the senses. To know a wine, it must be drunk; to know a role, it must be acted; to know a game, it must be played; to know a dance, it must be moved; to know a goal, it must be envisioned. Those whose sensory pathways are open, alert, and acute absorb more information from the environment than those whose pathways are withered, immune, and oblivious to sensory stimuli.

Furthermore, we are learning more about the impact of arts on improved mental functioning (Loring, 2001). Forming mental images is important in mathematics and engineering; social scientists solve problems through scenarios and role-playing; scientists build models; engineers use Cad-Cam;[2] mechanics learn through hands-on experimentation; artists experiment with colors and textures; musicians experiment by producing combinations of instrumental and vocal music.

Some students go through school and life oblivious to the textures, rhythms, patterns, sounds, and colors around them.

11. Creating, Imagining, Innovating

Human beings have the capacity to generate novel, original, clever, or ingenious products, solutions, and techniques—if that capacity is developed. Creative human beings try to conceive problem solutions differently, examining alternative possibilities from many angles. They tend to project themselves into different roles, using analogies and metaphorical thinking, starting with a vision and working backward, or imagining they are the objects being considered. Creative people take risks and frequently push the boundaries of their perceived limits (Perkins, 1985; Puccio & Murdock, 2001). Creative people are open to criticism. They hold up their products for others to judge and seek feedback in an ever-increasing effort to refine their technique. They are uneasy with the status quo. They constantly strive for greater fluency, elaboration, novelty, parsimony, simplicity, beauty, harmony, and balance.

Students, however, are often heard saying, "I can't draw"; "I was never very good at art"; "I can't sing a note"; "I'm not creative." Some people believe creative humans are just born that way; it's in their genes.

12. Responding with Wonderment and Awe

Describing the two hundred best and brightest of the All USA College Academic Team identified by USA Today, Briggs (1999) stated, "They are creative thinkers who have a passion for what they do." Efficacious people have not only an "*I can*" attitude, but also an "*I enjoy*" feeling. They seek problems to solve for themselves and to submit to others. They enjoy figuring things out; they delight in making up problems to solve on their own; and they request enigmas from others.

---

2. Editor's note: Computer-aided design—computer-aided manufacturing.

Some children and adults avoid problems and are "turned off" to learning. They make such comments as, "I was never good at these brain teasers"; "Its boring"; "When am I ever going to use this stuff?"; "Who cares?"; "I don't do thinking!" They perceive thinking as hard work.

Wondrous humans are curious. They commune with the world around them; they reflect on the changing formations of a cloud; they feel charmed by the opening of a bud; they sense the logical simplicity of mathematical order. Students can find beauty in a sunset, intrigue in the geometric of a spider web, and exhilaration at the iridescence of a hummingbird's wings. They see the congruity and intricacies in the derivation of a mathematical formula, recognize the orderliness and adroitness of a chemical change, and commune with the serenity of a distant constellation. Many people feel enthusiastic, passionate, even euphoric about learning, inquiring, and mastering.

13. Taking Responsible Risks

Some people seem to have an almost uncontrollable urge to go beyond established limits. They are uneasy about comfort; they "live on the edge of their competence." They seem compelled to place themselves in situations where they do not know what the outcome will be. They accept confusion, uncertainty, and the higher risks of failure as part of the normal process—and they view setbacks as interesting, challenging, and growth producing. They are spontaneous, willing to take a chance in the moment. However, they are not behaving impulsively. Their risks are educated. They draw on past knowledge, are thoughtful about consequences, and have a well-trained sense of what is appropriate. They know that all risks are not worth taking.

Some students seem reluctant to take risks. They hold back in games, new learning, and new friendships because their fear of failure is far greater than their sense of adventure. They are reinforced by that inner voice that says, "If you don't try it, you won't be wrong" or "If you try it and you are wrong, you will look stupid." The other voice that says, "If you don't try it, you will never know" is trapped in fear and mistrust. They have a need for certainty.

14. Finding Humor

Another unique attribute of being human is our sense of humor. The positive effects of laughter on psycho-logical functions include a drop in the pulse rate, the secretion of endorphins, and increased oxygen in the blood. Humor has been found to liberate creativity and provoke such higher level thinking skills as anticipation, finding novel relationships, visual imagery, and making analogies. People who engage in the mystery of humor have the ability to perceive situations from an original and often interesting vantage point. They tend to initiate humor more often, to place greater value on having a sense of humor, to appreciate and understand others' humor, and to be verbally playful when interacting with others. Having a whimsical frame of mind, they thrive on finding incongruity and perceiving absurdities, ironies, and satire; finding discontinuities; and being able to laugh at both situations and themselves (Dyer, 1997).

Some students find humor "in all the wrong places"—human differences, ineptitude, injurious behavior, vulgarity, violence, and profanity. They laugh at others, yet are unable to laugh at themselves.

15. Thinking Interdependently

Human beings are social animals. We congregate in groups, find it therapeutic to be listened to, draw energy from one another, and seek reciprocity. In groups we contribute our time and energy to tasks in which we would quickly tire if we worked alone. In fact, one of the cruelest forms of punishment is solitary confinement.

Cooperative humans realize that all of us together are more powerful—intellectually and physically—than any one individual. Probably the foremost disposition in our post-industrial society is the heightened ability to think in concert with others; to find ourselves increasingly more interdependent and sensitive to the needs of others. Problem solving has become so complex that no one person can go it alone. No one person has access to all the data needed to make critical decisions; no one person can consider as many alternatives as several people can.

Working in groups requires the ability to justify ideas and to test the feasibility of strategies on others. It also requires willingness and openness to accept feedback from a critical friend. Through this interaction the group and the individual continue to grow. Listening, consensus seeking, giving up one's own idea to work with someone else's, empathy, compassion, group leadership, knowing how to support group efforts, altruism—all are skills that make up collaborative human beings.

Some students may not have learned to work in groups; they have underdeveloped social skills. They feel isolated; they prefer their solitude.

16. Remaining Open to Continuous Learning

Many people are in a continuous learning mode. Their confidence in combination with their inquisitiveness allows them to search constantly for new and better ways. People with this habit of mind continually strive for improvement—always growing, always learning, always modifying and improving themselves. They seize problems, situations, tensions, conflicts, and circumstances as valuable opportunities to learn.

Some students confront learning opportunities with fear rather than wonder. They feel better when they know rather than when they learn. They defend their present biases, beliefs, and storehouses of knowledge rather than invite the unknown, the creative, and the inspirational. Being closed and certain may be comforting, while being doubtful and open produces fear.

From an early age, students are trained to believe that deep learning means figuring out the truth rather than developing capabilities for effective and thoughtful action. They have been taught to value certainty rather than doubt, to give answers rather than to inquire, to know which choice is correct rather than to explore alternatives.

Toward a New Vision: Learning to Behave Intelligently

These 16 habits of mind may serve as mental disciplines. When confronted with problematic situations, intelligent people habitually employ one or more of these habits of mind by asking themselves, "What is the most *intelligent thing* I can do right now?" For example:

- How can I learn from this? What are my resources? How can I draw on my past successes with problems like this? What do I already know about the problem? What resources do I have available or need to generate?
- How can I approach this problem *flexibly*? How might I look at the situation in another way? How can I draw upon my repertoire of problem-solving

strategies? How can I look at this problem from a fresh perspective?
- How can I illuminate this problem to make it clearer and more precise? Do I need to check out my data sources? How might I break this problem down into its component parts and develop a strategy for understanding and accomplishing each step?
- What do I know or not know? What questions do I need to ask? What strategies are in my mind now? What am I aware of in terms of my own beliefs, values, and goals with this problem? What feelings or emotions might be blocking or enhancing my progress?
- How does this problem affect others? Is there someone I can turn to for assistance? How can we solve it together, and what can I learn from others that would help me become a better problem solver?

SUMMARY AND CONCLUSIONS

The label "gifted" connotes a state of being. Either you have "it" or you don't. The label suggests that if you don't have "it," no amount of effort will ever help you acquire "it." This chapter suggests that, instead, we examine those learnable, teachable patterns of behaviors that describe intelligent action which, when practiced over time, can become habitual.

Children develop cognitive strategies and effort-based beliefs about their intelligence when they are continually pressed to raise questions and to accept challenges; to find solutions that are not immediately apparent; and to explain concepts, justify their reasoning, and seek information. The goal of education, therefore, should be to liberate and develop these habits of mind and the skills associated with them. When we hold children accountable for intelligent behavior, they take it as a signal that we think they are smart, and they come to accept this judgment. The paradox is that children become smart by being treated as if they already are intelligent (Resnick & Hall, 1998).

Drawn from research on human effectiveness, descriptions of remarkable performers, and analyses of the characteristics of efficacious people, 16 habits of mind were elaborated. They are characteristic of peak performers whether they be in homes, schools, athletic fields, the military, governments, churches, or corporations. These habits make marriages successful, learning continual, workplaces productive, and democracies enduring.

Some students identified as "gifted" are reluctant to take risks. They lack flexibility, are poor listeners, prefer to work in solitude, and are quick to jump to conclusions. Some students deemed "slow" however, are often insightful, venturesome, humorous, wondrous, and exploratory. Neither labels, genetics, scores on tests, nor numbers of right answers can adequately define giftedness. Rather, it is being in the habit of applying skillful thinking to perplexing problem situations. The habits of mind are the "right stuff" that make human beings gifted.

We are what we repeatedly do. Excellence, then, is not an act but a habit.

—Aristotle

QUESTIONS FOR THOUGHT AND DISCUSSION

1. Drawing upon what you know about effective, intellectually powerful human beings and Costa's chapter, how would you describe "giftedness" in behavioral, observable terms?

2. What is it about your (present or future) students that makes you believe they need to learn how to *think*? That is, what do you see them doing or saying that shows a need for instruction in thinking skills?

3. If you were to write a letter of recommendation describing the intellectual powers of one of your most promising students, what characteristics would you choose to elaborate?

4. Think about athletes, musicians, scientists, artists, CEOs, and others at their peak of achievement. According to Costa, what attributes have contributed to their high levels of performance?

REFERENCES

Beyer, B. (2001). What research suggests about teaching thinking skills. In A. Costa (Ed.), *Developing minds: A resource book for teaching thinking* (pp. 275–282). Alexandria, VA: Association for Supervision and Curriculum Development.

Briggs, T. W. (1999). Passion for what they do keeps alumni on first team. *U.S.A. Today,* February 25, pp. 1A–2A.

Coles, R. (1997). *The moral intelligence of children.* New York: Random House.

Costa, A. (Ed.). (1985). *Developing minds: A resource book for teaching thinking.* Alexandria, VA: Association for Supervision and Curriculum Development.

Costa, A. (2000). Describing habits of mind. In A. Costa & B. Kallick (Eds.), *Discovering and exploring habits of mind* (pp. 21–40). Alexandria, VA: Association for Supervision and Curriculum Development.

Costa, A., & Kallick, R. (Eds.). (2001). *Discovering and exploring habits of mind.* Alexandria, VA: Association for Supervision and Curriculum Development.

Covey, S. (1989). *The seven habits of highly effective people.* New York: Simon and Schuster.

de Bono, E. (1991). The CoRT thinking program. In A. Costa (Ed.), *Developing minds: Programs for teaching thinking* (pp. 27–32). Alexandria, VA: Association for Supervision and Curriculum Development.

Dyer, J. (1997). Humor as process. In A. Costa & R. Liebmann (Eds.), *Envisioning process as content: Toward a renaissance curriculum* (pp. 211–229). Thousand Oaks, CA: Corwin Press.

Ennis, R. (1985, October). Goals for critical thinking/reasoning curriculum. *Educational Leadership, 43*(2), 46.

Ennis, R. (2001). An outline of goals for a critical thinking curriculum and its assessment. In A. Costa (Ed.), *Developing minds: A resource book for teaching thinking* (pp. 44–46). Alexandria, VA: Association for Supervision and Curriculum Development.

Feuerstein, R., Rand, Y. M., Hoffman, M. B., & Miller, R. (1980). *Instrumental enrichment: An intervention program for cognitive modifiability.* Baltimore: University Park Press.

Fogarty, R. (1998). *Brain compatible classrooms.* Arlington Heights, IL: Skylight Training and Publishing.

Gardner, H. (1983). *Frames of mind: The theory of multiple intelligences.* New York: Basic Books.

Glatthorn, A., & Baron, J. (1985). The good thinker. In A. L. Costa (Ed.), *Developing minds: A resource book for teaching thinking* (pp. 49–53). Alexandria, VA: Association for Supervision and Curriculum Development.

Goleman, D. (1995). *Emotional intelligence: Why it can matter more than IQ.* New York: Bantam Books.

Loring, R. (2001). Music and skillful thinking. In A. Costa (Ed.), *Developing minds: A resource book for teaching thinking.* Alexandria, VA: Association for Supervision and Curriculum Development.

Marzano, R., & Pollock, J. (2001). Standards-based thinking and reasoning skills. In A. Costa (Ed.), *Developing minds: A resource book for teaching thinking* (pp. 29–34). Alexandria VA: Association for Supervision and Curriculum Development.

Perkins, D. (1985). What creative thinking is. In A. L. Costa (Ed.), *Developing minds: A resource book for teaching thinking* (pp. 85–88). Alexandria, VA: Association for Supervision and Curriculum Development.

Perkins, D. (1995). *Outsmarting IQ.* New York: The Free Press.

Perkins, D. N., Jay, E., & Tishman, S. (1993). Beyond abilities: A dispositional theory of thinking. *The Merrill-Palmer Quarterly, 39*(1), 1–21.

Puccio, G. and Murdock, M. (2001). Creative thinking: An essential life skill. In A. Costa (Ed.), *Developing minds: A resource book for teaching thinking.* Alexandria, VA: Association for Supervision and Curriculum Development.

Resnick, L. B., & Hall, M. W. (1998). Learning organizations for sustainable education reform. *Daedalus, 127,* 89–118.

Sternberg, R. (1984). *Beyond I.Q.: A triarchic theory of human intelligence.* New York: Cambridge University Press.

Sternberg, R. J. (1986). *Intelligence applied: Understanding and increasing your intellectual skills.* Orlando, FL: Harcourt Brace Jovanovich.

Sternberg, R., and Wagner, R. (n.d.) Understanding intelligence: What's in it for education? Paper submitted to the National Commission on Excellence in Education.

Swartz, R., and Parks, S. (1994). *Infusing critical and creative thinking into elementary instruction: A lesson design handbook.* Pacific Grove, CA: Critical Thinking Books and Software.

Tishman, S. (2000). Why teach habits of mind? In A. Costa & B. Kallick (Eds.), *Discovering and exploring habits of mind* (pp. 41–52). Alexandria, VA: Association for Supervision and Curriculum Development.

Treffinger, D., and Isaksen, S. (2001). Teaching for creative learning and problem solving. In A. Costa (Ed.), *Developing minds: A resource book for teaching thinking* (pp. 442–445). Alexandria, VA: Association for Supervision and Curriculum Development.

BIBLIOGRAPHY

Beyer, B. (1987). *Practical strategies for the teaching of thinking.* Boston: Allyn and Bacon.

Csikszentmihalyi, M. (1993). *The evolving self: A psychology for the third millennium.* New York: Harper Collins.

Resnick, L. (2001). Making America smarter: The real goal of school reform. In A. Costa (Ed.), *Developing minds: A resource book for teaching thinking* (pp. 3–6). Alexandria, VA: Association for Supervision and Curriculum Development.

Senge, P., Ross, R., Smith, B., Roberts, C., & Kleiner, A. (1994). *The fifth discipline fieldbook: Strategies and tools for building a learning organization.* New York: Doubleday/Currency.

26

Artistic Giftedness

ELLEN WINNER, *Boston College and Project Zero, Harvard Graduate School of Education*
GAIL MARTINO, *Gillette Advanced Technology Center, Boston*

It is common to distinguish between giftedness and talent. Children who are advanced in scholastic abilities or have a high IQ are labeled *gifted,* while those who show exceptional ability in an art form or an athletic area are called *talented.* In this chapter, we argue against such a distinction and refer to children with talent in an art form as gifted.

While there is no necessary link between a gift in art and a gift in terms of high IQ, children with high ability in an art form are similar to academically gifted children in three respects (Winner, 1996a). First, they are precocious. They master the first steps in their domain at an earlier than average age and learn more rapidly in that domain. Second, they have a "rage to master"—that is, they are intensely motivated to make sense of their domain and show an obsessive interest and ability to focus sharply in their area of high ability. In the visual arts, this means that they produce a large volume of work over a sustained period of time (Golomb, 1992; Milbrath, 1998; Pariser, 1997). And third, they "march to their own drummer," meaning that they do not just learn faster than ordinary children, they also learn differently. They learn virtually on their own, requiring minimum adult scaffolding, and often solve problems in their domain in novel, idiosyncratic ways.

Because these children solve problems in unusual ways, they are creative. But we distinguish sharply here between two levels of creativity: little-c and big-C creativity (Winner, 1997). Gifted children are creative in the little-c sense, meaning that they solve problems in novel ways and make discoveries about their domain on their own. Big-C creativity, or domain creativity, involves changing the domain.

According to Gardner (1993) and Simonton (1994), creators do not make domain-altering changes until they have worked for at least ten years in their area. Thus, children by definition cannot be domain creative. Take Picasso, for example. Although he drew a great deal as a child, his domain-altering contributions came from his adult works, not from his childhood drawings (Gardner, 1993).

Characteristics of Children Gifted in Visual Arts

Children who are considered "gifted" in drawing are not just more advanced than typical children in drawing milestones. Rather, they draw in a qualitatively different way. This has been demonstrated by Milbrath's (1998) longitudinal and cross-sectional study of gifted young artists. She followed eight artistically gifted children over ten years, and also compared a group of artistically gifted children between ages 4 and 14 to a normal control group. Using the terminology of Piaget (Piaget & Inhelder, 1969), Milbrath argued that artistically gifted children are guided by "figurative" rather than "operational" processes. Piaget distinguished between two kinds of knowledge: the ability to analyze and transform objects (called operative knowledge) and the ability to grasp the static physical properties of objects (called figurative knowledge). Operative knowledge involves interpretation; figurative knowledge involves representation (Feldman, 2000). According to Milbrath, artistically gifted children are more figurative in their approach to the world than are typical children.

Artistically gifted children actually *see* the world differently. To begin with, they encode visual information more accurately, and see the world less in terms of concepts and more in terms of shapes and visual surface features. Second, they have superior visual memories (see Rosenblatt & Winner, 1988, for corroborating evidence). And third, they attend more to the act of drawing itself; they can *see* when something looks wrong, and this leads to discoveries about how to represent the world on paper. Thus, in Milbrath's terms, these children are better at seeing, remembering, and doing. Typical children are guided more by their understanding of what they are trying to draw, and less by their grasp of its visual properties. In short, while typical children are constrained to draw what they *know* about objects, gifted children are able to override what they know and depict what they *see*.

Because artistically gifted children use figurative processes to represent (that is, they seem to be able to draw things as they appear, with all the distortions caused by point of view and perspective), their drawings typically appear highly realistic (Milbrath, 1998). This realism is a hallmark of gifted child art. The core indicator of giftedness in drawing is the ability to draw recognizable shapes at least one year before this skill normally emerges. While typical children begin to draw recognizable shapes representing objects in the world at around the age of three or four (Golomb, 1992; Kellogg, 1969; Matthews, 1984), gifted children have been noted to begin to draw representationally at the age of two. Figure 26.1 shows a striking contrast between the way in which a typical and an artistically gifted two-year-old drew apples. The typical two-year-old simply made a slash for each apple because he had not yet acquired the understanding that lines on the page represent the edges of objects. For him, a line simply stood for "thingness." The gifted two-year-old had grasped the concept of a line representing an edge, and produced a fluid line describing the contour of each apple.

Milbrath (1998) noted that a clear sign of artistic giftedness is the ability to use *line* to stand for *edge*, in contrast to typical children who use *line* to stand for *thing*. In Willats' (1981) terms, ordinary children use a denotation rule by which a one-dimensional picture primitive (i.e., a line) stands for a two-dimensional region or volume. Artistically gifted children bypass this rule. They also bypass another similar denotation rule formulated by Willats. While children ordinarily fill in planes to convey solidity (thereby

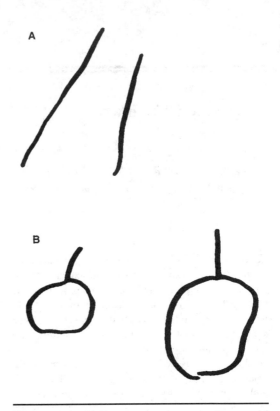

Figure 26.1   (a) Two apples drawn by 2-year-old on request; (b) Two apples drawn by artistically gifted 2-year-old on request.

Reprinted with permission of Ryan Sullivan.

using a 2-D primitive to stand for a 3-D volume), artistically gifted children emphasize the surface features of a plane by decorating its surface and retaining a line around its edge. In this way a plane is depicted correctly as a two-dimensional form.

Soon after gifted children begin to draw recognizable forms, they also begin to draw in a realistic manner. They are able to capture the precise shapes of objects; they add true-to-life details that most children would never add (e.g., gas tanks on cars); and they begin to represent the illusion of volume and depth. In place of the simple, schematic, flat, charming, child-like forms typically found in child art, one finds remarkable adult-like, differentiated, complex images that suggest an effort to understand and master how objects are structured. Gifted children draw realistic images quickly and with ease. They do not labor and erase. Instead, their lines are sure and confident (Gordon, 1987; Milbrath, 1998; Paine, 1987; Pariser, 1991, 1992/1993). The young Picasso, for example, could draw anything upon demand, and liked to start a figure from unusual places, for instance, by drawing a dog beginning with the ear (Richardson, 1991). A highly realistic pair of faces, copied by Millais at age eight from an adult work, is shown in Figure 26.2. Peter, the artistically gifted child documented by Winner (1996a), also started pictures from strange starting points—the hem of a dress, a shoulder, or a shoe—and nonetheless a seamless picture ultimately emerged.

The ability to draw realistically also means that gifted children's drawings capture the correct proportions of figures. Milbrath (1998) found that gifted children succeed in drawing human figures in proportion between the ages of four and ten. The non-gifted children that she studied still were unable to capture proportion by age fourteen (which was the oldest age at which she observed their drawings).

Numerous examples of children with precocious ability to draw realistically have been reported (e.g., Gardner, 1980; Golomb, 1992; Milbrath, 1998; Wilson & Wilson, 1976; Winner, 1996a; Winner & Pariser, 1985). One of the most striking examples of early realism is found in the work of Eytan, an Israeli child described by Golomb (1992). Eytan's family did not remember whether he scribbled, but the family does have drawings that he produced at two, an age when most children are just beginning to scribble. At two, Eytan drew recognizable shapes: people, tractors, fish, cars, etc. Normal children make their first tadpole-like representation of a human at about age three, and do not differentiate the head from the trunk until several years later. In contrast, Eytan began to draw humans with a differentiated head and trunk at age two years three months.

One way Eytan achieved realism was through the meticulous depiction of details, such as exhaust pipes on his vehicles. Another way he to achieved realism was through the depiction of volume and depth. Typically, children in Western culture do not begin to try to depict the third dimension until the middle elementary school years. By the age of two and one-half, Eytan was not content with drawing vehicles from their two-dimensional view, and invented ways to depict their volume, showing their side receding into depth. He first used an orthographic projection system to show more than the front or side of a vehicle. By three he had abandoned this system and instead showed multiple sides of a vehicle by attaching the

Figure 26.2 Pencil copy of an adult work drawn by John Everett Millais at age eight.

top and side faces to the front of a vehicle. After his third birthday, he used a mixture of three projection systems: horizontal and vertical oblique projection; isometric projection (in which the front view of a vehicle was its true rectangular shape, but the top and sides of his trucks were parallelograms); and divergent perspective, in which lines diverge outwards to show the front, top, and both sides of a vehicle. By four he showed an understanding of the perspectival rule that objects receding in the distance are reduced in size, and he was beginning to experiment with foreshortening. Figure 26.3 shows an attempt at perspective by Eytan at age three years, seven months.

According to Milbrath (1998), because artistically gifted children see the world in terms of its visible surface features, they are able to overcome the object-centered perspective that dominates typical children. Milbrath noted that artistically gifted children begin to make view-specific drawings long before ordinary children do so. This means that their drawings show figures in unusual positions (e.g., three-quarter views of faces by age seven, back views, profiles) as well as figures distorted and foreshortened by perspective. She observed, however, that while artistically gifted children use perspectival techniques at an early age, their drawings show mixed viewpoints (e.g., oblique projection mixed with linear perspective). These children do not appear to be able to make drawings with one single coordinated point of view until adolescence (Piagetian formal opérations). Research is needed to determine whether children could learn to draw with a single viewpoint at a pre-formal age with appropriate training. Given the fact that artistic savants such as Steven Wiltshire are able to use unified perspective despite being autistic and retarded, there are likely to be alternative routes to perspective besides operational understanding, a point on which Milbrath agrees.

Figure 26.3 Drawing of a truck by Eytan at age three years, seven months. From Claire Golomb, *The child's creation of a pictorial world.*

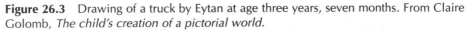

The ability to draw realistically at an earlier than average age also marks the childhoods of those who go on to become established artists. Gordon (1987) studied the childhood works of thirty-one Israeli artists and found that all could draw realistically. Sloane and Sosniak (1985) interviewed twenty sculptors about their childhoods, most of whom recalled drawing realistically at an early age. Numerous other well-known artists' early drawings have been singled out for their advanced realism: for example, Millais (Paine, 1987), Landseer (Goldsmith & Feldman, 1989), Seargent (Cox, 1992), and Picasso (Pariser, 1991).

Picasso provides a clear example of the ability to draw highly realistically at an early age. He claimed, perhaps falsely, that he bypassed the typical stage of early drawings in which children draw in a fanciful, playful, nonrealistic manner. "I have never done children's drawings. Never" (Richardson, 1991, p. 29). However, since we have no records of his works before the age of nine, it is not clear whether this is true. What is clear is that Picasso wanted to see himself as a prodigy. When he went to see a show of child art, he noted, "As a child I would never have been able to participate in a show of this kind: At age twelve, I drew like Raphael" (Richardson, 1991, p. 29). And he recalled specific examples of this adult-like style: "Even when I was very small, I remember one of my first drawings. I was perhaps six . . . In my father's house there was a statue of Hercules with his club in the corridor, and I drew Hercules. But it wasn't a child's drawing. It was a real drawing, representing Hercules with his club" (Richardson, 1991, p. 29).

Realism as an early indicator of artistic giftedness may well be culturally determined. In the West, at least from the Renaissance until the twentieth century, artists have striven to capture the illusion of space, volume, and depth (Gombrich, 1960). While gifted children probably begin to draw realistically long before they have much, if any, exposure to examples of Western realistic art, they have certainly been exposed to realistic images on billboards, magazines, and picture books. The most well-known non-Western artistic prodigy is Wang Yani, a Chinese child who painted in the Chinese brush and ink style at an adult-like level in the preschool years (Zhensun & Low, 1991). As can be seen in Figure 26.4, Wang Yani does not draw or paint in a realistic style, but rather in the style of classical Chinese painting. As young as four, Wang Yani had developed a sense of the adult art world, and could create the kind of art valued in her culture, for example, by art historians,

Figure 26.4 "Pull Harder," Painting by Wang Yani at age five.

Reprinted by permission of Wang Shiqiang.

museum curators, etc. Wang Yani uses the classical Chinese wash technique, and she paints in the loose, spontaneous, and abbreviated style of Chinese ink paintings. Thus, as Goldsmith and Feldman (1989) point out, the technical sophistication of her work reveals itself along dimensions different from those of Western children.

Alexandra Nechita, a Romanian-born artistic prodigy now in the United States, provides a similar example (Winner, 1997). She works in oil, on large canvases, some up to five feet by nine feet, and she paints quickly and compulsively, often completing several large paintings in one week. Her paintings are clearly imbued in the Western modernist tradition—Cubism, Fauvism, Expressionism. One can see in them the styles not only of Picasso, but also of Gorky, Kandinsky, and Miro (Figure 26.5).

The differences between Wang Yani and Alexandra Nechita are instructive. The domain—the body of works that make up the history of painting in one's culture—is shown here to exert as powerful an influence on child prodigies as on adult artists. Neither would have painted as they did without the influence of their respective traditions.

The similarities between the two child artists are just as instructive as their differences. Both have an uncanny sense of the adult art world of their culture, and both paint the kinds of paintings prized by their art worlds. Both have an astonishing mimetic ability. These two cases tell us not only about the power of the domain, but also about the strong role of the *field*—the gatekeepers, judges, curators, and art critics who determine whether a work is considered "creative" (Csikszentmihalyi, 1988). If Alexandra Nechita had somehow been able to develop her style in China, her works would almost certainly have been seen as odd, as distorted, as ugly, as unskillful, and as something to be discouraged. They would have looked nothing like the art that the adult field values. Because she painted in the West and in the twentieth century, where modernism and Picasso are revered, her art looks adultlike and has thus been deemed prodigious.

Further evidence that we place too high a value on early realism as a sign of artistic giftedness comes from Karpati (1994, 1997), who found that giftedness in design and construction did not predict a high level of ability to draw realistically. She concluded that different aspects of artistic talent are unrelated, and the ability to draw realistically is only one sign of such talent. There is, in fact, abundant evidence that artistically gifted children do not always draw

Figure 26.5 "Forgotten Values," Painting by 10-year-old Alexandra Nechita in a style reminiscent of Picasso.

Reprinted by permission of International Art Publishers, Costa Mesa, CA.

realistically. Gifted children often draw in cartoon style, and cartoons are a nonrealistic cultural convention (Wilson & Wilson, 1976). The childhood drawings of Toulouse Lautrec were not realistic but were in the style of grotesque and expressive caricatures (Pariser, 1999).

What unites all children with artistic gifts is thus not the ability or proclivity to draw realistically (though this is a common manifestation in the West), but rather the ability to master one or more of the culture's norms of artistry at a very early age. At the heart of artistic talent is the ability to master cultural conventions, whether the convention is realism in the case of Eytan or Millais, modernism's distortion in the case of Alexandra Nechita, grotesque caricature in the case of Lautrec, or allusionistic brush painting in the case of Wang Yani. It is a mistake to be blinded by our Western eyes and see realism as the prime sign of artistic talent, when realism is but one of many possible cultural conventions that artistically gifted children master so early and so independently.

Picasso viewed paintings as a logical sequence of explorations. "Paintings," he said, "are but research and experiment. I never do a painting as a work of art. All of them are researches. I search constantly and there is a logical sequence in all this research" (Liberman, 1960, p. 33). Many artistically gifted children seem to exemplify this approach. In their drawings, a single theme is explored over and over gain. This repeated practice in drawing one kind of subject means they are far more skilled in drawing their favored subject than in drawing other subjects. For Eytan, for instance, the theme was vehicles, and these were drawn far in advance of his human figures. Wang Yani painted only monkeys until the age of seven (Goldsmith, 1992), and was far better at rendering monkeys than horses or humans, just as Lautrec rendered horses better than birds or humans (Pariser, 1997). As Pariser (1997, p. 41) notes, the work of artistically gifted children is "thematically specialized."

Particularly in middle childhood and adolescence, artistically gifted children create imaginary settings and fantasy characters in their drawings, and their drawings depict episodes in the lives of these invented characters. This is the age when gifted children begin to create superheroes and science fiction characters modeled after the images they see in comic books. Wilson and Wilson (1976) noted that visual narrative need not be in the form of a series of frames, as in a comic strip. Each drawing functions as a shorthand for a complex plot. Or one episode may begin in one sketch book and then continue on disconnected pages. These fantasy worlds allow children an escape into a private world. According to one gifted child, "most people . . . just look at them and say 'that's a pretty picture' without understanding what the people are really like and the story behind them" (Wilson & Wilson, 1976, p. 46). Gifted children are often much more interested in inventing imaginary worlds in their drawings than in experimenting with form and design. In the process, they produce countless drawings, and thus gain fluency and technical skill (Wilson & Wilson, 1976).

There is conflicting evidence about whether the compositional strategies of artistically gifted children are advanced in comparison to those of typical children. According to the analyses of Pariser (1999), neither Picasso, Lautrec, nor Klee were advanced in the area of spatial rendering. An analysis of Klee's six-year-old drawings showed them to be at an adult level in realism (using the Goodenough Harris scale) but only at the six-year-old level in terms of organization of pictorial space (Porath, 1992).

However, Golomb (1992) found that artistically gifted children are more likely to organize their drawings according to the principle of asymmetrical balance, while typical children are likely to use the more obvious strategy of symmetrical balance. She found that younger typical children tended to align the parts of the drawing along either the horizontal or vertical axes, and gradually became able to organize their drawings symmetrically. But only children with artistic gifts used asymmetrical balance.

Milbrath (1998) also found that artistically gifted children can use asymmetrical balance. She found that the drawings by even her youngest gifted children were constructed according to symmetry as well as complex symmetry and asymmetrical balance. Both complex symmetry and asymmetrical balance use different dimensions as counterbalances. Thus, large size may be counterbalanced by a heavy color. In Figure 26.6, the large cat is balanced by the smaller ball of yarn which achieves weight because it is colored an intense yellow.

Milbrath hypothesized that artistically gifted children attend closely to the act of drawing itself, and thus can judge the visual weights of shapes, colors, empty spaces, and directional lines. She writes, "It is not proposed that young talented children are able to plan sophisticated compositions, but rather that they continually monitor what they are doing during the drawing process and react to what they see by placing elements in locations that counterbalance elements already drawn to achieve a stable organization." (Milbrath, 1998, p. 350).

It has been claimed that the normal course of artistic development follows a U-shaped curve, with artistic abilities high in the preschool years, then declining in the elementary school years, and rising again in the adolescent years, but only for those with gifts in the visual arts (Davis, 1997; Gardner & Winner, 1981). Systematic evidence for this position was provided by Davis, who elicited drawings from 140 participants: five-, eight-, and eleven-year-olds

Figure 26.6   Drawing by 8-year-old gifted child showing asymmetrical balance. The large cat is balanced by the small ball of yarn because the cat is uncolored and the yarn is bright yellow. The color gives the smaller shape more weight.

Reprinted by permission of Constance Milbrath and Cambridge University Press.

as well as adolescents and adults with and without artistic gifts. Davis asked her participants to make drawings of "happy," "sad," and "angry."

The 420 drawings produced were then judged in terms of their aesthetic properties. On a four-point scale, judges scored the drawings in terms of overall expression, overall composition, appropriate use of line to express the emotion, and appropriate use of composition to express the emotion. For example, a judge would have to consider whether an asymmetrically balanced drawing conveyed sadness more forcefully than did a symmetrically balanced one. The hypothesis tested was that drawings by five-year-olds would be more like those of adult artists on these dimensions than drawing by eight- and eleven-year-olds.

The findings supported this provocative hypothesis. Scores given to the drawings by adult artists were significantly higher than those given to all other drawings except for the drawings by the five-year-olds and by the adolescents with artistic gifts. The dimension on which the preschoolers performed most like the adult artists was that of overall expression. These findings demonstrate a decline in aesthetic properties of drawings after age five, a decline which flattens out and does not rise again among adolescents and adults with no artistic gifts, yielding an L-shaped curve. However, among adolescents and adults with artistic gifts, a strikingly different trajectory was found: Scores rose again in adolescent and adult artists to create a U-shaped curve. This study provides the first systematic evidence in support of the claim that the art of preschool children—but not older children—shares an aesthetic basis with the art of artists.

Origins of Artistic Gifts

The origin of giftedness is a subject of much debate. The lay person's view is that gifts of any kind are innate (Winner, 1996a). Recently, however, some cognitive psychologists have developed an antiinnatist position, arguing that high achievement in any area is due to motivation, hard work, perseverance, and what is termed *deliberate practice*—goal-directed work on what is difficult (Ericsson & Faivre, 1988; Ericsson, Krampe, & Tesch-Romer, 1993; Howe, 1990; Howe, Davidson, & Sloboda, 1998).

It is our position that hard work is necessary for the development of any gift. But there is no evidence that hard work is sufficient, and thus no evidence to allow us to rule out an innate component to artistic giftedness. Indeed, the strikingly early age of emergence of gifts in art, and the fact that high levels of skill make themselves known prior to formal training, are both strong pieces of indirect evidence for an innate component (Winner, 1996a).

Milbrath's (1998) careful comparison of the developmental trajectory of drawing in typical versus gifted children demonstrates that gifted children are not just faster, they are different. She documents how gifted drawers are more attuned than are typical children to the visual properties of what they draw. She also demonstrates that at any given point in drawing development, gifted children show much more variability in their drawing than do typical children, because gifted children are able to produce some (but not all) drawings at higher levels of development. She argued that this variability occurs because gifted drawers continually pose challenges for themselves. If the developmental trajectory of drawing differs in gifted versus typical children, it is likely that the difference is not simply due to the fact that gifted children make more drawings and thus practice more. The more plausible explanation is that the ability to attend more to the figurative properties of the world is an inborn gift, and it is this gift that then propels these children to want to draw, and to want to solve difficult drawing challenges.[1]

Milbrath's (1998) study provides clear support for the claim that along with artistic giftedness comes the desire to pose challenges for oneself. She found that her sample of typical adolescents drew human figures in three-quarters view only 15 percent of the time, whereas her sample of artistically gifted children used this orientation in half of their figure drawings by the age of six. These three-quarter views appeared abruptly between six and seven years of age. Peter, the

child studied by Winner (1996a), drew a self-portrait in three-quarters view at age six years, one month (see Figure 26.7). He also posed difficult drawing problems for himself, such as depicting people in motion (Figure 26.8), in unusual positions (Figure 26.9), a back view (Figure 26.10), and from an extremely foreshortened perspective (Figure 26.11).

Occasionally one finds examples of intensive work (deliberate practice) without a high degree of innate giftedness.

One example can be seen in urban preschools and elementary schools in China (Winner, 1989). Chinese children learn to draw through explicit, step-by-step instructions from the age of three. They are instructed in precisely how to draw a wide variety of images found in traditional Chinese painting, images such as bamboo, shrimp, goldfish, roosters, grapes, etc. They are taught what lines to make and in what order, and they learn by copying the teacher and from

Figure 26.7 Self-portrait in three-quarters view, by Peter at age six.

Reprinted with the permission of Lois Borelli.

---

1. See also Feldman (2000) for an elaboration of this argument.

Figure 26.8 Figure dancing over a waterfall by Peter at age seven years four months.

Reprinted with the permission of Lois Borelli.

Figure 26.9 Figure with hand on hips throwing a book by Peter age six and one-half.

Reprinted with the permission of Lois Borelli.

a book. This is also the method by which they are taught calligraphy. Because of the intensive training these children receive, their paintings appear very advanced, as shown, for example, in Figure 26.12. Entering a Chinese preschool, one might easily think one has entered a preschool for the artistically gifted! However, this impression will be readily corrected by the realization that none of these children were selected for artistic talent, and all of the children trained in this matter manage to produce highly skilled images. The paintings of Chinese children, while much more advanced in technical skill than those of Western children (who are typically given no explicit instruction in how to draw), nevertheless would never be confused with those of a true Chinese painting prodigy such as Yani. Thus once again we can see that intensive practice, and in this case explicit training, in drawing leads to high levels of skill, but that it cannot make ordinary children into artistic prodigies.

Families of both artistically and musically gifted children tend to be supportive and encouraging. However, families play a far more interventionist and active role in the case of the musically than the artistically gifted (Csikszentmihalyi, Rathunde, & Whalen, 1993). While musically gifted children typically enter a regimen of formal training at a young age, and realize the necessity of hard work and practice for the development of their talent, artistically gifted children often get little formal training in art. At least in the West, artistically gifted children are often suspicious of formal art education, believing such tutelage to be unnecessary and potentially destructive of their talent (Gardner, 1980). The typical art class in elementary and high school does not stimulate these children's art. It is a sad commentary on the way that art is typically taught in school that none of the sculptors studied by Sloane and Sosniak (1985) had anything good to say about their elementary or high school art

Figure 26.10   Figure drawn from the back by Peter at age five.

Reprinted with the permission of Lois Borelli.

classes. Winner and Pariser (1985) found that the artists they interviewed reported that what crystallized their identity as young artists was a professional artist who noted their ability. Contemporary Chinese artists show the same negative attitude towards their elementary school arts instructors (Winner, 1989). Thus, family and community appear more important than schools in the development of artistic ability. Not surprisingly then, artistically gifted children usually do their best, most inventive work out of school (Hurwitz, 1983; Wilson & Wilson, 1976).

Relationship between Childhood Giftedness and Adult Eminence

Highly gifted children often face a crisis at adolescence. Prodigies in music experience a midlife crisis at adolescence, when they become increasingly critical of their playing, and this crisis often results in dropping out of music. The same situation may be true of artistically gifted children. Adolescence is the time when prodigies must make the transition from technical perfection to innovation and big-C, domain creativity. Only those who can "reinvent themselves" will make the leap between childhood giftedness and adult creativity (Gardner, 1993). It is extremely difficult to predict those gifted children and prodigies who will make this transition, and those who will not (Simonton, 1994, 1999). We might predict that a six-year-old who can draw as realistically as a skilled

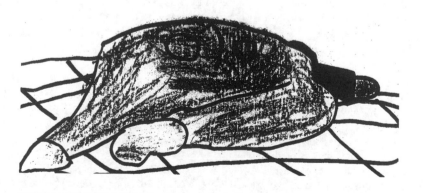

Figure 26.11   Foreshortened figure by Peter at age six years nine months.

Reprinted with the permission of Lois Borelli.

Figure 26.12 Painting by typical five-year-old Chinese child showing the high levels achievable through training alone. Note however that this painting, while skilled, pales in comparison to the painting shown in Figure 26.4 by Yani, an artistically gifted Chinese child who never received the typical Chinese step-by-step drawing training.

From the collection of the author.

adult will grow up to be the next Picasso. But again, if at twenty she is still just drawing with technical precision, and not doing anything innovative, she will fade from public view.

Consider the case of Alexandra Nechita. She is famous now as a child for painting in the style of Picasso. But will anyone take notice of her as an adult if she continues only to paint in the style of Picasso? Rostan, Pariser, and Gruber (1998) found that the childhood drawings of great artists (e.g., Picasso, Klee, Lautrec) were not distinguishable from drawings of our contemporary gifted child artists. Yet few if any of this contemporary group are likely to be-

come great artists. Clearly, while high ability is necessary, it is not sufficient. Degree of skill in childhood cannot by itself predict later creative eminence.

One reason why only a few artistically gifted children and prodigies make the transition to become domain creators as adults is that the funnel is small. There is simply not enough room at the top for all artistic prodigies to become domain-changing creative artists. And so there is an inevitable weeding out.

A second inevitable reason is that the skill of a prodigy is not the same as the skill of a big-C creator. A prodigy is someone who can easily and rapidly master a domain with expertise. A creator is someone who changes a domain. It is likely that personality factors play a major role in becoming a domain creator. Creators are restless, rebellious, and dissatisfied with the status quo (Simonton, 1994; Sulloway, 1996). And they have something new to say.

In a study of seven creative geniuses, Gardner (1993) suggested that a certain degree of tension or "asynchrony" is required for a prodigy to grow into an adult artist or musician who would be classified as creative, or even as a genius. Gardner (1992) argued that creative geniuses differ from prodigies in how well the individual synchronizes with his or her domain as it currently operates within the society. The prodigy typically exhibits talents that fit well with a domain. In contrast, the creative genius often initially exhibits talents that do not fully fit within the domain in which the individual works, and which do not fit with the established tastes of the field (e.g., critics, gallery owners, conductors).

Picasso painted realistically at an early age. But it is only because he began to paint in a revolutionary way and broke with established convention that we consider him a creative genius. The creative artist/musician takes risks and breaks with conventions. The gifted child, or child prodigy, does not. As Hurwitz (1983) points out, gifted children have invested a great deal of energy in mastering a set of skills, and are often unwilling, or unable, to experiment in the way that one must do in order to be creative.

In a study of art students, Getzels and Csikszentmihalyi (1976) found that the art students who went on to become recognized as creative artists did not differ from their art student peers in technical skill. Where they stood out was in their tendency and ability to *find* challenging problems. Such a problem-finding mentality was demonstrated by Picasso, who delighted in posing difficulties for himself, which he could then go on to solve (Richardson, 1991).

Sheer hard work also plays a role in determining whether a prodigy becomes a creative adult artist. The personality characteristics associated with success in any field are drive, tenacity, and the willingness to overcome obstacles (Gardner, 1980, 1993; Roe, 1953; Simonton, 1994). "I believe in nothing but work," said Picasso, who had tremendous energy and drive (Richardson, 1991, p. 48).

Finally, historical and socio-cultural factors determine who becomes classified as an adult creator or genius. No individual or artistic work is inherently creative or not. Instead, creativity is an emergent property formed by an interaction among the individual's gift, the state of the domain at the time when the individual begins to exhibit talent, and the tastes and judgments of the field (e.g., critics, curators, publishers) (Csikszentmihalyi, 1988; Gardner, 1992, 1993; Gardner & Wolf, 1988; Pariser, 1992/1993). There is a fair amount of serendipity involved: One needs to be born at a time when the field is ready to recognize one's talents.

SUMMARY AND CONCLUSIONS

This chapter discusses (1) characteristics of children gifted in the visual arts, (2) the origin of such giftedness, and (3) the relationship between childhood gifts in the visual arts and adult creativity in the visual arts.

Artistically gifted children are not just more advanced than typical children, they draw in a qualitatively different way. They are able to draw things as they appear, with all the distortions caused by point of view and perspective, and thus their drawings typically appear highly realistic. However, not all artistically gifted children draw in a precociously realistic manner. The cases of Wang Yani, a Chinese painting prodigy, and Alexandra Nechita, a Western child prodigy who paints in the style of Picasso, show that what unites all children with artistic gifts is not the ability or proclivity to draw realistically (though this is a common manifestation in the West), but rather the ability to master one or more of the culture's norms of artistry at a very early age.

Another way in which artistically gifted children differ from typical children is that they set themselves visual challenges to master in drawing. Drawings by gifted adolescents and adults are closer aesthetically to the drawings of preschoolers than they are to those by older children.

Evidence is mounted against the claim that high achievement in drawing is due simply to effort and motivation. The primary argument is that the developmental course of drawing differs qualitatively for gifted versus typical children. In addition, some children manifest a great deal of effort but do not achieve the levels of drawing prodigies.

Finally, with respect to the relationship between child prodigies and adult creators in the visual arts, it is noted that adolescence is the time when prodigies must make the transition from technical perfection to innovation and big-C, domain creativity. Only those who can "reinvent themselves" will make the leap between childhood giftedness and adult creativity.

QUESTIONS FOR THOUGHT AND DISCUSSION

1. a. Discuss the evidence that the drawing development of artistically gifted children proceeds on a different developmental path from that of typical children.

b. How does this relate to the (incorrect) argument that motivation and effort are sufficient to account for the drawings produced by artistically gifted children?

2. What is the difference between "little-c" and "big-C" creativity in the visual arts?

3. What is the evidence for and against the claim that drawing development follows a "U-shaped curve," with typical young children represented on the first high end of the U and artistically gifted adolescents represented on the second high end of the U?

4. Why is it too simplistic to say that only children with an early ability to draw realistically are gifted in the visual arts?

REFERENCES

Cox, M. (1992). *Children's drawings.* London: Penguin Books.

Csikszentmihalyi, M. (1988). Society, culture, and person: A systems view of creativity. In R. Sternberg (Ed.), *The Nature of creativity: Contemporary psychological perspectives.* New York: Cambridge University Press.

Csikszentmihalyi, M., Rathunde, K., & Whalen, S. (1993). *Talented teenagers: The roots of success and failure.* New York: Cambridge University Press.

Davis, J. H. (1997). Drawing's demise: U-shaped development in graphic symbolization. *Studies in Art Education, 38*(3), 132–157.

Ericsson, K. A., & Faivre, I. A. (1988). What's exceptional about exceptional abilities? In L. K. Obler & D. A. Fein (Eds.), *The exceptional brain: Neuropsychology of talent and special abilities* (pp. 436–473). New York: Guilford Press.

Ericsson, K. A., Krampe, R. T., & Tesch-Romer, C. (1993). The role of deliberate practice in the acquisition of expert performance. *Psychological Review, 100,* 3, 363–406.

Feldman, D. H. (2000). Figurative and operative processes in the development of artistic talent. *Human Development, 43,* 60–64.

Gardner, H. (1980). *Artful scribbles: The significance of children's drawings.* New York: Basic Books.

Gardner, H. (1992, February). *The "giftedness matrix" from a multiple intelligences perspective.* Paper presented at the Esther Katz Rosen Symposium on the development of Giftedness, University of Kansas.

Gardner, H. (1993). *Creating minds: An anatomy of creativity seen through the lives of Freud, Einstein, Picasso, Stravinsky, Eliot, Graham, and Gandhi.* New York: Basic Books.

Gardner, H., & Winner, E. (1981). Artistry and aphasia. In M. Sarno (Ed.), *Acquired aphasia.* New York: Academic Press.

Gardner, H., & Wolf, C. (1988). The fruits of asynchrony: A psychological examination of creativity. *Adolescent Psychiatry, 15,* 106–123.

Getzels, J. W., & Csikszentmihalyi, M. (1976). *The creative vision: A longitudinal study of problem finding in art.* New York: Wiley.

Goldsmith, L. (1992). Stylistic development of a Chinese painting prodigy. *Creativity Research Journal, 5,* 281–293.

Goldsmith, L., & Feldman, D. (1989). Wang Yani: Gifts well given. In W. C. Ho (Ed.), *Yani: The brush of innocence* (pp. 59–62). New York: Hudson Hills Press.

Golomb, C. (1992). *The child's creation of a pictorial world.* Berkeley: University of California Press.

Gombrich, E. H. (1960). *Art and illusion.* London: Phaidon Press.

Gordon, A. (1987). Childhood works of artists. *Israel Museum Journal, 6,* 75–82.

Howe, M. J. A. (1990). *The origins of exceptional abilities.* Oxford: Blackwell.

Howe, M. J. A., Davidson, J. W., & Sloboda, J. A. (1998). Innate talents: Reality or myth. *Brain and Behavioral Science, 21,* 430–431.

Hurwitz, A. (1983). *The gifted and talented in art: A guide to program planning.* Worcester, MA: Davis Publications.

Karpati, A. (1994). The Leonardo Program. In H. Kauppinen & M. Dicket (Eds.), *Trends in art education in diverse cultures* (pp. 95–102). Reston, VA: National Art Education Association.

Karpati, A. (1997). Detection and development of visual talent. *Journal of Aesthetic Education, 31*(4), 79–93.

Kellogg, R. (1969). *Analyzing children's art.* Palo Alto: National Press Books.

Liberman, A. (1960). *The artist in his studio.* New York: Viking Press.

Matthews, J. (1984). Children drawing: Are young children really scribbling? *Early Child Development and Care, 18,* 1–39.

Milbrath, C. (1998). *Patterns of artistic development in children: Comparative studies of talent.* Cambridge, UK: Cambridge University Press.

Paine, S. (Ed.). (1987). *Six children draw.* New York: Academic Press.

Pariser, D. (1991). Normal and unusual aspects of juvenile artistic development in Klee, Lautrec, and Picasso. *Creativity Research Journal, 4,* 457–472.

Pariser, D. (1992/1993). The artistically precocious child in different cultural contexts: Wang Yani and Toulouse-Lautrec. *Journal of Multicultural and Cross-cultural Research in Art Education, 10/11,* 49–72.

Pariser, D. (1997). Conceptions of children's artistic giftedness from modern and postmodern perspectives. *Journal of Aesthetic Education, 31*(4), 35–47.

Pariser, D. (1999). Looking for the muse in some of the right places: A review of Constance Milbrath's Patterns of Artistic Development. *American Journal of Education, 107*(2), 155–169.

Piaget, J., & Inhelder, B. (1969). *The psychology of the child.* New York: Basic Books.

Porath, M. (1992). Stage and structure in the development of children with various types of "giftedness." In R. Case (Ed.), *The mind's staircase: Exploring the conceptual underpinnings of children's thought and knowledge* (pp. 303–318). Hillsdale, NJ: Erlbaum.

Richardson, J. (1991). *A life of Picasso.* New York: Random House.

Roe, A. (1953). *The making of a scientist.* New York: Dodd Mead.

Rosenblatt, E., & Winner, E. (1988). Is superior visual memory a component of superior drawing ability? In L. Obler & D. Fein (Eds.). *The exceptional brain: Neuropsychology of talent and superior abilities* (pp. 341–363). New York: Guilford.

Rostan, S., Pariser, D., & Gruber, H. (1998). *What if Picasso, Lautrec and Klee were in my art class?* Paper presented at the American Educational Research Association, San Diego.

Simonton, D. K. (1994). *Greatness: Who makes history and why.* New York: Guilford Press.

Simonton, D. K. (1999). Talent and its development: An emergenic and epigenetic model. *Psychological Review, 106,* 435–457.

Sloane, K., & Sosniak, L. (1985). The development of accomplished sculptors. In B. Bloom (Ed.), *Developing talent in young people* (pp. 90–138). New York: Ballantine Books.

Sulloway, F. (1996). *Born to rebel: Birth order, family dynamics, and creative lives.* New York: Pantheon.

Willats, J. (1981). What do the marks in the picture stand for? The child's acquisition of systems of transformation and denotation. *Review of Research in Visual Arts Education, 13,* 18–33.

Wilson, B., & Wilson, M. (1976). Visual narrative and the artistically gifted. *Gifted Child Quarterly, 20,* 432–447.

Winner, E. (1989). How can Chinese children draw so well? *Journal of Aesthetic Education, 23,* 41–63.

Winner, E. (1996a). *Gifted children: Myths and realities.* New York: Basic Books.

Winner, E. (1997). Giftedness vs. creativity in the visual arts. *Poetics, 24(6),* 349–377.

Winner, E., & Pariser, D. (1985). Giftedness in the Visual arts. *Items, 31*(4), 65–69.

Zhensun, A., & Low, A. (1991). *A young painter: The life and paintings of Wang Yani—China's extraordinary young artist.* New York: Scholastic.

BIBLIOGRAPHY

Bamberger, J. (1982). Growing up prodigies: The mid-life crisis. In D. H. Feldman (Ed.), *Developmental approaches to giftedness* (pp. 265–279). San Francisco: Jossey-Bass.

Bastian, H. G. (1994). From the every-day world and the musical way of life of highly talented young instrumentalists. In K. A. Heller & E. A. Hany (Eds.), *Competence and responsibility: The Third European Conference of the European Council for High Ability* (Vol. 2, pp. 153–163). Seattle: Hogrefe & Huber.

Duncum, P. (1986). Breaking down the U-curve of artistic development. *Visual Arts Research, 12*(1), 43–54.

Gardner, H. (1983). *Frames of mind: The theory of multiple intelligences.* New York: Basic Books.

Hildreth, G. (1941). *The child mind in evolution.* New York: Kings Crown Press.

Kerschensteiner, G. (1905). *Die Entwicklung der zeichnerischen Begabung* (Development of drawing aptitude). Munich: Druck und Verlag von Carl Gerber.

Korzenick, D. (1995). The changing concept of artistic giftedness. In C. Golomb (Ed.), *The development of artistically gifted children* (pp. 1–30). Hillsdale, NJ: Erlbaum.

Lark-Horowitz, B., Lewis, H., & Luca, M. (1973). *Understanding children's art for better teaching* (2nd ed.). Columbus, OH: Merrill.

Miller, L. K. (1999). The savant syndrome: Intellectual impairment and exceptional skill. *Psychological Bulletin, 125,* 31–46.

Pariser, D., & Vandenberg, A. (1997). The mind of the beholder: Some provisional doubts about the U-curved aesthetic thesis. *Studies in Art Education, 38*(9), 155–170.

Richet, G. (1900). Note sur un cas remarquable de precocité musicale. IV Congrès Internationale de Psychologie. *Compte Rendu des Sciences,* 93–99.

Winner, E. (1996b). The rage to master: The decisive case for talent in the visual arts. In K. A. Ericsson (Ed.), *The road to excellence: The acquisition of expert performance in the arts and sciences, sports and games* (pp. 271–301). Hillsdale, NJ: Erlbaum.

Winner, E. (1998). Don't confuse necessity with sufficiency or science with policy. Commentary on Howe, M. J. A., Davidson, J. W., & Sloboda, J. A., Innate Talents: Reality or Myth. *Brain and Behavioral Science, 21,* 430–431.

27

Talent, Accomplishment, and Eminence

HERBERT J. WALBERG, *University of Illinois—Chicago*
DEBORAH B. WILLIAMS, *Chicago Public Schools*
SUSIE ZEISER, *University of Illinois—Chicago*

During the last quarter century, educational psychologists have completed and compiled the findings of more than 8,000 studies on how educational productivity factors during the first two or three decades of life influence academic learning. More efficient educational productivity in academic and related learning may allow more time to develop childhood and adolescent giftedness and adult eminence. The productivity factors that enhance academic learning, moreover, also appear to develop exceptional talent, since learning is a fundamental ingredient of notable human accomplishments. The theory of educational productivity based on meta-analysis of the outcomes of many studies (Walberg, 1984a, 1990; Walberg, Fraser, & Welch, 1986), coupled with the theory of human capital (Walberg & Stariha, 1992), emphasizes the importance of broad learning through the primary agencies of families, teachers, peer groups, mass media, and the efficient use of human time.

This chapter reviews corroborative findings as well as current primary research. It suggests that alterations in the productivity factors have proven beneficial for ordinary and extraordinary human achievement. It makes clear that the amount of time invested by parents, educators, coaches, and learners themselves multiplies the effects of educational and environmental factors to increase academic learning, talent development, and adult eminence.

Accordingly, to better realize human potential, efficient procedures are required. Efficiency streamlines the acquisition of basic skills and cultural literacy so that general education can be accomplished in less time and earlier in the life span. The time savings can result in greater supplies of time for the pursuit of general all-roundedness or specialized exceptionality. It is therefore reasonable, as Redmond, Mumford, and Teach (1993) found, that with this time saving, the resultant additional time could be spent planning and re-planning a project that would result in increased productivity and higher creativity. Piirto (1994) cites Simonton's (1988a, 1988b) concurrence that the early production of work by eminent creators results in impressive cumulative rates of output. Such time use allows for greater accomplishments, including transformation and novel application of existing knowledge (Walberg & Herbig, 1991; Walberg & Stariha, 1992; Walberg & Tsai, 1984). In the 1970s a select group of mathematically and scientifically precocious children were identified and guided by psychologist Julian Stanley of Johns Hopkins. The pace of their math and science education was accelerated, and they later enrolled in college at an early age. Preliminary results of a twenty-year follow-up of the Study for Mathematically Precocious Youth (SMPY) cohort I (those identified in the early 1970s) indicate that most of the participants have been successful. Many achieved advanced degrees and others rose to outstanding careers at an early age (Hendricks, 2000).

Educational Productivity

Research synthesis suggest that nine factors, when controlled for each other and other factors, consistently and strongly influence academic learning (Walberg, 1984a). These factors are the main direct influences on cognitive, affective, and behavioral learning in childhood and adolescence.

1. Ability or prior achievement as measured by the usual standardized tests.
2. Chronological age or stage of development.
3. Motivation or self-concept as indicated by perseverance on tasks.
4. Instructional time engaged in learning.
5. Quality of instruction, including both curricular and psychological aspects.
6. The curriculum of home life.
7. Classroom group environment.
8. Peer group selected outside school.
9. Exposure to mass media and popular culture, notably, television (which is the only factor inversely related to learning outcomes).

No single factor, however, accounts for great accomplishments. It is the combination and interaction of these factors, taken together, that appear to do so. High ability and large quantities of instructional time, for example, may have little effect on unmotivated students, on students whose home environment may discount the importance of school, or on those receiving poor-quality instruction.

Poor-quality instruction may be a result of non-identification. When high ability students are not provided appropriate enrichment, not only will their potential be under-capitalized, but they also may react with disruptive or nonproductive behaviors (Gallagher, 1994).

School, Home, and Peer Group

Constructive relations between parents and teachers are required for optimum performance (Bennett, 1987). The goals for intellectual development of the child, then, must be shared among these chief agents of education if instruction is to be maximally productive. One of the factors in thirty-eight schools recognized for consistent and significant gains in student achievement was that the administrators extended themselves to involve parents in the school and in their child's learning (Wolk, 2001). World-class test scores in culture-free subjects such as mathematics and science in Japan can be explained in part by this communality of interest. It has been observed, for example, that Asian families sometimes purchase not one, but two textbooks for their chil-

dren. The second textbook is for the mother to help her child be successful in school. Such dedication has huge effects on children's learning.

The first five of the above nine factors were included in the educational models of Bloom, Bruner, Carroll, and Glaser (see Walberg, 1984b). Syntheses of research, however, suggest that social/psychological factors, both inside and outside the school, significantly influence valued outcomes.

Factor 6, the curriculum of the home, refers to such activity as informed parent-child conversation and communication about everyday observations and events. These may include discussions or critical analysis of school-related discoveries, leisure reading, television programs, and friends. Among such serious efforts, as Walberg and Herbig (1991) point out, are the no less important expressions of affect and relatedness: happiness, laughter, caprice, and serenity.

Television's impact on academic skills depends not only on the amount of television watched, but also on the type of program and the age of the child (Reinking & Wu, 1990). Estimates suggest that American adolescents watch television around twenty-eight hours per week. After ten hours per week, however, television has deleterious influences on learning. The eighteen "excessive" hours per week might better be reallocated to other pursuits such as homework, leisure reading, projects, hobbies, and talent development.

Noncognitive Outcomes

Much research on productivity factors focused on cognitive outcomes. Still, these are hardly all of what educators and parents want from schooling. Raven's (1981) summary of surveys in Western countries, including England and the United States, suggests that attitudinal, social, and emotional goals are more important to educators, parents, and students than academic ones. Given a choice, Raven reports, all three groups rank cooperation, self-reliance, constructive attitudes, lifelong learning incentives, and critical thinking as more important than specific academic achievement reflected in school grades or standardized test scores. At the same time, no one has shown that cognitive mastery interferes with the less measurable outcomes of schooling; presumably the mastery of school subjects enhances self-concept, "learning to learn" skills, and the basic knowledge required for beginner's status in most academic and non-academic fields.

In a related noncognitive area, a recent study that compared the social status of highly gifted and moderately gifted students across academic and social settings found that level of giftedness does not play a major role in social status (Norman, Ramsay, Roberts, & Martray, 2000). This finding supports prior studies, which found that, in general, gifted students are no more or less adjusted than other students; rather, factors unrelated to giftedness often contribute to adjustment problems (Richardson & Benbow, 1990; Cornell, 1990).

Raven's findings and those of Norman et al. may underscore the value of active participation, interaction, and human relationships for learning in the home, the classroom, and friendship circles. These not only influence learning directly, but also indirectly influence ability and motivation, which, in turn, influence responsiveness to instruction (Walberg & Stariha, 1992). The dynamic and interactive qualities of our model of educational productivity suggest, then, that motivation and ability to learn will increase if we provide a great deal of exceptional instruction—with the support of the home, the active participation and cooperation of students in the classroom within a peer culture and popular culture that do not actively promote anti-intellectual values.

"Matthew Effects"

Research on the productivity model suggests that early educational advantages multiply (as the Matthew's Gospel story of the rich getting richer or what sociologists call "cumulative advantage"). In modern times, Merton (1968), in portraying distinguished scientific careers, described how the initial advantages of university study, work with eminent scientists, early publication, job placement, and citation combine multiplicatively to confer tastes, skills, habits, rewards, and further opportunities that cumulate to produce highly skewed productivity in scientific work. That is, relatively few scientists account for much of publications, citations, and discoveries. Similar processes and advantages appear to explain the precocity and accomplishments of talented children and adolescents who accumulate multiplicative advantages through the educational productivity factors. Still, unless they can maintain optimal conditions with respect to most of the factors, they may not reach and maintain world-class status (see Walberg & Tsai, 1984).

Motivation and Productivity

Although Herbert Simon's (1954) motivational theory pertains to foreign language learning, it appears to generalize and parsimoniously explain much of human learning and exceptional performance. Simon noted that in choosing frequent practice (that is, amount of self-instruction time), we eventually experience the learning activity as easier; with ease comes an increase in the pleasure of the activity; with an increase in pleasure comes greater desire for further learning. Knowledge of results, whether self-recognized or pointed out by others, enhances such motivation.

Sustained, concentrated effort over time appears to be one of the necessary factors of distinguished accomplishment. Catharine Cox (1926), who analyzed over 300 biographical accounts, found that eminent adults were characterized, in part, by persistence, intellectual energy, and unusual ambition—which all indicate motivation. Block (1971) also found impressive endurance of aspiration levels in his analysis of the Berkeley Growth Studies, a fifty-year longitudinal project. Kagan and Moss (1962) found that gifted children placed a high value on intellectual and cognitive activities, which also endured over time. Thus, accomplishment in adolescence and adult life may be attributable in part to sustained motivation and habits of perseverance acquired early in life.

Creativity, Activity, and Accomplishment

During the 1960s, creativity came to be misconstrued as an instant phenomenon. True enough, an apparently sudden insight may be a part of artistic and scientific discoveries. But insight is hardly sufficient by itself. Its coming to consciousness requires intense preparation, and most insights require vast testing and planning before they come to fruition. Therefore, though discovery may occur in an instant, distinguished accomplishment usually requires decades of preparation in the special field (Getzels & Csikszentmihalyi, 1976; Walberg & Herbig, 1991). For example, an entry in the journal of the great mathematician Karl Gauss reveals the progress of his discovery: "Finally, two days ago, I succeeded . . . . Like a sudden flash of lightning, the riddle happened to be solved. I myself cannot say what was the conducting thread which connected what I previously knew with what made my success possible" (Getzels & Jackson, 1962, p. 84). But for years Gauss had been working on a proof for this theorem, before everything came together at a single moment in time. Similarly, the great English scientist Isaac Newton believed that his record of discoveries was achieved "by always thinking about them."

A Knowledge Base

Amabile (1996) posits the following components in his theory of creativity: (1) domain-relevant skills or existing knowledge, (2) task motivation, and (3) creativity-relevant skills. Embedded in Amabile's creativity-relevant skills is the concept of exploring new pathways.

Of sixteen programs of research on creativity (Tardif & Sternberg, 1988), eleven cited the individual's use of existing knowledge for novel ideas as the most frequently observed cognitive characteristic of creativity. The necessity of the familiar component in creative discovery is supported by a large-scale review of psychological studies of eminent painters, writers, musicians, philosophers, religious leaders, and scientists, both past and present, as well as by prize-winning adolescents of today (Walberg, 1969). All reveal early, intense concentration and interest in previous work in their fields (Bloom, 1985).

Simon (1981) estimated that 70 hours of concentrated, prodigious work per week for ten years is required for expert mastery of a special field today. Recent evidence, even in the study of so-called idiot savants, suggests that social withdrawal leaves them enormous amounts of time to think about the fields in which they show brilliance (Howe & Smith, 1988). Showing, for example, that perfect pitch is a learned ability, Howe and Smith's work suggests that no person has ever managed to create outstanding accomplishments without undergoing a lengthy period of intense and careful preparation.

Although eminent creators sometimes produce inferior work, the amount of work produced generally varies directly with the quality of work produced (Albert, 1978; Barron, 1961; Simonton, 1984). It is interesting to note how extremely productive some highly creative people are. Bach composed an average of twenty pages of finished music per day; Picasso produced over 20,000 paintings, sculptures, and drawings; Poincaré published 500 papers and 30 books; Edison held 1093 patents; Freud had 300

publications, and Einstein 248 (Simonton, 1984). Only enduring motivation and perseverance can account for such prodigious production of outstanding works (Simonton, 1987; Ochse, 1990).

Knowledge, Experience, and Novelty

Acquisition of knowledge alone cannot completely account for eminent accomplishment. Creativity is something more than mere mastery (Walberg & Herbig, 1991). The growth of human capital and cultural progress requires more than mere transmission of knowledge and its embodiment in people; creativity refers ultimately to new knowledge, techniques, and applications that promote human welfare (Walberg, 1988).

In the search to identify the acquisition of this new knowledge, another definition of intelligence has evolved. While *cognition* refers to having skills, *metacognition* refers to awareness of and conscious control over those skills (Stewart & Tei, 1983). Metacognition has been defined as achieving a deep comprehension that synthesizes the knowledge of literal facts with creative thinking. It is a well-developed understanding and strategic use of one's own cognitive processes; knowing when and how to use one's thinking skills to understand and solve problems. Researchers have suggested that not only is there a link between metacognition and creativity (Boyce, VanTassel-Baska, Burruss, Sher, & Johnson, 1997; Feldhusen & Goh, 1995; Jausovec, 1994), but Davidson and Sternberg (1998) describe how metacognitive processes also contribute to problem solving, which can then lead to a "Eureka" moment.

Morgan (1953) reviewed a large number of definitions of creativity and demonstrated that the single most common element was novelty. Subsequently, Finke, Ward, and Smith (1992) identified two different kinds of processes leading to novelty: (1) *generating novel cognitive structures* via retrieving, associating, synthesizing, transforming, and constructing analogies; and (2) *exploring the creative implications of new structures,* that is, attribute finding, interpreting, and inferring. The first process produces novelty, and the second makes novelty effective, thereby leading to creativity. According to Csikszentmihalyi (1996) and Grudin (1990), social recognition and ethics are required for novelty to become creativity. Still, novelty or creativity has been accorded more mystery and inspiration than it probably deserves, and a parsimonious account deriving from the natural sciences may well serve as a working explanation and guide to practice.

In the theory of evolution, Darwin showed that new species evolve by trial and error; Skinner similarly showed that differential rewards or "positive reinforcements" determine what randomly emitted behavior is reinforced; and subsequent research on humans showed that given powerful enough needs and reinforcers, human behavior can also be strongly influenced, if not determined (Lea, 1978). Similarly, Campbell (1960) cogently argued that trial and error suffices to explain creative thought as well as other mental processes.

Campbell held that processes of blind variation and selective retention are "fundamental to all inductive achievements, to all genuine increases in knowledge, to all increases in fit of system to environment" (p. 380). For this reason, three conditions for creativity are necessary: a mechanism for introducing variation, a consistent selection process, and a mechanism for preserving and reproducing the selected variations" (p. 381). Campbell cites many illustrative examples of such creative trial and error in autobiographical works by such mathematicians and scientists as Mach, Poincaré and Hadamard, as well as works by psychologists such as Thurstone, Tolman, Hull, Miller and Dollard, and Mowrer.

The significance of the models of both Campbell and Simon lies in their parsimony and applicability to real-world problems and solutions. Notable in their work are the limitations and trade-offs in time, memory, and retrieval that constrain learning and thought.

Having a large fund of knowledge and experience confers advantages in discovering novel solutions, but such funds are hardly preconditions. Even novices can think of novel and workable ideas, particularly if they are encouraged to do so. Teachers and parents who understand and point out the possibilities of discovering and applying ideas may show novel applications of familiar ideas and experience—a good service, especially for exceptional students. In a national sample of high school students, those winning competitive awards in the arts and in science chose creativity over wealth and power as the most valued development in life (Walberg, 1969).

Eminent Men

Many of the ideas expressed here derive from our studies of eminent people (see Walberg & Stariha,

1992). Even though concerned about tomorrow's achievement, educators, psychologists, and others should also think about what they are doing today that may affect students' adult accomplishments. For more than two decades, we have been researching the early lives of people who achieved eminence in such fields as the visual arts, music, politics, and science. In our initial research, we studied the biographies of Leonardo da Vinci, Abraham Lincoln, Isaac Newton, and others (nearly all men). We and their biographers rated each person on the educative conditions of their families and schools that promoted their accomplishments.

It is the parents who, as the first adults to become aware of their child's talent, provide supplementary, meaningful activities (Walberg & Stariha, 1992), as well as support and guidance. As children, the eminent men showed intellectual competence and motivation, social and communication skills, general psychological wholesomeness, and both versatility and persevering concentration. Most were stimulated by cultural stimuli and materials related to their field of eminence and by teachers, parents, and other adults. Although most had clear parental expectations for their conduct, they also had the opportunity to explore on their own.

Large percentages of the sample were exposed to stimulating family, educational, and cultural conditions during childhood. Only slightly more than half were encouraged by parents, but a solid majority were encouraged by teachers and other adults and were exposed to many adults at an early age. Significantly more than half, 60%, were exposed to eminent persons during childhood.

About 80 percent were successful in school; the majority liked it; and less than a quarter had school problems. Seventy percent had clear parental expectations for their conduct; but nearly 90% were allowed to explore their environments on their own, obviously a delicate, important balance in child rearing and teaching.

Psychologists who have employed case studies and other methods to discover the conditions of creativity suggest similar traits and conditions. In addition, national surveys of accomplished adolescents who have won competitive awards for achievements in the arts and sciences suggested similar trends. Still, prior psychological studies concentrated on males, and the surveys employed the criterion of promising adolescent accomplishment rather than actual adult eminence.

Eminent Women

For these reasons, we made content analyses of biographies of 256 eminent women of this century. They include skater Sonja Henie, actress Ethel Barrymore, singer Mahalia Jackson, athlete Babe Didrikson Zaharias, business woman Helena Rubinstein, blind and deaf leader Helen Keller, poet Marianne Moore, painter Grandma Moses, reformer Margaret Sanger, educator and civil rights leader Mary McLeod Bethune, scientist Rachel Carson, suffragist Jeannette Rankin, and political leader Eleanor Roosevelt.

We wanted to depict childhood character and conditions of eminent women. One goal was to help identify and encourage distinguished accomplishments in others. We recognize, nonetheless, at least three problems: the shortcomings of biography, biases in our own ratings, and the possibility that the present may require different patterns of traits and conditions than did the past. Thus, our findings can be taken only as hints for the present and should be compared with other research and personal experience.

Childhood Traits

What was the most common psychological trait of eminent women shown during childhood? It was the same as that shown by eminent American and European men of previous centuries—intelligence. More than 50 percent of the women showed high intelligence in their early years. Equally for women as for men, the other top ranking traits were perseverance and work hard, especially in music and the visual arts.

Shared by more than three in ten girls, especially political activists and college administrators, was success in school. Seven in ten women, nonetheless, were not particularly successful academically. Many contemporary studies show little relation of academic grades to adult success for people with a given amount of education.

Parental and Other Social Influence

Because they can be altered, environmental influences are of practical interest. From about one-third to one-half of the women were taught directly or strongly encouraged by their fathers, mothers, or other adults. Seven in ten had clear parental expectations for their conduct, yet nearly one-fourth were allowed to explore on their own, and 32 percent learned much outside school.

Forty-six percent came from financially advantaged families, although more than half came from culturally advantaged families. More than one-third were extensively exposed to cultural materials and stimulation (not necessarily in their later fields of accomplishment). Roughly one-fifth of the sample (not necessarily overlapping groups) were exposed to one or more of the following advantages:

- The presence of many adults other than their parents;
- The presence of eminent adults other than their parents;
- Social milieux that were open and receptive to varied cultures;
- A revolutionary period in their future fields;
- Special tutoring;
- External incentives for accomplishment.

The rarest environmental condition was cultural emphasis on immediate gratification. Only 1 percent of the women grew up under this condition.

SUMMARY AND CONCLUSIONS

Research synthesis of over 8,000 studies suggests that the interaction of nine educational productivity factors is beneficial for realizing human potential. In addition, the critical element of *time* allows for reflection on knowledge, techniques, and applications that can lead to creativity or novelty. The amount of time invested by parents, educators, and other accomplished adults, as well as the efficient use of time invested in accelerated learning, are catalysts that can contribute to high accomplishment.

Our analyses of talented adolescents and the biographies of eminent men and women indicate that accomplished adults and young people in many fields share common traits. They are intelligent, hard-working, persistent, and follow through on activities, despite difficulties. Many are inquisitive and original enough to question conventions. Most of these traits were acquired early in life.

The accomplished adolescents and adults benefitted from encouragement, stimulation, and direct teaching provided by their parents, teachers, and other adults. Many lived in social environments receptive to varied ideas and cultures. Many were tutored and given special recognition for their early accomplishments.

It is the convergence of ability and motivational traits, the interaction of the educational productivity factors, the efficient use of time, and supportive environmental factors that promote human potential and accomplishment.

However, the common traits of accomplished people—intelligence, perseverance, and stimulating social environments—are hardly guarantees of adult success. Combinations of other traits and conditions undoubtedly play influential roles at various stages of childhood, adolescence, and adulthood. Luck and the vicissitudes of opportunity also play their parts. Nonetheless, the findings strongly suggest that parents, educators, and others should think carefully about how to encourage constructive psychological traits, and how to design stimulating conditions that are likely to enable boys and girls to fulfill their potential.

QUESTIONS FOR THOUGHT AND DISCUSSION

1. Look at the authors' nine educational productivity factors. Can you prioritize them in importance?

2. How would some of these educational productivity factors justify academic acceleration for gifted students?

3. How does the "Matthew Effect" help explain the accomplishments of gifted or talented children?

4. Consider recurrent traits of eminent men and women. How are they similar and different?

5. How might chance opportunities during childhood impact the realization of high achievement or eminence?

REFERENCES

Albert, R. S. (1978). Observations and suggestions regarding giftedness, familial influence and the achievement of eminence. *Gifted Child Quarterly, 22,* 201–211.

Amabile, T. M. (1996). *Creativity in context.* Boulder, CO: Westview Press.

Barron, F. (1961). Creative vision and expression in writing and painting. In D. W. McKinnon (Ed.), *The creative person* (pp. 231–247). Berkeley, CA: Institute of Personality Assessment Research, University of California.

Bennett, W. J. (1987). *What works: Research about teaching and learning* (2nd ed.). Washington, DC: U.S. Department of Education.

Block, J. (1971). *Lives through time.* Berkeley: Bancroft Books.

Bloom, B. S. (1985). Generalizations about talent development. In B. S. Bloom (Ed.), *Developing Talent in Young People.* New York: Ballantine.

Boyce, L. N., VanTassel-Baska J., Burruss, J. D., Sher, B. T., & Johnson, D. T. (1997). A problem-based curriculum: Parallel learning opportunities for students and teachers. *Journal for the Education of the Gifted, 20,* 363–379.

Campbell, D. T. (1960). Blind variation and selective retention in creative thought as in other knowledge processes. *Psychological Review, 67,* 380–400.

Cornell, D. G. (1990). High ability students who are unpopular with their peers. *Gifted Child Quarterly, 34,* 155–160.

Cox, C. M. (1926). *The early mental traits of three hundred geniuses.* Stanford, CA: Stanford University Press.

Csikszentmihalyi, M. (1996). *Creativity: Flow and the psychology of discovery and invention.* New York: HarperCollins.

Davidson, J. E., & Sternberg, R. J. (1998). Smart problem solving: How metacognition helps. In D. J. Hacker, J. Dunlosky, & A. C. Graeser (Eds.), *Metacognition in educational theory and practice* (pp. 47–68). Mahwah, NJ: Erlbaum.

Feldhusen, J. F., & Goh, B. E. (1995). Assessing and accessing creativity: An integrative review of theory, research, and development. *Creativity Research Journal, 8,* 231–247.

Finke, R. A., Ward, T. B., & Smith, S. M. (1992). *Creative cognition.* Boston: MIT Press.

Gallagher, J. J. (1994). Current and historical thinking on education for gifted and talented students. In P. O. Ross (Ed.), *National excellence: A case for developing America's talent.* Washington, DC: U.S. Department of Education.

Getzels, J. W., & Csikszentmihalyi, M. (1976). *The creative vision.* New York: Wiley.

Getzels, J. W., & Jackson, P. W. (1962). *Creativity and intelligence: Explorations with gifted students.* New York: Wiley.

Grudin, R. (1990). *The grace of great things: Creativity and innovation.* New York: Ticknor and Fields.

Hendricks, M. (2000). Yesterday's whiz kids. *Our Gifted Children, 76,* 8–14.

Howe, M. J., & Smith, J. (1988). Calendar calculating in "idiot savants": How do they do it? *British Journal of Psychology, 79*(3), 371–386.

Jausovec, N. (1994). Metacognition in creative problem solving. In M. A. Runco (Ed.), *Problem finding, problem solving, and creativity.* Norwood, NJ: Ablex.

Kagan, J., & Moss, H. A. (1962). *Birth to maturity.* New York: Wiley.

Lea, S. E. G. (1978). The psychology and economics of demand. *Psychological Bulletin, 85,* 441–466.

Merton, R. K. (1968). The Matthew effect in science. *Science, 159,* 56–63.

Morgan, D. N. (1953). Creativity today. *Journal of Aesthetics, 12,* 1–24.

Norman, A., Ramsay, S., Roberts, J., & Martray, C. (2000). Effect of social setting, self-concept, and relative age on the social status of moderately and highly gifted students. *Roeper Review, 23,* 34–39.

Ochse, R. (1990). *Before the gates of excellence: The determinants of creative genius.* New York: Cambridge University Press.

Piirto, J. (1994). *Talented children and adults: Their development and education.* New York: Macmillan College Publishing Company.

Raven, J. (1981). The most important problem in education is to come to terms with values. *Oxford Review of Education, 7,* 253–272.

Redmond, M. R., Mumford, M. D., & Teach, R. (1993). Putting creativity to work: Effects of leader behavior on subordinate creativity. *Organizational Behavior and Human Decision Processes, 55,* 120–151.

Reinking, D., & Wu, J. (1990). Reexamining the research on television and reading. *Reading Research and Instruction, 29,* 117–122.

Richardson, T. M., & Benbow, C. P. (1990). Long-term effects of acceleration on the social-emotional adjustment of mathematically precocious youths. *Journal of Educational Psychology, 82,* 464–470.

Simon, H. A. (1954). Some strategic considerations in the construction of social science models. In P. Lazarsfeld (Ed.), *Mathematical thinking in the social sciences.* Glencoe, IL: Free Press.

Simon, H. A. (1981). *Sciences of the artificial.* Cambridge: MIT Press.

Simonton, D. K. (1984). *Genius, creativity and leadership: Historiometric inquiries.* Cambridge: Harvard University Press.

Simonton, D. K. (1987). Developmental antecedents of achieved eminence. *Annals of Child Development, 5,* 131–169.

Simonton, D. K. (1988a). Creativity, leadership, and chance. In R. J. Sternberg (Ed.), *The nature of creativity.* New York: Cambridge University Press.

Simonton, D. K. (1988b). *Scientific genius: A psychology of science.* New York: Cambridge University Press.

Stewart, O., & Tei, O. (1983). Some implications of metacognition for reading instruction. *Journal of Reading, 26,* 36–43.

Tardif, T. Z., & Sternberg, R. J. (1988). What do we know about creativity? In R. J. Sternberg (Ed.), *The nature of creativity.* New York: Cambridge University Press.

Walberg, H. J. (1969). A portrait of the artist and scientist as young men. *Exceptional Children, 36,* 5–11.

Walberg, H. J. (1984a). Improving the productivity of America's schools. *Educational Leadership, 41,* 19–27.

Walberg, H. J. (1984b). *National abilities and economic growth.* Chicago: University of Illinois Office of Evaluation Research.

Walberg, H. J. (1988). Creativity and talent as learning. In R. J. Sternberg (Ed.), *The nature of creativity: contemporary psychological perspectives* (pp. 340–361). New York: Cambridge University Press.

Walberg, H. J. (1990). Productive teaching and instruction: Assessing the knowledge base. *Phi Delta Kappan, 71,* 470–478.

Walberg, H. J., Fraser, B. J., & Welch, W. W. (1986). A test of a model of educational productivity among senior high school students. *Journal of Educational Research, 79,* 133–139.

Walberg, H. J., & Herbig, M. P. (1991). Developing talent, creativity, and eminence. In N. Colangelo & G. A. Davis (Eds.), *Handbook of gifted education* (pp. 245–255). Boston: Allyn and Bacon.

Walberg, H. J., & Stariha, W. E. (1992). Productive human capital: Learning, creativity and eminence. *Creativity Research Journal, 5*(4), 323–340.

Walberg, H. J., & Tsai, S.-L. (1984). Matthew effects in education. *American Educational Research Journal, 20,* 359–374.

Wolk, R. (2001). Perspective—mission: Possible. *Teacher Magazine, 12*(8), 3.

28

When Does Giftedness Become Genius? And When Not?

DEAN KEITH SIMONTON, *University of California—Davis*

When Giftedness Becomes Genius: How Does Talent Achieve Eminence?

Lewis M. Terman's multivolume *Genetic Studies of Genius* has long been recognized as one of the classics in the literature on giftedness. Each volume of this monumental work contains important insights about the nature and development of intellectual giftedness across the life span. Yet we must recognize the reason why the set of five volumes must be referred to as "studies" rather than as a "study." The plural is mandated because Terman's *magnum opus* actually contains two rather different types of investigations.

The bulk of *Genetic Studies* is devoted to Terman's ambitious longitudinal study of gifted children. Volume 1 describes how the large sample of children were selected and then details their characteristics, such as family background, physical health, scholastic performance, interests and hobbies, and personality traits (Terman, 1925). Volume 3 examines the same children some years later to discern continuities and changes in their early development (Burks, Jensen, & Terman, 1930). Volume 4 looks at these "Termites" when they have become young adults at the thresholds of their careers (Terman & Oden, 1947). And finally, Volume 5, which was published posthumously (Terman & Oden, 1959), scrutinized this same intellectually gifted sample as it entered middle age, enabling the researchers to determine directly their adulthood achievements (see also Oden, 1968). In many respects this last volume is the most crucial, for Terman was by then obligated to show that those whom he identified as talented children did, in fact, become highly accomplished adults. Childhood gifts may even produce adulthood genius.

But we skipped Volume 2 (Cox, 1926), which is the only volume of the five that does not list Terman as a co-author. This 842-page tome was instead written by one of his doctoral students, Catharine Cox, who chose a rather contrary approach to the study of giftedness across the life span. Rather than identify a group of gifted children and then follow them through adulthood to see if they attained distinction in some significant domain, Cox decided to reverse the procedure: She would identify a group of obviously eminent adults and then peer into the biographies of their early childhood to find out whether they had displayed any signs of giftedness. Thus, Terman's longitudinal study of children was supplemented by Cox's retrospective study of adults. The explicit hope was that these two studies would obtain complementary results. Gifted children would become geniuses, and the geniuses would prove themselves to have been gifted children. Certainly, Terman had no regrets about including this aberrant study among the set. In his last years, when he was doing what he could to finish Volume 5, he firmly believed that giftedness and genius were intimately related. The concepts simply represented the two end points of an underlying process of talent development that stretched from birth until death.

But how valid is this belief? Does giftedness necessarily develop into genius? If not, why not? And conversely, does all genius exhibit giftedness in childhood? If not, again, why not? Note that this is a problem about which Terman himself expressed some concern. Not all of his gifted children made good, and he took great pains to explain these misfits and failures. Cox, too, was aware of this issue. Many of the 301 geniuses in her sample would not have qualified for inclusion in Terman's longitudinal study, a discrepancy that she tried to handle in various ways. Hence, the connection between childhood and adulthood talent may be more complex than the main argument of Genetic Studies of Genius would like us to think.

This chapter will discuss some of the intricacies involved. It will examine the consistencies and the incongruities that have arisen in longitudinal and retrospective studies of talent development. Quite frankly, I will pose more puzzles than provide firm solutions. The goal is simply to outline what we know so far and to indicate how far we must go before we know what we need to know.

Parallels and Paradoxes

Space is insufficient to discuss all the questions about the conversion of talent into eminence (see Simonton, 1994). Here I focus on three key research sites: intelligence, personality, and development. These three concern issues were first introduced in *Genetic Studies of Genius,* whether implicitly or explicitly.

Intelligence

Terman's sample was specifically selected according to performance on the Stanford-Binet intelligence test, which Terman had just developed a few years earlier. If a child earned an IQ score of 140 or better, he or she was identified as sufficiently gifted that the label "genius" might not be inappropriate. Indeed, the average IQ across the entire sample of over 1,500 children was about 150, a truly admirable figure. For Cox's 301 geniuses IQ scores were also calculated, only this time in an entirely different manner. Obviously, the Stanford-Binet cannot be administered to deceased subjects, and so Cox substituted a historiometric assessment for the psychometric one. Because the intelligence quotient is conceived as the ratio of mental age to chronological age (multiplied by 100), she and her fellow raters—which included Terman—applied this definition to biographical information about the ages at which members of her sample acquired certain skills and demonstrated certain accomplishments. Actually, Cox was following a procedure first introduced by Terman (1917) in a paper on the IQ of Francis Galton. Without going into the details, it suffices to say that her 301 geniuses also tended to be very bright, with IQ scores

also averaging around 150 (before introducing her "correction" for data reliability).

Both Terman and Cox thought of genius as a quantitative rather than qualitative attribute. The higher a person's IQ, the greater the intellectual talent, and hence the higher the level of genius. Accordingly, the IQ score should correlate highly with an individual's ultimate achievement. It did not turn out that way. In the Terman sample, not every gifted child became an eminent adult. Worse still, differences in IQ could not distinguish those who were successful from those who failed (Terman & Oden, 1959). The outcome was not much better for the Cox sample. Although she reported a small positive correlation between IQ and eminence, this correlation has been shown to be largely artifactual (Simonton, 1976). Subsequent research has obtained comparable results for both psychometric and historiometric samples (e.g., McClelland, 1973; Simonton, 1984c; cf. Barrett & Depinet, 1991). Only on rare occasions does variation in intellectual ability prove to be a conspicuous predictor of attained distinction (e.g., Simonton, 1986, 1991a). Why is it that a high IQ, however measured, does not always translate into adulthood genius?

Thresholds and Triangular Distributions. It often happens that intelligence functions as a necessary but not sufficient agent of achievement. Below a certain IQ—the figure is often put at around IQ 120—the probability of adulthood eminence is minimal, but beyond that threshold level further increases in IQ will not necessarily translate into proportional amounts of distinction (Barron & Harrington, 1981; Guilford, 1967; Simonton, 1985a). To be sure, an exceptionally high intellect may permit more attainments than an intellect somewhat less stratospheric (Benbow, 1992), but there are no guarantees. The outcome is a peculiar triangular distribution in which those with the highest levels of intelligence will display the greatest variation in attainment.

Curvilinear Relationships. It can get worse. Under certain conditions an individual might actually be penalized for possessing an excessively high IQ. For one thing, unusual precocity may interfere with the development of the social skills absolutely essential to the emergence of an adult capable of adapting to the world. The stories of intellectual prodigies who failed to realize their potential as adults for this very reason are sadly all too numerous. The case of William James Sidis provides the classic illustration (Montour, 1977). Moreover, social maturity aside, extremely brilliant individuals may often experience considerable difficulties trying to convince others of the value of their ideas. Too often they will "talk over the heads" of their potential audience. They find themselves dismissed as "high brow," "cerebral," "theoretical," "eccentric," "radical," or "avant garde." This liability is particularly damaging in domains where success depends on the cultivation of a broad constituency. A theoretical physicist can afford to be understood by only a handful of colleagues; a politician, entrepreneur, commander, or religious figure cannot.

In fact, one mathematical model predicts that for those areas of achievement where it is necessary to appeal to the masses, the relationship between IQ and effectiveness should be curvilinear, with a peak at around 119, a predicted peak that has been shown to be consistent with a considerable body of psychometric and historiometric research (Simonton, 1985a). Evidence also appears in the Terman and Cox samples. Very few of the Termites attained distinction in areas of leadership that required the individual to reach large masses of people. And in the Cox 301, those who did achieve a reputation of broad appeal—such as the U.S. presidents in her sample—exhibited much lower IQs than did the rest of her geniuses. It is possible to have too much of a good thing.

Multiple Intelligences. In the first few decades of the twentieth century, psychologists tended to view intelligence as a single, homogeneous construct. This unity has even been titled "Spearman's *g*" to reflect Spearman's (1927) advocacy of a single, general factor underlying performance on all tests of intellectual ability. Terman and Cox were not exceptions. They both implicitly subscribed to Samuel Johnson's (1781, p. 5) dictum that "the true Genius is a mind of large general powers, accidentally determined to some particular direction."

However, research since Terman, Cox, and Spearman suggests that intelligence is a far more complicated concept than any single-factor theory would lead us to suspect (Guilford, 1967; Sternberg, 1985). In Gardner's (1983) frequently discussed theory, for example, there are at least seven distinct intelligences: verbal, logical-mathematical, spatial-visual, bodily-kinesthetic, musical, intrapersonal, and interpersonal (but see Gardner, 1998). Accordingly, there should be at least seven kinds of intellectual giftedness, as well as seven varieties of genius. In fact, Gardner (1993) examined T. S. Eliot, Albert Einstein, Pablo Picasso, Martha Graham, Igor Stravinsky, Sigmund Freud, and Mahatma Gandhi as twentieth-century exemplars of these alternative intellects. Yet it is clear that the Stanford-Binet test on which Terman based his IQ scores is slanted heavily towards the first two or three of these intelligences. No wonder, then, that most of his children grew up to become professors, lawyers, doctors, and scientists rather than artists, choreographers, composers, psychoanalysts, or world leaders.

This problem still plagues some modern definitions of giftedness and genius. Children can still be selected for gifted programs on the basis of performance on narrowly defined psychometric instruments. And we still have people calling themselves "geniuses" because they score so many standard deviations above the mean on some equally limited test. Thus, an IQ of 132 admits you into Mensa, IQ 164 allows you to join Four Sigma, and IQ 228 makes you the brightest person in the world (viz. Marilyn Vos Savant). These conceptions of talent exalt one specific type of intellect and unfairly exclude the many equally valuable forms of intelligence.

Is this critique contradicted by the results of Cox's retrospective study? Not at all! Cox's operational definition of IQ was actually quite different from Terman's. In compiling evidence of childhood and adolescent precocity, she did not impose a one-size-fits-all conception of intelligence. Instead, she let each one of her 301 geniuses decide the specific intelligence on which they were going to be evaluated. Pascal's IQ was based largely on his early mathematical prowess, Mozart's on his being a musical prodigy, J. S. Mill's on his phenomenal analytical precocity, and so forth. None were penalized for being mediocre or even retarded in some cognitive domain captured by the Stanford-Binet. So Cox's IQs were implicitly predicated on the doctrine that there exist multiple forms of intelligence.

Skewed Distributions. Terman and Cox, following Galton (1869), believed that intellectual capacity, like so many psychological characteristics, is normally distributed in the population. And that assumption is valid, at least approximately (Burt, 1963). The frequency distribution of IQ scores indeed looks like the bell-shaped curve, with about two-thirds of the population having IQs within one standard deviation of the mean. Not only is the distribution roughly symmetrical, but virtually the entire human population will have an IQ score within four deviations from the mean. For instance, only one person out of a million can be admitted into the Mega Society, which requires an IQ of 176.

If intelligence enjoys an intimate relationship with achievement, then the distribution of achievements should also be approximately described by a normal distribution. But that is far from true. The discrepancy is best observed when we look at an objective index of accomplishment such as income, influence, or productivity (Burt, 1943; Price, 1963; Simonton, 1988a). Take creative output, for example. No matter what domain of creative activity we examine, the distribution of lifetime productivity is highly skewed, with a small proportion of the contributors creating the overwhelming proportion of the total contributions (Albert, 1975; Dennis, 1954a, 1954b, 1955). This skewed distribution is so well established that it has inspired the announcement of corresponding scientific laws (Lotka, 1926; Price, 1963). According to the Price Law, for instance, if k is the number of individuals active in a creative domain, then the square root of k gives the number in that elite group that is responsible for half of everything accomplished in the field (Price, 1963). To illustrate, of the 250 composers who have added something durable to the classical repertoire, the number of composers who are credited with half of that repertoire is 16 ($15.8 = \sqrt{250}$; Simonton, 1984b, Chapter 5). To show what this means more dramatically, suppose we translated this elitist distribution into the same terms as IQ scores, calling them "productivity quotients" or PQs (Simonton, 1988c, Chapter 4). Then the highest PQs would be almost 200 points higher than the highest IQs! We often speak of geniuses as giants in their fields: Imagine meeting a true giant whose height is 21 standard deviations above the population mean! That's the magnitude of distortion we are talking about here.

How can we explain this conspicuous discrepancy? There are actually several possible explanations (Simonton, 1988c, Chapter 4), but I would like to consider just one provocative account (Burt, 1943; Eysenck, 1995; Shockley, 1957). When trying to identify the predictors of some phenomena, behavioral scientists are accustomed to think in terms of additive models, where each cause makes an independent contribution to the effect; the total effect is simply the sum of the of the separate effects. Moreover, if the various components are normally distributed, any summation of those components will also be normally distributed. Yet outstanding talent may be a phenomenon that demands multiplicative interaction effects. All the diverse components of exceptional achievement—intellect, motivation, personality, developmental experiences, education, etc.—are multiplied together rather than merely added. Significantly, the multiplicative product of normally distributed variables yields a highly skewed lognormal distribution, in accord with what we see in distributions of lifetime achievements (see also Simonton, 1999b).

Such a multiplicative model is also compatible with the threshold and triangular distribution mentioned earlier. Individuals who are very low on just one of the contributing factors will not manifest any gifts as adults. Zero times any number is zero. Therefore, below the minimum intellectual requirement, we cannot expect genius to emerge. Yet additional increases in intelligence beyond that threshold value will not automatically increase the chances for success. The contribution of exalted intelligence to the overall product can be negated by deficiencies in other components of the product. In fact, this is precisely what happened to those in Terman's sample who ended up as adulthood underachievers. However high their IQs, some key factor was missing from their constitution.

In contrast, others with appreciably lower IQs may feature compensating factors that enable them to accomplish much more than Terman's unrealized talents. An instance may be found in William Shockley (Eysenck, 1995). As a child, Shockley was among the many children that Terman originally tested for possible inclusion in the longitudinal sample, but his IQ was not high enough to certify him as a psychometrically proven genius. So rather than become a gifted child, Shockley became a famous scientist instead, co-inventing the transistor and receiving the Nobel Prize for Physics! No member of Terman's sample achieved so high a level of acclaim. Clearly, Shockley had other things going for him that could easily compensate for a sub-genius IQ.

Personality

Cox was aware of the possibility of such tradeoffs. After gauging the personality characteristics of a subsample of 100 geniuses, she observed that drive and determination could more than compensate for a less than stratospheric IQ. In particular, she admitted that "high but not the highest intelligence, combined with the greatest degree of persistence, will achieve greater eminence than the highest degree of intelligence with somewhat less persistence" (Cox, 1926, p. 187). This motivational aspect of talent development is a *sine qua non* of success. Attainment requires an adult capable of overcoming the numerous frustrations and obstacles that always block the path to greatness. Even after notable achievers establish their reputations, their position is never secure, and failures will accompany successes throughout their lives (Simonton, 1977a, 1985b). Moreover, to attain distinction in any domain requires a childhood and adolescence packed with arduous training and practice. Research shows that potential talents have to grapple with their chosen domain several hours per day for a full decade before that latent capacity becomes actualized (Bloom, 1985; Ericsson, Krampe, & Tesch-Römer, 1993; Hayes, 1989; Simonton, 1991b, 2000). Such a commitment of time and energy is not for the weak of heart. Those of the Cox sample who became famous despite mediocre intellects obviously had this essential quality. Those of Terman's sample who failed to live up to expectations often missed this requirement (Terman & Oden, 1959).

Lack of zeal is not the only character flaw that may prevent a gifted child from becoming an adult genius. The personality profile needed to attain success in maturity is very complex, demanding that a developing talent be high on some traits and low on others (R. B. Cattell, 1963; Cox, 1926; Simonton, 1991a). Yet this profile for achievement is not necessarily selected for when IQ tests are used to identify talent. The classic studies by Getzels and Jackson (1962) and Wallach and Kogan (1965) illustrate this point rather well. Children picked on the basis of high IQs tend to have rather different personality profiles than those who are chosen according to their unusual performance on tests that purport to measure creativity. For instance, the latter tend to be more playful and humorous, to be less conventional in their ambitions, and to conform less in their attitudes about school and life.

But the most remarkable discrepancy has to do with psychopathology. Terman (1925) was almost preoccupied with the personality profiles of his precocious subjects. He wanted to counter the then prevalent view that genius was close to madness. He accordingly took great pains to show that his gifted children were not only not abnormal, but super-normal besides. Both psychologically and physically, the Termites were more healthy than average, not less. This demonstration seems misguided: There is some truth to Dryden's (1681, p. 6) famous lines "Great

Wits are sure to Madness near ally'd, / And thin Partitions do their Bounds divide."

I lack space to review relevant literature on behalf of this proposition, but that has been done by others anyway (e.g., Eysenck, 1995; Prentky, 1989; Richards, 1981). I will merely make the following four points. First, historiometric studies show that notable achievers exhibited incidence rates for various mental disorders that exceed the rates in the general population (Ellis, 1926; Ludwig, 1992, 1995; Martindale, 1972). Second, psychiatric studies found similarly high proportions of mental or emotional pathologies among famous contemporaries (Andreasen, 1987; Jamison, 1989). Third, psychometric studies of eminent individuals have found them to obtain high scores on the clinical subscales of various personality measures, such as the Minnesota Multiphasic Personality Inventory or the Eysenck Personality Questionnaire (Barron, 1969; Götz & Götz, 1979a, 1979b; MacKinnon, 1978; Rushton, 1990). Fourth, genetic studies of family pedigrees indicate that distinguished achievers are most likely to appear in lineages that display conspicuously high percentages of mental illness (Andreasen, 1987; Juda, 1949; Karlson, 1970).

All of this evidence corroborates the basic conclusion that genius-level talents probably reside at the delicate boundary between a healthy and an unhealthy personality. Furthermore, we have reason to believe that this precarious location is not incidental. There actually are certain advantages that accrue to individuals who lie at the edge. Such personalities are less conforming, more unconventional, even iconoclastic (Eysenck, 1995). They may experience manic periods full of optimistic activity that end up producing a large corpus of outstanding works (Jamison, 1993; Slater & Meyer, 1959). And they may entertain bizarre thoughts, crazy associations, or offbeat metaphors or analogies that enable them to arrive at path-breaking insights (Eysenck, 1995; Woody & Claridge, 1977). Of course, all of these tendencies can go too far; you can have too much of a bad thing. Those who inherit or acquire a disposition to go beyond the frontier into never-never land may never develop their gifts (Rothenberg, 1990). Or like Schumann or Van Gogh, they may not allow their talents to advance as far as they would have gone otherwise. Nonetheless, it's just as disastrous to talent development for a gifted individual never to break out of the shell of a conventional and courteous complacency.

I suspect that Terman's procedures for obtaining his original sample of gifted children militated against his identifying talents that had this essential component of potential greatness. He did not test the entire student population, but rather relied on teacher nominations to provide a first screening. One can only guess how many kids were not named because their teachers thought them a little weird rather than bright. Moreover, even if a few oddballs managed to get through this first filter, I wonder how many of them would have taken the tasks in the Stanford-Binet seriously enough to provide meaningful answers to the interviewer's probes? How many future geniuses would have had a good time offering bohemian and humorous answers that would earn them low scores on the test? Of course, we will never know. Yet maybe William Shockley was one of them!

Development

I want to dispel an impression that may have been inadvertently made in the previous section. I observed that the borderline pathology that contributes to the realization of intellectual talent may be inherited, for exceptional individuals often come from pathological family pedigrees. Hence, the family lines of "natural ability" documented by Galton (1869) seem to have been supplemented by family lines of "unnatural abilities." One might infer that where two such genetic lineages happen to intersect in precisely the proper proportions, giftedness becomes genius. However, this inference would be incorrect. Genius is not just born; it is also made—by the environment in which the talented youth emerges. Genetic endowment merely offers the raw materials on which the events and circumstances of childhood and adolescence must operate. Here, too, we can witness intriguing discrepancies between potential and actual talents. Below I focus on three sets of environmental influences that probably have received the most attention: (a) birth order, (b) traumatic events, and (c) education and training (Simonton, 1987).

Birth Order. Terman (1925) made the observation that first-borns seemed to be over-represented in his sample of gifted children. A similar pattern seems to hold for child prodigies as well (Feldman & Goldsmith, 1986). Furthermore, some early studies of adult notables suggest the same advantage of primogeniture, beginning with Galton's (1874) study of eminent British scientists (see, e.g., Albert, 1980;

Ellis, 1926). However, subsequent work indicates that the picture is not so simple. First-borns are more likely to attain distinction in some domains of achievement, while other ordinal positions are more prone to achieve success in rather different domains. Thus, where first-borns become famous scientific creators (Clark & Rice, 1982; Eiduson, 1962; Roe, 1952; Terry, 1989), later-borns become the notable artistic creators (Bliss, 1970; Clark & Rice, 1982), with the exception that the classical composers are more aligned with the scientists on this developmental event (Schubert, Wagner, & Schubert, 1977). An analogous distribution holds in leadership, where the first-borns provide the status quo politicians (Wagner & Schubert, 1977; Zweigenhaft, 1975), while the last-borns become the revolutionaries (Stewart, 1977, 1991). Of course, like all generalizations in the behavioral sciences, there are many exceptions. Nonetheless, the very existence of these departures ends up supporting a more general proposition: Later-borns who do go into science have a higher likelihood of becoming scientific revolutionaries who work to overthrow the established paradigms (Sulloway, 1996). Hence, the overall tendency is for first-borns to achieve eminence in highly prestigious positions that are well integrated with the Establishment, whereas later-borns are more likely to succeed as rebellious agents of a new order or even as advocates of disorder.

We need not discuss the reason for these divergent outcomes, except to say that this pattern fits nicely with Adler's (1938) classic theory of the first-born as the "dethroned king." The more important point to make here is that this tendency helps us appreciate why Terman's gifted children turned out the way they did. When first-borns predominate in a sample, we should expect a high percentage of doctors, lawyers, professors, and other professionals (Schachter, 1963), but a low percentage of artists, writers, and others who are less willing to conform to societal definitions of success. And that is how the story came out in the end. Moreover, this developmental pattern may also explain the very prominence of first-borns among the Termites in the first place. For one thing, first-borns may have been more likely to seek the scholastic attention that would have earned them a teacher nomination. Furthermore, the first-borns may have actually been more eager to earn additional academic kudos by performing well during the IQ screening. In fact, perhaps the trend for IQ to decline with ordinal position tells us more about attitudes than aptitudes (cf.

Zajonc, 1976, 1983). The later-borns may have less respect for the authorities who decide that these measures assess anything important, and may even prove too iconoclastic to accept the presumption that the questions have a single right answer.

Whatever the status of the last conjecture, one conclusion must be stressed. Birth order may not really decide the magnitude of adulthood distinction (cf. Helmreich, Spence, Beane, Lucker, & Matthews, 1980). Rather, ordinal position primarily determines the domain of achievement in which that distinction is attained. To call first-borns more successful because they are more likely to be identified as gifted children or because they become well-respected professionals serves only to perpetuate a first-born view of the world.

Traumatic Events. Empirical studies of eminent personalities repeatedly record that a large proportion experienced less than idyllic childhoods (Goertzel & Goertzel, 1962; Goertzel, Goertzel, & Goertzel, 1978). The family may have experienced tremendous fluctuations in economic and emotional well-being, and the home was often the locus of tragic occasions. Of the diverse ways that misfortunes can visit a talent's early development, the one that has received the most empirical attention has been orphanhood or parental loss (e.g., Albert, 1971; Eisenstadt, Haynal, Rentchnick, & De Senarclens, 1989). For both creators and leaders, the percentage of geniuses who lost one or both parents before reaching early adulthood is appreciably larger than what appears to hold in the general population or any other comparable group (e.g., Berrington, 1974; Martindale, 1972; Silverman, 1974; Walberg, Rasher, & Parkerson, 1980).

What makes statistics like these especially remarkable is the contrast with the far more benign home environments which Terman's group enjoyed as children and adolescents (Terman, 1925). His children were more likely to grow up in comfortable, intact families where everything transpired as in story books. Child prodigies, too, are more prone to emerge from such nurturant environments (Feldman & Goldsmith, 1986). What's the problem here? Why the discrepancy?

It may be that some form of "trials and tribulations" in early childhood and adolescence is an integral part of talent development. The beneficial impact may arise from three sources (Simonton, 1999a). First, such events may disrupt ordinary socialization practices to such an extent that the individual will find it less easy to conform to societal expectations. After all, parents play a big role in inculcating societal norms and values, both as instructors and as models. Second, the child may undergo a bereavement reaction that puts the developing talent into a permanent emotional disequilibrium that can only be alleviated by attaining fame and fortune (Eisenstadt, 1978). Third, the experience of traumatic events may facilitate the development of an emotional robustness that enables the individual to handle disappointments and frustrations far better than those who emerged from more tranquil family backgrounds (Simonton, 1994, chap. 6). These three sources are not necessarily mutually exclusive.

Before any parents try to do their kids a favor by making their childhoods more rough and tumble, some caveats are in order. In the first place, the advantage gained from an unhappy childhood or adolescence varies according to the domain of achievement (Simonton, 1999a). For example, although the rates of parental loss are higher among scientists than among the general population, the rates among literary creators are higher still (Berry, 1981). Evidently, artistic creativity requires more turmoil than does scientific creativity. In addition, the influence of traumatic events must be weighed against the personal resources that the youth possesses to overcome the sometimes severe emotional disabilities that can also ensue from a painful childhood or adolescence. Juvenile delinquents and suicidal depressives also may exhibit a high incidence of parental loss (Eisenstadt, 1978). Hence, there probably exists an optimal level of developmental stress for each youth. What might not be enough challenge for one developing talent, might be just right for a second, and far too much for a third. Thus, the many famous personalities who attained distinction without having to suffer orphanhood may be those for whom their development was optimized by less dramatic tests of character.

Whatever the complexities, I cannot help but think that most of Terman's children were not sufficiently challenged. They often seem to fit Dylan Thomas' remark that "There's only one thing that's worse than having an unhappy childhood, and that's having a too-happy childhood" (Ferris, 1977, p. 49).

Education and Training. Terman loved to boast about the academic success of his intellectually gifted children. They tended to get excellent grades and to obtain advanced degrees. Child prodigies, too, often make their first big splash in the newspapers by phenomenal displays of scholastic prowess. It not uncommon to read about brains who entered high school at ten and graduated at eleven with straight As and full scholarships to all of the Ivy League colleges.

Yet when we turn to those who actually made names for themselves, the role of education becomes more ambiguous. First of all, those who get excellent grades and high honors are not necessarily more likely to achieve distinction in their chosen fields; the correlations are either zero or very weakly positive (Cohen, 1984; Hudson, 1958; McClelland, 1973). As a consequence, there are many examples of unquestioned geniuses who showed themselves to be mediocre or even miserable scholars. Moreover, the relationship between the level of formal education and the realization of talent is not always straightforward. In fact, this became evident when the 301 members of the Cox (1926) sample were subjected to a more detailed analysis (Simonton, 1976, 1983a). If you plot the eminence scores that she derived from J. M. Cattell's (1903) rankings against the level of formal education obtained, and fit curves to the creators and leaders separately, very striking results emerge. For creative geniuses, the relationship between achieved eminence and formal education is described by an inverted-U curve, with a peak somewhere in the last half of undergraduate training. For leaders, in contrast, the connection is strictly negative. Yet in neither case can we conclude that adult accomplishment is a positive linear function of the level of education obtained. Other studies based on more contemporary samples lead to the same general conclusion. Higher degrees may not always be an advantage and may sometimes be a disadvantage (Simonton, 1984b, Chapter 4).

Of course, it is one matter to uncover a provocative empirical association, quite another to interpret its theoretical implications. In the present case, several explanations can be offered for curves like those just described (Simonton, 1994, 1999a). I will mention one obvious possibility. Formal education may not always make a positive contribution to talent development and may actually detract from the growth of certain kinds of talent.

On one hand, those who plan to become lawyers, doctors, professors, and other professionals—the kind of attainments that predominated in Terman's sample—have much more to benefit from advancing to higher degrees. Indeed, they may have no other choice!

On the other hand, most artistic creators, revolutionary scientists, and other more unconventional achievers may have much to lose and little to gain from continuing with more than a smattering of higher education. They may need enough formal training to acquire certain basic knowledge and skills, such as the ability to write well and to carry on an informed conversation. But beyond that, increased formal education may only interfere with more important pursuits. For instance, success in many fields is strongly correlated with voracious and omnivorous reading, an undisciplined activity that may suffer under increased academic demands (McCurdy, 1960; Simonton, 1984b, p. 74). In addition, many domains of achievement require the slow acquisition of highly specialized techniques that are not always taught—or taught well—in formal academic settings. Whatever the details, we must recall that it usually takes about ten years of intense study to master the materials of a domain. The implication is clear: When formal schooling is not directly contributing to that mastery, it is necessarily delaying that mastery. Distaste for that interference leads many talented young adults to become college dropouts—to their benefit.

When a developing talent must seek an education outside the educational system proper, one form of extracurricular training is especially important: mentoring. This was not a topic that attracted much attention from either Terman or Cox. Yet studies of talented youths show that mentoring is a crucial factor in their development (Bloom, 1985; Feldman & Goldsmith, 1986). The young talent must find a suitable teacher who is well matched to the youth's current capacity, and frequently change teachers as that capacity continues to grow. Furthermore, retrospective studies of eminent personalities reveal the impact of mentors, but with some critical differences that are often overlooked in the longitudinal literature (Simonton, 1983b, 1992b).

To begin with, mentors can have a detrimental effect on talent growth if they are driven to clone themselves through their students. It is partly for this reason that it is usually more advantageous to have multiple mentors rather than just one (Simonton, 1984a, 1992c).

In addition, the connection between mentor characteristics and successful talent development is often complex, with interaction effects, curvilinear relationships, and other niceties (Simonton, 1977b, 1984a, 1992c). For example, the most effective mentors tend to be those at the peak of their own careers, rather than those who are past their prime and thus are less receptive to new ideas.

Finally, we must also recognize that a developing talent may benefit from more impersonal relationships with predecessors in their domain of creative activity. Role models of eminent achievement can be admired and emulated at a distance, even when those paragons of excellence are deceased. This indirect mentoring can be just as powerful as one-on-one training (Simonton, 1975, 1984a, 1988b, 1992c). A figure like Albert Einstein had the portraits of three deceased predecessors hanging in his study— Newton, Faraday, and Maxwell. These three probably had far more influence on the development of Einstein's special talents than did any of his teachers. To borrow Newton's metaphor, they were the giants on whose shoulders Einstein stood.

Conceivably, many of Terman's children did not grow up to become highly distinguished adults because they failed to form the right linkages with those greats who represented the best in their particular area of talent. Without the deep desire to surpass admired predecessors, even the greatest gifts will seldom become genius.

SUMMARY AND CONCLUSIONS

This short essay can only offer a preliminary probe of a very profound enigma. Many critical questions have been necessarily ignored. We have not discussed, for example, the difficult question of gender and ethnic differences on the realization of latent talents (e.g., Simonton, 1996, 1998), nor have we treated the matter of how the "spirit of the times" (or *zeitgeist*) moderates the emergence and expression of genius (e.g., Simonton, 1992a, 1997). And we have omitted discussion of the possible role of crystallizing experiences, marginality, socioeconomic class, religious affiliation, and many other possibly critical developmental events (for further discussion, see Simonton, 1994, 1999a). Nevertheless, those topics that I have managed to cover should convey the developmental complexities behind the conversion of inherent into actual gifts. We are still a long way from understanding all the forces that impinge upon talent development. We are even farther from comprehending how all these forces converge and interact in the creation of an exceptional achiever. Future research must try to bring all these complexities together into a single life-span develop-

mental framework. Besides incorporating the large inventory of pertinent developmental influences, it must articulate all the interaction effects, curvilinear relationships, and other causal functions that greatly entangle the impact of these influences. Furthermore, this account must provide answers to two absolutely fundamental issues.

First, why is it that so many gifted children fail to realize their fullest potential as adults? In concrete terms, why did so many of Terman's children end up falling short of the highest expectations? Where did the developmental process go astray? What are the most common blind alleys? Which of these dead ends terminate one-way streets and which are cul de sacs in which a fortunate talent can reverse direction to reenter the main highway to success?

Second, how can it be that so many eminent adults displayed no obvious signs of giftedness in either childhood or adolescence? Why is it, for instance, that more than half of Cox's 301 geniuses had IQ scores below the minimum threshold required for entrance into the Terman sample? Is the developmental trajectory for these apparently unpromising children qualitatively different from that which guides the precocious who eventually make good?

The first issue is the enigma of the "nipped bud," the second that of the "late bloomer." These exceptional individuals are in many respects far more central to the emergence of a sound theoretical interpretation than the minority in the Cox sample who would have easily qualified for entrance into the Terman sample. The nipped buds and the late bloomers are anomalies that should help isolate the idiosyncrasies in the thin path in the garden between the promise of youth and the triumph of maturity. After all, nipped buds and late bloomers are far more common than those lucky few—like Pascal, Mozart, or J. S. Mill—whose transitions from giftedness to genius were comparatively smooth and untroubled. With a better understanding of these developmental discontinuities, we may someday learn how to ensure that the more auspicious path becomes the norm rather than the exception. Perhaps all the subjects of a future longitudinal study of gifted children will later qualify for inclusion in a subsequent retrospective study of genius adults.

Terman's classic *Genetic Studies of Genius* raises critical issues about the conversion of childhood giftedness into adulthood eminence. These issues arise, in part, because the results of his longitudinal study of intellectually gifted children contrast sharply with the results of Cox's retrospective study of 301 adult geniuses.

These apparent incompatibilities are then systematically scrutinized. First, the role of intelligence is examined, with special focus on the implications of thresholds, triangular distributions, curvilinear relationships, multiple intelligences, and skewed distributions. The critique then turns to the effects of personality traits, with special attention being paid to the impact of motivation and psychopathology—the "mad-genius" controversy. The next topic of contention concerns development. After touching upon the question of genetic endowment, discussion is directed at three sets of environmental factors: birth order, traumatic events, and education or training. In each case there emerge curious discrepancies between gifted children and genius adults.

The chapter concludes by posing two fundamental questions. First, why is it that so many gifted children fail to realize their full potential as adults? Second, how can it be that many eminent adults displayed no obvious signs of giftedness in either childhood or adolescence? The first question concerns the mystery of the "nipped bud," the second that of the "late bloomer." Only after we obtain complete answers to both of these questions will the development of giftedness and genius be fully understood.

QUESTIONS FOR THOUGHT AND DISCUSSION

1. One dictionary defines *genius* as a person with an IQ of 140 or more. What is wrong with this definition? What must be added to intelligence to obtain "genius," as the term is used by Simonton?

2. There's a saying that you can have too much of a good thing. According to Simonton's discussion of giftedness and genius, what would be some examples? Explain.

3. Make a list of criteria that you would use to identify a child as gifted. Make another list of criteria for identifying an adult as a "genius." How much overlap is there? Are there major discrepancies? Explain.

4. What factors upset the connection between childhood giftedness and adulthood genius? That is, why are some gifted children "nipped in the bud"? Why are some adult geniuses "late bloomers" who showed no exceptional potential in youth?

REFERENCES

Adler, A. (1938). *Social interest: A challenge to mankind* (J. Linton & R. Vaughan, Trans.). London: Faber & Faber.

Albert, R. S. (1971). Cognitive development and parental loss among the gifted, the exceptionally gifted and the creative. *Psychological Reports, 29,* 19–26.

Albert, R. S. (1975). Toward a behavioral definition of genius. *American Psychologist, 30,* 140–151.

Albert, R. S. (1980). Family positions and the attainment of eminence: A study of special family positions and special family experiences. *Gifted Child Quarterly, 24,* 87–95.

Andreasen, N. C. (1987). Creativity and mental illness: Prevalence rates in writers and their first-degree relatives. *American Journal of Psychiatry, 144,* 1288–1292.

Barrett, G. V., & Depinet, R. L. (1991). A reconsideration of testing for competence rather than for intelligence. *American Psychologist, 46,* 1012–1024.

Barron, F. (1969). *Creative person and creative process.* New York: Holt.

Barron, F., & Harrington, D. M. (1981). Creativity, intelligence, and personality. *Annual Review of Psychology, 32,* 439–476.

Benbow, C. P. (1992). Academic achievement in mathematics and science of students between ages 13 and 23: Are there differences among students in the top one percent of mathematical ability? *Journal of Educational Psychology, 84,* 51–61.

Berrington, H. (1974). Review article: The Fiery Chariot: Prime ministers and the search for love. *British Journal of Political Science, 4,* 345–369.

Berry, C. (1981). The Nobel scientists and the origins of scientific achievement. *British Journal of Sociology, 32,* 381–391.

Bliss, W. D. (1970). Birth order of creative writers. *Journal of Individual Psychology, 26,* 200–202.

Bloom, B. S. (Ed.). (1985). *Developing talent in young people.* New York: Ballantine Books.

Burks, B. S., Jensen, D. W., & Terman, L. M. (1930). *The promise of youth: Follow-up studies of a thousand gifted children.* Stanford, CA: Stanford University Press.

Burt, C. (1943). Ability and income. *British Journal of Educational Psychology, 12,* 83–98.

Burt, C. (1963). Is intelligence distributed normally? *British Journal of Statistical Psychology, 16,* 175–190.

Cattell, J. M. (1903). A statistical study of eminent men. *Popular Science Monthly, 62,* 359–377.

Cattell, R. B. (1963). The personality and motivation of the researcher from measurements of contemporaries and from biography. In C. W. Taylor & F. Barron (Eds.), *Scientific creativity: Its recognition and development* (pp. 119–131). New York: Wiley.

Clark, R. D., & Rice, G. A. (1982). Family constellations and eminence: The birth orders of Nobel Prize winners. *Journal of Psychology, 110,* 281–287.

Cohen, P. A. (1984). College grades and adult achievement: A research synthesis. *Research in Higher Education, 20,* 281–293.

Cox, C. (1926). *The early mental traits of three hundred geniuses.* Stanford, CA: Stanford University Press.

Dennis, W. (1954a). Bibliographies of eminent scientists. *Scientific Monthly, 79,* 180–183.

Dennis, W. (1954b). Productivity among American psychologists. *American Psychologist, 9,* 191–194.

Dennis, W. (1955). Variations in productivity among creative workers. *Scientific Monthly, 80,* 277–278.

Dryden, J. (1681). *Absalom and Achitophel: A poem.* London: Davis.

Eiduson, B. T. (1962). *Scientists: Their psychological world.* New York: Basic Books.

Eisenstadt, J. M. (1978). Parental loss and genius. *American Psychologist, 33,* 211–223.

Eisenstadt, J. M., Haynal, A., Rentchnick, P., & De Senarclens, P. (1989). *Parental loss and achievement.* Madison, CT: International Universities Press.

Ellis, H. (1926). *A study of British genius* (rev. ed.). Boston: Houghton Mifflin.

Ericsson, K. A., Krampe, R. T., & Tesch-Römer, C. (1993). The role of deliberate practice in the acquisition of expert performance. *Psychological Review, 100,* 363–406.

Eysenck, H. J. (1995). *Genius: The natural history of creativity.* Cambridge: Cambridge University Press.

Feldman, D. H., & Goldsmith, L. T. (1986). *Nature's gambit: Child prodigies and the development of human potential.* New York: Basic Books.

Ferris, P. (1977). *Dylan Thomas.* London: Hodder & Stoughton.

Galton, F. (1869). *Hereditary genius: An inquiry into its laws and consequences.* London: Macmillan.

Galton, F. (1874). *English men of science: Their nature and nurture.* London: Macmillan.

Gardner, H. (1983). *Frames of mind: A theory of multiple intelligences.* New York: Basic Books.

Gardner, H. (1993). *Creating minds: An anatomy of creativity seen through the lives of Freud, Einstein, Picasso, Stravinsky, Eliot, Graham, and Gandhi.* New York: Basic Books.

Gardner, H. (1998). Are there additional intelligences? The case for naturalist, spiritual, and existential intelligences. In J. Kane (Ed.), *Education, information, and transformation* (pp. 111–131). Upper Saddle River, NJ: Merrill.

Getzels, J., & Jackson, P. W. (1962). *Creativity and intelligence: Explorations with gifted students.* New York: Wiley.

Goertzel, M. G., Goertzel, V., & Goertzel, T. G. (1978). *300 eminent personalities: A psychosocial analysis of the famous.* San Francisco: Jossey-Bass.

Goertzel, V., & Goertzel, M. G. (1962). *Cradles of eminence.* Boston: Little, Brown.

Götz, K. O., & Götz, K. (1979a). Personality characteristics of professional artists. *Perceptual and Motor Skills, 49,* 327–334.

Götz, K. O., & Götz, K. (1979b). Personality characteristics of successful artists. *Perceptual and Motor Skills, 49,* 919–924.

Guilford, J. P. (1967). *The nature of human intelligence.* New York: McGraw-Hill.

Hayes, J. R. (1989). *The complete problem solver* (2nd ed.). Hillsdale, NJ: Erlbaum.

Helmreich, R. L., Spence, J. T., Beane, W. E., Lucker, G. W., & Matthews, K. A. (1980). Making it in academic psychology: Demographic and personality correlates of attainment. *Journal of Personality and Social Psychology, 39,* 896–908.

Hudson, L. (1958). Undergraduate academic record of Fellows of the Royal Society. *Nature, 182,* 1326.

Jamison, K. R. (1989). Mood disorders and patterns of creativity in British writers and artists. *Psychiatry, 52,* 125–134.

Jamison, K. R. (1993). *Touched with fire: Manic-depressive illness and the artistic temperament.* New York: Free Press.

Johnson, S. (1781). *The lives of the most eminent English poets* (Vol. 1). London: Bathurst.

Juda, A. (1949). The relationship between highest mental capacity and psychic abnormalities. *American Journal of Psychiatry, 106,* 296–307.

Karlson, J. I. (1970). Genetic association of giftedness and creativity with schizophrenia. *Hereditas, 66,* 177–182.

Lotka, A. J. (1926). The frequency distribution of scientific productivity. *Journal of the Washington Academy of Sciences, 16,* 317–323.

Ludwig, A. M. (1992). Creative achievement and psychopathology: Comparison among professions. *American Journal of Psychotherapy, 46,* 330–356.

Ludwig, A. M. (1995). *The price of greatness: Resolving the creativity and madness controversy.* New York: Guilford Press.

MacKinnon, D. W. (1978). *In search of human effectiveness.* Buffalo, NY: Creative Education Foundation.

Martindale, C. (1972). Father absence, psychopathology, and poetic eminence. *Psychological Reports, 31,* 843–847.

McClelland, D. C. (1973). Testing for competence rather than for "intelligence." *American Psychologist, 28,* 1–14.

McCurdy, H. G. (1960). The childhood pattern of genius. *Horizon, 2,* 33–38.

Montour, K. (1977). William James Sidis, the broken twig. *American Psychologist, 32,* 265–279.

Oden, M. H. (1968). The fulfillment of promise: 40-year follow-up of the Terman gifted group. *Genetic Psychology Monographs, 77,* 3–93.

Prentky, R. A. (1989). Creativity and psychopathology: Gambling at the seat of madness. In J. A. Glover, R. R. Ronning, & C. R. Reynolds (Eds.), *Handbook of creativity* (pp. 243–269). New York: Plenum Press.

Price, D. (1963). *Little science, big science.* New York: Columbia University Press.

Richards, R. (1981). Relationships between creativity and psychopathology: An evaluation and interpretation of the evidence. *Genetic Psychology Monographs, 103,* 261–324.

Roe, A. (1952). *The making of a scientist.* New York: Dodd, Mead.

Rothenberg, A. (1990). *Creativity and madness: New findings and old stereotypes.* Baltimore: Johns Hopkins University Press.

Rushton, J. P. (1990). Creativity, intelligence, and psychoticism. *Personality and Individual Differences, 11,* 1291–1298.

Schachter, S. (1963). Birth order, eminence, and higher education. *American Sociological Review, 28,* 757–768.

Schubert, D. S. P., Wagner, M. E., & Schubert, H. J. P. (1977). Family constellation and creativity: Firstborn predominance among classical music composers. *Journal of Psychology, 95,* 147–149.

Shockley, W. (1957). On the statistics of individual variations of productivity in research laboratories. *Proceedings of the Institute of Radio Engineers, 45,* 279–290.

Silverman, S. M. (1974). Parental loss and scientists. *Science Studies, 4,* 259–264.

Simonton, D. K. (1975). Sociocultural context of individual creativity: A transhistorical time-series analysis. *Journal of Personality and Social Psychology, 32,* 1119–1133.

Simonton, D. K. (1976). Biographical determinants of achieved eminence: A multivariate approach to the Cox data. *Journal of Personality and Social Psychology, 33,* 218–226.

Simonton, D. K. (1977a). Creative productivity, age, and stress: A biographical time-series analysis of 10 classical composers. *Journal of Personality and Social Psychology, 35,* 791–804.

Simonton, D. K. (1977b). Eminence, creativity, and geographic marginality: A recursive structural equation model. *Journal of Personality and Social Psychology, 35,* 805–816.

Simonton, D. K. (1983a). Formal education, eminence, and dogmatism: The curvilinear relationship. *Journal of Creative Behavior, 17,* 149–162.

Simonton, D. K. (1983b). Intergenerational transfer of individual differences in hereditary monarchs: Genes, role-modeling, cohort, or sociocultural effects? *Journal of Personality and Social Psychology, 44,* 354–364.

Simonton, D. K. (1984a). Artistic creativity and interpersonal relationships across and within generations. *Journal of Personality and Social Psychology, 46,* 1273–1286.

Simonton, D. K. (1984b). *Genius, creativity, and leadership: Historiometric inquiries.* Cambridge: Harvard University Press.

Simonton, D. K. (1984c). Leaders as eponyms: Individual and situational determinants of monarchal eminence. *Journal of Personality, 52,* 1–21.

Simonton, D. K. (1985a). Intelligence and personal influence in groups: Four nonlinear models. *Psychological Review, 92,* 532–547.

Simonton, D. K. (1985b). Quality, quantity, and age: The careers of 10 distinguished psychologists. *International Journal of Aging and Human Development, 21,* 241–254.

Simonton, D. K. (1986). Presidential personality: Biographical use of the Gough Adjective Check List. *Journal of Personality and Social Psychology, 51,* 149–160.

Simonton, D. K. (1987). Developmental antecedents of achieved eminence. *Annals of Child Development, 5,* 131–169.

Simonton, D. K. (1988a). Creativity, leadership, and chance. In R. J. Sternberg (Ed.), *The nature of creativity: Contemporary psychological perspectives* (pp. 386–426). New York: Cambridge University Press.

Simonton, D. K. (1988b). Galtonian genius, Kroeberian configurations, and emulation: A generational time-series analysis of Chinese civilization. *Journal of Personality and Social Psychology, 55,* 230–238.

Simonton, D. K. (1988c). *Scientific genius: A psychology of science.* Cambridge: Cambridge University Press.

Simonton, D. K. (1991a). Personality correlates of exceptional personal influence: A note on Thorndike's (1950) creators and leaders. *Creativity Research Journal, 4,* 67–78.

Simonton, D. K. (1991b). Emergence and realization of genius: The lives and works of 120 classical composers. *Journal of Personality and Social Psychology, 61,* 829–840.

Simonton, D. K. (1992a). Gender and genius in Japan: Feminine eminence in masculine culture. *Sex Roles, 27,* 101–119.

Simonton, D. K. (1992b). Leaders of American psychology, 1879–1967: Career development, creative output, and professional achievement. *Journal of Personality and Social Psychology, 62,* 5–17.

Simonton, D. K. (1992c). The social context of career success and course for 2,026 scientists and inventors. *Personality and Social Psychology Bulletin, 18,* 452–463.

Simonton, D. K. (1994). *Greatness: Who makes history and why.* New York: Guilford Press.

Simonton, D. K. (1996). Presidents' wives and First Ladies: On achieving eminence within a traditional gender role. *Sex Roles, 35,* 309–336.

Simonton, D. K. (1997). Foreign influence and national achievement: The impact of open milieus on Japanese civilization. *Journal of Personality and Social Psychology, 72,* 86–94.

Simonton, D. K. (1998). Achieved eminence in minority and majority cultures: Convergence versus divergence in the assessments of 294 African Americans. *Journal of Personality and Social Psychology, 74,* 804–817.

Simonton, D. K. (1999a). *Origins of genius: Darwinian perspectives on creativity.* New York: Oxford University Press.

Simonton, D. K. (1999b). Talent and its development: An emergenic and epigenetic model. *Psychological Review, 106,* 435–457.

Simonton, D. K. (2000). Creative development as acquired expertise: Theoretical issues and an empirical test. *Developmental Review, 20,* 283–318.

Slater, E., & Meyer, A. (1959). Contributions to a pathography of the musician: 1. Robert Schumann. *Confinia Psychiatrica, 2,* 65–94.

Spearman, C. (1927). *The abilities of man: Their nature and measurement.* New York: Macmillan.

Sternberg, R. J. (1985). *Beyond IQ: A triarchic theory of human intelligence.* New York: Cambridge University Press.

Stewart, L. H. (1977). Birth order and political leadership. In M. G. Hermann (Ed.), *The psychological examination of political leaders* (pp. 205–236). New York: Free Press.

Stewart, L. H. (1991). The world cycle of leadership. *Journal of Analytical Psychology, 36,* 449–459.

Sulloway, F. J. (1996). *Born to rebel: Birth order, family dynamics, and creative lives.* New York: Pantheon.

Terman, L. M. (1917). The intelligence quotient of Francis Galton in childhood. *American Journal of Psychology, 28,* 209–215.

Terman, L. M. (1925). *Mental and physical traits of a thousand gifted children.* Stanford, CA: Stanford University Press.

Terman, L. M., & Oden, M. H. (1947). *The gifted child grows up.* Stanford, CA: Stanford University Press.

Terman, L. M., & Oden, M. H. (1959). *The gifted group at mid-life.* Stanford, CA: Stanford University Press.

Terry, W. S. (1989). Birth order and prominence in the history of psychology. *Psychological Record, 39,* 333–337.

Wagner, M. E., & Schubert, H. J. P. (1977). Sibship variables and United States presidents. *Journal of Individual Psychology, 33,* 78–85.

Walberg, H. J., Rasher, S. P., & Parkerson, J. (1980). Childhood and eminence. *Journal of Creative Behavior, 13,* 225–231.

Wallach, M. A., & Kogan, N. (1965). *Modes of thinking in young children: A study of the creativity-intelligence distinction.* New York: Holt.

Woody, E., & Claridge, G. (1977). Psychoticism and thinking. *British Journal of Social and Clinical Psychology, 16,* 241–248.

Zajonc, R. B. (1976). Family configuration and intelligence. *Science, 192,* 227–235.

Zajonc, R. B. (1983). Validating the confluence model. *Psychological Bulletin, 93,* 457–480.

Zweigenhaft, R. L. (1975). Birth order, approval-seeking, and membership in Congress. *Journal of Individual Psychology, 31,* 205–210.

Psychological and Counseling Services

A critical feature of programs for the gifted is strong emphasis on psychological needs. Gifted students are no longer viewed simply as extraordinary and efficient learners, but as complex personalities with exceptional sensitivities and recurrent vulnerabilities. This section examines concepts related to counseling individuals, groups, and families of the gifted, as well as issues of motivation, underachievement, high-risk learners, and emotional and spiritual giftedness.

Despite Terman's opposite conclusion, many gifted children do have social and emotional problems. Nicholas Colangelo in Chapter 29 traces the need for counseling programs from Leta Hollingworth's early efforts to current counseling centers that feature personal, career, and family counseling. Today's counselors focus on such matters as underachievement and problems of gifted females, gifted minority students, and gifted students with disabilities. Colangelo elaborates on the complexities of gifted students' self-concept; career counseling and multipotentiality; group counseling and its benefits, topics, dynamics, and techniques; and family counseling, with its focus on sibling stresses, effects of labeling, and, most often, underachievement. His parent-school interaction model includes the four combinations of parents or schools being either concerned or uninterested in special programming for the gifted. While remedial counseling deals with problems as they arise, a good school counseling program, writes Colangelo, is developmentally grounded in students' cognitive and affective needs to understand their strengths and weaknesses, share their views and perceptions, learn interpersonal skills, and grow educationally.

In Chapter 30 Sidney M. Moon describes two types of family counseling for the families of gifted students. *Parent guidance* includes school counseling, school psychology, and career counseling. For example, the counseling addresses school issues such as counseling parents who believe their gifted child's academic needs are not met, helping parents to aid their bright child, and assisting with a child's social or emotional adjustment. Counseling models typically include (at least) an assessment of the child, information for parents, and recommendations for school programming. *Family therapy* deals with social and emotional difficulties of the gifted child, dysfunctional interactions among the child's family members, and problematic interactions with the school. For example, some foci are poor sibling relationships, difficulties in adolescence, underachievement, being gifted and having a learning disability, moving to a new area, and emotional or behavioral disorders. Treatment approaches vary, but all examine the gifted child's school performance and problems, family dynamics, and family-school interactions.

In Chapter 31, Michael M. Piechowski elaborates on the nature and implications of emotional and spiritual intelligence, whose high ends are emotional and spiritual giftedness. Emotional giftedness—a characteristic of many highly gifted students—includes high levels of moral sensitivity, intensity, and compassion. Piechowski presents many examples of spiritual experiences of adults and children, some before age five. Recurrent themes include feelings of ecstasy, timelessness, a sense of self beyond reality, personal techniques for heightened states of consciousness, and tolerance for adult ignorance of such phenomena. A central concept is *relational consciousness,* which refers to deep perceptiveness regarding how children relate to themselves, other people, and the world around them. A key thread is the current poor coordination between gifted education's development of talent and abilities, which, says Piechowski, includes competition and distancing people from each other, versus fostering personal growth, which includes the development of caring and altruistic attitudes.

In Chapter 32, Terry McNabb notes that strong intrinsic motivation is a core part of giftedness and achievement. Then she asks why some high ability students become underachievers and show low effort, low persistence, avoidance of challenges, and too low or too high self-expectations. Family problems, lack of classroom challenge, and boredom in school can reduce motivation. Locus of control theory and attribution theory—both social-cognitive theories—focus on students' perceptions of their ability and their feelings of control over educational outcomes. One dilemma is that, to some students, high effort means low ability. According to goal theory, students who view intelligence as *fixed* will see high performance as a measure of their ability; students who view intelligence as *malleable* will see learning as the route to increasing their capability. McNabb recommends that teachers emphasize the effort-outcome connection, encourage risk taking, use rewards sparingly, and model the incremental (malleable) view of intelligence.

Ten to 20 percent of high school dropouts test in the gifted range; 40 percent of the top high school graduates do not complete college. In Chapter 33, Sylvia B. Rimm identifies subtle pressures that contribute to underachievement in gifted students, for example, anti-intellectual and anti-gifted attitudes, classes that are rigid or too easy, an absence of education-oriented parent models, or a sibling who receives the title of "special." Some warning signs are procrastination, incomplete assignments, disorganization, inattention, and careless work. ADHD may or may not be present. Virtually all underachievers have low self-esteem, notes Rimm, followed by avoidance of academic tasks and, consequently, deficient skill development. Underachievers may be dependent or dominant, conforming or nonconforming, creating four behavior patterns. Rimm describes her six-step Trifocal model that can reverse underachievement. Remarkably, Rimm used subject and grade skipping and Future Problem Solving—highly challenging activities—to motivate underachievers.

In Chapter 34 Ken Seeley describes the paradox of student giftedness combined with high-risk behaviors, for example, truancy, violence, destructiveness, drug use, or criminality. Some risk factors are minor physical abnormalities, brain damage, a family history of criminal behavior or drug use, family conflict, early antisocial behavior, and academic failure. Some protective factors include being female, high intelligence, high resilience, a positive social orientation, healthy beliefs, and clear standards for behavior. Seeley reviews Cattell's two-part theory of intelligence, *fluid* (innate ability) and *crystallized* (learned information) intelligence, and contrasts a visual-spatial and an auditory-sequential learning style. Fluid intelligence combined with a visual-spatial learning style seems common among high-risk students. Another important concept is competence motivation. Important feelings of satisfaction and internal control stem from good achievement and they motivate further achievement. Seeley recommends assessing intelligence, learning style, competence, and motivation, for example, by evaluating family history and students' interests, values, self-perception, self-esteem, and social support.

29

Counseling Gifted Students

NICHOLAS COLANGELO, *The University of Iowa*

Since the first edition of the *Handbook* in 1991, there has been a continuing (and growing) emphasis on the counseling needs of gifted students. Counseling is built on the social-emotional issues of gifted students. As I stated in my introduction in 1991, meeting the learning (cognitive) needs of gifted students has dominated the field, while the recognition of the social-emotional needs has remained solid but not primary. Since the second edition of the *Handbook* in 1997, the National Association for Gifted Children has published a major report, *Task Force on Social-Emotional Issues for Gifted Students* co-chaired by Maureen Neihart and Nancy Robinson (2001). This task force report is a summary of the knowledge about the major social and emotional issues confronting gifted and talented youth and gives further national prominence to these issues. Over the years, there have been two main (and conflicting) views regarding the psychological well-being of gifted students (Neihart, 1999). One view is that gifted children are generally very well adjusted, at least as well adjusted as the general student population. In light of this view, there is little need for specialized school counseling for gifted students. Essentially, what gifted students need most is the typical counseling that is available in schools, and their needs for counseling are not dependent on their "giftedness" but on whatever aspects of their personalities may need attention.

The other view is that giftedness brings with it an array of intrapersonal and interpersonal issues that are unique to their "giftedness." Gifted students by their very advanced cognitive abilities and intensity of feelings deal with issues about self and others in ways that are different from those of the general population and therefore require specialized understand-ing. Interpersonally, gifted students are handed the task of adjusting to a peer culture that is often ambivalent, if not downright hostile, to those with intellectual talent. In this second view, counseling for the gifted is seen as a specialty. Counselors need to be aware of those unique needs of gifted students as they navigate the challenges of their development and the challenges of an environment of confusing and mixed messages. The assumption in this view is that while the majority of gifted students will and do make satisfactory psychological adjustment, there is a sizeable minority who are psychologically at risk and need counseling that is focused on their needs (Colangelo & Assouline, 2000).

The latter view is more helpful and accurate. From my experience and research, gifted students do have recurring and significant counseling needs based on their "giftedness." The focus of this chapter is on counseling needs of the gifted student and the role of the school counselor in addressing those needs. I recognize that counseling gifted students can take place in private practice and community mental health centers; however, my focus will be on the counseling that can be done in a school setting.

Historical Overview

A brief historical overview of counseling with gifted students will set the present-day context. The gifted-child movement in the United States can be traced back to Lewis M. Terman, whose pioneering longitudinal study of 1,528 gifted children formed the project titled *Genetic Studies of Genius* (Burks, Jensen, & Terman, 1930; Terman, 1925; Terman & Oden, 1947, 1959). The Terman studies grounded the study of giftedness in an empirical and psychometric tradition. Also, the work dispelled negative myths and traditions regarding the gifted. For example, Terman and his colleagues showed that gifted children were physically superior and psychologically and socially more stable than their intellectually average peers.

Because Terman's studies seemed to provide evidence that concern for gifted students' social/psychological needs was not necessary, any initial focus on counseling for gifted students was essentially derailed. However, since the sample from Terman's seminal studies is no longer considered representative of the broader gifted population, it is no longer valid to assume that there is a general absence of concern for the social-emotional well-being of the gifted student.

Terman's sample was identified by the Stanford-Binet intelligence test, and his sample was nearly exclusively white and middle-class youngsters (Holahan & Sears, 1995). The original group recommended for the Stanford-Binet testing was picked by teachers, and some teacher biases probably entered into the selection process even before the testing. Further, although Terman erased a number of myths, he created others, most notably the myth that gifted children are uniformly well adjusted and therefore do not need counseling services. Thus, counselors and those in related professions were not an integral part of gifted education during its early development (Kerr, 1986; Webb, Meckstroth, & Tolan, 1982).

Leta Hollingworth (1926, 1942) was the first to contribute evidence indicating that gifted children do have social and emotional needs meriting attention. Hollingworth also emphasized that the regular school environment did not meet the educational needs of the gifted. Rather, she wrote that the school environment was more likely to lead to apathy with these youngsters. She anticipated some of the emotional difficulties and peer problems that receive attention today. Especially, noting that there is often a gap between a gifted student's intellectual and emotional development, she stated, "To have the intellect of an adult and the emotions of a child combined in a childish body is to encounter certain difficulties" (Hollingworth, 1942, p. 282).

The 1950s witnessed some major attention to counseling gifted students and the establishment of research and guidance programs. John Rothney, a counselor educator, founded the Wisconsin Guidance Laboratory for Superior Students (University of Wisconsin—Madison), which was headed by

Rothney and later by Marshall Sanborn. The Guidance Laboratory, later named the Guidance Institute for Talented Students (GIFTS) was headed by Charles Pulvino, followed by Nicholas Colangelo and then Philip Perrone (Colangelo & Zaffrann, 1979).

John Curtis Gowan was a major force from the 1950s to 1970s in promoting counseling services for the gifted. A. Harry Passow and his students Abe Tannenbaum and Miriam Goldberg founded the Talented Youth Project in 1954, which had a strong counseling component. The 1960s and 1970s also witnessed increased sensitivity to issues and counseling needs of gifted women, minorities, and disadvantaged students.

The 1980s saw the establishment of the Supporting the Emotional Needs of Gifted (SENG) program by James T. Webb at Wright State University after the suicide of Dallas Egbert, a highly gifted seventeen-year-old. SENG has continued its focus on addressing the counseling and psychological needs of gifted students. The issues of depression and suicide among the gifted have continued to expand with the work of James Delisle at Kent State University (e.g., Delisle, 1992).

In 1982 Barbara Kerr established the Guidance Laboratory for Gifted and Talented at the University of Nebraska—Lincoln, to extend the work of both GIFTS and SENG (Myers & Pace, 1986). Linda Silverman, a psychologist, established the Gifted Child Development Center in Denver, Colorado. In 1988 The University of Iowa established the comprehensive Connie Belin National Center for Gifted Education (renamed The Connie Belin & Jacqueline N. Blank International Center for Gifted Education and Talent Development in 1995) with Nicholas Colangelo as director. The Belin-Blank Center has a strong focus on personal counseling, career guidance, family counseling, and psychological assessment. The clinical programs at the Belin-Blank Center are headed by Susan Assouline, associate director and school psychologist.

In an historical overview of counseling gifted students, Karen St. Clair (1989) divided counseling into several time periods:

1. *Early 1900s:* Some recognition of the counseling needs of gifted students, focusing on the work of Terman and Hollingworth.
2. *The 1950s:* A nondirective approach to counseling the gifted student, which acknowledged the

influence of Carl Rogers (1951) on the entire counseling profession.

3. *The 1960s:* the beginning of counseling the gifted in schools, where the role of the school counselor was emphasized in the development of all students with some special attention to gifted.

4. *The 1970s:* Program development for counseling gifted students emphasizing full-fledged programs of counseling in schools that focused not only on counseling sessions, but counseling programs, evaluations, and research relating to school counseling.

5. *The 1980s:* Diversity in counseling the gifted that indicated a decade of special issues in counseling, including focus on underachievement, females, and minority students. This period was also characterized by diversity in terms of models and approaches to counseling.

To St. Clair's review I add the following:

6. *The 1990s:* counseling provided a strong emphasis on gifted students with special needs. There was a focus on gifted students who were double labeled, that is, gifted and learning disabled. There was also a focus on providing programs (counseling and curriculum) that matched the dual exceptionalities of the students (see, e.g., Cash, 1999). Family and sexual identity issues were also important trends in this decade (Colangelo & Assouline, 2000).

7. *The 2000s and beyond:* in the next decade I anticipate a sharper concern for ethics and moral issues as well as a continued focus on the "emotional intelligence" of students. In addition there will be an expanding focus on international issues, as the vision of giftedness will include a global perspective. The NAGC *Task Force on Social-Emotional Issues for Gifted Students* (Neihart & Robinson, 2001) is a marker for the new century's attention to counseling needs.

Self-Concept

The interest in *self-concept,* which by no means began in the 1990s, saw a powerful revival during that decade. Almost everything "good" in school life seems related to a positive self-concept and almost all that is "at risk" has at least an aspect of negative self-concept associated with it. Dawes (1998) indicated

that pop psychology associates positive mental health with self-esteem (i.e., self-concept). His brief review indicates a number of destructive behaviors by adolescents and adults who seem to have quite positive evaluations of themselves. His insightful comments give cause to consider that simply having high self-esteem/self-concept does not ensure prosocial behavior, and that we must consider that students with high (positive) self-concepts may also perform actions with negative consequences.

The self-concept construct has deep historical roots in psychology and education. The self-concept can be viewed as a "powerful system of cognitive structures that is quite likely to mediate interpretation of and response to events and behaviors directed at or involving the individual" (Nurius, 1986, p. 435). The definition of self-concept has evolved from a "collection of self-views" (e.g., Rogers, 1951; Snygg & Combs, 1949) to general good and bad feelings about oneself (McGuire, 1984; Shavelson, Hubner, & Stanton, 1976) to recent theory and research on operationally defining the structures and contents of the self-concept (Colangelo & Assouline, 1995; Marsh, 1990; Nurius, 1986). Neihart (1999) states that self-concept is the collection of ideas that one has about oneself, an essential component of what is usually called personality.

Self-concept of gifted youngsters has received considerable attention over the past two decades (Neihart & Robinson, 2001; Plucker & Stocking, 2001). According to Neihart (1999), a number of studies concluded that there are no differences between gifted and nongifted students; however, other studies found differences in favor of gifted students, particularly when measuring self-concepts of one's academic abilities. These studies typically investigated (1) how gifted and average children's self-concepts compare (Hoge & Renzulli, 1993; Karnes & Wherry, 1981; Kelly & Colangelo, 1984; Loeb & Jay 1987); (2) whether self-concept is a developmental construct (Harter, 1982; Hoge & McSheffrey, 1991; Hoge & Renzulli, 1993; Karnes & Wherry, 1981; Marsh, 1992, 1993); and (3) how programming affects a child's self-concept (Kelly & Colangelo, 1984; Loeb & Jay, 1987; Maddux, Scheiber, & Bass, 1982).

Self-concept and *giftedness* represent complex constructs, and the study of each is made more difficult by theoretical controversies within each field. For example, the developmental nature and processes of self-concept have been debated (Harter, 1982; Karnes & Wherry, 1981; Ketcham & Snyder, 1977).

Additionally, there are concerns about the reliability and validity of multidimensional measures of self-concept (Marsh, 1990, 1993, 1994; Wylie, 1989). In the area of gifted education, the question of unidimensionality versus multidimensionality also permeates almost every aspect of the field.

Research lends credibility to the multidimensional nature of self-concept (see Plucker & Stocking, 2001). In a study investigating the self-concept of 563 gifted students spanning grades 3 to 11, Colangelo and Assouline (1995) found support for the general notion that the overall self-concept of gifted students is positive. However, there were peaks and valleys across the grade levels and the various domains as measured by the Piers-Harris Children's Self-Concept Scale. Most important for school counselors were the following findings:

1. General self-concept scores were high for elementary, middle, and high school gifted students; however, high school students had the lowest scores. High school girls, in particular showed the most significant drop in self-concept scores.
2. As gifted students progress in school, they become more anxious and feel more isolated.
3. The lowest scores of the 563 students in the study were in the domains of interpersonal skills and self-satisfaction.
4. The highest scores were in the domains of intellectual and school status.

Closely related to self-concept is the attitude that gifted students have toward their own giftedness. Three books—*On Being Gifted* (American Association for Gifted Children, 1978), *Gifted Children Speak Out* (Delisle, 1984), and *Gifted Kids Speak Out* (Delisle, 1987)—present testimonials from gifted children describing the impact of giftedness on their lives.

One conclusion drawn from these testimonials is that these children have mixed feelings about their giftedness. Research has provided some confirmation of this ambivalence. Colangelo and Kelly (1983) found that while gifted youngsters were positive about being labeled gifted, they perceived nongifted peers and teachers as having negative views of them. A study by Kerr, Colangelo, and Gaeth (1988) indicated that the attitude of gifted adolescents toward their own giftedness was multifaceted. Adolescents reported that being gifted was positive in terms of their own personal growth and in terms of academics. In terms of peer relations, however, they reported it to be negative. In a partial replication of the Kerr et al. study, Monaster, Chan, Walt, and Wiehe (1994) supported the finding that attitudes toward giftedness are multifaceted. In addition, Monaster and colleagues found that those who knew the gifted child well had positive attitudes toward the child, and that attitudes became more negative toward "giftedness" as respondents were removed from personal knowledge of a gifted youngster.

The Kerr et al. and Monaster et al. findings are very relevant for school counselors because the issues focus on human interaction. In individual counseling sessions, counselors can discuss issues such as: What does it mean to be gifted? What do I like about being gifted? What do I not like about being gifted? If I were not gifted, what would be better for me? If I were not gifted, what would be worse for me?

Career Counseling with Gifted

When gifted students are about to graduate from high school and they begin to plan for college and a career, parents and educators often get involved to be sure that the student "does not waste the gift." From my experience with this phenomenon, "not wasting the gift" translates into "making a decision that is reasonable to the adult." It seems there are a number of adults who believe that certain careers are worthy of a gifted student, and certain are not. Physician, lawyer, engineer, and physicist typically fall into the category of worthy, while elementary/secondary school teacher, social worker, school counselor, and nurse typically fall into a less worthy category.

Career planning for high ability students is not always smooth (Kaufmann, 1981; Kerr, 1985, 1991, 1998). Gifted students do not always know what they want to do for the "rest of their lives," and while they may have the academic ability to succeed in classes, this does not mean that they have the information to plan for a career. Ability and ambition do not always translate into planned or purposeful action.

Multipotentiality

One of the most discussed concepts in the giftedness literature is *multipotentiality* (Neihart & Robinson, 2001; Sajjadi, Rejskind, & Shore, 2001). As the term implies, it refers to individuals who have diverse talents (and interests also) and who could succeed at a high level in a number of different fields. The problem is how to make a decision, how to choose a path from so many realistic possibilities? While this may seem a problem one would gladly suffer, it is a significant problem for gifted students. "Multipotentialed young people may anguish over an abundance of choices available to them during career planning unless appropriate interventions are available" (Rysiew, Shore, & Leeb, 1998, p. 423). The most useful definition of *multipotential* comes from Frederickson and Rothney (1972), "the ability to select and develop any number of competencies to a high level" (p. vii). Without the stipulation of developing competencies *at a very high level,* the concept of multipotentiality loses any sense of meaningfulness. While there has been some discussion that the term should be reserved for abilities and not interests (see Rysiew, Shore, & Carson, 1994), there has been little disagreement in the field of gifted education as to the existence and importance of this concept in understanding giftedness.

While there is an absence of empirical data supporting the notion of multipotentiality, there have been considerable anecdotal and clinical reports regarding the concept (Rysiew, Shore, & Leeb, 1998). The only serious challenges to the usefulness and existence of multipotentiality have come from Achter, Lubinski, and Benbow (1996) and Achter, Benbow, and Lubinski (1997). Also, Sajjadi, Rejskind, and Shore (2001) indicate that while multipotentiality exists with gifted students, it may not be a significant problem for them.

Rysiew et al. (1998) outline some of the main problems or concerns in dealing with multipotentiality, especially as it deals with career choices:

1. Students find it hard to narrow to a single career since they have so many equally viable options.
2. Multipotential students also suffer from perfectionism; they look for the perfect or ideal career.
3. Students feel coerced by parents and others to make decisions based on status and high earning potential.
4. Students must make commitments that require long-term schooling (graduate, professional) and a delay of independence in terms of earning adequate salaries as well as starting families. These long-term "training" investments are also difficult to change once a student has worked for several years towards a particular career, even if there are serious doubts about the chosen career path.

Rysiew et al. (1998) review a number of writings regarding what counselors can do to help multipotential gifted students with career decisions. Among the recommendations are

a. A career should be explored as a way of life, a lifestyle rather than a particular job/position.
b. One does not have to limit oneself to one career; there can be career changes as well.
c. Use leisure activities as a way to continually develop areas of ability and interest apart from one's career.
d. Use career counseling as a value-based activity, exploring broad categories of life satisfaction.
e. Emphasize peer discussions and group work with other multipotential youth so that one can see that he or she is not alone with concerns.

Since 1988, the students selected for the Belin-Blank Center programs have participated in a Counseling Lab for Career Development. This career development program incorporates the recommendations listed by Rysiew et al. (1998). In particular, the values-based component of the Counseling Lab for Career Development has proven highly successful with secondary students.

Group Counseling

Gifted students are considerably smarter about coursework than about themselves. They have the ability to be insightful about themselves, but seldom the opportunity to articulate and share their insights. Counselors can offer no more powerful tool for the social and emotional growth of gifted students than group counseling. Group counseling is a rich arena that affords students a rare opportunity to share with one another their struggles and questions about growing up and what it means to be "gifted." But simply sitting around talking about feelings and values is not enough. Group counseling is a structured situation with a trained leader (e.g., a school counselor) who has knowledge of both gifted youngsters and group dynamics.

Why Group Counseling for Gifted Students?

All students grow by having opportunities to discuss feelings and perceptions in an atmosphere of trust and understanding. Also, students need to share with peers. To think of *peers* as one's age-mates trivializes the concept. A peer is more a "soul-mate" than an age-mate, someone who understands what you mean, has experienced what you are talking about, and can respond to you. Gifted students seldom have the opportunity to talk to one another about what it means to be gifted or how it feels to understand things that many age-mates cannot seem to grasp. These are subjects that educators do not encourage for discussion, and gifted students are bright enough to know it's best to keep such things to oneself.

Grouping gifted students for the sole purpose of helping them discuss, in a safe and open atmosphere, issues of a more personal and social nature gives them an opportunity to enjoy and grow from their peers. Most of the time gifted students hide who they are (Colangelo, 1991; Colangelo & Peterson, 1993). Group counseling is a situation in which they are encouraged to share themselves with others who understand and accept. I would guess that if gifted students were given a chance to meet as a small group for the purpose of self-discovery, for most of them this would be their first opportunity to share with true peers. If a rationale is needed for group counseling with gifted students, it is that in the course of school life such a situation will not arise naturally.

Topics for Group Counseling

A counselor may wonder what topics are useful or of interest to a group of gifted students meeting for group counseling sessions. These students will not find it difficult to generate discussion. In my experience with groups, the challenge is in ending the discussions rather than in starting them.

A counselor needs to set the atmosphere for a group. He or she must be clear on the ethics, purpose, rules, and norms. The overall purpose is for gifted students to be able to talk about themselves and learn about one another in an atmosphere of safety and respect. The following are some stems that a counselor may use in generating discussions:

1. What does it mean to be gifted? I have found exciting and varied discussions generated by such a question. Students will see it in different ways. Questions that help elaborate this topic are:
   a. What do your parents think it means to be gifted?
   b. What do your teachers think it means to be gifted?
   c. What do other kids in school think it means?

2. How is being gifted an advantage for you? How is it a disadvantage?
3. Have you ever deliberately hidden your giftedness? If so, how?

Colangelo (1991) described group discussions with gifted students in which they talked about "deliberate underachievement"—purposely getting lower grades so that their friends would be more accepting of them. Many gifted students will be able to articulate how they make decisions to avoid demonstrating their giftedness.

4. How is your participation in this group different from your regular school day?
   Colangelo (1991) also reported that students in groups talked about how "Finally, I can be myself" or "I can say what's on my mind without someone making fun of me or saying I'm a snob." What is different about being gifted and being a girl? Boy, Black, Hispanic, White, etc?

In studies reported by Colangelo and Kerr (1990) and Kerr and Colangelo (1988), it is obvious that gender and ethnicity are important variables related to giftedness. Questions I have found useful are

5. Would you rather be a gifted boy? Gifted girl? What does it mean to be gifted and Latino? Students will find it stimulating to discuss such issues. Also, they will achieve much better insight into gender and ethnic issues.
6. Is there a time in school (elementary, middle, high school) when it is easiest to be gifted? More difficult? Why? The foregoing questions are by no means exhaustive, and they will lead to other related questions and directions.

Dynamics and Techniques

The essence of group counseling is to transform students from *spectators* to *participants*. Although there is evidence of the positive effects of being a spectator in a group, its value pales compared to the value of being a participant. To be a spectator means to observe and listen, but to be only tangentially associated with the topic of discussion. A group is not effective when its members are primarily spectators.

A counselor can transform spectators into participants by taking opportunities to make any topic of discussion a connector to each group member.

Following is a specific example using the concepts of *vertical* and *horizontal* self-disclosures.

Let's say a student is talking about her feelings about having been labeled gifted. The counselor could ask her questions to help her elaborate on these feelings: "How long have you felt this way?" "Is it changing at all for you?" "Who knows that you felt this way?" All of these are good questions that help the student talk more about her feelings. These questions lead to what can be called *vertical* self-disclosure (Yalom, 1985) because they help "build" more information on how the student feels about labeling. As we build this mound of information, the rest of the students in the group are listening (perhaps nodding in agreement), being empathic, and so on. Their role is primarily that of spectators (albeit sympathetic and interested ones) in that they are observing this interaction between the one student and the counselor.

Using the same incident, the counselor could transform the group members from spectators to participants by moving from vertical to *horizontal* self-disclosure. Instead of asking for more information on the feelings about labeling, the counselor asks the student, "Who in this group do you think feels the same way you do?" or "Who in this group do you think feels most different from you about labeling?" These types of questions are *horizontal* in that they connect students to one another (Yalom, 1985). The students in the group are no longer simply spectators, listening to one girl talk about labeling. Instead, they are actively involved in their own feelings and perceptions about labeling. In every group, there will be countless opportunities to take what a student says and make *horizontal* connections. Every *horizontal* connection makes better use of group dynamics and generates more energy and participation. Group counseling is most vibrant when members are transformed from spectators to participants.

Another technique helps students to pay better attention to the processes in their group. At the end of every group session, the counselor can ask one student to "process for the group." What this means is to take the last three to five minutes of the session to articulate to everyone what he or she thought happened in the group. This group process time is an opportunity to share how the group went about its task for the session.

This simple technique accomplishes several important tasks. First, over time, it gives each student a chance to share what he or she saw happening in group. It also offers other students a chance to hear the perspective of one member. To paraphrase T. S. Eliot,

you can have the experience but miss the meaning. This technique minimizes the possibility of missing the meaning. Second, ending every session with group process time is a good way to summarize the session. Third, the group process time can often be an excellent stem for the start of the next group session. For instance, it is not uncommon in groups we have led for a student to start a session with, "When Bob did group process last week, he said some things that I saw very differently. I want to talk about how I saw them. . . ." The group session is off and running.

Group counseling is an effective means of helping gifted students in their social and emotional growth. It is rare that gifted students ever have opportunities for grouping when the primary purpose is personal growth rather than academics. See Colangelo & Peterson (1993) for a more extensive treatment of group counseling with the gifted.

Counseling with Families

The family has been recognized as a primary and critical component in the development of talent and the success of children in school.[1] Bloom's (1985; Bloom & Sosniak, 1981) seminal work on talent development made a compelling case for the demands on, as well as the influences of, the family in the development of talent.[2] Although research and writings on families of gifted students have increased in the last two decades (see reviews by Colangelo & Assouline, 1993; Moon & Hall, 1998; Neihart & Robinson, 2001), counseling with families is still an area of exceptional need and challenge.

In a special anniversary issue of *Roeper Review,* I emphasized that one of the most significant trends in gifted education over the next ten years would be a focus on families (Colangelo, 1988). Although there has been an increase in counseling families, counselors and therapists who work with families of gifted children rarely have expertise in the area of gifted (Moon & Hall, 1998; Wendorf & Frey, 1985). Their expertise is family counseling.

A major review of family issues appeared in 1983 by Colangelo and Dettmann. Recently, another major review on family counseling and family therapy was prepared by Moon and Hall (1998). A summary of the findings by Moon and Hall includes:

---

1. See Chapter 30 by Moon.
2. See Chapter 19 by Sosniak.

a. Parents of gifted have unique stressors and concerns brought about by the unique cognitive and personality characteristics of gifted children.

b. Parenting styles tend to be child-centered, with high expectations for education and achievement and a high value on cultural and intellectual activities.

c. While families of gifted children have been found to have generally close relationships, with flexibility and bonding, others have been found to experience stress, disorganization, and dysfunctional interactions.

d. Family therapists, while they are experts in family dynamics, do not have the expertise regarding the unique cognitive and affective characteristics of gifted children. With parents of gifted seeking guidance about family issues, family therapists (and school counselors) will need to complement their clinical expertise with knowledge of giftedness so that they can be effective helpers of these parents.

Sibling Relationships and the Label "Gifted"

School counselors should anticipate difficulties in families when a child is first labeled *gifted*. It is at this time that the family needs assistance. First, school counselors should be certain that parents clearly understand why their child has been identified as gifted. Many counselors hold parent discussion groups to clarify this issue. Second, counselors should help families anticipate changes as they attempt to adjust to the label. For siblings, the *gifted* label throws into question their role and their importance in the family (Chamrad, Robinson, Treder, & Janos, 1995; Neihart & Robinson, 2001).

Cornell and Grossberg (1986) found that in families with labeled gifted children, the non-labeled children are more prone to personality adjustment problems. Grenier (1985) reported increased competition and diminished cooperation by non-labeled siblings (see review by Jenkins-Friedman, 1992; Moon & Hall, 1998).

The good news is that the family will become accustomed to the label and positive adjustments are likely over time. Colangelo and Brower (1987) reported that, in time, the negative effects of labeling disappear. Counselors can effectively ease the initial strain and disruption by helping the family communicate openly about the gifted label. Also, families simply alerted to likely changes seem better able to take some strain and disruption in stride and thus appear to adjust even more quickly.

Giftedness as a Family Organizer

In working with families of gifted children, it is fair to ask, "To what extent is this issue simply what all families must confront, and to what extent is this issue unique because of the presence of a gifted child?" Giftedness in many families becomes an "organizer"—that is, a rationale for understanding behavior and actions (see Jenkins-Friedman, 1992).

In some families, behaviors are tolerated because the parents perceive that "this is how it is with a gifted child," or not tolerated because "such behavior should not come from a gifted child." The giftedness of a child can structure how parents relate to him or her as well as siblings (Moon & Hall, 1998). Many families feel they must put greater energy and resources into the development of a gifted child's talents. Negatives from such organizers can occur when a family loses balance with regard to the needs of other children. As in any case of exceptionality (e.g., a child with a disability), the giftedness can organize the energy and resources of a family, at times to the detriment of other aspects of the family.

A Family Counseling Program

At the Connie Belin & Jacqueline N. Blank International Center for Gifted Education and Talent Development (Belin-Blank Center), we have established a family counseling program to respond to the needs of families with a gifted child. The brief counseling approach lasts a maximum of five to six sessions per family. The focus is on helping the family develop its own strengths in the resolution of issues. Families receive services at no cost, and in return for these services they participate in research related to family counseling.

The majority of families who have participated in the Belin-Blank Center Clinic sought services for their gifted child's perceived underachievement. The perception is an important concept in the work that we do with families. In some cases, there truly was significant underachievement. In others, however, the notion of underachievement was the "symptom" that initiated the contact with the Belin-Blank Center Clinic. It was not so much a case of the student underachieving as an issue regarding parents expectations.

I have found that although a child's giftedness may be the stated reason for seeking counseling, there often are other issues within these families that have been subsumed under giftedness (e.g., marital discord, alcoholism, delinquency). When this is the case, the families are referred to a family counselor who can provide long-term therapy.

Parent-School Interactions

One of the most important issues confronting school counselors is the parent-school relationship (Colangelo & Dettmann, 1983, 1985; Dettmann & Colangelo, 1980; Moon & Hall, 1998; Neihart & Robinson, 2001). The underlying issue regarding this relationship is the role the school should take in providing special educational opportunities for gifted students. Colangelo and Dettmann (1982) developed a counseling model conceptualizing four types of parent-school interactions involving gifted students (Figure 29.1).

Type I (cooperation) is an interaction based on the attitude by both parents and schools that the school should be active in gifted education. The tendency here is for open sharing of information about the child and cooperation between parents and schools. Typically, the gifted are identified and given special educational opportunities commensurate with their needs. The underlying assumption by both parents and schools is that the most effective way to develop exceptional ability is through overt, special educational considerations based upon objective information concerning the student's learning needs (e.g., honors classes, advanced classes, resource rooms, independent projects, ability groupings, and grade skipping).

Type II (conflict) is an interaction based on conflicting attitudes by (active) parents and a (passive) school regarding the role of the school. Parents believe that their gifted child needs special programming by the school in order to develop his or her abilities. However, the school believes that the typical school curriculum is adequate to meet the needs of all youngsters, including the gifted. Also, it is typical for the school to believe that special programs should be a priority for students with disabilities. The school in this situation feels that parents are pushy and demand unnecessary attention for gifted youngsters. The parents feel they must be aggressive or the school will ignore the needs of their child.

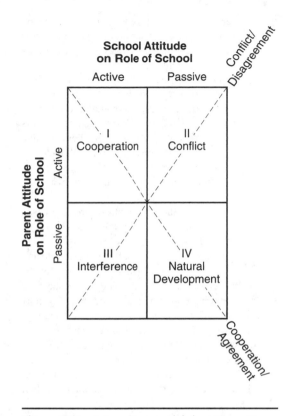

Figure 29.1 Interaction model depicting attitudes of parents and schools regarding the role of the school in gifted education.

Source: Reprinted by permission of the authors and publisher from N. Colangelo and D. F. Dettmann (1982). "A Conceptual Model of Four Types of Parent–School Interactions," *Journal for the Education of the Gifted,* Vol. 5, pp. 120–126, Figure 1.

Type II interactions often are the most difficult for parents and school. These schools tend to view gifted education as an albatross. Parents tend not to support the school and often blame the school for problems their child may have with boredom or lack of motivation and achievement. Parents sometimes encourage the child not to accept the school's evaluations and requirements (e.g., report card grades, classwork) as accurate assessments of his or her abilities.

I have found that parents usually take one of three approaches in this Type II conflict. One is that they continually fight the school. They may either demand meetings for further discussion or join forces with other parents to assert their position. In the second approach, parents take it upon themselves to provide the special programs needed by a child. These may include summer enrichment activities, museum trips, college courses, tutors, mentors, and sometimes even private schools. Obviously, this approach is limited by the educational background and financial resources of the parents. The third approach occurs when parents feel hopeless. They believe that they can have no real effect and that all they can do is complain. For many parents, the result is a withdrawal from direct communication with the school.

Type III (interference) interactions are also based on conflict, but with a reversal of the dynamics found in Type II. In Type III, the school actively wants to provide for the gifted child, but the parents do not agree. Parents are unsure if special programs for the gifted are helpful or necessary. They are concerned about what effect identification and labeling may have on their (gifted) child as well as on siblings who may not be so identified. They may be concerned that special recognition will damage their child's peer relationships. Parents also may view identification and special programs as an interference in the normal educational development of their child. Meanwhile, the school believes that the child *does* need special consideration and is willing to provide it. Of course, the school is often frustrated by the parents' refusal to let their child participate in the school's special program.

Type IV (natural development) interactions are based on agreement by both parents and schools that the role of the school should be passive. This belief is founded on the premise that high ability will take care of itself ("cream rises to the top") and that very little can be done meaningfully to nourish extraordinary ability. Essentially, both parents and schools view the typical school curriculum and extracurricular activities as providing enough challenge and variety to stimulate the development of high potential and ability. In Type IV interactions, parents and schools recognize and support the youngster's efforts but believe that the natural development of talent will take its course, if the talent is truly there.

Implications of Parent-School Interactions

The model in Figure 29.1 accounts for both *process* and *outcome*. The process relates to the nature of the interactions—cooperative or conflictual. The outcome relates to the four possible types of interactions

when parents and school communicate about the school's role in gifted education.

The model can be used as a diagnostic instrument for helping both parents and school staff understand their interactions. The model also provides counselors with a framework for understanding their interactions with parents and other school staff—thus gaining insight into *how* they will deal with issues regarding programming for gifted children. Counselors can use this model not only to determine the type of interaction that *exists* between the school and parents, but also to assess what type of interaction would be *preferred*.

Underachievement

Perhaps the most intense counseling focus has been on the underachieving gifted student.[3] In the Family Counseling program at the Connie Belin & Jacqueline N. Blank International Center for Gifted Education and Talent Development, underachievement has been the number one presenting problem. The issue of underachievement is confusing because of disagreement about its definition and the inconsistency of results from interventions (Delisle, 1992; Dowdall & Colangelo, 1982; Neihart & Robinson, 2001; Peterson & Colangelo, 1996; Reis, 1998; Whitmore, 1980).

Underachievement is seen as a discrepancy between assessed potential and actual performance. The discrepancy may be between two standardized measures (e.g., IQ and achievement tests), between a standardized measure and classroom performance (e.g., IQ and grades), or between two nonstandardized measures (e.g., teacher expectations and performance on daily assignments). The label "gifted underachiever" implies that a learner has a high level of potential (Reis, 1998). There are some measures, usually a standardized test, by which a student meets the criteria for giftedness, while actual school performance is well below the assessed potential.

There have been a number of attempts to categorize underachievers. Reis (1998) distinguished between *chronic* and *temporary* (situational) underachievement. Temporary underachievement is often in response to a situational stress or event (e.g., divorce, loss of a friend, problems with a teacher). A

---

3. See Chapter 33 by Rimm.

chronic underachiever is one who has a history and a pattern of underachievement, which appear to cut-across a particular incident or circumstance. (See also Peterson & Colangelo, 1996).

Whitmore (1980) proposed three types of under-achievers: *aggressive, withdrawn,* and *rebellious combination.* Aggressive students demonstrate disruption and rebellious behaviors; withdrawn under-achievers are bored and uninvolved. The third type is a combination of aggressive and withdrawn, and the underachiever vacillates between aggressive and withdrawn behaviors.

Delisle (1992) proposed the categories of *under-achiever* and *non-producer* and made an extensive comparison between the two categories.[4] For counselors, however, the most important distinction revolves around the counseling needs of the student. The non-producer has minimal counseling needs and is the type of student whose non-productive behaviors can be reversed "overnight" with minimal intervention. Underachieving behaviors require an extensive counseling program that may include family counseling. Most significantly, underachievement, according to Delisle, is a problem that demands a long-term solution.

To a school counselor, the discrepancy between scores is not as critical as the interpersonal dynamics involved in underachievement. Rather than looking at underachievement as a psychometric event, it can be seen as a relationship between the gifted student and teachers, parent(s), and sometimes peers. For some gifted students, underachievement is a way to express either a need for attention or a need for control over a situation.

Underachievement brings considerable attention from both teachers and parents, in extreme cases almost doting behavior. Adults are so concerned that gifted youngsters will not make good use of their gifts that they give a great deal of energy and time to the students (Peterson & Colangelo, 1996).

Counselors can break the attention-getting cycle by having parents and teaches avoid responding too strongly to the underachieving behavior or even ignoring it. They can give attention when the child achieves well and minimize attention when the child is not achieving. The equation is simple. If the child wants attention, he or she will soon learn that the attention is forthcoming only when certain achieving behaviors (and attitudes) are present. The child will want to do more of these kinds of behaviors because the reward is the attention.

A gifted youngster who uses underachievement as a means to gain control of a situation offers a more difficult challenge. For such youngsters, poor achievement is a way to show teachers and parents that they (the students) can do what they want. A typical reaction by teachers and parents to this kind of defiance is to attempt to force the student to do the task and do it at levels comparable to expectations. This situation can lead to a vicious and non-productive power struggle. The counselor can work with teachers and parents to help them quit the fight. It is likely the student will diminish the fight relationship if there is no one to fight with.

Minimizing the power struggle will allow more opportunity for the student to perform because he or she is free to do so. Group counseling can help gifted students better understand their behaviors and motives and learn new patterns of interactions. Importantly, it is in the rich atmosphere of a group of peers with a trained leader (school counselor) that a gifted youngster can explore motives and consequences of underachieving behavior.

Finally, it is important for the school counselor to use school records to understand gifted under-achievers, especially at the secondary level. In a comprehensive study of 153 gifted underachievers, in grades 7–12, Peterson and Colangelo (1996) found data on attendance, tardiness, course selection, and course grades, by gender and by age, that provided differential patterns that distinguished gifted students who achieved from those who under-achieved. Peterson and Colangelo reported that patterns of underachievement established in junior high school, though not impossible to alter in high school, tend to persist through high school. Records are ubiquitous in schools, and are a good resource for counselors.

While the issues surrounding underachievement are complex and research findings inconclusive and even contradictory, Reis (1998) provides a good summary of the current research on underachievement in the following eight points:

First, it appears that the beginnings of underachievement in many young people occur in elementary school.

Second, underachievement appears to be periodic and episodic, occurring some years and not others and in some classes but not others.

---

4. See Chapter 37 by Schultz and Delisle.

Third, a direct relationship seems to exist between inappropriate or too-easy content in elementary school and underachievement in middle or high school.

Fourth, parental issues interact with the behaviors of some underachievers, yet no clear pattern exists about the types of parental behaviors that cause underachievement.

Fifth, peers can play a major role in keeping underachievement from occurring in their closest friends, making peer groups an important part of preventing and reversing underachievement.

Sixth, busier adolescents who are involved in clubs, extracurricular activities, sports and religious activities are less likely to underachieve in school.

Seventh, many similar behavioral characteristics are exhibited by bright students who achieve and underachieve in school.

Eighth, there are some students who may underachieve as a direct result of an inappropriate and unmotivating curriculum.

Dual Exceptionalities

Much of the literature on underachievement either states or implies psychological undercurrents (e.g., intrapersonal, interpersonal, and family dynamics). While the psychological issues clearly have been shown to play a role in underachievement, it is critical to note that not all underachievement behaviors have a psychological root. The presence of learning and developmental disabilities has been shown to be associated with both giftedness and underachievement.[5]

The later 1980s and 1990s brought a new awareness to the field of gifted education: gifted students who also have disabilities, especially learning, developmental, and social-emotional disabilities (see Kaufmann & Castellanos, 2000; Neihart & Robinson, 2001). Dual exceptionalities may include autistic savant syndrome; developmental delays in speech, language, and motor coordination; disruptive behavior (including conduct and oppositional-defiant disorders); anxieties; and eating disorders (Moon & Hall, 1998). Gifted children also may have specific learning disorders (LD), and attention deficit/hyperactivity disorder (AD/HD) (Zentall, Moon, Hall, & Grskovic, 2001).

The most common behavior disorder in gifted children is ADHD (Moon & Hall, 1998; Zentall et al., 2001), which can interfere with academic and social functioning. For gifted with LD or ADHD, individualized testing will reflect patterns of inconsistency across talent areas (Moon & Hall, 1998). Multiple testing methods are typically needed to pinpoint areas of giftedness and disability (Moon & Dillon, 1995).

Dual exceptionality students are at risk for underachievement, since they have barriers to achieving at their level of giftedness. Such students can become easily frustrated (and frustrating) since their inability to perform or "behave" can bring about questions regarding their motivation and commitment. From our observations, it seems that dual exceptionalities are more common than most educators may think.

A battery of individualized tests is recommended to determine exceptionalities in cases where gifted students are underachieving in academics and unable to function effectively in the classroom. Dual exceptionalities require a team approach. School psychologists are in the best position to test and diagnose exceptionalities, while the school counselor (at times the school social worker) has the expertise for counseling students and families regarding the dual exceptionalities (Colangelo & Assouline, 2000).

School Counseling Programs for Gifted Students

School-based programs in counseling are important to the development of gifted students (see Neihart & Robinson, 2001). There are two ways to envision a school counseling program for gifted students: as *remedial* or as *developmental*. In the remedial approach, the emphasis is on problem solving and crisis intervention. In this approach, the counselor is primarily a "therapy expert" who intervenes in problem situations either to help solve the problem or to minimize the difficulty. The counselor is involved in staffing, referrals, and one-on-one counseling. Where there is group counseling, the students are selected because they share a common problem (e.g., underachievement, behavior problems), and the purpose is to correct the problem.

In the developmental approach, the counselor uses expertise to serve a therapeutic function and is available for problem solving, but therapy and problem solving are not the primary purpose. The real work of the developmentally oriented counselor is

---

5. See Chapter 41 by Silverman.

to establish an environment in school that is conducive to the educational growth of gifted students. Such an approach is predicated on knowledge of both affective and cognitive needs of gifted youngsters. The focus of individual counseling is to get to know students and help them better understand their own strengths and weaknesses as decision makers and formulators of their lives.

Group counseling focuses on sharing perceptions and learning more effective interpersonal skills. Group members do not necessarily have a common problem to resolve. Work with families is based not on a problem with their child, but on the recognition that gifted children pose a unique challenge to parents. Family work is based more on discussion groups with parents in which the parents share information and connect with other families.

I strongly advocate a developmental approach to counseling with gifted students. Giftedness is not a problem to be solved but a unique challenge to be nourished. In a therapy model, evidence of "problems" would be necessary to justify having a counselor with expertise in working with the gifted. However, a developmental approach does not depend on evidence that gifted youngsters are at risk.

A developmental counseling program requires the following components:

1. An articulated and coherent rationale;
2. A program of activities based on the affective and cognitive needs of youngsters;
3. Trained counselors who are well grounded not only in counseling, but also in giftedness;
4. A minimum of attention to rehabilitative (therapy) services, but a strong component of individual, family, and teacher consultations;
5. Input and participation from teachers, administrators, parents, and the youngsters who are served; and
6. A component for the continued professional development of counselors so that they may keep pace with the latest research and practices on the counseling needs of gifted youngsters.

SUMMARY AND CONCLUSIONS

Since the first edition of the *Handbook* there has been steady interest in the counseling needs of gifted students. With the publication of this third edition, there seems to be even more attention on counseling and the social-emotional needs of gifted students. Individual, group, and family counseling are predicated on the assumption and evidence that youngsters with exceptional ability and talents also have unique social and emotional needs.

These unique needs exist and interact in the successful or unsuccessful development of talent. Counseling is a necessary component in the successful development of talent. For counselors to be successful, they need knowledge and expertise both in counseling and in giftedness. A developmental counseling program in a school will foster both the cognitive and the affective growth of gifted youngsters.

QUESTIONS FOR THOUGHT AND DISCUSSION

1. What are some of the historical milestones in the growth of counseling services for gifted students?

2. How important is a positive self-concept in the development of gifted students? In programs for the gifted, how can we promote positive self-concepts?

3. Compare the benefits of individual counseling, group counseling, and family counseling in addressing the social and emotional needs of gifted students.

4. Explain the advantages and disadvantages for gifted students of remedial versus developmental counseling in schools.

5. Some believe that if the cognitive (educational) needs of gifted students are met in schools, then their social-emotional needs also are met. Explain your position on this belief.

REFERENCES

Achter, J. A., Benbow, C. P., & Lubinski, D. (1997). Rethinking multipotentiality among the intellectually gifted: A critical review and recommendations. *Gifted Child Quarterly, 41,* 5–15.

Achter, J. A., Lubinski, D., & Benbow, C. P. (1996). Multipotentiality among the intellectually gifted: It was never there and already it's vanishing. *Journal of Counseling Psychology, 43,* 65–76.

American Association for Gifted Children. (1978). *On being gifted.* New York: Walker & Company.

Bloom, B. S. (Ed.). (1985). *Developing talent in young people.* New York: Ballantine Books.

Bloom, B. S., & Sosniak, L. A. (1981). Talent development vs. schooling. *Educational Leadership, 39,* 86–94.

Burks, B. S., Jensen, D. W., & Terman, L. M. (1930). *Genetic studies of genius: Vol. 3. The promise of youth.* Stanford, CA: Stanford University Press.

Cash, A. B. (1999). The profile of gifted individuals with autism: The twice-exceptional learners. *Roeper Review, 22,* 22–27.

Chamrad, D. L., Robinson, N. M., Treder, R., & Janos, P. M. (1995). Consequences of having a gifted sibling: Myths and realities. *Gifted Child Quarterly, 39,* 135–145.

Colangelo, N. (1988). Families of gifted children: The next ten years. *Roeper Review, 11,* 16–18.

Colangelo, N. (1991). Counseling gifted students. In N. Colangelo & G. A. Davis (Eds.), *Handbook of gifted education* (pp. 273–284). Boston: Allyn and Bacon.

Colangelo, N., & Assouline, S. G. (1993). Families of gifted children: A research agenda. *Quest, 4,* 1–4.

Colangelo, N., & Assouline, S. G. (1995). Self-concept of gifted students: Patterns by self-concept, domain, grade level, and gender. In F. J. Monks (Ed.), *Proceedings from the 1994 European council on high ability conference* (pp. 66–74). New York: Wiley.

Colangelo, N., & Assouline, S. G. (2000). Counseling Gifted Students. In K. A. Heller, F. J. Monks, R. J. Sternberg, & R. F. Subotnik (Eds.), *International handbook of giftedness and talent* (2nd ed., pp. 595–607). Amsterdam: Elsevier.

Colangelo, N., & Brower, P. (1987). Labeling gifted youngsters: Long-term impact on families. *Gifted Child Quarterly, 31,* 75–78.

Colangelo, N., & Dettmann, D. F. (1982). A conceptual model of four types of parent-school interactions. *Journal for the Education of the Gifted, 5,* 120–126.

Colangelo, N., & Dettmann, D. F. (1983). A review of research on parents and families of gifted children. *Exceptional Children, 50,* 20–27.

Colangelo, N., & Dettmann, D. F. (1985). Families of gifted children. In S. Ehly, J. Conoly, & D. M. Rosenthal (Eds.), *Working with parents of exceptional children* (pp. 233–255). St. Louis: Mosby.

Colangelo, N., & Kelly, K. R. (1983). A study of student, parent, and teacher attitudes towards gifted programs and gifted students. *Gifted Child quarterly, 27,* 107–110.

Colangelo, N., & Kerr, B. A. (1990). Extreme academic talent: Profiles of perfect scorers. *Journal of Educational Psychology, 82,* 404–409.

Colangelo, N., & Peterson, J. S. (1993). Group counseling with gifted students. In L. S. Silverman (Ed.), *Counseling the gifted and talented* (pp. 111–129). Denver: Love.

Colangelo, N., & Zaffrann, R. T. (Eds.). (1979). *New voices in counseling the gifted.* Dubuque, IA: Kendall/Hunt.

Cornell, D. G., & Grossberg, I. W. (1986). Siblings of children in gifted programs. *Journal for the Education of the Gifted, 9,* 252–264.

Dawes, R. M. (1998). The social usefulness of self-esteem: A skeptical review. *The Harvard Mental Health Letter, 15*(4), 4–5.

Delisle, J. R. (1984). *Gifted children speak out.* New York: Walker.

Delisle, J. R. (1987). *Gifted kids speak out.* Minneapolis: Free Spirit.

Delisle, J. R. (1992). *Guiding the social and emotional development of gifted youth.* New York: Longman.

Dettmann, D. F., & Colangelo, N. (1980). A functional model for counseling parents of gifted students. *Gifted Child Quarterly, 24,* 139–147.

Dowdall, C. B., & Colangelo, N. (1982). Underachieving gifted students: Review and implications. *Gifted Child Quarterly, 26,* 179–184.

Frederickson, R. H., & Rothney, J. W. M. (Eds.). (1972). *Recognizing and assisting multipotential youth.* Columbus, OH: Merrill.

Grenier, M. E. (1985). Gifted children and other siblings. *Gifted Child Quarterly, 29,* 164–167.

Harter, S. (1982). The perceived competence scale for children. *Child Development, 53,* 87–97.

Hoge, R. D., & McSheffrey, R. (1991, December–January). An investigation of self-concept in gifted children. *Exceptional Children,* 238–245.

Hoge, R. D., & Renzulli, J. S. (1993). Exploring the link between giftedness and self-concept. *Review of Educational Research, 63,* 449–465.

Holahan, C. K., & Sears, R. S. (1995). *The gifted group in later maturity.* Stanford, CA: Stanford University Press.

Hollingworth, L. S. (1926). *Gifted children: Their nature and nurture.* New York: Macmillan.

Hollingworth, L. S. (1942). *Children above 180 IQ. Stanford-Binet.* New York: World Book.

Jenkins-Friedman, R. (1992). Families of gifted children and youth. In M. J. Fine & C. Carlson (Eds.), *Handbook of family school interventions: A systems perspective* (pp. 175–187). Boston: Allyn & Bacon.

Karnes, F. A., & Wherry, J. N. (1981). Self-concepts of gifted students as measured by the Piers-Harris children's self-concept scale. *Psychological Reports, 49,* 903–906.

Kaufmann, F. A. (1981). The 1964–1968 Presidential Scholar: A follow-up study. *Exceptional Children, 48,* 164–169.

Kaufmann, F. A., & Castellanos, F. X. (2000). Attention deficit/hyperactivity disorder in gifted students. In K. A. Heller, F. J. Monks, R. J. Sternberg, & R. F. Subotnik (Eds.), *International handbook of giftedness and talent* (2nd ed., pp. 621–633). Amsterdam: Elsevier.

Kelly, K. R., & Colangelo, N. (1984). Academic and social self-concepts of gifted, general, and special students. *Exceptional Children, 50,* 551–554.

Kerr, B. A. (1985). *Smart girls, gifted women.* Columbus, OH: Ohio Psychology Publications.

Kerr, B. A. (1986). Career counseling for the gifted: Assessments and interventions. *Journal of Counseling and Development, 64,* 602–604.

Kerr, B. A. (1991). *Handbook for counseling the gifted and talented.* Alexandria, VA: AACD Press.

Kerr, B. A. (Summer/Fall 1998). Career planning for gifted and talented youth. *Iowa Talented and Gifted Newsletter.*

Kerr, B. A., & Colangelo, N. (1988). The college plans of academically talented students. *Journal of Counseling and Development, 67,* 42–48.

Kerr, B. A., Colangelo, N., & Gaeth, J. (1988). Gifted adolescents' attitudes toward their giftedness. *Gifted Child Quarterly, 32,* 245–247.

Ketcham, B., & Snyder, R. T. (1977). Self-attitudes of the intellectually and socially advantaged student: Normative study of the Piers-Harris children's self-concept scale. *Psychological Reports, 40,* 111–116.

Loeb, R. C., & Jay, G. (1987). Self concept in gifted children: Differential impact in boys and girls. *Gifted Child Quarterly, 1,* 9–14.

Maddux, C. D., Scheiber, L. M., & Bass, J. E. (1982). Self-concept and social distance in gifted children. *Gifted Child Quarterly, 26,* 77–81.

Marsh, H. W. (1990). A multidimensional, hierarchical model of self-concept: Theoretical and empirical justification. *Educational Psychology Review, 2,* 77–172.

Marsh, H. W. (1992). Content specificity of relations between academic achievement and academic self-concept. *Journal of Educational Psychology, 84,* 35–42.

Marsh, H. W. (1993). The multidimensional structure of academic self-concept: Invariance over gender and age. *American Educational Research Journal, 30,* 841–860.

Marsh, H. W. (1994). Using the national longitudinal study of 1988 to evaluate theoretical models of self-concept: The self-description questionnaire. *Journal of Educational Psychology, 86,* 439–456.

McGuire, W. J. (1984). Search for self: Going beyond self-esteem and reactive self. In R. A. Zucher, J. Arnoff, & A. I. Rubin (Eds.), *Personality and the prediction of behavior* (pp. 73–120). New York: Academic Press.

Monaster, G. J., Chan, J. C., Walt, C., & Wiehe, J. (1994). Gifted adolescents' attitudes toward their giftedness: A partial replication. *Gifted Child Quarterly, 38,* 176–178.

Moon, S. M., & Hall, A. S. (1998). Family therapy with intellectually and creatively gifted children. *Journal of Marital and Family Therapy, 24,* 59–80.

Moon, S. M., & Dillon, D. R. (1995). Multiple exceptionalities: A case study. *Journal for the Education of the Gifted, 18,* 111–130.

Myers, R. S., & Pace, T. M. (1986). Counseling gifted and talented students: Historical perspectives and contemporary issues. *Journal of Counseling and Development, 64,* 548–551.

Neihart, M. (1999). The import of giftedness and psychological well-being: What does the empirical literature say? *Roeper Review, 22,* 10–17.

Neihart, M., & Robinson, N. (2001). *Task force on social-emotional issues for gifted students.* Washington, DC: National Association for Gifted Children.

Nurius, P. S. (1986). Reappraisal of the self-concept and implications for counseling. *Journal of Counseling Psychology, 33,* 429–438.

Peterson, J. S., & Colangelo, N. (1996). Gifted achievers and underachievers: A comparison of patterns found in school files. *Journal of Counseling and Development, 74,* 399–407.

Plucker, J. A., & Stocking, V. B. (2001). Looking outside and inside: Self-concept development of gifted adolescents. *Exceptional Children, 67*(4), 535–548.

Reis, S. (Winter 1998). Underachieving for some: Dropping out with dignity for others. *Communicator, 29*(1). Newsletter of the California Association for the Gifted.

Rogers, C. R. (1951). *Client-centered therapy.* Boston: Houghton-Mifflin.

Rysiew, K. J., Shore, B. M., & Carson, A. D. (1994). Multipotentiality and overchoice syndrome: Clarifying common usage. *Gifted and Talented International, 9*(2), 41–46.

Rysiew, K. J., Shore, B. M., & Leeb, R. T. (1998). Multipotentiality, giftedness and career choices: A review. *Journal of Counseling & Development, 77,* 423–430.

Sajjadi, S. H., Rejskind, F. G., & Shore, B. M. (2001). Is multipotentiality a problem or not? A new look at the data. *High Ability Studies, 12*(1), 27–43.

Shavelson, R. J., Hubner, J. J., & Stanton, G. C. (1976). Validation of construct interpretations. *Review of Educational Research, 46,* 407–441.

Snygg, D., & Combs, A. W. (1949). *Individual behaviors: A perceptual approach to behavior* (rev. ed.). New York: Harper.

St. Clair, K. L. (1989). Counseling gifted students: A historical review. *Roeper Review, 12,* 98–102.

Terman, L. M. (1925). *Genetic studies of genius (Vol. 1). Mental and physical traits of a thousand gifted children.* Stanford, CA: Stanford University Press.

Terman, L. M., & Oden, M. H. (1947). *Genetic studies of genius (Vol. 4). The gifted child grows up.* Stanford, CA: Stanford University Press.

Terman, L. M., & Oden, M. H. (1959). *Genetic studies of genius (Vol. 5). The gifted group at mid-life.* Stanford, CA: Stanford University Press.

Webb, J. T., Meckstroth, E. A., & Tolan, S. S. (1982). *Guiding the gifted child.* Columbus, OH: Ohio Psychology Press.

Wendorf, D. J., & Frey, J. (1985). Family therapy with intellectually gifted. *American Journal of Family Therapy, 13,* 31–37.

Whitmore, J. (1980). *Giftedness, conflict, and underachievement.* Boston: Allyn & Bacon.

Wylie, R. C. (1989). *Measures of self-concept.* Lincoln: University of Nebraska Press.

Yalom, I. D. (1985). *Theory and practice of group psychotherapy* (3rd ed.). New York: Basic Books.

Zentall, S. S., Moon, S. M., Hall, A. M., & Grskovic, J. A. (2001). Learning and motivational characteristics of boys with AD/HS and/or giftedness. *Exceptional Children, 67*(4), 499–519.

30

Counseling Families

SIDNEY M. MOON, *Purdue University*

The purpose of this chapter is to describe two types of family counseling for families of gifted children and adolescents: *parent guidance* and *family therapy*. These two categories of family counseling differ from each other in their theoretical orientation and purpose. I use the same pattern in describing each of the two types of family counseling. First, I describe the orientation and mental health disciplines associated with the counseling modality. Next, I describe the presenting problems that are most common with each type of family counseling. Finally, I discuss representative counseling models and strategies that have been used when counselors from each tradition are working with families of gifted children.

It is important to note that, in spite of repeated calls for more research on family issues (Colangelo, 1988; Moon, Kelly, & Feldhusen, 1997), neither type of family counseling has been extensively researched. Indeed, most of the literature on family counseling is characterized by informal clinical reports, case studies, and theoretical speculation. Hence, the material that follows is better grounded in clinical theory and practice than in empirical research.

Parent Guidance

There are several fields associated with parent guidance, including school counseling, school psychology, and career development. Most of these areas have a developmental perspective, rather than a therapeutic one. Practitioners are interested in fostering optimal development as much as, or more than, in diagnosing and correcting mental health problems. Their orientation is closer to that of educators than to

that of physicians. They are teachers rather than healers, guides and consultants instead of therapists. These fields have a heavy emphasis on assessment as a precursor, or prerequisite, to guidance interventions. They are oriented toward youth, rather than adults. They are focused on prevention of social/emotional problems through timely, early intervention. The most commonly used model in this type of counseling is assessment of individual traits and characteristics followed by interpretation of test results with recommendations for future action.

Applications to Families of Gifted Children

Presenting Problems. Counselors from the guidance traditions who work with families of gifted children most commonly address (a) school issues (Colangelo & Dettmann, 1983; Dettmann & Colangelo, 1980); (b) parenting concerns (Keirouz, 1990; Moon, Jurich, & Feldhusen, 1998); (c) and social/emotional development. In addition, family relationships have been addressed in the guidance literature on families of the gifted (see, e.g., Colangelo, 1988). However, presenting problems related to family relationships will be addressed here in the section on family therapy because family therapists specialize in working with relationships.

School Issues. Several surveys have indicated that school issues are a major concern for parents of gifted students (Alsop, 1997; Feldhusen & Kroll, 1985; Hackney, 1981; Moon et al., 1997). Many parents of academically talented children are confused about their role with the schools and uncertain about how to advocate appropriate educational services for their child (Colangelo & Dettmann, 1983; Hackney, 1981).

Early in their child's school career, parents may have high expectations of schools and feel disappointed and frustrated when those expectations are not met (Alsop, 1997; Feldhusen & Kroll, 1985). For example, a survey of 42 parents of young children (mean age = 6.9 years) who scored above IQ 130 (mean = 150) on the Stanford Binet L-M revealed that 61.7% expected their child to have a special teacher and 51.1% expected special classes, yet the most common opportunity the schools actually offered to their children was extensions of learning in the normal classroom (Alsop, 1997). Similarly, a survey of 385 parents whose children attended a Saturday enrichment program offered by a university revealed that 42% of parents of preschoolers, 47% of parents of children in grades 1–6, and 53% of parents of youth in grades 7–12 felt their children's needs were not being met in school (Feldhusen & Kroll, 1985). The unmet needs that parents perceived were academic rather than social. For example, at the elementary level 61.1% of parents felt their child's intellectual needs were not met, but only 15.2% felt their child's social needs were suffering. Clearly, many parents of gifted students do not believe their child is receiving an appropriate education in school.

Colangelo and Dettmann (1981) developed a conceptual model of types of parent-school interactions.[1] Their model predicts parental stress and conflict in situations where parent and school beliefs about gifted education differ. For example, conflict is likely when schools believe that the typical school curriculum is adequate to meet the needs of a gifted child but parents believe that special programming should be provided. Parents in this situation either advocate for gifted education services, feel that they themselves must provide the special programming their child needs, or develop feelings of hopelessness and powerlessness. All of these situations can be stressful for parents. A different type of conflict between parents and schools occurs when schools actively attempt to provide programs for gifted children, but parents resist because of value conflicts, discomfort with labeling, or unresolved issues related to their own giftedness (Colangelo & Dettmann, 1981; Ford, 1996). When school and parent beliefs are not congruent, school issues are likely to be the primary presenting problem in guidance work with parents of gifted children.

Parenting Concerns. Empirical research has documented that parents of gifted children have special concerns related to their child's giftedness (for a review, see Keirouz, 1990). A survey of 335 parents, school personnel, and counseling professionals indicated that all three groups of respondents felt that parents of gifted students need specialized guidance services (Moon et al., 1997). In an informal study of the effects of gifted children on families, Hackney (1981) found five areas of unique concern among parents: roles, self-views, family adaptations, neighborhood/community influences, and family-school interactions. Because of their child's precocity, the parents he interviewed had difficulty clarifying the differences between parental and child roles. They also felt anxiety, guilt, and pressure related to the responsibility of helping their talented child to actualize his or her potential. Similarly, a study of parents of gifted adolescents found that these parents felt very strong teaching responsibilities (Strom, Strom, Strom, & Collinsworth, 1994). The pressures these parents feel have some basis in reality, since several longitudinal studies have confirmed the importance of the family context in enabling gifted children to actualize their talents (Bloom, 1985; Csikszentmihalyi, Rathunde, & Whalen, 1993; Freeman, 2000).

It is important to keep in mind, however, that the concerns and pressures experienced by parents of gifted children are influenced by cultural contexts. For example, Chinese parents tend to feel great shame when their gifted child underachieves in school (Hsueh & Moon, 1998). In contrast, parents of some African American children in the United States can be threatened by high achievement, because they perceive that school achievement will draw their child away from family and community (Exum, 1983).

Social/Emotional Development. Finally, parents may seek counseling because they are concerned about their child's social and emotional development. Indeed, when parents, teachers, and counseling professionals were asked about the unique counseling needs of gifted students, all felt that gifted children had unique issues related to peer relationships, emotional adjustment, social adjustment, and stress management—issues that could be addressed by specialized counseling services (Moon et al., 1997). Although comparison studies using global measures of adjustment tend to show that gifted students are at least as well adjusted as their nongifted peers

---

1. See Chapter 29 by Colangelo.

(Neihart, 1999), some clinicians have found that their gifted clients have unique social or emotional issues related to characteristics such as asynchronous development, which can be addressed through developmental counseling (Mahoney, 1997; Silverman, 1993b; Silverman, 1993c). Parents of gifted children may also benefit from differentiated, preventative counseling focused on helping them help their child cope with stressors unique to giftedness (Baker, 1996; Genshaft, Greenbaum, & Borovksky, 1995; Hayes & Levitt, 1982; Silverman, 1993e).

Parent Guidance Counseling Models

Several university centers and a handful of clinicians specializing in work with gifted individuals have developed models for guidance work with parents of gifted children. Most such models include three components: (a) an assessment of the child's types and levels of academic abilities; (b) interpretation of the assessment; and (c) recommendations for parenting and school programming. Some models include additional components, such as advocacy with schools or a focus on social and emotional development. Three examples of parent guidance counseling models are described below.

Silverman's Developmental Model

Silverman (1993d) suggested a comprehensive developmental model for counseling the gifted that includes work with parents of gifted children, especially parents of young gifted children who are highly gifted. In this model, the gifted individual is seen as a complex, evolving system, and counseling with parents is focused on helping them provide a supportive environment for their child's process of self-actualization, as well as on preventing problems that can occur when the unique characteristics of gifted individuals are not understood. The goal is to facilitate optimal development, and the counseling model focuses as much on moral values, such as altruism and contribution to society, as it does on creativity and achievement.

When working with families, Silverman (1991, 1993a) analyzes parent concerns according to the support systems in her model. However, in her family counseling work the "self" component of her model is divided into two parts: the child and the parent. This enables her to deal separately with the giftedness and development of the child and the parents' own giftedness and development. More specifically, in her work with families she focuses on the following concerns:

1. Assessment of the child's giftedness and motivation;
2. Parental perceptions of competence, family relationships, provision of stimulation, and fostering of self-discipline;
3. School concerns such as grade placement and working with school personnel;
4. Peer relationships;
5. Information about community resources; and
6. Parental development, that is, counseling parents to help them understand their own giftedness and further their own development

This model is most appropriate for implementation by psychologists in private practice, because it is comprehensive and individualized.

The Counseling Center in Hamburg

The Hamburg counseling center began work in 1985 and has focused on parents of gifted children who are underachieving and/or have behavior problems (Wieczerkowski & Prado, 1991). The center focuses on five key tasks:

1. Giving diagnostic information, counseling, and guidance to parents and students on educational and psychological problems associated with giftedness;
2. Helping regular classroom teachers plan differentiated accommodations when confronted with behavioral difficulties of gifted children;
3. Providing information to parents;
4. Planning and carrying out seminars and courses for psychologists and teachers; and
5. Providing information to pediatricians and child guidance centers.

When working with parents, center staff first request parents to complete a background questionnaire. Then parents and children attend an initial intake session. During this session, the child is interviewed and assessed separately from the parents.

The rest of the counseling procedures are based on the results of the assessment. If the child is potentially gifted (IQ > 130), center staff provide parental guidance based on parental values and attitudes. For example, if the parents are trying to hold their child back or are having difficulty accepting their child's giftedness, they focus on providing the parent with information about the special needs of gifted children. If, on the other hand, the parents have accepted their child's special needs and are willing to support special measures to meet those needs, they make recommendations for how to do so. The most frequent concerns mentioned by parents at this center stem from school issues, that is, their child experiences boredom and lack of challenge at school, which reduces the child's motivation and/or creates social/emotional problems (Wieczerkowski & Prado, 1991). This center has developed detailed flow charts to guide their counseling process (see Figures 30.1, 30.2, and 30.3).

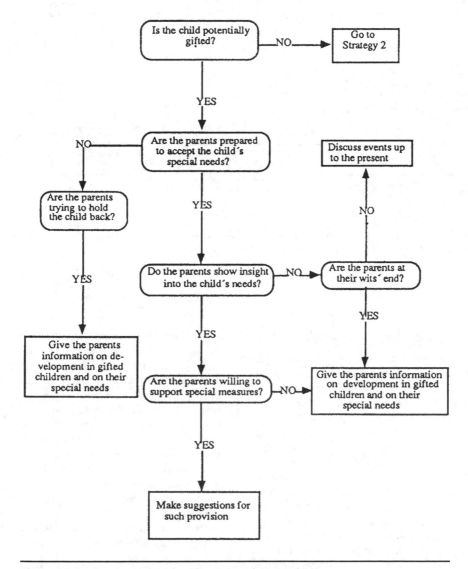

Figure 30.1 Strategy 1 for identification and counseling.

Source: From Wieczerkowski and Prado, 1991. Reprinted by permission of Taylor & Francis, Ltd., London *(http://www.tandf.co.uk/journals).*

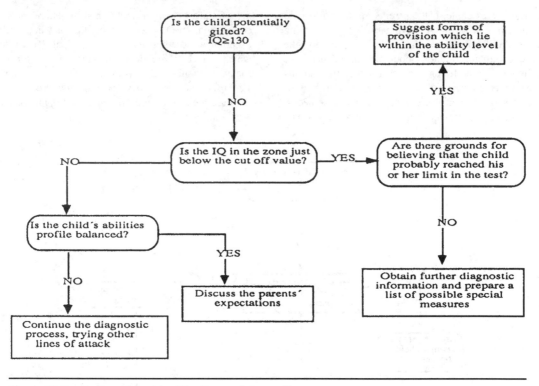

Figure 30.2 Strategy 2 for identification and counseling.

Source: From Wieczerkowski and Prado, 1991. Reprinted by permission of Taylor & Francis, Ltd., London *(http://www.tandf.co.uk/journals).*

Ball State School Psychology Clinic

The Ball State model (Gridley, 2001) was developed to provide comprehensive assessments of gifted students and assist parents in advocating for appropriate school services. It was implemented by school psychologists in training. Typically, evaluations of students spanned at least two days and took several hours. The evaluation consisted of a parent intake/interview and feedback as well as testing the students.

The test battery was individualized based on the age of the students, the referral issues, and concerns expressed by parents on the Background Information Questionnaire. The number of tests completed for each student ranged from five to twenty with a mean of ten. The most common number (the mode) of tests given was eight. All students were assessed for intelligence, achievement, learning styles, personality, and behavior. Some received specialized assessments such as continuous performance, projective, and/or memory tests.

Comprehensive written reports were completed for all evaluations. The clinic supervisor read every report and provided suggestions for changes and recommendations before giving feedback to parents. Feedback typically consisted of an interview with parents to explain the testing and provide recommendations. These recommendations ranged from suggestions for curriculum compacting and differentiation of programming to referral for individual counseling. Parents were also provided with sources and contacts in response to individual concerns. For most students tested, appropriate feedback and conferencing at the school was also completed. Some schools required more than one conference in order to provide appropriate programming.

Family Therapy

The field of family therapy is grounded in systems theory (Whitchurch & Constantine, 1993). Hence,

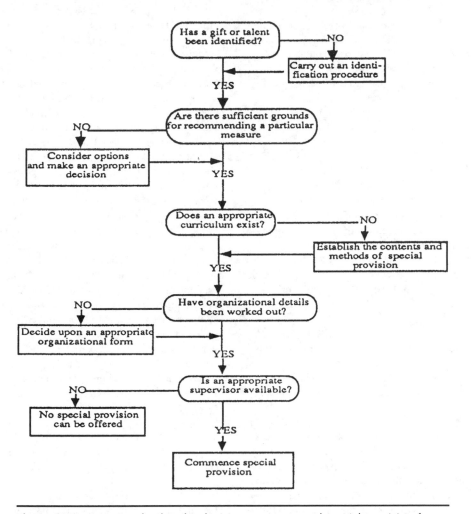

Figure 30.3 Steps involved in the decision to recommend special provision for the gifted.

Source: From Wieczerkowski and Prado, 1991. Reprinted by permission of Taylor & Francis, Ltd., London *(http://www.tandf.co.uk/journals).*

family therapists are interactionists. They see family problems as situated in the interactions among members of a family rather than in particular family members. In addition, they view causality as circular and reciprocal rather than as linear. For example, they are as interested in the way children affect parents as in the ways that parents influence their children.

In recent years, several writers have encouraged the application of systems thinking and family therapy to family-school interactions (Fine & Carlson, 1992) and counseling with families of gifted children

(Frey & Wendorf, 1985; Moon & Hall, 1998), but only a handful of individuals have made systematic attempts to differentiate family therapy for families of gifted children (Colangelo & Assouline, 2000; Wendorf & Frey, 1985). This may be because very few family therapists have been trained to work with families of the gifted (Moon & Hall, 1998). Alternatively, the fact that many families of gifted students are high functioning (Friedman, 1994) may account for the neglect. Historically, family therapists have focused on severe disorders, such as schizophrenia, and on low SES, multi-problem families, rather than on preventative counseling with functional, high SES families coping with unique stressors. Whatever the reason for the lack of attention to families of gifted children, the neglect is unfortunate because family therapy holds much promise as a counseling modality for families of gifted children.

Applications to Families of Gifted Children

Developmental Issues. All of the developmental presenting problems discussed in the section on parent guidance (parenting concerns, school issues, and social/emotional development) can be addressed by family therapists, although family therapy is not necessarily the approach of choice for these issues. Strengths of family therapists in addressing these concerns include (a) excellent understanding of family dynamics; (b) familiarity with principles of effective parenting; and (c) creative and complex counseling strategies.

The primary weaknesses of family therapists as primary preventative counselors for families of gifted children is that they usually do not receive extensive training in cognitive assessment or school issues. Since these are often the primary concerns of parents of gifted children, family therapists who wish to provide counseling for such families either need to seek additional training in these areas or to team up with professionals who have such training. They will, of course, also need to develop expertise in giftedness and the ways that giftedness impacts both the family system and social/emotional development (Coleman & Cross, 2000; Hsueh & Moon, 1998; Moon et al., 1998).

Family Relationships and Family Transitions. In contrast, family therapy is an excellent approach to family counseling when presenting problems involve family relationships or family transitions. As might be expected, family interactions and relationships have a strong influence on the social and emotional adjustment of gifted children (Sowa & May, 1997). Positive social and emotional adjustment and academic achievement are much more likely when family relationships are functional, that is, when the family environment balances a sense of belonging with encouragement of individual interests, identity, and autonomy (Csikszentmihalyi et al., 1993; Rathunde, 1996; Sowa & May, 1997). Family therapists are trained to help families create such positive

climates. Therefore, family therapy is recommended whenever environments are dysfunctional.

Sibling relationships can also benefit from family therapy, even when the overall family climate is positive, because there is evidence in the literature that sibling relationships can be influenced by giftedness. For example, labeling one child "gifted" can impact sibling relationships, perceptions, and experiences (Colangelo & Brower, 1987; Cornell & Grossberg, 1986; Grenier, 1985). In addition, when children perceive that they are more gifted than siblings in an area critical to parents, children may begin to suppress giftedness because of guilt feelings or loyalty conflicts (Glenn, 1995). Family therapists are trained to identify such systemic effects and could help families where giftedness has had a negative impact on sibling relationships.

In addition, family therapy can be helpful for functional families experiencing life cycle transitions. For example, there is evidence that the transition to adolescence can be difficult for families with a gifted child (Moon, Nelson, & Piercy, 1993). Although divorce and remarriage are common today, very little is known about how divorce, remarriage, or single parenting affect gifted children (Gelbrich & Kare, 1989; Rogers & Nielson, 1993). Family therapists receive extensive training in strategies for assisting families in coping with transitions, so it seems reasonable to assume that they could help families of gifted children cope effectively with the inevitable stresses associated with changes in family structure.

Underachievement. Family therapy has also been recommended when the presenting problem is the underachievement of a gifted child (Moon & Hall, 1998; Thomas, 1999; Zuccone & Amerikaner, 1986). Underachievement of gifted students in school is a complex phenomenon that can involve individual, home, and school factors, and usually involves factors from all three systems (Baker, Bridger, & Evans, 1998; Moon & Hall, 1998; Peters, Grager-Loidl, & Supplee, 2000; Reis & McCoach, 2000). *Individual factors* include low self-esteem, anxiety, impulsivity, depression, fears of failure or success, maladaptive attributional patterns, and poor self-regulation (Reis & McCoach, 2000). *School factors* include inappropriate curricula, learning style mismatches, teacher personalities, low teacher expectations, lack of teacher training in gifted education, punitive grading practices, and peers with negative school attitudes (Peters et al., 2000). *Family factors* associated with underachievement include conflict, disorganization, inconsistent parenting, permissive and/or authoritarian parenting styles, and parental devaluing of school and work (Reis & McCoach, 2000; Rimm, 1997; Rimm & Lowe, 1988).

Underachievement is not always associated with family dysfunction (Green, Fine, & Tollefson, 1988). In addition, it is unclear whether the family dysfunction that is sometimes associated with underachievement is a cause or an effect (Reis & McCoach, 2000). It may be that individual characteristics associated with underachievers, such as immaturity and aggression, create dysfunction in the family systems, as is often the case in families of children with AD/HD (Barkley, 1990).

Given the complexity of underachievement, interventions must be equally complex. As a result, there is debate in the literature about whether family therapy alone can be effective intervention for underachievement. Some recommend that interventions for underachievement simultaneously target all three systems. Rimm's TRIFOCAL model is an example of this approach (Rimm, 1995, 1997). Among those who advocate family counseling as a primary modality for intervening with underachievement, some contend that it is best to use a parent guidance model that encourages parent-school partnerships (Fine & Pitts, 1980). Others feel that the decision about which family counseling modality to use should depend on an initial assessment of the relative contribution of school and family factors. For example, Wendorf and Frey (1985) categorized families as either "problem families" or "clinical families." Problem families were marginally functional families that were overwhelmed by a poor school situation. These families received services like those described in the parent guidance models above, that is, assessment followed by conjoint sessions with school personnel to improve the child's school programming. Clinical families, on the other hand, were families with dysfunctional interaction patterns. These families were treated by Wendorf and Frey with structural-strategic family therapy.

There are also examples of effective family therapy with families that Wendorf and Frey would categorize as "problem" or nonclinical. For example, Thomas (1999) describes a creative application of narrative therapy to the case of a highly gifted boy who suddenly began underachieving, as well as developing social and behavior problems in the sixth grade. In this intriguing case, the narrative therapy

strategy of "externalizing the problem" (White & Epston, 1990) was used to interrupt dysfunctional patterns in both the individual and family systems. No work was done directly with the school system, yet positive changes in the child's behavior at school (as a result of the family therapy) led his English teacher to individualize her curriculum for him. This suggests that it may be possible to reverse underachievement through intervention with the family system even when the school system is involved in the etiology of the underachievement.

In summary, there is clearly a place for family therapy in interventions with underachieving gifted children and their families. However, more work needs to be done to determine how family therapy can be used most effectively with this population.

Twice-Exceptional Children. Families commonly seek therapy for children who are both gifted and disabled (Moon & Hall, 1998). Gifted children with cognitive and behavioral disabilities are often misunderstood both at home and at school (e.g., Moon, Zentall, Grskovic, Hall, & Stormont, 2001; Reis, Neu, & McGuire, 1997; Zentall, Moon, Hall, & Grskovic, in press). Their superior intellect combined with their inability to perform in one or more areas makes them vulnerable to social and emotional problems. Their families often feel helpless and frustrated. Parenting a twice-exceptional child is a challenge. To work effectively with families of children with neurological disabilities, family therapists need to be knowledgeable about both giftedness and the disability. Unfortunately, little work has been done to develop specific therapeutic approaches for families of gifted children with cognitive and behavioral disabilities, so little is known about the approaches and interventions that might be most effective.

The same is true for other populations of twice-exceptional children and adolescents. For example, although family therapists are trained to work with sexual issues, including gay and lesbian individuals/couples, no studies of family therapy with gifted adolescent gay, lesbian, or bisexual youth have yet been conducted. This is unfortunate, because a retrospective study of the adolescent experiences of eighteen gay, lesbian, or bisexual young adults with high ability found significant themes of danger, isolation, depression, and suicidal ideation (Peterson & Rischar, 2000). The "coming out" process was especially difficult for these individuals, so difficult that most (72%) did not do so until after they left home.

In addition, only 33% of the parents of the participants in this study were perceived as supportive of their child's sexual orientation. This strongly suggests that family therapy is warranted during the coming out period for gay, lesbian, and bisexual youth, even if the coming out process occurs during the young adult years.

Child Internalizing and Externalizing Disorders. Family therapy is also strongly recommended whenever gifted children or adolescents have emotional or behavioral disorders, both to determine the extent to which the problems might be related to family dynamics and to involve families in treatment. Again, however, no research has been conducted on family therapy with gifted individuals with mental health problems, so it is not clear whether such therapy needs to be differentiated for the child's giftedness (May, 2000). In case studies reported in the family therapy literature, high intelligence is sometimes noted as a characteristic of one or more clients (see, e.g., Conoley, 1987; Guerney & Guerney, 1989; Taichert, 1979). However, such case reports generally do not indicate that the therapy was differentiated because of the client's giftedness. It seems likely that therapy, like instruction, would be even more effective with gifted individuals if therapists differentiated their therapeutic approach to address the characteristics of gifted youth and their families.

Indeed, preliminary work at one university-based family therapy center suggests that not only is such differentiation needed, it may be a necessity (Bordeaux, 2001). Bordeaux found that mismatches in expectations between families of gifted children and therapists using a systemic, resource-based, postmodern approach to family therapy had to be made explicit and negotiated before therapy could proceed. This study suggests that programmatic, empirical research is needed to determine when and how family therapy should be differentiated for families of gifted youth.

Family Therapy Models

There are no empirically tested models to guide family therapy with families of gifted children. However, there are a few family therapists with expertise in giftedness who have published brief reports of their work with families of gifted children (Colangelo, 1997; Colangelo & Assouline, 1993; Frey &

Wendorf, 1985; Wendorf & Frey, 1985) and case studies of strategies that were effective with particular client families (Moon et al., 1993; Thomas, 1995, 1999). The work of these scientist-practitioners will be discussed in three categories: (a) systemic approaches, (b) postmodern approaches, and (c) integrated approaches.

Systemic Approaches

Belin-Blank Center Family Counseling and Assessment Program. The staff of the Connie Belin and Jacqueline N. Blank International Center for Gifted Education and Talent Development have developed a brief family therapy model for addressing relationship issues in families of gifted students (Colangelo, 1997; Colangelo & Assouline, 1993, 2000). The model is strength-based. It focuses on helping families identify their own strengths so they can solve their own problems. It is also brief. The counseling lasts a maximum of five to six sessions. Family dynamics are assessed using the Family Adaptability and Cohesion Evaluation Scales III (Olson, Portner, & Lavee, 1985) and the Family Environment Scale (Moos & Moos, 1994). In addition, self-concepts of all children in the family are assessed, using the Piers-Harris Children's Self-Concept Scale (Piers, 1984).

The Family FIRO model (Doherty & Colangelo, 1984; Doherty, Colangelo, Green, & Hoffman, 1985; Doherty, Colangelo, & Hovander, 1991) is used to conceptualize presenting problems and organize treatment (Colangelo & Assouline, 1993). According to the Family FIRO model, family issues can be categorized into a hierarchy of inclusion, control, and intimacy. When families present with issues in more than one of these categories, the hierarchy is followed. For example, if issues of inclusion are present, they are addressed before issues of control or intimacy. This model is implemented with families of gifted children in a family counseling program at the Belin-Blank Center that serves as a practicum for advanced doctoral students. Preliminary results suggest the model is very effective in helping practicum students prioritize issues when a family presents multiple issues. Also, the model has been effective in developing family counseling treatment plans.

Structural-Strategic Approaches. Several family therapists have reported success using traditional, structural-strategic family therapy interventions with families of gifted children (Conoley, 1987; Moon et al., 1993; Taichert, 1979; Wendorf & Frey, 1985; Zuccone & Amerikaner, 1986). Structural-strategic models of family therapy view the family as a system and social/emotional problems as residing in the family system, rather than in individual family members (Whitchurch & Constantine, 1993). Therapists who use this approach focus on assessing and changing family interaction patterns (Haley, 1988; Minuchin, 1974; Minuchin & Fishman, 1981; Piercy & Wetchler, 1996; Watzlawick, Weakland, & Fisch, 1974). The most detailed model of structural-strategic family therapy with families of the gifted comes from the work of Wendorf and Frey (1985) in the mid-1980s. This researcher-clinician team conducted a study of family dynamics in families of the gifted and developed a structural-strategic intervention model for working with such families.

Their clinical model began with a two-pronged assessment process (Wendorf & Frey, 1985). First, the gifted child's academic history was assessed with test scores, records of past achievement, and a clinical interview addressing current school programming and home-school relationships. This interview sometimes occurred at the school. Next, family dynamics were assessed with structural-strategic interview strategies that enabled the therapist to assess various aspects of the functioning of the family system including boundaries, hierarchy, subsystem functioning, and the family's developmental position in the family life cycle. Boundaries are invisible lines of demarcation around the family as a whole and/or subsets of family members (e.g., mother-father, father-daughter, etc., Piercy & Wetchler, 1996). Boundaries range from disengaged (little connection) to enmeshed (too close), with the most functional types providing a dynamic balance between closeness and autonomy (see also Csikszentmihalyi et al., 1993). One of the ways families become unhealthy is when two or more family members align themselves against a third. Hence, alignments are assessed in structural-strategic family therapy. Hierarchy is a boundary that separates the leader(s) of a system from system members (Piercy & Wetchler, 1996). In a family, it is usually optimal if parents are higher in the hierarchy, yet this optimal order can easily be reversed in families with gifted children who "parentify," that is, are given, or seek, too much parental-level authority. Hence, hierarchy is particularly important to assess in families with gifted children. At the conclusion of the clinical assessment

phase, families were divided into two categories: (a) problem families whose primary problem was between the home and school systems (b) clinical families whose primary problem was considered to be internal family dysfunctional based on the assessment of family system characteristics.

The problem families received parental guidance counseling similar to that described in the first half of this paper, with attention given to establishing appropriate subsystem boundaries and expectations. The clinical families received structural-strategic family therapy of varying durations from brief therapy (three to four sessions) to extended therapy (twenty or more sessions over several years). In general, these therapists began working with dysfunctional families of the gifted children, using structural family therapy techniques. Structural family therapists are not talk therapists. They are action and drama therapists. They work with entire families so they can see family interaction patterns acted out spontaneously in the therapy room and then intervene to change those patterns. Structural therapists usually initially join with the family using conversation about their problems, empathy, and metaphors to help the family feel understood and to accept the therapist as part of the family system. Then the therapist sets up "enactments," that is, conditions designed provoke family members into displaying their typical dysfunctional patterns of interaction in the therapy room. This stage of the therapy is often uncomfortable for clients, but it allows the therapist to see the interactional patterns and to coach the family directly on how to change those patterns, often bringing about rapid change. Family members see and experience different ways to interact, rather than just being told about them. In addition, after joining is complete, structural-strategic therapists use paradoxical, strategic techniques to help the family see their stuck patterns and to undo their defenses against change. One example of a paradoxical intervention is prescribing the symptom, that is, the therapist asks the family members to do more of the very thing they want to stop. Wendorf and Frey (1985) reported that these action-oriented techniques circumvented both intellectualizing tendencies and irrational beliefs and fears among their dysfunctional families with gifted children. They concluded that "these families' intellectualizing patterns may immobilize the family." They recommended "more action-oriented and/or strategic-based interventions . . . when this occurs" (Wendorf & Frey, 1985, p. 37).

Figure 30.4 Overview of three phases of treatment.

PHASE I: ASSESSMENT

Session	Type	Theoretical Framework	Intervention/Topics
1	F	Structural-Strategic	Initial interview protocol Observation
2	F	Family Life Cycle	Genogram Observation

PHASE II: TREATMENT

3	F	Family Life Cycle	Family history I
4	I	Talent Development	Peer relationships Interest assessment
5	F	Family Life Cycle	Family history II Griefwork
6	F	Family Life Cycle	Developmental stress Adolescence
7	F	Family Life Cycle	Developmental stress Adolescence
8	F	Structural-Strategic	Structural mapping
9	I	Talent Development	Satisfaction wheel Interest assessment
10	C	Structural-Strategic	Parenting team Letting go Communication skills
11	I	Talent Development	Walk through the day
12	C	Structural-Strategic	No violence contract Parenting team Letting go
13	I	Talent Development	Annoying behaviors
14	F	Structural-Strategic	Sequence tracking No violence contract
15	I	Talent Development	Graduation

PHASE III: TERMINATION/FOLLOW-UP

16	F	Structural-Strategic	Follow-up to #14
17	C	Structural-Strategic	Parenting team Letting go
18	F	Termination	Graduation

From Moon, Nelson, and Piercy. (1993). Reprinted by permission of The Hayworth Press.

KEY:

F = Family
C = Couple
I = Individual (Randy)

Imaginative, Postmodern Approaches. The primary proponent of postmodern approaches to family therapy has been Volker Thomas at Purdue University (Thomas, 1995; 1999). Thomas agrees that the intellectualizing tendencies of gifted families need to be circumvented, but proposes using fairy tales (Thomas, 1995) and creative narrative therapy strategies (Thomas, 1999) to do so. He feels that these imaginative and strength-based strategies fully utilize the creative resources of families of the gifted. For example, Thomas (1999) reported success using narrative therapy with the family of a highly gifted (IQ 165) and very creative boy who experienced a dramatic plunge into underachievement and social rejection in the sixth grade. David had developed a habit of rapid monologues that led others to tune him out, which in turn led David either to withdraw, feeling bad about himself, or to start fights with his peers. His parents felt helpless.

After traditional talk therapy was unsuccessful with this family, the therapist used a combination of play and narrative therapies to break the pattern. First, the therapist asked the family to give the destructive pattern a name. They decided to call it "the family bane." Then the therapists asked David to pick a toy that could represent "the family bane." David picked a rubber Dr. Seuss figure. This externalized the problem, a core narrative family therapy technique. The next step was to use the externalized object to interrupt the pattern. This was accomplished by having the "family bane" become a consultant to David, that is, come up with creative ideas that would keep David out of trouble both at home and at school. Over a period of weeks, these "consultations" were successful in mobilizing the creative resources of David and his family to solve their own problems.

Integrated Approaches. Therapists with training in both family therapy and giftedness are able to develop integrated approaches to therapy that combine the approaches of family therapy, parent guidance, and talent development psychology. For example, Moon et al. (1993) reported an eclectic approach to therapy with the family of a highly gifted adolescent that faced adjustment difficulties at home and school following a family move. The therapy in this case integrated structural-strategic family therapy, family life cycle therapy, and talent development counseling. The therapy included eighteen sessions with the three phases woven together throughout the therapeutic process (see Figure 30.4).

Structural-strategic therapy was used to join with the family, map and interrupt dysfunctional family interactions, adjust family boundaries, and improve the functioning of the parental and sibling subsystems. Family life cycle therapy was used to help the family process and adapt to stresses created by their recent move and young adolescence. Talent development strategies mobilized the gifted adolescent to continue to develop his abilities in his new environment. Integrated approaches are particularly appropriate when presenting problems are complex and involve individual, family, and school issues. Integrated approaches can be implemented by therapists, like myself, who have training in both family therapy and gifted education or by collaborative teams of therapists representing different disciplines.

SUMMARY AND CONCLUSIONS

Clearly, family counseling can benefit families of gifted children in many situations. Healthy families whose children are not receiving appropriate educational services can be helped by guidance counselors who are skilled at facilitating collaborative parent-school relationships. Parents of young highly gifted children who are uncertain or insecure in their roles as parents of an exceptional child need preventative family counseling. Families that are struggling with life cycle transitions, moves, or family conflict can benefit from family therapy, as can families of gifted children with emotional and behavioral disorders. Given the benefits that can accrue to families of gifted children from these various types of family counseling, there is a tremendous need for counseling professionals of all types to receive training in working with gifted and talented individuals. In addition, programmatic, empirical research is needed to determine how family counseling work should be differentiated for families of high ability youth, and which family counseling strategies are most effective with particular presenting problems.

QUESTIONS FOR THOUGHT AND DISCUSSION

1. Explain the difference between parent guidance and family therapy.

2. Imagine you have a bright but friendless and aggressive girl in your upper elementary class. Based on Moon's chapter, what help would you seek? Explain.

3. Look again at the three models of parent guidance explained by Moon. Which seems most appealing to you? Explain.

4. Look at the four models, or approaches, of family therapy. Which seems most appealing? Explain.

REFERENCES

Alsop, G. (1997). Coping or counseling: Families of intellectually gifted children. *Roeper Review, 20*(1), 28–34.

Baker, J. A. (1996). Everyday stressors of academically gifted adolescents. *Journal of Secondary Gifted Education, 7*(2), 356–368.

Baker, J. A., Bridger, R., & Evans, K. (1998). Models of underachievement among gifted preadolescents: The role of personal, family, and school factors. *Gifted Child Quarterly, 42*(1), 5–15.

Barkley, R. A. (1990). *Attention deficit hyperactivity disorder: A handbook for diagnosis and treatment.* New York: Guilford.

Bloom, B. S. (Ed.). (1985). *Developing talent in young people.* New York: Ballantine.

Bordeaux, B. (2001). Therapy with gifted clients: Honest disagreement is often a good sign of progress. *Unpublished manuscript,* Department of Child Development and Family Studies, Purdue University.

Colangelo, N. (1988). Families of gifted children: The next ten years. *Roeper Review, 11*(1), 16–18.

Colangelo, N. (1997). Counseling gifted students: Issues and practices. In N. Colangelo & G. A. Davis (Eds.), *Handbook of gifted education* (2nd ed., pp. 353–365). Boston: Allyn & Bacon.

Colangelo, N., & Assouline, A. (1993). Families of gifted children: A research agenda. *Quest, 4*(1), 1–4.

Colangelo, N., & Assouline, S. G. (2000). Counseling gifted students. In K. A. Heller, F. J. Monks, R. J. Sternberg, & R. F. Subotnik, (Eds.), *International handbook of giftedness and talent* (2nd ed., pp. 595–607). Amsterdam: Elsevier.

Colangelo, N., & Brower, P. (1987). Labeling gifted youngsters: Long-term impact on families. *Gifted Child Quarterly, 31,* 75–78.

Colangelo, N., & Dettmann, D. F. (1981). A conceptual model of four types of parent-school interactions. *Journal for the Education of the Gifted, 5,* 120–126.

Colangelo, N., & Dettmann, D. F. (1983). A review of research on parents and families of gifted children. *Exceptional Children, 50*(1), 20–27.

Coleman, L. J., & Cross, T. L. (2000). Social-emotional development and the personal experience of giftedness. In K. A. Heller, F. J. Monks, R. J. Sternberg, & R. F. Subotnik (Eds.), *International handbook of giftedness and talent* (2nd ed., pp. 203–212). Amsterdam: Elsevier.

Conoley, J. C. (1987). Strategic family intervention: Three cases of school-aged children. *School Psychology Review, 16*(4), 469–486.

Cornell, D. G., & Grossberg, I. N. (1986). Siblings of children in gifted programs. *Journal for the Education of the Gifted, 9,* 253–264.

Csikszentmihalyi, M., Rathunde, K., & Whalen, S. (1993). *Talented teenagers.* Cambridge: Cambridge University Press.

Dettmann, D. F., & Colangelo, N. (1980). A functional model for counseling parents of gifted students. *Gifted Child Quarterly, 24*(3), 158–161.

Doherty, W. J., & Colangelo, N. (1984). The family FIRO model: A modest proposal for organizing family treatment. *Journal of Marital and Family Therapy, 10*(1), 19–29.

Doherty, W. J., Colangelo, N., Green, A. M., & Hoffman, G. S. (1985). Emphases of the major family therapy models: A family FIRO analysis. *Journal of Marital and Family Therapy, 11,* 299–303.

Doherty, W. J., Colangelo, N., & Hovander, D. (1991). Priority setting in family change and clinical practice: The family FIRO model. *Family Process, 30*(2), 1–14.

Exum, H. A. (1983). Key issues in family counseling with gifted and talented black students. *Roeper Review, 5*(3), 28–31.

Feldhusen, J. F., & Kroll, M. D. (1985). Parent perceptions of gifted children's educational needs. *Roeper Review, 7*(4), 249–252.

Fine, M. J., & Carlson, C. (Eds.). (1992). *The handbook of family-school intervention: A systems perspective.* Boston: Allyn & Bacon.

Fine, M. J., & Pitts, R. (1980). Intervention with underachieving gifted children: Rationale and strategies. *Gifted Child Quarterly, 24*(2), 51–55.

Ford, D. Y. (1996). *Reversing underachievement among gifted black students: Promising practices and programs.* New York: Teachers College Press.

Freeman, J. (2000). Families: The essential context for gifts and talents. In K. A. Heller, F. J. Monks, R. J. Sternberg, & R. F. Subotnik (Eds.), *International handbook of giftedness and talent* (2nd ed., pp. 573–594). Amersterdam: Elsevier.

Frey, J., & Wendorf, D. J. (1985). Families of gifted children. In L. L'Abate (Ed.), *Handbook of family psychology and therapy* (Vol. 2, pp. 781–809). Homewood, IL: Dorsey Press.

Friedman, R. C. (1994). Upstream helping for low-income families of gifted students: Challenges and opportunities. *Journal of Educational and Psychological Consultation, 5,* 321–338.

Gelbrich, J. A., & Kare, E. K. (1989). The effects of single parenthood on school achievement in a gifted population. *Gifted Child Quarterly, 33,* 115–117.

Genshaft, J. L., Greenbaum, S., & Borovksky, S. (1995). Stress and the gifted. In J. L. Genshaft, M. Birely, & C. L. Hollinger (Eds.), *Serving gifted and talented students: A resource for school personnel* (pp. 257–286). Austin, TX: PRO-ED.

Glenn, L. S. (1995). Guilt and self-sacrifice: The plight of the better-off sibling. *Journal of Contemporary Psychotherapy, 25*(1), 61–75.

Green, K., Fine, M. J., & Tollefson, N. (1988). Family systems characteristics and underachieving gifted. *Gifted Child Quarterly, 32,* 267–272.

Grenier, M. E. (1985). Gifted children and other siblings. *Gifted Child Quarterly, 29,* 164–167.

Gridley, B. (2001). Personal Communication.

Guerney, L., & Guerney, B. (1989). Child relationship enhancement: Family therapy and parent education. *Person-Centered Review, 4,* 344–357.

Hackney, H. (1981). The gifted child, the family, and the school. *Gifted Child Quarterly, 25,* 51–54.

Haley, J. (1988). *Problem-solving therapy.* San Francisco: Jossey-Bass.

Hayes, D. G., & Levitt, M. (1982, Sept/Oct). Stress: An inventory for parents. *G/C/T,* 8.

Hsueh, W., & Moon, S. (1998). Families of gifted children in Taiwan: A comparative review of the literature. *Gifted and Talented International, 13,* 5–13.

Keirouz, K. S. (1990). Concerns of parents of gifted children: A research review. *Gifted Child Quarterly, 34,* 56–63.

Mahoney, A. S. (1997). In search of gifted identity: From abstract concept to workable counseling constructs. *Roeper Review, 20,* 222–227.

May, K. M. (2000). Gifted children and their families. *The Family Journal: Counseling and Therapy for Couples and Families, 8*(1), 58–60.

Minuchin, S. (1974). *Families and family therapy.* Cambridge: Harvard University Press.

Minuchin, S., & Fishman, H. C. (1981). *Family therapy techniques.* Cambridge: Harvard University Press.

Moon, S. M., & Hall, A. S. (1998). Family therapy with intellectually and creatively gifted children. *Journal of Marital and Family Therapy, 24*(1), 59–80.

Moon, S. M., Jurich, J. A., & Feldhusen, J. F. (1998). Families of gifted children: Cradles of development. In R. C. Friedman & K. B. Rogers (Eds.), *Talent in context: Historical and social perspectives on giftedness* (pp. 81–99). Washington, DC: American Psychological Association.

Moon, S. M., Kelly, K. R., & Feldhusen, J. F. (1997). Specialized counseling services for gifted youth and their families: A needs assessment. *Gifted Child Quarterly, 41,* 16–25.

Moon, S. M., Nelson, T. S., & Piercy, F. P. (1993). Family therapy with a highly gifted adolescent. *Journal of Family Psychotherapy, 4*(3), 1–16.

Moon, S. M., Zentall, S. S., Grskovic, J. A., Hall, A., & Stormont, M. (2001). Emotional and social characteristics of boys with AD/HD and/or giftedness: A comparative case study. *Journal for the Education of the Gifted, 24*(3), 207–247.

Moos, R. H., & Moos, B. S. (1994). *Family Environment Scale Manual* (3rd ed.). Palo Alto, CA: Consulting Psychologists Press.

Neihart, M. (1999). The impact of giftedness on psychological well-being: What does the empirical literature say. *Roeper Review, 22,* 10–17.

Olson, D. H., Portner, J., & Lavee, Y. (1985). *Family Adaptability and Cohesion Evaluation Scales III (FACES III).* Minneapolis: University of Minnesota.

Peters, W. A. M., Grager-Loidl, H., & Supplee, P. (2000). Underachievement in gifted children and adolescents: Theory and practice. In K. A. Heller, F. J. Monks, R. J. Sternberg, & R. F. Subotnik (Eds.), *International handbook of giftedness and talent* (2nd ed., pp. 609–620). Amsterdam: Elsevier.

Peterson, J., & Rischar, H. (2000). Gifted and gay: A study of the adolescent experience. *Gifted Child Quarterly, 44,* 231–246.

Piercy, F. P., & Wetchler, J. L. (1996). Structural, strategic, and systemic family therapies. In F. P. Piercy, D. H. Sprenkle, & J. L. Wetchler (Eds.), *Family therapy sourcebook* (pp. 50–78). New York: Guilford.

Piers, E. V. (1984). *Piers-Harris Children's Self-Concept Scale.* Los Angeles: Western Psychological Services.

Rathunde, K. (1996). Family context and talented adolescents' optimal experience in school-related activities. *Journal of Research on Adolescence, 6,* 605–628.

Reis, S. M., & McCoach, D. B. (2000). The underachievement of gifted students: What do we know and where do we go? *Gifted Child Quarterly, 44,* 152–170.

Reis, S. M., Neu, T. W., & McGuire, J. M. (1997). Case studies of high ability students with learning disabilities who have achieved. *Exceptional Children, 63,* 463–479.

Rimm, S. (1995). *Why bright kids get poor grades and what you can do about it.* New York: Crown.

Rimm, S. (1997). Underachievement syndrome: A national epidemic. In N. Colangelo & G. A. Davis (Eds.), *Handbook of gifted education* (2nd ed., pp. 416–434). Boston: Allyn & Bacon.

Rimm, S. B., & Lowe, B. (1988). Family environments of underachieving gifted students. *Gifted Child Quarterly, 32,* 353–359.

Rogers, J. A., & Nielson, A. B. (1993). Gifted children and divorce: A study of the literature on the incidence of divorce in families with gifted children. *Journal for the Education of the Gifted, 16,* 251–267.

Silverman, L. K. (1991). Family counseling. In N. Colangelo & G. A. Davis (Eds.), *Handbook of gifted education* (pp. 307–320). Boston: Allyn & Bacon.

Silverman, L. K. (1993a). Counseling families. In L. K. Silverman (Ed.), *Counseling the gifted and talented* (pp. 151–178). Denver, CO: Love.

Silverman, L. K. (1993b). Counseling needs and programs for the gifted. In K. A. Heller, F. J. Monks, & A. H. Passow (Eds.), *International handbook of research and development of giftedness and talent* (pp. 631–647). Oxford: Pergamon.

Silverman, L. K. (1993c). *Counseling the gifted and talented.* Denver, CO: Love.

Silverman, L. K. (1993d). A developmental model for counseling the gifted. In L. K. Silverman (Ed.), *Counseling the gifted and talented* (pp. 51–78). Denver: Love.

Silverman, L. K. (1993e). Techniques for preventive counseling. In L. K. Silverman (Ed.), *Counseling the gifted and talented* (pp. 81–109). Denver: Love.

Sowa, C. J., & May, K. M. (1997). Expanding Lazarus and Folkman's paradigm to the social and emotional adjustment of gifted children. *Gifted Child Quarterly, 41,* 36–43.

Strom, R., Strom, S., Strom, P., & Collinsworth, P. (1994). Parent competence in families with gifted children. *Journal for the Education of the Gifted, 18,* 39–54.

Taichert, L. C. (1979). Two adolescents at risk for schizophrenia: A family case study. *International Journal of Family Therapy, 7,* 138–148.

Thomas, V. (1995). Of thorns and roses: The use of the "Briar Rose" fairy tale in therapy with families of gifted children. *Contemporary Family Therapy, 17*(1), 83–91.

Thomas, V. (1999). David and the Family Bane: Therapy with a gifted child and his family. *Journal of Family Psychology, 10*(1), 15–24.

Watzlawick, P., Weakland, J. H., & Fisch, R. (1974).

Change: Principles of problem formation and problem resolution. New York: Norton.

Wendorf, D. J., & Frey, J. (1985). Family therapy with the intellectually gifted. *American Journal of Family Therapy, 13*(1), 31–38.

Whitchurch, C. G., & Constantine, L. L. (1993). Systems theory. In P. G. Boss, W. J. Doherty, R. LaRossa, W. R. Schumm, & S. K. Steinmetz (Eds.), *Sourcebook of family theories and methods: A contextual approach.* New York: Plenum.

White, M., & Epston, D. (1990). Narrative means to therapeutic ends. *Journal of Family Psychotherapy, 10*(1), 15–24.

Wieczerkowski, W., & Prado, T. M. (1991). Parental fears and expectations from the point of view of a counseling centre for the gifted. *European Journal for High Ability, 2,* 56–72.

Zentall, S. S., Moon, S. M., Hall, A. M., & Grskovic, J. A. (in press). Learning and motivational characteristics of boys with AD/HD and/or giftedness: A multiple case study. *Exceptional Children.*

Zuccone, C. F., & Amerikaner, M. (1986). Counseling gifted underachievers: A family systems approach. *Journal of Counseling and Development, 64,* 590–592.

31

Emotional and Spiritual Giftedness

MICHAEL M. PIECHOWSKI, *Northland College, Wisconsin*

The Emergence of EG and EI, and SG and SI

Sometimes things are suddenly simple. Recognition of genius (giftedness) led to the idea of intelligence as a measurable characteristic. Recognition of a special kind of giftedness called for a special kind of intelligence. Sometimes it is the other way round, the intelligence leads to giftedness. And sometimes the assessment instruments predate the recognition of an intelligence. This rivulet of abstract musing applies to the emergence of emotional and spiritual giftedness (EG and SG) and emotional and spiritual intelligence (EI and SI). Diving into these currents will carry us to one of the central issues in gifted education: the tension between talent development and personal growth.

The concept of emotional giftedness was first proposed by Roeper (1982) and later expanded by Piechowski (1991, 1997a, 1997b). The idea of emotional intelligence was first formulated by Salovey and Mayer (1990) and subsequently developed into a theory put to test by research (Mayer & Salovey, 1997; Mayer, Caruso, & Salovey, 1999, 2000; Mayer, Salovey, & Caruso, 2000a, 2000b; see Table 31.1). Ever since Goleman's (1995) *Emotional Intelligence* appeared, gifted people have been expressing their disappointment that Goleman did not say anything about the emotional intensity and sensitivity so characteristic of the lives of gifted and creative children and adults. In other words, he ignored the high end of emotional intelligence. Weep no more, o gifted youths and seniors alike! Faithful to the absolute principle of science that only that exists which can be measured, Mayer and his colleagues have developed an instrument, the Multifactor Emotional Intelligence

Scale, with which to measure the abilities that constitute emotional intelligence (Mayer, Caruso, & Salovey, 1999). The component skills of emotional intelligence are shown in Table 31.1—they define emotional intelligence as a set of abilities thus meeting the requirement for EI to be an intelligence. They tested, in a pilot study of eleven adolescents, the hypothesis that emotionally gifted adolescents ought to score high on the measure of emotional intelligence (Mayer, Perkins, Caruso, & Salovey, 2001). The hypothesis was confirmed; that is, the responses of high scorers typified emotional giftedness. They also found that a young person could show high emotional intelligence, even though verbal ability was only average. *Emotional giftedness* is the high end of emotional intelligence, with an identity distinct from intellectual giftedness.

As evidenced by the books and papers pouring out (e.g., Kurzweil, 1998; Noble, 2000, 2001; Sinetar, 2000; Zohar & Marshall, 2000), spiritual intelligence is a recent but rather catchy idea. Gardner (1999, 2000) considered the case for spiritual intelligence and decided against it; Emmons (1999), a mainstream psychologist, decided for it. Emmons wrote:

> because it is such a pervasive dimension of human life, spirituality revealed itself repeatedly through the phenomenon I was studying—personal goals, well-being, happiness, purpose, meaning, the psychology of possibility and human potential. . . . [To ignore this information] would have been the equivalent of committing academic malpractice. As a personality psychologist who professed a desire to understand the person in his or her entirety, I was guilty of ignoring what for many people is precisely what makes their life meaningful, valuable, and purposeful. I was ignoring people's attempts to contact a deep and authentic source of striving, goals

Table 31.1   The Emotional Intelligence Framework

Perception, Appraisal, and Expression of Emotions
- Ability to identify emotion in one's physical and psychological states
- Ability to identify emotion in other people and objects
- Ability to express emotions accurately, and to express needs related to those feelings
- Ability to discriminate between accurate and inaccurate, or honest and dishonest, expression of feelings

Emotional Facilitation of Thinking
- Ability to redirect and order one's thinking based on the feelings associated with objects, events, and other people
- Ability to generate or emulate vivid emotions to facilitate judgments and memories concerning feelings
- Ability to capitalize on mood swings to take multiple points of view; ability to integrate these mood-induced perspectives
- Ability to use emotional states to facilitate problem solving and creativity

Understanding and Analyzing Emotional Information; Employing Emotional Knowledge
- Ability to understand how different emotions are related
- Ability to perceive the causes and consequences of feelings
- Ability to interpret complex feelings, such as emotional blends and contradictory feeling states
- Ability to understand and to predict likely transitions between emotions

Regulation of Emotion
- Ability to be open to feelings, both pleasant and unpleasant
- Ability to monitor and reflect on emotions
- Ability to engage, prolong, or detach from an emotional state, depending upon its judged informativeness or utility
- Ability to manage emotion in oneself and others

Source: From Salovey, Bedell, Detweiler, and Mayer (2000).

that come closer to any other, in defining who people say they are (p. 7).

The instruments to measure spiritual constructs exist in abundance, such as the Spiritual Orientation Inventory, the Mystical Experiences Scale, the Peak Experience Scale, or the Spiritual Well-Being Scale, to name a few (MacDonald, LeClair, Holland, Alter, & Friedman, 1995; MacDonald, Friedman, & Kuentzel, 1999; MacDonald, Kuentzel, & Friedman, 1999). The ground was prepared, the Zeitgeist arrived and spiritual intelligence swam into the mainstream (Table 31.2).

Gardner's (2000) arguments against spiritual intelligence are unconvincing for the simple reason that he has not closely examined spiritually gifted people.

Table 31.2   Components of Spiritual Intelligence

1. The capacity to transcend the physical and material
2. The ability to experience heightened states of consciousness
3. The ability to sanctify everyday experience
4. The ability to utilize spiritual resources to solve problems
5. The capacity to be virtuous
6. The conscious recognition that physical reality is embedded in a larger multidimensional reality with which we interact, consciously and unconsciously, on a moment-to-moment basis
7. The conscious pursuit of psychological health, not only for ourselves but also for the sake of global community

Note. Components 1–5 are "core components" from Emmons (1999).
Components 6–7 are from Noble (2000).

His reservations also appear to stem from his lack of acquaintance with criteria for distinguishing charismatic spiritual leaders from evil ones. Yet such criteria have been available in Dabrowski's theory (Lysy & Piechowski, 1983; Piechowski, 1975, 1992, in press) and in Anthony, Ecker, and Wilber's (1987) analysis of how to discern authentic paths to inner transformation.

One must credit William James (1902/1936) with the recognition of religious virtuosi and spiritual athletes as individuals not only worthy of psychological study but a fortiori as "a study in human nature"—the subtitle of his *Varieties of Religious Experience*. He sought "the more developed minds," the "extremer examples" that can yield the "profounder information" (p. 476). In short, he was after spiritually gifted people.

Claims about emotional intelligence have substantial support in brain science (Damasio, 1994, 1999; Goleman, 1995; LeDoux, 1996), but emotional giftedness has not yet made it to the neurological laboratory. In contrast, spiritual giftedness has won laurels there (Newberg & d'Aquili, 2001). This being the case, it is only logical to conclude that the human brain is also the seat of spiritual intelligence.

Emotional Giftedness and Positive Maladjustment

To be emotionally gifted is to *dare* to act on one's awareness of what is happening with others by alleviating hunger, relieving emotional distress, opposing unfairness, and fighting injustice (Roeper, 1982). Gifted adolescents in particular, with their advanced thinking, see through pretense and double standards. Often they meet with opposition and ridicule. Not compromising one's ideals, resisting peer pressure, and being able to stand alone, Dabrowski (1970) called *positive maladjustment*. It is positive because it means being true to oneself and to the universal ideals of compassion, caring, and the conviction that each individual deserves consideration. Rooted in empathy and a sense of justice, such a stance is often in opposition to others' self-interest, prejudice, and ruthlessness. Therefore the two terms, *emotional giftedness* and *positive maladjustment* overlap.

Standing by one's beliefs and ideals is a common experience for gifted teens. Here are examples picked from responses to the Overexcitability Questionnaire

(Piechowski, 1979). To be true to oneself may at times require a person to stand alone. Two replies follow from students who were asked, "What situations bring you in conflict with others?". A sixteen-year-old girl said:

> My opinions are quite different from other students my age. This many times brings conflict between someone in my class and myself. For example, many kids in my class don't think drinking is dangerous and I do. I don't believe in it and I believe it is a waste of time. This sometimes causes a hassle. Another thing my classmates disagree with me on is styles. Many students buy clothes because they are "in style." I don't. If I like them I get them, if I hate them I leave them at the store, "in style" or not!

A young woman of eighteen reacted to her teachers' presumption of superiority:

> Sometimes I'm in conflict with my teachers because I won't go along with their superiority complexes. I won't accept their ideas all the time and I hate when they come at me with them and I better accept them or get them wrong on a test. Sometimes I found that they would give their view on a certain subject yet wouldn't listen to what my view is, for of course theirs is *right*.

Here are replies, two years apart, from a boy confronted with asking himself, "Who am I?" When he was fifteen, he wrote: "I feel that I am a person who is on the earth that is destined to use his abilities and talents to his fullest. This is simply what I think I really am." This is a typical, though erroneous, egocentric view of self-actualization as *self*-fulfillment. He gave it much thought over the next two years. At seventeen, he recognized a moral conflict between getting ahead and being considerate of others:

> The answer to this question has changed over the past few years. A few years ago I was a person who wanted things for himself. Now I am trying to change that person to a person who wants to contribute to others and the world not just himself. Obtaining this type of person in this world is not that easy. The one thing that is a roadblock is competition. Not necessarily losing to other people, but beating them. How can I compete to get into medical school when a doctor is supposed to build people's confidence and restore their sense of security? The process is self-defeating.

In their study, Mayer et al. (2001) noted that situations presented to the participants led those higher in emotional intelligence to defy their peers in order to protect others, an expression of positive maladjustment. They concluded that high emotional intelligence is isomorphic with emotional giftedness and positive maladjustment, two concepts that were shown to overlap to a large extent (Piechowski, 1997a). The convergence of the meanings of these different terms inspires confidence that emotional giftedness is not something elusive and hard to define, nor is high emotional intelligence. Thus, Pfeiffer's (2001) doubts to the contrary can be put to sleep.

Active Youth Today, Leaders Tomorrow

The initial descriptions of emotional giftedness relied on instances of children's actions taken individually. Silverman (1993) collected numerous observations of emotional sensitivity, compassion, and moral sensitivity in gifted children as young as two and a half and three years of age. Lovecky (1992, 1998) described many examples of empathic and moral action of gifted children on behalf of others as an expression of their values. In an example of positive maladjustment in a very young person, six-year old Madeline "decided to boycott all Miramax films because she didn't approve of the negative values in some of them. She felt she couldn't just go to the good films and ignore the rest but had to make a broader decision that reflected her values" (Lovecky, 1998).

Howard (1994) investigated the psychosocial development in five highly gifted five-year-old girls (140–154 IQ). These girls showed an advanced level of understanding of how human relationships work. They knew that people die but puppets don't, that a person may have conflicting feelings simultaneously (for example, feeling sad to leave a current home but happy to move to a new one), that overt behavior may not clearly reveal the feelings a person has inside, and that because personalities are based on inner feelings rather than simple actions, friendships take effort to maintain. Unlike other five-year-olds, they were not bound by appearance but were aware of the inner psychological reality in people. This type of understanding is usually found only in children twice their age or even older. These highly gifted preschoolers demonstrated their advanced understanding in their actions toward others, not just by being able to talk about it. The information gathered by Howard gives evidence that these gifted girls have most of, and probably all, the abilities listed in Table 31.1.

Stories of kids fighting crime, kids taking social action, and kids saving the environment can be found in Lewis (1992) and Waldman (2001). Ways to foster empathy and social responsibility are described by Barbara Lewis (1991) and Delisle (1996).

The instances of acts of empathy by outstanding children, like those cited above, can be easily multiplied, but there is more. There are gifted children who not only start campaigns for a good cause but who operate in a network of others devoted to helping others in impressive large scale endeavors. Justin Chapman (Chapman & Chapman, 2000), at the age of six, began a campaign against age discrimination. One has to admire the thorough information, the level of preparation, and the articulateness of expression in Justin Chapman's way of presenting the case for abandoning age discrimination against children, and gifted children especially. Jason Crowe, at the age of nine, launched *The Informer, a Neighborhood Newspaper for Kids and by Kids* in 1996,[1] in which he has been reporting on the actions of young gifted leaders from around the world. The mission of his paper, now a *Global Neighborhood Newspaper,* is "to share the good news about the great things kids are doing in their communities and in the world, to promote peace, and to change the unjust but popular image of youth." Jason's mission echoes the voices of teenagers who are well aware of the distorted image the society has of them as "a totally alien life-form" (S. Lewis, 1996).

The projects initiated by these gifted youngsters spring from their discovery of gaping needs around them and the awareness of the emotional impact of unmet needs on children. For instance

- Nadia Ben-Youssef, at thirteen, raised thousands of dollars for a school for deaf and blind, a home for abused children, Bosnian orphans, and Shriners' Hospital.
- Emily Kumpel, at thirteen, sent 56,000 books to children in South Africa. (Over 100,000 by 2001. She is now seventeen, and the list of her other activities is a page long.)

---

1. *The Informer, A Global Neighborhood Newspaper by Kids and for Kids.* J. D. Crowe, Editor & Publisher, 619 Rose Drive, Newburgh, IN 47630. Web sites: *http://members.sigecom.net/jdc,* and *www.peaceinc.org/ networking/cellocries/cellocries.htm.*

- Aubyn Burnside, at thirteen, started a program to give suitcases to kids who go to foster homes so they would not be humiliated by carrying their things in black garbage bags. In 1998 her project extended to twenty-seven states, by 2001 to all fifty states.
- In 1991, when still in the third grade, Michael Wiener started a campaign against second-hand smoke, then moved on to collect food for hungry people.
- Kelly Schlinsky, seventeen, started Books for Bedsides for children in hospitals—by 1998 she has collected and distributed 15,000 books.
- Laura Schlesinger, at twelve, started a bone marrow drive for leukemia victims, and began collecting eyeglasses and books for kids who could not afford them.
- Tabitha Joy Kulish, fourteen, raises money for healthier babies and as of the end of 1998 had put in 3000 volunteer hours (that's 75 full work days!).
- David Adamiec, fifteen, organized Kid Packs for children who are victims of domestic violence or whose parents are in jail. Boys get different Kid Packs than girls; younger children get different ones than older children. Each is worth about $120, and he distributes 100 to 160 a year. David Adamiec said: "These kids, on their way to foster care families, are terrified; and I can ease their fear a little. I really feel for these kids." Having received at least nine different awards, his comment was: "I have been awarded many honors lately. They were important to me at first; now I look at them as ways for the community to see that I am very serious about 'my kids.' When they see that I am on a mission for kids that sometimes do not have a voice, they give to my cause" (*The Informer,* 1999, Vol. 6, No. 2).
- Steven Cozza, a Boy Scout in Petaluma, California, himself not gay, at the age of twelve started Scouting for All to end discrimination against gays by the Boy Scouts (Gallagher, 2001) because he felt so deeply offended and angered by the B.S.A.'s policy of discrimination.

Jason Crowe, in addition to launching *The Informer* (at first as a source of money to give to cancer research), is involved in raising funds for the Children's International Peace-and-Harmony Statue, which he commissioned after reading about the Cellist of Sarajevo, Vedran Smailovic, who played the cello amidst falling artillery shells and bombs in the street where twenty-two people were killed in 1992 while waiting for bread. He has found a sculptor, David Kocka, and the statue will have the following inscription: "Kids are uniting and working together for multicultural harmony and international understanding to declare, 'No to war, and yes to harmony! No to genocide, and yes to human rights!' "[2]

In 1998, MIT organized a Junior Summit online of 1000 teams of 3200 participants age 10 to 16, from 139 countries to give kids a platform to identify problems and find ways to solve them. The Junior Summit is a continuing endeavor. In 1999 the youngsters wrote a letter to world leaders, "A New Millennium without Wars." The Junior Summit resulted in the formation of Nation1, an online global youth community. Progress toward peace would no doubt be faster if these young people were the leaders now.

The awards, local, national, and international, given to children and teenagers for their efforts to eliminate violence, war, hunger, poverty, and pollution are numerous: Kids' Hall of Fame, Hall of Fame of Caring America, Spirit of Community (Prudential), Points of Light, Youth Service of America, Young Hero, Youth in Action, Golden Rule, Outstanding Volunteer of the Year (VFW), Teen of the Year, and many others. They rarely make front page news. To its credit, *People* weekly has sections headed "Angels," "Do-Gooders," and "Crusaders" which sometimes feature young altruists and leaders. On television, Oprah's Angel Network gives awards for altruistic actions and projects.

The question that may be legitimately raised about good works is whether they represent emotional intelligence in the strict sense of the term, which is to say, as instances of intelligent action in the realm of emotions. Intelligent action relies on a set of abilities to process information toward solving problems at hand. Intelligent action in the realm of emotions involves perceiving, understanding, and managing emotions in oneself and others (Mayer & Salovey, 1997; Mayer, Salovey, & Caruso, 2000a). Interviewing the youngsters cited earlier could answer this question. However, lacking that, their actions suggest perception and understanding of an emotional problem in others followed by action to alleviate it. The latter

---

2. There are two Web sites: http://members.sigecom.net/jdc and www.peaceinc.org/networking/cellocries/cellocries.htm.

reflects an ability to manage emotions in others by helping them. The words of David Adamiec cited above express it well.

Standing Up for Moral Order and Overcoming Abuse

There are numerous examples of positive maladjustment and empathy that drive people to action. Conscientious objectors, social reformers, religious leaders, whistle blowers, peace workers, and eco-heroes are the exceptional individuals who see clearly that the exploitation of people is dehumanizing and must be stopped. They see that deprivation and poverty can be abolished, that poor health from malnutrition and lack of sanitary living conditions can be corrected, and that our environment has to be respected. These adult counterparts of the inspired teenagers mentioned earlier are described by Berkowitz (1987), Colby and Damon (1992), Craig (1985), Daloz, Keen, Keen, and Parks (1996), Everett (1986), Oliner and Oliner (1988), Wallace (1993), Witty, (1990), and others.

There are situations which suggest that the concept of emotional giftedness should be extended to include the capacity for emotional survival against all odds (Piechowski, 1997b). Studies of vulnerability, risk, and resilience have uncovered a small proportion of children and adolescents who cope well with the stress and disorganization brought on by alcoholic, psychotic, and abusive parents (Anthony, 1987). Many bright adolescents today cope with difficult lives in dangerous environments and are in great need of support and encouragement. What keeps them going and believing that they can find a better life are their personal strengths of intelligence, humor, plus their self-reliance, tenacity, perseverance, and their ability to fight back, to look on the bright side, and to forgive. Their future is uncertain, some will certainly overcome, others may not. What works against them is their tough persona and uneven school performance, and for this reason they are often excluded from gifted programs (Peterson, 1997).

Autobiographical accounts and studies of resilient people revealed several common characteristics that enabled their emotional survival and growth toward well-being. They had the ability to recognize, often quite young, that the mistreatment was unjustified. They felt different and marginal, and this realization helped them to dis-identify from their family. They were able to find alternative sources of support, even

very small, of which they made the best use (Higgins, 1994; Rubin, 1996). School is often the only safe haven for such children and a teacher's attention and kindness the only support. Resilient children have the capacity to benefit from the help offered; they seem to draw others to themselves.

On their long way toward healing their deep wounds, they all felt strongly it was their mission to help others, and they eventually did. It is praiseworthy in this context that the Prudential makes awards to children for being motivated to help others out of their own intense personal suffering (*The Informer*, Vol. 4, No. 9)

The resilient adults also discussed at length the question of forgiveness. They said that forgiveness can be offered only if the abusers recognize their responsibility for the damage they wrought and if their remorse is sincere. Genuine forgiveness, so that no residue of resentment remains, is not easily won. The capacity for forgiveness in emotionally gifted people is worthy of exploration. The research on forgiveness is growing (Enright & North, 1996).

Childhood Spirituality and Spiritual Giftedness

In discussions of emotional development, specifically in trying to understand the nature of inner transformation and the spiritual elements involved, the possibility of spiritual giftedness as a distinct category has been suggested. The reason for this question is fairly obvious—a genuine religious or spiritual experience is a powerful emotional event. Eleanor Roosevelt was motivated not only by her deep empathy but by a hidden life of prayer (Piechowski, 1990). Etty Hillesum, who perished in the Holocaust, through self-taught meditation developed an unexpected impulse toward prayer (Hillesum, 1985). Peace Pilgrim (1982) found all the answers within herself, which led her to an unshakable inner peace, radiant health, and "energy that never runs out." Both Etty and Peace had no religious training to speak of, yet from within their inner being came a spiritual search. They discovered that "everything we need is within us." They lived their lives at a deep emotional level (Piechowski, 1993).

I have received a number of reports of spiritual experiences from children and adults. There is a substantial research literature on childhood spirituality. A few examples are in the gifted literature (Feldman & Goldsmith, 1986; Harrison, 2000; Lovecky, 1992,

1998; Morelock, 1995; Noble, 2000), but the vast majority are outside of it, although here too, many of the respondents show evidence of being gifted: highly articulate, questioning, and energetic (Armstrong, 1984; Coles, 1990; Hay & Nye, 1998; Hoffman, 1992; Maxwell & Tschudin, 1990; Morse, 1990; Paffard, 1973; Robinson, 1977, 1978; Rubin, 1996; Young, 1977). There is thus sufficient evidence to admit spiritual giftedness as distinct from emotional giftedness (Piechowski, 1997, 2000, 2001a).

Despite the rising acknowledgment of spiritual interests and experiences in surveys (Hay, 2001), the social taboo on speaking about spiritual practices and experiences is strong and widespread (Hay & Nye, 1998). Some states, in fact, prohibit the use of guided imagery in schools for fear of it being an "occult" practice.

Data Sources

Edward Robinson (1977) in England and Edward Hoffman (1992) in the United States received adult recollections of childhood spiritual experiences, which can occur as early as the age of three or four, on occasion even earlier. Between them they examined about 850 such reports. Tobin Hart (personal communication, January 18, 2001) gathered over 150 reports of children describing their spiritual experiences, and Nye (1998) interviewed 38 children. There is a pool of over 1,000 such cases.

Spiritual experiences in childhood are fairly common, more so than in later years (Nye, 1998, Tamminen, 1991). Robinson (1977) examining 362 childhood experiences recalled by adults found that 10% occurred before age 5, 70% between ages of five and fifteen, and 19% after the age of fifteen. This and other studies are described more fully by Hay and Nye (1998) and Piechowski (2000).

These reports show that children are capable of having genuine spiritual experiences, similar in quality to adult ones. They can occur spontaneously—in nature or at home, in church or in the car—and they have enduring significance for the person's whole life. The families of some of these children were religious, others were not. Childhood spiritual experiences often initiate spiritual search later in life and endow a person with strength to endure reverses and tragic losses.

While the great majority of transcendental experiences are joyous, reassuring, and blissful, a certain number of such experiences are unsettling, some-

times even frightening. This type of experience is more likely to happen when a gifted child pursues difficult existential questions such as the meaning of death and nothingness, for which he or she cannot find authoritative assistance. This is a topic that requires a separate study.

Question of Authenticity

It is only natural to question the authenticity of these childhood accounts because memories can be distorted and subject to revision. Fortunately, there is strong evidence that children's memory is, in fact, very good (Sheingold & Tenney, 1982). More recent research demonstrated that children have a good recall of personally experienced events even as early as the end of the first year (Bauer, 1997; Fivush, 1997; Schneider & Pressley, 1997). Robinson (1977) has several examples of spiritual memories prior to eighteen months of age or even within the first year of life. The respondents themselves were emphatic that the experience was indelible, preverbal, and therefore not subject to interpreting, editing, and altering (Robinson, 1978; Piechowski, 2000).

Characteristic Themes

The themes that recur in the descriptions of childhood experiences have been illustrated by Robinson (1977), Murdock (1978), Hoffman (1992, 1998), and Piechowski (2000). They include experiences of ecstasy, timelessness, oneness with nature, pulsating energy and life force, God in everything, sense of self beyond physical reality and beyond one lifetime, and techniques of achieving heightened states of consciousness. There are also examples of *entelechy,* which is the concept of a vital force directing one's life, a strong will toward self-determination and fulfilling one's destiny (Lovecky, 1993).

Here is an example from early childhood. At the age of fifty-two a woman described how as a young child she was healed from an excruciatingly painful illness:

> At the age of three and a half I was very ill with rheumatic fever and rheumatic arthritis. One night, as I sobbed uncontrollably from the terrible pain, my grandmother gently told me, "Look up, and when the pain is bad, go to the stars."
>
> Later that night I again felt excruciating pain and decided to follow her advice. I gazed at the stars,

visible through my bedroom window. Suddenly I felt myself in the midst of a glowing, pulsating, slowly swirling light. I knew everything. I was everything. It was blissful beyond words. The next morning I felt immeasurably better, and my illness soon went away (Hoffman, 1992, p. 62).

A number of excerpts express the realization that one's individual essence or "I" is a consciousness that is separate from the body, which logically leads to the understanding that the "I" is changeless despite changes in the body; it is also changeless through successive lifetimes. The following excerpt is one of many such realizations (see also Feldman & Goldsmith, 1986; Hoffman, 1992; Piechowski, 2000).

When I was about 10 I had a strange experience which I still remember quite clearly. I was walking back from school and suddenly stood still as the realisation came over me, "My body is now that of a child—but it's not ME. Soon I shall have the body of a young girl and later of a woman—but it still won't be ME; I am apart from my body and always will be (Robinson, 1977, pp. 114–115).

Other instances describe the realization that in dissociation from one's body one can gain an expanded vision. It can be panoramic or even extending in all directions at once making material objects transparent (Piechowski, 2000). The interesting thing is that R. D. Davis (1994) described the "mind's eye" of the dyslexic to be a rapidly shifting location of the person's viewpoint, as if encircling an object in space and thus obtaining a 3-D view almost instantly. Atwater (1999, p. 76) interviewed a man who could see in 4-D, "looking at objects from all possible angles simultaneously." Thus, 4-D seeing is not limited to disembodied consciousness, as it were, but is a good instance of coming upon an extended human capacity in an unusual case only to find that there are people who have it as their natural endowment (see also Murphy, 1992).

Children's Techniques for Heightened Consciousness

More surprising than the spontaneous, wondrous transcendental experiences are children's own techniques for self-inducing a deep state of consciousness. Mentions of these techniques have appeared in accounts of adults recalling their experiences from childhood (Hoffman, 1992) and in interviews with children (Nye, 1998). They described how they practiced ways of entering a joyful state of deep peace, even bliss. Devotion expressed in intense prayer, pouring out the heart in longing for God, is the way of many great mystics. The childhood accounts contain descriptions of intense though wordless prayer, achieving a state of calmness by focusing on breathing, by focusing on a visual pattern in a tapestry or window, silent gazing in church, repeating a phrase, or concentrating on infinity. Only a gifted child could achieve a mystical state by concentrating on a mathematical concept. There are a number of instances of this ability on record. Here is an example:

When I was a second-grader in Catholic school, the teacher gave a homework assignment introducing the concept of zero. There were several problems in which zero was added to or subtracted from various numbers. Of course, the answer was that the number always remained the same . . . I sat alone in my room that night and stared with tears at this seemingly senseless problem.

I wondered, "How could I add something to a number and yet the number remained unchanged?" Suddenly, I *understood*—and had the first mystical experience of my life. The immensity of the concept of nothingness overwhelmed me. I was awed by the realization that mathematicians were brilliant enough to capture this immensity in a little symbol. I felt a sense of comfort and light (Hoffman, 1992, p. 115–116).

How young children arrive at these techniques is, to say the least, intriguing. One would think they are rare and unusual, but Nye (1998; Hay & Nye, 1998) found that children six and ten years old, from a regular English school, could at that age identify their strategies for reaching a state of heightened consciousness. Their techniques included mental and physical withdrawal, becoming absorbed and focused, seeking communication through prayer, pursuing a chain of questions about one's origin, the world's, and life's, and so on. A number of the children were clearly gifted. Only about 20 percent of them had families with an identified religious denomination, the others appeared to be without one.

Even more amazing is a child of three or four being able to go beyond thought and realize that his "I" had no form, or name, and no history, and that he was facing an emptiness that at the same time filled him with euphoric awareness. This account is not unique, but more likely to be found among adults. The striking thing about it is that the boy, at this young age, was able to practice a method that has a strong analogy to the Buddhist method of the Great Doubt designed to move the mind beyond all thought into a state of blissful nothingness (Piechowski, 2001b). It is a state of going beyond the self—the self either vanishes from awareness or becomes one with infinity.

Newberg and d'Aquili (2001) identified the neurological process by which the boundary from self to no-self is transcended with the resultant experience of oneness, timelessness, and infinity. This process "has evolved to allow us humans to transcend material existence and acknowledge and connect with a deeper, more spiritual part of ourselves perceived as an absolute, universal reality that connects us to all that is" (p. 9). This neurological state registers equally in advanced Tibetan Buddhist meditators and in Catholic nuns in deep contemplation.

Children's Wisdom and Adult Ignorance

A thread running through recollections of childhood spiritual experiences is the not infrequent negative reaction of adults' and the children's realization that the adults are ignorant. One respondent put it this way:

> I discovered that if I sat very still in my bed with my legs crossed and then fixed my eyes on a spot in the design of the Oriental rug, I entered a euphoric state. I had been taught prayers, but never experienced the same intensity of feeling with them.
>
> In simple terms, these meditative experiences led me to feel as a child that the grown-ups around me were out of touch with something and were deceiving themselves—and me—with unfounded opinions. As a result I often felt the need to retreat to a private reality among the woods and in nature (Hoffman, 1992, p. 96).

Or consider this example:

> I remember sitting in my mother's lap at the age of 5, while she affectionately explained that the idea of a God was a very nice and poetic way of explaining things, but just like a fairy tale. I felt embarrassed at what seemed abysmal blindness and ignorance and felt sorry for her (Robinson, 1977, p. 69).

Children learn quickly from one negative comment directed to them or to someone else that this subject is not to be talked about. The taboo is so strong that when children in Nye's study were asked how would they react if one of their classmates mentioned such an experience, they said that they wouldn't say anything or they would join others criticizing or ridiculing the child (Hay & Nye, 1998).

Not being able to share one's experience, or being told that one is lying, or that one should not talk about such things, leaves the child totally isolated. A number of adults recalled how confused and overwhelmed they felt, even in fear of their sanity. Only when they grew up, became more knowledgeable and the experience returned to them as a result of meditation, did they feel affirmed. Those to whom the experience is so strong and so compelling that nothing shakes their sense of its validity are truly fortunate.

The enduring significance of an early experience of this kind is the sense of something larger than oneself that gives assurance of safety and of having the wherewithal to withstand life's crises and trials. This assurance is one of the benefits that William James recognized in people who had religious experiences of a high order (James, 1902/1936). Another benefit was what he called "a temper of peace, and, in relation to others, a preponderance of loving affections." In other words, these people have undergone an inner transformation of the kind that Dabrowski made his theory about (Dabrowski, 1964, 1967; Piechowski, 1991, 1997, 2002).

Relational Consciousness

Nye (1998) proposed the concept of *relational consciousness* to capture the children's unusual level of consciousness or perceptiveness in regard to how they felt connected with the world around them, with people, with their own self, and with God. In conversations with Nye, the children showed a distinctly reflective consciousness (meta-cognition). She gives examples of children, six and ten years old, describing a strong sense of relationship to the natural world inspired by beauty in nature, examining their relationships with others, looking at their conscience, and wondering about their thought processes and how far they could lead them to find answers to their pressing existential and spiritual questions. Each child's spirituality had a "markedly individual character" reflecting the unique disposition of each child.

The spiritual character in many children's relational consciousness was evident in four dimensions:

1. *The Child:* God consciousness was evident in a child's mentioning experiences of God's presence, perceiving God's presence in literally everything, in praying to God person to person, and so on. It was also evident in children who asked questions of origin or how to explain the way the world is, in their rejection of God as an explanation for everything as too limited and too simplistic (these were six- and ten-year-olds). Thus the children are more sophisticated and mature in their conception of God than previously thought. Children's ideas of God tend not to be anthropomorphic (Petrovich, 1989). When children refer to God in anthropomorphic terms it is because they were so taught and because they know that these are the expected answers.

2. *The Child:* People consciousness was evident, for instance, in a boy's three wishes, which were for nasty people to become good, for the rich to give money to the poor, and for himself to be able to share it with someone else. In other instances it was a sensitive desire to exercise fairness toward a friend, or the idea that heaven would be a place with no unkindness. These examples show in these children a consciousness that is spiritual because it goes far beyond the idea of just being nice and getting along with others.

3. *The Child:* Self consciousness was evident in the realization that the child's identity is not just the physical body (from the experience of "popping out" of the body), puzzling over what it means to be dead and whether the present "I" will know it, and puzzling over where they came from and why they were here.

4. *The Child:* World consciousness was evident in the sense of wonder and the inspiration and joy the children drew from nature, newborn lambs, flowers, and the sky, which was felt to be holy, and from standing at night on a hill and looking down at the marvelous sight of the sea of lights of a shopping center.

The influences of home, religion, gender, class, or age were existing only in the background of the child's psyche. "The primary influences on a child's spirituality appeared to emanate from his or her personality" (Nye, 1998, p. 195). From the vocabulary, level of articulation, and intensity of thought in the material, she cited it was clear that several children were precocious and gifted.

The Philosophy of Gifted Education Conundrum

Examining spirituality makes the concept of relational consciousness of great import for gifted education. Relational consciousness, the sense of an all-embracing connectedness, is a higher-order concept unifying emotional and spiritual giftedness. Connectedness springs from the deepest source—the state of Absolute Unitary Being—that appears to potentially exist in all people as current brain studies seem to indicate (Goodman, 1990; Newberg & d'Aquili, 2001; *Newsweek,* May 7, 2001). Therefore to deny it, or to go against it, is to go against something that is not only essential but at the center of what makes us human.

Contrary to popular belief, American teenagers have a spiritual life, and that means not only girls, but boys, too:

> boys and men are a much more spiritual group than many of us might have ever imagined. Their belief—whether in God or an organized religion, or in a spiritual wellspring beyond themselves—is widespread and pronounced. For many boys, such a spiritual core is not only profoundly meaningful but also emotionally sustaining, leading to hopefulness and renewal when perhaps all other avenues and possibilities seemed compromised or lost. Even after my many years of close work with young men, I was struck, and indeed deeply moved, by the depth of the spiritual thread that ran through so many of their stories (Pollack, 2000, p. 87).

It should be no surprise that depression can be the flip side of emotional giftedness and the hunger for deeply meaningful connection with others. Jackson's (1998) study of depression of intellectually gifted and emotionally intense adolescents showed that they have a strong need for communion with others, for understanding and knowledge, and for active participation in the world—to work for the larger good. Lack of channels of expression and opportunities for action is very disturbing to them. Like most people, they prefer to associate with others with whom they can share insights and ideas. They are, as Maslow said of self-actualizing people, hungry for their own kind. But being somewhat of a rare species, it is harder for them to find their own kind. Being one of a kind leads to a sense of isolation, even the feeling of being an alien. In the vast majority of instances, they have to cope with this problem alone, not always successfully, which may lead to depression and suicide.

The concept of relational consciousness has many forerunners in psychology, although they address only two dimensions: relationships with others and the relationship with oneself. The two remaining dimensions—relationship with nature and relationship with a transcendent consciousness or transcendent Being—have not been included in most cases. The emphasis on relational awareness is present in Adler's social interest (Gemeinschaftsgefühl), in Rogers's client-centered counseling, in Maslow's self-actualization (e.g., traits of kindness to all individuals, democratic character structure, abhorrence of hostile and demeaning humor, deep relationships with others, etc.), in Bowlby's (1969) attachment theory, in relational psychology and ethics of responsibility (Gilligan, 1982), in connected knowing (Belenky, Clinchy, Goldberger, & Tarule, 1986), and in psychology of women (Miller, Stiver, Jordan, & Surrey, 1994). In education, its forerunners are the leaders in child-centered education: Quintilian, Comenius, Rousseau, Pestalozzi, Froebel, and Montessori, with Hollingworth and Roeper representing gifted education (Grant & Piechowski, 1999).

Roeper's education for self-actualization and interdependence (Roeper, 1990, 1995), Dabrowski's theory (Dabrowski, 1967; Piechowski, 1975, 1991, in press; Silverman, 1993), moral and spiritual sensitivity (Lovecky, 1997, 1998), and the concept of emotional giftedness (Roeper, 1982; Piechowski, 1991, 1997) are the principal expressions of a relational worldview in gifted education.

As a worldview, relational consciousness stands at the extreme opposite of individualism. Hay (2001) points out that the history of capitalism is a history of possessive and exploitive individualism. Its roots go back to Hobbes's *Leviathan* in 1651. Its engine is competition, its consequence distancing of people from each other—men especially—and spiritual alienation.

The task for education of the gifted is to achieve a balance between development of talents and abilities, its present dominant emphasis, and personal growth, which emphasizes the development of the whole child. The risk of an overemphasis on talent development is alienation (Grant & Piechowski, 1999).

Although Dai and Renzulli (2000) argued that talent development can promote personal growth, it is hardly guaranteed. On the contrary, attention to personal growth includes development of talents as an integral component of the emotional development of the whole person, therefore, it guarantees both.

If gifted education had a philosophy of education, which it manifestly lacks, it would struggle with this issue. It would have to confront the truth that developing a child's potential to the fullest is merely a slogan if it neglects emotional and spiritual development.

SUMMARY AND CONCLUSIONS

The concept of emotional giftedness predates the idea of emotional intelligence, and the concept of spiritual giftedness predates, implicitly, the idea of spiritual intelligence. Emotional giftedness finds expression in helping others when no one else would, alleviating distress, opposing unfairness, and fighting injustice. Numerous examples of gifted children initiating large-scale altruistic projects illustrate the concept of emotional giftedness. The resilience of children overcoming abuse is also included.

The concept of spiritual giftedness is old. However, the recognition of childhood spirituality is recent. Besides having adult-like experiences of ecstasy, timelessness, God in everything, and sense of self beyond physical reality, some children are able to discover their own techniques for achieving heightened consciousness.

There are many measures of spiritual intelligence, but only a handful of emotional intelligence. Both emotional and spiritual intelligence have a demonstrated neurological basis. The neurological component is also known for spiritual giftedness, but has yet to be demonstrated for emotional giftedness. Unifying both emotional and spiritual intelligence is the concept of relational consciousness, a sense of an overall connectedness, which has long-standing forerunners in psychology.

The idea of relational consciousness has vital implications for gifted education. It brings to light the basic issue in gifted education: how to achieve the proper balance in emphasis between talent development and personal growth. If the goal of education is to develop each child's potential to the fullest, how can it leave out emotional and spiritual development?

QUESTIONS FOR THOUGHT AND DISCUSSION

1. Discuss appropriate ways of responding to emotionally and spiritually sensitive children.

2. How ought one to respond when a child makes spiritual assertions that go contrary to the belief system of the community?

3. Explain the concept of "positive maladjustment."

4. What would be the consequences of emphasizing relational consciousness in the school as a community of learners?

5. Does the idea of relational consciousness get around the taboo against discussing spirituality? Explain.

REFERENCES

Anthony, D., Ecker, B., & Wilber, K. (Eds.) (1987). *Spiritual choices: The problem of recognizing authentic paths to inner transformation.* New York: Paragon House.

Anthony, E. J. (1987). Children at high risk for psychosis growing up successfully. In E. J. Anthony & B. Cohler (Eds.), *The invulnerable child.* New York: Guilford.

Armstrong, T. (1984). Transpersonal experience in childhood. *Journal of Transpersonal Psychology, 16,* 207–230.

Atwater, P. M. H. (1999). *Children of the new millennium.* New York: Three Rivers Press.

Bauer, P. J. (1997). Development of memory in early childhood. In N. Cowan (Ed.), *Development of memory in childhood* (pp. 83–111). Hove East Essex, UK: Psychology Press.

Belenky, M. F., Clinchy, B. M., Goldberger, N. R., & Tarule, J. M. (1986). *Women's ways of knowing: The development of self, voice, and mind.* New York: Basic Books.

Berkowitz, B. (1987). *Local heroes: The rebirth of heroism in America.* Lexington, MA: Lexington Books.

Bowlby, J. (1969). *Attachment and loss.* Vol. 1. *Attachment.* New York: Basic Books.

Chapman, J., & Chapman, E. (2000). Open doors to education. Annual Hollingworth Conference, May, 2000, Newton, MA.

Coles, R. (1990). *The spiritual life of children.* Boston: Houghton Mifflin.

Colby, A., & Damon, W. (1992). *Some do care: Contemporary lives of moral commitment.* New York: Free Press.

Craig, M. (1985). *Six modern martyrs.* New York: Crossroad.

Dabrowski, K. (1964). *Positive disintegration.* Boston: Little, Brown.

Dabrowski, K. (1967). *Personality-shaping through positive disintegration.* Boston: Little, Brown.

Dabrowski, K. (1970). *Mental growth through positive disintegration.* London: Gryf.

Dai, D. Y., & Renzulli, J. S. (2000). Dissociation and integration of talent development and personal growth: Comments and suggestions. *Gifted Child Quarterly, 44,* 247–251.

Daloz, L. A. P., Keen, C. H., Keen, J. P., Parks, S. D. (1996). *Common fire: Leading lives of commitment in a complex world.* Boston: Beacon Press.

Damasio, A. (1994). *Descartes' error: Emotion, reason and the human brain.* New York: Putnam.

Damasio, A. (1999). *The feeling of what happens: Body and emotion in the making of consciousness.* New York: Harcourt Brace.

Davis, R. D. (1994). *The gift of dyslexia.* New York: Perigee.

Delisle, D., & Delisle, J. (1996). *Growing good kids: 28 activities to enhance self-awareness, compassion, and leadership.* Minneapolis, MN: Free Spirit.

Emmons, R. A. (1999). *The psychology of ultimate concerns.* New York: Guilford.

Enright, R. D., & North, J. (Eds.). (1996). *Exploring forgiveness.* Madison, WI: University of Wisconsin Press.

Feldman, D. H., & Goldsmith, L. (1986). *Nature's gambit.* New York: Basic Books.

Fivush, R. (1997). Event memory in early childhood. In N. Cowan (Ed.), *The development of memory in childhood.* Hove, East Sussex, UK: Psychology Press, pp. 139–161.

Gallagher, J. (2001). Making a difference. *The Advocate,* May 22, 2001.

Gardner, H. (1999). *Intelligence reframed.* New York: Basic Books.

Gardner, H. (2000). A case against spiritual intelligence. *International Journal for the Psychology of Religion, 10,* 27–34.

Gilligan, C. (1982). *In a different voice: Psychological theory and women's development.* Cambridge: Harvard University Press.

Goodman, F. D. (1990). *Where the spirits ride the wind: Trance journeys and other ecstatic experiences.* Bloomington, IN: Indiana University Press.

Grant, B., & Piechowski, M. M. (1999). Theories and the good: Toward child-centered gifted education. *Gifted Child Quarterly, 43,* 4–12.

Goleman, D. (1995). *Emotional intelligence.* New York: Bantam.

Harrison, C. (2000). Out of the mouth of babes: Spiritual awareness and the young gifted child. *Advanced Development, 9,* 31–43.

Hay, D. (2001). Spirituality versus individualism: The challenge of relational consciousness. In J. Erricker, C. Ota, & C. Erricker (Eds.), *Spiritual education: Cultural, religious, and social differences.* Brighton, UK: Sussex Academic Press.

Hay, D., & Nye, R. (1998). *The spirit of the child.* London: Fount/HarperCollins.

Higgins, G. O. (1994). *Resilient adults: Overcoming a cruel past.* San Francisco: Jossey-Bass.

Hillesum, E. (1985). *An interrupted life: Diaries of Etty Hillesum, 1941–1943.* New York: Washington Square Press.

Hoffman, E. (1992). *Visions of innocence: Spiritual and inspirational experiences of childhood.* Boston: Shambhala.

Howard, D. D. (1994). A naturalistic study of the psychosocial development of highly gifted girls. Unpublished doctoral dissertation. University of Denver, Denver, Colorado.

Jackson, P. S. (1998). Bright star—black sky. A phenomenological study of depression as a window into the psyche of the gifted adolescent. *Roeper Review, 20,* 215–221.

James, W. (1902/1936). *The varieties of religious experience.* New York: Modern Library.

Kurzweil, R. (1998). *The age of spiritual machines.* New York: Penguin Audiobooks.

LeDoux, J. (1996). *The emotional brain.* New York: Simon & Schuster.

Lewis, B. (1991). *The kid's guide to social action.* Minneapolis, MN: Free Spirit.

Lewis, B. (1992). *Kids with courage.* Minneapolis, MN: Free Spirit.

Lewis, S. (1996). *"A totally alien life-form": Teenagers.* New York: The New Press.

Lovecky, D. V. (1992). Exploring social and emotional aspects of giftedness in children. *Roeper Review, 15,* 18–25.

Lovecky, D. V. (1993). The quest for meaning: Counseling issues with gifted children and adolescents. In L. K. Silverman (Ed.), *Counseling the gifted and talented.* Denver: Love.

Lovecky, D. V. (1997). Identity development in gifted children: Moral sensitivity. *Roeper Review, 20,* 90–94.

Lovecky, D. V. (1998). Spiritual sensitivity in gifted children. *Roeper Review, 20,* 178–183.

Lysy, K. Z., & Piechowski, M. M. (1983). Personal growth: An empirical study using Jungian and Dabrowskian measures. *Genetic Psychology Monographs, 108,* 267–320.

MacDonald, D. A., Friedman, H. L., & Kuentzel, J. G. (1999). A survey of measures of spiritual and transpersonal constructs: Part one—research update. *Journal of Transpersonal Psychology, 31,* 137–154.

MacDonald, D. A., Kuentzel, J. G., & Friedman, H. L. (1999). A survey of measures of spiritual and transpersonal constructs: Part two—additional instruments. *Journal of Transpersonal Psychology, 31,* 155–177.

MacDonald, D. A., LeClair, L., Holland, C. J., Alter, A. Friedman, H. L. (1995). A survey of measures of transpersonal constructs. *Journal of Transpersonal Psychology, 27,* 171–235.

Maxwell, P., & Tschudin, V. (1990). *Seeing the invisible: Modern religious and other transcendent experiences.* London: Penguin.

Mayer, J. D., & Salovey, P. (1997). What is emotional intelligence? In P. Salovey & D. J. Sluyter (Eds.), *Emotional development and emotional intelligence* (pp. 3–31). New York: Basic Books.

Mayer, J. D., Caruso, D. R., & Salovey, P. (1999). Emotional intelligence meets traditional standards for an intelligence. *Intelligence, 27,* 267–298.

Mayer, J. D., Caruso, D. R., & Salovey, P. (2000). Selecting a measure of emotional intelligence: The case for ability scales. In R. Bar-On & J. D. A. Parker (Eds.), *The handbook of emotional intelligence,* (pp. 320–342). San Francisco: Jossey-Bass.

Mayer, J. D., Perkins, D. M., Caruso, D. R., & Salovey, P. (2001). Emotional intelligence and giftedness. *Roeper Review, 23,* 131–137.

Mayer, J. D., Salovey, P., & Caruso, D. R. (2000a). Models of emotional intelligence. In R. Sternberg (Ed.), *Handbook of intelligence* (pp. 396–420). Cambridge: Cambridge University Press.

Mayer, J. D., Salovey, P., & Caruso, D. R. (2000b). Emotional intelligences as Zeitgeist, as personality, and as a mental ability. In R. Bar-On & J. D. A. Parker (Eds.), *The handbook of emotional intelligence* (pp. 92–117). San Francisco: Jossey-Bass.

Miller, J. B., Stiver, P. I., Jordan, J. V., & Surrey, J. L. (1994). The psychology of women: A relational approach. In J. Fadiman & R. Frager (Eds.). *Personality and personal growth* (3rd ed.). New York: HarperCollins.

Morelock, M. (1995). The profoundly gifted child in a family context. Unpublished doctoral dissertation. Medford, MA: Tufts University.

Morse, M. (1990). *Closer to the light: Learning from the near-death experiences of children.* New York: Ballantine.

Murdock, M. H. (1978). Meditation with young children. *Journal of Transpersonal Psychology, 10,* 29–44.

Murphy, M. (1992). *The future of the body: Explorations into the further evolution of human nature.* Los Angeles: Jeremy P. Tarcher.

Newberg, A., & d'Aquili, E. (2001). *Why God won't go away: Brain science and the biology of belief.* New York: Ballantine.

Noble, K. D. (2000). Spiritual intelligence: A new frame of mind. *Advanced Development, 9,* 1–29.

Noble, K. D. (2001). *Riding the windhorse: Spiritual intelligence and the growth of the self.* Cresskill, NJ: Hampton Press.

Nye, R. (1998). Psychological perspectives on children's spirituality. Ph.D. thesis. Nottingham: University of Nottingham.

Oliner, S. P., & Oliner, P. M. (1988). *The altruistic personality: Rescuers of Jews in Nazi Europe.* New York: The Free Press.

Paffard, M. (1973). *Inglorious Wordsworths: A study of some transcendental experiences in childhood and adolescence.* London: Hodder & Stoughton.

Peace Pilgrim (1982). *Peace Pilgrim: Her life and work in her own words.* Santa Fe, NM: Ocean Tree.

Peterson, J. S. (1997). Bright, tough, and resilient—and not in a gifted program. *Journal for Secondary Gifted Education, 8,* 121–136.

Petrovich, O. (1989). An examination of Piaget's theory of childhood artificialism. Ph.D. thesis. Oxford: University of Oxford.

Pfeiffer, S. I. (2001). Emotional intelligence: Popular but elusive construct. *Roeper Review, 23,* 138–142.

Piechowski, M. M. (1975). A theoretical and empirical approach to the study of development. *Genetic Psychology Monographs, 92,* 231–297.

Piechowski, M. M. (1979). Developmental potential. In N. Colangelo & R. T. Zaffrann (Eds.), *New voices in counseling the gifted.* (pp. 25–57). Dubuque, IA: Kendall/Hunt.

Piechowski, M. M. (1990). Inner growth and transformation in the life of Eleanor Roosevelt. *Advanced Development, 2,* 35–53.

Piechowski, M. M. (1991). Emotional development and emotional giftedness. In N. Colangelo & G. Davis, (Eds.), *Handbook of gifted education* (pp. 285–306). Boston: Allyn & Bacon.

Piechowski, M. M. (1992). Giftedness for all seasons: Inner peace in time of war. In N. Colangelo, S. G. Assouline, & D. L. Ambroson. (Eds.), *Talent development* (pp. 80–203). Proceedings of the Henry B. and Jocelyn Wallace National Research Symposium on Talent Development. Unionville, NY: Trillium Press.

Piechowski, M. M. (1993). Is inner transformation a creative process? *Creativity Research Journal, 6,* 89–98.

Piechowski, M. M. (1997a). Emotional giftedness: The measure of intrapersonal intelligence. In N. Colangelo & G. A. Davis (Eds.), *The handbook of gifted education* (2nd ed., 366–381). Boston: Allyn & Bacon.

Piechowski, M. M. (1997b). Emotional giftedness: An expanded view. *Apex, A New Zealand Journal of Gifted Education, 10,* 37–47.

Piechowski, M. M. (2000). Childhood experiences and spiritual giftedness. *Advanced Development, 9,* 65–90.

Piechowski, M. M. (2001a). Spiritual giftedness and the transpersonal dimension of experience. In N. Colangelo & S. G. Assouline (Eds.), at *Talent development* (393–397). Proceedings from the Wallace National Research Symposium on Talent Development. Scottsdale, AZ: Great Potential Press.

Piechowski, M. M. (2001b). Childhood spirituality. *Journal of Transpersonal Psychology, 33,* 1–15.

Piechowski, M. M. (2002). From William James to Maslow and Dabrowski: Excitability of character and self-actualization. In D. Ambrose, L. Cohen, & A. J. Tannenbaum (Eds.), *Creative intelligence: Toward a theoretic integration* (pp. 283–322). Cresskill, NJ: Hampton Press.

Pollack, W. (1998). *Real boys: Rescuing our sons from the myths of boyhood.* New York: Random House.

Pollack, W. (2000). *Real boys' voices.* New York: Random House.

Robinson, E. (1977). *The Original vision: A study of the religious experience of childhood.* Oxford: The Religious Experience Research Unit. Reprinted by Seabury Press, New York, 1983.

Robinson, E. (1978). *Living the questions.* Oxford: The Religious Experience Research Unit.

Roeper, A. (1982). How the gifted cope with their emotions. *Roeper Review, 5,* 21–24.

Roeper, A. (1990). *Educating children for life: The modern learning community.* Monroe, NY: Trillium.

Roeper, A. (1995). *Selected writings and speeches.* Minneapolis, MN: Free Spirit.

Rubin, L. (1996). *The transcendent child.* New York: Harper Perennial.

Salovey, P., & Mayer, J. D. (1990). Emotional intelligence. *Imagination, Cognition, and Personality, 9,* 185–211.

Salovey, P., Bedell, B. T., Detweiler, J. B., & Mayer, J. D. (2000). Current directions in emotional intelligence research. In M. Lewis & J. M. Haviland-Jones (Eds.), *Handbook of emotions* (2nd ed. pp. 504–520). New York: Guilford Press.

Schneider, W., & Pressley, M. (1997). *Memory development between two and twenty* (2nd ed.). Mahwah, NJ: Erlbaum.

Sheingold, K., & Tenney, Y. (1982). Memory for a salient childhood event. In U. Neisser (Ed.), *Memory observed.* New York: W. H. Freeman.

Silverman, L. K. (1993). The moral sensitivity of gifted children and the evolution of society. *Roeper Review, 17,* 110–116.

Silverman, L. K. (1993). The gifted individual. In L. K. Silverman (Ed.), *Counseling the gifted and talented* (pp. 3–28). Denver: Love.

Sinetar, M. (2000). *Spiritual intelligence.* Maryknoll, NY: Orbis.

Tamminen, K. (1991). *Religious development in childhood and youth: An empirical study.* Helsinki: Suomalainen Tiedeakatemia. (Cited in Hay & Nye, 1998.)

Waldman, J. (2001). *Teens with courage to give.* Berkeley: Conari Press.

Wallace, A. (1993). *Eco-heroes.* San Francisco: Mercury House.

Witty, M. (1990). Life history studies of committed lives. Unpublished Ph.D. dissertation. Northwestern University, Evanston, Illinois.

Young, S. H. (1977). *Psychic children.* Garden City, NY: Doubleday.

Zohar, D., & Marshall, I. (2000). *SQ: Connecting with our spiritual intelligence.* New York: Bloomsbury.

32

Motivational Issues: Potential to Performance

TERRY MCNABB, *Coe College, Iowa*

The role of motivation in academic achievement has been a subject of scientific inquiry for over forty-five years. Whether described as task commitment, persistence, intrinsic interest, challenge seeking, passion to learn, or effort expenditure, the concept of motivation is understood by researchers, educators, and lay people to represent the difference between *potential* and *performance*. The importance of motivation is especially salient for highly able students, for whom this difference can be substantial and extremely frustrating for parents, teachers, and the students themselves.

Understanding the role of motivation in both the behavior and the identification of gifted students is problematic. For example, in his three-ring conception of giftedness, Renzulli (1978) identified *task commitment* as one of three components (along with *above average ability* and *creativity*) of gifted behavior. Similarly, Winner (2000) identified a deep intrinsic motivation to master the domain in which the gift is present, along with precocity and independent learning, as three characteristics that define giftedness. Winner stated, "Intrinsic drive is part and parcel of an exceptional, inborn giftedness" (p. 163).

While both Renzulli's and Winner's models broaden the definition of giftedness beyond the traditional, psychometrically driven one used by Terman, the models cause some confusion in understanding underachievement (Gagné, 1991). If motivation is a necessary *condition* for giftedness, then what are we to think about students who are deemed capable of, but do not demonstrate, gifted behavior? At the crux of the underachievement issue is acknowledgment that high ability does not guarantee high achievement; giftedness does not guarantee gifted behavior.

A central question for educators and parents seems to be this: Assuming that children possess an intrinsic desire to learn, why do some high-ability children lose, suppress, or sidestep their intrinsic motivation? Further, what is meant, specifically, by *motivation,* and how can we better understand the psychological mechanisms that may contribute to low motivation?

Underachievement as a Motivation Problem

Academic underachievement is a complex phenomenon; indeed, in most situations it is likely to be the product of a constellation of variables, both endogenous and exogenous. Exogenous variables can include various environmental influences in both the child's home and school. Serious family problems can hinder a child's ability to give schoolwork the attention it requires, or the school environment may not allow the full expression of giftedness. Sometimes exceptional performance is hindered by limited course offerings or negative classroom interactions.

Many teachers have received inadequate instruction on the special needs of gifted students. For example, many gifted students prefer independent mastery of knowledge (Gottfried & Gottfried, 1996), yet teachers may not be aware of or use behaviors that support autonomy, such as those identified by Reeve and his colleagues (Reeve, Bolt, & Cai, 1999). Many children express their boredom in school through misbehavior, which, in turn, elicits negative reactions from teachers and reinforces the child's perception that his or her needs are unreasonable.

Finally, gifted students may be especially vulnerable to concerns about the social desirability of both giftedness and studiousness, and may submit to peer pressure to hide their gifts (Tannenbaum, 1983). More recent research suggests that academic achievement (along with athletic ability) is an important determinant of peer acceptance by other adolescents (Udvari & Rubin, 1996).

However, even when schools offer a challenging curriculum, when parents and teachers encourage academic excellence, and when no serious emotional problems are present, there remain a large number of high-ability students who suffer from one or more of the following academic problems: low effort, challenge avoidance, unreasonably low or unreasonably high self-expectations, low persistence at difficult tasks, or lack of joy in learning. It is this subgroup of students whose self-defeating behaviors likely are due to endogenous factors, and who can better be understood through the lens of motivational research.

The constellation of self-defeating behaviors described above may typify the student who lacks intrinsic motivation, defined as the tendency to engage in a behavior in the absence of external reward. As motivation research has proliferated over the past forty-five years, one focus has been on identifying specific academic behaviors that are associated with desirable academic outcomes. Research has generally targeted three behaviors—challenge seeking, persistence, and task enjoyment—as indicating the presence of intrinsic motivation. These behaviors are considered to be "adaptive" or "mastery-oriented" academic behaviors, and their opposites—challenge avoidance, giving up, and lack of enjoyment—are considered to be "maladaptive" or "helpless" academic behaviors.

In recent years, researchers have attempted to delineate the conditions under which adaptive and maladaptive behavior occurs. This focus on the situation-specific aspects of academic motivation departs from research that sees motivation as a stable personal characteristic. Specifically referring to research on motivation and gifted students, Clinkenbeard (1996) called on researchers to identify classroom variables that foster adaptive motivational behaviors. This focus on the context of motivation encourages the view that students are not simply "motivated" or "unmotivated." While they may not be motivated to meet the teacher's or the school's academic goals, they *are* motivated to meet their own psychological needs, and these needs can be directly influenced by the students' environment.

Since the publication of the second edition of this book, motivation researchers have begun to address the special issues of high-ability students directly.

Several well-developed and well-researched theories have shed light on the critical question of why some students with high academic ability do not meet or even attempt to meet, their potential. This chapter will trace the development of one specific "family" of social-cognitive theories of motivation as it has evolved over the past half-century, and suggest its implications for understanding underachievement in gifted students.[1]

Social-Cognitive Theories

Social-cognitive theories rest on the assumption that behavior stems from the way that people interpret and internalize information taken from their interaction with their social world. Further, many cognitive theories of achievement behavior are guided by the assumption that a child's *perception* of his or her ability is a better predictor of achievement-related behaviors than are objective measures of that ability (e.g., standardized test scores or grades). Research from many theoretical perspectives has supported this contention (Bandura, 1977; Covington, 1984; Harter, 1978; Nicholls, 1982; Parsons, 1982; Phillips, 1984; Weiner, 1979). Theories that derive from research on locus of control are especially useful in exploring why children who are academically exceptional behave as if they were not. Specifically, locus of control, attribution theory, and goal theory suggest explanations for what is preventing these children from exhibiting adaptive or mastery-oriented academic behaviors.

Locus of Control

In 1966, in the context of social learning theory, Julian Rotter identified the tendency of people to perceive that outcomes in a particular arena were either within or outside of their control. Further, this tendency predicted their expectations for future success in that area (Rotter, 1966). He called this construct *locus of control,* and it has since been applied to issues in numerous realms, including health, interpersonal relationships, and academics. People with an internal locus of control have been found to take more responsibility for their behavior and to demonstrate

---

1. For an extensive review of the research on achievement motivation and gifted students, see Dai, Moon, and Feldhusen (1998).

typical "expectancy shifts"; that is, to raise their expectations after experiencing success, and to lower their expectations following failure. People who have an external locus of control feel that forces outside themselves control their fortunes, and act as if there were little relationship between what they do and what happens to them. As a consequence, they exhibit "atypical" expectancy shifts, that is, low expectancy after success and high expectancy after failure, which are often manifested as low confidence in their own ability, even following success.

This pattern of expectancy shifts describes the behaviors of some underachievers. They appear to have either low or unrealistically high academic goals. For example, the student who avoids enrolling in an accelerated mathematics course despite high achievement test scores and high grades in previous math classes is demonstrating an atypical expectancy shift.

Rotter's theory has generated voluminous research into the antecedents, correlates, and consequences of a student's locus of control for academic subjects. It has been found that locus of control tends to be a generalized trait, but there is variation within and between domains or areas. For example, a student could exhibit an internal locus of control for athletic activities as well as an external locus of control for schoolwork; or have an internal locus for math but an external locus for English.

Locus of control is thought to derive from a person's reinforcement history, and is therefore sensitive to environmental variations. Research conducted in the early 1970s discovered that intrinsic motivation actually can be undermined by external reward, and that the mechanism through which this occurs is locus of control. Lepper, Green, and Nisbett (1973) conducted a program of research on the "overjustification hypothesis," in which children were given rewards for performing activities that they already enjoyed. Many experiments using varying types of rewards (i.e., verbal praise, candy, symbolic rewards) found that children showed *less* interest and enjoyment in an activity, which they had initially engaged in for its intrinsic interest, after being promised and given a reward for engaging in that same activity. The authors proposed that by imposing a reward on an already rewarding activity, the experiment shifted children's locus of control for that activity from internal to external. Later research by Amabile (1985), Amabile, Goldfarb, and Brackfield (1990), and Amabile, Hennessey, and Grossman (1986) showed that a similar phenomenon occurs when artists and authors are rewarded for their creative products; stories and artwork produced under contract were judged to be less creative than work produced without a promised reward.

The implications for gifted students seem clear. For those who are vulnerable to the undermining effect of reward (and we know little about why some students are and some are not), their loss of control over schoolwork would seem to begin as soon as grades are assigned. Constantly praised and rewarded for doing what comes naturally to them (i.e., excellent work), the students may come to depend on external evaluation, and worse, come to view their own behavior as driven by the external agent.

Although the controversy over the appropriate use of reward continues (see Cameron & Pierce, 1994), it seems clear that for some students, a loss of a sense of control over their own learning may be at the root of their underachievement.

Attribution Theory

Research on locus of control was absorbed, to a great degree, by Weiner's (1974, 1979) attribution theory. Weiner proposed that locus of control was one of two dimensions that characterized the explanations (or attributions) that students give for their success and failure in the classroom. According to Weiner, the four chief explanations that students give for academic outcomes relate to ability, effort, task difficulty, and luck. These four attributions vary not only in terms of their locus (internal or external), but also in terms of their stability or permanence (stable or unstable). Using these two dimensions, Weiner constructed a four-celled taxonomy (see Figure 32.1).

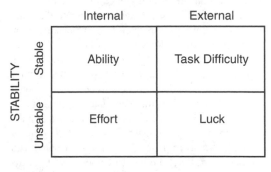

Figure 32.1 Four attributions that explain academic outcomes.

The major contribution of attribution theory to our understanding of academic achievement was thought to be its ability to link specific academic behaviors to particular attributions. Ability attributions for success were thought to be associated with high expectations for future success, challenge seeking, and persistence, while ability attributions for failure were thought to be associated with low expectations for future success, challenge avoidance, and low persistence. Students who believe that their failures are due to low ability also believe that future failures are likely. Diener and Dweck (1978) claimed that such students exhibit "learned helplessness" in academic settings. They see poor academic outcomes as outside of their control, since the outcomes are due to low ability, so they give up easily, avoid challenges, and dislike school.

Adaptive academic behaviors, then, were thought to be associated with ability attributions for success, but not for failure. As later research demonstrated, however, the consequences of ability attributions for successful outcomes are not so easily generalized.

Effort attributions, on the other hand, were thought to be associated with adaptive behaviors when used to explain failure. Because effort is generally perceived to be under one's control, it is changeable. Students who believe that their schoolwork can be improved through their own effort are likely to maintain high expectations for success and to try harder next time.

The way that students think about ability and effort, especially as these concepts relate to each other, has enormous implications for understanding high-ability students' motivation problems. By early adolescence, many children have developed a compensatory view of effort and ability; that is, they believe that smart kids don't have to try hard, and if you do have to try hard, you're not smart. Consider the implications of this belief, from an attribution theory perspective, for students who have been labeled and treated as "gifted" from a young age. Suppose that a student, on his first algebra test, receives a grade that he considers to be low (this could be a "B") after working very hard. Having made ability attributions for his good performance in math for his entire life as a result of being told repeatedly that he is "smart in math," he is now confronted with a situation in which he has to come up with an explanation for his "failure." The very fact that he had to work so hard on the test has already shaken his confidence in his ability. Many students in this situation begin to avoid situations in which they have to work hard, not out of laziness, but out of fear—to protect a self-concept of high ability.

Recent research has elaborated on the relationship between such failure avoidance and the beliefs students have about their abilities, casting doubt on the previous conclusions of attribution research about the unequivocally positive effects of ability attributions for success.

Goal Theories

Dweck and her colleagues (Dweck, 1986, 1991; Dweck & Leggett, 2000; Elliot & Dweck, 1988; Kamins & Dweck, 1999) proposed that adaptive achievement behaviors (challenge-seeking, high persistence in the face of obstacles, and positive affect) and maladaptive achievement behaviors (challenge avoidance, low persistence, and negative affect) have more to do with differences in students' classroom goals than with differences in their academic ability. Further, they contend that students' goals in academic situations are related to the way they think about their intelligence (see Figure 32.2).

According to Dweck, students hold either an *entity* view or an *incremental* view of intelligence. Students who have an entity view believe that intelligence is a fixed trait that they "have," and they are motivated to engage in activities that will give them favorable judgments of their ability. Operating from an entity viewpoint, students adopt *performance* goals, which focus on measuring and demonstrating their ability, and see achievement situations (performances) as tests of their competence. Consequently, being challenged and learning a lot are sacrificed in favor of "looking smart" (Mueller and Dweck, 1998). When they approach a learning situation about which they are confident, they will show adaptive learning behaviors. However, when they approach a situation about which they have low confidence (e.g., a new situation or one that has been challenging in the past), they exhibit maladaptive behaviors. "Entity theorists" tend to see ability and effort as inversely related, so they doubt their ability after high-effort successes.

Conversely, people who view their intelligence as malleable and a product of effort are called "incremental theorists." They see achievement situations as opportunities to increase their competence, and they orient toward activities that help them develop their intellect and skills. Incremental theorists have *learning* rather than performance goals, and

Theory of Intelligence	Goal Orientation	Confidence in Present Ability	Behavior Pattern
Entity theory (Intelligence is fixed)	**Performance goal** (Goal is to gain positive judgments/avoid negative judgments of competence)	**If high**→ but **If low**→	**Mastery-oriented** Seek challenge High persistence **Helpless** Avoid challenge Low persistence
Incremental theory (Intelligence is malleable)	**Learning goal** (Goal is to increase competence)	**If high**→ or **low**	**Mastery-oriented** Seek challenge (that fosters learning) High persistence

Figure 32.2   Dweck's model of achievement motivation.

Source: From "Motivational Processes Affecting Learning," by C. S. Dweck, 1986, *American Psychologist,* 41, p. 1041. Copyright 1986 by the American Psychological Association. Reprinted with permission.

they see effort and ability as positively related, so they focus on trying harder when they are challenged. Incremental theorists demonstrate adaptive academic behaviors, regardless of their level of confidence in a particular task.

Mueller and Dweck's (1998) research finds that students who receive praise for their intelligence are more likely to develop an entity view of intelligence and hold performance goals, compared with students who receive praise for their effort. The primary motivational goal of such entity students is to document their high ability levels through successful performances, which are most likely when tasks are not challenging. In addition, these students tend to exhibit low motivation following setbacks.

According to Dweck and Leggett (1988, p. 260):

Adaptive individuals effectively coordinate performance and learning goals. It is when an overconcern with proving their *adequacy* to themselves or to others leads individuals to ignore, avoid, or to abandon potentially valuable learning opportunities that problems arise.

Substitute *giftedness* for *adequacy* in the above quote, and the plight of the underachiever becomes clear. The aim of justifying the "gifted" label serves as a kind of self-handicapping for many high-ability children and reinforces the feelings of many gifted

children that their worth is determined by their performance. This sense of "contingent self-worth" is exacerbated when children receive feedback, even positive, that is directed toward a personal trait (like intelligence). These findings contradict long-held, entrenched beliefs of teachers and parents about the power of praise, and require a rethinking of the praise and terminology we use with gifted children.

It would seem difficult for a child who has been referred to as *gifted* for all of his or her childhood to develop an incremental view of intelligence. In fact, the child has probably heard innumerable messages that low-effort means high-ability ("That was so easy for you. You must be really smart," "You got that answer so quickly. You are really good at math"). By early adolescence a firm entity view may already be entrenched. Also by this time, being gifted is likely to be central to the child's identity, providing further incentive to protect the self-concept of high ability.

Unfortunately, as early adolescents enter junior high or middle school, they are often faced with greater academic challenges than they have previously encountered, many of them in novel situations where their confidence is shaky. Entity theorists, for whom the goal is a favorable evaluation of ability, must be confident of their ability before displaying it for judgment. But confidence is fragile, since exertion of effort calls ability into question. In this framework, self-defeating, self-handicapping behaviors like avoiding difficult courses, not studying for tests, and causing problems in class become easier to understand.

Research that conclusively ties children's perceptions of their giftedness to their achievement behaviors remains to be conducted. A better understanding of how high-ability children view effort will contribute greatly to understanding the high-ability, underachievement phenomenon. In the meantime, the preceding research suggests that teachers and parents can:

1. Emphasize the role of effort in learning by focusing on the process of learning rather than on its outcomes. This means measuring progress rather than absolute attainment, and encouraging self-assessment rather than external evaluation.
2. Sacrifice accuracy, occasionally, for risk taking.
3. Help students to see the relationship between their effort and outcomes.
4. Use rewards (including praise) sparingly, and only to reinforce behaviors that are not already rewarding. Help students to recognize the rewards intrinsic in working on a challenging task.
5. Model an incremental view of intelligence by emphasizing the importance of acquiring skills and downplaying normative performance.

SUMMARY AND CONCLUSIONS

Motivation to learn offers one explanation for the gap between gifted students' potential and their performance. Several social-cognitive theories of motivation, beginning with locus of control and attribution theories, discuss how students' understanding of and self-explanations for their behaviors can influence their future academic choices and performance. Recent research into the nature and consequences of students' goals in the classroom (performance versus learning) is especially useful in understanding one particular type of underachievement in gifted students. Specifically, when gifted students are more focused on preserving their identity as "gifted" than on increasing their competence, they may limit their potential by avoiding challenge. This research has important implications for teachers and parents, for example in their use of the "gifted" label, which may reduce some students' motivation to accept challenge.

QUESTIONS FOR THOUGHT AND DISCUSSION

1. Consider locus of control and attribution theory. What are the implications of these theories for using grades in school? Can teachers minimize the negative consequences of grades?

2. What classroom procedures or methods might promote an internal locus of control? What procedures and methods seem to encourage an external locus of control?

3. Explain *entity* versus *incremental* views of intelligence.

4. What are some implications of considering motivation as a prerequisite when identifying gifted students?

REFERENCES

Amabile, T. M. (1985). Motivation and creativity: Effects of motivational orientation on creative writers. *Journal of Personality and Social Psychology, 48,* 393–399.

Amabile, T. M., Goldfarb, P., & Brackfield, S. (1990). Social influences on creativity: Evaluation, coaction, and surveillance. *Creativity Research Journal, 3,* 6–21.

Amabile, T. M., Hennessey, B. A., & Grossman, B. S. (1986). Social influences on creativity: The effects of contracted-for reward. *Journal of Personality and Social Psychology, 50,* 14–23.

Bandura, A. (1977). Self-efficacy: Toward a unifying theory of behavioral change. *Psychological Review, 84,* 191–215.

Cameron, J., & Pierce, W. D. (1994). Reinforcement, reward, and intrinsic motivation: A meta-analysis. *Review of Educational Research, 64,* 363–403.

Clinkenbeard, P. R. (1996). Research on motivation and the gifted: Implications for identification, programming, and evaluation. *Gifted Child Quarterly, 40,* 220–221.

Covington, M. V. (1984). The self-worth theory of achievement motivation: Findings and educational implications. *Elementary School Journal, 85,* 5–20.

Dai, D. Y., Moon, S. M., & Feldhusen, J. F. (1998). Achievement motivation and gifted students: A social cognitive perspective. *Educational Psychologist, 33*(2/3), 45–63.

Diener, C. I., & Dweck, C. S. (1978). An analysis of learned helplessness: Continuous changes in performance, strategy and achievement cognitions following failure. *Journal of Personality and Social Psychology, 36,* 451–462.

Dweck, C. S. (1986). Motivational processes affecting learning. *American Psychologist, 41,* 1040–1048.

Dweck, C. S. (1991). Self-theories and goals: Their role in motivation, personality, and development. In R. A. Dienstbier (Ed.), *Nebraska symposium on motivation:*

Vol. 38. Perspectives on motivation (pp. 199–235). Lincoln: University of Nebraska Press.

Dweck, C. S., & Leggett, E. L. (1988). A social-cognitive approach to motivation and personality. *Psychological Review, 95,* 256–273.

Dweck, C. S., & Leggett, E. L. (2000). A social-cognitive approach to motivation and personality. In E. T. Higgins & W. W. Kruglanski (Eds.), *Motivational Science.* Ann Arbor: Psychology Press.

Elliot, E. S., & Dweck, C. S. (1988). Goals: An approach to motivation and achievement. *Journal of Personality and Social Psychology, 54,* 5–12.

Gagne, F. (1991). Toward a differentiated model of giftedness and talent. In N. Colangelo & G. Davis (Eds.), *Handbook of gifted education.* Boston: Allyn and Bacon.

Gottfried, A. E., & Gottfried, A. W. (1996). A longitudinal study of academic intrinsic motivation in intellectually gifted children: Childhood through early adolescence. *Gifted Child Quarterly, 40,* 179–183.

Harter, S. (1978). Effectance motivation reconsidered: Toward a developmental model. *Human Development, 21,* 34–64.

Kamins, M. L., & Dweck, C. S. (1999). Person versus process praise and criticism: Implications for contingent self-worth and coping. *Developmental Psychology, 35,* 835–847.

Lepper, M. R., Green, D., & Nisbett, R. E. (1973). Undermining children's intrinsic interest with extrinsic reward: A test of the overjustification hypothesis. *Journal of Personality and Social Psychology, 28,* 129–137.

Mueller, C. M., & Dweck, C. S. (1998). Praise for intelligence can undermine children's motivation and performance. *Journal of Personality and Social Psychology, 75,* 33–52.

Nicholls, J. G. (1982). Conceptions of ability and achievement motivation. In R. Ames & C. Ames (Eds.), *Research in motivation in education: Student motivation.* New York: Academic Press.

Parsons, J. E. (1982). Expectancies, values and academic behaviors. In J. T. Spence (Ed.), *Assessing achievement.* San Francisco: W. H. Freeman.

Phillips, D. (1984). The illusion of incompetence among high-achieving children. *Child Development, 55,* 2000–2016.

Reeve, J., Bolt, E., & Cai, Y. (1999). Autonomy-supportive teachers: How they teach and motivate students. *Journal of Educational Psychology, 91,* 537–548.

Renzulli, J. S. (1978). What makes giftedness? Reexamining a definition. *Phi Delta Kappan, 60,* 180–184, 261.

Rotter, J. B. (1966). Generalized expectancies for internal versus external control of reinforcement. *Psychological Monographs, 80,* (1, Whole number 609).

Tannenbaum, A. J. (1983). *Gifted children: Psychological and educational perspectives.* New York: Macmillan.

Udvari, S. J., & Rubin, K. H. (1996). Gifted and non-selected children's perceptions of academic achievement, academic effort and athleticism. *Gifted Child Quarterly, 40,* 211–219.

Weiner, B. (1979). A theory of motivation for some classroom experiences. *Journal of Educational Psychology, 71,* 3–25.

Weiner, B. (Ed.). (1974). *Achievement motivation and attribution theory.* Morristown, NJ: General Learning Press.

Winner, E. (2000). The origins and ends of giftedness. *American Psychologist, 55,* 159–169.

33

Underachievement: A National Epidemic

SYLVIA B. RIMM, *Case Western Reserve School of Medicine and the Family Achievement Clinic, Cleveland, Ohio*

Underachievement Syndrome continues in epidemic proportions in our country. Although it is impossible to determine precise percentages of gifted underachievers, the National Commission on Excellence in Education (1983) reported that half of gifted students do not perform to their tested abilities. High school dropout studies found that between 10 and 20% of those who do not complete high school are in the tested gifted range (Lajoie & Shore, 1981; Nyquist, 1973; Whitmore, 1980). Seeley (1993) estimated that between 15 and 40% are at risk for school underachievement. Underachievement of gifted students emerges dramatically again in college. Of the top 5% of this country's high school graduates, 40% do not complete college (DeLeon, 1989). The Carnegie Corporation's report, *Years of Promise* (1996), further certifies the seriousness of the underachievement problem in the United States. The report states:

> Make no mistake about it, underachievement is not a crisis of certain groups; it is not limited to the poor; it is not a problem afflicting other people's children. Many middle- and upper-income children are also falling behind intellectually. Indeed, by the fourth grade, the performance of most children in the United States is below what it should be for the nation and is certainly below the achievement levels of children in competing countries. (p. 2)

Being intellectually or creatively gifted does not assure educational or creative success or productivity. There are risks and pressures that accompany high intelligence that detour potentially high-achieving children toward defensive and avoidance patterns (Rimm, 2000). The determinants of whether gifted children move toward high achievement or fall into under-achieving patterns appear to be related to their home, school, and/or peer environments (Rimm, 1995).

The Pressures

The main pressures that gifted children feel include (1) the need to be extraordinarily intelligent, perfect, or "smartest"; (2) the wish to be extremely creative and unique, which they may translate as nonconformity; and (3) the concern with being admired by peers for appearance and popularity.

Although parents are often accused of pressuring their gifted children, these pressures typically arise because of the children's giftedness. Gifted children often internalize a sense of stress because adults in their environments have admired them for their academic accomplishments, their unusual ideas, and/or their appearance. While the profuse praise they receive reinforces their motivation, if too extreme or frequent it may cause them to feel as if important other people in their lives virtually demand them to accomplish the goals for which they are admired. Not only may they feel pressure to achieve, they may also acquire a dependence on attention and find it difficult to function without continuous praise and reinforcement (Deci, 1986; Hom, Gaskill, & Hutchins, 1988).

If school and home environments foster successful relationships between effort and outcomes, it is more likely that children will manage the internalized pressures and will incorporate them as motivations toward achievement (Rimm, 2000). School environments that foster underachievement would be those that either do not value high achievement or, conversely, set achievement outcomes too high. In either case, children may make appropriate efforts but do not gain satisfaction from their successful efforts. Some school circumstances that do not promote excellent school achievement include the following:

- An anti-intellectual school atmosphere that sets high priorities for athletics or social status but not for intellectual attainment or preparation for higher levels of education (Brown & Steinberg, 1990; U.S. Department of Education, 1993);
- An anti-gifted atmosphere that considers gifted programming elitist and emphasizes the importance of all students adjusting and fitting into the same mold;
- A rigid classroom environment that encourages all children to study identical materials at similar speeds or in similar styles; gifted children may teach others, but they are not provided challenging curriculum and thus experience boredom (Gallagher, Harradine, & Coleman, 1997; Reis, 1998; Rimm, 1995; Winebrenner, 2000);
- Teachers who rigidly fail to see the quality of children's work because of different values, personal power struggles, or cultural or racial prejudice; they cause children to feel unable to accomplish outcomes despite their efforts (Davis & Rimm, 1998; Rimm, 1980);
- An unidentified learning disability or attention deficit disorder: Thus dyslexia, dysgraphia, dyscalculia, or ADHD can mask students' giftedness and prevent children from experiencing the successful outcomes that should be related to appropriate efforts (Grimm, 1998; Leroux & Levitt-Perlman, 2000; Rimm, 1995, 2001b).

School environments that value children's accomplishments but only provide tasks that are too easy and do not encourage challenge or sustained efforts also foster underachievement. The schools value good grades and performance, and initially grades reflect excellent performance. Gifted children tend to feel positively about school, but they are not sufficiently challenged because the work is too easy. Reis and Purcell (1993) found that gifted children in elementary school already have accomplished 35 to 50% of the skills they will be taught in a specific grade before they have entered it. In a study of 871 academically gifted students in North Carolina, Gallagher and colleagues (1997) found that although most students felt challenged in special gifted classes and mathematics, only about half the students felt sufficiently challenged in science, language arts, and social studies. The middle school years were described as particularly unchallenging. Children learn that achievement is easy, that success is readily attainable, and that learning and study are effortless. Occasionally, they may comment about boredom or lack of challenge, but as long as grades continue to be high, they exhibit no behavioral problems.

When the curriculum becomes more complex or when students enter higher grades in which peer populations are more intellectually competitive, gifted children feel as though they are not as intelligent as they believed they were earlier. Some learn more appropriate study habits. Others hide from their threatening feelings. They worry that they are not as smart as they would like to be, and they invent or discover a whole group of rituals and excuses that prevent them from making further effort.

One college student thought her "brain cells might be dissolving." Another explained that something was missing, and he no longer felt special and, therefore, just gave up. Many bright high school students have reminded this author, "If you're smart, schoolwork should be easy." Peer messages about being "casual" or "cool" also reinforce a model of not making "too much" school effort. A fifth-grade boy's conclusion that he would like to "get all As without carrying a book" emphasizes that point well.

Procrastination, incomplete assignments, disorganization, inattention, and careless work become typical symptoms that characterize underachievement in these students. These symptoms will disappear only when the students are gradually persuaded to take the risk of making school effort. Only then will they find out that they are, indeed, highly capable. They also may learn to set more realistic goals. Their past school environments simply have not taught them the challenging *process* of achievement. Bias among teachers against accelerated curriculum and grade skipping often prevents schools from challenging these students (Rimm & Lovance, 1992).

Underachievement occurs when children's habits, efforts, and skills cause them to lose their sense of control over school outcomes. Teachers are less likely to identify these children as gifted because their intelligence or creativity may no longer be evident in the classroom. Even parents begin to doubt their children's abilities. They may recall that their children were "smart" at some point in the past, but now they may be willing to settle for very average and sometimes far below average achievement. Passing grades become acceptable.

Attention Deficit-Hyperactivity Disorders

Gifted underachievers with the characteristics of ADHD have also increased dramatically during the past ten years. Baum, Olenchak, and Owen (1998) suggest that some of the characteristics that are associated with giftedness, such as overexcitability, impulsiveness, accelerated learning pace, and high creativity, are being mistaken as characteristics of ADHD, and they suggest that teachers may be "missing the forest and only seeing the trees." Clinical observations seem to substantiate that the highly creative underachiever has difficulty coping with the repetitive nature of classroom tasks and searches for novelty in classroom assignments. As one young man described it, "Math would be more interesting if the answers to problems could be different each time." One problem may be that classroom teachers have a great deal more in-service training on the characteristics of ADHD than they do on the characteristics associated with creative giftedness and thus identify the problems rather than the strengths. Indeed, highly creative children may not be the easiest to teach.

Another problem may be that children are coming to school with a greater history of "screen time." Children who watch hours of television and spend many hours with computer games may become dependent on the overstimulation that the screen provides. Teachers are no match for the movement, change, color, music, and energy that television and computers provide. These children may appear inattentive in class because they have developed habits of attention that are dependent on rapid and changing visual movement and sound. Careful diagnosis of ADHD and appropriate treatment when necessary is a new focus in the treatment of underachievement.

High-Risk Home Environments

Family characteristics of underachievers have been described in several studies (Baker, Bridger, and Evans, 1998; Frasier, Passow, & Goldberg, 1958; French, 1959; Whitmore, 1980; Zilli, 1971). Rimm and Lowe (1988) targeted some critical differences between the families of 22 gifted underachievers and the findings from family studies of achievement and eminence. The findings are summarized and the main differences are highlighted in Tables 33.1, 33.2, and 33.3.

Parents of both groups showed concern about achievement for their children. However, the modeling of intrinsic and independent learning, positive

Table 33.1 Family Structural Characteristics

Characteristics	Eminence and Giftedness	Underachieving Gifted	Comparison
Size of family	Small	2.59 children	Similar
Birth order	More than half oldest	59% oldest	Similar
Only children	Percentage varied	27%	Similar to some, different from some
Adopted children in family	Not reported	23%	Not reported, probably different
Male/female	More males	More males	Similar
Specialness	Earned specialness	Specialness displaced for 81%; 18% never earned specialness	Different
Age of parents at marriage	Older parents fairly typical	Mother—30 Father—32	Similar
Education of parents	Higher education fairly typical	Mother—15.7 Father—17.9	Similar
Parent loss	Low parent divorce, some parent loss	Low parent divorce, some parent loss	Similar

Source: "Family Environments of Underachieving Gifted Students" by S. B. Rimm and B. Lowe, 1988, *Gifted Child Quarterly, 32*(4), Fall, pp. 353–359.

Table 33.2 Family Climate

Characteristics	Eminence and Giftedness	Underachieving Gifted	Comparison
Child centeredness	Child centered High adult personal interests	Child centered early; low adult personal interests	Similarities and differences
Discord and trauma vs. secure supportive families	Mixed findings: artists, authors more traumatic; scientists, mathematicians more secure	Considerable discord	Different
Parenting style	Mixed, but nonauthoritarian and consistent	Early liberal, then changed to 95% inconsistent "ogre" rituals	Different
Family relationships:			
Father/mother	Usually very good	68% good, 32% bad	Some differences
Child/mother	Usually good	59% poor	Different
Child/father	Usually good	63% poor	Different
Child/siblings	Usually good	45% poor	Different
Structure and organization	Consistent and predictable	Inconsistent: 95% indicated manipulating one or both parents	Different

Source: "Family Environments of Underachieving Gifted Students" by S. B. Rimm and B. Lowe, 1988, *Gifted Child Quarterly, 32*(4), Fall, pp. 353–359.

commitment to career, and respect for school were remarkably, though unintentionally, absent from families of underachieving gifted children. The enrichment and fun of early childhood were often replaced by a plethora of activities and lessons that were so time-consuming little energy was left for intrinsically interesting home learning, independent projects, or family game playing. Management of students' homework by parents resulted in dependent patterns and parent-child arguments.

Many parents of underachieving gifted children openly opposed teachers and school policies. Parents were involved in opposition to schools in 90% of the families. In some cases, parents' battles were—appropriately—based on lack of challenge. They rarely shared their own career interests with their children. Most fathers spoke quite negatively about their own work, even when they had invested many years in preparation for their high-level careers. Well-educated mothers who centered their lives on their children and volunteer activities often voiced frustration at their "nonprofessional" role. Green, Fine, and Tollefson (1988) also found that parents' attitudes toward their careers were related to their children's underachievement.

Unlike the families in the studies of giftedness and eminence (Bloom, 1985; MacKinnon, 1965; Walberg et al., 1981), the theme of family organization and consistent and predictable expectations for conduct was noticeably absent in the homes of the underachieving children studied by Rimm and Lowe (1988).[1] Differences between parents in the standards, limits, and expectations provided unclear guidelines. Ninety-five percent of the students (all but one) indicated that they could manipulate one or both parents much of the time, and the parents of these children confirmed their children's observations. The absence of consistent leadership among these parents was remarkable. Although most of the children spent their early childhoods with parents who considered their parenting techniques to be quite liberal and flexible, there was only one couple that maintained a consistent parenting philosophy. By the time their children were of school age, extreme differences in parenting styles emerged. In 95% of the families, one parent played the role of the parent who challenged

---

1. See Chapter 19 by Sosniak and Chapter 27 by Walberg, Williams, and Zeiser.

Table 33.3 Values Espoused and Modeled by Parents

Characteristics	Eminence and Giftedness	Underachieving Gifted	Comparison
Achievement orientation expressed	Valued work and achievement	Valued work and achievement	Similar
Grade expectations	Reasonable and unpressured	Reasonable and unpressured: Mothers—3.2 GPA Fathers—3.2 GPA	Similar
Early enrichment and activities	Provided	Provided	Similar
Social adjustment of children	Mixed	73% not well accepted by peers	Some differences
High energy of parents	Dramatically consistent	Mainly true	Some differences
Father's career	Mainly committed, positive and sharing interests	Considerable frustration with career or, if positive, not sharing interests	Different
Mother's career	Mainly homemakers, volunteers, busy and happy	Mainly homemakers, volunteers, busy but not satisfied	Different
Identification with same-sexed parent	Mixed research on identification, mainly positive for achievement with boys and girls with fathers	25% of males identified with father, 20% identified with mother	Different
School–home relationship	Mainly good and supportive Reasonable school adjustments	90% were oppositional, problem in school environments	Different
Homework independence	Independence plus additional independent learning projects; some parent monitoring	59% were homework dependent, absence of independent learning projects; oppositional monitoring	Different
Intrinsic learning	Frequently modeled by parents	Rarely modeled by parents	Different

Source: "Family Environments of Underachieving Gifted Students" by S. B. Rimm and B. Lowe, 1988, *Gifted Child Quarterly, 32*(4), Fall, pp. 353–359.

and disciplined, while the other took the role of protector. There was increasing opposition between parents as the challenger became more authoritarian and the rescuer became increasingly protective. In 54% of the families the father took the role of disciplinarian; in 41% the mother played the authoritarian role. These authoritarian/rescuer rituals are described by Rimm (1995) as "ogre" games.

When the children were asked which of their parents was easier, only five children (23%) indicated that their parents had similar expectations. Twenty-five percent of the boys thought their father was easier, and 50% chose their mother as the easier parent.

Three of the girls (60%) considered their father to be easier. Only one girl said her mother was easier.

According to their parents, 81% of the gifted underachievers were considered by their families to be "special." This sense of specialness was either attached to the parents' early discovery of their child's gifted abilities or based on a long-awaited birth or unusual circumstance. Later, that specialness was withdrawn, and the "special" attribution was given to another family member. Sometimes, the sense of specialness was lost as part of school adjustment (Rimm, 1990, 1996). Clinical interviews indicated that all of the children were given a great deal of early attention.

More than half (54%) had that attention withdrawn dramatically by a second sibling, who then received the "special" designation, or by a parent's remarriage to a stepparent. In 27% (6) of the cases, children without siblings adjusted poorly to sharing attention at school. In 18% (4) of the cases, children never established a sense of specialness because another sibling was already designated as having that role.

The following two examples provide insights into the trauma felt by children whose specialness is displaced:

Maureen, a gifted ninth grader, had been adopted. She was showered with extreme amounts of adult attention for the first six years of her life. Her younger sister was an unexpected birth child to her parents. Maureen was an underachiever throughout school and shared with the therapist that she could remember always resenting her younger sister, although she could not explain any reasons for her feelings.

Jonathan lost his feeling of specialness in high school. He was a high achiever until seventh grade, during which time he developed an illness that led his mother to home school him. He thrived with his mother's teaching. She was a graduate student at the time and arranged for Jonathan to audit several college courses. Jonathan actually completed the assignments and exams and earned A's for the two courses even though he was just an eighth grader. Other graduate students and the professor were impressed. Indeed, Jonathan felt unique.

After Jonathan returned to good health, his parents enrolled him in a public high school. It was his intention to achieve. However, he soon found himself arguing with teachers, deliberately not doing homework, and feeling dejected and angry with school. He became a leader of defiance, petitioned with other students to change the school, and became very negative in his classrooms.

As a sophomore, Jonathan came to the Family Achievement Clinic for counseling. He was determined to enlist this author in the capacity of therapist on his side against the school. When he was urged to put forth effort so his curriculum could be changed, he became momentarily silent, then asked if he should be like Ghandi in his resistance to the school. This therapist felt that an alliance had been formed with Jonathan, but he was still determined to return to college and skip the remainder of high school. He asked if he would be considered special at college, and he was told that at age fifteen, he would seem like a regular college student. Jonathan's face registered noticeable disappointment, and he accepted encouragement to return to high school.

Arrangements were made for Jonathan to attend another high school in the district so he would have a fresh start. Although he is now achieving reasonably well, he continues to need considerable encouragement. His creative writing, poetry, music, and art are critically important to his continued functioning in school and help him to feel somewhat special in a positive way.

In the Rimm and Lowe (1988) research, when the "special" designation was withdrawn, the early dependence on extreme amounts of attention had the effect of causing the children to feel "attention neglected." The search for a way to retrieve the special attention involved behaviors that parents and teachers often labeled as "spoiled" or "defiant." These children often behaved as if they had an attention deficit-hyperactivity disorder (Rimm, 2001b). Efforts by teachers and parents to "put these children back in their places" only increased the children's feelings of neglect and their defiant or nonproductive behaviors.

Sibling Rivalry

Siblings play an important role in underachievement. Frequently in the families of underachievers there are sisters or brothers who are "practically perfect." The underachievers feel invidiously compared even if parents make no comparisons.

Underachievers Among Achievers

Even in the research of the childhoods of successful women (Rimm, 1999), there were a few women in the study who admitted to temporary underachievement in childhood. For example, TV anchorwoman Donna Draves (pseudonym) remembers avoiding school subjects in which her brother performed well, particularly math, science, and athletics. In her gifted program, she was expected to do math independently, but preferred not doing it. When her teacher discovered she was not completing her math, she scolded Donna and insisted she get busy and catch up. The next day, Donna complained of a stomach ache and missed school. Her parents took her for medical examinations, but the stomach aches continued. Donna missed six weeks of school in the search for a diagnosis. No one, except her babysitter, realized that Donna was simply sick of math. Eventually, Donna tired of staying home and somehow recovered from her disabling stomachaches.

Sally Sahn (pseudonym), a media publicist, and her sister recalled their hatred of math as well. They achieved in verbal subjects but underachieved in math. Their dad would try to help them with the math, but more often than not would get frustrated and lose his temper. The girls both took that as a signal that they could go to Mom for math, and they could usually count on her doing the math for them.

New Jersey governor Christie Whitman, in her interview for the book *How Jane Won* (Rimm, 2001a), reluctantly acknowledged that she was somewhat of an underachiever in school. Although she never read this author's theories of underachievement, her description fit well with what occurs among many gifted underachievers. Governor Whitman explained her feelings in adolescence: "If I don't try, it's not that I'm dumb; it's that I didn't try." Eventually, the excitement of a college professor encouraged her to reverse her problem, and she became a high achiever in college and in life. Governor Whitman's comments confirm that within the underachiever is great potential for achievement once the underachiever sees hope of success.

Characteristics and Directions of Underachievement

The characteristic found most frequently and consistently among underachieving children is low self-esteem (Davis & Rimm, 1998; Fine & Pitts, 1980; Whitmore, 1980). Although the children acknowledge that they are intelligent, they do not believe themselves capable of accomplishing what their families or teachers expect of them. They may mask their low self-esteem with displays of bravado, rebellion, or highly protective defense mechanisms (Covington & Beery, 1976; Fine & Pitts, 1980; Rimm, 1995). For example, they may openly criticize the quality of the school or the talents of individual teachers, or claim that they "don't care" or "didn't really try" when they receive a mediocre test score or class grade.

Related to their low self-esteem is their sense of low personal control over their own lives (Rimm, 1995, 1996). If they fail at a task, they blame their lack of ability; if they succeed, they may attribute their success to luck. Thus, they may accept responsibility for failure, but not for success (Felton & Biggs, 1977). This attribution process in educational achievement has been related to the original theory of *learned helplessness* advanced by Seligman

(1975). If a child does not see a relationship between his efforts and the outcomes, he is likely to exhibit characteristics of learned helplessness and will no longer make an effort to achieve. Weiner (1974, 1980) also emphasized that children's subsequent performance will be strongly influenced by whether they attribute successes and failures to ability, effort, task difficulty, or luck. Attributing success to *effort* leads to further effort, while attributing success to *task ease* or *luck* does not.[2]

Low self-esteem leads the underachiever to nonproductive avoidance behaviors both at school and at home. For example, underachievers may avoid making a productive effort by asserting that school is irrelevant and they see no reason to study material only to receive a diploma. Students may further assert that when they are really interested in learning, they can do very well. They complain that teachers should make the work more interesting. These avoidance behaviors protect underachievers from admitting their feared lack of productive ability. If they study, they risk *confirming* their possible shortcomings to themselves and to important others. If they do not study, they can use the nonstudying as a rationale for the failure, thus protecting their precarious feelings of self-worth (Covington & Beery, 1976).

Extreme rebellion against authority, particularly school authority, provides another route to protect the underachiever. The student may be eager to tell teachers, the principal, the superintendent, even the board of education exactly how they ought to run the school (as did Jonathan). Faulting the school helps the underachiever avoid the responsibility of achieving by blaming the system.

Expectations of low grades and perfectionism, though apparent opposites, also serve as defense mechanisms for the underachieving child. Expecting low grades lowers the risk of failure. Setting goals that are impossibly high also provides safety for underachievers. They can use the "too high" goals as an excuse for not making efforts. By contrast, achieving children set realistic goals that are reachable, and failures are constructively used to indicate weaknesses needing attention.

Rimm (1995) described two main directions of responses. She found that underachievers exhibit their defenses by either dependent or dominant behaviors.

---

2. See Chapter 32 by McNabb.

Figure 33.1 shows these two directions. Conforming underachievers differ from those in the nonconforming category by their visibility. That is, conforming dependent and dominant students have characteristics that may lead to underachievement problems, but their underachievement is not as serious or apparent. Nonconforming dependent and dominant under-

achievers are already exhibiting serious problems. The prototypical names used in Figure 33.1—"Passive Paul," "Rebellious Rebecca," and so forth—are used to emphasize the main characteristics of these underachievers, but any one child typically exhibits a group of these symptoms. Rimm also points out that some underachievers exhibit both dependent

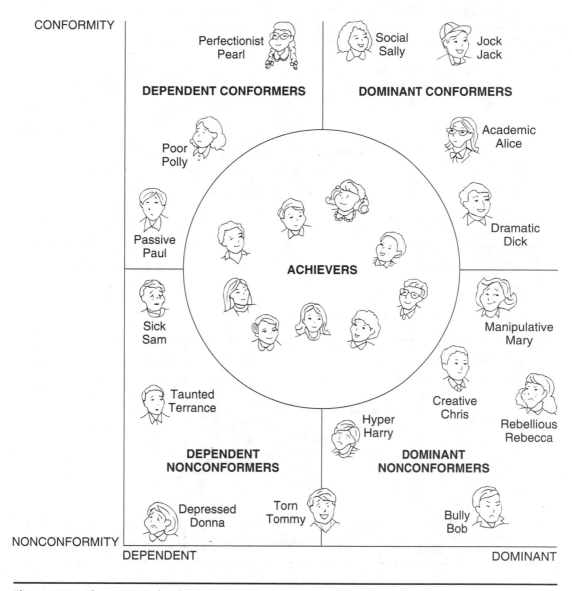

Figure 33.1 The inner circle of achievers.

Source: Underachievement Syndrome: Causes and Cures by Sylvia B. Rimm, 1986, Watertown, WI: Apple Publishing Company. Reprinted with permission.

and dominant qualities. Cornale (1988) found that by adolescence, most underachievers exhibit both dependent and dominant symptoms.

Reversal of Underachievement

The underachieving gifted child continues to underachieve because the home, school, or peer group unintentionally reinforces underachievement. The student is no longer motivated to achieve, and there may be deficiencies in skills necessary for achievement. Working below one's abilities affects both immediate educational success and eventual career achievement.

Although it is certainly difficult to reverse long-standing patterns of underachievement, Rimm's Trifocal Model has proven successful in approximately 80 percent of clinic cases (Rimm, 1995). She has found that the treatment of underachievement involves the collaboration of school and family in the implementation of six steps (see Figure 33.2).

1. Assessment;
2. Communication;
3. Changing the expectations of important others;
4. Role-model identification;
5. Correcting skill deficiencies; and
6. Modifications of reinforcements at home and school

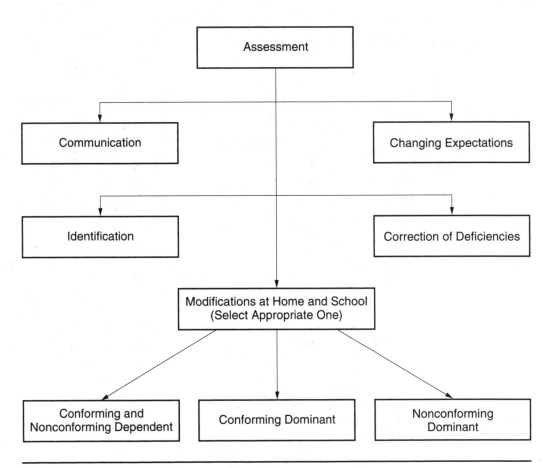

Figure 33.2 TRIFOCAL model for curing underachievement syndrome.

Source: Underachievement Syndrome: Causes and Cures by Sylvia B. Rimm, 1986, Watertown, WI: Apple Publishing Company. Reprinted with permission.

In addition to the use of the Trifocal model, parents and teachers should be equipped with "patience, dedication, and support" (Hoffman, Wasson, & Christianson, 1985).

Step 1: Assessment of Skills, Abilities, and Types of Underachievement

The first step in the underachievement reversal process is an assessment that involves the cooperation of the school psychologist, teacher of the gifted, and parents. It's critical that these people are aware of characteristics of gifted and creative children.

An *individual* intelligence test continues to be a highly recommended first assessment instrument. The venerable IQ number has the potential to communicate important expectations related to a child's abilities. Since gifted underachieving children have not been motivated, it is likely that *group* intelligence test scores have underestimated their intellectual potential. The underachievement also may have had a depressing effect on scores obtained by individual testing.

The WISC-R, WISC III, or the Stanford-Binet L-M must be individually administered by a psychologist. There are other individual intelligence tests that can be administered by a psychologist to evaluate learning potential for culturally diverse, nonverbal, non-English-speaking, blind, or deaf gifted children, who also need to be individually assessed. Some of these instruments are questionable in terms of their equivalence to the most conventionally accepted tests, namely the Wechsler and Binet scales, but all provide a reasonably acceptable predictor of a child's school-related capability. For culturally diverse children, scores may be lower than actual abilities.

During testing, the psychometrist should be especially aware of particular task-relevant characteristics of the child: symptoms of tension, attention to the task, perseverance at the task, responses to frustration, problem-solving approaches, defensiveness, and dependence on personal encouragement by the examiner. These reflect, in miniature, approaches to educational tasks that the child very likely uses in the classroom and home environments. Intelligence testing should be followed by individual achievement tests to assess clearly the child's strengths and deficits in basic skills, particularly reading and math. Achievement tests that do not require writing are a better measure for the many underachievers who have handwriting problems.

A creativity test or inventory, which can be administered by the teacher or by a psychologist, should also be part of the assessment. These produce not only a norm-referenced creativity score but also descriptions of abilities, characteristics, and interests that are relevant to understanding the child's personality, creative potential, and learning style. The GIFT and GIFFI tests include dimension scores in areas such as Independence, Self-confidence, Imagination, Interests, and Challenge-Inventiveness that provide important insights into understanding the student.

AIM (Achievement Identification Measure; Rimm, 1986), GAIM (Group Achievement Identification Measure; Rimm, 1987), and AIM-TO (Achievement Identification Measure-Teacher Observation; Rimm, 1988) are inventories developed to identify children's characteristics related to achievement or underachievement. GAIM can be used with students from grades 5 through 12. AIM is completed by parents, and AIM-TO is a teacher observation instrument. The latter two instruments also can be completed for any school-age student. The scores provide a description of the extent and type of underachievement. Dimension scores reveal whether the student is mainly dependent or dominant or combines a mixture of both. Scores also permit insights into parent consistency in messages about achievement. A description of the dimension scores is provided in Figure 33.3.

Finally, a parent interview also can be very helpful in identifying underachieving patterns unintentionally maintained at home or in school. Ideally, both parents should be at the interview. If only one appears, it would be important to ask about the other parent's relationship to the child.

Step 2: Communication

Communication between parents and teachers is an important component of the cure for underachievers. Either a parent or the teacher may initiate the first conference. The initiator should assure the other person of support rather than placing blame. If it appears to a teacher that the parents are not interested in or capable of consistent follow-through, the teacher should select another child advocate in the school with whom to work around the child's underachievement. Schools have facetiously labeled this adaption of the Trifocal model the "bifocal" model. Reversing the pattern without parental assistance is not as efficient but is nevertheless effective for many children. A

Competition

High scorers enjoy competition whether they win or lose. They are good sports and handle victories graciously. They do not give up easily.

Responsibility

High scorers are responsible in their home and schoolwork. They tend to be well organized and bring activities to closure. They have good study habits and understand that their efforts are related to their grades.

Achievement Communication

Children who score high are receiving clear and consistent messages from parents about the importance of learning and good grades. Their parents have communicated positive feelings about their own school experiences, and there is consistency between mother and father messages of achievement.

Independence/Dependence

High scorers are independent and understand the relationship between effort and outcomes. They are able to share attention at home and in the classroom.

Respect-Dominance

High scorers are respectful toward their parents and teachers. They are reasonably well-behaved at home and school. They value education. They are not deliberately manipulative.

Figure 33.3　Dimension scores for AIM, GAIM, and AIM-TO.

Source: Guidebook—Underachievement Syndrome: Causes and Cures, by S. Rimm, M. Cornale, R. Manos, and J. Behrend, 1989, Watertown, WI: Apple Publishing Company. Reprinted with permission.

counselor, gifted coordinator, resource teacher, or even another classroom teacher will often be an excellent child advocate.

The communication between parents and teachers should include a discussion of assessed abilities and achievements and the child's expressions of dependence or dominance. Teachers should communicate in clear English. Educators tend to employ jargon that mystifies intelligent adults who are not educators. Communication is especially important so that adults at home and at school do not fall into the trap of continually reinforcing the problem patterns (Rimm, 1995).

Step 3: Changing the Expectations of Important Others

Self, parent, teacher, peer, and sibling expectations are difficult to change. As noted above, IQ scores, if higher than anticipated, are very effective in modifying expectations. Anecdotal information also can provide convincing evidence of the child's abilities. For example, a teacher who is trying to convince an adolescent or parents of the adolescent's mathematical talent can explain that he or she solves problems in an unusually clever way or seems to learn math concepts more quickly than anyone else in the class. A psychologist who is trying to convince a teacher that a child has unusual talent can describe the unusual vocabulary or problem-solving skills that the child reveals during testing. Specific descriptions of special strengths are good evidence of giftedness.

It is important to underachieving children that parents and teachers be able to honestly say to them that they believe in the children's ability to achieve (Perkins & Wicas, 1971). The expectations of these important others are basic to the personal change in self-expectations that is necessary to reverse underachievement to high achievement.

Rimm and Lovance (1992) reported the effectiveness of grade skipping or subject acceleration in changing students' self-expectations. Although these were only components of the reversal of underachievement, they were very effective for building a gifted student's confidence and internal locus of control. Table 33.4 describes how both grade and subject skips were used in the prevention and reversal of underachievement. Following is a letter from an eighth grader who completely reversed his underachievement. Although many parenting and some

Table 33.4 Results of Subject and Grade Skipping

Summary of Case Events

Gender of Child	Presenting Problems	Wechsler FS IQ and Binet[a] Score (If Available)	Grades/Subjects Skipped to Date	Time for Adjustment (Teacher Perceptions)	Additional Therapy Required	Grade[e]	Projected Future Accelerations
F	Parent concern about boredom; behavior problems at home	147+[b] 151	Early placed kindergarten	One semester	Yes—brief[c]	1	NYD[f]
F	Parent concern about boredom	141	Early placed kindergarten Subject skipping	None	Yes—brief	6	NYD[f]
F	Behavior problems in preschool	139	Early placed kindergarten	One semester	Yes—brief	K	NYD[f]
M	Behavior problems at home and school	144 172	Skipped 1st grade	One quarter	Yes—brief	2	Math and reading skips or computer curriculum
M	Parent concern about boredom; peer adjustment problems; dependency	151+ 185+	Skipped 1st grade; math acceleration in 4th	One semester	Yes—brief	4	Further extreme math acceleration
F	Refusal to do school work	152+ 160+	Skipped 1st grade reading; 2nd grade math; other English, math, science, foreign language	One semester	Yes—occasional[d]	8	Subject skips and early graduation
M	Parent concern about boredom	141+ 173	Skipped 1st and 2nd grade reading, 2nd grade math; skipped last half of 1st grade; skipped 4th grade math	None	None	4	Subject and grade skips
F	Teacher concern about boredom	133+	Skipped last half of 2nd and first half of 3rd grade	None	None	7	None likely—AP courses available in high school
F	Unfinished work; disorganization; complaints of boredom; poor peer relations	127	Skipped 2nd grade; math accelerated later	One semester	Yes—1 semester	8	AP classes; NYD[f]

(continued)

Table 33.4   Continued

Summary of Case Events

Gender of Child	Presenting Problems	Wechsler FS IQ and Binet[a] Score (If Available)	Grades/Subjects Skipped to Date	Time for Adjustment (Teacher Perceptions)	Additional Therapy Required	Grade[e]	Projected Future Accelerations
M	Behavior problems at home and school; disorganization, unfinished work	149+	Skipped 3rd grade	One year	Yes—occasional	6	AP classes available in high school; NYD[f]
F	Parent and child concern about boredom	126+	Skipped 4th grade reading and math	None for reading; One quarter for math	Yes—brief	8	Possible grade skip in high school
F	Parent concern about boredom	139+	Skipped 2nd grade math, 4th grade reading; skipped 6th grade science	None	Yes—brief	6	Likely subject skips; NYD[f]
F	Teacher concern about boredom, perfectionism	135	Skipped 2nd grade math, 3rd grade reading; skipped 6th grade entirely	None	None	9	None likely—AP courses available in high school
M	Behavior problems, disorganization; incomplete work	149+	Skipped subjects in math, science, French, history, and Latin	One quarter	Yes—brief	10	Early graduation

Source: "The Use of Subject and Grade Skipping for the Prevention and Reversal of Underachievement," by S. B. Rimm, and K. J. Lovance, 1992, *Gifted Child Quarterly*, 36(2), pp. 100–105.

[a] Stanford-Binet, Form L-M
[b] Indicates ceiling scores
[c] Brief therapy refers to no more than 4 sessions.
[d] Several initial sessions followed by therapy sessions 2 or 3 times during the school year
[e] Grade at time of interview
[f] Not yet determined.

school changes were made for this young man, he attributed his success mainly to his subject skip to high school algebra.

> My life has changed through working with you because I realized that I was an underachiever. I started working to my ability and got to go to school at my high school a year early.
>
> Now every day I get to go to North and take Algebra 1. I have learned very much in terms of my education, self-confidence, and respect. I have become very good friends with my Algebra teacher and am getting very good grades in his class, something I didn't think I would do.
>
> I treat my parents with more respect because I have more respect for myself. I rarely get into trouble anymore, and at my middle school I haven't received any more referrals and am getting straight A's. I have more, better quality friends who are very trustworthy and nice.

Rimm and Olenchak (1991) found that involvement in Future Problem Solving proved helpful in the reversal of underachievement. It undoubtedly changed both self and peer expectations for the underachiever. It also helps underachievers to cope with the winning and losing aspects of team competition. Rimm (1995) finds group sessions effective for helping children change expectations. Figure 33.4 includes typical topics discussed or played out.

Jackson, Cleveland, and Mirenda (1975) showed in their longitudinal research with bright fourth-, fifth-, and sixth-grade underachievers that positive expectations by parents and teachers had a significant long-range effect on achievement in high school. Bloom's (1985) studies of talent development found that parents of research neurologists and mathematicians always expected their children to be very good students. An interesting true story that emphasizes the role of teacher expectation for achievement follows:

> It was the first teacher conference of the new year, a time when teachers may not yet know all the parents of their students. Ms. Dunn, a fourth-grade teacher, had two Janets in her class. One was an excellent student, positive, and well adjusted; the other had multiple problems and was very negative. When the second Janet's parents came for conference, Ms. Dunn mistook them for the first Janet's parents. She welcomed them with an enthusiastic description of their daughter's positive attitude, only to be greeted by their shocked expression. She immediately realized her mistake, but rather than embarrass herself and the parents, she continued her discussion about a "few areas" where Janet needed improvement.

Competition—Game Playing
Discussion of Feelings

Competition—Comparison to Sports

Peer Relations—Popularity vs. Friendship
Reading and Discussion—*It's Dumb to Be Smart*

Competition and Siblings
Reading and Discussion—*Brothers and Sisters*

Pressure—How to Cope and How Much Is Too Much

Leadership vs. "Bossyship"

Understanding Parents

Responsibility

Perfectionism

Creative Problem Solving

Figure 33.4 Topics for small-group sessions for students.

Source: Adapted from *Gifted Kids Have Feelings Too* by S. B. Rimm and *Exploring Feelings* by S. B. Rimm and C. Priest, 1990, Watertown, WI: Apple Publishing Company.

> The parents left the conference feeling more positive about their daughter than ever before and conveyed this excitement to their child. The next day, to Ms. Dunn's surprise, Janet entered school with a big smile and a positive attitude. Her self-confidence and her school efforts were completely transformed. She ended the school year with B's instead of the usual D's that had been typical of earlier report cards. A chance faux pas had led to a dramatic change for Janet. Yes, it really is a true story!

Because sibling competition is frequently a causal component of underachievement syndrome, changing the expectations of siblings may help. In the sibling rivalry that often exists, an achieving child may have assigned the role of "loser" to a brother or sister, and the anticipated change of that role may feel threatening to the "winner." An individual and personal communication to the "winner" about the expected change is helpful. Parents should provide the assurance that the sibling's changed status will not displace the achiever's role. Genetically and environmentally, a "whole smart family" is not only possible but also likely.

> Rachel, an eleventh-grade gifted high achiever, seemed to take a real pleasure in helping her ninth-grade underachieving brother get into trouble at home and in school. Although she mainly believed she was doing this because she loved her brother, it was also clear that she viewed the reversal of his long-standing underachievement problems as threatening to her own highest performance (Rimm, 1995).

Step 4: Role-Model Identification

A critical turning point for the underachieving child is the discovery of one or more role models for identification. All other treatments for underachievement pale in importance compared with strong identification with achieving models. As noted, Bloom's (1985; Bloom & Sosniak, 1981) biographical research with highly talented students showed that parents modeled the values and the lifestyles of successful achievers in the child's talent area. Research indicates that the best family environment for a gifted boy includes a father who is competent and strong, is pleased with his job, and permits his son to master tasks independently. Because this ideal situation is rarely provided for the gifted underachiever, parents and teachers need to manipulate the environment to encourage students to identify with appropriate role models. A long-term longitudinal study of culturally disadvantaged children who grew up on the island of Kauai indicated that role models are very important for successful young people (Werner, 1989).

Research on parent identification (Mussen & Rutherford, 1963) indicates that the selected parent identification figure is nurturant and powerful, and shares common characteristics with the child. As a warning, however, an underachieving adolescent sometimes selects a powerful, nurturant model that shares the *underachieving* characteristics of the adolescent. This person may then become a strong model for underachievement.

Underachieving children should be matched with achieving persons to serve as models for them. Such persons can serve in model capacities for more than one child. The model's actual role may be as tutor, mentor, companion, teacher, parent, sibling, counselor, psychologist, minister, scout leader, doctor, and

so on. One teacher may serve as a role model for many students. Although that may sound relatively simple, one teacher who was the only male on the faculty in his elementary school commented that he "was tired of being the only available role model for so many boys." Persons who may serve as appropriate role models may be invited to schools to talk to students about their careers. Videotaping these talks may provide a continuing role model for others.

Step 5: Correcting Skill Deficiencies

The underachieving gifted child almost always has skill deficiencies as a result of inattention in class, and poor work and study habits. However, because he or she is gifted the skill deficiencies may be easily overcome. This is less of a problem for very young children because the deficiencies are less likely to be extensive. Tutoring should be goal-directed, with movement to a higher reading or math group or acceptance into an accelerated class as the anticipated outcome. It should be of specified duration—for example, weekly for two months until the child takes a proficiency test—rather than ongoing. Ideally, an objective adult who recognizes the child's underachievement and giftedness should do the tutoring. Parents or siblings are seldom appropriate because the personal relationships are likely to cause the child additional pressure and dependency. Children have often described the assistance given by an older sibling as helpful but having a secondary effect of "making them feel dumb." The correction of skill deficiencies must be conducted carefully so that (1) the independent work of the underachieving child is reinforced by the tutor, (2) manipulation of the tutor by the child is avoided, and (3) the child senses the relationship between effort and the achievement outcomes. Charting progress during tutoring helps to confirm visually the rapid progress to both child and tutor.

Sometimes underachieving gifted students actually have learning disabilities. Other times their dependent patterns look like learning disabilities. Table 33.5 compares dependencies to disabilities and can provide teachers with a diagnostic guide for detecting actual disabilities. Sometimes underachieving children do have ADHD; sometimes they only appear to have the symptoms. Home and school environments can cause the symptoms of ADHD. The quiz in

Table 33.5   Ways to Discriminate between Dependence and Disability

Dependence	Disability
1. Child asks for explanations regularly despite differences in subject matter.	Child asks for explanations in particular subjects which are difficult.
2. Child asks for explanation of instructions regardless of style used, either auditory or visual.	Child asks for explanations of instructions only when given in one instruction style, either auditory or visual but not both.
3. Child's questions are not specific to material but appear to be mainly to gain adult attention.	Child's questions are specific to material, and once process is explained, child works efficiently.
4. Child is disorganized or slow in assignments but becomes much more efficient when a meaningful reward is presented as motivation.	Child's disorganization or slow pace continues despite motivating rewards.
5. Child works only when an adult is nearby at school and/or at home.	Child works independently once process is clearly explained.
6. Individually administered measures of ability indicate that the child is capable of learning the material. Individual tests improve with tester encouragement and support. Group measures may not indicate good abilities or skills.	Both individual and group measures indicate lack of specific abilities or skills. Tester encouragement has no significant effect on scores.
7. Child exhibits "poor me" body language (tears, helplessness, pouting, copying) regularly when new work is presented. Teacher or adult attention serves to ease the symptoms.	Child exhibits "poor me" body language only with instructions or assignments in specific disability areas and accepts challenges in areas of strength.
8. Parents report whining, complaining, attention getting, temper tantrums, and poor sportsmanship at home.	Although parents may find similar symptoms at home, they tend to be more sporadic than regular, particularly the whining and complaining.
9. Child's "poor me" behavior appears only with one parent and not with the other; only with some teachers and not with others. With some teachers or with the other parent, the child functions fairly well independently.	Although the child's "poor me" behaviors may only appear with one parent or with solicitous teachers, performance is not adequate even when behavior is acceptable.
10. Child learns only when given one-to-one instruction but will not learn in groups even when instructional mode is varied.	Although child may learn more quickly in a one-to-one setting, he/she will also learn efficiently in a group setting provided the child's disability is taken into consideration when instructions are given.

It is critical to realize that some children who are truly disabled have also become dependent. The key to distinguishing between disability and dependence is the child's response to adult support. If the child performs only with adult support when new material is presented, he/she is too dependent whether or not there is also a disability.

Source: Underachievement Syndrome: Causes and Cures by Sylvia B. Rimm, 1986, Watertown, WI: Apple Publishing Company. Reprinted with permission.

Figure 33.5 that families can take will show how environments can cause ADHD-like symptoms.

Step 6: Modification of Reinforcements at Home and School

Parent and teacher discussions will certainly identify some manipulative rituals that were discussed in the home and school etiology sections. These behaviors need to be modified by setting important long-term goals and some short-term objectives that can ensure immediate small successes for the child both at home and at school. These successful experiences may be temporarily reinforced by a variety of rewards.

Modifying reinforcements for homework and study are an important component of reversing

Before you decide that medication is the answer to your child's behaviors and concentration problems at home and school, ask yourself these questions.

1. Do you and your child's other parent(s) disagree on how to discipline your child?
2. Do you frequently find yourself being negative and angry with your child?
3. Do you lose your temper often and then apologize and hug your child afterward?
4. Do you find yourself in continuous power struggles with your child after which you feel quite helpless?
5. Do you find yourself sitting with your child to help with schoolwork because it wasn't finished in school and your child can't concentrate at home?
6. Do you find yourself disorganized and out of control much of the time?
7. Does your child spend two hours or more a day in front of the television or computer?
8. Is your workload so overwhelming that you have little time for quality parent-child time?
9. Does your child concentrate well in areas of special interest or high motivation?
10. Is your child's schoolwork too easy or too difficult?
11. Is your child involved in appropriate out of school activities for energy release?
12. Does your child function well in competition?

If your answer is yes to most of the first ten questions and no to the last two, your child's symptoms of attention disorders can likely be improved by home and school adjustments. More effective parenting and school changes will help you and your child and, unlike medication, will cause no negative side effects.

Figure 33.5 Self-Test for Parents

Source: Keys to Parenting the Gifted Child by S. B. Rimm, 2001, NY: Barrons Educational Series, reprinted with permission.

underachievement syndrome. However, this modification by itself will not be sufficient. Rimm (1995) also gives dozens of other recommendations for home and school changes in her books specifically written about underachievement syndrome.

The Importance of Interventions

Although it is true that maturity, mentors, and mates (M & M's) may help underachievers reverse their underachievement in adulthood, Peterson (2000) found that only 50% of high school underachievers completed four years of college. The accomplishments of these students did not match the higher achievements of students who were achievers in high school, nor did they attend the high-level colleges attended by the achieving students. That is both good news and bad news. The good news is that there is surely hope for gifted high school underachievers; the bad news is that the prognosis for underachievers is simply not as good as it is for achievers. Success rates were 80% for those underachievers who sought intervention at the Family Achievement Clinic. Success rates varied between 50 and 80 percent for schools that instituted the Trifocal model for gifted underachievers.

Clinical experiences with underachievers indicate that school, home, and peer environments can and should be modified to cure underachievement syndrome in gifted children. Although the reversal is difficult, the satisfaction felt by the child and family and the achievement of potential contributions to society make the extraordinary efforts worthwhile. The author of this chapter has been using the Trifocal model for twenty years and would like to close by sharing the results of a long-term, successful case.

John, a fourth-grade dependent underachiever, was disorganized and undisciplined in completing schoolwork in the classroom and at home. He had few friends, felt lonely, and was taunted on the playground, where he didn't fit in because he didn't like sports. He spent hours alone with his imaginary friends in his imaginary world, writing, playacting, and dressing up in costumes for his lonely performances. His grades were poor, he cried easily, and frequently lost his temper in frustration. Below is a letter from John, now grown up and achieving:

Dear Dr. Rimm,

I recently saw you on the Today Show and just had to write you. You were my psychologist back when I was in grade school. I went to school in Wisconsin back in the early 80's. You helped me through my underachievement issues that plagued my academic and social success. I owe most of the success that I now enjoy to you. You helped instill in me the confidence that I desperately needed to break free from my shell and allow myself to grow. I remember you told me to never be afraid of getting the wrong answer because that is how we learn; I remember you told me to continue and explore my creativity through writing and acting because that is how I would truly find my strengths; I remember how you taught me to manage my life strategically because this would help my confusion and random, inconsistent behavior. Finally, I remember that you told me to never be afraid to express myself no matter what others thought.

Dr. Rimm, in many ways you have been there for me over the past fifteen years because of what you taught me. I never became a famous writer, and I have never starred on Broadway, but I will soon have a degree from UW-Madison and attend law school. I have considered myself a leader since high school. I have held leadership roles in every single organization I have been involved with over the past ten years. I have been blessed with some of the best friends anyone could ask for—good, strong relationships that you helped me identify, seek out, and keep. I now consider my parents and brother my best friends and closest confidants, and I face the world with an uncompromising confidence that I will make a difference. Thank you, Dr. Rimm, for giving me the tools to make my dreams come true.

It is hard to raise and teach gifted underachievers, but within underachievers is the potential and usually the wish to achieve importance. When the defense mechanisms of underachievement are cut away, underachievers can indeed become superachievers. Educators, counselors, parents, and mentors are usually significant in intervening in these frustrating underachieving patterns.

SUMMARY AND CONCLUSIONS

Underachievement may stem from perceived too-strong academic pressure from parents; parents who are not education-oriented; parents who do not model independent learning and respect for school; inconsistent parent leadership; having a sibling who is "practically perfect"; a gifted student's wish to be creative, resulting in nonconformity; a school environment that overemphasize athletics or popularity; an academic curriculum that is unchallenging, and therefore unrewarding; anti-intellectual and anti-

gifted attitudes; or disabilities such as ADHD that mask the giftedness.

Some symptoms of underachievement include procrastination, incomplete assignments, disorganization, inattention, and careless work. These behaviors create skill deficiencies, causing gifted students to lose their sense of control over school outcomes. Low self-esteem is a consistent symptom of underachievers. Some prominent high-achievers in the Rimm studies occasionally underachieved.

To reverse underachievement, the Trifocal model includes the six steps of assessment of skills, abilities, and type of underachievement; good communication between parents and teachers; changing the expectations of important others; finding a model with which to identify; correcting skill deficiencies; and modifying reinforcements for homework and study, for example, by setting long-term goals and short-term objectives that ensure successes.

It is difficult to raise and teach gifted underachievers, but within these students is the potential and usually the wish to achieve importance. When the defense mechanisms of underachievement are cut away, underachievers can become superachievers. Educators, counselors, parents, and mentors are significant in intervening in these frustrating underachieving patterns.

QUESTIONS FOR THOUGHT AND DISCUSSION

1. Based on Rimm's descriptions, how might you identify gifted underachievers at the grade level you expect to teach?

2. What characteristics will help you to recognize that students are mainly *dependent* underachievers or *dominant* underachievers? In the classroom, how might you help each type of underachiever become better adjusted and a better achiever?

3. What help might you elicit from parents in order to reverse their child's underachievement?

4. If parents will not cooperate with you, how might you work with their underachieving gifted child to stimulate better adjustment and higher achievement?

5. Are you sometimes an underachiever? In what circumstances?

REFERENCES

Baker, J. A., Bridger, R., & Evans, K. (1998). Models of underachievement among gifted preadolescents: The role of personal, family, and school factors. *Gifted Child Quarterly, 42*(1), 5–15.

Baum, S., Olenchak, F. R., & Owen, S. V. (1998). Gifted students with attention deficits: Fact and/or fiction? Or, can we see the forest for the trees? *Gifted Child Quarterly, 42*(2), 96–104.

Bloom, B. S. (Ed.). (1985). *Developing talent in young people.* New York: Ballantine.

Bloom, B. S., & Sosniak, L. A. (1981). Talent development vs. schooling. *Educational Leadership, 39,* 86–94.

Brown, B. B., & Steinberg, L. (1990). Academic achievement and social acceptance: Skirting the "brain-nerd" connection. *Education Digest, 55*(7), 55–60.

Carnegie Corporation of New York. (1996). *Years of promise: A comprehensive learning strategy for America's children.* Executive Summary. New York: Carnegie Task Force of Learning.

Cornale, M. (1998). *Dependence and dominance in preadolescent academic underachievers.* Unpublished research paper, University of Wisconsin—Madison.

Covington, M. V., & Beery, R. G. (1976). *Self-worth and school learning.* New York: Holt.

Davis, G. A., & Rimm, S. B. (1998). *Education of the gifted and talented* (4th ed.). Boston: Allyn and Bacon.

Deci, E. L. (1986). Motivating children to learn: What can you do? *Learning 86, 14*(7), 42–44.

DeLeon, P. H. (1989, February). *Why we must attend to minority gifted: A national perspective.* Presented at the Johnson Foundation Wingspread Conference, Racine, Wisconsin.

Felton, G. S., & Biggs, B. E. (1977). *Up from underachievement.* Springfield, IL: Charles C. Thomas.

Fine, M. J., & Pitts, R. (1980). Intervention with underachieving gifted children: Rationale and strategies. *Gifted Child Quarterly, 24,* 51–55.

Frasier, A., Passow, A. H., & Goldberg, M. L. (1958). Curriculum research: Study of underachieving gifted. *Educational Leadership, 16,* 121–125.

French, J. L. (1959). *Education of the gifted: A book of readings.* New York: Holt.

Gallagher, J., Harradine, C. C., & Coleman, M. R. (1997). Challenge or boredom? Gifted students' views on their schooling. *Roeper Review, 19*(3), 132–136.

Green, K., Fine, M. J., & Tollefson, N. (1988). Family systems characteristics and underachieving gifted adolescent males. *Gifted Child Quarterly, 32,* 267–272.

Grimm, J. (1998). The participation of gifted students with disabilities in gifted programs. *Roeper Review,* 285–286.

Hoffman, J. L., Wasson, F. R., & Christianson, B. P. (1985, May–June). Personal development for the gifted underachiever. *G/C/T,* 12–14.

Hom, H. L., Jr., Gaskill, B., Hutchins, M. (1988). *Motivational orientation of the gifted student: Threat of evaluation and its impact on performance.* Paper presented at the meeting of the American Educational Research association, New Orleans, Louisiana.

Jackson, R. M., Cleveland, J. C., & Mirenda, P. F. (1975). The longitudinal effects of early identification and counseling of underachievers. *Journal of School Psychology, 13,* 119–128.

Lajoie, S. P., & Shore, B. M. (1981). Three myths? The over-representation of the gifted among dropouts, delinquents, and suicides. *Gifted Child Quarterly, 25,* 138–141.

Leroux, J. A., & Levitt-Perlman, M. (2000). The gifted child with attention deficit disorder: An identification and intervention challenge. *Roeper Review,* 171–176.

MacKinnon, D. W. (1965). Personality and the realization of creative potential. *American Psychologist, 20,* 273–281.

Mussen, P. H., & Rutherford, E. (1963). Parent-child relations and parental personality in relation to young children's sex-role preferences. *Child Development, 34,* 589–607.

National Commission on Excellence in Education. (1983). *A nation at risk: The imperative for educational reform.* Washington, DC: U.S. Government Printing Office.

Nyquist, E. (1973). *The gifted: The invisibly handicapped, or there is no heavier burden than a great potential.* Paper presented at the National Conference on the Gifted, Albany, New York.

Perkins, J. A., & Wicas, E. A. (1971). Group counseling with bright underachievers and their mothers. *Journal of Counseling Psychology, 18,* 273–278.

Peterson, J. S. (2000). A follow-up study of one group of achievers and underachievers four years after high school graduation. *Roeper Review, 22*(4), 217–224.

Reis, S. M., & Purcell, J. H. (1993). An analysis of content elimination and strategies used by elementary classroom teachers in the curriculum compacting process. *Journal for the Education of the Gifted, 16*(2), 147–170.

Reis, S. M. (1998). Underachievement for some—dropping out with dignity for others. *ITAG News,* Iowa Talented and Gifted Association Newsletter, *23*(4), 1, 12–15.

Rimm, S. B. (1980, September–October). Congratulations Miss Smithersteen you have proved that Amy isn't gifted. *G/C/T,* 23–24.

Rimm, S. B. (1986). *AIM: Achievement identification measure.* Watertown, WI: Educational Assessment Service.

Rimm, S. B. (1987). *GAIM: Group achievement identification measure.* Watertown, WI: Educational Assessment Service.

Rimm, S. B. (1988). *AIM-TO: Achievement Identification Measure-Teacher Observation.* Watertown, WI: Educational Assessment Service.

Rimm, S. B., & Lowe, B. (1988). Family environments of underachieving gifted students. *Gifted Child Quarterly, 32,* 353–359.

Rimm, S. B. (1990). A theory of relativity. *Gifted Child Today, 13*(3), 32–36.

Rimm, S. B. (1995). *Why bright kids get poor grades and what you can do about it.* New York: Crown.

Rimm, S. B. (1996). *How to parent so children will learn.* New York: Crown Publishers, Inc.

Rimm, S. B. (1999). *See Jane win.* New York: Crown Publishers, Inc.

Rimm, S. B. (2000). Why do bright children underachieve? The pressures they feel. *On Raising Kids* Newsletter. The Cleveland Clinic, Cleveland, OH, pp. 2–3.

Rimm, S. B. (2001a). *How Jane won.* New York: Crown Publishers, Inc.

Rimm, S. B. (2001b). *Keys to parenting the gifted child.* New York: Barrons Educational Series.

Rimm, S. B., & Lovance, K. J. (1992). The use of subject and grade skipping for the prevention and reversal of underachievement. *Gifted Child Quarterly, 36,* 100–105.

Rimm, S. B., & Olenchak, F. R. (1991). How FPS helps underachieving gifted students. *Gifted Child Today, 14,* 19–22.

Seeley, K. R. (1993). Gifted students at risk. In L. K. Silverman (Ed.), *Counseling the gifted and talented* (pp. 263–276). Denver CO: Love Publishing.

Seligman, M. E. (1975). *Helplessness: On depression, development and death.* San Francisco: Freeman.

Walberg, H., Tsai, S., Weinstein, T., Gabriel, C. L., Rasher, S. P., Rosencrans, T., Rovai, E., Ide, J., Truijillo, M., & Vukosavich, P. (1981). Childhood traits and environmental conditions of highly eminent adults. *Gifted Child Quarterly, 25,* 103–107.

Weiner, B. (1974). *Achievement motivation and attribution theory.* Morristown, NJ: General Learning Press.

Weiner, B. (1980). *Human motivation.* New York: Holt.

Werner, E. (1989). Children of the garden island. *Scientific American, 234*(1), 106–111.

Whitmore, J. R. (1980). *Giftedness, conflict, and underachievement.* Boston: Allyn and Bacon.

Winebrenner, S. (2000). *Teaching gifted kids in the regular classroom.* Minneapolis: Free Spirit Publishing.

Zilli, M. G. (1971). Reasons why the gifted adolescent underachievers and some of the implications of guidance and counseling of this problem. *Gifted Child Quarterly, 15,* 279–292.

34

High Risk Gifted Learners

KEN SEELEY, *Colorado Foundation for Families and Children, Denver*

The paradox is the source of the thinker's passion, and the thinker without a paradox is like a lover without feeling; a paltry mediocrity.
—Soren Kierkegaard (1813–1855)

The Paradox of High Risk Behaviors and Giftedness

The juxtaposition of high ability and high risk in children provides an organizing theme for this chapter. *Paradox* is typically viewed as seemingly contradictory conditions that may nonetheless be true. Paradoxes have been used in Eastern religions as a teaching approach to develop a student's intuitive skills. Having two opposites against each other—thesis and antithesis—helps to develop a synthesis that is not merely a compromise, but a new solution. In education and psychology, we see little use of paradox and ambiguity to advance understanding. Indeed, there seems to be a relentless commitment to simplify or reconcile differences in order to reach logical conclusions with straightforward explanations. High risk gifted students defy a simple explanation. We will see a certain logic in their behaviors, but a definite illogic in the way we attempt to educate and socialize them.

Talented children and youth who are disruptive, or violent, or delinquent, or just poor students are a paradox worthy of exploration in a search for new solutions or explanations. The solutions themselves may also be rich in paradox and ambiguities. This paradox will continue to confront us in developing high potential among youth whose behavior challenges our models, approaches, and understandings about intelligence and ability.

High Risk Defined

It is important to distinguish between "at-risk" and "high risk." These terms are often used interchangeably, but really mean different things. Most people are "at-risk" for something (e.g., cancer, heart attack, poor school performance, etc.). Family background or life circumstances often put some people at greater risk than others. This group is identified as "at-risk" for some bad outcome because of these preexisting conditions. High risk, on the other hand, requires that there be clear behavioral indicators that call attention to individuals immediately. For the purpose of this chapter, "high risk" is manifested in behaviors that include one or any combination of the following:

- Chronic truancy
- Disruptive behavior resulting in suspension or expulsion
- Behavior indicating the student is seriously withdrawn
- Behavior that is violent or destructive to self or others
- Running away from home
- Substance abuse
- Delinquent/criminal behavior.

While these behaviors are more frequent among adolescents, they also occur in younger children. There is also evidence that they occur more frequently during transitions, including home moves and school moves from kindergarten to first grade, elementary to middle school, and middle school to high school (Seeley & Shockley, 1997).

Research completed over the past thirty years has identified precursors of crime, violence, and substance abuse called *risk factors* as well as *protective factors* that buffer against the risk factors and inhibit the development of these health and behavior problems (Hawkins, Catalano, & Brewer, 1994). The notion that high risk behaviors are rooted in some predictable risk and protective factors that occur early in the life cycle is helpful as we explore the paradox of giftedness among high risk youth. David Hawkins and Richard Catalano are national leaders in the field of prevention. Their work, summarized in Table 34.1, provides our first framework for understanding and predicting high risk behaviors. It also provides a handy reference for the roots and causes of high risk behaviors from early childhood.

It is interesting to point out that academic failure is a risk factor for school-age children for crime, violence, and substance abuse. School failure is a stable predictor just after this early stage from about grade 4 onward. However, it appears that efforts to promote cognitive development at ages 4–6 can reduce risk. Academic failure for gifted students means serious underachievement and opens that entire area for exploration of causes and interventions.

Conceptions of Giftedness Among High Risk Students

For purposes of understanding high risk gifted students, four major concepts need to be explored. These are foundation of giftedness and include

- Intelligence
- Learning style
- Competence
- Motivation

Intelligence

The most relevant theory of intelligence that bears on high risk gifted youth is that proposed by Horn (1976) and Cattell (1971). Cattell proposed a two-factor model of human intelligence that includes fluid and crystallized intelligence. Through extensive factor analysis of primary mental abilities, Cattell described fluid intelligence as general reasoning ability, using the process of perceiving relations in figural and spatial material and perceptive and intuitive reasoning that uses a minimum of previously learned strategies or verbal mediation. Crystallized intelligence is developed through acculturation, education, training, and practice and is made up of abilities and knowledge such as verbal and quantitative reasoning, sequential memory, vocabulary, and reading comprehension. Crystallized intelligence "uses verbal mediation, sound inference, and sequential steps of logic in problem solving" (Harvey & Seeley, 1984, p. 76). Essentially, crystallized intelligence is rewarded in most public schools because it involves learning the rules, applying the rules, and giving back information to the teachers in the same forms that they gave to the student.

Horn (1976) described fluid ability as incidental learning, essentially an intelligence that is not taught

Table 34.1   Risk and Protective Factors in the Early Developmental Period (0–6 Years)

Risk Factors	*Protective Factors*
• Peri-natal difficulties	• Female gender
• Minor physical abnormalities	• High intelligence
• Brain damage	• Positive social orientation
• Family history of criminal behavior/substance abuse	• Resilient temperament
• Family management problems	• Social bonding to individuals
• Family conflict	• Healthy beliefs
• Early antisocial behavior	• Clear standards for behavior
• Academic failure	
• Favorable parental attitudes toward crime and substance abuse	

Source: Adapted from Hawkins, D., Catalano, R., and Brewer, D. (1994). *Preventing serious violent and chronic delinquency and crime.* Washington, DC: National Council on Crime and Delinquency.

or nurtured in schools. Gifted youth with high levels of fluid ability and low crystallized ability may appear to teachers as average or below students because they do not seem to follow the problem-solving rules that were taught, even if they can get the correct answer. Indeed, high fluid-ability students are sometimes accused of cheating because they can get the correct answers without going through the prescribed sequence of steps required by the teacher.

Cattell initially postulated that fluid intelligence was genetically determined, but Horn (1976) and many other researchers who accept the basic theory (e.g., Snow, 1981; Thorndike, 1963) disagree that fluid ability is innate. Silverman (1998) stated that "Cattell's theory of fluid and crystallized abilities strongly influenced Sternberg's (1985) triarchic theory of intelligence and became the basis of another major intelligence test: the Stanford Binet Intelligence Scale, Fourth Edition" (Thorndike, Hagen, & Sattler, 1986, p. 52).

The largest study ever undertaken on gifted delinquents revealed that these young offenders had high levels of fluid intelligence as measured by the WISC-R (Mahoney & Seeley, 1982; Seeley, 1984). It was their fluid ability that made the greatest contribution to their being identified as gifted.

Learning Style

A logical extension of the notion of high fluid ability among high risk gifted is that they can also be characterized as visual-spatial learners. It is a link worth exploring because of the connection between visual-spatial learners and underachievement. Silverman (1998) made the direct connection between fluid ability and visual-spatial learning style in her discussion of personality and learning styles of gifted children. She stated, ". . . there appear to be . . . two ways of knowing that need to be taken into account in educating gifted children: spatial or fluid abilities and sequential or crystallized abilities" (p. 52). These gifted spatial learners typically think in images, holistically, and not step by step. As a result they can learn difficult, complex material easily, but may be quickly confused by easy sequential tasks that they find difficult to master (West, 1991).

Spatial learners are often underachievers because of teachers' using and rewarding sequential tasks. Tests, state standards, and school curricula are typically set up for students with high crystallized ability. Gohm, Humphreys, and Yao (1998) found that students gifted in spatial ability "were not fully utilizing their academic capabilities, had interests that were less compatible with traditional coursework, received less college guidance from school personnel, were less motivated by the education experience, and aspired to, and achieved, lower levels of academic and occupational success" (p. 515).

Silverman (2002) makes several key points about gifted visual-spatial learners. "I think the biggest problem was that we never got the distinction between academic success and giftedness. When giftedness is defined as academic achievement, we not only miss individuals with unusual abilities, we also miss brilliant children with astronomical IQ scores" (Silverman, 2002).

Just as fluid and crystallized abilities may be viewed as ends of a continuum of intelligence, Silverman presents a two-factor learning style: visual-spatial learning opposing auditory-sequential learning. Because there is no "pure" or unilateral intelligence factor or learning style, students are a mix of fluid and crystallized abilities and visual-spatial and auditory-sequential learning styles.

Understanding the connections between the risk and resiliency factors and the type of intelligence and learning style should aid our assessment and programming for high risk gifted students. The evidence of high fluid ability among gifted delinquents (Mahoney & Seeley, 1982) and gifted school drop-outs (Seeley, 1987), coupled with higher visual-spatial learning styles connecting to underachievement (Gohm et al., 1998), gives us a good beginning for a theory of change about high risk gifted learners. Explaining the paradox helps us toward new solutions.

Competence

The term *competence* is used because if we used the typical concepts of *ability* or *achievement,* we would be limited and less inclusive. Our goal is to find a way to connect our understandings among intelligence, learning style, and motivation. The notion of competence is extremely helpful in making these connections.

John Raven, the Scottish psychologist, developed an expansive literature about competence, which he promotes as a new paradigm for assessment, teaching, learning, and educational research. In defining *competence,* Raven (1991) stated, "It means we must know an individual's values, preoccupations, or intentions before one attempts to assess his or her abilities. Important abilities demand time, energy and effort. As a result, people will only display them when they are undertaking activities which are important to them. It does not make sense to attempt to assess abilities except in relation to valued goals" (p. 49). Raven is critical of the narrow psychometric approaches used to assess ability and offers his own extensive explanations and models. He argues that one cannot assess abilities independent of values. Adopting competence measures of high risk gifted students moves us to a better understanding of their complex mix of abilities, challenges, values, and affect. The notion of competence helps us to understand a student's abilities linked to motivation.

Figure 34.1 presents a model of the connections between competence and motivation based on White's (1964) conception of competence or "effectance" motivation and the adaptive and maladaptive motivational patterns described by Dweck (1986). White's landmark work in personality development promotes the idea that our motivation is developed out of our attempts at mastery and how we perceive our competence as a result. If our self-perception is positive or successful, it stimulates a cycle of reinforcement that is self-perpetuating because it feeds motivation, which drives competence. On the other hand, if our mastery attempts fail, we perceive ourselves as incompetent; we become anxious about those situations and try to avoid them. This decreases motivation and diminishes overall competence into a self-perpetuating negative cycle. Thus, White's conception of effectance motivation described in Figure 34.1 helps explain the positive and negative cycles learners get into resulting from mastery attempts. These patterns can also affect one's internal or external locus of control. Failed mastery attempts not only decrease motivation, they contribute to externalizing the perception of control.

Figure 34.1 also includes some key concepts from the work of Carol Dweck (1986), as she also connects the ideas of competence, mastery, and motivation. Because gifted high risk students manifest many of their problems in these three areas, Dweck's ideas are important for understanding adaptive and maladaptive learning patterns. She states,

> Achievement motivation involves a particular class of goals—those involving competence—and these goals appear to fall into two classes: (a) learning goals in which individuals seek to increase their competence, to understand or master something new, and (b) performance goals, in which individuals seek to gain favorable judgments of their competence or avoid negative judgments of their competence (p. 1040).

The maladaptive pattern in Figure 34.1 shows that when mastery attempts fail, we see challenge avoidance, poor learning goals, and poor performance goals. This results in a feeling of helplessness, with low persistence in the face of challenging tasks. The mastery-oriented pattern suggests that for mastery attempts to succeed, they must be at the level of optimal challenge to produce perceived competence and to continue the positive cycle of high learning goals, high performance goals, and increased motivation.

The Synthesis Solution

Step 1, The Assessment

The interaction of these four major components, intelligence, learning style, competence, and motivation, along with the risk and protective factors, provide many implications for assessment. Standardized tests need to include measures of fluid ability with tasks that also measure visual-spatial ability. At times these overlap, depending on the test, but many visual-spatial abilities need to be assessed beyond those in IQ tests.

The assessment of competence, motivation, and the risk and protective factors implies a number of important steps often omitted from the gifted identification process. These additional assessments should include:

- A family social history
- Student interest inventory
- Personal interview with the student
- Writing sample to examine the student's values
- Tests of perceived competence and self-esteem (Susan Harter's Scales) (Harter, 1981, 1982, 1983, 1993; Harter, Waters, & Whitesall, 1998)
  - Self Perception Profiles
  - Social Support Scales
  - Scale of Intrinsic versus Extrinsic Orientation in the Classroom
  - Self-Perception for Learning Disabled Students
- Product reviews
- School attendance, suspensions, and office referrals.

The earlier in a student's life we can discover the coexistence of giftedness and high risk behaviors,

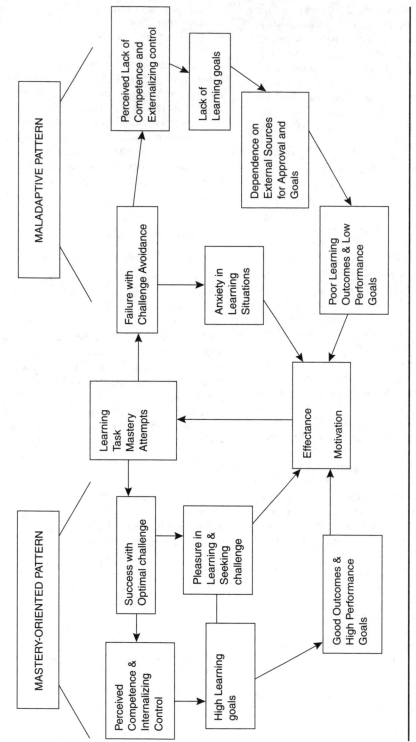

Figure 34.1 Competence and Motivation.

Source: Adapted from theories of competence and motivation of Robert White (1964) and Carol Dweck (1986).

the better are chances to develop the giftedness as a protective factor against the high risk behaviors. The paradox about the role of giftedness among high risk youth continues as an unresolved issue. Some see high ability as a protective factor because they infer good problem-solving skills and advanced insights will resolve conflict better. Others believe that the giftedness itself is a risk factor because of heightened sensitivities to negative conditions that produce bad behaviors. As a practical matter, it depends on the individual youth how the gifted characteristics interact with the risk factors. The results of a good comprehensive assessment should not only better describe the paradox but also help us prescribe corrective actions.

Step 2, Engagement

The capstone of the synthesis solution is assuring that students are engaged in school. We can assess and prescribe adaptations for gifted high risk students, but we must also engage them in school. Engagement is manifested in the amount of attention and effort students apply to schoolwork and homework, the emotions they experience while doing it, and the importance they place on doing well in school. "Student engagement has been found to be the single most robust predictor of students' performance and personal adjustment in school. This conclusion holds regardless of whether students come from families that are relatively advantaged or disadvantaged economically or socially" (Connell, 1998, p. 2). High levels of engagement can explain why some high risk students succeed academically regardless of gender or race or socioeconomic level (Finn, 1993; Connell, Spencer, & Aber, 1994).

Connell and Wellborn (1994) suggest that school engagement is defined by reaction to challenge, beliefs about self, and interpersonal supports. In building programs for high risk gifted students, we need to develop school engagement plans that include these three elements.

Reaction to Challenge. As described in Figure 34.1, the reaction to challenging work can ignite a positive or negative pattern. Following a good assessment, teachers should understand how to structure challenges that produce success and provide the benefits of perceived competence and motivation. This involves far more than giving the student easy work and then praising the mastery. The work must be challenging for that intrinsic pleasure of mastery and competence to trigger the effectance motivation cycle.

Beliefs about Self. Self-esteem is tied closely to academic achievement, problem solving, and success in school. Exploring these beliefs with students informally, as well as in the assessment, is important to finding causes and hopefully solutions to negative beliefs. Such beliefs are often grounded in an external locus of control and feelings of helplessness, denial, anger, blame, and anxiety. Designing positive experiences that build competence and mastery-oriented patterns can help these students become engaged.

Interpersonal Support. High risk students need to come to school and believe that they count in someone else's life—that it matters that they show up at school. Typically, a caring adult at school is the starting point for positive engagement. The caring adult must show respect for the student as well as general support. Interpersonal support can make high risk students feel that they belong, which may be the most crucial factor in the motivation and engagement process.

SUMMARY AND CONCLUSIONS

The paradox of high ability and high risk challenges our conceptions of giftedness and antisocial behavior. This chapter presents a framework for understanding the underlying dynamics of this ambiguity. The basic concepts of risk and protection are the cornerstone of prevention and intervention for all high risk populations, including gifted students. The connections among intelligence, learning style, competence, and motivation comprise the complex set of relationships that explains the paradox. High fluid ability versus crystallized ability and high visual-spatial versus auditory-sequential learning style are found among many high risk gifted youth. These fundamental conditions can have a great impact on the students' competence and motivation.

The solutions for these high risk youth begin with a good assessment that goes beyond typical identification practices. Understanding and promoting school engagement is the final part of the solution. As educators, we are not often in a position to eliminate the risk factors in the home and community. Poverty, abuse, delinquency, and family conflict often work against our best efforts to reach these students. However, developing giftedness in these students can be a way of improving their resilience to risk, which can help protect them from poor life circumstances.

It is becoming more apparent that different types of intelligence and learning styles may combine to put many gifted students at risk of school failure or other more serious bad outcomes. The hardened pedagogy that reinforces only the student mastery attempts that meet the crystallized, auditory-sequential teaching unfortunately misses an important group of students who understand their world differently and have the potential for making significant contributions. As we continue to grow into the twenty-first century, the loss of these non-linear thinkers is too great.

QUESTIONS FOR THOUGHT AND DISCUSSION

1. Look at Table 34.1. Do any of the *risk* factors apply to you or to persons you know? Explain. Do most of the *protective* factors apply to you? Explain.

2. Would you say you have a visual-spatial learning style, an auditory-sequential learning style, or a balance of both? Explain.

3. Consider Cattell's conception of fluid versus crystallized intelligence. How is this similar and different from standard conceptions of intelligence, as in the Wechsler Verbal and Performance IQs or Stanford-Binet single IQ?

4. Seeley's Synthesis Solution includes an extensive assessment in Step 1. Which of his suggested assessments seem most important? Least important? Explain.

5. How does Seeley recommend implementing Step 2, assuring engagement in school? Is this an easy step? Why or why not?

REFERENCES

Cattell, R. B. (1971). *Abilities: Their structure, growth and action.* Boston: Houghton Mifflin.

Connell, J. P. (1998). *The research assessment package for schools.* Rochester, NY: Institute for Research and Reform in Education.

Connell, J. P., Spencer, M. B., & Aber, J. L. (1994). Educational risk and resilience in African American youth. *Child Development, 65,* 493–506.

Connell, J. P., & Wellborn, J. G. (1994). *Engagement versus disaffection.* Rochester, NY: University of Rochester.

Dweck, C. (1986). Motivational processes affecting learning. *American Psychologist, 41,* 1040–1048.

Finn, J. D. (1993). *School engagement and students at risk.* Washington, DC: National Center for Education Statistics.

Gohm, C., Humphreys, L., & Yao, G. (1998). Underachievement among spatially gifted students. *American Educational Research Journal, 35,* 515–531.

Harter, S. (1981). A new self-report scale of intrinsic vs. extrinsic orientation in the classroom: Motivational and informational components. *Developmental Psychology, 17,* 300–312.

Harter, S. (1982). The Perceived Competence Scale for children. *Child Development, 49,* 788–789.

Harter, S. (1983). Developmental perspectives on self esteem. In M. Hetherington (Ed.), *Handbook of child psychology: Social and personality development* (Vol. 4). New York: Wiley.

Harter, S. (1993). Causes and consequences of low self esteem in children and adolescents. In R. F. Baumeister (Ed.), *Self esteem: The puzzle of low self regard.* New York: Plenum.

Harter, S., Waters, P., & Whitesall, N. R. (1998). Relational self-worth: Differences in perceived worth as a person across interpersonal contexts among adolescents. *Child Development, 69,* 756–766.

Harvey, S., & Seeley, K. (1984). An investigation of the relationships among intellectual and creative abilities, extracurricular activities, achievement, and giftedness in a delinquent population. *Gifted Child Quarterly, 28,* 73–79.

Hawkins, D., Catalano, R. F., & Brewer, D. (1994). *Preventing serious violent and chronic delinquency and crime.* Seattle: Developmental Research and Programs.

Horn, J. (1976). Human abilities: A review of research theory in the early 1970s. *Annual Review of Psychology, 27,* 436–485.

Mahoney, A., & Seeley, K. (1982). *A study of juveniles in a suburban court.* Technical Report. Washington DC: US Dept. of Justice.

Raven, J. (1991). *The tragic illusion: Educational testing.* Oxford: Oxford University Press.

Seeley, K. (1987). *High ability students at risk.* Denver CO: Clayton Foundation.

Seeley, K. (1984). Giftedness and delinquency in perspective. *Journal for the Education of the Gifted, 8,* 59–72.

Seeley, K., & Shockley, H. (1997). *Re-engaging youth in school.* Technical Report. Denver: Colorado Department of Public Safety.

Silverman, L. (1998). *Personality and learning styles in gifted children.* In J. VanTassel-Baska (Ed.), *Excellence in educating gifted and talented learners* (3rd ed.). Denver CO: Love Publishing.

Silverman, L. (2002). *Upside-down brilliance: The visual spatial learner.* Denver: DeLeon Publishing.

Snow, R. E. (1981). Toward a theory of aptitude for

learning. In M. P. Friedman, J. P. Das, & N. O'Conner (Eds.), *Intelligence and learning.* New York: Plenum.

Sternberg, R. (1985). *Beyond IQ: A triarchic theory of human intelligence.* New York: Cambridge University Press.

Thorndike, R. L. (1963). *The concepts of over and under achievement.* New York: Columbia University Press.

Thorndike, R. L., Hagen, E. P., & Sattler, J. M. (1986). *The Stanford Binet Intelligence Test: 4th Edition.* Technical Manual. New York: Riverside.

West, T. G. (1991). *In the mind's eye: Visual thinkers, gifted people with learning difficulties, computer images, and the ironies of creativity.* Buffalo NY: Prometheus Books.

White, R. (1964). *The abnormal personality* (3rd ed.). New York: Ronald Press.

PART V

Populations of Giftedness

Part VI looks at various populations of gifted students, whose special characteristics and problems present special challenges to educators of the gifted. A first thought-provoking chapter describes extremely bright youngsters, child prodigies, and savant syndrome. Then we turn to identifying, understanding, and meeting the educational and sometimes social and emotional needs of gifted young children, adolescents, girls and young women (and boys and young men), culturally diverse students, students with high spatial ability, and students with learning disabilities.

In Chapter 35 Martha J. Morelock and David H. Feldman describe three types of extremely precocious children. First, studies of high-IQ children include the landmark Terman studies (IQ 140+); Hollingworth's case studies of twelve children (IQ 180+); Gross's Australian study of fifteen children (IQ 160+); and Morelock's own study of eight children with IQs over 180—one of whom graduated college at age ten. Due to inappropriate school placements, children with extremely high IQs (almost always first-born) typically do have social and emotional problems. Second, child prodigies, by definition, perform at the level of a highly trained adult before age ten. The prodigies' high IQs do not explain their incredible domain-specific talent. Feldman's co-incidence theory describes the melding of favorable intraindividual, environmental, and historical forces. Third, savant syndrome is the logic-defying phenomena of spectacular music, art, math, "calendar-calculating," or mechanical ability in otherwise mentally handicapped persons. Savants seem to have rapid intuitive access to underlying rules and regularities of their domain. Emotion, however, is restricted.

Nancy Ewald Jackson in Chapter 36 defines *gifted behavior* in young children as excellent and rare, relative to peers, and demonstrable with reliable assessment methods, namely, ability tests and parent reports. Manifestations appear in precocious and sophisticated speaking and comprehension; sometimes in early reading and writing; and less often in precocious drawing. Children who display giftedness during preschool years are likely to continue to perform well. Children precocious in language often, but not always, later show gifts in other pattern-analysis areas such as math, music, chess, or computer languages. However, many older gifted children and eminent adults were not precocious in language. Intelligent parents create a favorable environment for learning and thinking, which tangles the effects of genes and environment. Effective parents help their children reflect on and extend their learning. However, early academic pressures seem to convey no lasting benefit. Jackson also reviews complexities in relating adult gifted behavior to childhood precocity.

In Chapter 37 Robert A. Schultz and James R. Delisle emphasize that gifted adolescents are "first and foremost" teenagers, much like all other teenagers. Their intensity and overexcitability can lead to remarkable achievement, but sometimes suicide. After self-selection—not identification—for a gifted program, the authors emphasize "space to grow." That is, gifted teenagers need respect and support (by "life preservers"), not critical judgment (by know-it-all "sages"). The authors describe underachievement as a myth—a mismatch of others' expectations and the adolescents' own passions. "Peer problems" may not exist—gifted adolescents simply prefer likeminded older students. Both personal and existential problems can be addressed with bibliotherapy. Perfectionism leads to poor self-concepts and the avoidance of challenging tasks; an antidote is a classroom atmosphere where risk taking is encouraged and mistakes are expected. "Gifting" is the mentorlike personal coaching of a student with high potential. To deal with multipotentiality, the authors recommend more exposure to the realities of each possible career.

According to Barbara A. Kerr and Megan Foley Nicpon in Chapter 38, gifted girls are closing the gap with boys in the academic arena. But problems include eating disorders, impossible ideals of beauty, and lower (e.g., math) achievement scores, which affect college admission. In childhood gifted girls are better adjusted than gifted boys, but both genders have social and emotional problems at the highest ability levels. Female self-esteem plunges during adolescence. While gifted girls out-achieve gifted boys in all subjects, males score higher on ACT tests, except for English. Young gifted girls have high career aspirations that resemble those of gifted boys, but in college they may switch majors and reduce their career goals. As adults, females suffer workplace discrimination and nonsupportive partners. With gifted boys, masculine stereotypes can depress high achievement and raise fears pertaining to being gay. Males exit fields as women become dominant in them, which reduces high school leadership and later career options. Texts and tests remain gender biased. Even feminist teachers treat boys and girls differently. Finally, the authors suggest ways to improve gender relationships, self-identity, and gender-fair teaching practices.

In Chapter 39 Donna Y. Ford addresses one of the most perplexing and sensitive issues in gifted education: the underrepresentation of culturally diverse students in gifted education programs and services. Ford outlines steps to recruit and retain larger numbers of gifted diverse students. She also describes factors that work against the representation of culturally diverse students in gifted education—particularly, the misunderstanding of cultural differences related to student beliefs, values, habits, and verbal and physical behavior. Together, these "differences" contribute to a "deficit" assumption by the majority culture, supported by overused and misused test scores. Ford recommends better definitions of giftedness and intelligence, adopting culturally sensitive tests and assessments, and building multicultural education programs for both staff and students. She also item-

izes numerous specific ideas for better understanding, working with, and teaching diverse students.

David Lubinski in Chapter 40 describes a gifted population that is underserved, often ignored, by current talent searches: students very high in spatial reasoning ability. Spatial ability is separate from tested math and verbal ability, and can lead to success in architecture, engineering, physical sciences, or many creative arts areas. A twenty-year longitudinal study by Lubinski and others used tests of verbal, mathematical, and spatial ability to illustrate how high school classes (most and least favorite), college majors, graduate school majors, and occupational outcomes all related systematically to students' scores on tests of verbal, math, and spatial ability. For example, college humanities/social science students scored highest in verbal ability, math/computer people scored highest in math ability, and electrical engineers scored highest in spatial ability. Lubinski recommends that Talent Searches evaluate spatial ability, that the school curriculum include more options for students high in spatial ability, and that counselors assess spatial ability and counsel students who score high.

In Chapter 41 Linda Kreger Silverman stresses a too-common problem of gifted students with learning disabilities. Because these bright students compensate for their learning disability and show adequate school performance, they usually do not qualify for gifted *or* special education programs. She explains the most common learning disabilities in gifted children: sensory integration dysfunction, AD/HD, auditory-processing disorder, visual-processing disorder, visual-processing deficits, dyslexia, and spatial disorientation. Silverman also addresses the twin challenges of detecting giftedness in students with learning disabilities and detecting learning disabilities in students who are gifted. Finally, she itemizes fourteen experienced insights for promoting success with twice exceptional students, for example: detect the learning disability early, use IEPs, allow liberal testing time, use available technology, use oral exams, teach to the child's strengths, and teach compensation strategies and keyboarding skills.

35

Extreme Precocity: Prodigies, Savants, and Children of Extraordinarily High IQ

MARTHA J. MORELOCK, *Elmira College*
DAVID H. FELDMAN, *Tufts University*

In this chapter, types of extremely precocious children are described, compared, and contrasted, and a taxonomy of extreme precocity is presented.

The Extremely Precocious Child

The Biblical story of Jesus, who, at the age of 12, astonished the rabbis with his understanding, is perhaps the first recorded allusion to an extremely precocious child.[1] It was not until the 1700s that detailed accounts of precocity appeared in what was a developing literature of child psychology (Hollingworth, 1942). The earliest, written in 1726, and later summarized by Barlow (1952), described the child Christian Friedrich Heinecken:

> Christian Friedrich Heinecken, a German, who was known as the "Infant of Lübeck," from the place where he was born in 1721, is said to have talked within a few hours after his birth. Besides his remarkable faculty for numbers, he is said to have known, at the age of one year, all the principal events related in the Pentateuch; at two was well acquainted with the historical events of the Bible; and at three had a knowledge of universal history and geography, Latin and French. People came from all parts to see him, and the King of Denmark had him brought to Copenhagen in 1724, in order to assure himself of the truth of what he had heard regarding him. But shortly after this, little Heinecken was taken ill and predicted his own death, which took place in 1725, at the tender age of four (Barlow, 1952, pp. 135–136).

Young Heinecken's life synopsis suggests an extraordinary ability to absorb and verbalize abstract knowledge. Although he lived before the development of IQ tests, his academic precocity is characteristic of the child of extraordinarily high IQ. But precocity comes in a number of guises. There are, for example, child prodigies whose extraordinary performance in particular fields rival that of highly trained adults. Such was the child musician and composer Wolfgang Amadeus Mozart (1756–1791) who, at the age of six, toured Europe with his father and sister exhibiting his mastery of the violin, piano, and organ (Barlow, 1952; Morelock & Feldman, 1999).

There are also astonishing cases like George and Charles—identical twin calendar calculators (Hamblin, 1966). George at the age of six and Charles at the age of nine could answer spontaneously questions such as, "On what day of the week was your third birthday?" "The year is 31275; on what day of the week will June 6 fall?" Given a date, these twins could give the day of the week over a span of 80,000 years, though their IQs only tested between 40 and 50. Although they could not count to 30, they swapped 20-digit prime numbers for amusement. They could easily factor the number 111 and remember 30 digits, but could not add.

Heinecken, Mozart, and George and Charles reflect the three major types of extremely precocious children found in the literature. Heinecken exemplifies the child of extraordinarily high IQ; Mozart was a supreme example of the child prodigy; and George and Charles are classified as savants. The sections below examine each of these of variations of extreme precocity.

---

1. This story may be found in the Bible, King James Version, Luke 2:46–47.

The Child of Extraordinarily High IQ

To understand the child of extraordinary IQ, it is necessary to understand something about the instrument that first defined and selected such children. Lewis M. Terman's Stanford-Binet Intelligence Scale, first appearing in 1916, extended and revised the 1908 Binet-Simon Scale, devised by the French psychologist Alfred Binet and T. Simon, his physician collaborator. The Binet-Simon Scale identified children who, unable to succeed in Paris public schools, needed special programs. Terman's scale, however, incorporated an innovation—a definition of human intelligence. He defined intelligence as ability to acquire and manipulate concepts—the symbols necessary for abstract thinking (Terman, 1975). Terman extended the instrument into higher levels of ability in late childhood, thereby paving the way for studies of the gifted (Segoe, 1975). Terman himself began the first broad-scale study of the gifted (Terman, 1925–1959), a longitudinal project following over 1,500 children with IQs of at least 140 into adulthood, middle age, and beyond. Terman's contemporary, Leta S. Hollingworth (1942), conducted the first in-depth study devoted solely to children of extraordinarily high IQ.

Leta Hollingworth and Children Above IQ 180

Hollingworth (1942) conducted case studies of twelve children (eight boys and four girls) testing above 180 IQ on the Stanford-Binet Intelligence Scale. She found that, although no one characteristic could be singled out as identifying accelerated development, early talking and reading most clearly differentiated these children from the average. Since the capacity for abstract, symbolic thought that Terman aimed at identifying was chiefly language-based conceptual facility, this is not a surprising finding. Early talking and reading are likely manifestations of high-level verbal-conceptual ability.

Hollingworth identified three major adjustment problems risked by children of above-180 IQ (Witty, 1951). First, they failed to develop desirable work habits in school settings geared to average children's capacities. In such settings, they spent considerable time in idleness and daydreaming. Consequently, they learned to dislike school. To remedy this, Hollingworth (1942) proposed acceleration through the normal elementary curriculum plus enrichment experiences providing knowledge about cultural evolution as manifested through the development of common things such as clothing, lighting, trains, etiquette, and so forth. She believed that by understanding how things had developed in the past, these children might become innovative thinkers themselves.

A second problem documented by Hollingworth was these children's difficulty in finding satisfying companionship and their consequent social isolation. While they typically attempted play with others, their efforts commonly failed since age-mates did not share their interests, vocabulary, or desire for more complex activities. Older children might satisfy the extraordinarily gifted child's need for intellectual rapport, but physically the younger child was at a disadvantage. Thus, Hollingworth believed that these children must be educated for leisure. She espoused games like chess or checkers, which could be enjoyed by people of all ages, potentially assisting in bridging social gaps.

Hollingworth's research suggested that children of extraordinarily high IQ are unlikely to be accepted as leaders by age-mates. Leaders, Hollingworth (1926) concluded, are likely to be "more intelligent, but not too much more intelligent, than the average of the group led" (p. 131). She believed that beyond IQ 160, children have little chance of being popular leaders in a regular school setting. To develop leadership skills, such children needed to be placed in special classes with others like themselves.

Emotional vulnerability was a third problem documented by Hollingworth. These children are able to understand and grapple with major philosophical and ethical issues before they are emotionally ready to do so. Hollingworth cautioned that adults must deal patiently with such vulnerabilities to avoid engendering lifelong emotional problems, concluding, "To have the intelligence of an adult and the emotions of a child combined in a childish body is to encounter certain difficulties" (Hollingworth, 1942, p. 282).

Children of Extraordinarily High IQ in Australia

It was 50 years after Hollingworth's research before another systematic in-depth study devoted to extraordinarily high IQ children appeared in the literature. Australian researcher Miraca U. M. Gross (1993) published research documenting the academic, social, and emotional development of fifteen children scoring at IQ 160+ in the eastern states of Australia. The group consisted of ten males and five females ranging in age from five years, three months, to thirteen years, five months. Only four of the children—all males—scored 175+ on the Stanford-Binet L-M, suggesting they were on a par with Hollingworth's children. Three of the children attained IQ scores of 200 or higher, prompting Gross to publish detailed individualized case studies about them (Gross, 1992). (Only one of Hollingworth's children had attained an IQ score of 200.) Gross looked at physical and psychosocial development, school history, and family characteristics. She collected results of achievement tests in reading, mathematics, and spelling. Many of the issues reported by Gross—for example, the trials of negotiating appropriate educational experiences and emotional and social difficulties stemming from inappropriate placements—echoed those first documented by Hollingworth.

An interesting aspect of this study is the use of psychosocial assessment instruments. Gross's use of the Coopersmith Self-Esteem Inventory (Coopersmith, 1981) revealed scores on the social self-peers subscale significantly below the mean of typical age-peers. The children's awareness that they were rejected and disliked by age-mates caused self-concept problems. Administration of Rest's (1986) Defining Issues Test (DIT), a test of moral judgment based on Kohlberg's stages of moral development, showed that these children exhibited accelerated levels of moral development. On questions of moral or ethical significance, the eight children to whom it was administered (ranging in age from ten to thirteen) resembled junior high, high school, or college students.[2]

Children of Extraordinarily High IQ in the Family Context: Families with Children Above 200 IQ

Morelock's (1994, 1995) in-depth study of extraordinarily high IQ children viewed these children from a developmental perspective. This research looked not only at child characteristics of mentality and personality, but also at the families giving rise to such extraordinary children. The investigation included some of the most profoundly gifted children, in IQ terms, ever studied. All of the children had IQ's of 180+; six had IQ scores well above 200. The children ranged from five through eleven years of age at the time of the interviews, and included seven

boys and one girl. One child, Michael Kearney, boasted the distinction of being, at age ten, the youngest person ever to have graduated from college (Kearney & Kearney, 1998; Morelock, 1995). Another, at the age of eight years, four months, achieved a score of 760 out of a possible 800 on the math portion of the SAT, winning the distinction of attaining the highest score for that test ever recorded at such an early age. One of Gross's (1993) subjects had set the former record, achieving the same score at the age of eight years, ten months. Only 1% of college-bound seventeen- and eighteen-year-olds in the United States attain a score of 750 or more. A third child and the only female in Morelock's group—an 11-year-old writing prodigy—wrote poetry rivaling that of professionals, not only in mastery and creative use of language, but also in her extraordinary spiritual, mystical, and psychological insights (Morelock, 1995).

The study examined family environment and transgenerational influences (Feldman & Goldsmith, 1986; Morelock, 1988, 1994, 1995). Additionally, the study looked at the phenomenological realities of the children and families through interviews with family members and individuals outside the family who had close interactions with the focus child (teachers, members of the extended families, psychologists, etc.). Aspects of family environment were assessed through the Moos Family Environment Scale (FES; Moos & Moos, 1994). Some intriguing trends emerged:

1. Family values and themes traced over the generations revealed themselves not only in parental child-rearing patterns, but even in children's language and mode of thought. It appears that heightened facility with language enables these children to absorb and express the values and modes of thought encoded in that language more readily than can average children. At an early age, they become sensitive distillers and reflectors of family values and themes. This is reflected in their behavior, talk, and thought processes.

2. Assessment with the Intellectual-Cultural Orientation subscale of the Moos Family Environment Scale (Moos & Moos, 1994) suggested that these families were more cohesive (the degree to which family members are committed to one another and help and support each other) and expressive (acting openly and expressing feelings directly) than average families. The expressiveness pertains not only to feelings but also to the free exchange and exploration

---

2. For an excellent and thorough review of the literature on cognitive development in exceptionally and profoundly gifted individuals, see Gross (2000).

of ideas. The families not only scored higher than average families on this subscale, but also higher than families of gifted children in former studies (who also scored above the norm) (Cornell, 1984).

The families scored lower than average on scales measuring orientation toward achievement or competition, participation in active social and recreational activities, degree of importance of clear organization and structure in family activities and responsibilities, and the extent to which set rules and procedures are used to run family life. Conflict occurred less in these families than in average families; while the extent to which family members were assertive, self-sufficient, and made their own decisions was higher than average.

3. A birth order trend emerged in these families regarding self-definition among siblings. Consistent with earlier studies of giftedness and talent (e.g., Feldman, 1991), children identified as profoundly gifted were first-borns. The second-borns tended to describe themselves in terms of what they could *do* rather than how they could think. Their talents were centered around products and performances—construction and mechanical or architectural design (with construction or mechanical toys), dancing, or artistic abilities. The seven-year-old younger brother of the writing prodigy declared, "I'm a doer, not a talker," and exhibited his mechanical designs and building constructions. Kearney's eight-year-old younger sister Maeghan, announced that she was the "creative" one in the family and took up drawing and the construction of doll clothes. The younger brother of the SAT-Math whiz also took up construction as a hobby, and delighted in showing the researcher a small building he had designed and his efforts at constructing a hot-air balloon. A younger sister of an eleven-year-old highly talented in mathematics, logical thought, and chess became an extraordinary dancer. Her brother reported that he was a "thinker" whereas she was an "applier."

Generally, the second-borns were much more at ease when demonstrating their active talent areas than when talking in an interview. This was distinctly unlike their older siblings, who delighted in verbally exploring concepts and inner feelings. Interestingly, the only family in which this general pattern failed to hold true was one that valued sports, athletics, and "doing things in the real world" to such an extent that it may have overridden the usual pattern. In this

particular family, the focus child reported that he wanted to be a professional athlete. His younger sister, who was only four at the time of the interview, was talented in drama, singing, and dance. Thus, both children were, at the time of the interviews, oriented toward more traditionally "second-born talents."

For second-borns, the product seemed the central reason for thinking; while for first-borns, the focus was intense, enjoyable exploration of thought and concepts. Second-borns gravitated toward areas in which they did not have to compete with older siblings.

Extraordinarily High IQ and Achievement

With the advent of the IQ scale, extraordinarily high IQ aroused expectations of extraordinary achievement. Hollingworth considered children testing above 180 IQ as "potential geniuses" (Witty, 1951). She saw in them the possibility of original contributions of outstanding and lasting merit. A 1984 study (Feldman, 1984) using Terman's (Terman, 1925–1959) original research files failed to bear out Hollingworth's expectations for achievement.[3]

---

3. We define genius in terms of developmental changes in bodies of knowledge. That is, a creative contribution meriting the designation of genius is one that transforms an entire domain of human knowledge. One of such caliber, for example, was Albert Einstein's theory of relativity, which did, indeed, transform the domain of physics (Feldman, 1980, 1994).

Feldman (1984) compared the lives of Terman's twenty-six above-180-IQ subjects with a group of lesser IQ (average group IQs: 185 versus 150) randomly selected from the original sample of over 1,500. Although there was some evidence that the above-180-IQ subjects were more successful, the difference was slight. A small number of distinguished men emerged from the group (e.g., an academic psychologist of international repute, a celebrated landscape architect, a judge, and a promising pollster who committed suicide at age 28), but the degree of distinction was not on a par with genius.

In a longitudinal study following 320 extraordinarily high-IQ adolescents (averaging over 180 in estimated IQs) over ten years into young adulthood (Lubinski, Webb, Morelock, & Benbow, 2001), subjects pursued doctoral degrees at rates over 50 times base-rate expectations, and several participants created noteworthy literary, scientific, or technical products by their early twenties.

In recent years, some have begun to argue that the IQ score is an index of asynchronous development (Morelock, 1992, 2000; Silverman, 1997). As such, it gauges the degree to which the rate of children's cognitive development is "in sync" with their rates of physical, social, and emotional development, as well as the extent to which children are facile in the manipulation of abstract symbols and concepts. According to proponents of the asynchronous development view, the IQ score is a diagnostic tool to assist in providing educational programming, counseling, and parenting that addresses children's varying developmental levels and needs—not a predictive tool for ferreting out potential achievers. Morelock's (1991) case study of "Jennie" was a progenitor of the asynchronous development view of giftedness.

A Sociohistorical Case Study of Asynchronous Development

In an in-depth case study of one extraordinarily high-IQ child, Morelock (1991, 2000) explored the emotional repercussions of a child's having a rate of cognitive development outpacing physical, social, and emotional development. Somewhere between the ages of three years, eight months, and four years, six months, "Jennie Cartwright" (a pseudonym) experienced a cognitive leap in her abstract reasoning abilities, as documented through Stanford-Binet L-M testings at those two ages (IQ 148; IQ 176). The cognitive changes were accompanied by intense existential questioning and marked emotional turmoil.[4]

Jennie's emotional turmoil during the period of the leap raised questions as to the emotional impact of such rapid changes. It also raised questions of the overall impact of the early and perhaps premature onset of abstract verbal-conceptual thinking in children's development, as is characteristic of high-IQ children. Jennie's development was cast in a Vygotskian framework to provide a theoretical explanation for the emotional vulnerability accompanying rapid cognitive development—when emotion and cognition become interrelated and children begin to have emotional reactions to the cognitive appraisal of events "too early" in life:

> As Jennie grappled with the sudden onslaught of increased abstract capacity, she was forced to deal with the emotional repercussions of her own thought. Thus, in Jennie's mind at age 4, God could not possibly be a loving God if He would refuse Heaven to anyone. And the terrible realization of her own mortality could not be softened by her mother's reassurances because "Nobody knows for sure . . . children die sometimes." Her emotional needs, like those of other 4-year-olds, included a trust in the strength and reliability of her parents and in the predictability of a secure world. However, her advanced cognitive capacities—or, from the Vygotskian perspective, the precocious logicalization of her thought processes and her increased ability to interpret and attribute meaning to experience—left her emotionally defenseless in the face of her own reason (Morelock, 2000, p. 68).

The repercussions of the asynchrony between Jennie's cognitive abilities and her emotional needs highlights the importance of looking at children of extraordinarily high IQ from the perspective of asynchronous development and its associated inner experience.[5] The case study inspired the evolution of the Columbus Group definition of giftedness. Based on asynchronous development, the group-formulated definition was first published in 1992 (Morelock, 1992). The case study appeared in its entirety eight years later (Morelock, 2000). The Columbus Group definition is articulated and debated in other literature (Gagné, 1997; Morelock, 1996, 1997a, 2000; Silverman, 1993, 1997).

Cognition and Imagination in Children of Extraordinarily High IQ

Children like Morelock's "Jennie" are characterized by the ability to reason abstractly at an early age. They can be logical and analytical. They use analogies and metaphors and transfer ideas between contexts.

---

4. Hollingworth (1942) documented leaps in IQ scores in the children she studied. One child, at age six years, seven months attained an IQ score of 163, while at eight years, he achieved an IQ of 192, prompting Hollingworth to note in her record that "the increase over the IQ obtained at the age of six is not unusual for a very young, very bright child, although it would be unusual for an average child" (p. 178).

5. Larisa V. Shavinina (1999) saw Jennie's cognitive leap as a manifestation of a "sensitive period" in development—a window of time during which conditions are optimal for cognitive development to proceed at a rapid pace and children are especially likely to actualize potentially extraordinary abilities.

Because they see beyond what most children their age can see, recognizing complexities of which other children are unaware, for these children the *simple* can be *complex*. Consequently, they have a need for precision in thought and expression. For such children, alternate meanings are myriad, and there is no way of knowing precisely which meaning a questioner intends. If asked, "Are you having a nice time?" such a child might answer, "What do you mean by a nice time?" At the same time, because these children grasp abstract material by finding underlying patterns, what is *complex* to others can be *simple* for them. They can have an early grasp of the essential element of an issue (Lovecky, 1994).

One five-year-old boy, "Peter Martin" (pseudonym; IQ 200+), discovered Stephen Hawking's book *A Brief History of Time,* which speculated on the origins of the universe. Fascinated with the book, he read it constantly, even falling asleep with it at night. About the same time, Peter saw a Sesame Street Christmas Special where Big Bird was worrying about how Santa Claus would get down all those chimneys. Peter applied the knowledge he had gained from Hawking's book to come up with a solution. Hawking theorized that if someone were able to enter a black hole, the person would become longer and thinner as he or she went deeper into the hole and further away from its boundary, the "event horizon." In addition, time would slow down. Peter reasoned that if Santa could direct and control the force of singularity (the force generated in the center of a black hole), he could make himself thin enough to get down chimneys. In addition, time would slow down so that he could get to all the houses in the world without any problem (Morelock, 1997b)!

The Prodigy

A *prodigy* is a child who, before the age of ten, performs at the level of a highly trained adult in some cognitively demanding domain (Feldman, 1991; Morelock & Feldman, 1999, 2000). As a uniquely defined category of extreme precocity, the prodigy came into being about two decades ago (Feldman, 1979)—in spite of the fact that "prodigy" has been used loosely to refer to extraordinary youngsters for many years. Historically, the term meant any unnatural occurrence portending change (Feldman, 1991). It referred to an entire range of phenomena extending across happenings notable as uncanny or extraordinary and the existence of humans or animals regarded as "freaks." Eventually, as the term began to refer more narrowly to extreme human precocity, the "sign" or "portent" aspect of its meaning was dropped, while the essential connotation of "unnatural" or "inexplicable" remained. Within this narrowed context, "prodigy" continued to be used to refer to a range of types of precocity (see Barlow, 1952).

With the advent of IQ and its general acceptance as the gauge of giftedness, prodigies were subsumed under the IQ umbrella (Feldman, 1979). Children composing sonatas at the age of six were assumed to have high IQs with penchants for given fields. While IQ began to dominate American concepts of giftedness, two studies of prodigies in the European literature failed to support IQ as the foundation for prodigiousness (Baumgarten, 1930; Revesz, 1925).

The Prodigy as Reflected in Research Literature[6]

Revesz and Erwin Nyiregyhazi. Revesz (1925) conducted a case study of the seven-year-old Hungarian musical prodigy Erwin Nyiregyhazi, using interviews; observations of Erwin in and out of performing situations; anecdotes from family, teachers, and acquaintances; and formal assessments (e.g., the 1908 Binet-Simon Scale).

Erwin was remarkable from an early age. By the age of two he reproduced tunes sung to him, and by the end of his third year he demonstrated perfect pitch by reproducing on the mouth organ any melody sung to him. At four he played the piano and composed. In his fifth year he began formal music lessons. From age six to twelve Erwin became a celebrity, playing before the British royal family and other audiences in Budapest and Vienna. Revesz favorably compared Erwin's abilities with those of other legendary prodigies and great musicians of the day.

---

6. A number of biographical or psycho-historical accounts have been published providing interesting insights into the life of the prodigy. See, for example, Kathleen Montour's (1977) "William James Sidis: The Broken Twig"; Norbert Wiener's 1953 autobiography, *Ex-Prodigy: My Childhood and Youth;* Amy Wallace's 1986 book (also about William James Sidis), *The Prodigy;* Fred Waitzkin's 1984 book, *Searching for Bobby Fischer: The World of Chess, Observed by the Father of a Child Prodigy;* and Kenneson's (1998) *Musical Prodigies.*

On the Binet-Simon scale, Erwin scored a mental age three years beyond his chronological age of seven, or by modern reckoning slightly above 140 IQ. Revesz, however, asserted that the test inadequately revealed Erwin's brilliant intellect, noting that the child "analyzed his own inner life in the manner of a trained psychologist" and "expressed himself with great caution and in remarkably pregnant phraseology" (Revesz, 1925, p. 42). In spite of Erwin's talents and exhibited brilliance, Revesz asserted that the prodigy was indeed, in every aspect other than his music, a child: "He played as children play, was fond of boyish exploits, and enjoyed them very much" (Revesz, 1925, p. 58).

Baumgarten's Nine Prodigies. Baumgarten (1930) studied nine child prodigies, including two pianists, two violinists, one orchestra conductor, one artist, one geographer, and one chess prodigy. Focusing on the children's whole personalities rather than only their achievements, she also examined patterns of abilities. Like Revesz, she wrote of the mixture of adult and child demonstrated by her subjects. They appeared ambitious, pragmatic, wary of those who might harm their careers, passionately devoted to their fields, unafraid of public performance, and desirous of using their gifts to benefit their families.

There were surprising contrasts between various abilities within subjects. Violinists and pianists demonstrated poor hand coordination in bending wire, drawing, and folding and cutting—though one girl violinist had a talent for drawing. A six-year-old boy showing difficulty in making a circle out of two or three sections or a pentagon from two sections was, at the same time, extraordinarily good at map drawing.

On standardized intelligence tests, the children performed well, but not with the degree of extraordinariness conveyed by their special talents. In contemporary IQ terms, the scores ranged from 120 to at least 160. Baumgarten concluded that her subjects' overall intellectual competence, as reflected in the test results, could not explain their outstanding performances in particular fields and that it was necessary to go beyond such testing to explain prodigious abilities—inheritance, temperament, family, education, environment, and culture must be examined.

Child Prodigies and Human Potential

A study of six prodigies begun in 1975 (Feldman, 1991, 1994; Goldsmith, 2000) included two chess players, a young mathematician, a musician-composer, a writer, and an "omnibus prodigy" showing prodigious achievement in a number of areas, but eventually focusing on music composition and performance.[7] What developed into an open-ended effort to observe, understand, and explain the prodigy phenomenon began as a psychological experiment designed to refute an esoteric point in cognitive-developmental psychology. The point in question was the Piagetian assertion that, universally, children's cognitive development proceeds in major predictable sequential stages grossly encompassing all of a child's thinking capacities at any given point in time. Accordingly, to account for prodigies' adult-level performance in specific fields, one would have to assume that their overall cognitive development was generally advanced beyond their years.

To test this assertion, four cognitive-developmental measures were administered to the two eight-year-old chess players and the ten-year-old musician-composer (Bensusan, 1976).[8] The results of the testing showed that these prodigies performed age-appropriately in logic, role-taking, spatial reasoning, and moral judgment. The Piagetian conceptualization of cognitive development was thus seriously challenged.

These findings, like those of Revesz and Baumgarten, suggest that prodigious abilities, rather than being the manifestation of a generalized endowment, are domain-specific. Association with these six prodigies and their families has extended beyond two

---

7. At the age of three and one-half when Adam, the omnibus prodigy, first entered the study, he was reported to read, write, speak several languages, study mathematics, and compose for the guitar (Feldman, 1980).

8. The four measures given were (1) Inhelder and Piaget's (1958) five chemicals task, a test of the level of acquisition of various concrete and formal logical operations; (2) a role-taking task devised by John Flavell (1968) and his associates at the University of Minnesota, the aim of which is to test social-cognitive development by assessing the level of ability to take another's point of view; (3) a map-drawing exercise, an adaptation of Piaget and Inhelder's (1948) layout diagram task (Snyder, Feldman, & La Rossa, 1976), which gives a general estimate of the level of the coordination of spatial-logical reasoning; and (4) a psychometric measure of level of moral judgment and reasoning prepared by James Rest (1986), based on Kohlberg's stages of moral development (Feldman, 1991).

decades, resulting in a theoretical framework, the *co-incidence theory,* that seeks to explain not only prodigious development, but also all human achievement.

Co-Incidence Theory

Co-incidence is the melding of the many sets of forces interacting in the development and expression of human potential (Feldman, 1994). These include intraindividual (e.g., biological and psychological), environmental (e.g., familial, societal, or cultural), and historical forces. They comprise at least four different time frames bearing on the prodigy's appearance and development: the individual's life span, the developmental history of the field or domain, historical and cultural trends impacting individuals and fields, and evolutionary time. Each of these is discussed briefly.

Life Span of the Individual. This time frame includes biological propensities predisposing an individual toward talented performance in certain fields. An example might be Gardner's (1993) concept of multiple brain-based intelligences (i.e., linguistic, musical, logical-mathematical, spatial, bodily-kinesthetic, interpersonal, and intrapersonal intelligences), each of which holds more or less potential for development within individuals. A child "at promise" for prodigious musical achievement is born with the intellectual, physical, and acoustic facilities necessary for extraordinary musical sensibility/performance.

Another factor in this time frame is the point in the child's physical, social, and emotional developmental history when he or she is introduced to a domain. Playing the violin, for example, requires a certain degree of dexterity. Some children may develop this dexterity earlier than others. The time of introduction to the instrument may thus be an important factor in whether violin playing becomes a source of pleasure or a source of frustration. Children's levels of social and emotional development may also play important roles in their receptivity to domains (Csikszentmihalyi & Robinson, 1986). An adolescent grappling with age-appropriate issues of peer acceptance and popularity may opt out of long hours of piano practice, choosing instead to spend time socializing with peers. In the case of one chess prodigy, the attractions of the peer group proved powerful enough to jeopardize an intense commitment to chess (Feldman, 1991; Goldsmith, 2000).

A family's likelihood of nurturing talent is another factor in this time frame. Mozart's musician-father possessed the musical ability to instruct his son. He valued music and was interested enough to spend hours tutoring his children and accompanying them on concert rounds, aside from opportunistic motives he also may have had.

Degree of parental support may be affected by a child's gender (Goldsmith, 1987). Historically, cultural undervaluing of feminine achievement has resulted in (1) less parental support for female would-be prodigies and (2) scarce documentation about girl prodigies.

Parental encouragement of talents may be influenced by values or child-rearing patterns passed down from prior generations. Transgenerational influences were apparently at work in the family of violinist Yehudi Menuhin. Menuhin's family, for centuries, had been shaped by a Hasidic Jewish tradition emphasizing music and the development of boy prodigies groomed to assume religious leadership as rabbis. The fervor of the Menuhins in encouraging Yehudi's prodigious talent may have been rooted in this tradition (Rolfe, 1978).

Developmental History of the Field. Bodies of knowledge develop and change over time. Consequently, performance requirements and opportunities change as well. The life span of a would-be prodigy coincides with some portion of a domain's developmental history, the joint existence of the two allowing for a particular expression of the child's potential. Prodigious achievement only occurs within domains accessible to children, meaning they require little prerequisite knowledge and are both meaningful and attractive to children. Media and techniques must be adaptable to children (e.g., child-size violins are necessary for child prodigy violinists). Given these prerequisites, music performance and chess are especially amenable to budding prodigies. Indeed, the largest proportion of child prodigies in recent decades emerges from these fields. Other fields produce comparatively few prodigies. There have been occasional writing prodigies, child prodigy visual artists (Goldsmith & Feldman, 1989), and on rare occasion a child prodigy in mathematics.

The delicate concordance of child ability and domain requirements for a particular area of achievement may shift as the prodigy develops. With entry into adolescence, new domains, previously inaccessible to the prodigy, become available for mastery (i.e., philosophy, art criticism, engineering, business, psychology, etc.) (Goldsmith, 2000). While these may call on abilities similar to the ones prodigies applied to their original domains of accomplishment, they may be engaging in their own way. Consequently, the prodigy may be enticed away from the original domain by new opportunities for learning and mastery.

Historical and Cultural Time Frame. This time frame reflects historical and cultural trends affecting opportunities for learning. Prodigious achievement is influenced by the cultural importance attached to various domains. The revived interest in science and math during the 1950s because of the Soviet satellite initiatives is one example.

Evolutionary Time Frame. Cultural and biological evolution provide the context within which all other factors in prodigy development interact. Through biological variation and natural selection, human capabilities come into being and either flourish or cease to exist. Parallel evolutionary forces operate on cultures and their artifacts. This flux influences options for the expression of potential.

Co-incidence and Prodigious Achievement

The child prodigy is the manifestation of a fortuitous concordance of the forces of coincidence in such a way as to maximize the expression of human potential. In each case of prodigiousness, there was, first of all, a child of unquestionably extraordinary native ability. This child was born into a family that recognized, valued, and fostered that ability. The child was exposed to the instruction of master teachers possessing superior knowledge of the domain and its history, and imparting that knowledge in a way most likely to engage the interest and sustain the commitment of the child. For the child's part, there was exhibited a combination of inner-directedness and a remarkably passionate commitment to the field of extraordinary achievement. Such commitment holds repercussions for family life, as shown in the following section.

Family Relationships

The family is the catalyst for the co-incidence process (Feldman, 1991). It is the prodigy's parents who must locate teachers and resources and assure the child's access. This may entail commuting or uprooting the family permanently to resettle closer to a mentor. Frequent changes may be required as the child outgrows a succession of mentors.

Close parental involvement results in a longer and more intense period of dependency for prodigies than in families with more typical children. Especially close family ties may be forged to protect a "special" child from an insensitive outside world.

The strong commitment to talent development shared by prodigies and their families means some sacrifice by other family members. Limited family resources may dictate that sibling talent goes unsupported. Or the prodigy's presence may influence the channeling of sibling potential. When Hepzibah Menuhin, Yehudi's younger sister, asked to learn to play the violin like her older brother, her parents encouraged her to play the piano instead—since Yehudi needed an accompanist. When Yalta, the youngest sibling, later showed interest in the piano, she was told to make herself useful around the house because the family didn't need another musician. Yet many believed Hepzibah and Yalta to be equally as talented as Yehudi (Rolfe, 1978).

The roles of families of prodigies change with time (Goldsmith, 2000). Adolescent prodigies, if they are to continue to grow, must begin to establish separate and autonomous lives with regard to both their talent areas and their psychosocial development. The family must facilitate this process of individuation by gradually relinquishing control.

The Savant

The phenomenon of the savant, like that of the high-IQ child and the child prodigy, has its own unique history. In 1887 Dr. J. Langdon Down of London coined the term "idiot savant" to refer to severely mentally handicapped persons displaying advanced levels of learning in narrowly circumscribed areas (Down, 1887). Although intriguing in its own right, the term failed to describe the individuals it labeled, since they are generally neither "idiots" nor "savants." In Down's time, "idiot" referred to individuals operating at the lowest level of retarded intellectual functioning, as classified by practitioners on the basis of evaluation of speech and language capabilities. With the advent of IQ tests, idiocy was translated as encompassing the lowest portion of the IQ scale, spanning an IQ range of 0 to 20.[9] In reality, however, the IQs of all known

---

9. The term *idiot* was used from 1910 to 1968 to refer to this portion of the IQ scale. In 1968, the World Health Organization adopted the term *profoundly retarded* to refer to this same range (Craft, 1979).

tested savants have been above 20—usually in the range of 40 to 70 (Treffert, 1989, 2000). The savant part of the term was a straightforward adaptation from the French word "to know" or "man of learning," which, although perhaps slightly more appropriate, was nevertheless a misnomer as well.[10]

Given the inappropriateness of the term as a whole and the pejorative connotation of the first part of it, Treffert (1989) proposed "savant syndrome"—or just "savant"—as a more desirable name for the phenomenon. He described the phenomenon, offering more precise classification terminology as well as a theoretical explanatory framework (Treffert, 1989, 2000).

Savant Syndrome—Definition and Description

Treffert defined savant syndrome as "an exceedingly rare condition in which persons with serious mental handicaps, either from mental retardation, Early Infant Autism or major mental illness (schizophrenia), have spectacular islands of ability or brilliance which stand in stark, markedly incongruous contrast to the handicap" (Treffert, 2000, p. 15). Some savants have skills that are remarkable simply in contrast to the handicap (talented savants, or savant I); while in rarer forms of the condition, the abilities would be spectacular even if viewed in a normal person (prodigious savants, or savant II).

Savant syndrome, which occurs six times as often in males as in females, can be either congenital or acquired by a normal person after injury or disease of the central nervous system. The skills can appear—and disappear—in an unexplained and sudden manner. Savant brilliance occurs only within very few areas: calendar calculating; music, chiefly limited to the piano; lightning calculating (the ability to do extraordinarily rapid mathematical calculations); art (painting, drawing, or sculpting); mechanical ability; prodigious memory (mnemonism); or, on rare occasion, unusual sensory discrimination (smell or touch) or extrasensory perception. Prodigious savants occur primarily within the areas of music, mathematics

(lightning and calendar calculating), and memory. Treffert (1989, 2000) reported that there have been only about 100 known prodigious savants in the world literature—twelve to fifteen of whom are currently living.

Characteristics of Savant Functioning

Savants display minimal abstract reasoning ability combined with almost exclusive reliance on concrete and literal patterns of expression and thought (Scheerer, Rothman, & Goldstein, 1945; Treffert, 2000), sometimes, with humorous results.

Peek (1996) reported several instructive incidents in the life of his savant son, Kim. On one occasion, Kim squinted at a camera while having his picture taken. When his father told him to open his eyes, Kim took his fingers and literally used them to "open" his eyes. On another occasion, a professor asked Kim what he knew about Abraham Lincoln. Kim reeled off Lincoln's date of birth, his death date, when and how he died, whom he had married, and his service in Congress. The professor interjected "Very good. Can you tell me his Gettysburg Address?" Kim responded "Will's House, 227 North West Front Street—but he only stayed there one night. He gave his speech the next day" (Peek, 1996, p. 77).

Kim, like all savants, cannot use language symbolically or conceptually. His thought processes are constrained by a concrete, fact-oriented mindset dominated by simple associations. When asked what "Follow in your father's footsteps" meant, Kim replied "Hold Dad's arm so you won't get lost in the airport" (Peek, 1996, p. 123).

Savants are incapable of metacognition (Scheerer, Rothman, & Goldstein, 1945; Treffert, 1989, 2000). Calendar calculators commonly respond correctly to queries (e.g., "On what day of the week did September 1, 1744, fall?") without being able to explain how they arrived at the correct response. Those able to articulate rule-based strategies tend to have higher IQs than do their counterparts (Hermelin & O'Connor, 1986). All savants have incredibly powerful memories narrowly limited to their domains of achievement.

Savants also have an immediate intuitive access to the underlying structural rules and regularities of their particular domain, be it music (Treffert, 1989, 2000), mathematical calculation (Hermelin & O'Connor, 1986; O'Connor & Hermelin, 1984), or art (O'Connor & Hermelin,

---

10. Bernard Rimland (1978) claimed that the *idiot* in *idiot savant* came from the French *idiot,* meaning "ill-informed or untutored." This interpretation captures the paradoxical nature of the phenomenon (i.e., "untutored man of learning") without confusing the issue with IQ-associated connotations.

1987). The domain-specific rules intuitively "known" by savants are the same rules applied by those with normal or high reasoning ability who are skilled in the same area. While savants function according to these rules and regularities, they have no metacognitive grasp of their own cognitive processes.

Savants can imitate, improvise, or embellish based on pre-established musical rules (Treffert, 2000). Hermelin, O'Connor, and Lee (1987) found that savants, by accessing a system of relevant rules and structures, can also invent music conforming to familiar patterns. The researchers concluded that this ability is independent of general intelligence.

Savants demonstrate a restricted range of emotion that precludes the experience of heightened passion, excitement, or sentiment. This restriction takes the form of generally flattened affect and—in the case of the performance of musical savants—shallow, imitative expressiveness lacking subtlety or innuendo (Treffert, 2000).

Using the Wechsler Adult Intelligence Scale (WAIS), Young (1995) investigated the psychometric performances of fifty-one savants recruited throughout Australia and the United States. The selection of savants included prodigious and talented savants as well as cases of "splinter skills"—levels of interest and competence only marginally above the level of general functioning. In contrast to the impression that savants manifest islands of extreme capability showcased against a backdrop of overly deficient intellect, Young found peaks and valleys in the cognitive profiles of her savants. Among her savants, sixteen had a subtest score at least one standard deviation above the general (non-savant) population mean, and a full 60% had at least 1 subtest one standard deviation above their Full-Scale Score. Highest scores were found on Block Design, Object Assembly, and Digit Span; while lowest accrued on Comprehension, Coding, and Vocabulary. These patterns are compatible with observed strengths and weaknesses of savant functioning documented in the literature (i.e., perceptual strengths and verbal/conceptual weaknesses). Tasks requiring successive or sequential processing (digit span, coding, and arithmetic) distinguished prodigious from talented subgroups, although sequential processing tasks did not differentially distinguish the type of skill (i.e., music, art, mathematics, etc.) Young concluded that while strengths in modes of processing may underlie the development of a skill, they do not influence the type of skill. In the savants' profiles, the Similarities subtest, which in the normal population loads on the Verbal Comprehension factor, was aligned more closely with the Perceptual Organization factor. Young concluded that her subjects approached this subtest using a different mode of information processing than does the normal population (Young, 1995; Morelock & Feldman, 2000).

Explaining the Prodigious Savant

In explaining the prodigious savant, Treffert (2000) posits that pre- or postnatal injury to the brain's left hemisphere results in right hemispheric compensatory growth, reflected in impairment of language and analytic thought, but heightened capacity for right-brain-dominated functions (e.g., musical and spatial abilities). Injury to the cerebral cortex causes memory functions to shift to a more primitive area of the brain (the corticostriatal system). Memory becomes nonassociative, habitual, emotionless, and nonvolitional—a conditioned response. The prodigious savant's extensive access to the structural rules of domains may be based on some inherited ancestral memory transmitted across generations and inherited separately from general intelligence.[11] Once the groundwork is laid for savant skills, intense concentration, obsessive repetition, social reinforcement for display of special abilities, and a drive to exercise those abilities produce the prodigious savant.

Snyder and his associates (Snyder, 1998; Snyder & Mitchell, 1999; Snyder & Thomas, 1997) propose another explanation, suggesting that, though not normally accessible, savant abilities exist in all of us. The normal brain is highly concept-driven: To cope with the stream of information from the outside, we categorize and conceptualize our experience, responding to it not in terms of the sensory details bombarding us, but in terms of conceptual mindsets. Thus, normal preschool children draw according to preset mental schema and abstracted patterns rather than with naturalistic, photographic detail. For example, a circle is used to represent a human face. A "concept-driven brain" confers advantage by allowing us to operate automatically, using unconscious mechanisms to sift

---

11. Treffert was not the first to suggest the possibility of genetically transmitted qualities of intellect. The idea has had a fair amount of support since, at least, Francis Galton's (1892) book *Hereditary Genius*. Brill (1940) proposed inherited transmission of domain-specific gifts as a factor in lightning calculator abilities.

through a world of unconscious information and arrive at final judgments and mindsets.

Savants, lacking this ability for conceptualization, are thrown back onto the lower levels of neural information—the raw information from which the rest of us abstract our conceptual schemes. Thus, savant artists draw with naturalistic detail, even when still at preschool age (Selfe, 1977); savant lightning calculators perform lightning-fast integer arithmetic (lengthy multiplication, division, factorization, and prime identification) (Smith, 1983); and savant musicians rely on perfect pitch (Miller 1989). All savants recall detail by accessing underlying processes common to all brains, but inaccessible to normal ones.

Snyder and Mitchell (1999) explain that apart from learning the nomenclature or the symbolic representation of numbers, integer arithmetic is simply the ability to separate groups into an equal number of elements, or to "equipartition." Equipartitioning is fundamental to some yet unknown aspect of mental processing—either analytical or perceptual. While mathematical savants tap a capacity for spatial equipartitioning (i.e., representing groups and patterns), musical savants equipartition time. Equipartitioning space and time in combination may be a mechanism that relates music and mathematics.

Juxtaposing the Extremes: The Child of Extraordinary IQ, the Prodigy, and the Savant

The types of extreme precocity discussed in this chapter can be characterized in terms of (1) degree of generalized abstract reasoning ability and (2) extent and nature of domain-specific ability. Morelock and Feldman's Taxonomy (see Table 35.1), which first appeared in the 1991 inaugural edition of this *Handbook*, compares and contrasts the various forms of precocity found in the research literature.

Table 35.1 Morelock/Feldman Taxonomy of Extreme Precocity

Type of Child	Characteristics
Extraordinarily high IQ—omnibus prodigy	Extraordinarily high abstract reasoning capability plus extraordinarily advanced domain-specific skills in multiplicity of domains. Performs at the level of a highly trained adult in multiple domains. Displays passionate involvement with numerous domains of prodigious achievement. Voracious appetite for academic knowledge.
Prodigy	Displays anywhere from above-average to extraordinarily high generalized abstract reasoning capability plus extraordinarily advanced domain-specific skill in a single domain. Performs at the level of a highly trained adult in a single domain. Displays passionate involvement with domain of prodigious achievement. May demonstrate voracious appetite for academic knowledge.
Extraordinarily high-IQ child	Extraordinarily high generalized abstract reasoning capability and possibly notable domain-specific skills in one or more areas. May be intensely drawn to a number of different areas. May have a problem committing to a single area of interest. Voracious appetite for academic knowledge.
Prodigious savant	Minimal generalized abstract reasoning capability and islands of extraordinarily advanced domain-specific skill in one or more areas. Appears driven to exercise domain-specific capabilities. Concrete thinker.

Note: These classifications reflect the types of extreme precocity found in the research literature to date. Certain groups, such as mental calculators and mnemonists, are anomalous in that they display anywhere from minimal to extraordinarily high generalized abstract reasoning ability along with their islands of advanced skill. When minimal generalized abstract reasoning capability exists, such persons are classified as prodigious savants. According to the definition here, however, they cannot be classified as prodigies—even at higher levels of abstract reasoning ability—because standards for highly trained adult performance do not exist in their areas of achievement. The generalized abstract reasoning capability referred to in this table is logical, verbal-conceptual facility.

SUMMARY AND CONCLUSIONS

Prodigies, savants, and children of extraordinarily high IQ are the three types of extreme precocity identified in the literature. Terman's 1916 Stanford-Binet Intelligence Scale enabled research into children with exceptionally strong verbal-conceptual abstract reasoning abilities (extraordinarily high-IQ children). But various forms of precocity were not clearly distinguished until years later. Thus, Barlow's (1952) *Mental Prodigies* included a hodgepodge of synoptic accounts under the heading of "prodigies." And prodigies" and "idiot savants" remained confused with and incompletely explained by IQ-related notions.

Hollingworth (1942) was the first to launch an in-depth study devoted to children of extraordinarily high IQ, documenting their needs for accelerated and enriched educational programming and their emotional vulnerability. Gross (1993) later documented self-concept problems and advanced moral reasoning among these children. Morelock's (1991, 2000) case study of "Jennie" used a sociohistorical perspective to frame the development of extraordinarily high-IQ children and inspired the construct of *asynchronous development.*

Feldman (1991) introduced a precise definition of "prodigy" and highlighted the *domain-specific* nature of prodigious talent, simultaneously challenging the power of either Piagetian conceptualizations *or* IQ to explain the prodigy phenomenon. A developmental theory (*Co-incidence*) was proposed to explain prodigious achievement.

In 1989, Treffert documented the types of "idiot savants" in the literature, differentiated between *talented* and *prodigious* savants, suggested an explanation for the phenomenon based on left hemispheric injury with compensatory neuronal growth in the right hemisphere, and proposed that the term *idiot savant* be dropped and replaced with *savant*. Snyder and his associates later proposed that savant abilities are natural to all human brains, but inaccessible to normally functioning, "concept-driven" ones.

Morelock and Feldman (1991) developed a taxonomy of extreme precocity, delineating and differentiating manifestations of extreme precocity. It appears in this chapter.

QUESTIONS FOR THOUGHT AND DISCUSSION

1. Consider the terms *gifted, prodigy, idiot savant, savant syndrome,* and *asynchronous development*. How has our understanding of various manifestations of extreme precocity been influenced by the names, definitions, and nuances attached to them over the last century?

2. Consider viewing children of extraordinarily high IQ either as "potential geniuses" or as experiencing "asynchronous development." How would each view affect the way society and the schools regard them and their needs?

3. Discuss how the following scenes from the 1988 film *Rain Man* movie reflect savant thinking and functioning.

  a. Raymond, an adult autistic savant, wants to cross a busy street. The sign says "Walk" and Raymond begins to cross. While crossing, the "Walk" sign changes to "Don't Walk." Raymond stops in the middle of the street—in spite of motorists blowing their horns and yelling at him.

  b. A lovely woman kisses Raymond, then asks, "How did that feel?" Raymond replies, "Wet."

4. If Raymond were endowed with a normal IQ, how might he have responded in each of the scenes?

5. Use Feldman's *co-incidence* theory to analyze the evolution of your own talents, interests, and achievements. What are your biologically based strengths? Do these match the talent domains available in your culture? Do your strengths match the values, talents, and interests in your family environment? Do you see *transgenerational influences* at work in your family? Which influences have most supported your talents?

REFERENCES

Barlow, F. (1952). *Mental prodigies*. New York: Philosophical Library.

Baumgarten, F. (1930). *Wünderkinder psychologische Untersuchungen*. Leipzig: Johann Ambrosius Barth.

Bensusan, R. (1976). *A study of cognitive early prodigious achievement development*. Unpublished master's thesis, Tufts University, Medford, Massachusetts.

Brill, A. A. (1940). Some peculiar manifestations of memory with special reference to lightning calculators. *Journal of Nervous and Mental Disease, 90,* 709–726.

Coopersmith, S. (1981). *The antecedents of self esteem*. Palo Alto, CA: Consulting Psychologists Press.

Cornell, D. G. (1984). *Families of gifted children*. Ann Arbor: UMI Research Press.

Craft, M. (Ed.). (1979). *Tredgold's mental retardation* (12th ed.). London: Bailliere Tindall.

Csikszentmihalyi, M., & Robinson, R. (1986). Culture, item, and the development of talent. In R. J. Steinberg & J. E. Davidson (Eds.), *Conceptions of giftedness* (pp. 264–284). New York: Cambridge University Press.

Down, J. L. (1887). *On some of the mental affections of childhood and youth*. London: Churchill.

Feldman, D. H. (1979). The mysterious case of extreme giftedness. In A. H. Passow (Ed.), *The gifted and the talented* (Seventy-eighth yearbook of the National Society for the Study of Education, pp. 335–351). Chicago: University of Chicago Press.

Feldman, D. H. (1980). *Beyond universals in cognitive development.* Norwood, NJ: Ablex.

Feldman, D. H. (1984). A follow-up of subjects scoring above 180 IQ in Terman's "Genetic studies of genius." *Exceptional Children, 50,* 518–523.

Feldman, D. H. (1994). *Beyond universals in cognitive development* (2nd ed.). Norwood, NJ: Ablex.

Feldman, D. H. (with Goldsmith, L. T.). (1991). *Nature's gambit: Child prodigies and the development of human potential.* New York: Teachers College Press.

Feldman, D. H., & Goldsmith, L. T. (1986). Transgenerational influences on the development of early prodigious behavior: A case study approach. In W. Fowler (Ed.), *Early experience and the development of competence: New directions for child development* (pp. 67–85). San Francisco: Jossey-Bass.

Flavell, J. H. (1968). *The development of role-taking and communication skills in children.* New York: Wiley.

Gagné, F. (1997). Critique of Morelock's (1996) definitions of giftedness and talent. *Roeper Review, 20,* 76–86.

Galton, F. (1892). *Heredity genius: An inquiry into its laws and consequences* (2nd ed.). New York: Appleton.

Gardner, H. (1993). *Frames of mind: The theory of multiple intelligences* (10th anniversary ed.). New York: Basic Books.

Goldsmith, L. T. (1987). Girl prodigies: Some evidence and some speculations. *Roeper Review, 10,* 74–82.

Goldsmith, L. T. (2000). Tracking trajectories of talent: Child prodigies growing up. In R. C. Friedman & B. Shore (Eds.), *Talents unfolding: Cognition and development* (pp. 89–117). Washington, DC: American Psychological Association.

Goldsmith, L. T., & Feldman, D. H. (1989). Wang Yani: Gifts well given. In W.-C. Ho (Ed.), *Yani: The brush of innocence* (pp. 50–62). New York: Hudson-Hills.

Gross, M. U. M. (1992). The early development of three profoundly gifted children of IQ 200. In P. S. Klein & A. J. Tannenbaum (Eds.), *To be young and gifted* (pp. 94–138). Norwood, NJ: Ablex.

Gross, M. U. M. (1993). *Exceptionally gifted children.* New York: Routledge.

Gross, M. U. M. (2000). Issues in the cognitive development of exceptionally and profoundly gifted individuals. In K. A. Heller, F. J. Monks, R. J. Sternberg, & R. F. Subotnik (Eds.), *International handbook of giftedness and talent* (2nd ed., pp. 179–192). New York: Elsevier.

Hamblin, D. J. (1966, March 18). They are idiot savants—Wizards of the calendar. *Life,* pp. 106–108.

Hermelin, B., & O'Connor, N. (1986). Idiot savant calendrical calculators: Rules and regularities. *Psychological Medicine, 16,* 1–9.

Hermelin, B., O'Connor, N., & Lee, S. (1987). Musical inventiveness of five idiot savants. *Psychological Medicine, 17,* 685–694.

Hollingworth, L. (1926). *Gifted Children: Their nature and nurture.* New Youk: Macmillan.

Hollingworth, L. (1942). *Children above 180 IQ Stanford-Binet—Origin and development.* Yonkers-on-Hudson, NY: World Book.

Inhelder, B., & Piaget, J. (1958). *The growth of logical thinking from childhood to adolescence.* New York: Basic Books.

Kearney, K., & Kearney, C. (1998). *Accidental genius.* Murphreesboro, TN: Woodshed Press.

Kenneson, C. (1998). *Musical prodigies.* Portland, OR: Amadeus Press.

Lovecky, D. (1994). Exceptionally gifted children: Different minds. *Roeper Review, 17,* 116–120.

Lubinski, D., Webb, R. M., Morelock, M. J., & Benbow, C. P. (2001). Top 1 in 10,000: A 10-year follow-up of the profoundly gifted. *Journal of Applied Psychology, 86,* 718–729.

Miller, L. K. (1989). *Musical savants: Exceptional skill in the mentally retarded.* Hillsdale, NJ: Erlbaum.

Montour, K. (1977). William James Sidis: The broken twig. *American Psychologist, 32,* 267–279.

Moos, R. H., & Moos, B. S. (1994). *Family environment scale manual: Development, application, research* (3rd ed.). Palo Alto, CA: Consulting Psychologists Press.

Morelock, M. J. (1988). *Transgenerational influences on the development of children's talents, gifts, and interests.* Unpublished master's thesis, Tufts University, Medford, MA.

Morelock, M. J. (1991). The case study of Jennie, a profoundly gifted child. Unpublished manuscript, Tufts University, Eliot-Pearson Department of Child Development, Medford, MA.

Morelock, M. J. (1992). Giftedness: The view from within. *Understanding Our Gifted, 4*(3), 11–14.

Morelock, M. J. (1994). *The profoundly gifted child in family context: Families with children above 200 IQ.* Unpublished manuscript, Tufts University, Medford, MA.

Morelock, M. J. (1995). *The profoundly gifted child in family context.* Unpublished doctoral dissertation, Tufts University, Medford, MA.

Morelock, M. J. (1996). On the nature of giftedness and talent: Imposing order on chaos. *Roeper Review, 19,* 4–12.

Morelock, M. J. (1997a). In response to Gagne's critique. *Roeper Review, 20,* 85–87.

Morelock, M. J. (1997b). Imagination, logic, and the exceptionally gifted child. *Roeper Review, 19,* A-1.

Morelock, M. J. (2000). A sociohistorical perspective on exceptionally high-IQ children. In R. C. Friedman & B. Shore (Eds.), *Talents unfolding: Cognition and development* (pp. 55–75). Washington, DC: American Psychological Association.

Morelock, M. J., & Feldman, D. H. (1991). Extreme Precocity. In N. Colangelo & G. A. Davis (Eds.), *Handbook of gifted education* (pp. 347–364). Boston: Allyn & Bacon.

Morelock, M. J., & Feldman, D. H. (1999). Prodigies. In M. A. Runco & S. R. Pritzker (Eds.), *Encyclopedia of creativity* (Vol. 2, pp. 449–456). Boston: Academic Press.

Morelock, M. J., & Feldman, D. H. (2000). Prodigies, savants and Williams Syndrome: Windows into talent and cognition. In K. A. Heller, F. J. Monks, R. J. Sternberg, & R. F. Subotnik (Eds.), *International handbook of giftedness and talent* (2nd ed., pp. 227–241). New York: Elsevier.

O'Connor, N., & Hermelin, B. (1984). Idiot savant calendrical calculators: Math or memory? *Psychological Medicine, 14,* 801–806.

O'Connor, N., & Hermelin, B. (1987). Visual and graphic abilities of the idiot savant artist. *Psychological Medicine, 17,* 79–80.

Peek, F. (1996). *The real Rain Man.* Salt Lake City, UT: Harkness.

Piaget, J., & Inheider, B. (1948). *The child's conception of space.* London: Routledge.

Rest, J. R. (1986). *Defining issues test: Manual.* Minneapolis: Center for Ethical Development, University of Minnesota.

Revesz, G. (1925). *The psychology of a music prodigy.* New York: Harcourt.

Rimland, B. (1978, August). Inside the mind of the autistic savant. *Psychology Today,* 68–80.

Rolfe, L. (1978). *The Menuhins: A family odyssey.* San Francisco: Panjandrum/Aris.

Scheerer, M., Rothman, E., & Goldstein, K. (1945). A case of "idiot savant": An experimental study of personality organization. *Psychology Monograph, 58,* 1–63.

Segoe, M. B. (1975). *Terman and the gifted.* Los Altos, CA: Kaufmann.

Selfe, L. (1977). Nadia: A case of extraordinary drawing ability in an autistic child. New York: Academic Press.

Shavinina, L. V. (1999). The psychological essence of the child prodigy phenomenon: Sensitive periods and cognitive experience. *Gifted Child Quarterly, 43,* 25–38.

Silverman, L. K. (Ed.). (1993). *Counseling the gifted and talented.* Denver CO: Love.

Silverman, L. K. (1997). The construct of asynchronous development. *Peabody Journal of Education, 72,* (3 & 4), 36–58.

Smith, S. B. (1983). *The great mental calculators: The psychology, methods, and lives of calculating prodigies, past and present.* New York: Columbia University Press.

Snyder, A. W. (1998). Breaking mindsets. *Mind and Language, 13,* 1–10.

Snyder, A. W., & Mitchell, D. J. (1999). Is integer arithmetic fundamental to mental processing? *Proceedings of the Royal Society, London, B, 266,* 587–592.

Snyder, A. W., & Thomas, M. (1997). Autistic artists give clues to cognition. *Perception, 26,* 93–96.

Snyder, S., Feldman, D. H., & La Rossa, C. (1976). *A manual for the administration and scoring of a Piaget-based map drawing task.* Tufts University, Medford, MA. Summarized in O. Johnson (Ed.) (1976), *Tests and measurements in child development: A handbook II.* San Francisco: Jossey-Bass.

Terman, L. M. (Ed.). (1925–1959). *Genetic studies of genius (Vols. 1–5).* Stanford, CA: Stanford University Press.

Terman, L. M. (1975). Human intelligence and achievement. In M. V. Seagoe (Ed.), *Terman and the gifted* (pp. 216–228). Los Altos, CA: Kaufmann.

Treffert, D. A. (1989). *Extraordinary people: Understanding "idiot savants."* New York: Harper.

Treffert, D. A. (2000). *Extraordinary people: Understanding savant syndrome.* Lincoln, NE: iuniverse.com.

Waitzkin, F. (1984). *Searching for Bobby Fischer: The world of chess, observed by the father of a child prodigy.* New York: Random House.

Wallace, A. (1986). *The prodigy.* New York: Dutton.

Weiner, N. (1953). *Ex-prodigy: My childhood and youth.* Cambridge: MIT Press.

Witty, P. (1951). *The gifted child.* Boston: Heath.

Young, R. (1995). *Savant Syndrome: Processes underlying extraordinary abilities.* Unpublished doctoral dissertation, University of Adelaide, South Australia.

36

Young Gifted Children

NANCY EWALD JACKSON, *The University of Iowa*

This chapter begins with descriptions of behaviors that might be called manifestations of intellectual giftedness in young children. Origins of gifted performance and the long-term predictive significance of these behaviors are considered next. Finally, I discuss the practical issue of how young children with intellectual gifts can be identified. For the purposes of this chapter, *young children* are from two through six years old and *infants* are below two years of age. Although I touch occasionally on questions about gifted performance in infancy, the primary focus is on young children and on connections between their behavior and giftedness later in childhood. Many examples are drawn from the literature on precocious reading, a form of gifted performance that is relatively common among bright young children (Jackson, 2000).

Throughout the chapter, I refer whenever possible to gifted behaviors rather than gifted children. It might be salutary for scholars in the field of giftedness to adopt the practice, now common among those who study individuals with disabilities, of "putting the person first" (Jackson, 1993). The literature provides little support for the assumption that giftedness in childhood is an enduring and unchanging property of the individual. Rather, different forms of giftedness emerge at different ages in different children (Gross, 1992; Horowitz, 1992; Jackson, 2000).

Manifestations of Giftedness in Young Children

What Is Gifted Performance in Young Children?

Sternberg and Zhang (1995) suggested that gifted performance must have all of five qualities: (1) It must be excellent, relative to the performance of peers who are the same age or who have had the same degree of instruction; (2) it must be rare among the same peers; (3) it must be demonstrable on some reliable and valid assessment instrument; (4) it must be productive or suggest potential for productivity; and (5) it must have some societal value.

Many behaviors that might be displayed by young children and infants meet Sternberg's first three criteria, including talking at seven months, using elaborate language or drawing recognizable pictures at thirty months, or reading fluently at four years. These performances are excellent relative to age norms, rare, and reliably demonstrable on validated standard instruments. Satisfying Sternberg and Zhang's last two criteria is more difficult.

"Productivity" implies work, and young children are not expected to be workers. Therefore, in a tradition that goes back to Terman (1925), psychologists, educators, and the general public often think of giftedness in children in terms of potential for adult productivity. A judgment that precocious talking, drawing, or reading indicates "potential for productivity" must be based on evidence from longitudinal studies (Jackson, 2000). However, a child's current behavior need not be evaluated by reference to its long-term predictive significance. While important, predictive significance can be assessed separately from any categorization of a young child's current behavior as *gifted*.

A more manageable way to evaluate the productivity of a young child's behaviors is to consider the extent to which an exceptional behavior pattern produces important immediate changes in the lives of the child and his or her family, teachers, and other companions. From this perspective, behaviors such as precocious talking and precocious reading easily qualify as productive, because they are important in everyday life in our society.

An eighteen-month-old who comprehends and produces sophisticated language lives in a social world dramatically different from the world of peers who cannot speak at length or comply with complex directions. Similarly, five-year-olds who read fluently and independently are able to learn in ways that are not yet open to other children their age. A preschooler's precocious talent in the graphic arts, music, or arithmetic also may make an immediate impact on the child's daily life, and therefore qualifies as productive (Kenneson, 1998; Milbrath, 1998; Pletan, Robinson, Berninger, & Abbott, 1995).

Sternberg and Zhang's (1995) final criterion, value, also can be applied to the behaviors of young children. In mainstream American culture, we value verbal sophistication, literacy, and numeracy in our children. These values are reflected in the content of educational television programs, preschool curricula, and popular children's toys and books. Other intellectual, artistic, social, and physical skills also are valued, but the definition of *excellence* and opportunities for children to develop a skill vary considerably across groups. Perhaps for this reason, research on the development of intellectual giftedness in young children has focused primarily on precocious oral language development and the early development of reading, writing, and arithmetic skills, with some case study literature (e.g., Feldman, 1986; Gross, 1992; Kenneson, 1998; Milbrath, 1998; Morelock & Feldman, 1993; Tannenbaum, 1992) documenting the early emergence of talent in music or the graphic arts. We shall touch on the latter literature only briefly.

Giftedness in Oral Language Production and Comprehension

Precocity in the production and comprehension of oral language has been noted consistently as an indicator of high verbal intelligence in children of preschool age and as a predictor of continued giftedness in linguistic performance (Crain-Thoreson & Dale, 1992; Tannenbaum, 1992). Identifying a child's language development as precocious is facilitated by the fact that language acquisition follows a set sequence; skills emerge in a predictable order, though at widely varying individual rates.

Linguistic precocity can be defined by performance on professionally administered standard tests of language comprehension and production, by analysis of tape-recorded language samples, and from parents' reports (Crain-Thoreson & Dale, 1992; Fenson et al., 1994). In one study, measures taken at twenty-four months that indicated continuing advanced development included vocabulary size and the length and grammatical complexity of a child's sentences (Crain-Thoreson & Dale, 1992). The various aspects of language often develop in synchrony with one another, but individual children may be especially advanced in some oral language skills, but not others (Fenson et al., 1994). For example, Henderson, Jackson, and Mukamal (1993) studied a two-year-old whose sentences were exceptionally long and grammatically complex, even though the words he used and topics discussed were not unusually sophisticated. Sentences produced by this child at age two years, seven months, included, "I'm going to show you the cranberry bread that mother baked in the oven" and "I want to leave the garlic there because haveta don't get paint on it."

In one study (Crain-Thoreson & Dale, 1992), parents of children whose language development was found to be advanced at ages twenty and twenty-four months reported that their children began talking at an average age of seven months and one week, which is consistent with other reports of precocious oral language development in children who have earned high intelligence test scores (e.g., Terman, 1925). However, the case study literature also includes reports of highly intelligent children, and adults of great intellectual achievement, who did not begin talking especially early. The report of a mother of one high-IQ boy reflected a recurring pattern in the case study literature—language production that did not begin early but progressed rapidly thereafter:

> Once he decided he was going to talk he went from single words to complete sentences with incredible speed and with virtually no transition stage. And there were very few pronunciation errors. . . . As for correctness of grammar, most children carry on for some time saying "he comed" or "I falled," but Ian only had these stages momentarily and then it was straight on into absolute accuracy (Gross, 1992, p. 115).

Gifted Performance in Reading and Writing

Children are expected to become skilled producers and comprehenders of oral language during their preschool years, but a minority demonstrate unusually gifted performance by becoming literate as well. Some of the most extremely precocious readers have been able to recognize a large number of words, and even sound out unfamiliar ones, before passing their third birthday (Fletcher-Flinn & Thompson, 2000; Henderson et al., 1993; Jackson, 1988a). Precocious readers may be able to read simple (or not-so-simple) texts on their own at the age of three or four years, comprehending what they have read (Jackson, 1988b, 1992a).

High verbal intelligence is neither necessary nor sufficient to make a child become a precocious reader, although highly intelligent children are more likely to begin reading early. Across a series of studies, children who learned to read before beginning first grade had an average IQ of about 130 (Jackson, 1992a). This is well above the average IQ of 100 for the population as a whole; in fact, an IQ of 130 is often the threshold for identifying a child as gifted. However, remember that if the average precocious reader has an IQ of about 130, one-half of precocious readers would have IQs below 130. Precocious readers often have IQs in the moderately above-average range, and the earliest readers are not always the children who are the most extremely advanced in verbal knowledge and reasoning ability (Jackson, 1992a; Jackson, Donaldson, & Cleland, 1988).

Cognitive Profiles of Precocious Readers. What other cognitive characteristics are associated with a child's becoming a precocious reader? There are no clear-cut answers to this question. Even when one knows something about the children's intellectual characteristics, it is difficult to determine exactly which toddlers will be precocious readers (Jackson, 1992a). For example, most children whose oral language development is extremely advanced at age two years do not become precocious readers by the time they are four, even when they come from homes in which their parents have supported their literacy development in appropriate ways (Crain-Thoreson & Dale, 1992). However, early talkers are likely to be superior readers by age six years (Dale, Crain-Thoreson, & Robinson, 1995).

Research on the intellectual characteristics of precocious readers suggests that their minds do some kinds of basic information processing with superior efficiency (Jackson, 1992a; Jackson & Myers, 1982). Perhaps individual differences in mental processing efficiency influence the pace with which children learn from the literacy-supporting experiences in their daily lives. Also, in working with precocious readers and their parents, one gets the impression that the children's interest and rapidly developing abilities shape parents' behavior at least as much as parents

lead their children (Fletcher-Flinn & Thompson, 2000; Henderson et al., 1993; Shavinina, 1999).

Interests. The interests of precocious readers are much like those of other children their age, except for their interests in reading and writing. These latter interests may be the result, rather than the cause, of exceptionally rapid development (Thomas, 1984). The reading-related interests of precocious readers tend to fall into two categories, which can be described as *literary* and *technical* interests. Literary interests include reading fiction and writing poems and stories. Technical interests include reading for information and drawing maps and diagrams. Boys tend to have more technical interests, girls more literary interests. This gender difference remains stable from the summer after kindergarten until late in elementary school (Jackson et al., 1988; Mills & Jackson, 1990). However, we do not know whether boys and girls *begin* learning to read for different reasons.

Reading Skill Patterns. Extensive studies of precocious readers' skill patterns have revealed that, at least by the time they have finished kindergarten and can comprehend text at or beyond the second-grade level, these children typically have a solid repertoire of skills. One need not worry that they have not learned to read "the right way." After a few years of reading, five- or six-year-old precocious readers typically have well-developed word identification skills that draw up on both knowledge of letter–sound correspondences and an ability to recognize words directly by sight (Jackson & Donaldson, 1989; Jackson, Donaldson, & Mills, 1993, Stainthorp & Hughes, 1998). The kinds of errors that precocious readers make in reading stories aloud are similar to the kinds of errors made by typical readers (Jackson, Donaldson, & Cleland, 1988). Precocious readers use information from context to help identify words, but they do not depend entirely on context for word identification (Jackson & Donaldson, 1989).

Precocious readers read both isolated words and text passages accurately, but the most striking feature of their skill repertoire is a tendency to read text very rapidly (Fletcher-Flinn & Thompson, 2000; Jackson & Donaldson, 1989; Jackson, 2000). One very young precocious reader also was extremely fast at reading word lists (Fletcher-Flinn & Thompson, 2000). Being a faster-than-average beginning reader is useful. Children who read through a passage quickly are likely to find it easier to comprehend. They still have the beginning of a sentence in mind by the time they reach the end, which makes it easier to "link up" and make sense of the whole (Breznitz & Share, 1992).

Precocious readers typically have developed their ability in ways that give them a firm foundation for future learning. However, this picture of precocious readers as well-rounded needs to be qualified in three ways. First, like many typical readers in a very early stage of reading acquisition, precocious readers in their preschool years, or those who are just a bit ahead of their kindergarten classmates, do not always have strong phonological decoding skills (Jackson & Coltheart, in press). Some precocious readers make an unusual degree of progress on the basis of sight-word reading skills alone, before they eventually figure out and start using the phonological system (Jackson, 1988b). Second, individual children who are all exceptionally advanced readers differ markedly from one another in the relative strengths of their various skills (Fletcher-Flinn & Thompson, 2000; Jackson et al., 1988; Jackson & Coltheart, in press; Jackson et al., 1993). Third, the school language arts curriculum for most kindergarten and primary classes encompasses a range of activities related to reading, spelling, and composition that is much broader than the set of skills measured in studies of precocious readers.

Precocious Writing and Spelling. The relation between precocity in reading and precocity in writing has not been studied extensively, and it seems to vary across children. Durkin (1966) described precocious readers as "pencil and paper kids" whose interest in reading, according to their parents' retrospective reports, seemed to flow from an even earlier interest in writing. Others also have described precocious readers like this (e.g., Jackson, 1988a). Some children create and systematically use non-standard spelling systems (e.g., spelling *giraffe* as *GRF*) before they become aware that what they write can be read (Read, 1971). However, there also are precocious readers whose spelling and writing skills do not emerge until several years after they begin to read words (e.g., Fletcher-Flinn & Thompson, 2000; Henderson et al., 1993; Jackson & Coltheart, in press).

Other Manifestations of Gifted Performance in Young Children

Children of preschool age who master reading, and sometimes writing, at an unusually early age might be expected to demonstrate other intellectual gifts as well. Learning to read an alphabetic language such as English requires analytic code-breaking skill of a sort that also should be useful in breaking the codes of other representational systems, such as mathematics and music.

Although Gardner (1983) has argued that linguistic, logical-mathematical, and musical "intelligences" are distinct, case studies of child prodigies and eminent adults suggest strong links between the skills used to learn alphabetic writing systems, mathematics, music, and computer languages (e.g., Csikszentmihalyi & Robinson, 1986; Gross, 1992; Feldman, 1986; Jackson, 1992a, 1992b; Tannenbaum, 1992). Similar analytic abilities may be involved in learning to sound out or spell words; play, read, and write music; or do elementary mathematics. Unusual skill in reading and music can emerge as early as age two or three years (e.g., Fletcher-Flinn & Thompson, 2000; Kenneson, 1998). Mathematical talent also may be evident to parents and identifiable by standard test performance during the preschool and kindergarten years (Pletan et al., 1995; Robinson, Abbott, Berninger, & Busse, 1996; Shavinina, 1999). Precocity in mathematics during early childhood may be more common among boys than girls (Robinson et al., 1996).

Gross (1992) reported case histories of three Australian boys with extremely high Stanford-Binet IQs that illustrate how gifted performance may occur in different domains as children grow up. All three boys were reading before their third birthday, and all showed precocious talent in mathematics. In their elementary school years, the boys' interests and precocious achievements spanned music, computer programming, Latin, physics, chess, and structural analysis of transportation systems. The analytic quality that linked one boy's interests across various domains is evident in the following observations:

> Ian always seemed to look for different things in reading . . . he's never been interested in fantasy or imaginative stories. The sort of things that excited him were factual books, books on computing or logic, or compendiums of math puzzles. He had a craze, at one stage, for "Choose Your Own Adventure" stories, because he liked working out the different permutations of changes and endings. But even in writing, he doesn't go in for imaginative stories. When he was 7 his teacher said to me that she would throw a party on the day he wrote an imaginative story because anything she asked him to do he would convert into a diagram, a maze, a flow-

chart, a timetable, calendar—everything had to be set out and analyzed. (Gross, 1992, pp. 123–124)

Other "pattern analyzers" like Ian have been described by several investigators (e.g., Shavinina, 1999). However, some highly intelligent children who were extremely precocious readers have had interests and abilities that were more specifically linguistic and literary (e.g., Jackson 1988a, 1992b). No child's gifted performance should be dismissed because he or she does not show other characteristics sometimes associated with that kind of performance.

Precocious talent in the graphic arts is mentioned less frequently in the case study literature than precocious reading, mathematics achievement, or musical talent. However, unusual degrees of representational skill have been reported in children of preschool age (Milbrath; 1998; Winner & Martino, 1993). Precocious talent in drawing may be a child's most striking demonstration of giftedness, but such talent also can co-occur with advanced performance on tests of visual-spatial reasoning and with reading precocity (Jackson, 1992a).

Although young children may demonstrate giftedness in various aspects of their artwork, the representation of space is especially interesting because children typically progress slowly through regular steps toward complete and integrated representations of three dimensions. Case (1992) argued that even the most precocious child artists are not extremely advanced in the way they represent space. However, Winner and Martino (1993) described several cases of precocity in spatial representation, including an Israeli boy who invented ways to represent depth in his drawings beginning at age two. Western children typically do not begin dealing with this problem until about age eight, and developmental theorists who emphasize the importance of maturational limits (e.g., Case, 1992) would be hard pressed to explain such precocity.

Milbrath (1998; see Porath & Arlin, 1997, for a similar view) suggested that very early talent in drawing can be described along two dimensions. Children who eventually will be identified as having exceptional talent in the visual arts are both precocious and qualitatively different in their early development. Precocity is evident in the advanced age at which they pass milestones, such as being able to draw a circle or represent the dimensions of space in a certain way. Qualitative difference, which may be more important, is apparent in the rich and realistic detail of their drawings. Milbrath argued that talent in the graphic arts involves the ability to work from exceptionally detailed perceptual memories of things seen. Even during their preschool years, children gifted in drawing ability seem to rely less on stereotyped cognitive schemas, such as those for a human figure or animal, and more on a perceptual memory of what a particular person or animal looked like at a particular moment.

Early Giftedness, Savant Syndrome, and Asperger's Syndrome

Gifted performances in areas such as reading, mathematics, and, to a lesser extent, music and drawing occur most often in children who also would earn high scores on tests of general or verbal intelligence. However, each of these talents also can occur in a peculiarly encapsulated form in what is known as *savant syndrome.*[1]

Savants, sometimes also referred to by the French term *idiots savants,* are individuals whose general intelligence is well below average, but who can perform brilliantly in particular areas. Many, but not all, savants are autistic. Savant readers are called *hyperlexics,* and they are likely to become able to sound out words, even unfamiliar nonsense words, before reaching school age, despite limited ability to use language for communication (Jackson & Coltheart, in press; Nation, 1999). Savant musicians, such as Eddie, studied by Miller (1989), typically become expert pianists at an early age despite low intelligence and the visual impairment particularly characteristic of this form of savant syndrome. Savant abilities are also evident in forms of mathematical calculation or in memory for tightly organized bodies of knowledge.

The skill and enthusiasm with which some highly intelligent young children master closed symbol systems by capitalizing on a sensitivity to rules and patterns is echoed in reports of savants' performances (Gross, 1992; Miller, 1989; Morelock & Feldman, 1993). The key difference between the two types of precocious achievers is in the lack of flexibility and generalizability of savants' talents. However, some savants have developed skills that would meet all of Sternberg's criteria for gifted performance (Morelock & Feldman, 1993).

---

1. See Chapter 35 by Morelock and Feldman.

A third group of children shares characteristics with both normal gifted children and autistic savants. These are children with Asperger's syndrome, a disorder whose defining characteristics include some of the atypical social behaviors seen in autism but which does not involve mental retardation. Neihart (2000) suggested that gifted children with Asperger's syndrome often show the verbal fluency, superior memory, early fascination with letters and numbers, and passionate enthusiasm for particular topics of study that also are seen in normal gifted children. Despite these similarities, certain autistic-like qualities of the behavior of the young child with Asperger's syndrome might be used to diagnose the condition. Early diagnosis of Asperger's syndrome is important because it enables an affected child to get needed help to develop social skills (Neihart, 2000).

Origin of Gifted Performances in Young Children

When a child demonstrates remarkably gifted performance, we wonder why that particular child has become exceptional in that particular way. One way of looking at this question is to try to identify the extent to which the behavior is an expression of a genetic predisposition or of an exceptionally supportive environment.

Imagine a child like the two-year-old reader Max (Henderson et al., 1993). On his second birthday, Max surprised his parents by reading a restaurant sign that said "Pizza." From that time on, his mother systematically encouraged his rapidly developing literacy. Perhaps Max's precocity reflected experiences provided by his parents. After all, his mother had been trained as a reading teacher. Although she had not consciously taught him to read before age two, she had supported his learning in many informal ways from infancy onward. On the other hand, Max's highly intelligent parents also had passed on genes that may have given him the potential to learn rapidly.

Genes and environment work together within families in ways that are impossible to disentangle unless one compares birth and adoptive families. For example, Max's parents' high intelligence, education, and literary interests probably influenced their choice to create a home environment in which the value of reading was clearly evident. Similarly, musical prodigies are likely to have both a genetic history of musical talent in their families and the experience of

early immersion in a rich musical environment (Kenneson, 1998).

Parents' genes can affect their children indirectly through the environments they create, as well as by transmission through egg and sperm (Scarr & McCartney, 1983). This mixing of heredity and environment is important when we try to plan interventions based on what has seemed to work well for parents and children who were only doing what came naturally to them. Parenting practices that have been associated with the development of gifted behavior will not necessarily produce gifted behavior if they are applied out of context.

Research on the development of precocious reading (Jackson, 1992a) illustrates the distinction between patterns of parental behavior naturally associated with gifted performance and the consequences of systematic attempts to create such performances. Children identified as precocious readers at age five or six years are likely to continue to be good readers, though not always exceptional ones (Mills & Jackson, 1990). However, intensive early instruction in reading and other academic skills typically does not have lasting effects (Coltheart, 1979; Rescorla, Hyson, & Hirsh-Pasek, 1991).

In observing how young gifted children interact with their parents, one often is struck simultaneously by the precocity of a child's current achievement and the skill with which the parent exploits opportunities to help the child reflect on and extend his or her learning. For example, the parent of a five-year-old who had been reading for several years told a story about her son's emerging skill in mathematics.

The boy surprised his mother by asking, "Do you know how much 3 times 8 is?"

She answered, "I think I do. Do you?"

He then replied, "Yes. It's 24. Do you know how I know? It's because 3 times 4 is 12."

Although this boy's independently developed understanding of mathematics is impressive, his mother's response is also noteworthy. She answered her son's question in a way that led him to express his knowledge and reasoning, rather than terminating the interchange by saying, "Yes, it's 24" (Jackson, 2000).

The dynamic interplay between a child's developing abilities and interests, and a parent's sensitive nurturing is evident in Moss's (1992) comparison of the teaching strategies of mothers of three- and four-year-olds with high and average Binet IQs. Moss videotaped each mother helping her child complete a puzzle and a peg game and engage in free play with blocks. The children with high IQs were more verbally fluent and able to engage their mothers in longer and more sophisticated conversations. They also demonstrated more self-regulation of their problem solving, perhaps as a response to their mothers' greater use of helping strategies such as predicting consequences of future actions and monitoring the activity by commenting on the appropriateness of moves. In contrast, mothers of children with average IQs were more likely to focus the child's attention on behavior related to getting back on task, rather than on ways of actually doing the task.

Moss interpreted her observations from a Vygotskyan perspective, suggesting that the mothers of children with high IQs were more likely to converse in ways that stretch a child's existing competence by structuring "a context in which the child is sensitively manipulated into finding his or her own solution" (p. 297). The kinds of behaviors demonstrated by the high-IQ children and their mothers are consistent with other findings suggesting that highly intelligent children have greater metacognitive, or thinking-about-thinking, skills than children of average intelligence (Jackson & Butterfield, 1986; Kanevsky, 1992; Shore, 2000).

Although an interaction style designed to encourage the child's ability to manage problem solving independently may characterize many interactions between children with intellectual gifts and their parents, the case study literature also suggests that parents of individuals who became eminent adults may incorporate specific agendas in their teaching. For example, Nobel-laureate physicist Richard Feynman (1988) reported that while he was still in his high chair, his father taught him to create patterns with colored tiles as an introduction to mathematics.

Middle-class Americans have become more and more concerned with fostering the development of academic skills in their preschool-age children (Zigler & Lang, 1985). This phenomenon may have contributed to the precocious emergence of reading in greater numbers of children who were ready to learn. However, early academic pressure does not seem to confer any lasting benefit on most children from middle class families, whether the pressure comes from home or a structured preschool program (Coltheart, 1979; Jackson, 1992a; Rescorla et al., 1991). The most sophisticated and enthusiastic precocious readers are likely to be children who have driven their parents and teachers to keep up with them (Jackson, 1992a; Fletcher-Flinn & Thompson, 2000).

Although gifted children sometimes are assumed to be the product of affluent homes, effective parent-child interactions can take place in any setting. For example, precocious readers come from a wide range of family backgrounds. Some have come from families rich in literacy but little else (Durkin, 1984; Torrey, 1979). Durkin found that most of the good readers from low-income African-American families in one urban school district had learned to read at home before beginning elementary school. In working with hundreds of parents of precocious readers, I have formed the impression that they tend to be excited, exceptionally thoughtful, and well-organized people who are strongly committed to supporting their children's development. Parents of precocious readers typically have supported their young children's developing literacy in activities such as reading with them and teaching letter names—but many parents provide the same kinds of support without their child making exceptionally rapid progress (Durkin, 1966; Jackson et al., 1988; Jackson & Roller, 1993).

Predictive Significance of Young Children's Gifted Performances

Methodological Issues

Giftedness, by definition, is rare. This fact alone makes it difficult to determine the long-term predictive significance of young children's demonstrations of giftedness. Longitudinal studies are expensive and difficult to manage, even when they include samples of only a few hundred children. One would need to study thousands of children to do a logically complete study, *in a sample representative of the population in general,* of relations between gifted performances in young children and gifted performances later on. Furthermore, the experience of participation in such a study could turn parents' and children's attention to issues studied by the investigators in ways that would make the sample unrepresentative. Therefore, efforts to understand the long-term predictive significance of gifted performances in early childhood probably will remain dependent on incomplete evidence gleaned from an assortment of imperfect approaches (Jackson, 2000).

One such incomplete approach is a simplification of the comprehensive longitudinal design described earlier. Records of major longitudinal studies, which were designed for other purposes, are scanned to identify children whose very early behavior was remarkable in some way or who later demonstrated some form of giftedness, typically high intelligence. Such studies (e.g., Willerman & Fiedler, 1974) have been useful. However, their records rarely contain the kind of information that is optimal for a study of the development of giftedness. For example, the researchers in such studies are not likely to have looked for or measured behaviors such as precocious reading.

A second approach is the retrospective case study. Children who have earned high intelligence test scores (e.g., Hollingworth, 1942; Terman & Oden, 1947) or demonstrated some other talent or prodigious achievement (e.g., Feldman, 1986; Milbrath, 1998; VanTassel-Baska, 1989) are identified, usually in elementary school. The children, their parents, and others are asked for retrospective accounts of the child's earliest years. However, memory for past events may be incomplete and distorted. Also, retrospective reports of the early childhoods of children who performed well at later ages tell us nothing about children who may have displayed similar behaviors in early childhood, but who were *not* later identified as gifted performers. Retrospective case studies of eminent adults have the same limitations, but to an even greater degree.

A third approach is to identify and follow the subsequent development of infants (Columbo, Shaddy, & Richman, 2000) or, more likely, very young children who already have demonstrated some form of giftedness such as precocious language use (Crain-Thoreson & Dale, 1992), precocious reading (Jackson & Myers, 1982; Mills & Jackson, 1990), or other precocious achievements (Roedell, Jackson, & Robinson, 1980; Robinson, Abbott, Berninger, Busse, & Mukhopadhyay, 1997). This focused approach is less costly than longitudinal studies of unselected groups of children. It complements retrospective studies by identifying children who behave in remarkable ways in their early years but may not qualify as gifted performers later on. Such studies could include comparison groups of children who did not display the remarkable early behavior of interest. However, even when such comparison groups are available, they cannot be assumed to be the same as the focal group in all but the gifted performance for which the focal group was selected. Such groups also may be too small to include cases of late-developing giftedness. Therefore, focused prospective longitudinal studies provide either potentially biased or no information about comparison children who become gifted performers without showing early signs of their talent.

Continuities and Changes in the Development of Gifted Performance

Limits of the research notwithstanding, the literature does suggest that infants who later will earn high IQ scores are more likely than others to become rapidly bored with repeated presentations of the same picture or sound, and will turn to novel stimuli more quickly than other children their age (Borkowski & Peck, 1986; Columbo et al., 2000; McCall & Carriger, 1993; Tannenbaum, 1992). As preschoolers, children who eventually will earn high IQs or high scores on out-of-level tests of mathematics and verbal reasoning are more likely than other children to have excellent memories, be advanced in language development (Terman & Oden, 1947), and read early (Terman & Oden, 1947; VanTassel-Baska, 1989). Furthermore, children who display these characteristics during their preschool years are likely to continue to perform well intellectually (Crain-Thoreson & Dale, 1992; Dale, Crain-Thoreson, & Robinson, 1995; Mills & Jackson, 1990; Robinson, 1993).

Demonstrations of gifted performance during the preschool years may be linked to later achievements that seem, at least superficially, to be quite different. As noted before, a child whose first remarkable accomplishment is early reading is not necessarily destined for a literary career. Instead, early reading ability sometimes may presage later interest and remarkable achievement in another symbol system such as music, mathematics, or computer science. This kind of nonobvious continuity in development is called *heterotypic continuity* (Kagan, 1971; see also Columbo, Shaddy, & Richman, 2000). Although the term has been used to describe many different aspects of development, it may be especially useful in thinking about the development of gifted performances across age.

Gifted performances are most likely to be evident in domains in which new forms of competence emerge as a result of a universal or culturally imposed timetable. For example, toddlers face the universal developmental task of mastering their native language. They also may encounter culture-specific symbol systems such as pictures and written language. At the age of two or three years, the children most likely to be identified as gifted performers in a literate society are those who talk, read, write, or draw unusually early or exceptionally well for their age. However, neither talking nor reading is a noteworthy accomplishment among eight-year-olds. Even though a child may continue to do these things exceptionally well, gifted performance may be more salient in domains such as mathematics or science to which the child has been introduced just recently (for examples, see Gross, 1992; Shavinina, 1999).

Later Development of Precocious and Nonprecocious Readers

Jackson (2000) proposed a conceptual model suggesting ways in which precocious readers may demonstrate precocious achievements in different ways at different ages. The kinds of achievement included in the model all have been observed in children. Except for literary production and verbal intelligence, all rest heavily in the mastery of closed symbol systems. Forms of precocious achievement were placed in the model according to their most likely age of emergence.

Reading precocity is reported often in case histories of eminent adults and children who have been selected for their remarkable accomplishments (Cox, 1926; Feldman, 1986). Reading precocity is especially common among children whose IQs are extraordinarily high (Hollingworth, 1942; Terman & Oden, 1947). However, estimates of the prevalence of reading precocity among moderately high IQ children have ranged widely from study to study (Terman & Oden, 1947; Ehrlich, 1978; Jackson, 1992a), perhaps because of differences in the degree of encouragement and instruction the children received in different communities and different eras.

Some very bright children do not learn to read early, even if they have had some encouragement (Jackson, 1992a; Jackson & Myers, 1982). High-IQ children and eminent adults occasionally have had great difficulty learning to read (Jackson, 1992a), but a more common pattern for bright children is to make rapid progress in reading after beginning at a typical age (Dale et al., 1995). At the same time, children who were precocious in beginning to read may slow down a bit in their elementary school years (Mills & Jackson, 1990).

The skills involved in beginning to identify words differ from those required of a mature reader of sophisticated text (e.g., Curtis, 1980). Those who had a head start because they learned very early to break the code of print may be overtaken by later bloomers who, once they also figure out the code, have the general world knowledge and language and reasoning skills required to comprehend increasingly advanced text. In one study of children who began reading early, the best predictor of individual differences in reading comprehension in fifth or sixth grade was the child's verbal intelligence, although how well the child could read just after kindergarten also predicted later comprehension (Mills & Jackson, 1990).

Precocious readers almost always remain at least average in their reading ability, and most stay well above average. However, their reading performance in fifth or sixth grade is much more likely to be within the range of their classmates' performance than it was in kindergarten (Mills & Jackson, 1990). Some investigators claim that precocious readers remain superior in reading achievement throughout their elementary school years, relative to children of comparable intelligence who were not early readers (Durkin, 1966; Pikulski & Tobin, 1989; Tobin & Pikulski, 1988). However, the meaning of these findings is hard to evaluate. Does an early start in reading in itself give a child a lasting advantage? Or do factors such as persistence, interest in learning, or parental support contribute both to the early emergence of reading and to continued good achievement? The general absence of long-term gains from experimental programs designed to create precocious readers (Coltheart, 1979) suggests that getting an early start in reading may not, in itself, be important for children who are not demographically or personally at risk for reading failure. A head start in reading may be more important for children from disadvantaged backgrounds, who have a special need to begin school with skills that will help them, and their teachers, recognize their ability (Durkin, 1984; Hansen & Farrell, 1995).

Identification of Young Children with Intellectual Gifts

Describing versus Identifying Gifted Performance

In previous sections we described aspects of gifted performance in young children. However, presenting a picture of what gifted performers are like is different from the task of identifying those children. When descriptions of the "typical" gifted young child become transformed into checklists of characteristics to use in deciding whether or not a child qualifies as gifted (e.g., Parkinson, 1990), a number of factors influence whether a characteristic will discriminate between gifted and less exceptional performers.

For example, most young gifted performers could be described as "intensely curious," "investigative," and "asks penetrating questions," but so could many young children not identified as gifted. Furthermore, a parent's judgment about what degree or kind of curiosity is unusual for a young child may differ from the judgment of a teacher or psychologist who has observed many children of that age. Perhaps this is why parents' perceptions of gifted performance are likely to have diagnostic utility for skills such as reading or mathematics, in which the difference between age-expected and exceptionally advanced behavior is widely known and easy to observe (e.g., Pletan et al., 1995; Roedell et al., 1980).

Also, concrete accomplishments are not necessarily a good basis for parents' claims of a young child's giftedness (Hodge & Kemp, 2000). For example, Louis and Lewis (1992) asked parents of children with a mean age of thirty-three months why they had brought their child to a specialized clinic for gifted children. Parents of children with higher tested IQs (mean = 149) were more likely to refer to their child's exceptional memory, imagination, and abstract thinking, whereas parents of the children with lower IQs (mean = 118) were more likely to mention their child's specialized knowledge of body parts, the alphabet, and or numbers. Unfortunately, interpretation of this and other similar findings is complicated by the fact that parents' perceptions may be strongly influenced by their own intellectual sophistication and education. In other words, Louis and Lewis' (1992) results may show only that smarter parents have smarter children.

SUMMARY AND CONCLUSIONS

Young children's gifted performances are most evident in those areas of development in which new skills that have social and practical importance are emerging, such as oral language and reading. Giftedness demonstrated during the preschool years may change form or disappear as a child matures, yet threads of developmental continuity may be detectable in the underlying abilities being expressed. It may never be possible to disentangle heredity from environment in accounting for the emergence of gifted performances, and the study of how giftedness develops has been restricted by practical and methodological factors.

Identifying gifted performances in young children involves dealing with issues different from those involved in the scientific study of the development of giftedness. Gifted performances in young children can be studied in terms of their current significance in the context of the child's everyday life. Understanding the development and long-term significance of these performances requires longitudinal research.

QUESTIONS FOR THOUGHT AND DISCUSSION

1. Imagine that two children in a seventh-grade gifted program, Jill and Rebecca, have equal IQ scores—but Jill had started talking at age six months. What differences, if any, might you expect in the academic performance of the two children due specifically to this early language difference?

2. Pablo Picasso's father gave up trying to find a tutor who could teach Picasso to read. Albert Einstein said little in school and was thought by some to be retarded. Explain.

3. Explain why some students with precocious language skills also excel in math, music, physics, or computers (or maybe chess or Latin)?

4. What characteristics are common and different among persons with savant syndrome, Asperger's syndrome, and "usual giftedness," as described by Jackson.

REFERENCES

Borkowski, J. G., & Peck, V. A. (1986). Causes and consequences of metamemory in gifted children. In R. J. Sternberg & J. E. Davidson (Eds.), *Conceptions of giftedness* (pp. 182–200). New York: Cambridge University Press.

Breznitz, Z., & Share, D. L. (1992). Effects of accelerated reading rate on memory for text. *Journal of Educational Psychology, 84,* 193–199.

Case, R. (1992). *The mind's staircase: Exploring the conceptual underpinnings of children's thought and knowledge.* Hillsdale, NJ: Lawrence Erlbaum Associates.

Coltheart, M. (1979). When can children learn to read—and when should they be taught? *Reading research: Advances in theory and practice* (Vol. 1, pp. 1–30). New York: Academic Press.

Columbo, J., Shaddy, D. J., & Richman, W. A. (2000). Cognition, development, and exceptional talent in infancy. In R. C. Friedman & B. M. Shore (Eds.), *Talents unfolding: Cognition and development* (pp. 123–148). Washington, DC: American Psychological Association.

Cox, C. M. (1926). *Genetic studies of genius: Vol. 2. The early mental traits of three hundred geniuses.* Palo Alto, CA: Stanford University Press.

Crain-Thoreson, C., & Dale, P. S. (1992). Linguistic precocity, preschool language, and emergent literacy. *Developmental Psychology, 28,* 421–429.

Csikszentmihalyi, M., & Robinson, R. E. (1986). Culture, time, and the development of talent. In R. J. Sternberg & J. E. Davidson (Eds.), *Conceptions of giftedness* (pp. 264–284). New York: Cambridge University Press.

Curtis, M. E. (1980). Development of components of reading skill. *Journal of Educational Psychology, 72,* 656–669.

Dale, P. S., Crain-Thoreson, C., & Robinson, N. M. (1995). Linguistic precocity and the development of reading: The role of extralinguistic factors. *Applied Psycholinguistics, 16,* 173–187.

Durkin, D. (1966). *Children who read early.* New York: Teachers College Press.

Durkin, D. (1984). *A study of poor black children who are successful readers* (Reading Education Report No. 33). Urbana, IL: Center for the Study of Reading, University of Illinois.

Ehrlich, V. Z. (1978). *The Astor program for gifted children.* New York: Columbia University Press.

Feldman, D. H. (1986). *Nature's gambit: Child prodigies and the development of human potential.* New York: Basic Books.

Fenson, L., Dale, P. S., Reznick, J. S., Bates, E., Thal, D. J., & Pethick, S. J. (1994). Variability in early communicative development. *Monographs of the Society for Research in Child Development, 59* (5, Serial No. 242).

Feynman, R. P. (1988). *"What do you care what other people think?" Further adventures of a curious character.* New York: Norton.

Fletcher-Flinn, C. M., & Thompson, G. B. (2000). Learning to read with underdeveloped phonemic awareness but lexicalized phonological recoding: A case study of a 3-year-old. *Cognition, 74,* 177–208.

Gardner, H. (1983). *Frames of mind.* New York: Basic Books.

Gross, M. U. M. (1992). The early development of three profoundly gifted children of IQ 200. In P. Klein & A. J. Tannenbaum (Eds.), *To be young and gifted* (pp. 94–140). Norwood, NJ: Ablex.

Hanson, R. A., & Farrell, D. (1995). The long-term effects on high-school seniors of learning to read in kindergarten. *Reading Research Quarterly, 30,* 908–933.

Henderson, S. J., Jackson, N. E., & Mukamal, R. A. (1993). Early development of language and literacy skills of an extremely precocious reader. *Gifted Child Quarterly, 37,* 46–50.

Hodge, K. A., & Kemp, C. R. (2000). Exploring the nature of giftedness in preschool children. *Journal for the Education of the Gifted, 24,* 46–73.

Hollingworth, L. S. (1942). *Children above 180 IQ.* New York: World Book.

Horowitz, F. D. (1992). A developmental view on the early identification of the gifted. In P. Klein & A. J. Tannenbaum (Eds.), *To be young and gifted* (pp. 73–93). Norwood, NJ: Ablex.

Jackson, N. E. (1988a). Case study of Bruce: A child with advanced intellectual abilities. In J. M. Sattler (Ed.), *Assessment of children* (3rd ed., pp. 676–678). San Diego: Sattler.

Jackson, N. E. (1988b). Precocious reading ability: What does it mean? *Gifted Child Quarterly, 32,* 200–204.

Jackson, N. E. (1992a). Precocious reading of English: Sources, structure, and predictive significance. In P. Klein & A. J. Tannenbaum (Eds.), *To be young and gifted* (pp. 171–203). Norwood, NJ: Ablex.

Jackson, N. E. (1992b). Understanding giftedness in young children: Lessons from the study of precocious readers. In N. Colangelo, S. G. Assouline, & D. L. Ambroson (Eds.), *Talent development: Proceedings from the 1991 Henry B. and Jocelyn Wallace National Research Symposium on Talent Development* (pp. 163–179). Unionville, NY: Trillium Press.

Jackson, N. E. (1993). Moving into the mainstream? Reflections on the study of giftedness. *Gifted Child Quarterly, 37,* 46–50.

Jackson, N. E. (2000). Strategies for modeling the development of giftedness in children: Reconciling theory and method. In R. C. Friedman & B. Shore (Eds.), *Talents within: Cognition and development* (pp. 27–54). Washington, DC: American Psychological Association.

Jackson, N. E., & Butterfield, E. C. (1986). A conception of giftedness designed to promote research. In R. J. Sternberg & J. E. Davidson (Eds.), *Conceptions of giftedness* (pp. 151–181). New York: Cambridge University Press.

Jackson, N. E., & Coltheart, M. (in press). *Routes to reading success and failure: Toward an integrated cognitive psychology of atypical reading.* Philadelphia: Taylor & Francis.

Jackson, N. E., & Donaldson, G. (1989). Precocious and second-grade readers' use of context in word identification. *Learning and Individual Differences, 1,* 255–281.

Jackson, N. E., Donaldson, G., & Cleland, L. N. (1988). The structure of precocious reading ability. *Journal of Educational Psychology, 80,* 234–243.

Jackson, N. E., Donaldson, G., & Mills, J. R. (1993). Components of reading skill in postkindergarten precocious readers and level-matched second graders. *Journal of Reading Behavior, 25,* 181–208.

Jackson, N. E., & Myers, M. G. (1982). Letter naming time, digit span, and precocious reading achievement. *Intelligence, 6,* 311–329.

Jackson, N. E., & Roller, C. M. (1993). *Reading with young children.* Storrs, CT: National Research Center on the Gifted and Talented. (Research-Based Decision Making Series No. 9302).

Kagan, J. (1971). *Change and continuity in infancy.* New York: Wiley.

Kanevsky, L. (1992). The learning game. In P. Klein & A. J. Tannenbaum (Eds.), *To be young and gifted* (pp. 204–241). Norwood, NJ: Ablex.

Kenneson, C. (1998). *Musical prodigies: Perilous journeys, remarkable lives.* Portland, OR: Amadeus Press.

Louis, B., & Lewis, M. (1992). Parental beliefs about giftedness in young children and their relationship to actual ability level. *Gifted Child Quarterly, 36,* 27–31.

McCall, R. B., & Carriger, M. S. (1993). A meta-analysis of infant habituation and recognition memory performance as predictors of later IQ. *Child Development, 64,* 57–79.

Milbrath, C. (1998). *Patterns of artistic development in children: Comparative studies of talent.* Cambridge: Cambridge University Press.

Miller, L. K. (1989). *Musical savants: Exceptional skills in the mentally retarded.* Hillsdale, NJ: Lawrence Erlbaum Associates.

Mills, J. R., & Jackson, N. E. (1990). Predictive significance of early giftedness: The case of precocious reading. *Journal of Educational Psychology, 82,* 410–419.

Morelock, M., & Feldman, D. (1993). Prodigies and savants: What they have to tell us about giftedness and human cognition. In K. A. Heller, F. J. Monks, & A. H. Passow (Eds.), *International handbook of research and development of giftedness and talent* (pp. 161–181). New York: Pergamon.

Moss, E. (1992). Early interactions and metacognitive development of gifted preschoolers. In P. Klein & A. J. Tannenbaum (Eds.), *To be young and gifted* (pp. 278–320). Norwood, NJ: Ablex.

Nation, K. (1999). Reading skills in hyperlexia: A developmental perspective. *Psychological Bulletin, 125,* 338–355.

Neihart, M. (2000). Gifted children with Asperger's syndrome. *Gifted Child Quarterly, 44,* 222–230.

Parkinson, M. L. (1990). Finding and serving gifted preschoolers. *Understanding Our Gifted, 2*(5), 1–13.

Pikulski, J. J., & Tobin, A. W. (1989). Factors associated with long-term reading achievement of early readers. In S. McCormick & J. Zutell (Eds.), *Cognitive and social perspectives for literacy research and instruction. Thirty-eighth yearbook of the National Reading Conference* (pp. 123–124). Chicago: National Reading Conference.

Pletan, M. D., Robinson, N. M., Berninger, V. W., & Abbott, R. D. (1995). Parents' observations of kindergartners who are advanced in mathematical reasoning. *Journal for the Education of the Gifted, 19,* 30–44.

Porath, M., & Arlin, P. K. (1997). Developmental approaches to artistic giftedness. *Creativity Research Journal, 10,* 241–250.

Read, C. (1971). Preschool children's knowledge of English phonology. *Harvard Educational Review, 41,* 1–34.

Rescorla, L., Hyson, M. C., & Hirsh-Pasek, K. (1991). *Academic instruction in early childhood: Challenge or pressure?* San Francisco: Jossey-Bass.

Robinson, N. M. (1993). Identifying and nurturing gifted, very young children. In K. A. Heller, F. J. Monks, & A. H. Passow (Eds.), *International handbook of research and development of giftedness and talent* (pp. 507–524). New York: Pergamon.

Robinson, N. M., Abbott, R. D., Berninger, V. W., & Busse, J. (1996). Structure of abilities in math-precocious young children: Gender similarities and differences. *Journal of Educational Psychology, 88,* 341–352.

Robinson, N. M., Abbott, R. D., Berninger, V. W., Busse, J., & Mukhopadhyay, S. (1997). Developmental changes in mathematically precocious young children: Longitudinal and gender effects. *Gifted Child Quarterly, 41,* 145–158.

Roedell, W. C., Jackson, N. E., & Robinson, H. B. (1980). *Gifted young children.* New York: Teachers College Press.

Scarr, S., & McCartney, K. (1983). How people make their own environments: A theory of genotype→environment effects. *Child Development, 54,* 424–435.

Shavinina, L. V. (1999). The psychological essence of the child prodigy phenomenon. *Gifted Child Quarterly, 43,* 25–38.

Stainthorp, R., & Hughes, D. (1998). Phonological sensitivity and reading: Evidence from precocious readers. *Journal of Research in Reading, 21,* 53–68.

ternberg, R. J., & Zhang, L. F. (1995). What do we mean by giftedness: A pentagonal implicit theory. *Gifted Child Quarterly, 39,* 88–94.

Tannenbaum, A. J. (1992). Early signs of giftedness: Research and commentary. In P. Klein & A. J. Tannenbaum (Eds.), *To be young and gifted* (pp. 3–32). Norwood, NJ: Ablex.

Terman, L. M. (1925). *Genetic studies of genius: Vol. 1. Mental and psychological traits of a thousand gifted children.* Palo Alto, CA: Stanford University Press.

Terman, L. M., & Oden, M. H. (1947). *Genetic studies of genius: Vol. 4. The gifted child grows up.* Palo Alto, CA: Stanford University Press.

Thomas, B. (1984). Early toy preferences of four-year-old readers and nonreaders. *Child Development, 55,* 424–430.

Tobin, A. W., & Pikulski, J. J. (1988). A longitudinal study of the reading achievement of early and non-early readers through sixth grade. In J. Readance & R. S. Baldwin (Eds.), *Dialogues in literacy research. Thirty-seventh yearbook of the National Reading Conference* (pp. 49–55). Chicago: National Reading Conference.

Torrey, J. W. (1979). Reading that comes naturally: The early reader. In T. G. Walker & G. E. Mackinnon (Eds.), *Reading research: Advances in theory and practice* (Vol. 1, pp. 117–144). New York: Academic Press.

VanTassel-Baska, J. (1989). Profiles of precocity: A three-year study of talented adolescents. In J. VanTassel-Baska & P. Olszewski-Kubilius (Eds.), *Patterns of influence on gifted learners: The home, the self, and the school* (pp. 29–39). New York: Teachers College Press.

Willerman, L., & Fiedler, M. F. (1974). Infant performance and intellectual precocity. *Child Development, 45,* 483–486.

Winner, E., & Martino, G. (1993). Giftedness in the visual arts and music. In K. A. Heller, F. J. Monks, & A. H. Passow (Eds.), *International handbook of research and development of giftedness and talent* (pp. 253–282). New York: Pergamon.

Zigler, E., & Lang, M. E. (1985). The emergence of "superbaby": A good thing? *Pediatric Nursing, 11,* 337–341.

BIBLIOGRAPHY

Burns, J. M., Collins, M. D. & Paulsell, J. C. (1991). A comparison of intellectually superior preschool accelerated readers and nonreaders: Four years later. *Gifted Child Quarterly, 35,* 118–124.

Cunningham, A. E., & Stanovich, K. E. (1997). Early reading acquisition and its relation to reading experience and ability 10 years later. *Developmental Psychology, 33,* 934–945.

Goldsmith, L. T. (2000). Tracking trajectories of talent: Child prodigies growing up. In R. C. Friedman & B. M. Shore (Eds.), *Talents unfolding: Cognition and development* (pp. 89–122). Washington, DC: American Psychological Association.

Robinson, N. M. (2000). Giftedness in very young children: How seriously should it be taken? In R. C. Friedman & B. M. Shore (Eds.), *Talents unfolding: Cognition and development* (pp. 7–26). Washington, DC: American Psychological Association.

Robinson, N. M., & Robinson, H. B. (1992). The use of standardized tests with young gifted children. In P. Klein & A. J. Tannenbaum (Eds.), *To be young and gifted* (pp. 141–170). Norwood, NJ: Ablex.

Shapiro, B. K., Palmer, F. B., Antell, S. E., Bilker, S., Ross, A., & Capute, A. J. (1989). Giftedness: Can it be predicted in infancy? *Clinical Pediatrics, 28,* 205–209.

Shore, B. M. (2000). Metacognition and flexibility: Qualitative differences in how gifted children think. In R. C. Friedman & B. M. Shore (Eds.), *Talents unfolding: Cognition and development* (pp. 167–188). Washington, DC: American Psychological Association.

Sternberg, R. J. (1993). Procedures for identifying intellectual potential in the gifted: A perspective on alternative "metaphors of mind." In K. A. Heller, F. J. Monks, & A. H. Passow (Eds.), *International handbook of research and development of giftedness and talent* (pp. 185–208). New York: Pergamon.

37

Gifted Adolescents

ROBERT A. SCHULTZ, *University of Toledo*
JAMES R. DELISLE, *Kent State University*

What distinguishes gifted adolescents from other adolescents is as individualistic and unique as is each of the students who wears this label. Often, the same characteristics and behaviors that were present when these adolescents were young—advanced vocabulary and thought patterns, emotional intensity, an awareness of the needs and fears of others—are still there in overabundance. Now, though, there may be an unsettling air of sophistication in these gifted young people.

Piechowski (1991), citing the work of Dabrowski (1964), calls these "overexcitabilities," which can envelop virtually every realm of an adolescent's life: intellectual, psychomotor, emotional, sensual, and imaginational. Each overexcitability, unique yet overlapping, pinpoints areas of arousal that cause the gifted adolescent to be noticed by others as "a cut above the rest" or "just a little different." Such overexcitability can be seen in adolescents like Catherine Murray who, at age seventeen, began the Global Teen Club, an international network of culturally diverse and socially aware teens; or Sarah Plunkett, a nineteen-year-old from Texas who has raised more than $600,000 for breast cancer awareness since the age of fourteen; or Matthew Sterling, a seventeen-year-old high school senior who took his own life five days before graduation, after discovering that someone else, not he, would be named valedictorian (Delisle, 1991).

That's right, suicide. No one ever said that emotional intensities and overexcitabilities all ended in rosy pictures and glowing reports of life successes. Like any other of life's important qualities—love, loyalty, compassion—there is a mixture of positive and negative to be found in each. Perhaps this admixture can best be expressed through the words of a gifted adolescent:

I'd never heard the phrase "transcend the human condition." But I knew that was what I longed to do. But once I did that, where would I go from there? . . . If I do transcend, are there other degrees or is there just one more? If there is just one more, maybe in its experience there is serenity at the end? (American Association for Gifted Children, 1978, pp. 18–19).

The adolescent years witness great upheavals in the emotional and physical characteristics of individuals. Often, parents and other adults focus on the potential problems associated with this seemingly chaotic time of human development. But adolescence also provides opportunities for gifted individuals to gain a sense of self and acknowledgement for their unique contributions to the world. At this point in life, a transition occurs from homebound childhood under the care and guidance of parents to a time of self-examination and exploration beyond the tethers of family and immediate neighborhood.

Gifted adolescents need support and respect for their budding self-inquiry. By listening carefully and observing situations that bring out a teenager's passions in life—music, reading, rock climbing, politics—the first important steps in talent awareness will have been satisfied: acknowledgement and respect for individuality.

The Role of Education in the Life of Gifted Adolescents

Because the majority of gifted identification at the secondary level is (or should be) through *self-selection,* a bigger concern than identification is the *development* of talents possessed by these able young people. As expressed by Betts (1991): "When working directly with gifted and talented students in a school setting, it becomes apparent that a broad range of experiences is necessary. Besides emphasizing the cognitive, it also is essential to include emotional and social development" (p. 143).

At this point, we could offer a whole set of prescriptions about how junior high and high schools should change to accommodate the intellectual and emotional needs of their most able students. However, as realists we sense that such prescriptions would be seen the way most prescriptions are: as overpriced solutions that leave a bad taste in the mouth.

Instead, we prefer to offer suggestions that could be accomplished with or without school support, in settings as different as Muleshoe, Texas, and Scarsdale, New York. The common themes that pervade these suggestions are two:

- Each requires initiative beyond the classroom from its student (and adult) participants;
- Each meshes two areas of importance to gifted adolescents: personal validation and intellectual challenge.

Finding Space to Grow

A major portion of the adolescent experience involves location, location, location! Just like realtors, gifted adolescents are on a constant quest to find space where their actions and emotions are accepted without judgment.

How is space provided for positive self-growth? Parents, teachers, and other caregivers can encourage positive decision making and support opportunities for gifted adolescents to challenge themselves. Respecting a decision made by a gifted teen encourages decisiveness and promotes self-learning, since consequences are encountered that perhaps were not considered; even if the decision makes adults cringe.

Ownership and responsibility are encouraged by the willingness of adults to act as *life preservers* rather than *sages*. What is the distinction? Sages tend to pooh-pooh decisions made by adolescents based on their own life experiences. "Been there, done that— and here's why it won't work. . . ." Unfortunately, spouting off all the things wrong with a choice often drives the adolescent decision maker underground. Rather than discussing potential options with caring adults, choices are made and experiences encountered through experimentation, without counsel (e.g., to-

bacco use, casual encounters with drugs, anatomy-by-Braille leading to possible teenage pregnancy, alcohol abuse). Adolescents most often avoid know-it-all sages, especially when the sage is more than a decade older than the teen.

On the other hand, life preservers hang around in plain sight, constantly available if needed. Acting as a life preserver means being respectful of an individual's self-worth and willingness to take risks in order to stretch and learn, while also being accessible for counsel without acting in a directive manner. Life preservers provide information for gifted adolescents to consider when grappling with a decision rather than prescriptively giving advice. They allow all the shades of gray that most gifted adolescents see to shine through, rather than reducing the picture to black and white or some rosy hue. Life preservers keep the conversation going, encouraging additional questions while enabling gifted adolescents to develop a sense of ownership and responsibility for their choices (see Figure 37.1).

Decisions leading to alcohol abuse, teen pregnancy, and drug and tobacco use remain possibilities. However, input from life preservers promotes stronger communication between teens and adults, thereby stemming the flow of underground decision making that leads to potentially self-damaging results.

The Myth of Underachievement

The luckless Charlie Brown, in a revelation of his innermost worries, confided to Linus that "There is no heavier burden than a great potential." So true, because when one is identified as "gifted," a whole array of extraordinary expectations conjoins that label. In fact, in the eyes of many, gifted students are often considered "underachievers" because they did not live up to the high, high standards that seem preordained when one is anointed a "gifted child."

Jim (one of your co-authors), calls this issue the "Aunt Peggy syndrome" in honor of one of his most annoying relatives. Here's Jim's story: "When I received my Ph.D. in educational psychology in 1981, I was the first person in our far, far extended family to have achieved that level of academic attainment. In celebration of my achievements (and to brag a little to their friends), my parents threw a congratulatory party for me. Friends and relatives I'd

Sage	Life Preserver
"I told you so."	"Let's see what we can learn from this."
"You're too young to be *really* in love."	"It's no fun to have your deep feelings toward someone ignored."
"It's not the end of the world if you get a 'B'."	"It sounds like you're disappointed with your performance."
"One day, this _____ (e.g. company, practice, firm) will be yours!"	"I respect your career choice and am happy you're pursuing your dreams."
"Do this."	"Here are some options; can you offer others?"
"It's not up for discussion."	"What do you think?"
"I'm disappointed in you."	"That probably wasn't the best choice. What other options were (are) there? Can we do something to remedy the situation?"
"You're so smart. You can be (do) anything you put your mind to."	"Let's explore some of your interests. Experience now will help you decide strengths and interests you may want to consider further."

Figure 37.1   Statements by sages and life preservers.

neither seen nor thought about in years attended, including Aunt Peggy. As she was sipping her cheap wine and recalling her images of me as an overweight ten-year-old (thanks, Aunt Peggy), she uttered a one-liner that will remain forever a family legend.

" 'Jim,' she said, 'we're all so proud of you— your achievements and your degree. But ya know?' she added, 'I always thought you'd become a *real* doctor—you know, the kind of doctor who really helps people.' "

Zap.

"In one tactless moment, Aunt Peggy had dismantled my pride, replacing it with self-doubts as to whether this Ph.D. was worth the years of toil it took to complete. In Aunt Peggy's mind then, and still today, I am an underachiever."

Unfortunately, Aunt Peggy is not just Jim's relative. And just as surely as her words had their impact on him, the Aunt Peggys in life will leave a mark on many gifted adolescents. It may be a shallow mark; its deepness toned down by the fact that Aunt Peggy's opinion, in reality, counts for very little. But what it lacks in depth it makes up for in length—"20 years later," Jim recalls, "I can still hear her voice, her disappointment in me."

This retelling of family folklore has a purpose. Sooner or later, in the lives of almost all gifted adolescents, they will be thought of as "underachievers" by someone or other who thought their lives should have taken a different direction. If this opinion becomes internalized, several scenarios could occur:

- The so-called underachiever begins to seek ways to make *everyone* happy, by running at breakneck speed in too many directions;
- The "underachiever" shuts down, figuring that by not performing *at all,* she or he can stave off the criticism that results when a goal attempted is not completely attained;
- The "underachiever" blows-off the criticism, disregarding either the words, their source, or both as just uninformed opinions about one's personal life choices.

This last option, the healthiest of the three, is not readily internalized despite some superficial bravado that would make it seem that it is. For gifted adolescents who sincerely question, deep down, whether their decisions were right or their performance acceptable, the threat of being perceived as an underachiever is enough to make them believe that Charlie Brown, if anything, understated the problems with "great potential."

Let's not leave the impression that all is lost, though. In a study of the life experiences of "underachieving" gifted adolescents, Bob (one of your coauthors) captured "Pete's" thoughtful argument:

> If you know you have an ability that nobody else does, you could underachieve; but only for yourself. Too many people judge each other at school. To play along and get along you have to hide—mutate to the class. And then the teacher—if you read them, it's easier to get by

hidden, to not be noticed and then just do your own thing. Interesting things come easier that way. Not being noticed frees up time for you to do what you are interested in instead of extra stuff put on you by others cause [*sic*] they think you can do more. (Schultz, 1999, pp. 146, 148)

Pete explains that it is not only possible, but preferable, to purposely "underachieve" (or "submerse" to use Bob's term) in order to concentrate on areas of interest outside of the school curriculum. Pete's story reveals that "underachievement" becomes more than a term comparing one's abilities with one's achievements. Indeed, it can be a coping mechanism to protect self-esteem and self-worth. "Underachievement," in this situation, is not underachievement at all!

As caregiving adults, we must take several steps to ensure the "survival of the fittest," intellectually speaking. First, we must begin to convince ourselves that, for the most part, *underachievement is a myth,* a convenient invention of twentieth-century pop psychology devised to make adolescents feel guilty and all others feel blameless for a student's lack of effort or progress in school. Adolescents are already ripe victims for self-doubt without adults adding the pressure that giftedness requires peak performance on a daily basis.

Next, we must recognize that every gifted adolescent will have a passion about one or more things, be it Roller Blading®, beachcombing, fly fishing, or embryology. By using these passions as vehicles to enhance learning in other, related areas (rather than as "rewards" for good behavior or high grades), gifted adolescents will receive the positive notoriety and self-confidence that accompanies unconditional acceptance of one's selected loves in life. Unless they are physically or emotionally harmful to self or others, or blatantly illegal or immoral, passions and the people who have them must be treated with respect. John Gardner (1961) once said that "the world needs both gifted plumbers and gifted philosophers, or neither our pipes nor our theories will hold water." A more reverential sentiment in tribute to passions has never been uttered.

When it comes to underachievement among gifted adolescents, the bottom line is that most of the books and articles written on this topic should be disregarded. Too often, you will find prescriptions on how to write student contracts, how to reserve rewards for special moments of success, and how to convince a fifteen-year-old that answering questions out of a social studies text that is older than he is really does make a difference in his learning. Almost nowhere, with the notable exceptions of Emerick (1988), Keighley (1996), Moore (1996), O'Grady (1995), and Schultz (1999), will you find what this gifted adolescent, typical among thousands, expresses so eloquently:

> I would have loved one of [my] teachers to recognize me and ask, "What are you thinking?" How I would have loved for my teacher to ask, "What's on your mind?" Instead I was called on to answer a question that I could not have cared less about, because it was hers, not mine (American Association for Gifted Children, 1978, p. 58).

Underachievement is in the eye of the beholder. See it as the paper tiger that it truly is.

Peerness: Acknowledging Commonality with Others

None of you reading this chapter has a peer group; neither do we. But before bemoaning our lot as rugged individualists, understand this: The reason none of us has a peer group is that there's *no such thing* as "a" peer group.

For some unknown reasons, and at some now-forgotten moment in time, the term *peer* became synonymous with *age-mate.* When this occurred, the era of "peer problems" for gifted children began. If a gifted nine-year-old didn't participate in school or free-time activities with other nine-year-olds, a problem with "peer relations" was said to exist. Never mind the reality that this very able nine-year-old got along with just about everyone *except* his or her age-mates, "peer problems" were still said to exist.

Talk about seeing a glass half-empty instead of half-full!

Newland (1976) saw the absurdity behind this error of logic and coined the term *peerness* to explain the situation that exists when the mental age and reasoning abilities of gifted children cause them to seek out the company of people who think and talk as they do—which, mostly, means people chronologically older than they are. Peerness affects both young children who seek soulmates, not just playmates, and gifted adolescents whose behaviors and social needs deal less with "Who's wearing what?" and "Who's dating who?" and more with the bigger issues of justice, fairness and responsibility. It's not that these adolescents don't enjoy an occasional burger and fries with age-mates, and they don't always wear their existential hearts on their sleeves, but gifted adolescents do benefit by associating with people of like minds who aren't afraid to let either their true emotions or their advanced vocabulary show—even if these people are older than the adolescents by several years.

Yet the myth persists that if sophomores don't hang out with other sophomores, something is wrong; something needs to be fixed. Before rushing headlong to remedy a problem that doesn't need a solution, make sure to ask these questions:

- Whose problem *is* this? If a gifted adolescent is content to have a peer group of older (and often, smaller in number) friends, does a problem really exist? And if so, who owns it?
- Is the gifted adolescent *unable* to make friends of his or her own age, or does she or he simply *choose* not to associate with classmates on a frequent basis?
- Does the gifted adolescent find fulfillment in solitary or small-group activities rather than in large, boisterous, and frequent social gatherings?

These questions should be asked *to* gifted adolescents by the persons concerned that a peer problems exists. With a little coaxing and some honest discussion, adults may find that they have one less worry about the care and feeding of that highly able adolescent whose interests and social preferences align more with our own than those of classmates.

However, for the vast majority of gifted adolescents, whose social problems are more in the eye of the beholder than anywhere else, it will be enough to introduce them to the concept of *peerness* and to acknowledge that, after high school, no one pegs social relationships to a specific chronological age. Those realities of growing up gifted, coupled with the exposure of gifted adolescents to others with similar styles and attributes (e.g., in honors classes, summer enrichment programs, or gifted programs) may be all the social skills instruction they need.

Isolation is the refuge of genius, not its goal, reminds Leta Hollingworth (1942). By allowing gifted adolescents to seek their own level of social contacts,

we validate two very important attributes: their uniqueness and their commonality with others.

Finding a Place of One's Own

Again, a story from your co-author, Jim: "The most capable student I ever met was a ten-year-old named Nathan who would get physically ill on Wednesday afternoons, just prior to leaving for his Hebrew class. It wasn't merely a dislike of this after-school school that bothered Nathan; his illness was prompted by something much more profound and personal. As he expressed it tearfully to me on the occasion of my discovering him vomiting in the boy's bathroom:

" 'My rabbi doesn't take me seriously. When I disagree with him or question something he says, he tells me I'm 'too young and stupid to have my own opinions about religion.'

"On the contrary, Nathan was asking the types of question that bother the analytical minds of gifted children: 'How do we know there's a God?' 'How do we know that Judaism is the 'right' religion?' 'If my mom remarries a non-Jew, what does that make me?' 'Shouldn't I be able to choose a religion when I'm older instead of being forced to have one while I'm a kid?'

"Unappreciated by an elder who was angered and perplexed by his maturity, Nathan turned inward, against himself, believing there was something wrong with him. None of his Hebrew school classmates seemed concerned about the issues that bothered Nathan, and that made him feel even more isolated and weird. Worst of all, he began to see himself as 'stupid,' obviously incapable of understanding something that both his classmates and his rabbi accepted at face value.

"Little did Nathan know that his questions and concerns were shared (and asked) by people he'd never heard of: Plato, Aristotle, Sartre, and Nietzsche. And only when I introduced him to a picture-book version of Thoreau's *Walden* did Nathan begin to believe that there was a bigger picture of the world than was afforded him through the concave lens of experiences he had had thus far. Nathan was a philosopher, and the only legitimate way to address and resolve his inner conflicts was to introduce him to the giants of philosophical thought: If it worked for Nathan, at 10, it can work for older gifted adolescents as well."

Methods of incorporating the great works from centuries past into rigorous and legitimate self-study are available in Ward (1980), White and Schlagger (1993), and Mehorter (1964), all of whom provide concrete outlines for introducing able students to universal questions and themes. Through this self-study (which is enhanced when students are able to discuss their questions with similarly disposed adults or age-mates), students not only learn about the foundations of world culture and knowledge, they also begin to see themselves within the personal reflections of others. The result is a deeper awareness of and bond with the intellectual rumblings that make one tick.

An additional resource, *The Courage of Conviction* (Berman, 1986), highlights the personal philosophies of prominent contemporaries such as the Dali Lama, Jane Goodall, Billy Graham, Mario Cuomo, Petra Kelly, and Steve Allen, who cites the importance of individual worth in this stunning quote by Jane Goodall:

> The way in which my own life touches those of so many others, those I know and thousands of those I don't, has strengthened my belief that each human has his or her own unique place in the ocean of existence. . . . At all different levels the ripples and currents pass or mingle, and some merge inextricably. With each merging a new force is created, itself as unique as the two beings that forged it. What joys the world would have lost if some of these forces had never been created, and what pain in other cases would it have been spared (Berman, 1986, p. 76).

A related area of study is bibliotherapy, defined by Schlichter and Burke (1994) as "a process of dynamic interaction between an individual and literature through facilitated dialogue . . . its focus is *not* on checking the reader's comprehension of the story but on helping individuals recognize, sort out, and evaluate their feeling responses to the literature" (p. 280). In bibliotherapy, the big questions are asked by characters as diverse as J. D. Salinger's Holden Caulfield, Judy Blume's Ramona Robinson, or Jonas in Lois Lowry's *The Giver,* and the issues range from existential crises to slumber party arguments. Frasier and McCannon (1981) and Piirto (1999) suggest books whose central characters are gifted adolescents, and White's (2001) *Philosophy for Kids* and Gaarder's (1996) *Sophie's World* provide the nourishment and intrigue philosophical thought triggers for teens reflecting on their place in the world.

Back to Nathan: After meeting with Nathan's rabbi and talking with her son, Nathan's mother decided to seek a new source for spiritual education. The new rabbi, more open to Nathan's questions and concerns, allowed Nathan to mature into a young man capable of dealing with life's inconsistencies.

Perfectionism: Enormous Expectations and Perilous Perceptions

Gifted adolescents displaying perfectionistic tendencies often rely on quantity rather than quality to feel a sense of accomplishment. "Ten awards is better than one award; Who's Who Among High School Students, National Merit Scholar, President of the Student Council, President of the Band, *and* President of the Sorority is better than being just one of these and doing the job well" (Piirto, 1999, p. 485).

The emotional stakes are raised with each judgment by self, peers, teachers, or parents as perfectionism blossoms into a full garden of thorny perceptions, expectations, and anticipated successes. Fear of failure grows as well, leading to gradual self-exclusion from challenging opportunities and denial of ability.

How can gifted individuals fight off the plight of perfectionism? It isn't likely that parents can effect change here. They probably unwittingly support and promote these tendencies. Bobby's experience is likely shared by many gifted adolescents. Parent's pride and lack of experience knowing what to do with a gifted child unchallenged by school contribute to a well-intentioned push toward perfection.

Much of the answer lies in the training of teachers and other provisions for a supportive classroom environment. Individuals trained to identify perfectionistic tendencies (in others and themselves) can begin to include options that nurture healthy risk-taking.

Although school life does not encompass all of an adolescent's learning experiences, teachers using open-ended strategies in a caring, respectful classroom environment can have a major impact on a student's sense of being. A classroom environment where risk taking is expected and mistakes are an accepted part of learning can deter and defuse perfectionism and competition. Students learn to work collaboratively, helping where needed, with the expectation that others will also provide assistance when asked. Self-respect and confidence rise as students learn individually, in teams, and from one another.

The teacher must use this model over a long period of time before savvy adolescents will accept this established classroom environment at face value. Too often, teachers expect immediate results and student acceptance, become frustrated when these are not encountered, and return to a more authoritarian position. Look at it from the teen/learner position:

> I thought maybe you watched *Stand and Deliver* or some other teaching movie over break and now you were going to become this wonderful caring individual. But, I also wondered how long until you went back to the same old, same old. Was I willing to put myself on the line and immediately buy-in? No way. I don't need another lesson in being cut off at the knees just when things are starting to become more interesting and fun. It's happened before, and probably will happen again (Schultz, 2001).

It takes time and concerted effort for adolescents and teachers to work out systematic change in the classroom. Open communication is key to gaining a sense of trust from either side of the proverbial desk.

Gifting the Gifted

Many of us understand the complexity behind "giftedness" from either being or living with a person bearing the label. For others, the label connotes something that was given, and therefore doesn't require any additional special treatment. "After all," the line of thinking often goes, "those who are gifted, whether it be in school, sports, or music, will develop and learn on their own." They are viewed as the elite—and elite often means privileged.

Being gifted, from a different perspective, requires that someone (or a series of "someones") has to help an individual become comfortable with personal differences and find a way (or ways) to fit into a seemingly uncaring and unforgiving society. To be fully aware of and comprehend the tendencies, differences, and difficulties that make a gifted individual unique from all others, some guidance and nurturing must take place by litterateurs identifiable as gifted individuals themselves. This is *gifting*.

Unlike mentorships, gifting requires more than talent in a specific field or profession. Gifting stretches personal as well as professional interactions as the novice and the artisan learn life skills from one another and grow interpersonally. The protégé is introduced to a way of life having limitless opportunities, rich with connections to others of like mind and soul.

Gifting comes from individuals who love learning and provide models of this passion for the protégé. Multiple interests and cross-disciplinary explorations undergird the foundation of the relationship. Indeed, the ancient guild system with its long-term apprenticeships and master-craftsman guides establishment of viable gifting opportunities.

Gifting can be recognized most readily in sports where coaches provide guidance to gifted athletes. Great coaches have tacit knowledge of their sport. They recognize fundamental strengths and provide guidance for even greater feats. Often, this success is beyond their own personal abilities—yet they willingly may sacrifice their own achievements to enable greatness in another. Bob Richards, a two-time Olympic Gold medalist pole vaulter, said it this way:

> Greatness is all around us! It's easy to be great because great people will help you. What is fantastic about all the conventions I go to is that the greatest in the business will come and share their ideas, their methods and their techniques with everyone else. I have seen the greatest salesmen open up and show young salesmen exactly how they did it. They don't hold back. I have also found it true in the world of sports.
>
> I'll never forget the time I was trying to break Dutch Warmerdam's record. I was about a foot below his record, so I called him on the phone. I said, "Dutch, can you help me? I've seemed to level off; I can't get any higher." He said, "Sure, Bob, come on up to visit me and I'll give you all I got." I spent three days with the master, the greatest pole vaulter in the world. For three days, Dutch gave me everything that he'd seen. There were things that I was doing wrong and he corrected them. To make a long story short, I went up eight inches. That great guy gave me the best that he had. I've found that sports champions and heroes willingly do this just to help you become great (As quoted in Ferguson, 1995, p. 3–1).

We see examples of the special relationship between an athlete and a coach in moments of triumph and defeat. Indeed, the Olympic games provide a showcase to observe glimpses of gifting in action. But gifting occurs in all areas of life, although clear description in the media and literature is often lacking.

The Hollow Promise of Talent Development

A central focus of service options in most school districts (and university settings) is that an exemplary product marks giftedness. In this sense, to remain in a gifted program, students have to display grades, papers, speeches, or other results which must be judged as noteworthy. To be gifted is to produce!

However, a few individuals have argued against this line of thinking. "Giftedness is a process, not a product," says Roeper (1995, p. 56). It involves complex interactions within the individual that cannot be scored by a percentile rank or standard deviation. These ratings only skim the surface of giftedness providing a snapshot of skill (or comparison of ability at a particular time). Giftedness is a condition causing individuals, at a very young age and thereafter, to question their being.

Think about your favorite author. Whether it be Keats, Tom Clancy, or Dr. Seuss, none of these individuals produced works of exemplary nature (that would identify them as gifted) early in their careers—let alone during their school days! It took a lifetime of study, of practice and thinking, to learn how to write in meaningful and engaging ways. How many of these individuals (or most other successful adults) would be excluded or removed from gifted and talented programs in public school due to a lack of product development at an early age?

Think of the pressure placed on an adolescent who has not found her or his self-spirit. A teenager abiding by and directed into action based on the expectations of others is in dire straits when the complexities of their mind and emotions stir up ideas that cannot be put into tangible form.

Can talents be developed? Sure. But we must not be casually lulled into believing that giftedness must have accountability attached to it. Giftedness is much more than a performance or product prepared on command. Giftedness is a state of being requiring broad examination of self and soul.

A Call to Action

One common characteristic of gifted adolescents is the *multipotential* many of them possess. An interest in many career directions, coupled with a proficiency to excel in multiple areas of endeavor, often complicates the process of focusing on a college major or a career direction. As stated by one student,

> When I look for a career in my future, the clouds really thicken. There are so many things I'd like to do and be, and I'd like to try them all; where to start is

the problem . . . I'd like to be a physical therapist, a foreign correspondent, a psychiatrist, an anthropologist, a linguist, a folk singer, an espionage agent, and a social worker (Sanborn, 1979, p. 285).

This lack of a singular career focus may appear, at first glance, to be a frivolous problem. After all, if one is blessed with an embarrassment of riches allowing for any number of vocational directions, what exactly is the problem?

As noted time and again by gifted adolescents (Delisle, 1987; Post-Kammer & Perrone, 1983), the dilemma comes when one realizes that the career direction selected is more than just making a "job choice." Involving years of advanced preparation with a singular focus, choosing a career path is a commitment that might require a decade beyond high school before one is allowed to practice the chosen profession. This is as true in the arts as it is in medicine or law or engineering, and this preparation phase often leaves even the brightest young person financially and emotionally dependent on others. In essence, this prolongs adolescence into the mid- or late twenties, by which time many contemporaries will already be earning decent salaries and living a more independent lifestyle.

Further, in choosing a career direction that involves an extended preparation phase, the gifted adolescent may question frequently whether he or she *really* wants to be a podiatrist or a civil engineer for the next thirty years. Despite evidence that most individuals will experience six or more job changes in their adult lives, highly skilled professionals seldom make a 180-degree shift in occupational focus. Once a podiatrist, always a podiatrist, even if you shift locations of employment from a general hospital to a specialized practice. Feet are feet, bridges are bridges, and talented adolescents fear that by selecting one area over others, they are dismissing the multiplicity of talents and interest that are part and parcel of being bright. A practicing trial lawyer who does tonsillectomies on the side? Doubtful. A concert pianist who moonlights as a social worker? Unlikely.

Secondary School GT Programming: A Modest Proposal

Cindy was an undergraduate work-study student at Kent State University. A gifted individual herself, Cindy shared many insights about giftedness that caused others to stop and wonder. As an example, Cindy's telling account of an often-overlooked aspect of gifted adolescence is crucial to gain an understanding of the life experiences of these individuals:

> It's not a problem of making decisions and taking risks. I need someone who's been there to show me the brakes and how and when to use them. We "gifties" get so caught up in . . . everything, but don't have a way of knowing when enough is enough! (personal communication, May 11, 1998).

Gifted adolescents often involve themselves in every imaginable activity in order to gain a sense of belonging—a space and place. Too often, these high-energy individuals lose touch with personal needs as they strive to meet the expectations of others. When is enough enough?

A curricular slot must be provided in the secondary school schedule where gifted adolescents meet with others of like ability to discuss experiences and be accepted for who they are. Peer acceptance and interaction are crucial for teenagers who differ from the status quo, and know it. All people need time with like-minded others and, therefore, should be automatically enrolled in a high school course slot specifically designed to provide continuity across the grade levels for the identified gifted as they progress through school. It can be called anything on the books, as long as:

- It is a requirement;
- It is staffed by an expert in gifted child education;
- It provides a safe haven for gifted adolescents in need of an accepting place in an otherwise potentially hostile environment for kids "a bit different" from their age-peers.

Just as snowflakes are similar yet oh-so-different, each individual contacted while trying to promote a social and emotional needs course will likely have a personal reaction hindering rather than endorsing the proposal, even if publicly acknowledging the thought as a good one. Questions such as "What about elitism? Isn't this another way of tracking? Just what would inclusion in this course mean for students excluded? Is it fair to them? What do we say to their parents? How will this course 'count' for university enrollment committees?" are just a few blockades.

You can see where this is heading.

The possibility of this curricular slot being made available is not very likely. Too many objections, too strong of a focus on more "needy" students, and the toll that accountability levies on schools, teachers, and students weigh heavily on the opposition side. But, being the hopeful dreamers we are, perhaps this option could best be implemented locally. Just like the tiny engine who thought he could, momentum may build eventually leading to all secondary schools meeting the often short-changed social and emotional needs of gifted adolescents.

SUMMARY AND CONCLUSIONS

This chapter on gifted adolescents was written in a style that reflects the minds of its subject—a bit irreverent, not altogether serious, and providing as many questions as answers. We hope that readers are able to glean the main points about these unique, yet remarkably similar students: that they deserve to express their opinions and lifestyle choices; that they want to succeed as surely as we want them to (albeit, in some different areas of focus); and that despite their advanced intellects and stunning powers of mind, they are still teenagers concerned about zits and dates and cars and clothes and college. In many ways, gifted adolescents are the "us" we were several decades ago, seeking similar challenges, dreaming thoughts of omnipotence. If we treat them with the same degree of personal respect that we wanted from others when we were twelve or seventeen or twenty-one, we will be on the right path in providing them with appropriate guidance and support.

QUESTIONS FOR THOUGHT AND DISCUSSION

1. When you were a teenager, did you find more "sages" than "life preservers"? Explain.

2. Explain why Schultz and Delisle see underachievement as (a) submersion or (b) lack of interest (passion).

3. What is "gifting"?

4. Pick one section of this chapter that made great sense to you. Discuss.

REFERENCES

American Association for Gifted Children. (1978). *On being gifted*. New York: Walker.

Berman, S. (1986). *The courage of conviction.* New York: Dodd, Mead.

Betts, G. T. (1991). The autonomous learner model for the gifted and talented. In N. Colangelo & G. A. Davis (Eds.), *Handbook of gifted education* (pp. 142–153). Boston: Allyn & Bacon.

Dabrowski, K. (1964). *Positive disintegration.* Boston: Little, Brown.

Delisle, J. (1987). *Gifted kids speak out.* Minneapolis, MN: Free Spirit.

Delisle, J. (1991). *Kidstories: Biographies of twenty young people you'd like to know.* Minneapolis, MN: Free Spirit.

Emerick, L. J. (1988). *Academic underachievement among the gifted: Students' perceptions of factors relating to the reversal of the academic underachievement pattern.* Unpublished doctoral dissertation, University of Connecticut, Storrs.

Ferguson, H. E. (1995). *The edge* (rev. ed.). Cleveland, OH: Getting the Edge Co.

Frasier, M., & McCannon, C. (1981). Using bibliotherapy with gifted children. *Gifted Child Quarterly, 25,* 81–85.

Gaarder, J. (1996). *Sophie's world.* New York: Berkley.

Gardner, J. W. (1961). *Excellence: Can we be equal and excellent too?* New York: Harper.

Hollingworth, L. S. (1942). *Gifted children above 180 IQ Stanford Binet: Origin and development.* New York: World Book.

Keighley, T. (1996). *The odyssey: Reaching an understanding of academically underachieving gifted students' perceptions of boredom.* Unpublished master's thesis, Simon Fraser University, British Columbia, Canada.

Mehorter, J. T. (1964). *Self and society: An independent study course for gifted high school students.* Ph.D. dissertation, University of Virginia. Dissertation Abstracts International, 25, 3879-A. (University Microfilms #64-10909).

Moore, B. J. (1996). *Three case studies of gifted students who underachieve in high school.* Unpublished doctoral dissertation, University of Virginia, Charlottesville.

Newland, T. E. (1976). *The gifted in socio-educational perspective.* Englewood Cliffs, NJ: Prentice-Hall.

O'Grady, A. L. (1995). *The onset of academic underachievement among gifted adolescents: Causal attributions and the perceived effect of early interventions.* Unpublished doctoral dissertation, University of Connecticut, Storrs.

Piechowski, M. M. (1991). Emotional development and emotional giftedness. In N. Colangelo & G. A. Davis (Eds.), *Handbook of gifted education* (pp. 285–306). Boston: Allyn & Bacon.

Piirto, J. (1999). *Talented children and adults: Their development and education* (2nd ed.). New York: Macmillan.

Post-Kammer, P., & Perrone, P. A. (1983). Career perceptions of talented individuals: A follow-up study. *Vocational Guidance Quarterly, 31,* 203–211.

Roeper, A. (1995). *Annemarie Roeper: Selected writings and speeches.* Minneapolis, MN: Free Spirit.

Sanborn, M. (1979). Career development: Problems of gifted and talented students. In N. Colangelo & R. Zaffrann (Eds.), *New voices in counseling the gifted* (pp. 294–300). Dubuque, IA: Kendall/Hunt.

Schlichter, C. L., & Burke, M. (1994). Using books to nurture the social and emotional development of gifted students. *Roeper Review, 16,* 280–283.

Schultz, R. A. (1999). *Illuminating learner realities: Perceptions, expectations, and experiences of gifted underachievers in a secondary school classroom.* Unpublished doctoral dissertation. Kent State University, Kent, Ohio.

Schultz, R. A. (2001). [High school student responses to changes in core teaching style]. Unpublished raw data.

Ward, V. S. (1980). *Differential education for the gifted.* Ventura, CA: National/State Leadership Training Institute, Ventura County Superintendent of Schools.

White, D. A., & Schlaggar, S. (1993, July–August). Gifted sixth graders and primary source philosophy. *Gifted Child Today,* 25–29.

White, D. A. (2001). *Philosophy for kids.* Waco, TX: Prufrock Press.

38

Gender and Giftedness

BARBARA A. KERR, *Arizona State University*
MEGAN FOLEY NICPON, *Arizona State University*

Gender roles have changed throughout the world, creating one of the most profound transformations in the history of human society. As these new roles evolve, the ways in which we guide and mentor gifted girls and boys are changing as well. This chapter will review how gender affects the development of gifted children and suggests ways to prevent inequitable practices from blocking the fulfillment of talent.

In the United States, girls have closed the gender gap with boys in many ways (Campbell & Clewell, 1999). Eighth-grade girls have caught up with boys in math achievement, despite researchers' predictions from a mere ten years ago that biological differences would preclude girls from the highest attainments in mathematics. Bright girls are taking challenging biology, chemistry, and physics classes in almost the same numbers as bright boys. The many efforts to help girls to raise their career aspirations, attempt course work of greater rigor, and claim leadership positions have been strikingly successful. As many young gifted women as gifted men now plan careers in medicine, law, and many other fields once dominated by males. Girls now hold a majority of high school leadership positions, and women's athletics have brought fame to female athletes in unprecedented numbers.

As girls and women become more active in formerly male domains, they often assume the problems that have traditionally been the province of males: substance abuse, violence, and self-destructiveness (Phillips, 1998). In addition to these newly acquired difficulties, achieving girls and women struggle with societal images of the "perfect" woman with impossible ideals of physical beauty. This struggle to be physically perfect can develop into bulimia or anorexia, two disorders with the highest mortality rate of any mental illness (National Institute of Mental Health, 1993). Ninety percent of people with eating disorders are women.

Internal and external barriers to the attainment of gifted females' goals continue to persist in society (Leroux, 1994). Lower achievement test scores still exclude gifted women from colleges and academic opportunities. The math achievement gap at the top range of scores has not changed much (Campbell & Clewell, 1999), and college women continue to endure a virulent culture of romance that forces them into competition for relationships with high prestige males (Holland & Eisenhart, 1990). Once in the workplace, bright women often find that discrimination is subtle; barriers are manifested in such things as the dearth of childcare, inflexible scheduling, and lack of mentoring. Furthermore, young professional women often find that their partners do not support their ambitions or goals. As a result, gifted women continue to subvert their own dreams, compromising their goals and aspirations in an attempt to compose a lifestyle that will work for all the members of their families (Tomlinson-Keasey, 1999).

The great gender revolution has also had a tremendous effect on gifted males. Gifted boys are often held to rigid stereotypes of masculinity (Kerr & Cohn, 2001). Underachievement continues to be a major problem for gifted boys. Colangelo, Kerr, Christensen, and Maxey (1993) found nine times more male than female gifted underachievers in a national study of achievement test scores. Underachievement may be a way in which gifted boys define their masculinity. When talented boys are held back and denied gifted education, they often become bored, difficult children. While females aspire to leadership positions in their schools, young men often detach, fearing the stigma of participating in girl-led and girl-dominated groups (Fiscus, 1997).

Differences and Similarities between Gifted Girls and Gifted Boys

Developmental Differences

Giftedness is evident at an earlier age in girls than in boys because gifted girls are more likely to show developmental advancement in a variety of areas (Silverman, 1986). For example, gifted girls are likely to speak earlier, read earlier, and write earlier than gifted boys. In comparison to their own gender, high-IQ girls tend to be taller, stronger, and healthier than girls of average IQ (Terman & Oden, 1935). Nevertheless, gifted girls still feel generally less physically competent than gifted boys (Chan, 1988).

Similarly, gifted boys are taller, stronger, and healthier than average boys (Terman & Oden, 1935) and are likely to have earlier large muscle development and therefore are more active and physically competent than gifted girls (Kerr & Cohn, 2001). However, they are likely to be less advanced in language development than gifted girls, and less likely to be precocious readers (Silverman, 1986).

Ability and Achievement

Gifted girls outperform gifted boys in classroom achievement throughout the school years, maintaining higher grades in all subjects (Kerr, 1997). Again, boys are much more likely to underachieve than girls; underachievers' classroom performance tends to be less than would be expected by intelligence and achievement tests. Sometimes, this is the result of bias in achievement tests that overestimates the talent of boys, and other times it is the result of deliberate camouflage of talents, as shall be seen later in this chapter.

Nevertheless, there continue to be differences favoring boys at the highest levels of achievement on standardized achievement tests. In 1988, on the American College Testing (ACT) exams taken during the senior year of high school, 61% of students scoring above the 95th percentile on the composite score were male, and 72% of students scoring in the 99th percentile on the composite score were male (Kerr & Colangelo, 1988). On the four subtests, males outperformed females in the mathematics, natural sciences,

and social studies areas; only on the English subtest did females outperform males. There were three times as many males who earned perfect math scores, five times as many males who earned perfect natural sciences scores, and two and one-half times as many males who earned perfect social studies scores (Colangelo & Kerr, 1991). Although the gap is narrowing, it appears that in math and science gifted males tend to hold the lead in achievement test scores after tenth grade.

The lower composite scores for females on the ACT seem to be strongly related to course taking. Laing, Engen, and Maxey (1987) provided convincing evidence that much of the variance in ACT scores is accounted for by curriculum. Gifted adolescent females, at least until recently, apparently took not only fewer and less challenging math and science courses than gifted males, but also fewer and less challenging social studies courses.

In a study examining self-efficacy's relationship to mathematical ability and achievement, Pajares (1996) reported that in a sample of gifted students, girls outperformed boys on math tasks, but there was no difference in self-efficacy between the sexes. Although performance scores should have warranted a greater self-efficacy for girls, that was not the case. Additionally, girls were less overconfident in the ability to solve the math problems than boys—their self-beliefs more accurately reflected their ability. This may be harmful for girls in light of the argument that some overestimation of ability is helpful because it increases persistence and effort.

The onset of adolescence brings changes in gifted girls' aspirations, expectations, attitudes, and achievement. The changes that occur for gifted girls today are subtler than those that occurred in the past; however, the theme of many gifted females' lives continues to be one of declining involvement with former achievement goals. The changes are most evident in academic achievement test scores, course taking, and other academically related behaviors. That is, by their sophomore year of college, many gifted women have changed their majors to less challenging disciplines; by senior year they may have changed to lower career goals; and by five years after college graduation, they may have compromised their original dreams entirely (Kerr, 1997).

For gifted boys and young men, it is quite a different story. Career development tends to be linear for academically talented boys, with career aspirations, particularly in math and science, leading to academic majors and jobs in related areas. However, gifted boys, too, disengage from earlier goals by becoming less enthusiastic, or even disillusioned about their career choices (Arnold, 1993). A striking theme in the lives of gifted men is an unimaginative vocationalism that often leads to a loss of interest in occupation and a quiet acceptance of an ordinary life (Kerr & Cohn, 2001).

Sex Role Socialization

Gifted girls are more similar to gifted boys than to average girls in their interests, attitudes, and aspirations. Gifted girls apparently enjoy a wide variety of play activities, including many that are traditionally associated with boys: outdoor games and recreation, adventurous play, sports, and problem-solving activities. They also frequently maintain feminine interests, such as playing with dolls and reading girls' magazines (Silverman, 1986; Terman & Oden, 1935). They are likely to be more open to playing with both girls and boys, and are likely to enjoy adventurous, active play that is usually preferred by boys. They often play with toys in a more complex way, inventing new games with even the most passive feminine toys (e.g., doing surgery on a Barbie or marrying her off to a Lego robot).

Gifted boys also seem to enjoy a wide variety of play. However, they are not afforded the same liberties in their choices as are girls. For gifted boys, androgynous play interests are dangerous in a homophobic society. Therefore, despite the fact that many gifted boys are indeed sensitive, nurturing, and caring, they are usually restricted to boys' activities out of fear of appearing too feminine (Pollack, 1998).

Research that has examined the socialization of eminent women and men shows that the women remember girlhoods full of exploration, adventure, and voracious reading (Kerr, 1997). As girls, eminent women spent an unusually large amount of time in solitary activities. Eminent men also spent a great deal of time alone; however, solitariness is not as strong a theme in their lives as it is in those of eminent women. A surprising number of eminent men had lost a father; it has been suggested that their resourceful response to this loss may have enhanced their creativity (Csikszentmihalyi, 1996).

Career Aspirations

Although sex-role-stereotyped career interests are well established by second grade in the general population of girls and boys, gifted girls may have career interests more similar to those of gifted boys (Silverman, 1986; Terman & Oden, 1935). Also, gifted girls tend to be less rigid in their sex role identification than average girls (Terman & Oden, 1935; Hay & Bakken, 1991; Kerr, 1997). Young gifted girls have high aspirations and vivid career fantasies (Kerr, 1997). Highly gifted girls, such as the top 1% of National Merit scholars, usually maintained high career aspirations in adolescence (Kaufmann, 1981). Until recently, moderately gifted girls, such as those scoring in the upper 5% on IQ and achievement tests, tended to have declining career aspirations during adolescence (Fox, 1976; Kerr, 1983, 1985). However, more recently this trend has changed; gifted girls' aspirations continue to climb, and at this point their career goals are just as high as those of gifted boys. For example, gifted adolescent girls are naming college majors and career goals that are frequently nontraditional for women (Kerr & Colangelo, 1988).

Although there are now equal numbers of gifted females interested in math, natural sciences, and health sciences as gifted males, they continue to avoid pursuing careers in the physical sciences, computer science, and engineering (Campbell & Clewell, 1999). This may relate to basic gender differences in career aspirations.

The major differences between the aspirations of gifted girls and gifted boys are the stronger altruistic and social motivations for girls, and stronger economic and achievement motivations for boys. Gifted girls nearly always want careers that make people's lives better, or that make the world safer or more beautiful. Gifted boys, still socialized to be providers, are just as idealistic as girls; however, they often choose careers that will satisfy their ideals and lead to high salaries and high status.

Kelly (1992) indicated that gifted adolescents do not have higher career maturity than non-gifted adolescents, suggesting that the gifted also require interventions during school that expose them to various career opportunities. His findings also suggest that gifted boys have a greater need for occupational information than gifted girls. Hollinger (1991) suggested that these interventions be highly individualized for each gifted student and address the conflicting messages of multipotentiality and gender-role stereotypes that influence career decision making.

Adjustment and Self-Esteem

When examining the very highest levels of ability, both gifted boys and gifted girls may experience more adjustment problems than average children. Terman and Oden (1935) and Hollingworth (1926) noted, fairly predictably, that the highest IQ children in general suffered more adjustment problems, probably as a result of their profoundly deviant intellectual abilities. However, this does not appear to be true for moderately gifted children. In the moderately gifted range, approximately the 95th percentile on intelligence and achievement tests, gifted boys and girls are as healthy mentally as they are physically. Gifted children before age eleven are strikingly confident; they assert themselves in groups and will argue for their opinions. They have high self-efficacy, believing they are good at many things, particularly schoolwork. At both five years old and eight years old, they have strong self-concepts (Chan, 1988). They have high opinions of their physical selves, their academic selves, and their social selves.

The majority of moderately gifted girls, like gifted boys, remain well adjusted during adolescence (Kerr, 1997; Terman & Oden, 1935; Webb, 1993). However, gifted adolescent girls may experience social anxiety and decreases in self-confidence. This first appeared in Groth's (1969) cross-sectional study that showed an abrupt psychological shift at age fourteen from wishes related to achievement and self-esteem, to wishes related to love and belonging. Her study showed that younger gifted girls tended to dream about success in school activities and accomplishments; older gifted girls dreamed of popularity and intimate friendships. In another study (Kelly & Colangelo, 1984), researchers found that while gifted boys were superior to average boys in academic and social self-concepts, gifted girls were not similarly higher than average girls. Therefore, gifted boys seem to maintain their high self-esteem throughout the teen years, but gifted girls do not.

In Kerr, Colangelo, and Gaeth's (1988) study of adolescents' attitudes toward their own giftedness, gifted girls were evidently quite concerned about the impact of their giftedness on the attitudes of others. Although most of them believed that there were some social advantages to being gifted, females saw more disadvantages than their male peers to being gifted. There was a deep ambivalence about the label *gifted* as well as concern about negative images others might hold of that label.

Gifted boys' concern about giftedness is subtle (Kerr & Cohn, 2001). They strive to show that they are regular guys, despite their intelligence. Most gifted boys learn early that it is acceptable for them to be gifted if they are also athletically competent; therefore, many work to be excellent at the most popular sports, such as football and basketball. Those gifted adolescent boys who cannot shine on the playing fields may be doomed to be labeled *nerds* and *brains*. In many cases, even these boys can develop a "machismo" based on their extraordinary technical ability, becoming admired by other students for their pyrotechnics on computers.

Issues of Special Concern to Gifted Boys

Kindergarten Redshirting

"Redshirting" is the sports practice of holding back an athlete's academic progress in college so that he can play an extra year. Perhaps one of the most destructive practices for gifted boys is "kindergarten redshirting," in which parents delay a child's entrance into kindergarten by a year or more. Kindergarten redshirting has become a popular practice, one that has grown in recent years (Brent, May, & Kundert, 1996). However, there is persuasive evidence that it is, in fact, harmful to a gifted boy's educational, emotional, and social development.

Parents usually redshirt gifted boys so that they can be more competitive athletically, even though they may also claim social and developmental reasons for holding their sons back. Sometimes kindergarten redshirting reflects parents' fears about bullying. They don't want their son to be at a disadvantage among bigger kids, and they are frightened by media reports of ruthless bullying in the schools.

Teachers and administrators also tend to favor holding boys back from school entrance, particularly when their birth dates fall near the cutoff. They are thinking of the average boy, who is slower to develop intellectually and socially than the average girl. However, boys who are gifted tend to read earlier than average boys. They also tend to be more socially and emotionally advanced than average boys. If they come from a middle or upper socioeconomic background, they even tend to be bigger, healthier, and stronger. Unfortunately, many educators do not recognize these great developmental differences and make the same recommendations for all boys, regardless of their talent.

Despite its frequency, there is no data to support the practice of kindergarten redshirting gifted boys; instead, it may be harmful for many reasons. First, bright boys may be better off entering kindergarten at a younger age than average boys, especially if they already have preschool experience (Gullo & Burton, 1992). Second, the belief that older children are more academically successful is simply unfounded. Although older average children attain higher academic achievement than younger average children, younger gifted children generally do better in their classes than older average children. Third, any social disadvantage of being younger usually disappears for average children by about first grade, and this disadvantage can fade for the gifted boy as well (Spitzer, Cupp, & Parke, 1995). When a gifted boy has difficulty relating to his peers, it is more likely because his classmates are too young for him rather than too old for him. A young gifted boy with good social skills will usually be popular with older children. It is true that a boy's giftedness may place him at a social disadvantage when he is among his classmates, but it is the intellectual difference, not the age difference, that causes the asynchrony.

Redshirting can depress both academic and social performance later on in school. In one study, boys who were delayed from entering kindergarten were more likely to be referred for a learning or psycho-educational evaluation, and less likely to be referred for a gifted education evaluation than boys who weren't held back (DeMeis & Stearns, 1992).

It appears that this bad practice, based almost entirely on masculine stereotyping, harms rather than helps gifted boys. A redshirted gifted boy is likely to become a big, bored, unhappy bully who bosses other boys into submission, either by pushing them around physically, when they don't play games by the rules that only he can understand, or by raining contempt upon kids he perceives to be willfully ignorant.

Bartleby Syndrome and Underachievement

"Bartleby Syndrome" is a puzzling pattern of under-achieving behaviors—a congenial refusal to do homework or to complete classroom tasks (Kerr & Cohn, 2001). The name of the syndrome is based on a character in a short story by Herman Melville who gently refuses to fulfill assignments with the phrase, "I prefer not to." Gifted boys between the third and fifth grade often begin to underachieve when they learn that it isn't cool among their male peers to be the best student in the class (Wolfle, 1991). These boys are usually friendly and mild-mannered and seem to have no good reason to underachieve.

Teachers like them and are mystified when a boy who has previously been high achieving and productive suddenly stops performing. Parents are puzzled, frustrated, and angry.

There are several gender-related explanations for Bartleby Syndrome. One may be that gentle under-achievement of this sort is an easy way for a boy to establish his newly developing masculine identity. By resisting his teachers' wishes—particularly if the teacher is a female—he can separate himself from her as a mother figure. Another possible explanation may be that many gifted boys would rather frustrate their parents and teachers than antagonize bullies. Mild-mannered underachievement is an excellent way to cope with bullies; the gifted boy may be less of a target for the bully's mocking and teasing. A third possible explanation for Bartleby Syndrome is boredom. A gifted boy who was redshirted may have enjoyed getting good grades and performing, as long as he was young enough to take simple pleasure in being better than everybody else. However, a gifted boy may come to believe that feeling a true sense of accomplishment, a true testing of their limits may never happen. In a society that glorifies men breaking the barrier, pushing the limits, going the distance, a young boy who thinks he may never have the opportunity to prove his worth may simply give up—like Bartleby.

It is important that Bartleby-like behaviors be identified and nipped in the bud. Of course, the optimum is to discover topics and areas of interest that stimulate the boy's sense of excitement about learning and achieving, and to build on that motivation (Webb, Meckstroth, & Tolan, 1982). Teachers can help prevent Bartleby Syndrome by talking honestly about boys and underachievement at the beginning of the school year. The best prevention of under-achievement, whether related to Bartleby Syndrome or not, is to have education that is stimulating, appropriate, and flexible—even in the regular classroom (Rogers, 2001).

Alienation and Disengagement

Adolescence used to be a time of initiation into manhood; however, there are few initiation rites for today's adolescent male (Gilmore, 1990). These rituals were society's way of integrating boys into the adult community, preparing them to defend their community, infusing them with a sense of belonging and meaning, and preparing them to find their vocation.

Without these meaningful, symbolic ceremonies, today's young men have few appropriate ways of establishing their identity as men (Pittman, 1993).

When a boy does not feel a part of the community into which he was born, or worse, when he sees that he is not a part of any community at all, he may become dangerously alienated. Many gifted boys have felt different and alone for much of their childhood and have felt deprived of adult male company. For example, a major concern of the gifted boys in the Free Spirit study (Alvino, 1991) was that their dads did not do enough with them. This time without a male role model, such as a father, may contribute to feelings of isolation in the gifted boy.

The possibility that the gifted boy may not receive recognition for his approaching manhood may prompt existential depression and a sense of alienation. He may see the shallowness of the behaviors of those around him and despair over hypocrisy. He may be painfully aware that few other boys share his idealism and his search for meaning. When a brilliant boy has no one to guide him in his quest for his place in the world, he may come to believe that there is no place for him at all.

This depression may also engulf him when he becomes fully aware of the evils and wrongs of the world and sees no way that he can be a part of combating them. The gifted boy is often aware of the complexities and tragedies of the world, such as the destruction of the earth's forests, the spread of AIDS, and the continuing religious and ethnic wars. Because he understands these complexities, he may not see how he can make a difference. Existential depression is often the consequence of feeling that one's search for meaning is fruitless (Webb, 1993). Part of a young man's initiation into manhood is learning his particular role in making the world a better place. Without a meaningful goal, the gifted may simply wonder in despair whether or not he will ever find his place.

Some gifted boys are fortunate enough to have a school group or a youth group led by a caring and visionary male leader who can take the role of initiator and mentor. Others may have fathers or other male family members who do communicate with the gifted boy about his journey. However, too many gifted boys do without leaders or mentors and flounder for years in search of manhood, often jumping from cause to cause, never understanding why they remain unsatisfied.

Besides these reasons for alienation, other factors may account for the disengagement of gifted adolescent boys. A study by the National Association of Secondary School Principals showed that girls now dominate in school leadership activities (Fiscus, 1997). Females are now much more likely than males to hold offices in student government, departmental clubs, and virtually all after-school activities except sports. Student advisers in the study simply believed that girls were more effective in relationships with the administration and that the faculty was more responsive to the female leaders. When faculty and students in the study were questioned in detail, faculty gave a number of reasons why they believed that girls were leading and boys were disengaging.

Many spoke of boys' unwillingness to engage in student leadership because too many school activities were social rather than political—the males did not want to plan dances. Student leadership, according to many boys, is a "girl thing." For many decades, gifted boys dominated student leadership. But schools have increased their emphasis on raising girls' aspirations and assertiveness, and the result has been a flood of girls into leadership, and an exodus of boys.

It may be true that faculty encourage girls more. However, the study suggests that boys themselves are making the choice to disengage. The reason may be based on the tendency for any activity that is primarily engaged in by females to have lower status (Kerr, 1997). Even from an early age, parents, family, neighbors and teachers often discourage boys from any feminine activity. For gifted boys, the dominance of girls in student leadership poses a dilemma. Gifted boys have usually been socialized to be involved, high achievers. They are aware that the best colleges look closely for leadership and service activities along with academic excellence. Despite this awareness, many choose to disengage. Thus, it appears that they are willing to jeopardize their chances for a high quality education to avoid being involved in a "girl thing." As a result, gifted young women are now in the majority in freshman classes at many prestigious colleges and universities (Koerner, 1999), and gifted young men are more likely to be consigned to second-tier colleges. Disengagement and the abdication from school leadership and service positions are the high price gifted boys pay to maintain their masculinity.

Career Decisions in Adulthood

From kindergarten through the professions, as females enter an activity in greater numbers, the status of that activity has gone down. Interestingly, it is not a gradual process. Once the ratio of females to males approaches one-half, the males suddenly exit the field in large numbers. This is happening across the country in college majors such as biology, in professions such as law and psychology, and in many leadership activities after college (Koerner, 1999). Although women are entering business and politics more than ever before, these two fields presently continue to attract males—possibly because of their sustained majority status in these fields.

Although the gifted male in college has not given up his math and science interests, he is in danger of giving up something much more important: his opportunity to choose a career based on his most deeply held values. Most gifted men, no matter how strong their interests in creative arts, languages, humanities, or literature, have give up these interests because they do not seem lucrative—or perhaps manly—enough (Colangelo & Kerr, 1991). The majority of gifted men choose college majors from among the same four areas: engineering, pre-med, pre-law, and business. The unimaginative majors of gifted men often lead to dissatisfaction in adulthood, with little hope of changing careers because of the enormous investment of time and money that goes into higher-status occupations. Gifted men may end up overworked and unavailable to their families as they pursue what they have been taught to pursue: status, power, and riches.

Relationships as Achievements

Many gifted boys attempt to attain happiness through the "Pursuit of the Perfect 10." This was how James Alvino (1991) labeled the tendency of some gifted boys to believe it absolutely necessary to have a perfect girlfriend. Men and boys are persuaded by the media that a beautiful woman is the key to happiness and high status. For gifted boys who are often already intensely achievement-oriented, a relationship with a girl becomes one more achievement. The perfect girlfriend should, of course, be slender, beautiful, pleasing, friendly, a good listener, and not too much of an achiever in her own right.

In our society, women generally marry their intellectual superiors or their intellectual equals. Men tend to marry their intellectual equals or their intellectual inferiors (Kerr, 1985). Many gifted men seem convinced that a woman's attractiveness can make up for her lack of intellectual ability. Not only is the lack of intellectual ability in a woman not seen as a liability by gifted boys and men, it is sometimes seen as an asset by men who are threatened by competition with a female. In high school, the achievement-oriented gifted boy may try very hard to attract a girl just because she is pretty, particularly if other boys also seek after her.

Despite extraordinary changes in the career expectations of women, many college men have yet to acknowledge the changes in gender roles that women's expectations now imply. In an interesting case of whether the glass is 70% full or 30% empty, Dey, Astin, and Korn (1996) showed how the percent of men who endorse the item, "The activities of married women are best confined to the home and family," dropped from 66.5% to 30.8% over twenty-five years. The percent of women who endorsed this item changed from 44.3% in 1966 to 19% in 1996. Dey and his colleagues seem to praise this as progress; however, the fact remains that three out of every ten men that a college woman may meet may expect that after marriage she will "confine" herself to caring for him and his children. It is likely that even more men who publicly endorse equity in relationships secretly wish for a more traditional lifestyle.

Nevertheless, there are many gifted boys and men who don't want to play the game of the Perfect 10. They would like the company of a girl, but they don't know how to find a girl who is an equal or a woman with whom they can have serious conversations. In addition, they may be puzzled or intimidated by the newly assertive, powerful young women in their classes. These young men often hover around the edges of social groups, not wishing to engage with females, but are just as unhappy about being alone.

For gay gifted young men, there is an additional overwhelming problem—homophobia and gay bashing (NAGC Task Force, 2000). In homophobic, conservative communities, gay boys know that their lives are literally in danger if they are discovered. They not only stay in the closet most of the time, but they may also go through the painful process of dating girls and pretending to want a girlfriend (Kerr & Cohn, 2001). They, too, are victims of the cult of the Perfect 10—the prettier the girl they are able to date, the safer they are from suspicion and attack.

Gay gifted boys will struggle with dual problems of being gifted and gay, perhaps trying to hide both, and losing themselves in the process. Those who suspect that they are gay, but who do not know yet, will defer that knowledge as long as possible. They fear that if it is true, they must live life with the double stigma of being gay and gifted. And others who are simply gifted but not gay may fear that their sensitivity, unusual interests, and cultural concerns are signs that they are gay.

Issues of Special Concern to Gifted Girls

The Self-Esteem Plunge

Beginning in 1991 with the American Association of University Women report about the plunge in girls' self-esteem during the teenage years, many researchers have investigated this phenomenon. For example, Brown and Gilligan (1992) wrote passionately about their study of gifted girls' loss of confidence. Others have documented the increase of eating disorders, substance abuse, and sexually transmitted diseases among teenage girls, all of which influence girls' self-esteem (Phillips, 1998).

Unfortunately, many people believe that gifted girls are somehow protected from these crises by their intelligence. The majority of gifted girls continue to receive high grades and to have very high levels of involvement in extracurricular activities, so on the outside, their self-esteem appears to be intact. However, they too are vulnerable to a loss of self-esteem and to risky behaviors that can jeopardize their goals and dreams (Kerr & Robinson Kurpius, 1999). In fact, gifted girls' concept of themselves in all dimensions—physical, academic, and social—slides (Czeschlik & Rost, 1994). Further, their special sensitivities and acute powers of observation of social cues may make them even more vulnerable to self-esteem losses in comparison to other girls (Lea-Wood & Clunies-Ross, 1995). This failure to believe in their ability can even lead gifted girls to avoid coursework if they think it requires considerable effort for which they believe they lack the ability (Eccles, 1985, 1987).

How does the rapid change in the self-esteem of gifted girls come about? The roles of family, societal, and school expectations, achievement tests and grades, and girls' attitudes toward themselves have all been examined in an effort to understand what happens to adolescent gifted girls. For example, gifted girls, particularly in traditional families and cultures, are expected to do an "about face" in adolescence. Until puberty, intelligence in a girl is considered a positive characteristic, and little girls are encouraged in their schoolwork and precocious behavior. However, with adolescence comes the expectation that the gifted girl will turn her attention to becoming an attractive potential mate. Few cultures perceive intelligence as an attractive characteristic in a woman; as stated previously, men tend to marry their equals or inferiors in ability (Kerr, 1997). As a result, most bright girls adjust to society's expectations of them. Girls carefully observe media portrayals of women and seek to emulate the makeup and dress of television and musical stars. Gifted girls may focus their intelligence and creativity on diets, shopping, and grooming. They may become social engineers, manipulating their peer group with Machiavellian skill to increase their status and popularity.

At-Risk Behaviors

Although the incidence of severe behavioral problems is much lower in gifted girls than in average- or low-ability girls, they do engage in behaviors that put them at risk. At-risk behaviors include bulimia and anorexia, drug and alcohol abuse, and unsafe sex and unwanted pregnancies. In gifted girls, these behaviors take on different meanings than with the general population of girls (Kerr & Robinson Kurpius, 1999). Eating disorders are often an extension of adolescent gifted girls' high need for achievement. When society demands a thin, attractive body as opposed to an educated mind, these girls may attempt to become the thinnest girls in the school. Drug and alcohol abuse are compounded by gifted girls' ability to hide their problem behaviors, to create cover stories, and to distract adults with academic achievement. Even alcohol abuse can be a kind of achievement for the gifted girl who wants to prove her ability to out-drink the boys. On the other hand, unsafe sex and unwanted pregnancies are sometimes the result of gifted girls wanting to prove their femininity. Sexual precocity may bring acceptance from a social group that would otherwise exclude her.

Inequity in the Classroom

Portrayals of girls and women in academic materials are comparable to media portrayals. Sadker and Sadker (1994) analyzed the content of commonly used math, language arts, and history books and found that girls and women were greatly underrepresented, with two to four times as many males as females depicted. Furthermore, only eleven women's names were mentioned in a popular 631-page history textbook. Items on achievement tests, particularly in science and math, consisted of problems that were more interesting to boys than to girls. These included items about machines, wagering ("If you had a poker hand that had two aces . . ."), and sports that tend to be of less interest to girls. Girls perform worse than boys on these items, but score higher on items with the same level of difficulty that pertain to issues of interest to them: nature and animals, arts and crafts, and people.

Adolescent gifted girls may also be at a disadvantage in the classroom because of teacher attitudes. Siegle and Reis (1998) found that teachers perceive their gifted girls as working harder and producing better quality work than gifted boys, but still assign higher grades to the boys. Girls then seem to accept their teachers' judgments, and evaluate themselves as less able than boys in mathematics and science. Cooley, Chauvin, and Karnes (1984) found similar stereotyping, with teachers in gifted classrooms perceiving the boys as having superior critical thinking skills and problem-solving abilities, and perceiving the girls as having superior creative writing abilities. It is interesting that although most teachers are opposed to sex-role stereotyping, and most make an effort to avoid stereotyping in general, they still tend to see gifted boys as enjoying math more, as well as being better at it, than girls (Secada, Fennema, & Adajian, 1995).

Adolescent gifted girls may also be at a disadvantage in the classroom because of inequitable instruction. According to Sadker and Sadker (1985), boys receive more attention from teachers than girls throughout their education. Boys are called on more often in the classroom than girls. They are more frequently rewarded for calling out answers while girls are more frequently reprimanded for the same response. Boys also receive more informative and complex responses. Sadker and Sadker found that girls receive bland, "accepting" responses from teachers, whereas boys receive praise and criticism. Boys receive more instructional attention; for example, they get detailed advice on the correct approach to tasks. On the other hand, girls are simply given the right answers.

These differential teacher responses do not seem to be the result of deliberate discrimination on teachers' parts; even staunchly feminist teachers exhibit similar patterns. Differential instruction seems to be both a response to different behaviors of boys and girls, and a reflection of underlying socialized attitudes that are mostly unconscious. Similar studies have not been done specifically with gifted children or in the context of gifted education programs. Nevertheless, it is likely that gifted girls suffer from differential treatment just as average girls do.

The Culture of Romance and the Decline of Aspirations

According to the research of Holland and Eisenhart (1990) and Arnold (1993), a culture of romance that is inimical to female achievement and aspirations still thrives in coeducational colleges and universities. According to Holland and Eisenhart, the culture of romance dictates that every young woman must achieve a relationship with a high-prestige male. In fact, a relationship with a high-prestige male may be the only way that a gifted woman can attain the admiration of her peers. Apparently, excellent academic performance and involvement in leadership activities mean little to her peer group. Unless she has a supportive family, encouraging teachers, and concerned mentors, a gifted young woman may come to rely only upon her peer group for affirmation and approval. Among the bright young women surveyed, Holland and Eisenhart found that 80% of their conversations concerned relationships with men and preparation for activities with men.

At the same time that she is receiving relentless pressure to engage in romantic relationships, the gifted young woman may be losing confidence in her intellectual abilities. The scientific community has long been concerned that so many young women drop out of math, science, technology, and engineering after their freshman year (Campbell & Clewell, 1999). One mediocre grade in a beginning course may discourage gifted women from persisting, probably because of the tendency of females to attribute this "failure" to lack of ability. She is much more likely than her gifted male peers to abandon her math and science interests, no matter how strong they once were, and is less likely to pursue graduate training in these fields.

By the time a gifted young woman has graduated from college, she is likely to have lowered her estimate of her own intelligence, to have changed majors to a less challenging area, and to have lowered her career aspirations (Arnold, 1993). After college, she is more likely to follow her boyfriend or husband to his job than to have him follow her. She is the one most likely to have the major childrearing responsibilities. And although it is now the norm for gifted women to combine work and family, gifted women continue to be more likely to give up full-time work for part-time and to give up leadership positions than are gifted men (Kerr, 1997). The culture of romance may be the most powerful force in deterring gifted women from their goals. Yet interventions are few and far between for gifted girls and women, despite the need for programs to keep girls motivated toward their goals (McCormick & Wolf, 1993).

Achieving Gender Equity for Gifted Students

By the time gifted males and females have reached adulthood, the development of their talent has been profoundly shaped by their gender. For different reasons, they have often "compromised away" the promise of their giftedness. Except for those boys and girls who have the courage and support to challenge gender roles, most gifted boys and girls do succumb to society's image of what constitutes achievement. Teachers and counselors can help support gifted boys and girls in their journey toward their goals by encouraging gender equity in the classroom, modeling and teaching good gender relations, and helping gifted boys and girls to define their own unique masculinity and femininity.

Gifted young people need help from counselors and mentors to plan a future that includes both work and relationships (Hollinger & Fleming, 1992, 1993). Unfortunately, gifted boys and girls have stereotypical fantasies about their future lives (Kerr, 1998). Women dream of dual career bliss, while men still seem to nourish the hope that they might find a woman who wants to stay home and take care of them and the children. Gifted college men are hoping for relationships that will be nearly impossible to find, and college women have as their goals romantic yet egalitarian relationships for which they have no roadmaps. Gifted young men, heterosexual or homosexual, need relationship education that centers on finding love that is an experience in communication and intimacy rather than an achievement like a grade or a score. Gifted women need help transcending the culture of romance, finding the courage to stay true to their goals, and seek partners who respect their career plans. Mentors of gifted students can help by discussing freely their own diffi-

cult choices, and by modeling egalitarian solutions to future dual career dilemmas.

Both gifted young men and young women may sabotage their own education and life plans by trying to fit too well into the gender roles that have been prescribed for them. Bright boys should be forewarned of the consequences of becoming underachieving Bartlebys just to prove their masculinity. They need comprehensive preventive programs for underachievement (Fehrenback, 1993). Similarly, girls need to understand the consequences of compromising their mental and physical health by attempting to attain an impossible ideal of beauty and popularity (Reis, 1995). Girls and boys can learn to accomplish their own goals, rather than to accomplish the goals of others. Educators and counselors can prevent compromised dreams by helping girls and boys discover their own meaning of femininity and masculinity, and by helping both girls and boys to make their choices based on their most deeply held values.

Noble, Subotnik, and Arnold (1999) proposed, "To thine own self be true," with a new model of talent development that can help gifted young people understand how giftedness is uniquely defined for each individual as a combination of intelligence, achievement, and the distance one must travel to arrive at one's goals. When each gifted boy is free to create his unique masculinity, and each gifted girl is free to create her unique femininity, they will also be liberated to fulfill their dreams.

SUMMARY AND CONCLUSIONS

The psychosocial challenges of gifted men and women reflect the current struggle in society to define gender roles. On the one hand, the gender gap is closing, with more women now than ever finding success in previously male dominated fields. On the other hand, gifted women continue to compromise their own talents and career aspirations, and gifted men still struggle with issues of masculinity, relationships, and career satisfaction.

There are issues of special concern for gifted boys, such as kindergarten redshirting (the practice of holding back gifted boys from beginning school), Bartleby Syndrome (failing to attend to academic tasks previously enjoyed), disengagement and alienation leading to compromising career decisions in adulthood, and relationships as achievements in order to prove masculinity. There are also special issues for gifted girls, such as decreased self-esteem, at-risk behaviors (eating disorders, substance abuse, and unsafe sex), inequity in the classroom, and the culture of romance (obtaining status through relationships with males).

Several suggestions were made for teachers and counselors who work with gifted boys and girls that address these concerns. For example, gender equity should be practiced and taught in the classroom. For gifted young people to thrive, they need assistance in planning futures that encompass both work and relationships. These are initial steps that will help prevent gifted boys and girls from sabotaging their own education and life plans in order to fit into the gender roles that society has prescribed for them.

QUESTIONS FOR THOUGHT AND DISCUSSION

1. Describe physical development, ability, and achievement differences between males and females, as presented by Kerr and Nicpon.

2. Describe the value conflicts that lead many bright female students to lower their college and career aspirations.

3. How do gifted boys' perceptions of gender roles affect their education and career?

4. Why is "kindergarten redshirting" damaging for gifted boys?

5. Explain the "Bartleby Syndrome."

REFERENCES

Alvino, J. (1991). An investigation into the needs of gifted boys. *Roeper Review, 13,* 174–180.

Arnold, K. D. (1993). Academically talented women in the 1980's: The Illinois Valedictorian Project. In K. D. Hulbert & D. L. Schuster (Eds.), *Women's lives through time: Educated American women of the twentieth century* (pp. 393–414). San Francisco: Jossey-Bass.

Brent, D., May, D. C., & Kundert, D. K. (1996). The incidence of delayed school entry: A twelve year review. *Early Education and Development, 7,* 1122–1135.

Brown, L., & Gilligan, C. (1992) *At the crossroads.* Cambridge: Harvard University Press.

Campbell, P., & Clewell, B. C. (1999, September 15). Science, math and girls: Still a long way to go. *Education Week,* 50–51.

Chan, L. K. S. (1988). The perceived competence of intellectually talented students. *Gifted Child Quarterly, 32,* 310–315.

Colangelo, N., & Kerr, B. A. (1991). Extreme academic talent: Profiles of perfect scorers. *Journal of Educational Psychology, 82,* 404–410.

Colangelo, N., Kerr, B., Christensen, P., & Maxey, J. (1993). A comparison of gifted underachievers and gifted high achievers. *Gifted Child Quarterly, 37,* 155–160.

Cooley, D., Chauvin, J. C., & Karnes, F. A. (1984). Gifted females: A comparison of male and female teachers. *Roeper Review, 6,* 164–167.

Czeschlik, T., & Rost, D. H. (1994). Socio-emotional adjustment in elementary school boys and school girls: Does giftedness make a difference? *Roeper Review, 16,* 294–297.

Csikzentmihalyi, M. (1996). *Creativity: Flow and the psychology of discovery and invention.* New York: Harper-Collins.

DeMeis, J. L., & Stearns, E. S. (1992). Relationship of school entrance age to academic and social performance. *Journal of Educational Research, 86,* 20–27.

Dey, E. L., Astin, J., & Korn, J. (1996). Betrayal by the academy: Sexual harassment of women college faculty. *Journal of Higher Education 67,* 149–173.

Eccles, J. S. (1985). Why doesn't Jane run? Sex differences in educational and occupational patterns. In F. D. Horowitz & M. O'Brien (Eds.), *The gifted and talented: Developmental perspectives* (pp. 251–295). Washington, DC: American Psychological Association.

Eccles, J. S. (1987). Gender roles and women's achievement related decisions. *Psychology of Women Quarterly, 11,* 135–172.

Fehrenback, C. R. (1993). Underachieving gifted students. Intervention programs that work. *Roeper Review, 16,* 88–90.

Fiscus, L. (1997). Survey says: Gender issues survey. *Leadership, 7,* 17–21.

Fox, L. H. (1976, August). *Changing behaviors and attitudes of gifted girls.* Paper presented at the annual meeting of the American Psychological Association, Washington, DC.

Gilmore, D. (1990). *Manhood in the making.* New Haven: Yale University Press.

Groth, N. (1969). *Vocational development for gifted girls.* ERIC Document ED 941737. Reston, VA: ERIC.

Gullo, D. F., & Burton, C. B. (1992). Age of entry, preschool experience, and sex as antecedents of academic readiness in kindergarten. *Early Childhood Research Quarterly, 7,* 175–186.

Hay, C. A., & Bakken, L. (1991). Gifted sixth-grade girls: Similarities and differences in attitudes among gifted girls, non-gifted peers, and their mothers. *Roeper Review, 13,* 158–160.

Holland, D. C., & Eisenhart, M. A. (1990). *Educated in romance: Women, achievement, and college culture.* Chicago: University of Chicago.

Hollinger, C. L. (1991). Facilitating the career development of gifted young women. *Roeper Review, 13,* 135–139.

Hollinger, C. L., & Fleming, E. S. (1992). A longitudinal examination of life choices of gifted and talented young women. *Gifted Child Quarterly, 36,* 207–212.

Hollinger, C. L., & Fleming, E. S. (1993). Project CHOICE: The emerging roles and careers of gifted women. *Roeper Review, 15,* 156–160.

Hollingworth, L. S. (1926). *Gifted children: Their nature and nurture.* New York: Macmillan.

Kaufmann, F. (1981). The 1964–1968 Presidential Scholars: A follow-up study. *Exceptional Children, 48,* 2.

Kelly, K. (1992). Career maturity of young gifted adolescents: A replication study. *Journal for the education of the gifted, 16,* 36–45.

Kelly, K., & Colangelo, N. (1984). Academic and social self-concepts of gifted, general, and special students. *Exceptional Children, 50,* 551–554.

Kerr, B. A. (1983). Raising the career aspirations of gifted girls. *Vocational Guidance Quarterly, 32,* 37–43.

Kerr, B. A. (1985). *Smart girls, gifted women.* Columbus: Ohio Psychology Press.

Kerr, B. A. (1997). *Smart girls: A new psychology of girls, women and giftedness* (rev. ed.). Scottsdale, AZ: Gifted Psychology Press.

Kerr, B. A. (1998, March). When dreams differ: Gender relations on the college campus. *Chronicle of Higher Education.* Washington, DC.

Kerr, B. A., & Cohn, S. J. (2001). *Smart boys: Talent, manhood, and the search for meaning.* Scottsdale, AZ: Gifted Psychology Press.

Kerr, B. A., & Colangelo, N. (1988). The college plans of academically talented students. *Journal of Counseling and Development, 67,* 42–49.

Kerr, B. A., Colangelo, N., & Gaeth, J. (1988). Gifted adolescents' attitudes toward their own giftedness. *Gifted Child Quarterly, 32,* 245–247.

Kerr, B. A., & Robinson Kurpius, S. E. (1999). Brynhilde's Fire: Talent, risk and betrayal in the lives of gifted girls. In J. LeRoux (Ed.), *Connecting the gifted community worldwide* (pp. 261–271). Ottawa: World Council on Gifted and Talented.

Koerner, B. I. (1999, February 8). Where the boys aren't. *U.S. News and World Report Online,* 1–8. Retrieved from http://www.usnews.com/.

Laing, J., Engen, H., & Maxey, J. (1987). *The relationship of high school coursework to corresponding ACT assessment scores.* (ACT Research Report 87-3). Iowa City, IA: American College Testing Program.

Lea-Wood, S. S., & Clunies-Ross, G. (1995). Self-esteem of gifted adolescent girls in Australian schools. *Roeper Review, 17,* 195–197.

Leroux, J. A. (1994). A tapestry of values: Gifted women speak out. *Gifted Education International, 9*(3), 167–171.

McCormick, M. E., & Wolf, J. S. (1993). Intervention programs for gifted girls. *Roeper Review, 16,* 85–87.

NAGC Task Force on Social and Emotional Needs. (2000). Washington, DC: National Association for Gifted Children.

National Institute of Mental Health. (1993). *Eating Disorders.* NIH Publication No. 93-3477. Washington, DC: U.S. Department of Health and Human Services.

Noble, K. D., Subotnik, R. F., & Arnold, K. D. (1999). To thine own self be true: A new model of female talent development. *Gifted Child Quarterly, 43,* 140–149.

Pajares, F. (1996). Self-efficacy beliefs and mathematical problem-solving of gifted students. *Contemporary Educational Psychology, 21,* 325–344.

Phillips, L. (1998). *The girls report.* New York: National Council for Research on Women.

Pittman, F. (1993). *Man enough: Fathers, sons, and the search for masculinity.* New York: Perigee.

Pollack, W. (1998). *Real boys: Rescuing our sons from the myths of boyhood.* New York: Holt.

Reis, S. M. (1995). Talent ignored, talent diverted: The cultural context underlying giftedness in females. *Gifted Child Quarterly, 39,* 162–170.

Rogers, K. B. (2001). *Re-forming gifted education: Matching the program to the child.* Scottsdale, AZ: Gifted Psychology Press.

Sadker, M., & Sadker, D. (1985, October). *Interventions that promote equity and effectiveness in student-teacher interaction.* Paper presented at the annual meeting of the American Educational Research Association, Chicago.

Sadker, M., & Sadker, D. (1994). *Failing at fairness: How America's schools cheat girls.* New York: Charles Scribner's Sons.

Secada, W., Fennema, E., Adajian, L. B. (1995). *New directions for equity in mathematics education.* New York: Cambridge University Press.

Siegle, D., & Reis, S. M. (1998). Gender differences in teacher and student perceptions of gifted students' ability and effort. *Gifted Child Quarterly, 42,* 39–47.

Silverman, L. K. (1986). What happens to the gifted girl? In C. J. Maker (Ed.), *Critical issues in gifted education: Defensible programs for the gifted* (pp. 43–89). Rockville, MD: Aspen.

Spitzer, S., Cupp, R., & Parke, R. D. (1995). School entrance age, social acceptance, and self-perceptions in kindergarten and 1st grade. *Early Childhood Research Quarterly, 19,* 433–450.

Terman, L. M., & Oden, M. H. (1935). *Genetic studies of genius: Vol. 3. The promise of youth.* Stanford, CA: Stanford University Press.

Tomlinson-Keasey, C. (1999). Gifted women's lives. In N. Colangelo & S. G. Assouline (Eds.), *Talent development.* Scottsdale, AZ: Gifted Psychology Press.

Webb, J. T. (1993). Nurturing social-emotional development of gifted children. In K. A. Heller, F. J. Monks, & A. H. Passow (Eds.), *International handbook of research and development of giftedness and talent* (pp. 525–538).

Oxford: Pergamon Press.

Webb, J. T., Meckstroth, E. A., & Tolan, S. S. (1982). *Guiding the gifted child.* Scottsdale, AZ: Gifted Psychology Press.

Wolfle, J. A. (1991). Underachieving gifted males: Are we missing the boat? *Roeper Review, 13,* 181–185.

39

Equity and Excellence: Culturally Diverse Students in Gifted Education

DONNA Y. FORD, *The Ohio State University*

Lacking both incentive and opportunity, the probabilities are very great that, however superior one's gifts may be, he will rarely live a life of high achievement. Follow-up studies of highly gifted young Negroes . . . reveal a shocking waste of talent—a waste that adds an incalculable amount to the price of prejudice in this country.
—Educational Policies Commission (1950, p. 33)

$\mathbf{A}$s the quote suggests, a mind is not only a terrible thing to waste,[1] a mind is a terrible thing to erase. Advocates of gifted education recognize that we are wasting and erasing gifts and talents when we do not recognize the strengths of gifted students.

Although dated, the most comprehensive data on the demographics of gifted programs come from the U.S. Department of Education (1993), which reported that African-American, Hispanic-American, and Native-American students are underrepresented in gifted programs by 50% to 70%. Specifically, while Black students represented approximately 16% of the school population, they comprised approximately 8% of gifted programs; Hispanic-American students comprised 9% of the school population, but about 5% of gifted education; and Native-American students comprised 1% of the school population, but 0.3% of gifted education. After conducting a review of the several reports on this topic, I drew two conclusions (Ford, 1998a, 1998b). First, despite considerable effort, our field has made little progress in improving the overall representation of diverse students in gifted education; second, while our field has

recognized this underrepresentation issue for decades, certain diverse students are more underrepresented than ever before in gifted education (see Table 39.1).

These data demand the question: Why are diverse students underrepresented—consistently and grossly underrepresented—in gifted education programs? What factors contribute to difficulties in recruiting and retaining diverse students in gifted education?

The primary premise of this chapter is that the underrepresentation of diverse students in gifted education centers on two central issues: (1) the debate between excellence and equity, which is grounded in a "deficit perspective" about culturally diverse populations; and (2) educators' lack of understanding of cultural diversity. These factors effectively hinder educators from recognizing the gifts and talents of students who are different from the dominant or mainstream culture.

Barriers to Recruiting and Retaining Culturally Diverse Students in Gifted Education

Several authors have focused on barriers to recruiting and retaining diverse students in gifted programs. Explanations fall into at least two major categories: (1) issues related to cultural misunderstanding, and (2) issues related to testing and assessment.

Why do diverse students persist in being underrepresented in gifted education? Most publications point to problems related to testing and assessment. But surely, the tests are not totally to blame. While a majority of publications point to testing and

---

1. Motto of the United Negro College Fund.

Table 39.1 Special Education Data on Trends in the Representation of Diverse Students in Gifted Education Programs, 1978 to 1992.

Student Population	1978	1980	1982	1984	1992
Hispanic American	6.8	9.0	8.6	13.2	13.7
	5.15	5.4	4.0	7.2	7.9
	(u = 25%)	(u = 40%)	(u = 53%)	(u = 45%)	(u = 42%)
American Indian	.8	.7	.5	.8	1.0
	.3	.3	.3	.3	.5
	(u = 62%)	(u = 57%)	(u = 40%)	(u = 62%)	(u = 50%)
Asian American	1.4	2.2	2.6	3.7	4.0
	3.4	4.4	4.7	6.8	7.0
	(o = 59%)	(o = 50%)	(o = 45%)	(o = 46%)	(o = 43%)
African American	15.7	20.1	25.8	24.5	21.1
	10.3	11.1	11.0	12.9	12.0
	(u = 33%)	(u = 45%)	(u = 57%)	(u = 47%)	(u = 41%)

Notes: Top number indicates the percentage of total student population; middle number represents percentage in gifted education; U = under-represented; O = over-represented.

Source: Ford (1996).

assessment issues, issues surrounding testing and assessment are just a symptom of the problem. Specifically, my experiences suggest that the primary barrier is the pervasive deficit orientation that prevails in society and our schools. After examining this deficit orientation, I will discuss *symptoms* of this orientation, such as the low referral rates of diverse students for gifted education services, and the heavy reliance (sometimes, exclusive reliance) on tests that inadequately capture the strengths and cultural orientations of diverse students. I also discuss how educators' lack of understanding of cultural diversity hinders their ability to recognize the strengths of diverse students.

Cultural Misunderstanding

Before discussing how cultural misunderstanding hinders the recruitment and retention of diverse students in gifted education, a discussion of the concept of "culture" is in order. Culture is a social system that represents an accumulation of beliefs, attitudes, habits, values, and practices that serve as a filter through which a group of people view and respond to the world in which they live (Shade, Kelly, & Oberg, 1997). Nobles (1990) stated that culture represents the rules and frames of reference that provide a group and

the individuals within that group with a design for living. Lynch (1992a) stated that culture is like a second skin, and it profoundly impacts our behaviors. Culture is a set of invisible patterns that become normal ways of acting, feeling, and being for a particular group (Hall, 1989). For example, cultural practices, beliefs, and values differ on such variables as family structure (e.g., nuclear versus extended; patriarchal versus matriarchal), competition versus cooperation, conceptions of beauty, conceptions of friendship, health practices, hygiene practices, views about authority, concepts of time, and notions regarding spirituality.

Boykin (1994) delineated cultural styles and strengths of African Americans that influence teaching and learning. His theory, supported by other scholars (e.g., Shade et al., 1997), indicates that Black students tend to be verbal and vocal (oral tradition), physically active (verve and movement), creative (expressive individualism), communal (social bonds are important; prefer cooperation to competition), adept at reading the behaviors of others (harmony), and sensitive and emotional (affective) (see Table 39.2).

Perceptions about differences among students manifest themselves in various ways, and they exert a powerful influence in educational settings. A common saying among African Americans is "The less we know about each other, the more we make up."

Table 39.2   Cultural Styles/Strengths of African Americans.

Spirituality

A conviction that nonmaterial, religious forces influence people's everyday lives; acceptance of a nonmaterial higher force that pervades all of life's affairs.

Harmony

The notion that one's fate is interrelated with other elements in the scheme of things so that humankind and nature are harmonically conjoined; harmony—one's functioning is tightly linked to nature's order.

Movement

An emphasis on the interweaving of movement, rhythm, music, and dance, which are considered central to psychological health.

A need to move—physical over-excitability; expresses self nonverbally.

Verve

A propensity for relatively high levels of stimulation to action that is energetic and lively.

Affect

An emphasis on emotions and feelings, together with a special sensitivity to emotional cues and a tendency to be emotionally responsive.

Communalism

A commitment to social connectedness—social bonds and responsibilities transcend individual privileges; a commitment to the fundamental interdependence of people and to the importance of social bonds and relationships; need for affiliation and social acceptance/approval.

Oral Tradition

A preference for oral modes of communication—speaking and listening are treated as performances. Oral virtuosity—use metaphorically colorful, graphic forms of spoken language.

Speaking is a performance. Enjoy oral traditions—storytelling, embellishments, jokes, etc.

Expressive Individualism

Seeks and cultivates a distinctive personality; a proclivity for spontaneity, and genuine personal expression; denotes the uniqueness of personal expression, personal style; risk taker, independent, impulsive.

Social Time Perspective

The event is more important than the time; the here and now is important. May not adhere to time limitations imposed by others.

For instance, if a teacher does not understand how some cultural groups value cooperation or communalism over competition (see Boykin, 1994; Shade et al., 1997), that teacher may perceive the diverse child who prefers cooperation as being "too social." Communalism is a commitment to social relationships and social learning (e.g., working in groups, helping others, etc.). It is a "we, us, our" philosophical orientation. Likewise, if teachers do not understand that some students come from cultures that value the oral tradition, they may neither recognize nor appreciate the strengths of students who prefer speaking to writing and reading. They may not rec-

ognize that students who speak nonstandard English can still have strong verbal skills. Thus, teachers may not refer culturally and linguistically diverse students for gifted education services if they equate giftedness with verbal, reading, and/or writing proficiency.

The matrix in Table 39.3 presents a cultural filter that uses Boykin's (1994) framework to help educators to see that the characteristics and strengths of African Americans can become a liability in schools where educators have little understanding of and respect for cultural differences. In their report entitled *A New Window for Looking at Gifted Children*, Frasier et al. (1995) came to a similar conclusion—we must

Table 39.3 Giftedness in Cultural Context: Problems Related to Identifying and Serving Gifted Black Students.

Characteristics of Giftedness	Cultural Filter	Manifestations of Giftedness Based on Cultural Filters	Possible Interpretations of Gifted Black Student Characteristics
Large memory; acquires and retains information quickly	Harmony—Adept at reading verbal and nonverbal behaviors, observant and read environment well Affective—Sensitive; sense of justice	• Quick to see discrepancies, inconsistencies, injustices • Remembers negative events more than positive events	Overly sensitive; overly preoccupied with negative events; difficult to please or appease
Inquisitive—Searches for significance and meaning	Social time perspective—Needs a context, a reason for learning Harmony—Adept at reading the environment	• Quick to note lack of relevance in assignments, rules, and so forth • Frustrated by irrelevance and lack of context and meaning	Questions perceived as a challenge; feedback and concerns are perceived as too critical and judgmental
Intrinsic motivation; task commitment	Social time perspective—Social, seeks relevance, valence	Most engaged when tasks are personally rewarding and meaningful	Extrinsically motivated
Seeks cause-effect relations	Harmony—Seeks order and logic; traditions are important	Sees things that others do not; insightful, perceptive; asks "why?" as much as "why not?"	Rude, stubborn, arrogant, too demanding
Heightened sensitivity; concerned about equity and justice	Affective—Worries about humanitarian concerns, primarily immediate social issues in home, neighborhood, and school	Confronts rather than accepts inequities (e.g., questions, resists, protests, refuses to accept the *status quo*)	Defensive, overly sensitive; narrow-sighted, self-centered (personal concerns outweigh larger social issues)
Advanced, large vocabulary; verbal proficiency	Oral tradition—Expresses self with openness and honesty; forthright	• May use words to manipulate, to present double messages • May use words and language considered inappropriate in school settings • Talkative	Verbal skills, advanced vocabulary, and content (*what*) of messages not recognized due to delivery mode (*how* statements are made)
Creative, inventive, divergent thinkers	Expressive individualism—Wants to be seen as an individual within a group; creative; innovative	• Dislikes structure, routine • Dares to be different; risk taker; enjoys challenges • Sees things that others do not; sees many alternatives; resourceful	Disruptive, trouble maker, class clown; nonconforming, weird; indecisive

(continued)

Table 39.3 Continued

Characteristics of Giftedness	Cultural Filter	Manifestations of Giftedness Based on Cultural Filters	Possible Interpretations of Gifted Black Student Characteristics
Empathic, strong interpersonal skills	Affective—Feelings influence thoughts and behaviors	Sensitive to rejection, fear of isolation, strong need for positive social relations and student-centered classrooms	Too social, too emotional and needy
Interpersonal; desire for social acceptance and approval	Harmony—Self and one's environment are one (inter-connected)	• Sensitive to negative feedback or unconstructive criticism • Strong desire to belong, to fit in	Socially incompetent (too social, too emotional and needy); follower rather than leader; overly dependent
Independent, prefer to rely on self or to work alone	Communal, family-oriented; cooperative; social, group-oriented ("we" rather than "I")	Less motivated in competitive situations; more engaged in cooperative situations	Lack independence and initiative, too dependent on others; overly conforming
Strong sense of humor	Expressive individualism; oral tradition	• Likes to play with words and ideas; enjoys puns; clever • Uses humor to improve social relations • Uses metaphorically colorful, graphic language	Cruel, sarcastic, insensitive, class clown, attention seeker
Diverse interests	Verve—Energetic; eclectic, multipotential	• Inquisitive, willing to take risks & flirt with temptations • May not show strengths in one area • Attention easily diverted	Unfocused, disorganized, easily distracted; flat profile—Major strengths not recognized
Intense concentration	Social time—Time is expended and measured by relevance and meaning; time not measured by hands on a clock	• May not want to be disturbed or interrupted • May have difficulty managing & allocating time • Likes to take time rather than be ruled by schedules	Stubborn or single-minded; disorganized
High energy	Movement and verve (intense)	• Frustrated and bored by inactivity • Highly engaged during active learning and experiential activities • Physical	Hyperactive, out of control, aggressive; behavioral problem

510

learn more about diverse gifted students in order to effectively identify and serve them (also see Frasier & Passow, 1996).

Essentially, the matrix indicates that ideas about cultural diversity influence definitions, policies, and practices. Too often, differences are equated with deficits. Herrnstein and Murray (1994) revived the deficit orientation in *The Bell Curve*. Among other grievous errors (e.g., equating IQ with actual intelligence; viewing intelligence as static and almost totally inherited; misinterpreting correlation as causation, etc.), the authors overinterpreted and misinterpreted results of studies on the intelligence of African-American children. They ulti-mately drew the fatalistic conclusion that African Americans are intellectually and culturally inferior to other cultural and ethnic groups. This premise is harmful and unsound, and has no place in educational settings.

Deficit Thinking and Cultural Misunderstanding: Influences on Assessment, Policy, and Practice

A person's color is the first thing we see, but the last thing we talk about (Lynch, 1992a, 1999b). Menchaca (1997) traced the evolution of deficit thinking, and demonstrated how it influenced segregation in schools (e.g., *Plessy v. Fergusen*, 1896) and resistance to desegregation during the Civil Rights era and today. Deficit thinking carries connotations of genetic inferiority, and one group is held up as being superior to another. Groups that are perceived as different from the evaluator are deemed inferior in some way. This ideology focuses on students' shortcomings rather than strengths. Below, I discuss how deficit orientations influence a myriad of educational practices and limit diverse students' access to gifted education.

Extensive Reliance on Tests. Test scores play a dominant role in identification and placement decisions. More than 90 percent of school districts use intelligence or achievement test scores for placement decision (Colangelo & Davis, 1997; Davis & Rimm, 1997). This near-exclusive reliance on test scores for placement decisions keeps the demographics of gifted programs primarily White and middle class. Yet, educators frequently justify their decisions to use tests because they are "objective." Essentially, tests have become smokescreens that help us to don a cloak of objectivity, which ultimately helps decision makers to abdicate any responsibility for the outcomes.

Students who score at the requisite level in terms of IQ (often 130 is the minimum) or achievement (often 95th percentile or higher) qualify for gifted education services. Unfortunately, diverse students tend to score lower than White students on traditional standardized intelligence and achievement tests. Data indicate that Black and Hispanic students score about one deviation below White students on standardized intelligence tests (Sattler, 1992). More specifically, on the WISC-R, the mean IQ for Black students is 86.4, 91.9 for Hispanic students, and 102.3 for White students (see Mercer, 1979). On the Kaufman-Assessment Battery for Children (K-ABC), the mean IQ for Black students is 95.0, 95.8 for Hispanic students, and 102.0 for White students (Kaufman & Kaufman, 1983); (see Tables 39.1 and 39.2). Further, when socio-economic status (SES) is controlled, the gap in test scores continues but decreases. That is, when SES is similar, the traditional standard deviation gap decreases on the WISC-R and K-ABC by almost half. On the K-ABC, Black children score six IQ points lower than White students; and on the WISC-R, Black students score nine points lower than White students.

The data are not much different with aptitude tests. In terms of the SAT, Black students score 123 points lower than White students on the math subscale and 95 points lower on the verbal subscale. Likewise, Hispanic students score 89 points lower than Whites on the math subscale, and 70 points lower on the verbal subscale.

Given the persistent gap in the intelligence, aptitude, and achievement test scores of African American, Hispanic American, and White students, one must ask why educators continue to rely extensively or exclusively on such tests for recruitment purposes. This is not just a question of access; it is also a question of equity. One instrument must not dictate our decision making; this practice misuses or abuses the test and the integrity of the assessment process. On this note, the National Association for Gifted Children (1997) published a position statement urging educators to use more than one test to make educational and placement decisions about gifted students, and to seek equity in their identification and assessment instruments, policies, and procedures. Just as important, the standards of the American Psychological Association

(1999) call for the use of more than one instrument when making educational decisions.

Why do we continue to use these tests so exclusively and extensively, particularly when they have negatively affected diverse students? There are at least three explanations: (1) the fault rests with the test (e.g., test bias); (2) the fault rests with the educational environment (e.g., poor instruction and lack of access to high quality education contributes to poor test scores); or (3) the fault rests with (or within) the students (e.g., they are cognitively inferior or "culturally deprived").

The first two viewpoints consider the influence of the environmental or external forces on test performance. Therefore, if the test is being questioned, alternative tests and assessment tools will be considered and adopted. Further, if the quality of the instruction and resources are poor or inadequate, then educators recognize that test scores are likely to be low.

Conversely, the last explanation rests in deficit thinking; it points to shortcomings within the students and, thus, it blames the victim. Educators who support this view abdicate any responsibility for minority students' lower test scores because of the belief that genetics exclusively or primarily determine intelligence, and that intelligence is static—that genes are destiny. Such advocates are also likely to believe that the environment (e.g., families) in which culturally diverse students are reared is inferior to those of other groups. Both views result from a deficit-oriented philosophy that hinders educators from seeing the potential of diverse students and prevents them from working effectively with such students.

IQ-Based Definitions and Theories. Educators continue to define giftedness unidimensionally—as a function of high IQ scores. Thus, definitions and theories are based extensively on the results of intelligence tests. IQ or test-driven definitions often ignore the strengths of those who are culturally diverse, who are linguistically diverse, who live in poverty, or who are poor test takers. These students may very well be capable, but lack experiences deemed necessary for school success, as explained earlier. According to Helms (1992), cultural styles affect test performance. For example, verve can make it difficult for students to sit through and maintain attention during lengthy assessments; harmony can contribute to poorer performance if the assessor is perceived by the student as uncaring or hostile; and communalism may contribute to students wishing to help others and, therefore, being distracted about their friend's progress on the test.

Achievement-Based Definitions and Theories. Along with high intelligence test scores, giftedness is often defined in terms of high achievement, as measured by achievement tests and/or grades. Gifted students are expected to demonstrate their ability. Such definitions and theories, of course, ignore the reality that gifted students can and do underachieve. Gifted underachievers may be teachers' greatest nightmare because the students have the ability to excel, but they do not. When we equate giftedness with achievement, we ignore an important reality—gifted children may lack motivation, may have a conflict between need for achievement and need for affiliation, and may have personal problems that hinder their productivity and interest in school. Compounding these realities is another reality—diverse students face social injustices (e.g., discrimination, stereotypes, negative peer pressures, etc.) that can contribute to underachievement. Performance on achievement tests is influenced by the quality of students' learning experiences at home and school. If expectations and standards are low for diverse students (e.g., due to cultural misunderstanding and/or deficit thinking), the quality of the curriculum and instruction will suffer.

Inadequate Policies and Practices. Procedural and policy issues also contribute to the underrepresentation of diverse students in gifted education. For instance, a policy may require that the gifted education screening first begin with a teacher referral. Because teachers (including culturally diverse teachers) underrefer diverse students for gifted education services (Ford, 1996; Saccuzzo, Johnson, & Guertin, 1994), this policy is problematic. I have found many Black students, for example, with high test scores who are underrepresented in gifted education because teachers did not refer them for screening (Ford, 1996). Thus, when teacher referral is the first (or only) recruitment step, diverse students are likely to be underrepresented. Certainly, teacher referrals are quite subjective; they rest heavily on expectations and perceptions of students.

An additional policy may require that students have a certain GPA to be referred to, or to remain in, the gifted program. The implications and impact of this policy are clear—since a disproportionate percentage of diverse students underachieve, their opportunities to be identified as gifted are diminished.

Equity versus Excellence Debate

The aforementioned barriers are empowered by debates over excellence versus equity, as if the two cannot co-exist. This debate begs the question, "If we increase diversity in the gifted program, will the quality of programs suffer (i.e., excellence)?" I am often asked by teachers and administrators, "If underachieving gifted students are identified and served, will this "water down" the gifted education class?" I am convinced that beliefs—conscious or unconscious—about inferiority lie at the heart of this question.

Recommendations for Change

Schools must eliminate barriers to the participation of economically disadvantaged and minority students in

services for students with outstanding talents . . . and must develop strategies to serve students from underrepresented groups.
> —(U.S. Department of Education, 1993, p. 28)

Increasing the participation of diverse students in gifted education requires more than finding the "right" test. To effectively recruit and retain diverse students in gifted education, educators must shed deficit thinking. As Einstein once said, "The world we have created is a product of our thinking. We cannot change things until we change our thinking." As Table 39.4 illustrates, no time is better than the present to move away from traditional practices and beliefs that have been counterproductive to our field when it comes to culturally diverse students. What follows are some suggestions for promoting equity and excellence in gifted education.

Table 39.4   A Comparison of Traditional versus Contemporary Beliefs and Practices.

Traditional Beliefs and Practices	Contemporary Beliefs and Practices
Identification—Focus is on a convergent answer. Is the child gifted? (yes/no response required)	Assessment—Focus is on a divergent answer. How is the child gifted and what are his/her needs? This is diagnostic and prescriptive.
Identification—Focus is on students earning a certain number on an intelligence or achievement test.	Assessment—Focus in on developing a profile of students' strengths and shortcomings.
Giftedness—Represented by a high IQ score or achievement percentile.	Giftedness—viewed as multidimensional.
Measurement—The best (most valid and reliable) measure of giftedness is a test(s).	Measurement—Giftedness must be assessed in multiple ways due to its multimodal nature.
Measurement—One measure/test is sufficient.	Measurement—Multiple sources are essential to develop a profile.
Ability is rewarded.	Effort and achievement are rewarded.
Ability must be demonstrated.	Talent development and potential are recognized.
Etiology—Genetics primarily determine giftedness.	Etiology—The environment and genetics determine giftedness. We must look at characteristics.
Students are in a gifted program. Gifted education is a place.	Students receive gifted education services. Gifted education is not a place.
Excellence versus equity debate.	Excellence and equity are not mutually exclusive.
Gifted education is a privilege.	Gifted education is a need.

Adopt Contemporary Definitions and Theories

The U.S. Department of Education's (USDE, 1993) most recent definition of *gifted* broadens notions of giftedness with its attention to potential and to talent development. Further, it acknowledges that giftedness is a social construct and a relative construct. Educators are urged to carefully choose their comparisons based on similar experiences and backgrounds. Unlike other definitions, the USDE definition recognizes that giftedness also exists among children living in ghettos, barrios, and hollows. Unfortunately, as with other definitions and theories, practical, valid, and reliable instruments have yet to be developed to assess these proactive and contemporary theories of intelligence. My hope is that this will be rectified in the near future.

A number of theories of intelligence and giftedness exist, but two capture the strengths, abilities, and promise of gifted diverse learners, Sternberg's (1985) Triarchic Theory of Intelligence and Gardner's (1983) Theory of Multiple Intelligences.[2] These two comprehensive, flexible, and inclusive theories contend that giftedness is a social construct that manifests itself in many ways and means different things to different cultural groups. The theorists acknowledge the multifaceted, complex nature of intelligence and how current tests (which are too simplistic and static) fail to do justice to this construct.

Adopt Culturally Sensitive Instruments

To date, the most promising instruments for assessing the strengths of culturally diverse students are such nonverbal tests of intelligence as the Naglieri Non-Verbal Abilities Test and Raven's Progressive Matrices, which are considered less culturally loaded than traditional tests (Saccuzzo, Johnson, & Guertin, 1994). Accordingly, these are more likely to capture the cognitive strengths of culturally diverse students. Saccuzzo et al. identified substantially more Black and Hispanic students using the Raven's than using a traditional test, and reported that "50 percent of the non-White children who had failed to qualify based on a WISC-R qualified with the Raven" (p. 10). They went on to state that "the Raven is a far better

measure of pure potential than tests such as the WISC-R, whose scores depend heavily on acquired knowledge" (p. 10).

Educators should understand that "nonverbal" tests assess intelligence nonverbally. This is not to say that students are "nonverbal" (i.e., cannot talk); rather, the tests give students opportunities to demonstrate their intelligence without the confounding influence of language, vocabulary, and academic exposure. Gardner, Sternberg, and others contend that some gifted individuals do not have strong verbal or linguistic skills, as may be the case with musically gifted students, creatively gifted students, spatially gifted students, and those having a great deal of practical or social intelligence. Thus, we must find ways to assess the strengths, the gifts of these capable students. At this time, nonverbal tests hold much promise for identifying such students—one test and one type of test cannot possibly measure the many types of intelligences that exist.

In addition to adopting culturally sensitive instruments, educators must consider the following when interpreting test results:

a. Use subgroups' norms (e.g., does the test manual report differences in test performance for diverse groups? Do diverse groups perform differently from White students on the tests?);
b. Analyze all test scores for trends (e.g., are early test scores higher than later test scores? Are achievement tests scores significantly different from intelligence test scores for diverse groups?);
c. Analyze differences in subtests within the tests (e.g., do certain groups score higher on performance versus verbal subscales?).

The most recent testing standards provide more detailed precautions and recommendations regarding culturally sensitive, equitable assessment (American Psychological Association, 1999).

Identify and Serve Underachievers and Low Socio-Economic Status Students

Underachievement is learned. Children are not born underachieving. If one equates giftedness with high achievement, however, gifted underachievers will be underreferred for gifted education. When designing programs that address underachievement, educators must tailor strategies to the needs of diverse students. These strategies include *supportive, intrinsic,* and *remedial* strategies.

---

2. See Chapter 7 by Sternberg and Chapter 8 by von Károlyi, Ramos-Ford, and Gardner.

Supportive strategies affirm the worth of diverse students. They include:

- Providing opportunities for students to discuss concerns with teachers and counselors;
- Addressing issues of motivation, self-perception, and self-efficacy;
- Accommodating learning styles; modifying teaching styles (e.g., abstract, concrete, visual, auditory);
- Using mastery learning;
- Decreasing competitive, norm-referenced learning environments;
- Using cooperative learning and group work;
- Using positive reinforcement and praise;
- Seeking affective and student-centered classrooms;
- Setting high expectations for students;
- Using multicultural education and counseling techniques and strategies;
- Involving mentors and role models;
- Involving family members in substantive ways.

Intrinsic strategies help students develop internal motivation; they are designed to increase academic engagement and self-efficacy. Thus, we must:

- Provide students with constructive and consistent feedback; feedback they can learn from to change their behaviors and improve academically;
- Give choices by focusing on students' interests;
- Provide for active and experiential learning (e.g., role plays, simulations, case studies, projects, internships);
- Use bibliotherapy and biographies to motivate and inspire students;
- Use mentorships and role models to show students that they can succeed;
- Adopt an education that is multicultural; this is an education that is culturally relevant and personally meaningful, an education that provides insight and self-understanding.

Finally, we must provide remedial strategies, when necessary. These strategies include implementing academic counseling (e.g., tutoring, study skills, test-taking skills) and teaching time management and organization; using individual and small group instruction; and using learning contracts and learning journals.

Improve Quality of Education

Closing the achievement gap between White and diverse students takes more than testing. The prevalent achievement gap is not an irreversible reality. Just as the gap narrowed once, during the 1970s and 1980s, it can narrow again. Policymakers are being irresponsible if they lead the public into thinking that testing and accountability will close the gap. Rather, substantive recommendations include:

- Increasing the participation of minority students in challenging courses;
- Investing in professional development for teachers;
- Implementing comprehensive research-based models for school improvement;
- Reducing class sizes;
- Focusing on preventing (i.e., expanding high quality preschool programs and opportunities);
- Addressing inequities and discrepancies in curriculum, instruction, resources, and facilities;
- Raising teachers' expectations of diverse students
- Providing extended learning time and intensive support for struggling students;
- Strengthening family involvement efforts;
- Increasing the number and percent of highly qualified teachers in diverse settings.

Provide Multicultural Preparation for Educators

With forecasts projecting a growing minority student population, teachers must bear a greater responsibility for demonstrating multicultural competence (Ford, Grantham, & Harris, 1998; Ford & Harris, 1999, 2000; Ford et al., 2000). Preparation for multicultural education among all school personnel may increase the recruitment and retention of diverse students in gifted education. Lynch (1992b) noted that "achieving cross-cultural competence requires that we lower our defenses, take risks, and practice behaviors that may feel unfamiliar and uncomfortable. It requires a flexible mind, an open heart, and a willingness to accept alternative perspectives. It may mean changing the way we think, what we say, and how we behave" (p. 35).

To become more culturally competent, educators must at least (1) engage in critical self-examination to explore their attitudes and perceptions concerning cultural diversity, and the influence of these attitudes and perceptions on diverse students' achievement and educational opportunities; (2) acquire and use accurate information about culturally diverse groups (e.g., histories, cultural styles, norms, values, traditions, customs, etc.) to inform and improve teaching and learning; (3) learn how to infuse multicultural perspectives and materials into curriculum and instruction to maximize the academic, cognitive, social-emotional, and cultural development of all students; and (4) build partnerships with diverse families, communities, and organizations. In teacher education programs and staff development initiatives, we must prepare future and current teachers to work with culturally diverse students.

Provide a Multicultural Education for Gifted Students

Just as gifted students are gifted 24 hours of the day, culturally diverse students are culturally diverse 24 hours of the day. With this in mind, many scholars emphasize the need for all students to have a multicultural education (e.g., Banks, 1999; Ford, 1998a; Ford, Grantham, & Harris, 1998; Ford & Harmon, 2001; Ford & Harris, 2000). Students have the right to see themselves reflected (and affirmed) in the curriculum. At the very least, this means that teachers must expose students to high quality multicultural books and materials, create lesson plans that focus on multicultural

themes and concepts, and expose students to culturally diverse role models (e.g., using biographies and having speakers visit classrooms). What resources accurately and effectively teach about slavery? What materials and resources offer multiple perspectives on the Trail of Tears? How can we ensure that all subject areas (including math and science) have a multicultural focus?

As described in Table 39.5, Banks (1999) outlined four levels to infusing multicultural content into the curriculum: the contributions approach, additive approach, transformation approach, and social action approach. Teachers must try to teach at the highest levels so that students have a substantive understanding and appreciation of diverse populations.

Harris and I (Ford & Harris, 1999) extended the Banks model by incorporating Bloom's taxonomy. We contend that an education for gifted students must challenge them as gifted individuals and cultural beings at the highest level of Bloom's taxonomy and Banks' model. Consequently, Harris and I created the Ford-Harris matrix (also known as the Bloom-Banks matrix). As Table 39.6 illustrates, it is

Table 39.5   Levels of Integration of Multicultural Content into Curriculum.

Level 4 **The Social Action Approach**	Students make decisions on important social issues and take actions to help solve them. Students become empowered to make meaningful contributions to the resolution of social issues and problems.
Level 3 **The Transformation Approach**	The structure of the curriculum is changed to enable students to view concepts, issues, events, and themes from the perspectives of different cultural groups. Students are provided multiple perspectives and viewpoints on issues, concepts, topics, and events. They are encouraged to be empathic and consider events through more than one pair of lenses.
Level 2 **The Additive Approach**	Content, concepts, themes, and perspectives are added to the curriculum without changing its structure. For example, teachers may add a book to the curriculum, or add a diverse scientist to the list of famous scientists that students will study in a unit. Changes to the curriculum often occur during certain times (e.g., Black History Month) rather than throughout the year. Multiculturalism is not an integral part of the curriculum—it is an add-on. Consequently, students fail to understand how the predominant culture interacts with and is related to culturally diverse groups.
Level 1 **The Contributions Approach**	Teachers focus on heroes, holidays, and discrete cultural elements when teaching about diverse cultures and topics. For example, students may study teepees in a unit on Native Americans; they may learn about Kwanzaa when studying about African Americans. Or students study foods and holidays. As a result, students acquire a superficial understanding of culturally diverse groups.

Source: Adapted from Banks (1999).

Table 39.6 **Ford-Harris Matrix Using Bloom-Banks Model: Definition/Description of Categories.**

	Knowledge	Comprehension	Application	Analysis	Synthesis	Evaluation
Contributions	Students are taught and know facts about cultural artifacts, events, groups, and other cultural elements.	Students show an understanding of information about cultural artifacts, groups, etc.	Students can apply information learned on cultural artifacts, events, etc.	Students are taught to analyze (e.g., compare and contrast) information about cultural artifacts, groups, etc.	Students are required to create a new product from the information on cultural artifacts, groups, etc.	Students are taught to evaluate facts and information based on cultural artifacts, groups, etc.
Additive	Students are taught concepts and themes about cultural groups.	Students are taught cultural concepts and themes.	Students are required to apply information learned about cultural concepts and themes.	Students are taught to analyze important cultural concepts and themes.	Students are asked to synthesize important information on cultural concepts and themes.	Students are taught to critique cultural concepts and themes.
Transformation	Students are given information on important cultural elements, groups, etc., and can understand this information from different perspectives.	Students are taught to understand and can demonstrate an understanding of important cultural concepts and themes from different perspectives.	Students are asked to apply their understanding of important concepts and themes from different perspectives.	Students are taught to examine important cultural concepts and themes from more than one perspective.	Students are required to create a product based on their new perspective or the perspective of another group.	Students are taught to evaluate or judge important cultural concepts and themes from different viewpoints (e.g., minority group).
Social action	Based on information on cultural artifacts, etc., students make recommendations for social action.	Based on their understanding of important concepts and themes, students make recommendations for social action.	Students can apply their understanding of important social and cultural issues; they make recommendations and take action on these issues.	Students are required to analyze social and cultural issues from different perspectives; they take action on these issues.	Students create a plan of action to address social and cultural issue(s); they seek important social change.	Students critique important social and cultural issues, and seek to make national and/or international change.

Note: Actions taken on the *social action* level can range from immediate and small scale (e.g., classroom and school level) to moderate (e.g., community or regional level) to large scale (state, national, and international levels). Likewise, students can make recommendations for action or actually take social action.

possible for every teacher in every subject area to create lesson plans that challenge students cognitively and multiculturally.

Develop Home-School Partnerships

In theory, school districts consider family involvement central to student achievement. In practice, few schools consistently and aggressively build partnerships with diverse families (Ford, 1996). During the first week of school and constantly thereafter, teachers and administrators must make sure that diverse families know that the school district offers gifted education services. They must understand referral and screening measures and procedures, and know how placement decisions are made. Just as important, diverse families must understand the purpose and benefits of gifted education. Efforts by schools must be aggressive and proactive; school personnel need to go into diverse communities (e.g., visit homes), attend minority-sponsored events, and seek the support of minority churches and corporations to build home-school partnerships.

Equally important, efforts should focus on family education—holding workshops and meetings to educate diverse parents how to meet the needs of their gifted children and advocate for them. As I have noted elsewhere (Ford, 1996), culturally diverse parents need strategies for helping their children cope with peer pressures and social injustices, for maintaining achievement, and for staying motivated and goal-oriented in the face of social injustices.

Ongoing Evaluation

No easy or quick fixes can increase opportunities for diverse students to have access to gifted education services. Educators at all levels (e.g., teachers, administrators) and in all positions (e.g., counselors, psychologists) must constantly evaluate and re-evaluate their efforts to recruit and retain diverse students in gifted education. This examination must focus on instruments, definitions, policies and procedures, curriculum and instruction, and staff development. Armed with such information, schools can be proactive in opening doors that have been historically closed to diverse students.

The success schools achieve at diversifying or "desegregating" gifted education depends heavily on critical self-examination, and on a willingness to move beyond the equity versus excellence debate and beyond deficit thinking. As Borland (1996) suggested, gifted education must begin to question and examine its fundamental premises and practices to see if they remain (or ever were) valid. Students in the gifted program should closely represent the community's demographics. The reasons for disparities must be evaluated and rectified.

SUMMARY AND CONCLUSIONS

There is a wealth of talent and intelligence in this field of gifted education, but I worry that we are using it to defend yesterday, not to imagine and build tomorrow. (Borland, 1996).

Clearly, controversy exists regarding why diverse students are underrepresented in gifted education. The controversy focuses on whether the causes include deficiencies in the children and their families, or discriminatory practices of schools and society that restrict the search for, and discovery of, minority talent. Giftedness is a social construct; therefore, inclusiveness is the philosophy of choice for ensuring equity and excellence. For the sake of children, we must err on the side of inclusion rather than exclusion.

The persistent and pervasive underrepresentation of diverse students in gifted education is likely to have devastating, long-lasting effects. We can attribute much of this difficulty to deficit thinking, which limits access and opportunity. Likewise, doing what is in the best interest of diverse students has been hampered by debates between equity and excellence. How many more diverse children must suffer while we debate this issue? What changes are we willing to make in the new millennium?

The goal of every educator must be to find and nurture all gifted students. This goal is non-negotiable.

QUESTIONS FOR THOUGHT AND DISCUSSION

1. Look at the cultural differences Ford explains in Table 39.2 (also the second column of Tables 39.3 and 39.4). Which three cultural styles might damage a minority student's school performance the most? Why? Which three would be the most helpful? Why?

2. What are some sensible alternatives to ability and achievement tests for recruitment?

3. a. Which would be most important, multicultural education programs for staff or students? Explain.

    b. Look again at Tables 39.5 and 39.6. What should be the goals of a *good* multicultural education program?

4. Explain what Ford means by *supportive, intrinsic,* and *remedial* strategies.

REFERENCES

American Psychological Association. (1999). *Standards for educational and psychological testing.* Washington, DC: Author.

Banks, J. A. (1999). *Introduction to multicultural education* (2nd ed.). Boston: Allyn and Bacon.

Borland, J. H. (1996). Gifted education and the threat of irrelevance. *Journal for the Education of the Gifted, 16,* 129–147.

Boykin, A. W. (1994). Afrocultural expression and its implications for schooling. In E. R. Hollins, J. E. King, & W. C. Hayman (Eds.), *Teaching diverse populations: Formulating a knowledge base* (pp. 225–273). New York: State University of New York Press.

Colangelo, N. & Davis, G. A. (Eds.). (1997). *Handbook of gifted education* (2nd ed.). Boston: Allyn and Bacon.

Davis, G. A., & Rimm, S. B. (1998). *Education of the gifted and talented* (4th ed.). Boston: Allyn and Bacon.

Educational Policies Commission. (1950). *Education of the gifted.* Washington, DC: National Education Association and American Association of School Administrators.

Ford, D. Y. (1996). *Reversing underachievement among gifted Black students: Promising practices and programs.* New York: Teachers College Press.

Ford, D. Y. (1998a). *Factors affecting the career decision making of minority teachers in gifted education.* Storrs, CT: National Research Center on the Gifted and Talented, University of Connecticut.

Ford, D. Y. (1998b). The underrepresentation of minority students in special education: Problems and promises in recruitment and retention. *Journal of Special Education, 32*(1), 4–14.

Ford, D. Y., Grantham, T. C., & Harris III, J. J. (1998). Multicultural gifted education: A wakeup call to the profession. *Roeper Review, 19,* 72–78.

Ford, D. Y., & Harmon, D. A. (2001). Equity and excellence: Providing access to gifted education for culturally diverse students. *Journal of Secondary Gifted Education, 12*(3), 141–147.

Ford, D. Y., & Harris III, J. J. (1999). *Multicultural gifted education.* New York: Teachers College Press.

Ford, D. Y., & Harris III, J. J. (2000). A framework for infusing multicultural curriculum into gifted education. *Roeper Review, 23,* 4–10.

Ford, D. Y., Howard, T. C., Harris III, J. J., & Tyson, C. A. (2000). Creating culturally responsive classrooms for gifted minority students. *Journal for the Education of the Gifted, 23,* 397–427.

Frasier, M. M., Martin, D., Garcia, J., Finely, V. S., Frank, E., Krisel, S., & King, L. L. (1995). *A new window for looking at gifted children.* Storrs, CT: National Research Center on the Gifted and Talented, University of Connecticut.

Frasier, M. M., & Passow, A. H. (1996). *Toward a new paradigm for identifying talent potential.* National Research Center on the Gifted and Talented, University of Connecticut.

Gardner, H. (1983). *Frames of mind: The theory of multiple intelligences.* New York: Basic Books.

Hall, E. T. (1989). Unstated features of the cultural context of learning. *Educational Forum, 54,* 21–34.

Helms, J. E. (1992). Why is there no study of cultural equivalence in standardized cognitive ability testing? *American Psychologist, 47,* 1083–1101.

Herrnstein, R. I., & Murray, C. (1994). *The bell curve.* New York: Free Press.

Kaufman, A. S., & Kaufman, N. L. (1983). *Interpretative manual for the Kaufman Assessment Battery for Children (K-ABC).* Circle Pines, MN: American Guidance Service.

Lynch, E. W. (1992a). Developing cross-cultural competence. In E. W. Lynch & M. J. Hanson (Eds.), *Developing cross-cultural competence: A guide for working with young children and their families* (pp. 34–64). Baltimore: Brookes.

Lynch, E. W. (1992b). From culture shock to cultural learning. In E. W. Lynch & M. J. Hanson (Eds.), *Developing cross-cultural competence: A guide for working with young children and their families* (pp. 19–33). Baltimore: Brookes.

Menchaca, M. (1997). Early racist discourses: The roots of deficit thinking. In R. Valencia (Ed.), *The evolution of deficit thinking* (pp. 13–40). New York: Falmer.

Mercer, J. R. (1979). *System of Multicultural Pluralistic Assessment.* San Antonio: Psychological Corporation.

Nobles, W. W. (1990, January). *Infusion of African and African American culture.* Keynote address at the annual conference, Academic and Cultural Excellence: An Investment in Our Future, Detroit Public Schools, Detroit, MI.

Plessy v. Ferguson, 163, U.S. 537, 16 S. Ct. 1138; 41 L. Ed. 256 (1896).

Saccuzzo, D. P., Johnson, N. E., & Guertin, T. L. (1994). *Identifying underrepresented disadvantaged gifted and talented children: A multifaceted approach* (Vols. 1 & 2). San Diego: San Diego State University.

Sattler, J. H. (1992). *Assessment of children* (3rd ed., revised). San Diego, CA: Sattler.

Shade, B. J., Kelly, C., & Oberg, M. (1997). *Creating culturally responsive classrooms.* Washington, DC: American Psychological Association.

Sternberg, R. J. (1985). *Beyond IQ: A triarchic theory of human intelligence.* Cambridge, MA: Cambridge University Press.

U.S. Department of Education. (1993). *National excellence: A case for developing America's talent.* Washington, DC, Author.

40

Exceptional Spatial Abilities[1]

DAVID LUBINSKI, *Vanderbilt University*

A marked escalation of knowledge about the psychological underpinnings of intellectual precocity and gifted education has occurred over the past thirty years. Elements of much of this growth may be traced to Julian C. Stanley, who in 1971 launched a project that changed the landscape of gifted education permanently. At a time when many social scientists were following Kuhn's (1962) recommendations for scientific revolutions, by jettisoning the "normal science" of their disciplines and proposing "paradigm shifts," Stanley (1996; Keating & Stanley, 1972; Stanley, Keating, & Fox, 1974) did something different. He chose to stand on the strong shoulders of his intellectual predecessors, Leta Hollingworth (1926, 1942) and Lewis Terman (Terman et al., 1925–1959), to reach new heights by building on what they gave us.

Stanley did not reject what the construct of general intelligence had to offer gifted education. Rather, he assimilated this powerful dimension of psychological diversity and extended the psychometric approach to major group factors for identifying and developing more specific (less general) intellectual strengths. At the outset, because of his interest and experience in identifying and developing scientific talent, Stanley studied mathematical reasoning ability (Keating & Stanley, 1972; Stanley et al., 1974). But by 1980, his Study of Mathematically Precocious Youth (SMPY) devoted an equal amount of attention

to verbal reasoning ability (Benbow & Stanley, 1983; George, Cohn, & Stanley, 1979; Keating, 1976; Stanley, George, & Solano, 1977). To study long-term outcomes and the development of talent across the lifespan, SMPY, now based at Vanderbilt University, is currently tracking over 5,000 intellectually precocious youth, identified before age 13, through talent searches as being in the top 1% in verbal or mathematical reasoning ability (Lubinski & Benbow, 1994).[2]

Identifying intellectually precocious youth through assessment tools initially designed for college-bound high school seniors is one of applied psychology's major success stories (Benbow & Stanley, 1996; Lubinski, 1996, 2000; Stanley, 2000). It equips educators and counselors with the information and data they need to differentially plan educational programs that are developmentally appropriate for bright youth. Age 13 assessments using out-of-level tests such as SAT-Math and SAT-Verbal provide an ability profile that is quite diagnostic (Benbow & Lubinski, 1996; Benbow & Stanley, 1996). For example, SMPY's longitudinal findings of the contrasting developmental trajectories displayed by differential mathematical-verbal reasoning strengths have contributed fundamental understandings of exceptional developmental patterns and proclivities (Achter, Lubinski, & Benbow, 1996; Achter, Lubinski, Benbow, & Eftekhari-Sanjani, 1999; Lubinski & Benbow, 2000; Lubinski, Webb, Morelock, & Benbow, 2001). These can meaningfully effect practice. In addition, the potential of these findings to

1. I am indebted to Camilla Benbow and Julian C. Stanley for commenting on an earlier version of this chapter. Support for this article was provided by a grant from the National Science Foundation (MDR 8855625), an anonymous donor, and a Templeton Award for Positive Psychology.

2. See Chapter 15 by Lupkowski-Shoplik, Benbow, Assouline, and Brody.

inform educational policy is slowly emerging (Benbow & Stanley, 1996; Lubinski, Benbow, Shea, Eftekhari-Sanjani, & Halvorson, 2001).

Yet over the last ten years, particularly compelling evidence also has has emerged to demonstrate the importance of assessing other personal attributes in this special population. College entrance exams carry comparable construct validity for both intellectually precocious youth and college-bound high school seniors (Benbow & Stanley, 1996; Benbow & Lubinski, 1996), but so do other conceptually distinct instruments. For example, conventional interest and values questionnaires initially designed for adults have, among intellectually precocious young adolescents, uncovered marked individual differences (Achter et al., 1996), stability over 15- and 20-year intervals (Lubinski, Benbow, & Ryan, 1995; Lubinski, Schmidt, & Benbow, 1996), and construct (including predictive) validity (Schmidt, Lubinski, & Benbow, 1998). They help educators and counselors make better recommendations when working with gifted youth. A recent longitudinal study (Achter et al., 1999), for example, revealed the validity of such preference questionnaires over SAT-Math and SAT-Verbal scores in forecasting educational outcomes (four-year degree area) over a ten-year interval, age 13 to age 23. Collectively, these positive findings on nonintellectual attributes motivated a model for conceptualizing a multidimensional approach to talent identification and development. This model is discussed here, paying particular attention to spatial ability.[3]

Theory of Work Adjustment

Although the Theory of Work Adjustment (TWA) was initially developed to conceptualize work adjustment in adult populations (Dawis & Lofquist, 1984; Lofquist & Dawis, 1991), it has broader implications. Lubinski and Benbow (2000) extended its use to organizing the above ability/preference findings to create a multidimensional approach to talent development and to provide a model for conceptualizing lifelong learning. According to TWA, *optimal* learning and work environments are defined by the co-occurrence of two broad dimensions of correspondence. The first is *satisfactoriness* (a match between ability and ability requirements) and the second is *satisfaction* (a match between preferences and the rewards typical of learning and work environments).[4]

Spatial Ability

The next logical step suggested by this model is reaching out to a population of intellectually precocious youth that are currently underserved by modern talent searches. Excellent evidence suggests that a population of intellectually precocious youth, those with especially high spatial reasoning ability, is neglected (Gohm, Humphreys, & Yao, 1998; Humphreys, Lubinski, & Yao, 1993; Humphreys & Lubinski, 1996). They are an inconspicuous population. Unlike mathematical and verbal precocity, their distinctiveness involves talent in nonverbal ideation, and it is not given many opportunities to reveal itself (or be developed) in traditional school settings. Often, such individuals are also personologically more introverted and unassuming. Because there is a significantly smaller correlation between socioeconomic status and spatial ability, relative to mathematical or verbal ability, this special population comes disproportionately from lower SES levels, which increases the likelihood that such talent will not be recognized. Collectively, these considerations point to a pool of students with unmet *personal* needs and a loss of human potential for many kinds of *societal* needs.

Figure 40.1 contains a model of cognitive abilities. There are three primary abilities. The spatial/mechanical component is distinct from verbal and mathematical reasoning abilities, the abilities most frequently assessed by current academic testing programs. Spatial ability is infrequently assessed. The correlations of spatial/mechanical measures are typically in the neighborhood of .60 or .70 with mathematical and verbal reasoning measures (Humphreys, Lubinski, & Yao, 1993). Therefore, approximately half of the students in the top 1% of spatial/mechanical ability are not identified for talent search opportunities because of the exclusive reliance on math and

---

3. For a deeper historical appreciation of this construct, with particular emphasis on its educational-vocational importance, readers are referred to Smith (1964); for a more modern treatment, see Lohman (1988, 1994).

4. For further explication of this model, and how it connects with other theoretical frameworks, see Lubinski and Benbow (2000); for applied practice in gifted education, see Benbow and Lubinski (1997).

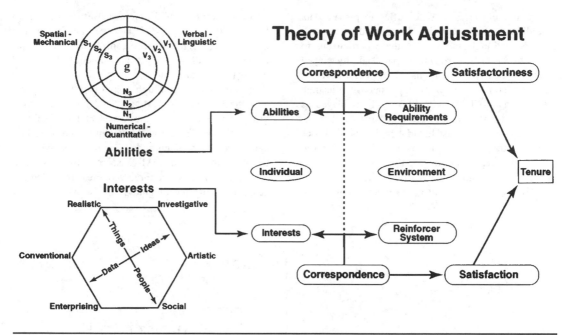

Figure 40.1 The Theory of Work Adjustment (right) combined with the radex scaling of cognitive abilities (upper left) and the RIASEC hexagon of interests (lower left) for conceptualizing personal attributes relevant to learning and work. The letters within the cognitive ability arrangement denote different regions of concentration whereas their accompanying numbers increase as a function of complexity. Contained within the RIASEC is a simplification of this hexagon. Following Prediger (1982), it amounts to a two-dimensional structure of independent dimensions: people/things and data/ideas, which underlie RIASEC. The dotted line running down the individual and environment sectors of TWA illustrates that TWA places equal emphasis on assessing the personal attributes (abilities and interests) and assessing the environment (ability requirements and reward structures). Taken from Lubinski and Benbow (2000).

verbal measures (Shea, Lubinski, & Benbow, 2001). That is, many of these unidentified students with top 1% spatial ability would not score exceptionally high on college entrance exams exclusively restricted to reasoning with numbers and words. Their gifts are in areas involving reasoning with figures and shapes, the kind of reasoning that characterizes architecture, engineering, the physical sciences, and many of the creative arts.

A variety of studies address the need to identify spatially talented students (see Gohm et al., 1998; Humphreys et al., 1993; Humphreys & Lubinski, 1996). One recently published study coming out of SMPY (Shea et al., 2001) is particularly compelling. In this investigation, 563 participants identified in the late 1970s were tracked longitudinally for 20 years. At the time of their initial identification (age 13), these participants were given the Differential Aptitude Test (DAT; Bennett, Seashore, & Wesman, 1974). Because they were selected for longitudinal tracking based on their SAT scores, this made it possible to document their developmental trajectory as a function of the three major cognitive abilities in Figure 40.1 (mathematical, spatial, and verbal ability). In what follows, we will focus on a spatial ability composite (DAT-C) formed by the equal weighting of DAT Space Relations and DAT Mechanical Reasoning.[5]

---

5. For a more detailed description of this study, which includes incremental validity analyses of each of the three ability measures (SAT-M, SAT-V, and DAT-C) relative to the other two, readers are referred to the original source (Shea et al., 2001).

For our purposes, it will suffice to present data regarding the high school, college, graduate school, and occupational outcomes of these participants to illustrate the critical role that spatial ability played in their educational/vocational choices and development. Of course, this will simultaneously illustrate the role that SAT-M and SAT-V abilities played as well. Specifically, data is presented first on participants' favorite and least favorite high school classes (based on their five-year follow up). This is followed by their undergraduate degree field (ten-year follow up), graduate school degree field (twenty-year follow up), and occupational group membership at age

33 (also twenty-year follow up). Before moving to Figures 40.2 through 40.6, however, an explanation of how these figures are organized is needed, because they follow a unique method of displaying multivariate data.

In Figures 40.2 through 40.6, open circles represent the bivariate SAT-M × SAT-V means for each group. The SAT-M is on the X-axis, and the SAT-V is on the Y-axis. The arrows projecting from these circles represent the magnitude (length) and sign (direction) of the mean DAT-C scores. In these and subsequent figures, the three variables are scaled the same, allowing the magnitude of the spatial ability

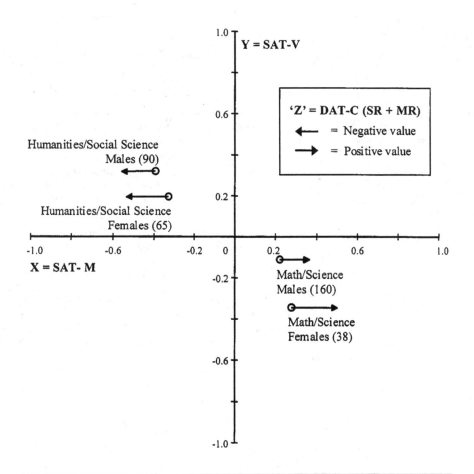

Figure 40.2 Trivariate means for favorite high-school-class groups. Ability variables are all on the same scale. Means are based on within-sex standardization using all participants. Group *N*s are provided in parentheses. Taken from Shea et al. (2001).

means to be ascertained by direct comparison with the X-axis. For example, in Figure 40.2, left-facing arrows represent DAT-C group means less than the grand mean for each sex (based on all participants), right-facing arrows represent DAT-C group means greater than the grand mean. The distribution of group centroids can be more fully appreciated by mentally rotating the left-facing arrows downward ("below" the page) and the right-facing arrows upward ("above" the page) around an imaginary Z-axis. This Z-axis should be rotated such that it is independent of both X and Y (i.e., at a 90° angle to them). Viewed this way, the arrowheads represent the group centroids (or trivariate means), and comparisons

among all groups on all three abilities can be made simultaneously in three-dimensional space.

Now with respect to Figure 40.2, favorite high school class, here is what Shea and colleagues (2001) found. Both males and females in the math/science group (i.e., math/science was their favorite class) tended to have stronger math and spatial ability and lower verbal ability, relative to their gender-equivalent peers who belong to the humanities and social science group (i.e., those whose favorite class was in humanities or social science). The inverse pattern holds for the humanities/social science groups (i.e., those whose favorite course was in this area), where males' and females' within-sex standardized means

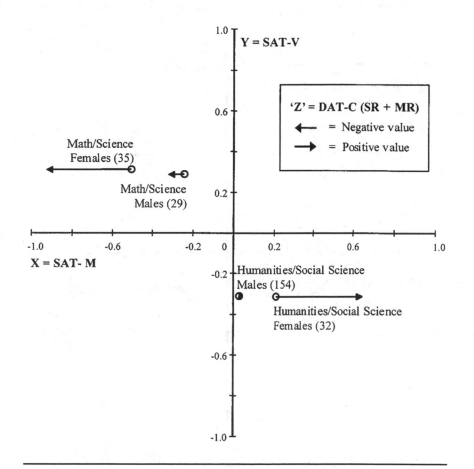

Figure 40.3 Trivariate means for least favorite high school class groups. Ability variables are all on the same scale. Means are based on within-sex standardization using all participants. Group *N*s are provided in parentheses. Taken from Shea et al. (2001).

for SAT-M and DAT-C are below those for the entire sample of 563 participants and the within-sex SAT-V group means are greater. (It is important to keep in mind, however, when comparing these groups that they are all highly able individuals. That is, differences reflect *relative* differences in strength.) Comparing the male and female groups, the patterns observed are strikingly similar. An important sex difference, however, is that the majority of males in this analysis (64%) chose a math or science class as their favorite, while a minority of females (37%) did so. Yet the other relation held.

For least favorite class (Figure 40.3), the trends seen in the previous figure are reversed, but for females the two centroids are much farther apart than those for the males. For males, mean differences in

verbal ability primarily distinguish these math/science and humanities/social science groups, with the latter group having a substantially smaller SAT-V mean but small differences between groups in SAT-M and DAT-C means. The female groups clearly differ on all three means. The female math/science least-favorite group has lower mathematical and spatial within-sex means and a larger verbal mean, whereas the humanities/social science least-favorite group shows the reverse ability pattern. A sex difference in choice of least favorite course is again evident. Among males, the majority (84%) chose a humanities or social science as their least favorite, while a slight minority of females (48%) did so.

Shifting focus now from high school to college, Figure 40.4 displays trivariate means for the eight

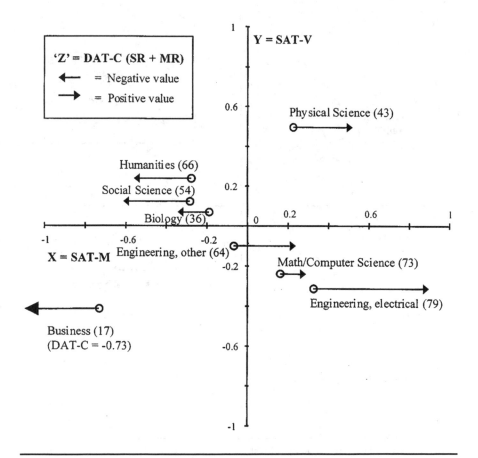

Figure 40.4 Trivariate means for conferred bachelor degree groups. Ability variables are all on the same scale. Means are based on standardization using all participants. Group *N*s are provided in parentheses. Taken from Shea et al. (2001).

bachelor's degree groups. Participants who majored in mathematics, computer science, or electrical engineering showed greater mathematical and spatial abilities, while those majoring in the humanities, social sciences, and biology were relatively more verbally able. The physical science majors tend to be relatively more able in all three ability domains, while the business majors are relatively less able than all other groups in all three abilities. (Note that for the business group, the large arrowhead illustrates that the magnitude of this group's relative weakness in spatial ability, which is actually twice as great as that indicated by the displayed length.) The "other engineering" group seems to be characterized by higher DAT-C scores relative to their SAT-M and SAT-V scores. Overall, these patterns are consistent with

prior expectations—engineering requires more spatial ability, business relatively little.

Trivariate means for the eight graduate-degrees groups are found in Figure 40.5. As with the undergraduate degree means, these centroids are consistent with prior findings. The humanities/social science group obtained the highest SAT-V mean, the math/computer science group has the highest SAT-M mean, and the electrical engineering group has the highest DAT-C mean.

Upon close scrutiny, however, it can be seen that consideration of all three abilities, conjointly, greatly facilitates the task of distinguishing group membership. For instance, the math/computer science and other-engineering group can be distinguished only in terms of mathematical ability, while spatial ability

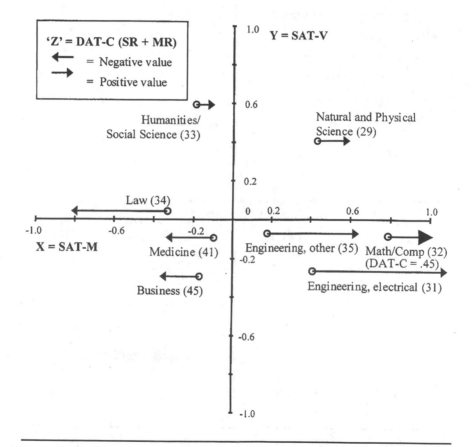

Figure 40.5 Trivariate means for conferred graduate degree groups. Ability variables are all on the same scale. Means are based on standardization using all participants. Group *N*s are provided in parentheses. Taken from Shea et al. (2001).

provides the greatest separation between the other-engineering group and medicine. In turn, the medical students' centroid is best distinguished from the humanities/social science group by lower verbal ability. The separation between the law group and the electrical engineering group is quite large when all three abilities are considered simultaneously. (Note again that the large arrowhead for the math/computer science group indicates a spatial ability mean twice the magnitude of that indicated by the displayed length.)

Occupational group data are displayed in Figure 40.6. Despite significant migration across categories from undergraduate or graduate degree groups to occupational groups, the pattern in previous figures is maintained here. Again, the importance of spatial

ability is evident from an analysis of these data. Comparing the engineering and medicine groups, for instance, the SAT-M provides little differentiation, but the DAT-C and, to a lesser extent, SAT-V seem to account for the separation between these centroids. Likewise, what distinguishes the law group from the business group (in fact from all of these groups) appears to be the law group's relatively lower spatial-ability mean.

Overall, this developmentally sequenced five-figure series illustrates the importance of spatial visualization in structuring important outcomes in the lives of these participants throughout their educational and vocational development. Clearly, many highly able students are missed by current talent search practices,

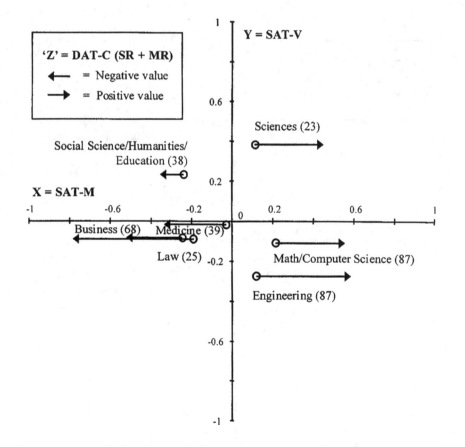

Figure 40.6 Trivariate means for occupational groups at age 33. Ability variables are scaled on a uniform metric. Means are based on standardization using all participants. Group *N*s are provided in parentheses. Taken from Shea et al. (2001).

and they are at risk for underachievement (Gohm et al., 1998; Humphreys et al., 1993). Many young adolescents scoring, say, within the 75th to 95th percentile in mathematical and verbal reasoning measures, but who possess exceptional gifts in spatial visualization, are currently missed by talent searches. In disciplines that place a premium on nonverbal ideation, such students would readily "compensate" for their *relatively* low math and verbal abilities with their exceptional talent in spatial visualization. They also would likely do fine in summer residential programs for spatially talented youth. But, of course, there are essentially no special opportunities for spatially gifted students in the 75–95 percent math/verbal ability range at summer residential programs for intellectually talented youth or even in their regular schools. But there should be.

Unique Needs

Ackerman (1996; Ackerman & Heggestad, 1997) has shown that mathematical, spatial, and verbal abilities covary in unique ways with educational and vocational interests as well as personality dimensions. And this finding has been replicated with intellectually precocious young adolescents (Schmidt et al., 1998). Ackerman's model of intellectual development construes expertise and skill development as a function of interests, personality, and intelligence-as-process (PPIK), and provides a developmental foundation for concepts and findings inspired by TWA (Lubinski & Benbow, 2000). One important implication derived from the empirical findings of both PPIK and TWA is that selecting students based exclusively on either mathematical, spatial, or verbal ability engenders group differences in a host of nonintellectual personal attributes. For example, spatial ability covaries negatively with social interests but positively with mechanical interests, while verbal ability has the inverse pattern.

To be sure, talent identification programs must be aware of the importance of spatial abilities for selecting young adolescents for learning opportunities tailored to their unique strengths and interests, that is, for "appropriate developmental placement" (Lubinski & Benbow, 2000), because many of these students are not currently being identified. Clearly, a spatial ability instrument should be added to the talent search procedure. However, once these students are identified, counselors and educators need to be aware of the unique patterns of individuality (interests and values)

that co-occur with selecting high-math, high-verbal, and high-spatial students (Lubinski & Benbow, 2000). These three groups, selected by their high potential in distinct cognitive abilities, manifest contrasting profiles of nonintellectual attributes across interests, personality, and values. Because of the unique sensitivities and the developmental trajectories that result from these differences (Lubinski, 1996, 2000), distinct academic *and* nonacademic needs are certain to characterize each group (Gohm et al., 1998; Humphreys et al., 1993; Humphreys & Lubinski, 1996).

SUMMARY AND CONCLUSIONS

Augmenting Talent Search Procedures

We need to create systematic procedures for identifying spatially talented young adolescents. Spatially talented kids gravitate to environments and hobbies that involve opportunities to build, create, manipulate, and shape materials and objects (Humphreys et al., 1993). Their preferred hobbies (relative to their mathematically and verbally precocious peers) all appear to involve objects that are created, shaped, or transformed (Gohm et al., 1998; Humphreys et al., 1993): artwork, assembling, building, cooking, designing, drawing, gardening, inventing, painting, repairing, and others.

In school settings, architectural design classes, computer laboratories, wood and metal shops, workshops in the creative arts, and physical science laboratories are good places to look for them. Implementing a talent search for students who distinguish themselves in these settings is likely to uncover a number of young adolescents with highly developed spatial abilities. There are many spatial visualization measures available for doing so (Bennett, Seashore, & Wesman, 1974; Carroll, 1993; Eliot, 1987; Eliot & Smith, 1983; Stumpf, 2000; Stumpf & Eliot, 1999).

Curriculum Changes

Spatially talented kids tend to display an uneven pattern of grades. They tend to excel in course work that contains a large hands-on component, for example, creative arts, laboratory bench work, or technical shops. In designing appropriate developmental placement opportunities for spatially talented students, it is ideal to have a large component of manual manipulation in the curriculum. Working with "materials" or "things" readily found in agriculture, architecture, computer simulation, engineering (robotics), and bench work in the physical sciences and creative arts are ideal settings for developing their talent. Given the unique interest pattern that characterizes spatially talented kids, it might even be good to suggest options to them in other educational contexts. For example, in English literature classes it might be profitable to have options such as reading the biographies of Edison or Curie as well as other distinguished laboratory scientists and inventors to facilitate their appreciation of literature (Humphreys et al., 1993; Humphreys & Lubinski, 1996). Certainly, summer residential programs for these students need to involve many hands-on experiences relative to more "bookish" ones.

Educational Counseling

In addition to identifying spatially talented young adolescents and providing developmentally appropriate learning opportunities, educational counselors need to understand the role spatial ability plays in immediate choice and long-term development in other areas. The five developmentally sequenced figures reviewed here illustrate how spatial ability structures educational-vocational outcomes of participants in the top half of the top 1% in general intellectual ability. From an individual differences point of view (Dawis, 1992, 2001; Tyler, 1992), the models that counseling psychologists have used for conceptualizing educational-vocational choice, and performance after choice, have stressed the importance of focusing on strengths or the salient features of one's individuality (Achter & Lubinski, in press; Dawis, 1992, 2001; Tyler, 1992; Williamson, 1965). Whether systematic or not, this appears to be precisely what these SMPY participants were doing (Figures 40.2 through 40.6).

Counselors need to incorporate spatial ability assessments (more routinely) into their practice for advising students not only to consider certain learning environments, but also for pointing out environments that they are likely to find particularly challenging and perhaps overwhelming. Spatially talented students with relatively modest quantitative and verbal reasoning abilities are at risk for academic underachievement, because the standard educational curriculum requires them to operate in learning environments that stress reasoning with numbers and words. Also, quantitative and verbally talented students with relatively modest spatial ability need to know that their developmental potential varies across the educational-vocational spectrum. Intellectually precocious students with relatively modest spatial ability are likely to find that environments that place a premium on deep, conceptual nonverbal ideation (thinking about shapes and figures) are particularly challenging, especially compared to how they typically find most academic settings. Knowing both one's strengths and relative weaknesses is important.

Spatial ability is an inconspicuous and under-appreciated dimension of cognitive functioning; as it has all along, it will continue to operate whether or not we choose to measure it (Humphreys et al., 1993; Smith, 1964). However, if we continue to neglect its importance in education and counseling, at least two things are certain: frustration will be encountered in some mathematically and verbally talented students, while some spatially gifted students will underdevelop their potential.

Standing on Stanley

Just as Julian C. Stanley stood on the shoulders of Leta Hollingworth and Lewis Terman to reveal the importance of going beyond the construct of general intelligence by measuring the specific mathematical and verbal reasoning abilities of intellectually precocious youth, it is time for modern procedures to take the next logical step. It is clear that measures of spatial visualization, initially designed for high school students and young adults, have construct validity for intellectually precocious youth. The evidence is clear that seeking out this special population and implementing a talent search using measures of spatial-visualization will pay high dividends. At the very least, we need to identify the approximately 50% of the top 1% of spatially talented students who are lost currently by modern talent search procedures. This will not only better meet the needs of this special population, but also, by facilitating their development, the human capital needed to maintain and advance our ever-changing technical world will be insured. Finally, on a more basic theoretical level, launching such an effort will contribute to a more comprehensive understanding of exceptional forms of intellectual precocity and lifelong learning (Lubinski & Benbow, 2000).

QUESTIONS FOR THOUGHT AND DISCUSSION

1. What damage may have been (and is) done by Talent Searches and other gifted identification procedures that ignore spatial ability?

2. Can you explain the meaning and significance of Figures 40.2 through 40.6? Can you easily visualize each graph in three-dimensional space? Why might you have trouble?

3. Explain Lubinski's Theory of Work Adjustment. Do you agree with his interpretations of its importance? Explain.

4. What curriculum implications are evident based on understanding spatial abilities?

REFERENCES

Achter, J. A., & Lubinski, D. (in press). Fostering optimal development in intellectually talented populations. In W. B. Walsh (Ed.), *Counseling psychology and optimal human functioning.* Hillsdale, NJ: Erlbaum.

Achter, J. A., Lubinski, D., & Benbow, C. P. (1996). Multipotentiality among intellectually gifted: "It was never there and already it's vanishing." *Journal of Counseling Psychology, 43,* 65–76.

Achter, J. A., Lubinski, D., Benbow, C. P., & Eftekhari-Sanjani, H. (1999). Assessing vocational preferences among intellectually gifted adolescents adds incremental validity to abilities: A discriminant analysis of educational outcomes over a 10-year interval. *Journal of Educational Psychology, 91,* 777–786.

Ackerman, P. L. (1996). A theory of adult intellectual development: Process, personality, interests, and knowledge. *Intelligence, 22,* 227–257.

Ackerman, P. L., & Heggestad, E. D. (1997). Intelligence, personality, and interests: Evidence for overlapping traits. *Psychological Bulletin, 121,* 218–245.

Benbow, C. P., & Lubinski, D. (Eds.), (1996). *Intellectual talent: Psychometric and social issues.* Baltimore: Johns Hopkins University Press.

Benbow, C. P., & Lubinski, D. (1997). Intellectually talented children: How can we best meet their needs? In N. Colangelo & G. A. Davis (Eds.), *Handbook of gifted education* (2nd ed., pp. 155–169). Boston: Allyn and Bacon.

Benbow, C. P., & Stanley, J. C. (1983). *Academic precocity: Aspects of its development.* Baltimore: Johns Hopkins University Press.

Benbow, C. P., & Stanley, J. C. (1996). Inequity in equity: How "equity" can lead to inequity for high-potential students. *Psychology, Public Policy, and Law, 2,* 249–292.

Bennett, G. K., Seashore, H. G., & Wesman, A. G. (1974). *Manual for the Differential Aptitude Tests* (5th ed.). New York: Psychological Corporation.

Carroll, J. B. (1993). *Human cognitive abilities: A survey of factor-analytic studies.* Cambridge: Cambridge University Press.

Dawis, R. V. (1992). The individual differences tradition in counseling psychology. *Journal of Counseling Psychology, 39,* 7–19.

Dawis, R. V. (2001). Toward a psychology of values. *The Counseling Psychologist, 29,* 458–465.

Dawis, R. V., & Lofquist, L. H. (1984). *A psychological theory of work adjustment.* Minneapolis: University of Minnesota Press.

Eliot, J. C. (1987). *Models of psychological space: Psychometric, developmental, and experimental approaches.* New York: Springer-Verlag.

Eliot, J. C., & Smith, I. M. (1983). *An international dictionary of spatial tests.* Windsor, England: NFER-Nelson.

George, W. C., Cohn, S. J., & Stanley, J. C. (1979). *Educating the gifted: Acceleration and enrichment.* Baltimore: Johns Hopkins University Press.

Gohm, C. L., Humphreys, L. G., & Yao, G. (1998). Underachievement among spatially gifted students. *American Educational Research Journal, 35,* 515–531.

Hollingworth, L. S. (1926). *Gifted children.* New York: Macmillan.

Hollingworth, L. S. (1942). *Children above 180 IQ.* New York: World Book.

Humphreys, L. G., & Lubinski, D. (1996). Assessing spatial visualization: An underappreciated ability for many school and work settings. In C. P. Benbow & D. Lubinski (Eds.), *Intellectual talent: Psychometric and social issues.* Baltimore: Johns Hopkins University Press.

Humphreys, L. G., Lubinski, D., & Yao, G. (1993). Utility of predicting group membership and the role of spatial visualization in becoming an engineer, physical scientist, or artist. *Journal of Applied Psychology, 78,* 250–261.

Keating, D. P. (1976). *Intellectual talent: Research and development.* Baltimore: Johns Hopkins University Press.

Keating, D. P., & Stanley, J. C. (1972). Extreme measures for the exceptionally gifted in mathematics and science. *Educational Researcher, 1,* 3–7.

Kuhn, T. S. (1962). *The structure of scientific revolutions.* Chicago: University of Chicago Press.

Lofquist, L. H., & Dawis, R. V. (1991). *Essentials of person environment correspondence counseling.* Minneapolis: University of Minnesota Press.

Lohman, D. F. (1988). Spatial abilities as traits, processes, and knowledge. In R. J. Sternberg (Ed.), *Advances in the psychology of human intelligence* (Vol. 4, pp. 181–248). Hillsdale, NJ: Erlbaum.

Lohman, D. F. (1994). Spatially gifted, verbally inconvenienced. In N. Colangelo, S. G. Assouline, & D. L. Ambroson (Eds.), *Proceedings of the Henry B. and Jocelyn Wallace National Research Symposium on Talent Development* (2nd ed., pp. 25–264). Dayton, OH: Ohio Psychology Press.

Lubinski, D. (1996). Applied individual differences research and its quantitative methods. *Psychology, Public Policy, and Law, 2*, 187–203.

Lubinski, D. (2000). Scientific and social significance of assessing individual differences: "Sinking shafts at a few critical points." *Annual Review of Psychology, 51*, 405–444.

Lubinski, D., & Benbow, C. P. (1994). The Study of Mathematically Precocious Youth: The first three decades of a planned 50-year study of intellectual talent. In R. F. Subotnik & K. D. Arnold (Eds.), *Beyond Terman: Contemporary longitudinal studies of giftedness and talent* (pp. 255–281). Norwood, NJ: Ablex.

Lubinski, D., & Benbow, C. P. (2000). States of excellence. *American Psychologist, 55*, 137–150.

Lubinski, D., Benbow, C. P., & Ryan, J. (1995). Stability of vocational interests among the intellectually gifted from adolescence to adulthood: A 15-year longitudinal study. *Journal of Applied Psychology, 80*, 196–200.

Lubinski, D., Benbow, C. P., Shea, D. L., Eftekhari-Sanjani, H., & Halvorson, M. B. J. (2001). Men and woman at promise for scientific excellence: Similarity not dissimilarity. *Psychological Science, 12*, 309–317.

Lubinski, D., Schmidt, D. B., & Benbow, C. P. (1996). A 20-year stability analysis of the Study of Values for intellectually gifted individuals from adolescence to adulthood. *Journal of Applied Psychology, 81*, 443–451.

Lubinski, D., Webb, R. M., Morelock, M. J., & Benbow, C. P. (2001). Top 1 in 10,000: A 10-year follow-up of the profoundly gifted. *Journal of Applied Psychology, 86*, 718–729.

Prediger, D. J., (1982). Dimensions underlying Holland's hexagon: Missing link between interests and occupations? *Journal of Vocational Behavior, 21*, 259–287.

Schmidt, D. B., Lubinski, D., & Benbow, C. P. (1998). Validity of assessing educational-vocational preference dimensions among intellectually talented 13-year olds. *Journal of Counseling Psychology, 45*, 436–453.

Shea, D. L., Lubinski, D., & Benbow, C. P. (2001). Importance of assessing spatial ability in intellectually talented young adolescents: A 20-year longitudinal study. *Journal of Educational Psychology, 93*, 604–614.

Smith, I. M. (1964). *Spatial ability: Its educational and social significance.* San Diego: Knapp.

Stanley, J. C. (1996). In the beginning: The Study of Mathematically Precocious Youth. In C. P. Benbow & D. Lubinski (Eds.) *Intellectual talent: Psychometric and social issues* (pp. 225–235). Baltimore: Johns Hopkins University Press.

Stanley, J. C. (2000). Helping students learn only what they don't already know. *Psychology, Public Policy, and Law, 8*, 216–222.

Stanley, J. C., George, W. C., & Solano, C. H. (1977). *The gifted and the creative: A fifty-year perspective.* Baltimore: Johns Hopkins University Press.

Stanley, J. C., Keating, D. P., & Fox, L. H. (1974). *Mathematical talent: Discovery, description, and development.* Baltimore: Johns Hopkins University Press.

Stumpf, H. (2000). On the predictive validity of the Scholastic Assessment Test I (SAT I) and the Spatial Test Battery (STB) with respect to teacher evaluations of performance in CTY and CAA mathematics and science courses (Summer 1999). *Technical Report No. 25, Center for Talented Youth.* Baltimore: Johns Hopkins University.

Stumpf, H., & Eliot, J. C. (1999). A structural analysis of spatial ability in academically talented students. *Learning and Individual Differences, 11*, 137–151.

Terman, L. M., et al. (1925–1959). *Genetic studies of genius* (Vols. 1–5). Stanford: Stanford University Press.

Tyler, L. E. (1992). Counseling psychology—Why? *Professional Psychology: Research and Practice, 23*, 342–344.

Williamson, E. G. (1965). *Vocational counseling.* New York: McGraw-Hill.

41

Gifted Children with Learning Disabilities

LINDA KREGER SILVERMAN, *Gifted Development Center and the Institute for the Study of Advanced Development, Denver*

How can a child be both exceptionally able and "dis-abled"? This appears to be a contradiction in terms. The paradoxical combination of giftedness and learning disabilities has been viewed as "entirely incompatible and irreconcilable in any single child" (Tannenbaum & Baldwin, 1983, p. 12). Yet, the incidence of learning disabilities in the gifted population is at least as high as the incidence in the general population (10–15%), and some preliminary investigations suggest that the risk of learning disorders increases as a function of IQ (Silverman, 2002). In a study of 241 children with IQ scores in excess of 160, 40 of the fathers (16%) were reported as having dyslexia or other learning difficulties (Rogers & Silverman, 1997). Children in the highest IQ ranges often have attention deficit symptoms, sensory integration issues, or both. Some suffer from dyslexia (reading disability), dysgraphia (writing disability), Asperger's Syndrome (severe impairment of social interaction), or combinations of symptoms that do not clearly fit any diagnostic category.

Recognition of this group has been hindered by the common perception that giftedness equates with academic achievement. For example, Hagen (1980) recommended that in determining placement in gifted programs, major weight should be given to "demonstrated achievement, because it is the best single predictor of future achievement" (pp. 39–40). A bright child who is slow at learning to read, or fails to memorize the multiplication facts, or has difficulty paying attention in school, or cannot master handwriting, is not likely to be regarded as gifted. And when a student obtains high scores on tests or is outstanding at reading, mathematics, or oral communication, exceptional ability may be obvious, but the co-existence of

a learning disorder may not be evident. Indeed, poor performance in any area is usually considered volitional and attributed to lack of effort, "laziness," lack of discipline, inattentiveness, or lack of interest. Such a student is likely to be labeled an "underachiever" and blamed instead of helped. A major cause of underachievement in the gifted appears to be undetected learning disabilities (Silverman, 1989).

It is possible for giftedness to co-exist with nearly all disabilities—even retardation, if one includes savants.[1] There are gifted children who are deaf or hard of hearing, blind or partially sighted, paraplegic, with cerebral palsy, with debilitating diseases, who have missing limbs or have lost the use of limbs, or have other physical impairments. Individuals with physical disabilities are often treated as if they lack intelligence. Attention is paid to their deficiencies, rather than to the development of their gifts. Wheelchair-bound adults have experienced people talking louder and slower to them, with simpler vocabulary, as if they were hearing impaired and senile. Individuals with cerebral palsy are often highly intelligent, but find that their imperfect motor control is mistakenly interpreted as retardation. Continuously being treated as unintelligent takes its toll on self-esteem. Some disabled persons never come to recognize their own intelligence or believe in their capabilities.

Strong parental advocacy, public awareness programs, and federal legislation have gone a long way in improving the quality of life, mobility, educational and employment opportunities, and protection of

---

1. See Chapter 35 by Morelock and Feldman.

physically challenged children and adults. However, there is a group of disabled children who remain virtually defenseless. These children are physically healthy and highly intelligent, but poorly coordinated, dyslexic, dysgraphic, anxious, or hyperactive. They are often teased by their classmates, misunderstood by their teachers, disqualified for gifted programs due to their deficiencies, and unserved by special education because of their strengths. Twice-exceptional learners can become casualties of a system that refuses to acknowledge their existence, fails to identify them, and does not support their strengths or assist them with their weaknesses. Too often, they are left on their own to cope with their differences.

The Most Prevalent Learning Disabilities in the Gifted

The following learning disabilities have surfaced most frequently at our Gifted Development Center, which specializes in assessing children with dual exceptionality:

Sensory integration dysfunction

Attention deficit hyperactivity disorder (ADHD)

Auditory processing disorder

Visual processing deficits

Dyslexia

Spatial disorientation (Silverman, 2002)

Each of these syndromes is explained below.

Sensory Integration Dysfunction

Sensory integration is the organization of sensation, enabling the brain to construct meaning of experience (Ayres, 1979). Sensory integration *dysfunction* involves fine motor difficulties (e.g., writing and drawing), gross motor difficulties (e.g., riding a bicycle and catching a ball), or sensory modulation issues (e.g., intense reactions to sound, touch, light, smell, and taste). The most common signs are sensory defensiveness (e.g., stiffening up when being held), physical awkwardness and lack of muscle tone, not developing hand dominance before school age, and the inability to cross the midline (i.e., use one's right hand left of center). The symptoms for gifted children, however, tend to be more subtle. Some gifted

children are excellent athletes, but cannot write. Some lack physical energy and trunk strength, making it nearly impossible for them to sit up straight. Some have no problem with physical coordination, but are in a constant state of sensory overload. They wince at the sound of the vacuum cleaner, squint in fluorescent light, react strongly to perfumes and hairsprays, gag except with certain foods, wear only loose clothing, startle easily when approached from behind, or panic in crowded places. And some chew on their clothing because they are understimulated and in constant need of sensory stimulation.

Because the ability to integrate and make sense of sensory input is the neurological foundation for most functions, it follows that "sensory integrative dysfunctions are the basis for many, but not all learning disorders" (Ayres, 1979, p. 184). Sensory integration dysfunction is frequently observed in children and adults with a variety of disabilities, such as Asperger's Syndrome, autism, Nonverbal Learning Disorder, dyslexia, and ADHD (Roley, Blanche, & Schaaf, 2001). Since many symptoms of ADHD and sensory integration dysfunction overlap, an intense program of research is currently underway to determine psychophysiological and behavioral differences between the two syndromes (Mangeot et al., in press).

Attention Deficit Hyperactivity Disorder

There are two types of attention deficits: hyperactive/impulsive and inattentive (distractible). They often co-occur as a mixed type. Since ADHD is commonly thought of as hyperactivity, highly active boys are most likely to be labeled with this syndrome. The inattentive type, which does not involve extraneous movement, is likely to be overlooked. The diagnosis of ADHD is highly controversial, particularly in gifted education because so many gifted children are labeled ADHD and placed on medication. Although the question has been raised repeatedly, "Is it ADHD *or* giftedness?" (e.g., Cramond, 1994; Baum, Olenchak, & Owen, 1998; Webb & Latimer, 1993), recent investigators have studied ADHD *and* giftedness. Gifted children with ADHD have been found to be cognitively advanced, like other gifted children, but socially and emotionally immature and with poor self-regulation (Kaufmann & Castellanos, 2000; Lovecky, 2000, in press; Moon, Zentall, Grskovic, Hall, & Stormont, 2001).

Although the popular view is that ADHD is over-diagnosed in the gifted, it is equally plausible that

ADHD is underdiagnosed in this population. Gifted children with attention deficits can concentrate for long periods of time in their areas of interest, and they are often well-behaved and attentive in one-on-one situations with adults, such as in an individual assessment. However, they find it nearly impossible to focus their attention when they are not intellectually engaged (Kutner, 1999), and the hyperactive types have a difficult time controlling themselves in the classroom.

While the more typical form of ADHD usually manifests before the age of seven, the inattentive type may not surface until junior high school or later. It closely resembles depression, and may respond to antidepressants. The inattentive type of ADHD is extremely difficult to diagnose, particularly in gifted girls. They may seem "spacey," but they compensate well enough to succeed in elementary school. They find it harder to concentrate and organize themselves as they approach adolescence and adulthood. They may not remember what they read, nor understand what is needed to complete their schoolwork. Children with untreated ADHD are likely to be friendless, because they have a hard time reading social cues and and are not good at self-monitoring. Hyperactive children are usually rejected by their peers, while inattentive types are generally ignored or neglected by peers (Wheeler & Carlson, 1994).

It is possible that the gifted are more at risk than other groups for sensory integration and inconsistent attention due to birthing issues. Gifted children tend to have a larger than average head circumference (Hitchfield, 1973), which complicates the birthing process, especially in firstborns. Any factor that cuts off oxygen to the newborn's brain during birth can cause sensory or attention deficits. Exceptionally long labor, a cord wrapped around any part of the child's body, meconium (infant's first stool) in the amniotic fluid, fetal distress, more than four hours of pitocin used to induce labor, and emergency C-sections all appear to be risk factors correlated with ADHD, sensory motor integration dysfunction, Nonverbal Learning Disorder, and the autistic spectrum.

A high incidence of birth complications has been found in the case histories of 600 exceptionally gifted children (Silverman, 2002). "During birth, because of the normal position of the baby's head, the blood supply to the left hemisphere is more likely to be temporarily cut off" (Ornstein, 1997, p. 84). Many of the learning disorders of gifted children stem from left hemispheric weaknesses, which respond best to early

intervention. Sensory motor issues, auditory weaknesses, and linguistic delays need to be detected and treated during the critical period of early childhood to ensure optimal development.

Auditory Processing Disorder

Auditory processing disorder is often associated with recurrent otitis media (chronic ear infections). Children who suffered more than nine ear infections during the first three years of life are more likely to experience difficulty attending in class, comprehending stories, learning phonics, and succeeding with typical school tasks (Feagans, 1986). Otitis media is often asymptomatic, particularly in toddlers who have a high pain tolerance (Downs, 1985). Its major symptom is irritability. Otitis media is more difficult to diagnose in the gifted, because these children often have a high pain tolerance, they usually compensate well enough to succeed in the primary grades, and they tend to be irritable for many other reasons besides ear infections. Tests of auditory acuity usually fail to reveal decibel loss; on the contrary, some gifted children seem to have hyperacuity (Silverman, 2002). Even though their hearing may be fine, their listening skills are impaired. There is considerable overlap between the symptoms of auditory processing disorder and the inattentive type of ADHD, and ADHD specialists often request information about a child's ear infection history.

Giftedness can mask severe auditory weaknesses. One gifted toddler held his mother's face in his hands and intently studied her face whenever she spoke. In school, he watched his teacher's face just as intently. It wasn't until second grade that he was identified as having a 98% hearing loss (C. J. Maker, personal communication, July 8, 1998). In average children, the main symptom of an auditory weakness is lack of facility with expressive language. Not so with the gifted. Even when gifted children have suffered conductive hearing loss due to numerous ear infections in early childhood, they usually learn to speak within appropriate age norms. Their abstract reasoning allows them to fill in the missing sounds with a high degree of accuracy. They may be late talkers in comparison to their siblings, or they may have problems with articulation or dysfluency, but they rarely exhibit the types of language difficulties seen in children of average intelligence.

Additional symptoms of auditory processing disorder include fluctuating attention, asking to have questions repeated, copying their neighbors to find out what they are supposed to do, mispronouncing words, difficulty remembering instructions, speaking loudly, turning up the volume on electronic equipment, or covering their ears in noisy settings. These symptoms are often erroneously attributed to ADHD or "immaturity."

Many bright children with auditory processing disorder excel at oral communication, but face their greatest challenge with written expression. Poor auditory processing interferes with the development of motor sequences and has been linked to motor-output problems in gifted children, such as poor handwriting (Silverman, 2000b). Recent brain research (e.g., Kimura, 1993) suggests that the part of the brain responsible for speech is also responsible for fine motor control. "The left hemisphere came to possess a virtual monopoly on control of the motor systems involved in linguistic expression, whether by speech or writing" (Springer & Deutsch, 1998, p. 305). Average children with auditory processing disorder are compromised in both areas, but gifted children may manifest problems only in the motor sequences involved in handwriting.

Visual Processing Deficits

High abstract reasoning ability can also disguise visual processing weaknesses. Many gifted children talk their way through visual tasks, verbally mediating the tasks when they lack visual efficiency (Silverman, 2000a). They may shut one eye when doing close work. These symptoms are not obvious in a classroom setting, but they become apparent to observant diagnosticians during individual assessment.

Additional typical symptoms of visual processing deficits include double vision; blurred vision; rubbing eyes or closing an eye; sitting very close to the television set or placing one's face very close to a book; fatigue and headaches during sustained visual tasks; omitting letters and words, or losing one's place when reading; difficulty copying from the board; and difficulty with writing and spelling (Hellerstein, 1990). With average students, these symptoms tend to interfere with learning, and the child is more likely to be evaluated. However, a gifted child with visual difficulties often succeeds in the early grades and escapes detection.

Rebecca Hutchins (2000), a behavioral optometrist, theorizes that early readers (children who teach themselves to read before age six) may be cognitively ready for the task, but the "ocular motor system is not yet developed enough to perform smooth tracking" (p. 161). Some of these children acquire poor visual skills and need a few months of vision exercises to retrain their eyes for improved efficiency. Some early readers suddenly stop reading when the print becomes smaller. This is a tell-tale sign of visual stress. If the child resumes reading when offered larger print books, a vision evaluation is warranted.

Visual and auditory issues for gifted children may involve either acuity or central nervous system processing, or both. Hutchins (2000) likens the situation to hardware and software. Regular auditory and vision evaluations examine the hardware—the health of the eyes and ears—but may fail to detect a problem with the software—the processing of auditory or visual information. An audiogram, tympanogram, bone conduction test, and air conduction test will determine if audition is adequate: if the full range of sound is getting into the central nervous system. But a test such as the Central Auditory Processing Battery is necessary to determine what happens to the auditory impulse after it reaches the brain. Similarly, a typical vision exam will determine if a person has 20/20 acuity, good eye health, no problems with crossed eyes, or other ocular issues. It is necessary to have a different type of examination, from a behavioral optometrist, to determine if the child's eyes are tracking properly, able to fixate accurately, fusing information from both eyes into a single image, focusing efficiently, and flexible enough to support learning (Hutchins, 2000).

Dyslexia

It is frustrating and humiliating for a bright child who grasps advanced concepts to fall behind classmates in mastering reading. This is the plight of gifted dyslexics. Dyslexia is a marked impediment in the development of reading skills. It is characterized by phonological impairments and associated with an assortment of processing deficits (von Károlyi, 2001). Reading relies heavily on left-hemispheric abilities (Springer & Deutsch, 1998), and several experts have suggested that the left-hemispheric deficits of dyslexics are accompanied by right hemispheric, visual-spatial strengths (Davis &

Marshall, 2000; Geschwind & Galaburda, 1987; Orton, 1925; West, 1991).

An essential quality of normal visual-spatial learners is the ability to think three-dimensionally, enabling the perception of a form in space from many different angles (Silverman, 2002). This is a necessary skill for architects, pilots, engineers, artists, mechanics, and in many areas of science, mathematics, and technology. However, this skill can interfere with the early mastery of reading. Some dyslexic children report that they see letters and numbers in 3-D, so that an "o" looks like a donut and can roll all over the page (Ringle, Miller, & Anderson, 2000). If the orientation of letters can shift, the letters b, d, p, and q are easy to confuse. They are all the same form—flipped or rotated.

Many of the most inventive minds in history, such as Albert Einstein, Thomas Edison, and Leonardo da Vinci, apparently had dyslexic symptoms (West, 1991). Davis and Marshall (2000) contend that this not a coincidence: "The same mental thought processes that give rise to genius also are at the root of dyslexia" (p. 167). Dyslexics think mainly in pictures instead of words and have vivid imaginations. They see solutions to problems in their "mind's eye," but they do not take a series of linear steps to arrive at their solutions, so it is impossible for them to "show their work."

If supported, the visualization capacity of gifted dyslexics can lead to high levels of creativity. Unfortunately, their giftedness is overshadowed by their deficits. "A nine-year-old who cannot read is usually not seen as a candidate for accelerated coursework" (Davis & Marshall, 2000, p. 167). This observation is echoed by other researchers: "Educators are often so preoccupied with a child's failures, they simply do not look for sparks of extraordinary potential" (Tannenbaum & Baldwin, 1983, p. 12).

Dyslexia is often accompanied by dysgraphia, as well as problems with spelling, calculation, rote memorization, auditory short-term memory, and language mechanics. These skills are essential to scholastic success, particularly in elementary school. However, they are not essential to life success in our technological era. Most of the difficulties encountered by gifted dyslexics are basic skills that can be handled by computers. Their extraordinary visualization capabilities and abstract reasoning are needed for advancements in science, engineering, mathematics, and technology.

In today's world, employment opportunities abound for dyslexics.

Once the imagistic, 3-D thought process of the dyslexic is understood, and adaptive technology is employed, the gifted dyslexic can also become an excellent student.

Spatial Disorientation

There are a number of syndromes that involve an inability to negotiate space adequately. They range from simple weaknesses that may be gender-related to serious right hemispheric impairments. Males excel at making mental maps, and can usually retrace their steps in unfamiliar settings, whereas females tend to pay more attention to details and are less likely to create a visual-spatial schematic in their minds to orient themselves (Levy, 1982). Many highly gifted women get lost easily. Dyslexics, who tend to have superb visual-spatial capacities, often experience right-left confusion.

In many ways, Nonverbal Learning Disorder is the mirror image of dyslexia. Children with this syndrome have serious problems with visual-spatial organization, nonverbal problem-solving skills, and psychomotor efficiency. These deficits are accompanied by strengths in decoding written language, spelling, verbal classification, and verbal output (Harnadek & Rourke, 1994). Gifted children with Nonverbal Learning Disorder tend to be whizzes with words. Verbose and given to monologues, they talk *at* the listener instead of *with* the listener. Their speech may lack intonation; they miss social cues; they tend to be clumsy; they lack mechanical aptitude; they get lost easily; they have poor visual and tactile perception; they are unable to visualize; they have difficulty adapting to new situations; and they rely on verbal rules of conduct. One of the principal methods of diagnosing Nonverbal Learning Disorder is when the Verbal (V) IQ on a Wechsler Intelligence Scale is significantly higher than the Performance (P) IQ. However, it is necessary to rule out visual processing deficits first, since these can also cause significant discrepancies between V and P scores.

Spatial strengths and spatial deficits can co-exist. Gifted children with Asperger's Syndrome or *prosopagnosia* (the inability to recognize faces) may perform extraordinarily well on the Block Design subtest of the Wechsler scales, which measures abstract visual-spatial reasoning, but be unsuccessful at putting together puzzles in the Object Assembly subtest. Some of these children arrange the face puzzle by the shapes of the pieces, irrespective of content—failing to notice that, for example, they have placed the lips above the nose. Minor spatial weaknesses are quite common in the gifted population, whereas serious weaknesses are signs of various neurological disorders and lesions, and need to be diagnosed with a complete neuropsychological battery.

Assessing Twice Exceptional Children

The interaction effect between giftedness and learning disorders is not well understood. Gifted individuals are more complex than others; when they struggle, their issues are more difficult to diagnose. And when their weaknesses are subtracted from their strengths, the extent of their abilities is not fully appreciated. It is important to analyze the pattern of strengths independently from the pattern of weaknesses in order to comprehend the full picture of dual exceptionality. Otherwise, the strengths and weaknesses negate each other, and the child appears "average." Unfortunately, few professionals have sufficient training and experience with both exceptionalities to be able to interpret their complex profiles. It takes a good detective to ferret out the gifts, as well as to pinpoint the deficits.

Detecting Giftedness

Gifted/learning-disabled children tend to have unusual discrepancies between their strengths and weaknesses—much more so than other students. On the WISC-III, a 4-point scatter between highest and lowest subtest scores is considered significant at the .05 level (Sattler, 1992). There are twice-exceptional children with a 15-point scatter (5 standard deviations). Placement in gifted programs usually depends on Full Scale IQ scores—averages of these highly discrepant subtest scores. The inappropriateness of averaging such scores is discussed in *The Diagnostic and Statistical Manual of Mental Disorders, Fourth Edition* (DSM-IV):

> When there is *significant scatter* in the subtest scores, the profile of strengths and weaknesses, rather than the mathematically derived full-scale IQ, will more accurately reflect the person's learning abilities. When there is a marked discrepancy across verbal and performance

scores, averaging to obtain a full-scale IQ score can be misleading (American Psychiatric Association, 1994, p. 40).

In addition, the Verbal and Performance IQ scores can severely underestimate the cognitive strengths of twice-exceptional children. On the Verbal side, a low average score (7–9) in Arithmetic cancels out a highly gifted score (17–19) in Vocabulary, and on the Performance side, a low-average score in Coding (eye-hand coordination and speed) eclipses a highly gifted score in Block Design (visual-spatial reasoning). Many children with gifted abilities combined with serious deficiencies fail to qualify for gifted programs because of rigid adherence to Verbal, Performance, or Full Scale IQ cut-off scores.

Gifted children with learning disabilities are also excluded from gifted programs because of the widespread use of tests with inordinate time limits, such as the Wechsler Intelligence Scale for Children, Third Edition (WISC-III) and the Wechsler Preschool and Primary Scale of Intelligence, Revised (WPPSI-R). This issue has been addressed several times by Alan Kaufman, the major interpreter of the Wechsler tests.

> Giving bonus points for speed to preschool children [on the WPPSI-R] seems silly from every developmental and common-sense perspective (Kaufman, 1992, p. 156).
>
> The biggest negatives for gifted assessment are the new emphasis on problem-solving speed on the WPPSI-R; the substantially increased stress on performance time in the WISC-III compared to the WISC-R; and the low stability coefficients for a majority of WPPSI-R and WISC-III subtests (Kaufman, 1992, p. 158).
>
> The impact of problem-solving speed on a person's WISC-III IQ is substantial. . . . Children with reflective cognitive styles will be penalized on highly speeded items, as will children with coordination difficulties. Gifted children may score well below the cutoff needed to qualify for an enrichment program when the WISC-III is administered if they tend to be reflective or have even a mild coordination problem. Similarly, learning-disabled children may fail to score in the average range, even if they have normal intelligence, because of the speed factor (Kaufman, 1993, p. 350).

The problems created by bonus points for speed increase with the age of the student. If an eight-year-old gets every single item correct, but fails to earn bonus points for speed, it is only possible to obtain a score of 14 on Picture Arrangement (PA), 16 on Block Design (BD), and 14 on Object Assembly (OA). (The maximum score is 19.) At the age of twelve, the highest possible scores without bonus points are 8 on PA, 9 on BD, and 9 on OA—all below the 50th percentile. At the age of 16, the highest possible scores are 6 on PA, 7 on BD, and 7 on OA (Kaufman, 1993). Thus when disabled children are retested at an older age, their IQ scores are likely to decrease, due to these increased processing speed demands.

Psychologists usually consider the most recent test the best measure of a child's abilities. However, given the degree to which bonus points adversely affect scores for older students, it is likely that IQ tests administered when the child was younger will provide more accurate estimates of the child's abilities. When available, these should be given greater weight in placement decisions.

Subtests of the WISC-III do not all have equal value in determining giftedness. Those with the highest loadings on general intelligence are Vocabulary (.80), Information (.78), Similarities (.76), Arithmetic (.76), Block Design (.71), and Comprehension (.68) (Kaufman, 1994). As these are the best measures of abstract reasoning, they are much better predictors of success in gifted programs than the Full Scale IQ score. They constitute the Verbal IQ score plus Block Design, and most of them (with the exception of Block Design and Arithmetic) are untimed. Arithmetic is partially timed, and is highly affected by distractibility, auditory processing disorder, sequential deficits, processing speed issues, and anxiety. If there is a large discrepancy between Arithmetic and the other Verbal subtest scores, then the Verbal Comprehension Index, which includes all the Verbal subtests except Arithmetic, will provide a better estimate of the child's intellectual power.

Visual-spatial learners may not score well on these verbally loaded measures. They tend to score slightly higher on Performance than Verbal IQ, and significantly higher on Block Design than on Digit Span (Silverman, 2002). The Block Design score is the best indicator of visual-spatial abilities on the WISC-III. Children with auditory processing disorder also are more likely to succeed on the nonverbal items.

Many gifted children with learning disabilities perform better on measures of achievement than on measures of ability. When a twice-exceptional child achieves in the gifted range on any section of an achievement test, this should be taken as sufficient proof of giftedness—despite lower scores on IQ tests. Achievement tests, such as the Woodcock-Johnson,

have more liberal time limits than the Wechsler scales. This enables gifted children to demonstrate more of their real capabilities. However, this is a "Catch-22," since eligibility for special education services depends on the IQ score being significantly higher than the achievement score. Gifted children with processing speed or motor coordination deficits cannot possibly demonstrate the true level of their abilities on a heavily timed IQ test, so they are prevented from qualifying for special education provisions. The Stanford-Binet Intelligence Scale, Revision V, promises to be a more suitable instrument for assessing gifted/learning-disabled children, because it has a much higher ceiling than the WISC-III and is largely untimed.

And then there are gifted children with learning disabilities who have such severe test anxiety that they cannot perform well on either ability or achievement measures. If children suffer from both auditory and visual information processing deficits, or sensory integration dysfunction, or untreated ADHD, it is quite possible that all test scores will be depressed. In these cases, the children's vocabulary (e.g., "well, actually . . ."), their contributions in class discussions, their sophisticated concepts, their moral sensitivity, their extensive knowledge in a given domain (such as computers), and the presence of giftedness in siblings should all be taken into account and given greater weight in placement decisions than test scores.

Detecting Disabilities

Twice-exceptional children are frequently misdiagnosed because:

- Their scores are averaged, masking both their strengths and weaknesses;
- They are compared to the norms for average children instead of to their own strengths;
- Their lower scores may not be significantly below the norm;
- Their ability to compensate often inflates their lower scores;
- The magnitude of the disparities between their strengths and weaknesses is not fully taken into account (Silverman, 2000b).

Diagnosticians in the helping professions usually look at test scores from a normative perspective. School psychologists, audiologists, occupational therapists, optometrists, and speech pathologists are trained to compare a child's performance with the norms for average children. If a child performs within the normal range, no disability is revealed. Children with dramatic discrepancies may be overlooked if their lowest scores fall within the broad range of "normal." For example, a child with 19s (99.9th percentile) on Similarities, Vocabulary, and Block Design, who attains a 6 on Coding (>4 s.d. disparity), would not be identified as learning disabled, because 6 (9th percentile) is at the low end of the average range.

To understand gifted children with learning disabilities, it is necessary to ask an entirely different diagnostic question: *"To what extent does the discrepancy between the child's strengths and weaknesses cause frustration and interfere with the full development of the child's potential?"* This is an intrapersonal rather than a normative view of test interpretation, and it is critical in working with this population (Silverman, 1998, 2000b).

Two key diagnostic indicators of giftedness combined with learning disorders are: (1) significant (2 s.d.) disparities between strengths and weaknesses, with some subtest scores in at least the superior range; and (2) succeeding on the harder items, while missing the easier items. When both are present, it is likely that the child is twice exceptional.

A classic pattern associated with learning disabilities is the "ACID" test, consisting of low scores in *A*rithmetic, *C*oding, *I*nformation, and *D*igit Span, compared with other subtests. This is a better litmus test for average children with learning disabilities than for the gifted, because gifted/learning-disabled children often obtain high scores on Information (Schiff, Kaufman, & Kaufman, 1981), which is richly loaded with abstract reasoning. Arithmetic and Digit Span make up the Freedom from Distractibility Index on the WISC-III, but mathematically gifted children with ADHD are often "so adept at recalling, using, and hearing numbers that Arithmetic and Digit Span subtests may be among their highest scores" (Lovecky, 2000, p. 1).

Assessing ADHD in the gifted is highly complex and requires knowledge of both attention deficits and giftedness. Before a positive diagnosis of ADHD is made, the following must be ruled out: "Inattention in the classroom may also occur when children with high intelligence are placed in academically *under-stimulating environments*" (American Psychiatric Association, 1994, p. 83, emphasis in original). Gifted children with confirmed ADHD are able to concentrate much better when the work is more diffi-cult (therefore, more engaging) than when it is too easy. A child whose activity, impulsivity, and distractibility are beyond the norm of a group of gifted children in an appropriately challenging environment is more likely to be truly ADHD than a gifted child who exhibits symptoms of ADHD within a heterogeneous classroom.

Gifted individuals may not demonstrate typical manifestations of Attention Deficit Hyperactivity Disorder, Asperger's Syndrome, manic depression, dyslexia, etc. High intelligence enables a person to compensate sufficiently to disguise weaknesses. But compensation is inconsistent. It fails to operate if one is fatigued, frightened, ill, stressed, or in an unfamiliar situation (Silverman, 2000b). And when the bar is set too low, twice-exceptional children can "get by" in the early years of school. Their weaknesses do not gain attention until the workload increases. High abstract reasoning elevates scores in weaker areas, preventing the detection of learning disorders. Compensation is the joker that masks the full extent of disabilities in the gifted; it always must be taken into account in the assessment process.

Dual Exceptionality in the Classroom

The most common symptom of dual exceptionality encountered by teachers is an extremely bright child who hates to write. Writing disability goes by many names: sensory integration dysfunction, motor output problems, developmental coordination disorder, and dysgraphia—a subset of dyspraxia. In the following list of symptoms (from Silverman, 1991, 2002). the generic "he" is used because many more boys suffer from this syndrome than girls.

Diagnostic Checklist of Writing Disability

1. Is his writing posture awkward?
2. Does he hold his pencil strangely?
3. Can you see the tension run through his hand, arm, furrowed brow?
4. Does it take him much longer to write than anyone else his age?
5. Does he fatigue easily and want to quit?
6. Does he space his letters on the paper in an unusual way (too close, too far apart, no spaces between words)?
7. Does he form his letters oddly (e.g., starting letters at the top that others would start at the bottom)?

8. Does he mix upper- and lower-case letters?
9. Does he mix cursive and manuscript?
10. Are his cursive letters disconnected?
11. Does he prefer manuscript to cursive?
12. Does his lettering lack fluidity?
13. Does he still reverse letters after age 7?
14. Is his handwriting illegible?
15. Is his spelling terrible?
16. Does he avoid writing words he can't spell?
17. Does he leave off the endings of words?
18. Does he confuse singulars and plurals?
19. Does he mix up small words, like "the" and "they"?
20. Does he leave out soft sounds, like the "d" in gardener?
21. Is his grasp of phonics weak?

Students who exhibit at least half of these signs are likely to suffer from dysgraphia. Gifted underachievers need to be assessed for writing disability. For centuries, dysgraphic children have been treated as though they were purposely defiant, and were punished accordingly throughout the grades. In a formal grievance filed because her daughter had been barred from the Honors Program, the mother of a fourteen-year-old wrote:

> I have explained to Mrs. S that [my daughter] has a handwriting disability and is extremely nervous around the other students when there is pressure to perform. I have asked that she be allowed to take tests in a private place and to use a computer or laptop. These requests have been denied. In fact, even with homework, the teacher has denied the use of the computer, stating that she wanted to see the work in [my daughter's] own handwriting, which is very difficult to decipher.

We create underachievement when we refuse to allow disabled children the tools they need to succeed. Children who struggle with writing need access to keyboards. Alpha Smarts are inexpensive. *Keyboarding is an important life skill in the twenty-first century, whereas handwriting has little employment value.* As schools become aware of this societal shift, twice-exceptional children will find more success in the classroom.

Strategies for Success

1. First and foremost, learning disabilities must be detected as early as possible. Early identification allows early intervention. Most remedial efforts need to be put in place before a child is nine.

2. Gifted children with learning disabilities need Individual Educational Plans (IEPs) that take into account both exceptionalities. The IEP should address the development of the child's strengths as well as adaptations for the child's weaknesses.

3. Because processing speed is usually compromised in disabled learners, timed tests should be avoided. Students can qualify to take college board exams and other standardized tests with more liberal time limits if slow processing speed can be documented through individual assessment.

4. More emphasis should be placed on the child's strengths than on the weaknesses. Children who are taught to their strengths are often able to find ways to get around their deficits.

5. Children with writing disabilities should be taught keyboarding skills and allowed to use a computer for all written assignments. If motor impairment is so severe that they cannot master keyboarding, then a voice-activated computer, such as Dragon Naturally Speaking, should be employed.

6. Compensation strategies should be actively taught to twice-exceptional learners. Some compensation strategies include carrying around a day-planner, making lists, visualizing, using a word processor with a spell-check, having a quiet place at home to study, tape recording lectures, using earphones to block out auditory distractions, and having a place to retreat when overstimulated.

7. Many gifted/learning-disabled children think in pictures instead of words. Overhead projectors, demonstrations, and hands-on experiences are vital to their learning.

8. Nonsequentiality is another common ingredient in the profiles of gifted children with learning disabilities. They do not learn in a step-by-step fashion like most learners. It is important to accept correct answers, even if the child cannot show his or her work.

9. Many of these children are "whole-part" learners. They need to see the big picture in their minds and be allowed to figure out on their own how to get to the result.

10. Visualization techniques should be used liberally. Children can be asked to picture concepts in their minds as they are being taught. They may have to be taught to visualize; but if they develop this strength, it will serve them in all subjects.

11. Assistive technology should be considered, such as an Alpha Smart, calculator, or Franklin speller.

12. Writing assignments often need to be shortened, and oral exams may have to substitute for some written exams. In some cases, children will need to dictate their work to a parent or aide.

13. For disabled learners, grades should not be lowered due to mechanical difficulties (e.g., spelling, punctuation, grammar, capitalization, and sentence structure). Schoolwork needs to be graded on the quality of content.

14. If they learn complex work easily, yet struggle with simple material, twice-exceptional children will need advanced concepts, even though they have not mastered the easier work. Acceleration is often more effective than remediating weaknesses.

SUMMARY AND CONCLUSIONS

More gifted children suffer from learning disabilities than anyone suspects. Many underachievers are actually twice-exceptional. Learning disabilities can depress IQ scores significantly, preventing twice-exceptional children from qualifying for gifted programs. Giftedness facilitates compensation, which can prevent accurate diagnosis and recognition of disabilities. Compensation is unstable, and fails to operate when a person is fatigued, ill, or under stress. Early identification and intervention, assistive technology, and compensation strategies are keys to success for twice-exceptional children. Detection and amelioration of disabilities can dramatically improve the quality of life. Gifted children with learning disabilities can be highly successful with recognition and intervention.

QUESTIONS FOR THOUGHT AND DISCUSSION

1. How common are learning disabilities in the gifted?

2. Explain the symptoms of three or four of the most prevalent learning disorders in the gifted population.

3. Why are twice-exceptional children frequently misdiagnosed?

4. How can a classroom teacher recognize twice-exceptional children?

5. What might be Silverman's most important recommendations for helping gifted children with learning disabilities to succeed in school? Explain.

REFERENCES

American Psychiatric Association. (1994). *Diagnostic and statistical manual of mental disorders* (4th ed.). Washington, DC: Author.

Ayres, A. J. (1979). *Sensory integration and the child.* Los Angeles: Western Psychological Services.

Baum, S. M., Olenchak, F. R., & Owen, S. V. (1998). Gifted students with attention deficits: Fact and/or fiction? Or, Can we see the forest for the trees? *Gifted Child Quarterly, 42,* 96–104.

Cramond, B. (1994). ADHD and creativity: What is the connection? *Journal of Creative Behavior, 28,* 193–210.

Davis, R. D., & Marshall, A. (2000). Dyslexia and the seeds of genius. In K. Kay (Ed.), *Uniquely gifted: Identifying and meeting the needs of twice exceptional learners* (pp. 167–171). Gilsum, NH: Avocus.

Downs, M. P. (1985). Effects of mild hearing loss on auditory processing. *Otolaryngologic Clinics of North America, 18,* 337–343.

Feagans, L. (1986). Otitis media: A model for long term effects with implications for intervention. In J. Kavanaugh (Ed.), *Otitis media and child development.* Parkton, MD: York Press.

Geschwind, N., & Galaburda, A. (1987). *Cerebral lateralization.* Cambridge: MIT Press.

Hagen, E. (1980). *Identification of the gifted.* New York: Teachers College Press.

Harnadek, M. C. S., & Rourke, B. P. (1994). Principal identifying features of the syndrome of nonverbal learning disabilities in children. *Journal of Learning Disabilities, 27,* 144–154.

Hellerstein, L. F. (1990). The gift of vision. *Understanding Our Gifted, 2*(6), 1, 8–10.

Hitchfield, E. M. (1973). *In search of promise.* London: Longman.

Hutchins, R. E. (2000). Visual processing deficits in the gifted. In K. Kay (Ed.), *Uniquely gifted: Identifying and meeting the needs of twice-exceptional learners* (pp. 160–162). Gilsum, NH: Avocus.

Kaufman, A. S. (1992). Evaluation of the WISC-III and WPPSI-R for gifted children. *Roeper Review, 14,* 154–158.

Kaufman, A. S. (1993). King WISC the third assumes the throne. *Journal of School Psychology, 31,* 345–354.

Kaufman, A. S. (1994). *Intelligent testing with the WISC-III.* New York: Wiley.

Kaufmann, F., & Castellanos, F. X. (2000). Attention Deficit/Hyperactivity Disorder and gifted students. In

K. A. Heller, F. J. Monks, R. J. Sternberg, & R. F. Subotnik (Eds.), *International handbook of giftedness and talent* (2nd ed., pp. 621–632). Amsterdam: Elsevier.

Kimura, D. (1993). *Neuromotor mechanisms in human communication.* New York: Oxford University Press.

Kutner, D. R. (1999). Blurred brilliance: What ADHD looks like in gifted adults. *Advanced Development, 8,* 87–96.

Levy, J. (1982, November). *Brain research: Myths and realities for the gifted male and female.* Paper presented at the Illinois Gifted Education Conference, Chicago.

Lovecky, D. V. (2000). *Gifted children with AD/HD.* ERIC Fact Sheet EC 307734. Retrieved from: http://ericec.org/fact/lovecky.html.

Lovecky, D. V. (in press). *Gifted children with attention deficits: Different minds.* London: Jessica Kingsley.

Mangeot, S., Miller, L. J., McIntosh, D. N., McGrath-Clarke, J., Simon, J., Hagerman, R. J., & Goldson, E. (in press). Sensory modulation dysfunction in children with Attention Deficit Hyperactivity Disorder. *Developmental Medicine and Child Neurology.*

Moon, S. M., Zentall, S. S., Grskovic, J. A., Hall, A., & Stormont, M. (2001). Social and emotional characteristics of boys with AD/HD and/or giftedness: A comparative case study. *Journal for the Education of the Gifted, 24*(3), 207–247.

Ornstein, R. (1997). *The right mind: Making sense of the hemispheres.* New York: Harcourt.

Orton, S. T. (1925). "Word blindness" in school children. *Archives of Neurology and Psychiatry, 14,* 581–613.

Ringle, J., Miller, S., & Anderson, R. (2000). *Reading achievement results integrating Davis Learning Strategies in the special education and special reading classroom. Year 1—1999–2000.* Report for Sherrard Elementary School. Sherrard, IL: Authors.

Rogers, K. B., & Silverman, L. K. (1997, November 7). *Personal, medical, social and psychological factors in 160+ IQ children.* National Association for Gifted Children, Little Rock, AR. Available: *www.gifted development.com.*

Roley, S., Blanche, E. I., & Schaaf, R. C. (Eds.). (2001). *Understanding the nature of sensory integration with diverse populations.* San Antonio, TX: Therapy Skill Builders.

Sattler, J. M. (1992). *Assessment of children* (3rd ed., revised). San Diego, CA: Sattler.

Schiff, M. M., Kaufman, A. S., & Kaufman, N. L. (1981). Scatter analysis of WISC-R profiles for learning disabled children with superior intelligence. *Journal of Learning Disabilities, 14,* 400–404.

Silverman, L. K. (1989). Invisible gifts, invisible handicaps. *Roeper Review, 12,* 37–42.

Silverman, L. K. (1991). Help for the hidden handicapped. *Highly Gifted Children, 7*(2), 10–11.

Silverman, L. K. (1998). Through the lens of giftedness. *Roeper Review, 20,* 204–210.

Silverman, L. K. (2000a, October). Diagnosing and treating visual perceptual issues in gifted children. Invited address. *Proceedings of the College of Optometrists in Vision Development Annual Meeting,* Reno, NV.

Silverman, L. K. (2000b). The two-edged sword of compensation: How the gifted cope with learning disabilities. In K. Kay (Ed.), *Uniquely gifted: Identifying and meeting the needs of twice exceptional learners* (pp. 153–159). Gilsum, NH: Avocus.

Silverman, L. K. (2002). *Upside-down brilliance: The visual-spatial learner.* Denver: DeLeon Publishing.

Springer, S. P., & Deutsch, G. (1998). *Left brain/right brain: Perspectives from cognitive neuroscience* (5th ed.). New York: W. H. Freeman.

Tannenbaum, A. J., & Baldwin, L. J. (1983). Giftedness and learning disability: A paradoxical combination. In L. H. Fox, L. Brody, & D. Tobin (Eds.), *Learning-disabled/gifted children: Identification and programming.* Baltimore University Park Press.

von Károlyi, C. (2001). Visual-spatial strength in dyslexia: Rapid discrimination of impossible figures. *Journal of Learning Disabilities, 34*(4), 173–213.

Webb, J. T., & Latimer, D. (1993, July). ADHD and children who are gifted. *Eric Digest,* EDO-ED-93-5.

West, T. G. (1991). *In the mind's eye: Visual thinkers, gifted people with learning difficulties, computer images, and the ironies of creativity.* Buffalo, NY: Prometheus.

Wheeler, J., & Carlson, C. L. (1994). The social functioning of children with ADD with hyperactivity and without hyperactivity: A comparison of their peer relations and social deficits. *Journal of Emotional and Behavioral Disorders, 2,* 2–12.

PART VII

Special Topics

This section includes several important areas of gifted education that make this textbook comprehensive. We examine the development of gifted education in some other countries, look at educating teachers of the gifted, and consider students with exceptional spatial abilities. We also look at special applications of today's technology—computers for the gifted. We end our volume with two topics that widen our view of gifted education even further: legal issues and procedures and U.S. government perspectives on gifted education.

Miraca U. M. Gross in Chapter 42 summarizes developments in England, Scotland, Australia, and Russia. A history of aristocracy—unearned privilege—in England causes some resentment of gifted programs. In Scotland education is highly valued as a route to security and upward mobility. In both countries, the 1990s saw growth in positive attitudes and legal steps on behalf of highly able students. For example, England's 1997 *Excellence in Schools* report mandated strong steps on behalf of the gifted, and a 1999 *Excellence in Cities* program requires identification and programming in 450 inner-city secondary schools. Similarly, the Edinburgh, Scotland, 2001 document *Framework for the Education of Gifted and Talented Pupils* requires identification, acceleration, ability grouping, enrichment, and IEPs. Many Australians—including teachers—hold strong egalitarian attitudes, including resentment of too-bright students. Nonetheless, professional development programs are changing teachers' attitudes, and marvelous programs are in place. Russia has long trained its talented math and science students. Currently, gifted programs include arts and humanities.

In Chapter 43 Laurie J. Croft summarizes the critical role of teachers of the gifted, and especially their enthusiastic personality, flexible and varied teaching styles, their training and preparation beyond that required even for excellent teachers—and their own giftedness. A sample of traits unique to effective teachers of the gifted includes humor, imagination, diplomacy, openness to innovation, ability to challenge and inspire, a broad repertoire of curriculum differentiation techniques, and tolerance for gifted students' excitability, competitiveness, and emotionality. She discusses details of curriculum differentiation in the categories of *types* (grouping, acceleration, enrichment), *content, process* (virtually always emphasizing high-level thinking skills), *models* (well-represented in this book), student *products,* and *environment* (physical and affective, including consideration of learning styles). Croft also elaborates on several roles of teachers of the gifted: counselor to gifted students, consultant to other teachers, and coordinator of gifted identification and programming for a district. Finally, she elaborates on professional preparation, especially undergraduate teacher training endorsement in gifted education.

Nicholas Colangelo, Susan G. Assouline, Clar M. Baldus, and Jennifer K. New in Chapter 44 discuss problems and benefits of rural schools—not only in farm areas, but in remote communities in New England, Alaska, and the Southwest. An overriding theme is that gifted programs in rural areas are rare, due to small enrollments (therefore few gifted students), small budgets, staff untrained in gifted education, and unsupportive rural values. Other disadvantages also relate to isolation—from cultural opportunities, universities (for teacher training), professional models and mentors, major libraries, and other schools. AP classes are rare. Strengths include small class size, mixed-age classes, more individualized attention, low dropout rates, community service and support, and student participation in many activities. Urban schools now copy some of these benefits. A move toward consolidation, after about 1930, decreased the number of rural schools, along with their benefits. Successful gifted programs virtually always have teachers and/or administrators with vision and commitment, gifted students who need the attention, and a flexible program with high standards.

Michael C. Pyryt in Chapter 45 uses Treffinger's six-category model for nurturing talents to elaborate on uses of computer technology with gifted students. Briefly, with *individualizing basics* Pyryt explains how to use the Internet to assess learning styles, learn about gifted education, or explore any subject area. Under *appropriate enrichment*, he mentions using the Internet to develop such process skills as creativity and critical thinking. *Effective acceleration*, both in pace and content, easily lends itself to self-paced computer-based learning. *Independence and self-direction* also are built-in to individual explorations over the Internet. *Personal and social growth* are aided, for example, with e-mail mentorships, peer contacts around the world, and by acquiring perseverance and high ethics. *Careers and futures* includes Internet information on career development. Finally, Pyryt warns about such technology misuses as software piracy, unlawful access to or destruction of information, sending viruses, and pornography.

In Chapter 46 Frances A. Karnes and Ronald G. Marquardt review legal issues and procedures in gifted education—a topic they pioneered and that previously had existed only at the fringes of gifted education. The authors stress that disputes are best and most cheaply resolved at the lowest possible level. Starting at the bottom, with *negotiation* one works up the chain of command from program staff to the principal, superintendent, and then school board. *Mediation* helps decide issues at the state board of education level, followed by more costly and adversarial *due process* procedures and then state or federal *courts*. The authors present thoughtful ideas, recommendations, and court cases related to these following recurring issues: early admission to school, providing gifted programs, racial balance, awarding high school credit to younger students, transferring students to schools with a suitable G/T program, rights of gifted students with disabilities, teacher certification, liability for injury, fraud and misrepresentation, rights of home schooled gifted children, and others.

In Chapter 47 Patricia O'Connell completes this third edition of the *Handbook of Gifted Education* with her chapter on the role of the federal government in gifted education. O'Connell stipulates that at best the federal government has given sputtering attention to the education of gifted and talented students. She briefly outlines the federal involvement acknowledging that the federal role in education, let alone gifted education, is based on conflicting beliefs and not on clearly prescribed responsibilities. After the Marland Report of 1972 the U.S. Congress created the Office of Gifted and Talented in the U.S. Office of Education and continued this until 1981. In 1988 Congress passed the Jacob K. Javits Gifted and Talented Students Education Act and this serves as the current federal program. The Javits program has remained intact but not greatly expanded and still serves as the only direct federal involvement in gifted education.

42

International Perspectives

MIRACA U. M. GROSS, *University of New South Wales, Sydney, Australia*

Shortly before his death in 1996, my colleague and friend A. Harry Passow wrote the International Perspectives chapter for the second edition of this handbook. I was honored by Nick Colangelo and Gary Davis' invitation to serve in Harry's stead, and write the chapter you are now reading.

In developing state or national programs for gifted and talented children, educators and politicians require three qualities that Harry possessed in abundance: wisdom, foresight and balance. Indeed, Harry Passow was one of the wisest, farthest-seeing, and most balanced people I have known.

In analyzing some of the key issues underpinning and affecting gifted education not only in the United States but internationally, Harry proposed that one of the primary dilemmas was the tension between the desire for educational equity and the need for educational excellence. With his usual thoughtful care for language, and his insightful capacity to cut to the core of a question, Harry proposed that the issue was not one of excellence *versus* equity, but rather excellence *vis-à-vis* equity (Passow, 1997).

Vis-à-vis means "face to face." It places topics or issues in relation to each other rather than in opposition. In nineteenth-century England, a *vis-à-vis* was a carriage in which the occupants sat facing each other. Although they were looking in opposite directions, they were engaged on the same journey, and their placement facilitated discussion.

Harry's point was that many premises or practices that at first glance seem to be oppositional may in fact complement each other and, if used in conjunction, may provide a more comprehensive and richly textured approach to educating the gifted and talented. Too often, we still debate the merits of inclusion *versus* ability grouping, acceleration *versus* enrichment, subjective identification procedures *versus* ability and achievement testing, and the commitment of time and resources to students with intellectual disabilities *versus* the commitment of time and resources to students who are intellectually gifted. How might our attitudes and practices change if we replaced the too often voiced *versus* with *vis-à-vis* to acknowledge that there is a place for multiple views or practices?

This chapter is not intended to provide a comprehensive overview of gifted education developments internationally. This is not possible in the space available. This chapter will focus on three nations in which significant change has occurred in the last few years through structured efforts to accommodate a range of philosophies and practices in gifted education—a willingness to adopt the *vis-à-vis* philosophy, rather than the *versus*—and a fourth nation that currently faces this challenge.

Developments in England

If one follows the developments in the field of gifted and talented children's education for the past five years, one is left with a feeling of cautious optimism. Provision remains patchy and there is still resentment about resources being targeted at the most able from some teachers, schools and Local Education Authorities (LEAs), but I think it is true to say that attitudes to gifted and talented children have improved among the general public and the government (Froggatt, in press).

For positive change to occur in any nation's attitudes toward, and provisions for, intellectually gifted students, there must be substantial support at both community and governmental level. The strong class-consciousness, which has traditionally pervaded

British society, with the associated resentment of advantages, which are seen as primarily inherited rather than earned, such as membership in the titled nobility, family wealth, and high intellectual ability, has led to an unwillingness to spend scarce resources on assisting intellectually gifted students, who are perceived as already advantaged.

However, the last few years of the 1990s were characterized by a growing awareness and concern in the educational community, that academically gifted students, particularly those in inner-city schools, are educationally disadvantaged. Although traditionally the Labour Party in Britain, with its staunchly egalitarian social agenda, has shown little interest in gifted children, under Prime Minister Tony Blair, who took office in 1997, the "New Labour" philosophies have incorporated a concern that "able" and "highly able" pupils, like other pupils, should be assisted to develop their potential.

Koshy (personal communication, 2001) suggested that it was the publication of Her Majesty's Government Inspector's (HMI) report entitled *The Education of Very Able Children in Maintained Schools* in 1992 that provided the first spark of serious interest in gifted education. This was followed in 1993 by two national conferences to promote the report and build on good practice. There was, however, no immediate major improvement. A report by the Department for Education and Employment (DfEE) in 1994 reflected the tone of the conferences and report, but did little to provide concrete support for able students and their teachers. Additionally, Froggatt comments that these reports and conferences focused on the upper 20% of students in schools; there was little discussion of *levels* of high ability and almost no acknowledgment of students whose needs cannot easily be met in the inclusion classroom. From 1992 onward, school inspections conducted by OFSTED (Office of Standards and Training in Education) regularly highlighted weaknesses in classroom provision for able pupils; however, undergraduate teacher training courses provided virtually no information on how to recognize or respond to able students, and there was a paucity of inservice or professional development programs in gifted education for practicing teachers.

In February 1995, a British BBC television program called *Too Clever by Half* highlighted the dilemma of six-year-old Ahmed Luquman who was studying senior high school mathematics at home because his parents could not find a school that could cater to his special needs. The program explored some of the academic and social difficulties experienced by extremely gifted children seeking education within the state system, and showed footage of one of the regular weekend courses offered by the Support Society for Children of High Intelligence (CHI), a voluntary organization that advocates for the special needs of intellectually gifted children. This program, which was shown nationally, had considerable influence in alerting education authorities to the plight of the highly gifted and to the needs of gifted students from immigrant populations.

The first indication of possible large-scale government support came in 1996 in the form of the Labour Party's draft policy on education. The policy based its platform on two arguments, which Borland (1989) characterizes as the "national resource" and the "special education" rationales. The former rationale holds that gifted children must be cultivated as a powerful community resource to ensure the economic survival of the nation. The "special education" rationale proposes that, like other exceptional children, gifted children differ significantly from the majority of their age-peers and will not reach their full potential unless schools modify their curriculum substantially. Traditionally, those two philosophies have been seen as oppositional; however, Labour's policy harnessed both, allowing them to be seen *vis-à-vis,* complementing rather than contradicting each other.

The Labour policy highlighted the cultural bias against intellectually gifted students, particularly those in the top 2–3% of the ability range. It proposed that Local Education Authorities (LEAs) should draw up and implement policies on the needs of gifted children and that each school should state, in its prospectus, the arrangements that it proposed for identifying and providing for its most able students.

The policy endorsed various forms of acceleration and suggested that extension classes would be useful. It endorsed the development of links between secondary schools (which serve students aged approximately twelve–eighteen) and universities and the provision of mentors for the most able. It advocated the strengthening of links with voluntary organizations such as CHI, the National Association for Gifted Children (NAGC), and the National Association for Curriculum Enrichment and Extension (NACE).

When Labour came into power in 1997, the Prime Minister stated that the education of highly able children would become an educational priority for his government, and he identified England's anti-intellectual cultural bias and fears of elitism as the main problems to be overcome in responding more effectively to these children's needs. The government published a White Paper entitled *Excellence in Schools* (Department for Education and Employment, 1997), which mandated many of the proposals contained in the draft policy of the previous year.

A series of radical education initiatives commenced in 1999 with the launch of the *Excellence in Cities* program, a three-year initiative targeted primarily at the most able 5–10% of secondary school students in 450 inner city schools in England's largest industrial cities (Education and Employment Committee, 1999). Initially, 20 out of 140 LEAs, and later another 30, were provided with substantial funding attached to the following conditions.

- Each LEA should appoint an advisor with special responsibility for the education of gifted and talented students.
- All secondary schools should appoint a coordinator for gifted and talented programs.
- Each school should identify the most able 5–10% of its students.
- Schools should develop a distinct teaching and learning program for the identified students.

Schools were advised that identification procedures should be multifaceted and should incorporate both objective and subjective indicators of high ability rather than rely on teacher nomination alone, as had previously been common practice. "Schools will need to take a robust and consistent approach to the identification of their gifted and talented cohorts, making use of available test and assessment data alongside a range of other evidence such as subject-specific checklists of high-ability indicators and analysis of pupils' work. They will need to take care to identify and include able children who are currently underachieving, as well as those who are already relatively high attainers" (Education and Employment Committee, 1999, p. v).

Similarly, the report attempts to balance an acknowledgment of the proven effectiveness of ability grouping as established by international research (see research reviews by Rogers, 1991; Kulik & Kulik, 1997; Gross, 1997b) with the historically influenced reluctance to re-establish special "streams."[1] However, it encourages various forms of ability grouping and requires schools that remain committed to an exclusively mixed-ability approach to provide objective evidence of the effectiveness of this procedure.

> A distinct programme is not necessarily a separate programme: Schools will not be expected to establish a separate stream and it should be possible to deliver much of the program through effective differentiation in existing classes, including mixed-ability settings. But those schools that currently follow an exclusively mixed-ability approach will be expected to give very serious consideration to a mixed economy, drawing on a much wider range of models including setting [ability grouping] and fast-tracking, in response to the varying needs of their able pupil cohort. The guidance will specifically encourage setting [ability grouping] in maths, science and modern foreign languages. Schools that remain wedded to a mixed-ability approach will be expected to demonstrate high performance by their able pupils relative to those in other, similar, schools (Education and Employment Committee, 1999, p. vi).

A major initiative developed under the aegis of *Excellence in Cities* has been the construction of World Class Tests in mathematics and problem-solving for gifted nine-year-old and thirteen-year-old students. The tests are designed to assist with the identification of mathematically gifted children and children who excel in many aspects of problem solving. The government's Qualifications and Curriculum Authority (QCA) has evaluated the tests in England and overseas to ensure that they are sufficient challenging to discriminate among the top 10% of students. An invitational seminar held in London in February 2001, brought together experts in the assessment of children of high ability from Australia, New Zealand, the United Kingdom, and the United States to discuss the construction and implementation of the tests.

Certainly, the current provisions for special assistance for academically gifted students appear to attract rather more community and educational support in England than has been evident for some years. However, there are still ambiguities in the terminologies employed by education authorities and even by support organizations, with "able," "more able," "exceptionally able," "gifted," and even "exceptionally gifted" being used almost interchangeably in many articles and initiatives. As a result, educators frequently argue about which students comprise the population under examination, what proportion of the

---

1. See Chapter 21 by Kulik.

population they comprise, and which children should be included.

For example, Eyres (1999), tracing the development of gifted programs within the Oxford LEA between 1987 and 1997, reported the LEA's reluctance to define *giftedness* "a matter of considerable controversy." He noted their concern about the effects of labeling children as *gifted* and their resultant decision "to avoid creating a clearly defined section of the pupil cohort called "the gifted" but, rather, to employ the term "more able." It was intended that "more able" would serve as "a relative term used in relation to specific school cohorts rather than a nominal national cohort" (p. 14). One of the problems arising from such a decision is that a student may be defined as "more able" and eligible for special services in one school but not in others—precisely the problem encountered by gifted students in the United States who move between school districts that employ different percentages in their definitions of giftedness or talent.

Additionally, little understanding is evident of the intellectual differences between moderately, highly, and exceptionally gifted students and the range of differentiated procedures with which schools can respond to their learning and social needs (Froggatt, in press).

Developments in Scotland

Scotland, one of four nations of the United Kingdom of Great Britain, has its own systems of education, law, and government. Until the beginning of the twentieth century, the economic gap between "rich" and "poor" was even wider in Scotland than in England, and education was regarded as valuable not only in itself, but also as a hedge against poverty and a vehicle for upward mobility. The curriculum in Scottish schools was unusually academically rigorous (Kellas, 1968), and students who achieved highly were admired and valued by the community—particularly if they came from economically disadvantaged families.

This respect for high ability was, however, tempered with a belief that academic success should not be ostentatiously displayed; modesty and even self-deprecation were prized. In Scotland it is still viewed as slightly improper to express pride in one's own ability or success, or even the ability or success of one's children.

Until the early 1960s, Scotland had a stratified system of secondary education somewhat similar to

that of England. This was disbanded in favour of a comprehensive approach to education in which all students were educated in mixed-ability settings. However, while the inclusion setting is viewed as more "equitable," there has been an ongoing concern that highly able students, particularly those from disadvantaged backgrounds, are being denied an education commensurate with their ability.

In June 1999, the City Council of Edinburgh, Scotland's capital, brought together 60 primary and secondary school principals for a full-day seminar on issues in the education of gifted children. The seminar revealed high levels of concern about academic underachievement, which was viewed as endemic among gifted pupils. The principals sought guidance on objective, as well as subjective, procedures through which gifted pupils could be identified, and they asked for further inservice on the development of differentiated curricula and special programs. The seminar ended with a call from the principals for an evaluative review of the Council's policy on the education of able students.

In 2001, the Council published a ground-breaking new *Framework for the Education of Gifted and Talented Pupils,* referred to as the *Strategy.* The former policy, entitled *The Education of Able Pupils Primary 6–Secondary 2* (Scottish Office of Education, 1993), failed to define clearly the population under consideration and used the terms "able," "more able," and "highly able" indiscriminately and often interchangeably. By contrast, the new Strategy adopts the Gagné definition[1] of giftedness and talent and focuses on students whose ability in at least one domain, or achievement in at least one field of performance, places them in the top 10% of their age-peers. It discusses environmental and personalogical causes of academic underachievement and the need to identify and respond appropriately to underachievement. It acknowledges that pupils at different levels of intellectual giftedness may require different interventive responses.

A significant feature of the Strategy is its advocacy of a wide range of identification procedures and interventions.

- It advocates a multifaceted approach to identification that incorporates tests of cognitive ability and standardized tests of achievement as well as a range

---

[1] See Chapter 5 by Gagné.

of subjective nomination procedures such as teacher, parent, peer, and self-nomination. It acknowledges the problems of ceiling effects in testing and requires that pupils who score in the top 10% of their age-cohort be reassessed on tests designed for older students. It acknowledges the proven effectiveness of parent nomination, particularly in the early years of school.

- It supports several types of acceleration, including curriculum compacting; early entry to primary school, secondary school, and university; grade-advancement; and single subject acceleration.
- It supports the development of a range of ability grouped settings, including cluster groups, pullout programs, special classes, and specialist schools.
- It requires that enrichment and fast-paced, academically challenging work in the mainstream classroom become an essential element of schools' provisions for gifted students regardless of what additional programs are set in place.
- It requires that an Individual Educational Program be developed for each identified gifted or talented student.

This seems to be an unusually comprehensive policy that synthesizes a range of identification procedures and interventions, which are too often seen as antithetical rather than complementary. However, an educational community's acceptance of new policies or procedures depends on the degree to which teachers and principals are encouraged to feel ownership of the ideas proposed. The City of Edinburgh Council has committed itself to the task of inservicing all teaching staff on the requirements of the Strategy and the educational research that underpins it. Further, short-term training programs have been developed for principals and assistant principals who will have primary responsibility for implementing the organizational initiatives.

Developments in Australia

Australia is a federation of eight states and territories, which together make up a population of 18 million. The government school system within each state is centrally administered. For example, the Department of Education and Training in New South Wales, Australia's most populous state, serves more than 750,000 students in 2,200 schools across the state. Because of this centralization, the policy on gifted education developed by an individual state, and the funds it is willing to commit to gifted education, impact on gifted students statewide. Education is funded by the federal government, but the states have relative autonomy in terms of how they spend these funds. Almost 30% of Australian children are educated in nongovernment (private) schools.

Given the constraints of space it is not possible to discuss the full range of provisions and services offered to gifted and talented students in the various states. I will, however, present an analysis of trends that have developed over the last few years. It should be noted that, in Australia, talent in sports, and the performing arts has traditionally been admired and fostered, whereas socio-political attitudes towards high intellectual ability have been less positive. Accordingly, I will focus on changes in attitudes towards, and provisions for, intellectually and academically gifted students.

Australia shares the egalitarian philosophies of Scotland and England—not surprising given the nation's development in the late 1700s as a British penal colony. Indeed, the Australian wariness of high intellectual ability goes even further, frequently translating into open resentment or even hostility (Gross, 1993). Combined with a genuine concern for the underdog and the desire to "equalize upwards" by assisting those disadvantaged by intellectual, social, or physical handicaps, there has traditionally been a strong impulse to "level down" by hindering the advancement of those "unfairly" endowed with high intellectual or academic potential. So accepted is this practice that it even has a name—"cutting down the tall poppies." A number of influential research studies have recorded Australian adolescents' rejection of highly able classmates (e.g., Carrington, 1993).

Disturbingly, this predisposition is reflected in the attitudes of many Australian teachers. Carrington and Bailey (2000) surveyed 942 university students training to be K to sixth-grade teachers and 528 training to be seventh- to twelfth-grade teachers. The study sought preservice teachers' reactions towards various hypothetical students who differed according to their levels of ability, their studiousness, and their gender.

Preservice teachers training to teach in K–6 schools considered children of average ability to be significantly more desirable than gifted children and showed a clear preference for their future students *not* to be studious! Preservice teachers training to teach in middle and high schools also strongly preferred students not to be studious, but they made less of a distinction on the basis of ability. For these trainee teachers, it was how ability was blended with effort and gender that made the difference. For example, gifted girls who applied themselves to study were viewed as less acceptable than gifted girls who did not study.

With regard to the gender of the preservice teachers, many of the significant ability/studiousness/gender interactions involved a simple reversal in preferences between the sexes. Female teachers were more tolerant towards gifted boys—as long as they did not study—than towards gifted girls, while the male teachers preferred gifted non-studious girls. Carrington and Bailey comment, perceptively, that the preservice secondary teachers were only marginally older than some of the teenagers they would be teaching in a few years' time. Perhaps they were carrying into their professional lives some of the social attitudes that influenced them in their personal relationships. For whatever reasons, the researchers noted that the attitudes held towards gifted students both by adolescents and by trainee teachers were uncomfortably similar. It appears that to be bright and studious—and particularly to be bright, studious, and female—does not augur well for social acceptability either by one's peers or one's teachers in Australia.

However, Australian research shows that it is possible to elicit strong positive changes in teachers' attitudes towards gifted students and gifted education through professional development programs and inservice courses that provide factual information about the needs and characteristics of academically gifted and talented students. A study of 70 teachers undertaking an extended program of professional development comprising 80 contact hours of lectures, seminars, and workshops showed strong positive attitudinal shifts towards a range of issues in gifted education as measured by pre- and post-test assessment using the Gagné and Nadeau (1985) attitude scale (Gross, 1994). Effect sizes of 1.2 and 1.3 for the factors of ability grouping and acceleration, respectively, indicate remarkably powerful attitudinal shifts, given the participants' initial wariness regarding the efficacy of these two interventions. The idea of moving gifted children away from chronological peers through ability grouping or grade advancement concerns many teachers, even those who support, in principle, the need for specialized programs.

Even short-term inservice can produce positive attitudinal change. The Gagné-Nadeau Attitude Scale was given as a pre- and post-test to 200 New South Wales teachers undertaking single-day (six hour) inservice courses that provided an introduction to a range of issues in gifted education (Gross, 1997a). Even in this short time frame, statistically significant changes in attitude were noted on four of the six factors of the scale. As with the earlier study, strongly positive changes were noted in teachers' attitudes towards acceleration and ability grouping.

It is noteworthy that the use of these two procedures, which are among the most contentious issues in gifted education—VanTassel-Baska (1992) calls them the "lightning rod issues"—is most common in New South Wales and Victoria, the two states that have the highest prevalence both of university-based undergraduate and postgraduate courses in gifted education and of teacher inservice programs systematically offered by their state education departments. Twenty-six schools (seventh–twelfth grade) in Victoria offer an accredited Select Entry Accelerated Learning Program to a cohort of gifted students. This program allows these students to complete their six years of secondary schooling in five years through telescoping the first two or three years. The Select Entry schools vary in the number of subjects in which they offer accelerated progress. During their final year at school, students in this program normally undertake an Extension Study set at a high level as part of their Victorian Certificate of Education (Kronborg, 2000).

Acceleration of academically gifted students is much more comprehensively used in New South Wales than in any other state. Since 1991, more than 9000 gifted and talented students have been accelerated in New South Wales through grade advancement, single-subject acceleration, or early entrance, with a high degree of success.

Until the state's education legislation changed in 1990 with the development of the Education Reform Act, students were legally required to spend seven years in elementary school, regardless of their level of intellectual ability or their academic or social readiness to enter secondary education. The Education Reform Act removed this requirement, and, as a consequence, the NSW Government included a special focus on acceleration in its 1991 policy NSW Government *Strategy on the Education of Gifted and Talented Students*. Also, the NSW Board of Studies (the state curriculum authority) developed a complementary document *Guidelines for Accelerated Progress* that adapted existing international guidelines (Proctor, Black, & Feldhusen, 1986) for Australian use. This provided teachers with an official policy on acceleration, combined with a practical structure and a set of model strategies that had proven effective overseas. These two teacher-friendly documents, combined with the Department of School Education's decision to commit significant funding over the period 1992–1993 to inservice teachers on the practical use of acceleration for gifted students, ensured acceptance and use of the "new" procedures. Inservicing teachers on new techniques empowers them to use these techniques. It should be noted that teachers in other Australian states, who have not received such inservice, are much more reluctant to accelerate gifted students for fear of causing social or emotional damage or distress to these students.

The second "lightning rod issue," ability grouping, arouses strong feelings in Australia, particularly among the militant teachers' industrial unions. Mark Carey of the Australian Education Network describes the provision of special programs for intellectually gifted students as "educational apartheid" and "the segregation of the 'gifted and talented' from the great unwashed" (1994, p. 18). In August 1997, the New South Wales Teachers' Federation called on the state government to "reduce and eliminate [*sic*]" the government-run Selective High Schools for academically gifted students on the grounds that "the increased welfare/discipline problems at comprehensive high schools [are] caused by the removal of their local, positive role models" (NSW Teachers Federation, 1997, p. 12). This claim is difficult to sustain as fewer than 5% of students attending New South Wales secondary schools are enrolled in Selective High Schools, but it is indicative of the resentment felt by many teachers against what they perceive as an elitist stratification of schooling.

New South Wales' 23 Selective and Agricultural High Schools serve academically gifted students in seventh through twelfth grade. Entrance to these schools is through a battery of ability and off-level achievement tests, as well as ranked nominations by the principal and teachers of the student's primary school. The academic success and facilitative social environment of the "Selectives" are widely recognized, and competition to gain entry is high, with several applicants for each vacancy. Sixty-six New South Wales elementary schools offer one or two Opportunity Classes, full-time self-contained classes for intellectually gifted children. These, however, are mainly placed at the fifth- and sixth-grade level, and

very little ability grouping provision is made for gifted students in earlier grades.

Some years ago Braggett (1993) analyzed the relationships between the political ideologies espoused by different Australian state governments and the degree to which special provision for academically gifted students is valued or permitted. Traditionally, states governed by the Australian Labour Party have pursued policies of inclusion, with gifted and talented students educated in the mixed-ability classroom. States governed by the Liberal Party have been more willing to implement policies in which structured programs of ability grouping exist alongside inclusion settings—the *vis-à-vis* rather than the *versus* perspective. However, while in New South Wales the striking expansion of Selective High Schools, Opportunity Classes, acceleration opportunities, and teacher inservice programs were implemented under a Liberal government, the incoming Labour government permitted the continuation of the special schools and special classes and, indeed, recently announced the proposed establishment of additional ability-grouped classes for gifted students in comprehensive (mixed-ability) secondary schools in 2002.

South Australia has three special interest secondary schools for Students of High Intellectual Potential (SHIP) and six primary schools (K–7) have ability-grouped programs for academically gifted students. In Western Australia, a small number of secondary schools provide ability-grouped programs for gifted students in the first two years, while the Primary Extension and Challenge Program (PEAC) caters through part-time grouping to students in fifth–seventh grades who achieve above the 90th percentile of age-peers on achievement tests.

Australian teachers have, until recently, been reluctant to employ standardized testing of ability or achievement to identify academically gifted students (Gross, 1993). However, this reluctance is beginning to break down, in part because a number of states have implemented "basic skills" testing to identify students at risk of school failure, and this has allowed teachers to see for themselves some of the advantages of objective assessment.

In 1997, the Gifted Education Research, Resource and Information Centre (GERRIC) at the University of New South Wales, in association with the Belin-Blank International Center for Gifted Education and Talent Development at The University of Iowa, initiated the highly successful Australian Primary Talent Search (APTS). The goal of talent searches is to identify, through above-level testing, students who need further educational challenge to fully realize their potential.

APTS, which is offered each year, assesses students in third–sixth grades who have already been identified as academically gifted by EXPLORE, a multiple-choice test developed by American College Testing for eighth-grade students. EXPLORE measures students' academic aptitude in four key learning areas, English, mathematics, reading comprehension, and science reasoning.

APTS enables gifted and talented students to demonstrate unusual academic strengths in any or all of these four key learning areas by taking an academically challenging test at a level that is not generally used in primary school. Students' families receive two copies of an individualized score report and a written interpretation of results; many families choose to give the second copy of the report to their child's school. This information can be used by schools to determine appropriate curricular and programming modifications. Anecdotal reports received by GERRIC over the last four years (e.g., Mackie, 2001) indicate that increasing numbers of schools are using the reports in this way.

More than 6000 third–sixth grade students in every state have been tested through APTS, and more than 50% have scored above the mean for eighth grade students in at least one of the four subject areas. The Australian Secondary School Educational Talent Search (ASSETS), which GERRIC will inaugurate in 2002, will assess academically gifted students in seventh–ninth grades on the ACT tests of math, science reasoning, reading comprehension, and English, which are used in the United States to assess twelfth-grade students preparing for college entrance.

In Australia, attitudes towards intellectually gifted students, and provisions for them, differ significantly from state to state. However, over the last five years it has become somewhat more common for education systems to widen their range of program structures, employing grouping and acceleration as well as inclusion, and to include some form of objective assessment to complement the traditional nomination procedures to identify academically gifted students.

Developments in Russia

Grigorenko (2000) began her discussion of the changes in Russia's provisions for gifted students with the metaphor of a math problem in which students are presented with the scenario of two trains that must travel on common tracks, but they will either collide or arrive safely depending on the speeds at which they are driven. The students' task is to calculate the optimal speed at which the trains can travel to reach their destinations safely.

In Grigorenko's cleverly sustained metaphor, Train 1 represents "the inertia of the traditional centralized and controlled educational system," while Train 2 symbolizes "the momentum established by recent developments beginning in the late 1980s." "The trains departed from different places but at some point they must pass through the same switch. The chances are that they can collide, pass each other without rendering an explosion, or unlike it goes in the maths problem, get assembled in a single train" (p. 735).

The traditional Russian system of education adopted the "natural resources" philosophy of gifted education, which taught that the abilities of gifted students must be developed and harnessed so they could be placed at the service of the community. A system of increasingly rigorous competitions was developed to identify academically gifted students, whose talents were then developed through specialized schooling. The focus was on mathematics, physics, and general science rather than on arts and the humanities; nonetheless, their gifted education programs in math and science were exemplary.

Grigorenko (2000) commented that within this system gifted students received little social or emotional support, parents were rarely consulted on their children's education, and since few cities had day schools for the gifted, many gifted adolescents were placed in boarding schools far from home. However, gifted education was financially supported by the state, and gifted students in general attended better schools with teachers who were experts in their field. Diplomas from the more prestigious schools virtually guaranteed entry to the most esteemed universities, and high-achieving students had access to more prestigious and better-paying jobs.

The last decade of the twentieth century saw major changes. Although some of the special schools for gifted young mathematicians and scientists still remain, the newer system has produced "an explosion of different programs" (Grigorenko, 2000, p. 737), with many different types of schools and a greater emphasis on individualized instruction. A somewhat decreased interest in math and science has been balanced by a broader focus on the arts, social sciences, and humanities.

However, perhaps the most striking change occurred through alterations in Russia's financial status, which resulted in the withdrawal of almost all financial support from specialized programs for the gifted. This has both arisen from and accelerated a shift from the "national resource" philosophy to the "special education" perspective, which holds that special abilities should be fostered because the gifted, in common with other children, have the right to develop their abilities to the full. Grigorenko noted that the older system fostered special talents because it benefited from them; however, now that the system is unable to employ these talents, the original motivation for developing them has weakened. She advises that the primary rationale for gifted education must now be "the good of the child"—a perspective that will remove parents from their traditionally passive role and require that they become active participants in talent development. She also insists that teacher training must shift from what she views as an overemphasis on content knowledge, towards an awareness of child and adolescent psychology, including an awareness of research in the education and psychology of the gifted.

As an illustration of how Russian education is "opening up," Callisto, McChesney, and Simmons (2000) described "The Russian School in America," a regular three-month visitation program through which a group of Russian students and their teachers live in the United States and learn about American customs, culture, and lifestyles while continuing their Russian studies.

As with many ground-breaking initiatives, the introductory programs have proceeded on a trial and error basis. Pilot programs found that when Russian students were "mainstreamed" in American classes their understanding and use of English improved, but academically they fell significantly behind their age-peers who remained in Russia. By contrast, when the Russian students studied with Russian teachers, separately from their American host students, the acculturation process suffered. The solution, which has proven highly successful, is a synthesis of both models; each morning, the Russian students attend American classes following the schedules of their host students, while in the afternoon they work together taught by Russian teachers who follow the Russian National Curriculum. This allows them to experience American education and culture while en-

suring that they do not fall behind their classmates, with whom they will still be working on their return to Russia.

The Braxton County School District in West Virginia has hosted more than 250 students from the city of Korolev, home of the Russian Space Mission Control Center. Until 1992, Korolev was a "secret city" whose existence was camouflaged by its being given the same name as an existing city, Kaliningrad (Callisto, McChesney, & Simmons, 2000). The development of a program of cultural and educational exchange between a city such as Korolev and an American school district less than a decade after the end of the Cold War illustrates the profound shift in Russian attitudes towards the purpose of education.

SUMMARY AND CONCLUSIONS

England, Scotland, Australia, and Russia have undergone significant change in the last few years, both in their attitudes to the education of academically gifted students and in the procedures through which these students are identified and served.

The first three nations have, in a sense, self-manufactured the process of change through an awareness of weaknesses in previous educational policy and practice. Russia, by contrast, has had educational change thrust upon her as a result of political and financial upheaval. Nonetheless, the growth of services to the gifted in Australia and Great Britain has resulted from structured efforts to accommodate a range of philosophies and practices in gifted education—a willingness to adopt the *vis-à-vis* philosophy, rather than the *versus*—while Grigorenko affirms the need for Russia to harness the best of both the old and the new systems if it is to survive the challenge of the future.

Strong government leadership is essential if the process of change in gifted education is to be structured, appropriately funded, and systematically evaluated. The educational and lay communities must accept the need for change and engage in it. All four nations agree that teachers must be trained or at least inserviced, on effective identification procedures and defensible, research-based practices of program development and curriculum differentiation. As Benbow and Stanley (1996) warned, the education of gifted and talented students should not be governed by educational fads and social fallacies.

Most important for the development of effective services to the gifted, however, are the qualities advised and exemplified by Harry Passow—wisdom, foresight, and, above all, balance.

QUESTIONS FOR THOUGHT AND DISCUSSION

1. In your district or education system, what issues or principles in gifted education are seen as oppositional or mutually exclusive? Can you develop effective arguments to help these issues to be viewed *vis-à-vis* (face-to-face; together), rather than as mutually exclusive?

2. Write a brief comparison/definition of the (e.g., Russian) "natural resource" and the (e.g., British, American) "special education" philosophies. Which do you support? Explain?

3. Why are some teachers in England reluctant to identify and give special educational services to their ablest students? Is there a similar reluctance among teachers in your district or education system? Are the reasons similar? Explain.

4. Choose one of the countries discussed in this chapter. What could your district or education system learn from this nation's experiences or practices in gifted education? What could this nation learn from your system's experiences or practices?

REFERENCES

Benbow, C. P., & Stanley, J. C. (1996). Inequity in equity: How "equity" can lead to inequality for high-potential students. *Psychology, Public Policy and Law, 2*(2), 249–292.

Borland, J. H. (1989). *Planning and implementing programs for the gifted.* New York: Teachers College Press.

Braggett, E. J. (1993). Programs and practises for identifying and nurturing giftedness and talent in Australia and New Zealand. In K. A. Heller, F. J. Monks & A. H. Passow (Eds.), *International handbook of research and development of giftedness and talent* (815–832). Oxford: Pergamon.

Callisto, T. A., McChesney, D. W., & Simmons, V. G. (2000). A Russian school in the hills. In M. I. Stein (Ed.), *Creativity's global correspondents—2000* (pp. 111–121). Delray Beach, FL: Winslow Press.

Carey, M. (1994). New fashioned apartheid. *Education Links, 47,* 18–22.

Carrington, N. (1993). Australian adolescent attitudes towards academic brilliance. *Australasian Journal of Gifted Education, 2*(2), 10–15.

Carrington, N., & Bailey, S. (2000). How do preservice teachers view gifted students? Evidence from a New South Wales study. *Australasian Journal of Gifted Education, 9*(1), 18–22.

City of Edinburgh Council. (2001). *A framework for the education of gifted and talented pupils.* Edinburgh: City of Edinburgh Council.

Department for Education and Employment. (1997). *Excellence in schools.* London: Her Majesty's Stationery Office.

Department of Education and Employment. (1994). *The education of the able child.* Norwich: Her Majesty's Stationery Office.

Education and Employment Committee. (1999). *Government's response to the Third Report from the Committee, Session 1998–1999: Highly able children.* London: Her Majesty's Stationery Office.

Eyres, D. (1999). Ten years of provision for the gifted in Oxfordshire ordinary schools: Insights into policy and practice. *Gifted and Talented International, 14*(1), 12–20.

Froggatt, A. (in press). Developments in gifted and talented education from 1995 to 2001. *Newsletter of the Support Society for Children of High Intelligence, July.* London: CHI.

Gagné, F., & Nadeau, L. (1985). Dimensions of attitudes towards giftedness. In A. H. Roldan (Ed.), *Gifted and talented children, youth and adults: Their social perspectives and culture* (148–170). Monroe, NY: Trillium Press.

Grigorenko, E. L. (2000). Russian gifted education in technical disciplines: Tradition and transformation. In K. Heller, F. Monks, R. J. Sternberg, & R. F. Subotnik (Eds.), *International handbook of giftedness and talent* (2nd ed., pp. 735–742). Oxford: Pergamon.

Gross, M. U. M. (1993). *Exceptionally gifted children.* London: Routledge.

Gross, M. U. M. (1994). Changing teacher attitudes to gifted students through inservice training. *Gifted International, 9*(1), 15–21.

Gross, M. U. M. (1997a). Changing teacher attitudes towards gifted children: An early but essential step. In J. Chan, R. Li, & J. Spinks (Eds.), *Maximizing potential: Lengthening and strengthening our stride* (3–22). Hong Kong: World Council for Gifted and Talented Children.

Gross, M. U. M. (1997b). How ability grouping turns big fish into little fish—or does it? Of optical illusions and optimal environments. *Australasian Journal of Gifted Education, 6*(2), 18–30.

Kellas, J. G. (1968). *Modern Scotland: The nation since 1870.* London: Praeger.

Koshy, V. (2001). Personal communication from Dr. Valsa Koshy, Brunel University, England.

Kronborg, L. (2000). Victorian report. *Australasian Journal of Gifted Education, 9*(1), 61–62.

Kulik, J. A., & Kulik, C.-L. C. (1997). Ability grouping. In N. Colangelo & G. A. Davis (Eds.), *Handbook of gifted education* (2nd ed., pp. 230–242). Boston: Allyn and Bacon.

Mackie, L. (2001, Summer). APTS: What's the point? *GERRIC News,* 6.

New South Wales Teachers Federation. (1997). Opposing the Carr Labor Government policy on selective high schools. *Education, 216,* 12.

NSW Board of Studies. (1991). *Guidelines for accelerated progression.* Sydney: NSW Board of Studies.

NSW Government. (1991). *NSW Government strategy on the education of gifted and talented students.* Sydney: Ministry for School, Education and Youth Affairs.

Passow, A. H. (1997). International perspectives on gifted education. In N. Colangelo & G. A. Davis (Eds.), *Handbook of gifted education* (2nd ed., pp. 528–535). Boston: Allyn and Bacon.

Proctor, T. B., Black, K. N., & Feldhusen, J. F. (1986). Guidelines for grade advancement of precocious children. *Roeper Review, 9*(1), 25–27.

Rogers, K. B. (1991). *The relationship of grouping practices to the education of the gifted and talented learner.* Storrs, CT: National Research Center on the Gifted and Talented, University of Connecticut.

Scottish Office of Education. (1993). *The education of able pupils P6–S2.* Edinburgh: Her Majesty's Stationery Office.

VanTassel-Baska, J. (1992). Educational decision-making on acceleration and grouping. *Gifted Child Quarterly, 36*(2), 68–72.

43

Teachers of the Gifted: Gifted Teachers

LAURIE J. CROFT, *The University of Iowa*

In the final years of the twentieth century, educational reports announced the results of considerable empirical research. Teachers make a difference. Math teachers count. Science teachers, in fact as well as in theory, spark interests that last a lifetime. History teachers and their subjects are memorable. According to the National Commission on Teaching and America's Future (1996), "good teachers literally save lives . . . by loving students, helping them imagine the future, and insisting that they meet high expectations and standards" (p. iii). This chapter explores current research in general education about the importance of teachers, especially the unique importance of teachers in gifted education.

Gifted students appear to be more profoundly impacted by their teachers' attitudes and actions than are other students. Although their teachers must possess the same characteristics and competencies of all good teachers, the most successful teachers of the gifted develop areas of specific expertise not required in general education. The roles played by teachers of the gifted go far beyond the role of the classroom teacher, and effective and comprehensive professional development opportunities facilitate the transformation from successful teacher to gifted teacher.

Twenty-First Century Teachers

In contrast to the trite assertion that "those who can, do; those who can't, teach," the Institute for Educational Leadership (2001) declared that "student learning depends first, last, and always on the quality of teachers" (p. 1). The competencies and characteristics attributed to excellent teachers have begun to assume almost Herculean proportions. Teachers need professional expertise in subject matter and pedagogy. Teachers with deep conceptual understanding of their subject area ask higher-level questions, better engage students, and enable students to apply and transfer knowledge (Rigden, 2000).

The Role of the Teacher in Student Achievement

Teacher influence on student achievement is complex, but research (Cohen & Hill, 2000; Darling-Hammond, 2000; Weglinsky, 2000) has demonstrated that:

- Investments in well-qualified teachers are more highly correlated with improvements in student achievement than are any other use of educational resources;
- Differences in teacher qualifications account for more than 90% of the variations in student mathematic and reading achievement;
- Even more than subject-area coursework, teachers' completion of education courses and subject-methods courses are consistently related to increased student achievement;
- A complete program of certification through a teacher-education program results in student gains;
- Math students whose teachers participate in professional development in working with diverse populations outperform their peers by more than a full grade level;
- Math students whose teachers are involved in professional development in facilitating higher-order thinking skills outperform peers by 40% of a grade level;

- Science students whose teachers participate in professional development in laboratory skills outperform peers by more than 40% of a grade level;
- Students whose teachers facilitate hands-on learning outperform peers by more than 70% of a grade level in math and 40% of a grade level in science.

A frequently cited study by William Sanders (Sanders & Horn, 1998; Stone, n.d.) explored data from the Tennessee Value-Added Assessment System and found that the single most important factor in the academic growth of students is teacher effectiveness.

From General Education to Gifted Education

The current reform movement in general education has important ramifications for gifted education. Describing the symbiotic relationship between general education and gifted education, Parker (1996) suggested, "Where there is excellence in general education, gifted education will more likely flourish; where gifted education flourishes, there is increased potential for excellence in general education" (p. 159). The current movement, however, has described characteristics and competencies of exemplary—that is, gifted—teachers without explicit or implicit consideration of teachers of the gifted. The National Board for Professional Teaching Standards (NBPTS; 2001), for example, has proposed National Board certification as the standard for excellence in teaching. The NBPTS asserts that commitment to student learning is best reflected through "knowledge of [e.g., multiple intelligence] theories and . . . experiences in classrooms [that] have taught teachers that each student has different strengths, even gifts." This philosophical emphasis fails to recognize that "there may be multiple areas of giftedness, but to be gifted still requires a remarkably high standard" (Colangelo, 2001, p.2).

Different Perceptions of the Role of the Teacher

The reconceptualization of the role of the teacher suggests that "teachers are now asked to generate sufficiently varied and powerful pedagogies so that the inevitably different interests and learning styles of each and every child will be tapped and put to maximum use" (Lagemann, 1993, p. 1). The focus on "interests" and "learning styles," however, does not reflect a commitment to maximizing the intellectual abilities of gifted students. While in general education, "knowledge of the material to be taught is essential to good teaching" (Darling-Hammond, 2000, p. 5), "subject matter knowledge is a positive influence up to some level of basic competence *but is less important thereafter*" [italics added] (p. 4). "Deep understanding" (Rigden, 2000, para. 5) of content is recommended for teachers at their level of teaching and, "preferably, for one grade level above their teaching level" (para. 11). However, teachers who are prepared to provide grade-level content, or even content one grade-level higher, are not prepared to provide effective education for intellectually gifted students.

Intellectually Gifted Students

When discussing the needs of gifted children, "we are talking about students who are so advanced beyond the normal curriculum that they need significantly higher level curriculum and instruction to truly challenge them and produce [a] high level of achievement. . . . That curriculum and instruction must be a level, pace, depth, and complexity that would be inappropriate and frustrating for children of average ability" (Feldhusen, 1994, p. 232). Only 41% of all teachers, however, feel very well prepared to implement innovative teaching methods, a prerequisite for challenging intellectually gifted students. Only 20% of all teachers feel very well prepared to meet the needs of gifted learners (National Commission on Teaching and America's Future, 1996). It remains clear that "what is necessary and sufficient for the nongifted is necessary but *insufficient* for the gifted, who need more and different learning experiences" (Tannenbaum, 1983, p. 461).

Some curricular methods, including enrichment, inquiry, discovery, problem solving, enhancing creativity, and focusing on professional end products as the standard for student achievement, are effective with both general education students and academically gifted students. But acceleration, homogeneous ability grouping, and high-level differentiated curricular programming are uniquely appropriate for gifted education. Good general education teachers, because they do not understand the needs of gifted children, are frequently not successful teachers of the gifted (Ferrell, Kress, & Croft, 1988; Gallagher, 2000).

Gifted Students and Their Teachers

Students identified for gifted programs have described the qualities that they believe are essential for the successful teacher of the gifted (Lewis, 1982):

- "The difference between a normal teacher and a gifted teacher is that a gifted teacher is very much like her kids."
- "A gifted teacher needs to be more than a normal teacher. She needs more talent and imagination."
- "Other teachers teach us things. Gifted teachers teach us how to think about things."
- "We need teachers who help us, not haunt us."
- "It's easy to know what you want in a teacher—it's hard to know how to get it."

Intellectually gifted students provide the anecdotal evidence suggested by empirical research. Students spend some 10,000 hours of their lives in schools; they are the personalities behind the student-achievement statistics. They sense, for example, the varying levels of teacher enthusiasm for gifted classes. According to Bransky (1987), while teachers of the gifted indicated positive to enthusiastic reactions to a gifted program, general education teachers' reactions varied widely. Approximately one-third of the latter teachers indicated a generally positive response, but more teachers were negative than enthusiastic. Many were indifferent.

Students also perceive the differences between teachers who have participated in professional development opportunities in gifted education and teachers who have not. Studies suggest that students rate trained teachers significantly higher in skills such as facilitating higher-level thought processes, focusing on higher-level learning experiences, relying less on lectures and more on discussions, and placing less emphasis on extrinsic rewards for learning. Teachers themselves report similar differences between successful teachers of the gifted and successful general education teachers (Hansen & Feldhusen, 1994).

Teachers of the gifted differ significantly in the kinds of high standards they set for their students, and in the ways they encourage students to achieve perfection. Teachers of the gifted reportedly enjoy trying new approaches to the teaching-learning process, and they value the creativity expressed by young learners. They more often affirm that education provides students with the foundation for growth throughout life and for making productive contributions to society. Significantly more often than general education teachers, teachers of the gifted express a commitment to building positive working relationships with their students (Ferrell, Kress, & Croft, 1988; Hansen & Feldhusen, 1994).

Teachers of the Gifted

Isolating the characteristics and competencies unique to effective teachers of the gifted is a challenge. Many of the attributes delineated in research in gifted education correspond to characteristics necessary for any teaching success. The National Association for Gifted Children (NAGC) has attempted to meet the challenge and define standards for educators working with gifted children. NAGC expressed a commitment to the "right of all persons to have educational opportunities to maximize their potential" (Parker, 1996, p. 159).

Highly successful teachers of the gifted understand and meet the needs of gifted students in a variety of ways. Through their careful differentiation of classroom experiences for gifted students, they demonstrate an awareness of the positive, and the sometimes negative, ramifications of students' unique characteristics. Their perception of curriculum and programming needs includes:

- Understanding student needs within the contexts of both giftedness and the field of study;
- Facilitating independent study;
- Scheduling for rapid comprehension, an ability that enables fast pacing and discovery learning, with an occasional tendency to race through content without depth of understanding;
- Emphasizing complexity over simplicity;
- Facilitating the achievement of ever more challenging curricular goals;
- Using differentiated and fair grading practices;
- Establishing a learner-centered environment and some freedom of choice in content, process, product, and environment;
- Encouraging collaborative learning and mutual support between teacher and students;

- Establishing policies beneficial to gifted students; even "reinterpreting" school policies that are detrimental to needs of gifted students.

Insights into the affective needs of gifted students encourage highly successful teachers to:

- Inspire and motivate students;
- Reduce tension and anxiety for students who are frequently perfectionists;
- Plan for high levels of excitability, including high energy and powerful emotions, as well as disruptive humor and extreme competitiveness;
- Encourage patterns of divergent and original thinking;
- Help students overcome tendencies toward disorganization, inattentiveness, and/or social ineptness;
- Recognize student perceptiveness, often expressed as the awareness of truth and justice, but also as intolerance and rigidity;
- Appreciate high levels of sensitivity, expressed both in compassion and easily hurt feelings.

(See, e.g., Chan, 2001; Clark, 1997; Ferrell, Kress, & Croft, 1988; Gallagher, 2000; Henry, 1991; Hunt & Seney, 2001; Joffe, 2001; Kitano & Landry, 2001; Landvogt, 2001; Maker & Nielson, 1995; Mingus, 1999; Shore, Cornell, Robinson, & Ward, 1991; Westberg, 1995; Whitlock & DuCette, 1989.)

Teacher Competencies in the Classroom

The different attitudes and attributes associated with successful teachers of the gifted correlate with distinct teacher competencies, including effective student identification and a broad repertoire of techniques for meaningful curricular differentiation. Clearly, teachers assume the primary role in articulating and enacting an appropriate curriculum for their students. The complex teaching process interacts with students' intellectual abilities, motivation and persistence.

Many classroom teachers in general education have difficulty conceptualizing appropriately challenging activities that emphasize student needs, interests, and learning preferences. Research suggests that gifted students spend much of their time in passive classroom activities, often experiencing advanced content or challenging curricular units less than once per month (Archambault et al., 1993). This is further substantiated by the recollections of outstanding research neurologists, who noted that "exciting or stimulating classes were few and far between." Even the advanced classes in their specific domains of ability were often "undistinguished" and "really deadly" (Bloom, 1985, p. 377).

Recent studies from the National Research Center on the Gifted and Talented have found no instructional or curricular differentiation in 84% of the activities experienced by elementary school high-ability students in major content areas. When teachers received direct in-service instruction in curriculum compacting, they were able to eliminate from 24% to 70% of what they typically taught. This confirmed earlier findings that much of the assigned work for bright students has been previously mastered. Even when classroom teachers were able to select students who needed curricular modifications, however, they had little time to develop appropriate replacement activities. (Renzulli, Smith, & Reis, 1982; Westberg, Archambault, Dobyns, & Salvin, 1993).

Identification of Gifted Students

Classroom teachers without training in gifted education generally have less success in identifying gifted students than do teachers with specialized preparation. Yet the identification of intellectual ability is the educator competency that predicates all other successful services. General education teachers fail to identify many high-ability children, especially those from economically or culturally divergent backgrounds or those with learning disabilities. In fact, teachers with little or no background in gifted education often express beliefs and attitudes antithetical to appropriate identification:

- "A truly gifted kid is not really bored."
- "They are all articulate and enthusiastic and creative."
- "He's probably gifted, but he's a first-class jerk" (Peterson & Margolin, 1997, p. 87).

Other misconceptions include beliefs that gifted children uniformly demonstrate conformity to classroom rules, good behavior, and superior performance in all academic areas. In truth, gifted children are not always popular with their peers, do not have academically talented siblings, and do not come from families with well-educated or professional parents (Dawson, 1997; Rohrer, 1995).

Teachers with specific training and coursework about gifted students comprehend, advocate, and utilize essential factors implicit in gifted-student identification (Ford & Trotman, 2001; Stanley, 1984):

- The use of multiple measures of ability;
- Recognition of the strengths of students who are culturally or ethnically diverse;
- The use of above-level testing, avoiding the "ceilings" encountered by many gifted children;
- A focus on relevant subject subscores rather than composite scores;
- Recognition of degrees of talent;
- The use of diagnostic testing to plan prescriptive instruction;
- Awareness that the formal assessment of the gifted is a "qualitatively different experience," as gifted children become deeply engaged in the testing process, enjoying the challenge of providing elaborate details to as many questions as possible. (Osborn, 1999).

Educators of the gifted develop an understanding of the critical importance of discovering talent. Children must be "recognized as talented in order to develop a talent . . . [but] talent alone is no guarantee of future success. Every potential talent needs to be cultivated and nurtured with great discipline for many years if it is to be applied usefully" (Csikszentmihalyi, Rathunde, & Whalen, 1993, p. 1).

Differentiation in the Classroom

The classroom competencies necessary for successful teachers of the gifted do include those ascribed to all good teachers. However, additional distinct skills emerge as critical to the process of cultivating outstanding intellectual ability. Central to these abilities is a commitment to the general concept of *differentiation*—a substantial adaptation in goals/objectives, resources, teaching procedures, evaluation procedures, and attention to learning styles and environments (Gallagher, 1975; Passow, 1983).

General guidelines for differentiated curriculum include more information, greater depth, higher-level thinking skills, nontraditional subjects and experiences, faster pace, self-directed learning, and commitment to future learning. Because "individuals who differ by virtue of enduring characteristics . . . require . . . patterns of developmental education distinguishably different in form and substance" (Ward,

1985, p. 7), educators need to identify the salient characteristics of their population of gifted students, determine corresponding educational needs, and develop appropriate means to meet those needs.

By responding to the characteristics and needs of the particular gifted population, teachers enact programs that become models of "defensible differentiation" (Borland, 1989, p. 172). Too many activities that are reserved for small classes of gifted students would be comprehensible to, enjoyed by, and beneficial to most students. Defensible differentiation should be based on a consensus as "to what gifted students should learn that they would not learn in the mainstream" (p. 176). Successful teachers of the gifted allow capable students to critically analyze meaningful content at a pace that the students find challenging. Successful teachers do *not* require more of the same kind of learning mastered in the mainstream curriculum. From the perspective of teachers trained in gifted education, curricular modification should "accomplish more than is accomplished by [an] underlying administrative arrangement alone (that is, the act of putting kids together)." Differentiation should be a substantive adaptation: "curricular transformation as distinct from curricular transportation" (Shore, Cornell, Robinson, & Ward, 1991, p. 96).

Types of Differentiation: Grouping, Acceleration, and Enrichment. Three general types of differentiation encompass the efforts to link the characteristics and needs of gifted learners with program adaptations by teachers. *Grouping* high-ability students together clearly can be beneficial; teachers can target the appropriate level of instruction needed for student learning. Successful teachers of the gifted recognize that their students make greater academic gains when interacting with intellectual peers than they do in more heterogeneous classrooms.[1] Options for grouping include self-contained gifted classrooms, pull-out programs, cluster grouping, across-grade grouping, and within-class flexible grouping. All require different expertise from the teacher.

Educators with training and expertise in gifted education are in the best position to guide decisions about which grouping strategies best meet local student needs. Because grouping has political as well as

---

1. See Chapter 21 by Kulik.

pragmatic implications, however, decisions are often made by school or district administrators who may be juggling competing interests. While grouping facilitates the other types of differentiation, teachers find themselves challenged to adopt grouping plans in increasingly heterogeneous classrooms (Davalos & Griffin, 1999; Hughes, 1999).

Other adaptations revolve around acceleration and enrichment, which are complementary components of comprehensive differentiated curriculum. *Acceleration* has been predicated on certain educational assumptions: Each level of instruction possesses an established logical sequence of materials, tasks, skills, and acquired knowledge; the average or typical rate of progress desired for most students has been established; and intellectually gifted students are capable of more rapid progress through the discipline. Accelerated students, regardless of age or grade, rapidly move through sequential sets of concepts and skills normally prescribed for older learners, effectively promoting the student into a higher level within a subject area or into a higher grade. Acceleration has strong research support as a unique adaptation for gifted students and is recommended more often than any other single practice in gifted education (Shore, Cornell, Robinson, & Ward, 1991).

In comparison, *enrichment* is a more horizontal intervention. Teachers introduce any content or process distinct from what is usually included in a particular subject and grade. These activities allow students to expand their knowledge base while remaining with age-mates and within the parameters of the normal sequence of a subject area. As an adaptation suitable for all students, enrichment facilitates original student investigations; productive and critical thinking in content areas; moral and ethical reasoning; and advanced levels of analysis, synthesis, and evaluation. With its different focus, enrichment ideally enhances student ability to analyze and solve problems; introduces students to new interests; stimulates originality, initiative, and self-direction; and develops a growing sense of social consciousness (Southern & Jones, 1991).

Teachers using a blend of the general types of differentiation enable "the gifted learner [to] proceed at a faster pace, to a higher level of content and more abstract and evaluative thinking than his or her age peers" (Fox, 1979, p. 215). Passow (1979) asserted that "good educational acceleration is always enriching . . . and solid enrichment programs always advance the student's learning of new and relevant material and are consequently accelerating" (p. 188). Empirical research has suggested that homogeneous grouping, as well as combinations of acceleration and enrichment, lead to more successful learning than does any approach employed alone (Shore, Cornell, Robinson, & Ward, 1991).

Elements of Curriculum Differentiation in the Classroom. Within these general types of differentiation, teachers modify one or more of four elements impacting the transmission of curriculum: content, process, product, and environment (Maker & Nielson, 1995). As teachers of the gifted gain knowledge, maturity, and experience in the field, they begin to shape flexible and responsive adaptations to gifted students' needs in creative combinations of all four areas. *The capability of developing, implementing, and evaluating defensibly differentiated curriculum is a key characteristic unique to teachers of the gifted.*

Content. The teaching-and-learning of meaningful content—facts, concepts, and ideas essential to understand subject matter—is the fundamental goal of the educational system. Within the context of subject-area content, giftedness can be understood in part in terms of increasingly expert performance in domains of aptitude. "The process of mastery of successive stages in a specific field is . . . a joint exchange between the individual student and the accumulated wisdom of others who have greater mastery of the domain" (Feldman, 1982, p. 35). Greater expertise and the expression of talent are associated with the knowledge of substantial amounts of factual and conceptual knowledge in the discipline, ability to easily retrieve relevant information, and sophisticated strategies for mentally organizing the discipline (Rabinowitz & Glaser, 1985).

To ensure continuous educational progress, successful teachers use the structure of a discipline to establish the framework for conceptual understanding. They include one or more of the following content modifications (Ford & Trotman, 2001; Gallagher, 1998; Maker & Nielson, 1995; Parks, 2001; Shore, Cornell, Robinson, & Ward, 1991):

- Novelty;
- Sophistication;
- Methodologies unique to the discipline;
- Biographical explorations of creative and productive individuals;
- Multicultural resources and perspectives;

- Career education;
- Metacognitive strategies.

Process. The process—the methods, activities, and questions—that successful teachers use to present content represents much of the artistry in teaching. Coleman (1994) describes the essence of "being a teacher" of the gifted as far more than just presenting technical knowledge. Successful processes implemented in teaching the gifted involve acting, interacting, reacting, and spontaneously revising the intended curriculum in response to the needs of remarkably agile student minds. Teachers of the gifted participate in extensive professional development so they may internalize suggestions for process modification in the gifted classroom. (See, e.g., Callahan, 2001; Dunn & Milgram, 1993; Joffe, 2001; Kelble, Howard, & Tapp, 1994; Kennedy, 1995; Maker & Nielson, 1996; Tomlinson, 1999.)

Curriculum Models. Curriculum models provide teachers with systematic ways to deliver content, as well as organizational schema for appropriately differentiated units. Models are applied in whole or in part, depending on school context. But a thorough understanding of the purpose, nuances, and efficacy of any model is essential. Interestingly, teachers report using Bloom's *Taxonomy of Educational Objectives: Cognitive Domain* more than any other model (Rash & Miller, 2000), but Bloom's Taxonomy is not an example of defensible differentiation. Designed for general education, it is an essential strategy for all learners, but is insufficient as a unitary strategy to enhance learning for intellectually gifted children. The familiarity with, understanding of, and ability to apply a variety of complex curriculum models reflects a level of professional expertise that significantly distinguishes gifted teachers from colleagues in general education.

Examples of models used by educators of the gifted include:

- Betts' Autonomous Learner Model;
- Feldhusen's Purdue Three-Stage Enrichment Model for Elementary Gifted Learners; Purdue Secondary Model for Gifted and Talented Youth;
- Gallagher's adaptations of Problem-Based Learning;
- Gardner's Multiple Intelligences;
- Guilford's Structure of Intellect (adapted by Meeker);
- Parnes' Creative Problem Solving;

- Renzulli's Enrichment Triad;
- Schlicter's Talents Unlimited;
- Stanley's Study of Mathematically Precocious Youth;
- Sternberg's Triarchic Model;
- VanTassel-Baska's Integrated Curriculum Model.

Product. Curriculum models, philosophical preferences, learning styles, and the discipline or field of study all recommend products—the outcomes of instruction—that demonstrate student learning and understanding. The standards for assessment of gifted-student learning should be based on development of deeper subject understanding and expertise, rather than on comparisons of achievement with others of the same age. Successful teachers of gifted children are aware that gifted children should not have to produce more regular work than their age peers. In addition to testing, other types of products are important in gifted programs. Independent research findings, portfolios, oral presentations, and creative expressions of understanding all relate to varying objectives revolving around higher-level understandings. Products created by gifted students should be authentic products designed for real audiences and should be "transformative," reflecting the ways in which students apply new knowledge, more often than summative (Dettmer, 1985; Maker & Nielson, 1995).

Environment. The educational environment includes both physical and affective components. The physical and affective adaptations to all educational environments should stem as much as possible from program objectives and student needs. Recommendations related to the gifted classroom emphasize the centrality of the learner.

General education teachers frequently acknowledge students as gifted because of their compliance with what the teachers perceive to be ideal student attitudes and behaviors (Peterson & Margolin, 1997). Price and Milgram (1993), however, reported that gifted adolescents express distinct learning preferences within their physical environment. Gifted students vary widely in their preferences and abilities to learn best in settings that are quiet—or allow for music and other auditory stimuli; well lit—or less brightly lit; warm—or cool; and formal, with traditionally arranged desks—or informal, with options for seating, working, free movement, and even snacking. Students also vary in preferences for working alone or working with groups of different sizes. The use of gifted students as peer tutors and group leaders is rarely the most appropriate or equitable way to guarantee learning for any of the group members.

Regarding the affective environment, teachers of the gifted explicitly introduce strategies to promote acceptance of oneself, peers, and others; to develop effective social skills and group processes; and to become meaningfully involved with the larger community (Hunt & Seney, 2001; Maker & Nielson, 1995). Ford and Trotman (2001) stress the importance of creating an environment in which gifted students, including those who are culturally and ethnically diverse, feel challenged and safe to explore and express their uniqueness.

Importantly, research has indicated variations in the educational environment based on the learner's level of talent development. Regardless of the age of the learner and independent of the field of study, successful teachers of gifted students who are novices in an area are supportive, encouraging, and enthusiastic. They emphasize the excitement of the subject with both expectations of progress and prompt positive feedback. Successful teachers also facilitate student discovery of larger disciplinary patterns and processes, and encourage student experimentation.

When gifted students attain sufficient expertise, however, they require a qualitatively different environment. The next phase of talent development is characterized by the greater discipline required to achieve a high level of performance. Teachers (and private tutors) with very high levels of ability in the subject establish environments that emphasize practice, habits of precision, and substantial progress (Bloom, 1985; Sosniak, 1985, 1999).[2] "These teachers [give students] a perspective in the field, including the meaning and purpose in the field in its largest dimensions" (Bloom, 1985, p. 522). For students who have attained greater levels of expertise in subject areas, very different roles are required of teachers who are successful in facilitating continued educational progress.

Roles for Educators of the Gifted

The roles required of many educators of the gifted frequently supersede the cultural ethos familiar to classroom teachers. Teachers generally create a

culture characterized by great personal autonomy in their classrooms and by the interplay of their individualistic styles of interaction with their students. Much of the satisfaction derived from teaching emerges from daily successes. Most teachers of the gifted, however, do not have full-time positions in self-contained classrooms. They more frequently meet with other teachers' students on a part-time and pull-out basis. Their appointment may be a percentage of a full-time equivalent. They may travel to various schools, borrowing space in which to meet with students. As specialists, teachers of the gifted serve as counselors to gifted students, as consultants with sometimes less enthusiastic colleagues, and even as formal or informal program coordinators.

The Counselor

Feldhusen (1995) noted that the gifted need special support to help them develop a better understanding of their abilities; to better equip them to deal with the personal and social challenges of their giftedness; to set appropriately challenging career goals; and to plan realistic educational routes to those goals. Because teachers trained in gifted education often possess the greatest understanding of the nature and needs of intellectually gifted students, they express concern, patience, and willingness to listen to student concerns, all critical to meeting student needs. Teachers of the gifted can promote positive rather than punitive reactions to gifted behaviors, including high levels of activity, independence, and underachievement, all examples of conduct that can provoke other teachers. Teachers of the gifted can also help develop each student's sense of self as a gifted and unique individual, especially important to gifted girls and to gifted students from traditionally underrepresented groups (Borland, 1989; Dunn & Milgram, 1993; Ford & Trotman, 2001).

The Consultant

While teachers of the gifted may average as much as 20 minutes per day on counseling activities, they spend approximately 25 minutes per day consulting with colleagues in the general education classroom (Rash & Miller, 2000). In some districts, the role of the teacher of the gifted is one designated specifically as a consultant—a resource specialist rather than a teacher. Generally, consultation includes advising colleagues on areas of concern, providing special materials, and conducting demonstration lessons

---

2. See Chapter 19 by Sosniak.

in colleagues' classrooms. Collaboration may also involve the development, implementation, and modification of curriculum, or assisting classroom teachers with independent projects and investigations (Gallagher, 2001; Kirschenbaum, Armstrong, & Landrum, 1999; Robinson & Ringlaber, 1992).

The Coordinator

The teacher of the gifted may also serve in the capacity of formal or informal program coordinator, a more political and potentially less popular role than that of colleague-consultant. As program coordinator, the teacher has the responsibility of advising and leading the district in defining the gifted population to be served and in developing a cohesive program linked to the general education curriculum. Coordinators require skills in public relations and public speaking, to say nothing of diplomacy. As the coordinator of gifted education, the teacher is also expected to have the skills to provide meaningful in-service training to colleagues and to advocate for the needs of gifted students. Importantly, although "gifted education has had and continues to have a role as a laboratory for testing, refining, and disseminating ideas . . . applicable to general education," it falls to well-educated teachers of the gifted to advocate for and "meet the unique needs of gifted students" (Tomlinson, Coleman, Allan, Udall, & Landrum, 1996, p. 167).

Professional Development for Gifted Teachers

The characteristics, competencies, and multiple roles associated with teachers of the gifted are not explicitly enhanced through traditional teacher education programs. Classroom teachers who have concerns for their gifted students dedicate significant amounts of time and personal resources to develop the expertise necessary to meet the needs of these special students. Continuing professional development in gifted education is the key to the transformation of good teachers into gifted teachers.

The State of the States in Gifted Education

Research has confirmed that professional development changes teacher attitudes; enhances teachers'

sense of self-efficacy, that is, the belief in their capability to organize and enact appropriate activities; and promotes greater proficiency, the understanding and application of relevant competencies (Ropp, 1999; Shore & Kaizer, 1989). The most recent *State of the States in Gifted and Talented Education Report* (Council of State Directors of Programs for the Gifted, 1999), however, found that only 3 of 43 responding states indicated that classroom teachers have more than 3 contact hours in either preservice or inservice training in gifted education. Only Nevada, West Virginia, and Iowa currently report an undergraduate endorsement in gifted education. Kentucky is currently the only state requiring professional development in gifted education for all classroom teachers. At least 30 states mandate the identification of gifted students, and 26 states mandate special programming for gifted students. Twenty-six states also require endorsement for teachers working with gifted students, but curiously, they are not the same 26. At least 8 states that require special programming for gifted students do not require any special training of the teachers who provide that programming. At least 19 states do not require any training in gifted education, even for teachers who work primarily with gifted students.

Novice versus Expert Teachers of the Gifted

Preservice and novice teachers without training in gifted education demonstrate unsophisticated attitudes and less effective strategies when they interact with gifted students. Student teachers focus on issues such as classroom management, being liked by their students, and being evaluated positively by their supervisors. They express empathy for low-achieving students and a preference for working with them. Even when they indicate a commitment to differentiation for high-ability learners, their lesson plans do not reflect the complexity inherent in effective differentiation. Novices express confidence in the centrality of the teacher in the classroom, the value of heterogeneous cooperative learning, and in the completion of assignments as the measure of success. They "tend to create a chilling and less supportive social-emotional environment for students" who are underachievers or simply less compliant (Ribich & Barone, 1998).

Unlike novices, expert teachers of the gifted focus on student-initiated learning, responsive differentiated strategies appropriate to the curricular material, theoretically based and cohesive programs rather than disconnected activities, competitions, or other provisions. Expert teachers are committed to the importance of their students' interests, seeking ways to help children express their areas of passion, both in school and in the larger community (Hanninen, 1988; Tomlinson et al., 1994).

Professional Development Programs in Gifted Education

The National Association for Gifted Children (1998) stated that "gifted learners are entitled to be served by professionals who have specialized preparation in gifted education, expertise in appropriate differentiated content and instructional methods, involvement in ongoing professional development, and who possess exemplary personal and professional traits." While graduate degrees in gifted education are available in several states, specialized preparation for teachers who work most directly with gifted children typically revolves around a state endorsement program, often including local inservice opportunities, workshops, courses, and conferences. Professional development opportunities are a confluence of several streams of expertise:

- A balance of pedagogical theory and practice in gifted education and in subject areas;
- Advanced content in subject areas, including complex performance goals reflected in national standards;
- Links among teachers' existing knowledge, schools' program objectives, and best practices for differentiating curricula to meet the needs of intellectually gifted learners;
- Historical and contemporary issues in gifted education, from the nature of intelligence and its assessment to the continuum of essential services for diverse gifted students, taught through direct instruction, videos, individualized and independent learning, small-group discussions, field experiences, and peer coaching;
- Observations of gifted teachers facilitating the development of the extraordinary abilities of gifted students.

(See, e.g., Cashion & Sullenger, 2000; Gallagher, 2001; Karnes & Lewis, 1996; Karnes, Stephens, & Whorton, 2000; Parker, 1996; Reis & Westberg, 1994; Shore & Kaizer, 1989; Taplin, 1996.)

An Endorsement in Gifted Education

Since 1981, The Connie Belin & Jacqueline N. Blank International Center for Gifted Education and Talent Development, a part of The University of Iowa College of Education, has facilitated the professional development of approximately 2,500 educators through courses or workshops in gifted education. The Connie Belin & Jacqueline N. Blank Fellowship Program for Teacher Training in Gifted Education provides intensive residential professional development to a cadre of classroom teachers from different areas of general education. The educators selected for participation in the summer program are new to the area of gifted education. With a group of enthusiastic and supportive colleagues, mentored by leaders in gifted education, they are immersed in an experience crafted to help them critically explore their attitudes toward gifted students; better understand the theoretical underpinnings of a wide variety of psychological and programming issues in gifted education; link personal areas of expertise to plans for the application of best practices in their classrooms and schools; and actively observe gifted students in a wide range of content areas.

As measured by pre-post test comparisons, participants in the Fellowship have demonstrated consistent development in more positive attitudes toward gifted children and significant increases in knowledge about the education of gifted children. Individual comments bring the experience to life:

- "This has opened my eyes in ways beyond the gifted arena—but, of course, it will mean that my sensitivity will be even greater to the needs and identification of gifted students. I hope I will be able to be an influential leader in the advocacy of gifted programs as I progress in the field."
- "There is an art and a science to teaching. I have always known intuitively that the needs of gifted students are different, but I lacked concrete background and why and how to facilitate programming. This experience has revitalized my interest because I feel so much smarter—like there is so much more than can and has to be done!"

Since Iowa adopted an endorsement in gifted education, the Belin-Blank Center has offered all of the coursework necessary to fulfill the requirements for greater understanding the psychological needs of gifted students; developing and implementing programming interventions for high-ability learners; the administration of gifted programs; and the completion of a practicum experience. Courses model a wide variety of implementation strategies, including independent learning and distance learning. New content emphases include neuroscientific implications for gifted education, curricular differentiation through technology, opportunities to link content with differentiated pedagogical strategies, gifted program evaluation, and staff development. The Advanced placement (AP) Teacher Training Institute has implemented a one-hour option for secondary teachers who want to augment their understanding of the AP program with greater understanding of gifted students.

SUMMARY AND CONCLUSIONS

Comprehensive and effective professional development opportunities help dedicated teachers transform successful characteristics and competencies into gifted education practice. Teachers of the gifted play unique and varied roles within schools, but traditional teacher education programs are just beginning to consider providing preservice teachers with some of the knowledge they will need to work effectively with gifted learners. Teachers generally enter the field without access to other colleagues to serve as mentors, and frequently without colleagues who share their concerns and visions for excellence. The benefits of professional development include not only the theory and practical applications of a broad range of information, but also a network of supportive colleagues.

The characteristics and competencies of successful teachers of the gifted are not identical to the attributes of other successful teachers. Research both within and outside the field of gifted education clearly demonstrates the pivotal role that prepared teachers play with high achievers: Gifted students require teachers who have a special constellation of knowledge and abilities that facilitate progress through complex and challenging content. Curricular differentiation, the accurate diagnosis of the diverse needs of gifted learners, and the concomitant prescription for appropriate interventions are essential. Teachers make the difference.

QUESTIONS FOR THOUGHT AND DISCUSSION

1. What evidence would be most persuasive in your district to convince local stakeholders that "student learning depends first, last, and always on the quality of teachers"?

2. Analyze and evaluate the characteristics of successful teachers of the gifted.

3. Select one of the roles played by a teacher of the gifted and create an appropriate job description for that role.

4. What is it that teachers of the gifted do that is different from "regular" teaching?

REFERENCES

Archambault, F. X., Westberg, K. L., Brown, S. W., Hallmark, B. W., Zhang, W., & Emmons, C. L. (1993). Classroom practices used with gifted third and fourth grade students. *Journal for the Education of the Gifted, 1,* 103–119.

Bloom, B. S. (1985). Generalizations about talent development. In B. S. Bloom (Ed.). *Developing talent in young people* (pp. 507–549). New York: Ballantine Books.

Borland, J. H. (1989). *Planning and implementing programs for the gifted.* New York: Teachers College Press.

Bransky, T. (1987). Specific program information: A key to attitudes about the gifted education program. *Gifted Child Quarterly, 31,* 20–24.

Callahan, C. (2001). Evaluating learners and program outcomes in gifted education. In F. A. Karnes & S. M. Bean (Eds.), *Methods and materials for teaching the gifted* (pp. 253–298). Waco, TX: Prufrock Press.

Cashion, M., & Sullenger, K. (2000). "Contact us next year": Tracing teachers' use of gifted practices. *Roeper Review, 23,* 18–21.

Chan, D. W. (2001). Characteristics and competencies of teachers of gifted learners: The Hong Kong teacher perspective. *Roeper Review, 23,* 197–202.

Clark, B. (1997). *Growing up gifted* (5th ed.). Upper Saddle River, NJ: Merrill.

Cohen, D. K. & Hill, H. C. (2000). Instructional policy and classroom performance: The mathematics reform in California. *Teachers College Record, 102,* 294–343.

Colangelo, N. (2001, fall). Message from the director. *Vision, 10*(2), 2.

Coleman, L. J. (1994). "Being a teacher": Emotions and optimal experience while teaching gifted children. *Gifted Child Quarterly, 38,* 146–152.

Council of State Directors of Programs for the Gifted. (1999). *The 1998–1999 state of the states gifted and tal-*

ented education report. Longmont, CO: Council of State Directors of Programs for the Gifted.

Csikszentmihalyi, M., Rathunde, K., & Whalen, S. (1993). *Talented teenagers: The roots of success and failure.* Cambridge: Cambridge University Press.

Darling-Hammond, L. (2000). Teacher quality and student achievement: A review of state policy evidence [Electronic version]. *Education Policy Analysis Archives, 8*(1). Retrieved from http://epaa.asu.edu/epaa/v8n1/.

Davalos, R., & Griffin, G. (1999). The impact of teachers' individualized practices on gifted students in rural, heterogeneous classrooms. *Roeper Review, 21,* 308–314.

Dawson, V. L. (1997). In search of the wild bohemian: Challenges in the identification of the creatively gifted. *Roeper Review, 19,* 148–152.

Dettmer, P. (1985). Attitudes of school role groups toward learning needs of gifted students. *Roeper Review, 7,* 252–255.

Dunn, R., & Milgram, R. M. (1993). Learning styles of gifted students in diverse cultures. In R. M. Milgram, R. Dunn, & G. E. Price (Eds.), *Teaching and counseling gifted and talented adolescents: An international learning style perspective* (pp. 4–23). Westport, CT: Praeger.

Feldhusen, J. F. (1994). A case for developing America's talent: How we went wrong and where we go now. *Roeper Review, 16,* 231–233.

Feldhusen, J. F. (1995). Talent development during the high school years. *Gifted Education International, 10*(2), 60–64.

Feldman, D. H. (1982). A developmental framework for research with gifted children. In D. H. Feldman (Ed.), *Developmental approaches to giftedness and creativity, No. 17: New directions for child development* (pp. 31–45). San Francisco: Jossey-Bass.

Ferrell, B., Kress, M., & Croft, J. (1988). Characteristics of teachers in a full day gifted program. *Roeper Review, 10,* 136–139.

Ford, D. Y., & Trotman, M. F. (2001). Teachers of gifted students: Suggested multicultural characteristics and competencies. *Roeper Review, 23,* 235–239.

Fox, L. H. (1979). Sexism, democracy, and the acceleration versus enrichment controversy. In W. C. George, S. J. Cohn, & J. C. Stanley (Eds.), *Educating the gifted: Acceleration and enrichment* (pp. 215–217). Baltimore: Johns Hopkins University Press.

Gallagher, J. J. (1975). *Teaching the gifted child* (2nd ed.). Boston: Allyn and Bacon.

Gallagher, J. J. (1998). Accountability for gifted students. *Phi Delta Kappan, 79,* 739–742.

Gallagher, J. J. (2000). Unthinkable thoughts: Education of gifted students. *Gifted Child Quarterly, 44,* 5–12.

Gallagher, J. J. (2001). Personnel preparation and secondary education programs for gifted students. *Journal for the Education of the Gifted, 11,* 133–138.

Hanninen, G. E. (1988). A study of teacher training in gifted education. *Roeper Review, 10,* 139–144.

Hansen, J. B., & Feldhusen, J. F. (1994). Comparison of trained and untrained teachers of gifted students. *Gifted Child Quarterly, 38,* 115–121.

Henry, M. E. (1991). Expectations of teachers and students: A gifted classroom observed. *Gifted Education International, 7*(2), 69–75.

Hughes, L. (1999). Action research and practical inquiry: How can I meet the needs of the high-ability student within my regular education classroom? *Journal for the Education of the Gifted, 22,* 282–297.

Hunt, B. G., & Seney, R. W. (2001). Planning the learning environment. In F. A. Karnes & S. M. Bean (Eds.), *Methods and materials for teaching the gifted* (pp. 43–89). Waco, TX: Prufrock Press.

Institute for Educational Leadership. (2001). *Leadership for student learning: Redefining the teacher as leader.* Washington, D.C.: Author.

Joffe, W. S. (2001). Investigating the acquisition of pedagogical knowledge: Interviews with a beginning teacher of the gifted. *Roeper Review, 23,* 219–226.

Karnes, F. A., & Lewis, J. D. (1996). Staff development through videotapes in gifted education. *Roeper Review, 19,* 106–110.

Karnes, F. A., Stephens, K. R., & Whorton, J. E. (2000). Certification and specialized competencies for teachers in gifted education programs. *Roeper Review, 22,* 201–202.

Kelble, E. S., Howard, R. E., & Tapp, J. B. (1994). Enhancing physical science instruction for gifted elementary students: Developing teacher confidence and skill. *Roeper Review, 16,* 162–166.

Kennedy, D. M. (1995). Plain talk about creating a gifted-friendly classroom. *Roeper Review, 17,* 232–234.

Kirschenbaum, R. J., Armstrong, D. C., & Landrum, M. S. (1999). Resource consultation model in gifted education to support talent development in today's inclusive schools. *Gifted Child Quarterly, 43,* 39–47.

Kitano, M. K., & Landry, H. (Eds.). (2001). Instructional cases: Learning from the dilemmas of practicing teachers. *Roeper Review, 23,* 206–218.

Lagemann, E. C. (1993). For the record: Reinventing the teacher's role [Electronic version]. *Teachers College Record, 95*(1), 1–7. Retrieved from http://www.tcrecord.org/Content.asp?ContentID=99.

Landvogt, J. (2001). Affecting eternity: Teaching for talent development. *Roeper Review, 23,* 190–196.

Lewis, J. F. (1982). Bulldozers or chairs? Gifted students describe their ideal teacher. *Gifted Child Today, 23,* 16–19.

Maker, C. J., & Nielson, A. B. (1995). *Teaching models in education of the gifted.* Austin, TX: Pro-Ed.

Maker, C. J., & Nielson, A. B. (1996). *Curriculum development and teaching strategies for gifted learners* (2nd ed.). Austin, TX: Pro-Ed.

Mingus, T. T. Y. (1999). What constitutes a nurturing environment for the growth of mathematically gifted students? *School Science and Mathematics, 99,* 286–293.

National Association for Gifted Children. (1998). *Pre-K–Grade 12 Gifted Program Standards* [Electronic version]. Retrieved from http://www.nagc.org/webprek12.htm.

National Board for Professional Teaching Standards. (2001). *Standards* [Electronic version]. Retrieved from http://www.nbpts.org/.

National Commission on Teaching and America's Future. (1996). *What matters most: Teaching for America's future* [Electronic version]. New York: Author. Retrieved from http://www.nctaf.org/publications/whatmattersmost.html.

Osborn, J. B. (1999). *Assessing gifted children: Advocacy for gifted and talented education in New York.* Retrieved from http://www.agateny.org/resources/agc.htm.

Parks, S. (2001). Materials and methods for teaching analytical and critical thinking skills in gifted education. In F. A. Karnes & S. M. Bean (Eds.), *Methods and materials for teaching the gifted* (pp. 301–367). Waco, TX: Prufrock Press.

Parker, J. P. (1996). NAGC standards for personnel preparation in gifted education: A brief history. *Gifted Child Quarterly, 40,* 158–164.

Passow, A. H. (1979). A look around and a look ahead. In A. H. Passow (Ed.), *The gifted and the talented: Their education and development, Part 1* (pp. 439–456). Chicago: University of Chicago Press.

Passow, A. H. (1983). The four curricula of the gifted and talented: Toward a total learning environment. In B. M. Shore, F. Gagné, S. Larivée, R. H. Tali, & R. E. Tremblay (Eds.), *Face to face with giftedness* (pp. 379–394). New York: Trillium.

Peterson, J. S., & Margolin, L. (1997). Naming gifted children: An example of unintended "reproduction." *Journal for the Education of the Gifted, 21,* 82–100.

Price, G. E., & Milgram, R. M. (1993). The learning styles of gifted adolescents around the world: Differences and similarities. In R. M. Milgram, R. Dunn, & G. E. Price (Eds.), *Teaching and counseling gifted and talented adolescents: An international learning style perspective* (pp. 230–247). Westport, CT: Praeger.

Rabinowitz, M., & Glaser, R. (1985). Cognitive structure and process in highly competent performance. In F. D. Horowitz & M. O'Brien (Eds.), *The gifted and talented: Developmental perspectives* (pp. 75–98). Washington, DC: American Psychological Association.

Rash, P. K., & Miller, A. D. (2000). A survey of practices of teachers of the gifted. *Roeper Review, 22,* 192–194.

Reis, S. M., & Westberg, K. L. (1994). The impact of staff development on teachers' ability to modify curriculum for gifted and talented students. *Gifted Child Quarterly, 38,* 127–135.

Renzulli, J. S., Smith, L. H., & Reis, S. M. (1982). Curriculum compacting: An essential strategy for working with gifted students. *The Elementary School Journal, 82*(3), 185–194.

Ribich, F., & Barone, W. (1998). Semantically different: Preservice teachers' reactions to the gifted student concept. *Journal of Educational Research, 91,* 308–312.

Rigden, D. (2000). Implications of standards for teacher preparation. *Council for Basic Education: Online Edition, 45*(3). Retrieved from http://www.c-b-e.org/be/iss0011/a1ridgen.htm.

Robinson, A., & Ringlaben, R. (1992). Ideas with impact: Consultant teacher. *Journal for the Education of the Gifted, 16,* 83–87.

Rohrer, J. C. (1995). Primary teacher conceptions of giftedness: Image, evidence, and nonevidence. *Journal for the Education of the Gifted, 18,* 269–283.

Ropp, M. M. (1999). Exploring individual characteristics associated with learning to use computers in preservice teacher preparation. *Journal of Research on Computing in Education, 31,* 402–424.

Sanders, W. L., & Horn, S. P. (1998). Research findings from the Tennessee Value-Added Assessment System (TVAAS) database: Implications for educational evaluation and research. *Journal of Personnel Evaluation in Education, 12,* 247–256.

Shore, B. M., Cornell, D. G., Robinson, A., & Ward, V. S. (1991). *Recommended practices in gifted education: A critical analysis.* New York: Teachers College Press.

Shore, B. M., & Kaizer, C. (1989). The training of teachers for gifted pupils. *Canadian Journal of Education, 14*(1), 74–87.

Sosniak, L. (1985). Phases of learning. In B. S. Bloom (Ed.), *Developing talent in young people* (pp. 409–438). New York: Ballantine Books.

Sosniak, L. A. (1999). An everyday curriculum for the development of talent. *Journal of Secondary Gifted Education, 10*(4), 166–172.

Southern, W. T., & Jones, E. D. (1991). Academic acceleration: Background and issues. In W. T. Southern & E. D. Jones (Eds.), *The academic acceleration of gifted children* (pp. 1–28). New York: Teachers College Press.

Stanley, J. C. (1984). Use of general and specific aptitude measures in identification: Some principles and certain cautions. *Gifted Child Quarterly, 28,* 177–180.

Stone, J. E. (n.d.). Value-added assessment: An accountability revolution. Retrieved from http://www.edexcellence.net/better/tchrs/16.htm.

Tannenbaum, A. J. (1983). *Gifted children: Psychological and educational perspectives.* New York: Macmillan.

Taplin, M. (1996). Student teachers providing programmes for gifted and talented children: A cooperative venture between university and schools. *Gifted Education International, 11*(2), 95–99.

Tomlinson, C. A. (1999). *The differentiated classroom: Responding to the needs of all learners.* Alexandria, VA: Association for Supervision and Curriculum Development.

Tomlinson, C. A., Coleman, M. R., Allan, S., Udall, A., & Landrum, M. (1996). Interface between gifted education and general education: Toward communication, cooperation and collaboration. *Gifted Child Quarterly, 40,* 165–171.

Tomlinson, C. A., Tomchin, E. M., Callahan, C. M., Adams, C. M., Pizzat-Tinnin, P., Cunningham, C. M., Moore, B., Lutz, L., Roberson, C., Eiss, N., Landrum, M., Hunsaker, S., & Imbeau, M. (1994). Practices of preservice teachers related to gifted and other academically diverse learners. *Gifted Child Quarterly, 38,* 106–114.

Ward, V. S. (1985). Giftedness and personal development: Theoretical considerations. *Roeper Review, 8,* 6–10.

Weglinsky, H. (2000). *How teaching matters: Bringing the classroom back into discussions of teacher quality* [Electronic version]. Princeton, NJ: Educational Testing Service and the Milken Family Foundation. Retrieved from http://www.ets.org/research/pic/teamat.pdf.

Westberg, K. L. (1995). Meeting the needs of the gifted in the regular classroom: The practices of exemplary teachers and schools. *Gifted Child Today, 18*(1), 27–29.

Westberg, K. L., Archambault, F. X., Dobyns, S. M., & Salvin, T. J. (1993). The classroom practices observation study. *Journal for the Education of the Gifted, 16,* 120–146.

Whitlock, M. S., & DuCette, J. P. (1989). Outstanding and average teachers of the gifted: A comparative study. *Gifted Child Quarterly, 33,* 15–21.

44

Gifted Education in Rural Schools

NICHOLAS COLANGELO, *The University of Iowa*
SUSAN G. ASSOULINE, *The University of Iowa*
CLAR M. BALDUS, *The University of Iowa*
JENNIFER K. NEW, *Synapse Learning, Iowa City*

With regard to gifted students, "luck" of geography should not dictate the opportunities to identify and enhance talent.

—Colangelo, 2001

The educational opportunities of gifted and talented young people living in rural areas and small towns in the United States deserves to be of concern and interest to America's educators. Rural gifted students are everywhere. Every state has rural areas and rural schools: 50% of all public schools in the United States are in small towns and rural areas, and 39% of all public school students—nearly 17,500,000—live in small towns and rural areas (National Center for Education Statistics, 1998). This chapter focuses on the convergence of two national issues: ruralness and giftedness. Although the issue of gifted education in rural schools is a new topic, ironically, the pioneers of gifted education, Lewis Terman and Leta Hollingworth, were from rural areas.[1]

The literature on gifted education in rural schools is as sparse as a rural population. Seal and Harman (1995) reported on a task force indicating that students in rural settings are less likely to be classified as gifted since there are so few such programs. Spicker, Southern, and Davis (1987) discussed size as well as traditional rural values as barriers to providing educational opportunities to gifted students. Jones and Southern (1992) found similar issues, in that size and financial support made it difficult to have gifted programs. Cross and Dixon (1998) in an overview of issues regarding gifted education in rural areas, identified the challenges of sparse resources and minimal support for identifying gifted students. A recent study by Gentry, Rizza, and Gable (2001) compares attitudes of gifted students from rural, suburban, and urban areas. The authors reported that gifted students from rural schools perceived less challenge, interest, and generally less enjoyment in classes compared to their suburban and urban peers.

It should be noted that rural schools have many inherent strengths, such as small class size, low dropout rates, community support, teacher autonomy, and opportunities for students to participate in many activities (Gentry, Rizza, & Gable, 2001; Whooley, 1999). Although these strengths have not yet translated into advantages for gifted students in rural schools, they can become advantages. Two major national reports from the Connie Belin & Jacqueline N. Blank International Center for Gifted Education and Talent Development (Belin-Blank Center), *Gifted Education in Rural Schools: A National Assessment* (Colangelo et al., 1999) and *Gifted Voices from Rural America* (Colangelo, Assouline, & New, 2001), both focus on the needs of gifted students in rural schools and on the strengths of rural schools in meeting these needs. This chapter relies on a synthesis of the two national reports by the Belin-Blank Center and interviews with gifted students and teachers from rural schools.

---

1. For a historical timeline on gifted education and gifted education in rural schools, see Colangelo, Assouline, & New (1999). *Gifted Education in Rural Schools: A National Assessment.*

We first address rural education within a context of community issues, including an operational definition of *rural*. Issues of gifted education in rural schools are also covered, including challenges and benefits associated with being a gifted student in a rural school.

> *I like the stuff that I hate. I like that I know everybody. I like that people know me and my family. That it's safe and no one locks their doors at night. But some of that stuff drives me crazy too. I don't like it that few people have very open minds—this is a fairly conservative place. There's little diversity, not many viewpoints.*
>
> —Catherine Maki, twelfth grade, Candor, New York, describing the pros and cons of living in a small town.

Rural Communities and Rural Education

Definition of Rural

Establishing a definition of *rural* sounds simple enough. However, we have found it to be a complicated task. Most reports on rural issues contain an explanation of how the authors grappled with this definition. Even the federal government and its myriad of offices—to which we turned for precedents—does not use a single definition. Rather, different federal offices use different meanings and often eschew the term altogether in favor of the more homogenous *nonmetropolitan*. Instead of defining what rural *is*, this term lumps together everything it is *not*. Our frustration over the elusive nature of this word puts us in good company.

The American Heritage College Dictionary's entry provides one common element to the definition of rural in that it is "of the country" and "relating to farming; agriculture." While the word commonly suggests a tractor in a field, New England's fishing villages, logging towns of the Pacific Northwest, and the Southwest's desert region populated by American Indian reservations and Mexican-American communities are also rural. Each of these is a rural area, albeit nonfarming in nature. Each plays a significant role in our national heritage.

Federal Definitions

Among the federal offices that have definitions of *rural,* the Census Bureau's two definitions are commonly used. In its decennial survey, the Bureau defines *rural* as a residual category of places "outside urbanized areas in open country, or in communities with less than 2,500 inhabitants," with a population density of "less than 1,000 inhabitants per square mile" (Stern, 1994, p. 4). In its monthly household sample surveys, however, the Census Bureau uses the term *nonmetropolitan* instead of *rural*. *Nonmetropolitan* refers to counties "outside of, or not integrated with, large population concentrations of 50,000 or more" (Stern, 1994, p. 4).

Another federal office, the Economic Research Service (ERS) of the U.S. Department of Agriculture organizes its classification by counties. There are ten ERS categories, ranging from the central areas of very large cities at 0, to "completely rural" areas that are not adjacent to any sort of town or city at 9.

The National Center for Education Statistics (NCES, 1998) provides yet another definition and perhaps the one most relevant to education researchers. Differentiating by community type, the NCES has a five-level definition moving from *central city* to *rural*. Each community type is defined, in part, by its relation to a *metropolitan statistical area*.

An Operational Definition

As Daryl Hobbs (1994) commented, "The term nonmetropolitan is a residual; it is what is left over after the metropolitan areas have been taken out. . . . The concept of rurality once had significant economic, social, and political associations, but the nonmetropolitan concept that replaced it is primarily, though perhaps not totally, geographic" (pp. 7–8). We are interested in that more traditional "concept of rurality." We believe this concept still has currency. In trying to tool an operational definition, we have sought one that is as pliable and inclusive as possible, allowing us to investigate the nature of schools in a variety of rural settings, each with their own unique economic, social, and political characteristics.

Each of the four previous definitions was developed to fit the specific needs and purposes of the respective governmental offices, for example, NCES. These definitions also reflect the considerable resources available to such offices for data collection. For the purpose of this chapter we define public school districts with 2,000 or fewer students as being "rural and small schools" (from Colangelo et al., 1999). This definition, while imperfect, captures the vast majority of schools that meet the multiple standards of *rural.*

Demographics

Rural issues are clearly national issues. Every state has rural schools (only Washington, D.C., does not have a school considered rural; National Center for Education Statistics, 1998). There are concentrations of rural schools in the United States. Figure 44.1 (NCES, 1988) indicates the percentage of students attending public small/rural schools across the nation.

Many facets of rural life impinge on schools. Demographically, the number of people who live in rural areas has been shrinking since the last century. During the Civil War, for example, four of five Americans lived in communities of 2,500 or less. Today, over three-quarters of the population live in metro areas, and fewer than one-fourth live in rural places (Herzog & Pittman, 1995).

Another imbalance exists within the rural population itself, this one in terms of age. The number of working adults and children is proportionally smaller in rural areas, while the rural elderly population is increasing. This is partly a result of the increase in retirement communities, which will only grow as the Baby Boom generation ages. The equation of a shrinking population on one end of the age spectrum and a growing one on the other end does not bode well for rural schools, since education funds are often linked to enrollment, and older voters are not always avid supporters of education. In addition, recently arrived retirees tend to be less vested in local schools, having no personal memories of or connections to the schools through their own experiences or those of children and grandchildren.

Economics

The economies of rural communities also impact schools. No longer based on agriculture or natural resources, such as logging or oil, rural economies have radically altered after decades of stability. In the 1990s, for example, farming employed fewer than one in ten rural workers (Stern, 1994); at the same time, the manufacturing and service industries have expanded significantly in rural locales. We can no longer make assumptions about the income of a rural community, and yet to understand the state of a community's schools and its children we must know where its money comes from. According to Hobbs (1994), a community's economic base affects its so-

cial organization, social class structure, demographic composition, leadership, and wealth. And all of this affects children and the schools.

One thing that hasn't changed for rural economies is that they remain dependent on a single industry, although the industry may have shifted from mining to manufacturing, or from fishing to retirement service. Any study of an industry that goes from boom to bust illustrates the devastating effects that a lack of economic diversity can have on a community. Take, for example, the bleak depression that surrounded many small communities in the Midwest following the farm crisis of the 1980s or the widespread unemployment that hit parts of the Northwest after environmental concern triggered cutbacks in the timber industry in the early 1990s.

Although poverty's hold on rural America has gradually loosened during the last century, rural children continue to bear the brunt of it (see Beeson & Strange, 2000). And every farm crisis or timber cutback is especially hard on this segment of the population. In 1993, for example, more than one-third of the rural Americans who were in poverty were children under the age of 18 (Herzog & Pittman, 1995). This is partly due to the instability of employment in rural areas, a situation that is not significantly better than that found in many inner cities. Although overall unemployment is lower in rural areas than in inner cities, jobs are often short-term, seasonal, and part-time (Hobbs, 1994). Such work not only undermines stability, it also limits a family's benefits, including health insurance for children, access to unemployment compensation, and retraining programs. As with inner cities, the jobs that exist in rural locales are usually low-paying, and are increasingly service-related (e.g., restaurants, motels, retail). There are far fewer managerial, professional, and technical jobs in rural areas than in metropolitan areas.

This trend parallels or results in the migration of more highly skilled and educated residents, who leave small communities in search of higher-paying jobs. Every migration of a talented young person is the loss of a community's investment in education. When the would-be doctors, teachers, and entrepreneurs move away, they take with them both their promise for the future and twelve-years' worth of education. For rural schools, where the price-per-pupil expenditure is often higher than in metropolitan schools (due partly to the much greater cost of transportation) and where few new people migrate *to* the community, this is a significant loss (Beeson & Strange, 2000).

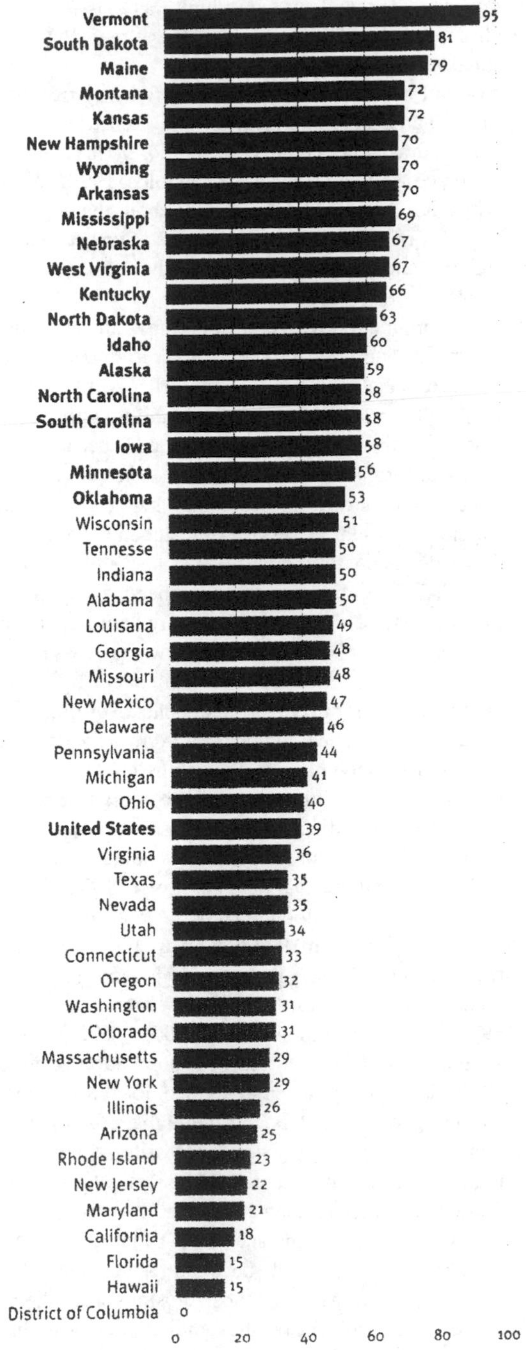

Figure 44.1 Percentage of Public School Students in Small Town/Rural Areas, by State: 1993–94.

Source: National Center for Education Statistics, 1998.

Top-20 rural states are in bold.

I don't think I could live in a big city, but I'm not sure I could live here either. The only reason would be to be near my parents if they needed me. I have a strong tie with the mountain and our property but not to the area.
—Jubal Slone, twelfth grade, Gate City, VA

Education

These economic conditions impact children and their schools, as reflected in differences between rural and metropolitan areas in a number of statistics. Rural students, for example, do not earn college degrees at the same rate as their metropolitan peers (Stern, 1994). Although the high school completion rate of rural students has gradually risen during the past several decades, the gap between rural and metropolitan students for college completion has grown larger. In 1960, the discrepancy of the college completion rate for these two groups was 3.4%; by 1990 it was 9.5% (Herzog & Pittman, 1995).

Although some studies show that rural students are not as well prepared for college as their metropolitan peers (Herzog & Pittman, 1995), their success in higher education and, later, in the work world are linked closely to the climate of their community. "Expectations for students and teachers will vary widely from one type of rural community to the next. The standards for those expectations are most likely tied to the experience of the adults. If there are few professional role models and if most of the adults are first generation high school graduates, the expectations will be very different than those in a community where, because of culture or location, high percentages of adults have some college or post-high school education," writes Paul Nachtigal (1994, p. 27). This is not promising news for communities that are losing their most talented residents.

Schools

Rural schools have a complex history. For many small and isolated communities they have been a focal point of activity, serving not only as a place for the education of children, but also as a meeting space for political and social affairs. Townships have traditionally taken pride and ownership in their schools, viewing them as a defining and shared centerpiece. Like many facets of education, rural schools have been victim to cyclical schools of thought. At the end of the twentieth century, for example, many of the mainstays of small schools were being heralded by the education establishment; smaller class size, mixed grades, and the community as classroom are all popular methods today. At other times, however, small and rural schools have been under attack, accused of being backward and insufficiently rigorous. In the name of modernization and industrialization, many rural schools have been closed in favor of larger, consolidated systems (Reynolds, 1999). While critics have sometimes been right about the deficiencies of rural schools, they have more often been shortsighted and unconcerned with the best form of education for rural students.

In conjunction with consolidation, standardization became a central tenet of education reformers. As students, especially in large, urban schools, were more frequently grouped by age and ability rather than taught together in multi-age groupings, it became necessary to formalize a set curriculum. The central principle of standardization was that a single curriculum should be presented to same-age students working at the same pace with a qualified teacher. Since smaller schools had neither sufficient numbers of students of the same age or ability level nor more than a couple of teachers, at most, consolidation was necessary to achieve the reformists' goals. The advent of school buses made the movement of students over great distances more practical than before. Across the country, schools from neighboring townships joined together to form larger institutions. In the process, at least one school became extinct for each consolidation.

The march for "bigger, better" schools has continued throughout the twentieth century. In 1930, for example, there were about 128,000 school districts in the United States; in 1996 there were just 14,883 districts (NCES, 1998). Between 1940 and 1990, the total number of public elementary schools declined 69%—from approximately 200,000 to 62,037—despite a 70% increase in the U.S. population (Cotton, 1996). Even today, when many people—both experts and lay people—understand the damage that can be done to a community when it loses its school, closings still occur. The impetus for consolidation is now more often financial than curricular. In West Virginia, for example, 258 of the state's K–12 public schools, or 26 percent, closed between 1990 and 1998 (Strange, 1998). Many of those closings were the result of a requirement by the state's School Building Authority that schools meet minimum size criteria before qualifying for construction funding. Today, small schools and districts continue to fight consolidation, though paradoxically, they sometimes rely on it as the only way to exist.

Consolidation continues despite convincing evidence that (1) small school size is associated with lower high school dropout rates; (2) socio-economically disadvantaged students perform better in small schools; and (3) student participation is dramatically higher in small schools (Cotton, 1996). Ironically, consolidation continues at the same time that large urban districts are increasingly interested in creating schools-within-schools and other creative ways of forming smaller educational communities.

Qualities of Rural Schools

Many analysts have commented on how the cultural gap between rural and metropolitan areas has diminished as a result of such factors as commuting, cable television, and regional shopping malls (e.g., Hobbs, 1994). Still, schools in rural areas possess some unique qualities. For example, they are relatively isolated, situated geographically far from resources such as cultural centers, universities, large libraries, and even other schools. Teachers in these buildings don't have ready access to universities that can augment their training, nor are materials near at hand to research or expand curricula. Students have less exposure to a range of professions than their suburban peers. Small classes also limit the chances that a student with special needs will have a classmate with similar aptitudes or interests. These and related challenges will be revisited in the discussion of gifted education in rural schools.

Benefits of Rural Education

Although it is important to realize the many deficits under which rural schools operate, it is equally key to remember the many benefits they offer. Some positive components of rural schools include small class size, mixed-age classrooms, schools-within-schools, and community service. Indeed, as mentioned earlier, urban schools are now copying some of the most successful elements of their rural counterparts. Ironically, many of these positive features were diminished by consolidation, a process that forced rural schools to grow bigger and to lose ties to their communities.

A survey of rural educators yielded many responses emphasizing the benefits of small schools (Colangelo, Assouline, & New, 1999). Teachers, superintendents, parents, students, and association presidents all stressed the following benefits of small schools:

- A higher level of child-adult contact
- More individualized learning
- Learning through community involvement
- Participation in multiple school events

These benefits are the norm, not the exception. There is greater opportunity (and need) for students in small schools to participate on teams, serve in student government, and play an active part in clubs.

Students in smaller schools also have an increased sense of belonging. Among the teachers and administrators interviewed, many of them commented on the ease they had in discussing a particular student's progress and needs with other faculty, sometimes creating individualized plans for students with special needs and interests. Such spontaneous and flexible planning isn't as possible in a larger school, where the bureaucracy is usually more rigid and the larger enrollment simply means less time per student.

Gifted Education

Like trends in rural education, gifted education has experienced a see-saw effect of interest and lack of interest on the part of the educational establishment. Whether seen as an invaluable commodity to be well-funded and nourished, or as an elitist group draining money from more worthwhile projects, there have been strong reactions to gifted education in the United States. Over the years, theories and research have increased the awareness of and interest in gifted education. However, arriving at a definition for *gifted* has been as perplexing as defining *rural* schools. The National Assessment report (Colangelo et al., 1999) describes *giftedness* as exceptional potential and/or performance in one or more socially valued areas.

A Crossroads

Similar to rural education, gifted education has not always benefited from reform policies. Notably, the recent move towards detracking (abolishing accelerated and advanced courses) and the increased use of cooperative learning have been considered hindrances to gifted students by many experts in the field.

These trends are coupled with the ever-present concern regarding elitism. In our attempts to give everyone a fair chance, or to "level the playing field," American schools are often guilty of ignoring the talents and needs of their most able students. Some critics go so far as to argue that American schools are markedly anti-intellectual. In *Out of Our Minds,* Howley, Howley, and Pendarvis (1995) say that "the dark side of society's commitment to provide everyone with a standard, functional schooling . . . [is] the destruction of talent, and not only (or even principally) among the gifted" (p. 142). Gifted students are expected to succeed, whatever the obstacles, without the benefits of special help. They, along with their parents and teachers, are often accused of being elitist and of pilfering resources from students who have greater needs.

The State of Gifted Education in Rural and Small Schools

When examining rural education side by side with gifted education, some striking similarities appear. Both have borne the brunt of educational fads, and both have received relatively little funding and national attention. Today, we have a much better idea of what is happening to serve our most able inner-city students, and we have models of successful programming for these students. Nothing on a similar scale, however, is available for parents and educators working to improve the schooling of gifted rural students. While we know that rural schools are dedicated to helping gifted students, there has been little attempt to provide adequate assistance or develop a national network to serve these students.

Schools in rural areas and small towns also have many advantages, which provide benefits that small schools provide to *all* students. The advantages most frequently mentioned include considerable individualized attention, familiarity and trust among members of the school community, opportunities for involvement in a wide range of activities despite skill level (e.g., the school newspaper, sports teams, and student council), and participation and commitment by parents and community members.

Many gifted students comment on the benefits of both a small school and a small town. Will Nedved, from small-town Garner, Iowa, said that his senior year independent study project on opera was possible because all of the teachers in the building knew and trusted him. "I set up a plan for my project and presented it to my teachers," said Will. "Because they knew I could work well on my own, they didn't hesitate to let me go for it. It was the most exciting, chal-

lenging thing I did in high school" (Colangelo et al., 1999). Nedved eventually won a $5,000 Scholastic Art and Writing Award and was invited to Washington, D.C., to present his opera. Likewise, Tom Skuzinski, a National Merit Finalist from Reed City, Michigan, said that he really appreciated the support and security offered by his small community: "I sometimes received congratulatory notes from people in town who I didn't even know," he recalled fondly (Colangelo et al., 1999, p. 37). While these students might have profited from a wider range of peers and greater academic offerings in a larger school, they clearly enjoyed the advantages of their small schools (Colangelo et al., 1999).

In rural schools, the immediate impact for gifted students depends on changes within the rural schools. In recognizing this, our focus is not to urbanize, or suburbanize, rural schools in the name of gifted education, but to advocate educational opportunities for gifted students while preserving the integrity of rural schools.

Literature on Gifted and Rural

The Belin-Blank Center at The University of Iowa has produced two extensive reports focusing on issues of gifted students in rural schools: *Gifted Education in Rural Schools: A National Assessment* (Colangelo et al., 1999) and *Gifted Voices from Rural America* (Colangelo et al., 2001). However, these recent undertakings are exceptions to the national reports on education. Unlike the comprehensive reports and histories that have been written separately about gifted education and rural education, there are generally no other such roadmaps to follow on the topic of how our most academically advantaged and talented students are being served in America's small and rural schools. Relatively little has been written on the combined topics of giftedness and rural education. In *The Gifted in Socio-Educational Perspective,* Newland (1976) allotted one chapter to the obstacles of providing challenges to gifted students in rural areas and outlined some alternatives. Almost two decades later, Spicker (1992; Spicker & Poling, 1993) and Piirto (1994) also briefly addressed the needs of rural and gifted youth, very much echoing the observations of Newland.

Technology is one of two main themes that reoccurs in articles addressing the gifted in rural areas. Increasingly, authors are interested in describing methods of delivering advanced materials to isolated gifted students via the Internet, e-mail, teleconferencing, or other means. The other common theme falls under the heading of a *profile article*—that is, an article outlining the challenges that face both gifted students and those adults involved in their education, often focusing on the progress of an individual or program.

The ideas in technology-centered articles are often as quickly outdated as the programs and hardware they describe. Although technology in general is an increasingly popular method for serving rural gifted students, the various methods for transmitting information and coursework are ever-changing, causing a unique set of challenges. The fast-paced nature of technology, including the spread of the Internet and the advancement of hardware, makes it a difficult topic to cover in any writing that will have more than a year's staying power.

The issue of timeliness also affects the second group of articles, those that profile specific programs. As Colangelo et al. (2001) indicated, when they tried to contact gifted rural programs that had been mentioned in their 1999 report, "None of the respondents had anything to report. Every school had long since dropped its programs, usually because the key people responsible for inspiring and directing them had long since departed from the scene, as had the funds needed for the extra support" (p. 24).

Challenges

As mentioned, the Belin-Blank Center is producing a series of reports examining how gifted students are served in rural schools. The 1999 *Gifted Education in Rural Schools: A National Assessment* provided an overview of both gifted and rural education and how the two have interacted and overlapped. Some of these issues have been noted in this chapter. In addition, the report presents a series of charts and statistics highlighting conditions affecting schools and youths in the twenty most rural states. As part of the report, a survey of rural educators was conducted to better understand the quality of life in rural schools as it pertains to giftedness. As indicated in the report, the challenges faced today by rural schools attempting to serve their gifted and talented students are numerous. Few of the fifty schools surveyed for the 1999 report had either gifted programs or, in the case of high schools, Advanced Placement courses.

In many instances, students were identified as gifted, often due to state laws requiring such identification, but little or no programming was available. Many students indicated that the services they were offered seemed tacked onto their regular schedules and were perceived more as excuses to get out of class than as positive, worthwhile opportunities.

Teachers, administrators, students, and government statistics report that the following are among the most common challenges:

- A lack of community resources, such as museums, libraries, and professional mentors to augment school resources and facilities;
- A lack of a sizeable peer base for gifted students;
- A lack of time for student involvement in additional programming, such as community college courses;
- Difficulties in hiring teachers, especially those with advanced training and experience;
- Lack of Advanced Placement classes and an overemphasis on community college classes for gifted students;
- Lack of training for teachers and administrators on issues of gifted education;
- Limited curricula due to small student populations and the need for remedial courses that compete for teacher time and resources;
- Accusations of "elitism" by community members;
- A sense of isolation for teachers dedicated to trying new methods and/or serving gifted and talented students.

The superintendent has two kids in the gifted and talented program, and one of our principals has a daughter in the program. So they are very supportive of it. But the faculty is a different story. Some faculty members are intimidated by gifted kids. They don't see why special services are necessary, or they resent not being able to teach those children. Gifted children have special needs, and the higher their ability, the more emotional problems they have. Many faculty members don't understand this.
—Jane Sly, teacher and gifted
program coordinator, Cochran, GA

Overcoming the Challenges: Rural Gifted Voices of Success

Gifted voices from rural america, the 2001 report prepared by the Belin-Blank Center, focuses on unique schools and educators who creatively faced challenges commonly experienced by rural and small-town schools. These educators developed effective programs to serve their gifted and talented students while maintaining their rural identity. Six schools from across the United States were included in these profiles: Jackson River Governor's School, Virginia; Kenai Peninsula Borough School District, Alaska; Native American Preparatory School, New Mexico; Nevada City School of the Arts, California; Idalia High School, Colorado; Akron-Westfield Community School District, Iowa.

What do these success stories have in common?

• A teacher/administrator with vision and tremendous personal commitment;
• Programs that provided standards and flexibility for the development of exceptional talent;
• Students who were exceptional and needed the special programs;
• Rural/small-town areas with limited options.

It must be noted, though, that these schools do not serve *all* students and *all* forms of giftedness. Given their size and limited resources, each of these educational communities has chosen its niche. Often, there is a special teacher who leads the way, with talents that serve as a base for a program. In other cases, the unique nature and background of the local community decide the direction and needs of a school. The results are wonderful and applause-worthy. Yet students in the school with the strong writing program, for example, have few options for math and science, while students in the districts that have banded together to create science and technology offerings often do not have a similar special program for the arts.

SUMMARY AND CONCLUSIONS

There is still much work to accomplish in order to build better programs to serve some of America's most able students—gifted youth who live in rural places. As we identify challenges, let's also celebrate rural and small schools creatively serving their gifted students, and we look to them to further that goal. The major objective needs to be the integration of gifted education into rural schools, while preserving their inherent advantages. It is a goal worth our time and energies.

QUESTIONS FOR THOUGHT AND DISCUSSION

1. What are some of the challenges in defining a school as "rural"?

2. Explain some of the inherent advantages of a rural school district.

3. While millions of students attend rural schools, the issues of rural schools are seen as "invisible." Why is this so?

4. Some people in rural areas view gifted education as a threat. Why would gifted education be a threat to rural schools?

5. The philosophy in this chapter is that gifted education can be integrated into rural schools without threatening its "ruralness." What is meant by this? Do you agree it can be done? Do you agree with the authors?

REFERENCES

Beeson, E., & Strange, M. (2000). Why rural matters: The needs for every state to take action on rural education. *Journal of Research in Rural Education, 16,* 63–69.

Colangelo, N. (2001). Gifted education in rural schools. Keynote Presentation at the Wallace Family National Conference on Gifted Education in Rural Schools at The University of Iowa, Iowa City, IA.

Colangelo, N., Assouline, S. G., & New, J. K. (1999). *Gifted education in rural schools: A national assessment.* Iowa City, IA: The Connie Belin & Jacqueline N. Blank International Center for Gifted Education and Talent Development, The University of Iowa.

Colangelo, N., Assouline, S. G., & New, J. K. (2001). *Gifted voices from rural America.* Iowa City, IA: The Connie Belin & Jacqueline N. Blank International Center for Gifted Education and Talent Development, The University of Iowa.

Cotton, K. (1996). School size, school climate, and school performance. *School Improvement Research Series, SIRS [On-Line].* Close up #20 Portland, OR: Northwest Regional Educational Laboratory.

Cross, T. L., & Dixon, F. A. (1998). On gifted students in rural schools. *NASSP Bulletin, 82,* 119–124.

Gentry, M., Rizza, M. G., & Gable, R. K. (2001). Gifted students' perceptions of their class activities: Differences among rural, urban, and suburban student attitudes. *Gifted Child Quarterly, 45,* 115–129.

Herzog, M. J. R., & Pittman, R. B. (1995). Home, family, and community: Ingredients in the rural education equation. *Phi Delta Kappan,* 113–118.

Hobbs, D. (1994). The rural context for education: Adjusting the images. In G. Karim & N. Weate (Eds.), *Toward the 21st century: A rural education anthology. Rural school development outreach project. Volume 1* (pp. 5–22). (ERIC Document No.: ED401073). [Oak

Brook, IL]: NCRL; [Washington, DC]: U.S. Department of Education, Office of Educational Research and Improvement, Educational Resources Information Center.

Howley, C., Howley, A., & Pendarvis, E. (1995). *Out of our minds: Anti-intellectualism and talent development in American schooling.* New York: Teachers College Press.

Jones, E. D., & Southern, W. T. (1992). Programming, grouping, and acceleration in rural school districts: A survey of attitudes and practices. *Gifted Child Quarterly, 36,* 112–117.

Nachtigal, P. (1994). Rural education in a period of transition: Are the public schools up to the task? In G. Karim & N. Weate (Eds.), *Toward the 21st century: A rural education anthology. Rural school development outreach project. Volume 1* (pp. 23–35). (ERIC Document No.: ED401073). [Oak Brook, IL]: NCRL; [Washington, DC]: U.S. Department of Education, Office of Educational Research and Improvement, Educational Resources Information Center, c. 1994.

National Center for Education Statistics. (1998). *The schools and staffing survey (SASS) and teacher follow-up survey (TFS) CD-ROM: Electronic codebook and public-use data for three cycles of SASS and TFS.* Washington, DC: U.S. Department of Education, Office of Educational Research and Improvement.

Newland, T. E. (1976). *The gifted in socio-educational perspective.* Englewood Cliffs, NJ: Prentice-Hall.

Piirto, J. (1994). *Talented children and adults: Their development and education.* New York: Macmillan.

Reynolds, D. R. (1999). *There goes the neighborhood: Rural school consolidation at the grass roots in early twentieth-century.* Iowa City, IA: The University of Iowa Press.

Seal, K. R., & Harmon, H. L. (1995). Realities in rural school reform. *Phi Delta Kappan, 77,* 119–124.

Spicker, H. H. (1992). Identifying and enriching rural gifted children. *Educational Horizons, 70,* 60–65.

Spicker, H. H., & Poling, N. (1993). *Identifying rural disadvantaged gifted students. Project SPRING.* Washington, DC: Department of Education.

Spicker, H. H., Southern, W. T., & Davis, B. I. (1987). The rural gifted child. *Gifted Child Quarterly, 31,* 155–157.

Stern, J. (Ed.). (1994). *The condition of education in rural schools.* Washington, DC: U.S. Department of Education Office of Educational Research and Improvement.

Strange, M. (1998). Does consolidation deny rural kids equal access? *Ruralmatters: The Rural Challenge News,* 5–6. [http://www.ruralchallengepolicy.org/rm/rmspring98/spring05.html.]

Whooley, E. (1999). A raw deal for rural schools. *NEA Today, 17,* (6), 8–16.

45

Technology and the Gifted

MICHAEL C. PYRYT, *University of Calgary, Canada*

This chapter describes ways of using technology to nurture the potential of intellectually gifted students. The major ways that technology instruction can enhance experiences for gifted individuals are by increasing personal productivity, exposing students to emerging innovations, and providing more learner control in the instructional environment (Berger & McIntire, 1998). Generally, an eclectic approach is recommended, since no single formula will work for all gifted students and all schools. The challenge of providing appropriate technology-based training is one of integrating types of giftedness, domain-specific knowledge, learner characteristics, instructional environment, and visions of what gifted individuals should become (Pyryt, 1991). Many conceptions of giftedness (Colangelo & Davis, 1991, 1997; Renzulli, 1986; Sternberg & Davidson, 1986) are available to guide educators regarding possible visions of gifted education.

Six Categories of Instructional Experiences

Treffinger's (1986) Individualized Programming Planning Model (IPPM) provides a framework for discussing technology-based applications. The IPPM approach is an eclectic one that attempts to nurture the development of independent learners. This is achieved through promoting cognitive competence and process development in a supportive learning environment. The IPPM approach considers the selection of appropriate educational experiences to be the responsibility of both the regular classroom teacher and the G/T specialist. The model also recognizes that both in-school and out-of-school experiences can

benefit gifted students. The IPPM approach organizes instructional experiences along six major foci: individualized basics, appropriate enrichment, effective acceleration, independence and self-direction, personal and social growth, and careers and future. The following sections will describe examples of how technology can enhance each of these components.

Individualized Basics

The Individualized Basics component of the IPPM approach acknowledges that students' learning styles and interests affect the way they learn. The learning style system of Dunn, Dunn, and Price (1985) provides a comprehensive system for understanding an individual's preferred learning style. It is possible to use the Internet to determine one's learning style. The site www.learningstyle.com provides an assessment of an individual's preferred environmental, emotional, sociological, and physical learning conditions. Contract Activity Packages (Dunn, 1993) can be devised to accommodate a student's preferred learning style. For example, in a science unit on the planets students may have the opportunity to learn about the solar system by reading a text, by watching a video, or by interacting with computer software. Computer-assisted instruction is especially beneficial for students with tactile-kinesthetic learning styles (Dunn, Dunn, & Price, 1985).

A wonderful Internet resource for anyone interested in gifted education is www.hoagiesgifted.com. This comprehensive website incorporates links to useful educational resources. For example, students studying geography and their teachers would benefit from exploring the National Geographic expeditions website at www.nationalgeographic.com/xpeditions.

This website features the fourteen National Geography Standards and provides interactive multimedia exploration of a variety of geographic concepts. Students of history or literature can visit www.biography.com to obtain biographical information about historical or literary figures. Berger (2001) also provides an annotated listing of websites to expand gifted students' awareness of history and government.

Appropriate Enrichment

Stanley (1979) criticized typical enrichment activities provided for gifted students as either consisting of busywork or being irrelevant to their academic needs. The IPPM approach seeks to make enrichment appropriate by exposing students to topics outside the regular curriculum, by allowing them to develop process skills and by facilitating their pursuit of independent research projects.

As an eclectic model, the IPPM approach incorporates Renzulli's (1977) enrichment triad model, which has been refined over the past twenty years (Renzulli & Reis, 1986, 1997).[1] Type I Enrichment, General Exploratory Activities, provides opportunities to explore topics outside the prescribed curriculum. Curriculum specialists examine the curriculum to determine possible areas for further exploration. In mathematics, for example, topics in statistics such as linear regression or factor analysis might be unique areas of study in mathematics that are not covered in the K–12 curriculum. A compendium of online statistical textbooks, software descriptions, and teaching resources is available at www.execpc.com/~helberg/statistics.html.

Type II Enrichment, Group Training Activities, focuses on developing process skills. There is a variety of websites that are helpful for encouraging the developing of Type II skills. The Creativity Web (http://members.ozemail.com.au/~caveman/Creative/index2.html) synthesizes much of the knowledge base related to developing creativity. The website provides an annotated description and links to 59 software products designed to enhance creative thinking abilities.

Odyssey of the Mind (Micklus, 1984) is a competition-based approached for developing creative abilities. Students who participate in this program participate in a variety of creative challenges as part of local, state, provincial, national, or international competitions. Some of the problems such as building balsa wood structures that support the most weight and mechanical design problems would be beneficial for students gifted in mathematics and science. The Odyssey of the Mind website (www.odysseyofthemind.org) provides an overview as well as practice problems.

A variety of resources for the training of critical thinking can be found at the Center for Critical Thinking website (www.criticalthinking.org). These include definitions of the components of critical thinking, rationale for integrating critical thinking into the curriculum, sample lesson plans, and publication information.

The IPPM approach also views the development of research skills as a fundamental aspect of appropriate enrichment. Type III Enrichment, Individual and Small Group Investigation of Real Problems, provides the opportunity for students to have self-selected independent inquiry experiences. The goal of a Type III project is the production of original knowledge. To the extent possible, the individual emulates the methodology used by practicing professionals.

Technology can greatly facilitate the knowledge production process. The gifted student would begin by using an electronic database to obtain relevant references, typically text-based, for the topic. Web-based resources could be obtained through using a comprehensive search engine available at www.dogpile.com or www.metacrawler.com. Once the information is collected, it must be analyzed to determine the current knowledge base and areas that need to be studied. The use of "tool skills" such as word processing could be helpful in organizing the body of knowledge. Once the methodology is determined and data collected, a statistical analysis software package could be used to perform the data analysis. Once the data is analyzed and interpreted, presentation software such as Powerpoint could be used to produce a sophisticated display of the research project from initial conceptualization through final results.

Effective Acceleration

The IPPM approach supports the use of accelerative strategies to ensure that those students who learn content rapidly are given instruction at an appropriate pace. One of the most promising approaches for accelerating the pace of instruction is the use

---

1. See Chapter 14 by Renzulli and Reis.

of Diagnostic Testing followed by Prescriptive Instruction (DT-PI). This technique, pioneered by Julian Stanley (1978, 1998), involves pretesting to determine a student's level of knowledge, analyzing errors to determine instructional needs, designing and implementing an instructional program to meet these needs, retesting, using an alternate form of the initial test to determine mastery, and proceeding to the next level using the same approach (Benbow & Lubinski, 1997). This approach has been successfully used to promote acceleration in both mathematics and science (Stanley & Stanley, 1986). During an intense three-week summer institute, intellectually able students ages eleven–fifteen were able to learn the equivalent of a year of high school biology, chemistry, or both using the DT-PI approach. Stanley (1998) suggested that computer programs could greatly facilitate the Diagnostic Testing–Prescriptive Instruction process.

Computer-based training instructional designs rely on task analysis (Carrier & Jonassen, 1988; Hannum, 1988; Roblyer, 1988; Wager & Gagné, 1988). It is possible to specify prerequisite skills needed for subsequent achievement by ordering the skills along a learning hierarchy (Gagné, 1985). Software designed for gifted students should incorporate a content analysis of the discipline that includes a sequenced hierarchy of skills needed to master a discipline. The instructional designer of the software should focus on identifying higher-order skills that incorporate other skills. For example, the ability to solve two variable equations incorporates the ability to solve one variable equation. Educators concerned with selecting software for gifted students should be extremely wary of courseware programs that involve the demonstration of many minute skills which are not hierarchically organized in order to complete a course.

Another strategy for effective acceleration is *subject-matter acceleration.* Students who show strengths in particular subjects such as mathematics or science would accelerate in those subjects. There are several ways to accomplish subject matter acceleration. The easiest but most dangerous is to allow an individual or small group of students to work on advanced material in their regular classrooms. Unless written into an Individualized Education Plan (IEP), there is danger that the student may have to repeat the material the following year. Another possibility would be for the student to physically study the subject at the appropriate grade level. The third grader with advanced math skills could take fourth grade

math in the fourth grade room. This approach works best when similar subject matter classes are scheduled at the same time.

Another possibility for subject matter acceleration is the use of fast-paced classes. In such classes, content is covered at a more rapid pace so that at least two years of material is covered in one year. The Study of Mathematically Precocious Youth (SMPY) at Johns Hopkins University has demonstrated the effectiveness of fast-paced classes in mathematics (Bartkovich & George, 1980; Benbow, Perkins, & Stanley, 1983; George & Denham, 1976) and science (Lynch, 1990; Mezynski, Stanley, & McCoart, 1983; Stanley & Stanley, 1986).

Subject matter acceleration can also be implemented via distance learning courses such as those developed by Stanford University's Educational Program for Gifted Youth (EPGY) (Ravaglia, Suppes, Stillinger, & Alper, 1995). The current EPGY CD-Rom courseware programs are extensions of the pioneering work of Suppes (1980), who enabled highly gifted students ages ten–fifteen with IQs mostly above 165 to complete Computer-Assisted Instructional courses at their own pace from home through terminal access to the Stanford University's mainframe computer. In a pilot project using EPGY material, a group of eighteen eighth graders mastered 1.5 grade years in five months of instruction (Gilbert-Macmillan, 2000). Another example of subject matter acceleration using technology was the successful implementation of a university-level course in polymer chemistry with gifted high school students attending the Mississippi Governor's School.

At the high school level, the use of credit by examination is also an effective way to accelerate one's progress. One example of this approach is the Advanced Placement (AP) Program (Hanson, 1980). Students earn university credit based on their scores on an AP examination. A grade of "3" on a 5-point scale will lead to the granting of credit at most universities. Selective universities require a grade of "4" or "5" before awarding credit. For students gifted in mathematics and science, there are examinations in calculus, computer science, biology, chemistry, and physics. The Advanced Placement Program provides content descriptions of the objectives that will be assessed on the AP examinations. Nearly 10,000 high schools worldwide offer courses geared to the content assessed on the AP examinations. Universities offer courses in summer institutes that prepare secondary teachers to instruct a specific AP course.

Longitudinal studies support the effectiveness of AP courses for mathematically gifted students. Brody, Assouline, and Stanley (1990) found that number of AP credits was the only statistically significant predictor of GPA, semesters on the Dean's list, and graduation honors in their study of early entrants at Johns Hopkins University. AP courses have been computerized through EPGY (Ravaglia, Acacio de Barros, & Suppes, 1995). A very positive development is the announcement of the plans to create online AP courses at The University of Iowa (Fisher, 2000).

For some students, early entrance to universities (one or two years earlier than normal), part-time university courses, correspondence courses, and distance learning opportunities provide effective acceleration experiences. Students who are identified through talent searches benefit from early entrance experiences (Brody, 1998; Brody, Assouline & Stanley, 1990; Olszewski-Kubilius, 1995; Stanley, 1985a, 1985b; Stanley & McGill, 1986). The development of online courses at the university level is changing the nature of the admission/enrollment process.

Independence and Self-Direction

Another integral part of the IPPM approach is the deliberate attempt to foster independence and self-direction. Treffinger and Barton (1988) provide an approach for fostering independence based on five teaching styles: command, task, peer-partner, teacher-pupil contract, and self-directed. The styles vary in terms of the four major components of an instructional system: determination of goals and objectives, assessment of entering behavior, instructional activities, and evaluation plan. In the final, self-directed style, the teacher allows the student to control all four components of the instructional system. The transition from the teacher-directed command style to self-directed learning is viewed as a gradual process that is implemented over the course of school year.

Access to technologies such as the worldwide web should promote more self-direction and independence. Students will have ongoing experiences in determining which subject-based websites they want to explore and then evaluating their usefulness.

Personal and Social Growth

The IPPM approach recognizes the importance of personal and social growth and the development of positive self-concepts, positive regard for the processes of growth and development, and commitment to ethical principles. Pyryt and Mendaglio (1996/1997) view self-concept development as integrally linked to an individual's perceptions of the evaluations by significant others, social comparison processes, and attributions. The major vehicles for self-concept development are observations of one's own behavior and communication with significant others. The major technological channel for self-concept enhancement is via electronic communication.

The use of e-mail broadens the social milieu. Through the program BESTS Friends, which evolved from a collaboration between the Universities of Iowa, Calgary, and New South Wales (Assouline, Colangelo, Gross, & Pyryt, 1999), students in the United States, Canada, and Australia have the opportunity to interact with each other electronically. This should reduce feelings of social isolation if there are no intellectual peers in one's home area. Electronic communication also promotes a greater sense of community since an individual is only "an e-mail away" regardless of geographic distance.

The use of discussion groups or LISTSERVs also reduces isolation, since individuals have the opportunity to communicate with others having similar interests. Various discussion groups in gifted education (families, underachievement, curriculum, and other issues) can be found on the Hoagies website (www.hogiesgifted.com). Online course technology also provides opportunities for synchronous and asynchronous modes. In the synchronous communication mode, individuals all have the opportunity to discuss issues in a selected time setting. In the asynchronous mode, individuals can post and receive information at their leisure. Electronic communication also provides a vehicle for collaboration and productivity that enables students to work on projects collaboratively at a distance. Group projects help create interdependence (Strop, 2000).

Exposure to mentors and role models can also enhance one's self-image (Zorman, 1993). Electronic communication provides an opportunity for mentoring relationships to be established at a distance. Exposure to the biographies of productive individuals will help gifted students identify perseverance as a major factor in success. Websites such as www.biography.com provide numerous examples of the need to persevere in order to succeed.

Given the many controversies in science and ethical dilemmas that scientific discovery may engender, training in ethics is especially important for potential scientists (Passow, 1957; Pyryt, 1979; Pyryt, Masharov, & Feng, 1993; Tannenbaum, 1979). There are numerous sources of information about ethical issues on the Internet. For example, the Centre for Applied Ethics at the University of British Columbia (www.cae.ubc.ca) has links to numerous ethics websites on the Internet. It is also possible to download the ethical codes of conduct adopted by various professional organizations.

Careers and Futures

The IPPM model recognizes the need for exploring career possibilities and coping with the uncertainty of societal change. Pyryt (1998) examined career development for the gifted in terms of challenges and needs. Gifted students may be challenged by their multipotentiality, that is, their capability of succeeding at many possible careers. They may be pressured by their parents or teachers to choose certain occupations. They will need to understand the financial and personal investment that obtaining the proper credentials to become practicing professionals will entail. They need to appreciate the lifestyle that various professionals lead. Finally, they need to recognize that new technologies may change the nature of their occupation.

To cope with these challenges, Pyryt (1998) suggested the development of several process skills. These process skills are self-awareness, self-concept development, creative problem-solving, interpersonal effectiveness training, time/stress management, and sex-role awareness. All of these process skills are consistent with the IPPM approach.

There is a overwhelming amount of information available on the Internet regarding career development. A good starting place would be www.yahoo.com, a popular search engine to evocational education and career education sites. If one wanted to acquire some of the books described in the previous section, or find out about books available on careers in any area, one could visit www.amazon.com, the largest bookstore on the Internet. Professionals seing syntheses of the latest research on career dveopment can go to coe.ohiostate.edu/cete/ericacve/index.html, the ERIC Clearinghouse on Adult, Career, and Vocational Education (ERIC/ACVE) located at the Center on Education and Training (CETE) at The Ohio State University. This site provides access to ERIC digests in the areas of career education (childhood through adult), adult and continuing education, and vocational and technical education, including employment and training. The University of Alberta has numerous links through its Career and Placement Services (www.ualberta.ca/~caps) website. Their current monthly "Hotsites" has links to 34 websites dealing with all aspects of career planning and work search.

The Dark Side of Technology

Although this chapter highlights the positive ways that technology can be used to nurture the potential of intellectually gifted individuals, it is important to discuss some potential problems that must be addressed. The first issue is the absolute insistence on ethics and integrity in utilizing computer technology. Gifted students are capable of computer crimes such as software piracy, unlawful access to classified information, computer alteration of records, and virus infestation. Some gifted individuals appear to be more motivated by the intellectual challenge of hacking into a forbidden site than bound by a sense of concern for the implications of their actions.

A second issue is the need for "controlled curiosity" when logging onto the Internet. There is a potential to be overwhelmed by the vast amount of information available. There is much inappropriate information available on the Internet, such as directions for making Molotov Cocktails and pornographic websites. Some of these sites may be accessed unintentionally. Gifted individuals need to have a focus for their Internet explorations and a plan for remaining focused.

A third issue is the need to refrain from believing that all worthwhile information is contained on the Internet and there is no longer a need to visit libraries. Although more and more full-text journal articles are accessible through the Internet, much information remains available only through manual searching.

Although LISTSERVs are beneficial vehicles for communication, they need to be used judiciously since they can generate enormous amounts of dubious information. One needs to carefully select the particular LISTSERVs that one belongs to. Otherwise, processing one's electronic mail will be tedious and unproductive.

Finally, educators need to remember that there is an affective dimension to giftedness that can be enhanced through positive human interaction. Although positive relationships can be developed through electronic communication, such relationships won't replace a mother's love, a teacher's confidence, or a friend's smile.

SUMMARY AND CONCLUSIONS

The possibilities for the use of technology with gifted students have increased dramatically over the past decade. The development of integrated software, powerful hardware, and Internet expansion has kept computer technology on the forefront of an educational revolution. I believe that the possibilities for computer-based instruction with gifted individuals are limited only by our visions. The challenge will be to integrate our technological capabilities with our dreams.

This chapter provided an overview of how technology could be used with gifted students to foster the key components of Treffinger's (1981, 1986) Individualized Programming Planning Model (IPPM). The IPPM approach was adopted for illustration because it is a flexible programming system that is designed to nurture talents on an individualized basis. It also recognizes that designing appropriate educational experiences for gifted students is the responsibility of both the regular classroom teacher and a resource facilitator. The chapter assumes that appropriateness of any technological experience is dependent upon learner characteristics, domain-specific knowledge, technological features, instructional environment, and vision of desired outcomes. It also assumes that gifted individuals should develop the necessary technological skills to enable them to conduct inquiry using methodology that emulates the methods of practicing professionals. Two elementary technology tools that gifted individuals must master include accessing the Internet and using e-mail to communicate. The intricacies of computer-assisted instruction courseware are discussed. In addition, some of the problematic features of using technology with gifted students are highlighted.

QUESTIONS FOR THOUGHT AND DISCUSSION

1. How could computers and the Internet be used within Renzulli's (Chapter 14) Enrichment Triad Model?

2. What are some affective (personal and social growth, ethics and values) benefits related to the use of the Internet by gifted students?

3. Pyryt mentioned several websites. Which seem exciting and worth exploring? Explain.

4. How does technology fit in with your vision of gifted education?

REFERENCES

Assouline, S. G., Colangelo, N., Gross, M. U. M., & Pyryt, M. C. (1999, November). *International Talent Search Results: Comparison with TIMMS.* Paper presented at the meeting of the National Association for Gifted Children, November, 1999, Albuquerque, New Mexico.

Bartkovich, K. G., & George, W. C. (1980). *Teaching the gifted in the mathematics classroom.* Washington, DC: National Educational Association.

Benbow, C. P., & Lubinski, D. (1997). Intellectually talented children: How can we meet their needs? In N. Colangelo & G. A. Davis (Eds.), *Handbook of gifted education* (2nd ed., pp. 155–169). Boston, MA: Allyn and Bacon.

Benbow, C. P., Perkins, S., & Stanley, J. C. (1983). Mathematics taught at a fast pace: A longitudinal evaluation of SMPY's first class. In C. P. Benbow & J. C. Stanley (Eds.), *Academic precocity: Aspects of its development* (pp. 51–78). Baltimore: Johns Hopkins University Press.

Berger, S. (2001). We the people—Using interest as motivator. *Understanding Our Gifted, 13,* 23–25.

Berger, S. L., & McIntire, J. (1998). Technology-based instruction for young gifted children. In J. F. Smutny (Ed.), *The young gifted child: Potential and promise, an anthology* (pp. 535–546). Cresskill, NJ: Hampton Press.

Brody, L. E. (1998). The talent searches: A catalyst for change in higher education. *Journal of Secondary Gifted Education, 9,* 124–133.

Brody, L. E., Assouline, S. G., & Stanley, J. C. (1990). Five years of early entrants: Predicting achievement in college. *Gifted Child Quarterly, 34,* 138–142.

Carrier, C. A., & Jonassen, D. H. (1988). Adapting courseware to accommodate individual differences. In D. H. Jonassen (Ed.), *Instructional design for microcomputer courseware* (pp. 203–226). Hillsdale, NJ: Erlbaum.

Colangelo, N., & Davis, G. A. (Eds.). (1991). *Handbook of gifted education.* Boston, MA: Allyn and Bacon.

Colangelo, N., & Davis, G. A. (Eds.). (1997). *Handbook of gifted education* (2nd ed.). Boston, MA: Allyn and Bacon.

Dunn, R. (1993). Teaching gifted adolescents through their learning style strengths. In R. Milgram, R. Dunn, & G. E. Price (Eds.), *Teaching and counseling gifted and talented adolescents: An international perspective* (pp. 37–68). Westport, CT: Praeger.

Dunn, R., Dunn, K., & Price, G. E. (1985). *Learning style inventory manual.* Lawrence, KS: Price Systems.

Fisher, J. (2000, Spring). Wallace to provide AP classes for rural Iowa students. *Vision, 8*(2), 6.

Gagné, R. M. (1985). *The conditions of learning* (4th ed.). New York: Holt, Rinehart, & Winston.

George, W. C., & Denham, S. A. (1976). Curriculum experimentation for the mathematically talented. In D. P. Keating (Ed.), *Intellectual talent: Research and development* (pp. 103–131). Baltimore: Johns Hopkins University Press.

Gilbert-Macmillan, K. (2000). Computer-based distance learning for gifted students: The EPGY experience. *Understanding Our Gifted, 12,* 17–20.

Hannum, W. (1988). Designing courseware to fit subject matter structure. In D. H. Jonassen (Ed.), *Instructional design for microcomputer courseware* (pp. 275–296). Hillsdale, NJ: Erlbaum.

Hanson, H. P. (1980). Twenty-five years of the Advanced Placement program: Encouraging able students. *College Board Review, 115,* 8–12, 35.

Lynch, S. J. (1990). Fast paced science for the academically talented: Issues of age and competence. *Science Education, 74,* 585–596.

Mezynski, K., Stanley, J. C., & McCoart, R. F. (1983). Helping youths score well on AP examinations in physics, chemistry, and calculus. In C. P. Benbow & J. C. Stanley (Eds.), *Academic precocity: Aspects of its development* (pp. 86–112). Baltimore: Johns Hopkins University Press.

Micklus, C. S. (1984). *Odyssey of the mind.* Glassboro, NJ: Creative Competitions, Inc.

Olszewski-Kubilius, P. (1995). A summary of research regarding early entrance to college. *Roeper Review, 18,* 121–125.

Passow, A. H. (1957). Developing a science program for rapid learners. *Science Education, 41,* 104–112.

Pyryt, M. C. (1979). Helping scientifically gifted children. *Science and children, 16*(6), 16–17.

Pyryt, M. C. (1991). Promising directions for computer-based training with gifted individuals. In T. M. Shlechter (Ed.), *Problems and promises of computer-based training* (pp. 139–150). Norwood, NJ: Ablex.

Pyryt, M. C. (1998). Career education for the gifted and talented: Complexities and recommendations. *AGATE, 12*(1), 13–17.

Pyryt, M. C., Masharov, Y. P., & Feng, C. (1993). Programs and strategies for nurturing talents/gifts in science and technology. In K. A. Heller, F. J. Mönks, & A. H. Passow (Eds.), *International handbook of research and development of giftedness and talent* (pp. 453–471). Oxford: Pergamon.

Pyryt, M. C., & Mendaglio, S. (1996/1997). The many facets of self-concept: Insights from the Pyryt-Mendaglio Self-Perception Survey. *Exceptionality Education Canada, 6*(2), 75–83.

Ravaglia, R., Acacio de Barros, J., & Suppes, P. (1995). Computer-based instruction brings advanced placement physics to gifted students. *Computers in Physics, 9,* 380–386.

Ravaglia, R., Suppes, P., Stillinger, C., & Alper, T. M. (1995). Computer-based mathematics and physics for gifted students. *Gifted Child Quarterly, 39,* 7–13.

Renzulli, J. S. (1977). *The enrichment triad model: A guide for developing defensible programs for the gifted and talented.* Mansfield Center, CT: Creative Learning Press.

Renzulli, J. S. (Ed.). (1986). *Systems and models for developing programs for the gifted and talented.* Mansfield Center, CT: Creative Learning Press.

Renzulli, J. S., & Reis, S. M. (1986). The enrichment triad/revolving door model: A schoolwide plan for the development of creative productivity. In J. S. Renzulli (Ed.), *Systems and models for developing programs for the gifted and talented* (pp. 216–266). Mansfield Center, CT: Creative Learning Press.

Renzulli, J. S., & Reis, S. M. (1997). The schoolwide enrichment model: New directions for developing high-end learning. In N. Colangelo & G. A. Davis (Eds.), *Handbook of gifted education* (2nd ed., pp. 136–154). Boston: Allyn and Bacon.

Roblyer, M. D. (1988). Fundamental problems and principles of designing effective courseware. In D. H. Jonassen (Ed.), *Instructional design for microcomputer courseware* (pp. 7–33). Hillsdale, NJ: Erlbaum.

Stanley, J. C. (1978). SMPY's DT-PI model: Diagnostic testing followed by prescriptive instruction. *Intellectually Talented Youth Bulletin, 4*(10), 7–8.

Stanley, J. C. (1979). The study and facilitation of talent for mathematics. In A. H. Passow (Ed.), *The gifted and talented: Their education and development* (pp. 169–185). (Seventy-eighth Yearbook of the National Society for the Study of Education, Part I.) Chicago: University of Chicago Press.

Stanley, J. C. (1985a). Young entrants to college: How did they fare? *College and University, 60,* 219–228.

Stanley, J. C. (1985b). How did six highly accelerated gifted students fare in graduate school? *Gifted Child Quarterly, 29,* 180.

Stanley, J. C. (1998, May). *Helping students learn only what they don't already know.* Paper presented at the Fourth Biennial Henry B. & Jocelyn Wallace National Research Symposium on Talent Development, University of Iowa, Iowa City.

Stanley, J. C., & McGill, A. M. (1986). More about "Young entrants to colleges: How did they fare?" *Gifted Child Quarterly, 30,* 70–73.

Stanley, J. C., & Stanley, B. S. K. (1986). High-school biology, chemistry, or physics learned well in three weeks. *Journal of Research in Science Teaching, 23,* 237–250.

Sternberg, R. J., & Davidson, J. E. (Eds.). (1986). *Conceptions of giftedness.* New York: Cambridge University Press.

Strop, J. (2000). The affective side of the Internet. *Understanding Our Gifted, 12,* 28–29.

Suppes, P. (1980). The future of computers in education. In R. P. Taylor (Ed.), *The computer in the school: Tutor, tool, tutee* (pp. 248–261). New York: Teachers College Press.

Tannenbaum, A. J. (1979). Pre-Sputnik to post-Watergate concern about the gifted. In A. H. Passow (Ed.), *The gifted and talented: Their education and development* (pp. 5–27). (Seventy-eighth Yearbook of the National Society for the Study of Education, Part I.) Chicago: University of Chicago Press.

Treffinger, D. J. (1981). *Blending gifted education with the total school program.* Honeoye, NY: Center for Creative Learning.

Treffinger, D. J. (1986). Fostering effective independent learning through individualized programming. In J. S. Renzulli (Ed.), *Systems and models for for developing programs for the gifted and talented* (pp. 429–460). Mansfield Center, CT: Creative Learning Press.

Treffinger, D. J., & Barton, B. L. (1988). Fostering independent learning. *G/C/T, 11*(1), 28–30.

Wager, W., & Gagné, R. M. (1988). Designing computer-aided instruction. In D. H. Jonassen (Ed.), *Instructional design for microcomputer courseware* (pp. 35–60). Hillsdale, NJ: Erlbaum.

Zorman, R. (1993). Mentoring and role modeling programs for the gifted. In K. A. Heller, F. J. Mönks, & A. H. Passow (Eds.), *International handbook of research and development of giftedness and talent* (pp. 727–741). Oxford: Pergamon.

46

Gifted Education and Legal Issues: Procedures and Recent Decisions

FRANCES A. KARNES, *University of Southern Mississippi*
RONALD G. MARQUARDT, *University of Southern Mississippi*

Procedures and Recent Decisions

The most significant aspect of the legal framework in which gifted education operates is that, unlike the statutory legal protection provided the disabled student, there is no federal government mandate requiring school districts to provide special programs for gifted students. Consequently, gifted education proponents must look to state governments to establish the legal foundation to protect the interest of gifted students.

State governments take a variety of approaches in establishing the gifted education legal milieu. Approximately three-fifths of the states have passed a statutory mandate requiring special instruction for the gifted, with the balance of the states choosing the "permissive" route (Council of State Directors of Programs for the Gifted, 1994). The permissive statutory path simply means that school districts may, but are not legally required to, provide programs for the gifted. As explained later in this chapter, whether a state has a mandate in place is often a crucial factor in resolving legal disputes. The National Association for Gifted Children (1994) has issued a Position Paper on mandated educational opportunities, although not legally binding (see Appendix). States also vary in the degree of state funding for gifted education, which often has legal consequences.

The reliance on the states for protection of gifted students makes monitoring legal developments in gifted education difficult. The number of states, the variety of legal procedural mazes operating in the states, and the fact that most states do not publish hearing officer and trial court decisions make the tracking of legal disputes burdensome.

In the past, researchers were relegated to state appellate court decisions, statutes, administrative regulations, and whatever bits and pieces could be garnered from state gifted education associations, professionals in the field, and parents. No systematic collection procedures existed to observe and record the resolutions to the variety of legal conflicts occurring in gifted education. Today, a body of literature (see References at the end of this chapter) and computer-assisted legal research make the investigation task easier. New problems and cases continue to emerge, however, so the research task is ongoing.

Procedures for Resolving Legal Issues

Methods for settling legal conflicts in gifted education range from informal discussions to state supreme court decisions. An axiom in this legal arena is that the best solution is to resolve the dispute at the lowest possible level. As the complainant proceeds up the ladder—through negotiation, mediation, due process, administrative review, and the courts—costs and delays expand exponentially. If a matter reaches litigation, financial concerns take on great significance.

Negotiation

Within each school system there should be approved local, county, or parish board of education policies established to resolve general educational issues.

Such policies usually apply to concerns regarding gifted education. A general rule of thumb is to begin solving an issue at the source and proceed up the designated chain of command. For example, if the issue were in regard to assessment and eligibility criteria for admission to a program, one would begin with the person having responsibility for the testing. If there were disagreements over the program in which the gifted student was placed, discussion would begin with the person responsible for placement and/or programming. When agreement cannot be reached at this first point, it should be taken to the next levels, which are usually the principal, the superintendent, and then the school board. In large school districts, there may be additional intermediate steps.

The person who is dissatisfied should gather the relevant documents: state laws pertaining to gifted education and related issues; state board of education rules and regulations; and local, county, or parish board rules and regulations. If there have been court cases and/or due process hearings, these should be reviewed unless they involve privileged information. In addition to a thorough review of the above, accurate records of all meetings, phone calls, and other points of contact as to the time, place, persons present, discussion, and decisions made should be assembled. After each meeting, a letter should be sent to those involved, with a summary and a written request for verification within a designated amount of time.

Additional guidelines for negotiation, as well as other steps in resolving an issue, are to be sure that facts are correct, not hearsay, and that the records are kept of each action taken. Current state laws; state board of education policies, rules, and regulations; and local, county, or parish board policies should provide the facts needed to understand the legal parameters.

Mediation

Twenty-one states have *mediation* available to resolve issues in gifted education. This process may be used if negotiation has not produced the anticipated results through the board of education level (Karnes, Troxclair, & Marquardt, 1998a). Alaska, California, Kansas, New Mexico, Pennsylvania, and South Dakota have mediation provided at the state level, either through legislative action or regulations. The gifted are included with special education students for mediation in Alabama, Connecticut, Louisiana, Nevada, Oregon, and Tennessee. However, Connecticut provides for mediation only in regard to identification of the gifted. At the local level, mediation is in place in Arkansas, the District of Columbia, Hawaii, North Dakota, Michigan, Utah, Virginia, Washington, and West Virginia.

Mediation is a process by which disputes are resolved in an informal manner with a minimum of time, money, and emotional and psychological stress (Karnes & Marquardt, 1991a). Parents and educators may request to use the process through the state board of education or another state-designated agency. The mediation meeting can be scheduled within a short period of time and with a trained impartial mediator.

The mediator should have training in mediation, good written and oral communication skills, and excellent interpersonal skills. The mediator, after hearing both sides of the issue, writes a mediation agreement with the assistance and the cooperation of both parties. The written document should be clearly worded with the specifics of what should be undertaken, who is responsible, the date at which it must be completed, and the name of the person who will monitor the process. Copies are given to both parties to sign and keep, and one is forwarded to the state agency that has responsibility for mediation.

Due Process

If mediation is not available or if an agreement cannot be reached through mediation, then in 26 states procedural *due process* may be employed (Karnes, Troxclair, & Marquardt, 1998a). This is available under different provisions. In states where the gifted are given the same rights as the disabled, due process is usually included within special education law and/or rules and regulations. There are a few other ways that states provide due process for the gifted. The most common is through general state due process procedures for all students, including the gifted; another means is through provisions specific to the gifted.

Commonalities and differences are apparent in reviewing procedural due process for the gifted. Among the most common features are written prior notice as to the date and time of the meeting, an electronic or written transcript of the meeting, having an open or closed meeting, having the student in question in attendance, having attorneys present, and expert witnesses on both sides to offer testimony. Differences occur in the level of the initial hearing, the jurisdiction, the selection and training of the hearing officers, and the route of appeal.

When a due process meeting has been completed, the hearing officer writes a report based on his or her interpretation of the evidence and within the parameters of local, state, and federal laws, rules, regulations, and policies. The hearing officer solely makes the decision regarding the dispute. Copies are forwarded to the appropriate parties and to persons in the state agencies responsible for due process—usually the state superintendent of education. In the initial investigation of due process and the gifted, Karnes and Marquardt (1991a) discovered that over 100 hearings have been conducted. In 1998, Karnes, Troxclair, and Marquardt (1998b) reported twenty-six due process hearings from 1992–1995. The issues included appropriate placement and/or programming, program eligibility and/or identification, compensation, and miscellaneous other issues.

Mediation and procedural due process differ in several ways. The latter is more costly in time and money, and it is more adversarial. Mediation offers the opportunity for both parties to write an agreement, while in due process the hearing officer writes the final document. The hearing officer makes the decision by which both parties must abide, unless an appeal is made.

The appeal process differs slightly from state to state. The most common is to appeal to the state superintendent of education, or to another person within the state department of education.

Karnes and Marquardt (1991a) discussed the possible inherent conflict in a due process structure and provided a more equitable model. In addition, they presented guidelines for states needing to establish and/or change procedural due process.

Courts

If the appeal to the state agency is not satisfactory, the parents or school officials may decide to take the matter to state or federal courts. Most educational matters are governed by state laws or rules and regulations and would be heard in the state courts. Federal courts are the appropriate forum in cases involving federal law and constitutional provisions. There are several points to keep in mind while making a decision to go to court. The complainant must know the current law(s), and understand that court cases are costly in time, money, and emotions. It may take years for the

courts to make a ruling, and the attorneys' fees and court costs are very high. Persons having undertaken the court route described it as emotionally and psychologically draining, whether the case is settled in their favor or not (Karnes & Marquardt, 1991a, 2001).

Another rule of thumb is to hire an attorney with knowledge of educational law; the state bar association may have information on the topic. Before a commitment is made, be sure to know how the costs will be determined. Will there be a flat fee, an hourly rate, or a combination? There can be big differences.

Legal Issues

Certain legal issues consistently reappear on the gifted education landscape. Space does not permit an analysis of every form of dispute, but the following are major conflicts that often arise between parents and school districts.

Early Admission

A recurring legal issue in gifted education is early admission to public school. Many states have statutes that specify that the child must reach a chronological age by a certain date, usually September 1, to enter the first year of school. School administrators are reluctant to ignore the age statute for fear of running afoul of state law and/or policy and procedures.

The best approach to overcoming that age barrier is to check the statute to see if it permits exceptions. Many states have written in the law circumstances that allow early admission. Some states, for example, allow a child transferring from another state who has been attending school to be admitted in the new state of residence. A few other states allow a child to be admitted early upon the showing that the child is mentally and physically ready to attend school.

Most states, however, rely heavily on requiring the child to be a designated age by September 1. Therefore, parents seeking early admission must find some way to circumvent the statute. The first step, of course, is to follow the designated maze through the school administration and school board procedures and, if necessary, to exhaust the administrative review process, including the state board of education. In most states, completion of this administrative gauntlet is a prerequisite for seeking judicial relief.

The model case in early admission is *Doe v. Petal Municipal School District* (1984). In this case, the parents had their four-year-old daughter tested at a local college, and she was determined to be physically, emotionally, and mentally prepared to enter the first grade. In fact, the child was reading at the third-grade level. Standing as a barrier to the child's admission was the Mississippi school admission law that stated that a child must be six years old by September 1 for admission to the first grade. (At that time, the state did not support public kindergartens.) After exhausting all administrative remedies, the father, a local attorney, took his plea to the county youth court.

Because the father had prepared his case well by obtaining the evidence that his daughter was ready to enter school, the county court judge issued an order to the school board to admit the child. The order provided the school district with the requisite legal protection it needed. Because in Mississippi, as in most states, youth court cases are handled secretly, and the files are sealed, the child was protected from harmful publicity.

In *Wright v. Ector County Independent School District* (1993), the mother sought early admission of her son into first grade. He had completed kindergarten in a private school, but was too young by two months to be admitted to the first grade in a public school. The county board of education had adopted a blanket policy of no admission to first grade until the age of six. Ms. Wright argued twice unsuccessfully before the school board and once before the trial court. Although she argued several points of law, the appellate court also denied her child early admission to first grade (Karnes & Marquardt, 2001).

Provision of Programs

Many parents resort to the courts in an attempt to force a school district to provide gifted education programs. Unless the state mandates that school districts provide gifted education opportunities, these suits brought by parents will, for the most part, be unsuccessful.

For example, if a district located in a nonmandated state chooses not to provide gifted education instruction, the courts have uniformly rejected parental claims that their gifted children have been denied state or federal constitutional protections, such as due process of law or equal protection under the law. Gifted children are not a constitutionally

protected class, nor have parents been successful in convincing courts to agree that state general education statutes or constitutional provisions dictate special instruction for gifted children. Instead, courts take the approach that these general education statutes mean that the child must be given the opportunity to attend school and that the educational experts will determine curriculum.

The best case embodying the above principles is the New York case, *Bennett v. New Rochelle School District* (1985). New Rochelle identified 109 gifted students for its newly established gifted education program. Unfortunately, the district only had funds to support 37 students, so a lottery drawing was used to select students for the program. A parent (Bennett) whose gifted daughter was not a lottery winner sued the district claiming that the school district's actions violated state statutory and constitutional law and the Equal Protection Clause of the Federal Constitution. The New York educational statute reads that districts "should develop programs to insure that children reach their full academic potential" (*Bennett v. New Rochelle School District*, 1985). Bennett also claimed that the lottery process violated the Equal Protection Clauses of the New York and United States Constitutions.

These claims were rejected by the New York trial and appellate courts. The appellate court held that the word *should* in the statute provided the district discretion as to curriculum offerings. New York does not mandate that gifted education be provided to identified gifted children, and the use of the word *should*, rather than *shall*, left room for the district to have flexibility in serving the educational needs of the gifted. Bennett lost on the equal protection claims as well. The court indicated that lotteries had been used in other educational matters in the past, and the New York Department of Education had given prior approval to the district's gifted program and procedures.

Broadley v. Board of Education (1994) is another example of why states need to have specific laws for not only identification, but also for specific services. The parents of Neil Broadley sued the local board of education to hopefully force the school to give him individualized gifted instruction. The statutes in Connecticut dealing with the gifted were permissive and stated that districts may provide programming for the gifted but were not mandated to do so.

The Broadleys argued that the gifted were classified as exceptional children under the law and were entitled to individualized instruction. The trial court granted a summary judgment favoring the school system.

Appealing the case, the Broadleys were heard in the supreme court of the state, but their arguments were rejected. The court distinguished the state's obligation to two groups, the gifted and the disabled. The language of the law focusing on appropriate services stated *shall* for the disabled and *may* for the gifted. Neil Broadley was not entitled to special individualized instruction (Karnes & Marquardt, 2001).

The court seemingly did not wish to substitute its will for the expertise of professional educators. Karnes and Marquardt (1991a) tracked several cases in which parents attempted to use ambiguous statutes or constitutional clauses—and all were unsuccessful in the courts. From a legal standpoint, it is much better for a specific state mandate to be passed by the state legislature *requiring* districts to serve the needs of its gifted students.

Racial Balance in Gifted Programs

Another problem for gifted education administrators is the maintenance of a proper racial balance in gifted programs. At the outset of many programs, there was a tendency to use only IQ to select students for admission to gifted programs. These tests provided administrators a convenient and quantitative method to justify admission. Placing too great an emphasis on the standard intelligence test, however, frequently resulted in overlooking gifted minority students (*Vaughns v. Board of Education of Prince George County,* (1985); *Montgomery v. Starkville Municipal School District* (1977)).

Consequently, racial imbalance in gifted programs often became one issue among many raised by plaintiffs in district-wide desegregation suits. In an attempt to correct this imbalance, court desegregation orders have forced school districts to develop a variety of procedures for identifying gifted children. Normally, districts involved in desegregation suits are required to adopt such admission criteria as teacher, parent, and self nominations, grades, and a variety of standardized and nonstandardized assessments. To be certain that their districts make a good-faith effort to avoid future discrimination, many administrators offer staff development for teachers to aid them in identifying gifted minority children. An advisory committee representing the constituent groups is helpful, to make certain that minorities have input into the district's gifted program.

The famous Denver desegregation case, *Keyes v. School District No. 1* (1995), is a good example of a school district's attempt to adopt a variety of procedures to enhance minority participation. The district adopted a variety of testing procedures, conducted interviews, allowed peer nominations, and took other meaningful steps to make certain the selection process for the gifted program was fair. This is an excellent case to read to gain insight into the tools that can be adopted by a district to make certain that a gifted program is not being run in a discriminatory manner.

Three cases typify the ongoing race-based litigation involving gifted programs: *Manning v. The School Board of Hillsborough County* (1999), *Jacksonville Branch, NAACP v. Duval County School Board* (1999), and *The Thomas County Branch of the NAACP v. Thomasville School District* (1999). The two Florida cases in Hillsborough and Duval Counties involved desegregation suits attempting to remove the school districts from federal court supervision and declare a unitary, in contrast to a dual black and white, school system. Duval County was successful, but Hillsborough County, despite major changes in the operation of its gifted program, was not.

Hillsborough County, however, had taken steps to increase minority participation in its gifted programs. When, in 1991, the state of Florida allowed school districts to vary from the state-mandated 130 IQ score in selecting students for gifted programs, Hillsborough County reduced its minimum IQ score to 115 and allowed program administrators to consider a student's academic achievement and other personality characteristics in the selection process.

While the minority participation did not increase dramatically after the new selection criteria were put in place, the federal judge concluded that the racial imbalance in the gifted program was not racially motivated. Hillsborough's failure to escape federal court supervision, at this time, was not because of discrimination in its education programs, but because of its failure to cure vestiges of past discrimination in school assignments, adequacy of facilities, and other miscellaneous factors.

The *Thomasville School District* (1999) case presented an issue the authors had never before encountered in gifted litigation. In this Georgia case, the plaintiffs were attempting to get two preliminary rulings from a federal court: a finding that the plaintiffs had suffered sufficient injury for the court to hear the case and a declaration from the judge that the case would be certified as a class action under Rule 23 of the Federal Rules of Civil Procedure.

This latter issue regarding the creation of the class action was the new one in the authors' research, and it could have considerable importance in gifted education litigation. A procedure allowed in the federal courts and in many state courts, a class action allows plaintiffs to group their claims in a single case in order to increase court efficiency and reduce the expenses of the plaintiffs. A third advantage of a class action in a lengthy education-related suit is that even though some members of the class graduate before the case is completed, the case does not become moot as there are other plaintiffs still involved in the case. The *Thomasville* plaintiffs had myriad racially based claims against the school district, including the claims of three parents that the district operated a segregated gifted program. The federal trial settled the two issues by finding that the plaintiffs had suffered injury and that the various education-related claims had sufficient numbers and similarity to constitute a class action.

A fourth case, *Rosenfeld v. Montgomery County Public Schools* (1999), concerns a developing issue in the operation of gifted programs: reverse discrimination. While *Rosenfeld* is among the first of its type to reach the courts (Karnes & Marquardt, 2001), similar cases are sure to follow. School districts need to make certain that when they institute measures to increase minority participation, the procedures are academically sound and can withstand a legal challenge.

In matters of racial balance, concerned parents have another avenue of resolution besides the traditional approaches of negotiation, mediation, due process, and litigation. Because racial discrimination violates federal laws, parents can file a complaint that a gifted program is discriminatory with the U.S. Department of Education's Office for Civil Rights (OCR). OCR protects persons from discrimination based on race, sex, disability, or age. It investigates complaints and, if discrimination is discovered, will insist that the school district modify its procedures to comply with federal law. Failure to comply may result in the withholding of federal funds from the district.

A study of OCR letters of findings covering the years 1985 to 1990 found forty-six complaints dealing with gifted education programs (Karnes & Marquardt, 1993). The analysis of thirty-eight letters of findings from 1992–1995 produced four general categories: admission to gifted programs; identification of gifted students; placement in gifted programs; and procedures involving notification/communication/testing of gifted children (Karnes, Troxclair, & Marquardt, 1997). In almost every instance, the school district—after some negotiation—was able to convince OCR that it was operating a nondiscriminatory program and received a "school district is in compliance" determination. Nonetheless, the OCR process provides federally protected gifted students and their proponents another avenue to solve disputes and escape the burden of going to court.

Carnegie Units

The awarding of Carnegie units for successfully completed high school courses for graduation varies from state to state. Some states allow seventh- and eighth-grade students to enroll in courses usually designated for those in grades nine through twelve, but will not award them Carnegie units toward graduation. These courses are taught by teachers certified to teach the high school–level academic content, require the same textbooks, and apply the same standards in grading. Three families described their plight in working with local and state school districts and boards; there were positive outcomes in two of the situations (Karnes & Marquardt, 1991b). With twenty-two states empowered to grant Carnegie units to students upon the successful completion of advanced courses prior to admission to high school, and with an additional eight states allowing the local districts to make the decision, the issue of awarding Carnegie units for high school courses taken before the ninth grade will remain in the forefront.

Transfer of Students

When a gifted student's academic, intellectual, or talent needs are not being met by a public elementary or secondary school, one possible option is to transfer the student to another district offering the needed advanced program. Several parents have undertaken this unusual step to resolve the lack of adequate instruction. A family in Mississippi had been denied a transfer, previously promised, after seeking legal counsel and going to court (Karnes & Marquardt, 1991b). They were so determined to receive an appropriate education for their elementary gifted daughter they decided to sell their home in the county district and purchase another in a local district offering a gifted program. They stated that they would repeat the process, if they had to, in order to meet her educational needs.

A family in Illinois was given a transfer through annexing the family farm to the property of the adjacent school district (*Davis v. Regional Board of School Trustees* (1987)). After the school board denied the petition for transfer of the family home, the trial court granted the request of the parents and the appellate court upheld the decision of the trial court. The children were then afforded an appropriate education according to their abilities.

The State of Iowa allows all children due process hearings to determine the appropriateness of instruction, and parents of the gifted have employed this provision to seek instructional remedies. In two hearings, districts were ordered to provide tuition for the students to transfer to another district; in three others, the districts were given the choice of adjusting instruction or paying the cost of transferring the students. In only one situation was the family denied the transfer for their gifted child (Karnes & Marquardt, 1991a).

Transfers *within* a district can also be an issue in gifted litigation. For example, the parents of Melissa Dean requested the Punxsutawney, Pennsylvania, School District to transfer their daughter, a seventh-grade gifted student, to a new school building (Karnes & Marquardt, 2000). Melissa complained of respiratory difficulties and other medical problems while attending classes at her current school, the Jefferson Building. The school district refused the transfer, but after protracted legal skirmishing, including a due process hearing, an appeal to the Pennsylvania Special Education Appeals Panel, and a Pennsylvania Commonwealth Court case (*Punxsutawney Area School District v. Dean, 1995*), Melissa prevailed on the transfer issue. During the legal skirmishing, Melissa received some home schooling, but because of the prolonged nature of the proceeding she was out of school for two months. Evidently, the district misread the applicable law to the extent that the Commonwealth Court judge granted Melissa a compensatory education award, a type of remedy that is often difficult to win.

Appropriate Instruction

Once a gifted program is started, tension frequently arises between the school district and the parents as to the appropriateness of the instruction provided to the gifted student. In states using the special education model, an Individualized Education Plan (IEP) is written for each child after consultation with teachers, counselors, parents, and the student. The IEP, tailored for each child, would include a range of possibilities, for example, grade acceleration, advanced study in a particular academic area, off-campus instruction, or resource programs.

Resource programs allow districts to set aside a particular time each week when gifted students meet in a classroom and receive specialized instruction. These programs are economically efficient, allowing the district to serve a large number of gifted students. To some parents, however, these programs lack the degree of individualized instruction they believe their child should receive.

The resource program approach was the legal issue in what remains today the seminal case in gifted education, the Pennsylvania case, *Centennial School District v. Commonwealth Department of Education* (1988). Centennial used the resource approach to serve its gifted students, reserving ninety minutes each week to provide specialized instruction for students selected for the gifted program. Pennsylvania law placed gifted and disabled children under the *exceptional children* rubric, and the resource program allowed the district to meet the state mandate that gifted students be identified and given appropriate instruction.

A student in the Centennial School District was identified as intellectually gifted and having outstanding abilities in reading and mathematics. Believing he was not receiving appropriate instruction in the resource program in these two subject areas, his parents requested that the district provide him with instruction to serve his special talents in the regular classroom. The school district refused, fearful that if the district were forced to develop individualized instruction for him, other students would demand specialized instruction to serve their special aptitudes. The resource program, the district claimed, was the only economically feasible approach to fulfilling the state mandate to serve gifted children.

Under Pennsylvania law his family had a right to request a due process hearing, and the impartial hearing officer ruled in favor of the student. Centennial appealed the decision to the state Department of Education, but the Department agreed with the hearing officer's ruling. The district then appealed its case in the Commonwealth Court of Pennsylvania, but lost again. Undaunted, the district appealed to the Pennsylvania Supreme Court.

The decision is one that supports gifted education, but is tempered by economic reality (Marquardt &

Karnes, 1989). Correctly interpreting the (exceptional children) statutory mandate to require an IEP for each student, the supreme court first stated that appropriate education for the gifted meant that the student's educational experience had to be tailored to the needs of the student. A resource program, the court concluded, lacked the individualized instruction required under state law.

The second thrust of the decision held that this individualized instruction need not "maximize" each gifted child's abilities. The school district was required to provide an individualized, appropriate curriculum to its gifted children, but did not have to allocate additional resources to do so. Pennsylvania's school districts were required to serve the needs of the gifted students through the curriculum and instructional staff the districts had in place. Compliance with the state's mandate did not mean each district has to become a "Harvard or a Princeton" to develop fully the abilities of its most academically gifted students.

The *Centennial* case provides a judicial precedent that gifted education proponents can use to support the demand for individualized, appropriate education for gifted students, particularly in states statutorily mandating that districts provide gifted education.

Huldah A. v. Easton Area School District (1992) and *Brownsville Area School District v. Student X* (1999) relate to the *Centennial* decision. Interestingly, Hulda A.'s father, in direct contrast to the *Centennial* case, wanted Hulda to be kept in a resource program containing gifted students rather than being placed in the district's special enrichment classes that also had non-gifted students enrolled. Resource programs were used in the Easton District until the student reached the eighth grade, then the gifted student was placed in the special enrichment courses.

At a due process hearing, Huldah's father requested the district pay for an independent evaluation of Huldah, but the hearing officer denied the request and ordered the district's Multidisciplinary Team to write a report for Huldah's Individual Education Program Team. Still seeking an independent evaluation of Huldah, the father then appealed to the Pennsylvania Special Education Appeals Panel, which agreed with the hearing officer that the school district did not have to pay for an independent evaluation of Huldah and, in addition, ruled the district did not have to pay the father's attorney's fees. An appeal to the Pennsylvania Commonwealth Court had much the same outcome, with the court denying the attorney's fees request as well as the father's request for compensation for providing extra instruction for

Huldah during the time the matter was being resolved.

Centennial played a more influential role in the *Brownsville Area School District v. Student X* (1999). Student X ranked in the top 5% of all kindergarten students in the nation in math, reading, and language, but the Pennsylvania district did not have any accelerated or enrichment program in place for the child. When Student X reached the fifth grade, the district did establish an Individualized Education Plan (IEP), but no subject-specific gifted instruction was provided. Five years later, the parents requested a new IEP, but when presented with the plan, they refused to sign it and asked for a due process hearing.

The hearing officer concluded that the district was not providing an appropriate education for Student X and ordered the district to prepare a different IEP. He also awarded Student X 1,954 hours of compensatory education that could be completed within a six-year period. When the district appealed to the state Special Education Appeals Panel, the panel upheld the hearing officer's decision.

An appeal by the district to the Pennsylvania Commonwealth Court provided the district some monetary relief. The court held the Special Education Appeals Panel had exceeded its authority in stating that the compensatory education could be completed at a college or university, and, citing *Centennial* as a precedent, concluded that the compensatory education would have to be fulfilled within the curriculum provided by the district. Special tutors, college or university tuition, etc., would be outside of the limits of the compensatory education award.

Gifted and Disabled

Two interesting cases illustrate a developing area of gifted education law, the situation in which a child has been identified as gifted and disabled. In *Conrad Weiser Area School District v. Department of Education* (1992), the student had a learning disability, and in *Fowler v. Unified School District No. 259* (1995), the case involved a deaf child.

The significant question in *Conrad Weiser* was whether a child who had a high IQ and great intellectual ability could qualify for special education services. While the child was doing well in school, he did have difficulty in writing. The district rejected the parents' plea for special instruction, claiming that the student's success in the regular classroom precluded his request for special education services. When the matter reached the trial court, however, the judge held that Pennsylvania law (22 Pa. Code §342.1[ii]) provided for special education services when a child experienced a discrepancy between achievement and mental ability, and the law included a divergence in competency in writing and the child's intellectual level. Since the child had been identified as having a learning disability in written expression, he was entitled to special education services.

When the local school district provided no gifted education services to Michael Fowler, a ten-year-old deaf child who had been identified as having superior intellectual ability, his parents enrolled Michael at Wichita Collegiate, a private school. The parents then requested the Wichita School District to provide interpretive services for Michael at the private school. The district refused for financial reasons, stating that the district's policy was to place all deaf children in Caldwell School where the children could receive interpretive services more economically. The catch was, of course, that there were no gifted programs at Caldwell. During the controversy, a new IEP was designed and it recommended that Michael spend 180 minutes a week in a gifted resource room. While the district agreed to create such a room for Michael at Caldwell, school officials stated that he would be the only child in the room. Realizing that Michael would not have the advantage of interacting with other gifted children, the parents requested a due process hearing concerning the issue of providing special education services at Wichita Collegiate. The hearing officer ordered the district to provide interpretive services, a district review officer reversed that decision, but when the case reached a federal court, the judge held that Michael was entitled to interpretative services at Wichita Collegiate. The district did not have to pay Michael's tuition to Wichita Collegiate, but the judge concluded that federal law required interpretive services be provided to deaf students attending both private and public schools. Cost to the district could not be a factor, the judge concluded, because the needs of the child prevailed over the financial concerns of the school district.

In regard to applicable law, parents of children who are gifted and disabled generally use the federal Individuals with Disabilities Act as a basis for their claims. This law is often more protective and more supportive of children than a state's gifted education statute. And when the facts of a case allow the federal statute to be joined with a state's gifted education law, the parents have even a stronger legal framework to obtain appropriate instruction for their child.

Teacher Certification

Teacher certification in gifted education presents a legal dilemma for gifted education proponents. On one hand, certification furnishes legal security for gifted education teachers in times of personnel reduction and serves as a safeguard against the hiring of untrained teachers for gifted education positions. The downside is that gifted education advocates do not wish to see the lack of certified teachers become a stumbling block to initiating or continuing gifted programs.

In *Johnson v. Cassell* (1989), Robert Johnson applied for a gifted education position in the Hampshire County, West Virginia, school district. Johnson possessed a master's degree, certification in gifted education (as required by law in West Virginia), and eleven years' teaching experience in gifted education. The candidate hired had no graduate training, no certification, and no gifted education experience. After exhausting his administrative remedies, Johnson sued the district in the local trial court, lost, and appealed to the West Virginia Court of Appeals.

The appeals court noted that West Virginia law provided school boards discretion in personnel decision, but the refusal to hire Johnson carried that discretion too far. The court ruled that the board's action was arbitrary and capricious and awarded Johnson the position.

A second West Virginia case, *Egan v. Board of Education* (1991), reinforced the *Johnson* decision when a West Virginia Court of Appeals determined that Sarah Egan, who was in the process of obtaining gifted education certification, but who had no experience in teaching gifted students, should replace a teacher hired for a gifted education position in the Taylor County School District. Egan possessed a master's degree and certification in grades kindergarten through eighth grade. The person selected for the gifted position held a bachelor's degree, certification in grades one through six, and experience as a full-time and substitute teacher of the gifted, but had made no attempt to obtain certification. Assisting in the appellate court's decision was the fact that Egan had finished the gifted certification process by the time the case percolated up from the trial court to the court of appeals. The court of appeals held that the school board had abused its discretion when it hired the less credentialed teacher and awarded Egan the position, back pay, attorney's fees, and other benefits.

A 1990 Pennsylvania case illustrates how the legal outcome can differ when a state does not require certification for gifted teachers. In *Dallap v. Sharon City School District* (1987, 1990), Vicky Linger, a gifted education coordinator, was retained while several more senior teachers lost their positions. Linger had developed the curriculum for the gifted students and evidently had established contacts throughout the community to support the program. To remove Linger from the gifted position, the superintendent concluded, would be "educationally unsound" (*Dallap v. Sharon City School District,* 1990). She did not have, nor did the coordinator's position require, gifted education certification.

Dallap and several other more senior teachers sued the district and, after seven years of litigation, prevailed. After the case had made its way up through the lower courts, the Pennsylvania Supreme Court ruled that Linger be replaced by a more senior teacher.

Pennsylvania law, the court concluded, required that seniority in a subject area be the key factor in personnel reductions. While recognizing that Linger had been with the program since its inception and that she had considerable knowledge and experience in gifted education, the court held that because her certification was in English, the retention decision should be based on seniority in that subject area. If she had had certification in gifted education, seniority in this classification of teachers would have been the benchmark for the personnel determination.

A similar case, but with a more positive outcome for the gifted education teacher, occurred in a Pennsylvania case, *Dilley v. Slippery Rock Area School District* (1993). As in *Dallap,* a declining enrollment forced the Slippery Rock School District to reduce personnel. Dilley, who had seniority over the gifted education specialist, Kathleen Nachtman, saw his position diminished from full time to half time. Using *Dallap* as a precedent, Dilley claimed that since he had seven years seniority more than Nachtman, he should be given the gifted education post. However, the Commonwealth court held that Dilley was stretching the seniority factor too far. The gifted education job description required computer training, and Dilley did not possess computer skills. But more importantly, the district had sought, and received, a program specialist certification for Nachtman. Dilley, of course, had no such certification, and this allowed the court to distinguish this case from the *Dallap* litigation. Therefore, despite having less seniority than Dilley, the trained and ex-

perienced gifted education professional was able to retain her position.

Transportation

Woodland Hills School District v. Commonwealth Department of Education (1986), another Pennsylvania case, presents a clear victory for advocates of public school busing of gifted students to instructional sites. Decided on Pennsylvania's busing statutes, the judge recognized the problems that working parents face in arranging midday transportation for their children.

Pennsylvania statutorily mandates that an appropriate education be provided to exceptional children. Included under the rubric of *exceptional* are disabled and gifted students. Pennsylvania law also allows a child to attend a private school but receive special education services at a public school site. Private school disabled children were bused to a public school site for midday educational services, but private school gifted students did not receive public transportation.

The school district justified not busing the gifted children in that gifted education teachers traveled to public schools to present gifted instruction. Under that state's general busing statute, the district was only required to provide equal busing treatment to all students. By busing public and private disabled children to instructional sites and not busing either public or private gifted students, the district claimed it was abiding by the statute.

Unable to convince the district to change its policy, parents of gifted private school children filed a complaint with the Pennsylvania Department of Education. The Department of Education ruled against the district, citing a statute specific to special education. Because gifted students fell into the special education category private school gifted students would have to be bused to the public schools for instruction.

Woodland Hills disagreed and filed suit against the Pennsylvania Department of Education. The Commonwealth Court agreed with the Department of Education that gifted children fit under the special education statute, and using a recognized rule of statutory construction held that a specific statute should take priority over a general law. The specific statute, the court concluded, required Woodland Hills to provide transportation to the private school students. Given that many parents would have difficulty in leaving work to transport their children in the middle of the day, the court's decision had a practical aspect as well as an equal treatment component.

Parents of gifted children seeking reimbursement for transportation expenses in two later cases, *Ellis v. Chester-Upland School District* (1994) and *New Brighton Area School District v. Matthew Z* (1997) were not as successful. Monique Ellis was identified as a gifted child, and she requested that the Chester-Upland School District, in Pennsylvania, pay her tuition and transportation expenses to a private school in Delaware. After a hearing officer and the Special Education Appeals Panel denied the requests, Monique's mother went to court. The trial judge held that Pennsylvania law does not provide for payment of out-of-state tuition or transportation costs for gifted children, even if there were a question of whether Monique was receiving an appropriate education within the Chester-Upland School District.

Matthew Z sought tuition and transportation expenses to a nearby college. Matthew, an eleventh-grade gifted student, wished to take science courses at Geneva College, but the district refused to pay his tuition and transportation expenses. The dispute eventually reached the Pennsylvania Commonwealth Court and the trial judge, citing *Centennial* (discussed earlier) as a precedent, held that the district only had to provide Matthew instruction using the educational resources within the district. There was no requirement under Pennsylvania law, the judge concluded, that the school had to pay tuition and transportation expenses to a college.

Tort Liability

Summer residence programs, field trips, and transportation to and from instructional sites present opportunities for accidents. Moreover, because gifted students are intellectually advanced, parents and school personnel often assume they are as physically and mentally mature as adults. Case law suggests this is not the circumstance and that teachers, counselors, and program directors must take preventive steps to make certain accidents do not occur.

A brief survey of selected case law illustrates the need for vigilance in protecting gifted children. For example, as a reward for her good academic work, a third-grade child was given the privilege of bringing a television cart from storage to the classroom. As the child rolled the cart down the hall, the television toppled, killing the 7-year-old child (*Dieringer v. Plain Township* (1985)). In another tragedy, two children attending the governor's school in South Carolina drowned while on a field trip to the beach ("Missing Boy's Body Is Found," 1986).

Four children in a Washington, D.C., summer gifted program were severely burned when chemicals exploded while the children were making sparklers in a laboratory experiment (Sargent, 1985). One of the children, Stewart Ugelow, described his injuries and recovery in Jill Krementz's book *How It Feels to Fight for Your Life* (1989). The parents of Derek Howell sued the D.C. public schools (*District of Columbia v. Howell* (1992)) and American University. The Howells won an eight-million-dollar judgment in the Superior Court of the District of Columbia.

A child enrolled in a residential program had to be airlifted to have leg surgery when a lack of communication following an accident exacerbated the child's injury (*Martinez v. Western Carolina University* (1980)). Gifted education professionals should read this case—it depicts how *not* to handle an accident situation in a residence program.

Finally, at issue in *O'Campo v. The School Board of Dade County* (1991) was when a school district's duty of care to a gifted child began during the school day. School officials instructed eleven-year-old Angelina O'Campo to be at Coral Way Elementary School at 6:55 A.M. to await transportation to South Miami Elementary School to attend a special arts program for gifted students. Coral Way was not open at that early hour, and no faculty were present to monitor her. Sadly, one morning while waiting for the transportation, she was attacked and raped. In the resulting suit by Angelina against the board to recover compensation for emotional, physical, and mental injuries, the school district argued that the district had no duty to protect Angelina from criminal acts by third parties. Citing a lack of previous acts of violence at Coral Way, the district also argued that it should not be held liable because school officials were not on notice that this was a dangerous area.

The trial court agreed with the district, but the Florida Court of Appeals reversed, stating that the district had a general duty of care when school officials were entrusted with the care of a child. The case was remanded to the trial court for jury determination of whether there was a breach of duty in this case. Trial court outcomes are generally not reported in formal court reports, and there is no record of the *O'Campo* case going back into the Florida appellate court system.

Fraud and Misrepresentation

Although the *O'Neill v. Margorie Walters School for Gifted Children* (1985) court case on fraud and misrepresentation has not been settled, it brings this issue into the arena of gifted education. The owner of a private elementary school advertised that teachers were certified in gifted education, indicated that the program was based on individualized instruction, and stated the curriculum was appropriate for gifted students. Several sets of parents disagreed and took the proprietor to court.

The application of this type of situation to gifted education in public elementary and secondary education is apparent. However, a few questions may help districts avoid the accusation of fraud and misrepresentation. Are gifted students in specialized programs in fact receiving differentiated instruction? In states where certification/endorsement in gifted education is required, do all teachers working in special programs meet the state requirements?

Parents, teachers, administrators, school boards, and other concerned citizens may want to examine written materials and public oral statements regarding programs and services in comparison to the reality of such. Some districts and states have attorneys review all official written education documents before they are circulated.

Home Schooling

When parents are dissatisfied with the education of their bright child, they will seek appropriate alternatives, one of which is home schooling. There are a number of questions to be asked pertaining to the gifted and the provision for their education in a home setting. If the district provides transportation to gifted programs, should the parents expect the same for their child in a home education program? If the school has a gifted program, may the child attend during the time that the specialized education takes place? If the local or state budget provides for differentiated materials or equipment, is the home-schooled child entitled to a prorated share? Is the student entitled to any instructional assistance from the teacher of the gifted? Should the child be involved in field experiences or extracurricular activities designated for the gifted and sponsored by the district?

Home schooling has never been found to be the focus of a due process hearing or a court case involving a gifted child. However, the fact that an increasing number of gifted children are homeschooled may make it a future legal issue.

SUMMARY AND CONCLUSIONS

The most expeditious way to solve a dispute is through negotiation, mediation, or a due process hearing. In other words, exhaust all the informal and quasi-formal means to resolving a dispute before seeking relief from the expensive, often frustrating, and cumbersome world of lawyers and courts.

But sometimes litigation is inevitable. Unless an issue can be handled in the federal courts, as with disability, race, age, or gender discrimination, the case will be heard in the state court system. Reliance on state courts means that it is extremely important that the states have clearly written legislation and administrative regulation in place to guide the courts. Judges are reluctant to incorporate protection for gifted students from general educational statutes and vague constitutional provisions.

The reliance on state courts to resolve legal issues means the court decisions rendered in a state are binding precedents in that state, but are not controlling in other states. Therefore, it is difficult to establish a national body of case law that might be described as *what the law is in gifted education.*

Nevertheless, some general legal conclusions can be extrapolated from existing case and statutory law. States should have early admission statutes in place that allow for the administrative processing of exceptions to a chronological age requirement. When states begin gifted programs, they should be certain that funds exist to serve all students identified as gifted; having a group of students identified as gifted and only serving a select group of them is an invitation to lawsuits. School personnel should develop an individualized educational plan for each child, keeping in mind the resources they have within the district to aid the student. When an appropriate education is not provided at the local level in public schools, parents may seek the option of school transfer.

Teacher certification in gifted education protects the integrity of gifted education. Even the courts that are most deferential to allowing educators and school boards control over hiring and firing decisions can understand that a certificated teacher possesses competency over a teacher having no training in gifted education.

Court decisions also reveal certain matters in which gifted education professionals must remain constantly vigilant in order to keep themselves and their programs out of court. Gifted educators must assume a standard of care to their students, including an obligation to foresee dangerous situations and to promptly obtain competent medical care when accidents occur. The same vigilance is necessary to prevent gifted programs from becoming limited to the cultural and racial majority in a school district. Districts must incorporate procedures to identify the gifted from all segments of the community.

Regarding home schooling, questions pertaining to attending school only during the time of the gifted program, being given transportation, and prorating the teacher unit and instructional supplies are only a few yet to be answered.

Another issue that has not been resolved is the awarding of Carnegie units for advanced courses completed prior to admission to high school. States not allowing this practice should examine the manner in which this issue has been decided in other states. If younger students have completed advanced courses with the same content and under a certified teacher, it would appear unfair not to award credit toward high school graduation.

Extreme caution must be taken by local and state educational agencies and boards, as well as public, private, and parochial schools, in describing all aspects of their gifted education programs in printed form. Promulgated policies and procedures must be based in reality. The issue of fraud and misrepresentation may be the Achilles' heel of gifted education.

APPENDIX

Position Paper: Mandated Educational Opportunities for Gifted and Talented Students (1994)

The National Association for Gifted Children (NAGC) periodically issues policy statements that deal with issues, policies, and practices that have an impact on the education of gifted and talented students. Policy statements represent the official convictions of the organization.

All policy statements approved by the NAGC Board of Directors are consistent with the organization's belief that education in a democracy must respect the uniqueness of all individuals, the broad range of cultural diversity present in our society, and similarities and differences in learning characteristics that can be found within any group of students. NAGC is fully committed to national goals that advocate both excellence and equity for all students, and we believe that the best way to achieve these goals is through differentiated educational opportunities, resources, and encouragement for all students.

The National Association for Gifted children supports mandating services to meet the unique needs of gifted and talented children.

Numerous studies, including the federal report *National Excellence: A Case for Developing America's Talent,* released in November 1993, have documented that needs of our nation's gifted and talented students are not being met. Programs for these students are currently often viewed as extracurricular and are available only on limited basis in some school systems, money permitting. The needs of gifted and talented students have been well documented by research and federal studies.

To educate all our children and allow America to compete in a global economy and all fields of human endeavor, the nation must provide an environment in which gifted and talented students, along with all of our children, can reach their full potential.

National Association for Gifted Children
707 L Street, Suite 550
Washington, D.C. 20036

QUESTIONS FOR THOUGHT AND DISCUSSION

1. Why is it important to resolve gifted education disputes at the "lowest level"?

2. Review the legal issues in this chapter. Which three or four are likely the most pressing in your state? Which seem of least concern? Explain.

3. What are the differences between the federal legal protections given to students with disabilities versus gifted students?

4. In your state, can a student receive special services as both gifted and having a disability? (How could you find out?)

5. In your state, are services for the gifted *required* or *permitted*? Explain.

REFERENCES

Council of State Directors of Programs for the Gifted. (1994). *The 1994 state of the states gifted and talented education report.* Austin, TX: Author.

Karnes, F. A., & Marquardt, R. G. (2000). The Pennsylvania Supreme Court decision on gifted education. *Gifted Child Quarterly, 32,* 360–361.

Karnes, F. A., & Marquardt, R. G. (1991a). *Gifted children and the law: Mediation, due process and court cases.* Scottsdale, AZ: Gifted Psychology Press.

Karnes, F. A., & Marquardt, R. G. (1991b). *Gifted children and legal issues in education: Parents' stories of hope.* Scottsdale, AZ: Gifted Psychology Press.

Karnes, F. A., & Marquardt, R. G. (1993). Pathways to solutions: Using conflict resolution in matters of the gifted and talented. *Gifted Child Today 16,* 38–41.

Karnes, F. A., & Marquardt, R. G. (2001). *Gifted children and legal issues: An update.* Scottsdale, AZ: Gifted Psychology Press.

Karnes, F. A., Troxclair, D. A., & Marquardt, R. G. (1997). The Office for Civil Rights and the gifted: An update. *Roeper Review, 19,* 162–163.

Karnes, F. A., Troxclair, D. A., & Marquardt, R. G. (1998a). A survey of mediation opportunities in gifted education. *Gifted Child Today, 21*(3), 46–47, 49.

Karnes, F. A., Troxclair, D. A., & Marquardt, R. G. (1998b). Legal aspects of gifted education: Due process in gifted education. *Roeper Review, 20,* 297–301.

Krementz, J. (1989). *How it feels to fight for your life.* Boston: Little, Brown.

Marquardt, R. G., & Karnes, F. A. (1989). The courts and gifted education. *West's Education Law Reporter, 50,* 9–14.

Missing boy's body is found. (1986, June 30). *The Evening Post,* p. A-1.

National Association for Gifted Children. (1994). Position paper: Mandated educational opportuniites for gifted and talented students. Washington, DC: Author.

Sargent, E. D. (1985, August 13). Science lab blast injures 4 D.C. pupils. *Washington Post,* pp. A-1, A-8.

COURT CASES

Bennett v. New Rochelle School District, 497 N.Y.S.2d 72 (App. Div. 1985).

Broadley v. Board of Education, 639 A.2d 502 (Conn. 1994).

Brownsville Area School District v. Student X, 729 A.2d 198 (Pa. Commw. Ct. 1999).

Centennial School District v. Commonwealth Department of Education, 517 Pa. 540, 539A.2d 785 (1988).

Conrad Weiser Area School District v. Department of Education, 603 A.2d 701 (Pa. Commw. Ct. 1992).

Dallap v. Sharon City School District, 105 Pa. Common-wealth, 346, 524 A.2d 546 (1987); 524 A.2d 546 (1987); 524 Pa. 260, 571 A.2d 368 (1990).

Davis v. Regional Board of School Trustees, 507 N.E.2d 1350 (Ill. App. 1987).

Dieringer v. Plain Township (Unreported 1985 Ohio Trial Court case).

Dilley v. Slippery Rock Area School District, 155 Pa. Commonwealth 357, 625 A.2d 153 (1993).

District of Columbia v. Howell, 607 A.2d 501 (D.C. App. 1992).

Doe v. Petal Municipal School District, Forrest County, Miss. (Unreported Opinion) (1984).

Egan v. Board of Education, 406 S.E.2d 733 (W. Va. Ct. App. 1991).

Ellis v. Chester-Upland School District, 651 A.2d 616 (Pa. Commw. Ct. 1994).

Fowler v. Unified School District No. 259, 900 F. Supp. 1540 (D. Kan. 1995).

Huldah A. v. Easton Area School District, 601 A.2d 860 (Pa. Commw. Ct. 1992).

Jacksonville Branch, NAACP v. Duval County School Board, Case No. 85-316-Civ-J-10C, 1999 U.S. Dist LEXIS 15711 (M.D. Fla. May 27, 1999).

Johnson v. Cassell, 387 S. E.2d 553 (W. Va. 1989).

Keyes v. School District No. 1, 902 F. Supp. 1274 (D. Colo. 1995).

Manning v. The School Board of Hillsborough County, 24 F. Supp. 2d 1277 (M.D. Fla. 1999).

Martinez v. Western Carolina University, 49 N.C. App. 234, 271 S. E.2d 91 (1980).

Montgomery v. Starkville Municipal Separate School District, 665 F. Supp. 487 (N.D. Miss. 1977).

New Brighton Area School District v. Matthew Z., 697 A.2d 1056 (Pa. Commw. Ct. 1997).

O'Campo v. The School Board of Dade County, 589 So. 2d 323 (Fla. Dist. Ct. App. 1991).

O'Neill v. Margorie Walters School for Gifted Children, 466 So. 2d 1295 (La. 1985).

Punxsutawney Area School District v. Dean, 663 A.2d. 831 (Pa. Commw. Ct. 1995).

Rosenfeld v. Montgomery County Public Schools, 41 F. Supp. 2d 581 (D. Md. 1999).

The Thomas County Branch of the NAACP v. Thomasville School District, 187 F.R.D. 690 (M.D. Ga. 1999).

Vaughns v. Board of Education of Prince George County, 758 F.2d 983 (4th Cir. 1985).

Woodland Hills School District v. Commonwealth Department of Education, 101 Pa. Commonwealth 506, 516 A.2d 875 (1986).

Wright v. Ector County Independent School District, 867 S.W.2d 863 (Tex. App. Ct. 1993).

47

Federal Involvement in Gifted and Talented Education

PATRICIA O'CONNELL, *Javits Program, U.S. Department of Education*

Over the past fifty years, sputtering attention has been paid at the federal level to the education of gifted and talented students. When there has been an interest in this student population, it has been embedded in the broader educational concerns of the nation. As a result, the arguments and rationales of special services for gifted and talented students have varied over time, depending on the larger sociopolitical issues of the day.

This chapter addresses federal policy on gifted and talented education over the past fifty years, and analyzes the current education reform debate and its impact on services for gifted and talented students.

Before discussing federal involvement in gifted and talented education, it is important to acknowledge the conflicting beliefs in the United States about the role the federal government should take in education throughout the nation. The U.S. Constitution does not mention education as a federal responsibility, and it declares that all areas not discussed explicitly in the Constitution are the responsibility of states and local communities. Up until recently, the federal government's main involvement in K–12 education was in supplementing states' and local districts' efforts to educate students at risk of educational failure. Gifted and talented education programs have always been a state and local responsibility.

The Sputnik Era

In the fall of 1957, the Soviet Union launched the first Sputnik satellite, simultaneously launching intense debate in this country about the quality of American education. Many voices claimed that the United States was losing the Cold War because of our inadequate educational system, in particular our "manpower"

preparation in mathematics and the sciences. It was believed that the most able students needed a more rigorous secondary education and broader access to higher educational opportunities. Many critics of the system decried progressive education's influence, as carried out by followers of John Dewey, and claimed that this approach focused more on the social development of students than on rigorous academic preparation. The U.S. public believed that the United States was in peril from outside forces if the education system was not improved.

As a result, Congress passed the National Defense Education Act of 1958, the first major federal legislation supporting education. Title V of this Act gave assistance to states by providing funding for testing programs to identify able students, and for counseling and guidance to encourage students to develop their aptitudes and attend college, particularly in mathematics and the sciences.

During this era, the rhetoric supporting programs for able students emerged from passionate concerns about our "race" with the Soviet Union and our ability to win the Cold War. Channeling able students into mathematics and the sciences was the way to improve our relative standing with the Soviet Union. The focus was on national need, not on self-fulfillment, and on the most able students, not the entire student body. With the success of the U.S. space program and the end of the Sputnik "crisis," support for able students waned.

The Rights of Special Children

The 1960s and 1970s saw the rise in demands for rights of individuals within U.S. institutions, particularly the disenfranchised. Major support for poor, educationally disadvantaged students was initiated as a part of the Great Society legislation and came to be known as Title I. In addition, a series of court cases found that children with handicaps were undereducated in U.S. schools. Court decisions led to a push for federal legislation to protect the rights of exceptional children in public schools. In early versions of the draft legislation for exceptional children, gifted and talented students were included as a category of exceptionality. At some point, language including gifted and talented students was removed from the draft legislation. Instead, Congress asked for a study on the status of gifted and talented education in the nation to:

(a) Determine the extent to which special educational assistance programs are necessary or useful to meet the needs of gifted and talented children; (b) show which existing Federal educational assistance programs are being used to meet the needs of gifted and talented children; (c) evaluate how existing Federal education assistance programs can be more effectively used to meet these needs; and (d) recommend which new programs, if any, are needed to meet these needs (U.S. Department of Health, Education and Welfare, 1972; p. V).

The ensuing report to Congress, known as the Marland Report (U.S. Department of Health, Education, and Welfare, 1972), was named after then Commissioner of Education, Sydney Marland. It found that existing services for these students were all but nonexistent and went on to claim:

There is an enormous individual and social cost when talent among the Nation's children and youth goes undiscovered and undeveloped. These students cannot ordinarily excel without assistance.

Identification of the gifted is hampered not only by costs of appropriate testing—when these methods are known and adopted—but also by apathy and even hostility among teachers, administrators, guidance counselors and psychologists.

Gifted and Talented children are, in fact, deprived and can suffer psychological damage and permanent impairment of their abilities to function well which is equal to or greater than the similar deprivations suffered by any other population with special needs served by the Office of Education (p. 3).

In response to this report, the 93rd Congress passed legislation that created an Office of Gifted and Talented in the U.S. Office of Education and provided modest funding ($2.5 million) to support research and development projects, as well as grants to state and local agencies.

In keeping with the rhetoric of the times, which focused on student rights and equal opportunity, arguments for gifted and talented education centered on the need to help students develop their potential for their own well-being. The arguments also accused schools of creating unfriendly environments for the brightest students, thus indicating that these students required special advocacy and programs in order for their needs to be met. These are many of the same arguments that were used for other special populations, including students who were economically disadvantaged, bilingual, migrant, and so on. The basic assumption at the time was that the regular education program was adequate to meet the needs of most children, but that there were special-needs students who required additional attention and support.

The federal program for gifted and talented students continued until passage of the Omnibus Budget Reconciliation Act of 1981. Caught in the recurring dispute over the appropriate federal role in education, the modest funds of the federal gifted and talented program were consolidated with nineteen other programs into a block grant and sent out to states to spend at their own discretion.

Current Reform Initiatives and Federal Policy

In 1988, the Congress reestablished a small federal program on gifted and talented education. The Jacob K. Javits Gifted and Talented Students Education Act of 1988 (P.L. 100-297) provided support for national demonstration grants, a national research and development center, and national leadership activities. The legislation specified that the program place special emphasis on economically disadvantaged students, limited-English-proficient students, and students with disabilities who are gifted and talented. It stated:

The Federal Government can best carry out the limited but essential role of stimulating research and development and personnel training, and providing a national focal point of information and technical assistance, that is necessary to ensure that our Nation's schools are able to meet the special educational needs of gifted and talented students, and thereby serve a profound national interest.

The Javits Gifted and Talented Students Education Program was created as a part of the most intensive and sustained school reform movement in the history of the nation. Since the 1983 publication of *A Nation at Risk: The Imperative for Educational Reform* (U.S. Department of Education, 1983) there have been sustained efforts to improve U.S. education. In 1989, President George Bush and the nation's governors met to develop a set of national goal providing, for the first time, a unified set of expectations for all of American education. The essential message of these goals was that there should be higher standards for all children and that our education system should be the best in the world. Of particular interest for students with outstanding talents is Goal 3 of the National Education Goals, which states:

> By the year 2000, all students will leave grades 4, 8, and 12 having demonstrated competency over challenging subject matter including English, mathematics, science, foreign languages, civics and government, economics, arts, history, and geography, and every school in America will insure that all students learn to use their minds well, so that they may be prepared for responsible citizenship, further learning, and productive employment in our Nation's modern economy.
>
> (A) The objectives for this goal are that:
>
> (i) The academic performance of all students at the elementary and secondary levels will increase significantly in every quartile, and the distribution of minority students in each quartile will more closely reflect the student population as a whole;
>
> (ii) The percentage of all students who demonstrate the ability to reason, solve problems, apply knowledge, and write and communicate effectively will increase substantially. (U.S. Department of Education, 1995, p.70)

The underlying assumption of this goal is that students at all levels of accomplishment, including the most talented, need to be performing at higher levels—in essence, the mission of the Javits Program.

The National Education Goals presented a broad framework for national direction in education. In policy circles, the next debate centered on *how* to accomplish the massive task of improving all of education as envisioned in the National Education Goals. In response, the Congress passed several important pieces of legislation in 1994. GOALS 2000: Educate America Act (U.S. Department of Education, 1994) provided funds to states to develop standards, frameworks, and assessments for what students should

know and be able to do that were more demanding than current practice. In addition, the Elementary and Secondary Education Act (ESEA) was reauthorized with substantial changes in the focus of K–12 education programs to incorporate the belief that all children can achieve higher academic standards. This represented a shift from a focus on reinforcement of basic skills for at-risk populations that was emphasized in previous legislation. Instead, the Improving America's Schools Act of 1994, (U.S. Congress, 1994), as ESEA was renamed, called for acceleration and enrichment as strategies to improve the educational attainment of students. Students in at-risk circumstances were expected to meet the same performance standards as other students. Through this legislation, strategies that were typically the hallmark of programs for gifted and talented students were promoted for students most at risk of school failure. It suggested that *all* students need conceptually complex curriculum, problem-solving skills, instruction in the arts, and enrichment and acceleration. Further, all students had to be assessed based, on the same standards.

National Excellence: A Case for Developing America's Talent

In an attempt to define the place of gifted and talented education within the context of education reform, in 1993 the U.S. Department of Education published a national report on the status of gifted and talented education. *National Excellence: A Case for Developing America's Talent* offered a portrait of how the nation is presently serving gifted and talented students, and suggested the direction in which the nation should head to improve educational opportunities for these students. The report stated:

> The United States is squandering one of its most precious resources—the gifts, talents, and high interests of many of its students. In a broad range of intellectual and artistic endeavors, these youngsters are not challenged to do their best work. This problem is especially severe among economically disadvantaged and minority students, who have access to fewer advanced educational opportunities and whose talents often go unnoticed (p. 1).

The report made the case that, although effective programs for gifted and talented students exist around the country, most are limited in scope and substance and most gifted and talented students spend most of their time in school in regular classrooms where few, if any, provisions are made for them.

To improve educational opportunities for talented students, the report made the following recommendations:

- Establish challenging curriculum standards;
- Establish high-level learning opportunities;
- Ensure access to early childhood education;
- Expand opportunities for disadvantaged and minority children;
- Encourage appropriate teacher training and technical assistance; and
- Match world performance.

In *The National Excellence Report* (1993), the U.S. Department of Education articulated the belief that gifted and talented education fits within the larger educational concerns of the nation. It offered arguments based on national interest, as well as on the need to develop each individual to his or her full potential, especially students who do not currently have access to many advanced educational opportunities. These twin concerns are argued in the context of the need for all of education to be more substantial and rigorous.

No Child Left Behind

In 2001, Congress passed President George W. Bush's education plan, the No Child Left Behind Act of 2001 (NCLB), which reauthorizes the Elementary and Secondary Education Act and covers most of the federal programs for K–12 education. It builds on the previous reauthorization, which began the shift in federal programs to emphasize high standards and challenging opportunities for at-risk students, but goes far beyond prior legislation by insisting on accountability and results; providing more choice for parents and students, particularly those in low-performing schools; offering more flexibility for states and LEAs in the use of federal funds; and placing a strong emphasis on reading for young children. The new legislation offers the most sweeping change in federal education policy in a generation.

Among the most significant features of No Child Left Behind (U.S. Department of Education, 2001) are the following:

Accountability: States are required to implement statewide accountability systems covering all public schools and students. These systems must be based on challenging state standards in reading and mathematics, annual testing of students in grades 3–8, and annual statewide progress objectives ensuring that all groups of students reach proficiency within 12 years. Results will be broken out by poverty, race, ethnicity, disability, and limited English proficiency. School districts and schools that fail to make adequate yearly progress toward statewide proficiency goals will, over time, be subject to improvement, corrective action, and restructuring measures.

Choice: For students in persistently failing schools, LEAs must permit low-income students to use Title I funds to obtain supplemental educational services from public or private sector providers selected by parents and students.

Greater flexibility: Authority is provided to states and LEAs to transfer up to 50% of the funding they receive in four major state grant programs to any one of the programs, or to Title I. The covered programs include Teacher Quality State Grants, Educational Technology, Innovative Programs, and Safe and Drug-Free Schools.

Reading: A substantial increase in funding will support scientifically-based reading programs in the early grades.

No Child Left Behind continues the Javits Program as a source of support for research and development in gifted and talented education, and provides even more emphasis on serving poor and minority students. What is the potential impact of NCLB on students performing at high levels? One important result will be that there is better information on student achievement in reading and mathematics in grades 3–8. Parents and teachers will be able to make better, more objective judgments on students' progress in these two core subjects. In addition, low-income students who are performing at advanced levels can be identified. Further, states are provided with significant autonomy in the deployment of the increased funding that has been provided, so states with a commitment to services for advanced learners can build this into their plans in some federally funded programs.

SUMMARY AND CONCLUSIONS

Education continues to be an important and expanding concern of the federal government. While states continue to have primary responsibility for education in the nation, the federal government is expanding its role by demanding accountability and results for all students. The Javits Program continues to provide direction on ways to close the achievement gap for students performing at high levels.

QUESTIONS FOR THOUGHT AND DISCUSSION

1. Why do you think the federal government historically has taken a minimal role in gifted education?

2. The federal government's role in gifted education began as a response to the cold war and Sputnik. What do you consider the driving forces behind the federal role in gifted education today?

3. What role do you think gifted education needs to have in the push for education reform?

4. The Javits Program is currently the federal program for gifted education. Javits has limited focus and priorities. Do you think the priorities should remain as they are or should the Javits Program be expanded to include other priorities? What new priorities should be added? If the program should be kept in its current form, why?

REFERENCES

U.S. Congress. (1994). *Improving America's Schools Act of 1994* (Public Law 103-882). Washington, DC: Author.

U.S. Congress. (2001). *No Child Left Behind Act of 2001* (H.R.1). Washington, DC: Author.

U.S. Department of Education. (1983). *A nation at risk: The imperative for educational reform.* Washington, DC: Author.

U.S. Department of Education. (1993). *National Excellence: A case for developing America's talent.* Washington, DC: Author.

U.S. Department of Education. (1994). *Goals 2000: A world class education for every child.* Washington, DC: Author.

U.S. Department of Education. (1995). Teachers and GOALS 2000: Leading a journey toward high standards for all students. Washington, DC: Author.

U.S. Department of Education. (2001). *No Child Left Behind: Executive Summary.* Washington, DC: Author.

U.S. Department of Health, Education, and Welfare. (1972). *Education of the gifted and talented.* Washington, DC: Author.

JOURNALS IN GIFTED EDUCATION

Creativity Research Journal
Lawrence Erlbaum Associates, Inc.
Journal Subscription Department
10 Industrial Avenue
Mahwah, NJ 07430-2262
(201) 236-9500; (800) 926-6579
FAX: (201) 760-3735

ERIC Clearinghouse on Disabilities and Gifted Education
The Council for Exceptional Children (CEC)
1110 N. Glebe Rd.
Arlington, VA 22201-5704
(800) 328-0272 (V/TTY)

Exceptional Children
The Council for Exceptional Children
1920 Association Drive
Reston, VA 20191-1589
(888) CEC-SPED
(Local Voice Line: (703) 620-3660;
TTY: (703) 264-9446
FAX (703) 264-9494

Gifted and Talented International
World Council for Gifted and Talented
Children Publications Office
College of William and Mary
Center for Gifted Education
P.O. Box 8795
Williamsburg, VA 23187-8795
(757) 221-2185
FAX: (757) 221-2184

Gifted Child Quarterly
National Association for Gifted Children
1707 L Street NW Suite 550
Washington, DC 20036
(202) 785-4268
FAX: (202) 785-4248

Gifted Child Today
Prufrock Press
P.O. Box 8813

Waco, TX 76714-8813
(800) 998-2208
FAX: (800) 240-0333

High Ability Studies
Taylor & Francis
Journal Customer Service Center
Suite 800, 325 Chestnut Street
Philadelphia, PA 19106
(800) 354-1420
FAX: (215) 625-8914

Intelligence: A Multidisciplinary Journal
Elsevier Science
655 Avenue of the Americas
New York, NY 10010-5107
(212) 633-3730; (888) 437-4636
FAX: (212) 633-3680

Journal for the Education of the Gifted
Prufrock Press
P.O. Box 8813
Waco, TX 76714-8813
(800) 998-2208
FAX: (800) 240-0333

Journal of Secondary Gifted Education
Prufrock Press
P.O. Box 8813
Waco, TX 76714-8813
(800) 998-2208
FAX:(800) 240-0333

MENSA Research Journal
MENSA Education & Research
Foundation
1229 Corporate Drive West
Arlington, TX 76006-6103
(817) 607-0060 ext. 111

Parenting for High Potential
National Association for Gifted Children

1707 L Street NW Suite 550
Washington, DC 20036
(202) 785-4268
FAX: (202) 785-4248

Roeper Review
The Roeper Institute
P.O. Box 329
Bloomfield Hills, MI 48303-0329
Roeper Review: (248) 203-7321
Roeper Institute: (248) 203-7300

Teaching Exceptional Children
The Council for Exceptional Children
1920 Association Drive
Reston, VA 20191-1589
(888) CEC-READ
Local Voice Line: (703) 620-3660;
TTY: (703) 264-9446)

The Australasian Journal of Gifted Education
Dr. Wilma Vialle
Faculty of Education
University of Wollongong
Wollongong NSW 2522
Phone: 61 2 4221-4434
FAX: 61 2 4221 4657

Journal of Creative Behavior
Creative Education Foundation
1050 Union Road #4
Buffalo, NY 14224
(716) 675-3181
FAX: (716) 675-3209

Understanding Our Gifted
Open Space Communications, Inc.
1900 Folsom Suite 108
Boulder, CO 80302
(303) 444-7020
FAX (303) 545-6505;
(800) 494-6178